Foundations of Databases

Foundations of
Databases

Serge Abiteboul

INRIA–Rocquencourt

Richard Hull

University of Southern California

Victor Vianu

University of California–San Diego

Addison-Wesley Publishing Company

Reading, Massachusetts • Menlo Park, California
New York • Don Mills, Ontario • Wokingham, England
Amsterdam • Bonn • Sydney • Singapore
Tokyo • Madrid • San Juan • Milan • Paris

Sponsoring Editor: Lynne Doran Cote
Associate Editor: Katherine Harutunian
Senior Production Editor: Helen M. Wythe
Cover Designer: Eileen R. Hoff
Manufacturing Coordinator: Evelyn M. Beaton
Cover Illustrator: Toni St. Regis
Production: Superscript Editorial Production Services (Ann Knight)
Composition: Windfall Software (Paul C. Anagnostopoulos, Marsha Finley,
    Jacqueline Scarlott), using ZzTeX
Copy Editor: Patricia M. Daly
Proofreader: Cecilia Thurlow

The procedures and applications presented in this book have been included for their instructional value. They have been tested with care but are not guaranteed for any purpose. The publisher does not offer any warranties or representations, nor does it accept any liabilities with respect to the programs and applications.

Many of the designations used by manufacturers and sellers to distinguish their products are claimed as trademarks. Where those designations appear in this book, and Addison-Wesley was aware of a trademark claim, the designations have been printed in initial caps or all caps.

Library of Congress Cataloging-in-Publication Data
Abiteboul, S. (Serge)
    Foundations of databases : the logical level / Serge Abiteboul.
    Richard Hull, Victor Vianu.
        p.   cm.
    Includes bibliographical references and index.
    ISBN 0-201-53771-0
    1. Database management.   I. Hull, Richard, 1953–.   II. Vianu,
    Victor.   III. Title.
    QA76.9.D3A26   1995
    005.74'01—dc20 94-19295
CIP

1 2 3 4 5 6 7 8 9 10–MA–98 97 96 95 94

FTW
AJB 7/89

Alice:	*Whom are you going to dedicate the book to?*
Vittorio:	*How about our parents?*
Riccardo:	*Yes, and our spouses . . .*
Sergio:	*. . . and the kids . . .*
Alice:	*Hold it, that's a dozen people already! Don't you guys have some common ancestor?!*
All:	*You're right! We* also *dedicate it to Seymour Ginsburg.*

Preface

Database theory is a relative newcomer to the field of computer science. Early data management systems were based on techniques from several classical areas of computer science, ranging from hardware and operating systems to data structures and programming languages. In the early seventies, a leap of abstraction from file systems produced relational databases and its accompanying theory, with logic as the catalyst. We believe that database theory has matured—that it has emerged as an elegant and robust part of science with its own identity. As such, it embodies its own peculiar brand of wisdom that deserves to be communicated not just to insiders, but to the computer science community at large.

In a nutshell, a database management system is a software system that enables the creation, maintenance, and use of large amounts of data. In contrast with many programming applications, the logical data structure—the "database schema"—used to structure a given data set is usually much smaller than the volume of that set. Furthermore, the data is persistent, evolving over time and surviving multiple invocations of the database management software. To increase usability, concurrent access to the data is usually supported with specialized protocols that guarantee a form of noninterference between interleaved transactions. Importantly, modern database management systems embody a distinction between the *logical level* and the *physical level*. The logical level focuses on an abstract representation of the data, along with languages to create, query and modify it; the physical level focuses on the underlying implementation, including the physical layout used to store the data, the indexing and clustering schemes, and the concurrency and recovery protocols.

Database theory has developed primarily around the logical level of databases. (A notable exception is concurrency control, which is not addressed in this volume.) A core of fundamental material on the relational model has become well established. It consists primarily of three paradigms for query languages (algebraic, calculus-based, and deductive) and the theory of dependencies. The theory of query languages, including issues of expressiveness and complexity specific to databases, is well developed. The marriage between databases and logic programming produced deductive databases, with the main focus on the deductive query languages. Dependency theory focused initially on formalizing and applying the disparate integrity constraints that commonly arise in practice, and it went on to relate constraints with query optimization and to develop a unifying perspective for them.

As a field, database theory draws on several areas, including mathematical logic, complexity, and programming languages. But the database context brings with it different assumptions, perspectives, and emphases. Relations can be viewed as predicates in the sense of logic, and the relational calculus as a specialization of the first-order predicate calculus. However, the database area emphasizes finite structures and has developed the notions of "domain independence" and "safety" to capture intuitive properties related to this finitude. The questions and techniques in dependency theory borrow heavily from logic, with a focus on practically motivated, relatively weak classes of sentences. Query languages provide an interesting contrast with conventional, imperative programming languages. Query languages typically embody a set-at-a-time focus as opposed to an object-at-a-time focus. Also, they are largely declarative in nature, and failing that, are more applicative than imperative. Because of the emphasis on tractability in the face of large volumes of data, there is considerable interest in query languages that do not have full computational power, which gives rise to a rich interplay between query languages and complexity theory. Specialized notions of complexity have arisen, stemming from the practical reality of large volumes of data and the theoretical interest in different query languages. Also, the important notion of "genericity," which captures a form of abstraction stemming from the separation of the logical and physical levels, has led to new perspectives on complexity theory, involving formalisms that circumvent the ordering of input data implicit in traditional Turing machines.

Exciting new research directions have continued to emerge in database theory, stemming primarily from unanswered questions about query languages and from an interest in expanding beyond the limitations of the relational model. Current research includes investigations motivated by connections with object-orientation, artificial intelligence, and graphics interfaces. And as the database field matures, it, in turn, influences adjacent areas in computer science, notably finite model theory, programming languages, and logic programming.

A Note on Style

This book deals with the theory that has developed around the logical level of databases. It has two main objectives: to provide a focused presentation of the core material and to present the essence of the advanced material in a unified framework. Some of the advanced material has never before been presented in book form. The presentation style is quite rigorous, in that precise definitions and statements of results are provided. However, our overriding concern was to make things simple to the reader, to get across the intuition and elegance of the concepts and proofs, rather than adhere to very strict criteria of rigor. Numerous examples, figures, and exercises should help clarify the development. Some of the proofs emphasize intuition and leave out much of the detail; we called such a proof a "crux." In this way we have tried to achieve a balance between formalism and intuition. As we went along, a two-tier style emerged, with a tendency towards more rigor in the exposition of the core material and more intuition in the presentation of advanced and tangential topics.

The book is aimed at an eclectic audience. Most broadly, it should be a useful resource for any computer scientist or mathematician who wishes to find out what database theory is about. Database researchers and practitioners should find it useful as a reference to both classical material and to advanced topics, otherwise scattered in sometimes hard-to-read papers. As a textbook, it is aimed at graduate students and seniors who would use the book as the main text in a database theory course or as complementary material in a database systems course. The book is fairly self-contained. Some needed background is provided concisely in the preliminaries, and the reader is told where more can be found.

We have attempted to make life easier for the database aficionado by adapting the material consistently to the database framework. This saves the reader the work of translating to the database framework, a task which is at best distracting and at worst tedious and confusing. Perhaps the most substantial difference from the conventional presentation arises in the case of logic programming, where the deductive database point of view has dramatic impact. Mostly, things become much simpler because there are no function symbols. However, for some questions, such as expressive power and complexity, the conventional approach is simply inapplicable. The book also maintains a strong focus on database theory issues—tangential material from adjacent areas has been kept to an absolute minimum.

Results are attributed to their sources in bibliographical notes, included at the end of each chapter.

Organization of This Book

The outline of this book is as follows. Part A contains preliminaries, and a brief introduction to databases and the relational model.

The basic material on relational query languages is developed in Part B. Throughout the entire presentation of query languages, we develop in parallel the three query language paradigms: algebraic, calculus-based, and deductive. The presentation starts with conjunctive queries, which lie at the core of virtually all query languages, both formal and commercial, and have particularly nice properties that make them the prototypical well-behaved class of queries. We use conjunctive queries as a vehicle to introduce many of the main issues in query languages, which will recur throughout the book. More powerful languages are then obtained by gradually enriching the conjunctive queries by adding negation, recursion, and finally negation and recursion combined. At each stage, we examine the basic properties of the newly obtained classes of queries and contrast them with queries considered previously. Adding union and negation yields three equivalent languages: relational calculus (first-order logic without function symbols), relational algebra, and non-recursive datalog¬.

The languages with recursion are studied in Part D. Adding recursion to the conjunctive queries yields datalog. Recursion in combination with negation produces datalog¬ (with the various associated semantics for negation), and other languages, all the way to the *fixpoint* and *while* queries. Included here is a presentation of the logic programming paradigm in the framework of databases, with implementation techniques, including top-down, bottom-up, and heuristics for optimization.

Dependency theory is presented in Part C. The emphasis is on functional, join, and inclusion dependencies, which are widely encountered in practice. We use these classes of dependencies to illustrate the main issues. A larger perspective on more general dependencies is also provided. Uses of dependencies in query optimization and schema design are presented.

More advanced material on the expressiveness and complexity of query languages is presented in Part E. The goal is to highlight the aspects of computability and complexity specific to databases. This includes complexity measures for queries and results on the connection between languages and complexity classes. In particular, the notion of query is formalized carefully, and languages that express all queries are exhibited. Some advanced techniques like 0-1 laws and games, are presented in an informal and self-contained way, with the aim of making them easily accessible to readers with a limited background in logic.

Finally, several advanced topics are briefly surveyed in Part F. They include incomplete information, complex objects and object-oriented databases, and dynamic aspects. These share the characteristic that they are less settled, and possibly more controversial than the other topics covered. Our aim is to identify the main concepts and issues in each of these areas, that are likely to generate a substantial portion of the database theory research in the coming years. The style is more informal, in the manner of a survey, with most proofs omitted and pointers provided to current research.

Teaching from This Book

To teach from this book, several paths can be followed. The diagram on page xi indicates dependencies among chapters. Solid arrows indicate prerequisites. Dashed arrows indicate preferred, but not mandatory, order among chapters. As a sample, here are some possible menus:

- The Classic: a basic database theory course covering the classical material would center around Parts B and C. Chapter 10 and parts of Chapter 9 of Part C are somewhat more advanced and could be skipped. If time allows, some of Chapter 12 and a selection of Part F might be covered.

- Feast of Query Languages: a course on the theory of query languages would start with a quick review of the basic material on classical languages (Part B), and continue with Parts D and E. If time allows, some material on languages for complex objects and object-oriented databases (Part F) could be covered.

- Gourmet Sampling of Database Theory: a course for people with theoretical appetites that emphasizes the specificity of database theory. Logicians wishing to explore the connection between finite-model theory and databases will be interested in Parts C and E. Those interested in descriptive complexity will find Part E closest to their hearts. Researchers in logic programming will prefer Part D, particularly Chapters 12, 13, and 15. People with a background in theoretical artificial intelligence will find Parts D and F of particular interest. Rule-based systems are related to Chapter 14 (see also parts of Chapter 22). Programming language people will be interested in much of the material on query languages, including Chapters 20 and 21 in Part F.

- Fast-Food Database Theory: a course for applied database students that is meant to provide informal exposure to some of the basic results of database theory. This would include assorted topics, with an informal presentation emphasizing the examples, results, and intuition provided in the text, rather than the proofs. A possible syllabus would include Part B; parts of Chapters 8, 9, and 11 in Part C; Chapter 12 and parts of Chapter 15 in Part D; and selected chapters of Part F.

Numerous exercises have been included, and they are essentially of three categories. Routine exercises (unmarked) require easy manipulation of the basic concepts and results. Harder exercises are marked with a (★). Another category of exercises is meant to complement the material in the text and often contains results from related research articles. These exercises are usually on the hard side, and some may constitute term projects. These exercises are marked with a (♠).

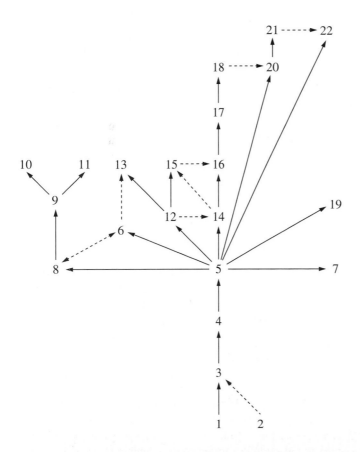

Acknowledgments

We are grateful to several people for their many comments and fruitful discussions on the material of this book: Dennis Allard, Nicole Bidoit, Catriel Beeri, Luca Cabibbo, Sophie Cluet, Claude Delobel, Guozhu Dong, Sophie Gamerman, Françoise Gire, Gösta Grahne, Erich Graedel, Stéphane Grumbach, Gerd Hillebrand, Dean Jacobs, Paris Kanellakis, Phokion Kolaitis, Leonid Libkin, Tova Milo, Jan Paredaens, Raghu Ramakrishnan, Michel Scholl, Jianwen Su, Jan Van den Bussche, Moshe Y. Vardi, and Emmanuel Waller. We are especially thankful to the following people, who served as formal reviewers of part or all of the manuscript: Luca Cabibbo, Jan Chomicki, Jeffrey F. Naughton, Daniel J. Rosenkrantz, Jan Paredaens, Raghu Ramakrishnan, Jianwen Su, Jan Van den Bussche, Dirk Van Gucht, Moshe Y. Vardi, and Marianne Winslett.

We also wish to thank our students from ENS–Paris, ENST–Paris, UCSD, USC, and CU-Boulder who suffered through early versions of the book and tested exercises. In particular, we thank Tim Bailey, Ti-Pin (Ben) Chang, Martha Escobar-Molano, Sergio Lifschitz, Alvaro Monge, Huda Omran, and Gang Zhou.

We are very grateful for the extensive support and assistance we received from the staff at Addison-Wesley, including notably Lynne Doran Cote, Katherine Harutunian, and Peter Shepard on the editorial side, and Helen Wythe on the production side; and the staff of Superscript Editorial Production Services. We also thank Eileen Hoff and Toni St. Regis for helping to develop and executing the cover illustration.

We would also like to acknowledge the continuing support of the NSF and the ES-PRIT Program. Finally, the Verso Research Project at INRIA–Rocquencourt provided a warm and stimulating environment for much of our collaborative work.

SA, RH, VV
Paris

Contents

P A R T

 Antechamber

The primary focus in this book is to present part of the theory underlying the design and use of very popular systems—namely, the database systems. A brief presentation of the main features of these systems is provided in the first chapter.

The second chapter gives a brief review of the main theoretical tools and results that are used in this volume including some basics from naive set theory and standard computer science material from language, complexity, and computability theories. We also survey aspects of mathematical logic.

In the third chapter, we reach the core material of the book. We introduce the relational model and present the basic notation that will be used throughout the book.

1 Database Systems

Alice:	*I thought this was a theory book.*
Vittorio:	*Yes, but good theory needs the big picture.*
Sergio:	*Besides, what will you tell your grandfather when he asks what you study?*
Riccardo:	*You can't tell him that you're studying the fundamental implications of genericity in database queries.*

Computers are now used in almost all aspects of human activity. One of their main uses is to manage information, which in some cases involves simply holding data for future retrieval and in other cases serving as the backbone for managing the life cycle of complex financial or engineering processes. A large amount of data stored in a computer is called a *database*. The basic software that supports the management of this data is called a *database management system* (dbms). The dbms is typically accompanied by a large and evergrowing body of application software that accesses and modifies the stored information. The primary focus in this book is to present part of the theory underlying the design and use of these systems. This preliminary chapter briefly reviews the field of database systems to indicate the larger context that has led to this theory.

1.1 The Main Principles

Database systems can be viewed as mediators between human beings who want to use data and physical devices that hold it (see Fig. 1.1). Early database management was based on explicit usage of *file systems* and customized application software. Gradually, principles and mechanisms were developed that insulated database users from the details of the physical implementation. In the late 1960s, the first major step in this direction was the development of *three-level architecture*. This architecture separated database functionalities into physical, logical, and external levels. (See Fig. 1.2. The three views represent various ways of looking at the database: multirelations, universal relation interface, and graphical interface.)

The separation of the logical definition of data from its physical implementation is central to the field of databases. One of the major research directions in the field has been the development and study of abstract, human-oriented models and interfaces for specifying the structure of stored data and for manipulating it. These models permit the user to concentrate on a logical representation of data that resembles his or her vision of the reality modeled by the data much more closely than the physical representation.

3

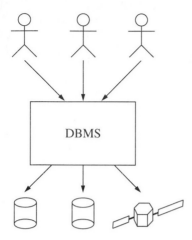

Figure 1.1:   Database as mediator between humans and data

Several logical *data models* have been developed, including the hierarchical, network, relational, and object oriented. These include primarily a *data definition language* (DDL) for specifying the structural aspects of the data and a *data manipulation language* (DML) for accessing and updating it. The separation of the logical from the physical has resulted in an extraordinary increase in database usability and programmer productivity.

Another benefit of this separation is that many aspects of the physical implementation may be changed without having to modify the abstract vision of the database. This substantially reduces the need to change existing application programs or retrain users.

The separation of the logical and physical levels of a database system is usually called the *data independence principle*. This is arguably the most important distinction between file systems and database systems.

The second separation in the architecture, between external and logical levels, is also important. It permits different perspectives, or *views*, on the database that are tailored to specific needs. Views hide irrelevant information and restructure data that is retained. Such views may be simple, as in the case of automatic teller machines, or highly intricate, as in the case of computer-aided design systems.

A major issue connected with both separations in the architecture is the trade-off between human convenience and reasonable performance. For example, the separation between logical and physical means that the system must compile queries and updates directed to the logical representation into "real" programs. Indeed, the use of the relational model became widespread only when query optimization techniques made it feasible. More generally, as the field of physical database optimization has matured, logical models have become increasingly remote from physical storage. Developments in hardware (e.g., large and fast memories) are also influencing the field a great deal by continually changing the limits of feasibility.

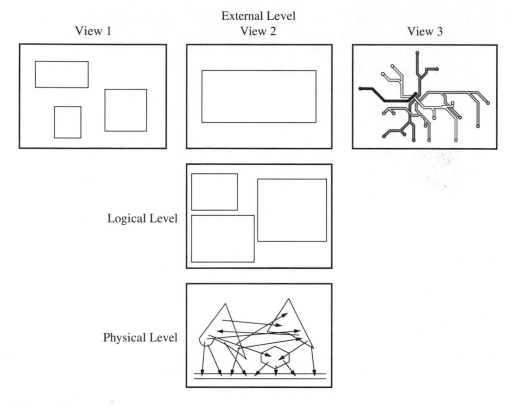

Figure 1.2: Three-level architecture of database systems

1.2 Functionalities

Modern dbms's include a broad array of functionalities, ranging from the very physical to the relatively abstract. Some functionalities, such as database recovery, can largely be ignored by almost all users. Others (even among the most physical ones, such as indexing) are presented to application programmers in abstracted ways.

The primary functionalities of dbms's are as follows:

Secondary storage management: The goal of dbms's is the management of large amounts of shared data. By *large* we mean that the data is too big to fit in main memory. Thus an essential task of these systems is the management of secondary storage, which involves an array of techniques such as indexing, clustering, and resource allocation.

Persistence: Data should be persistent (i.e., it should survive the termination of a particular database application so that it may be reused later). This is a clear divergence from standard programming, in which a data structure must be coded in a file to live beyond the execution of an application. Persistent programming languages (e.g., persistent C^{++}) are now emerging to overcome this limitation of programming languages.

Concurrency control: Data is shared. The system must support simultaneous access to shared information in a harmonious environment that controls access conflicts and presents a coherent database state to each user. This has led to important notions such as *transaction* and *serializability* and to techniques such as two-phase locking that ensure serializability.

Data protection: The database is an invaluable source of information that must be protected against human and application program errors, computer failures, and human misuse. *Integrity checking mechanisms* focus on preventing inconsistencies in the stored data resulting, for example, from faulty update requests. Database *recovery* and *back-up* protocols guard against hardware failures, primarily by maintaining snapshots of previous database states and logs of transactions in progress. Finally, *security control* mechanisms prevent classes of users from accessing and/or changing sensitive information.

Human-machine interface: This involves a wide variety of features, generally revolving around the logical representation of data. Most concretely, this encompasses DDLs and DMLs, including both those having a traditional linear format and the emerging visual interfaces incorporated in so-called fourth-generation languages. Graphically based tools for database installation and design are popular.

Distribution: In many applications, information resides in distinct locations. Even within a local enterprise, it is common to find interrelated information spread across several databases, either for historical reasons or to keep each database within manageable size. These databases may be supported by different systems (interoperability) and based on distinct models (heterogeneity). The task of providing transparent access to multiple systems is a major research topic of the 1990s.

Compilation and optimization: A major task of database systems is the translation of the requests against the external and logical levels into executable programs. This usually involves one or more compilation steps and intensive optimization so that performance is not degraded by the convenience of using more friendly interfaces.

Some of these features concern primarily the physical data level: concurrency control, recovery, and secondary storage management. Others, such as optimization, are spread across the three levels.

Database theory and more generally, database models have focused primarily on the description of data and on querying facilities. The support for designing application software, which often constitutes a large component of databases in the field, has generally been overlooked by the database research community. In relational systems applications can be written in C and extended with embedded SQL (the standard relational query language) commands for accessing the database. Unfortunately there is a significant distance between the paradigms of C and SQL. The same can be said to a certain extent about fourth-generation languages. Modern approaches to improving application programmer productivity, such as object-oriented or active databases, are being investigated.

1.3   Complexity and Diversity

In addition to supporting diverse functionalities, the field of databases must address a broad variety of uses, styles, and physical platforms. Examples of this variety include the following:

Applications: Financial, personnel, inventory, sales, engineering design, manufacturing control, personal information, etc.

Users: Application programmers and software, customer service representatives, secretaries, database administrators (dba's), computer gurus, other databases, expert systems, etc.

Access modes: Linear and graphical data manipulation languages, special purpose graphical interfaces, data entry, report generation, etc.

Logical models: The most prominent of these are the network, hierarchical, relational, and object-oriented models; and there are variations in each model as implemented by various vendors.

Platforms: Variations in host programming languages, computing hardware and operating systems, secondary storage devices (including conventional disks, optical disks, tape), networks, etc.

Both the quality and quantity of variety compounds the complexity of modern dbms's, which attempt to support as much diversity as possible.

Another factor contributing to the complexity of database systems is their longevity. Although some databases are used by a single person or a handful of users for a year or less, many organizations are using databases implemented over a decade ago. Over the years, layers of application software with intricate interdependencies have been developed for these "legacy" systems. It is difficult to modernize or replace these databases because of the tremendous volume of application software that uses them on a routine basis.

1.4   Past and Future

After the advent of the three-level architecture, the field of databases has become increasingly abstract, moving away from physical storage devices toward human models of information organization. Early dbms's were based on the network and hierarchical models. Both provide some logical organization of data (in graphs and trees), but these representations closely mirror the physical storage of the data. Furthermore, the DMLs for these are primitive because they focus primarily on navigation through the physically stored data.

In the 1970s, Codd's relational model revolutionized the field. In this model, humans view the data as organized in relations (tables), and more "declarative" languages are provided for data access. Indexes and other mechanisms for maintaining the interconnection between data are largely hidden from users. The approach became increasingly accepted as implementation and optimization techniques could provide reasonable response times in spite of the distance between logical and physical data organization. The relational model also provided the initial basis for the development of a mathematical investigation of databases, largely because it bridges the gap between data modeling and mathematical logic.

Historically dbms's were biased toward business applications, and the relational model best fitted the needs. However, the requirements for the management of large, shared amounts of data were also felt in a variety of fields, such as computer-aided design and expert systems. These new applications require more in terms of structures (more complex than relations), control (more dynamic environments), and intelligence (incorporation of knowledge). They have generated research and developments at the border of other fields. Perhaps the most important developments are the following:

Object-oriented databases: These have come from the merging of database technology, object-oriented languages (e.g., C++), and artificial intelligence (via semantic models). In addition to providing richer logical data structures, they permit the incorporation of behavioral information into the database schema. This leads to better interfaces and a more modular perspective on application software; and, in particular, it improves the programmer's productivity.

Deductive and active databases: These originated from the fusion of database technology and, respectively, logic programming (e.g., Prolog) and production-rule systems (e.g., OPS5). The hope is to provide mechanisms that support an abstract view of some aspects of information processing analogous to the abstract view of data provided by logical data models. This processing is generally represented in the form of rules and separated from the control mechanism used for applying the rules.

These two directions are catalysts for significant new developments in the database field.

1.5   Ties with This Book

Over the past two decades, database theory has pursued primarily two directions. The principal one, which is the focus of this book, concerns those topics that can meaningfully be discussed within the logical and external layers. The other, which has a different flavor and is not discussed in this book, is the elegant theory of concurrency control.

The majority of this book is devoted to the study of the relational model. In particular, relational query languages and language primitives such as recursion are studied in depth. The theory of dependencies, which provides the formal foundation of integrity constraints, is also covered. In the last part of the book, we consider more recent topics whose theory is generally less well developed, including object-oriented databases and behavioral aspects of databases.

By its nature, theoretical investigation requires the careful articulation of all assumptions. This leads to a focus on abstract, simplified models of much more complex practical situations. For example, one focus in the early part of this book is on conjunctive queries. These form the core of the *select-from-where* clause of the standard language in database systems, SQL, and are perhaps the most important class of queries from a practical standpoint. However, the conjunctive queries ignore important practical components of SQL, such as arithmetic operations.

Speaking more generally, database theory has focused rather narrowly on specific areas that are amenable to theoretical investigation. Considerable effort has been directed toward the expressive power and complexity of both query languages and dependencies, in which close ties with mathematical logic and complexity theory could be exploited. On the other hand, little theory has emerged in connection with physical query optimization, in which it is much more difficult to isolate a small handful of crucial features upon which a meaningful theoretical investigation can be based. Other fundamental topics are only now receiving attention in database theory (e.g., the behavioral aspects of databases).

Theoretical research in computer science is driven both by the practical phenomena that it is modeling and by aesthetic and mathematical rigor. Although practical motivations are touched on, this text dwells primarily on the mathematical view of databases and presents many concepts and techniques that have not yet found their place in practical systems. For instance, in connection with query optimization, little is said about the heuristics that play such an important role in current database systems. However, the homomorphism theorem for conjunctive queries is presented in detail; this elegant result highlights the essential nature of conjunctive queries. The text also provides a framework for analyzing a broad range of abstract query languages, many of which are either motivated by, or have influenced, the development of practical languages.

As we shall see, the data independence principle has fundamental consequences for database theory. Indeed, much of the specificity of database theory, and particularly of the theory of query languages, is due to this principle.

With respect to the larger field of database systems, we hope this book will serve a dual purpose: (1) to explain to database system practitioners some of the underlying principles and characteristics of the systems they use or build, and (2) to arouse the curiosity of theoreticians reading this book to learn how database systems are actually created.

Bibliographic Notes

There are many books on database systems, including [Dat86, EN89, KS91, Sto88, Ull88, Ull89b, DA83, Vos91]. A (now old) bibliography on databases is given in [Kam81]. A good introduction to the field may be found in [KS91], whereas [Ull88, Ull89b] provides a more in-depth presentation.

The relational model is introduced in [Cod70]. The first text on the logical level of database theory is [Mai83]. More recent texts on the subject include [PBGG89], which focuses on aspects of relational database theory; [Tha91], which covers portions of dependency theory; and [Ull88, Ull89b], which covers both practical and theoretical aspects of the field. The reader is also referred to the excellent survey of relational database theory in [Kan88], which forms a chapter of the *Handbook of Theoretical Computer Science* [Lee91].

Database concurrency control is presented in [Pap86, BHG87]. Deductive databases are covered in [Bid91a, CGT90]. Collections of papers on this topic can be found in [Min88a]. Collections of papers on object-oriented databases are in [BDK92, KL89, ZM90]. Surveys on database topics include query optimization [JK84a, Gra93], deductive databases [GMN84, Min88b, BR88a], semantic database models [HK87, PM88], database programming languages [AB87a], aspects of heterogeneous databases [BLN86, SL90], and active databases [HW92, Sto92]. A forthcoming book on active database systems is [DW94].

2 Theoretical Background

Alice:	*Will we ever get to the real stuff?*
Vittorio:	*Cine nu cunoaşte lema, nu cunoaşte teorema.*
Riccardo:	*What is Vittorio talking about?*
Sergio:	*This is an old Romanian saying that means, "He who doesn't know the* lemma *doesn't know the* teorema."
Alice:	*I see.*

This chapter gives a brief review of the main theoretical tools and results that are used in this volume. It is assumed that the reader has a degree of maturity and familiarity with mathematics and theoretical computer science. The review begins with some basics from set theory, including graphs, trees, and lattices. Then, several topics from automata and complexity theory are discussed, including finite state automata, Turing machines, computability and complexity theories, and context-free languages. Finally basic mathematical logic is surveyed, and some remarks are made concerning the specializing assumptions typically made in database theory.

2.1 Some Basics

This section discusses notions concerning binary relations, partially ordered sets, graphs and trees, isomorphisms and automorphisms, permutations, and some elements of lattice theory.

A *binary relation* over a (finite or infinite) set S is a subset R of $S \times S$, the cross-product of S with itself. We sometimes write $R(x, y)$ or $x R y$ to denote that $(x, y) \in R$.

For example, if Z is a set, then inclusion ($\subseteq$) is a binary relation over the power set $\mathcal{P}(Z)$ of Z and also over the *finitary power set* $\mathcal{P}^{\text{fin}}(Z)$ of Z (i.e., the set of all finite subsets of Z). Viewed as sets, the binary relation $\leq$ on the set $\mathbf{N}$ of nonnegative integers properly contains the relation $<$ on $\mathbf{N}$.

We also have occasion to study n-ary relations over a set S; these are subsets of S^n, the cross-product of S with itself n times. Indeed, these provide one of the starting points of the relational model.

A binary relation R over S is *reflexive* if $(x, x) \in R$ for each $x \in S$; it is *symmetric* if $(x, y) \in R$ implies that $(y, x) \in R$ for each $x, y \in S$; and it is *transitive* if $(x, y) \in R$ and $(y, z) \in R$ implies that $(x, z) \in R$ for each $x, y, z \in S$. A binary relation that is reflexive, symmetric, and transitive is called an *equivalence relation*. In this case, we associate to each $x \in S$ the *equivalence class* $[x]_R = \{y \in S \mid (x, y) \in R\}$.

An example of an equivalence relation on **N** is *modulo* for some positive integer n, where $(i, j) \in \text{mod}_n$ if the absolute value $|i - j|$ of the difference of i and j is divisible by n.

A *partition* of a nonempty set S is a family of sets $\{S_i \mid i \in I\}$ such that (1) $\cup_{i \in I} S_i = S$, (2) $S_i \cap S_j = \emptyset$ for $i \neq j$, and (3) $S_i \neq \emptyset$ for $i \in I$. If R is an equivalence relation on S, then the family of equivalence classes over R is a partition of S.

Let E and E' be equivalence relations on a nonempty set S. E is a *refinement* of E' if $E \subseteq E'$. In this case, for each $x \in S$ we have $[x]_E \subseteq [x]_{E'}$, and, more precisely, each equivalence class of E' is a disjoint union of one or more equivalence classes of E.

A binary relation R over S is *irreflexive* if $(x, x) \notin R$ for each $x \in S$.

A binary relation R is *antisymmetric* if $(y, x) \notin R$ whenever $x \neq y$ and $(x, y) \in R$. A *partial order* of S is a binary relation R over S that is reflexive, antisymmetric, and transitive. In this case, we call the ordered pair (S, R) a *partially ordered set*. A *total order* is a partial order R over S such that for each $x, y \in S$, either $(x, y) \in R$ or $(y, x) \in R$.

For any set Z, the relation $\subseteq$ over $\mathcal{P}(Z)$ is a partially ordered set. If the cardinality $|Z|$ of Z is greater than 1, then this is not a total order. $\leq$ on **N** is a total order.

If (S, R) is a partially ordered set, then a *topological sort* of S (relative to R) is a binary relation R' on S that is a total order such that $R' \supseteq R$. Intuitively, R' is compatible with R in the sense that $x R y$ implies $x R' y$.

Let R be a binary relation over S, and **P** be a set of properties of binary relations. The **P***-closure* of R is the smallest binary relation R' such that $R' \supseteq R$ and R' satisfies all of the properties in **P** (if a unique binary relation having this specification exists). For example, it is common to form the transitive closure of a binary relation or the reflexive and transitive closure of a binary relation. In many cases, a closure can be constructed using a recursive procedure. For example, given binary relation R, the transitive closure R^+ of R can be obtained as follows:

1. If $(x, y) \in R$ then $(x, y) \in R^+$;
2. If $(x, y) \in R^+$ and $(y, z) \in R^+$ then $(x, z) \in R^+$; and
3. Nothing is in R^+ unless it follows from conditions (1) and (2).

For an arbitrary binary relation R, the reflexive, symmetric, and transitive closure of R exists and is an equivalence relation.

There is a close relationship between binary relations and graphs. The definitions and notation for graphs presented here have been targeted for their application in this book. A *(directed) graph* is a pair $G = (V, E)$, where V is a finite set of *vertexes* and $E \subseteq V \times V$. In some cases, we define a graph by presenting a set E of edges; in this case, it is understood that the vertex set is the set of endpoints of elements of E.

A *directed path* in G is a nonempty sequence $p = (v_0, \ldots, v_n)$ of vertexes such that $(v_i, v_{i+1}) \in E$ for each $i \in [0, n-1]$. This path is from v_0 to v_n and has length n. An *undirected path* in G is a nonempty sequence $p = (v_0, \ldots, v_n)$ of vertexes such that $(v_i, v_{i+1}) \in E$ or $(v_{i+1}, v_i) \in E$ for each $i \in [0, n-1]$. A (directed or undirected) path is *proper* if $v_i \neq v_j$ for each $i \neq j$. A *(directed or undirected) cycle* is a (directed or undirected, respectively) path $v_0, \ldots, v_n$ such that $v_n = v_0$ and $n > 0$. A directed cycle is proper if $v_0, \ldots, v_{n-1}$ is a proper path. An undirected cycle is proper if $v_0, \ldots, v_{n-1}$ is a proper path and $n > 2$. If G has a cycle from v, then G has a proper cycle from v. A graph $G = (V, E)$ is *acyclic* if it has no cycles or, equivalently, if the transitive closure of E is irreflexive.

Any binary relation over a finite set can be viewed as a graph. For any finite set Z, the graph $(\mathcal{P}(Z), \subseteq)$ is acyclic. An interesting directed graph is (M, L), where M is the set of metro stations in Paris and $(s_1, s_2) \in L$ if there is a train in the system that goes from s_1 to s_2 without stopping in between. Another directed graph is (M, L'), where $(s_1, s_2) \in L'$ if there is a train that goes from s_1 to s_2, possibly with intermediate stops.

Let $G = (V, E)$ be a graph. Two vertexes u, v are *connected* if there is an undirected path in G from u to v, and they are *strongly connected* if there are directed paths from u to v and from v to u. Connectedness and strong connectedness are equivalence relations on V. A (*strongly*) *connected component* of G is an equivalence class of V under (strong) connectedness. A graph is (strongly) connected if it has exactly one (strongly) connected component.

The graph (M, L) of Parisian metro stations and nonstop links between them is strongly connected. The graph $(\{a, b, c, d, e\}, \{(a, b), (b, a), (b, c), (c, d), (d, e), (e, c)\})$ is connected but not strongly connected.

The *distance* $d(a, b)$ of two nodes a, b in a graph is the length of the shortest path connecting a to b [$d(a, b) = \infty$ if a is not connected to b]. The *diameter* of a graph G is the maximum finite distance between two nodes in G.

A *tree* is a graph that has exactly one vertex with no in-edges, called the *root*, and no undirected cycles. For each vertex v of a tree there is a unique proper path from the root to v. A *leaf* of a tree is a vertex with no outedges. A tree is connected, but it is not strongly connected if it has more than one vertex. A *forest* is a graph that consists of a set of trees. Given a forest, removal of one edge increases the number of connected components by exactly one.

An example of a tree is the set of all descendants of a particular person, where (p, p') is an edge if p' is the child of p.

In general, we shall focus on directed graphs, but there will be occasions to use undirected graphs. An *undirected graph* is a pair $G = (V, E)$, where V is a finite set of vertexes and E is a set of two-element subsets of V, again called *edges*. The notions of path and connected generalize to undirected graphs in the natural fashion.

An example of an undirected graph is the set of all persons with an edge $\{p, p'\}$ if p is married to p'. As defined earlier, a tree $T = (V, E)$ is a directed graph. We sometimes view T as an undirected graph.

We shall have occasions to *label* the vertexes or edges of a (directed or undirected) graph. For example, a *labeling* of the vertexes of a graph $G = (V, E)$ with label set L is a function $\lambda : V \to L$.

Let $G = (V, E)$ and $G' = (V', E')$ be two directed graphs. A function $h : V \to V'$ is a *homomorphism* from G to G' if for each pair $u, v \in V$, $(u, v) \in E$ implies $(h(u), h(v)) \in E'$. The function h is an *isomorphism* from G to G' if h is a one-one onto mapping from V to V', h is a homomorphism from G to G', and h^{-1} is a homomorphism from G' to G. An *automorphism* on G is an isomorphism from G to G. Although we have defined these terms for directed graphs, they generalize in the natural fashion to other data and algebraic structures, such as relations, algebraic groups, etc.

Consider the graph $G = (\{a, b, c, d, e\}, \{(a, b), (b, a), (b, c), (b, d), (b, e), (c, d), (d, e), (e, c)\})$. There are three automorphisms on G: (1) the identity; (2) the function that maps c to d, d to e, e to c and leaves a, b fixed; and (3) the function that maps c to e, d to c, e to d and leaves a, b fixed.

Let S be a set. A *permutation* of S is a one-one onto function $\rho : S \to S$. Suppose that $x_1, \ldots, x_n$ is an arbitrary, fixed listing of the elements of S (without repeats). Then there is a natural one-one correspondence between permutations ρ on S and listings $x_{i_1}, \ldots, x_{i_n}$ of elements of S without repeats. A permutation ρ' is *derived* from permutation ρ by an *exchange* if the listings corresponding to ρ and ρ' agree everywhere except at some positions i and $i + 1$, where the values are exchanged. Given two permutations ρ and ρ', ρ' can be derived from ρ using a finite sequence of exchanges.

2.2 Languages, Computability, and Complexity

This area provides one of the foundations of theoretical computer science. A general reference for this area is [LP81]. References on automata theory and languages include, for instance, the chapters [BB91, Per91] of [Lee91] and the books [Gin66, Har78]. References on complexity include the chapter [Joh91] of [Lee91] and the books [GJ79, Pap94].

Let Σ be a finite set called an *alphabet*. A *word* over alphabet Σ is a finite sequence $a_1 \ldots a_n$, where $a_i \in \Sigma$, $1 \leq i \leq n$, $n \geq 0$. The *length* of $w = a_1 \ldots a_n$, denoted $|w|$, is n. The empty word $(n = 0)$ is denoted by ϵ. The *concatenation* of two words $u = a_1 \ldots a_n$ and $v = b_1 \ldots b_k$ is the word $a_1 \ldots a_n b_1 \ldots b_k$, denoted uv. The concatenation of u with itself n times is denoted u^n. The set of all words over Σ is denoted by Σ^*. A *language* over Σ is a subset of Σ^*. For example, if $\Sigma = \{a, b\}$, then $\{a^n b^n \mid n \geq 0\}$ is a language over Σ. The concatenation of two languages L and K is $LK = \{uv \mid u \in L, v \in K\}$. L concatenated with itself n times is denoted L^n, and $L^* = \bigcup_{n \geq 0} L^n$.

Finite Automata

In databases, one can model various phenomena using words over some finite alphabet. For example, sequences of database events form words over some alphabet of events. More generally, everything is mapped internally to a sequence of bits, which is nothing but a word over alphabet $\{0, 1\}$. The notion of computable query is also formalized using a low-level representation of a database as a word.

An important type of computation over words involves *acceptance*. The objective is to accept precisely the words that belong to some language of interest. The simplest form of acceptance is done using *finite-state automata* (fsa). Intuitively, fsa process words by scanning the word and remembering only a bounded amount of information about what has already been scanned. This is formalized by computation allowing a finite set of states and transitions among the states, driven by the input. Formally, an fsa M over alphabet Σ is a 5-tuple $\langle S, \Sigma, \delta, s_0, F \rangle$, where

- S is a finite set of *states*;
- δ, the *transition function*, is a mapping from $S \times \Sigma$ to S;

- s_0 is a particular state of S, called the *start* state;
- F is a subset of S called the *accepting* states.

An fsa $\langle S, \Sigma, \delta, s_0, F \rangle$ works as follows. The given input word $w = a_1 \ldots a_n$ is read one symbol at a time, from left to right. This can be visualized as a tape on which the input word is written and an fsa with a head that reads symbols from the tape one at a time. The fsa starts in state s_0. One move in state s consists of reading the current symbol a in w, moving to a new state $\delta(s, a)$, and moving the head to the next symbol on the right. If the fsa is in an accepting state after the last symbol in w has been read, w is accepted. Otherwise it is rejected. The language accepted by an fsa M is denoted $L(M)$.

For example, let M be the fsa

δ	0	1
even	even	odd
odd	odd	even

$\langle \{\text{even,odd}\}, \{0, 1\}, \delta, \text{even}, \{\text{even}\} \rangle$,   with

The language accepted by M is

$$L(M) = \{w \mid w \text{ has an even number of occurrences of } 1\}.$$

A language accepted by some fsa is called a *regular language*. Not all languages are regular. For example, the language $\{a^n b^n \mid n \geq 0\}$ is not regular. Intuitively, this is so because no fsa can remember the number of a's scanned in order to compare it to the number of b's, if this number is large enough, due to the boundedness of the memory. This property is formalized by the so-called *pumping lemma* for regular languages.

As seen, one way to specify regular languages is by writing an fsa accepting them. An alternative, which is often more convenient, is to specify the shape of the words in the language using so-called regular expressions. A regular expression over Σ is written using the symbols in Σ and the operations concatenation, $*$ and $+$. (The operation $+$ stands for union.) For example, the foregoing language $L(M)$ can be specified by the regular expression $((0^*10^*)^2)^* + 0^*$. To see how regular languages can model things of interest to databases, think of employees who can be affected by the following events:

hire, transfer, quit, fire, retire.

Throughout his or her career, an employee is first hired, can be transferred any number of times, and eventually quits, retires, or is fired. The language whose words are allowable sequences of such events can be specified by a regular expression as *hire (transfer)* (quit + fire + retire)*. One of the nicest features of regular languages is that they have a dual characterization using fsa and regular expressions. Indeed, Kleene's theorem says that a language L is regular iff it can be specified by a regular expression.

There are several important variations of fsa that do not change their accepting power. The first allows scanning the input back and forth any number of times, yielding *two-way automata*. The second is *nondeterminism*. A nondeterministic fsa allows several possible next states in a given move. Thus several computations are possible on a given input. A word is accepted if there is at least one computation that ends in an accepting state. Nondeterministic fsa (nfsa) accept the same set of languages as fsa. However, the number of states in the equivalent deterministic fsa may be exponential in the number of states of the nondeterministic one. Thus nondeterminism can be viewed as a convenience allowing much more succinct specification of some regular languages.

Turing Machines and Computability

Turing machines (TMs) provide the classical formalization of computation. They are also used to develop classical complexity theory. Turing machines are like fsa, except that symbols can also be overwritten rather than just read, the head can move in either direction, and the amount of tape available is infinite. Thus a move of a TM consists of reading the current tape symbol, overwriting the symbol with a new one from a specified finite *tape alphabet*, moving the head left or right, and changing state. Like an fsa, a TM can be viewed as an acceptor. The language accepted by a TM M, denoted $L(M)$, consists of the words w such that, on input w, M halts in an accepting state. Alternatively, one can view TM as a generator of words. The TM starts on empty input. To indicate that some word of interest has been generated, the TM goes into some specified state and then continues. Typically, this is a nonterminating computation generating an infinite language. The set of words so generated by some TM M is denoted $G(M)$. Finally, TMs can also be viewed as computing a function from input to output. A TM M computes a partial mapping f from Σ^* to Σ^* if for each $w \in \Sigma^*$: (1) if w is in the domain of f, then M halts on input w with the tape containing the word $f(w)$; (2) otherwise M does not halt on input w.

A function f from Σ^* to Σ^* is *computable* iff there exists some TM computing it. Church's thesis states that any function computable by some reasonable computing device is also computable in the aforementioned sense. So the definition of computability by TMs is robust. In particular, it is insensitive to many variations in the definition of TM, such as allowing multiple tapes. A particularly important variation allows for nondeterminism, similar to nondeterministic fsa. In a nondeterministic TM (NTM), there can be a choice of moves at each step. Thus an NTM has several possible computations on a given input (of which some may be terminating and others not). A word w is accepted by an NTM M if there exists at least one computation of M on w halting in an accepting state.

Another useful variation of the Turing machine is the *counter machine*. Instead of a tape, the counter machine has two stacks on which elements can be pushed or popped. The machine can only test for emptiness of each stack. Counter machines can also define all computable functions. An essentially equivalent and useful formulation of this fact is that the language with integer variables $i, j, \ldots$, two instructions *increment(i)* and *decrement(i)*, and a looping construct *while i > 0 do*, can define all computable functions on the integers.

Of course, we are often interested in functions on domains other than words—integers are one example. To talk about the computability of such functions on other domains, one goes through an encoding in which each element d of the domain is represented as a word

$enc(d)$ on some fixed, finite alphabet. Given that encoding, it is said that f is computable if the function $enc(f)$ mapping $enc(d)$ to $enc(f(d))$ is computable. This often works without problems, but occasionally it raises tricky issues that are discussed in a few places of this book (particularly in Part E).

It can be shown that a language is $L(M)$ for some acceptor TM M iff it is $G(M)$ for some generator TM M. A language is *recursively enumerable* (r.e.) iff it is $L(M)$ [or $G(M)$] for some TM M. L being r.e. means that there is an algorithm that is guaranteed to say eventually *yes* on input w if $w \in L$ but may run forever if $w \notin L$ (if it stops, it says *no*). Thus one can never know for sure if a word is not in L.

Informally, saying that L is recursive means that there is an algorithm that always decides in finite time whether a given word is in L. If $L = L(M)$ and M always halts, L is *recursive*. A language whose complement is r.e. is called *co-r.e.* The following useful facts can be shown:

1. If L is r.e. and co-r.e., then it is recursive.
2. L is r.e. iff it is the domain of a computable function.
3. L is r.e. iff it is the range of a computable function.
4. L is recursive iff it is the range of a computable nondecreasing function.[1]

As is the case for computability, the notion of recursive is used in many contexts that do not explicitly involve languages. Suppose we are interested in some class of objects called thing-a-ma-jigs. Among these, we want to distinguish widgets, which are those thing-a-ma-jigs with some desirable property. It is said that it is *decidable* if a given thing-a-ma-jig is a widget if there is an algorithm that, given a thing-a-ma-jig, decides in finite time whether the given thing-a-ma-jig is a widget. Otherwise the property is *undecidable*. Formally, thing-a-ma-jigs are encoded as words over some finite alphabet. The property of being a widget is decidable iff the language of words encoding widgets is recursive.

We mention a few classical undecidable problems. The *halting problem* asks if a given TM M halts on a specified input w. This problem is undecidable (i.e., there is no algorithm that, given the description of M and the input w, decides in finite time if M halts on w). More generally it can be shown that, in some precise sense, all nontrivial questions about TMs are undecidable (this is formalized by *Rice's theorem*). A more concrete undecidable problem, which is useful in proofs, is the *Post correspondence problem* (PCP). The input to the PCP consists of two lists

$$u_1, \ldots, u_n; \qquad v_1, \ldots, v_n;$$

of words over some alphabet Σ with at least two symbols. A solution to the PCP is a sequence of indexes $i_1, \ldots, i_k$, $1 \leq i_j \leq n$, such that

$$u_{i_1} \ldots u_{i_k} = v_{i_1} \ldots v_{i_k}.$$

---

[1] f is nondecreasing if $|f(w)| \geq |w|$ for each w.

The question of interest is whether there is a solution to the PCP. For example, consider the input to the PCP problem:

$$
\begin{array}{cccc@{\qquad}cccc}
u_1 & u_2 & u_3 & u_4 & v_1 & v_2 & v_3 & v_4 \\
aba & bbb & aab & bb & a & aaa & abab & babba.
\end{array}
$$

For this input, the PCP has the solution 1, 4, 3, 1; because

$$
u_1 u_4 u_3 u_1 = ababbaababa = v_1 v_4 v_3 v_1.
$$

Now consider the input consisting of just u_1, u_2, u_3 and v_1, v_2, v_3. An easy case analysis shows that there is no solution to the PCP for this input. In general, it has been shown that it is undecidable whether, for a given input, there exists a solution to the PCP.

The PCP is particularly useful for proving the undecidability of other problems. The proof technique consists of *reducing* the PCP to the problem of interest. For example, suppose we are interested in the question of whether a given thing-a-ma-jig is a widget. The reduction of the PCP to the widget problem consists of finding a computable mapping f that, given an input i to the PCP, produces a thing-a-ma-jig $f(i)$ such that $f(i)$ is a widget iff the PCP has a solution for i. If one can find such a reduction, this shows that it is undecidable if a given thing-a-ma-jig is a widget. Indeed, if this were decidable then one could find an algorithm for the PCP: Given an input i to the PCP, first construct the thing-a-ma-jig $f(i)$, and then apply the algorithm deciding if $f(i)$ is a widget. Because we know that the PCP is undecidable, the property of being a widget cannot be decidable. Of course, any other known undecidable problem can be used in place of the PCP.

A few other important undecidable problems are mentioned in the review of context-free grammars.

Complexity

Suppose a particular problem is solvable. Of course, this does not mean the problem has a *practical* solution, because it may be prohibitively expensive to solve it. Complexity theory studies the difficulty of problems. Difficulty is measured relative to some resources of interest, usually time and space. Again the usual model of reference is the TM. Suppose L is a recursive language, accepted by a TM M that always halts. Let f be a function on positive integers. M is said to use time bounded by f if on every input w, M halts in at most $f(|w|)$ steps. M uses space bounded by f if the amount of tape used by M on every input w is at most $f(|w|)$. The set of recursive languages accepted by TMs using time (space) bounded by f is denoted TIME(f) (SPACE(f)). Let $\mathcal{F}$ be a set of functions on positive integers. Then TIME($\mathcal{F}$) = $\bigcup_{f \in \mathcal{F}}$ TIME(f), and SPACE($\mathcal{F}$) = $\bigcup_{f \in \mathcal{F}}$ SPACE(f). A particularly important class of bounding functions is the polynomials *Poly*. For this class, the following notation has emerged: TIME(*Poly*) is denoted PTIME, and SPACE(*Poly*) is denoted PSPACE. Membership in the class PTIME is often regarded as synonymous to tractability (although, of course, this is not reasonable in all situations, and a case-by-case judgment should be made). Besides the polynomials, it is of interest to consider lower bounds, like logarithmic space. However, because the input itself takes more than logarithmic space to write down, a separation of the input tape from the tape used throughout the computation must be made. Thus the input is given on a read-only tape, and a separate worktape is added. Now let LOGSPACE consist of the recursive languages L that are accepted by some such TM using on input w an amount of worktape bounded by $c \times \log(|w|)$ for some constant c.

Another class of time-bounding functions we shall use is the so-called *elementary* functions. They consist of the set of functions

$$Hyp = \{hyp_i \mid i \geq 0\}, \quad \text{where} \quad \begin{aligned} hyp_0(n) &= n \\ hyp_{i+1}(n) &= 2^{hyp_i(n)}. \end{aligned}$$

The *elementary languages* are those in TIME(Hyp).

Nondeterministic TMs can be used to define complexity classes as well. An NTM uses time bounded by f if all computations on input w halt after at most $f(|w|)$ steps. It uses space bounded by f if all computations on input w use at most $f(|w|)$ space (note that termination is not required). The set of recursive languages accepted by some NTM using time bounded by a polynomial is denoted NP, and space bounded by a polynomial is denoted by NPSPACE. Are nondeterministic classes different from their deterministic counterparts? For polynomial space, Savitch's theorem settles the question by showing that PSPACE = NPSPACE (the theorem actually applies to a much more general class of space bounds). For time, things are more complicated. Indeed, the question of whether PTIME equals NP is the most famous open problem in complexity theory. It is generally conjectured that the two classes are distinct.

The following inclusions hold among the complexity classes described:

$$\text{LOGSPACE} \subseteq \text{PTIME} \subseteq \text{NP} \subseteq \text{PSPACE} \subset \text{TIME}(Hyp) = \text{SPACE}(Hyp).$$

All nonstrict inclusions are conjectured to be strict.

Complexity classes of languages can be extended, in the same spirit, to complexity classes of computable functions. Here we look at the resources needed to compute the function rather than just accepting or rejecting the input word.

Consider some complexity class, say $C = \text{TIME}(\mathcal{F})$. Such a class contains all problems that can be solved in time bounded by some function in $\mathcal{F}$. This is an upper bound, so C clearly contains some easy and some hard problems. How can the hard problems be distinguished from the easy ones? This is captured by the notion of *completeness* of a problem in a complexity class. The idea is as follows: A language K in C is complete in C if solving it allows solving all other problems in C, also within C. This is formalized by the notion of *reduction*. Let L and K be languages in C. L is reducible to K if there is a computable mapping f such that for each w, $w \in L$ iff $f(w) \in K$. The definition of reducibility so far guarantees that solving K allows solving L. How about the complexity? Clearly, if the reduction f is hard then we do not have an acceptance algorithm in C. Therefore the complexity of f must be bounded. It might be tempting to use C as the bound. However, this allows all the work of solving L within the reduction, which really makes K irrelevant. Therefore the definition of completeness in a class C requires that the complexity of the reduction function be lower than that for C. More formally, a recursive language is complete in C by C' reductions if for each $L \in C$ there is a function f in C' reducing L to K. The class C' is often understood for some of the main classes C. The conventions we will use are summarized in the following table:

Type of Completeness	Type of Reduction
P completeness	LOGSPACE reductions
NP completeness	PTIME reductions
PSPACE completeness	PTIME reductions

Note that to prove that a problem L is complete in C by C' reductions, it is sufficient to exhibit another problem K that is known to be complete in C by C' reductions, and a C' reduction from K to L. Because the C'-reducibility relation is transitive for all customarily used C', it then follows that L is itself C complete by C' reductions. We mention next a few problems that are complete in various classes.

One of the best-known NP-complete problems is the so-called *3-satisfiability (3-SAT)* problem. The input is a propositional formula in conjunctive normal form, in which each conjunct has at most three literals. For example, such an input might be

$$(\neg x_1 \vee \neg x_4 \vee \neg x_2) \wedge (x_1 \vee x_2 \vee x_4) \wedge (\neg x_4 \vee x_3 \vee \neg x_1).$$

The question is whether the formula is satisfiable. For example, the preceding formula is satisfied with the truth assignment $\xi(x_1) = \xi(x_2) = false$, $\xi(x_3) = \xi(x_4) = true$. (See Section 2.3 for the definitions of propositional formula and related notions.)

A useful PSPACE-complete problem is the following. The input is a quantified propositional formula (all variables are quantified). The question is whether the formula is true. For example, an input to the problem is

$$\exists x_1 \forall x_2 \forall x_3 \exists x_4 [(\neg x_1 \vee \neg x_4 \vee \neg x_2) \wedge (x_1 \vee x_2 \vee x_4) \wedge (\neg x_4 \vee x_3 \vee \neg x_1)].$$

A number of well-known games, such as GO, have been shown to be PSPACE complete.

For PTIME completeness, one can use a natural problem related to context-free grammars (defined next). The input is a context-free grammar G and the question is whether $L(G)$ is empty.

Context-Free Grammars

We have discussed specification of languages using two kinds of acceptors: fsa and TM. Context-free grammars (CFGs) provide different approach to specifying a language that emphasizes the generation of the words in the language rather than acceptance. (Nonetheless, this can be turned into an accepting mechanism by *parsing*.) A CFG is a 4-tuple $\langle N, \Sigma, S, P \rangle$, where

- N is a finite set of *nonterminal symbols*;
- Σ is a finite alphabet of *terminal symbols*, disjoint from N;

- S is a distinguished symbol of N, called the *start symbol*;
- P is a finite set of *productions* of the form $\xi \to w$, where $\xi \in N$ and $w \in (N \cup \Sigma)^*$.

A CFG $G = \langle N, \Sigma, S, P \rangle$ defines a language $L(G)$ consisting of all words in Σ^* that can be *derived* from S by repeated applications of the productions. An application of the production $\xi \to w$ to a word v containing ξ consists of replacing one occurrence of ξ by w. If u is obtained by applying a production to some word v, this is denoted by $u \Rightarrow v$, and the transitive closure of $\Rightarrow$ is denoted $\overset{*}{\Rightarrow}$. Thus $L(G) = \{w \mid w \in \Sigma^*, S \overset{*}{\Rightarrow} w\}$. A language is called *context free* if it is $L(G)$ for some CFG G. For example, consider the grammar $\langle \{S\}, \{a, b\}, S, P \rangle$, where P consists of the two productions

$$S \to \epsilon,$$
$$S \to aSb.$$

Then $L(G)$ is the language $\{a^n b^n \mid n \geq 0\}$. For example the following is a derivation of $a^2 b^2$:

$$S \Rightarrow aSb \Rightarrow a^2 Sb^2 \Rightarrow a^2 b^2.$$

The specification power of CFGs lies between that of fsa's and that of TMs. First, all regular languages are context free and all context-free languages are recursive. The language $\{a^n b^n \mid n \geq 0\}$ is context free but not regular. An example of a recursive language that is not context free is $\{a^n b^n c^n \mid n \geq 0\}$. The proof uses an extension to context-free languages of the pumping lemma for regular languages. We also use a similar technique in some of the proofs.

The most common use of CFGs in the area of databases is to view certain objects as CFGs and use known (un)decidability properties about CFGs. Some questions about CFGs known to be decidable are (1) emptiness [is $L(G)$ empty?] and (2) finiteness [is $L(G)$ finite?]. Some undecidable questions are (3) containment [is it true that $L(G_1) \subseteq L(G_2)$?] and (4) equality [is it true that $L(G_1) = L(G_2)$?].

2.3   Basics from Logic

The field of mathematical logic is a main foundation for database theory. It serves as the basis for languages for queries, deductive databases, and constraints. We briefly review the basic notions and notations of mathematical logic and then mention some key differences between this logic in general and the specializations usually considered in database theory. The reader is referred to [EFT84, End72] for comprehensive introductions to mathematical logic, and to the chapter [Apt91] in [Lee91] and [Llo87] for treatments of Herbrand models and logic programming.

Although some previous knowledge of logic would help the reader understand the content of this book, the material is generally self-contained.

Propositional Logic

We begin with the *propositional calculus*. For this we assume an infinite set of *propositional variables*, typically denoted $p, q, r, \ldots$, possibly with subscripts. We also permit the special *propositional constants true* and *false*. (*Well-formed*) *propositional formulas* are constructed from the propositional variables and constants, using the unary connective *negation* ($\neg$) and the binary connectives *disjunction* ($\vee$), *conjunction* ($\wedge$), *implication* ($\rightarrow$), and *equivalence* ($\leftrightarrow$). For example, p, $(p \wedge (\neg q))$ and $((p \vee q) \rightarrow p)$ are well-formed propositional formulas. We generally omit parentheses if not needed for understanding a formula.

A *truth assignment* for a set V of propositional variables is a function $\xi : V \rightarrow \{true, false\}$. The *truth value* $\varphi[\xi]$ of a propositional formula φ under truth assignment ξ for the variables occurring in φ is defined by induction on the structure of φ in the natural manner. For example,

- $true[\xi] = true$;
- if $\varphi = p$ for some variable p, then $\varphi[\xi] = \xi(p)$;
- if $\varphi = (\neg \psi)$ then $\varphi[\xi] = true$ iff $\psi[\xi] = false$;
- $(\psi_1 \vee \psi_2)[\xi] = true$ iff at least one of $\psi_1[\xi] = true$ or $\psi_2[\xi] = true$.

If $\varphi[\xi] = true$ we say that $\varphi[\xi]$ is true and that φ is true under ξ (and similarly for false).

A formula φ is *satisfiable* if there is at least one truth assignment that makes it true, and it is *unsatisfiable* otherwise. It is *valid* if each truth assignment for the variables in φ makes it true. The formula $(p \vee q)$ is satisfiable but not valid; the formula $(p \wedge (\neg p))$ is unsatisfiable; and the formula $(p \vee (\neg p))$ is valid.

A formula φ *logically implies* formula ψ (or ψ is a *logical consequence of* φ), denoted $\varphi \models \psi$ if for each truth assignment ξ, if $\varphi[\xi]$ is true, then $\psi[\xi]$ is true. Formulas φ and ψ are (*logically*) *equivalent*, denoted $\varphi \equiv \psi$, if $\varphi \models \psi$ and $\psi \models \varphi$.

For example, $(p \wedge (p \rightarrow q)) \models q$. Many equivalences for propositional formulas are well known. For example,

$$(\varphi_1 \rightarrow \varphi_2) \equiv ((\neg \varphi_1) \vee \varphi_2); \quad \neg(\varphi_1 \vee \varphi_2) \equiv (\neg \varphi_1 \wedge \neg \varphi_2);$$
$$(\varphi_1 \vee \varphi_2) \wedge \varphi_3 \equiv (\varphi_1 \wedge \varphi_3) \vee (\varphi_2 \wedge \varphi_3); \quad \varphi_1 \wedge \neg \varphi_2 \equiv \varphi_1 \wedge (\varphi_1 \wedge \neg \varphi_2);$$
$$(\varphi_1 \vee (\varphi_2 \vee \varphi_3)) \equiv ((\varphi_1 \vee \varphi_2) \vee \varphi_3).$$

Observe that the last equivalance permits us to view $\vee$ as a polyadic connective. (The same holds for $\wedge$.)

A *literal* is a formula of the form p or $\neg p$ (or *true* or *false*) for some propositional variable p. A propositional formula is in *conjunctive normal form* (CNF) if it has the form $\psi_1 \wedge \cdots \wedge \psi_n$, where each formula ψ_i is a disjunction of literals. *Disjunctive normal form* (DNF) is defined analogously. It is known that if φ is a propositional formula, then there is some formula ψ equivalent to φ that is in CNF (respectively DNF). Note that if φ is in CNF (or DNF), then a shortest equivalent formula ψ in DNF (respectively CNF) may have a length exponential in the length of φ.

First-Order Logic

We now turn to *first-order predicate calculus*. We indicate the main intuitions and concepts underlying first-order logic and describe the primary specializations typically made for database theory. Precise definitions of needed portions of first-order logic are included in Chapters 4 and 5.

First-order logic generalizes propositional logic in several ways. Intuitively, propositional variables are replaced by predicate symbols that range over n-ary relations over an underlying set. Variables are used in first-order logic to range over elements of an abstract set, called the *universe of discourse*. This is realized using the quantifiers $\exists$ and $\forall$. In addition, function symbols are incorporated into the model. The most important definitions used to formalize first-order logic are first-order language, interpretation, logical implication, and provability.

Each first-order language L includes a set of variables, the propositional connectives, the quantifiers $\exists$ and $\forall$, and punctuation symbols ")", "(", and ";". The variation in first-order languages stems from the symbols they include to represent constants, predicates, and functions. More formally, a first-order language includes

    (a) a (possibly empty) set of *constant* symbols;

    (b) for each $n \geq 0$ a (possibly empty) set of *n-ary predicate symbols*;

    (c) for each $n \geq 1$ a (possibly empty) set of *n-ary function symbols*.

In some cases, we also include

    (d) the equality symbol $\approx$, which serves as a binary predicate symbol,

and the propositional constants *true* and *false*. It is common to focus on languages that are finite, except for the set of variables.

A familiar first-order language is the language L_N of the nonnegative integers, with

    (a) constant symbol $\mathbf{0}$;

    (b) binary predicate symbol $\leq$;

    (c) binary function symbols $+$, $\times$, and unary $\mathbf{S}$ (successor);

and the equality symbol.

Let L be a first-order language. *Terms* of L are built in the natural fashion from constants, variables, and the function symbols. An *atom* is either *true*, *false*, or an expression of the form $R(t_1, \ldots, t_n)$, where R is an n-ary predicate symbol and $t_1, \ldots, t_n$ are terms. Atoms correspond to the propositional variables of propositional logic. If the equality symbol is included, then atoms include expressions of the form $t_1 \approx t_2$. The family of (*well-formed predicate calculus*) *formulas* over L is defined recursively starting with atoms, using the Boolean connectives, and using the quantifiers as follows: If φ is a formula and x a variable, then $(\exists x \varphi)$ and $(\forall x \varphi)$ are formulas. As with the propositional case, parentheses are omitted when understood from the context. In addition, $\vee$ and $\wedge$ are viewed as polyadic connectives. A term or formula is *ground* if it involves no variables.

Some examples of formulas in L_N are as follows:

$$\forall x (\mathbf{0} \leq x), \quad \neg (x \approx \mathbf{S}(x)),$$
$$\neg \exists x (\forall y (y \leq x)), \quad \forall y \forall z (x \approx y \times z \rightarrow (y \approx \mathbf{S}(\mathbf{0}) \lor z \approx \mathbf{S}(\mathbf{0}))).$$

(For some binary predicates and functions, we use infix notation.)

The notion of the scope of quantifiers and of *free* and *bound* occurrences of variables in formulas is now defined using recursion on the structure. Each variable occurrence in an atom is free. If φ is $(\psi_1 \lor \psi_2)$, then an occurrence of variable x in φ is free if it is free as an occurrence of ψ_1 or ψ_2; and this is extended to the other propositional connectives. If φ is $\exists y \psi$, then an occurrence of variable $x \neq y$ is free in φ if the corresponding occurrence is free in ψ. Each occurrence of y is bound in φ. In addition, each occurrence of y in φ that is free in ψ is said to be in the *scope* of $\exists y$ at the beginning of φ. A *sentence* is a well-formed formula that has no free variable occurrences.

Until now we have not given a meaning to the symbols of a first-order language and thereby to first-order formulas. This is accomplished with the notion of *interpretation*, which corresponds to the truth assignments of the propositional case. Each interpretation is just one of the many possible ways to give meaning to a language.

An *interpretation* of a first-order language L is a 4-tuple $\mathcal{I} = (U, \mathcal{C}, \mathcal{P}, \mathcal{F})$ where U is a nonempty set of abstract elements called the *universe* (*of discourse*), and $\mathcal{C}, \mathcal{P}$, and $\mathcal{F}$ give meanings to the sets of constant symbols, predicate symbols, and function symbols. For example, $\mathcal{C}$ is a function from the constant symbols into U, and $\mathcal{P}$ maps each n-ary predicate symbol p into an n-ary relation over U (i.e., a subset of U^n). It is possible for two distinct constant symbols to map to the same element of U.

When the *equality symbol* denoted $\approx$ is included, the meaning associated with it is restricted so that it enjoys properties usually associated with equality. Two equivalent mechanisms for accomplishing this are described next.

Let $\mathcal{I}$ be an interpretation for language L. As a notational shorthand, if c is a constant symbol in L, we use $c^{\mathcal{I}}$ to denote the element of the universe associated with c by $\mathcal{I}$. This is extended in the natural way to ground terms and atoms.

The usual interpretation for the language $L_{\mathbf{N}}$ is $\mathcal{I}_{\mathbf{N}}$, where the universe is $\mathbf{N}$; $\mathbf{0}$ is mapped to the number 0; $\leq$ is mapped to the usual less than or equal relation; $\mathbf{S}$ is mapped to successor; and $+$ and $\times$ are mapped to addition and multiplication. In such cases, we have, for example, $[\mathbf{S}(\mathbf{S}(\mathbf{0}) + \mathbf{0}))]^{\mathcal{I}_{\mathbf{N}}} \approx 2$.

As a second example related to logic programming, we mention the family of *Herbrand interpretations* of $L_{\mathbf{N}}$. Each of these shares the same universe and the same mappings for the constant and function symbols. An assignment of a universe, and for the constant and function symbols, is called a *preinterpretation*. In the Herbrand preinterpretation for $L_{\mathbf{N}}$, the universe, denoted $U_{L_{\mathbf{N}}}$, is the set containing $\mathbf{0}$ and all terms that can be constructed from this using the function symbols of the language. This is a little confusing because the terms now play a dual role—as terms constructed from components of the language L, and as elements of the universe $U_{L_{\mathbf{N}}}$. The mapping $\mathcal{C}$ maps the constant symbol $\mathbf{0}$ to $\mathbf{0}$ (considered as an element of $U_{L_{\mathbf{N}}}$). Given a term t in U, the function $\mathcal{F}(\mathbf{S})$ maps t to the term $\mathbf{S}(t)$. Given terms t_1 and t_2, the function $\mathcal{F}(+)$ maps the pair (t_1, t_2) to the term $+(t_1, t_2)$, and the function $\mathcal{F}(\times)$ is defined analogously.

The set of ground atoms of $L_{\mathbf{N}}$ (i.e., the set of atoms that do not contain variables) is sometimes called the *Herbrand base* of $L_{\mathbf{N}}$. There is a natural one-one correspondence between interpretations of L_N that extend the Herbrand preinterpretation and subsets of the Herbrand base of L_N. One Herbrand interpretation of particular interest is the one that mimics the usual interpretation. In particular, this interpretation maps $\leq$ to the set $\{(t_1, t_2) \mid (t_1^{\mathcal{I}_N}, t_2^{\mathcal{I}_N}) \in \leq^{\mathcal{I}_N}\}$.

We now turn to the notion of satisfaction of a formula by an interpretation. The definition is recursive on the structure of formulas; as a result we need the notion of variable assignment to accommodate variables occurring free in formulas. Let L be a language and $\mathcal{I}$ an interpretation of L with universe U. A *variable assignment* for formula φ is a partial function μ : variables of $L \to U$ whose domain includes all variables free in φ. For terms t, $t^{\mathcal{I},\mu}$ denotes the meaning given to t by $\mathcal{I}$, using μ to interpret the free variables. In addition, if μ is a variable assignment, x is a variable, and $u \in U$, then $\mu[x/u]$ denotes the variable assignment that is identical to μ, except that it maps x to u. We write $I \models \varphi[\mu]$ to indicate that $\mathcal{I}$ *satisfies* φ under μ. This is defined recursively on the structure of formulas in the natural fashion. To indicate the flavor of the definition, we note that $\mathcal{I} \models p(t_1, \ldots, t_n)[\mu]$ if $(t_1^{\mathcal{I},\mu}, \ldots, t_n^{\mathcal{I},\mu}) \in p^{\mathcal{I}}$; $\mathcal{I} \models \exists x \psi[\mu]$ if there is some $u \in U$ such that $\mathcal{I} \models \psi[\mu[x/u]]$; and $\mathcal{I} \models \forall x \psi[\mu]$ if for each $u \in U$, $I \models \psi[\mu[x/u]]$. The Boolean connectives are interpreted in the usual manner. If φ is a sentence, then no variable assignment needs to be specified.

For example, $\mathcal{I}_N \models \forall x \exists y (\neg(x \approx y) \lor x \leq y)$; $\mathcal{I}_N \not\models S(0) \leq 0$; and

$$\mathcal{I}_N \models \forall y \forall z (x \approx y \times z \to (y \approx S(0) \lor z \approx S(0)))[\mu]$$

iff $\mu(x)$ is 1 or a prime number.

An interpretation $\mathcal{I}$ is a *model* of a set Φ of sentences if $\mathcal{I}$ satisfies each formula in Φ. The set Φ is *satisfiable* if it has a model.

Logical implication and equivalence are now defined analogously to the propositional case. Sentence φ logically implies sentence ψ, denoted $\varphi \models \psi$, if each interpretation that satisfies φ also satisfies ψ. There are many straightforward equivalences [e.g., $\neg(\neg\varphi) \equiv \varphi$ and $\neg\forall x \varphi \equiv \exists x \neg\varphi$]. Logical implication is generalized to sets of sentences in the natural manner.

It is known that logical implication, considered as a decision problem, is not recursive. One of the fundamental results of mathematical logic is the development of effective procedures for determining logical equivalence. These are based on the notion of *proofs*, and they provide one way to show that logical implication is r.e. One style of proof, attributed to Hilbert, identifies a family of *inference rules* and a family of *axioms*. An example of an inference rule is *modus ponens*, which states that from formulas φ and $\varphi \to \psi$ we may conclude ψ. Examples of axioms are all *tautologies* of propositional logic [e.g., $\neg(\varphi \lor \psi) \leftrightarrow (\neg\varphi \land \neg\psi)$ for all formulas φ and ψ], and *substitution* (i.e., $\forall x \varphi \to \varphi_t^x$, where t is an arbitrary term and φ_t^x denotes the formula obtained by simultaneously replacing all occurrences of x free in φ by t). Given a family of inference rules and axioms, a *proof* that set Φ of sentences implies sentence φ is a finite sequence $\psi_0, \psi_1, \ldots, \psi_n = \varphi$, where for each i, either ψ_i is an axiom, or a member of Φ, or it follows from one or more of the previous ψ_j's using an inference rule. In this case we write $\Phi \vdash \varphi$.

The soundness and completeness theorem of Gödel shows that (using *modus ponens* and a specific set of axioms) $\Phi \models \varphi$ iff $\Phi \vdash \varphi$. This important link between $\models$ and $\vdash$ permits the transfer of results obtained in model theory, which focuses primarily on interpretations and models, and proof theory, which focuses primarily on proofs. Notably, a central issue in the study of relational database dependencies (see Part C) has been the search for sound and complete proof systems for subsets of first-order logic that correspond to natural families of constraints.

The model-theoretic and proof-theoretic perspectives lead to two equivalent ways of incorporating equality into first-order languages. Under the model-theoretic approach, the equality predicate $\approx$ is given the meaning $\{(u, u) \mid u \in U\}$ (i.e., normal equality). Under the proof-theoretic approach, a set of *equality axioms* EQ_L is constructed that express the intended meaning of $\approx$. For example, EQ_L includes the sentences $\forall x, y, z(x \approx y \wedge y \approx z \rightarrow x \approx z)$ and $\forall x, y(x \approx y \rightarrow (R(x) \leftrightarrow R(y)))$ for each unary predicate symbol R.

Another important result from mathematical logic is the compactness theorem, which can be demonstrated using Gödel's soundness and completeness result. There are two common ways of stating this. The first is that given a (possibly infinite) set of sentences Φ, if $\Phi \models \varphi$ then there is a finite $\Phi' \subseteq \Phi$ such that $\Phi' \models \varphi$. The second is that if each finite subset of Φ is satisfiable, then Φ is satisfiable.

Note that although the compactness theorem guarantees that the Φ in the preceding paragraph has a model, that model is not necessarily finite. Indeed, Φ may only have infinite models. It is of some solace that, among those infinite models, there is surely at least one that is countable (i.e., whose elements can be enumerated: $a_1, a_2, \ldots$). This technically useful result is the Löwenheim-Skolem theorem.

To illustrate the compactness theorem, we show that there is no set Ψ of sentences defining the notion of connectedness in directed graphs. For this we use the language L with two constant symbols, a and b, and one binary relation symbol R, which corresponds to the edges of a directed graph. In addition, because we are working with general first-order logic, both finite and infinite graphs may arise. Suppose now that Ψ is a set of sentences that states that a and b are connected (i.e., that there is a directed path from a to b in R). Let $\Sigma = \{\sigma_i \mid i > 0\}$, where σ_i states "a and b are at least i edges apart from each other." For example, σ_3 might be expressed as

$$\neg R(a, b) \wedge \neg \exists x_1 (R(a, x_1) \wedge R(x_1, b)).$$

It is clear that each finite subset of $\Psi \cup \Sigma$ is satisfiable. By the compactness theorem (second statement), this implies that $\Psi \cup \Sigma$ is satisfiable, so it has a model (say, $\mathcal{I}$). In $\mathcal{I}$, there is no directed path between (the elements of the universe identified by) a and b, and so $\mathcal{I} \not\models \Psi$. This is a contradiction.

Specializations to Database Theory

We close by mentioning the primary differences between the general field of mathematical logic and the specializations made in the study of database theory. The most obvious specialization is that database theory has not generally focused on the use of functions on data values, and as a result it generally omits function symbols from the first-order languages used. The two other fundamental specializations are the focus on finite models and the special use of constant symbols.

An interpretation is *finite* if its universe of discourse is finite. Because most databases are finite, most of database theory is focused exclusively on finite interpretations. This is closely related to the field of finite model theory in mathematics.

The notion of logical implication for finite interpretations, usually denoted $\models_{fin}$, is not equivalent to the usual logical implication $\models$. This is most easily seen by considering the compactness theorem. Let $\Phi = \{\sigma_i \mid i > 0\}$, where σ_i states that there are at least i distinct elements in the universe of discourse. Then by compactness, $\Phi \not\models false$, but by the definition of finite interpretation, $\Phi \models_{fin} false$.

Another way to show that $\models$ and $\models_{fin}$ are distinct uses computability theory. It is known that $\models$ is r.e. but not recursive, and it is easily seen that $\models_{fin}$ is co-r.e. Thus if they were equal, $\models$ would be recursive, a contradiction.

The final specialization of database theory concerns assumptions made about the universe of discourse and the use of constant symbols. Indeed, throughout most of this book we use a fixed, countably infinite set of constants, denoted **dom** (for domain elements). Furthermore, the focus is almost exclusively on finite Herbrand interpretations over **dom**. In particular, for distinct constants c and c', all interpretations that are considered satisfy $\neg c \approx c'$.

Most proofs in database theory involving the first-order predicate calculus are based on model theory, primarily because of the emphasis on finite models and because the link between $\models_{fin}$ and $\vdash$ does not hold. It is thus informative to identify a mechanism for using traditional proof-theoretic techniques within the context of database theory. For this discussion, consider a first-order language with set **dom** of constant symbols and predicate symbols $R_1, \ldots, R_n$. As will be seen in Chapter 3, a database *instance* is a finite Herbrand interpretation **I** of this language. Following [Rei84], a family $\Sigma_{\mathbf{I}}$ of sentences is associated with **I**. This family includes the axioms of equality (mentioned earlier) and

Atoms: $R_i(\vec{a})$ for each $\vec{a}$ in $R_i^{\mathbf{I}}$.

Extension axioms: $\forall \vec{x}(R_i(\vec{x}) \leftrightarrow (\vec{x} \approx \vec{a}_1 \vee \cdots \vee \vec{x} \approx \vec{a}_m))$, where $\vec{a}_1, \ldots, \vec{a}_m$ is a listing of all elements of $R_i^{\mathbf{I}}$, and we are abusing notation by letting $\approx$ range over vectors of terms.

Unique Name axioms: $\neg c \approx c'$ for each distinct pair c, c' of constants occurring in **I**.

Domain Closure axiom: $\forall x(x \approx c_1 \vee \cdots \vee x \approx c_n)$, where $c_1, \ldots, c_n$ is a listing of all constants occurring in **I**.

A set of sentences obtained in this manner is termed an *extended relational theory*.

The first two sets of sentences of an extended relational theory express the specific contents of the relations (predicate symbols) of **I**. Importantly, the Extension sentences ensure that for any (not necessarily Herbrand) interpretation $\mathcal{J}$ satisfying $\Sigma_{\mathbf{I}}$, an n-tuple is in $R_i^{\mathcal{J}}$ iff it equals one of the n-tuples in $R_i^{\mathbf{I}}$. The Unique Name axiom ensures that no pair of distinct constants is mapped to the same element in the universe of $\mathcal{J}$, and the Domain Closure axiom ensures that each element of the universe of $\mathcal{J}$ equals some constant occurring in **I**. For all intents and purposes, then, any interpretation $\mathcal{J}$ that models $\Sigma_{\mathbf{I}}$ is isomorphic to **I**, modulo condensing under equivalence classes induced by $\approx^{\mathcal{J}}$. Importantly, the following link with conventional logical implication now holds: For any set Γ of sentences, $\mathbf{I} \models \Gamma$ iff $\Sigma_{\mathbf{I}} \cup \Gamma$ is satisfiable. The perspective obtained through this connection with classical logic is useful when attempting to extend the conventional relational model (e.g., to incorporate so-called incomplete information, as discussed in Chapter 19).

The Extension axioms correspond to the intuition that a tuple $\vec{a}$ is in relation R only if it is explicitly included in R by the database instance. A more general formulation of this intuition is given by the *closed world assumption* (CWA) [Rei78]. In its most general formulation, the CWA is an inference rule that is used in proof-theoretic contexts. Given a set Σ of sentences describing a (possibly nonconventional) database instance, the CWA states that one can infer a negated atom $R(\vec{a})$ if $\Sigma \nvdash R(\vec{a})$ [i.e., if one cannot prove $R(\vec{a})$ from Σ using conventional first-order logic]. In the case where Σ is an extended relational theory this gives no added information, but in other contexts (such as deductive databases) it does. The CWA is related in spirit to the *negation as failure* rule of [Cla78].

3 The Relational Model

Alice:	*What is a relation?*
Vittorio:	*You studied that in math a long time ago.*
Sergio:	*It is just a table.*
Riccardo:	*But we have several ways of viewing it.*

A *database model* provides the means for specifying particular data structures, for constraining the data sets associated with these structures, and for manipulating the data. The specification of structure and constraints is done using a *data definition language* (DDL), and the specification of manipulation is done using a *data manipulation language* (DML). The most prominent structures that have been used for databases to date are graphs in the network, semantic, and object-oriented models; trees in the hierarchical model; and relations in the relational model.

DMLs provide two fundamental capabilities: *querying* to support the extraction of data from the current database; and *updating* to support the modification of the database state. There is a rich theory on the topic of querying relational databases that includes several languages based on widely different paradigms. This theory is the focus of Parts B, D, and E, and portions of Part F of this book. The theory of database updates has received considerably less attention and is touched on in Part F.

The term *relational model* is actually rather vague. As introduced in Codd's seminal article, this term refers to a specific data model with relations as data structures, an algebra for specifying queries, and no mechanisms for expressing updates or constraints. Subsequent articles by Codd introduced a second query language based on the predicate calculus of first-order logic, showed this to be equivalent to the algebra, and introduced the first integrity constraints for the relational model—namely, functional dependencies. Soon thereafter, researchers in database systems implemented languages based on the algebra and calculus, extended to include update operators and to include practically motivated features such as arithmetic operators, aggregate operators, and sorting capabilities. Researchers in database theory developed a number of variations on the algebra and calculus with varying expressive power and adapted the paradigm of logic programming to provide a third approach to querying relational databases. The story of integrity constraints for the relational model is similar: A rich theory of constraints has emerged, and two distinct but equivalent perspectives have been developed that encompass almost all of the constraints that have been investigated formally. The term *relational model* has thus come to refer to the broad class of database models that have relations as the data structure and that incorporate some or all of the query capabilities, update capabilities, and integrity constraints mentioned earlier. In this book we are concerned primarily with the relational model in this broad sense.

Relations are simple data structures. As a result, it is easy to understand the conceptual underpinnings of the relational model, thus making relational databases accessible to a broad audience of end users. A second advantage of this simplicity is that clean yet powerful declarative languages can be used to manipulate relations. By *declarative*, we mean that a query/program is specified in a high-level manner and that an efficient execution of the program does not have to follow exactly its specification. Thus the important practical issues of compilation and optimization of queries had to be overcome to make relational databases a reality.

Because of its simplicity, the relational model has provided an excellent framework for the first generation of theoretical research into the properties of databases. Fundamental aspects of data manipulation and integrity constraints have been exposed and studied in a context in which the peculiarities of the data model itself have relatively little impact. This research provides a strong foundation for the study of other database models, first because many theoretical issues pertinent to other models can be addressed effectively within the relational model, and second because it provides a variety of tools, techniques, and research directions that can be used to understand the other models more deeply.

In this short chapter, we present formal definitions for the data structure of the relational model. Theoretical research on the model has grown out of three different perspectives, one corresponding most closely to the natural usage of relations in databases, another stemming from mathematical logic, and the third stemming from logic programming. Because each of these provides important intuitive and notational benefits, we introduce notation that encompasses the different but equivalent formulations reflecting each of them.

3.1 The Structure of the Relational Model

An example of a relational database is shown in Fig. 3.1[1]. Intuitively, the data is represented in tables in which each row gives data about a specific object or set of objects, and rows with uniform structure and intended meaning are grouped into tables. Updates consist of transformations of the tables by addition, removal, or modification of rows. Queries allow the extraction of information from the tables. A fundamental feature of virtually all relational query languages is that the result of a query is also a table or collection of tables.

We introduce now some informal terminology to provide the intuition behind the formal definitions that follow. Each table is called a relation and it has a name (e.g., *Movies*). The columns also have names, called attributes (e.g, *Title*). Each line in a table is a tuple (or record). The entries of tuples are taken from sets of constants, called domains, that include, for example, the sets of integers, strings, and Boolean values. Finally we distinguish between the database schema, which specifies the structure of the database; and the database instance, which specifies its actual content. This is analogous to the standard distinction between type and value found in programming languages (e.g., an

---

[1] *Pariscope* is a weekly publication that lists the cultural events occurring in Paris and environs.

Movies	Title	Director	Actor
	The Trouble with Harry	Hitchcock	Gwenn
	The Trouble with Harry	Hitchcock	Forsythe
	The Trouble with Harry	Hitchcock	MacLaine
	The Trouble with Harry	Hitchcock	Hitchcock
	...	...	...
	Cries and Whispers	Bergman	Andersson
	Cries and Whispers	Bergman	Sylwan
	Cries and Whispers	Bergman	Thulin
	Cries and Whispers	Bergman	Ullman

Location	Theater	Address	Phone Number
	Gaumont Opéra	31 bd. des Italiens	47 42 60 33
	Saint André des Arts	30 rue Saint André des Arts	43 26 48 18
	Le Champo	51 rue des Ecoles	43 54 51 60
	...	...	...
	Georges V	144 av. des Champs-Elysées	45 62 41 46
	Les 7 Montparnassiens	98 bd. du Montparnasse	43 20 32 20

Pariscope	Theater	Title	Schedule
	Gaumont Opéra	Cries and Whispers	20:30
	Saint André des Arts	The Trouble with Harry	20:15
	Georges V	Cries and Whispers	22:15
	...	...	...
	Les 7 Montparnassiens	Cries and Whispers	20:45

Figure 3.1:   The **CINEMA** database

identifier X might have type *record A : int, B : bool endrecord* and value *record A : 5, B : true endrecord*).

We now embark on the formal definitions. We assume that a countably infinite set **att** of *attributes* is fixed. For a technical reason that shall become apparent shortly, we assume that there is a total order $\leq_{att}$ on **att**. When a set U of attributes is listed, it is assumed that the elements of U are written according to $\leq_{att}$ unless otherwise specified.

For most of the theoretical development, it suffices to use the same domain of values for all of the attributes. Thus we now fix a countably infinite set **dom** (disjoint from **att**), called the underlying *domain*. A *constant* is an element of **dom**. When different attributes should have distinct domains, we assume a mapping *Dom* on **att**, where *Dom*(A) is a set called the domain of A.

We assume a countably infinite set **relname** of relation names disjoint from the previous sets. In practice, the structure of a table is given by a relation name and a set of attributes. To simplify the notation in the theoretical treatment, we now associate a *sort* (i.e., finite set of attributes) to each relation name. (An analogous approach is usually taken in logic.) In particular, we assume that there is a function *sort* from **relname** to $\mathcal{P}^{\text{fin}}(\textbf{att})$ (the *finitary powerset* of **att**; i.e., the family of finite subsets of **att**). It is assumed that *sort* has the property that for each (possibly empty) finite set U of attributes, $sort^{-1}(U)$ is infinite. This allows us to use as many relation names of a given sort as desired. The *sort* of a relation name is simply $sort(R)$. The *arity* of a relation name R is $arity(R) = |sort(R)|$.

A *relation schema* is now simply a relation name R. We sometimes write this as $R[U]$ to indicate that $sort(R) = U$, or $R[n]$, to indicate that $arity(R) = n$. A *database schema* is a nonempty finite set **R** of relation names. This might be written $\textbf{R} = \{R_1[U_1], \ldots, R_n[U_n]\}$ to indicate the relation schemas in **R**.

For example, the database schema **CINEMA** for the database shown in Fig. 3.1 is defined by

$$\textbf{CINEMA} = \{Movies, \ Location, \ Pariscope\}$$

where relation names *Movies*, *Location*, and *Pariscope* have the following sorts:

$$
\begin{aligned}
sort(Movies) &= \{Title, \ Director, \ Actor\} \\
sort(Location) &= \{Theater, \ Address, \ Phone \ Number\} \\
sort(Pariscope) &= \{Theater, \ Title, \ Schedule\}.
\end{aligned}
$$

We often omit commas and set brackets in sets of attributes. For example, we may write

$$sort(Pariscope) = Theater \ Title \ Schedule.$$

The formalism that has emerged for the relational model is somewhat eclectic, because it is intimately connected with several other areas that have their own terminology, such as logic and logic programming. Because the slightly different formalisms are well entrenched, we do not attempt to replace them with a single, unified notation. Instead we will allow the coexistence of the different notations; the reader should have no difficulty dealing with the minor variations.

Thus there will be two forks in the road that lead to different but largely equivalent formulations of the relational model. The first fork in the road to defining the relational model is of a philosophical nature. Are the attribute names associated with different relation columns important?

3.2 Named versus Unnamed Perspectives

Under the *named* perspective, these attributes are viewed as an explicit part of a database schema and may be used (e.g., by query languages and dependencies). Under the *unnamed* perspective, the specific attributes in the sort of a relation name are ignored, and only the arity of a relation schema is available (e.g., to query languages).

In the named perspective, it is natural to view tuples as functions. More precisely, a *tuple* over a (possibly empty) finite set U of attributes (or over a relation schema $R[U]$) is a total mapping u from U to **dom**. In this case, the *sort* of u is U, and it has *arity* $|U|$. Tuples may be written in a linear syntax using angle brackets—for example, $\langle A : 5, \ B : 3 \rangle$. (In general, the order used in the linear syntax will correspond to $\leq_{\text{att}}$, although that is not necessary.) The unique tuple over $\emptyset$ is denoted $\langle \rangle$.

Suppose that u is a tuple over U. As usual in mathematics, the value of u on an attribute A in U is denoted $u(A)$. This is extended so that for $V \subseteq U$, $u[V]$ denotes the tuple v over V such that $v(A) = u(A)$ for each $A \in V$ (i.e., $u[V] = u|_V$, the restriction of the function u to V).

With the unnamed perspective, it is more natural to view a tuple as an element of a Cartesian product. More precisely, a *tuple* is an ordered n-tuple ($n \geq 0$) of constants (i.e., an element of the Cartesian product $\mathbf{dom}^n$). The arity of a tuple is the number of coordinates that it has. Tuples in this context are also written with angle brackets (e.g., $\langle 5, \ 3 \rangle$). The ith coordinate of a tuple u is denoted $u(i)$. If relation name R has arity n, then a *tuple* over R is a tuple with arity $arity(R)$.

Because of the total order $\leq_{\text{att}}$, there is a natural correspondence between the named and unnamed perspectives. A tuple $\langle A_1 : a_1, A_2 : a_2 \rangle$ (defined as a function) can be viewed (assuming $A_1 \leq_{\text{att}} A_2$) as an ordered tuple with $(A_1 : a_1)$ as a first component and $(A_2 : a_2)$ as a second one. Ignoring the names, this tuple may simply be viewed as the ordered tuple $\langle a_1, a_2 \rangle$. Conversely, the ordered tuple $t = \langle a_1, a_2 \rangle$ may be interpreted as a function over the set $\{1, 2\}$ of integers with $t(i) = a_i$ for each i. This correspondence will allow us to blur the distinction between the two perspectives and move freely from one to the other when convenient.

3.3   Conventional versus Logic Programming Perspectives

We now come to the second fork in the road to defining the relational model. This fork concerns how relation and database instances are viewed, and it is essentially independent of the perspective taken on tuples. Under the *conventional* perspective, a *relation* or *relation instance* of (or over) a relation schema $R[U]$ (or over a finite set U of attributes) is a (possibly empty) finite set I of tuples with sort U. In this case, I has *sort* U and *arity* $|U|$. Note that there are two instances over the empty set of attributes: $\{\}$ and $\{\langle \rangle\}$.

Continuing with the conventional perspective, a *database instance* of database schema $\mathbf{R}$ is a mapping $\mathbf{I}$ with domain $\mathbf{R}$, such that $\mathbf{I}(R)$ is a relation over R for each $R \in \mathbf{R}$.

The other perspective for defining instances stems from logic programming. This perspective is used primarily with the ordered-tuple perspective on tuples, and so we focus on that here. Let R be a relation with arity n. A *fact* over R is an expression of the form $R(a_1, \ldots, a_n)$, where $a_i \in \mathbf{dom}$ for $i \in [1, n]$. If $u = \langle a_1, \ldots, a_n \rangle$, we sometimes write $R(u)$ for $R(a_1, \ldots, a_n)$. Under the *logic-programming* perspective, a *relation (instance)* over R is a finite set of facts over R. For a database schema $\mathbf{R}$, a *database instance* is a finite set $\mathbf{I}$ that is the union of relation instances over R, for $R \in \mathbf{R}$. This perspective on instances is convenient when working with languages stemming from logic programming, and it permits us to write database instances in a convenient linear form.

The two perspectives provide alternative ways of describing essentially the same data. For instance, assuming that $sort(R) = AB$ and $sort(S) = A$, we have the following four representations of the same database:

Named and Conventional
$I(R) = \{f_1, f_2, f_3\}$

$$
\begin{array}{ll}
f_1(A) = a & f_1(B) = b \\
f_2(A) = c & f_2(B) = b \\
f_3(A) = a & f_3(A) = a
\end{array}
$$

$I(S) = \{g\}$

$$g(A) = d$$

Unnamed and Conventional
$I(R) = \{\langle a, b \rangle, \langle c, b \rangle, \langle a, a \rangle\}$
$I(S) = \{\langle d \rangle\}$

Named and Logic Programming
$\{R(A:a, B:b), \ R(A:c, B:b), \ R(A:a, B:a), \ S(A:d)\}$

Unnamed and Logic Programming
$\{R(a,b), \ R(c,b), \ R(a,a), \ S(d)\}.$

Because relations can be viewed as sets, it is natural to consider, given relations of the same sort, the standard set operations *union* ($\cup$), *intersection* ($\cap$), and *difference* ($-$) and the standard set comparators $\subset$, $\subseteq$, $=$, and $\neq$. With the logic-programming perspective on instances, we may also use these operations and comparators on database instances.

Essentially all topics in the theory of relational database can be studied using a fixed choice for the two forks. However, there are some cases in which one perspective is much more natural than the other or is technically much more convenient. For example, in a context in which there is more than one relation, the named perspective permits easy and natural specification of correspondences between columns of different relations whereas the unnamed perspective does not. As will be seen in Chapter 4, this leads to different but equivalent sets of natural primitive algebra operators for the two perspectives. A related example concerns those topics that involve the association of distinct domains to different relation columns; again the named perspective is more convenient. In addition, although relational dependency theory can be developed for the unnamed perspective, the motivation is much more natural when presented in the named perspective. Thus during the course of this book the choice of perspective during a particular discussion will be motivated primarily by the intuitive or technical convenience offered by one or the other.

In this book, we will need an infinite set **var** of *variables* that will be used to range over elements of **dom**. We generalize the notion of tuple to permit variables in coordinate positions: a *free tuple* over U or $R[U]$ is (under the named perspective) a function u from U to **var** $\cup$ **dom**. An *atom* over R is an expression $R(e_1, \ldots, e_n)$, where $n = arity(R)$ and

e_i is *term* (i.e., $e_i \in$ **var** $\cup$ **dom** for each $i \in [1, n]$). Following the terminology of logic and logic programming, we sometimes refer to a fact as a *ground* atom.

3.4   Notation

We generally use the following symbols, possibly with subscripts:

Constants	a, b, c
Variables	x, y
Sets of variables	X, Y
Terms	e
Attributes	A, B, C
Sets of attributes	U, V, W
Relation names (schemas)	$R, S; R[U], S[V]$
Database schemas	**R, S**
Tuples	t, s
Free tuples	u, v, w
Facts	$R(a_1, \ldots, a_n), R(t)$
Atoms	$R(e_1, \ldots, e_n), R(u)$
Relation instances	I, J
Database instances	**I, J**

Bibliographic Notes

The relational model is founded on mathematical logic (in particular, predicate calculus). It is one of the rare cases in which substantial theoretical development preceded the implementation of systems. The first proposal to use predicate calculus as a query language can be traced back to Kuhns [Kuh67]. The relational model itself was introduced by Codd [Cod70]. There are numerous commercial database systems based on the relational model. They include IBM's DBZ, [A+76], INGRES [SWKH76], and ORACLE [Ora89], Informix, and Sybase.

Other data models have been proposed and implemented besides the relational model. The most prominent ones preceding the relational model are the hierarchical and network models. These and other models are described in the books [Nij76, TL82]. More recently, various models extending the relational model have been proposed. They include semantic models (see the survey [HK87]) and object-oriented models (see the position paper [ABD+89]). In this book we focus primarily on the relational model in a broad sense. Some formal aspects of other models are considered in Part F.

B Basics: Relational Query Languages

The area of query languages, and more generally providing access to stored data, is one of the most important topics in databases and one of the most deeply studied ones in database theory. This part introduces three paradigms that have been developed for querying relational databases. Each yields a family of query languages, and there are close connections among the different families.

The first paradigm provides simple algebraic operations for manipulating relations to construct answers to queries. This yields a language called relational *algebra*. It uses three operators tailored specially for the relational model, in addition to the natural set operators. The second paradigm is logic based. It is a variant of the predicate calculus of first-order logic, called relational *calculus*, and has expressive power equivalent to the algebra. The third paradigm stems from logic programming. Its most prominent representative in databases is *datalog*, which can be viewed as logic programming without function symbols.

The three paradigms yield languages that enjoy fundamental properties that have become standard for virtually all database access languages. First, they are *set-at-a-time*, in the sense that they focus on identifying and uniformly manipulating sets of tuples rather than identifying tuples individually and using loops to manipulate groups of tuples. Second, they are *associative* in that tuples are identified through a specification of their properties rather than by chasing pointers. And third, they are abstract, high-level languages that are separated from the physical storage of the data and from the specific algorithms that are used to implement them.

The relational algebra is conceptually a "procedural" language because queries are specified by a sequence of operations that constructs the answer. The relational calculus and datalog are conceptually "declarative" because the tuples in the answer are specified by properties they satisfy, with no reference to an algorithm for producing them. However, in modern database implementations the optimized translation of queries from any of the three languages may have little resemblance to the original; in this sense all three are essentially declarative.

In this part and Part D we introduce a variety of query languages based on the three paradigms. This is done in a natural progression, starting with simple, commonly asked queries and building up to very powerful ones. At each stage, we provide equivalent languages in the three paradigms. In this part we focus on the simplest queries and incorporate negation into them. In Part D we incorporate recursion into the languages.

The simplest queries are based on extracting certain values as soon as a simple pattern of tuples is found in the database. These are discussed in Chapter 4. In terms of the calculus, the corresponding language is based on conjunction and existential quantification; hence the term *conjunctive queries.* Although these queries are simple, they constitute the vast majority of relational database queries arising in practice. In addition, conjunctive queries have many pleasing theoretical properties. For instance, there is an elegant characterization of two conjunctive queries being equivalent (discussed in Chapter 6). Chapter 4 also considers the inclusion of a union (or disjunction) capability into these languages, yielding the *conjunctive queries with union.*

In Chapter 5, the conjunctive queries (with union) are extended with *negation.* Adding negation (or set difference, in the algebraic paradigm) yields the full relational calculus and relational algebra. The calculus and algebra turn out to be equivalent; this is one of the earliest significant results in database theory. An equivalent language is also obtained from the datalog version of the conjunctive queries. In general, the positive results for conjunctive queries fail with the relational calculus. In Chapter 5 we also touch on the subject of infinite databases with finite representation and, in particular, the emerging area of "constraint databases."

Chapter 6 considers the conjunctive queries and the relational calculus from the perspective of static analysis (in the sense of programming languages). An elegant theorem shows that properties such as containment and equivalence are decidable for the conjunctive queries. Interestingly, these properties are undecidable for relational calculus. Query optimization is also considered in Chapter 6. The focus is on conjunctive queries (most practical and early theoretical work on optimization has been focused on these as well). Three topics in optimization are considered. First, some of the fundamental approaches taken by practical optimizers are considered. Second, the theory for testing equivalence of conjunctive queries is extended to develop a technique for minimizing the number of joins needed to compute a conjunctive query. Third, a family of interesting results concerning a natural subclass of conjunctive queries is presented based on a theory of "acyclic hypergraphs." (More recent work on optimizing recursive datalog queries is presented in Chapter 13.)

This concludes the presentation of the basic theory of the simple query languages. The theory of query languages is again taken up in Part D, which considers languages with recursion and resumes the parallel development along the three paradigms. Expressiveness and complexity of query languages are discussed in Part E.

Some connections between the abstract languages described in Chapters 4 and 5 and practical languages are considered in Chapter 7. We focus largely on SQL, which has become the industry standard for relational database access, and we briefly describe two visual languages, QBE and Access.

4 Conjunctive Queries

Alice:	*Shall we start asking queries?*
Sergio:	*Very simple ones for the time being.*
Riccardo:	*But the system will answer them fast.*
Vittorio:	*And there is some nice theory.*

In this chapter we embark on the study of queries for relational databases, a rich topic that spans a good part of this book. This chapter focuses on a limited but extremely natural and commonly arising class of queries called *conjunctive queries*. Five equivalent versions of this query family are presented here: one from each of the calculus and datalog paradigms, two from the algebra paradigm, and a final one that has a more visual form. In the context of conjunctive queries, the three nonalgebraic versions can be viewed as minor syntactic variants of each other; but these similarities diminish as the languages are generalized to incorporate negation and/or recursion. This chapter also discusses query composition and its interaction with user views, and it extends conjunctive queries in a straightforward manner to incorporate union (or disjunction).

The conjunctive queries enjoy several desirable properties, including, for example, decidability of equivalence and containment. These results will be presented in Chapter 6, in which a basic tool, the Homomorphism Theorem, is developed. Most of these results extend to conjunctive queries with union.

In the formal framework that we have developed in this book, we distinguish between a *query*, which is a syntactic object, and a *query mapping*, which is the function defined by a query interpreted under a specified semantics. However, we often blur these two concepts when the meaning is clear from the context. In the relational model, query mappings generally have as domain the family of all instances of a specified relation or database schema, called the *input schema*; and they have as range the family of instances of an *output schema*, which might be a database schema or a relation schema. In the latter case, the relation name may be specified as part of the syntax of the query or by the context, or it may be irrelevant to the discussion and thus not specified at all. We generally say that a query (mapping) is *from* (or *over*) its input schema *to* its output schema. Finally, two queries q_1 and q_2 over $\mathbf{R}$ are *equivalent*, denoted $q_1 \equiv q_2$, if they have the same output schema and $q_1(\mathbf{I}) = q_2(\mathbf{I})$ for each instance $\mathbf{I}$ over $\mathbf{R}$.

This chapter begins with an informal discussion that introduces a family of simple queries and illustrates one approach to expressing them formally. Three versions of conjunctive queries are then introduced, and all of them have a basis in logic. Then a brief

37

(4.1)   Who is the director of "Cries and Whispers"?

(4.2)   Which theaters feature "Cries and Whispers"?

(4.3)   What are the address and phone number of the Le Champo?

(4.4)   List the names and addresses of theaters featuring a Bergman film.

(4.5)   Is a film directed by Bergman playing in Paris?

(4.6)   List the pairs of persons such that the first directed the second in a movie, and vice versa.

(4.7)   List the names of directors who have acted in a movie they directed.

(4.8)   List pairs of actors that acted in the same movie.

(4.9)   On any input produce ⟨"Apocalypse Now", "Coppola"⟩ as the answer.

(4.10)   Where can I see "Annie Hall" or "Manhattan"?

(4.11)   What are the films with Allen as actor or director?

(4.12)   What films with Allen as actor or director are currently featured at the Concorde?

(4.13)   List all movies that were directed by Hitchcock or that are currently playing at the Rex.

(4.14)   List all actors and director of the movie "Apocalypse Now."

Figure 4.1:   Examples of conjunctive queries, some of which require union

digression is made to consider query composition and database views. The algebraic perspectives on conjunctive queries are then given, along with the theorem showing the equivalence of all five approaches to conjunctive queries. Finally, various forms of union and disjunction are added to the conjunctive queries.

4.1   Getting Started

To present the intuition of conjunctive queries, consider again the **CINEMA** database of Chapter 3. The following correspond to conjunctive queries:

(4.1)   Who is the director of "Cries and Whispers"?

(4.2)   Which theaters feature "Cries and Whispers"?

(4.3)   What are the address and phone number of the Le Champo?

These and other queries used in this section are gathered in Fig. 4.1. Each of the queries just given calls for extracting information from a single relation. In contrast, queries (4.4) through (4.7) involve more than one relation.

In queries (4.1–4.4 and 4.6–4.9), the database is asked to find values or tuples of values for which a certain pattern of data holds in the database, and in query (4.5) the database is asked whether a certain pattern of data holds. We shall see that the patterns can be described simply in terms of the existence of tuples that are connected to each other by equality of some of their coordinates. On the other hand, queries (4.9) through (4.14) cannot be expressed in this manner unless some form of disjunction or union is incorporated.

EXAMPLE 4.1.1   Consider query (4.4). Intuitively, we express this query by stating that

> **if** there are tuples r_1, r_2, r_3 respectively in relations
>   *Movies, Pariscope, Location* **such that**
>   the *Director* in r_1 is "Bergman"
>   **and** the *Titles* in tuple r_1 and r_2 are the same
>   **and** the *Theaters* in tuple r_2 and r_3 are the same
> **then** we want the *Theater* and *Address* coordinates from tuple r_3.

In this formulation we essentially use variables that range over tuples. Although this is the basis of the so-called (*relational*) *tuple calculus* (see Exercise 5.23 in the next chapter), the focus of most theoretical investigations has been on the *domain calculus*, which uses variables that range over constants rather than tuples. This also reflects the convention followed in the predicate calculus of first-order logic. Thus we reformulate the preceding query as

> **if** there are tuples $\langle x_{ti}, \text{"Bergman"}, x_{ac}\rangle$, $\langle x_{th}, x_{ti}, x_s\rangle$, and $\langle x_{th}, x_{ad}, x_p\rangle$,
>   respectively, in relations *Movies, Pariscope,* and *Location*
> **then** include the tuple $\langle Theater : x_{th}, \ Address : x_{ad}\rangle$ in the answer,

where $x_{ti}, x_{ac}, \ldots$ are variables. Note that the equalities specified in the first formulation are achieved implicitly in the second formulation through multiple occurrences of variables.

The translation of this into the syntax of *rule-based conjunctive queries* is now obtained by

$$ans(x_{th}, x_{ad}) \leftarrow Movies(x_{ti}, \text{"Bergman"}, x_{ac}), \ Pariscope(x_{th}, x_{ti}, x_s),$$
$$Location(x_{th}, x_{ad}, x_p)$$

where *ans* (for "answer") is a relation over {*Theater, Address*}. The atom to the left of the $\leftarrow$ is called the rule *head*, and the set of atoms to the right is called the *body*.

The preceding rule may be abbreviated as

$$ans(x_{th}, x_{ad}) \leftarrow Movies(x_{ti}, \text{"Bergman"}, \_), \ Pariscope(x_{th}, x_{ti}, \_),$$
$$Location(x_{th}, x_{ad}, \_)$$

where _ is used to replace all variables that occur exactly once in the rule. Such variables are sometimes called *anonymous*.

In general, a rule-based conjunctive query is a single rule that has the form illustrated in the preceding example. The semantics associated with rule-based conjunctive queries ensures that their interpretation corresponds to the more informal expressions given in the preceding example. Rule-based conjunctive queries can be viewed as the basic building block for datalog, a query language based on logic programming that provides an elegant syntax for expressing recursion.

A second paradigm for the conjunctive queries has a more visual form and uses tables

Movies	Title		Director	Actor	
	_The Seventh Seal		Bergman		

Pariscope	Theater	Title		Schedule	
	_Rex	_The Seventh Seal			

Location	Theater	Address		Phone number	
	P._Rex	P._1 bd. Poissonnière			

Figure 4.2:   A query in QBE

with variables and constants. Although we present a more succinct formalism for this paradigm later in this chapter, we illustrate it in Fig. 4.2 with a query presented in the syntax of the language Query-By-Example (QBE) (see also Chapter 7). The identifiers starting with a _ designate variables, and P. indicates what to output. Following the convention established for QBE, variable names are chosen to reflect typical values that they might take. Note that the coordinate entries left blank correspond, in terms of the rule given previously, to distinct variables that occur exactly once in the body and do not occur in the head (i.e., to anonymous variables).

The third version of conjunctive queries studied in this chapter is a restriction of the predicate calculus; as will be seen, the term *conjunctive query* stems from this version. The fourth and fifth versions are algebraic in nature, one for the unnamed perspective and the other for the named perspective.

4.2   Logic-Based Perspectives

In this section we introduce and study three versions of the conjunctive queries, all stemming from mathematical logic. After showing the equivalence of the three resulting query languages, we extend them by incorporating a capability to express equality explicity, thereby yielding a slightly more powerful family of languages.

Rule-Based Conjunctive Queries

The rule-based version of conjunctive queries is now presented formally. As will be seen later, the rule-based paradigm is well suited for specifying queries from database schemas to database schemas. However, to facilitate the comparison between the different variants of the conjunctive queries, we focus first on rule-based queries whose targets are relation schemas. We adopt the convention of using the name *ans* to refer to the name of the target relation if the name itself is unimportant (as is often the case with relational queries).

DEFINITION 4.2.1 Let **R** be a database schema. A *rule-based conjunctive query* over **R** is an expression of the form

$$ans(u) \leftarrow R_1(u_1), \ldots, R_n(u_n)$$

where $n \geq 0$, $R_1, \ldots, R_n$ are relation names in **R**; *ans* is a relation name not in **R**; and $u, u_1, \ldots, u_n$ are free tuples (i.e., may use either variables or constants). Recall that if $v = \langle x_1, \ldots, x_m \rangle$, then '$R(v)$' is a shorthand for '$R(x_1, \ldots, x_n)$'. In addition, the tuples $u, u_1, \ldots, u_n$ must have the appropriate arities (i.e., u must have arity of *ans*, and u_i must have the arity of R_i for each $i \in [1, n]$). Finally, each variable occurring in u must also occur at least once in $u_1, \ldots, u_n$. The set of variables occurring in q is denoted $var(q)$.

Rule-based conjunctive queries are often more simply called *rules*. In the preceding rule, the subexpression $R_1(u_1), \ldots, R_n(u_n)$ is the *body* of the rule, and '$ans(u)$' is the *head*. The rule here is required by the definition to be *range restricted* (i.e., each variable occurring in the head must also occur in the body). Although this restriction is followed in most of the languages based on the use of rules, it will be relaxed in Chapter 18.

Intuitively, a rule may be thought of as a tool for deducing new facts. If one can find values for the variables of the rule such that the body holds, then one may deduce the head fact. This concept of "values for the variables in the rules" is captured by the notion of "valuation." Formally, given a finite subset V of **var**, a *valuation* v over V is a total function v from V to the set **dom** of constants. This is extended to be identity on **dom** and then extended to map free tuples to tuples in the natural fashion.

We now define the semantics for rule-based conjunctive queries. Let q be the query given earlier, and let **I** be an instance of **R**. The *image* of **I** under q is

$$q(\mathbf{I}) = \{v(u) \mid v \text{ is a valuation over } var(q) \text{ and } v(u_i) \in \mathbf{I}(R_i),$$
$$\text{for each } i \in [1, n]\}.$$

The *active domain* of a database instance **I**, denoted $adom(\mathbf{I})$, is the set of all constants occurring in **I**, and the active domain $adom(I)$ of relation instance I is defined analogously. In addition, the set of constants occurring in a query q is denoted $adom(q)$. We use $adom(q, \mathbf{I})$ as an abbreviation for $adom(q) \cup adom(\mathbf{I})$.

Let q be a rule and **I** an input instance for q. Because q is range restricted, it is easily verified that $adom(q(\mathbf{I})) \subseteq adom(q, \mathbf{I})$ (see Exercise 4.2). In other words, $q(\mathbf{I})$ contains only constants occurring in q or in **I**. In particular, $q(\mathbf{I})$ is finite, and so it is an instance.

A straightforward algorithm for evaluating a rule q is to consider systematically all valuations with domain the set of variables occurring in q, and range the set of all constants occurring in the input or q. More efficient algorithms may be achieved, both by performing symbolic manipulations of the query and by using auxiliary data structures such as indexes. Such improvements are considered in Chapter 6.

Returning to the intuition, under the usual perspective a fundamental difference between the head and body of a rule $R_0 \leftarrow R_1, \ldots, R_n$ is that body relations are viewed as being stored, whereas the head relation is not. Thus, referring to the rule given earlier, the values of relations $R_1, \ldots, R_n$ are known because they are provided by the input instance

I. In other words, we are given the extension of $R_1, \ldots, R_n$; for this reason they are called *extensional* relations. In contrast, relation R_0 is not stored and its value is computed on request by the query; the rule gives only the "intension" or definition of R_0. For this reason we refer to R_0 as an *intensional* relation. In some cases, the database instance associated with $R_1, \ldots, R_n$ is called the *extensional database* (edb), and the rule itself is referred to as the *intensional database* (idb). Also, the defined relation defined relation is sometimes referred to as an *idb relation*.

We now present the first theoretical property of conjunctive queries. A query q over **R** is *monotonic* if for each **I, J** over **R**, $\mathbf{I} \subseteq \mathbf{J}$ implies that $q(\mathbf{I}) \subseteq q(\mathbf{J})$. A query q is *satisfiable* if there is some input **I** such that $q(\mathbf{I})$ is nonempty.

PROPOSITION 4.2.2   Conjunctive queries are monotonic and satisfiable.

Proof   Let q be the rule-based conjunctive query

$$ans(u) \leftarrow R_1(u_1), \ldots, R_n(u_n).$$

For monotonicity, let $\mathbf{I} \subseteq \mathbf{J}$, and suppose that $t \in q(\mathbf{I})$. Then for some valuation v over $var(q)$, $v(u_i) \in \mathbf{I}(R_i)$ for each $i \in [1, n]$, and $t = v(u)$. Because $\mathbf{I} \subseteq \mathbf{J}$, $v(u_i) \in \mathbf{J}(R_i)$ for each i, and so $t \in q(\mathbf{J})$.

For satisfiability, let **d** be the set of constants occurring in q, and let $a \in \mathbf{dom}$ be new. Define **I** over the relation schemas R of the rule body so that

$$\mathbf{I}(R) = (\mathbf{d} \cup \{a\})^{arity(R)}$$

[i.e., the set of all tuples formed from $(\mathbf{d} \cup \{a\})$ having arity $arity(R)$]. Finally, let v map each variable in q to a. Then $v(u_i) \in \mathbf{I}(R_i)$ for $i \in [1, n]$, and so $v(u) \in q(\mathbf{I})$. Thus q is satisfiable. ∎

The monotonicity of the conjunctive queries points to limitations in their expressive power. Indeed, one can easily exhibit queries that are nonmonotonic and therefore not conjunctive queries. For instance, the query "Which theaters in New York show only Woody Allen films?" is nonmonotonic.

We close this subsection by indicating how rule-based conjunctive queries can be used to express yes-no queries. For example, consider the query

(4.5)   Is there a film directed by Bergman playing in Paris?

To provide an answer, we assume that relation name *ans* has arity 0. Then applying the rule

$$ans() \leftarrow Movies(x, \text{"Bergman"}, y), Pariscope(z, x, w)$$

returns the relation $\{\langle\rangle\}$ if the answer is yes, and returns $\{\}$ if the answer is no.

Tableau Queries

If we blur the difference between a variable and a constant, the body of a conjunctive query can be seen as an instance. This leads to a formulation of conjunctive queries called "tableau", which is closest to the visual form provided by QBE.

DEFINITION 4.2.3 The notion of *tableau* over a schema **R** (*R*) is defined exactly as was the notion of instance over **R** (*R*), except that both variables and constants may occur. A *tableau query* is simply a pair (**T**, *u*) [or (*T*, *u*)] where **T** is a tableau and each variable in *u* also occurs in **T**. The free tuple *u* is called the *summary* of the tableau query.

The summary tuple *u* in a tableau query (**T**, *u*) represents the tuples included in the answer to the query. Thus the answer consists of all tuples *u* for which the pattern described by **T** is found in the database.

EXAMPLE 4.2.4 Let **T** be the tableau

Movies	*Title*	*Director*	*Actor*
	x_{ti}	"Bergman"	x_{ac}

Pariscope	*Theater*	*Title*	*Schedule*
	x_{th}	x_{ti}	x_s

Location	*Theater*	*Address*	*Phone Number*
	x_{th}	x_{ad}	x_p

The tableau query (**T**, ⟨*Theater* : x_{th}, *Address* : x_{ad}⟩) expresses query (4.4). If the unnamed perspective on tuples is used, then the names of the attributes are not included in *u*.

The notion of valuation is extended in the natural fashion to map tableaux[1] to instances. An *embedding* of tableau **T** into instance **I** is a valuation *v* for the variables occurring in **T** such that *v*(**T**) ⊆ **I**. The semantics for tableau queries is essentially the same as for rule-based conjunctive queries: The output of (**T**, *u*) on input **I** consists of all tuples *v*(*u*) where *v* is an embedding of **T** into **I**.

Aside from the fact that tableau queries do not indicate a relation name for the answer, they are syntactically close to the rule-based conjunctive queries. Furthermore, the alternative perspective provided by tableaux lends itself to the development of several natural results. Perhaps the most compelling of these arises in the context of the chase (see

---

[1] One *tableau*, two *tableaux*.

Chapter 8), which provides an elegant characterization of two conjunctive queries yielding identical results when the inputs satisfy certain dependencies.

A family of restricted tableaux called *typed* have been used to develop a number of theoretical results. A tableau query $q = (T, u)$ under the named perspective, where T is over relation schema R and $sort(u) \subseteq sort(R)$, is typed if no variable of T or t is associated with two distinct attributes in q. Intuitively, the term 'typed' is used because it is impossible for entries from different attributes to be compared. The connection between typed tableaux and conjunctive queries in the algebraic paradigm is examined in Exercises 4.19 and 4.20. Additional results concerning complexity issues around typed tableau queries are considered in Exercises 6.16 and 6.21 in Chapter 6. Typed tableaux also arise in connection with data dependencies, as studied in Part C.

Conjunctive Calculus

The third formalism for expressing conjunctive queries stems from predicate calculus. (A review of predicate calculus is provided in Chapter 2, but the presentation of the calculus in this and the following chapter is self-contained.)

We begin by presenting conjunctive calculus queries that can be viewed as syntactic variants of rule-based conjunctive queries. They involve simple use of conjunction and existential quantification. As will be seen, the full conjunctive calculus, defined later, allows unrestricted use of conjunction and existential quantification. This provides more flexibility in the syntax but, as will be seen, does not increase expressive power.

Consider the conjunctive query

$$ans(e_1, \ldots, e_m) \leftarrow R_1(u_1), \ldots, R_n(u_n).$$

A conjunctive calculus query that has the same semantics is

$$\{e_1, \ldots, e_m \mid \exists x_1, \ldots, x_k (R_1(u_1) \wedge \cdots \wedge R_n(u_n))\},$$

where $x_1, \ldots, x_k$ are all the variables occurring in the body and not the head. The symbol $\wedge$ denotes conjunction (i.e., "and"), and $\exists$ denotes existential quantification (intuitively, $\exists x \ldots$ denotes "there exists an x such that $\ldots$"). The term 'conjunctive query' stems from the presence of conjunctions in the syntax.

EXAMPLE 4.2.5   In the calculus paradigm, query (4.4) can be expressed as follows:

$$\{x_{th}, \ x_{ad} \mid \exists x_{ti} \, \exists x_{ac} \, \exists x_s \, \exists x_p \, (Movies(x_{ti}, \text{"Bergman"}, x_{ac})$$
$$Pariscope(x_{th}, x_{ti}, x_s)$$
$$Location(x_{th}, x_{ad}, x_p))\}.$$

Note that some but not all of the existentially quantified variables play the role of anonymous variables, in the sense mentioned in Example 4.1.1.

The syntax used here can be viewed as a hybrid of the usual set-theoretic notation, used to indicate the form of the query output, and predicate calculus, used to indicate what should be included in the output. As discussed in Chapter 2, the semantics associated with calculus formulas is a restricted version of the conventional semantics found in first-order logic.

We now turn to the formal definition of the syntax and semantics of the (full) conjunctive calculus.

DEFINITION 4.2.6 Let **R** be a database schema. A (*well-formed*) *formula* over **R** for the conjunctive calculus is an expression having one of the following forms:

   (a) an atom over **R**;

   (b) $(\varphi \wedge \psi)$, where φ and ψ are formulas over **R**; or

   (c) $\exists x \varphi$, where x is a variable and φ is a formula over **R**.

In formulas we permit the abbreviation of $\exists x_1 \ldots \exists x_n$ by $\exists x_1, \ldots, x_n$.

The usual notion of "free" and "bound" occurrences of variables is now defined. An occurrence of variable x in formula φ is *free* if

   (i) φ is an atom; or

   (ii) $\varphi = (\psi \wedge \xi)$ and the occurrence of x is free in ψ or ξ; or

   (iii) $\varphi = \exists y \psi$, x and y are distinct variables, and the occurrence of x is free in ψ.

An occurrence of x in φ is *bound* if it is not free. The set of *free variables* in φ, denoted $free(\varphi)$, is the set of all variables that have at least one free occurrence in φ.

DEFINITION 4.2.7 A *conjunctive calculus query* over database schema **R** is an expression of the form

$$\{e_1, \ldots, e_m \mid \varphi\},$$

where φ is a conjunctive calculus formula, $\langle e_1, \ldots, e_m \rangle$ is a free tuple, and the set of variables occurring in $\langle e_1, \ldots, e_m \rangle$ is exactly $free(\varphi)$. If the named perspective is being used, then attributes can be associated with output tuples by specifying a relation name R of arity m. The notation

$$\{\langle e_1, \ldots, e_m \rangle : A_1 \ldots A_m \mid \varphi\}$$

can be used to indicate the sort of the output explicitly.

To define the semantics of conjunctive calculus queries, it is convenient to introduce some notation. Recall that for finite set $V \subset$ **var**, a *valuation* over V is a total function ν from V to **dom**. This valuation will sometimes be viewed as a syntactic expression of the form

$$\{x_1/a_1, \ldots, x_n/a_n\},$$

where $x_1, \ldots, x_n$ is a listing of V and $a_i = v(x_i)$ for each $i \in [1, n]$. This may also be interpreted as a set. For example, if x is not in the domain of v and $c \in \mathbf{dom}$, then $v \cup \{x/c\}$ denotes the valuation with domain $V \cup \{x\}$ that is identical to v on V and maps x to c.

Now let $\mathbf{R}$ be a database schema, φ a conjunctive calculus formula over $\mathbf{R}$, and v a valuation over *free*(φ). Then $\mathbf{I}$ *satisfies* φ under v, denoted $\mathbf{I} \models \varphi[v]$, if

(a) $\varphi = R(u)$ is an atom and $v(u) \in \mathbf{I}(R)$; or

(b) $\varphi = (\psi \wedge \xi)$ and[2] $\mathbf{I} \models \psi[v|_{free(\psi)}]$ and $\mathbf{I} \models \xi[v|_{free(\xi)}]$; or

(c) $\varphi = \exists x \psi$ and for some $c \in \mathbf{dom}$, $\mathbf{I} \models \psi[v \cup \{x/c\}]$.

Finally, let $q = \{e_1, \ldots, e_m \mid \varphi\}$ be a conjunctive calculus query over $\mathbf{R}$. For an instance $\mathbf{I}$ over $\mathbf{R}$, the *image* of $\mathbf{I}$ under q is

$$q(\mathbf{I}) = \{v(\langle e_1, \ldots, e_n \rangle) \mid \mathbf{I} \models \varphi[v] \text{ and } v \text{ is a valuation over } free(\varphi)\}.$$

The *active domain* of a formula φ, denoted *adom*(φ), is the set of constants occurring in φ; and as with queries q, we use *adom*$(\varphi, \mathbf{I})$ to abbreviate *adom*$(\varphi) \cup adom(\mathbf{I})$. An easy induction on conjunctive calculus formulas shows that if $\mathbf{I} \models \varphi[v]$, then the range of v is contained in *adom*$(\mathbf{I})$ (see Exercise 4.3). This implies, in turn, that to evaluate a conjunctive calculus query, one need only consider valuations with range contained in *adom*$(\varphi, \mathbf{I})$ and, hence, only a finite number of them. This pleasant state of affairs will no longer hold when disjunction or negation is incorporated into the calculus (see Section 4.5 and Chapter 5).

Conjunctive calculus formulas φ and ψ over $\mathbf{R}$ are *equivalent* if they have the same free variables and, for each $\mathbf{I}$ over $\mathbf{R}$ and valuation v over *free*$(\varphi) =$ *free*(ψ), $\mathbf{I} \models \varphi[v]$ iff $\mathbf{I} \models \psi[v]$. It is easily verified that if φ and ψ are equivalent, and if Ψ' is the result of replacing an occurrence of φ by ψ in conjunctive calculus formula Ψ, then Ψ and Ψ' are equivalent (see Exercise 4.4).

It is easily verified that for all conjunctive calculus formulas φ, ψ, and ξ, $(\varphi \wedge \psi)$ is equivalent to $(\psi \wedge \varphi)$, and $(\varphi \wedge (\psi \wedge \xi))$ is equivalent to $((\varphi \wedge \psi) \wedge \xi)$. For this reason, we may view conjunction as a polyadic connective rather than just binary.

We next show that conjunctive calculus queries, which allow unrestricted nesting of $\exists$ and $\wedge$, are no more powerful than the simple conjunctive queries first exhibited, which correspond straightforwardly to rules. Thus the simpler conjunctive queries provide a normal form for the full conjunctive calculus. Formally, a conjunctive calculus query $q = \{u \mid \varphi\}$ is in *normal form* if φ has the form

$$\exists x_1, \ldots, x_m (R_1(u_1) \wedge \cdots \wedge R_n(u_n)).$$

Consider now the two *rewrite* (or *transformation*) *rules* for conjunctive calculus queries:

Variable substitution: replace subformula

$$\exists x \ \psi \ \text{ by } \ \exists y \ \psi_y^x,$$

---

[2] $v|_V$ for variable set V denotes the restriction of v to V.

if y does not occur in ψ, where ψ_y^x denotes the formula obtained by replacing all free occurrences of x by y in ψ.

Merge-exists: replace subformula

$$(\exists y_1, \ldots, y_n \psi \wedge \exists z_1, \ldots, z_m \xi) \text{ by } \exists y_1, \ldots, y_n, z_1, \ldots, z_m (\psi \wedge \xi)$$

if $\{y_1, \ldots, y_n\}$ and $\{z_1, \ldots, z_m\}$ are disjoint, none of $\{y_1, \ldots, y_n\}$ occur (free or bound) in ξ, and none of $\{z_1, \ldots, z_m\}$ occur (free or bound) in ψ.

It is easily verified (see Exercise 4.4) that (1) application of these transformation rules to a conjunctive calculus formula yields an equivalent formula, and (2) these rules can be used to transform any conjunctive calculus formula into an equivalent formula in normal form. It follows that:

LEMMA 4.2.8 Each conjunctive calculus query is equivalent to a conjunctive calculus query in normal form.

We now introduce formal notation for comparing the expressive power of query languages. Let $\mathcal{Q}_1$ and $\mathcal{Q}_2$ be two query languages (with associated semantics). Then $\mathcal{Q}_1$ is *dominated* by $\mathcal{Q}_2$ (or, $\mathcal{Q}_1$ is *weaker than* $\mathcal{Q}_2$), denoted $\mathcal{Q}_1 \sqsubseteq \mathcal{Q}_2$, if for each query q_1 in $\mathcal{Q}_1$ there is a query q_2 in $\mathcal{Q}_2$ such that $q_1 \equiv q_2$. $\mathcal{Q}_1$ and $\mathcal{Q}_2$ are *equivalent*, denoted $\mathcal{Q}_1 \equiv \mathcal{Q}_2$, if $\mathcal{Q}_1 \sqsubseteq \mathcal{Q}_2$ and $\mathcal{Q}_2 \sqsubseteq \mathcal{Q}_1$.

Because of the close correspondence between rule-based conjunctive queries, tableau queries, and conjunctive calculus queries in normal form, the following is easily verified (see Exercise 4.15).

PROPOSITION 4.2.9 The rule-based conjunctive queries, the tableau queries, and the conjunctive calculus are equivalent.

Although straightforward, the preceding result is important because it is the first of many that show equivalence between the expressive power of different query languages. Some of these results will be surprising because of the high contrast between the languages.

Incorporating Equality

We close this section by considering a simple variation of the conjunctive queries presented earlier, obtained by adding the capability of explicitly expressing equality between variables and/or constants. For example, query (4.4) can be expressed as

$$ans(x_{th}, x_{ad}) \leftarrow Movies(x_{ti}, x_d, x_{ac}), x_d = \text{``Bergman''}$$
$$Pariscope(x_{th}, x_{ti}, x_s), \ Location(x_{th}, x_{ad}, x_p)$$

and query (4.6) can be expressed as

$$ans(y_1, y_2) \leftarrow Movies(x_1, y_1, z_1), \ Movies(x_2, y_2, z_2), \ y_1 = z_2, \ y_2 = z_1.$$

It would appear that explicit equalities like the foregoing can be expressed by conjunctive queries without equalities by using multiple occurrences of the same variable or constant. Although this is basically true, two problems arise. First, unrestricted rules with equality may yield infinite answers. For example, in the rule

$$ans(x, y) \leftarrow R(x), y = z$$

y and z are not tied to relation R, and there are infinitely many valuations satisfying the body of the rule. To ensure finite answers, it is necessary to introduce an appropriate notion of range restriction. Informally, an unrestricted rule with equality is *range restricted* if the equalities require that each variable in the body be equal to some constant or some variable occurring in an atom $R(u_i)$; Exercise 4.5 explores the notion of range restriction in more detail. A *rule-based conjunctive query with equality* is a range-restricted rule with equality.

A second problem that arises is that the equalities in a rule with equality may cause the query to be unsatisfiable. (In contrast, recall that rules without equality are always satisfiable; see Proposition 4.2.2.) Consider the following query, in which R is a unary relation and a, b are distinct constants.

$$ans(x) \leftarrow R(x), x = a, x = b.$$

The equalities present in this query require that $a = b$, which is impossible. Thus there is no valuation satisfying the body of the rule, and the query yields the empty relation on all inputs. We use $q^{\emptyset:\mathbf{R}, R}$ (or $q^{\emptyset}$ if $\mathbf{R}$ and R are understood) to denote the query that maps all inputs over $\mathbf{R}$ to the empty relation over R. Finally, note that one can easily check if the equalities in a conjunctive query with equality are unsatisfiable (and hence if the query is equivalent to $q^{\emptyset}$). This is done by computing the transitive closure of the equalities in the query and checking that no two distinct constants are required to be equal. Each satisfiable rule with equality is equivalent to a rule without equality (see Exercise 4.5c).

One can incorporate equality into tableau queries in a similar manner by adding separately a set of required equalities. Once again, no expressive power is gained if the query is satisfiable. Incorporating equality into the conjunctive calculus is considered in Exercise 4.6.

4.3   Query Composition and Views

We now present a digression that introduces the important notion of query composition and describe its relationship to database views. A main result here is that the rule-based conjunctive queries with equality are closed under composition.

Consider a database $\mathbf{R} = \{R_1, \ldots, R_n\}$. Suppose that we have a query q (in any of the preceding formalisms). Conceptually, this can be used to define a relation with new relation name S_1, which can be used in subsequent queries as any ordinary relation from $\mathbf{R}$. In particular, we can use S_1 in the definition of a new relation S_2, and so on. In this context, we could call each of $S_1, S_2, \ldots$ *intensional* (in contrast with the extensional relations of $\mathbf{R}$).

This perspective on query composition is expressed most conveniently within the rule-based paradigm. Specifically, a *conjunctive query program* (with or without equality) is a sequence P of rules having the form

$$S_1(u_1) \leftarrow body_1$$
$$S_2(u_2) \leftarrow body_2$$
$$\vdots$$
$$S_m(u_m) \leftarrow body_m,$$

where each S_i is distinct and not in $\mathbf{R}$; and for each $i \in [1, m]$, the only relation names that may occur in $body_i$ are $R_1, \ldots, R_n$ and $S_1, \ldots, S_{i-1}$. An instance $\mathbf{I}$ over $\mathbf{R}$ and the program P can be viewed as defining values for all of $S_1, \ldots, S_m$ in the following way: For each $i \in [1, m]$, $[P(\mathbf{I})](S_i) = q_i(\lfloor P(\mathbf{I})\rfloor)$, where q_i is the ith rule and defines relation S_i in terms of $\mathbf{I}$ and the previous S_j's. If P is viewed as defining a single output relation, then this output is $[P(\mathbf{I})](S_m)$. Analogous to rule-based conjunctive queries, the relations in $\mathbf{R}$ are called *edb* relations, and the relations occurring in rule heads are called *idb* relations.

EXAMPLE 4.3.1   Let $\mathbf{R} = \{Q, R\}$ and consider the conjunctive query program

$$S_1(x, z) \leftarrow Q(x, y), R(y, z, w)$$
$$S_2(x, y, z) \leftarrow S_1(x, w), R(w, y, v), S_1(v, z)$$
$$S_3(x, z) \leftarrow S_2(x, u, v), Q(v, z).$$

Figure 4.3 shows an example instance $\mathbf{I}$ for $\mathbf{R}$ and the values that are associated to S_1, S_2, S_3 by $P(\mathbf{I})$.

It is easily verified that the effect of the first two rules of P on S_2 is equivalent to the effect of the rule

$$S_2(x, y, z) \leftarrow Q(x_1, y_1), R(y_1, z_1, w_1), x = x_1, w = z_1,$$
$$R(w, y, v), Q(x_2, y_2), R(y_2, z_2, w_2), v = x_2, z = z_2.$$

Alternatively, expressed without equality, it is equivalent to

$$S_2(x, y, z) \leftarrow Q(x, y_1), R(y_1, w, w_1), R(w, y, v), Q(v, y_2), R(y_2, z, w_2).$$

Note how variables are renamed to prevent undesired "cross-talk" between the different rule bodies that are combined to form this rule. The effect of P on S_3 can also be expressed using a single rule without equality (see Exercise 4.7).

It is straightforward to verify that if a permutation P' of P (i.e., a listing of the elements of P in a possibly different order) satisfies the restriction that relation names in a rule body must be in a previous rule head, then P' will define the same mapping as P. This kind of consideration will arise in a richer context when stratified negation is considered in Chapter 15.

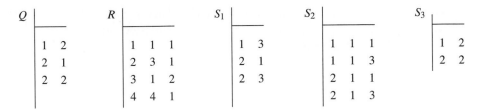

Figure 4.3:   Application of a conjunctive query program

EXAMPLE 4.3.2   Consider the following program P:

$$T(a, x) \leftarrow R(x)$$
$$S(x) \leftarrow T(b, x).$$

Clearly, P always defines the empty relation S, so it is not equivalent to any rule-based conjunctive query without equality. Intuitively, the use of the constants a and b in P masks the use of equalities, which in this case are contradictory and yield an unsatisfiable query.

Based on the previous examples, the following is easily verified (see Exercise 4.7).

THEOREM 4.3.3 (Closure under Composition)   If conjunctive query program P defines final relation S, then there is a conjunctive query q, possibly with equality, such that on all input instances $\mathbf{I}$, $q(\mathbf{I}) = [P(\mathbf{I})](S)$. Furthermore, if P is satisfiable, then q can be expressed without equality.

The notion of programs is based on the rule-based formalism of the conjunctive queries. In the other versions introduced previously and later in this chapter, the notation does not conveniently include a mechanism for specifying names for the output of intermediate queries. For the other formalisms we use a slightly more elaborate notation that permits the specification of these names. In particular, all of the formalisms are compatible with a functional, purely expression-based paradigm:

$$\textbf{let} \quad S_1 = q_1 \qquad \textbf{in}$$

$$\textbf{let} \quad S_2 = q_2 \qquad \textbf{in}$$

$$\vdots$$

$$\textbf{let} \quad S_{m-1} = q_{m-1} \quad \textbf{in}$$

$$q_m$$

and with an imperative paradigm in which the intermediate query values are assigned to relation variables:

$$S_1 := q_1;$$
$$S_2 := q_2;$$
$$\vdots$$
$$S_{m-1} := q_{m-1};$$
$$S_m := q_m.$$

It is clear from Proposition 4.2.9 and Theorem 4.3.3 that the conjunctive calculus and tableau queries with equality are both closed under composition.

Composition and User Views

Recall that the top level of the three-level architecture for databases (see Chapter 1) consists of user *views* (i.e., versions of the data that are restructured and possibly restricted images of the database as represented at the middle level). In many cases these views are specified as queries (or query programs). These may be *materialized* (i.e., a physical copy of the view is stored and maintained) or *virtual* (i.e., relevant information about the view is computed as needed). In the latter case, queries against the view generate composed queries against the underlying database, as illustrated by the following example.

EXAMPLE 4.3.4   Consider the view over schema {*Marilyn, Champo-info*} defined by the following two rules:

$$Marilyn(x_t) \leftarrow Movies(x_t, x_d, \text{``Monroe''})$$
$$Champo\text{-}info(x_t, x_s, x_p) \leftarrow Pariscope(\text{``Le Champo''}, x_t, x_s),$$
$$Location(\text{``Le Champo''}, x_a, x_p).$$

The conjunctive query "What titles in *Marilyn* are featured at the Le Champo at 21:00?" can be expressed against the view as

$$ans(x_t) \leftarrow Marilyn(x_t), \ Champo\text{-}info(x_t, \text{``21:00''}, x_p).$$

Assuming that the view is virtual, evaluation of this query is accomplished by considering the composition of the query with the view definition. This composition can be rewritten as

$$ans(x_t) \leftarrow Movies(x_t, x_d, \text{``Monroe''}),$$
$$Pariscope(\text{``Le Champo''}, x_t, \text{``21:00''})$$
$$Location(\text{``Le Champo''}, x_a, x_p).$$

An alternative expression specifying both view and query now follows. (Expressions from the algebraic versions of the conjunctive queries could also be used here.)

$$Marilyn := \{x_t \mid \exists x_d(Movies(x_t, x_d, \text{"Monroe"}))\};$$

$$Champo\text{-}info := \{x_t, x_s, x_p \mid \exists x_a(Location(\text{"Le Champo"}, x_t, x_s)$$
$$\wedge \; Location(\text{"Le Champo"}, x_a, x_p))\};$$

$$ans := \{x_t \mid Marilyn(x_t) \wedge \exists x_p(Champo\text{-}info(x_t, \text{"21:00"}, x_p))\}.$$

This example illustrates the case in which a query is evaluated over a single view; evaluation of the query involves a two-layer composition of queries. If a series of nested views is defined, then query evaluation can involve query compositions having two or more layers.

4.4   Algebraic Perspectives

The use of algebra operators provides a distinctly different perspective on the conjunctive queries. There are two distinct algebras associated with the conjunctive queries, and they stem, respectively, from the named, ordered-tuple perspective and the unnamed, function-based perspective. After presenting the two algebras, their equivalence with the conjunctive queries is discussed.

The Unnamed Perspective: The SPC Algebra

The algebraic paradigm for relational queries is based on a family of unary and binary operators on relation instances. Although their application must satisfy some typing constraints, they are polymorphic in the sense that each of these operators can be applied to instances of an infinite number of arities or sorts. For example, as suggested in Chapter 3, the union operator can take as input any two relation instances having the same sort.

Three primitive algebra operators form the *unnamed conjunctive algebra*: selection, projection, and cross-product (or Cartesian product). This algebra is more often referred to as the *SPC algebra*, based on the first letters of the three operators that form it. (This convention will be used to specify other algebras as well.) An example is given before the formal definition of these operators.

EXAMPLE 4.4.1   We show how query (4.4) can be built up using the three primitive operators. First we use selection to extract the tuples of *Movies* that have Bergman as director.

$$I_1 := \sigma_{2=\text{"Bergman"}}(Movies)$$

Next a family of "wide" (six columns wide, in fact) tuples is created by taking the cross-product of I_1 and *Pariscope*.

$$I_2 := I_1 \times Pariscope$$

Another selection is performed to focus on the members of I_2 that have first and fifth columns equal.

$$I_3 := \sigma_{1=5}(I_2)$$

In effect, the cross-product followed by this selection finds a matching of tuples from I_1 and *Pariscope* that agree on the *Title* coordinates.

At this point we are interested only in the theaters where these films are playing, so we use projection to discard the unneeded columns, yielding a unary relation.

$$I_4 := \pi_4(I_3)$$

Finally, this is paired with *Location* and projected on the *Theater* and *Address* columns to yield the answer.

$$I_5 := \pi_{2,3}(\sigma_{1=2}(I_4 \times Location))$$

The development just given uses SPC expressions in the context of a simple imperative language with assignment. In the pure SPC algebra, this query is expressed as

$$\pi_{2,3}(\sigma_{1=2}(\pi_4(\sigma_{1=5}(\sigma_{2=\text{"Bergman"}}(Movies) \times Pariscope)) \times Location)).$$

Another query that yields the same result is

$$\pi_{4,8}(\sigma_{4=7}(\sigma_{1=5}(\sigma_{2=\text{"Bergman"}}(Movies \times Pariscope \times Location)))).$$

This corresponds closely to the conjunctive calculus query of Example 4.2.5.

Although the algebraic operators have a procedural feel to them, algebraic queries are used by most relational database systems as high-level specifications of desired output. Their actual implementation is usually quite different from the original form of the query, as will be discussed in Section 6.1.

We now formally define the three operators forming the SPC algebra.

Selection: This can be viewed as a "horizontal" operator. The two primitive forms are $\sigma_{j=a}$ and $\sigma_{j=k}$, where j, k are positive integers and $a \in \mathbf{dom}$. [In practice, we usually surround constants with quotes (" ").] The operator $\sigma_{j=a}$ takes as input any relation instance I with arity $\geq j$ and returns as output an instance of the same arity. In particular,

$$\sigma_{j=a}(I) = \{t \in I \mid t(j) = a\}.$$

The operator $\sigma_{j=k}$ for positive integers j, k is defined analogously for inputs with arity $\geq \max\{j, k\}$. This is sometimes called *atomic* selection; generalizations of selection will be defined later.

Projection: This "vertical" operator can be used to delete and/or permute columns of a relation. The general form of this operator is $\pi_{j_1,\ldots,j_n}$, where $j_1, \ldots, j_n$ is a possibly empty sequence of positive integers (the empty sequence is written [ ]), possibly with repeats. This operator takes as input any relation instance with arity $\geq$ $\max\{j_1, \ldots, j_n\}$ (where the max of $\emptyset$ is 0) and returns an instance with arity n. In particular,

$$\pi_{j_1,\ldots,j_n}(I) = \{\langle t(j_1), \ldots, t(j_n)\rangle \mid t \in I\}.$$

Cross-product (or Cartesian product): This operator provides the capability for combining relations. It takes as inputs a pair of relations having arbitrary arities n and m and returns a relation with arity $n + m$. In particular, if $arity(I) = n$ and $arity(J) = m$, then

$$I \times J = \{\langle t(1), \ldots, t(n), s(1), \ldots, s(m)\rangle \mid t \in I \text{ and } s \in J\}.$$

Cross-product is associative and noncommutative and has the nonempty 0-ary relation $\{\langle\rangle\}$ as left and right identity. Because it is associative, we sometimes view cross-product as a polyadic operator and write, for example, $I_1 \times \cdots \times I_n$.

We extend the cross-product operator to tuples in the natural fashion—that is $u \times v$ is a tuple with arity $= arity(u) + arity(v)$.

The SPC algebra is the family of well-formed expressions containing relation names and one-element unary constants and closed under the application of the selection, projection, and cross-product operators just defined. Each expression is considered to be defined over a given database schema and has an associated output arity. We now give the formal, inductive definition.

Let **R** be a database schema. The *base SPC (algebra) queries* and output arities are

Input relation: Expression R; with arity equal to $arity(R)$.

Unary singleton constant: Expression $\{\langle a\rangle\}$, where $a \in$ **dom**; with *arity* equal to 1.

The family of *SPC (algebra) queries* contains all base SPC queries and, for SPC queries q_1, q_2 with arities α_1, α_2, respectively,

Selection: $\sigma_{j=a}(q_1)$ and $\sigma_{j=k}(q_1)$ whenever $j, k \leq \alpha_1$ and $a \in$ **dom**; these have arity α_1.

Projection: $\pi_{j_1,\ldots,j_n}(q_1)$, where $j_1, \ldots, j_n \leq \alpha_1$; this has arity n.

Cross product: $q_1 \times q_2$; this has arity $\alpha_1 + \alpha_2$.

In practice, we sometimes use brackets to surround algebraic queries, such as $[R \times \sigma_{1=a}(S)](\mathbf{I})$. In addition, parentheses may be dropped if no ambiguity results.

The *semantics* of these queries is defined in the natural manner (see Exercise 4.8).

The SPC algebra includes unsatisfiable queries, such as $\sigma_{1=a}(\sigma_{1=b}(R))$, where $arity(R) \geq 1$ and $a \neq b$. This is equivalent to $q^{\emptyset}$.

As explored in Exercise 4.22, permitting as base SPC queries constant queries that are not unary (i.e., expressions of the form $\{\langle a_1\rangle, \ldots, \langle a_n\rangle\}$) yields expressive power greater than the rule-based conjunctive queries with equality. This is also true of selection formulas in which disjunction is permitted. As will be seen in Section 4.5, these capabilities are subsumed by including an explicit union operator into the SPC algebra. Permitting negation in selection formulas also extends the expressive power of the SPC algebra (see Exercise 4.27b).

Before leaving SPC algebra, we mention three operators that can be simulated by the primitive ones. The first is intersection ($\cap$), which is easily simulated (see Exercise 4.28). The other two operators involve generalizations of the selection and cross-product operators. The resulting algebra is called the *generalized SPC algebra*. We shall introduce a normal form for generalized SPC algebra expressions.

The first operator is a generalization of selection to permit the specification of multiple conditions. A *positive conjunctive selection formula* is a conjunction $F = \gamma_1 \wedge \cdots \wedge \gamma_n$ ($n \geq 1$), where each conjunct γ_i has the form $j = a$ or $j = k$ for positive integers j, k and $a \in$ **dom**; and a *positive conjunctive selection operator* is an expression of the form σ_F, where F is a positive conjunctive selection formula. The intended typing and semantics for these operators is clear, as is the fact that they can be simulated by a composition of selections as defined earlier.

The second operator, called *equi-join*, is a binary operator that combines cross-product and selection. A (well-formed) equi-join operator is an expression of the form $\bowtie_F$ where $F = \gamma_1 \wedge \cdots \wedge \gamma_n$ ($n \geq 1$) is a conjunction such that each conjunct γ_i has the form $j = k$. An equi-join operator $\bowtie_F$ can be applied to any pair I, J of relation instances, where the $arity(I) \geq$ the maximum integer occurring on the left-hand side of any equality in F, and $arity(J) \geq$ the maximum integer occurring on the right-hand side of any equality in F. Given an equi-join expression $I \bowtie_F J$, let F' be the result of replacing each condition $j = k$ in F by $j = arity(I) + k$. Then the semantics of $I \bowtie_F J$ is given by $\sigma_{F'}(I \times J)$. As with cross-product, equi-join is also defined for pairs of tuples, with an undefined output if the tuples do not satisfy the conditions specified.

We now develop a normal form for SPC algebra. We stress that this normal form is useful for theoretical purposes and, in general, represents a costly way to compute the answer of a given query (see Chapter 6).

An SPC algebra expression is in *normal form* if it has the form

$$\pi_{j_1,\ldots,j_n}(\{\langle a_1 \rangle\} \times \cdots \times \{\langle a_m \rangle\} \times \sigma_F(R_1 \times \cdots \times R_k)),$$

where $n \geq 0$; $m \geq 0$; $a_1, \ldots, a_m \in$ **dom**; $\{1, \ldots, m\} \subseteq \{j_1, \ldots, j_n\}$; $R_1, \ldots, R_k$ are relation names (repeats permitted); and F is a positive conjunctive selection formula.

PROPOSITION 4.4.2 For each (generalized) SPC query q there is a generalized SPC query q' in normal form such that $q \equiv q'$.

The proof of this proposition (see Exercise 4.12) is based on repeated application of the following eight *equivalence-preserving SPC algebra rewrite rules* (or *transformations*).

Merge-select: replace $\sigma_F(\sigma_{F'}(q))$ by $\sigma_{F \wedge F'}(q)$.

Merge-project: replace $\pi_{\vec{j}}(\pi_{\vec{k}}(q))$ by $\pi_{\vec{l}}(q)$, where $l_i = k_{j_i}$ for each term l_i in $\vec{l}$.

Push-select-through-project: replace $\sigma_F(\pi_{\vec{j}}(q))$ by $\pi_{\vec{j}}(\sigma_{F'}(q))$, where F' is obtained from F by replacing all coordinate values i by j_i.

Push-select-through-singleton: replace $\sigma_{1=j}(\langle a \rangle \times q)$ by $\langle a \rangle \times \sigma_{(j-1)=a}(q)$.

Associate-cross: replace $((q_1 \times \cdots \times q_n) \times q)$ by $(q_1 \times \cdots q_n \times q)$, and replace $(q \times (q_1 \times \cdots q_n))$ by $(q \times q_1 \times \cdots q_n)$.

Commute-cross: replace $(q \times q')$ by $\pi_{\vec{j}\vec{j}'}(q' \times q)$, where $\vec{j} = arity(q') + 1, \ldots, arity(q') + arity(q)$, and $\vec{j}' = 1, \ldots, arity(q')$.

Push-cross-through-select: replace $(\sigma_F(q) \times q')$ by $\sigma_F(q \times q')$, and replace $(q \times \sigma_F(q'))$ by $\sigma_{F'}(q \times q')$, where F' is obtained from F by replacing all coordinate values i by $i + arity(q)$.

Push-cross-through-project: replace $(\pi_{\vec{j}}(q) \times q')$ by $\pi_{\vec{j}}(q \times q')$, and replace $(q \times \pi_{\vec{j}}(q'))$ by $\pi_{\vec{j}'}(q \times q')$, where $\vec{j}'$ is obtained from $\vec{j}$ by replacing all coordinate values i by $i + arity(q)$.

For a set S of rewrite rules and algebra expressions q, q', write $q \rightarrow_S q'$, or simply $q \rightarrow q'$ if S is understood from the context, if q' is the result of replacing a subexpression of q according to one of the rules in S. Let $\overset{*}{\rightarrow}_S$ denote the reflexive, transitive closure of $\rightarrow_S$.

A family S of rewrite rules is *sound* if $q \rightarrow_S q'$ implies $q \equiv q'$. If S is sound, then clearly $q \overset{*}{\rightarrow}_S q'$ implies $q \equiv q'$.

It is easily verified that the foregoing set of rewrite rules is sound and that for each SPC query q there is a normal form SPC query q' such that q' is in normal form, and $q \overset{*}{\rightarrow} q'$ (see Exercise 4.12).

In Section 6.1, we describe an approach to optimizing the evaluation of conjunctive queries using rewrite rules. For example, in that context, the merge-select and merge-project transformations are helpful, as are the *inverses* of the push-cross-through-select and push-cross-through-project.

Finally, note that an SPC query may require, as the result of transitivity, the equality of two distinct constants. Thus there are unsatisfiable SPC queries equivalent to $q^\emptyset$. This is analogous to the logic-based conjunctive queries with equality. It is clear, using the normal form, that one can check whether an SPC query is $q^\emptyset$ by examining the selection formula F. The set of SPC queries that are not equivalent to $q^\emptyset$ forms the *satisfiable SPC algebra*.

The Named Perspective: The SPJR Algebra

In Example 4.4.1, the relation I_3 was constructed using selection and cross-product by the expression $\sigma_{1=5}(I_1 \times Pariscope)$. As is often the case, the columns used in this selection are labeled by the same attribute. In the context of the named perspective on tuples, this suggests a natural variant of the cross-product operator (and of the equi-join operator) that is called *natural join* and is denoted by $\bowtie$. Informally, the natural join requires the tuples that are concatenated to agree on the common attributes.

EXAMPLE 4.4.3 The natural join of *Movies* and *Pariscope* is

> *Movies* ⋈ *Pariscope*
>> = {u with sort *Title Director Actor Theater Schedule* |
>>> for some $v \in$ Movies and $w \in$ Pariscope,
>>>> $u[\textit{Title Director Actor}] = v$ and $u[\textit{Theater Title Schedule}] = w$}
>> = $\pi_{1,2,3,4,6}(\textit{Movies} \bowtie_{1=2} \textit{Pariscope})$

(assuming that the sort of the last expression corresponds to that of the previous expression). More generally, using the natural analog of projection and selection for the named perspective, query (4.4) can be expressed as

$$\pi_{\textit{Theater,Address}}((\sigma_{\textit{Director}=\text{“Bergman”}}(\textit{Movies}) \bowtie \textit{Pariscope}) \bowtie \textit{Location}).$$

As suggested by the preceding example, natural join can be used in the named context to replace certain equi-joins arising in the unnamed context. However, a problem arises if two relations sharing an attribute A are to be joined but without forcing equality on the A coordinates, or if a join is to be formed based on the equality of attributes not sharing the same name. For example, consider the query

(4.8) List pairs of actors that acted in the same movie.

To answer this, one would like to join the *Movies* relation with itself but matching only on the *Title* column. This will be achieved by first creating a copy *Movies′* of *Movies* in which the attribute *Director* has been renamed to *Director′* and *Actor* to *Actor′*; joining this with *Movies*; and finally projecting onto the *Actor* and *Actor′* columns. Renaming is also needed for query (4.6) (see Exercise 4.11).

The *named conjunctive algebra* has four primitive operators: *selection*, essentially as before; *projection*, now with repeats not permitted; *(natural) join*; and *renaming*. It is thus referred to as the *SPJR algebra*. As with the SPC algebra, we define the individual operators and then indicate how they are combined to form a typed, polymorphic algebra. In each case, we indicate the sorts of input and output. If a relation name is needed for the output, then it is assumed to be chosen to have the correct sort.

Selection: The selection operators have the form $\sigma_{A=c}$ and $\sigma_{A=B}$, where $A, B \in$ **att** and $a \in$ **dom**. These operators apply to any instance I with $A \in sort(I)$ [respectively, $A, B \in sort(I)$] and are defined in analogy to the unnamed selection, yielding an output with the same sort as the input.

Projection: The projection operator has the form $\pi_{A_1,...,A_n}$, $n \geq 0$ (repeats not permitted) and operates on all inputs having sort containing $\{A_1, \ldots, A_n\}$, producing output with sort $\{A_1, \ldots, A_n\}$.

(Natural) join: This operator, denoted ⋈, takes arbitrary inputs I and J having sorts V

and W, respectively, and produces an output with sort equal to $V \cup W$. In particular,

$$I \bowtie J = \{t \text{ over } V \cup W \mid \text{for some } v \in I \text{ and } w \in J,$$
$$t[V] = v \text{ and } t[W] = w\}.$$

When $sort(I) = sort(J)$, then $I \bowtie J = I \cap J$, and when $sort(I) \cap sort(J) = \emptyset$, then $I \bowtie J$ is the cross-product of I and J. The join operator is associative, commutative, and has the nonempty 0-ary relation $\{\langle\rangle\}$ as left and right identity. Because it is associative, we sometimes view join as a polyadic operator and write, for example, $I_1 \bowtie \cdots \bowtie I_n$.

As with cross-product and equi-join, natural join is extended to operate on pairs of tuples, with an undefined result if the tuples do not match on the appropriate attributes.

Renaming: An *attribute renaming* for a finite set U of attributes is a one-one mapping from U to **att**. An attribute renaming f for U can be described by specifying the set of pairs $(A, f(A))$, where $f(A) \neq A$; this is usually written as $A_1 A_2 \ldots A_n \to B_1 B_2 \ldots B_n$ to indicate that $f(A_i) = B_i$ for each $i \in [1, n]$ $(n \geq 0)$. A *renaming operator* for inputs over U is an expression δ_f, where f is an attribute renaming for U; this maps to outputs over $f[U]$. In particular, for I over U,

$$\delta_f(I) = \{v \text{ over } f[U] \mid \text{for some } u \in I, v(f(A)) = u(A) \text{ for each } A \in U\}.$$

EXAMPLE 4.4.4   Let I, J be the two relations, respectively over R, S, given in Fig. 4.4. Then $I \bowtie J$, $\sigma_{A=1}(I)$, $\delta_{BC \to B'A}(J)$, and $\pi_A(I)$ are also shown there. Let K be the one-tuple relation $\langle A : 1, C : 9 \rangle$. Then $\pi_{A,B}(I \bowtie K)$ coincides with $\sigma_{A=1}(I)$ and $J \bowtie K = \{\langle A : 1, B : 8, C : 9 \rangle\}$.

The *base* SPJR algebra queries are:

Input relation: Expression R; with *sort* equal to $sort(R)$.

Unary singleton constant: Expression $\{\langle A : a \rangle\}$, where $a \in$ **dom**; with *sort* A.

The remainder of the syntax and semantics of the SPJR algebra is now defined in analogy to those of the SPC algebra (see Exercise 4.8).

EXAMPLE 4.4.5   Consider again Fig. 4.4. Let **I** be the instance over $\{R, S\}$ such that $\mathbf{I}(R) = I$ and $\mathbf{I}(S) = J$. Then $[R]$ is a query and the answer to that query, denoted $R(\mathbf{I})$, is just I. Figure 4.4 also gives the values of $S(\mathbf{I})$, $[R \bowtie S](\mathbf{I})$, $[\sigma_{A=1}(R)](\mathbf{I})$, $[\delta_{BC \to B'A}(S)](\mathbf{I})$, and $[\pi_A(R)](\mathbf{I})$. Let $K_A = \{\langle A : 1 \rangle\}$ and $K_C = \{\langle C : 9 \rangle\}$. Then $[K_A]$ and $[K_C]$ are constant queries, and $[K_A \bowtie K_C]$ is a query that evaluates (on all inputs) to the relation K of Example 4.4.4.

As with the SPC algebra, we introduce a natural generalization of the selection operator for the SPJR algebra. In particular, the notions of *positive conjunctive selection formula* and *positive conjunctive selection operator* are defined for the context in complete

R	A	B
	1	2
	4	2
	6	6
	7	7
	1	7
	1	6

S	B	C
	2	3
	2	5
	6	4
	8	9

$[R \bowtie S]$	A	B	C
	1	2	3
	1	2	5
	4	2	3
	4	2	5
	6	6	4
	1	6	4

$[\sigma_{A=1}(R)]$	A	B
	1	2
	1	7
	1	6

$[\delta_{BC \to B'A}(S)]$	B'	A
	2	3
	2	5
	6	4
	8	9

$[\pi_A(R)]$	A
	1
	4
	6
	7

Figure 4.4:   Examples of SPJR operators

analogy to the unnamed case. Including this operator yields the *generalized SPJR algebra*.

A normal form result analogous to that for the SPC algebra is now developed. In particular, an SPJR algebra expression is in *normal form* if it has the form

$$\pi_{B_1,\dots,B_n}(\{\langle A_1 : a_1\rangle\} \bowtie \cdots \bowtie \{\langle A_m : a_m\rangle\} \bowtie \sigma_F(\delta_{f_1}(R_1) \bowtie \cdots \bowtie \delta_{f_k}(R_k))),$$

where $n \geq 0$; $m \geq 0$; $a_1, \dots, a_m \in \mathbf{dom}$; each of $A_1, \dots, A_m$ occurs in $B_1, \dots, B_n$; the A_i's are distinct; $R_1, \dots, R_k$ are relation names (repeats permitted); δ_{f_j} is a renaming operator for $sort(R_j)$ for each $j \in [1, k]$ and no A_i's occur in any $\delta_{f_j}(R_j)$; the sorts of $\delta_{f_1}(R_1), \dots, \delta_{f_k}(R_k)$ are pairwise disjoint; and F is a positive conjunctive selection formula. The following is easily verified (see Exercise 4.12).

PROPOSITION 4.4.6   For each (generalized) SPJR query q, there is a generalized SPJR query q' in normal form such that $q \equiv q'$.

The set of SPJR queries not equivalent to $q^\emptyset$ forms the *satisfiable SPJR algebra*.

Equivalence Theorem

We now turn to the main result of the chapter, showing the equivalence of the various formalisms introduced so far for expressing conjunctive queries. As shown earlier, the three logic-based versions of the conjunctive queries are equivalent. We now show that the SPC and SPJR algebras are also equivalent to each other and then obtain the equivalence of the algebraic languages and the three logic-based languages.

LEMMA 4.4.7   The SPC and SPJR algebras are equivalent.

Crux   We prove the inclusion SPC algebra $\sqsubseteq$ SPJR algebra; the converse is similar (see Exercise 4.14). Let q be the following normal form SPC query:

$$\pi_{j_1,\dots,j_n}(\{\langle a_1\rangle\} \times \cdots \times \{\langle a_m\rangle\} \times \sigma_F(R_1 \times \cdots \times R_k)).$$

We now describe an SPJR query q' that is equivalent to q; q' has the following form:

$$\pi_{A_{j_1},\dots,A_{j_n}}(\{\langle A_1 : a_1\rangle\} \bowtie \cdots \bowtie \{\langle A_m : a_m\rangle\} \bowtie \sigma_G(\delta_{f_1}(R_1) \bowtie \cdots \bowtie \delta_{f_k}(R_k))).$$

We use the renaming functions so that the attributes of $\delta_{f_t}(R_t)$ are $A_s, \dots, A_{s'}$, where $s, \dots, s'$ are the coordinate positions of R_t in the expression $R_1 \times \cdots \times R_k$ and modify F into G accordingly. In a little more detail, for each $r \in [1, k]$ let $\beta(t) = m + \Sigma_{s=0}^{t} arity(R_s)$, and let $A_{m+1}, \dots, A_{\beta(k)}$ be new attributes. For each $t \in [1, k]$, choose δ_{f_t} so that it maps the ith attribute of R_t to the attribute $A_{\beta(t-1)+i}$. To define G, first define the function γ from coordinate positions to attribute names so that $\gamma(j) = A_{m+j}$, extend γ to be the identity on constants, and extend it further in the natural manner to map unnamed selection formulas to named selection formulas. Finally, set $G = \gamma(F)$. It is now straightforward to verify that $q' \equiv q$. ∎

   It follows immediately from the preceding lemma that the satisfiable SPC algebra and the satisfiable SPJR algebra are equivalent.
   The equivalence between the two algebraic languages and the three logic-based languages holds with a minor caveat involving the empty query $q^{\emptyset}$. As noted earlier, the SPC and SPJR algebras can express $q^{\emptyset}$, whereas the logic-based languages cannot, unless extended with equality. Hence the equivalence result is stated for the satisfiable SPC and SPJR algebras.
   Theorem 4.3.3 (i.e., the closure of the rule-based conjunctive queries under composition) is used in the proof of this result. The closures of the SPC and SPJR algebras under composition are, of course, immediate.

THEOREM 4.4.8   (Equivalence Theorem) The rule-based conjunctive queries, tableau queries, conjunctive calculus queries, satisfiable SPC algebra, and satisfiable SPJR algebra are equivalent.

Proof   The proof can be accomplished using the following steps:

   (i) satisfiable SPC algebra $\sqsubseteq$ rule-based conjunctive queries; and
   (ii) rule-based conjunctive queries $\sqsubseteq$ satisfiable SPC algebra.

   We briefly consider how steps (i) and (ii) might be demonstrated; the details are left to the reader (Exercise 4.15). For (i), it is sufficient to show that each of the SPC algebra operations can be simulated by a rule. Indeed, then the inclusion follows from the fact that rule-based conjunctive queries are closed under composition by Theorem 4.3.3 and that satisfiable rules with equality can be expressed as rules without equality. The simulation of algebra operations by rules is as follows:

1. $P \times Q$, where P and Q are not constant relations, corresponds to $ans(\vec{x}, \vec{y}) \leftarrow P(\vec{x}), Q(\vec{y})$, where $\vec{x}$ and $\vec{y}$ contain no repeating variables; in the case when P (Q) are constant relations, $\vec{x}$ ($\vec{y}$) are the corresponding constant tuples.

2. $\sigma_F(R)$ corresponds to $ans(\vec{x}) \leftarrow R(\sigma_F(\vec{y}))$, where $\vec{y}$ consists of distinct variables, $\sigma_F(\vec{y})$ denotes the vector of variables and constants obtained by merging variables of $\vec{y}$ with other variables or with constants according to the (satisfiable) selection formula F, and $\vec{x}$ consists of the distinct variables in $\sigma_F(\vec{y})$.

3. $\pi_{j_1 \dots j_n}(R)$ corresponds to $ans(x_{j_1} \dots x_{j_n}) \leftarrow R(x_1 \dots x_m)$, where $x_1, \dots, x_m$ are distinct variables.

Next consider step (ii). Let $ans(\vec{x}) \leftarrow R_1(\vec{x}_1), \dots, R_n(\vec{x}_n)$ be a rule. There is an equivalent SPC algebra query in normal form that involves the cross-product of $R_1, \dots, R_n$, a selection reflecting the constants and repeating variables occurring in $\vec{x}_1, \dots, \vec{x}_n$, a further cross-product with constant relations corresponding to the constants in $\vec{x}$, and finally a projection extracting the coordinates corresponding to $\vec{x}$. ■

An alternative approach to showing step (i) of the preceding theorem is explored in Exercise 4.18.

4.5 Adding Union

As indicated by their name, conjunctive queries are focused on selecting data based on a conjunction of conditions. Indeed, each atom added to a rule potentially adds a further restriction to the tuples produced by the rule. In this section we consider a natural mechanism for adding a disjunctive capability to the conjunctive queries. Specifically, we add a *union* operator to the SPC and SPJR algebras, and we add natural analogs of it to the rule-based and tableau-based paradigms. Incorporating union into the conjunctive calculus raises some technical difficulties that are resolved in Chapter 5. This section also considers the evaluation of queries with union and introduces a more restricted mechanism for incorporating a disjunctive capability.

We begin with some examples.

EXAMPLE 4.5.1 Consider the following query:

(4.10) Where can I see "Annie Hall" or "Manhattan"?

Although this cannot be expressed as a conjunctive query (see Exercise 4.22), it is easily expressed if union is added to the SPJR algebra:

$$\pi_{Theater}(\sigma_{Title=\text{``Annie Hall''}}(Pariscope) \cup \sigma_{Title=\text{``Manhattan''}}(Pariscope)).$$

An alternative formulation of this uses an extended selection operator that permits disjunctions in the selection condition:

$$\pi_{Theater}(\sigma_{Title=\text{``Annie Hall''}\vee Title=\text{``Manhattan''}}(Pariscope)).$$

As a final algebraic alternative, this can be expressed in the original SPJR algebra but permitting nonsingleton constant relations as base expressions:

$$\pi_{Theater}(Pariscope \bowtie \{\langle Title: \text{``Annie Hall''}\rangle, \langle Title: \text{``Manhattan''}\rangle\}).$$

The rule-based formalism can accommodate this query by permitting more than one rule with the same relation name in the head and taking the union of their outputs as the answer:

$$ans(x_t) \leftarrow Pariscope(x_t, \text{``Annie Hall''}, x_s)$$
$$ans(x_t) \leftarrow Pariscope(x_t, \text{``Manhattan''}, x_s).$$

Consider now the following query:

(4.11)   What are the films with Allen as actor or director?

This query can be expressed using any of the preceding formalisms, except for the SPJR algebra extended with nonsingleton constant relations as base expressions (see Exercise 4.22).

Let I_1, I_2 be two relations with the same arity. As standard in mathematics, $I_1 \cup I_2$ is the relation having this arity and containing the union of the two sets of tuples. The definition of the *SPCU algebra* is obtained by extending the definition of the SPC algebra to include the *union* operator. The *SPJRU algebra* is obtained in the same fashion, except that union can only be applied to expressions having the same sort.

The SPCU and SPJRU algebras can be generalized by extending the selection operator (and join, in the case of SPC) as before. We can then define *normal forms* for both algebras, which are expressions consisting of one or more normal form SPC (SPJR) expressions combined using a polyadic union operator (see Exercise 4.23). As suggested by the previous example, disjunction can also be incorporated into selection formulas with no increase in expressive power (see Exercise 4.22).

Turning now to rule-based conjunctive queries, the simplest way to incorporate the capability of union is to consider sets of rules all having the same relation name in the head. These queries are evaluated by taking the union of the output of the individual rules.

This can be generalized without increasing the expressive power by incorporating something analogous to query composition. A *nonrecursive datalog program* (*nr-datalog program*) over schema **R** is a set of rules

$$S_1 \leftarrow body_1$$
$$S_2 \leftarrow body_2$$
$$\vdots$$
$$S_m \leftarrow body_m,$$

where no relation name in **R** occurs in a rule head; the same relation name may appear in more than one rule head; and there is some ordering $r_1, \ldots, r_m$ of the rules so that the relation name in the head of r_i does not occur in the body of a rule r_j whenever $j \leq i$.

The term 'nonrecursive' is used because recursion is not permitted. A simple example of a recursive rule is

$$ancestor(x, z) \leftarrow parent(x, y), \ ancestor(y, z).$$

A fixpoint operator is used to give the semantics for programs involving such rules. Recursion is the principal topic of Part D.

As in the case of rule-based conjunctive query programs, the query is evaluated on input **I** by evaluating each rule in (one of) the order(s) satisfying the foregoing property and forming unions whenever two rules have the same relation name in their heads. Equality atoms can be added to these queries, as they were for the rule-based conjunctive queries.

In general, a nonrecursive datalog program P over **R** is viewed as having a database schema as target. Program P can also be viewed as mapping from **R** to a single relation (see Exercise 4.24).

Turning to tableau queries, a *union of tableaux query* over schema **R** (or R) is an expression of the form $(\{\mathbf{T}_1, \ldots, \mathbf{T}_n\}, u)$, where $n \geq 1$ and $(\mathbf{T}_i, u)$ is a tableau query over **R** for each $i \in [1, n]$. The semantics of these queries is obtained by evaluating the queries $(\mathbf{T}_i, u)$ independently and then taking the union of their results. Equality is incorporated into these queries by permitting each of the queries $(\mathbf{T}_i, u)$ to have equality.

We can now state (see Exercise 4.25) the following:

THEOREM 4.5.2   The following have equivalent expressive power:

1. the nonrecursive datalog programs (with single relation target),
2. the SPCU queries,
3. the SPJRU queries.

The union of tableau queries is weaker than the aforementioned languages with union. This is essentially because the definition of union of tableau queries does not allow separate summary rows for each tableau in the union. With just one summary row, the nonrecursive datalog query

$$ans(a) \leftarrow$$
$$ans(b) \leftarrow$$

cannot be expressed as a union of tableaux query.

As with conjunctive queries, it is easy to show that the conjunctive queries with union and equality are closed under composition.

Union and the Conjunctive Calculus

At first glance, it would appear that the power of union can be added to the conjunctive calculus simply by permitting *disjunction* (denoted $\vee$) along with conjunction as a binary connective for formulas. This approach, however, can have serious consequences.

EXAMPLE 4.5.3   Consider the following "query":

$$q = \{x, y, z \mid R(x, y) \vee R(y, z)\}.$$

Speaking intuitively, the "answer" of q on nonempty instance I will be (using a slight abuse of notation)

$$q(I) = (I \times \mathbf{dom}) \cup (\mathbf{dom} \times I).$$

This is an infinite set of tuples and thus not an instance according to the formal definition.

Informally, the query q of the previous example is not "safe." This notion is one of the central topics that needs to be resolved when using the first-order predicate calculus as a relational query language, and it is studied in Chapter 5. We return there to the issue of adding union to the conjunctive calculus (see also Exercise 4.26).

Bibliographic Notes

Codd's pioneering article [Cod70] on the relational model introduces the first relational query language, a named algebra. The predicate calculus was adapted to the relational model in [Cod72b], where it was shown to be essentially equivalent to the algebra. The conjunctive queries, in the calculus paradigm, were first introduced in [CM77]. Their equivalence with the SPC algebra is also shown there.

Typed tableau queries appeared as a two-dimensional representation of a subset of the conjunctive queries in [ASU79b] along with a proof that all typed restricted SPJ algebra expressions over one relation can be expressed using them. A precursor to the typed tableau queries is found in [ABU79], which uses a technique related to tableaux to analyze the join operator. [ASU79a, ASSU81, CV81] continued the investigation of typed tableau queries; [SY80] extends tableau queries to include union and a limited form of difference; and [Klu88] extends them to include inequalities and order-based comparators. Tableau queries have also played an important role in dependency theory; this will be discussed in Part C.

Many of the results in this chapter (including, for example, the equivalence of the SPC and SPJR algebras and closure of conjunctive queries under composition) are essentially part of the folklore.

Exercises

Exercise 4.1 Express queries (4.1–4.3) and (4.5–4.9) as (a) rule-based conjunctive queries, (b) conjunctive calculus queries, (c) tableau queries, (d) SPC expressions, and (e) SPJR expressions.

Exercise 4.2 Let **R** be a database schema and q a rule.

    (a) Prove that $q(\mathbf{I})$ is finite for each instance **I** over **R**.

    (b) Show an upper bound, given instance **I** of **R** and output arity for conjunctive query q, for the number of tuples that can occur in $q(\mathbf{I})$. Show that this bound can be achieved.

Exercise 4.3 Let **R** be a database schema and **I** an instance of **R**.

    (a) Suppose that φ is a conjunctive calculus formula over **R** and ν is a valuation for $free(\varphi)$. Prove that $\mathbf{I} \models \varphi[\nu]$ implies that the image of ν is contained in $adom(\mathbf{I})$.

    (b) Prove that if q is a conjunctive calculus query over **R**, then only a finite number of valuations need to be considered when evaluating $q(\mathbf{I})$. (Note: The presence of existential quantifiers may have an impact on the set of valuations that need to be considered.)

Exercise 4.4

    (a) Let φ and ψ be equivalent conjunctive calculus formulas, and suppose that Ψ' is the result of replacing an occurrence of φ by ψ in conjunctive calculus formula Ψ. Prove that Ψ and Ψ' are equivalent.

    (b) Prove that the application of the rewrite rules *rename* and *merge-exists* to a conjunctive calculus formula yields an equivalent formula.

    (c) Prove that these rules can be used to transform any conjunctive calculus formula into an equivalent formula in normal form.

Exercise 4.5

    (a) Formally define the syntax and semantics of rule-based conjunctive queries with equality and conjunctive calculus queries with equality.

    (b) As noted in the text, logic-based conjunctive queries with equality can generally yield infinite answers if not properly restricted. Give a definition for *range-restricted* rule-based and conjunctive calculus queries with equality that ensures that queries satisfying this condition always yield a finite answer.

    (c) Prove for each rule-based conjunctive query with equality q that either $q \equiv q^{\emptyset}$ or $q \equiv q'$ for some rule-based conjunctive query q' without equality. Give a polynomial time algorithm that decides whether $q \equiv q^{\emptyset}$, and if not, constructs an equivalent rule-based conjunctive query q'.

    (d) Prove that each rule-based conjunctive query with equality but no constants is equivalent to a rule-based conjunctive query without equality.

Exercise 4.6 Extend the syntax of the conjunctive calculus to include equality. Give a syntactic condition that ensures that guarantees that the answer to a query q on **I** involves only constants from $adom(q, \mathbf{I})$ and such that the answer can be obtained by considering only valuations whose range is contained in $adom(q, \mathbf{I})$.

Exercise 4.7   Give a proof of Theorem 4.3.3.

Exercise 4.8

(a) Give a formal definition for the semantics of the SPC algebra.
(b) Give a formal definition for the syntax and semantics of the SPJR algebra.

Exercise 4.9   Consider the algebra consisting of all SPJR queries in which constants do not occur.

(a) Define a normal form for this algebra.
(b) Is this algebra closed under composition?
(c) Is this algebra equivalent to the rule-based conjunctive queries without constants or equality?

Exercise 4.10   Under the named perspective, a selection operator is *constant based* if it has the form $\sigma_{A=a}$, where $A \in$ **att** and $a \in$ **dom**. Prove or disprove: Each SPJR algebra expression is equivalent to an SPJR algebra expression all of whose selection operators are constant based.

Exercise 4.11   Prove that queries (4.6 and 4.8) cannot be expressed using the SPJ algebra (i.e., that renaming is needed).

Exercise 4.12

(a) Prove that the set of SPC transformations presented after the statement of Proposition 4.4.2 is sound (i.e., preserves equivalence).
(b) Prove Proposition 4.4.2.
(c) Prove that each SPJR query is equivalent to one in normal form. In particular, exhibit a set of equivalence-preserving SPJR algebra transformations used to demonstrate this result.

Exercise 4.13

(a) Prove that the nonempty 0-ary relation is the left and right identity for cross product and for natural join.
(b) Prove that for a fixed relation schema S, there is an identity for union for relations over S. What if S is not fixed?
(c) Let S be a relational schema. For the binary operations $\alpha \in \{\bowtie, \cup\}$, does there exist a relation I such that $I \alpha J = I$ for each relation J over S?

Exercise 4.14   Complete the proof of Lemma 4.4.7 by showing the inclusion SPJR algebra $\subseteq$ SPC algebra.

Exercise 4.15

(a) Prove Proposition 4.2.9.
(b) Complete the proof of Theorem 4.4.8.

Exercise 4.16   Consider the problem of defining restricted versions of the SPC and SPJR algebras that are equivalent to the rule-based conjunctive queries without equality. Find natural restricted versions, or explain why they do not exist.

Exercise 4.17 Let q be a tableau query and q' the SPC query corresponding to it via the translation sketched in Theorem 4.4.8. If q has r rows and q' has j joins of database (nonconstant) relations, show that $j = r - 1$.

♠ **Exercise 4.18**

(a) Develop an inductive algorithm that translates a satisfiable SPC query q into a tableau query by associating a tableau query to each subquery of q.

(b) Do the same for SPJR queries.

(c) Show that if q is a satisfiable SPC (SPRJ) query with n joins (not counting joins involving constant relations), then the tableau of the corresponding tableau query has $n + 1$ rows.

♠ **Exercise 4.19** [ASU79b] This exercise examines the connection between typed tableaux and a subset of the SPJ algebra. A *typed restricted* SPJ algebra expression over R is an SPJR algebra expression that uses only $[R]$ as base expressions and only constant-based selection (i.e., having the form $\sigma_{A=a}$ for constant a), projection, and (natural) join as operators.

(a) Describe a natural algorithm that maps typed restricted SPJ queries q over R into equivalent typed tableau queries $q' = (T, u)$ over R, where $|T| = $ (the number of join operations in q) $+ 1$.

(b) Show that $q = (\{\langle x, y_1\rangle, \langle x_1, y_1\rangle, \langle x_1, y\rangle\}, \langle x, y\rangle)$ is not the image of any typed restricted SPJ query under the algorithm of part (a).

★ (c) [ASSU81] Prove that the tableau query q of part (b) is not equivalent to any typed restricted SPJ algebra expression.

Exercise 4.20 [ASU79b] A typed tableau query $q = (T, u)$ with T over relation R is *repeat restricted* if

1. If $A \in sort(u)$, then no variable in $\pi_A(T) - \{u(A)\}$ occurs more than once in T.
2. If $A \notin sort(u)$, then at most one variable in $\pi_A(T)$ occurs more than once in T.

Prove that if $q = (T, u)$ is a typed repeat-restricted tableau query over R, then there is a typed restricted SPJ query q' such that the image of q' under the algorithm of Exercise 4.19 part (a) is q.

Exercise 4.21 Extend Proposition 4.2.2 to include disjunction (i.e., union).

Exercise 4.22 The following query is used in this exercise:

(4.15) Produce a binary relation that includes all tuples $\langle t, $ "excellent"$\rangle$ where t is a movie directed by Allen, and all tuples $\langle t, $ "superb"$\rangle$ where t is a movie directed by Hitchcock.

(a) Show that none of queries (4.10–4.15) can be expressed using the SPC or SPJR algebras.

A *positive selection formula* for the SPC and SPJR algebras is a selection formula as before, except that disjunction can be used in addition to conjunction. Define the *S+PC algebra* to be the SPC algebra extended to permit arbitrary positive selection operators; and define the *S+PJR algebra* analogously.

(b) Determine which of queries (4.10–4.15) can be expressed using the S+PJR algebra.

Define the *SPC-1* algebra* to be the SPC algebra, except that nonsingleton unary constant relations can be used as base queries; and define the *SPC-n* algebra* to be the SPC algebra, except that nonsingleton constant relations of arbitrary arity can be used as base queries. Define the *SPJR-1** and *SPJR-n** algebras analogously.

(c) Determine which of queries (4.10–4.15) can be expressed using the SPJR-1* and SPJR-n* algebras.

(d) Determine the relative expressive powers of the S+PC, SPC-1*, SPC-n*, and SPCU algebras.

Exercise 4.23   Give precise definitions for normal forms for the SPCU and SPJRU algebras, and prove that all expressions from these algebras have an equivalent in normal form.

Exercise 4.24   An nr-datalog program P is in *normal form* if all relation names in rule heads are identical. Prove that each nonrecursive datalog query with single relation target has an equivalent in normal form.

Exercise 4.25   Prove Theorem 4.5.2.

★ **Exercise 4.26**   Recall the discussion in Section 4.5 about disjunction in the conjunctive calculus.

(a) Consider the query $q = \{x \mid \varphi(x)\}$, where

$$\varphi(x) \equiv R(x) \wedge \exists y, z(S(y, x) \vee S(x, z)).$$

Let $\mathbf{I}$ be an instance over $\{R, S\}$. Using the natural extension of the notion of *satisfies* to disjunction, show for each subformula ψ of φ that there exists a valuation ν for *free*(ψ) such that $\mathbf{I} \models \psi[\nu]$ iff there exists a valuation ν' for *free*(ψ) such that (1) the range of ν' is contained in *adom*$(\mathbf{I})$ and (2) $\mathbf{I} \models \psi[\nu']$. Conclude that this query can be evaluated by considering only valuations whose range is contained in *adom*$(\mathbf{I})$.

(b) The *positive existential (relational) calculus* is the relational calculus query language in which query formulas are constructed using $\wedge, \vee, \exists$. Define a condition on positive existential calculus queries that guarantees that the answer involves only constants from *adom*$(q, \mathbf{I})$ and such that the answer can be obtained by considering only valuations whose range is contained in *adom*$(q, \mathbf{I})$. Extend the restriction for the case when equality is allowed in the calculus.

(c) Prove that the family of restricted positive existential calculus queries defined in the previous part has expressive power equivalent to the rule-based conjunctive queries with union and that this result still holds if equality is added to both families of queries.

Exercise 4.27

(a) Consider as an additional algebraic operation, the *difference*. The semantics of $q - q'$ is given by $[q - q'](\mathbf{I}) = q(\mathbf{I}) - q'(\mathbf{I})$. Show that the difference cannot be simulated in the SPCU or SPJRU algebras. (*Hint:* Use the monotonicity property of these algebras.)

(b) Negation can be added to (generalized) selection formulas in the natural way—that is, if γ is a selection formula, then so is $(\neg\gamma)$. Give a precise definition for the syntax and semantics of selection with negation. Prove that the SPCU algebra cannot simulate selections of the form $\sigma_{\neg 1=2}(R)$ or $\sigma_{\neg 1=a}(R)$.

Exercise 4.28 Show that intersection can be expressed in the SPC algebra.

★ **Exercise 4.29**

(a) Prove that there is no redundant operation in the set $\chi = \{\sigma, \pi, \times, \cup\}$ of unnamed algebra operators (i.e., for each operator α in the set, exhibit a schema and an algebraic query q over that schema such that q cannot be expressed with $\chi - \{\alpha\}$).

(b) Prove the analogous result for the set of named operators $\{\sigma, \pi, \bowtie, \delta, \cup\}$.

Exercise 4.30 An *inequality atom* is an expression of the form $x \neq y$ or $x \neq a$, where x, y are variables and a is a constant. Assuming that the underlying domain has a total order, a *comparison atom* is an expression of the form $x\theta y$, $x\theta a$, or $a\theta x$, where θ ranges over $<, \leq, >$, and $\geq$.

(a) Show that the family of rule-based conjunctive queries with equality and inequality strictly dominates the family of rule-based conjunctive queries with equality.

(b) Assuming that the underlying domain has a total order, describe the relationships between the expressive powers of the family of rule-based conjunctive queries with equality; the family of rule-based conjunctive queries with equality and inequality; the family of rule-based conjunctive queries with equality and comparison atoms; and the family of rule-based conjunctive queries with equality, inequality, and comparison atoms.

(c) Develop analogous extensions and results for tableau queries, the conjunctive calculus, and SPC and SPJR algebras.

★ **Exercise 4.31** For some films, we may not want to store any actor name. Add to the domain a constant $\perp$ meaning unknown information. Propose an extension of the SPJR queries to handle unknown information (see Chapter 19).

5 Adding Negation: Algebra and Calculus

Alice: *Conjunctive queries are great. But what if I want to see a movie that doesn't feature Woody Allen?*

Vittorio: *We have to introduce negation.*

Sergio: *It is basically easy.*

Riccardo: *But the calculus is a little feisty.*

A s indicated in the previous chapter, the conjunctive queries, even if extended by union, cannot express queries such as the following:

(5.1) What are the Hitchcock movies in which Hitchcock did not play?

(5.2) What movies are featured at the Gaumont Opera but not at the Gaumont les Halles?

(5.3) List those movies for which all actors of the movie have acted under Hitchcock's direction.

This chapter explores how negation can be added to all forms of the conjunctive queries (except for the tableau queries) to provide the power needed to express such queries. This yields languages in the various paradigms that have the same expressive power. They include relational algebra, relational calculus, and nonrecursive datalog with negation. The class of queries they express is often referred to as the *first-order queries* because relational calculus is essentially first-order predicate calculus without function symbols. These languages are of fundamental importance in database systems. They provide adequate power for many applications and at the same time can be implemented with reasonable efficiency. They constitute the basis for the standard commercial relational languages, such as SQL.

In the case of the algebras, negation is added using the set difference operator, yielding the language(s) generally referred to as *relational algebra* (Section 5.1). In the case of the rule-based paradigm, we consider negative literals in the bodies of rules, which are interpreted as the absence of the corresponding facts; this yields *nonrecursive datalog¬* (Section 5.2).

Adding negation in the calculus paradigm raises some serious problems that require effort and care to resolve satisfactorily. In the development in this chapter, we proceed in two stages. First (Section 5.3) we introduce the calculus, illustrate the problematic issues of "safety" and domain independence, and develop some simple solutions for them. We also show the equivalence between the algebra and the calculus at this point. The material in this section provides a working knowledge of the calculus that is adequate for understanding the study of its extensions in Parts D and E. The second stage in our study of the calculus (Section 5.4) focuses on the important problem of finding syntactic restrictions on the calculus that ensure domain independence.

The chapter concludes with brief digressions concerning how aggregate functions can be incorporated into the algebra and calculus (Section 5.5), and concerning the emerging area of constraint databases, which provide a natural mechanism for representing and manipulating infinite databases in a finite manner (Section 5.6).

From the theoretical perspective, the most important aspects of this chapter include the demonstration of the equivalence of the algebra and calculus (including a relatively direct transformation of calculus queries into equivalent algebra ones) and the application of the classical proof technique of structural induction used on both calculus formulas and algebra expressions.

5.1   The Relational Algebras

Incorporating the *difference* operator, denoted '$-$', into the algebras is straightforward. As with union and intersection, this can only be applied to expressions that have the same sort, in the named case, or arity, in the unnamed case.

EXAMPLE 5.1.1   In the named algebra, query (5.1) is expressed by

$$\pi_{Title}\sigma_{Director=\text{“Hitchcock”}}(Movies) - \pi_{Title}\sigma_{Actor=\text{“Hitchcock”}}(Movies).$$

The *unnamed relational algebra* is obtained by adding the difference operator to the SPCU algebra. It is conventional also to permit the *intersection* operator, denoted '$\cap$' in this algebra, because it is simulated easily using cross-product, select, and project or using difference (see Exercise 5.4). Because union is present, nonsingleton constant relations may be used in this algebra. Finally, the selection operator can be extended to permit negation (see Exercise 5.4).

The *named relational algebra* is obtained in an analogous fashion, and similar generalizations can be developed.

As shown in Exercise 5.5, the family of unnamed algebra operators $\{\sigma, \pi, \times, \cup, -\}$ is nonredundant, and the same is true for the named algebra operators $\{\sigma, \pi, \bowtie, \delta, \cup, -\}$. It is easily verified that the algebras are not monotonic, nor are all algebra queries satisfiable (see Exercise 5.6). In addition, the following is easily verified (see Exercise 5.7):

PROPOSITION 5.1.2   The unnamed and named relational algebras have equivalent expressive power.

The notion of *composition* of relational algebra queries can be defined in analogy to the composition of conjunctive queries described in the previous chapter. It is easily verified that the relational algebras, and hence the other equivalent languages presented in this chapter, are closed under composition.

5.2   Nonrecursive Datalog with Negation

To obtain a rule-based language with expressive power equivalent to the relational algebra, we extend nonrecursive datalog programs by permitting negative literals in rule bodies. This yields the *nonrecursive datalog with negation* also denoted *nonrecursive datalog$^\neg$* and *nr-datalog$^\neg$*.

A *nonrecursive datalog$^\neg$* (*nr-datalog$^\neg$*) rule is a rule of the form

$$q : \quad S(u) \leftarrow L_1, \ldots, L_n,$$

where S is a relation name, u is a free tuple of appropriate arity, and each L_i is a *literal* [i.e., an expression of the form $R(v)$ or $\neg R(v)$, where R is a relation name and v is a free tuple of appropriate arity and where S does not occur in the body]. This rule is *range restricted* if each variable x occurring in the rule occurs in at least one literal of the form $R(v)$ in the rule body. Unless otherwise specified, all datalog$^\neg$ rules considered are assumed to be range restricted.

To give the *semantics* of the foregoing rule q, let **R** be a relation schema that includes all of the relation names occurring in the body of the rule q, and let **I** be an instance of **R**. Then the *image* of **I** under q is

$$q(\mathbf{I}) = \{v(u) \mid v \text{ is a valuation and for each } i \in [1, n],$$
$$v(u_i) \in \mathbf{I}(R_i), \text{ if } L_i = R_i(u_i), \text{ and}$$
$$v(u_i) \notin \mathbf{I}(R_i), \text{ if } L_i = \neg R_i(u_i)\}.$$

In general, this image can be expressed as a difference $q_1 - q_2$, where q_1 is an SPC query and q_2 is an SPCU query (see Exercise 5.9).

Equality may be incorporated by permitting literals of the form $s = t$ and $s \neq t$ for terms s and t. The notion of *range restriction* in this context is defined as it was for rule-based conjunctive queries with equality. The semantics are defined in the natural manner.

To obtain the full expressive power of the relational algebras, we must consider sets of nr-datalog$^\neg$ rules; these are analogous to the nr-datalog programs introduced in the previous chapter. A *nonrecursive datalog$^\neg$ program* (with or without equality) over schema **R** is a sequence

$$S_1 \leftarrow body_1$$
$$S_2 \leftarrow body_2$$
$$\vdots$$
$$S_m \leftarrow body_m$$

of nr-datalog$^\neg$ rules, where no relation name in **R** occurs in a rule head; the same relation name may appear in more than one rule head; and there is some ordering $r_1, \ldots, r_m$ of the rules so that the relation name in the head of a rule r_i does not occur in the body of a rule r_j whenever $j \leq i$. The *semantics* of these programs are entirely analogous to the semantics of nr-datalog programs. An *nr-datalog¬ query* is a query defined by some nr-datalog¬ program with a specified target relation.

EXAMPLE 5.2.1 Assume that each movie in *Movies* has one director. Query (5.1) is answered by

$$ans(x) \leftarrow Movies(x, \text{ "Hitchcock"}, z),$$
$$\neg Movies(x, \text{ "Hitchcock"}, \text{ "Hitchcock"}).$$

Query (5.3) is answered by

$$Hitch\text{-}actor(z) \leftarrow Movies(x, \text{ "Hitchcock"}, z)$$
$$not\text{-}ans(x) \leftarrow Movies(x, y, z), \neg Hitch\text{-}actor(z)$$
$$ans(x) \leftarrow Movies(x, y, z), \neg not\text{-}ans(x).$$

Care must be taken when forming nr-datalog¬ programs. Consider, for example, the following program, which forms a kind of merging of the first two rules of the previous program. (Intuitively, the first rule is a combination of the first two rules of the preceding program, using variable renaming in the spirit of Example 4.3.1.)

$$bad\text{-}not\text{-}ans(x) \leftarrow Movies(x, y, z), \neg Movies(x', \text{ "Hitchcock"}, z)$$
$$Movies(x', \text{ "Hitchcock"}, z'),$$
$$ans(x) \leftarrow Movies(x, y, z), \neg bad\text{-}not\text{-}ans(x)$$

Rather than expressing query (5.3), it expresses the following:

(5.3′)   (Assuming that all movies have only one director) list those movies for which all actors of the movie acted in *all* of Hitchcock's movies.

It is easily verified that each nr-datalog¬ program with equality can be simulated by an nr-datalog¬ program not using equality (see Exercise 5.10). Furthermore (see Exercise 5.11), the following holds:

PROPOSITION 5.2.2 The relational algebras and the family of nr-datalog¬ programs that have single relation output have equivalent expressive power.

5.3 The Relational Calculus

Adding negation in the calculus paradigm yields an extremely flexible query language, which is essentially the predicate calculus of first-order logic (without function symbols). However, this flexibility brings with it a nontrivial cost: If used without restriction, the calculus can easily express queries whose "answers" are infinite. Much of the theoretical development in this and the following section is focused on different approaches to make the calculus "safe" (i.e., to prevent this and related problems). Although considerable effort is required, it is a relatively small price to pay for the flexibility obtained.

This section first extends the syntax of the conjunctive calculus to the full calculus. Then some intuitive examples are presented that illustrate how some calculus queries can violate the principle of "domain independence." A variety of approaches have been developed to resolve this problem based on the use of both semantic and syntactic restrictions.

This section focuses on semantic restrictions. The first step in understanding these is a somewhat technical definition based on "relativized interpretation" for the semantics of (arbitrary) calculus queries; the semantics are defined relative to different "underlying domains" (i.e., subsets of **dom**). This permits us to give a formal definition of domain independence and leads to a family of different semantics for a given query.

The section closes by presenting the equivalence of the calculus under two of the semantics with the algebra. This effectively closes the issue of expressive power of the calculus, at least from a semantic point of view. One of the semantics for the calculus presented here is the "active domain" semantics; this is particularly convenient in the development of theoretical results concerning the expressive power of a variety of languages presented in Parts D and E.

As noted in Chapter 4, the calculus presented in this chapter is sometimes called the *domain calculus* because the variables range over elements of the underlying domain of values. Exercise 5.23 presents the *tuple calculus*, whose variables range over tuples, and its equivalence with the domain calculus and the algebra. The tuple calculus and its variants are often used in practice. For example, the practical languages SQL and Quel can be viewed as using tuple variables.

Well-Formed Formulas, Revisited

We obtain the relational calculus from the conjunctive calculus with equality by adding negation ($\neg$), disjunction ($\vee$), and universal quantification ($\forall$). (Explicit equality is needed to obtain the full expressive power of the algebras; see Exercise 5.12.) As will be seen, both disjunction and universal quantification can be viewed as consequences of adding negation, because $\varphi \vee \psi \equiv \neg(\neg\varphi \wedge \neg\psi)$ and $\forall x\varphi \equiv \neg\exists x\neg\varphi$.

The formal definition of the syntax of the relational calculus is a straightforward extension of that for the conjunctive calculus given in the previous chapter. We include the full definition here for the reader's convenience. A *term* is a constant or a variable. For a given input schema **R**, the *base formulas* include, as before, atoms over **R** and equality (inequality) atoms of the form $e = e'$ ($e \neq e'$) for terms e, e'. The (*well-formed*) *formulas* of the relational calculus over **R** include the base formulas and formulas of the form

(a) $(\varphi \wedge \psi)$, where φ and ψ are formulas over **R**;

(b) $(\varphi \vee \psi)$, where φ and ψ are formulas over **R**;

(c) $\neg\varphi$, where φ is a formula over **R**;

(d) $\exists x\varphi$, where x is a variable and φ a formula over **R**;

(e) $\forall x\varphi$, where x is a variable and φ a formula over **R**.

As with conjunctive calculus,

$\exists x_1, x_2, \ldots, x_m \varphi$ abbreviates $\exists x_1 \exists x_2 \ldots \exists x_m \varphi$, and

$\forall x_1, x_2, \ldots, x_m \varphi$ abbreviates $\forall x_1 \forall x_2 \ldots \forall x_m \varphi$.

It is sometimes convenient to view the binary connectives $\wedge$ and $\vee$ as polyadic connectives. In some contexts, $e \neq e'$ is viewed as an abbreviation of $\neg(e = e')$.

It is often convenient to include two additional logical connectives, *implies* ($\rightarrow$) and *is equivalent to* ($\leftrightarrow$). We view these as syntactic abbreviations as follows:

$$\varphi \rightarrow \psi \equiv \neg\varphi \vee \psi$$
$$\varphi \leftrightarrow \psi \equiv (\varphi \wedge \psi) \vee (\neg\varphi \wedge \neg\psi).$$

The notions of *free* and *bound* occurrences of variables in a formula, and of *free*(φ) for formula φ, are defined analogously to their definition for the conjunctive calculus. In addition, the notion of *relational calculus query* is defined, in analogy to the notion of conjunctive calculus query, to be an expression of the form

$\{\langle e_1, \ldots, e_m \rangle : A_1, \ldots, A_m \mid \varphi\}$, in the named perspective,

$\{e_1, \ldots, e_m \mid \varphi\}$, in the unnamed perspective,

or if the sort is understood from the context,

where $e_1, \ldots, e_m$ are terms, repeats permitted, and where the set of variables occurring in $e_1, \ldots, e_m$ is exactly *free*(φ).

EXAMPLE 5.3.1 Suppose that each movie has just one director. Query (5.1) can be expressed in the relational calculus as

$$\{x_t \mid \exists x_a Movies(x_t, \text{``Hitchcock''}, x_a) \wedge$$
$$\neg Movies(x_t, \text{``Hitchcock''}, \text{``Hitchcock''})\}.$$

Query (5.3) is expressed by

$$\{x_t \mid \exists x_d, x_a \, Movies(x_t, x_d, x_a) \wedge$$
$$\forall y_a \, (\exists y_d Movies(x_t, y_d, y_a)$$
$$\rightarrow \exists z_t \, Movies(z_t, \text{``Hitchock''}, y_a))\}.$$

The first conjunct ensures that the variable x_t ranges over titles in the current value of *Movies*, and the second conjunct enforces the condition on actors of the movie identified by x_t.

"Unsafe" Queries

Before presenting the alternative semantics for the relational calculus, we present an intuitive indication of the kinds of problems that arise if the conventional definitions from predicate calculus are adapted directly to the current context.

The fundamental problems of using the calculus are illustrated by the following expressions:

(*unsafe-1*) $\{x \mid \neg Movies(\text{"Cries and Whispers"}, \text{"Bergman"}, x)\}$

(*unsafe-2*) $\{x, y \mid Movies(\text{"Cries and Whispers"}, \text{"Bergman"}, x)$

$\vee \; Movies(y, \text{"Bergman"}, \text{"Ullman"})\}.$

If the usual semantics of predicate calculus are adapted directly to this context, then the query (*unsafe-1*) produces all tuples $\langle a \rangle$ where $a \in \mathbf{dom}$ and $\langle$"Cries and Whispers", "Bergman", $a\rangle$ is not in the input. Because all input instances are by definition finite, the query yields an infinite set on all input instances. The same is true of query (*unsafe-2*), even though it does not use explicit negation.

An intuitively appealing approach to resolving this problem is to view the different relation columns as typed and to insist that variables occurring in a given column range over only values of the appropriate type. For example, this would imply that the answer to query (*unsafe-1*) is restricted to the set of actors. This approach is not entirely satisfactory because query answers now depend on the domains of the types. For example, different answers are obtained if the type *Actor* includes all and only the current actors [i.e., persons occurring in $\pi_{Actor}(Movies)$] or includes all current *and potential* actors. This illustrates that query (*unsafe-1*) is not independent of the underlying domain within which the query is interpreted (i.e., it is not "domain independent." The same is true of query (*unsafe-2*).

Even if the underlying domain is finite, users will typically not know the exact contents of the domains used for each variable. In this case it would be disturbing to have the result of a user query depend on information not directly under the user's control. This is another argument for permitting only domain-independent queries.

A related but more subtle problem arises with regard to the interpretation of quantified variables. Consider the query

(*unsafe-3*) $\{x \mid \forall y R(x, y)\}.$

The answer to this query is necessarily finite because it is a subset of $\pi_1(R)$. However, the query is not domain independent. To see why, note that if y is assumed to range over all of $\mathbf{dom}$, then the answer is always the empty relation. On the other hand, if the underlying domain of interpretation is finite, it is possible that the answer will be nonempty. (This occurs, for example, if the domain is $\{1, \ldots, 5\}$, and the input for R is $\{\langle 3, 1\rangle, \ldots \langle 3, 5\rangle\}$.) So again, this query depends on the underlying domain(s) being used (for the different variables) and is not under the user's control.

There is a further difficulty of a more practical nature raised by query (*unsafe-3*). Specifically, if the intuitively appealing semantics of the predicate calculus are used, then the naive approach to evaluating quantifiers leads to the execution of potentially infinite procedures. Although the proper answer to such queries can be computed in a finite manner (see Theorem 5.6.1), this is technically intricate.

The following example indicates how easy it is to form an unsafe query mistakenly in practice.

EXAMPLE 5.3.2   Recall the calculus query answering query (5.3) in Example 5.3.1. Suppose that the first conjunct of that query is omitted to obtain the following:

$$\{x_t \mid \forall y_a (\exists y_d Movies(x_t, y_d, y_a)$$
$$\rightarrow \exists z_t Movies(z_t, \text{``Hitchcock''}, y_a))\}.$$

This query returns all titles of movies that have the specified property and also all elements of **dom** not occurring in $\pi_{Title}(Movies)$. Even if x_t were restricted to range over the set of actual and potential movie titles, it would not be domain independent.

Relativized Interpretations

We now return to the formal development. As the first step, we present a definition that will permit us to talk about calculus queries in connection with different underlying domains.

Under the conventional semantics associated with predicate calculus, quantified variables range over all elements of the underlying domain, in our case, **dom**. For our purposes, however, we generalize this notion to permit explicit specification of the underlying domain to use (i.e., over which variables may range).

A *relativized instance* over schema **R** is a pair $(\mathbf{d}, \mathbf{I})$, where **I** is an instance over **R** and $adom(\mathbf{I}) \subseteq \mathbf{d} \subseteq \mathbf{dom}$. A calculus formula φ is *interpretable* over $(\mathbf{d}, \mathbf{I})$ if $adom(\varphi) \subseteq \mathbf{d}$. In this case, if v is a valuation over *free*(φ) with range contained in **d**, then **I** *satisfies* φ for v *relative* to **d**, denoted $\mathbf{I} \models_{\mathbf{d}} \varphi[v]$, if

(a) $\varphi = R(u)$ is an atom and $v(u) \in \mathbf{I}(R)$;

(b) $\varphi = (s = s')$ is an equality atom and $v(s) = v(s')$;

(c) $\varphi = (\psi \wedge \xi)$ and[1] $\mathbf{I} \models_{\mathbf{d}} \psi[v|_{free(\psi)}]$ and $\mathbf{I} \models_{\mathbf{d}} \xi[v|_{free(\xi)}]$;

(d) $\varphi = (\psi \vee \xi)$ and $\mathbf{I} \models_{\mathbf{d}} \psi[v|_{free(\psi)}]$ or $\mathbf{I} \models_{\mathbf{d}} \xi[v|_{free(\xi)}]$;

(e) $\varphi = \neg\psi$ and $\mathbf{I} \not\models_{\mathbf{d}} \psi[v]$ (i.e., $\mathbf{I} \models_{\mathbf{d}} \psi[v]$ does not hold);

(f) $\varphi = \exists x \psi$ and for some $c \in \mathbf{d}$, $\mathbf{I} \models_{\mathbf{d}} \psi[v \cup \{x/c\}]$; or

(g) $\varphi = \forall x \psi$ and for each $c \in \mathbf{d}$, $\mathbf{I} \models_{\mathbf{d}} \psi[v \cup \{x/c\}]$.

The notion of "satisfies ... relative to" just presented is equivalent to the usual notion of satisfaction found in first-order logic, where the set **d** plays the role of the universe of discourse in first-order logic. In practical database settings it is most natural to assume that the underlying universe is **dom**; for this reason we use specialized terminology here.

Recall that for a query q and input instance **I**, we denote $adom(q) \cup adom(\mathbf{I})$ by $adom(q, \mathbf{I})$, and the notation $adom(\varphi, \mathbf{I})$ for formula φ is defined analogously.

We can now define the relativized semantics for the calculus. Let **R** be a schema, $q = \{e_1, \ldots, e_n \mid \varphi\}$ a calculus query over **R**, and $(\mathbf{d}, \mathbf{I})$ a relativized instance over **R**. Then

---

[1] $v|_V$ for variable set V denotes the restriction of v to V.

the *image* of **I** under q *relative to* **d** is

$$q_{\mathbf{d}}(\mathbf{I}) = \{v(\langle e_1, \ldots, e_n \rangle) \mid \mathbf{I} \models_{\mathbf{d}} \varphi[v],$$
$$v \text{ is a valuation over } free(\varphi) \text{ with range} \subseteq \mathbf{d}\}.$$

Note that if **d** is infinite, then this image may be an infinite set of tuples.

As a minor generalization, for arbitrary $\mathbf{d} \subseteq \mathbf{dom}$, the *image* of q on **I** relative to **d** is defined by[2]

$$q_{\mathbf{d}}(\mathbf{I}) = q_{\mathbf{d} \cup adom(q, \mathbf{I})}(\mathbf{I}).$$

EXAMPLE 5.3.3   Consider the query

$$q = \{x \mid R(x) \wedge \exists y(\neg R(y) \wedge \forall z(R(z) \vee z = y))\}$$

Then

$$q_{\mathbf{dom}}(I) = \{\} \text{ for any instance } I \text{ over } R$$
$$q_{\{1,2,3,4\}}(J_1) = \{\} \text{ for } J_1 = \{\langle 1 \rangle, \langle 2 \rangle\} \text{ over } R$$
$$q_{\{1,2,3,4\}}(J_2) = J_2 \text{ for } J_2 = \{\langle 1 \rangle, \langle 2 \rangle, \langle 3 \rangle\} \text{ over } R$$
$$q_{\{1,2,3,4\}}(J_3) = \{\} \text{ for } J_3 = \{\langle 1 \rangle, \langle 2 \rangle, \langle 3 \rangle, \langle 4 \rangle\} \text{ over } R$$
$$q_{\{1,2,3,4\}}(J_4) = J_4 \text{ for } J_4 = \{\langle 1 \rangle, \langle 2 \rangle, \langle 3 \rangle, \langle 5 \rangle\} \text{ over } R.$$

This illustrates that under an interpretation relative to a set **d**, a calculus query q on input **I** may be affected by $|\mathbf{d} - adom(q, \mathbf{I})|$.

It is important to note that the semantics of algebra and datalog$^\neg$ queries q evaluated on instance **I** are independent of whether **dom** or some subset **d** satisfying $adom(q, \mathbf{I}) \subseteq \mathbf{d} \subseteq \mathbf{dom}$ is used as the underlying domain.

The Natural and Active Domain Semantics for Calculus Queries

The relativized semantics for calculus formulas immediately yields two important semantics for calculus queries. The first of these corresponds most closely to the conventional interpretation of predicate calculus and is thus perhaps the intuitively most natural semantics for the calculus.

DEFINITION 5.3.4   For calculus query q and input instance **I**, the *natural* (or *unrestricted*) interpretation of q on **I**, denoted $q_{nat}(\mathbf{I})$, is $q_{\mathbf{dom}}(\mathbf{I})$ if this is finite and is undefined otherwise.

---

[2] Unlike the convention of first-order logic, interpretations over an empty underlying domain are permitted; this arises only with empty instances.

The second interpretation is based on restricting quantified variables to range over the active domain of the query and the input. Although this interpretation is unnatural from the practical perspective, it has the advantage that the output is always defined (i.e., finite). It is also a convenient semantics for certain theoretical developments.

DEFINITION 5.3.5   For calculus query q and input instance $\mathbf{I}$, the *active domain* interpretation of q on $\mathbf{I}$, denoted $q_{adom}(\mathbf{I})$, is $q_{adom(q,\mathbf{I})}(\mathbf{I})$. The family of mappings obtained from calculus queries under the active domain interpretation is denoted CALC_{adom}.

EXAMPLE 5.3.6   Recall query (*unsafe-2*). Under the natural interpretation on input the instance $\mathbf{I}$ shown in Chapter 3, this query yields the undefined result. On the other hand, under the active domain interpretation this yields as output (written informally) ({actors in "Cries and Whispers"} $\times$ $adom(\mathbf{I})$) $\cup$ ($adom(\mathbf{I})$ $\times$ {movies by Bergman featuring Ullman}), which is finite and defined.

Domain Independence

As noted earlier, there are two difficulties with the natural interpretation of the calculus from a practical point of view: (1) it is easy to write queries with undefined output, and (2) even if the output is defined, the naive approach to computing it may involve consideration of quantifiers ranging over an infinite set. The active domain interpretation solves these problems but generally makes the answer dependent on information (the active domain) not readily available to users. One approach to resolving this situation is to restrict attention to the class of queries that yield the same output on all possible underlying domains.

DEFINITION 5.3.7   A calculus query q is *domain independent* if for each input instance $\mathbf{I}$, and each pair $\mathbf{d}, \mathbf{d}' \subseteq \mathbf{dom}$, $q_{\mathbf{d}}(\mathbf{I}) = q_{\mathbf{d}'}(\mathbf{I})$. If q is domain independent, then the *image* of q on input instance $\mathbf{I}$, denoted simply $q(\mathbf{I})$, is $q_{\mathbf{dom}}(\mathbf{I})$ [or equivalently, $q_{adom}(\mathbf{I})$]. The family of mappings obtained from domain-independent calculus queries is denoted CALC_{di}.

In particular, if q is domain independent, then the output according to the natural interpretation can be obtained by computing the active domain interpretation. Thus,

LEMMA 5.3.8 $\text{CALC}_{di} \sqsubseteq \text{CALC}_{adom}$.

EXAMPLE 5.3.9   The two calculus queries of Example 5.3.1 are domain independent, and the query of Example 5.3.2 is not (see Exercise 5.15).

Equivalence of Algebra and Calculus

We now demonstrate the equivalence of the various languages introduced so far in this chapter.

Theorem 5.3.10 (Equivalence Theorem)   The domain-independent calculus, the calculus under active domain semantics, the relational algebras, and the family of nr-datalog¬ programs that have single-relation output have equivalent expressive power.

Proposition 5.2.2 shows that nr-datalog¬ and the algebras have equivalent expressive power. In addition, Lemma 5.3.8 shows that $\text{CALC}_{di} \sqsubseteq \text{CALC}_{adom}$. To complete the proof, we demonstrate that

   (i) algebra $\sqsubseteq \text{CALC}_{di}$ (Lemma 5.3.11)
   (ii) $\text{CALC}_{adom} \sqsubseteq$ algebra (Lemma 5.3.12).

Lemma 5.3.11   For each unnamed algebra query, there is an equivalent domain-independent calculus query.

Proof   Let q be an unnamed algebra query with arity n. We construct a domain-independent query $q' = \{x_1, \ldots, x_n \mid \varphi_q\}$ that is equivalent to q. The formula φ_q is constructed using an induction on subexpressions of q. In particular, for subexpression E of q, we define φ_E according to the following cases:

   (a) E is R for some $R \in \mathbf{R}$: φ_E is $R(x_1, \ldots, x_{arity(R)})$.
   (b) E is $\{u_1, \ldots, u_m\}$, where each u_j is a tuple of arity α: φ_E is

$$(x_1 = u_1(1) \wedge \cdots \wedge x_\alpha = u_1(\alpha)) \vee \cdots \vee (x_1 = u_m(1) \wedge \cdots \wedge x_\alpha = u_m(\alpha)).$$

   (c) E is $\sigma_F(E_1)$: φ_E is $\varphi_{E_1} \wedge \psi_F$, where ψ_F is the formula obtained from F by replacing each coordinate identifier i by variable x_i.
   (d) E is $\pi_{i_1, \ldots, i_n}(E_1)$: φ_E is

$$\exists y_{i_1}, \ldots, y_{i_n}((x_1 = y_{i_1} \wedge \cdots \wedge x_n = y_{i_n}) \wedge \exists y_{j_1} \ldots \exists y_{j_l} \varphi_{E_1}(y_1, \ldots, y_{arity(E_1)})),$$

   where $j_1, \ldots, j_l$ is a listing of $[1, arity(E_1)] - \{i_1, \ldots, i_n\}$.
   (e) E is $E_1 \times E_2$: φ_E is $\varphi_{E_1} \wedge \varphi_{E_2}(x_{arity(E_1)+1}, \ldots, x_{arity(E_1)+arity(E_2)})$.
   (f) E is $E_1 \cup E_2$: φ_E is $\varphi_{E_1} \vee \varphi_{E_2}$.
   (g) E is $E_1 - E_2$: φ_E is $\varphi_{E_1} \wedge \neg \varphi_{E_2}$.

We leave verification of this construction and the properties of q' to the reader (see Exercise 5.13a). ∎

Lemma 5.3.12   For each calculus query q, there is a query in the unnamed algebra that is equivalent to q under the active domain interpretation.

Crux   Let $q = \{x_1, \ldots, x_n \mid \varphi\}$ be a calculus query over $\mathbf{R}$. It is straightforward to develop a unary algebra query E_{adom} such that for each input instance $\mathbf{I}$,

$$E_{adom}(\mathbf{I}) = \{\langle a \rangle \mid a \in adom(q, \mathbf{I})\}.$$

Next an inductive construction is performed. To each subformula $\psi(y_1, \ldots, y_m)$ of φ this associates an algebra expression E_ψ with the property that (abusing notation slightly)

$$\{y_1, \ldots, y_m \mid \psi\}_{adom(q,\mathbf{I})}(\mathbf{I}) = E_\psi(\mathbf{I}) \cap (adom(q, \mathbf{I}))^m.$$

[This may be different from using the active domain semantics on ψ, because we may have $adom(\psi, \mathbf{I}) \subset adom(q, \mathbf{I})$.] It is clear that E_φ is equivalent to q under the active domain semantics.

We now illustrate a few cases of the construction of expressions E_ψ and leave the rest for the reader (see Exercise 5.13b). Suppose that ψ is a subformula of φ. Then E_ψ is constructed in the following manner:

    (a) $\psi(y_1, \ldots, y_m)$ is $R(t_1, \ldots, t_l)$, where each t_i is a constant or in $\vec{y}$: Then $E_\psi \equiv \pi_{\vec{k}}(\sigma_F(R))$, where $\vec{k}$ and F are chosen in accordance with $\vec{y}$ and $\vec{t}$.

    (b) $\psi(y_1, y_2)$ is $y_1 \neq y_2$: E_ψ is $\sigma_{1\neq2}(E_{adom} \times E_{adom})$.

    (c) $\psi(y_1, y_2, y_3)$ is $\psi'(y_1, y_2) \vee \psi''(y_2, y_3)$: E_ψ is $(E_{\psi'} \times E_{adom}) \cup (E_{adom} \times E_{\psi''})$.

    (d) $\psi(y_1, \ldots, y_m)$ is $\neg\psi'(y_1, \ldots, y_m)$: E_ψ is $(E_{adom} \times \cdots \times E_{adom}) - E_{\psi'}$. ∎

5.4 Syntactic Restrictions for Domain Independence

As seen in the preceding section, to obtain the natural semantics for calculus queries, it is desirable to focus on domain independent queries. However, as will be seen in the following chapter (Section 6.3), it is undecidable whether a given calculus query is domain independent. This has led researchers to develop syntactic conditions that ensure domain independence, and many such conditions have been proposed.

Several criteria affect the development of these conditions, including their generality, their simplicity, and the ease with which queries satisfying the conditions can be translated into the relational algebra or other lower-level representations. We present one such condition here, called "safe range," that is relatively simple but that illustrates the flavor and theoretical properties of many of these conditions. It will serve as a vehicle to illustrate one approach to translating these restricted queries into the algebra. Other examples are explored in Exercises 5.25 and 5.26; translations of these into the algebra are considerably more involved.

This section begins with a brief digression concerning equivalence preserving rewrite rules for the calculus. Next the family CALC$_{sr}$ of safe-range queries is introduced. It is shown easily that the algebra $\sqsubseteq$ CALC$_{sr}$. A rather involved construction is then presented for transforming safe-range queries into the algebra. The section concludes by defining a variant of the calculus that is equivalent to the conjunctive queries with union.

1	$\varphi \wedge \psi$	$\leftrightarrow$	$\psi \wedge \varphi$
2	$\psi_1 \wedge \cdots \wedge \psi_n \wedge (\psi_{n+1} \wedge \psi_{n+2})$	$\leftrightarrow$	$\psi_1 \wedge \cdots \wedge \psi_n \wedge \psi_{n+1} \wedge \psi_{n+2}$
3	$\varphi \vee \psi$	$\leftrightarrow$	$\psi \vee \varphi$
4	$\psi_1 \vee \cdots \vee \psi_n \vee (\psi_{n+1} \vee \psi_{n+2})$	$\leftrightarrow$	$\psi_1 \vee \cdots \vee \psi_n \vee \psi_{n+1} \vee \psi_{n+2}$
5	$\neg(\varphi \wedge \psi)$	$\leftrightarrow$	$(\neg\varphi) \vee (\neg\psi)$
6	$\neg(\varphi \vee \psi)$	$\leftrightarrow$	$(\neg\varphi) \wedge (\neg\psi)$
7	$\neg(\neg\varphi)$	$\leftrightarrow$	φ
8	$\exists x\varphi$	$\leftrightarrow$	$\neg\forall x\neg\varphi$
9	$\forall x\varphi$	$\leftrightarrow$	$\neg\exists x\neg\varphi$
10	$\neg\exists x\varphi$	$\leftrightarrow$	$\forall x\neg\varphi$
11	$\neg\forall x\varphi$	$\leftrightarrow$	$\exists x\neg\varphi$
12	$\exists x\varphi \wedge \psi$	$\leftrightarrow$	$\exists x(\varphi \wedge \psi)$ (x not free in ψ)
13	$\forall x\varphi \wedge \psi$	$\leftrightarrow$	$\forall x(\varphi \wedge \psi)$ (x not free in ψ)
14	$\exists x\varphi \vee \psi$	$\leftrightarrow$	$\exists x(\varphi \vee \psi)$ (x not free in ψ)
15	$\forall x\varphi \vee \psi$	$\leftrightarrow$	$\forall x(\varphi \vee \psi)$ (x not free in ψ)
16	$\exists x\varphi$	$\leftrightarrow$	$\exists y\varphi_y^x$ (y not free in φ)
17	$\forall x\varphi$	$\leftrightarrow$	$\forall y\varphi_y^x$ (y not free in φ)

Figure 5.1:   Equivalence-preserving rewrite rules for calculus formulas

Equivalence-Preserving Rewrite Rules

We now digress for a moment to present a family of rewrite rules for the calculus. These preserve equivalence regardless of the underlying domain used to evaluate calculus queries. Several of these rules will be used in the transformation of safe-range queries into the algebra.

Calculus formulas φ, ψ over schema **R** are *equivalent*, denoted $\varphi \equiv \psi$, if for each **I** over **R**, $\mathbf{d} \subseteq \mathbf{dom}$, and valuation ν with range $\subseteq \mathbf{d}$

$$\mathbf{I} \models_{\mathbf{d} \cup adom(\varphi,\mathbf{I})} \varphi[\nu] \text{ if and only if } \mathbf{I} \models_{\mathbf{d} \cup adom(\psi,\mathbf{I})} \psi[\nu].$$

(It is verified easily that this generalizes the notion of equivalence for conjunctive calculus formulas.)

Figure 5.1 shows a number of equivalence-preserving rewrite rules for calculus formulas. It is straightforward to verify that if ψ transforms to ψ' by a rewrite rule and if φ' is the result of replacing an occurrence of subformula ψ of φ by formula ψ', then $\varphi' \equiv \varphi$ (see Exercise 5.14).

Note that, assuming $x \notin free(\psi)$ and $y \notin free(\varphi)$,

$$\exists x\varphi \wedge \forall y\psi \equiv \exists x\forall y(\varphi \wedge \psi) \equiv \forall y\exists x(\varphi \wedge \psi).$$

EXAMPLE 5.4.1   Recall from Chapter 2 that a formula φ is in *prenex normal form* (PNF) if it has the form $\%_1 x_1 \ldots \%_n x_n \psi$, where each $\%_i$ is either $\forall$ or $\exists$, and no quantifiers occur in ψ. In this case, ψ is called the *matrix* of formula φ.

A formula ψ without quantifiers or connectives $\rightarrow$ or $\leftrightarrow$ is in *conjunctive normal form* (CNF) if it has the form $\xi_1 \wedge \cdots \wedge \xi_m$ $(m \geq 1)$, where each conjunct ξ_j has the form $L_1 \vee \cdots \vee L_k$ $(k \geq 1)$ and where each L_l is a literal (i.e., atom or negated atom). Similarly, a formula ψ without quantifiers or connectives $\rightarrow$ or $\leftrightarrow$ is in *disjunctive normal form* (DNF) if it has the form $\xi_1 \vee \cdots \vee \xi_m$, where each disjunct ξ_j has the form $L_1 \wedge \cdots \wedge L_k$ where each L_l is a literal (i.e., atom or negated atom).

It is easily verified (see Exercise 5.14) that the rewrite rules can be used to transform an arbitrary calculus formula into an equivalent formula that is in PNF with a CNF matrix, and into an equivalent formula that is in PNF with a DNF matrix.

Safe-Range Queries

The notion of safe range is presented now in three stages, involving (1) a normal form called SRNF, (2) a mechanism for determining how variables are "range restricted" by subformulas, and (3) specification of a required global property of the formula.

During this development, it is sometimes useful to speak of calculus formulas in terms of their parse trees. For example, we will say that the formula $(R(x) \wedge \exists y(S(y, z)) \wedge \neg T(x, z))$ has 'and' or $\wedge$ as a root (which has an atom, an $\exists$, and a $\neg$ as children).

The normalization of formulas puts them into a form more easily analyzed for safety without substantially changing their syntactic structure. The following equivalence-preserving rewrite rules are used to place a formula into *safe-range normal form* (SRNF):

Variable substitution: This is from Section 4.2. It is applied until no distinct pair of quantifiers binds the same variable and no variable occurs both free and bound.

Remove universal quantifiers: Replace subformula $\forall \vec{x} \psi$ by $\neg \exists \vec{x} \neg \psi$. (This and the next condition can be relaxed; see Example 5.4.5.)

Remove implications: Replace $\psi \rightarrow \xi$ by $\neg \psi \vee \xi$, and similarly for $\leftrightarrow$.

Push negations: Replace

    (i) $\neg\neg\psi$ by ψ

    (ii) $\neg(\psi_1 \vee \cdots \vee \psi_n)$ by $(\neg\psi_1 \wedge \cdots \wedge \neg\psi_n)$

    (iii) $\neg(\psi_1 \wedge \cdots \wedge \psi_n)$ by $(\neg\psi_1 \vee \cdots \vee \neg\psi_n)$

    so that the child of each negation is either an atom or an existentially quantified formula.

Flatten 'and's, 'or's, and existential quantifiers: This is done so that no child of an 'and' is an 'and,' and similarly for 'or' and existential quantifiers.

The SRNF formula resulting from applying these rules to φ is denoted $\text{SRNF}(\varphi)$. A formula φ (query $\{\vec{e} \mid \varphi\}$) is in SRNF if $\text{SRNF}(\varphi) = \varphi$.

EXAMPLE 5.4.2 The first calculus query of Example 5.3.1 is in SRNF. The second calculus query is not in SRNF; the corresponding SRNF query is

$$\{x_t \mid \exists x_d, x_a Movies(x_t, x_d, x_a) \wedge$$
$$\neg \exists y_a (\exists y_d Movies(x_t, y_d, y_a)$$
$$\wedge \neg \exists z_t Movies(z_t, \text{``Hitchcock''}, y_a))\}.$$

Transforming the query of Example 5.3.2 into SRNF yields

$$\{x_t \mid \neg \exists y_a (\exists y_d Movies(x_t, y_d, y_a)$$
$$\wedge \neg \exists z_t Movies(z_t, \text{``Hitchcock''}, y_a))\}.$$

We now present a syntactic condition on SRNF formulas that ensures that each variable is "range restricted," in the sense that its possible values all lie within the active domain of the formula or the input. If a quantified variable is not range restricted, or if one of the free variables is not range restricted, then the associated query is rejected. To make the definition, we first define the set of *range-restricted variables* of an SRNF formula using the following procedure, which returns either the symbol $\bot$, indicating that some quantified variable is not range restricted, or the set of free variables that is range restricted.

ALGORITHM 5.4.3 (Range restriction (rr))

Input: a calculus formula φ in SRNF

Output: a subset of the free variables of φ or[3] $\bot$

> **begin**
>   **case** φ **of**
>
> $\qquad\qquad R(e_1, \ldots, e_n) \;:\; rr(\varphi) = $ the set of variables in $\{e_1, \ldots, e_n\}$;
>
> $\qquad\qquad x = a \text{ or } a = x \;:\; rr(\varphi) = \{x\}$;
>
> $\qquad\qquad \varphi_1 \wedge \varphi_2 \;:\; rr(\varphi) = rr(\varphi_1) \cup rr(\varphi_2)$;
>
> $\qquad\qquad \varphi_1 \wedge x = y \;:\; rr(\varphi) = \begin{cases} rr(\psi) & \text{if } \{x, y\} \cap rr(\psi) = \emptyset, \\ rr(\psi) \cup \{x, y\} & \text{otherwise}; \end{cases}$
>
> $\qquad\qquad \varphi_1 \vee \varphi_2 \;:\; rr(\varphi) = rr(\varphi_1) \cap rr(\varphi_2)$;
>
> $\qquad\qquad \neg \varphi_1 \;:\; rr(\varphi) = \emptyset$;
>
> $\qquad\qquad \exists \vec{x} \varphi_1 \;:\; \textbf{if } \vec{x} \subseteq rr(\varphi_1)$
>
> $\qquad\qquad\qquad\qquad\qquad \textbf{then } rr(\varphi) = rr(\varphi_1) - \vec{x}$
>
> $\qquad\qquad\qquad\qquad\qquad \textbf{else return } \bot$
>
>   **end case**
> **end** ∎

---

[3] In the following, for each Z, $\bot \cup Z = \bot \cap Z = \bot - Z = Z - \bot = \bot$. In addition, we show the case of binary 'and's, etc., but we mean this to include polyadic 'and's, etc. Furthermore, we sometimes use '$\vec{x}$' to denote the set of variables occurring in $\vec{x}$.

Intuitively, the occurrence of a variable x in a base relation or in an atom of the form $x = a$ restricts that variable. This restriction is propagated through $\wedge$, possibly lost in $\vee$, and always lost in $\neg$. In addition, each quantified variable must be restricted by the subformula it occurs in.

A calculus query $\{u \mid \varphi\}$ is *safe range* if $rr(\text{SRNF}(\varphi)) = free(\varphi)$. The family of safe-range queries is denoted by CALC_{sr}.

EXAMPLE 5.4.4   Recall Examples 5.3.1 and 5.4.2. The first query of Example 5.3.1 is safe range. The first query of Example 5.4.2 is also safe range. However, the second query of Example 5.4.2 is not because the free variable x_t is not range restricted by the formula.

Before continuing, we explore a generalization of the notion of safe range to permit universal quantification.

EXAMPLE 5.4.5   Suppose that formula φ has a subformula of the form

$$\psi \equiv \forall \vec{x} (\psi_1(\vec{x}) \to \psi_2(\vec{y})),$$

where $\vec{x}$ and $\vec{y}$ might overlap. Transforming into SRNF (and assuming that the parent of ψ is not $\neg$), we obtain

$$\psi' \equiv \neg \exists \vec{x} (\psi_1(\vec{x}) \wedge \neg \psi_2(\vec{y})).$$

Now $rr(\psi')$ is defined iff

(a) $rr(\psi_1) = \vec{x}$, and

(b) $rr(\psi_2)$ is defined.

In this case, $rr(\psi') = \emptyset$. This is illustrated by the second query of Example 5.3.1, that was transformed into SRNF in Example 5.4.2.

Thus SRNF can be extended to permit subformulas that have the form of ψ without materially affecting the development.

The calculus query constructed in the proof of Lemma 5.3.11 is in fact safe range. It thus follows that the algebra $\sqsubseteq \text{CALC}_{sr}$.

As shown in the following each safe range query is domain independent (Theorem 5.4.6). For this reason, if q is safe range we generally use the natural interpretation to evaluate it; we may also use the active domain interpretation.

Finally, it will be shown in the following that all of CALC_{sr}, CALC_{di}, and CALC_{adom} are equivalent. When the particular choice is irrelevant to the discussion, we use the term *relational calculus* to refer to any of these three equivalent query languages.

From Safe Range to the Algebra

We now present the main result of this section (namely, the translation of safe-range queries into the named algebra). Speaking loosely, this translation is relatively direct in the sense that the algebra query E constructed for calculus query q largely follows the structure of q. As a result, evaluation of E will in most cases be more efficient than using the algebra query that is constructed for q by the proof of Lemma 5.3.12.

Examples of the construction used are presented after the formal argument.

THEOREM 5.4.6 $CALC_{sr} \equiv$ the relational algebra. Furthermore, each safe-range query is domain independent.

The proof of this theorem involves several steps. As seen earlier, the algebra $\sqsubseteq$ $CALC_{sr}$. To prove the other direction, we develop a translation from safe-range queries into the named algebra. Because the algebra is domain independent, this will also imply the second sentence of the theorem.

To begin, let φ be a safe-range formula in SRNF. An occurrence of a subformula ψ in φ is *self-contained* if its root is $\wedge$ or if

(i) $\psi = \psi_1 \vee \cdots \vee \psi_n$ and $rr(\psi) = rr(\psi_1) = \cdots = rr(\psi_n) = free(\psi)$;

(ii) $\psi = \exists \vec{x}\, \psi_1$ and $rr(\psi) = free(\psi_1)$; or

(iii) $\psi = \neg \psi_1$ and $rr(\psi) = free(\psi_1)$.

A safe-range, SRNF formula φ is in[4] *relational algebra normal form* (RANF) if each subformula of φ is self-contained.

Intuitively, if ψ is a self-contained subformula of φ that does not have $\wedge$ as a root, then all free variables in ψ are range restricted within ψ. As we shall see, if φ is in RANF, this permits construction of an equivalent relational algebra query E_φ using an induction from leaf to root.

We now develop an algorithm RANF that transforms safe-range SRNF formulas into RANF. It is based on the following rewrite rules:

(R1) Push-into-or: Consider the subformula

$$\psi = \psi_1 \wedge \cdots \wedge \psi_n \wedge \xi,$$

where

$$\xi = \xi_1 \vee \cdots \vee \xi_m.$$

Suppose that $rr(\psi) = free(\psi)$, but $rr(\xi_1 \vee \cdots \vee \xi_m) \neq free(\xi_1 \vee \cdots \vee \xi_m)$. Nondeterministically choose a subset $i_1, \ldots, i_k$ of $1, \ldots, n$ such that

$$\xi' = (\xi_1 \wedge \psi_{i_1} \wedge \cdots \wedge \psi_{i_k}) \vee \cdots \vee (\xi_m \wedge \psi_{i_1} \wedge \cdots \wedge \psi_{i_k})$$

---

[4] This is a variation of the notion of RANF used elsewhere in the literature; see Bibliographic Notes.

satisfies $rr(\xi') = free(\xi')$. (One choice of $i_1, \ldots, i_k$ is to use all of $1, \ldots, n$; this necessarily yields a formula ξ' with this property.) Letting $\{j_1, \ldots, j_l\} = \{1, \ldots, n\} - \{i_1, \ldots, i_k\}$, set

$$\psi' = \text{SRNF}(\psi_{j_1} \wedge \cdots \wedge \psi_{j_l} \wedge \xi').$$

The application of SRNF to ξ' only has the effect of possibly renaming quantified variables[5] and of flattening the roots of subformulas $\xi_p \wedge \psi_{i_1} \wedge \cdots \wedge \psi_{i_k}$, where ξ_p has root $\wedge$; analogous remarks apply. The rewrite rule is to replace subformula ψ by ψ' and possibly apply SRNF to flatten an $\vee$, if both $l = 0$ and the parent of ψ is $\vee$.

(R2) Push-into-quantifier: Suppose that

$$\psi = \psi_1 \wedge \cdots \wedge \psi_n \wedge \exists \vec{x} \xi,$$

where $rr(\psi) = free(\psi)$, but $rr(\xi) \neq free(\xi)$. Then replace ψ by

$$\psi' = \text{SRNF}(\psi_{j_1} \wedge \cdots \wedge \psi_{j_l} \wedge \exists \vec{x} \xi'),$$

where

$$\xi' = \psi_{i_1} \wedge \cdots \wedge \psi_{i_k} \wedge \xi$$

and where $rr(\xi') = free(\xi')$ and $\{j_1, \ldots, j_l\} = \{1, \ldots, n\} - \{i_1, \ldots, i_k\}$. The rewrite rule is to replace ψ by ψ' and possibly apply SRNF to flatten an $\exists$.

(R3) Push-into-negated-quantifier: Suppose that

$$\psi = \psi_1 \wedge \cdots \wedge \psi_n \wedge \neg \exists \vec{x} \xi,$$

where $rr(\psi) = free(\psi)$, but $rr(\xi) \neq free(\xi)$. Then replace ψ by

$$\psi' = \text{SRNF}(\psi_1 \wedge \cdots \wedge \psi_n \wedge \neg \exists \vec{x} \xi'),$$

where

$$\xi' = \psi_{i_1} \wedge \cdots \wedge \psi_{i_k} \wedge \xi$$

and where $rr(\xi') = free(\xi')$ and $\{i_1, \ldots, i_k\} \subseteq \{1, \ldots, n\}$. That ψ' is equivalent to ψ follows from the observation that the propositional formulas $p \wedge q \wedge \neg r$ and $p \wedge q \wedge \neg (p \wedge r)$ are equivalent. The rewrite rule is to replace ψ by ψ'.

The algorithm RANF for applying these rewrite rules is essentially top-down and recursive. We sketch the algorithm now (see Exercise 5.19).

---

[5] It is assumed that under SRNF renamed variables are chosen so that they do not occur in the full formula under consideration.

ALGORITHM 5.4.7 (Relational Algebra Normal Form (RANF))

Input: a safe-range calculus formula φ in SRNF

Output: a RANF formula φ' equivalent to φ

> **begin**
> > **while** some subformula ψ (with its conjuncts possibly reordered) of φ satisfies the premise of R1, R2, or R3
> > **do**
> > > **case** R1: (left as exercise)
> > > > R2: (left as exercise)
> > > > R3: Let $\psi = \psi_1 \wedge \cdots \wedge \psi_n \wedge \neg \exists \vec{x} \xi$
> > > > and $\psi_{i_1}, \ldots, \psi_{i_k}$ satisfy the conditions of R3;
> > > > $\alpha := \text{RANF}(\psi_1 \wedge \cdots \wedge \psi_n)$;
> > > > $\beta := \text{RANF}(\text{SRNF}(\psi_{i_1} \wedge \cdots \wedge \psi_{i_k} \wedge \xi))$;
> > > > $\psi' := \alpha \wedge \neg \exists \vec{x} \beta$;
> > > > $\varphi :=$ result of replacing ψ by ψ' in φ;
> > > **end case**
> > **end while**
> **end**

The proof that these rewrite rules can be used to transform a safe-range SRNF formula into a RANF formula has two steps (see Exercise 5.19). First, a case analysis can be used to show that if safe-range φ in SRNF is not in RANF, then one of the rewrite rules (R1, R2, R3) can be applied. Second, it is shown that Algorithm 5.4.7 terminates. This is accomplished by showing that (1) each successfully completed call to RANF reduces the number of non-self-contained subformulas, and (2) if a call to RANF on ψ invokes other calls to RANF, the input to these recursive calls has fewer non-self-contained subformulas than does ψ.

We now turn to the transformation of RANF formulas into equivalent relational algebra queries. We abuse notation somewhat and assume that each variable is also an attribute. (Alternatively, a one-one mapping *var-to-att* : **var** $\rightarrow$ **att** could be used.) In general, given a RANF formula φ with free variables $x_1, \ldots, x_n$, we shall construct a named algebra expression E_φ over attributes $x_1, \ldots, x_n$ such that for each input instance **I**, $E_\varphi(\mathbf{I}) = \{x_1, \ldots, x_n \mid \varphi\}(\mathbf{I})$. (The special case of queries $\{e_1, \ldots, e_n \mid \varphi\}$, where some of the e_i are constants, is handled by performing a join with the constants at the end of the construction.)

A formula φ is in *modified RANF* if it is RANF, except that each polyadic 'and' is ordered and transformed into binary 'and's, so that atoms $x = y$ ($x \neq y$) are after conjuncts that restrict one (both) of the variables involved and so that each free variable in a conjunct of the form $\neg \xi$ occurs in some preceding conjunct. It is straightforward to verify that each RANF formula can be placed into modified RANF. Note that each subformula of a modified RANF formula is self-contained.

Let RANF formula φ be fixed. The construction of E_φ is inductive, from leaf to root, and is sketched in the following algorithm. The special operator **diff**, on inputs R and S where $att(S) \subset att(R)$, is defined by

$$R \textbf{ diff } S = R - (R \bowtie S).$$

(Many details of this transformation, such as the construction of renaming function f, projection list $\vec{k}$, and selection formula F in the first entry of the case statement, are left to the reader; see Example 5.4.9 and Exercise 5.19.)

ALGORITHM 5.4.8 (Translation into the Algebra)

Input: a formula φ in modified RANF

Output: an algebra query E_φ equivalent to φ

> **begin**
> > **case** φ **of**
>
> $R(\vec{e})$ $\delta_f(\pi_{\vec{k}}(\sigma_F(R)))$
>
> $x = a$ $\{\langle x : a \rangle\}$
>
> $\psi \wedge \xi$ if ξ is $x = x$, then E_ψ
> > if ξ is $x = y$ (with x, y distinct), then
> > > $\sigma_{x=y}(E_\psi)$, if $\{x, y\} \subseteq free(\psi)$
> > > $\sigma_{x=y}(E_\psi \bowtie \delta_{x \to y} E_\psi)$, if $x \in free(\psi)$ and $y \notin free(\psi)$
> > > $\sigma_{x=y}(E_\psi \bowtie \delta_{y \to x} E_\psi)$, if $y \in free(\psi)$ and $x \notin free(\psi)$
> >
> > if ξ is $x \neq y$, then $\sigma_{x \neq y}(E_\psi)$
> > if $\xi = \neg \xi'$, then
> > > $E_\psi \textbf{ diff } E_{\xi'}$, if $free(\xi') \subset free(\psi)$
> > > $E_\psi - E_{\xi'}$, if $free(\xi') = free(\psi)$
> >
> > otherwise, $E_\psi \bowtie E_\xi$
>
> $\neg \psi$ $\{\langle\rangle\} - E_\psi$
> > (in the case that $\neg\psi$ does not have 'and' as parent)
>
> $\psi_1 \vee \cdots \vee \psi_n$ $E_{\psi_1} \cup \cdots \cup E_{\psi_n}$
>
> $\exists x_1, \ldots, x_n \psi(x_1, \ldots, x_n, y_1, \ldots, y_m)$
> > $\pi_{y_1, \ldots, y_m}(E_\psi)$
>
> > **end case**
> **end**

Finally, let $q = \{x_1, \ldots, x_n \mid \varphi\}$ be safe range. Because the transformations used for SRNF and RANF are equivalence preserving, without loss of generality we can assume that φ is in modified RANF. To conclude the proof of Theorem 5.4.6, it must be shown that q and E_φ are equivalent. In fact, it can be shown that for each instance $\mathbf{I}$ and each $\mathbf{d}$ satisfying $adom(q, \mathbf{I}) \subseteq \mathbf{d} \subseteq \mathbf{dom}$,

$$q_{\mathbf{d}}(\mathbf{I}) = E_\varphi(\mathbf{I}).$$

This will also yield that q is domain independent.

Let **I** and **d** be fixed. A straightforward induction can be used to show that for each subformula $\psi(y_1, \ldots, y_m)$ of φ and each variable assignment ν with range **d**,

$$\mathbf{I} \models_\mathbf{d} \psi[\nu] \Leftrightarrow \langle \nu(y_1), \ldots, \nu(y_m) \rangle \in E_\psi(\mathbf{I})$$

(see Exercise 5.19.) This completes the proof of Theorem 5.4.6.

EXAMPLE 5.4.9   (a) Consider the query

$$q_1 = \{\langle a, x, y \rangle : A_1 A_2 A_3 \mid \exists z (P(x, y, z) \vee [R(x, y) \wedge$$
$$([S(z) \wedge \neg T(x, z)] \vee [T(y, z)])])\}.$$

The formula of q_1 is in SRNF. Transformation into RANF yields

$$\exists z (P(x, y, z) \vee [R(x, y) \wedge S(z) \wedge \neg T(x, z)] \vee [R(x, y) \wedge T(y, z)]).$$

Assuming the schemas $P[B_1 B_2 B_3]$, $R[C_1 C_2]$, $S[D]$, and $T[F_1 F_2]$, transformation of this into the algebra yields

$$E = \pi_{x, y}(\delta_{B_1 B_2 B_3 \to xyz}(P)$$
$$\cup ((\delta_{C_1 C_2 \to xy}(R) \bowtie \delta_{D \to z}(S)) \text{ diff } \delta_{F_1 F_2 \to yz}(T))$$
$$\cup (\delta_{C_1 C_2 \to xy}(R) \bowtie \delta_{F_1 F_2 \to yz}(T))).$$

Finally, an algebra query equivalent to q_1 is

$$\{\langle A_1 : a \rangle\} \bowtie \delta_{xy \to A_2 A_3}(E).$$

(b) Consider the query

$$q_2 = \{x \mid \exists y [R(x, y) \wedge \forall z (S(z, a) \to T(y, z))$$
$$\wedge \exists v, w (\neg T(v, w) \wedge w = b \wedge v = x)]\}.$$

Transforming to SRNF, we have

$$\exists y [R(x, y) \wedge \neg \exists z (S(z, a) \wedge \neg T(y, z)) \wedge \exists v, w (\neg T(v, w) \wedge w = b \wedge v = x)].$$

Transforming to RANF and reordering the conjunctions, we obtain

$$\exists y [\exists v, w (R(x, y) \wedge w = b \wedge v = x \wedge \neg T(v, w)) \wedge \neg \exists z (R(x, y) \wedge S(z, a) \wedge \neg T(y, z))].$$

Assuming schemas $R[A_1, A_2]$, $S[B_1, B_2]$, and $T[C_1, C_2]$, the equivalent algebra query is obtained using the program

$$E_1 := (\delta_{A_1 A_2 \to xy}(R) \bowtie \{\langle w : b \rangle\});$$
$$E_2 := (\sigma_{v=x}(E_1 \bowtie \delta_{x \to v}(E_1))) \text{ diff } \delta_{C_1 C_2 \to vw}(T);$$
$$E_3 := \pi_{x,y}(E_2);$$
$$E_4 := \pi_{x,y}(\delta_{A_1 A_2 \to xy}(R) \bowtie \delta_{B_1 \to z}(\pi_{B_1}(\sigma_{B_2=a}(S)))) \text{ diff } \delta_{C_1 C_2 \to yz}(T));$$
$$E_5 := \pi_x(E_3 - E_4).$$

The Positive Existential Calculus

In Chapter 4, disjunction was incorporated into the rule-based conjunctive queries, and union was incorporated into the tableau, SPC, and SPJR queries. Incorporating disjunction into the conjunctive calculus was more troublesome because of the possibility of infinite "answers." We now apply the tools developed earlier in this chapter to remedy this situation.

A *positive existential* (*calculus*) *query* is a domain-independent calculus query $q = \{e_1, \ldots, e_n \mid \varphi\}$, possibly with equality, in which the only logical connectives are $\wedge$, $\vee$, and $\exists$. It is decidable whether a query q with these logical connectives is domain independent; and if so, q is equivalent to a safe-range query using only these connectives (see Exercise 5.16). The following is easily verified.

THEOREM 5.4.10 The positive existential calculus is equivalent to the family of conjunctive queries with union.

5.5 Aggregate Functions

In practical query languages, the underlying domain is many-sorted, with sorts such as boolean, string, integer, or real. These languages allow the use of comparators such as $\leq$ between database entries in an ordered sort and "aggregate" functions such as **sum**, **count**, or **average** on numeric sorts. In this section, aggregate operators are briefly considered. In the next section, a novel approach for incorporating arithmetic constraints into the relational model will be addressed.

Aggregate operators operate on collections of domain elements. The next example illustrates how these are used.

EXAMPLE 5.5.1 Consider a relation *Sales*[*Theater*, *Title*, *Date*, *Attendance*], where a tuple $\langle th, ti, d, a \rangle$ indicates that on date d a total of a people attended showings of movie ti at theater th. We assume that {*Theater*, *Title*, *Date*} is a key, i.e., that two distinct tuples cannot share the same values on these three attributes. Two queries involving aggregate functions are

(5.4)   For each theater, list the total number of movies that have been shown there.

(5.5)   For each theater and movie, list the total attendance.

Informally, the first query might be expressed in a pidgin language as

$$\{\langle th,c\rangle \mid th \text{ is a theater occurring in } Sales$$
$$\text{and } c = |\pi_{Title}(\sigma_{Theater=th}(Sales))|\}$$

and the second as

$$\{\langle th, ti, s\rangle \mid \langle th, ti\rangle \text{ is a theater-title pair appearing in } Sales$$
$$\text{and } s \text{ is the sum that includes each occurrence of each } a\text{-value in}$$
$$\sigma_{Theater=th \wedge Title=ti}(Sales)\}$$

A subtlety here is that this second query cannot be expressed simply as

$$\{\langle th, ti, s\rangle \mid \langle th, ti\rangle \text{ is a theater-title pair appearing in } Sales$$
$$\text{and } s = \Sigma\{a \in \pi_{Attendance}(\sigma_{Theater=th \wedge Title=ti}(Sales))\}\}$$

since a value a has to be counted as many times as it occurs in the selection. This suggests that a more natural setting for studying aggregate functions would explicitly include *bags* (or multisets, i.e., collections in which duplicates are permitted) and not just sets, a somewhat radical departure from the model we have used so far.

The two queries can be expressed as follows using aggregate functions in an algebraic language:

$$\pi_{Theater;\ \mathbf{count}(Title)}(Sales)$$

$$\pi_{Theater,Title;\ \mathbf{sum}(Attendance)}(Sales).$$

We now briefly present a more formal development. To simplify, the formalism is based on the unnamed perspective, and we assume that $\mathbf{dom} = \mathbf{N}$, i.e., the set of non-negative integers. We stay within the relational model although as noted in the preceding example, a richer data model with bags would be more natural. Indeed, the complex value model that will be studied in Chapter 20 provides a more appropriate context for considering aggregate functions.

We shall adopt a somewhat abstract view of aggregate operators. An *aggregate function* f is defined to be a family of functions $f_1, f_2, \ldots$ such that for each $j \geq 1$ and each relation schema S with $arity(S) \geq j$, $f_j : Inst(S) \rightarrow \mathbf{N}$. For instance, for the **sum** aggregate function, we will have $\mathbf{sum}_1$ to sum the first column and, in general, $\mathbf{sum}_i$ to sum the ith one. As in the case of **sum**, we want the f_i to depend only on the content of the column to which they are applied, where the "content" includes not only the set of elements in the column, but also the number of their occurrences (so, columns are viewed as bags). This requirement is captured by the following *uniformity property* imposed on each aggregate function f:

Suppose that the ith column of I and the jth of J are identical, i.e., for each a, there are as many occurrences of a in the ith column of I and in the jth column of J. Then $f_i(I) = f_j(J)$.

All of the commonly arising aggregate functions satisfy this uniformity property. The uniformity condition is also used when translating calculus queries with aggregates into the algebra with aggregates.

We next illustrate how aggregate functions can be incorporated into the algebra and calculus (we do not discuss how this is done for nr-datalog¬, since it is similar to the algebra.) Aggregate functions are added to the algebra using an extended projection operation. Specifically, the projection function for aggregate function f on relation instance I is defined as follows:

$$\pi_{j_1,\ldots,j_m;f(k)}(I) = \{\langle a_{j_1}, \ldots, a_{j_m}, f_k(\sigma_{j_1=a_{j_1} \wedge \cdots \wedge j_m=a_{j_m}}(I))\rangle \mid \langle a_1, \ldots, a_n\rangle \in I\}.$$

Note that the aggregate function f_k is applied separately to each group of tuples in I corresponding to a different possible value for the columns $j_1, \ldots, j_m$.

Turning to the calculus, we begin with an example. Query (5.5) can be expressed in the extended calculus as

$$\{th, ti, s \mid \exists d_1, a_1(Sales(th, ti, d_1, a_1)$$
$$\wedge s = \mathbf{sum}_2\{d_2, a_2 \mid Sales(th, ti, d_2, a_2)\})\}$$

where $\mathbf{sum}_2$ is the aggregate function summing the second column of a relation. Note that the subexpression $\{d_2, a_2 \mid Sales(th, ti, d_2, a_2)\}$ has free variables th and ti that do not occur in the target of the subexpression. Intuitively, different assignments for these variables will yield different values for the subexpression.

More formally, aggregate functions are incorporated into the calculus by permitting *aggregate terms* that have the form $f_j\{\vec{x} \mid \psi\}$, where f is an aggregate function, $j \leq arity(\vec{x})$ and ψ is a calculus formula (possibly with aggregate terms). When defining the extended calculus, care must be taken to guarantee that aggregate terms do not recursively depend on each other. This can be accomplished with a suitable generalization of safe range. This generalization will also ensure that free variables occurring in an aggregate term are range restricted by a subformula containing it. It is straightforward to define the semantics of the generalized safe-range calculus with aggregate functions. One can then show that the extensions of the algebra and safe-range calculus with the same set of aggregate functions have the same expressive power.

5.6 Digression: Finite Representations of Infinite Databases

Until now we have considered only finite instances of relational databases. As we have seen, this introduced significant difficulty in connection with domain independence of calculus queries. It is also restrictive in connection with some application areas that involve temporal or geometric data. For example, it would be convenient to think of a rectangle in the real plane as an infinite set of points, even if it can be represented easily in some finite manner.

In this short section we briefly describe some recent and advanced material that uses logic to permit the finite representation of infinite databases. We begin by presenting an alternative approach to resolving the problem of safety, that permits queries to have answers that are infinite but finitely representable. We then introduce a promising generalization of the relational model that uses constraints to represent infinite databases, and we describe how query processing can be performed against these in an efficient manner.

An Alternative Resolution to the Problem of Safety

As indicated earlier, much of the research on safety has been directed at syntactic restrictions to ensure domain independence. An alternative approach is to use the natural interpretation, even if the resulting answer is infinite. As it turns out, the answers to such queries are recursive and have a finite representation.

For this result, we shall use a finite set $\mathbf{d} \subset \mathbf{dom}$, which corresponds intuitively to the active domain of a query and input database; and a set $C = \{c_1, \ldots, c_m\}$ of m distinct "new" symbols, which will serve as placeholders for elements of $\mathbf{dom} - \mathbf{d}$. Speaking intuitively, the elements of C sometimes act as elements of $\mathbf{dom}$, and so it is not appropriate to view them as simple variables.

A *tuple with placeholders* is a tuple $t = \langle t_1, \ldots, t_n \rangle$, where each t_i is in $\mathbf{d} \cup C$. The *semantics* of such t relative to $\mathbf{d}$ are

$$sem_{\mathbf{d}}(t) = \{\rho(t) \mid \rho \text{ is a one-one mapping from } \mathbf{d} \cup C$$
$$\text{that leaves } \mathbf{d} \text{ fixed and maps } C \text{ into } \mathbf{dom} - \mathbf{d}\}.$$

The following theorem, stated without proof, characterizes the result of applying an arbitrary calculus query using the natural semantics.

THEOREM 5.6.1   Let $q = \{e_1, \ldots, e_n \mid \varphi\}$ be an arbitrary calculus query, such that each quantifier in φ quantifies a distinct variable that is not free in φ. Let $C = \{c_1, \ldots, c_m\}$ be a set of m distinct "new" symbols not occurring in $\mathbf{dom}$, but viewed as domain elements, where m is the number of distinct variables in φ. Then for each input instance $\mathbf{I}$,

$$q_{\mathbf{dom}}(\mathbf{I}) = \cup\{sem_{adom(q,\mathbf{I})}(t) \mid t \in q_{adom(q,\mathbf{I}) \cup C}(\mathbf{I})\}.$$

This shows that if we apply a calculus query (under the natural semantics) to a finite database, then the result is recursive, even if infinite. But is the set of infinite databases described in this manner closed under the application of calculus queries? The affirmative answer is provided by an elegant generalization of the relational model presented next (see Exercise 5.31).

Constraint Query Languages

The following generalization of the relational model seems useful to a variety of new applications. The starting point is to consider infinite databases with finite representations based on the use of constraints. To begin we define a generalized n-tuple as a conjunction of constraints over n variables. The constraints typically include $=$, $\neq$, $\leq$, etc. In some sense, such a constraint can be viewed as a finite representation of a (possibly infinite) set of (normal) n-tuples (i.e., the valuations of the variables that satisfy the constraint).

EXAMPLE 5.6.2 Consider the representation of rectangles in the plane. Suppose first that rectangles are given using 5-tuples (n, x_1, y_1, x_2, y_2), where n is the name of the rectangle, (x_1, y_1) are the coordinates of the lower left corner, and (x_2, y_2) are the coordinates of the upper right. The set of points $\langle u, v \rangle$ in such a rectangle delimited by x_1, y_1, x_2, y_2 is given by the constraint

$$x_1 \le u \le x_2 \wedge y_1 \le v \le y_2.$$

Now the names of intersecting rectangles from a relation R are given by

$$\{\langle n_1, n_2 \rangle \mid \exists\, x_1, y_1, x_2, y_2, x_1', y_1', x_2', y_2', u, v$$
$$(R(n_1, x_1, y_1, x_2, y_2) \wedge (x_1 \le u \le x_2 \wedge y_1 \le v \le y_2) \wedge$$
$$R(n_2, x_1', y_1', x_2', y_2') \wedge (x_1' \le u \le x_2' \wedge y_1' \le v \le y_2'))\}.$$

This is essentially within the framework of the relational model presented so far, except that we are using an infinite base relation $\le$. There is a level of indirection between the representation of a rectangle (a, x_1, y_1, x_2, y_2) and the actual set of points that it contains.

In the following constraint formalism, a named rectangle can be represented by a "generalized tuple" (i.e., a constraint). For instance, the rectangle of name a with corners $(0.5, 1.0)$ and $(1.5, 5.5)$ is represented by the constraint

$$z_1 = a \wedge 0.5 \le z_2 \wedge z_2 \le 1.5 \wedge 1.0 \le z_3 \wedge z_3 \le 5.5.$$

This should be viewed as a finite syntactic representation of an infinite set of triples. A triple $\langle z_1, z_2, z_3 \rangle$ satisfying this constraint indicates that the point of coordinates (z_2, z_3) is in a rectangle with name z_1.

One can see a number of uses in allowing constraints in the language. First, constraints arise naturally for domains concerning measures (price, distance, time, etc.). The introduction of time has already been studied in the active area of temporal databases (see Section 22.6). In other applications such as spatial databases, geometry plays an essential role and fits nicely in the realm of constraint query languages.

One can clearly obtain different languages by considering various domains and various forms of constraints. Relational calculus, relational algebra, or some other relational languages can be extended with, for instance, the theory of real closed fields or the theory of dense orders without endpoints. Of course, a requirement is the decidability of the resulting language.

Assuming some notion of constraints (to be formalized soon), we now define somewhat more precisely the constraint languages and then illustrate them with two examples.

DEFINITION 5.6.3 A *generalized n-tuple* is a finite conjunction of constraints over variables $x_1, \ldots, x_n$. A *generalized instance* of arity n is a finite set of generalized n-tuples (the corresponding formula is the disjunction of the constraints).

Suppose that I is a generalized instance. We refer to I as a *syntactic* database and to the set of conventional tuples represented by I as the *semantic* database.

We now present two applications of this approach, one in connection with the reals and the other with the rationals.

We assume now that the constants are interpreted over a real closed field (e.g., the reals). The constraints are polynomial inequality constraints [i.e., inequalities of the form $p(x_1, \ldots, x_n) \geq 0$, where p is a polynomial]. Two 3-tuples in this context are

$$(3.56 \times x_1^2 + 4.0 \times x_2 \geq 0) \wedge (x_3 - x_1 \geq 0)$$
$$(x_1 + x_2 + x_3 \geq 0).$$

One can evaluate queries algebraically bottom-up (i.e., at each step of the computation, the result is still a generalized instance). This is a straightforward consequence of Tarski's decision procedure for the theory of real closed fields. A difficulty resides in projection (i.e., quantifier elimination). The procedure for projection is extremely costly in the size of the query. However, for a fixed query, the complexity *in the size of the syntactic database* is reasonable (in NC).

We assume now that the constants are interpreted over a countably infinite set with a binary relation $\leq$ that is a dense order (e.g., the rationals). The constraints are of the form $x \theta y$ or $x \theta c$, where x, y are variables, c is a constant, and θ is among $\leq, <, =$. An example of a 3-tuple is

$$(x_1 \leq x_2) \wedge (x_2 < x_3).$$

Here again, a bottom-up algebraic evaluation is feasible. Indeed, evaluation is in AC$_0$ in the size of the syntactic database (for a fixed query).

In the remainder of this book, we consider standard databases and not generalized ones.

Bibliographic Notes

One of the first investigations of using predicate calculus to query relational database structures is [Kuh67], although the work by Codd [Cod70, Cod72b] played a tremendous role in bringing attention to the relational model and to the relational algebra and calculus. In particular, [Cod72b] introduced the equivalence of the calculus and algebra to the database community. That paper coined the phrase *relational completeness* to describe the expressive power of relational query languages: Any language able to simulate the algebra is called relationally complete. We have not emphasized that phrase here because subsequent research has suggested that a more natural notion of completeness can be described in terms of Turing computability (see Chapter 16).

Actually, a version of the result on the equivalence of the calculus and algebra was known much earlier to the logic community (see [CT48, TT52]) and is used to show Tarski's algebraization theorem (e.g., see [HMT71]). The relation between relational algebras and cylindric algebras is studied in [IL84] (see Exercise 5.36). The development of algebras equivalent to various calculus languages has been a fertile area for database theory. One such result presented in this chapter is the equivalence of the positive existential calculus and the SPCU algebra [CH82]; analogous results have also been developed for the relational calculus extended with aggregate operators [Klu82], the complex value model [AB88] (studied in Chapter 20), the Logical Data Model [KV84], the directory model [DM86a, DM92], and formalizations of the hierarchy and network models using database logic [Jac82].

Notions related to domain independence are found as early as [Low15] in the logic community; in the database community the first paper on this topic appears to be [Kuh67], which introduced the notion of *definite* queries. The notion of domain independence used here is from [Fag82b, Mak81]; the notions of definite and domain independent were proved equivalent in [ND82]. A large number of classes of domain-independent formulas have been investigated. These include the safe [Ull82b], safe DRC [Ull88], range separable [Cod72b], allowed [Top87] (Exercise 5.25), range restricted [Nic82] (Exercise 5.26), and evaluable [Dem82] formulas. An additional investigation of domain independence for the calculus is found in [ND82]. Surveys on domain independence and various examples of these classes can be found in [Kif88, VanGT91]. The focus of [VanGT91] is the general problem of practical translations from calculus to algebra queries; in particular, it provides a translation from the set of evaluable formulas into the algebra. It is also shown there that the notions of evaluable and range restricted are equivalent. These are the most general syntactic conditions in the literature that ensure domain independence. The fact that domain independence is undecidable was first observed in [DiP69]; this is detailed in Chapter 6.

Domain independence also arises in the context of dependencies [Fag82b, Mak81] and datalog [Dec86, Top87, RBS87, TS88]. The issue of extending domain independence to incorporate functions (e.g., arithmetic functions, or user-defined functions) is considered in [AB88, Top91, EHJ93]. The issue of extending domain independence to incorporate freely interpreted functions (such as arise in logic programming) is addressed in [Kif88]. Syntactic conditions on (recursive) datalog programs with arithmetic that ensure safety are developed in [RBS87, KRS88a, KRS88b, SV89]. Issues of safety in the presence of function or order symbols are also considered in [AH91]. Aggregate functions were first incorporated into the relational algebra and calculus in [Klu82]; see also [AB88].

The notion of safe range presented here is richer than safe, safe DRC, and range separable and weaker than allowed, evaluable, and range restricted. It follows the spirit of the definition of allowed presented in [VanGT91] and safe range in [AB88]. The transformations of the safe-range calculus to the algebra presented here follows the more general transformations in [VanGT91, EHJ93]. The notion of "relational algebra normal form" used in those works is more general than the notion by that name used here.

Query languages have mostly been considered for finite databases. An exception is [HH93]. Theorem 5.6.1 is due to [AGSS86]. An alternative proof and extension of this result is developed in [HS91].

Programming with constraints has been studied for some time in topic areas ranging from linear programming to AI to logic programming. Although the declarative spirit of both constraint programming and database query languages leads to a natural marriage, it is only recently that the combination of the two paradigms has been studied seriously [KKR90]. This was probably a consequence of the success of constraints in the field of logic programming (see, e.g., [JL87] and [Lel87, Coh90] for surveys). Our presentation was influenced by [KKR90] (calculii for closed real fields with polynomial inequalities and for dense order with inequalities are studied there) as well as by [KG94] (an algebra for constraint databases with dense order and inequalities is featured there). Recent works on constraint database languages can be found in [Kup93, GS94].

Exercises

Exercise 5.1   Express queries (5.2 and 5.3) in (1) the relational algebras, (2) nonrecursive datalog¬, and (3) domain-independent relational calculus.

Exercise 5.2   Express the following queries against the *CINEMA* database in (1) the relational algebras, (2) nonrecursive datalog¬, and (3) domain-independent relational calculus.

   (a) Find the actors cast in at least one movie by Kurosawa.
   (b) Find the actors cast in every movie by Kurosawa.
   (c) Find the actors cast only in movies by Kurosawa.
   (d) Find all pairs of actors who act together in at least one movie.
   (e) Find all pairs of actors cast in exactly the same movies.
   (f) Find the directors such that every actor is cast in one of his or her films.

(Assume that a film is uniquely identified by its title.)

Exercise 5.3   Prove or disprove (assuming $X \subseteq sort(P) = sort(Q)$):

   (a) $\pi_X(P \cup Q) = \pi_X(P) \cup \pi_X(Q)$;
   (b) $\pi_X(P \cap Q) = \pi_X(P) \cap \pi_X(Q)$.

Exercise 5.4

   (a) Give formal definitions for the syntax and semantics of the unnamed and named relational algebras.
   (b) Show that in the unnamed algebra $\cap$ can be simulated using (1) the difference operator $-$; (2) the operators $\times, \pi, \sigma$.
   (c) Give a formal definition for the syntax and semantics of selection operators in the unnamed algebra that permit conjunction, disjunction, and negation in their formulas. Show that these selection operators can be simulated using atomic selection operators, union, intersect, and difference.
   ★ (d) Show that the SPCU algebra, in which selection operators with negation in the formulas are permitted, cannot simulate the difference operator.
   ★ (e) Formulate and prove results analogous to those of parts (b), (c), and (d) for the named algebra.

Exercise 5.5

   (a) Prove that the unnamed algebra operators $\{\sigma, \pi, \times, \cup, -\}$ are nonredundant.
   (b) State and prove the analogous result for the named algebra.

Exercise 5.6

   (a) Exhibit a relational algebra query that is not monotonic.
   (b) Exhibit a relational algebra query that is not satisfiable.

Exercise 5.7   Prove Proposition 5.1.2 (i.e., that the unnamed and named relational algebras have equivalent expressive power).

Exercise 5.8   (Division) The *division* operator, denoted $\div$, is added to the named algebra as follows. For instances I and J with $sort(J) \subseteq sort(I)$, the value of $I \div J$ is the set of tuples $r \in \pi_{sort(I)-sort(J)}(I)$ such that $(\{r\} \bowtie J) \subseteq I$. Use the division to express algebraically the query, "Which theater is featuring all Hitchcock movies?". Describe how nr-datalog$^{\neg}$ can be used to simulate division. Describe how the named algebra can simulate division. Is division a monotonic operation?

Exercise 5.9   Show that the semantics of each nr-datalog$^{\neg}$ rule can be described as a difference $q_1 - q_2$, where q_1 is an SPC query and q_2 is an SPCU query.

Exercise 5.10   Verify that each nr-datalog$^{\neg}$ program with equality can be simulated by one without equality.

Exercise 5.11   Prove Proposition 5.2.2. *Hint:* Use the proof of Theorem 4.4.8 and the fact that the relational algebra is closed under composition.

★ **Exercise 5.12**

    (a) Prove that the domain-independent relational calculus without equality is strictly weaker than the domain-independent relational calculus. *Hint:* Suppose that calculus query q without equality is equivalent to $\{x \mid R(x) \wedge x \neq a\}$.

    (b) Show that q can be translated into an algebra query q' that is constructed without using a constant base relation and such that all selections are on base relation expressions. Argue that on each input relation I over R, each subexpression of q' evaluates to either I^n for some $n \geq 0$, or to the empty relation for some $n \geq 0$.

Exercise 5.13

    (a) Complete the proof of Lemma 5.3.11.

    (b) Complete the proof of Lemma 5.3.12.

Exercise 5.14

    (a) Prove that the rewrite rules of Figure 5.1 preserve equivalence.

    (b) Prove that these rewrite rules can be used to transform an arbitrary calculus formula into an equivalent formula in PNF with CNF matrix. State which rewrite rules are needed.

    (c) Do the same as (b), but for DNF matrix.

    (d) Prove that the rewrite rules of Figure 5.1 are not complete in the sense that there are calculus formulas φ and ψ such that (1) $\varphi \equiv \psi$, but (2) there is no sequence of applications of the rewrite rules that transforms φ into ψ.

Exercise 5.15   Verify the claims of Example 5.3.9.

Exercise 5.16

    (a) Show that it is decidable, given a relational calculus query q (possibly with equality) whose only logical connectives are $\wedge$, $\vee$, and $\exists$, whether q is domain independent.

    (b) Show that each positive existential query is equivalent to one whose formula is in PNF with either CNF or DNF matrix and that they can be expressed in the form

$\{e_1, \ldots, e_n \mid \psi_1 \vee \cdots \vee \psi_m\}$, where each ψ_j is a conjunctive calculus formula with $free(\psi_j) =$ the set of variables occurring in $e_1, \ldots, e_n$. Note that this formula is safe range.

(c) Prove Theorem 5.4.10.

Exercise 5.17   Use the construction of the proof of Theorem 5.4.6 to transform the following into the algebra.

(a) $\{\langle\rangle \mid \exists x (R(x) \wedge \exists y (S(x, y) \wedge \neg \exists z (T(x, y, a))))\}$

(b) $\{w, x, y, z \mid (R(w, x, y) \vee R(w, x, z)) \wedge (R(y, z, w) \vee R(y, z, x))\}$

Exercise 5.18   For each of the following queries, indicate whether it is domain independent and/or safe range. If it is not domain independent, give examples of different domains yielding different answers on the same input; and if it is safe range, translate it into the algebra.

(a) $\{x, y \mid \exists z [T(x, z) \wedge \exists w T(w, x, y)] \wedge x = y\}$

(b) $\{x, y \mid [x = a \vee \exists z (R(y, z)] \wedge S(y))\}$

(c) $\{x, y \mid [x = a \vee \exists z (R(y, z))] \wedge S(y) \wedge T(x)\}$

(d) $\{x \mid \forall y (R(y) \rightarrow S(x, y))\}$

(e) $\{\langle\rangle \mid \exists x \forall y (R(y) \rightarrow S(x, y))\}$

(f) $\{x, y \mid \exists z T(x, y, z) \wedge \exists u, v ([(R(u) \vee S(u, v)) \wedge R(v)]$
    $\rightarrow [\exists w (T(x, w, v) \wedge T(u, v, y))])\}$

★ **Exercise 5.19**   Consider the proof of Theorem 5.4.6.

(a) Give the missing parts of Algorithm 5.4.7.

(b) Show that Algorithm 5.4.7 is correct and terminates on all input.

(c) Give the missing parts of Algorithm 5.4.8 and verify its correctness.

(d) Given $q = \{\langle x_1, \ldots, x_n \rangle \mid \varphi\}$ with φ in modified RANF, show for each instance **I** and each **d** satisfying $adom(q, \mathbf{I}) \subseteq \mathbf{d} \subseteq \mathbf{dom}$ that $q_\mathbf{d}(\mathbf{I}) = E_\varphi(\mathbf{I})$.

Exercise 5.20   Consider the proof of Theorem 5.4.6.

(a) Present examples illustrating how the nondeterministic choices in these rewrite rules can be used to help optimize the algebra query finally produced by the construction of the proof of this lemma. (Refer to Chapter 6 for a general discussion of optimization.)

(b) Consider a generalization of rules (R1) and (R2) that permits using a set of indexes $\{j_1, \ldots, j_l\} \subseteq \{1, \ldots, n\} - \{i_1, \ldots, i_k\}$. What are the advantages of this generalization? What restrictions must be imposed to ensure that Algorithm 5.4.8 remains correct?

Exercise 5.21   Develop a direct proof that $\text{CALC}_{adom} \sqsubseteq \text{CALC}_{sr}$. *Hint:* Given calculus query q, first build a formula $\xi_{adom}(x)$ such that $\mathbf{I} \models \xi_{adom}(x)[v]$ iff $v(x) \in adom(q, \mathbf{I})$. Now perform an induction on subformulas.

★ **Exercise 5.22**   [Coh86] Let R have arity n. Define the *gen(erator)* operator so that for instance I of R, indexes $1 \leq i_1 < \cdots < i_k \leq n$, and constants $a_1, \ldots, a_k$,

$$gen_{i_1:a_1,\ldots,i_k:a_k}(I) = \pi_{j_1,\ldots,j_l}(\sigma_{i_1 = a_1 \wedge \cdots \wedge i_k = a_k}(I)),$$

where $\{j_1, \ldots, j_l\}$ is a listing in order of (some or all) indexes in $\{1, \ldots, n\} - \{i_1, \ldots, i_k\}$. Note that the special case of $gen_{1:b_1, \ldots, n:b_n}(I)$ can be viewed as a test of $\langle b_1, \ldots, b_n \rangle \in I$; and $gen_{[\,]}(I)$ is a test of whether I is nonempty. In some research in AI, the primitive mechanism for accessing relations is based on generators that are viewed as producing a stream of tuples as output. For example, the query $\{\langle x, y, z \rangle \mid R(x, y) \wedge S(y, z)\}$ can be computed using the algorithm

> **for each** tuple $\langle x, y \rangle$ generated by $gen_{1:x, 2:y}(R)$
>   **for each** value $\langle z \rangle$ generated by $gen_{1:y}(S)$
>   **output** $\langle x, y, z \rangle$
>   **end for each**
> **end for each**

     Develop an algorithm for translating calculus queries into programs using generators. Describe syntactic restrictions on the calculus that ensure that your algorithm succeeds.

♠ **Exercise 5.23** [Cod72b] (Tuple calculus.) We use a set **tvar** of sorted tuple variables. The *tuple calculus* is defined as follows. If t is a tuple variable and A is an attribute in the sort of t, $t.A$ is a *term*. A constant is also a *term*. The atomic formulas are either of the form $R(t)$ with the appropriate constraint on sorts, or $e = e'$, where e, e' are terms. Formulas are constructed as in the standard relational calculus. For example, query (5.1) is expressed by the tuple calculus query

$$\{t\!:\!title \mid \exists s\!:\!title, director, actor[Movie(s) \wedge t.title = s.title$$

$$\wedge\ s.director = \text{``Hitchcock''}]$$

$$\wedge\ \neg\exists u\!:\!title, director, actor[Movie(u) \wedge u.title = s.title$$

$$\wedge\ u.actor = \text{``Hitchcock''}]\}.$$

Give a formal definition for the syntax of the tuple calculus and for the relativized interpretation, active domain, and domain-independent semantics. Develop an analog of safe range. Prove the equivalence of conventional calculus and tuple calculus under all of these semantics.

Exercise 5.24 Prove that the relational calculus and the family of nr-datalog$^\neg$ programs with single-relation output have equivalent expressive power by using direct simulations between the two families.

♠ **Exercise 5.25** [Top87] Let **R** be a database schema, and define the binary relation *gen(erates)* on variables and formulas as follows:

$gen(x, \varphi)$	if $\varphi = R(u)$ for some $R \in \mathbf{R}$ and $x \in free(\varphi)$
$gen(x, \neg\varphi)$	if $gen(x, pushnot(\neg\varphi))$
$gen(x, \exists y\varphi)$	if x, y are distinct and $gen(x, \varphi)$
$gen(x, \forall y\varphi)$	if x, y are distinct and $gen(x, \varphi)$
$gen(x, \varphi \vee \psi)$	if $gen(x, \varphi)$ and $gen(x, \psi)$
$gen(x, \varphi \wedge \psi)$	if $gen(x, \varphi)$ or $gen(x, \psi)$,

where $pushnot(\neg\varphi)$ is defined in the natural manner to be the result of pushing the negation into the next highest level logical connective (with consecutive negations cancelling each other) unless φ is an atom (using the rewrite rules 5, 6, 7, 10, and 11 from Fig. 5.1). A formula φ is *allowed*

(i) if $x \in free(\varphi)$ then $gen(x, \varphi)$;

(ii) if for each subformula $\exists y \psi$ of φ, $gen(y, \psi)$ holds; and

(iii) if for each subformula $\forall y \psi$ of φ, $gen(y, \neg\psi)$ holds.

A calculus query is *allowed* if its formula is allowed.

(a) Exhibit a query that is allowed but not safe range.

★ (b) Prove that each allowed query is domain independent.

In [VanGT91, EHJ93] a translation of allowed formulas into the algebra is presented.)

★ **Exercise 5.26**   [Nic82] The notion of "range-restricted" queries, which ensures domain independence, is based on properties of the normal form equivalents of queries. Let $q = \{\vec{x} \mid \varphi\}$ be a calculus query, and let $\varphi_{DNF} = \%\vec{y}(D_1 \vee \cdots \vee D_n)$ be the result of transforming φ into PNF with DNF matrix using the rewrite rules of Fig. 5.1; and similarly let $\varphi_{CNF} = \%\vec{z}(C_1 \wedge \cdots \wedge C_m)$ be the result of transforming φ into PNF with CNF matrix. The query q is *range restricted* if

(i) each free variable x in φ occurs in a positive literal (other than $x = y$) in every D_i;

(ii) each existentially quantified variable x in φ_{DNF} occurs in a positive literal (other than $x = y$) in every D_i where x occurs; and

(iii) each universally quantified variable x in φ_{CNF} occurs in a negative literal (other than $x \neq y$) in every C_j where x occurs.

Prove that range-restricted queries are domain independent. (In [VanGT91] a translation of the range-restricted queries into the algebra is presented.)

Exercise 5.27   [VanGT91] Suppose that $R[Product, Part]$ holds project numbers and the parts that are used to make them, and $S[Supplier, Part]$ holds supplier names and the parts that they supply. Consider the queries

$$q_1 = \{x \mid \forall y (R(100, y) \rightarrow S(x, y))\}$$
$$q_2 = \{\langle\rangle \mid \exists x \forall y (R(100, y) \rightarrow S(x, y))\}$$

(a) Prove that q_1 is not domain independent.

(b) Prove that q_2 is not allowed (Exercise 5.25) but it is range restricted (Exercise 5.26) and hence domain independent.

(c) Find an algebra query q' equivalent to q_2.

Exercise 5.28   [Klu82] Consider a database schema with relations $Dept[Name, Head, College]$, $Faculty[Name, Dname]$, and $Grad[Name, MajorProf, GrantAmt]$, and the query

For each department in the Letters and Science College, compute the total graduate student support for each of the department's faculty members, and produce as output a relation that includes all pairs $\langle d, a \rangle$ where d is a department in the Letters and Science College, and a is the average graduate student support per faculty member in d.

Write algebra and calculus queries that express this query.

Exercise 5.29   We consider constraint databases involving polynomial inequalities over the reals. Let $I_1 = \{(9x_1^2 + 4x_2 \geq 0)\}$ be a generalized instance over AB, where x_1 ranges over A

and x_2 ranges over B, and let $I_2 = \{(x_3 - x_1 \geq 0)\}$ over AC. Express $I_1 \bowtie I_2$ as a generalized instance.

★ **Exercise 5.30**   Recall Theorem 5.6.1.

   (a) Let finite $\mathbf{d} \subset \mathbf{dom}$ be fixed, C be a set of new symbols, and t be a tuple with placeholders. Describe a generalized tuple (in the sense of constraint databases) t' whose semantics are equal to $sem_{\mathbf{d}}(t)$.

   (b) Show that the family of databases representable by sets of tuples with placeholders is closed under the relational calculus.

♠ **Exercise 5.31**   Prove Theorem 5.6.1.

Exercise 5.32   [Mai80] (Unrestricted algebra) For this exercise we permit relations to be finite or infinite. Consider the *complement* operator ^{c} defined on instances I of arity n by $I^c = \mathbf{dom}^n - I$. (The analogous operator is defined for the named algebra.) Prove that the calculus under the natural interpretation is equivalent to the algebra with operators $\{\sigma, \pi, \times, \cup, ^c\}$.

★ **Exercise 5.33**   A total mapping τ from instances over $\mathbf{R}$ to instances over S is *C-generic* for $C \subseteq \mathbf{dom}$, iff for each bijection ρ over $\mathbf{dom}$ that is the identity on C, τ and ρ commute. That is, $\tau(\rho(\mathbf{I})) = \rho(\tau(\mathbf{I}))$ for each instance $\mathbf{I}$ of $\mathbf{R}$. The mapping τ is *generic* if it is C-generic for some finite $C \subseteq \mathbf{dom}$. Prove that each relational algebra query is generic—in particular, that each algebra query q is $adom(q)$-generic.

♠ **Exercise 5.34**   Let R be a unary relation name. A *hyperplane query* over R is a query of the form $\sigma_F(R \times \cdots \times R)$ (with 0 or more occurrences of R), where F is a conjunction of atoms of the form $i = j, i \neq j, i = a$, or $i \neq a$ (for indexes i, j and constant a). A formula F of this form is called a *hyperplane formula*. A *hyperplane-union query* over R is a query of the form $\sigma_F(R \times \cdots \times R)$, where F is a disjunction of hyperplane formulas; a formula of this form is called a *hyperplane-union* formula.

   (a) Show that if q is an algebra query over R, then there is an $n \geq 0$ and a hyperplane-union query q' such that for all instances I over R, if $|I| \geq n$ and $adom(I) \cap adom(q) = \emptyset$, then $q(I) = q'(I)$.

The query *even* is defined over R as follows: $even(I) = \{\langle\rangle\}$ (i.e., yes) if $|I|$ is even; and $even(I) = \{\}$ (i.e., no) otherwise.

   (b) Prove that there is no algebra query q over R such that $q \equiv even$.

Exercise 5.35   [CH80b] (Unsorted algebra) An *h-relation* (for heterogeneous relation) is a finite set of tuples not necessarily of the same arity.

   (a) Design an algebra for h-relations that is at least as expressive as relational algebra.

   ★ (b) Show that the algebra in (a) can be chosen to have the additional property that if q is a query in this algebra taking standard relational input and producing standard relational output, then there is a standard algebra query q' such that $q' \equiv q$.

♠ **Exercise 5.36**   [IL84] (Cylindric algebra) Let n be a positive integer, $R[A_1, \ldots, A_n]$ a relation schema, and C a (possibly infinite) set of constants. Recall that a *Boolean algebra* is a 6-tuple $(\mathcal{B}, \vee, \wedge, ^-, \bot, \top)$, where $\mathcal{B}$ is a set containing $\bot$ and $\top$; $\vee, \wedge$ are binary operations on $\mathcal{B}$; and $^-$ is a unary operation on $\mathcal{B}$ such that for all $x, y, z \in \mathcal{B}$:

   (a) $x \vee y = y \vee x$;

(b) $x \wedge y = y \wedge x$;

(c) $x \vee (y \wedge z) = (x \vee y) \wedge (x \vee z)$;

(d) $x \wedge (y \vee z) = (x \wedge y) \vee (x \wedge z)$;

(e) $x \wedge \bot = \bot$;

(f) $x \vee \top = \top$;

(g) $x \wedge \bar{x} = \bot$;

(h) $x \vee \bar{x} = \top$; and

(i) $\bot \neq \top$.

For a Boolean algebra, define $x \leq y$ to mean $x \wedge y = x$.

(a) Show that $\langle \mathcal{R}_C, \cup, \cap, ^c, \emptyset, C^n \rangle$ is a Boolean algebra where $\mathcal{R}_C$ is the set of all (possibly infinite) R-relations over constants in C and ^{c} denotes the unary *complement* operator, defined so that $I^c = C^n - I$. In addition, show that $I \leq J$ iff $I \subseteq J$.

Let the diagonals d_{ij} be defined by the statement, "for each i, j, $d_{ij} = \sigma_{A_i = A_j}(C^n)$"; and let the ith cylinder C_i be defined for each I by the statement, "$C_i I$ is the relation over $\mathcal{R}_C$ defined by

$$C_i I = \{t \mid \pi_{A_1 \dots A_{i-1} A_{i+1} \dots A_n}(t) \in \pi_{A_1 \dots A_{i-1} A_{i+1} \dots A_n}(I) \text{ and } t(A_i) \in C\}.\text{"}$$

(b) Show the following properties of cylindric algebras: (1) $C_i \emptyset = \emptyset$; (2) $x \leq C_i x$; (3) $C_i(x \cap C_i y) = C_i x \cap C_i y$; (4) $C_i C_j x = C_j C_i x$; (5) $d_{ii} = C^n$; (6) if $i \neq j$ and $i \neq k$, then $d_{jk} = C_i(d_{ji} \cap d_{ik})$; (7) if $i \neq j$, then $C_i(d_{ij} \cap x) \cap C_i(d_{ij} \cap \bar{x}) = \emptyset$.

(c) Let h be the mapping from any (possibly infinite) relation S with $sort(S) \subset A_1 \dots A_n$ with entries in C to a relation over R obtained by extending each tuple in S to $A_1 \dots A_n$ in all possible ways with values in C. Prove that (1) $h(R_1 \bowtie R_2) = h(R_1) \cap h(R_2)$ and (2) if $A_1 \in sort(R)$, then $h(\pi_{A_1}(R)) = C_1 h(R_1)$.

6 Static Analysis and Optimization

Alice:	*Do you guys mean* real *optimization?*
Riccardo:	*Well, most of the time it's local maneuvering.*
Vittorio:	*But sometimes we go beyond incremental reform . . .*
Sergio:	*. . . with provably global results.*

This chapter examines the conjunctive and first-order queries from the perspective of static analysis (in the sense of programming languages). It is shown that many properties of conjunctive queries (e.g., equivalence, containment) are decidable although they are not decidable for first-order queries. Static analysis techniques are also applied here in connection with query optimization (i.e., transforming queries expressed in a high-level, largely declarative language into equivalent queries or machine instruction programs that are arguably more efficient than a naive execution of the initial query).

To provide background, this chapter begins with a survey of practical optimization techniques for the conjunctive queries. The majority of practically oriented research and development on query optimization has been focused on variants of the conjunctive queries, possibly extended with arithmetic operators and comparators. Because of the myriad factors that play a role in query evaluation, most practically successful techniques rely heavily on heuristics.

Next the chapter presents the elegant and important *Homomorphism Theorem*, which characterizes containment and equivalence between conjunctive queries. This leads to the notion of tableau "minimization": For each tableau query there is a unique (up to isomorphism) equivalent tableau query with the smallest number of rows. This provides a theoretical notion of true optimality for conjunctive queries. It is also shown that deciding these properties and minimizing conjunctive queries is NP-complete in the size of the input queries.

Undecidability results are then presented for the first-order queries. Although related to undecidability results for conventional first-order logic, the proof techniques used here are necessarily different because all instances considered are finite by definition. The undecidability results imply that there is no hope of developing an algorithm that performs optimization of first-order queries that is complete. Only limited optimization of first-order queries involving difference is provided in most systems.

The chapter closes by returning to a specialized subset of the conjunctive queries based on *acyclic joins*. These have been shown to enjoy several interesting properties, some yielding insight into more efficient query processing.

Chapter 13 in Part D examines techniques for optimizing datalog queries.

6.1   Issues in Practical Query Optimization

Query optimization is one of the central topics of database systems. A myriad of factors play a role in this area, including storage and indexing techniques, page sizes and paging protocols, the underlying operating system, statistical properties of the stored data, statistical properties of anticipated queries and updates, implementations of specific operators, and the expressive power of the query languages used, to name a few. Query optimization can be performed at all levels of the three-level database architecture. At the physical level, this work focuses on, for example, access techniques, statistical properties of stored data, and buffer management. At a more logical level, algebraic equivalences are used to rewrite queries into forms that can be implemented more efficiently.

We begin now with a discussion of rudimentary considerations that affect query processing (including the usual cost measurements) and basic methods for accessing relations and implementing algebraic operators. Next an optimization approach based on algebraic equivalences is described; this is used to replace a given algebraic expression by an equivalent one that can typically be computed more quickly. This leads to the important notion of query evaluation plans and how they are used in modern systems to represent and choose among many alternative implementations of a query. We then examine intricate techniques for implementing multiway joins based on different orderings of binary joins and on join decomposition.

The discussion presented in this section only scratches the surface of the rich body of systems-oriented research and development on query optimizers, indicating only a handful of the most important factors that are involved. Nothing will be said about several factors, such as the impact of negation in queries, main-memory buffering strategies, and the implications of different environments (such as distributed, object oriented, real time, large main memory, and secondary memories other than conventional disks). In part due to the intricacy and number of interrelated factors involved, little of the fundamental theoretical research on query optimization has found its way into practice. As the field is maturing, salient aspects of query optimization are becoming isolated; this may provide some of the foothold needed for significant theoretical work to emerge and be applied.

The Physical Model

The usual assumption of relational databases is that the current database state is so large that it must be stored in secondary memory (e.g., on disk). Manipulation of the stored data, including the application of algebraic operators, requires making copies in primary memory of portions of the stored data and storing intermediate and final results again in secondary memory. By far the major time expense in query processing, for a single-processor system, is the number of disk pages that must be swapped in and out of primary memory. In the case of distributed systems, the communication costs typically dominate all others and become an important focus of optimization.

Viewed a little more abstractly, the physical level of relational query implementation involves three basic activities: (1) generating streams of tuples, (2) manipulating streams of tuples (e.g., to perform projections), and (3) combining streams of tuples (e.g., to perform joins, unions, and intersections). Indexing methods, including primarily B-trees and hash indexes, can be used to reduce significantly the size of some streams. Although not discussed here, it is important to consider the cost of maintaining indexes and clusterings as updates to the database occur.

Main-memory buffering techniques (including the partitioning of main memory into segments and paging policies such as deleting pages based on policies of least recent use and most recent use) can significantly impact the number of page I/Os used.

Speaking broadly, an *evaluation plan* (or *access plan*) for a query, a stored database state, and a collection of existing indexes and other data structures is a specification of a sequence of operations that will compute the answer to the query. The term evaluation plan is used most often to refer to specifications that are at a low physical level but may sometimes be used for higher-level specifications. As we shall see, query optimizers typically develop several evaluation plans and then choose one for execution.

Implementation of Algebraic Operators

To illustrate the basic building blocks from which evaluation plans are constructed, we now describe basic implementation techniques for some of the relational operators.

Selection can be realized in a straightforward manner by a scan of the argument relation and can thus be achieved in linear time. Access structures such as B-tree indexes or hash tables can be used to reduce the search time needed to find the selected tuples. In the case of selections with single tuple output, this permits evaluation within essentially constant time (e.g., two or three page fetches). For larger outputs, the selection may take two or three page fetches per output tuple; this can be improved significantly if the input relation is *clustered* (i.e., stored so that all tuples with a given attribute value are on the same or contiguous disk pages).

Projection is a bit more complex because it actually calls for two essentially different operations: *tuple rewriting* and *duplicate elimination*. The tuple rewriting is typically accomplished by bringing tuples into primary memory and then rewriting them with coordinate values permuted and removed as called for. This may yield a listing of tuples that contains duplicates. If a pure relational algebra projection is to be implemented, then these duplicates must be removed. One strategy for this involves sorting the list of tuples and then removing duplicates; this takes time on the order of $n \log n$. Another approach that is faster in some cases uses a hash function that incorporates all coordinate values of a tuple.

Because of the potential expense incurred by duplicate elimination, most practical relational languages permit duplicates in intermediate and final results. An explicit command (e.g., *distinct*) that calls for duplicate elimination is typically provided. Even in languages that support a pure algebra, it may be more efficient to leave duplicates in intermediate results and perform duplicate elimination once as a final step.

The equi-join is typically much more expensive than selection or projection because two relations are involved. The following naive *nested loop* implementation of $\bowtie_F$ will take time on the order of the product $n_1 \times n_2$ of the sizes of the input relations I_1, I_2:

$J := \emptyset;$
for each u **in** I_1
    for each v **in** I_2
        if u and v are joinable **then** $J := J \cup \{u \bowtie_F v\}$.

Typically this can be improved by using the *sort-merge* algorithm, which independently sorts both inputs according to the join attributes and then performs a simultaneous scan of both relations, outputting join tuples as discovered. This reduces the running time to the order of $\max(n_1 \log n_1 + n_2 \log n_2,$ size of output).

In many cases a more efficient implementation of join can be accomplished by a variant of the foregoing nested loop algorithm that uses indexes. In particular, replace the inner loop by indexed retrievals to tuples of I_2 that match the tuple of I_1 under consideration. Assuming that a small number of tuples of I_2 match a given tuple of I_1, this computes the join in time proportional to the size of I_1. We shall consider implementations of multiway joins later in this section and again in Section 6.4. Additional techniques have been developed for implementing richer joins that include testing, e.g., relationships based on order ($\leq$).

Cross-product in isolation is perhaps the most expensive algebra operation: The output necessarily has size the product of the sizes of the two inputs. In practice this arises only rarely; it is much more common that selection conditions on the cross-product can be used to transform it into some form of join.

Query Trees and Query Rewriting

Alternative query evaluation plans are usually generated by rewriting (i.e., by local transformation rules). This can be viewed as a specialized case of program transformation. Two kinds of transformations are typically used in query optimization: one that maps from the higher-level language (e.g., the algebra) into the physical language, and others that stay within the same language but lead to alternative, equivalent implementations of a given construct.

We present shortly a family of rewriting rules that illustrates the general flavor of this component of query optimizers (see Fig. 6.2). Unlike true optimizers, however, the rules presented here focus exclusively on the algebra. Later we examine the larger issue of how rules such as these are used to find optimal and near-optimal evaluation plans.

We shall use the SPC algebra, generalized by permitting positive conjunctive selection and equi-join. A central concept used is that of *query tree*, which is essentially the parse tree of an algebraic expression. Consider again Query (4.4), expressed here as a rule:

$$ans(x_{th}, x_{ad}) \leftarrow Movies(x_{ti}, \text{``Bergman''}, x_{ac}), \ Pariscope(x_{th}, x_{ti}, x_s),$$
$$Location(x_{th}, x_{ad}, x_p).$$

A naive translation into the generalized SPC algebra yields

$$q_1 = \pi_{4,8}\sigma_{2=\text{``Bergman''}}((Movies \bowtie_{1=2} Pariscope) \bowtie_{4=1} Location).$$

The query tree of this expression is shown in Fig. 6.1(a).

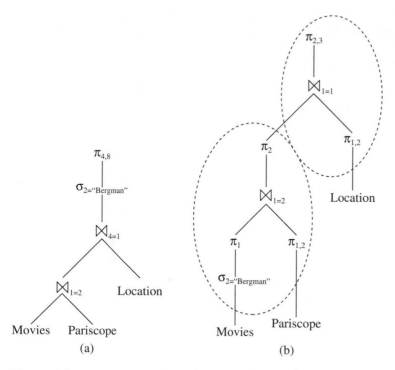

Figure 6.1:   Two query trees for Query (4.4) from Chapter 4

To provide a rough idea of how evaluation costs might be estimated, suppose now that *Movies* has 10,000 tuples, with about 5 tuples per movie; *Pariscope* has about 200 tuples, and *Location* has about 100 tuples. Suppose further that in each relation there are about 50 tuples per page and that no indexes are available.

Under a naive evaluation of q_1, an intermediate result would be produced for each internal node of q_1's query tree. In this example, then, the join of *Movies* and *Pariscope* would produce about $200 \times 5 = 1000$ tuples, which (being about twice as wide as the input tuples) will occupy about 40 pages. The second equi-join will yield about 1000 tuples that fit 18 to a page, thus occupying about 55 pages. Assuming that there are four Bergman films playing in one or two theaters each, the final answer will contain about six tuples. The total number of page fetches performed here is about 206 for reading the input relations (assuming that no indexes are available) and 95 for working with the intermediate relations. Additional page fetches might be required by the join operations performed.

Consider now the query q_2 whose query tree is illustrated in Fig. 6.1(b). It is easily verified that this is equivalent to q_1. Intuitively, q_2 was formed from q_1 by "pushing" selections and projections as far "down" the tree as possible; this generally reduces the size of intermediate results and thus of computing with them.

In this example, assuming that all (i.e., about 20) of Bergman's films are in *Movies*, the selection on *Movies* will yield about 100 tuples; when projected these will fit onto a single page. Joining with *Pariscope* will yield about six tuples, and the final join with *Location* will again yield six tuples. Thus only one page is needed to hold the intermediate results constructed during this evaluation, a considerable savings over the 95 pages needed by the previous one.

It is often beneficial to combine several algebraic operators into a single implemented operation. As a general rule of thumb, it is typical to materialize the inputs of each equi-join. The equi-join itself and all unary operations directly above it in the query tree are performed before output. The dashed ovals of Fig. 6.1(b) illustrate a natural grouping that can be used for this tree. In practical systems, the implementation and grouping of operators is typically considered in much finer detail.

The use of different query trees and, more generally, different evaluation plans can yield dramatically different costs in the evaluation of equivalent queries. Does this mean that the user will have to be extremely careful in expressing queries? The beauty of query optimization is that the answer is a resounding no. The user may choose any representation of a query, and the system will be responsible for generating several equivalent evaluation plans and choosing the least expensive one. For this reason, even though the relational algebra is conceptually procedural, it is implemented as an essentially declarative language.

In the case of the algebra, the generation of evaluation plans is typically based on the existence of rules for transforming algebraic expressions into equivalent ones. We have already seen rewrite rules in the context of transforming SPC and SPJR expressions into normal form (see Propositions 4.4.2 and 4.4.6). A different set of rules is useful in the present context due to the focus on optimizing the execution time and space requirements.

In Fig. 6.2 we present a family of representative rewrite rules (three with inverses) that can be used for performing the transformations needed for optimization at the logical level. In these rules we view cross-product as a special case of equi-join in which the selection formula is empty. Because of their similarity to the rules used for the normal form results, several of the rules are shown only in abstract form; detailed formulation of these, as well as verification of their soundness, is left for the reader (see Exercise 6.1). We also include the following rule:

Simplify-identities: replace $\pi_{1,...,arity(q)}q$ by q; replace $\sigma_{i=i}q$ by q; replace $q \times \{\langle\rangle\}$ by q; replace $q \times \{\}$ by $\{\}$; and replace $q \bowtie_{1=1 \wedge \cdots \wedge arity(q)=arity(q)} q$ by q.

Generating and Choosing between Evaluation Plans

As suggested in Fig. 6.2, in most cases the transformations should be performed in a certain direction. For example, the fifth rule suggests that it is always desirable to push selections through joins. However, situations can arise in which pushing a selection through a join is in fact much more costly than performing it second (see Exercise 6.2). The broad variety of factors that influence the time needed to execute a given query evaluation plan make it virtually impossible to find an optimal one using purely analytic techniques. For this reason, modern optimizers typically adopt the following pragmatic strategy: (1) generate a possibly large number of alternative evaluation plans; (2) estimate the costs of ex-

$$\sigma_F(\sigma_{F'}(q)) \quad\leftrightarrow\quad \sigma_{F \wedge F'}(q)$$
$$\pi_{\bar{j}}(\pi_{\bar{k}}(q)) \quad\leftrightarrow\quad \pi_{\bar{j}}(q)$$
$$\sigma_F(\pi_{\bar{j}}(q)) \quad\leftrightarrow\quad \pi_{\bar{j}}(\sigma_{F'}(q))$$
$$q_1 \bowtie q_2 \quad\leftrightarrow\quad q_2 \bowtie q_1$$
$$\sigma_F(q_1 \bowtie_G q_2) \quad\rightarrow\quad \sigma_F(q_1) \bowtie_G q_2$$
$$\sigma_F(q_1 \bowtie_G q_2) \quad\rightarrow\quad q_1 \bowtie_G \sigma_{F'}(q_2)$$
$$\sigma_F(q_1 \bowtie_G q_2) \quad\rightarrow\quad q_1 \bowtie_{G'} q_2$$
$$\pi_{\bar{j}}(q_1 \bowtie_G q_2) \quad\rightarrow\quad \pi_{\bar{j}}(q_1) \bowtie_{G'} q_2$$
$$\pi_{\bar{j}}(q_1 \bowtie_G q_2) \quad\rightarrow\quad q_1 \bowtie_{G'} \pi_{\bar{k}}(q_2)$$

Figure 6.2:   Rewriting rules for SPC algebra

ccuting them; and (3) select the one of lowest cost. The database system then executes the selected evaluation plan.

In early work, the transformation rules used and the method for evaluation plan generation were essentially intermixed. Motivated in part by the desire to make database systems extensible, more recent proposals have isolated the transformation rules from the algorithms for generating evaluation plans. This has the advantages of exposing the semantics of evaluation plan generation and making it easier to incorporate new kinds of information into the framework.

A representative system for generating evaluation plans was developed in connection with the Exodus database toolkit. In this system, techniques from AI are used and, a set of transformation rules is assumed. During processing, a set of partial evaluation plans is maintained along with a set of possible locations where rules can be applied. Heuristics are used to determine which transformation to apply next, so that an exhaustive search through all possible evaluation plans can be avoided while still having a good chance of finding an optimal or near-optimal evaluation plan. Several of the heuristics include weighting factors that can be tuned, either automatically or by the dba, to reflect experience gained while using the optimizer.

Early work on estimating the cost of evaluation plans was based essentially on "thought experiments" similar to those used earlier in this chapter. These analyses use factors including the size of relations, their expected statistical properties, selectivity factors of joins and selections, and existing indexes. In the context of large queries involving multiple joins, however, it is difficult if not impossible to predict the sizes of intermediate results based only on statistical properties. This provides one motivation for recent research on using random and background sampling to estimate the size of subquery answers, which can provide more reliable estimates of the overall cost of an evaluation plan.

Sideways Information Passing

We close this section by considering two practical approaches to implementing multiway joins as they arise in practical query languages.

Much of the early research on practical query optimization was performed in connection with the System R and INGRES systems. The basic building block of the query languages used in these systems (SQL and Quel, respectively) takes the form of "select-from-where" clauses or blocks. For example, as detailed further in Chapter 7, Query (4.4) can be expressed in SQL as

> **select**   *Theater, Address*
> **from**   *Movies, Location, Pariscope*
> **where**   *Director* = "Bergman"
>   **and** *Movies.Title = Pariscope.Title*
>   **and** *Pariscope.Theater = Location.Theater.*

This can be translated into the algebra as a join between the three relations of the **from** part, using join condition given by the **where** and projecting onto the columns mentioned in the **select**. Thus a typical select-from-where block can be expressed by an SPC query as

$$\pi_{\bar{j}}(\sigma_F(R_1 \times \cdots \times R_n)).$$

With such expressions, the System R query optimizer pushes selections that affect a single relation into the join and then considers evaluation plans based on *left-to-right* joins that have the form

$$(\ldots (R_{i_1} \bowtie R_{i_2}) \bowtie \cdots \bowtie R_{i_n})$$

using different orderings $R_{i_1}, \ldots, R_{i_n}$. We now present a heuristic based on "sideways information passing," which is used in the System R optimizer for eliminating some possible orderings from consideration. Interestingly, this heuristic has also played an important role in developing evaluation techniques for recursive datalog queries, as discussed in Chapter 13.

To describe the heuristic, we rewrite the preceding SPC query as a (generalized) rule that has the form

$(*)$ $ans(u) \leftarrow R_1(u_1), \ldots, R_n(u_n), C_1, \ldots, C_m,$

where all equalities of the selection condition F are incorporated by using constants and equating variables in the free tuples $u_1, \ldots, u_n$, and the expressions $C_1, \ldots, C_m$ are conditions in the selection condition F not captured in that way. (This might include, e.g., inequalities and conditions based on order.) We shall call the $R_i(u_i)$'s *relation atoms* and the C_j's *constraint atoms*.

EXAMPLE 6.1.1   Consider the rule

$$ans(z) \leftarrow P(a, v), Q(b, w, x), R(v, w, y), S(x, y, z), v \leq x,$$

where a, b denote constants. A common assumption in this case is that there are few values for v such that $P(a, v)$ is satisfied. This in turn suggests that there will be few triples (v, w, y) satisfying $P(a, v) \wedge R(v, w, y)$. Continuing by transitivity, then, we also expect there to be few 5-tuples (v, w, y, x, z) that satisfy the join of this with $S(x, y, z)$.

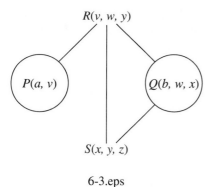

6-3.eps

Figure 6.3:　A sip graph

More generally, the *sideways information passing graph*, or *sip graph*, of a rule ρ that has the form (∗) just shown has vertexes the set of relation atoms of a rule, and includes an undirected edge between atoms $R_i(u_i)$, $R_j(u_j)$ if u_i and u_j have at least one variable in common. Furthermore, each node with a constant appearing is specially marked. The sip graph for the rule of Example 6.1.1 is shown in Fig. 6.3.

Let us assume that the sip graph for a rule ρ is connected. In this case, a sideways information passing *strategy* (*sip strategy*) for ρ is an ordering $A_1, \ldots, A_n$ of the atoms in the rule, such that for each $j > 1$, either

(a) a constant occurs in A_j;

(b) A_j is a relational atom and there is at least one $i < j$ such that $\{A_i, A_j\}$ is an edge of the sip graph of (ρ); or

(c) A_j is a constraint atom and each variable occurring in A_j occurs in some atom A_i for $i < j$.

EXAMPLE 6.1.2　A representative sample of the several sip strategies for the rule of Example 6.1.1 is as follows:

$$P(a, v), Q(b, w, x), v \le x, R(v, w, y), S(x, y, z)$$
$$P(a, v), R(v, w, y), S(x, y, z), v \le x, Q(b, w, x)$$
$$Q(b, w, x), R(v, w, y), P(a, v), S(x, y, z), v \le x.$$

A sip strategy for the case in which the sip graph of rule ρ is not connected is a set of sip strategies, one for each connected component of the sip graph. (Incorporation of constraint atoms whose variables lie in distinct components is left for the reader.) The System R optimizer focuses primarily on joins that have connected sip graphs, and it considers only those join orderings that correspond to sip strategies. In some cases a more efficient evaluation plan can be obtained if an arbitrary tree of binary joins is permitted; see Exercise 6.5. While generating sip strategies the System R optimizer also considers alternative implementations for the binary joins involved and records information about the orderings that the partial results would have if computed. An additional logical-level technique used in System R is illustrated in the following example.

EXAMPLE 6.1.3   Let us consider again the rule

$$ans(z) \leftarrow P(a, v), R(v, w, y), S(x, y, z), v \leq x, Q(b, w, x).$$

Suppose that a left-to-right join is performed according to the sip strategy shown. At different intermediate stages certain variables can be "forgotten," because they are not used in the answer, nor are they used in subsequent joins. In particular, after the third atom the variable y can be projected out, after the fourth atom v can be projected out, and after the fifth atom w and x can be projected out. It is straightforward to formulate a general policy for when to project out unneeded variables (see Exercise 6.4).

Query Decomposition: Join Detachment and Tuple Substitution

We now briefly discuss the two main techniques used in the original INGRES system for evaluating join expressions. Both are based on decomposing multiway joins into smaller ones.

While again focusing on SPC queries of the form

$$\pi_{\bar{j}}(\sigma_F(R_1 \times \cdots \times R_n))$$

for this discussion, we use a slightly different notation. In particular, tuple variables rather than domain variables are used. We consider expressions of the form

(∗∗) $ans(s) \leftarrow R_1(s_1), \ldots, R_n(s_n), C_1, \ldots, C_m, T,$

where $s, s_1, \ldots, s_n$ are tuple variables; $C_1, \ldots, C_n$ are Boolean conditions referring to coordinates of the variables $s_1, \ldots, s_n$ (e.g., $s_1.3 = s_4.1 \vee s_2.4 = a$); and T is a *target condition* that gives a value for each coordinate of the target variable s. It is generally assumed that none of $C_1, \ldots, C_n$ has $\wedge$ as its parent connective.

A condition C_j is called *single variable* if it refers to only one of the variables s_i. At any point in the processing it is possible to apply one or more single-variable conditions to some R_i, thereby constructing an intermediate relation R_i' that can be used in place of R_i. In the INGRES optimizer, this is typically combined with other steps.

Join detachment is useful for separating a query into two separate queries, where the second refers to the first. Consider a query that has the specialized form

$$ans(t) \leftarrow P_1(p_1), \ldots, P_m(p_m), C_1, \ldots, C_k, T,$$

(†) $Q(q),$

$$R_1(r_1), \ldots, R_n(r_n), D_1, \ldots, D_l,$$

where conditions $C_1, \ldots, C_k, T$ refer only to variables $t, p_1, \ldots, p_n, q$ and $D_1, \ldots, D_l$ refer only to $q, r_1, \ldots, r_n$. It is easily verified that this is equivalent to the sequence

$$temp(q) \leftarrow Q(q), R_1(r_1), \ldots, R_n(r_n), D_1, \ldots, D_l$$
$$ans(t) \leftarrow P_1(p_1), \ldots, P_m(p_m), temp(q), C_1, \ldots, C_k, T.$$

In this example, variable q acts as a "pivot" around which the detachment is performed. More general forms of join detachment can be developed in which a set of variables serves as the pivot (see Exercise 6.6).

   Tuple substitution chooses one of the underlying relations R_j and breaks the n-variable join into a set of $(n-1)$-variable joins, one for each tuple in R_j. Consider again a query of form (**) just shown. The tuple substitution of this on R_i is given by the "program"

> **for each** r **in** R_i **do**
> $$ans(s) +\leftarrow R_1(s_1), \ldots, R_{i-1}(s_{i-1}), R_{i+1}(s_{i+1}), \ldots, R_n(s_n),$$
> $$(C_1, \ldots, C_m, T)[s_i/r].$$

Here we use $+\leftarrow$ to indicate that *ans* is to accumulate the values stemming from all tuples r in (the value of) R_i; furthermore, r is substituted for s_i in all of the conditions.

   There is an obvious trade-off here between reducing the number of variables in the join and the number of tuples in R_i. In the INGRES optimizer, each of the R_i's is considered as a candidate for forming the tuple substitution. During this process single-variable conditions may be applied to the R_i's to decrease their size.

6.2   Global Optimization

The techniques for creating evaluation plans presented in the previous section are essentially *local* in their operation: They focus on clusters of contiguous nodes in a query tree. In this section we develop an approach to the *global* optimization of conjunctive queries. This allows a transformation of an algebra query that removes several joins in a single step, a capability not provided by the techniques of the previous section. The global optimization technique is based on an elegant Homomorphism Theorem.

The Homomorphism Theorem

For two queries q_1, q_2 over the same schema **R**, q_1 is *contained* in q_2, denoted $q_1 \subseteq q_2$, if for each **I** over **R**, $q_1(\mathbf{I}) \subseteq q_2(\mathbf{I})$. Clearly, $q_1 \equiv q_2$ iff $q_1 \subseteq q_2$ and $q_2 \subseteq q_1$. The Homomorphism Theorem provides a characterization for containment and equivalence of conjunctive queries.

   We focus here on the tableau formalism for conjunctive queries, although the rule-based formalism could be used equally well. In addition, although the results hold for tableau queries over database schemas involving more than one relation, the examples presented focus on queries over a single relation.

R	A	B
	x	y
	x	y

R	A	B
	x	y_1
	x_1	y_1
	x_1	y
	x	y

R	A	B
	x	y_1
	x_1	y_1
	x_1	y_2
	x_2	y_2
	x_2	y
	x	y

R	A	B
	x	y_1
	x_1	y
	x	y

$q_0 = (T_0, \langle x, y \rangle)$ $q_1 = (T_1, \langle x, y \rangle)$ $q_2 = (T_2, \langle x, y \rangle)$ $q_\omega = (T_\omega, \langle x, y \rangle)$

(a)   (b)   (c)   (d)

Figure 6.4: Tableau queries used to illustrate the Homomorphism Theorem

Recall the notion of *valuation*—a mapping from variables to constants extended to be the identity on constants and generalized to free tuples and tableaux in the natural fashion. Valuations are used in the definition of the semantics of tableau queries. More generally, a *substitution* is a mapping from variables to variables and constants, which is extended to be the identity on constants and generalized to free tuples and tableaux in the natural fashion. As will be seen, substitutions play a central role in the Homomorphism Theorem.

We begin the discussion with two examples. The first presents several simple examples of the Homomorphism Theorem in action.

EXAMPLE 6.2.1   Consider the four tableau queries shown in Fig. 6.4. By using the Homomorphism Theorem, it can be shown that $q_0 \subseteq q_1 \subseteq q_2 \subseteq q_\omega$.

To illustrate the flavor of the proof of the Homomorphism Theorem, we argue informally that $q_1 \subseteq q_2$. Note that there is substitution θ such that $\theta(T_2) \subseteq T_1$ and $\theta(\langle x, y \rangle) = \langle x, y \rangle$ [e.g., let $\theta(x_1) = \theta(x_2) = x_1$ and $\theta(y_1) = \theta(y_2) = y_1$]. Now suppose that I is an instance over AB and that $t \in q_1(I)$. Then there is a valuation v such that $v(T_1) \subseteq I$ and $v(\langle x, y \rangle) = t$. It follows that $\theta \circ v$ is a valuation that embeds T_2 into I with $\theta \circ v(\langle x, y \rangle) = t$, whence $t \in q_2(I)$.

Intuitively, the existence of a substitution embedding the tableau of q_2 into the tableau of q_1 and mapping the summary of q_2 to the summary of q_1 implies that q_1 is *more restrictive* than q_2 (or more correctly, *no less restrictive* than q_2.) Surprisingly, the Homomorphism Theorem states that this is also a necessary condition for containment (i.e., if $q \subseteq q'$, then q is more restrictive than q' in this sense).

The second example illustrates a limitation of the techniques discussed in the previous section.

R	A	B
	x	x
	x	y_1
	y_1	y_2
	$\vdots$	$\vdots$
	y_{n-1}	y_n
	y_n	x
	x	

$q = (T, u)$

(a)

R	A	B
	x	x
	x	

$q' = (T', u)$

(b)

Figure 6.5:   Pair of equivalent tableau queries

EXAMPLE 6.2.2   Consider the two tableau queries shown in Fig. 6.5. It can be shown that $q \equiv q'$ but that q' cannot be obtained from q using the rewrite rules of the previous section (see Exercise 6.3) or the other optimization techniques presented there.

Let $q = (\mathbf{T}, u)$ and $q' = (\mathbf{T}', u')$ be two tableau queries over the same schema $\mathbf{R}$. A *homomorphism* from q' to q is a substitution θ such that $\theta(\mathbf{T}') \subseteq \mathbf{T}$ and $\theta(u') = u$.

THEOREM 6.2.3 (Homomorphism Theorem)   Let $q = (\mathbf{T}, u)$ and $q' = (\mathbf{T}', u')$ be tableau queries over the same schema $\mathbf{R}$. Then $q \subseteq q'$ iff there exists a homomorphism from $(\mathbf{T}', u')$ to $(\mathbf{T}, u)$.

Proof   Suppose first that there exists a homomorphism θ from q' to q. Let $\mathbf{I}$ be an instance over $\mathbf{R}$. To see that $q(\mathbf{I}) \subseteq q'(\mathbf{I})$, suppose that $w \in q(\mathbf{I})$. Then there is a valuation v that embeds $\mathbf{T}$ into $\mathbf{I}$ such that $v(u) = w$. It is clear that $\theta \circ v$ embeds $\mathbf{T}'$ into $\mathbf{I}$ and $\theta \circ v(u') = w$, whence $w \in q'(\mathbf{I})$ as desired.

For the opposite inclusion, suppose that $q \subseteq q'$ [i.e., that $(\mathbf{T}, u) \subseteq (\mathbf{T}', u')$]. Speaking intuitively, we complete the proof by applying both q and q' to the "instance" $\mathbf{T}$. Because q will yield the free tuple u, q' also yields u (i.e., there is an embedding θ of $\mathbf{T}'$ into $\mathbf{T}$ that maps u' to u). To make this argument formal, we construct an instance $\mathbf{I_T}$ that is isomorphic to $\mathbf{T}$.

Let V be the set of variables occurring in $\mathbf{T}$. For each $x \in V$, let a_x be a new distinct constant not occurring in $\mathbf{T}$ or $\mathbf{T}'$. Let μ be the valuation mapping each x to a_x, and let $\mathbf{I_T} = \mu(\mathbf{T})$. Because μ is a bijection from V to $\mu(V)$, and because $\mu(V)$ has empty intersection with the constants occurring in $\mathbf{T}$, the inverse μ^{-1} of μ is well defined on $adom(\mathbf{I_T})$.

It is clear that $\mu(u) \in q(\mathbf{I_T})$, and so by assumption, $\mu(u) \in q'(\mathbf{I_T})$. Thus there is a valuation v that embeds $\mathbf{T}'$ into $\mathbf{I_T}$ such that $v(u') = \mu(u)$. It is now easily verified that $v \circ \mu^{-1}$ is a homomorphism from q' to q. ∎

Permitting a slight abuse of notation, we have the following (see Exercise 6.8).

COROLLARY 6.2.4   For tableau queries $q = (\mathbf{T}, u)$ and $q' = (\mathbf{T}', u')$, $q \subseteq q'$ iff $u \in q'(\mathbf{T})$.

We also have

COROLLARY 6.2.5   Tableau queries q, q' over schema $\mathbf{R}$ are equivalent iff there are homomorphisms from q to q' and from q' to q.

In particular, if $q = (\mathbf{T}, u)$ and $q' = (\mathbf{T}', u')$ are equivalent, then u and u' are identical up to one-one renaming of variables.

Only one direction of the preceding characterization holds if the underlying domain is finite (see Exercise 6.12). In addition, the direct generalization of the theorem to tableau queries with equality does not hold (see Exercise 6.9).

Query Optimization by Tableau Minimization

Although the Homomorphism Theorem yields a decision procedure for containment and equivalence between conjunctive queries, it does not immediately provide a mechanism, given a query q, to find an "optimal" query equivalent to q. The theorem is now applied to obtain just such a mechanism.

We note first that there are simple algorithms for translating tableau queries into (satisfiable) SPC queries and vice versa. More specifically, given a tableau query, the corresponding generalized SPC query has the form $\pi_{\bar{j}}(\sigma_F(R_1 \times \cdots \times R_k))$, where each component R_i corresponds to a distinct row of the tableau. For the opposite direction, one algorithm for translating SPC queries into tableau queries is first to translate into the normal form for generalized SPC queries and then into a tableau query. A more direct approach that inductively builds tableau queries corresponding to subexpressions of an SPC query can also be developed (see Exercise 4.18). Analogous remarks apply to SPJR queries.

The goal of the optimization presented here is to minimize the number of rows in the tableau. Because the number of rows in a tableau query is one more than the number of joins in the SPC (SPJR) query corresponding to that tableau (see Exercise 4.18c), the tableau minimization procedure provides a way to minimize the number of joins in SPC and SPJR queries.

Surprisingly, we show that an optimal tableau query equivalent to tableau query q can be obtained simply by eliminating some rows from the tableau of q.

We say that a tableau query $(\mathbf{T}, u)$ is *minimal* if there is no query $(\mathbf{S}, v)$ equivalent to $(\mathbf{T}, u)$ with $|\mathbf{S}| < |\mathbf{T}|$ (i.e., where $\mathbf{S}$ has strictly fewer rows than $\mathbf{T}$).

We can now demonstrate the following.

R	A	B	C
u_1	x_2	y_1	z
u_2	x	y_1	z_1
u_3	x_1	y	z_1
u_4	x	y_2	z_2
u_5	x_2	y_2	z
u	x	y	z

Figure 6.6: The tableau (T, u)

THEOREM 6.2.6 Let $q = (\mathbf{T}, u)$ be a tableau query. Then there is a subset $\mathbf{T}'$ of $\mathbf{T}$ such that $q' = (\mathbf{T}', u)$ is a minimal tableau query and $q' \equiv q$.

Proof Let $(\mathbf{S}, v)$ be a minimal tableau that is equivalent to q. By Corollary 6.2.5, there are homomorphisms θ from q to $(\mathbf{S}, v)$ and λ from $(\mathbf{S}, v)$ to q. Let $\mathbf{T}' = \theta \circ \lambda(\mathbf{S})$. It is straightforward to verify that $(\mathbf{T}', u) \equiv q$ and $|\mathbf{T}'| \leq |\mathbf{S}|$. By minimality of $(\mathbf{S}, v)$, it follows that $|\mathbf{T}'| = |\mathbf{S}|$, and $(\mathbf{T}', u)$ is minimal. ∎

Example 6.2.7 illustrates how one might minimize a tableau by hand.

EXAMPLE 6.2.7 Let R be a relation schema of sort ABC and (T, u) the tableau over R in Fig. 6.6. To minimize (T, u), we wish to detect which rows of T can be eliminated. Consider u_1. Suppose there is a homomorphism θ from (T, u) onto itself that eliminates u_1 [i.e., $u_1 \notin \theta(T)$]. Because any homomorphism on (T, u) is the identity on u, $\theta(z) = z$. Thus $\theta(u_1)$ must be u_5. But then $\theta(y_1) = y_2$, and $\theta(u_2) \in \{u_4, u_5\}$. In particular, $\theta(z_1) \in \{z_2, z\}$. Because u_3 involves z_1, it follows that $\theta(u_3) \neq u_3$ and $\theta(y) \neq y$. But the last inequality is impossible because y is in u so $\theta(y) = y$. It follows that row u_1 cannot be eliminated and is in the minimal tableau. Similar arguments show that u_2 and u_3 cannot be eliminated. However, u_4 and u_5 can be eliminated using $\theta(y_2) = y_1, \theta(z_2) = z_1$ (and identity everywhere else). The preceding argument emphasizes the global nature of tableau minimization.

The preceding theorem suggests an improvement over the optimization strategies described in Section 6.1. Specifically, given a (satisfiable) conjunctive query q, the following steps can be used:

1. Translate q into a tableau query.
2. Minimize the number of rows in the tableau of this query.
3. Translate the result into a generalized SPC expression.
4. Apply the optimization techniques of Section 6.1.

$$
\begin{array}{c|ccc}
R & A & B & C \\
\hline
 & x & 5 & z_1 \\
 & x_1 & 5 & z_2 \\
 & x_1 & 5 & z \\
\hline
u & x & 5 & z \\
\end{array}
$$

Figure 6.7:   Tableau equivalent to q

As illustrated by Examples 6.2.2, 6.2.7, and 6.2.8, this approach has the advantage of performing global optimizations that typical query rewriting systems cannot achieve.

EXAMPLE 6.2.8   Consider the relation schema R of sort ABC and the SPJR query q over R:

$$
\pi_{AB}(\sigma_{B=5}(R)) \bowtie \pi_{BC}(\pi_{AB}(R) \bowtie \pi_{AC}(\sigma_{B=5}(R))).
$$

The tableau (T, u) corresponding to it is that of Fig. 6.7. To minimize (T, u), we wish to find a homomorphism that "folds" T onto a subtableau with minimal number of rows. (If desired, this can be done in several stages, each of which eliminates one or more rows.) Note that the first row cannot be eliminated because every homomorphism is the identity on u and therefore on x. A similar observation holds for the third row. However, the second row can be eliminated using the homomorphism that maps z_2 to z and is the identity everywhere else. Thus the minimal tableau equivalent to (T, u) consists of the first and third rows of T. An SPJR query equivalent to the minimized tableau is

$$
\pi_{AB}(\sigma_{B=5}(R)) \bowtie \pi_{BC}(\sigma_{B=5}(R)).
$$

Thus the optimization procedure resulted in saving one join operation.

Before leaving minimal tableau queries, we present a result that describes a strong correspondence between equivalent minimal tableau queries. Two tableau queries $(\mathbf{T}, u)$, $(\mathbf{T}', u')$ are *isomorphic* if there is a one-one substitution θ that maps variables to variables such that $\theta((\mathbf{T}, u)) = (\mathbf{T}', u')$. In other words, (T, u) and (T', u') are the same up to renaming of variables. The proof of this result is left to the reader (see Exercise 6.11).

PROPOSITION 6.2.9   Let $q = (\mathbf{T}, u)$ and $q' = (\mathbf{T}', u')$ be minimal and equivalent. Then q and q' are isomorphic.

Complexity of Tableau Decision Problems

The following theorem shows that determining containment and equivalence between tableau queries is NP-complete and tableau query minimization is NP-hard.

THEOREM 6.2.10 The following problems, given tableau queries q, q', are NP-complete:

  (a) Is $q \subseteq q'$?
  (b) Is $q \equiv q'$?
  (c) Suppose that the tableau of q is obtained by deleting free tuples of the tableau of q'. Is $q \equiv q'$ in this case?

These results remain true if q, q' are restricted to be single-relation typed tableau queries that have no constants.

Proof The proof is based on a reduction from the "exact cover" problem to the different tableau problems. The *exact cover* problem is to decide, given a set $X = \{x_1, \ldots, x_n\}$ and a collection $S = \{S_1, \ldots, S_m\}$ of subsets of X, whether there is an exact cover of X by S (i.e., a subset S' of S such that each member of X occurs in exactly one member of S'). The exact cover problem is known to be NP-complete.

We now sketch a polynomial transformation from instances $\mathcal{E} = (X, S)$ of the exact cover problem to pairs $q_{\mathcal{E}}, q'_{\mathcal{E}}$ of typed tableau queries. This construction is then applied in various ways to obtain the NP-completeness results. The construction is illustrated in Fig. 6.8.

Let $\mathcal{E} = (X, S)$ be an instance of the exact cover problem, where $X = \{x_1, \ldots, x_n\}$ and $S = \{S_1, \ldots, S_m\}$. Let $A_1, \ldots, A_n, B_1, \ldots, B_m$ be a listing of distinct attributes, and let R be chosen to have this set as its sort. Both $q_{\mathcal{E}}$ and $q'_{\mathcal{E}}$ are over relation R, and both queries have as summary $t = \langle A_1 : a_1, \ldots, A_n : a_n \rangle$, where $a_1, \ldots, a_n$ are distinct variables.

Let $b_1, \ldots, b_m$ be an additional set of m distinct variables. The tableau $T_{\mathcal{E}}$ of $q_{\mathcal{E}}$ has n tuples, each corresponding to a different element of X. The tuple for x_i has a_i for attribute A_i; b_j for attribute B_j for each j such that $x_i \in S_j$; and a new, distinct variable for all other attributes.

Let $c_1, \ldots, c_m$ be an additional set of m distinct variables. The tableau $T'_{\mathcal{E}}$ of $q'_{\mathcal{E}}$ has m tuples, each corresponding to a different element of S. The tuple for S_j has a_i for attribute A_i for each i such that $x_i \in S_j$; $c_{j'}$ for attribute $B_{j'}$ for each j' such that $j' \neq j$; and a new, distinct variable for all other attributes.

To illustrate the construction, let $\mathcal{E} = (X, S)$ be an instance of the exact cover problem, where $X = \{x_1, x_2, x_3, x_4\}$ and $S = \{S_1, S_2, S_3\}$ where

$$S_1 = \{x_1, x_3\}$$
$$S_2 = \{x_2, x_3, x_4\}$$
$$S_3 = \{x_2, x_4\}.$$

The tableau queries q_{ξ} and q'_{ξ} corresponding to (X, S) are shown in Fig. 6.8. (Here the

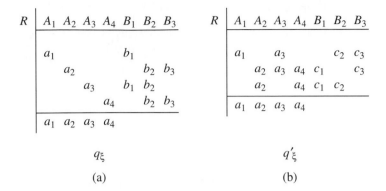

Figure 6.8 tableau (a):

R	A_1	A_2	A_3	A_4	B_1	B_2	B_3
	a_1				b_1		
		a_2				b_2	b_3
			a_3		b_1	b_2	
				a_4		b_2	b_3
	a_1	a_2	a_3	a_4			

$$q_\xi$$

(a)

Figure 6.8 tableau (b):

R	A_1	A_2	A_3	A_4	B_1	B_2	B_3
	a_1		a_3			c_2	c_3
		a_2	a_3	a_4	c_1		c_3
		a_2		a_4	c_1	c_2	
	a_1	a_2	a_3	a_4			

$$q'_\xi$$

(b)

Figure 6.8: Tableau queries corresponding to an exact cover

blank entries indicate distinct, new variables.) Note that $\xi = (X, \mathcal{S})$ is satisfiable, and $q'_\xi \subseteq q_\xi$.

More generally, it is straightforward to verify that for a given instance $\xi = (X, \mathcal{S})$ of the exact cover problem, X has an exact cover in $\mathcal{S}$ iff $q'_\xi \subseteq q_\xi$. Verification of this, and of parts (b) and (c) of the theorem, is left for Exercise 6.16. ■

A subclass of the typed tableau queries for which containment and equivalence is decidable in polynomial time is considered in Exercise 6.21.

Although an NP-completeness result often suggests intractability, this conclusion may not be warranted in connection with the aforementioned result. The complexity there is measured relative to the size of the *query* rather than in terms of the underlying stored *data*. Given an n-way join, the System R optimizer may potentially consider $n!$ evaluation strategies based on different orderings of the n relations; this may be exponential in the size of the query. In many cases, the search for a minimal tableau (or optimal left-to-right join) may be justified because the data is so much larger than the initial query. More generally, in Part D we shall examine both "data complexity" and "expression complexity," where the former focuses on complexity relative to the size of the data and the latter relative to the size of queries.

6.3 Static Analysis of the Relational Calculus

We now demonstrate that the decidability results for conjunctive queries demonstrated in the previous section do not hold when negation is incorporated (i.e., do not hold for the first-order queries). In particular, we present a general technique for proving the undecidability of problems involving static analysis of first-order queries and demonstrate the undecidability of three such problems.

We begin by focusing on the basic property of satisfiability. Recall that a query q is *satisfiable* if there is some input $\mathbf{I}$ such that $q(\mathbf{I})$ is nonempty. All conjunctive queries are satisfiable (Proposition 4.2.2), and if equality is incorporated then satisfiability is not guaranteed but it is decidable (Exercise 4.5). This no longer holds for the calculus.

To prove this result, we use a reduction of the Post Correspondence Problem (PCP) (see Chapter 2) to the satisfiability problem. The reduction is most easily described in terms of the calculus; of course, it can also be established using the algebras or nr-datalog¬.

At first glance, it would appear that the result follows trivially from the analogous result for first-order logic (i.e., the undecidability of satisfiability of first-order sentences). There is, however, an important difference. In conventional first-order logic (see Chapter 2), both finite and infinite interpretations are considered. Satisfiability of first-order sentences is co-recursively enumerable (co-r.e.) but not recursive. This follows from Gödel's Completeness Theorem. In contrast, in the context of first-order queries, only finite instances are considered legal. This brings us into the realm of finite model theory. As will be shown, satisfiability of first-order queries is recursively enumerable (r.e.) but not recursive. (We shall revisit the contrast between conventional first-order logic and the database perspective, i.e., finite model theory, in Chapters 9 and 10.)

THEOREM 6.3.1 Satisfiability of relational calculus queries is r.e. but not recursive.

Proof   To see that the problem is r.e., imagine an algorithm that, when given query q over **R** as input, generates all instances **I** over **R** and tests $q(\mathbf{I}) = \emptyset$ until a nonempty answer is found.

To show that satisfiability is not recursive, we reduce the PCP to the satisfiability problem. In particular, we show that if there were an algorithm for solving satisfiability, then it could be used to construct an algorithm that solves the PCP.

Let $\mathcal{P} = (u_1, \ldots, u_n; v_1, \ldots, v_n)$ be an instance of the PCP (i.e., a pair of sequences of nonempty words over alphabet $\{0,1\}$). We describe now a (domain independent) calculus query $q_\mathcal{P} = \{\langle\rangle \mid \varphi_\mathcal{P}\}$ with the property that $q_\mathcal{P}$ is satisfiable iff $\mathcal{P}$ has a solution.

We shall use a relation schema **R** having relations *ENC(ODING)* with sort $[A, B, C, D, E]$ and *SYNCH(RONIZATION)* with sort $[F, G]$. The query $q_\mathcal{P}$ shall use constants $\{0, 1, \$, c_1, \ldots, c_n, d_1, \ldots, d_n\}$. (The use of multiple relations and constants is largely a convenience; the result can be demonstrated using a single ternary relation and no constants. See Exercise 6.19.)

To illustrate the construction of the algorithm, consider the following instance of the PCP:

$$u_1 = 011, \ u_2 = 011, \ u_3 = 0; \quad v_1 = 0, \ v_2 = 11, \ v_3 = 01100.$$

Note that $s = (1, 2, 3, 2)$ is a solution of this instance. That is,

$$u_1 u_2 u_3 u_2 = 0110110011 = v_1 v_2 v_3 v_2.$$

Figure 6.9 shows an input instance $\mathbf{I}_s$ over **R** which encodes this solution and satisfies the query $q_\mathcal{P}$ constructed shortly.

In the relation *ENC* of this figure, the first two columns form a *cycle*, so that the 10

solved as follows: For each query $q = \{x_1, \ldots, x_n \mid \varphi\}$, this is unsatisfiable if and only if it is equivalent to the empty query $q^\emptyset$. This demonstrates that equivalence is not decidable. The undecidability of containment also follows from this.

For domain independence, let ψ be a sentence whose truth value depends on the underlying domain. Then $\{x_1, \ldots, x_n \mid \varphi \wedge \psi\}$ is domain independent if and only if φ is unsatisfiable. ■

The preceding techniques can also be used to show that "true" optimization cannot be performed for the first-order queries (see Exercise 6.20d).

6.4   Computing with Acyclic Joins

We now present a family of interesting theoretical results on the problem of computing the projection of a join. In the general case, if both the data set and the join expression are allowed to vary, then the time needed to evaluate such expressions appears to be exponential. The measure of complexity here is a combination of both "data" and "expression" comlexity, and is somewhat non-standard; see Part D. Interestingly, there is a special class of joins, called *acyclic*, for which this evaluation is polynomial. A number of interesting properties of acyclic joins are also presented.

For this section we use the named perspective and focus exclusively on *flat project-join* queries of the form

$$q = \pi_X(R_1 \bowtie \cdots \bowtie R_n)$$

involving projection and natural join. For this discussion we assume that $\mathbf{R} = R_1, \ldots, R_n$ is a fixed database schema, and we use $\mathbf{I} = (I_1, \ldots, I_n)$ to refer to instances over it.

One of the historical motivations for studying this problem stems from the *pure universal relation assumption (pure URA)*. An instance $\mathbf{I} = (I_1, \ldots, I_n)$ over schema $\mathbf{R}$ satisfies the pure URA if $\mathbf{I} = (\pi_{R_1}(I), \ldots, \pi_{R_n}(I))$ for some "universal" instance I over $\cup_{j=1}^n R_j$. If $\mathbf{I}$ satisfies the pure URA, then $\mathbf{I}$ can be stored, and queries against the corresponding instance I can be answered using joins of components in $\mathbf{I}$. The URA will be considered in more depth in Chapter 11.

Worst-Case Results

We begin with an example.

EXAMPLE 6.4.1   Let $n > 0$ and consider the relations $R_i[A_i A_{i+1}]$, $i \in [1, n-1]$, as shown in Fig. 6.10(a). It is easily seen that the natural join of $R_1, \ldots, R_{n-1}$ is exponential in n and thus exponential in the size of the input query and data.

Now suppose that n is odd. Let R_n be as in Fig. 6.10(b), and consider the natural join of $R_1, \ldots, R_n$. This is empty. On the other hand, the join of any i of these for $i < n$ has size

R_i	A_i	A_{i+1}
	0	a
	0	b
	1	a
	1	b
	a	0
	a	1
	b	0
	b	1

R_n	A_n	A_1
	0	a
	0	b
	1	a
	1	b
	a	0
	a	1
	b	0
	b	1

(a)　　　　　　　　　　(b)

Figure 6.10:　Relations to illustrate join sizes

exponential in i. It follows that the algorithms of the System R and INGRES optimizers take time exponential in the size of the input and output to evaluate this query.

The following result implies that it is unlikely that there is an algorithm for computing projections of joins in time polynomial in the size of the query and the data.

THEOREM 6.4.2　It is NP-complete to decide, given project-join expression q_0 over **R**, instance **I** of **R**, and tuple t, whether $t \in q_0(\mathbf{I})$. This remains true if q_0 and **I** are restricted so that $|q_0(\mathbf{I})| \leq 1$.

Proof　The problem is easily seen to be in NP. For the converse, recall from Theorem 6.2.10(a) that the problem of tableau containment is NP-complete, even for single-relation typed tableaux having no constants. We reduce this to the current problem. Let $q = (T, u)$ and $q' = (T', u')$ be two typed constant-free tableau queries over the same relation schema. Recall from the Homomorphism Theorem that $q \subseteq q'$ iff there is a homomorphism of q' to q, which holds iff $u \in q'(T)$.

Assume that the sets of variables occurring in q and in q' are disjoint. Without loss of generality, we view each variable occurring in q to be a constant. For each variable x occurring in q', let A_x be a distinct attribute. For free tuple $v = (x_1, \ldots, x_n)$ in T', let I_v over $A_{x_1}, \ldots, A_{x_n}$ be a copy of T, where the ith attribute is renamed to A_{x_i}. Letting $u' = \langle u'_1, \ldots, u'_m \rangle$, it is straightforward to verify that

$$q'(T) = \pi_{A_{u'_1}, \ldots, A_{u'_m}} (\bowtie \{I_v \mid v \in T'\}).$$

In particular, $u \in q'(T)$ iff u is in this projected join.

To see the last sentence of the theorem, let $u = \langle u_1, \ldots, u_m \rangle$ and use the query

$$\pi_{A_{u'_1}, \ldots, A_{u'_m}} (\bowtie \{I_v \mid v \in T'\} \bowtie \{\langle A_{u'_1} : u_1, \ldots, A_{u'_m} : u_m \rangle\}). \quad \blacksquare$$

Theorem 6.2.10(a) considers complexity relative to the size of queries. As applied in the foregoing result, however, the queries of Theorem 6.2.10(a) form the basis for constructing a database instance $\{I_v \mid v \in T'\}$. In contrast with the earlier theorem, the preceding result suggests that computing projections of joins is intractable relative to the size of the query, the stored data, and the output.

Acyclic Joins

In Example 6.4.1, we may ask what is the fundamental difference between $R_1 \bowtie \cdots \bowtie R_{n-1}$ and $R_1 \bowtie \cdots \bowtie R_n$? One answer is that the relation schemas of the latter join form a cycle, whereas the relation schemas of the former do not.

We now develop a formal notion of acyclicity for joins and four properties equivalent to it. All of these are expressed most naturally in the context of the named perspective for the relational model. In addition, the notion of acyclicity is sometimes applied to database schemas $\mathbf{R} = \{R_1, \ldots, R_n\}$ because of the natural correspondence between the schema $\mathbf{R}$ and the join $R_1 \bowtie \cdots \bowtie R_n$.

We begin by describing four interesting properties that are equivalent to acyclicity. Let $\mathbf{R} = \{R_1, \ldots, R_n\}$ be a database schema, where each relation schema has a different sort. An instance $\mathbf{I}$ of $\mathbf{R}$ is said to be *pairwise consistent* if for each pair $j, k \in [1, n]$, $\pi_{R_j}(I_j \bowtie I_k) = I_j$. Intuitively, this means that no tuple of I_j is "dangling" or "lost" after joining with I_k. Instance $\mathbf{I}$ is *globally consistent* if for each $j \in [1, n]$, $\pi_{R_j}(\bowtie \mathbf{I}) = I_j$ (i.e., no tuple of I_j is dangling relative to the full join). Pairwise consistency can be checked in PTIME, but checking global consistency is NP-complete (Exercise 6.25). The first property that is equivalent to acyclicity is:

Property (1): Each instance $\mathbf{I}$ that is pairwise consistent is globally consistent.

Note that the instance for schema $\{R_1, \ldots, R_{n-1}\}$ of Example 6.4.1 is both pairwise and globally consistent, whereas the instance for $\{R_1, \ldots, R_n\}$ is pairwise but not globally consistent.

The second property we consider is motivated by query processing in a distributed environment. Suppose that each relation of $\mathbf{I}$ is stored at a different site, that the join $\bowtie \mathbf{I}$ is to be computed, and that communication costs are to be minimized. A very naive algorithm to compute the join is to send each of the I_j to a specific site and then form the join. In the general case this may cause the shipment of many unneeded tuples because they are dangling in the full join.

The *semi-join* operator can be used to alleviate this problem. Given instances I, J over R, S, then semi-join of I and J is

$$I \ltimes J = \pi_R(I \bowtie J).$$

It is easily verified that $I \bowtie J = (I \ltimes J) \bowtie J = (J \ltimes I) \bowtie I$. Furthermore there are many cases in which computing the join in one of these ways can reduce data transmission costs if I and J are at different nodes of a distributed database (see Exercise 6.24).

Suppose now that $\mathbf{R}$ satisfies Property (1). Given an instance $\mathbf{I}$ distributed across the network, one can imagine replacing each relation I_j by its semi-join with other relations of

R_1	A	B	C
	0	3	2
	0	1	2
	3	1	2
	1	1	3

R_2	B	C	D	E
	3	2	1	0
	1	2	3	0
	1	3	1	0

R_3	B	C	D	G
	3	2	1	4
	1	2	3	2
	1	3	1	0
	1	3	1	1

R_4	C	D	E	F
	2	1	1	4
	2	3	0	1
	3	1	0	2
	3	1	0	3

Figure 6.11:   Instance for Example 6.4.3

I. If done cleverly, this might be done with communication cost polynomial in the size of **I**, with the result of the replacements satisfying pairwise consistency. Given Property (1), all relations can now be shipped to a common site, safe in the knowledge that no dangling tuples have been shipped.

More generally, a *semi-join program* for **R** is a sequence of commands

$$R_{i_1} := R_{i_1} \ltimes R_{j_1};$$
$$R_{i_2} := R_{i_2} \ltimes R_{j_2};$$
$$\vdots$$
$$R_{i_p} := R_{i_p} \ltimes R_{j_p};$$

(In practice, the original values of R_{i_j} would not be overwritten; rather, a scratch copy would be made.) This is a *full reducer* for **R** if for each instance **I** over **R**, applying this program yields an instance **I**′ that is globally consistent.

EXAMPLE 6.4.3   Let $\mathbf{R} = \{ABC, BCDE, BCDG, CDEF\} = \{R_1, R_2, R_3, R_4\}$ and consider the instance **I** of **R** shown in Fig. 6.11. **I** is not globally consistent; nor is it pairwise consistent.

A full reducer for this schema is

$$R_2 := R_2 \ltimes R_1;$$
$$R_2 := R_2 \ltimes R_4;$$
$$R_3 := R_3 \ltimes R_2;$$
$$R_2 := R_2 \ltimes R_3;$$
$$R_4 := R_4 \ltimes R_2;$$
$$R_1 := R_1 \ltimes R_2;$$

Note that application of this program to **I** has the effect of removing the first tuple from each relation.

We can now state the second property:

Property (2): **R** has a full reducer.

It can be shown that the schema $\{R_1, \ldots, R_{n-1}\}$ of Example 6.4.1 has a full reducer, but $\{R_1, \ldots, R_n\}$ does not (see Exercise 6.26).

The next property provides a way to view a schema as a tree with certain properties. A *join tree* of a schema **R** is an undirected tree $T = (\mathbf{R}, E)$ such that

(i) each edge (R, R') is labeled by the set of attributes $R \cap R'$; and

(ii) for every pair R, R' of distinct nodes, for each $A \in R \cap R'$, each edge along the unique path between R and R' includes label A.

Property (3): **R** has a join tree.

For example, two join trees of the schema **R** of Figure 6.11 are $T_1 = (\mathbf{R}, \{(R_1, R_2),$ $(R_2, R_3), (R_2, R_4)\})$ and $T_2 = (\mathbf{R}, \{(R_1, R_3), (R_3, R_2), (R_2, R_4)\})$. (The edge labels are not shown.)

The fourth property we consider focuses entirely on the database schema **R** and is based on a simple algorithm, called the *GYO algorithm*.[1] This is most easily described in terms of the hypergraph corresponding to **R**. A *hypergraph* is a pair $\mathcal{F} = (V, F)$, where V is a set of vertexes and F is family of distinct nonempty subsets of V, called *edges* (or *hyperedges*). The *hypergraph* of schema **R** is the pair $(U, \mathbf{R})$, where $U = \cup \mathbf{R}$. In what follows, we often refer to a database schema **R** as a hypergraph. Three schemas and their hypergraphs are shown in Fig. 6.12.

A hypergraph is *reduced* if there is no pair f, f' of distinct edges with f a proper subset of f'. The *reduction* of $\mathcal{F} = (V, F)$ is $(V, F - \{f \in F \mid \exists f' \in F \text{ with } f \subset f'\})$. Suppose that **R** is a schema and **I** over **R** satisfies the pure URA. If $R_j \subset R_k$, then $I_j = \pi_{R_j}(I_k)$, and thus I_j holds redundant information. It is thus natural in this context to assume that **R**, viewed as a hypergraph, is reduced.

An *ear* of hypergraph $\mathcal{F} = (V, F)$ is an edge $f \in F$ such that for some distinct $f' \in F$, no vertex of $f - f'$ is in any other edge or, equivalently, such that $f \cap (\cup(F - \{f\})) \subseteq f'$. In this case, f' is called a *witness* that f is an ear. As a special case, if there is an edge f of $\mathcal{F}$ that intersects no other edge, then f is also considered an ear.

For example, in the hypergraph of Fig. 6.12(b), edge ABC is an ear, with witness ACE. On the other hand, the hypergraph of Fig. 6.12(a) has no ears.

We now have

ALGORITHM 6.4.4 (GYO Algorithm)

Input: Hypergraph $\mathcal{F} = (V, F)$

Output: A hypergraph involving a subset of edges of $\mathcal{F}$

Do until $\mathcal{F}$ has no ears:
1. Nondeterministically choose an ear f of $\mathcal{F}$.
2. Set $\mathcal{F} := (V', F - \{f\})$, where $V' = \cup(F - \{f\})$. ∎

The output of the GYO algorithm is always reduced.

---

[1] This is so named in honor of M. Graham and the team C. T. Yu and M. Z. Ozsoyoglu, who independently came to essentially this algorithm.

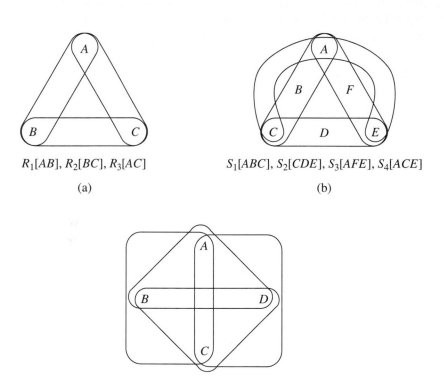

$R_1[AB]$, $R_2[BC]$, $R_3[AC]$

(a)

$S_1[ABC]$, $S_2[CDE]$, $S_3[AFE]$, $S_4[ACE]$

(b)

$T_1[ABC]$, $T_2[BCD]$, $T_3[ABD]$, $T_4[ACD]$

(c)

Figure 6.12:   Three schemas and their hypergraphs

A hypergraph is *empty* if it is $(\emptyset, \emptyset)$. In Fig. 6.12, it is easily verified that the output of the GYO algorithm is empty for part (b), but that parts (a) and (c) have no ears and so equal their output under the algorithm. The output of the GYO algorithm is independent of the order of steps taken (see Exercise 6.28).

We now state the following:

Property (4): The output of the GYO algorithm on **R** is empty.

Speaking informally, Example 6.4.1 suggests that an absence of cycles yields Properties (1) to (4), whereas the presence of a cycle makes these properties fail. This led researchers in the late 1970s to search for a notion of acyclicity for hypergraphs that both generalized the usual notion of acyclicity for conventional undirected graphs and was equivalent to one or more of the aforementioned properties. For example, the conventional notion of hypergraph acyclicity from graph theory is due to C. Berge; but it turns out that this condition is necessary but not sufficient for the four properties (see Exercise 6.32).

We now define the notion of acyclicity that was found to be equivalent to the four aforementioned properties. Let $\mathcal{F} = (V, F)$ be a hypergraph. A *path* in $\mathcal{F}$ from vertex v to vertex v' is a sequence of $k \geq 1$ edges $f_1, \ldots, f_k$ such that

(i) $v \in f_1$;

(ii) $v' \in f_k$;

(iii) $f_i \cap f_{i+1} \neq \emptyset$ for $i \in [1, k - 1]$.

Two vertexes are *connected* in $\mathcal{F}$ if there is a path between them. The notions of *connected pair of edges*, *connected component*, and *connected hypergraph* are now defined in the usual manner.

Now let $\mathcal{F} = (V, F)$ be a hypergraph, and $U \subseteq V$. The *restriction* of $\mathcal{F}$ to U, denoted $\mathcal{F}|_U$, is the result of forming the reduction of $(U, \{f \cap U \mid f \in F\} - \{\emptyset\})$.

Let $\mathcal{F} = (V, F)$ be a reduced hypergraph, let f, f' be distinct edges, and let $g = f \cap f'$. Then g is an *articulation set* of $\mathcal{F}$ if the number of connected components of $\mathcal{F}|_{V-g}$ is greater than the number of connected components of $\mathcal{F}$. (This generalizes the notion of articulation point for ordinary graphs.)

Finally, a reduced hypergraph $\mathcal{F} = (V, F)$ is *acyclic* if for each $U \subseteq V$, if $\mathcal{F}|_U$ is connected and has more than one edge then it has an articulation set; it is *cyclic* otherwise. A hypergraph is *acyclic* if its reduction is.

Note that if $\mathcal{F} = (V, F)$ is an acyclic hypergraph, then so is $\mathcal{F}|_U$ for each $U \subseteq V$.

Property (5): The hypergraph corresponding to **R** is acyclic.

We now present the theorem stating the equivalence of these five properties. Additional equivalent properties are presented in Exercise 6.31 and in Chapter 8, where the relationship of acyclicity with dependencies is explored.

THEOREM 6.4.5   Properties (1) through (5) are equivalent.

Proof   We sketch here arguments that $(4) \Rightarrow (2) \Rightarrow (1) \Rightarrow (5) \Rightarrow (4)$. The equivalence of (3) and (4) is left as Exercise 6.30(a).

We assume in this proof that the hypergraphs considered are connected; generalization to the disconnected case is straightforward.

$(4) \Rightarrow (2)$: Suppose now that the output of the GYO algorithm on $\mathbf{R} = \{R_1, \ldots, R_n\}$ is empty. Let $S_1, \ldots, S_n$ be an ordering of $\mathbf{R}$ corresponding to a sequence of ear removals stemming from an execution of the GYO algorithm, and let T_i be a witness for S_i for $i \in [1, n - 1]$. An induction on n ("from the inside out") shows that the following is a full reducer (see Exercise 6.30a):

I	A_1	A_2	$\ldots$	A_p	B_1	$\ldots$	B_q
	1	0	$\ldots$	0	1	$\ldots$	1
	0	1	$\ldots$	0	2	$\ldots$	2
	$\vdots$	$\vdots$	$\vdots$	$\vdots$	$\vdots$	$\vdots$	$\vdots$
	0	0	$\ldots$	1	p	$\ldots$	p

Figure 6.13: Instance for proof of Theorem 6.4.5

$$T_1 := T_1 \bowtie S_1;$$
$$T_2 := T_2 \bowtie S_2;$$
$$\vdots$$
$$T_{n-1} := T_{n-1} \bowtie S_{n-1};$$
$$S_{n-1} := S_{n-1} \bowtie T_{n-1};$$
$$\vdots$$
$$S_2 := S_2 \bowtie T_2;$$
$$S_1 := S_1 \bowtie T_1;$$

(2) ⇒ (1): Suppose that **R** has a full reducer, and let **I** be a pairwise consistent instance of **R**. Application of the full reducer to **I** yields an instance **I'** that is globally consistent. But by pairwise consistency, each step of the full reducer leaves **I** unchanged. It follows that **I** = **I'** is globally consistent.

(1) ⇒ (5): This is proved by contradiction. Suppose that there is a hypergraph that satisfies Property (1) but violates the definition of *acyclic*. Let $\mathbf{R} = \{R_1, \ldots, R_n\}$ be such a hypergraph where n is minimal among such hypergraphs and where the size of $U = \cup \mathbf{R}$ is minimal among such hypergraphs with n edges.

It follows easily from the minimality conditions that **R** is reduced. In addition, by minimality no vertex (attribute) in U is in only one edge (relation schema).

Consider now the schema $\mathbf{R}' = \{R_2 - R_1, \ldots, R_n - R_1\}$. Two cases arise:

Case 1: $\mathbf{R}'$ is connected. Suppose that $R_1 = \{A_1, \ldots, A_p\}$ and $U - R_1 = \{B_1 \ldots, B_q\}$. Consider the instance I over U shown in Fig. 6.13. Define $\mathbf{I} = \{I_1, \ldots, I_n\}$ so that

$$I_j = \pi_{R_j}(I) \text{ for } j \in [2, n], \text{ and}$$
$$I_1 = \pi_{R_1}(I) \cup \{\langle 0, 0, \ldots, 0 \rangle\}.$$

Using the facts that $\mathbf{R}'$ is connected and that each vertex of **R** occurs in at least two edges, it is straightforward to verify that **I** is pairwise consistent but not globally consistent, which is a contradiction (see Exercise 6.30b).

Case 2: $\mathbf{R}'$ is not connected. Choose a connected component of $\mathbf{R}'$ and let $\{S_1, \ldots, S_k\}$ be the set of edges of $\mathbf{R} - \{R_1\}$ involved in that connected component. Let $S = \cup_{i=1}^{k} S_i$ and let $R'_1 = R_1 \cap S$. Two subcases arise:

Subcase 2.a: $R'_1 \subseteq S_j$ for some $j \in [1, k]$. If this holds, then $R'_1 \cap S_j$ is an articulation set for $\mathbf{R}$, which is a contradiction (see Exercise 6.30b).

Subcase 2.b: $R'_1 \nsubseteq S_j$ for each $j \in [1, k]$. In this case $\mathbf{R}'' = \{S_1, \dots, S_k, R'_1\}$ is a reduced hypergraph with fewer edges than $\mathbf{R}$. In addition, it can be verified that this hypergraph satisfies Property (1) (see Exercise 6.30b). By minimality of n, this implies that $\mathbf{R}''$ is acyclic. Because it is connected and has at least two edges, it has an articulation set. Two nested subcases arise:

Subcase 2.b.i: $S_i \cap S_j$ is an articulation pair for some i, j. We argue in this case that $S_i \cap S_j$ is an articulation pair for $\mathbf{R}$. To see this, let $x \in R'_1 - (S_i \cap S_j)$ and let y be a vertex in some other component of $\mathbf{R}''|_{S-\{S_i \cap S_j\}}$. Suppose that $R_{i_1}, \dots, R_{i_l}$ is a path in $\mathbf{R}$ from y to x. Let R_{i_p} be the first edge in this path that is not in $\{S_1, \dots, S_k\}$. By the choice of $\{S_1, \dots, S_k\}$, $R_{i_p} = R_1$. It follows that there is a path from y to x in $\mathbf{R}''|_{S-\{S_i \cap S_j\}}$, which is a contradiction. We conclude that $\mathbf{R}$ has an articulation pair, contradicting the initial assumption in this proof.

Subcase 2.b.ii: $R'_1 \cap S_i$ is an articulation pair for some i. In this case $R_1 \cap S_i$ is an articulation pair for $\mathbf{R}$ (see Exercise 6.30b), again yielding a contradiction to the initial assumption of the proof.

(5) $\Rightarrow$ (4): We first show inductively that each connected reduced acyclic hypergraph $\mathcal{F}$ with at least two edges has at least two ears. For the case in which $\mathcal{F}$ has two edges, this result is immediate. Suppose now that $\mathcal{F} = (V, F)$ is connected, reduced, and acyclic, with $|F| > 2$. Let $h = f \cap f'$ be an articulation set of $\mathcal{F}$. Let $\mathcal{G}$ be a connected component of $\mathcal{F}|_{V-h}$. By the inductive hypothesis, this has at least two ears. Let g be an ear of $\mathcal{G}$ that is different from $f - h$ and different from $f' - h$. Let g' be an edge of $\mathcal{F}$ such that $g = g' - h$. It is easily verified that g' is an ear of $\mathcal{F}$ (see Exercise 6.30b). Because $\mathcal{F}|_{V-h}$ has more than two connected components, it follows that $\mathcal{F}$ has at least two ears.

Finally, suppose that $\mathcal{F} = (V, F)$ is acyclic. If there is only one edge, then the GYO algorithm yields the empty hypergraph. Suppose that it has more than one edge. If $\mathcal{F}$ is not reduced, the GYO algorithm can be applied to reduce it. If $\mathcal{F}$ is reduced, then by the preceding argument $\mathcal{F}$ has an ear, say f. Then a step of the algorithm can be applied to yield $\mathcal{F}|_{\cup(\mathcal{F}-\{f\})}$. This is again acyclic. An easy induction now yields the result. ∎

Recall from Theorem 6.4.2 that computing projections of arbitrary joins is probably intractable if both query and data size are considered. The following shows that this is not the case when the join is acyclic.

COROLLARY 6.4.6 If $\mathbf{R}$ is acyclic, then for each instance $\mathbf{I}$ over $\mathbf{R}$, the expression $\pi_X(\bowtie \mathbf{I})$ can be computed in time polynomial in the size of $\mathbf{IR}$, the input, and the output.

Proof Because the computation for each connected component of $\mathbf{R}$ can be performed separately, we assume without loss of generality that $\mathbf{R}$ is connected. Let $\mathbf{R} = (R_1, \dots, R_n)$ and $\mathbf{I} = (I_1, \dots, I_n)$. First apply a full reducer to $\mathbf{I}$ to obtain $\mathbf{I}' = (I'_1, \dots, I'_n)$. This takes time polynomial in the size of the query and the input; the result is globally consistent; and $\bowtie \mathbf{I} = \bowtie \mathbf{I}'$.

Because **R** is acyclic, by Theorem 6.4.5 there is a join tree T for **R**. Choose a root for T, say R_1. For each subtree T_k of T with root $R_k \neq R_1$, let $X_k = X \cap (\cup\{R \mid R \in T_k\})$, and $Z_k = R_k \cap$ (the parent of R_k). Let $J_k = I'_k$ for $k \in [1, n]$. Inductively remove nodes R_k and replace instances J_k from leaf to root of T as follows: Delete node R_k with parent R_m by replacing J_m with $J_m \bowtie \pi_{X_k Z_k} J_k$. A straightforward induction shows that immediately before nonleaf node R_k is deleted, then $J_k = \pi_{X_k R_k}(\bowtie_{R_l \in T_k} I'_l)$. It follows that at the end of this process the answer is $\pi_X J_1$ and that at each intermediate stage each instance J_k has size bounded by $|I'_k| \cdot |\pi_X(\bowtie \mathbf{II}_k)|$ (see Exercise 6.33). ■

Bibliographic Notes

An extensive discussion of issues in query optimization is presented in [Gra93]. Other references include [JK84a, KS91, Ull89b]. Query optimization for distributed databases is surveyed in [YC84]. Algorithms for binary joins are surveyed in [ME92].

The paper [SAC+79] describes query optimization in System/R, including a discussion of generating and analyzing multiple evaluation plans and a thorough discussion of accessing tuples from a single relation, as from a projection and selection. System/R is the precursor of IBM's DB2 database management system. The optimizer for INGRES introduces query decomposition, including both join detachment and tuple substitution [WY76, SWKH76].

The use of semi-joins in query optimization was first introduced in INGRES [WY76, SWKH76] and used for distributed databases in [BC81, BG81]. Research on optimizing buffer management policies includes [FNS91, INSS92, NCS91, Sto81]. Other system optimizers include those for Exodus [GD87], distributed INGRES [ESW79], SDD-1 [BGW+81], and the TI Open Object-Oriented Data Base [BMG93].

[B+88] presents the unifying perspective that physical query implementation can be viewed as generation, manipulation, and merging of streams of tuples and develops a very flexible toolkit for constructing dbms's. A formal model incorporating streams, sets, and parallelism is presented in [PSV92].

The recent work [IK90] focuses on finding optimal and near-optimal evaluation plans for n-way joins, where n is in the hundreds, using simulated annealing and other techniques. Perhaps most interesting about this work are characterizations of the space of evaluation plans (e.g., properties of evaluation plan cost in relation to natural metrics on this space).

Early research on generation and selection of query evaluation plans is found in [SAC+79, SWKH76]. Treatments that separate plan generation from transformation rules include [Fre87, GD87, Loh88]. More recent research has proposed mechanisms for generating *parameterized* evaluation plans; these can be generated at compile time but permit the incorporation of run-time information [GW89, INSS92]. An extensive listing of references to the literature on estimating the costs of evaluation plans is presented in [SLRD93]. This article introduces an estimation technique based on the computation of series functions that approximates the distribution of values and uses regression analysis to estimate the output sizes of select-join queries.

Many forward-chaining expert systems in AI also face the problem of evaluating what amounts to conjunctive queries. The most common technique for evaluating conjunctive queries in this context is based on a sequential generate-and-test algorithm. The paper

[SG85] presents algorithms that yield optimal and near-optimal orderings under this approach to evaluation.

The technique of tableau query minimization was first developed in connection with database queries in [CM77], including the Homomorphism Theorem (Theorem 6.2.3) and Theorem 6.2.6. Theorem 6.2.10 is also due to [CM77]; the proofs sketched in the exercises are due to [SY80] and [ASU79b]. Refinements of this result (e.g., to subclasses of typed tableau queries) are presented in [ASU79b, ASU79a].

The notion of tableau homomorphism is a special case of the notion of *subsumption* used in resolution theorem proving [CL73]. That work focuses on clauses (i.e., disjunctions of positive and negative literals), and permits function symbols. A clause $C = (L_1 \vee \cdots \vee L_n)$ *subsumes* a clause $D = (M_1 \vee \cdots \vee M_k)$ if there is a substitution σ such that $C\sigma$ is a subclause of D. A generalized version of tableau minimization, called *condensation*, also arises in this connection. A condensation of a clause $C = (L_1 \vee \cdots \vee L_n)$ is a clause $C' = (L_{i_1} \vee \cdots \vee L_{i_m})$ with m minimal such that $C' = C\theta$ for some substitution θ. As observed in [Joy76], condensations are unique up to variable substitution.

Reference [SY80] studies restricted usage of difference with SPCU queries, for which several positive results can be obtained (e.g., decidability of containment; see Exercise 6.22).

The undecidability results for the relational calculus derive from results in [DiP69] (see also [Var81]). The assumption in this chapter that relations be finite is essential. For instance, the test for containment is co-r.e. in our context whereas it is r.e. when possibly infinite structures are considered. (This is by reduction to the validity of a formula in first-order predicate logic with equality using the Gödel Completeness Theorem.

The complexity of query languages is studied in [CH82, Var82a] and is considered in Part E of this volume.

As discussed in Chapter 7, practical query languages typically produce *bags* (also called multisets; i.e., collections whose members may occur more than once). The problem of containment and equivalence of conjunctive queries under the bag semantics is considered in [CV93]. It remains open whether containment is decidable, but it is Π_2^p-hard. On the other hand, two conjunctive queries are equivalent under the bag semantics iff they are isomorphic.

Acyclic joins enjoyed a flurry of activity in the database research community in the late 1970s and early 1980s. As noted in [Mal86], the same concept has been studied in the field of statistics, beginning with [Goo70, Hab70]. An early motivation for their study in databases stemmed from distributed query processing; the notions of join tree and full reducers are from [BC81, BG81]; see also [GS82, GS84, SS86]. The original GYO algorithm was developed in [YO79] and [Gra79]; we use here a variant due to [FMU82]. The notion of globally consistent is studied in [BR80, HLY80, Ris82, Var82b]; see also [Hul83]. Example 6.4.1 is taken from [Ull89b]. The paper [BFM+81] introduced the notion of acyclicity presented here and observed the equivalence to acyclicity of several previously studied properties, including those of having a full reducer and pairwise consistency implying global consistency; this work is reported in journal form in [BFMY83].

A linear-time test for acyclicity is developed in [TY84]. Theorem 6.4.2 and Corollary 6.4.6 are due to [Yan81].

The notion of Berge acyclic is due to [Ber76a]. [Fag83] investigates several notions of acyclicity, including the notion studied in this chapter and Berge acyclicity. Further investigation of these alternative notions of acyclicity is presented in [ADM85, DM86b, GR86]. Early attempts to develop a notion of acyclic that captured desirable database characteristics include [Zan76, Gra79].

The relationship of acyclicity with dependencies is considered in Chapter 8.

Many variations of the universal relation assumption arose in the late 1970s and early 1980s. We return to this topic in Chapter 11; surveys of these notions include [AP82, Ull82a, MRW86].

Exercises

Exercise 6.1

(a) Give detailed definitions for the rewrite rules proposed in Section 6.1. In other words, provide the conditions under which they preserve equivalence.

(b) Give the step-by-step description of how the query tree of Fig. 6.1(a) can be transformed into the query tree of Fig. 6.1(b) using these rewrite rules.

Exercise 6.2 Consider the transformation $\sigma_F(q_1 \bowtie_G q_2) \rightarrow \sigma_F(q_1) \bowtie_G q_2$ of Fig. 6.2. Describe a query q and database instance for which applying this transformation yields a query whose direct implementation is dramatically more expensive than that of q.

Exercise 6.3

(a) Write generalized SPC queries equivalent to the two tableau queries of Example 6.2.2.

(b) Show that the optimization of this example cannot be achieved using the rewrite rules or multiway join techniques of System/R or INGRES discussed in Section 6.1.

(c) Generate an example analogous to that of Example 6.2.2 that shows that even for typed tableau queries, the rewrite rules of Section 6.1 cannot achieve the optimizations of the Homomorphism Theorem.

Exercise 6.4 Present an algorithm that identifies when variables can be projected out during a left-to-right join of a sip strategy.

Exercise 6.5 Describe a generalization of sip strategies that permits evaluation of multiway joins according to an arbitrary binary tree rather than using only left-to-right join processing. Give an example in which this yields an evaluation plan more efficient than any left-to-right join.

Exercise 6.6 Consider query expressions that have the form (†) mentioned in the discussion of join detachment in Section 6.1.

(a) Describe how the possibility of applying join detachment depends on how equalities are expressed in the conditions (e.g., Is there a difference between using conditions '$x.1 = y.1, y.1 = z.1$' versus '$x.1 = z.1, z.1 = y.1$'?). Describe a technique for eliminating this dependence.

(b) Develop a generalization of join detachment in which a set of variables serves as the pivot.

Exercise 6.7 [WY76]

    (a) Describe some heuristics for choosing the atom $R_i(s_i)$ for forming a tuple substitution. These may be in the context of using tuple substitution and join detachment for the resulting subqueries, or they may be in a more general context.

    (b) Develop a query optimization algorithm based on applying single-variable conditions, join detachment, and tuple substitution.

Exercise 6.8 Prove Corollary 6.2.4.

Exercise 6.9

    (a) State the direct generalization of Theorem 6.2.3 for tableau queries with equality, and show that it does not hold.

    (b) State and prove a correct generalization of Theorem 6.2.3 that handles tableau queries with equality.

Exercise 6.10 For queries q, q', write $q \subset q'$ to denote that $q \subseteq q'$ and $q \not\equiv q'$. The meaning of $q \supset q'$ is defined analogously.

    (a) Exhibit an infinite set $\{q_0, q_1, q_2, \ldots\}$ of typed tableau queries involving no constants over a single relation with the property that $q_0 \subset q_1 \subset q_2 \subset \ldots$.

    (b) Exhibit an infinite set $\{q'_0, q'_1, q'_2, \ldots\}$ of (possibly nontyped) tableau queries involving no constants over a single relation such that $q'_i \not\subseteq q'_j$ and $q'_j \not\subseteq q'_i$ for each pair $i \neq j$.

    (c) Exhibit an infinite set $\{q''_0, q''_1, q''_2, \ldots\}$ of (possibly nontyped) tableau queries involving no constants over a single relation with the property that $q''_0 \supset q''_1 \supset q''_2 \supset \ldots$.

    (d) Do parts (b) and (c) for typed tableau queries that may contain constants.

    ★ (e) [FUMY83] Do parts (b) and (c) for typed tableau queries that contain no constants.

Exercise 6.11 [CM77] Prove Proposition 6.2.9.

Exercise 6.12

    (a) Prove that if the underlying domain **dom** is finite, then only one direction of the statement of Theorem 6.2.3 holds.

    (b) Let $n > 1$ be arbitrary. Exhibit a pair of tableau queries q, q' such that under the assumption that **dom** has n elements, $q \subseteq q'$, but there is no homomorphism from q' to q. In addition, do this using typed tableau queries.

    (c) Show for arbitrary $n > 1$ that Theorem 6.2.6 and Proposition 6.2.9 do not hold if **dom** has n elements.

Exercise 6.13 Let R be a relation schema of sort ABC. For each of the following SPJR queries over R, construct an equivalent tableau (see Exercise 4.19), minimize the tableau, and construct from the minimized tableau an equivalent SPJR query with minimal number of joins.

    (a) $\pi_{AC}[\pi_{AB}(R) \bowtie \pi_{BC}(R)] \bowtie \pi_A[\pi_{AC}(R) \bowtie \pi_{CB}(R)]$

    (b) $\pi_{AC}[\pi_{AB}(R) \bowtie \pi_{BC}(R)] \bowtie \pi_{AB}(\sigma_{B=8}(R)) \bowtie \pi_{BC}(\sigma_{A=5}(R))$

    (c) $\pi_{AB}(\sigma_{C=1}(R)) \bowtie \pi_{BC}(R) \bowtie \pi_{AB}[\sigma_{C=1}(\pi_{AC}(R)) \bowtie \pi_{CB}(R)]$

♠ **Exercise 6.14** [SY80]

(a) Give a decision procedure for determining whether one union of tableaux query is contained in another one. *Hint:* Let the queries be $q = (\{\mathbf{T}_1, \dots, \mathbf{T}_n\}, u)$ and $q' = (\{\mathbf{S}_1, \dots, \mathbf{S}_m\}, v)$; and prove that $q \subseteq q'$ iff for each $i \in [1, n]$ there is some $j \in [1, m]$ such that $(\mathbf{T}_i, u) \subseteq (\mathbf{S}_j, v)$. (The case of queries equivalent to $q^\emptyset$ must be handled separately.)

A union of tableaux query $(\{\mathbf{T}_1, \dots, \mathbf{T}_n\}, u)$ is *nonredundant* if there is no distinct pair i, j such that $(\mathbf{T}_i, u) \subseteq (\mathbf{T}_j, u)$.

(b) Prove that if $(\{\mathbf{T}_1, \dots, \mathbf{T}_n\}, u)$ and $(\{\mathbf{S}_1, \dots, \mathbf{S}_m\}, v)$ are nonredundant and equivalent, then $n = m$; for each $i \in [1, n]$ there is a $j \in [1, n]$ such that $(\mathbf{T}_i, u) \equiv (\mathbf{S}_j, v)$; and for each $j \in [1, n]$ there is a $i \in [1, n]$ such that $(\mathbf{S}_j, v) \equiv (\mathbf{T}_i, u)$.

(c) Prove that for each union of tableaux query q there is a unique (up to renaming) equivalent union of tableaux query that has a minimal total number of atoms.

Exercise 6.15 Exhibit a pair of typed restricted SPJ algebra queries q_1, q_2 over a relation R and having no constants, such that there is no conjunctive query equivalent to $q_1 \cup q_2$. *Hint:* Use tableau techniques.

♠ **Exercise 6.16** [SY80]

(a) Complete the proof of part (a) of Theorem 6.2.10.

(b) Prove parts (b) and (c) of that theorem. *Hint:* Given ξ and $q_\xi = (T_\xi, t)$ and $q'_\xi = (T'_\xi, t)$ as in the proof of part (a), set $q''_\xi = (T_\xi \cup T'_\xi, t)$. Show that ξ is satisfiable iff $q''_\xi \equiv q'_\xi$.

(c) Prove that it is NP-hard to determine, given a pair q, q' of typed tableau queries over the same relation schema, whether q is minimal and equivalent to q'. Conclude that optimizing conjunctive queries, in the sense of finding an equivalent with minimal number of atoms, is NP-hard.

Exercise 6.17 [ASU79b] Prove Theorem 6.2.10 using a reduction from 3-SAT (see Chapter 2) rather than from the exact cover problem.

Exercise 6.18 [ASU79b]

(a) Prove that determining containment between two typed SPJ queries of the form $\pi_X(\bowtie_{i=1}^n (\pi_{X_i} R))$ is NP-complete. *Hint:* Use Exercise 6.16.

(b) Prove that the problem of finding, given an SPJ query q of the form $\pi_X(\bowtie_{i=1}^n (\pi_{X_i} R))$, an SPJ query q' equivalent to q that has the minimal number of join operations among all such queries is NP-hard.

Exercise 6.19

(a) Complete the proof of Theorem 6.3.1.

(b) Describe how to modify that proof so that q_P uses no constants.

(c) Describe how to modify the proof so that no constants and only one ternary relation is used. *Hint:* Speaking intuitively, a tuple $t = \langle a_1, \dots, a_5 \rangle$ of *ENC* can be simulated as a set of tuples $\{\langle b_t, b_1, a_1 \rangle, \dots, \langle b_t, b_5, a_5 \rangle\}$, where b_t is a value not used elsewhere and $b_1, \dots, b_5$ are values established to serve as integers $1, \dots, 5$.

(d) Describe how, given instance $\mathcal{P}$ of the PCP, to construct an nr-datalog$^\neg$ program that is satisfiable iff $\mathcal{P}$ has a solution.

Exercise 6.20   This exercise develops further undecidability results for the relational calculus.

(a) Prove that containment and equivalence of range-safe calculus queries are co-r.e.

(b) Prove that domain independence of calculus queries is co-r.e. *Hint:* Theorem 5.6.1 is useful here.

(c) Prove that containment of safe-range calculus queries is undecidable.

(d) Show that there is no algorithm that always halts and on input calculus query q gives an equivalent query q' of minimum length. Conclude that "complete" optimization of the relational calculus is impossible. *Hint:* If there were such an algorithm, then it would map each unsatisfiable query to a query with formula (of form) $\neg(a = b)$.

♠ **Exercise 6.21**   [ASU79a, ASU79b] In a typed tableau query (T, u), a *summary variable* is a variable occurring in u. A *repeated nonsummary variable* for attribute A is a nonsummary variable in $\pi_A(T)$ that occurs more than once in T. A typed tableau query is *simple* if for each attribute A, there is a repeated nonsummary variable in $\pi_A(T)$, then no other constant or variable in $\pi_A(T)$ occurs more than once $\pi_A(T)$. Many natural typed restricted SPJ queries translate into simple tableau queries.

(a) Show that the tableau query over $R[ABCD]$ corresponding to

$$\pi_{AC}(\pi_{AB}(R) \bowtie \pi_{BC}(R)) \bowtie (\pi_{AB}(R) \bowtie \pi_{BD}(R))$$

is *not* simple.

(b) Exhibit a simple tableau query that is not the result of transforming a typed restricted SPJ query under the algorithm of Exercise 4.19.

(c) Prove that if (T, u) is simple, $T' \subseteq T$, and (T', u) is a tableau query, then (T', u) is simple.

(d) Develop an $O(n^4)$ algorithm that, on input a simple tableau query q, produces a minimal tableau query equivalent to q.

(e) Develop an $O(n^3)$ algorithm that, given simple tableau queries q, q', determines whether $q \equiv q'$.

(f) Prove that testing containment for simple tableau queries is NP-complete.

♠ **Exercise 6.22**   [SY80] Characterize containment and equivalence between queries of the form $q_1 - q_2$, where q_1, q_2 are SPCU queries. *Hint:* First develop characterizations for the case in which q_1, q_2 are SPC queries.

Exercise 6.23   Recall from Exercise 5.9 that an arbitrary nonrecursive datalog$^\neg$ rule can be described as a difference $q_1 - q_2$, where q_1 is an SPC query and q_2 is an SPCU query.

(a) Show that Exercise 5.9 cannot be strengthened so that q_2 is an SPC query.

(b) Show that containment between pairs of nonrecursive datalog$^\neg$ rules is decidable. *Hint:* Use Exercise 6.22.

(c) Recall that for each nr-datalog program P with a single-relation target there is an equivalent nr-datalog program P' such that all rule heads have the same relation name (see Exercise 4.24). Prove that the analogous result does not hold for nr-datalog⁻ programs.

Exercise 6.24

   (a) Verify that $I \bowtie J = (I \ltimes J) \bowtie J$.

   (b) Analyze the transmission costs incurred by the left-hand and right-hand sides of this equation, and describe conditions under which one is more efficient than the other.

Exercise 6.25   [HLY80] Prove that the problem of deciding, given instance **I** of database schema **R**, whether **I** is globally consistent is NP-complete.

Exercise 6.26   Prove the following without using Theorem 6.4.5.

   (a) The database schema $\mathbf{R} = \{AB, BC, CA\}$ has no full reducer.

   (b) For arbitrary $n > 1$, the schema $\{R_1, \ldots, R_{n-1}\}$ of Example 6.4.1 has a full reducer.

   (c) For arbitrary (odd or even) $n > 1$, the schema $\{R_1, \ldots, R_n\}$ of Example 6.4.1 has no full reducer.

Exercise 6.27

   (a) Draw the hypergraph of the schema of Example 6.4.3.

   (b) Draw the hypergraph of Fig. 6.12(b) in a fashion that suggests it to be acyclic.

Exercise 6.28   Prove that the output of Algorithm 6.4.4 is independent of the nondeterministic choices.

Exercise 6.29   As originally introduced, the GYO algorithm involved the following steps:

Nondeterministically perform either step,
     until neither can be applied
  1. If $v \in V$ is in exactly one edge $f \in F$
     then $\mathcal{F} := (V - \{v\}, (F - \{f\}) \cup \{f - \{v\}\}) - \{\emptyset\})$.
  2. If $f \subseteq f'$ for distinct $f, f' \in F$,
     then $\mathcal{F} := (V, F - \{f\})$.

The result of applying the original GYO algorithm to a schema **R** is the *GYO reduction* of **R**.

   (a) Prove that the original GYO algorithm yields the same output independent of the nondeterministic choices.

   (b) [FMU82] Prove that Algorithm 6.4.4 given in the text yields the empty hypergraph on **R** iff the GYO reduction of **R** is the empty hypergraph.

Exercise 6.30   This exercise completes the proof of Theorem 6.4.5.

   (a) [BG81] Prove that (3) $\Leftrightarrow$ (4).

   (b) Complete the other parts of the proof.

Exercise 6.31   [BFMY83] **R** has the *running intersection property* if there is an ordering $R_1, \ldots, R_n$ of **R** such that for $2 \le i \le n$ there exists $j_i < i$ such that $R_i \cap (R_1 \cup \cdots \cup R_{i-1}) \subseteq R_{j_i}$. In other words, the intersection of each R_i with the union of the previous $R'_j s$ is contained in one of these. Prove that **R** has the running intersection property iff **R** is acyclic.

Exercise 6.32   [BFMY83] A *Berge cycle* in a hypergraph $\mathcal{F}$ is a sequence $(f_1, v_1, f_2, v_2, \ldots, f_n, v_n, f_{n+1})$ such that

(i) $v_1, \ldots, v_n$ are distinct vertexes of $\mathcal{F}$;

(ii) $f_1, \ldots, f_n$ are distinct edges of $\mathcal{F}$, and $f_{n+1} = f_1$;

(iii) $n \geq 2$; and

(iv) $v_i \in f_i \cap f_{i+1}$ for $i \in [1, n]$.

A hypergraph is *Berge cyclic* if it has a Berge cycle, and it is *Berge acyclic* otherwise.

(a) Prove that Berge acyclicity is necessary but not sufficient for acyclicity.

(b) Show that any hypergraph in which two edges have two nodes in common is Berge cyclic.

Exercise 6.33   [Yan81] Complete the proof of Corollary 6.4.6.

7 Notes on Practical Languages

Alice:	*What do you mean by practical languages?*
Riccardo:	**select from where**.
Alice:	*That's it?*
Vittorio:	*Well, there are of course lots of bells and whistles.*
Sergio:	*But basically, this forms the core of most practical languages.*

In this chapter we discuss the relationship of the abstract query languages discussed so far to three representative commercial relational query languages: Structured Query Language (SQL), Query-By-Example (QBE), and Microsoft Access. SQL is by far the dominant relational query language and provides the basis for languages in extensions of the relational model as well. Although QBE is less widespread, it illustrates nicely the basic capabilities and problems of graphic query languages. Access is a popular database management system for personal computers (PCs) and uses many elements of QBE.

Our discussion of the practical languages is not intended to provide a complete description of them, but rather to indicate some of the similarities and differences between theory and practice. We focus here on the central aspects of these languages. Many features, such as string-comparison operators, iteration, and embeddings into a host language, are not mentioned or are touched on only briefly.

We first present highlights of the three languages and then discuss considerations that arise from their use in the real world.

7.1 SQL: The Structured Query Language

SQL has emerged as *the* preeminent query language for mainframe and client-server relational dbms's. This language combines the flavors of both the algebra and the calculus and is well suited for the specification of conjunctive queries.

This section begins by describing how conjunctive queries are expressed using SQL. We then progress to additional features, including nested queries and various forms of negation.

Conjunctive Queries in SQL

Although there are numerous variants of SQL, it has become the standard for relational query languages and indeed for most aspects of relational database access, including data definition, data modification, and view definition. SQL was originally developed under the

143

name Sequel at the IBM San Jose Research Laboratory. It is currently supported by most of the dominant mainframe commercial relational systems, and increasingly by relational dbms's for PCs.

The basic building block of SQL queries is the *select-from-where* clause. Speaking loosely, these have the form

select   *<list of fields to select>*
from   *<list of relation names>*
where   *<condition>*

For example, queries (4.1) and (4.4) of Chapter 4 are expressed by

select   *Director*
from   *Movies*
where   *Title* = 'Cries and Whispers';

select   *Location.Theater, Address*
from   *Movies, Location, Pariscope*
where   *Director* = 'Bergman'
        and *Movies.Title = Pariscope.Title*
        and *Pariscope.Theater = Location.Theater*;

In these queries, relation names themselves are used to denote variables ranging over tuples occurring in the corresponding relation. For example, in the preceding queries, the identifier *Movies* can be viewed as ranging over tuples in relation *Movies*. Relation name and attribute name pairs, such as *Location.Theater*, are used to refer to tuple components; and the relation name can be dropped if the attribute occurs in only one of the relations in the **from** clause.

The **select** keyword has the effect of the relational algebra *projection* operator, the **from** keyword has the effect of the *cross-product* operator, and the **where** keyword has the effect of the *selection* operator (see Exercise 7.3). For example, the second query translates to (using abbreviated attribute names)

$$\pi_{L.Th,A}(\sigma_{D='\text{Bergman}'\wedge M.Ti=P.Ti\wedge P.Th=L.Th}(Movies \times Location \times Pariscope)).$$

If all of the attributes mentioned in the **from** clause are to be output, then * can be used in place of an attribute list in the **select** clause. In general, the **where** condition may include conjunction, disjunction, negation, and (as will be seen shortly) nesting of select-from-where blocks. If the **where** clause is omitted, then it is viewed as having value *true* for all tuples of the cross-product. In implementations, as suggested in Chapter 6, optimizations will be used; for example, the **from** and **where** clauses will typically be merged to have the effect of an *equi-join* operator.

In SQL, as with most practical languages, duplicates may occur in a query answer.

Technically, then, the output of an SQL query may be a *bag* (also called "multiset")— a collection whose members may occur more than once. This is a pragmatic compromise with the pure relational model because duplicate removal is rather expensive. The user may request that duplicates be removed by inserting the keyword **distinct** after the keyword **select**.

If more than one variable ranging over the same relation is needed, then variables can be introduced in the **from** clause. For example, query (4.7), which asks for pairs of persons such that the first directed the second and the second directed the first, can be expressed as

select *M1.Director, M1.Actor*
from   *Movies M1, Movies M2*
where *M1.Director* = *M2.Actor*
          and *M1.Actor* = *M2.Director*;

In the preceding example, the *Director* coordinate of *M1* is compared with the *Actor* coordinate of *M2*. This is permitted because both coordinates are (presumably) of type **character string**. Relations are declared in SQL by specifying a relation name, the attribute names, and the scalar types associated with them. For example, the schema for *Movies* might be declared as

create table *Movies*
       (*Title* **character**[60]
       Director **character**[30]
       Actor **character**[30]);

In this case, *Title* and *Director* values would be comparable, even though they are character strings of different lengths. Other scalar types supported in SQL include integer, small integer, float, and date.

Although the select-from-where block of SQL has a syntactic flavor close to the relational calculus (but using tuple variables rather than domain variables), from a technical perspective the SQL semantics are firmly rooted in the algebra, as illustrated by the following example.

EXAMPLE 7.1.1   Let $\{R[A], S[B], T[C]\}$ be a database schema, and consider the following query:

select *A*
from   *R, S, T*
where *R.A* = *S.B* **or** *R.A* = *T.C*;

A direct translation of this into the SPJR algebra extended to permit disjunction in selection formulas (see Exercise 4.22) yields

$$\pi_A(\sigma_{A=B \vee A=C}(R \times S \times T)),$$

which yields the empty answer if S is empty or if T is empty. Thus the foregoing SQL query is not equivalent to the calculus query:

$$\{x \mid R(x) \wedge (S(x) \vee T(x))\}.$$

A correct translation into the conjunctive calculus (with disjunction) query is

$$\{w \mid \exists x, y, z(R(x) \wedge S(y) \wedge T(z) \wedge x = w \wedge (x = y \vee x = z))\}.$$

_____

Adding Set Operators

The select-from-where blocks of SQL can be combined in a variety of ways. We describe first the incorporation of the set operators (**union**, **intersect**, and **difference**). For example, the query

(4.14)   List all actors and director of the movie "Apocalypse Now."

can be expressed as

(**select**	*Actor Participant*
from	*Movies*
where	*Title* = 'Apocalypse Now')
union	
(**select**	*Director Participant*
from	*Movies*
where	*Title* = 'Apocalypse Now');

In the first subquery the output relation uses attribute *Participant* in place of *Actor*. This illustrates renaming of attributes, analogous to relation variable renaming. This is needed here so that the two relations that are unioned have compatible sort.

   Although **union**, **intersect**, and **difference** were all included in the original SQL, only **union** is in the current SQL2 standard developed by the American National Standards Institute (ANSI). The two left out can be simulated by other mechanisms, as will be seen later in this chapter.

   SQL also includes a keyword **contains**, which can be used in a selection condition to test containment between the output of two nested select-from-where expressions.

Nested SQL Queries

Nesting permits the use of one SQL query within the **where** clause of another. A simple illustration of nesting is given by this alternative formulation of query (4.4):

select   *Theater*
from   *Pariscope*
where   *Title*   **in**
                              (**select**   *Title*
                              from   *Movies*
                              where   *Director* = 'Bergman');

The preceding example tests membership of a unary tuple in a unary relation. The keyword **in** can also be used to test membership for arbitrary arities. The symbols < and > are used to construct tuples from attribute expressions. In addition, because negation is permitted in the **where** clause, set difference can be expressed. Consider the query

List title and theater for movies being shown in only one theater.

This can be expressed in SQL by

select   *Title, Theater*
from   *Pariscope*
where   ⟨*Title, Theater*⟩   **not in**
                                    (**select**   *P1.Title, P1.Theater*
                                    from   *Pariscope P1, Pariscope P2*
                                    where   *P1.Title = P2.Title*
                                             and not (*P1.Theater = P2.Theater*));

Expressing First-Order Queries in SQL

We now discuss the important result that SQL is relationally "complete," in the sense that it can express all relational queries expressible in the calculus. Recall from Chapter 5 that the family of nr-datalog¬ programs is equivalent to the calculus and algebra. We shall show how to simulate nr-datalog¬ using SQL. Intuitively, the result follows from the facts that

(a) each rule can be simulated using the *select-from-where* construct;

(b) multiple rules defining the same predicate can be simulated using **union**; and

(c) negation in rule bodies can be simulated using **not in**.

We present an example here and leave the formal proof for Exercise 7.4.

EXAMPLE 7.1.2   Consider the following query against the **CINEMA** database:

Find the theaters showing every movie directed by Hitchcock.

An nr-datalog¬ program expressing the query is

$$Pariscope'(x_{th}, x_{title}) \leftarrow Pariscope(x_{th}, x_{title}, x_{sch})$$
$$Bad\_th(x_{th}) \quad\quad \leftarrow Movies(x_{title}, Hitchcock, x_{act}),$$
$$Location(x_{th}, x_{loc}, x_{ph}),$$
$$\neg Pariscope'(x_{th}, x_{title})$$
$$Answer(x_{th}) \quad\quad \leftarrow Location(x_{th}, x_{loc}, x_{ph}), \neg Bad\_th(x_{th}).$$

In the program, *Bad_th* holds the list of "bad" theaters, for which one can find a movie by Hitchcock that the theater is not showing. The last rule takes the complement of *Bad_th* with respect to the list of theaters provided by *Location*.

An SQL query expressing an nr-datalog¬ program such as this one can be constructed in two steps. The first is to write SQL queries for each rule separately. In this example, we have

Pariscope':   **select**   *Theater, Title*
                from   *Pariscope*;

Bad_th: **select**   *Theater*
           from   *Movies, Location*
           where   *Director* = 'Hitchcock'
                  and $\langle Theater, Title\rangle$ **not in**
                                    (select *
                                    from   *Pariscope'*);

Answer: **select**   *Theater*
           from   *Location*
           where   *Theater*   **not in**
                                (select *
                                from   *Bad_th*);

The second step is to combine the queries. In general, this involves replacing nested queries by their definitions, starting from the *answer* relation and working backward. In this example, we have

select   *Theater*
from   *Location*
where   *Theater*   **not in**
                        (select   *Theater*
                        from   *Movies, Location*
                        where   *Director* = 'Hitchcock'
                                and $\langle Theater, Title\rangle$ **not in**
                                          (select   *Theater, Title*
                                          from   *Pariscope*));

In this example, each *idb* (see Section 4.3) relation that occurs in a rule body occurs negatively. As a result, all variables that occur in the rule are bound by *edb* relations, and so the *from* part of the (possibly nested) query corresponding to the rule refers only to *edb* relations. In general, however, variables in rule bodies might be bound by positively occurring *idb* relations, which cannot be used in any *from* clause in the final SQL query. To resolve this problem, the nr-datalog⁻ program should be rewritten so that all positively occurring relations in rule bodies are *edb* relations (see Exercise 7.4a).

View Creation and Updates

We conclude our consideration of SQL by noting that it supports both view creation and updates.

SQL includes an explicit mechanism for view creation. The relation *Champo-info* from Example 4.3.4 is created in SQL by

create view   *Le Champo* **as**
   select   *Pariscope.Title, Schedule, Phone*
   from   *Pariscope, Location*
   where   *Pariscope.Theater* = 'Le Champo'
       and *Location.Theater* = 'Le Champo.'

Views in SQL can be accessed as can normal relations and are useful in building up complex queries.

As a practical database language, SQL provides commands for updating the database. We briefly illustrate these here; some theoretical aspects concerning updates are presented in Chapter 22.

SQL provides three primitive commands for modifying the contents of a database—**insert**, **delete**, and **update** (in the sense of modifying individual tuples of a relation). The following can be used to insert a new tuple into the *Movies* database:

insert into *Movies*
   values ('Apocalypse Now,' 'Coppola,' 'Duvall');

A set of tuples can be deleted simultaneously:

delete   *Movies*
   where   *Director* = 'Hitchcock';

Tuple update can also operate on sets of tuples (as illustrated by the following) that might be used to correct a typographical error:

update *Movies*
   set   *Director* = 'Hitchcock'
   where   *Director* = 'Hickcook';

The ability to insert and delete tuples provides an alternative approach to demonstrating the relational completeness of SQL. In particular, subexpressions of an algebra expression can be computed in intermediate, temporary relations (see Exercise 7.6). This approach does not allow the same degree optimization as the one based on views because the SQL interpreter is required to materialize each of the intermediate relations.

7.2   Query-by-Example and Microsoft Access

We now turn to two query languages that have a more visual presentation. The first, Query-by-Example (QBE), presents a visual display for expressing conjunctive queries that is close to the perspective of tableau queries. The second language, Access, is available on personal computers; it uses elements of QBE, but with a more graphical presentation of join relationships.

QBE

The language Query-By-Example (QBE) was originally developed at the IBM T. J. Watson Research Center and is currently supported as part of IBM's Query Management Facility. As illustrated at the beginning of Chapter 4, the basic format of QBE queries is fundamentally two-dimensional and visually close to the tableau queries. Importantly, a variety of features are incorporated into QBE to give more expressive power than the tableau queries and to provide data manipulation capabilities. The development of QBE is remarkable in that it demonstrates how far its visual, tableau-based paradigm can be extended to support general data access, manipulation, and definition capabilities.

As seen in Fig. 4.2, which expresses query (4.4), QBE uses strings with prefix _ to denote variables and other strings to denote constants. If the string is preceded by P., then the associated coordinate value forms part of the query output. QBE provides a partial union capability by permitting the inclusion in a query of multiple tuples having a P. prefix in a single relation. For example, Fig. 7.1 expresses the query

(4.12)   What films with Allen as actor or director are currently featured at the Concorde?

Importantly, the underlying semantics of QBE are similar to that of SQL, and this query will yield the empty answer if either of $\sigma_{Director=\text{"Allen"}}Movies$ or $\sigma_{Actor=\text{"Allen"}}Movies$ is empty (see Example 7.1.1).

QBE also includes a capability of *condition boxes*, which can be viewed as an extension of the incorporation of equality atoms into tableau queries.

QBE does not provide a mechanism analogous to SQL for nesting of queries. It is hard to develop an appropriate visual representation of such nesting within the QBE framework, in part due to the lack of scoping rules. More recent extensions of QBE address this issue by incorporating, for example, hierarchical windows. QBE also provides mechanisms for both view definition and database update.

Negation can be incorporated into QBE queries in a variety of ways. The use of database update is an obvious mechanism, although not especially efficient. Two restricted

Movies	Title	Director	Actor
	_X	Allen	
	_Y		Allen

Pariscope	Theater	Title	Schedule
	Concorde	P._X	
	Concorde	P._Y	

Figure 7.1:   One form of union in QBE

Movies	Title	Director	Actor
¬	_Z	Bergman	

Pariscope	Theater	Title	Schedule
	P._champio ¬Concorde	_Z	

Figure 7.2:   A query with negation in QBE

forms of negation are illustrated in Fig. 7.2, which expresses the following query: (assuming that each film has only one director) what theaters, other than the Concorde, feature a film *not* directed by Bergman? The ¬ in the *Pariscope* relation restricts attention to those tuples with *Theater* coordinate not equal to Concorde, and the ¬ preceding the tuple in the *Movies* relation is analogous to a negative literal in a datalog rule and captures a limited form of ¬∃ from the calculus; in this case it excludes all films directed by Bergman. When such negation is used, it is required that all variables that occur in a row preceded by ¬ also appear in positive rows. Other restricted forms of negation in QBE include using negative literals in condition boxes and supporting an operator analogous to relational division (as defined in Exercise 5.8).

The following example shows more generally how view definition can be used to obtain relational completeness.

EXAMPLE 7.2.1   Recall the query and nr-datalog¬ program of Example 7.1.2. As with SQL, the QBE query corresponding to an nr-datalog¬ will involve one or more views for each rule (see Exercise 7.5). For this example, however, it turns out that we can compute the effect of the first two rules with a single QBE query. Thus the two stages of the full query are shown in Fig. 7.3, where the symbol *I.* indicates that the associated tuples are to be inserted into the answer. The creation of the view *Bad_th* is accomplished using the

Stage I:

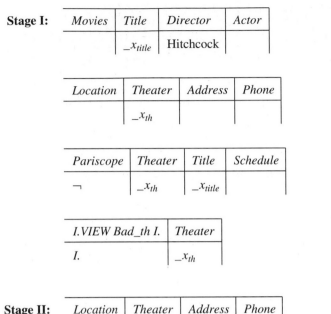

Movies	Title	Director	Actor
	$\_x_{title}$	Hitchcock	

Location	Theater	Address	Phone
	$\_x_{th}$		

Pariscope	Theater	Title	Schedule
¬	$\_x_{th}$	$\_x_{title}$	

I.VIEW Bad_th I.	Theater
I.	$\_x_{th}$

Stage II:

Location	Theater	Address	Phone
	$\_x_{th}$		

Bad_th	Theater
¬	$\_x_{th}$

Answer	Theater
I.	$\_x_{th}$

Figure 7.3:   Illustration of relational completeness of QBE

---

expression *I.VIEW Bad_th I.*, which both creates the view and establishes the attribute names for the view relation.

Microsoft Access: A Query Language for PCs

A number of dbms's for personal computers have become available over the past few years, such as DBASE IV, Microsoft Access, Foxpro, and Paradox. Several of these support a version of SQL and a more visual query language. The visual languages have a flavor somewhat different from QBE. We illustrate this here by presenting an example of a query from the Microsoft Access dbm's.

Access provides an elegant graphical mechanism for constructing conjunctive queries. This includes a tabular display to indicate the form and content of desired output tuples, the use of single-attribute conditions within this display (in the rows named "Criteria" and "or"), and a graphical presentation of join relationships that are to hold between relations used to form the output. Fig. 7.4 shows how query (4.4) can be expressed using Access.

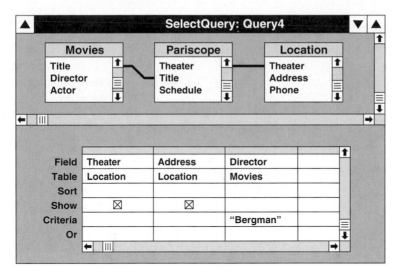

Figure 7.4: Example query in Access

(Although not shown in the figure, join conditions can also be expressed using single-attribute conditions represented as text.)

Limited forms of negation and union can be incorporated into the condition part of an Access query. For more general forms of negation and union, however, the technique of building views to serve as intermediate relations can be used.

7.3 Confronting the Real World

Because they are to be used in practical situations, the languages presented in this chapter incorporate a number of features not included in their formal counterparts. In this section we touch on some of these extensions and on fundamental issues raised by them. These include domain independence, the implications of incorporating many-sorted atomic objects, the use of arithmetic, and the incorporation of aggregate operators.

Queries from all of the practical languages described in this chapter are domain independent. This is easily verified from the form of queries in these languages: Whenever a variable is introduced, the relation it ranges over is also specified. Furthermore, the specific semantics associated with **or**'s occurring in **where** clauses (see Example 7.1.1) prevent the kind of safety problem illustrated by query *unsafe-2* of Section 5.3.

Most practical languages permit the underlying domain of values to be many-sorted—for example, including distinct scalar domains for the types integer, real, character string, etc., and some constructed types, such as date, in some languages. (More recent systems, such as POSTGRES, permit the user to incorporate abstract data types as well.) For most of the theoretical treatment, we assumed that there was one underlying domain of values, **dom**, which was shared equally by all relational attributes. As noted in the discussion of

SQL, the typing of attributes can be used to ensure that comparisons make sense, in that they compare values of comparable type. Much of the theory developed here for a single underlying domain can be generalized to the case of a *many-sorted* underlying domain (see Exercise 7.8).

Another fundamental feature of practical query languages is that they offer value comparators other than equality. Typically most of the base sorts are totally ordered. This is the case for the integers or the strings (under the lexicographical ordering). It is therefore natural to introduce $\leq, \geq, <, >$ as comparators. For example, to ask the query, "What can we see at the Le Champo after 21:00," we can use

$$ans(x_t) \leftarrow Pariscope(\text{"Le Champo,"} x_t, x_s), \ x_s > \text{"21:00"};$$

and, in the algebra, as

$$\pi_{Title}(\sigma_{Theater=\text{"Le Champo"} \wedge Schedule > \text{"21:00"}} Pariscope).$$

Exercise 4.30 explores the impact of incorporating comparators into the conjunctive queries. Many languages also incorporate string-comparison operators.

Given the presence of integers and reals, it is natural to incorporate arithmetic operators. This yields a fundamental increase in expressive power: Even simple counting is beyond the power of the calculus (see Exercise 5.34).

Another extension concerns the incorporation of *aggregate* operators into the practical languages (see Section 5.5). Consider, for example, the query, "How many films did Hitchcock direct?". In SQL, this can be expressed using the query

select   **count(distinct** *Title*)
from   *Movies*
where   *Director* = 'Hitchcock';

(The keyword **distinct** is needed here, because otherwise SQL will not remove duplicates from the projection onto *Title*.) Other aggregate operators typically supported in practical languages include **sum, average, minimum**, and **maximum**.

In the preceding example, the aggregate operator was applied to an entire relation. By using the **group by** command, aggregate operators can be applied to clusters of tuples, each common values on a specified set of attributes. For example, the following SQL query determines the number of movies directed by each director:

select   *Director*, **count(distinct** *Title*)
from   *Movies*
group by   *Director*;

The semantics of *group by* in SQL are most easily understood when we study an extension of the relational model, called the complex object (or nested relation) model, which models grouping in a natural fashion (see Chapter 20).

Bibliographic Notes

General descriptions of SQL and QBE may be found in [EN89, KS91, Ull88]; more details on SQL can be found in [C$^+$76], and on QBE in [Zlo77]. Another language similar in spirit to SQL is Quel, which was provided with the original INGRES system. A description of Quel can be found in [SWKH76]. Reference [OW93] presents a survey of QBE langauges and extensions. A reference on Microsoft Access is [Cam92]. In Unix, the command *awk* provides a basic relational tool.

Formal semantics for SQL are presented in [NPS91]. Example 7.1.1 is from [GT91]. Other proofs that SQL can simulate the relational calculus are presented in [PBGG89, Ull88]. Motivated by the fact that SQL outputs bags rather than sets, [CV93] studies containment and equivalence of conjunctive queries under the bag semantics (see "Bibliographic Notes" in Chapter 6).

Aggregate operators in query languages are studied in [Klu82].

SQL has become the standard relational query language [57391, 69392]; reference [GW90] presents the original ANSI standard for SQL, along with commentary about particular products and some history. SQL is available on most main-frame relational dbms's, including, for example, IBM's DB2, Oracle, Informix, INGRES, and Sybase, and in some more recent database products for personal computers (e.g.,Microsoft Access, dBASE IV). QBE is available as part of IBM's product QMF (Query Management Facility). Some personal computer products support more restricted graphical query languages, including Microsoft Access and Paradox (which supports a form-based language).

Exercises

Exercise 7.1   Write SQL, QBE, and Access queries expressing queries (4.1 to 4.14) from Chapter 4. Start by expressing them as nr-datalog$^\neg$ programs.

Exercise 7.2   Consider again the queries (5.2 and 5.3) of Chapter 5. Express these in SQL, QBE, and Access.

Exercise 7.3   Describe formally the mapping of SQL select-from-where blocks into the SPJR algebra.

♠ **Exercise 7.4**

(a) Let P be an nr-datalog$^\neg$ program. Describe how to construct an equivalent program P' such that each predicate that occurs positively in a rule body is an *edb* predicate.

(b) Develop a formal proof that SQL can simulate nr-datalog$^\neg$.

Exercise 7.5   Following Example 7.2.1, show that QBE is relationally complete.

Exercise 7.6

(a) Assuming that R and S have compatible sorts, show how to compute in SQL the value of $R - S$ into the relation T using **insert** and **delete**.

(b) Generalize this to show that SQL is relationally complete.

Exercise 7.7 In a manner analogous to Exercise 7.6, show that Access is relationally complete.

★ **Exercise 7.8** The intuition behind the typed restricted PSJ algebra is that each attribute has a distinct type whose elements are incomparable with the types of other attributes. As motivated by the practical query languages, propose and study a restriction of the SPJR algebra analogous to the typed restricted PSJ algebra, but permitting more than one attribute with the same type. Does the equivalence of the various versions of the conjunctive queries still hold? Can Exercise 6.21 be generalized to this framework?

C Constraints

As presented so far, there is little in the relational model that can be used to indicate the intended meaning of tuples stored in a database. Although this provides database designers and users with great flexibility, the inability to represent so-called *meta-data* can also lead to a variety of problems. For example, it is hard to develop understandable and usable schemas for complex database applications because of the somewhat simplistic nature of the model. Furthermore, the lack of information on the properties of the stored data often leads to inefficient implementations.

In response to these problems, a framework for adding semantics to the relational model has been developed. This is accomplished by incorporating *integrity constraints* (i.e., properties that are supposed to be satisfied by all instances of a database schema). Some of the early research included the study of integrity constraints expressed by essentially arbitrary sentences from first-order logic. However, feasibility considerations have led to the study of more restricted classes of constraints, usually called *dependencies*. A simple example is that of *key dependency*. For instance, we expect that in a relation concerning personnel data, the Social Security number will serve as a "key" (i.e., the Social Security number will uniquely identify tuples in the relation).

The fundamental motivation for the study of dependencies is to incorporate more semantics into the relational model. An alternative is to develop more sophisticated database models with richer constructs than the relational model, yielding schemas conveying explicitly more of the semantics associated with the data. One family of such models, called semantic data models, and its relationship to the relational model are discussed in Chapter 11. A more general family, called object-oriented database models, is studied in Chapter 21 of Part F.

With the development of new models, dependency theory has become somewhat out of fashion. However, we believe that the results presented in this part remain important. The functional, join, and inclusion dependencies are fundamental to the understanding of the more elaborate constructs found in modern database models. Their study in the simple context of the relational model captures the essence of such constructs. Some results presented in this part have also found applications to various fields, such as deductive databases. Finally, some of the techniques that are developed are interesting in their own right and highlight in a nutshell key aspects of computer science.

A broad theory of dependencies has been developed for the relational model.[1] Several natural kinds of dependencies were introduced, often using an *ad hoc* notation, and studied in depth. Subsequently, a framework stemming primarily from mathematical logic was developed that provides a unifying view of virtually all of them. The single most important theoretical question examined in connection with dependencies is that of (*logical*) *implication*: Given a set Σ of dependencies and a dependency σ, if an instance satisfies Σ does it necessarily satisfy σ as well? The implication problem turns out to be a key technical issue in most situations in which dependencies are used. It has been studied primarily from two perspectives. One is focused on developing algorithms for determining implication and on studying the complexity of this problem for different classes of dependencies. The other perspective is focused on the development of *inference rules* that can be used to construct proofs that a dependency is implied.

Dependencies are intimately related to several other important topics in various database contexts. A driving force for the study of dependencies has been schema design. The goal is to select the most appropriate schema for a particular database application. Under one approach, a schema from a semantic data model is transformed into a relational schema with dependencies. An alternative approach starts with a "universal relation" and applies *decomposition* to create new relations that satisfy certain *normal forms*. Other areas of theoretical research have been to study query optimization techniques in the presence of dependencies and the interaction between dependencies and data restructuring. Results include the use of dependencies to optimize conjunctive queries and the study of how dependencies are carried from a database to a view.

All of the dependencies studied in this part are *static*, in the sense that they describe properties that should be satisfied by all possible instances of a schema regardless of the past and future. Research has also been performed in connection with *dynamic dependencies*, which describe properties of the evolution of the database; these are considered briefly in Chapter 22.

The first chapter of this part presents the practical motivations for the incorporation of dependencies into the relational model and then examines the basic themes of dependency theory in connection with two fundamental kinds of dependencies (namely, *functional* and *join* dependencies). This chapter also introduces the *chase*, an elegant tool for optimizing conjunctive queries in the presence of dependencies and for determining implication for dependencies. The second chapter introduces *inclusion dependencies*. Although positive results are obtained for these dependencies considered in isolation, several negative results hold when they are considered with functional dependencies. The third chapter presents a unifying framework for dependencies based on a perspective from mathematical logic. The final chapter of this part considers dependency theory in connection with several issues of database design.

---

[1] To keep theoreticians in business, some say.

8 Functional and Join Dependency

Alice:	*Your model reduces the most interesting information to something flat and boring.*
Vittorio:	*You're right, and this causes a lot of problems.*
Sergio:	*Designing the schema for a complex application is tough, and it is easy to make mistakes when updating a database.*
Riccardo:	*Also, the system knows so little about the data that it is hard to obtain good performance.*
Alice:	*Are you telling me that the model is bad?*
Vittorio:	*No, wait, we are going to fix it!*

This chapter begins with an informal discussion that introduces some simple dependencies and illustrates the primary motivations for their development and study. The two following sections of the chapter are devoted to two of the simple kinds of dependencies; and the final section introduces the chase, an important tool for analyzing these dependencies and their effect on queries.

Many of the early dependencies introduced in the literature use the named (as opposed to unnamed) perspective on tuples and relations. Dependency theory was one of the main reasons for adopting this perspective in theoretical investigations. This is because dependencies concern the semantics of data, and attribute names carry more semantics than column numbers. The general view of dependencies based on logic, which is considered in Chapter 10, uses the column-number perspective, but a special subcase (called *typed*) retains the spirit of the attribute-name perspective.

8.1 Motivation

Consider the database shown in Fig. 8.1. Although the schema itself makes no restrictions on properties of data that might be stored, the intended application for the schema may involve several such restrictions. For example, we may know that there is only one director associated with each movie title, and that in *Showings*, only one movie title is associated with a given theater-screen pair.[1] Such properties are called *functional dependencies* (fd's) because the values of some attributes of a tuple uniquely or *functionally* determine the values of other attributes of that tuple. In the syntax to be developed in this chapter, the

---

[1] Gone are the days of seeing two movies for the price of one!

Movies	Title	Director	Actor
	The Birds	Hitchcock	Hedren
	The Birds	Hitchcock	Taylor
	Bladerunner	Scott	Hannah
	Apocalypse Now	Coppola	Brando

Showings	Theater	Screen	Title	Snack
	Rex	1	The Birds	coffee
	Rex	1	The Birds	popcorn
	Rex	2	Bladerunner	coffee
	Rex	2	Bladerunner	popcorn
	Le Champo	1	The Birds	tea
	Le Champo	1	The Birds	popcorn
	Cinoche	1	The Birds	Coke
	Cinoche	1	The Birds	wine
	Cinoche	2	Bladerunner	Coke
	Cinoche	2	Bladerunner	wine
	Action Christine	1	The Birds	tea
	Action Christine	1	The Birds	popcorn

Figure 8.1:   Sample database illustrating simple dependencies

dependency in the *Movies* relation is written as

$$Movies : Title \rightarrow Director$$

and that of the *Showings* relation is written as

$$Showings : Theater\ Screen \rightarrow Title.$$

Technically, there are sets of attributes on the left- and right-hand sides of the arrow, but we continue with the convention of omitting set braces when understood from the context.

When there is no confusion from the context, a dependency $R : X \rightarrow Y$ is simply denoted $X \rightarrow Y$. A relation I *satisfies* a functional dependency $X \rightarrow Y$ if for each pair s, t of tuples in I,

$$\pi_X(s) = \pi_X(t) \text{ implies } \pi_Y(s) = \pi_Y(t).$$

An important notion in dependency theory is *implication*. One can observe that any relation satisfying the dependency

(a) $Title \rightarrow Director$

also has to satisfy the dependency

(b) $Title, Actor \rightarrow Director.$

We will say that dependency (a) implies dependency (b).

A *key dependency* is an fd $X \rightarrow U$, where U is the full set of attributes of the relation. It turns out that dependency (b) is equivalent to the key dependency *Title, Actor* $\rightarrow$ *Title, Director, Actor*.

A second fundamental kind of dependency is illustrated by the relation *Showings*. A tuple (th, sc, ti, sn) is in *Showings* if theater *th* is showing movie *ti* on screen *sc* and if theater *th* offers snack *sn*. Intuitively, one would expect a certain independence between the *Screen-Title* attributes, on the one hand, and the *Snack* attribute, on the other, for a given value of *Theater*. For example, because (Cinoche, 1, The Birds, Coke) and (Cinoche, 2, Bladerunner, wine) are in *Showings*, we also expect (Cinoche, 1, The Birds, wine) and (Cinoche, 2, Bladerunner, Coke) to be present. More precisely, if a relation I has this property, then

$$I = \pi_{Theater, Screen, Title}(I) \bowtie \pi_{Theater, Snack}(I).$$

This is a simple example of a *join dependency* (jd) which is formally expressed by

$$Showings : \bowtie[\{Theater, Screen, Title\}, \{Theater, Snacks\}].$$

In general, a jd may involve more than two attribute sets. *Multivalued dependency* (mvd) is the special case of jd's that have at most two attribute sets. Due to their naturalness, mvd's were introduced before jd's and have several interesting properties, which makes them worth studying on their own.

As will be seen later in this chapter, the fact that the fd *Title* $\rightarrow$ *Director* is satisfied by the *Movies* relation implies that the jd

$$\bowtie[\{Title, Director\}, \{Title, Actor\}]$$

is also satisfied. We will also study such interaction between fd's and jd's.

So far we have considered dependencies that apply to individual relations. Typically these dependencies are used in the context of a database schema, in which case one has to specify the relation concerned by each dependency. We will also consider a third fundamental kind of dependency, called *inclusion dependency* (ind) and also referred to as "referential constraint." In the example, we might expect that each title currently being shown (i.e., occurring in the *Showings* relation) is the title of a movie (i.e., also occurs in the *Movies* relation). This is denoted by

$$Showings[Title] \subseteq Movies[Title].$$

In general, ind's may involve sequences of attributes on both sides. Inclusion dependencies will be studied in depth in Chapter 9.

Data dependencies such as the ones just presented provide a formal mechanism for expressing properties expected from the stored data. If the database is known to satisfy a set of dependencies, this information can be used to (1) improve schema design, (2) protect data by preventing certain erroneous updates, and (3) improve performance. These aspects are considered in turn next.

Schema Design and Update Anomalies

The task of designing the schema in a large database application is far from being trivial, so the designer has to receive support from the system. Dependencies are used to provide information about the semantics of the application so that the system may help the user choose, among all possible schemas, the most appropriate one.

There are various ways in which a schema may not be appropriate. The relations *Movies* and *Showings* illustrate the most prominent kinds of problems associated with fd's and jd's:

Incomplete information: Suppose that one is to insert the title of a new movie and its director without knowing yet any actor of the movie. This turns out to be impossible with
the foregoing schema, and it is an *insertion anomaly*. An analogue for deletion, a *deletion anomaly*, occurs if actor Marlon Brando is no longer associated with the movie
"Apocalypse Now." Then the tuple ⟨Apocalypse Now, Coppola, Brando⟩ should be
deleted from the database. But this has the additional effect of deleting the association
between the movie "Apocalypse Now" and the director Coppola from the database,
information that may still be valid.

Redundancy: The fact that Coke can be found at the Cinoche is recorded many times.
Furthermore, suppose that the management of the Cinoche decided to sell Pepsi instead of Coke. It is not sufficient to modify the tuple ⟨Cinoche, 1, The Birds, Coke⟩
to ⟨Cinoche, 1, The Birds, Pepsi⟩ because this would lead to a violation of the jd. We
have to modify several tuples. This is a *modification anomaly*. Insertion and deletion
anomalies are also caused by redundancy.

Thus because of a bad choice for the schema, updates can lead to loss of information, inconsistency in the data, and more difficulties in writing correct updates. These problems can be prevented by choosing a more appropriate schema. In the example, the relation *Movies* should be "decomposed" into two relations *M-Director[Title, Director]* and *M-Actor[Title, Actor]*, where *M-Director* satisfies the fd *Title* → *Director*. Similarly, the relation *Showings* should be replaced by two relations *ST-Showings[Theater, Screen, Title]* and *S-Showings[Theater, Snack]*, where *ST-Showings* satisfies the fd *Theater, Screen* → *Title*. This approach to schema design is explored in Chapter 11.

Data Integrity

Data dependencies also serve as a filter on proposed updates in a natural fashion: If a database is expected to satisfy a dependency σ and a proposed update would lead to the violation of σ, then the update is rejected. In fact, the system supports transactions. During a transaction, the database can be in an inconsistent state; but at the end of a transaction, the system checks the integrity of the database. If dependencies are violated, the whole transaction is rejected (*aborted*); otherwise it is accepted (*validated*).

Efficient Implementation and Query Optimization

It is natural to expect that knowledge of structural properties of the stored data be useful in improving the performances of a system for a particular application.

At the physical level, the satisfaction of dependencies leads to a variety of alternatives for storage and access structures. For example, satisfaction of an fd or jd implies that a relation can be physically stored in decomposed form. In addition, satisfaction of a key dependency can be used to reduce indexing space.

A particularly striking theoretical development in dependency theory provides a method for optimizing conjunctive queries in the presence of a large class of dependencies. As a simple example, consider the query

$$ans(d, a) \leftarrow Movies(t, d, a'), Movies(t, d', a),$$

which returns tuples $\langle d, a \rangle$, where actor a acted in a movie directed by d. A naive implementation of this query will require a join. Because *Movies* satisfies *Title* $\rightarrow$ *Director*, this query can be simplified to

$$ans(d, a) \leftarrow Movies(t, d, a),$$

which can be evaluated without a join. Whenever the pattern of tuples $\{\langle t, d, a' \rangle, \langle t, d', a \rangle\}$ is found in relation *Movies*, it must be the case that $d = d'$, so one may as well use just the pattern $\{\langle t, d, a \rangle\}$, yielding the simplified query. This technique for query optimization is based on the chase and is considered in the last section of this chapter.

8.2 Functional and Key Dependencies

Functional dependencies are the most prominent form of dependency, and several elegant results have been developed for them. Key dependencies are a special case of functional dependencies. These are the dependencies perhaps most universally supported by relational systems and used in database applications. Many issues in dependency theory have nice solutions in the context of functional dependencies, and these dependencies lie at the origin of the decomposition approach to schema design.

To specify a class of dependencies, one must define the syntax and the semantics of the dependencies of concern. This is done next for fd's.

DEFINITION 8.2.1 If U is a set of attributes, then a *functional dependency* (fd) over U is an expression of the form $X \rightarrow Y$, where $X, Y \subseteq U$. A *key dependency* over U is an fd of the form $X \rightarrow U$. A relation I over U *satisfies* $X \rightarrow Y$, denoted $I \models X \rightarrow Y$, if for each pair s, t of tuples in I, $\pi_X(s) = \pi_X(t)$ implies $\pi_Y(s) = \pi_Y(t)$. For a set Σ of fd's, I *satisfies* Σ, denoted $I \models \Sigma$, if $I \models \sigma$ for each $\sigma \in \Sigma$.

A functional dependency over a database schema **R** is an expression $R : X \to Y$, where $R \in \mathbf{R}$ and $X \to Y$ is a dependency over $sort(R)$. These are sometimes referred to as *tagged* dependencies, because they are "tagged" by the relation that they apply to. The notion of satisfaction of fd's by instances over **R** is defined in the obvious way. In the remainder of this chapter, we consider only relational schemas. All can be extended easily to database schemas.

The following simple property provides the basis for the decomposition approach to schema design. Intuitively, it says that if a certain fd holds in a relation, one can store instead of the relation two projections of it, without loss of information. More precisely, the original relation can be reconstructed by joining the projections. Such joins have been termed "lossless joins" and will be discussed in some depth in Section 11.2.

PROPOSITION 8.2.2   Let I be an instance over U that satisfies $X \to Y$ and $Z = U - XY$. Then $I = \pi_{XY}(I) \bowtie \pi_{XZ}(I)$.

Proof   The inclusion $I \subseteq \pi_{XY}(I) \bowtie \pi_{XZ}(I)$ holds for all instances I. For the opposite inclusion, let r be a tuple in the join. Then there are tuples $s, t \in I$ such that $\pi_{XY}(r) = \pi_{XY}(s)$ and $\pi_{XZ}(r) = \pi_{XZ}(t)$. Because $\pi_X(r) = \pi_X(t)$, and $I \models X \to Y$, $\pi_Y(r) = \pi_Y(t)$. It follows that $r = t$, so r is in I. ∎

Logical Implication

In general, we may know that a set Σ of fd's is satisfied by an instance. A natural question is, What other fd's are necessarily satisfied by this instance? This is captured by the following definition.

DEFINITION 8.2.3   Let Σ and Γ be sets of fd's over an attribute set U. Then Σ *(logically)* *implies* Γ, denoted $\Sigma \models_U \Gamma$ or simply $\Sigma \models \Gamma$, if U is understood from the context, if for all relations I over U, $I \models \Sigma$ implies $I \models \Gamma$. Two sets Γ, Σ are *(logically)* *equivalent*, denoted $\Gamma \equiv \Sigma$, if $\Gamma \models \Sigma$ and $\Sigma \models \Gamma$.

EXAMPLE 8.2.4   Consider the set $\Sigma_1 = \{A \to C, B \to C, CD \to E\}$ of fd's over $\{A, B, C, D, E\}$. Then[2] a simple argument allows to show that $\Sigma_1 \models AD \to E$. In addition, $\Sigma_1 \models CDE \to C$. In fact, $\emptyset \models CDE \to C$ (where $\emptyset$ is the empty set of fd's).

Although the definition just presented focuses on fd's, this definition will be used in connection with other classes of dependencies studied here as well.

---

[2] We generally omit set braces from singleton sets of fd's.

The *fd closure* of a set Σ of fd's over an attribute set U, denoted $\Sigma^{*,U}$ or simply Σ^* if U is understood from the context, is the set

$$\{X \rightarrow Y \mid XY \subseteq U \text{ and } \Sigma \models X \rightarrow Y\}.$$

It is easily verified that for any set Σ of fd's over U and any sets $Y \subseteq X \subseteq U$, $X \rightarrow Y \in \Sigma^{*,U}$. This implies that the closure of a set of fd's depends on the underlying set of attributes. It also implies that $\Sigma^{*,U}$ has size greater than $2^{|U|}$. (It is bounded by $2^{2|U|}$ by definition.) Other properties of fd closures are considered in Exercise 8.3.

Determining Implication for fd's Is Linear Time

One of the key issues in dependency theory is the development of algorithms for testing logical implication. Although a set Σ of fd's implies an exponential (in terms of the number of attributes present in the underlying schema) number of fd's, it is possible to test whether Σ implies an fd $X \rightarrow Y$ in time that is linear in the size of Σ and $X \rightarrow Y$ (i.e., the space needed to write them).

A central concept used in this algorithm is the *fd closure* of a set of attributes. Given a set Σ of fd's over U and attribute set $X \subseteq U$, the fd closure of X under Σ, denoted $(X, \Sigma)^{*,U}$ or simply X^* if Σ and U are understood, is the set $\{A \in U \mid \Sigma \models X \rightarrow A\}$. It turns out that this set is independent of the underlying attribute set U (see Exercise 8.6).

EXAMPLE 8.2.5   Recall the set Σ_1 of fd's from Example 8.2.4. Then $A^* = AC$, $(AB)^* = ABC$, and $(AD)^* = ACDE$. The family of subsets X of U such that $X^* = X$ is $\{\emptyset, C, D, E, AC, BC, CE, DE, ABC, ACE, ADE, BCE, BDE, CDE, ABCE, ACDE, BCDE, ABCDE\}$.

The following is easily verified (see Exercise 8.4):

LEMMA 8.2.6   Let Σ be a set of fd's and $X \rightarrow Y$ an fd. Then $\Sigma \models X \rightarrow Y$ iff $Y \subseteq X^*$.

Thus testing whether $\Sigma \models X \rightarrow Y$ can be accomplished by computing X^*. The following algorithm can be used to compute this set.

ALGORITHM 8.2.7

Input: a set Σ of fd's and a set X of attributes.

Output: the closure X^* of X under Σ.

    1. *unused* := Σ;
    2. *closure* := X;
    3. repeat until no further change:
        if $W \rightarrow Z \in$ *unused* and $W \subseteq$ *closure* then
            i. *unused* := *unused* $- \{W \rightarrow Z\}$;
            ii. *closure* := *closure* $\cup Z$
    4. output *closure*.

PROPOSITION 8.2.8   On input Σ and X, Algorithm 8.2.7 computes $(X, \Sigma)^*$.

Proof   Let U be a set of attributes containing the attributes occurring in Σ or X, and let *result* be the output of the algorithm. Using properties established in Exercise 8.5, an easy induction shows that *result* $\subseteq X^*$.

For the opposite inclusion, note first that for attribute sets Y, Z, if $Y \subseteq Z$ then $Y^* \subseteq Z^*$. Because $X \subseteq result$, it now suffices to show that *result*$^* \subseteq result$. It is enough to show that if $A \in U - result$, then $\Sigma \not\models result \to A$. To show this, we construct an instance I over U such that $I \models \Sigma$ but $I \not\models result \to A$ for $A \in U - result$. Let $I = \{s, t\}$, where $\pi_{result}(s) = \pi_{result}(t)$ and $s(A) \neq t(A)$ for each $A \in U - result$. (Observe that this uses the fact that the domain has at least two elements.) Note that, by construction, for each fd $W \to Z \in \Sigma$, if $W \subseteq result$ then $Z \subseteq result$. It easily follows that $I \models \Sigma$. Furthermore, for $A \in U - result$, $s(A) \neq t(A)$, so $I \not\models result \to A$. Thus $\Sigma \not\models result \to A$, and *result*$^* \subseteq result$. ∎

The algorithm provides the means for checking whether a set of dependencies implies a single dependency. To test implication of a *set* of dependencies, it suffices to test independently the implication of each dependency in the set. In addition, one can check that the preceding algorithm runs in time $O(n^2)$, where n is the length of Σ and X. As shown in Exercise 8.7, this algorithm can be improved to linear time. The following summarizes this development.

THEOREM 8.2.9   Given a set Σ of fd's and a single fd σ, determine whether $\Sigma \models \sigma$ can be decided in linear time.

Several interesting properties of fd-closure sets are considered in Exercises 8.11 and 8.12.

Axiomatization for fd's

In addition to developing algorithms for determining logical implication, the second fundamental theme in dependency theory has been the development of inference rules, which can be used to generate symbolic proofs of logical implication. Although the inference rules do not typically yield the most efficient mechanisms for deciding logical implication, in many cases they capture concisely the essential properties of the dependencies under study. The study of inference rules is especially intriguing because (as will be seen in the next section) there are several classes of dependencies for which there is no finite set of inference rules that characterizes logical implication.

Inference rules and algorithms for testing implication provide alternative approaches to showing logical implication between dependencies. In general, the existence of a finite set of inference rules for a class of dependencies is a stronger property than the existence of an algorithm for testing implication. It will be shown in Chapter 9 that

- the existence of a finite set of inference rules for a class of dependencies implies the existence of an algorithm for testing logical implication; and

- there are dependencies for which there is no finite set of inference rules but for which there is an algorithm to test logical implication.

We now present the inference rules for fd's.

FD1: (reflexivity) If $Y \subseteq X$, then $X \rightarrow Y$.

FD2: (augmentation) If $X \rightarrow Y$, then $XZ \rightarrow YZ$.

FD3: (transitivity) If $X \rightarrow Y$ and $Y \rightarrow Z$, then $X \rightarrow Z$.

The variables X, Y, Z range over sets of attributes. The first rule is sometimes called an *axiom* because it is degenerate in the sense that no fd's occur in the antecedent.

The inference rules are used to form proofs about logical implication between fd's, in a manner analogous to the proofs found in mathematical logic. It will be shown that the resulting proof system is "sound" and "complete" for fd's (two classical notions to be recalled soon). Before formally presenting the notion of proof, we give an example.

EXAMPLE 8.2.10 The following is a proof of $AD \rightarrow E$ from the set Σ_1 of fd's of Example 8.2.4.

σ_1 :	$A \rightarrow C$	$\in \Sigma_1$,
σ_2 :	$AD \rightarrow CD$	from σ_1 using FD2,
σ_3 :	$CD \rightarrow E$	$\in \Sigma_1$,
σ_4 :	$AD \rightarrow E$	from σ_2 and σ_3 using FD3.

Let U be a set of attributes. A *substitution* for an inference rule ρ (relative to U) is a function that maps each variable appearing in ρ to a subset of U, such that each set inclusion indicated in the antecedent of ρ is satisfied by the associated sets. Now let Σ be a set of fd's over U and σ an fd over U. A *proof* of σ from Σ using the set $\mathcal{I} = \{$FD1, FD2, FD3$\}$ is a sequence of fd's $\sigma_1, \ldots, \sigma_n = \sigma$ ($n \geq 1$) such that for each $i \in [1, n]$, either

(a) $\sigma_i \in \Sigma$, or

(b) there is a substitution for some rule $\rho \in \mathcal{I}$ such that σ_i corresponds to the consequent of ρ, and such that for each fd in the antecedent of ρ the corresponding fd is in the set $\{\sigma_j \mid 1 \leq j < i\}$.

The fd σ is *provable* from Σ using $\mathcal{I}$ (relative to U), denoted $\Sigma \nvdash \sigma$ or $\Sigma \vdash \sigma$ if $\mathcal{I}$ is understood from the context, if there is a proof of σ from Σ using $\mathcal{I}$.

Let $\mathcal{I}$ be a set of inference rules. Then

$\mathcal{I}$ is *sound* for logical implication of fd's if $\Sigma \nvdash \sigma$ implies $\Sigma \models \sigma$,

$\mathcal{I}$ is *complete* for logical implication of fd's if $\Sigma \models \sigma$ implies $\Sigma \nvdash \sigma$.

We will generalize these definitions to other dependencies and other sets of inference rules.

In general, a finite sound and complete set of inference rules for a class $\mathcal{C}$ of dependencies is called a (finite) *axiomatization* of $\mathcal{C}$. In such a case, $\mathcal{C}$ is said to be (finitely) *axiomatizable*.

We now state the following:

THEOREM 8.2.11   The set {FD1, FD2, FD3} is sound and complete for logical implication of fd's.

Proof   Suppose that Σ is a set of fd's over an attribute set U. The proof of soundness involves a straightforward induction on proofs $\sigma_1, \ldots, \sigma_n$ from Σ, showing that $\Sigma \models \sigma_i$ for each $i \in [1, n]$ (see Exercise 8.5).

For the proof of completeness, we show that $\Sigma \models X \rightarrow Y$ implies $\Sigma \vdash X \rightarrow Y$. As a first step, we show that $\Sigma \vdash X \rightarrow X^*$ using an induction based on Algorithm 8.2.7. In particular, let *closure$_i$* be the value of *closure* after i iterations of step 3 for some fixed execution of that algorithm on input Σ and X. We set *closure$_0$* $= X$. Suppose inductively that a proof $\sigma_1, \ldots, \sigma_{k_i}$ of $X \rightarrow$ *closure$_i$* has been constructed. [The case for $i = 0$ follows from FD1.] Suppose further that $W \rightarrow Z$ is chosen for the $(i + 1)^{\text{st}}$ iteration. It follows that $W \subseteq$ *closure$_i$* and *closure$_{i+1}$* $=$ *closure$_i$* $\cup Z$. Extend the proof by adding the following steps:

$$
\begin{aligned}
\sigma_{k_i+1} &= W \rightarrow Z & \text{in } \Sigma \\
\sigma_{k_i+2} &= \textit{closure}_i \rightarrow W & \text{by FD1} \\
\sigma_{k_i+3} &= \textit{closure}_i \rightarrow Z & \text{by FD3} \\
\sigma_{k_i+4} &= \textit{closure}_i \rightarrow \textit{closure}_{i+1} & \text{by FD2} \\
\sigma_{k_i+5} &= X \rightarrow \textit{closure}_{i+1} & \text{by FD3}
\end{aligned}
$$

At the completion of this construction we have a proof $\sigma_1, \ldots, \sigma_n$ of $X \rightarrow X^*$. By Lemma 8.2.6, $Y \subseteq X^*$. Using FD1 and FD3, the proof can be extended to yield a proof of $X \rightarrow Y$. ∎

Other inference rules for fd's are considered in Exercise 8.9.

Armstrong Relations

In the proof of Proposition 8.2.8, an instance I is created such that $I \models \Sigma$ but $I \not\models X \rightarrow A$. Intuitively, this instance witnesses the fact that $\Sigma \not\models X \rightarrow A$. This raises the following natural question: Given a set Σ of fd's over U, is there a *single* instance I that satisfies Σ and that violates every fd not in Σ^*? It turns out that for each set of fd's, there is such an instance; these are called *Armstrong relations*.

PROPOSITION 8.2.12   If Σ is a set of fd's over U, then there is an instance I such that, for each fd σ over U, $I \models \sigma$ iff $\sigma \in \Sigma^*$.

Crux   Suppose first that $\Sigma \not\models \emptyset \rightarrow A$ for any A (i.e., $\emptyset^* = \emptyset$). For each set $X \subseteq U$ satisfying $X = X^*$, choose an instance $I_X = \{s_X, t_X\}$ such that $s_X(A) = t_X(A)$ iff $A \in X$. In addition, choose these instances so that $adom(I_X) \cap adom(I_Y) = \emptyset$ for $X \neq Y$. Then

$$\cup \{I_X \mid X \subset U \text{ and } X = X^*\}$$

is an Armstrong relation for Σ.

If $\emptyset^* \neq \emptyset$, then the instances I_X should be modified so that $\pi_A(I_X) = \pi_A(I_Y)$ for each X, Y and $A \in \emptyset^*$. ∎

In some applications, the domains of certain attributes may be finite (e.g., *Sex* conventionally has two values, and *Grade* typically consists of a finite set of values). In such cases, the construction of an Armstrong relation may not be possible. This is explored in Exercise 8.13.

Armstrong relations can be used in practice to assist the user in specifying the fd's for a particular application. An interactive, iterative specification process starts with the user specifying a first set of fd's. The system then generates an Armstrong relation for the fd's, which violates all the fd's not included in the specification. This serves as a worst-case counterexample and may result in detecting additional fd's whose satisfaction should be required.

8.3 Join and Multivalued Dependencies

The second kind of simple dependency studied in this chapter is *join dependency* (jd), which is intimately related to the join operator of the relational algebra. As mentioned in Section 8.1, a basic motivation for join dependency stems from its usefulness in connection with relation decomposition. This section also discusses *multivalued dependency* (mvd), an important special case of join dependency that was historically the first to be introduced.

The central results and tools for studying jd's are different from those for fd's. It has been shown that there is no sound and complete set of inference rules for jd's analogous to those for fd's. (An axiomatization for a much larger family of dependencies will be presented in Chapter 10.) In addition, as shown in the following section, logical implication for jd's is decidable. The complexity of implication is polynomial for a fixed database schema but becomes NP-hard if the schema is considered part of the input. (An exact characterization of the complexity remains open.)

The following section also presents an interesting correspondence between mvd's and acyclic join dependencies (i.e., those based on joins that are acyclic in the sense introduced in Chapter 6).

A major focus of the current section is on mvd's; this is because of several positive results that hold for them, including axiomatizability of fd's and mvd's considered together.

Join Dependency and Decomposition

Before defining join dependency, we recall the definition of natural join. For attribute set U, sets $X_1, \ldots, X_n \subseteq U$, and instances I_j over X_j for $j \in [1, n]$, the (*natural*) *join* of the I_j's is

$$\bowtie_{j=1}^{n} \{I_j\} = \{s \text{ over } \cup X_j \mid \pi_{X_j}(s) \in I_j \text{ for each } j \in [1, n]\}.$$

A join dependency is satisfied by an instance I if it is equal to the join of some of its projections.

DEFINITION 8.3.1   A *join dependency* (jd) over attribute set U is an expression of the form $\bowtie[X_1, \ldots, X_n]$, where $X_1, \ldots, X_n \subseteq U$ and $\cup_{i=1}^n X_i = U$. A relation I over U satisfies $\bowtie[X_1, \ldots, X_n]$ if $I = \bowtie_{j=1}^n \{\pi_{X_j}(I)\}$.

A jd σ is *n-ary* if the number of attribute sets involved in σ is n. As discussed earlier, the relation *Showings* of Fig. 8.1 satisfies the 2-ary jd

$$\bowtie[\{Theater, Screen, Title\}, \{Theater, Snacks\}].$$

The 2-ary jd's are also called *multivalued dependencies* (mvd's). These are often denoted in a style reminiscent of fd's.

DEFINITION 8.3.2   If U is a set of attributes, then a *multivalued dependency* (mvd) over U is an expression of the form $X \twoheadrightarrow Y$, where $X, Y \subseteq U$. A relation I over U satisfies $X \twoheadrightarrow Y$ if $I \models \bowtie[XY, X(U - Y)]$.

In the preceding definition, it would be equivalent to write $\bowtie[XY, (U - Y)]$; we choose the foregoing form to emphasize the importance of X. For instance, the jd

$$\bowtie[\{Theater, Screen, Title\}, \{Theater, Snack\}]$$

can be written as an mvd using

$$Theater \twoheadrightarrow Screen, Title, \quad \text{or equivalently,} \quad Theater \twoheadrightarrow Snack.$$

Exercise 8.16 explores the original definition of satisfaction of an mvd.

Figure 8.2 shows a relation schema SDT and an instance that satisfies a 3-ary jd. This relation focuses on snacks, distributors, and theaters. We assume for this example that a tuple (s, d, p, t) is in SDT if the conjunction of the following predicates is true:

$P_1(s, d, p)$:   Snack s is supplied by distributor d at price p.

$P_2(d, t)$:   Theater t is a customer of distributor d.

$P_3(s, t)$:   Snack s is bought by theater t.

Under these assumptions, each instance of SDT must satisfy the jd:

$$\bowtie[\{Snack, Distributor, Price\}, \{Distributor, Theater\}, \{Snack, Theater\}].$$

For example, this holds for the instance in Fig. 8.2. Note that if tuple ⟨coffee, Smart, 2.35, Cinoche⟩ were removed, then the instance would no longer satisfy the jd because ⟨coffee, Smart, 2.35⟩, ⟨coffee, Cinoche⟩, and ⟨Smart, Cinoche⟩ would remain in the appropriate projections. We also expect the instances of SDT to satisfy *Snack, Distributor* → *Price*.

It can be argued that schema SDT with the aforementioned constraint is unnatural in the following sense. Intuitively, if we choose such a schema, the presence of a tuple

SDT	Snack	Distributor	Price	Theater
	coffee	Smart	2.35	Rex
	coffee	Smart	2.35	Le Champo
	coffee	Smart	2.35	Cinoche
	coffee	Leclerc	2.60	Cinoche
	wine	Smart	0.80	Rex
	wine	Smart	0.80	Cinoche
	popcorn	Leclerc	5.60	Cinoche

Figure 8.2:   Illustration of join dependency

$\langle s, d, p, t \rangle$ seems to indicate that t buys s from d. If we wish to record just the information about who buys what, who sells what, and who sells to whom, a more appropriate schema would consist of three relations $SD[Snack, Distributor, Price]$, $ST[Snack, Theater]$, and $DT[Distributor, Theater]$ corresponding to the three sets of attributes involved in the preceding jd. The jd then guarantees that no information is lost in the decomposition because the original relation can be reconstructed by joining the projections.

Join Dependencies and Functional Dependencies

The interaction of fd's and jd's is important in the area of schema design and user interfaces to the relational model. Although this is explored in more depth in Chapter 11, we present here one of the first results on the interaction of the two kinds of dependencies.

PROPOSITION 8.3.3   Let U be a set of attributes, $\{X, Y, Z\}$ be a partition of U, and Σ be a set of fd's over U. Then $\Sigma \models \bowtie[XY, XZ]$ iff either $\Sigma \models X \to Y$ or $\Sigma \models X \to Z$.

Crux   Sufficiency follows immediately from Proposition 8.2.2. For necessity, suppose that Σ does not imply either of the fd's. Then $Y - X^* \neq \emptyset$ and $Z - X^* \neq \emptyset$, say $C \in Y - X^*$ and $C' \in Z - X^*$. Consider the two-element instance $I = \{u, v\}$ where, $u(A) = v(A) = 0$ if A is in X^* and $u(A) = 0, v(A) = 1$ otherwise. Clearly, I satisfies Σ and one can verify that $\pi_{XY}(I) \bowtie \pi_{XZ}(I)$ contains a tuple w with $w(C) = 0$ and $w(C') = 1$. Thus w is not in I, so I violates $\bowtie[XY, XZ]$. ∎

Axiomatizations

As will be seen later (Theorem 8.4.12), there is a decision procedure for jd's in isolation, and for jd's and fd's considered together. Here we consider axiomatizations, first for jd's in isolation and then for fd's and mvd's taken together.

We state first the following result without proof.

THEOREM 8.3.4   There is no axiomatization for the family of jd's.

In contrast, there is an axiomatization for the class of fd's and multivalued dependencies. Note first that implication for fd's is independent of the underlying set of attributes (i.e., if $\Sigma \cup \{\sigma\}$ is a set of fd's over U and $V \supseteq U$, then $\Sigma \models \sigma$ relative to U iff $\Sigma \models \sigma$ relative to V; see Exercise 8.6). An important difference between fd's and mvd's is that this is not the case for mvd's. Thus the inference rules for mvd's must be used in connection with a fixed underlying set of attributes, and a variable (denoted U) referring to this set is used in one of the rules.

The following lists the four rules for mvd's alone and an additional pair of rules needed when fd's are incorporated.

MVD0: (complementation) If $X \twoheadrightarrow Y$, then $X \twoheadrightarrow (U - Y)$.

MVD1: (reflexivity) If $Y \subseteq X$, then $X \twoheadrightarrow Y$.

MVD2: (augmentation) If $X \twoheadrightarrow Y$, then $XZ \twoheadrightarrow YZ$.

MVD3: (transitivity) If $X \twoheadrightarrow Y$ and $Y \twoheadrightarrow Z$, then $X \twoheadrightarrow (Z - Y)$.

FMVD1: (conversion) If $X \to Y$, then $X \twoheadrightarrow Y$.

FMVD2: (interaction) If $X \twoheadrightarrow Y$ and $XY \to Z$, then $X \to (Z - Y)$.

THEOREM 8.3.5   The set {FD1, FD2, FD3, MVD0, MVD1, MVD2, MVD3, FMVD1, FMVD2} is sound and complete for logical implication of fd's and mvd's considered together.

Crux   Soundness is easily verified. For completeness, let an underlying set U of attributes be fixed, and assume that $\Sigma \not\vdash \sigma$, where $\sigma = X \to Y$ or $\sigma = X \twoheadrightarrow Y$.

The *dependency set* of X is $dep(X) = \{Y \subseteq U \mid \Sigma \vdash X \twoheadrightarrow Y\}$. One first shows that

1. $dep(X)$ is a Boolean algebra of sets for U.

That is, it contains U and is closed under intersection, union, and difference (see Exercise 8.17). In addition,

2. for each $A \in X^+$, $\{A\} \in dep(X)$,

where X^+ denotes $\{A \in U \mid \Sigma \vdash X \to A\}$.

A *dependency basis* of X is a family $\{W_1, \ldots, W_m\} \subseteq dep(X)$ such that (1) $\bigcup_{i=1}^{n} W_i = U$; (2) $W_i \neq \emptyset$ for $i \in [1, n]$; (3) $W_i \cap W_j = \emptyset$ for $i, j \in [1, n]$ with $i \neq j$; and (4) if $W \in dep(X)$, $W \neq \emptyset$, and $W \subseteq W_i$ for some $i \in [1, n]$, then $W = W_i$. One then proves that

3. there exists a unique dependency basis of X.

Now construct an instance I over U that contains all tuples t satisfying the following conditions:

(a) $t(A) = 0$ for each $A \in X^+$.

(b) If W_i is in the dependency basis and $W_i \neq \{A\}$ for each $A \in X^+$, then $t(B) = 0$ for all $B \in W_i$ or $t(B) = 1$ for all $B \in W_i$.

It can be shown that $I \models \Sigma$ but $I \not\models \sigma$ (see Exercise 8.17). ∎

This easily implies the following (see Exercise 8.18):

COROLLARY 8.3.6   The set {MVD0, MVD1, MVD2, MVD3} is sound and complete for logical implication of mvd's considered alone.

8.4   The Chase

This section presents the chase, a remarkable tool for reasoning about dependencies that highlights a strong connection between dependencies and tableau queries. The discussion here is cast in terms of fd's and jd's, but as will be seen in Chapter 10, the chase generalizes naturally to a broader class of dependencies. At the end of this section, we explore important applications of the chase technique. We show how it can also be used to determine logical implication between sets of dependencies and to optimize conjunctive queries.

The following example illustrates an intriguing connection between dependencies and tableau queries.

EXAMPLE 8.4.1   Consider the tableau query (T, t) shown in Fig. 8.3(a). Suppose the query is applied only to instances I satisfying some set Σ of fd's and jd's. The chase is based on the following simple idea. If v is a valuation embedding T into an instance I satisfying Σ, $v(T)$ must satisfy Σ. Valuations that do not satisfy Σ are therefore of no use. The chase is a procedure that eliminates the useless valuations by changing (T, t) itself so that T, viewed as an instance, satisfies Σ. We will show that the tableau query resulting from the chase is then equivalent to the original on instances satisfying Σ. As we shall see, this can be used to optimize queries and test implication of dependencies.

Let us return to the example. Suppose first that $\Sigma = \{B \to D\}$. Suppose (T, t) is applied to an instance I satisfying Σ. In each valuation embedding T into I, it must be the case that z and z' are mapped to the same constant. Thus in this context one might as well replace T by the tableau where $z = z'$. This transformation is called "applying the fd $B \to D$" to (T, t). It is easy to see that the resulting tableau query is in fact equivalent to the identity, because T contains an entire row of distinguished variables.

Consider next an example involving both fd's and jd's. Let Σ consist of the following two dependencies over $ABCD$: the jd $\bowtie[AB, BCD]$ and the fd $A \to C$. In this example we argue that for each I satisfying these dependencies, $(T, t)(I) = I$ or, in other words, in the context of input instances that satisfy the dependencies, the query (T, t) is equivalent to the identity query $(\{t\}, t)$.

Let I be an instance over $ABCD$ satisfying the two dependencies. We first explain why $(T, t)(I) = (T', t)(I)$ for the tableau query (T', t) of Fig. 8.3(b). It is clear that $(T', t)(I) \subseteq (T, t)(I)$, because T' is a superset of T. For the opposite inclusion, suppose that v is a valuation for T with $v(T) \subseteq I$. Then, in particular, both $v(\langle w, x, y, z' \rangle)$ and $v(\langle w', x, y', z \rangle)$ are in I. Because $I \models \bowtie[AB, BCD]$, it follows that $v(\langle w, x, y', z \rangle) \in I$. Thus $v(T') \subseteq I$ and $v(t) \in (T', t)(I)$. The transformation from (T, t) to (T', t) is termed "applying the jd $\bowtie[AB, BCD]$," because T' is the result of adding a member of $\pi_{AB}(T) \bowtie$

	A	B	C	D
T	w	x	y	z'
	w'	x	y'	z
t	w	x	y	z

	A	B	C	D
T'	w	x	y	z'
	w'	x	y'	z
	w	x	y'	z
t	w	x	y	z

	A	B	C	D
T''	w	x	y	z'
	w'	x	y	z
	w	x	y	z
t	w	x	y	z

(a) The tableau query (T, t) (b) (One) result of applying the jd $\bowtie[AB, BCD]$ (c) Result of applying the fd $A \rightarrow C$

Figure 8.3:   Illustration of the chase

$\pi_{BCD}(T)$ to T. We shall see that, by repeated applications of a jd, one can eventually "force" the tableau to satisfy the jd.

The tableau T'' of Fig. 8.3(c) is the result of chasing (T', t) with the fd $A \rightarrow C$ (i.e., replacing all occurrences of y' by y). We now argue that $(T', t)(I) = (T'', t)(I)$. First, by Theorem 6.2.3, $(T', t)(I) \supseteq (T'', t)(I)$ because there is a homomorphism from (T', t) to (T'', t). For the opposite inclusion, suppose now that $v(T') \subseteq I$. This implies that v embeds the first tuple of T'' into I. In addition, because $v(\langle w, x, y, z'\rangle)$ and $v(\langle w, x, y', z\rangle)$ are in I and $I \models A \rightarrow C$, it follows that $v(y) = v(y')$. Thus $v(\langle w', x, y, z\rangle) = v(\langle w', x, y', z\rangle) \in I$, and $v(\langle w, x, y, z\rangle) = v(\langle w, x, y', z\rangle) \in I$, [i.e., v embeds the second and third tuples of T'' into I, such that $v(T'') \subseteq I$]. Note that (T'', t) is the result of identifying a pair of variables that caused a violation of $A \rightarrow C$ in T'. We will see that by repeated applications of an fd, one can eventually "force" a tableau to satisfy the fd. Note that in this case, chasing with respect to $A \rightarrow C$ has no effect before chasing with respect to $\bowtie[AB, BCD]$.

Finally, note that by the Homomorphism Theorem 6.2.3 of Chapter 6, $(T'', t) \equiv (\{t\}, t)$. It follows, then, that for all instances I that satisfy $\{A \rightarrow C, \bowtie[AB, BCD]\}$, (T, t) and $(\{t\}, t)$ yield the same answer.

Defining the Chase

As seen in Example 8.4.1, the chase relates to equivalence of queries over a family of instances satisfying certain dependencies. For a family $\mathcal{F}$ of instances over $\mathbf{R}$, we say that q_1 is *contained* in q_2 *relative to* $\mathcal{F}$, denoted $q_1 \subseteq_{\mathcal{F}} q_2$, if $q_1(\mathbf{I}) \subseteq q_2(\mathbf{I})$ for each instance $\mathbf{I}$ in $\mathcal{F}$. We are particularly interested in families $\mathcal{F}$ that are defined by a set Σ of dependencies (in the current context, fd's and jd's). Let Σ be a set of (functional and join) dependencies over $\mathbf{R}$. The *satisfaction family* of Σ, denoted $sat(\mathbf{R}, \Sigma)$ or simply $sat(\Sigma)$ if $\mathbf{R}$ is understood from the context, is the family

$$sat(\Sigma) = \{\mathbf{I} \text{ over } \mathbf{R} \mid \mathbf{I} \models \Sigma\}.$$

Query q_1 is contained in q_2 *relative to* Σ, denoted $q_1 \subseteq_\Sigma q_2$, if $q_1 \subseteq_{sat(\Sigma)} q_2$. Equivalence relative to a family of instances ($\equiv_\mathcal{F}$) and to a set of dependencies ($\equiv_\Sigma$) are defined similarly.

The chase is a general technique that can be used, given a set of dependencies Σ, to transform a tableau query q into a query q' such that $q \equiv_\Sigma q'$. The chase is defined as a nondeterministic procedure based on the successive application of individual dependencies from Σ, but as will be seen this process is "Church-Rosser" in the sense that the procedure necessarily terminates with a unique end result. As a final step in this development, the chase will be used to characterize equivalence of conjunctive queries with respect to a set Σ of dependencies ($\equiv_\Sigma$).

In the following, we let R be a fixed relation schema, and we focus on sets Σ of fd's and jd's over R and tableau queries with no constants over R. The entire development can be generalized to database schemas and conjunctive queries with constants (Exercise 8.27) and to a considerably larger class of dependencies (Chapter 10).

For technical convenience, we assume that there is a total order $\leq$ on the set **var**. Let R be a fixed relation schema and suppose that (T, t) is a tableau query over R. The chase is based on the successive application of the following two rules:

fd rule: Let $\sigma = X \to A$ be an fd over R, and let $u, v \in T$ be such that $\pi_X(u) = \pi_X(v)$ and $u(A) \neq v(A)$. Let x be the lesser variable in $\{u(A), v(A)\}$ under the ordering $\leq$, and let y be the other one (i.e., $\{x, y\} = \{u(A), v(A)\}$ and $x < y$). The *result of applying* the fd σ to u, v in (T, t) is the tableau query $(\theta(T), \theta(t))$, where θ is the substitution that maps y to x and is the identity elsewhere.

jd rule: Let $\sigma = \bowtie [X_1, \ldots, X_n]$ be a jd over R, let u be a free tuple over R not in T, and suppose that $u_1, \ldots, u_n \in T$ satisfy $\pi_{X_i}(u_i) = \pi_{X_i}(u)$ for $i \in [1, n]$. Then the *result of applying* the jd σ to $(u_1, \ldots, u_n)$ in (T, t) is the tableau query $(T \cup \{u\}, t)$.

Following the lead of Example 8.4.1, the following is easily verified (see Exercise 8.24a).

PROPOSITION 8.4.2 Suppose that Σ is a set of fd's and jd's over R, $\sigma \in \Sigma$, and q is a tableau query over R. If q' is the result of applying σ to some tuples in q, then $q' \equiv_\Sigma q$.

A *chasing sequence* of (T, t) by Σ is a (possibly infinite) sequence

$$(T, t) = (T_0, t_0), \ldots, (T_i, t_i), \ldots$$

such that for each $i \geq 0$, (T_{i+1}, t_{i+1}) (if defined) is the result of applying some dependency in Σ to (T_i, t_i). The sequence is *terminal* if it is finite and no dependency in Σ can be applied to it. The last element of the terminal sequence is called its *result*. The notion of *satisfaction* of a dependency is extended naturally to tableaux. The following is an important property of terminal chasing sequences (Exercise 8.24b).

LEMMA 8.4.3 Let (T', t') be the result of a terminal chasing sequence of (T, t) by Σ. Then T', considered as an instance, satisfies Σ.

Because the chasing rules do not introduce new variables, it turns out that the chase procedure always terminates. The following is easily verified (Exercise 8.24c):

LEMMA 8.4.4   Let (T, t) be a tableau query over R and Σ a set of fd's and jd's over R. Then each chasing sequence of (T, t) by Σ is finite and is the initial subsequence of a terminal chasing sequence.

An important question now is whether the results of different terminal chasing sequences are the same. This turns out to be the case. This property of chasing sequences is called the *Church-Rosser property*. We provide the proof of the Church-Rosser property for the chase at the end of this section (Theorem 8.4.18).

Because the Church-Rosser property holds, we can define without ambiguity the result of chasing a tableau query by a set of fd's and jd's.

DEFINITION 8.4.5   If (T, t) is a tableau query over R and Σ a set of fd's and jd's over R, then the *chase* of (T, t) by Σ, denoted $chase(T, t, \Sigma)$, is the result of some (any) terminal chasing sequence of (T, t) by Σ.

From the previous discussion, $chase(T, t, \Sigma)$ can be computed as follows. The dependencies are picked in some arbitrary order and arbitrarily applied to the tableau. Applying an fd to a tableau query q can be performed within time polynomial in the size of q. However, determining whether a jd can be applied to q is NP-complete in the size of q. Thus the best-known algorithm for computing the chase is exponential (see Exercise 8.25). However, the complexity is polynomial if the schema is considered fixed.

Until now, besides the informal discussion in Section 8.1, the *chase* remains a purely syntactic technique. We next state a result that shows that the chase is in fact determined by the semantics of the dependencies in Σ and not just their syntax.

In the following proposition, recall that by definition, $\Sigma \equiv \Sigma'$ if $\Sigma \models \Sigma'$ and $\Sigma' \models \Sigma$. The proof, which we omit, uses the Church-Rosser property of the chase (see also Exercise 8.26).

PROPOSITION 8.4.6   Let Σ and Σ' be sets of fd's and jd's over R, and let (T, t) be a tableau query over R. If $\Sigma \equiv \Sigma'$, then $chase(T, t, \Sigma)$ and $chase(T, t, \Sigma')$ coincide.

We next consider several important uses of the chase that illustrate the power of this technique.

Query Equivalence

We consider first the problem of checking the equivalence of tableau queries in the presence of a set of fd's and jd's. This allows, for example, checking whether a tableau query can be replaced by a simpler tableau query when the dependencies are satisfied. Suppose now that (T', t') and (T'', t'') are two tableau queries and Σ a set of fd's and jd's such that $(T', t') \equiv_\Sigma (T'', t'')$. From the preceding development (Proposition 8.4.2), it follows that

$$chase(T', t', \Sigma) \equiv_\Sigma (T', t') \equiv_\Sigma (T'', t'') \equiv_\Sigma chase(T'', t'', \Sigma).$$

We now show that, in fact, $chase(T', t', \Sigma) \equiv chase(T'', t'', \Sigma)$. Furthermore, this condition is sufficient as well as necessary.

To demonstrate this result, we first establish the following more general fact.

THEOREM 8.4.7 Let $\mathcal{F}$ be a family of instances over relation schema R that is closed under isomorphism, and let (T_1, t_1), (T_2, t_2), (T_1', t_1'), and (T_2', t_2') be tableau queries over R. Suppose further that for $i = 1, 2$,

  (a) $(T_i', t_i') \equiv_\mathcal{F} (T_i, t_i)$ and
  (b) T_i', considered as an instance, is in $\mathcal{F}$.[3]

  Then $(T_1, t_1) \subseteq_\mathcal{F} (T_2, t_2)$ iff $(T_1', t_1') \subseteq (T_2', t_2')$.

Proof The if direction is immediate. For the only-if direction, suppose that $(T_1, t_1) \subseteq_\mathcal{F} (T_2, t_2)$. It suffices by the Homomorphism Theorem 6.2.3 to exhibit a homomorphism that embeds (T_2', t_2') into (T_1', t_1'). Because T_1', considered as an instance, is in $\mathcal{F}$,

$$t_1' \in (T_1', t_1')(T_1') \Rightarrow t_1' \in (T_1, t_1)(T_1') \Rightarrow t_1' \in (T_2, t_2)(T_1') \Rightarrow t_1' \in (T_2', t_2')(T_1').$$

It follows that there is a homomorphism h such that $h(T_2') \subseteq T_1'$ and $h(t_2') = t_1'$. Thus $(T_1', t_1') \subseteq (T_2', t_2')$. This completes the proof. ∎

Together with Lemma 8.4.3, this implies the following:

THEOREM 8.4.8 Let (T_1, t_1) and (T_2, t_2) be tableau queries over R and Σ a set of fd's and jd's over R. Then

  1. $(T_1, t_1) \subseteq_\Sigma (T_2, t_2)$ iff $chase(T_1, t_1, \Sigma) \subseteq chase(T_2, t_2, \Sigma)$.
  2. $(T_1, t_1) \equiv_\Sigma (T_2, t_2)$ iff $chase(T_1, t_1, \Sigma) \equiv chase(T_2, t_2, \Sigma)$.

Query Optimization

As suggested in Example 8.4.1, the chase can be used to optimize tableau queries in the presence of dependencies such as fd's and jd's. Given a tableau query (T, t) and a set Σ of fd's and jd's, $chase(T, t, \Sigma)$ is equivalent to (T, t) on all instances satisfying Σ. A priori, it is not clear that the new tableau is an improvement over the first. It turns out that the chase using fd's can never yield a more complicated tableau and, as shown in Example 8.4.1, can yield a much simpler one. On the other hand, the chase using jd's may yield a more complicated tableau, although it may also produce a simpler one.

We start by looking at the effect on tableau minimization of the chase using fd's. In the following, we denote by $min(T, t)$ the tableau resulting from the minimization of

---

[3] More precisely, T' considered as an instance is in $\mathcal{F}$ means that some instance isomorphic to T' is in $\mathcal{F}$.

the tableau (T, t) using the Homomorphism Theorem 6.2.3 for tableau queries, and by $|min(T, t)|$ we mean the cardinality of the tableau of $min(T, t)$.

LEMMA 8.4.9   Let (T, t) be a tableau query and Σ a set of fd's. Then $|min(chase(T, t, \Sigma))| \leq |min(T, t)|$.

Crux   By the Church-Rosser property of the chase, the order of the dependencies used in a chase sequence is irrelevant. Clearly it is sufficient to show that for each tableau query (T', t') and $\sigma \in \Sigma$, $|min(chase(T', t', \sigma))| \leq |min(T', t')|$. We can assume without loss of generality that σ is of the form $X \to A$, where A is a single attribute.

Let $(T'', t'') = chase(T', t', \{X \to A\})$, and let θ be the *chase homomorphism* of a chasing sequence for $chase(T', t', \{X \to A\})$, i.e., the homomorphism obtained by composing the substitutions used in that chasing sequence (see the proof of Theorem 8.4.18). We will use here the Church-Rosser property of the chase (Theorem 8.4.18) as well as a related property stating that the homomorphism θ, like the result, is also the same for all chase sequences (this follows from the proof of Theorem 8.4.18).

By Theorem 6.2.6, there is some $S \subseteq T'$ such that (S, t') is a minimal tableau query equivalent to (T', t'); we shall use this as the representative of $min(T', t')$. Let h be a homomorphism such that $h(T', t') = (S, t')$. Consider the mapping f on (T'', t'') defined by $f(\theta(x)) = \theta(h(x))$, where x is a variable in (T', t'). If we show that f is well defined, we are done. [If f is well defined, then f is a homomorphism from (T'', t'') to $\theta(S, t') = (\theta(S), t'')$, and so $(T'', t'') \supseteq \theta(S, t')$. On the other hand, the $\theta(S) \subseteq \theta(T') = T''$, and so $(T'', t'') \subseteq \theta(S, t')$. Thus, $(T'', t'') \equiv \theta(S, t') = \theta(min(T', t'))$, and so $|min(T'', t'')| = |min(\theta(min(T', t')))| \leq |\theta(min(T', t'))| \leq |min(T', t')|$.]

To see that f is well defined, suppose $\theta(x) = \theta(y)$. We have to show that $\theta(h(x)) = \theta(h(y))$. Consider a terminal chasing sequence of (T', t') using $X \to A$, and $(u_1, v_1), \ldots, (u_n, v_n)$ as the sequence of pairs of tuples used in the sequence, yielding the chase homomorphism θ. Consider the sequence $(h(u_1), h(v_1)), \ldots, (h(u_n), h(v_n))$. Clearly if $X \to A$ can be applied to (u, v), then it can be applied to $(h(u), h(v))$, unless $h(u(A)) = h(v(A))$. Let $(h(u_{i_1}), h(v_{i_1})), \ldots, (h(u_{i_k}), h(v_{i_k}))$ be the subsequence of these pairs for which $X \to A$ can be applied. It can be easily verified that there is a chasing sequence of $(h(T'), t')$ using $X \to A$ that uses the pairs $(h(u_{i_1}), h(v_{i_1})), \ldots, (h(u_{i_k}), h(v_{i_k}))$, with chase homomorphism θ'. Note that for all x', y', if $\theta(x') = \theta(y')$ then $\theta'(h(x')) = \theta'(h(y'))$. In particular, $\theta'(h(x)) = \theta'(h(y))$. Because $h(T') \subseteq T'$, θ' is the chase homomorphism of a chasing sequence $\sigma_1, \ldots, \sigma_k$ of (T', t'). Let θ'' be the chase homomorphism formed from a terminal chasing sequence that extends $\sigma_1, \ldots, \sigma_k$. Then $\theta''(h(x)) = \theta''(h(y))$. Finally, by the uniqueness of the chase homomorphism, $\theta'' = \theta$, and so $\theta(h(x)) = \theta(h(y))$ as desired. This concludes the proof. ∎

It turns out that jd's behave differently than fd's with respect to minimization of tableaux. The following shows that the chase using jd's may yield simpler but also more complicated tableaux.

	A	B	C	D
T	w	x	y'	z'
	w'	x	y	z
t	w	x	y	z

	A	B	C	D
T'	w	x	y	z'
	w'	x'	y'	z
t'	w	x	y	z

	A	B	C	D
T''	w'	x	y	z'
	w	x'	y'	z
	w'	x	y'	z
	w	x'	y	z'
t''	w	x	y	z

(a) The tableau query (T, t) (b) The tableau query (T', t') (c) The tableau query
$chase(T', t', \{\bowtie[AB, CD]\})$

Figure 8.4:   Minimization and the chase using jd's

EXAMPLE 8.4.10   Consider the tableau query (T, t) shown in Fig. 8.4(a) and the jd $\sigma = \bowtie$ $[AB, BCD]$. Clearly (T, t) is minimal, so $|min(T, t)| = 2$. Next consider $chase(T, t, \sigma)$. It is easy to check that $\langle w, x, y, z \rangle \in chase(T, t, \sigma)$, so $chase(T, t, \sigma)$ is equivalent to the identity and

$$|min(chase(T, t, \sigma))| = 1.$$

Next let (T', t') be the tableau query in Fig. 8.4(b) and $\sigma = \bowtie[AB, CD]$. Again (T', t') is minimal. Now $chase(T', t', \sigma)$ is represented in Fig. 8.4(c) and is minimal. Thus

$$|min(chase(T', t', \sigma))| = 4 > |min(T', t')|.$$

Despite the limitations illustrated by the preceding example, the chase in conjunction with tableau minimization provides a powerful optimization technique that yields good results in many cases. This is illustrated by the following example and by Exercise 8.28.

EXAMPLE 8.4.11   Consider the SPJ expression

$$q = \pi_{AB}(\pi_{BCD}(R) \bowtie \pi_{ACD}(R)) \bowtie \pi_{AD}(R),$$

where R is a relation with attributes $ABCD$. Suppose we wish to optimize the query on databases satisfying the dependencies

$$\Sigma = \{B \rightarrow D, D \rightarrow C, \bowtie[AB, ACD]\}.$$

The tableau (T, t) corresponding to q is represented in Fig. 8.5(a). Note that (T, t) is minimal. Next we chase (T, t) using the dependencies in Σ. The chase using the fd's in Σ does not change (T, t), which already satisfies them. The chase using the jd

	A	B	C	D
T	w'	x	y'	z'
	w	x'	y'	z'
	w	x''	y''	z
t	w	x	y	z

(a) The tableau query
(T, t) corresponding to q

	A	B	C	D
T''	w'	x	y'	z'
	w	x'	y'	z
	w	x''	y'	z
t''	w	x	y	z

(c) The tableau query
$(T'', t'') = chase(T', t', \{B \to D, D \to C\})$

	A	B	C	D
T'	w'	x	y'	z'
	w	x'	y'	z'
	w	x''	y''	z
	w	x'	y''	z
	w	x''	y'	z'
t'	w	x	y	z

(b) The tableau query
$(T', t') = chase(T, t, \{\bowtie[AB, ACD]\})$

	A	B	C	D
T'''	w'	x	y'	z
	w	x'	y'	z
t'''	w	x	y	z

(d) The tableau query
$(T''', t''') = min(T'', t'')$

Figure 8.5:   Optimization of SPJ expressions by tableau minimization and the chase

$\bowtie[AB, ACD]$ yields the tableau (T', t') in Fig. 8.5(b). Now the fd's can be applied to (T', t') yielding the tableau (T'', t'') in Fig. 8.5(c). Finally (T'', t'') is minimized to (T''', t''') in Fig. 8.5(d). Note that (T''', t''') satisfies Σ, so the chase can no longer be applied. The SPJ expression corresponding to (T''', t''') is $\pi_{ABD}(\pi_{BCD}(R) \bowtie \pi_{ACD}(R))$. Thus, the optimization of q resulted in saving one join operation. Note that the new query is not simply a subexpression of the original. In general, the shape of queries can be changed radically by the foregoing procedure.

The Chase and Logical Implication

We consider a natural correspondence between dependency satisfaction and conjunctive query containment. This correspondence uses tableaux to represent dependencies. We will see that the chase provides an alternative point of view to dependency implication.

First consider a jd $\sigma = \bowtie[X_1, \ldots, X_n]$. It is immediate to see that an instance I satisfies σ iff $q_\sigma(I) \subseteq q_{id}(I)$, where

$$q_\sigma = [X_1] \bowtie \cdots \bowtie [X_n]$$

and q_{id} is the identity query. Both q_σ and q_{id} are PSJR expressions. We can look at alternative formalisms for expressing q_σ and q_{id}. For instance, the *tableau query of* σ is (T_σ, t), where for some $t_1, \ldots, t_n$,

- t is a free tuple over R with a distinct variable for each coordinate,
- $T_\sigma = \{t_1, \ldots, t_n\}$,
- $\pi_{X_i}(t_i) = \pi_{X_i}(t)$ for $i \in [1, n]$, and
- the other coordinates of the t_i's hold distinct variables.

It is again easy to see that $q_\sigma = (T_\sigma, t)$, so $I \models \sigma$ iff $(T_\sigma, t)(I) \subseteq (\{t\}, t)(I)$.

For fd's, the situation is only slightly more complicated. Consider an fd $\sigma' = X \to A$ over U. It is easy to see that $I \models \sigma'$ iff $(T_{\sigma'}, t_{\sigma'})(I) \subseteq (T_{\sigma'}, t'_{\sigma'})(I)$, where

	X	A	$(U - AX)$
$T_{\sigma'}$	u	x	v_1
	u	x'	v_2
$t_{\sigma'}$	x	x'	

	X	A	$(U - AX)$
$T_{\sigma'}$	u	x	v_1
	u	x'	v_2
$t'_{\sigma'}$	x	x	

where u, v_1, v_2 are vectors of distinct variables and x, x' are distinct variables occurring in none of these vectors. The *tableau query* of σ' is $(T_{\sigma'}, t_{\sigma'})$.

Again observe that $(T_{\sigma'}, t_{\sigma'})$, (T_σ, t_σ) can be expressed as PSJR expressions, so fd satisfaction also reduces to containment of PSJR expressions. It will thus be natural to look more generally at all dependencies expressed as containment of PSJR expressions. In Chapter 10, we will consider the general class of *algebraic dependencies* based on containment of these expressions.

Returning to the chase, we next use the tableau representation of dependencies to obtain a characterization of logical implication (Exercise 8.29). This result is generalized by Corollary 10.2.3.

THEOREM 8.4.12 Let Σ and $\{\sigma\}$ be sets of fd's and jd's over relation schema R, let (T_σ, t_σ) be the tableau query of σ, and let T be the tableau in $chase(T_\sigma, t_\sigma, \Sigma)$. Then $\Sigma \models \sigma$ iff

(a) $\sigma = X \to A$ and $|\pi_A(T)| = 1$, that is, the projection over A of T is a singleton; or

(b) $\sigma = \bowtie[X_1, \ldots, X_n]$ and $t_\sigma \in T$.

This implies that determining logical implication for jd's alone, and for fd's and jd's taken together, is decidable. On the other hand, tableau techniques are also used to obtain the following complexity results for logical implication of jd's (see Exercise 8.30).

THEOREM 8.4.13

   (a) Testing whether a jd and an fd imply a jd is NP-complete.

   (b) Testing whether a set of mvd's implies a jd is NP-hard.

Acyclic Join Dependencies

In Section 6.4, a special family of joins called acyclic was introduced and was shown to enjoy a number of desirable properties. We show now a connection between those results, join dependencies, and multivalued dependencies.

   A jd $\bowtie[X_1, \ldots, X_n]$ is *acyclic* if the hypergraph corresponding to $[X_1, \ldots, X_n]$ is acyclic (as defined in Section 6.4).

   Using the chase, we show here that a jd is acyclic iff it is equivalent to a set of mvd's. The discussion relies on the notation and techniques developed in the discussion of acyclic joins in Section 6.4.

   We shall use the following lemma.

LEMMA 8.4.14   Let $\sigma = \bowtie\mathbf{X}$ be a jd over U, and let $X, Y \subseteq U$ be disjoint sets. Then the following are equivalent:

   (i) $\sigma \models X \twoheadrightarrow Y$;

   (ii) there is no $X_i \in \mathbf{X}$ such that $X_i \cap Y \neq \emptyset$ and $X_i \cap (U - XY) \neq \emptyset$;

   (iii) Y is a union of connected components of the hypergraph $\mathbf{X}|_{U-X}$.

Proof   Let $Z = U - XY$. Let τ denote the mvd $X \twoheadrightarrow Y$, and let (T_τ, t_τ) be the tableau query corresponding to τ. Let $T_\tau = \{t_Y, t_Z\}$ where $t_Y[XY] = t_\tau[XY]$ and $t_Z[XZ] = t_\tau[XZ]$ and distinct variables are used elsewhere in t_Y and t_Z.

   We show now that (i) implies (ii). By Theorem 8.4.12, $t_\tau \in T = chase(T_\tau, t_\tau, \sigma)$. Let $X_i \in \mathbf{X}$. Suppose that t is a new tuple created by an application of σ during the computation of T. Then $t[X_i]$ agrees with $t'[X_i]$ for some already existing tuple. An induction implies that $t_\tau[X_i] = t_Y[X_i]$ or $t_\tau[X_i] = t_Z[X_i]$. Because t_Y and t_Z agree only on X, this implies that X_i cannot intersect with both Y and Z.

   That (ii) implies (iii) is immediate. To see that (iii) implies (i), consider an application of the jd $\bowtie\mathbf{X}$ on T_τ, where $X_i \in \mathbf{X}$ is associated with t_Y if $X_i - X \subseteq Y$, and X_i is associated with t_Z otherwise. This builds the tuple t_τ, and so by Theorem 8.4.12, $\sigma \models X \twoheadrightarrow Y$. ∎

   We now have the following:

THEOREM 8.4.15   A jd σ is acyclic iff there is a set Σ of mvd's that is equivalent to σ.

Proof   (**only if**) Suppose that $\sigma = \bowtie\mathbf{X}$ over U is acyclic. By Theorem 6.4.5, this implies that the output of the GYO algorithm on $\mathbf{X}$ is empty. Let $X_1, \ldots, X_n$ be an enumeration of $\mathbf{X}$ in the order of an execution of the GYO algorithm. In particular, X_i is an ear of the hypergraph formed by $\{X_{i+1}, \ldots, X_n\}$.

For each $i \in [1, n-1]$, let $P_i = \cup_{j \in [1,i]} X_j$ and $Q_i = \cup_{j \in [i+1,n]} X_j$. Let $\Sigma = \{[P_i \cap Q_i] \twoheadrightarrow Q_i \mid i \in [1, n-1]\}$. By Lemma 8.4.14 and the choice of sequence $X_1, \ldots, X_n$, $\sigma \models \Sigma$. To show that $\Sigma \models \sigma$, we construct a chasing sequence of (T_σ, t_σ) using Σ that yields t_σ. This chase shall inductively produce a sequence $t_1, \ldots, t_n$ of tuples, such that $t_i[P_i] = t_\sigma[P_i]$ for $i \in [1, n]$.

We begin by setting t_1 to be the tuple of T_σ that corresponds to X_1. Then $t_1[P_1] = t_\sigma[P_1]$ because $P_1 = X_1$. More generally, given t_i with $i \geq 1$, the mvd $[P_i \cap Q_i] \twoheadrightarrow Q_i$ on t_i and the tuple corresponding to X_{i+1} can be used to construct tuple t_{i+1} with the desired property. The final tuple t_n constructed by this process is t_σ, and so $\Sigma \models \sigma$ as desired.

(**if**) Suppose that $\sigma = \bowtie \mathbf{X}$ over U is equivalent to the set Σ of mvd's but that σ is not acyclic. From the definition of acyclic, this implies that there is some $W \subseteq U$ such that $\mathbf{Y} = \mathbf{X}|_W$ has no articulation pair. Without loss of generality we assume that $\mathbf{Y}$ is connected.

Let $\mathbf{Y} = \{Y_1, \ldots, Y_m\}$. Suppose that $s_1, \ldots$ are the tuples produced by some chasing sequence of (T_σ, t_σ). We argue by induction that for each $k \geq 1$, $s_k[W] \in \pi_W(T_\sigma)$. Suppose otherwise, and let s_k be the first where this does not hold. Suppose that s_k is the result of applying an mvd $X \twoheadrightarrow Y$ in Σ. Without loss of generality we assume that $X \cap Y = \emptyset$. Let $Z = U - XY$. Because s_k results from $X \twoheadrightarrow Y$, there are two tuples s' and s'' either in T_σ or already produced, such that $s_k[XY] = s'[XY]$ and $s_k[XZ] = s''[XZ]$. Because s_k is chosen to be least, there are tuples t_i and t_j in T_σ, which correspond to X_i and X_j, respectively, such that $s'[W] = t_i[W]$ and $s''[W] = t_j[W]$.

Because t_i and t_j correspond to X_i and X_j, for each attribute $A \in U$ we have $t_i[A] = t_j[A]$ iff $A \in X_i \cap X_j$. Thus $X \cap W \subseteq X_i \cap X_j$.

Because $s_k[W] \neq t_i[W]$, $W - XZ \neq \emptyset$, and because $s_k[W] \neq t_j[W]$, $W - XY \neq \emptyset$. Now, by Lemma 8.4.14, because $X \twoheadrightarrow Y$ is implied by σ, there is no $X_k \in \mathbf{X}$ such that $X_k \cap Y \neq \emptyset$ and $X_k \cap Z \neq \emptyset$. It follows that $\mathbf{Y}|_{W-X}$ is disconnected. Finally, let $Y = X_i \cap W$ and $Y' = X_j \cap W$. Because $X \cap W \subseteq X_i \cap X_j$, it follows that $Y \cap Y'$ is an articulation set for $\mathbf{Y}$, a contradiction. ∎

We conclude with a complexity result about acyclic jd's. The first part follows from the proof of the preceding theorem and the fact that the GYO algorithm runs in polynomial time. The second part, stated without proof, is an interesting converse of the first part.

PROPOSITION 8.4.16

(a) There is a PTIME algorithm that, given an acyclic jd σ, produces a set of mvd's equivalent to σ.

(b) There is a PTIME algorithm that, given a set Σ of mvd's, finds a jd equivalent to Σ or determines that there is none.

The Chase Is Church-Rosser

To conclude this section, we provide the proof that the results of all terminal chasing sequences of a tableau query q by a set Σ of fd's and jd's are identical. To this end, we first introduce tools to describe correspondences between the free tuples occurring in the different elements of chasing sequences.

Let $(T, t) = (T_0, t_0), \ldots, (T_n, t_n)$ be a chasing sequence of (T, t) by Σ. Then for each $i \in [1, n]$, the *chase homomorphism* for step i, denoted θ_i, is an assignment with domain $var(T_i)$ defined as follows:

(a) If (T_{i+1}, t_{i+1}) is the result of applying the fd rule to (T_i, t_i), which replaces all occurrences of variable y by variable x, then θ_{i+1} is defined so that $\theta_{i+1}(y) = x$ and θ_{i+1} is the identity on $var(T_i) - \{y\}$.

(b) If (T_{i+1}, t_{i+1}) is the result of applying the jd rule to (T_i, t_i), then θ_{i+1} is the identity on $var(T_i)$.

The *chase homomorphism* of this chasing sequence is $\theta = \theta_1 \circ \cdots \circ \theta_n$. If $w \in (T \cup \{t\})$, then the tuple *corresponding* to w in (T_i, t_i) is $w_i = \theta_1 \circ \cdots \circ \theta_i(w)$. It may arise that $u_i = v_i$ for distinct tuples u, v in T. Observe that $\theta_1 \circ \cdots \circ \theta_i(T) \subseteq T_i$ and that, because of the jd rule, the inclusion may be strict.

We now have the following:

LEMMA 8.4.17   Suppose that $I \models \Sigma$, v is a substitution over $var(T)$, $v(T) \subseteq I$, and $(T_0, t_0), \ldots, (T_n, t_n)$ is a chasing sequence of (T, t) by Σ. Then

$$v(w_i) = v(w) \text{ for each } i \in [1, n] \text{ and each } w \in (T \cup \{t\}),$$

and $v(T_i) \subseteq I$ for each $i \in [1, n]$.

Crux   Use an induction on the chasing sequence (Exercise 8.24d). ∎

Observe that this also holds if I is a tableau over R that satisfies Σ, which is what we use next. We now have the following:

THEOREM 8.4.18   Let (T, t) be a tableau query over R and Σ a set of fd's and jd's over R. Then the results of all terminal chasing sequences of (T, t) by Σ are identical.

Proof   Let (T', t') and (T'', t'') be the results of two terminal chasing sequences on (T, t) using Σ, and let θ', θ'' be the chase homomorphisms of these chasing sequences. For each tuple $w \in T$, let w' denote the tuple of T' that corresponds to w, and similarly for w'', T''.

By construction, $\theta''(T) \subseteq T''$ and $\theta''(t) = t''$. Because $T'' \models \Sigma$ and $\theta''(T) \subseteq T''$, $\theta''(T') \subseteq T''$ by Lemma 8.4.17 considering the chasing sequence leading to T'. The same argument shows that $\theta''(w') = w''$ for each w in T and $\theta''(t') = t''$. By symmetry, $\theta'(T'') \subseteq T'$, $\theta'(w'') = w'$ for each w in T and $\theta'(t'') = t'$.

We next prove that

(*) θ'' is an isomorphism from (T', t') to (T'', t'').

Let w'' be in T'' for some w in T. Then

$$\theta' \circ \theta''(w'') = \theta''(\theta'(w'')) = \theta''(w') = w''.$$

Observe that each variable x in $var(T'')$ occurs in w'', for some w in T. Thus $\theta' \circ \theta''$ is the identity over $var(T'')$. We therefore have

$$\theta' \circ \theta''(T'') = T''.$$

By symmetry, $\theta'' \circ \theta'$ is the identity over $var(T')$ and

$$\theta'' \circ \theta'(T') = T'.$$

Thus $|T''| = |T'|$. Because $\theta''(T') \subseteq T''$, $\theta''(T') = T''$ and θ'' is an isomorphism from (T', t') to (T'', t''), so (*) holds.

To conclude, we prove that

$(**)$ $\qquad\qquad\qquad\qquad \theta''$ is the identity over $var(T')$.

We first show that for each pair x, y of variables occurring in T,

$(\dagger)$ $\qquad\qquad\qquad\qquad \theta''(x) = \theta''(y)$ iff $\theta'(x) = \theta'(y)$.

Suppose that $\theta''(x) = \theta''(y)$. Then for some tuples $u, v \in T$ and attributes A, B, we have $u(A) = x$, $v(B) = y$ and $u''(A) = \theta''(x) = \theta''(y) = v''(B)$. Next $\theta'(x) = u'(A)$ and $\theta'(y) = v'(B)$. Because θ' is an isomorphism from (T'', t'') to (T', t') and $\theta'(u'') = u'$, $\theta'(v'') = v'$, it follows that $u'(A) = v'(B)$. Hence $\theta'(x) = u'(A) = v'(B) = \theta'(y)$ as desired. The if direction follows by symmetry.

Now let $x \in var(T')$. To prove $(**)$ and the theorem, it now suffices to show that $\theta''(x) = x$. Let

$$\mathcal{A}' = \{y \in var(T) \mid \theta'(y) = \theta'(x)\},$$
$$\mathcal{A}'' = \{y \in var(T) \mid \theta''(y) = \theta''(x)\}.$$

First $(\dagger)$ implies that $\mathcal{A}' = \mathcal{A}''$. Furthermore, an induction on the chasing sequence for (T', t') shows that for each $z \in \mathcal{A}'$, $\theta'(z)$ is the least (under the ordering on **var**) element of $\mathcal{A}'$, and similarly for (T'', t''). Thus θ' and θ'' map all elements of $\mathcal{A}'$ and $\mathcal{A}''$ to the same variable z. Because $x \in var(T')$, it follows that $z = x$ so, in particular, $\theta'(x) = \theta''(x) = x$. ∎

Bibliographic Notes

On a general note, we first mention that comprehensive presentations of dependency theory can be found in [Var87, FV86]. A more dense presentation is provided in [Kan91]. Dependency theory is also the topic of the book [Tha91].

Research on general integrity constraints considered from the perspective of first-order logic is presented in [GM78]. Other early work in this framework includes [Nic78], which observes that fd's and mvd's have a natural representation in logic, and [Nic82], which considers incremental maintanence of integrity constraints under updates to the underlying state.

Functional dependencies were introduced by Codd [Cod72b]. The axiomatization is due to [Arm74]. The problem of implication is studied in [BB79, Mai80]. Several alternative formulations of fd implication, including formulation in terms of the propositional calculus perspective (see Exercise 8.22), are mentioned in [Kan91]; they are due to [SDPF81, CK85, CKS86].

Armstrong relations were introduced and studied in [Fag82b, Fag82a, BDFS84]. Interesting practical applications of Armstrong relations are proposed in [SM81, MR85]. The idea is that, given a set Σ of fd's, the system presents an Armstrong relation for Σ with natural column entries to a user, who can then determine whether Σ includes all of the desired restrictions.

The structure of families of instances specified by a set of fd's is studied in [GZ82, Hul84].

Multivalued dependencies were discovered independently in [Zan76, Fag77b, Del78]. They were generalized in [Ris77, Nic78, ABU79]. The axiomatization of fd's and mvd's is from [BFH77]. A probabilistic view of mvd's in terms of conditional independence is presented in [PV88, Pea88]. This provides an alternative motivation for the study of such dependencies.

The issue of whether there is an axiomatization for jd's has a lengthy history. As will be detailed in Chapter 10, the family of full typed dependencies subsumes the family of jd's, and an axiomatization for these was presented in [BV84a, YP82]; see also [SU82]. More focused axiomatizations, which start with jd's and end with jd's but use slightly more general dependencies at intermediate stages, are presented in [Sci82] and [BV85]; see also [BV81b]. Reference [BV85] also develops an axiomatization for join dependencies based on Gentzen-style proofs (see, e.g., [Kle67]); proofs in this framework maintain a form of scratch paper in addition to a sequence of inferred sentences. Finally, [Pet89] settled the issue by establishing that there is no axiomatization (in the sense defined in Section 8.2) for the family of jd's.

As noted in Chapter 6, acyclic joins received wide interest in the late 1970s and early 1980s so Theorem 8.4.15 was demonstrated in [FMU82]. Proposition 8.4.16 is from [GT83].

An ancestor to the chase can be found in [ABU79]. The notion of chase was articulated in [MMS79]. Related results can be found in [MSY81, Var83]. The relationship between the chase and both tableau queries and logical implication was originally presented in [MMS79] and builds on ideas originally introduced in [ASU79b, ASU79a]. The chase technique is extended to more general dependencies in [BV84c]; see also Chapter 10. The connection between the chase and the more general theorem-proving technique of resolution with paramodulation (see [CL73]) is observed and analyzed in [BV80b]. The chase technique is applied to datalog programs in [RSUV89, RSUV93].

Exercises

Exercise 8.1 Describe the set of fd's, mvd's, and jd's that are tautologies (i.e., dependencies that are satisfied by all instances) for a relation schema R.

Exercise 8.2 Let Σ_1 be as in Example 8.2.4. Prove that $\Sigma_1 \models AD \to E$ and $\Sigma_1 \models CDE \to C$.

Exercise 8.3 Let U be a set of attributes, and let Σ, Γ be sets of dependencies over U. Show that

    (a) $\Sigma \subseteq \Sigma^*$.

    (b) $(\Sigma^*)^* = \Sigma^*$.

    (c) If $\Gamma \subseteq \Sigma$, then $\Gamma^* \subseteq \Sigma^*$.

State and prove analogous results for fd closures of attribute sets.

Exercise 8.4 Prove Lemma 8.2.6.

Exercise 8.5 Let U be a set of attributes and Σ a set of fd's over U. Prove the soundness of FD1, FD2, FD3 and show that

$$\text{If } \Sigma \vdash X \to Y \text{ and } \Sigma \vdash X \to Z, \text{ then } \Sigma \vdash X \to YZ.$$

Exercise 8.6 Let Σ be a set of fd's over U.

    (a) Suppose that $X \subseteq U$ and $U \subseteq V$. Show that $(X, \Sigma)^{*,U} = (X, \Sigma)^{*,V}$. *Hint:* Use the proof of Proposition 8.2.8.

    (b) Suppose that $XY \subseteq U$, and $U \subseteq V$. Show that $\Sigma \models_U X \to Y$ iff $\Sigma \models_V X \to Y$.

♠**Exercise 8.7** [BB79] Describe how to improve the efficiency of Algorithm 8.2.7 to linear time. *Hint:* For each unused fd $W \to Z$ in Σ, record the number attributes of W not yet in *closure*. To do this efficiently, maintain a list for each attribute A of those unused fd's of Σ for which A occurs in the left-hand side.

Exercise 8.8 Give a proof of $AB \to F$ from $\Sigma = \{AB \to C, A \to D, CD \to EF\}$ using $\{FD1, FD2, FD3\}$.

Exercise 8.9 Prove or disprove the soundness of the following rules:

    FD4: (pseudo-transitivity) If $X \to Y$ and $YW \to Z$, then $XW \to Z$.

    FD5: (union) If $X \to Y$ and $X \to Z$, then $X \to YZ$.

    FD6: (decomposition) If $X \to YZ$, then $X \to Y$.

    MVD4: (pseudo-transitivity) If $X \twoheadrightarrow Y$ and $YW \twoheadrightarrow Z$, then $XW \twoheadrightarrow Z - Y$.

    MVD5: (union) If $X \twoheadrightarrow Y$ and $X \twoheadrightarrow Z$, then $X \twoheadrightarrow YZ$.

    MVD6: (decomposition) If $X \twoheadrightarrow Y$ and $X \twoheadrightarrow Z$, then $X \twoheadrightarrow Y \cap Z$, $X \twoheadrightarrow Y - Z$, and $X \twoheadrightarrow Z - Y$.

    bad-FD1: If $XW \to Y$ and $XY \to Z$, then $X \to (Z - W)$.

    bad-MVD1: If $X \twoheadrightarrow Y$ and $Y \twoheadrightarrow Z$, then $X \twoheadrightarrow Z$.

    bad-FMVD1: If $X \twoheadrightarrow Y$ and $XY \to Z$, then $X \to Z$.

(The use of the hint is optional.)

Exercise 8.10   Continuing with Exercise 8.9,

(a) [BFH77] Find a two-element subset of {FD1, FD2, FD3, FD4, FD5, FD6} that is sound and complete for inferring logical implication of fd's.

(b) Prove that there is exactly one two-element subset of {FD1, FD2, FD3, FD4, FD5, FD6} that is sound and complete for inferring logical implication of fd's.

Exercise 8.11   [Arm74] Let U be a fixed set of attributes. An attribute set $X \subseteq U$ is *saturated* with respect to a set Σ of fd's over U if $X = X^*$. The family of saturated sets of Σ with respect to U is $satset(\Sigma) = \{X \subseteq U \mid X \text{ is saturated with respect to } \Sigma\}$.

(a) Show that $satset = satset(\Sigma)$ satisfies the following properties:

> **S1**: $U \in satset$.
> **S2**: If $Y \in satset$ and $Z \in satset$, then $Y \cap Z \in satset$.

★ (b) Suppose that $satset$ is a family of subsets of U satisfying properties (**S1**) and (**S2**). Prove that $satset = satset(\Gamma)$ for some set Γ of fd's over U. *Hint:* Use $\Gamma = \{Y \rightarrow Z \mid$ for each $X \in satset$, if $Y \subseteq X$ then $Z \subseteq X\}$.

Exercise 8.12   Let Σ and Γ be sets of fd's over U. Using the notation of Exercise 8.11,

(a) Show that $satset(\Sigma \cup \Gamma) = satset(\Sigma) \cap satset(\Gamma)$.

(b) Show that $satset(\Sigma^* \cap \Gamma^*) = satset(\Sigma) \wedge satset(\Gamma)$, where for families $\mathcal{F}, \mathcal{G}$, the *wedge* of $\mathcal{F}$ and $\mathcal{G}$ is $\mathcal{F} \wedge \mathcal{G} = \{X \cap Y \mid X \in \mathcal{F} \text{ and } Y \in \mathcal{G}\}$.

(c) For $V \subseteq U$, define $\pi_V \Sigma = \{X \rightarrow Y \in \Sigma \mid XY \subseteq V\}$. For $V \subseteq U$ characterize $satset(\pi_V(\Sigma^*))$ (where this family is defined with respect to V).

Exercise 8.13

(a) Exhibit a set Σ_1 of fd's over $\{A, B\}$ such that each Armstrong relation for Σ has at least three distinct values occurring in the A column. Exhibit a set Σ_2 of fd's over $\{A, B, C\}$ such that each Armstrong relation for Σ has at least four distinct values occurring in the A column.

(b) [GH83, BDFS84] Let Σ be a set of fd's over U. Recall the notion of saturated set from Exercise 8.11. For an instance I over U, the *agreement set* of I is $agset(I) = \{X \subseteq U \mid \exists s, t \in I \text{ such that } s(A) = t(A) \text{ iff } A \in X\}$. For a family $\mathcal{F}$ of subsets of U, the *intersection closure* of $\mathcal{F}$ is $intclo(\mathcal{F}) = \{\bigcap_{i=1}^{n} X_i \mid n \geq 0 \text{ and each } X_i \in \mathcal{F}\}$ (where the empty intersection is defined to be U). Prove that I is an Armstrong relation for Σ iff $intclo(agset(I)) = satset(\Sigma)$.

Exercise 8.14   [Mai80] Let Σ be a set of fd's over U, $X \rightarrow Y \in \Sigma$, and let A be an attribute. A is *extraneous* in $X \rightarrow Y$ with respect to Σ if either

(a) $(\Sigma - \{X \rightarrow Y\}) \cup \{X \rightarrow (Y - A)\} \models X \rightarrow Y$; or

(b) $(\Sigma - \{X \rightarrow Y\}) \cup \{(X - A) \rightarrow Y\} \models X \rightarrow Y$.

Develop an $O(n^2)$ algorithm that takes as input a set Σ of fd's and produces as output a set $\Sigma' \equiv \Sigma$, where Σ' has no extraneous attributes.

Exercise 8.15   Show that there is no set Σ of jd's and fd $X \rightarrow A$ such that $\Sigma \models X \rightarrow A$. *Hint:* Show that for any instance I there exists an instance I' such that $I \subseteq I'$ and $I' \models \Sigma$. Then choose I violating $X \rightarrow A$.

Exercise 8.16   [Fag77b, Zan76] This exercise refers to the original definition of mvd's. Let U be a set of attributes and $X, Y \subseteq U$. Given an instance I over U and a tuple $x \in \pi_X(I)$, the *image* of x on Y in I is the set $image_Y(x, I) = \pi_Y(\sigma_{X=x}(I))$ of tuples over Y. Prove that $I \models X \twoheadrightarrow Y$ iff

$$\text{for each } x \in \pi_X(I) \text{ and each } z \in image_Z(x, I), \ image_Y(x, I) = image_Y(xz, I),$$

where $Z = U - XY$ and xz denotes the tuple w over XZ such that $\pi_X(w) = x$ and $\pi_Z(w) = z$.

★ **Exercise 8.17**   [BFH77] Complete the proof of Theorem 8.3.5. *Hint:* Of course, the inference rules can be used when reasoning about I. The following claims are also useful:

Claim 1: If $A \in X^+$, then $I \models \emptyset \rightarrow A$.

Claim 2: If $A, B \in W_i$ for some $i \in [1, n]$, then $I \models A \rightarrow B$.

Claim 3: For each $i \in [1, n]$, $I \models \emptyset \twoheadrightarrow W_i$.

Exercise 8.18   Prove Corollary 8.3.6.

Exercise 8.19   [Kan91] Consider the following set of inference rules:

MVD7: $X \twoheadrightarrow U - X$.

MVD8: If $Y \cap Z = \emptyset$, $X \twoheadrightarrow Y$, and $Z \twoheadrightarrow W$, then $X \twoheadrightarrow W - Y$.

FMVD3: If $Y \cap Z = \emptyset$, $X \twoheadrightarrow Y$, and $Z \rightarrow W$, then $X \rightarrow Y \cap W$.

Prove that {MVD7, MVD2, MVD8} are sound and complete for inferring implication for mvd's, and that {FD1, FD2, FD3, MVD7, MVD2, MVD8, FMVD1, FMVD3} are sound and complete for inferring implication for fd's and mvd's considered together.

Exercise 8.20   [Bee80] Let Σ be a set of fd's and mvd's, and let $m(\Sigma) = \{X \twoheadrightarrow Y \mid X \twoheadrightarrow Y \in \Sigma\} \cup \{X \twoheadrightarrow A \mid A \in Y \text{ for some } X \rightarrow Y \in \Sigma\}$. Prove that

(a) $\Sigma \models X \rightarrow Y$ implies $m(\Sigma) \models X \twoheadrightarrow Y$; and

(b) $\Sigma \models X \twoheadrightarrow Y$ iff $m(\Sigma) \models X \twoheadrightarrow Y$.

Hint: For (b) do an induction on proofs using the inference rules.

Exercise 8.21   For sets Σ and Γ of dependencies over U, Σ *implies* Γ *for two-element instances*, denoted $\Sigma \models_2 \Gamma$, if for each instance I over U with $|I| \leq 2$, $I \models \Sigma$ implies $I \models \Gamma$.

(a) [SDPF81] Prove that if $\Sigma \cup \{\sigma\}$ is a set of fd's and mvd's, then $\Sigma \models_2 \sigma$ iff $\Sigma \models \sigma$.

(b) Prove that the equivalence of part (a) does not hold if jd's are included.

(c) Exhibit a jd σ such that there is no set Σ of mvd's with $\sigma \equiv \Sigma$.

◆ **Exercise 8.22**   [SDPF81] This exercise develops a close connection between fd's and mvd's, on the one hand, and a fragment of propositional logic, on the other. Let U be a fixed set of attributes. We view each attribute $A \in U$ as a propositional variable. For the purposes of this exercise, a *truth assignment* is a mapping $\xi : U \rightarrow \{T, F\}$ (where T denotes *true* and F denotes *false*). Truth assignments are extended to mappings on subsets X of U by $\xi(X) = \wedge_{A \in X} \xi(A)$. A truth assignment ξ *satisfies* an fd $X \to Y$, denoted $\xi \models X \to Y$, if $\xi(X) = T$ implies $\xi(Y) = T$. It satisfies an mvd $X \twoheadrightarrow Y$, denoted $\xi \models X \twoheadrightarrow Y$, if $\xi(X) = T$ implies that either $\xi(Y) = T$ or $\xi(U - Y) = T$. Given a set $\Sigma \cup \{\sigma\}$ of fd's and mvd's, Σ implies σ *in the propositional calculus*, denoted $\Sigma \models_{\text{prop}} \sigma$, if for each truth assignment ξ, $\xi \models \Sigma$ implies $\xi \models \sigma$. Prove that for all sets $\Sigma \cup \{\sigma\}$ of fd's and mvd's, $\Sigma \models \sigma$ iff $\Sigma \models_{\text{prop}} \sigma$.

★ **Exercise 8.23**   [Bis80] Exhibit a set of inference rules for mvd's that are sound and complete in the context in which an underlying set of attributes is not fixed.

♠ **Exercise 8.24**

     (a) Prove Proposition 8.4.2.

     (b) Prove Lemma 8.4.3.

     (c) Prove Lemma 8.4.4. What is the maximum size attainable by the tableau in the result of a terminal chasing sequence?

     (d) Prove Lemma 8.4.17.

♠ **Exercise 8.25**

     (a) Describe a polynomial time algorithm for computing the chase of a tableau query by Σ, assuming that Σ contains only fd's.

     (b) Show that the problem of deciding whether a jd can be applied to a tableau query is NP-complete if the schema is considered variable, and polynomial if the schema is considered fixed. *Hint:* Use Exercise 6.16.

     (c) Prove that it is NP-hard, given a tableau query (T, t) and a set Σ of fd's and jd's, to compute $chase(T, t, \Sigma)$ (this assumes that the schema is part of the input and thus not fixed).

     (d) Describe an exponential time algorithm for computing the chase by a set of fd's and jd's. (Again the schema is not considered fixed.)

Exercise 8.26   Prove Proposition 8.4.6. *Hint:* Rather than modifying the proof of Theorem 8.4.18, prove as a lemma that if $\Sigma \models \sigma$, then $chase(T, t, \Sigma) = chase(T, t, \Sigma \cup \{\sigma\})$.

Exercise 8.27

     (a) Verify that the results concerning the chase generalize immediately to the context in which database schemas as opposed to relation schemas are used.

     (b) Describe how to generalize the chase to tableau in which constants occur, and state and prove the results about the chase and tableau queries. *Hint:* If the chase procedure attempts to equate two distinct constants (a situation not occurring before), we obtain a particular new tableau, called T_{false}, which corresponds to the query producing an empty result on all input instances.

Exercise 8.28   For each of the following relation schemas R, SPJ expressions q over R, and dependencies Σ over R, simplify q knowing that it is applied only to instances over R satisfying Σ. Use tableau minimization and the chase.

     (a) $sort(R) = ABC$, $q = \pi_{AC}(\pi_{AB}(\sigma_{A=2}(R) \bowtie \pi_{BC}(R)) \bowtie \pi_{AB}(\sigma_{B=8}(R) \bowtie \pi_{BC}(R))$,
        $\Sigma = \{A \to C, B \to C\}$

     (b) $sort(R) = ABCD$, $q = \pi_{BC}(R) \bowtie \pi_{ABD}(R)$, $\Sigma = \{B \twoheadrightarrow CD, B \twoheadrightarrow D\}$

     (c) $sort(R) = ABCD$, $q = \pi_{ABD}(R) \bowtie \pi_{AC}(R)$, $\Sigma = \{A \to B, B \twoheadrightarrow C\}$.

♠ **Exercise 8.29** Prove Theorem 8.4.12.

♠ **Exercise 8.30** Prove Theorem 8.4.13(a) [BV80a] and Theorem 8.4.13(b) [FT83].

Exercise 8.31 [MMS79] Describe an algorithm based on the chase for

(a) computing the closure of an attribute set X under a set Σ of fd's and jd's (where the notion of closure is extended to include all fd's implied by Σ); and

(b) computing the dependency basis (see Section 8.3) of a set X of attributes under a set Σ of fd's and jd's (where the notion of dependency basis is extended to include fd's in the natural manner).

Exercise 8.32 [GH86] Suppose that the underlying domain **dom** has a total order $\leq$. Let $U = \{A_1, \ldots, A_n\}$ be a set of attributes. For each $X \subseteq U$, define the partial order $\leq_X$ over the set of tuples of X by $t \leq_X t'$ iff $t(A) \leq t'(A)$ for each $A \in X$. A *sort set dependency* (SSD) over U is an expression of the form $s(X)$, where $X \subseteq U$. An instance I over U satisfies $s(X)$, denoted $I \models s(X)$, if $\leq_X$ is a total order on $\pi_X(I)$.

(a) Show that the following set of inference rules is sound and complete for finite logical implication between SSDs:
    SSD1: If A is an attribute, then $s(A)$.
    SSD2: If $s(X)$ and $Y \subseteq X$, then $s(Y)$.
    SSD3: If $s(X)$, $s(Y)$ and $s(X \triangle Y)$, then $s(XY)$ [where $X \triangle Y$ denotes $(X - Y) \cup (Y - X)$, i.e., the symmetric difference of X and Y].

(b) Exhibit a polynomial time algorithm for inferring logical implication between sets of SSDs.

(c) Describe how SSDs might be used in connection with indexes.

9 Inclusion Dependency

Vittorio:	*Fd's and jd's give some structure to relations.*
Alice:	*But there are no connections between them.*
Sergio:	*Making connections is the next step . . .*
Riccardo:	*. . . with some unexpected consequences.*

The story of inclusion dependencies starts in a manner similar to that for functional dependencies: Implication is decidable (although here it is PSPACE-complete), and there is a simple set of inference rules that is sound and complete. But the story becomes much more intriguing when functional and inclusion dependencies are taken together. First, the notion of logical implication will have to be refined because the behavior of these dependencies taken together is different depending on whether infinite instances are permitted. Second, both notions of logical implication are nonrecursive. And third, it can be proven in a formal sense that no "finite" axiomatization exists for either notion of logical implication of the dependencies taken together. At the end of this chapter, two restricted classes of inclusion dependencies are discussed. These are significant because they arise in modeling certain natural relationships such as those encountered in semantic data models. Positive results have been obtained for inclusion dependencies from these restricted classes considered with fd's and other dependencies.

Unlike fd's or jd's, a single inclusion dependency may refer to more than one relation. Also unlike fd's and jd's, inclusion dependencies are "untyped" in the sense that they may call for the comparison of values from columns (of the same or different relations) that are labeled by different attributes. A final important difference from fd's and jd's is that inclusion dependencies are "embedded." Speaking intuitively, to satisfy an inclusion dependency the presence of one tuple in an instance may call for the presence of another tuple, of which only some coordinate values are determined by the dependency and the first tuple. These and other differences will be discussed further in Chapter 10.

9.1 Inclusion Dependency in Isolation

To accommodate the fact that inclusion dependencies permit the comparison of values from different columns of one or more relations, we introduce the following notation. Let R be a relation schema and $X = A_1, \ldots, A_n$ a *sequence* of attributes (possibly with repeats) from R. For an instance I of R, the *projection* of I onto the sequence X, denoted $I[X]$, is the n-ary relation $\{\langle t(A_1), \ldots, t(A_n) \rangle \mid t \in I\}$.

The syntax and semantics of inclusion dependencies is now given by the following:

DEFINITION 9.1.1   Let **R** be a relational schema. An *inclusion dependency* (ind) over **R** is an expression of the form $\sigma = R[A_1, \ldots, A_m] \subseteq S[B_1, \ldots, B_m]$, where

(a) R, S are (possibly identical) relation names in **R**,

(b) $A_1, \ldots, A_m$ is a sequence of distinct attributes of $sort(R)$, and

(c) $B_1, \ldots, B_m$ is a sequence of distinct attributes of $sort(S)$.

An instance **I** of **R** *satisfies* σ, denoted $\mathbf{I} \models \sigma$, if

$$\mathbf{I}(R)[A_1, \ldots, A_m] \subseteq \mathbf{I}(S)[B_1, \ldots, B_m].$$

Satisfaction of a set of ind's is defined in the natural manner.

To illustrate this definition, we recall an example from the previous chapter.

EXAMPLE 9.1.2   There are two relations: *Movies* with attributes *Title, Director, Actor* and *Showings* with *Theater, Screen, Title, Snack*; and we have an ind

$$Showings[Title] \subseteq Movies[Title].$$

The generalization of ind's to permit repeated attributes on the left-or right-hand side is considered in Exercise 9.4.

The notion of *logical implication* between sets of ind's is defined in analogy with that for fd's. (This will be refined later when fd's and ind's are considered together.)

Rules for Inferring ind Implication

The following set of inference rules will be shown sound and complete for inferring logical implication between sets of ind's. The variables X, Y, and Z range over sequences of distinct attributes; and R, S, and T range over relation names.

IND1: (reflexivity) $R[X] \subseteq R[X]$.

IND2: (projection and permutation) If $R[A_1, \ldots, A_m] \subseteq S[B_1, \ldots, B_m]$, then $R[A_{i_1}, \ldots, A_{i_k}] \subseteq S[B_{i_1}, \ldots, B_{i_k}]$ for each sequence $i_1, \ldots, i_k$ of distinct integers in $\{1, \ldots, m\}$.

IND3: (transitivity) If $R[X] \subseteq S[Y]$ and $S[Y] \subseteq T[Z]$, then $R[X] \subseteq T[Z]$.

The notions of proof and of provability (denoted $\vdash$) using these rules are defined in analogy with that for fd's.

THEOREM 9.1.3   The set $\{\text{IND1, IND2, IND3}\}$ is sound and complete for logical implication of ind's.

Proof   Soundness of the rules is easily verified. For completeness, let Σ be a set of ind's over database schema $\mathbf{R} = \{R_1, \ldots, R_n\}$, and let $\sigma = R_a[A_1, \ldots, A_m] \subseteq R_b[B_1, \ldots, B_m]$

R	A	B
	1	0
	2	1
	3	2
	4	3
	⋮	⋮

(a)

R	A	B
	1	1
	2	1
	3	2
	4	3
	⋮	⋮

(b)

Figure 9.1: Instances used for distinguishing $\models_{\text{fin}}$ and $\models_{\text{unr}}$

DEFINITION 9.2.1 A set Σ of dependencies over **R** *implies without restriction* a dependency σ, denoted $\Sigma \models_{\text{unr}} \sigma$, if for each unrestricted instance **I** of **R**, **I** $\models \Sigma$ implies **I** $\models \sigma$. A set Σ of dependencies over **R** *finitely implies* a dependency σ, denoted $\Sigma \models_{\text{fin}} \sigma$, if for each (finite) instance **I** of **R**, **I** $\models \Sigma$ implies **I** $\models \sigma$.

If finite and unrestricted implication coincide, or if the kind of implication is understood from the context, then we may use $\models$ rather than $\models_{\text{fin}}$ or $\models_{\text{unr}}$. This is what we implicitly did so far by using $\models$ in place of $\models_{\text{fin}}$.

Of course, if $\Sigma \models_{\text{unr}} \sigma$, then $\Sigma \models_{\text{fin}} \sigma$. The following shows that the converse need not hold:

THEOREM 9.2.2

(a) There is a set Σ of fd's and ind's and an ind σ such that $\Sigma \models_{\text{fin}} \sigma$ but $\Sigma \not\models_{\text{unr}} \sigma$.

(b) There is a set Σ of fd's and ind's and an fd σ such that $\Sigma \models_{\text{fin}} \sigma$ but $\Sigma \not\models_{\text{unr}} \sigma$.

Proof For part (a), let R be binary with attributes A, B; let $\Sigma = \{A \rightarrow B, R[A] \subseteq R[B]\}$; and let σ be $R[B] \subseteq R[A]$. To see that $\Sigma \models_{\text{fin}} \sigma$, let I be a finite instance of R that satisfies Σ. Because $I \models A \rightarrow B$, $|\pi_A(I)| \geq |\pi_B(I)|$ and because $I \models R[A] \subseteq R[B]$, $|\pi_B(I)| \geq |\pi_A(I)|$. It follows that $|\pi_A(I)| = |\pi_B(I)|$. Because I is finite and $\pi_A(I) \subseteq \pi_B(I)$, it follows that $\pi_B(I) \subseteq \pi_A(I)$ and $I \models R[B] \subseteq R[A]$.

On the other hand, the instance shown in Fig. 9.1(a) demonstrates that $\Sigma \not\models_{\text{unr}} \sigma$.

For part (b), let Σ be as before, and let σ be the fd $B \rightarrow A$. As before, if $I \models \Sigma$, then $|\pi_A(I)| = |\pi_B(I)|$. Because $I \models A \rightarrow B$, each tuple in I has a distinct A-value. Thus the number of B-values occurring in I equals the number of tuples in I. Because I is finite, this implies that $I \models B \rightarrow A$. Thus $\Sigma \models_{\text{fin}} \sigma$. On the other hand, the instance shown in Fig. 9.1(b) demonstrates that $\Sigma \not\models_{\text{unr}} \sigma$. ∎

It is now natural to reconsider implication for fd's, jd's, and inds taken separately and in combinations. Are unrestricted and finite implication different in these cases? The answer is given by the following:

Theorem 9.2.3 Unrestricted and finite implication coincide for fd's and jd's considered separately or together and for ind's considered alone.

Proof Unrestricted implication implies finite implication by definition. For fd's and jd's taken separately or together, Theorem 8.4.12 on the relationship between chasing and logical implication can be used to obtain the opposite implication. For ind's, Theorem 9.1.3 shows that finite implication and provability by the ind inference rules are equivalent. It is easily verified that these rules are also sound for unrestricted implication. Thus finite implication implies unrestricted implication for ind's as well. ∎

The notion of finite versus unrestricted implication will be revisited in Chapter 10, where dependencies are recast into a logic-based formalism.

Implication Is Undecidable for fd's + ind's

As will be detailed in Chapter 10, fd's and ind's (and most other relational dependencies) can be represented as sentences in first-order logic. By Gödel's Completeness Thoerem implication is recursively enumerable for first-order logic. It follows that unrestricted implication is r.e. for fd's and ind's considered together. On the other hand, finite implication for fd's and ind's taken together is co-r.e. This follows from the fact that there is an effective enumeration of all finite instances over a fixed schema; if $\Sigma \not\models_{\text{fin}} \sigma$, then a witness of this fact will eventually be found. When unrestricted and finite implication coincide, this pair of observations is sufficient to imply decidability of implication; this is not the case for fd's and ind's.

The Word Problem for (Finite) Monoids

The proof that (finite) implication for fd's and ind's taken together is undecidable uses a reduction from the word problem for monoids, which we discuss next.

A monoid is a set with an associative binary operation ∘ defined on it and an identity element ε. Let Γ be a finite alphabet and Γ^* the *free monoid* generated by Γ (i.e., the set of finite words with letters in Γ with the concatenation operation). Let $E = \{\alpha_i = \beta_i \mid i \in [1..n]\}$ be a finite set of equalities, and let e be an additional equality $\alpha = \beta$, where $\alpha_i, \beta_i, \alpha, \beta \in \Gamma^*$. Then E *(finitely) implies* e, denoted $E \models_{\text{unr}} e$ ($E \models_{\text{fin}} e$), if for each (finite) monoid M and homomorphism $h : \Gamma^* \to M$, if $h(\alpha_i) = h(\beta_i)$ for each $i \in [1..n]$, then $h(\alpha) = h(\beta)$. The *word problem* for (finite) monoids is to decide, given E and e, whether $E \models_{\text{unr}} e$ ($E \models_{\text{fin}} e$). Both the word problem for monoids and the word problem for finite monoids are undecidable.

Using this, we have the following:

Theorem 9.2.4 Unrestricted and finite implication for fd's and ind's considered together are undecidable. In particular, let Σ range over sets of fd's and ind's. The following sets are not recursive:

(a) $\{(\Sigma, \sigma) \mid \sigma \text{ an ind and } \Sigma \models_{\text{unr}} \sigma\}$; $\{(\Sigma, \sigma) \mid \sigma \text{ an ind and } \Sigma \models_{\text{fin}} \sigma\}$;

(b) $\{(\Sigma, \sigma) \mid \sigma \text{ an fd and } \Sigma \models_{\text{unr}} \sigma\}$; and $\{(\Sigma, \sigma) \mid \sigma \text{ an fd and } \Sigma \models_{\text{fin}} \sigma\}$.

Crux   We prove (a) using a reduction from the word problem for (finite) monoids to the (finite) implication problem for fd's and ind's. The proof of part (b) is similar and is left for Exercise 9.5. We first consider the unrestricted case.

Let Γ be a fixed alphabet. Let $E = \{\alpha_i = \beta_i \mid i \in [1, n]\}$ be a set of equalities over Γ^*, and let e be another equality $\alpha = \beta$. A *prefix* is defined to be any prefix of $\alpha_i, \beta_i, \alpha$, or β (including the empty string ε, and full words α_1, β_1, etc.). A single relation R is used, which has attributes

   (i) A_γ, for each prefix γ;

   (ii) A_x, A_y, A_{xy};

   (iii) A_{ya}, for each $a \in \Gamma$; and

   (iv) A_{xya}, for each $a \in \Gamma$;

where x and y are two fixed symbols.

To understand the correspondence between constrained relations and homomorphisms over monoids, suppose that there is a homomorphism h from Γ^* to some monoid M. Intuitively, a tuple of R will hold information about two elements $h(x), h(y)$ of M (in columns A_x, A_y, respectively) and their product $h(x) \circ h(y) = h(xy)$ (in column A_{xy}). For each a in Γ, tuples will also hold information about $h(ya)$ and $h(xya)$ in columns A_{ya}, A_{xya}. More precisely, the instance $I_{M,h}$ corresponding to the monoid M and the homomorphism $h : \Gamma^* \to M$ is defined by

$$I_{M,h} = \{t_{u,v} \mid u, v \in \Gamma^*\},$$

where for each $u, v \in \Gamma^*$, $t_{u,v}$ is the tuple such that

$$t_{u,v}(A_x) = h(u), \qquad t_{u,v}(A_y) = h(\gamma), \text{ for each prefix } \gamma,$$

$$t_{u,v}(A_y) = h(v), \qquad t_{u,v}(A_{ya}) = h(va), \text{ for each } a \in \Gamma,$$

$$t_{u,v}(A_{xy}) = h(uv), \qquad t_{u,v}(A_{xya}) = h(uva), \text{ for each } a \in \Gamma.$$

Formally, to force the correspondence between the relations and homomorphisms over monoids, we use a set Σ of dependencies. In other words, we wish to find a set Σ of dependencies that characterizes precisely the instances over R that correspond to some homomorphism h from Γ^* to some monoid M. The key to the proof is that this can be done using just fd's and ind's. Strictly speaking, the dependencies of (8) in the following list are not ind's because an attribute is repeated in the left-hand side. As discussed in Exercise 9.4(e), the set of dependencies used here can be modified to a set of proper ind's that has the desired properties. In addition, we use fd's with an empty left-hand side, which are sometimes not considered as real fd's. The use of such dependencies is not crucial. A slightly more complicated proof can be found that uses only fd's with a nonempty left-hand side. The set Σ is defined as follows:

1. $\emptyset \to A_\gamma$ for each prefix γ;
2. $A_x A_y \to A_{xy}$;
3. $A_y \to A_{ya}$, for each $a \in \Gamma$;
4. $R[A_\varepsilon] \subseteq R[A_y]$;
5. $R[A_\gamma, A_{\gamma a}] \subseteq R[A_y, A_{ya}]$, for each $a \in \Gamma$ and prefix γ;
6. $R[A_{xy}, A_{xya}] \subseteq R[A_y, A_{ya}]$, for each $a \in \Gamma$;
7. $R[A_x, A_{ya}, A_{xya}] \subseteq R[A_x, A_y, A_{xy}]$, for each $a \in \Gamma$;
8. $R[A_y, A_\varepsilon, A_y] \subseteq R[A_x, A_y, A_{xy}]$; and
9. $R[A_{\alpha_i}] \subseteq R[A_{\beta_i}]$, for each $i \in [1, n]$.

The ind σ is $R[A_\alpha] \subseteq R[A_\beta]$.

Let I be an instance satisfying Σ. Observe that I has to satisfy a number of implied properties. In particular, one can verify that I also satisfies the following property:

$$R[A_{xya}] \subseteq R[A_{ya}] \subseteq R[A_y] = R[A_{xy}] \subseteq R[A_x]$$

and that $adom(I) \subseteq I[A_x]$.

We now show that $\Sigma \models_{\text{unr}} \sigma$ iff $E \models_{\text{unr}} e$. We first show that $E \not\models_{\text{unr}} e$ implies $\Sigma \not\models_{\text{unr}} \sigma$. Suppose that there is a monoid M and homomorphism $h : \Gamma^* \to M$ that satisfies the equations of E but violates the equation e. Consider $I_{M,h}$ defined earlier. It is straightforward to verify that $I \models \Sigma$ but $I \not\models \sigma$.

For the opposite direction, suppose now that $E \models_{\text{unr}} e$, and let I be a (possibly infinite) instance of R that satisfies Σ. To conclude the proof, it must be shown that $I[A_\alpha] \subseteq I[A_\beta]$. (Observe that these two relations both consist of a single tuple because of the fd's with an empty left-hand-side.)

We now define a function $h : \Gamma^* \to adom(I)$. We will prove that h is a homomorphism from Γ^* to a free monoid whose elements are $h(\Gamma^*)$ and that satisfies the equations of E (and hence, e). We will use the fact that the monoid satisfies e to derive that $I[A_\alpha] \subseteq I[A_\beta]$.

We now give an inductive definition of h and show that it has the property that $h(v) \in I[A_y]$ for each $v \in \Gamma^*$.

Basis: Set $h(\varepsilon)$ to be the element in $I[A_\varepsilon]$. Note that $h(\varepsilon)$ is also in $I[A_y]$ because $R[A_\varepsilon] \subseteq R[A_y] \in \Sigma$.

Inductive step: Given $h(v)$ and $a \in \Gamma$, let $t \in I$ be such that $t[A_y] = h(v)$. Define $h(va) = t(A_{ya})$. This is uniquely determined because $A_y \to A_{ya} \in \Sigma$. In addition, $h(va) \in I[A_y]$ because $R[A_x, A_{ya}, A_{xya}] \subseteq R[A_x, A_y, A_{xy}] \in \Sigma$.

We next show by induction on v that

($\dagger$) $\langle h(u), h(v), h(uv) \rangle \in I[A_x, A_y, A_{xy}]$ for each $u, v \in \Gamma^*$.

For a fixed u, the basis (i.e., $v = \varepsilon$) is provided by the fact that $h(u) \in I[A_y]$ and the ind $R[A_y, A_\varepsilon, A_y] \subseteq R[A_x, A_y, A_{xy}] \in \Sigma$. For the inductive step, let $\langle h(u), h(v), h(uv) \rangle \in$

$I[A_x, A_y, A_{xy}]$ and $a \in \Gamma$. Let $t \in I$ be such that $t[A_x, A_y, A_{xy}] = \langle h(u), h(v), h(uv) \rangle$. Then by construction of h, $h(va) = t(A_{ya})$, and from the ind $R[A_{xy}, A_{xya}] \subseteq R[A_y, A_{ya}]$, we have $h(uva) = t(A_{xya})$. Finally, the ind $R[A_x, A_{ya}, A_{xya}] \subseteq R[A_x, A_y, A_{xy}]$ implies that $\langle h(u), h(va), h(uva) \rangle \in I[A_x, A_y, A_{xy}]$ as desired.

Define the binary operation $\circ$ on $h(\Gamma^*)$ as follows. For $a, b \in h(\Gamma^*)$, let

$$a \circ b = c \text{ if for some } t \in I, t[A_x, A_y, A_{xy}] = \langle a, b, c \rangle.$$

There is such a tuple by (†) and c is uniquely defined because $A_x, A_y \to A_{xy} \in \Sigma$. Furthermore, by (†), for each u, v, $h(u) \circ h(v) = h(uv)$. Thus for $h(u), h(v), h(w)$ in $h(\Gamma^*)$,

$$(h(u) \circ h(v)) \circ h(w) = h(uvw) = (h(u) \circ h(v)) \circ h(w),$$

and

$$h(u) \circ h(\varepsilon) = h(u)$$

so $(h(\Gamma^*), \circ)$ is a monoid. In addition, h is a homomorphism from the free monoid over Γ^* to the monoid $(h(\Gamma^*), \circ)$.

It is easy to see that $I[A_{\alpha_i}] = \{h(\alpha_i)\}$ and $I[A_{\beta_i}] = \{h(\beta_i)\}$ for $i \in [1, n]$. Let i be fixed. Because $R[A_{\alpha_i}] \subseteq R[A_{\beta_i}]$, $h(\alpha_i) = h(\beta_i)$. Because $E \models_{unr} e$, $h(\alpha) = h(\beta)$. Thus $I[A_\alpha] = \{h(\alpha)\} = \{h(\beta)\} = I[A_\beta]$. It follows that $I \models_{unr} R[A_\alpha] \subseteq R[A_\beta]$ as desired.

This completes the proof for the unrestricted case. For the finite case, note that everything has to be finite: The monoid is finite, I is finite, and the monoid $h[\Gamma^*]$ is finite. The rest of the argument is the same. ∎

The issue of decidability of finite and unrestricted implication for classes of dependencies is revisited in Chapter 10.

9.3   Nonaxiomatizability of fd's + ind's

The inference rules given previously for fd's, mvd's and ind's can be viewed as "inference rule schemas," in the sense that each of them can be instantiated with specific attribute sets (sequences) to create infinitely many ground inference rules. In these cases the family of inference rule schemas is finite, and we informally refer to them as "finite axiomatizations."

Rather than formalizing the somewhat fuzzy notion of inference rule schema, we focus in this section on families $\mathcal{R}$ of ground inference rules. A (*ground*) *axiomatization* of a family $\mathcal{S}$ of dependencies is a set of ground inference rules that is sound and complete for (finite or unrestricted) implication for $\mathcal{S}$. Two properties of an axiomatization $\mathcal{R}$ will be considered, namely: (1) $\mathcal{R}$ is recursive, and (2) $\mathcal{R}$ is k-ary, in the sense (formally defined later in this section) that each rule in $\mathcal{R}$ has at most k dependencies in its condition.

Speaking intuitively, if $\mathcal{S}$ has a "finite axiomatization," that is, if there is a finite family $\mathcal{R}'$ of inference rule schemas that is sound and complete for $\mathcal{S}$, then $\mathcal{R}'$ specifies a ground axiomatization for S that is both recursive and k-ary for some k. Two results are demonstrated in this section: (1) There is no recursive axiomatization for finite implication of fd's and ind's, and (2) there is no k-ary axiomatization for finite implication of fd's and ind's. It is also known that there is no k-ary axiomatization for unrestricted implication of fd's and ind's. The intuitive conclusion is that the family of fd's and ind's does not have a "finite axiomatization" for finite implication or for unrestricted implication.

To establish the framework and some notation, we assume temporarily that we are dealing with a family $\mathcal{F}$ of database instances over a fixed database schema $\mathbf{R} = \{R_1, \ldots, R_n\}$. Typically, $\mathcal{F}$ will be the set of all finite instances over $\mathbf{R}$, or the set of all (finite or infinite) instances over $\mathbf{R}$. All the notions that are defined are *with respect to $\mathcal{F}$*. Let S be a family of dependencies over $\mathbf{R}$. (At present, S would be the set of fd's and ind's over $\mathbf{R}$.) Logical implication $\models$ among dependencies in S is defined with respect to $\mathcal{F}$ in the natural manner. In particular, $\models_{\mathrm{unr}}$ and $\models_{\mathrm{fin}}$ are obtained by letting $\mathcal{F}$ be the set of unrestricted or finite instances.

A *(ground) inference rule* over S is an expression of the form

$$\rho = \text{if } S \text{ then } s,$$

where $S \subseteq S$ and $s \in S$.

Let $\mathcal{R}$ be a set of rules over $\mathbf{R}$. Then $\mathcal{R}$ is *sound* if each rule in $\mathcal{R}$ is sound. Let $\Sigma \cup \{\sigma\} \subseteq S$ be a set of dependencies over $\mathbf{R}$. A *proof* of σ from Σ using $\mathcal{R}$ is a finite sequence $\sigma_1, \ldots, \sigma_n = \sigma$ such that for each $i \in [1, n]$, either (1) $\sigma_i \in \Sigma$, or (2) for some rule 'if S then s' in $\mathcal{R}$, $\sigma_i = s$ and $S \subseteq \{\sigma_1, \ldots, \sigma_{i-1}\}$. We write $\Sigma \vdash_{\mathcal{R}} \sigma$ (or $\Sigma \vdash \sigma$ if $\mathcal{R}$ is understood) if there is a proof of σ from Σ using $\mathcal{R}$. Clearly, if each rule in $\mathcal{R}$ is sound, then $\Sigma \vdash \sigma$ implies $\Sigma \models \sigma$. The set $\mathcal{R}$ is *complete* if for each pair (Σ, σ), $\Sigma \models \sigma$ implies $\Sigma \vdash_{\mathcal{R}} \sigma$. A *(sound and complete) axiomatization* for logical implication is a set $\mathcal{R}$ of rules that is sound and complete.

The aforementioned notions are now generalized to permit all schemas $\mathbf{R}$. In particular, we consider a set $\mathcal{R}$ of rules that is a union $\cup\{\mathcal{R}_{\mathbf{R}} \mid \mathbf{R} \text{ is a schema}\}$. The notions of sound, proof, etc. can be generalized in the natural fashion.

Note that with the preceding definition, every set S of dependencies has a sound and complete axiomatization. This is provided by the set $\mathcal{R}$ of all rules of the form

$$\text{if } S \text{ then } s,$$

where $S \models s$. Clearly, such trivial axiomatizations hold no interest. In particular, they are not necessarily effective (i.e., one may not be able to tell if a rule is in $\mathcal{R}$, so one may not be able to construct proofs that can be checked). It is thus natural to restrict $\mathcal{R}$ to be recursive.

We now present the first result of this section, which will imply that there is no recursive axiomatization for finite implication of fd's and ind's. In this result we assume that the dependencies in S are sentences in first-order logic.

PROPOSITION 9.3.1 Let S be a class of dependencies. If S has a recursive axiomatization for finite implications, then finite implication is decidable for S.

Crux   Suppose that S has a recursive axiomatization. Consider the set

$$Implic = \{(S, s) \mid S \subseteq \mathcal{S}, s \in \mathcal{S}, \text{ and } S \models_{\text{fin}} s\}.$$

First note that the set *Implic* is r.e.; indeed, let $\mathcal{R}$ be a recursive axiomatization for $\mathcal{S}$. One can effectively enumerate all proofs of implication that use rules in $\mathcal{R}$. This allows one to enumerate *Implic* effectively. Thus *Implic* is r.e. We argue next that *Implic* is also co-r.e. To conclude that a pair (S, s) is not in *Implic*, it is sufficient to exhibit a finite instance satisfying S and violating s. To enumerate all pairs (S, s) not in *Implic*, one proceeds as follows. The set of *all* pairs (S, s) is clearly r.e., as is the set of all instances over a fixed schema. Repeat for all positive integers n the following. Enumerate the first n pairs (S, s) and the first n instances. For each (S, s) among the n, check whether one of the n instances is a counterexample to the implication $S \models s$, in which case output (S, s). Clearly, this procedure enumerates the complement of *Implic*, so *Implic* is co-r.e. Because it is both r.e. and co-r.e., *Implic* is recursive, so there is an algorithm testing whether (S, s) is in *Implic*. ∎

It follows that there is no recursive axiomatization for finite implication of fd's and ind's. [To see this, note that by Theorem 9.2.4, logical implication for fd's and ind's is undecidable. By Proposition 9.3.1, it follows that there can be no finite axiomatization for fd's and ind's.] Because implication for jd's is decidable (Theorem 8.4.12), but there is no axiomatization for them (Theorem 8.3.4), the converse of the preceding proposition does not hold.

Speaking intuitively, the preceding development implies that there is no finite set of inference rule schemas that is sound and complete for finite implication of fd's and ind's. However, the proof is rather indirect. Furthermore, the approach cannot be used in connection with unrestricted implication, nor with classes of dependencies for which finite implication is decidable (see Exercise 9.9). The notion of k-ary axiomatization developed now shall overcome these objections.

A rule 'if S then s' is k-ary for some $k \geq 0$ if $|S| = k$. An axiomatization $\mathcal{R}$ is k-ary if each rule in $\mathcal{R}$ is l-ary for some $l \leq k$. For example, the instantiations of rules FD1 and IND1 are 0-ary, those of rules FD2 and IND2 are 1-ary, and those of FD3 and IND3 are 2-ary. Theorem 9.3.3 below shows that there is no k-ary axiomatization for finite implication of fd's and ind's.

We now turn to an analog in terms of logical implication of k-ary axiomatizability. Again let S be a set of dependencies over $\mathbf{R}$, and let $\mathcal{F}$ be a family of instances over $\mathbf{R}$. Let $k \geq 0$. A set $\Gamma \subseteq \mathcal{S}$ is:

closed under implication with respect to $\mathcal{S}$ if $\sigma \in \Gamma$ whenever

$$(a) \; \sigma \in \mathcal{S} \text{ and (b) } \Gamma \models \sigma$$

closed under k-ary implication with respect to $\mathcal{S}$ if $\sigma \in \Gamma$ whenever

$$(a) \; \sigma \in \mathcal{S}, \text{ and for some } \Sigma \subseteq \Gamma, (b_1) \; \Sigma \models \sigma \text{ and } (b_2) \; |\Sigma| \leq k.$$

Clearly, if Γ is closed under implication, then it is closed under k-ary implication for each $k \geq 0$, and if Γ is closed under k-ary implication, then it is closed under k'-ary implication for each $k' \leq k$.

PROPOSITION 9.3.2 Let **R** be a database schema, $\mathcal{S}$ a set of dependencies over **R**, and $k \geq 0$. Then there is a k-ary axiomatization for $\mathcal{S}$ iff whenever $\Gamma \subseteq \mathcal{S}$ is closed under k-ary implication, then Γ is closed under implication.

Proof Suppose that there is a k-ary axiomatization for $\mathcal{S}$, and let $\Gamma \subseteq \mathcal{S}$ be closed under k-ary implication. Suppose further that $\Gamma \models \sigma$ for some $\sigma \in \mathcal{S}$. Let $\sigma_1, \ldots, \sigma_n$ be a proof of σ from Γ using $\mathcal{R}$. Using the fact that $\mathcal{R}$ is k-ary and that Γ is closed under k-ary implication, a straightforward induction shows that $\sigma_i \in \Gamma$ for $i \in [1, n]$.

Suppose now that for each $\Gamma \subseteq \mathcal{S}$, if Γ is closed under k-ary implication, then Γ is closed under implication. Set

$$\mathcal{R} = \{\text{'if } S \text{ then } s' \mid S \subseteq \mathcal{S}, s \in \mathcal{S}, |S| \leq k, \text{ and } S \models s\}.$$

To see that $\mathcal{R}$ is complete, suppose that $\Gamma \models \sigma$. Consider the set $\Gamma^* = \{\gamma \mid \Gamma \vdash_{\mathcal{R}} \gamma\}$. From the construction of $\mathcal{R}$, Γ^* is closed under k-ary implication. By assumption it is closed under implication, and so $\Gamma \vdash_{\mathcal{R}} \sigma$ as desired. ∎

In the following, we consider finite implication, so $\mathcal{F}$ is the set of finite instances.

THEOREM 9.3.3 For no k does there exist a k-ary sound and complete axiomatization for finite implication of fd's and ind's taken together. More specifically, for each k there is a schema **R** for which there is no k-ary sound and complete axiomatization for finite implication of fd's and ind's over **R**.

Proof Let $k \geq 0$ be fixed. Let **R** = $\{R_0, \ldots, R_k\}$ be a database schema where $sort(R_i) = \{A, B\}$ for each $i \in [0, k]$. In the remainder of this proof, addition is always done modulo $k + 1$. The dependencies $\Sigma = \Sigma_a \cup \Sigma_b$ and σ are defined by

(a) $\Sigma_a = \{R_i : A \rightarrow B \mid i \in [0, k]\}$;
(b) $\Sigma_b = \{R_i[A] \subseteq R_{i+1}[B] \mid i \in [0, k]\}$; and
(c) $\sigma = R_0[B] \subseteq R_k[A]$.

Let Γ be the union of Σ with all fd's and ind's that are tautologies (i.e., that are satisfied by all finite instances over **R**).

In the remainder of the proof, it is shown that (1) Γ is not closed under finite implication, but (2) Γ is closed under k-ary finite implication. Proposition 9.3.2 will then imply that the family of fd's and ind's has no k-ary sound and complete axiomatization for **R**.

First observe that Γ does not contain σ, so to show that Γ is not closed under finite implication, it suffices to demonstrate that $\Sigma \models_{\text{fin}} \sigma$. Let **I** be a finite instance of **R** that satisfies Σ. By the ind's of Σ, $|\mathbf{I}(R_i)[A]| \leq |\mathbf{I}(R_{i+1})[B]|$ for each $i \in [0, k]$, and by the fd's of Σ, $|\mathbf{I}(R_i)[B]| \leq |\mathbf{I}(R_i)[A]|$ for each $i \in [0, k]$. From this we obtain

$$|\mathbf{I}(R_0)[A]| \leq |\mathbf{I}(R_1)[B]| \leq |\mathbf{I}(R_1)[A]|$$
$$\leq \qquad \cdots$$
$$\leq |\mathbf{I}(R_k)[B]| \leq |\mathbf{I}(R_k)[A]| \leq |\mathbf{I}(R_0)[B]| \leq |\mathbf{I}(R_0)[A]|.$$

In particular, $|\mathbf{I}(R_k)[A]| = |\mathbf{I}(R_0)[B]|$. Since $\mathbf{I}$ is finite and we have $\mathbf{I}(R_k)[A] \subseteq \mathbf{I}(R_0)[B]$ and $|\mathbf{I}(R_k)[A]| = |\mathbf{I}(R_0)[B]|$, it follows that $\mathbf{I}(R_0)[B] \subseteq \mathbf{I}(R_k)[A]$ as desired.

We now show that Γ is closed under k-ary finite implication. Suppose that $\Delta \subseteq \Gamma$ has no more than k elements ($|\Delta| \leq k$). It must be shown that if γ is an fd or ind and $\Delta \models_{\text{fin}} \gamma$, then $\gamma \in \Gamma$. Because Σ contains $k + 1$ ind's, any subset Δ of Γ that has no more than k members must omit some ind δ of Σ. We shall exhibit an instance $\mathbf{I}$ such that $\mathbf{I} \models \gamma$ iff $\gamma \in \Gamma - \{\delta\}$. (Thus $\mathbf{I}$ will be an Armstrong instance for $\Gamma - \{\delta\}$.) It will then follow that $\Gamma - \{\delta\}$ is closed under finite implication. Because $\Delta \subseteq \Gamma - \{\delta\}$, this will imply that for each fd or ind γ, if $\Delta \models_{\text{fin}} \gamma$, then $\Gamma - \{\delta\} \models_{\text{fin}} \gamma$, so $\gamma \in \Gamma$.

Because Σ is symmetric with regard to ind's, we can assume without loss of generality that δ is the ind $R_k[A] \subseteq R_0[B]$. Assuming that $\mathbf{N} \times \mathbf{N}$ is contained in the underlying domain, define $\mathbf{I}$ so that

$$\mathbf{I}(R_0) = \{\langle(0, 0), (0, k + 1)\rangle, \ \langle(1, 0), (1, k + 1)\rangle, \ \langle(2, 0), (1, k + 1)\rangle\}$$

and for each $i \in [1, k]$,

$$\mathbf{I}(R_i) = \{\langle(0, i), (0, i - 1)\rangle, \ \langle(1, i), (1, i - 1)\rangle, \ldots,$$
$$\langle(2i + 1, i), (2i + 1, i - 1)\rangle, \ \langle(2i + 2, i), (2i + 1, i - 1)\rangle\}.$$

Figure 9.2 shows $\mathbf{I}$ for the case $k = 3$.

We now show for each fd and ind γ over $\mathbf{R}$ that $\mathbf{I} \models \gamma$ iff $\gamma \in \Gamma - \delta$. Three cases arise:

1. γ is a tautology. Then this clearly holds.

2. γ is an fd that is not a tautology. Then γ is equivalent to one of the following for some $i \in [0, k]$:

$$\begin{array}{ll} R_i : A \rightarrow B, & R_i : B \rightarrow A, \\ R_i : \emptyset \rightarrow A, & R_i : \emptyset \rightarrow B, \\ \text{or} & R_i : \emptyset \rightarrow AB. \end{array}$$

If γ is $R_i : A \rightarrow B$, then $\gamma \in \Gamma$ and clearly $\mathbf{I} \models \gamma$. In the other cases, $\gamma \notin \Gamma$ and $\mathbf{I} \not\models \gamma$.

3. γ is an ind that is not a tautology. Considering now which ind's $\mathbf{I}$ satisfies, note that the only pairs of nondisjoint columns of relations in $\mathbf{I}$ are

$$\mathbf{I}(R_0)[A], \mathbf{I}(R_1)[B];$$
$$\mathbf{I}(R_1)[A], \mathbf{I}(R_2)[B]; \quad \ldots;$$
$$\mathbf{I}(R_{k-1})[A], \mathbf{I}(R_k)[B].$$

$\mathbf{I}(R_0)$	A	B
	(0,0)	(0,4)
	(1,0)	(1,4)
	(2,0)	(1,4)

$\mathbf{I}(R_1)$	A	B
	(0,1)	(0,0)
	(1,1)	(1,0)
	(2,1)	(2,0)
	(3,1)	(3,0)
	(4,1)	(3,0)

$\mathbf{I}(R_2)$	A	B
	(0,2)	(0,1)
	(1,2)	(1,1)
	(2,2)	(2,1)
	(3,2)	(3,1)
	(4,2)	(4,1)
	(5,2)	(5,1)
	(6,2)	(5,1)

$\mathbf{I}(R_3)$	A	B
	(0,3)	(0,2)
	(1,3)	(1,2)
	(2,3)	(2,2)
	(3,3)	(3,2)
	(4,3)	(4,2)
	(5,3)	(5,2)
	(6,3)	(6,2)
	(7,3)	(7,2)
	(8,3)	(7,2)

Figure 9.2:   An Armstrong relation for $\Gamma - \delta$

Furthermore, $\mathbf{I} \not\models R_{i+1}[B] \subseteq R_i[A]$ for each $i \in [0, k]$; and $\mathbf{I} \models R_i[A] \subseteq R_{i+1}[B]$. This implies that $\mathbf{I} \models \gamma$ iff $\gamma \in \Gamma - \{\delta\}$, as desired. ■

In the proof of the preceding theorem all relations used are binary, and all fd's and ind's are *unary*, in the sense that at most one attribute appears on either side of each dependency. In proofs that there is no k-ary axiomatization for unrestricted implication of fd's and ind's, some of the ind's used involve at least two attributes on each side. This cannot be improved to unary ind's, because there is a 2-ary sound and complete axiomatization for unrestricted implication of unary ind's and arbitrary fd's (see Exercise 9.18).

9.4   Restricted Kinds of Inclusion Dependency

This section explores two restrictions on ind's for which several positive results have been obtained. The first one focuses on sets of ind's that are acyclic in a natural sense, and the second restricts the ind's to having only one attribute on either side. The restricted dependencies are important because they are sufficient to model many natural relationships, such as those captured by semantic models (see Chapter 11). These include subtype relationships of the kind "every student is also a person."

This section also presents a generalization of the chase that incorporates ind's. Because ind's are embedded, chasing in this context may lead to infinite chasing sequences. In the context of acyclic sets of ind's, however, the chasing sequences are guaranteed to terminate. The study of infinite chasing sequences will be taken up in earnest in Chapter 10.

Ind's and the Chase

Because ind's may involve more than one relation, the formal notation of the chase must be extended. Suppose now that $\mathbf{R}$ is a database schema, and let $q = (\mathbf{T}, t)$ be a tableau query over $\mathbf{R}$. The fd and jd rules are generalized to this context in the natural fashion.

We first present an example and then describe the rule that is used for ind's.

EXAMPLE 9.4.1   Consider the database schemas consisting of two relation schemas P, Q with $sort(P) = ABC$, $sort(Q) = DEF$, the dependencies

$$Q[DE] \subseteq P[AB] \qquad \text{and} \qquad P : A \to B,$$

and the tableau $\mathbf{T}$ shown in Fig. 9.3. Consider $\mathbf{T}_1$ and $\mathbf{T}_2$ in the same figure. The tableau $\mathbf{T}_1$ is obtained by applying to $\mathbf{T}$ the ind rule given after this example. The intuition is that the tuples $\langle x, y_i \rangle$ should also be in the P-relation because of the ind. Then $\mathbf{T}_2$ is obtained by applying the fd rule. Tableau minimization can be applied to obtain $\mathbf{T}_3$.

The following rule is used for ind's.

ind rule: Let $\sigma = R[X] \subseteq S[Y]$ be an ind, let $u \in \mathbf{T}(R)$, and suppose that there is no free tuple $v \in \mathbf{T}(S)$ such that $v[Y] = u[X]$. In this case, we say that σ is *applicable* to $R(u)$. Let w be a free tuple over S such that $w[Y] = u[X]$ and w has distinct new variables in all coordinates of $sort(S) - Y$ that are greater than all variables occurring in q. Then "the" result of applying σ to $R(u)$ is $(\mathbf{T}', t)$, where

- $\mathbf{T}'(P) = \mathbf{T}(P)$ for each relation name $P \in \mathbf{R} - \{S\}$, and
- $\mathbf{T}'(S) = \mathbf{T}(S) \cup \{w\}$.

For a tableau query q and a set Σ of ind's, it is possible that two terminal chasing sequences end with nonisomorphic tableau queries, that there are no finite terminal chasing sequences, or that there are both finite terminal chasing sequences and infinite chasing sequences (see Exercise 9.12). General approaches to resolving this problem will be considered in Chapter 10. In the present discussion, we focus on acyclic sets of ind's, for which the chase always terminates after a finite number of steps.

Acyclic Inclusion Dependencies

DEFINITION 9.4.2   A family Σ of ind's over $\mathbf{R}$ is *acyclic* if there is no sequence $R_i[X_i] \subseteq S_i[Y_i]$ ($i \in [1, n]$) of ind's in Σ where for $i \in [1, n]$, $R_{i+1} = S_i$ for $i \in [1, n-1]$, and $R_1 = S_n$. A family Σ of dependencies has *acyclic* ind's if the set of ind's in Σ is acyclic.

$\mathbf{T}(P)$	A	B	C

$\mathbf{T}(Q)$	D	E	F
	x	y_1	z
	x	y_2	x
t	y_1	x	

$\mathbf{T}_1(P)$	A	B	C
	x	y_1	w_1
	x	y_2	w_2

$\mathbf{T}_1(Q)$	D	E	F
	x	y_1	z
	x	y_2	x
t	y_1	x	

$\mathbf{T}_2(P)$	A	B	C
	x	y_1	w_1
	x	y_1	w_2

$\mathbf{T}_2(Q)$	D	E	F
	x	y_1	z
	x	y_1	x
t	y_1	x	

$\mathbf{T}_3(P)$	A	B	C
	x	y_1	w_1

$\mathbf{T}_3(Q)$	D	E	F
	x	y_1	x
t	y_1	x	

Figure 9.3:   Chasing with ind's

The following is easily verified (see Exercise 9.14):

PROPOSITION 9.4.3   Let q be a tableau query and Σ a set of fd's, jd's, and acyclic ind's over **R**. Then each chasing sequence of q by Σ terminates after an exponentially bounded number of steps.

For each tableau query q and set Σ of fd's, jd's, and acyclic ind's, let *chase*(q, Σ) denote the result of some arbitrary chasing sequence of q by Σ. (One can easily come up with some syntactic strategy for arbitrarily choosing this sequence.)

Using an analog to Lemma 8.4.3, one obtains the following result on tableau query containment (an analog to Theorem 8.4.8).

THEOREM 9.4.4   Let q, q' be tableau queries and Σ a set of fd's, jd's, and acyclic ind's over **R**. Then $q \subseteq_\Sigma q'$ iff *chase*$(q, \Sigma) \subseteq$ *chase*(q', Σ).

Next we consider the application of the chase to implication of dependencies. For database schema $\mathbf{R}$ and ind $\sigma = R[X] \subseteq S[Y]$ over $\mathbf{R}$, the *tableau query* of σ is $q_\sigma = (\{R(u_\sigma)\}, \langle u_\sigma \rangle)$, where u_σ is a free tuple all of whose entries are distinct. For example, given $R[ABCD]$, $S[EFG]$, and $\sigma = R[BC] \subseteq S[GE]$, $q_\sigma = (\{R(x_1, x_2, x_3, x_4)\}, \langle x_1, x_2, x_3, x_4 \rangle)$. In analogy with Theorem 8.4.12, we have the following for fd's, jd's, and acyclic ind's.

THEOREM 9.4.5   Let Σ be a set of fd's, jd's, and acyclic ind's over database schema $\mathbf{R}$ and let $\mathbf{T}$ be the tableau in $chase(q_\sigma, \Sigma)$. Then $\Sigma \models_{unr} \sigma$ iff

(a) For fd or jd σ over $\mathbf{R}$, $\mathbf{T}$ satisfies the conditions of Theorem 8.4.12.

(b) For ind $\sigma = R[X] \in S[Y]$, $u_\sigma[X] \in \mathbf{T}(S)[Y]$.

This yields the following:

COROLLARY 9.4.6   Finite and unrestricted implication for sets of fd's, jd's, and acyclic ind's coincide and are decidable in exponential time.

An improvement of the complexity here seems unlikely, because implication of an ind by an acyclic set of ind's is NP-complete (see Exercise 9.14).

Unary Inclusion Dependencies

A *unary inclusion dependency* (uind) is an ind in which exactly one attribute appears on each side. The uind's arise frequently in relation schemas in which certain columns range over values that correspond to entity types (e.g., if $SS\#$ is a key for the *Person* relation and is also used to identify people in the *Employee* relation).

As with arbitrary ind's, unrestricted and finite implication do not coincide for fd's and uind's (proof of Theorem 9.2.2). However, both forms of implication are decidable in polynomial time. In this section, the focus is on finite implication. We present a sound and complete axiomatization for finite implication of fd's and uind's (but in agreement with Theorem 9.3.3, it is not k-ary for any k).

For uind's considered in isolation, the inference rules for ind's are specialized to yield the following two rules, which are sound and complete for (unrestricted and finite) implication. Here A, B, and C range over attributes and R, S, and T over relation names:

UIND1: (reflexivity) $R[A] \subseteq R[A]$.
UIND2: (transitivity) If $R[A] \subseteq S[B]$ and $S[B] \subseteq T[C]$, then $R[A] \subseteq T[C]$.

To capture the interaction of fd's and uind's in the finite case, the following family of rules is used:

C: (cycle rules) For each positive integer n,

$$\text{if}\begin{cases} R_1 : A_1 \rightarrow B_1, \\ R_2[A_2] \subseteq R_1[B_1], \\ \dots, \\ R_n : A_n \rightarrow B_n, \text{ and} \\ R_1[A_1] \subseteq R_n[B_n] \end{cases} \quad \text{then}\begin{cases} R_1 : B_1 \rightarrow A_1, \\ R_1[B_1] \subseteq R_2[A_2], \\ \dots, \\ R_n : B_n \rightarrow A_n, \text{ and} \\ R_n[B_n] \subseteq R_1[A_1]. \end{cases}$$

The soundness of this family of rules follows from a straightforward cardinality argument. More generally, we have the following (see Exercise 9.16):

THEOREM 9.4.7 The set {FD1, FD2, FD3, UIND1, UIND2} along with the cycle rules (C) is sound and complete for finite implication of fd's and uind's. Furthermore, finite implication is decidable in polynomial time.

Bibliographic Notes

Inclusion dependency is based on the notion of referential integrity, which was known to the broader database community during the 1970s (see, e.g., [Dat81]). A seminal paper on the theory of ind's is [CFP84], in which inference rules for ind's are presented and the nonaxiomatizability of both finite and unrestricted implication for fd's and ind's is demonstrated. A non-k-ary sound and complete set of inference rules for finite implication of fd's and ind's is presented in [Mit83b]. Another seminal paper is [JK84b], which also observed the distinction between finite and unrestricted implication for fd's and ind's, generalized the chase to incorporate fd's and ind's, and used this to characterize containment between conjunctive queries. Related work is reported in [LMG83].

Undecidability of (finite) implication for fd's and ind's taken together was shown independently by [CV85] and [Mit83a]. The proof of Theorem 9.2.4 is taken from [CV85]. (The undecidability of the word problem for monoids is from [Pos47], and of the word problem for finite monoids is from [Gur66].)

Acyclic ind's were introduced in [Sci86]. Complexity results for acyclic ind's include that implication for acyclic ind's alone is NP-complete [CK86], and implication for fd's and acyclic ind's has an exponential lower bound [CK85].

Given the PSPACE complexity of implication for ind's and the negative results in connection with fd's, unary ind's emerged as a more tractable form of inclusion dependency. The decision problems for finite and unrestricted implication for uind's and fd's taken together, although not coextensive, both lie in polynomial time [CKV90]. This extensive paper also develops axiomatizations of both finite and unrestricted logical implication for unary ind's and fd's considered together, and develops results for uind's with some of the more general dependencies studied in Chapter 10.

Typed ind's are studied in [CK86]. In addition to using traditional techniques from dependency theory, such as chasing, this work develops tools for analyzing ind's using equational theories.

Ind's in connection with other dependencies are also studied in [CV83].

Exercises

Exercise 9.1   Complete the proof of Proposition 9.1.5.

Exercise 9.2   Complete the proof of Theorem 9.1.7.

Exercise 9.3   [CFP84] (In this exercise, by a slight abuse of notation, we allow fd's with sequences rather than sets of attributes.) Demonstrate the following:

(a) If $|\vec{A}| = |\vec{B}|$, then $\{R[\vec{A}\vec{C}] \subseteq S[\vec{B}\vec{D}], S : \vec{B} \rightarrow \vec{D}\} \models_{unr} R : \vec{A} \rightarrow \vec{C}$.

(b) If $|\vec{A}| = |\vec{B}|$, then $\{R[\vec{A}\vec{C}] \subseteq S[\vec{B}\vec{D}], R[\vec{A}\vec{E}] \subseteq S[\vec{B}\vec{F}], S : \vec{B} \rightarrow \vec{D}\} \models_{unr} R[\vec{A}\vec{C}\vec{E}] \subseteq S[\vec{B}\vec{D}\vec{F}]$.

(c) Suppose that $|\vec{A}| = |\vec{B}|$; $\Sigma = \{R[\vec{A}\vec{C}] \subseteq S[\vec{B}\vec{D}], R[\vec{A}\vec{E}] \subseteq S[\vec{B}\vec{D}], S : \vec{B} \rightarrow \vec{D}\}$; and $\mathbf{I} \models \Sigma$. Then $u[\vec{C}] = u[\vec{E}]$ for each $u \in \mathbf{I}(R)$.

Exercise 9.4   As defined in the text, we require in ind $R[A_1, \ldots, A_m] \subseteq S[B_1, \ldots, B_m]$ that the A_i's and B_i's are distinct. A *repeats-permitted inclusion dependency* (rind) is defined as was inclusion dependency, except that repeats are permitted in the attribute sequences on both the left- and right-hand sides.

(a) Show that if Σ is a set of ind's, σ a rind, and $\Sigma \models_{unr} \sigma$, then σ is equivalent to an ind.

(b) Exhibit a set Σ of ind's and fd's such that $\Sigma \models_{unr} R[AB] \subseteq S[CC]$. Do the same for $R[AA] \subseteq R[BC]$.

♠ (c) [Mit83a] Consider the rules

> IND4: If $R[A_1A_2] \subseteq S[BB]$ and $R[\vec{C}] \subseteq T[\vec{D}]$, then $R[\vec{C}'] \subseteq T[\vec{D}]$, where $\vec{C}'$ is obtained from C by replacing one or more occurrences of A_2 by A_1.

> IND5: If $R[A_1A_2] \subseteq S[BB]$ and $T[\vec{C}] \subseteq R[\vec{D}]$, then $T[\vec{C}] \subseteq R[\vec{D}']$, where $\vec{D}'$ is obtained from D by replacing one or more occurrences of A_2 by A_1.

> Prove that the inference rules {IND1, IND2, IND3, IND4, IND5} are sound and complete for finite implication of sets of rind's.

(d) Prove that unrestricted and finite implication coincide for rind's.

(e) A *left-repeats-permitted inclusion dependency* (l-rind) is a rind for which there are no repeats on the right-hand side. Given a set $\Sigma \cup \{\sigma\}$ of l-rind's over $\mathbf{R}$, describe how to construct a schema $\mathbf{R}'$ and ind's $\Sigma' \cup \{\sigma'\}$ over $\mathbf{R}'$ such that $\Sigma \models \sigma$ iff $\Sigma' \models \sigma'$ and $\Sigma \models_{fin} \sigma$ iff $\Sigma' \models_{fin} \sigma'$.

(f) Do the same as in part (e), except for arbitrary rind's.

Exercise 9.5   [CV85] Prove part (b) of Theorem 9.2.4. *Hint:* In the proof of part (a), extend the schema of R to include new attributes $A_{\alpha'}$, $A_{\beta'}$, and $A_{y'}$; add dependencies $A_y \rightarrow A_{y'}$, $R[A_\alpha, A_{\alpha'}] \subseteq R[A_y, A_{y'}]$, $R[A_\beta, A_{\beta'}] \subseteq R[A_y, A_{y'}]$; and use $A_{\alpha'} \rightarrow A_{\beta'}$ as σ.

Exercise 9.6

(a) Develop an alternative proof of Theorem 9.3.3 in which δ is an fd rather than an ind.

(b) In the proof of Theorem 9.3.3 for finite implication, the dependency σ used is an ind. Using the same set Σ, find an fd that can be used in place of σ in the proof.

Exercise 9.7   Prove that there is no k for which there is a k-ary sound and complete axiomatization for finite implication of fd's, jd's, and ind's.

★ **Exercise 9.8** [SW82] Prove that there is no k-ary sound and complete set of inference rules for finite implication of emvd's.

Exercise 9.9 Recall the notion of sort-set dependency (ssd) from Exercise 8.32.

(a) Prove that finite and unrestricted implication coincide for fd's and ssd's considered together. Conclude that implication for fd's and ssd's is decidable.

★ (b) [GH86] Prove that there is no k-ary sound and complete set of inference rules for finite implication of fd's (key dependencies) and ssd's taken together.

Exercise 9.10

(a) [CFP84] A set of ind's is *bounded* by k if each ind in the set has at most k attributes on the left-hand side and on the right-hand side. Show that logical implication for bounded sets of ind's is decidable in polynomial time.

(b) [CV83] An ind is *typed* if it has the form $R[\vec{A}] \subseteq S[\vec{A}]$. Exhibit a polynomial time algorithm for deciding logical implication between typed ind's.

Exercise 9.11 Suppose that some attribute domains may be finite.

(a) Show that {IND1, IND2, IND3} remains sound in the framework.

(b) Show that if one-element domains are permitted, then {IND1, IND2, IND3} is not complete.

(c) Show for each $n > 0$ that if all domains are required to have at least n elements, then {IND1, IND2, IND3} is not complete.

Exercise 9.12 Suppose that no restrictions are put on the order of application of ind rules in chasing sequences.

(a) Exhibit a tableau query q and a set Σ of ind's and two terminal chasing sequences of q by Σ that end with nonisomorphic tableau queries.

(b) Exhibit a tableau query q and a set Σ of ind's, a terminal chasing sequence of q by Σ, and an infinite chasing sequence of q by Σ.

(c) Exhibit a tableau query q and a set Σ of ind's such that q has no finite terminal chasing sequence by Σ.

♠ **Exercise 9.13** [JK84b] Recall that for tableau queries q and q' and a set Σ of fd's and jd's over R, $q \subseteq_\Sigma q'$ if for each instance I that satisfies Σ, $q(I) \subseteq q'(I)$. In the context of ind's, this containment relationship may depend on whether infinite instances are permitted or not. For tableau queries q, q' and a set Σ of dependencies over $\mathbf{R}$, we write $q \subseteq_{\Sigma,\text{fin}} q'$ ($q \subseteq_{\Sigma,\text{unr}} q'$) if $q(\mathbf{I}) \subseteq q'(\mathbf{I})$ for each finite (unrestricted) instance $\mathbf{I}$ that satisfies Σ.

(a) Show that if Σ is a set of fd's and jd's, then $\subseteq_{\Sigma,\text{fin}}$ and $\subseteq_{\Sigma,\text{unr}}$ coincide.

(b) Exhibit a set Σ of fd's and ind's and tableau queries q, q' such that $q \subseteq_{\Sigma,\text{fin}} q'$ but $q \not\subseteq_{\Sigma,\text{unr}} q'$.

Exercise 9.14

(a) Prove Proposition 9.4.3.

(b) Prove Theorem 9.4.4.

(c) Let q be a tableau query and Σ a set of fd's, jd's, and ind's over $\mathbf{R}$, where the set of ind's in Σ is acyclic; and suppose that q', q'' are the final tableaux of two terminal chasing sequences of q by Σ (where the order of rule application is not restricted). Prove that $q \equiv q'$.

(d) Prove Theorem 9.4.5.

(e) Prove Corollary 9.4.6.

Exercise 9.15

(a) Exhibit an acyclic set Σ of ind's and a tableau query q such that *chase*(q, Σ) is exponential in the size of Σ and q.

(b) [CK86] Prove that implication of an ind by an acyclic set of ind's is NP-complete. *Hint:* Use a reduction from the problem of Permutation Generation [GJ79].

(c) [CK86] Recall from Exercise 9.10(b) that an ind is *typed* if it has the form $R[\vec{A}] \subseteq S[\vec{A}]$. Prove that implication of an ind by a set of fd's and an acyclic set of typed ind's is NP-hard. *Hint:* Use a reduction from 3-SAT.

♠ **Exercise 9.16**   [CKV90] In this exercise you will prove Theorem 9.4.7. The exercise begins by focusing on the unirelational case; for notational convenience we omit the relation name from uind's in this context.

Given a set Σ of fd's and uind's over R, define $G(\Sigma)$ to be a multigraph with node set R and two colors of edges: a red edge from A to B if $A \rightarrow B \in \Sigma$, and a black edge from A to B is $B \subseteq A \in \Sigma$. If A and B have red (black) edges in both directions, replace them with an undirected red (black) edge.

(a) Suppose that Σ is closed under the inference rules. Prove that $G(\Sigma)$ has the following properties:
   1. Nodes have red (black) self-loops, and the red (black) subgraph of $G(\Sigma)$ is transitively closed.
   2. The subgraphs induced by the strongly connected components of $G(\Sigma)$ contain only undirected edges.
   3. In each strongly connected component, the red (black) subset of edges forms a collection of node disjoint cliques (the red and black partitions of nodes could be different).
   4. If $A_1 \ldots A_m \rightarrow B$ is an fd in Σ and $A_1, \ldots, A_m$ have common ancestor A in the red subgraph of $G(\Sigma)$, then $G(\Sigma)$ contains a red edge from A to B.

(b) Given a set Σ of fd's and uind's closed under the inference rules, use $G(\Sigma)$ to build counterexample instances that demonstrate that $\Sigma \not\vdash \sigma$ implies $\Sigma \not\models_{\text{fin}} \sigma$ for fd or uind σ.

(c) Use the rules to develop a polynomial time algorithm for inferring finite implication for a set of fd's and uind's.

(d) Generalize the preceding development to arbitrary database schemas.

Exercise 9.17

(a) Let $k > 1$ be an integer. Prove that there is a database schema $\mathbf{R}$ with at least one unary relation $R \in \mathbf{R}$, and a set Σ of fd's and ind's such that
   (i) for each $\mathbf{I} \models \Sigma$, $|\mathbf{I}(R)| = 0$ or $|\mathbf{I}(R)| = 1$ or $|\mathbf{I}(R)| \geq k$.
   (ii) for each $l \geq k$ there is an instance $\mathbf{I}_l \models \Sigma$ with $|\mathbf{I}(R)| = l$.

(b) Prove that this result cannot be strengthened so that condition (i) reads
   (i) (i') for each $\mathbf{I} \models \Sigma$, $|\mathbf{I}(R)| = 0$ or $|\mathbf{I}(R)| = 1$ or $|\mathbf{I}(R)| = k$.

♠ **Exercise 9.18** [CKV90]

(a) Show that the set of inference rules containing {FD1, FD2, FD3, UIND1, UIND2} and

FD-UIND1: If $\emptyset \rightarrow A$ and $R[B] \subseteq R[A]$, then $\emptyset \rightarrow B$.

FD-UIND1: If $\emptyset \rightarrow A$ and $R[B] \subseteq R[A]$, then $R[A] \subseteq R[B]$.

is sound and complete for unrestricted logical implication of fd's and uind's over a single relation schema R.

(b) Generalize this result to arbitrary database schemas, under the assumption that in all instances, each relation is nonempty.

10 A Larger Perspective

Alice: *fd's, jd's, mvd's, ejd's, emvd's, ind's—it's all getting very confusing.*
Vittorio: *Wait! We'll use logic to unify it all.*
Sergio: *Yes! Logic will make everything crystal clear.*
Riccardo: *And we'll get a better understanding of dependencies that make sense.*

The dependencies studied in the previous chapters have a strong practical motivation and provide a good setting for studying two of the fundamental issues in dependency theory: deciding logical implication and constructing axiomatizations.

Several new dependencies were introduced in the late 1970s and early 1980s, sometimes motivated by practical examples and later motivated by a desire to understand fundamental theoretical properties of unirelational dependencies or to find axiomatizations for known classes of dependencies. This process culminated with a rather general perspective on dependencies stemming from mathematical logic: Almost all dependencies that have been introduced in the literature can be described as logical sentences having a simple structure, and further syntactic restrictions on that structure yield natural subclasses of dependencies. The purpose of this chapter is to introduce this general class of dependencies and its natural subclasses and to present important results and techniques obtained for them.

The general perspective is given in the first section, along with a simple application of logic to obtain the decidability of implication for a large class of dependencies. It turns out that the chase is an invaluable tool for analyzing implication; this is studied in the second section. Axiomatizations for important subclasses have been developed, again using the chase; this is the topic of the third section. We conclude the chapter with a provocative alternative view of dependencies stemming from relational algebra.

The classes of dependencies studied in this chapter include complex dependencies that would not generally arise in practice. Even if they did arise, they are so intricate that they would probably be unusable—it is unlikely that database administrators would bother to write them down or that software would be developed to use or enforce them. Nevertheless, it is important to repeat that the perspective and results discussed in this chapter have served the important function of providing a unified understanding of virtually all dependencies raised in the literature and, in particular, of providing insight into the boundaries between tractable and intractable problems in the area.

10.1   A Unifying Framework

The fundamental property of all of the dependencies introduced so far is that they essentially say, "The presence of some tuples in the instance implies the presence of certain other tuples in the instance, or implies that certain tuple components are equal." In the case of jd's and mvd's, the *new* tuples can be completely specified in terms of the *old* tuples, but for ind's this is not the case. In any case, all of the dependencies discussed so far can be expressed using first-order logic sentences of the form

$$(*) \qquad \forall x_1 \ldots \forall x_n \left[\varphi(x_1, \ldots, x_n) \rightarrow \exists z_1 \ldots \exists z_k \psi(y_1, \ldots, y_m) \right],$$

where $\{z_1, \ldots, z_k\} = \{y_1, \ldots, y_m\} - \{x_1, \ldots, x_n\}$, and where φ is a (possibly empty) conjunction of atoms and ψ a nonempty conjunction. In both φ and ψ, one finds *relation atoms* of the form $R(w_1, \ldots, w_l)$ and *equality atoms* of the form $w = w'$, where each of the $w, w', w_1, \ldots, w_l$ is a variable.

Because we generally focus on sets of dependencies, we make several simplifying assumptions before continuing (see Exercise 10.1a). These include that (1) we may eliminate equality atoms from φ without losing expressive power; and (2) we can also assume without loss of generality that no existentially quantified variable participates in an equality atom in ψ. Thus we define an *(embedded) dependency* to be a sentence of the foregoing form, where

1. φ is a conjunction of relation atoms using all of the variables $x_1, \ldots, x_n$;
2. ψ is a conjunction of atoms using all of the variables $z_1, \ldots, z_k$; and
3. there are no equality atoms in ψ involving existentially quantified variables.

A dependency is *unirelational* if at most one relation name is used, and it is *multirelational* otherwise. To simplify the presentation, the focus in this chapter is almost exclusively on unirelational dependencies. Thus, unless otherwise indicated, the dependencies considered here are unirelational.

We now present three fundamental classifications of dependencies.

Full versus embedded: A *full* dependency is a dependency that has no existential quantifiers.

Tuple generating versus equality generating: A *tuple-generating dependency* (tgd) is a dependency in which no equality atoms occur; an *equality-generating dependency* (egd) is a dependency for which the right-hand formula is a *single* equality atom.

Typed versus untyped: A dependency is *typed* if there is an assignment of variables to column positions such that (1) variables in relation atoms occur only in their assigned position, and (2) each equality atom involves a pair of variables assigned to the same position.

It is sometimes important to distinguish dependencies with a single atom in the right-hand formula. A dependency is *single head* if the right-hand formula involves a single atom; it is *multi-head* otherwise.

The following result is easily verified (Exercise 10.1b).

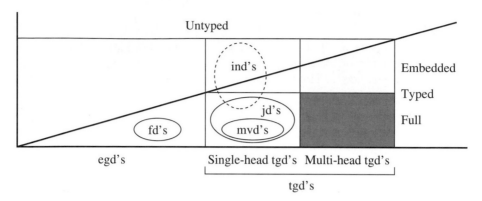

Figure 10.1: Dependencies

PROPOSITION 10.1.1   Each (typed) dependency is equivalent to a set of (typed) egd's and tgd's.

It is easy to classify the fd's, jd's, mvd's, ejd's, emvd's and ind's studied in Chapters 8 and 9 according to the aforementioned dimensions. All except the last are typed. During the late 1970s and early 1980s the class of typed dependencies was studied in depth. In many cases, the results obtained for dependencies and for typed dependencies are equivalent. However, for negative results the typed case sometimes requires more sophisticated proof techniques because it imposes more restrictions.

A classification of dependencies along the three axes is given in Fig. 10.1. The gray square at the lower right indicates that each full multihead tgd is equivalent to a set of single-head tgd's. The intersection of ind's and jd's stems from trivial dependencies. For example, $R[AB] \subseteq R[AB]$ and $\bowtie[AB]$ over relation $R(AB)$ are equivalent [and are syntactically the same when written in the form of $(*)$].

There is a strong relationship between dependencies and tableaux. Tableaux provide a convenient notation for expressing and working with dependencies. (As will be seen in Section 10.4, the family of typed dependencies can also be represented using a formalism based on algebraic expressions.) The tableau representation of two untyped egd's is shown in Figs. 10.2(a) and 10.2(b). These two egd's are equivalent. Note that all egd's can be expressed as a pair $(T, x = y)$, where T is a tableau and $x, y \in var(T)$. If $(T, x = y)$ is typed, unirelational, and x, y are in the A column of T, then this is referred to as an A-*egd*.

Parts (c) and (d) of Fig. 10.2 show two full tgd's that are equivalent. This is especially interesting because, considered as tableau queries, (T', t) properly contains (T, t) (see Exercise 10.4). As suggested earlier, each full tgd is equivalent to some set of full single-head tgd's. In the following, when considering full tgd's, we will assume that they are single head.

Part (e) of Fig. 10.2 shows a typed tgd that is not single head. To represent these within

	A	B	C
S	x	y	w_1
	y	w_2	z
	z	y	w_3
	$x = z$		

	A	B	C
S'	x	y	w_1
	y	w_2	u
	u	y	w_3
	y	w_4	z
	z	y	w_5
	$x = z$		

(a) $(S, x = z)$　　　　　　　(b) $(S', x = z)$

	A	B
T	x	y_1
	x_1	y_1
	x_1	y
t	x	y

	A	B
T'	x	y_1
	x_1	y_1
	x_1	y_2
	x_2	y_2
	x_2	y
t	x	y

	A	B
T_1	x	y_1
	x_1	y_1
	x_1	y_2
	x'	y_2
T_2	x	y_3
	x'	y_3

(c) (T, t)　　　　(d) (T', t)　　　　(e) (T_1, T_2)

Figure 10.2:　Five dependencies

the tableau notation, we use an ordered pair (T_1, T_2), where both T_1 and T_2 are tableaux. This tgd is not equivalent to any set of single-head tgd's (see Exercise 10.6b).

Finite versus Unrestricted Implication Revisited

We now reexamine the issues of finite versus unrestricted implication using the logical perspective on dependencies. Because all of these lie within first-order logic, $\models_{\text{fin}}$ is co-r.e. and $\models_{\text{unr}}$ is r.e. (see Chapter 2). Suppose that $\Sigma = \{\sigma_1, \ldots, \sigma_n\}$ is a set of dependencies and $\{\sigma\}$ a dependency. Then $\Sigma \models_{\text{unr}} \sigma$ ($\Sigma \models_{\text{fin}} \sigma$) iff there is no unrestricted (finite) model of $\sigma_1 \wedge \cdots \wedge \sigma_n \wedge \neg\sigma$. If these are all full dependencies, then they can be rewritten in prenex normal form, where the quantifier prefix has the form $\exists^*\forall^*$. (Here each of the σ_i is universally quantified, and $\neg\sigma$ contributes the existential quantifier.) The family of sentences that have a quantifier prefix of this form (and no function symbols) is called the *initially extended Bernays-Schönfinkel class*, and it has been studied in the logic community since the 1920s. It is easily verified that finite and unrestricted satisfiability coincide for sentences in this class (Exercise 10.3). It follows that finite and unrestricted implication coincide for full dependencies and, as discussed in Chapter 9, it follows that implication is decidable. On the other hand, because fd's and uind's are dependencies, we know from Theorem 9.2.4 that the two forms of implication do not coincide for (embedded) dependencies, and both are nonrecursive. Although not demonstrated here, these results have been extended to the family of embedded multivalued dependencies (emvd's).

To summarize:

THEOREM 10.1.2

1. For full dependencies, finite and unrestricted implication coincide and are decidable.

2. For (typed) dependencies, finite and unrestricted implication do not coincide and are both undecidable. In fact, this is true for embedded multivalued dependencies. In particular, finite implication is not r.e., and unrestricted implication is not co-r.e.

10.2 The Chase Revisited

As suggested by the close connection between dependencies and tableaux, chasing is an invaluable tool for characterizing logical implication for dependencies. In this section we first use chasing to develop a test for logical implication of arbitrary dependencies by full dependencies. We also present an application of the chase for determining how full dependencies are propagated to views. We conclude by extending the chase to work with embedded dependencies. In this discussion we focus almost entirely on typed dependencies, but it will be clear that the arguments can be modified to the untyped case.

Chasing with Full Dependencies

We first state without proof the natural generalization of chasing by fd's and jd's (Theorem 8.4.12) to full dependencies (see Exercise 10.8). In this context we begin either with a tableau T, or with an arbitrary tgd (T, T') or egd $(T, x = y)$. The notion of *applying* a full dependency to this is defined in the natural manner. Lemma 8.4.17 and the notation developed for it generalize naturally to this context, as does the following analog of Theorem 8.4.18:

THEOREM 10.2.1   If Σ is a set of full dependencies and T is a tableau (τ a dependency), then chasing $T(\tau)$ by Σ yields a unique finite result, denoted $chase(T, \Sigma)$ ($chase(\tau, \Sigma)$).

Logical implication of (full or embedded) dependencies by sets of full dependencies will now be characterized by a straightforward application of the techniques developed in Section 8.4 (see Exercise 10.8). A dependency τ is *trivial* if

(a) τ is an egd $(T, x = x)$; or

(b) τ is a tgd (T, T') and there is a substitution θ for T' such that $\theta(T') \subseteq T$ and θ is the identity on $var(T) \cap var(T')$.

Note that if τ is a *full* tgd, then (b) simply says that $T' \subseteq T$.

A dependency τ is a *tautology* for finite (unrestricted) instances if each finite (unrestricted) instance of appropriate type satisfies τ—that is, if $\emptyset \models_{fin} \tau$ ($\emptyset \models_{unr} \tau$). It is easily verified that a dependency is a tautology iff it is trivial.

The following now provides a simple test for implication by full typed dependencies:

THEOREM 10.2.2 Let Σ be a set of full typed dependencies and τ a typed dependency. Then $\Sigma \models \tau$ iff $chase(\tau, \Sigma)$ is trivial.

Recall that the chase relies on a total order $\leq$ on **var**. For egd $(T, x = y)$ we assume that $x < y$ and that these are the least and second to least variables appearing in the tableau; and for full tgd (T, t), $t(A)$ is least in $T(A)$ for each attribute A. Using this convention, we can obtain the following:

COROLLARY 10.2.3 Let Σ be a set of full typed dependencies.

(a) If $\tau = (T, x = y)$ is a typed egd, then $\Sigma \models \tau$ iff x and y are identical or $y \notin var(chase(T, \Sigma))$.

(b) If $\tau = (T, t)$ is a full typed tgd, then $\Sigma \models \tau$ iff $t \in chase(T, \Sigma)$.

Using the preceding results, it is straightforward to develop a deterministic exponential time algorithm for testing implication of full dependencies. It is also known that for both the typed and untyped cases, implication is complete in EXPTIME. (Note that, in contrast, logical implication for arbitrary sets of initially extended Bernays-Schöfinkel sentences is known to be complete in nondeterministic EXPTIME.)

Dependencies and Views

On a bit of a tangent, we now apply the chase to characterize the interaction of full dependencies and user views. Let $\mathbf{R} = \{R_1, \ldots, R_n\}$ be a database schema, where R_j has associated set Σ_j of full dependencies for $j \in [1, n]$. Set $\Sigma = \{R_i : \sigma \mid \sigma \in \Sigma_i\}$. Note that the elements of Σ are tagged by the relation name they refer to. Suppose that a view is defined by algebraic expression $E : \mathbf{R} \rightarrow S[V]$. It is natural to ask what dependencies will hold in the view. Formally, we say that $\mathbf{R} : \Sigma$ *implies* $E : \sigma$, denoted $\mathbf{R} : \Sigma \models E : \sigma$, if $E(\mathbf{I})$ satisfies σ for each $\mathbf{I}$ that satisfies Σ. The notion of $\mathbf{R} : \Sigma \models E : \Gamma$ for a set Γ is defined in the natural manner.

To illustrate these notions in a simple setting, we state the following easily verified result (see Exercise 10.10).

PROPOSITION 10.2.4 Let $(R[U], \Sigma)$ be a relation schema where Σ is a set of fd's and mvd's, and let $V \subseteq U$. Then

(a) $R : \Sigma \models [\pi_V(R)] : X \rightarrow A$ iff $\Sigma \models X \rightarrow A$ and $XA \subseteq V$.

(b) $R : \Sigma \models [\pi_V(R)] : X \twoheadrightarrow Y$ iff $\Sigma \models X \twoheadrightarrow Z$ for some $X \subseteq V$ and $Y = Z \cap V$.

Given a database schema $\mathbf{R}$, a family Σ of tagged full dependencies over $\mathbf{R}$, a view expression E mapping $\mathbf{R}$ to $S[V]$, and a full dependency γ, is it decidable whether $\mathbf{R} : \Sigma \models E : \gamma$? If E ranges over the full relational algebra, the answer is no, even if the only dependencies considered are fd's.

THEOREM 10.2.5   It is undecidable, given database schema $\mathbf{R}$, tagged fd's Σ, algebra expression $E : \mathbf{R} \to S$ and fd σ over S, whether $\mathbf{R} : \Sigma \models E : \sigma$.

Proof   Let $\mathbf{R} = \{R[U], S[U]\}$, $\sigma = R : \emptyset \to U$ and $\Sigma = \{\sigma\}$. Given two algebra expressions $E_1, E_2 : S \to R$, consider

$$E = R \cup [E_1(S) - E_2(S)] \cup [E_2(S) - E_1(S)]$$

Then $\mathbf{R} : \Sigma \models E : \sigma$ iff $E_1 \equiv E_2$. This is undecidable by Corollary 6.3.2. ■

In contrast, we now present a decision procedure, based on the chase, for inferring view dependencies when the view is defined using the SPCU algebra.

THEOREM 10.2.6   It is decidable whether $\mathbf{R} : \Sigma \models E : \gamma$, if E is an SPCU query and $\Sigma \cup \{\gamma\}$ is a set of (tagged) full dependencies.

Crux   We prove the result for SPC queries that do not involve constants, and leave the extension to include union and constants for the reader (Exercise 10.12).

Let $E : \mathbf{R} \to S[V]$ be an SPC expression, where $S \notin \mathbf{R}$. Recall from Chapter 4 (Theorem 4.4.8; see also Exercise 4.18) that for each such expression E there is a tableau mapping $\tau_E = (\mathbf{T}, t)$ equivalent to E.

Assume now that Σ is a set of full dependencies and γ a full tgd. (The case where γ is an egd is left for the reader.) Let the tgd γ over S be expressed as the tableau (W, w). Create a new free instance $\mathbf{Z}$ out of $(\mathbf{T}, t)$ and W as follows: For each tuple $u \in W$, set $\mathbf{T}_u = \nu(\mathbf{T})$ where valuation ν maps t to u, and maps all other variables in $\mathbf{T}$ to new distinct variables. Set $\mathbf{Z} = \cup_{u \in W} \mathbf{T}_u$. It can now be verified that $\mathbf{R} : \Sigma \models E : \gamma$ iff $w \in E(chase(\mathbf{Z}, \Sigma))$. ■

In the case where $\Sigma \cup \{\gamma\}$ is a set of fd's and mvd's and the view is defined by an SPCU expression, testing the implication of a view dependency can be done in polynomial time, if jd's are involved the problem is NP-complete, and if full dependencies are considered the problem is EXPTIME-complete.

Recall from Section 8.4 that a *satisfaction family* is a family $sat(\mathbf{R}, \Sigma)$ for some set Σ of dependencies. Suppose now that SPC expression $E : R[U] \to S[V]$ is given, and that Σ is a set of full dependencies over R. Theorem 10.2.6, suitably generalized, shows that the family Γ of full dependencies implied by Σ for view E is recursive. This raises the natural question: Does $E(sat(R, \Sigma)) = sat(\Gamma)$, that is, does Γ completely characterize the image of $sat(R, \Sigma)$ under E? The affirmative answer to this question is stated next. This result follows from the proof of Theorem 10.2.6 (see Exercise 10.13).

THEOREM 10.2.7   If Σ is a set of full dependencies over $\mathbf{R}$ and $E : \mathbf{R} \to S$ is an SPC expression without constants, then there is a set Γ of full dependencies over S such that $E(sat(\mathbf{R}, \Sigma)) = sat(S, \Gamma)$.

Suppose now that $E : R[U] \to S[V]$ is given, and Σ is a *finite set* of dependencies. Can a *finite* set Γ be found such that $E(sat(R, \Sigma)) = sat(S, \Gamma)$? Even in the case where E is a simple projection and Σ is a set of fd's, the answer to this question is sometimes negative (Exercise 10.11c).

Chasing with Embedded Dependencies

We now turn to the case of (embedded) dependencies. From Theorem 10.1.2(b), it is apparent that we cannot hope to generalize Theorem 10.2.2 to obtain a decision procedure for (finite or unrestricted) implication of dependencies. As initially discussed in Chapter 9, the chase need not terminate if dependencies are used. All is not lost, however, because we are able to use the chase to obtain a proof procedure for testing unrestricted implication of a dependency by a set of dependencies.

For nonfull tgd's, we shall use the following rule. We present the rule as it applies to tableaux, but it can also be used on dependencies.

tgd rule: Let T be a tableau, and let $\sigma = (S, S')$ be a tgd. Suppose that there is a valuation θ for S that embeds S into T, but no extension θ' to $var(S) \cup var(S')$ of θ such that $\theta'(S') \subseteq T$. In this case σ can be *applied* to T.

   Let $\theta_1, \ldots, \theta_n$ be a list of all valuations having this property. For each $i \in [1, n]$, (nondeterministically) choose a *distinct extension*, i.e., an extension θ'_i to $var(S) \cup var(S')$ of θ_i such that each variable in $var(S') - var(S)$ is assigned a distinct new variable greater than all variables in T. (The same variable is not chosen in two extensions $\theta'_i, \theta'_j, i \neq j$.)

   The *result of applying* σ to T is $T \cup \{\theta'_i(S') \mid i \in [1, n]\}$.

This rule is nondeterministic because variables not occurring in T are chosen for the existentially quantified variables of σ. We assume that some fixed mechanism is used for selecting these variables when given T, (S, S'), and θ.

   The notion of a chasing sequence $T = T_1, T_2, \ldots$ of a tableau (or dependency) by a set of dependencies is now defined in the obvious manner. Clearly, this sequence may be infinite.

EXAMPLE 10.2.8   Let $\Sigma = \{\tau_1, \tau_2, \tau_3\}$, where

	A	B	C	D
T	w	x		
	w		y	
t		x	y	

$$\tau_1$$

	A	B	C	D
T'	w		y	z
		x	y	
t'	w	x		z

$$\tau_2$$

	A	B	C	D
T''		x		z
		x		z'
		$z = z'$		

$$\tau_3$$

A	B	C	D	
x_1	x_2	x_3	x_4	
x_1	x_5	x_6	x_7	
x_{10}	x_2	x_6	x_{12}	application
x_{11}	x_5	x_3	x_{13}	of τ_1

(a)

A	B	C	D	
x_1	x_2	x_3	x_4	
x_1	x_5	x_6	x_7	
x_{10}	x_2	x_6	x_4	application
x_{11}	x_5	x_3	x_7	of τ_3

(b)

A	B	C	D	
x_1	x_2	x_3	x_4	
x_1	x_5	x_6	x_7	
x_{10}	x_2	x_6	x_4	
x_{11}	x_5	x_3	x_7	
x_1	x_5	x_{20}	x_4	
x_{11}	x_2	x_{21}	x_7	
x_1	x_2	x_{22}	x_7	application
x_{10}	x_5	x_{23}	x_4	of τ_2

(c)

A	B	C	D	
x_1	x_2	x_3	x_4	
x_1	x_5	x_6	x_4	
x_{10}	x_2	x_6	x_4	
x_{11}	x_5	x_3	x_4	
x_1	x_5	x_{20}	x_4	
x_{11}	x_2	x_{21}	x_4	
x_1	x_2	x_{22}	x_4	application
x_{10}	x_5	x_{23}	x_4	of τ_3

(d)

Figure 10.3: Parts of a chasing sequence

We show here only the relevant variables of τ_1, τ_2, and τ_3; all other variables are assumed to be distinct. Here $\tau_3 \equiv B \rightarrow D$.

In Fig. 10.3, we show some stages of a chasing sequence that demonstrates that $\Sigma \models_{unr} A \rightarrow D$. To do that, the chase begins with the tableau $\{\langle x_1, x_2, x_3, x_4 \rangle, \langle x_1, x_5, x_6, x_7 \rangle\}$. Figure 10.3 shows the results of applying τ_1, τ_3, τ_2, τ_3 in turn (left to right). This sequence implies that $\Sigma \models_{unr} A \rightarrow D$, because variables x_4 and x_7 are identified.

Consider now the typed tgd's:

	A	B	C	D
T'''	w	x		z
	w		y	
t''		x	y	z

τ_4

	A	B	C	D
T''''	w	x		
	w		y	
t'''	w	x	y	

τ_5

The chasing sequence of Fig. 10.3 also implies that $\Sigma \models_{\text{unr}} \tau_4$, because (x_{10}, x_2, x_6, x_4) is in the second tableau. On the other hand, we now argue that $\Sigma \not\models_{\text{unr}} \tau_5$. Consider the chasing sequence beginning as the one shown in Fig. 10.3, and continuing by applying the sequence $\tau_1, \tau_3, \tau_2, \tau_3$ repeatedly. It can be shown that this chasing sequence will not terminate and that (x_1, x_2, x_6, v) does not occur in the resulting infinite sequence for any variable v (see Exercise 10.16). It follows that $\Sigma \not\models_{\text{unr}} \tau_5$; in particular, the infinite result of the chasing sequence is a counterexample to this implication. On the other hand, this chasing sequence does not alone provide any information about whether $\Sigma \models_{\text{fin}} \tau_5$. It can be shown that this also fails.

To ensure that all relevant dependencies have a chance to influence a chasing sequence, we focus on chasing sequences that satisfy the following conditions:

(1) Whenever an egd is applied, it is applied repeatedly until it is no longer applicable.

(2) No dependency is "starved" (i.e., each dependency that is applicable infinitely often is applied infinitely often).

Even if these conditions are satisfied, it is possible to have two chasing sequences of a tableau T by typed dependencies, where one is finite and the other infinite (see Exercise 10.14).

Now consider an infinite chasing sequence $T_1 = T, T_2, \ldots$. Let us denote it by $\overline{T, \Sigma}$. Because egd's may be applied arbitrarily late in $\overline{T, \Sigma}$, for each n, tuples of T_n may be modified as the result of later applications of egd's. Thus we cannot simply take the union of some tail $T_n, T_{n+1}, \ldots$ to obtain the result of the chase. As an alternative, for the chasing sequence $\overline{T, \Sigma} = T_1, T_2, \ldots$, we define

$$chase(\overline{T, \Sigma}) = \{u \mid \exists n \; \forall m > n (u \in T_m)\}.$$

This is nonempty because (1) the "new" variables introduced by the tgd rule are always greater than variables already present; and (2) when the egd rule is applied, the newer variable is replaced by the older one.

By generalizing the techniques developed, it is easily seen that the (possibly infinite) resulting tableau satisfies all dependencies in Σ. More generally, let Σ be a set of dependencies and σ a dependency. Then one can show that $\Sigma \models_{\text{unr}} \sigma$ iff for some chasing sequence $\overline{\sigma, \Sigma}$ of σ using Σ, $chase(\overline{\sigma, \Sigma})$ is trivial. Furthermore, it can be shown that

- if for some chasing sequence $\overline{\sigma, \Sigma}$ of σ using Σ, $chase(\overline{\sigma, \Sigma})$ is trivial, then it is so for *all* chasing sequences of σ using Σ; and

- for each chasing sequence $\overline{\sigma, \Sigma} = T_1, \ldots, T_n, \ldots$ of σ using Σ, $chase(\overline{\sigma, \Sigma})$ is trivial iff T_i is trivial for some i.

This shows that, for practical purposes, it suffices to generate some chasing sequence of σ using Σ and stop as soon as some tableau in the sequence becomes trivial.

10.3 Axiomatization

A variety of axiomatizations have been developed for the family of dependencies and for subclasses such as the full typed tgd's. In view of Theorem 10.1.2, sound and complete recursively enumerable axiomatizations do not exist for finite implication of dependencies. This section presents an axiomatization for the family of full typed tgd's and typed egd's (which is sound and complete for both finite and unrestricted implication). A generalization to the embedded case (for unrestricted implication) has also been developed (see Exercise 10.21). The axiomatization presented here is closely related to the chase. In the next section, a very different kind of axiomatization for typed dependencies is discussed.

We now focus on the full typed dependencies (i.e., on typed egd's and full typed tgd's). The development begins with the introduction of a technical tool for forming the composition of tableaux queries. The axiomatization then follows.

Composition of Typed Tableaux

Suppose that $\tau = (T, t)$ and $\sigma = (S, s)$ are two full typed tableau queries over relation schema R. It is natural to ask whether there is a tableau query $\tau \bullet \sigma$ corresponding to the composition of τ followed by σ—that is, with the property that for each instance I over R,

$$(\tau \bullet \sigma)(I) = \sigma(\tau(I))$$

and, if so, whether there is a simple way to construct it. We now provide an affirmative answer to both questions. The syntactic composition of full typed tableau mappings will be a valuable tool for combining pairs of full typed tgd's in the axiomatization presented shortly.

Let $T = \{t_1, \ldots, t_n\}$ and $S = \{s_1, \ldots, s_m\}$. Suppose that tuple w is in $\sigma(\tau(I))$. Then there is an embedding ν of $s_1, \ldots, s_m$ into $\tau(I)$ such that $\nu(s) = w$. It follows that for each $j \in [1, m]$ there is an embedding μ_j of T into I, with $\mu_j(t) = \nu(s_j)$. This suggests that the tableau of $\tau \bullet \sigma$ should have mn tuples, with a block of n tuples for each s_j.

To be more precise, for each $j \in [1, m]$, let T_{s_j} be $\theta_j(T)$, where θ_j is a substitution that maps $t(A)$ to $s_j(A)$ for each attribute A of R and maps each other variable of T to a new, distinct variable not used elsewhere in the construction. Now set

$$[S](T, t) \equiv \cup \{T_{s_j} \mid j \in [1, m]\} \quad \text{and} \quad \tau \bullet \sigma \equiv ([S](T, t), s).$$

The following is now easily verified (see Exercise 10.18):

PROPOSITION 10.3.1 For full typed tableau queries τ and σ over R, and for each instance I of R, $\tau \bullet \sigma(I) = \sigma(\tau(I))$.

EXAMPLE 10.3.2 The following table shows two full typed tableau queries and their composition.

	A	B	C
T	x	y	z'
	x	y'	z
	x	y'	z''
t	w	x	y

	A	B	C
S	u	v	w'
	u'	v	w
s	u	v	w

	A	B	C
	u	v	p_1
	u	p_2	w'
	u	p_2	p_3
	u'	v	p_4
	u'	p_5	w
	u'	p_5	p_6
	u	v	w

$$\tau \qquad\qquad \sigma \qquad\qquad \tau \bullet \sigma$$

It is straightforward to verify that the syntactic operation of composition is associative.

Suppose that τ and σ are full typed tableau queries. It can be shown by simple chasing arguments that $\{\tau, \sigma\}$ and $\{\tau \bullet \sigma\}$ are equivalent as sets of dependencies. It follows that full typed tgd's are closed under finite conjunction, in the sense that each finite set of full typed tgd's over a relation schema R is equivalent to a single full typed tgd. This property does not hold in the embedded case (see Exercise 10.20).

An Axiomatization for Full Typed Dependencies

For full typed tgd's, $\tau = (T, t)$ and $\sigma = (S, s)$, we say that τ *embeds into* σ denoted $\tau \hookrightarrow \sigma$, if there is a substitution ν such that $\nu(T) \subseteq S$ and $\nu(t) = s$. Recall from Chapter 4 that $\tau \supseteq \sigma$ (considered as tableau queries) iff $\tau \hookrightarrow \sigma$. As a result we have that if $\tau \hookrightarrow \sigma$, then $\tau \models \sigma$, although the converse does not necessarily hold. Analogously, for A-egd's $\tau = (T, x = y)$ and $\sigma = (S, v = w)$, we define $\tau \hookrightarrow \sigma$ if there is a substitution ν such that $\nu(T) \subseteq S$, and $\nu(\{x, y\}) = \{v, w\}$. Again, if $\tau \hookrightarrow \sigma$, then $\tau \models \sigma$.

We now list the axioms for full typed tgd's:

FTtgd1: (triviality) For each free tuple t without constants, $(\{t\}, t)$.

FTtgd2: (embedding) If τ and $\tau \hookrightarrow \sigma$, then σ.

FTtgd3: (composition) If τ and σ, then $\tau \bullet \sigma$.

The following rules focus exclusively on typed egd's:

Tegd1: (triviality) If $x \in var(T)$, then $(T, x = x)$.

Tegd2: (embedding) If τ and $\tau \hookrightarrow \sigma$, then σ.

The final rules combining egd's and full typed tgd's use the following notation. Let $R[U]$ be a relation schema. For $A \in U$, $\overline{A}$ denotes $U - \{A\}$. Given typed A-egd $\tau = (T, x = y)$ over R, define free tuples u_x, u_y such that $u_x(A) = x$, $u_y(A) = y$ and $u_x[\overline{A}] = u_y[\overline{A}]$ consists of distinct variables not occurring in T. Define two full typed tgd's $\tau_x = (T \cup \{u_y\}, u_x)$ and $\tau_y = (T \cup \{u_x\}, u_y)$.

FTD1: (conversion) If $\tau = (T, x = y)$, then τ_x and τ_y.

FTD2: (composition) If (T, t) and $(S, x = y)$, then $([S](T, t), x = y)$.

We now have the following:

THEOREM 10.3.3 The set {FTtgd1, FTtgd2, FTtgd3, Tegd1, Tegd2, FTD1, FTD2} is sound and complete for (finite and unrestricted) logical implication of full typed dependencies.

Crux   Soundness is easily verified. We illustrate completeness by showing that the FTtgd rules are complete for tgd's. Suppose that $\Sigma \models \tau = (T, t)$, where Σ is a set of full typed tgd's and (T, t) is full and typed. By Theorem 10.2.2 there is a chasing sequence of T by Σ yielding T' with $t \in T'$. Let $\sigma_1, \ldots, \sigma_n$ $(n \geq 0)$ be the sequence of elements of Σ used in the chasing sequence. It follows that $t \in \sigma_n(\ldots (\sigma_1(T)) \ldots)$, and by Proposition 10.3.1, $t \in (\sigma_1 \bullet \cdots \bullet \sigma_n)(T)$. This implies that $(\sigma_1 \bullet \cdots \bullet \sigma_n) \hookrightarrow (T, t)$. A proof of τ from Σ is now obtained by starting with σ_1 (or $(\{s\}, s)$ if $n = 0$), followed by $n - 1$ applications of FTtgd3 and one application of FTtgd2 (see Exercise (10.18b). ∎

The preceding techniques and the chase can be used to develop an axiomatization of unrestricted implication for the family of all typed dependencies.

10.4   An Algebraic Perspective

This section develops a very different paradigm for specifying dependencies based on the use of algebraic expressions. Surprisingly, the class of dependencies formed is equivalent to the class of typed dependencies. We also present an axiomatization that is rooted primarily in algebraic properties rather than chasing and tableau manipulations.

We begin with examples that motivate and illustrate this approach.

EXAMPLE 10.4.1   Let $R[ABCD]$ be a relation schema. Consider the tgd τ of Fig. 10.4 and the algebraic expression

$$\pi_{AC}(\pi_{AB}(R) \bowtie \pi_{BC}(R)) \subseteq \pi_{AC}(R).$$

It is straightforward to verify that for each instance I over $ABCD$,

$$I \models \tau \text{ iff } \pi_{AC}(\pi_{AB}(I) \bowtie \pi_{BC}(I)) \subseteq \pi_{AC}(I).$$

Now consider dependency σ. One can similarly verify that for each instance I over $ABCD$,

$$I \models \sigma \text{ iff } \pi_{AC}(\pi_{AB}(I) \bowtie \pi_{BC}(I)) \subseteq \pi_{AC}(\pi_{AD}(I) \bowtie \pi_{CD}(I)).$$

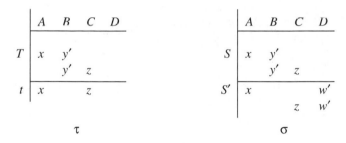

Figure 10.4:   Dependencies of Example 10.4.1

The observation of this example can be generalized in the following way. A *project-join* (PJ) expression is an algebraic expression over a single relation schema using only projection and natural join. We describe next a natural recursive algorithm for translating PJ expressions into tableau queries (see Exercise 10.23). (This algorithm is also implicit in the equivalence proofs of Chapter 4.)

ALGORITHM 10.4.2

Input: a PJ expression E over relation schema $R[A_1, \ldots, A_n]$

Output: a tableau query (T, t) equivalent to E

Basis: If E is simply R, then return $(\{\langle x_1, \ldots, x_n \rangle\}, \langle x_1, \ldots, x_n \rangle)$.

Inductive steps:

      1. If E is $\pi_X(q)$ and the tableau query of q is (T, t), then return $(T, \pi_X(t))$.

      2. Suppose E is $q_1 \bowtie q_2$ and the tableau query of q_i is (T_i, t_i) for $i \in [1, 2]$.

            Let X be the intersection of the output sorts of q_1 and q_2. Assume without loss of generality that the two tableaux use distinct variables except that $t_1(A) = t_2(A)$ for $A \in X$. Then return $(T_1 \cup T_2, t_1 \bowtie t_2)$.

Suppose now that (T, T') is a typed dependency with the property that for some free tuple t, (T, t) is the tableau associated by this algorithm with PJ expression E, and (T', t) is the tableau associated with PJ expression E'. Suppose also that the only variables common to T and T' are those in t. Then for each instance I, $I \models (T, T')$ iff $E(I) \subseteq E'(I)$.

This raises three natural questions: (1) Is the family of PJ inclusions equivalent to the set of typed tgd's? (2) If not, can this paradigm be extended to capture all typed tgd's? (3) Can this paradigm be extended to capture typed egd's as well as tgd's?

The answer to the first question is no (see Exercise 10.24).

The answer to the second and third questions is yes. This relies on the notion of *extended relations* and *extended project-join expressions*. Let $R[A_1, \ldots, A_n]$ be a relation schema. For each $i \in [1, n]$, we suppose that there is an infinite set of attributes $A_i^1, A_i^2, \ldots$, called *copies* of A_i. The *extended schema* of R is the schema $\overline{R}[A_1^1, \ldots, A_n^1, A_1^2, \ldots, A_n^2, \ldots]$. For an instance I of R, the *extended instance* of $\overline{R}$ corresponding to I, denoted $\overline{I}$, has one "tuple" $\overline{u}$ for each tuple $u \in I$, where $\overline{u}(A_i^j) = u(A_i)$ for each $i \in [1, n]$ and $j > 0$.

	A	B	C	D
T	x		z	w'
			z'	w'
	x'		z'	w
T'	x	y'		
		y'	z	w

$$\tau$$

	A	B	C	D
T	x		z	w'
			z'	w'
	x'		z'	w
	$x = x'$			

$$\sigma$$

Figure 10.5:   tgd and egd of Example 10.4.3

An *extended project-join expression* over R is a PJ expression over $\overline{R}$ such that a projection operator is applied first to each occurrence of $\overline{R}$. (This ensures that the evaluation and the result of such expressions involve only finite objects.) Given two extended PJ expressions E and E' with the same target sort, and instance I over R, $E(I) \subseteq_e E'(I)$ denotes $E(\overline{I}) \subseteq E'(\overline{I})$.

An *algebraic dependency* is a syntactic expression of the form $E \subseteq_e E'$, where E and E' are extended PJ expressions over a relation schema R with the same target sort. An instance I over R *satisfies* $E \subseteq_e E'$ if $E(I) \subseteq_e E'(I)$—that is, if $E(\overline{I}) \subseteq E'(\overline{I})$.

This is illustrated next.

EXAMPLE 10.4.3   Consider the dependency τ of Fig. 10.5. Let

$$E = \pi_{ACD^1}(\overline{R}) \bowtie \pi_{C^1D^1}(\overline{R}) \bowtie \pi_{A^1C^1D}(\overline{R}).$$

Here we use $A, A^1, \dots$ to denote different copies the attribute A, etc.

It can be shown that, for each instance I over $ABCD$, $I \models \tau$ iff $E_1(\overline{I}) \subseteq_e E_2(\overline{I})$, where

$$E_1 = \pi_{ACD}(E)$$
$$E_2 = \pi_{ACD}(\pi_{AB^1}(\overline{R}) \bowtie \pi_{B^1CD}(\overline{R})).$$

(See Exercise 10.25).

Consider now the functional dependency $A \to BC$ over $ABCD$. This is equivalent to $\pi_{ABC}(\overline{R}) \bowtie \pi_{AB^1C^1}(\overline{R}) \subseteq_e \pi_{ABCB^1C^1}(\overline{R})$.

Finally, consider σ of Fig. 10.5. This is equivalent to $F_1 \subseteq_e F_2$, where

$$F_1 = \pi_{AA^1}(E)$$
$$F_2 = \pi_{AA^1}(\overline{R}).$$

We next see that algebraic dependencies correspond precisely to typed dependencies.

THEOREM 10.4.4   For each algebraic dependency, there is an equivalent typed dependency, and for each typed dependency, there is an equivalent algebraic dependency.

Crux   Let $R[A_1, \ldots, A_n]$ be a relation schema, and let $E \subseteq_e E'$ be an algebraic dependency over R, where E and E' have target sort X. Without loss of generality, we can assume that there is k such that the sets of attributes involved in E and E' are contained in $\widehat{U} = \{A_1^1, \ldots, A_n^1, \ldots, A_1^k, \ldots, A_n^k\}$. Using Algorithm 10.4.2, construct tableau queries $\tau = (T, t)$ and $\tau' = (T', t')$ over $\widehat{U}$ corresponding to E and E'. We assume without loss of generality that τ and τ' do not share any variables except that $t(A) = t'(A)$ for each $A \in X$.

Consider T (over $\widehat{U}$). For each tuple $s \in T$ and $j \in [1, k]$,

- construct an atom $R(x_1, \ldots, x_n)$, where $x_i = s(A_i^j)$ for each $i \in [1, n]$;
- construct atoms $s(A_i^j) = s(A_i^{j'})$ for each $i \in [1, n]$ and j, j' satisfying $1 \le j < j' \le k$.

Let $\varphi(x_1, \ldots, x_p)$ be the conjunction of all atoms obtained from τ in this manner. Let $\psi(y_1, \ldots, y_q)$ be constructed analogously from τ'. It can now be shown (Exercise 10.26) that $E \subseteq_e E'$ is equivalent to the typed dependency

$$\forall x_1 \ldots x_p(\varphi(x_1, \ldots, x_p) \to \exists z_1 \ldots z_r \psi(y_1, \ldots, y_q)),$$

where $z_1, \ldots, z_r$ is the set of variables in $\{y_1, \ldots, y_q\} - \{x_1, \ldots, x_p\}$.

For the converse, we generalize the technique used in Example 10.4.3. For each attribute A, one distinct copy of A is used for each variable occurring in the A column. ∎

An Axiomatization for Algebraic Dependencies

Figure 10.6 shows a family of inference rules for algebraic dependencies. Each of these rules stems from an algebraic property of join and project, and only the last explicitly uses a property of extended instances. (It is assumed here that all expressions are well formed.)

The use of these rules to infer dependencies is considered in Exercises 10.31, and 10.32.

It can be shown that:

THEOREM 10.4.5   The family $\{AD1, \ldots, AD8\}$ is sound and complete for inferring unrestricted implication of algebraic dependencies.

To conclude this discussion of the algebraic perspective on dependencies, we consider a new operation, direct product, and the important notion of faithfulness.

AD1: (Idempotency of Projection)
    (a) $\pi_X(\pi_Y E) =_e \pi_X E$
    (b) $\pi_{sort(E)} E =_e E$

AD2: (Idempotency of Join)
    (a) $E \bowtie \pi_X E =_e E$
    (b) $\pi_{sort(E)}(E \bowtie E') \subseteq_e E$

AD3: (Monotonicity of Projection)
    If $E \subseteq_e E'$ then $\pi_X E \subseteq_e \pi_X E'$

AD4: (Monotonicity of Join)
    If $E \subseteq_e E'$, then $E \bowtie E'' \subseteq_e E' \bowtie E''$

AD5: (Commutativity of Join)
    $E \bowtie E' =_e E' \bowtie E$

AD6: (Associativity of Join)
    $(E \bowtie E') \bowtie E'' =_e E \bowtie (E' \bowtie E'')$

AD7: (Distributivity of Projection over Join)
    Suppose that $X \subseteq sort(E)$ and $Y \subseteq sort(E')$. Then
    (a) $\pi_{X \cup Y}(E \bowtie E') \subseteq_e \pi_{X \cup Y}(E \bowtie \pi_Y E')$.
    (b) If $sort(E) \cap sort(E') \subseteq Y$, then equality holds in (a).

AD8: (Extension)
    If $X \subseteq sort(\overline{R})$ and A, A' are copies of the same attribute, then
    $\pi_{AA'}\overline{R} \bowtie \pi_{AX}\overline{R} =_e \pi_{AA'X}\overline{R}$.

Figure 10.6: Algebraic dependency axioms

Faithfulness and Armstrong Relations

We show now that sets of typed dependencies have Armstrong relations,[1] although these may sometimes be infinite. To accomplish this, we first introduce a new way to combine instances and an important property of it.

Let R be a relation schema of arity n. We blur our notation and use elements of **dom** $\times$ **dom** as if they were elements of **dom**. Given tuples $u = \langle x_1, \ldots, x_n \rangle$ and $v = \langle y_1, \ldots, y_n \rangle$, we define the *direct product* of u and v to be

$$u \otimes v = \langle (x_1, y_1), \ldots, (x_n, y_n) \rangle.$$

The *direct product* of two instances I, J over R is

$$I \otimes J = \{u \otimes v \mid u \in I, v \in J\}.$$

This is generalized to form k-ary direct product instances for each finite k. Furthermore, if $\mathcal{J}$ is a (finite or infinite) index set and $\{I_j \mid j \in \mathcal{J}\}$ is a family of instances over R, then $\otimes\{I_j \mid j \in \mathcal{J}\}$ denotes the (possibly infinite) direct product of this family of instances.

---

[1] Recall that given a set Σ of dependencies over some schema R, an Armstrong relation for Σ is an instance I over R that satisfies Σ and violates every dependency not implied by Σ.

A dependency σ is *faithful* if for each family $\{I_j \mid j \in \mathcal{J}\}$ of nonempty instances,

$$\otimes\{I_j \mid j \in \mathcal{J}\} \models \sigma \text{ if and only if } \forall j \in \mathcal{J}, I_j \models \sigma.$$

(The restriction that the instances be nonempty is important—if this were omitted then no nontrivial dependency would be faithful.)

The following holds because the $\otimes$ operator commutes with project, join, and "extension" (see Exercise 10.29).

PROPOSITION 10.4.6 The family of typed dependencies is faithful.

We can now prove that each set of typed dependencies has an Armstrong relation.

THEOREM 10.4.7 Let Σ be a set of typed dependencies over relation R. Then there is a (possibly infinite) instance I_Σ such that for each typed dependency σ over R, $I_\Sigma \models \sigma$ iff $\Sigma \models_{\text{unr}} \sigma$.

Proof Let Γ be the set of typed dependencies over R not in Σ^*. For each $\gamma \in \Gamma$, let I_γ be a nonempty instance that satisfies Σ but not γ. Then $\otimes\{I_\gamma \mid \gamma \in \Gamma\}$ is the desired relation. ∎

This result cannot be strengthened to yield finite Armstrong relations because one can exhibit a finite set of typed tgd's with no finite Armstrong relation.

Bibliographic Notes

The papers [FV86, Kan91, Var87] all provide excellent surveys on the motivations and history of research into relational dependencies; these have greatly influenced our treatment of the subject here.

Because readers could be overwhelmed by the great number of dependency theory terms we have used a subset of the terminology. For instance, the typed single-head tgd's (that were studied in depth) are called *template* dependencies. In addition, the typed unirelational dependencies that are considered here were historically called *embedded implicational dependencies* (eid's); and their full counterparts were called *implicational dependencies* (id's). We use this terminology in the following notes.

After the introduction of fd's and mvd's, there was a flurry of research into special classes of dependencies, including jd's and ind's. *Embedded* dependencies were first introduced in [Fag77b], which defined embedded multivalued dependencies (emvd's); these are mvd's that hold in a projection of a relation. Embedded jd's are defined in the analogous fashion. This is distinct from *projected* jd's [MUV84]—these are template dependencies that correspond to join dependencies, except that some of the variables in the summary row may be distinct variables not occurring elsewhere in the dependency. Several other specialized dependencies were introduced. These include *subset dependencies* [SW82], which generalize mvd's; *mutual dependencies* [Nic78], which say that a relation is a 3-ary join;

generalized mutual dependencies [MM79]; *transitive dependencies* [Par79], which generalize fd's and mvd's; *extended transitive dependencies* [PPG80], which generalize mutual dependencies and transitive dependencies; and *implied dependencies* [GZ82], which form a specialized class of egd's. In many cases these classes of dependencies were introduced in attempts to provide axiomatizations for the emvd's, jd's, or superclasses of them. Although most of the theoretical work studies dependencies in an abstract setting, [Sci81, Sci83] study families of mvd's and ind's as they arise in practical situations.

The proliferation of dependencies spawned interest in the development of a unifying framework that subsumed essentially all of them. Nicolas [Nic78] is credited with first observing that fd's, mvd's, and others have a natural representation in first-order logic. At roughly the same time, several researchers reached essentially the same generalized class of dependencies that was studied in this chapter. [BV81a] introduced the class of tgd's and egd's, defined using the paradigm of tableaux. Chasing was studied in connection with both full and embedded dependencies in [BV84c]. Reference [Fag82b] introduced the class of typed dependencies, essentially the same family of dependencies but presented in the paradigm of first-order logic. Simultaneously, [YP82] introduced the algebraic dependencies, which present the same class in algebraic terms. A generalization of algebraic dependencies to the untyped case is presented in [Abi83].

Related general classes of dependencies introduced at this time are the *general dependencies* [PJ81], which are equivalent to the full typed tgd's, and *generalized dependency constraints* [GJ82], which are the full dependencies.

Importantly, several kinds of constraints that lie outside the dependencies described in this chapter have been studied in the literature. Research on the use of arbitrary first-order logic sentences as constraints includes [GM78, Nic78, Var82b]. A different extension of dependencies based on partitioning relationships, which are not expressible in first-order logic, is studied in [Cos87]. Another kind of dependency is the *afunctional dependency* of [BP83], which, as the name suggests, focuses on the portions of an instance that violate an fd. The *partition dependencies* [CK86] are not first-order expressible and are powerful; interestingly, finite and unrestricted implication coincide for this class of dependencies and are decidable in PTIME. *Order* [GH83] and *sort-set dependencies* [GH86] address properties of instances defined in terms of orderings on the underlying domain elements. There is provably no finite axiomatization for order dependencies, or for sort-set dependencies and fd's considered together (Exercise 9.8).

Another broad class of constraints not included in the dependencies discussed in this chapter is *dynamic* constraints, which focus on how data change over time [CF84, Su92, Via87, Via88]; see Section 22.6.

As suggested by the development of this chapter, one of the most significant theoretical directions addressed in connection with dependencies has been the issue of decidability of implication. The separation of finite and unrestricted implication, and the undecidability of the implication problem, were shown independently for typed dependencies in [BV81a, CLM81]. Subsequently, these results were independently strengthened to projected jd's in [GL82, Var84, YP82]. Then, after nearly a decade had elapsed, this result was strengthened to include emvd's [Her92].

On the other hand, the equivalence of finite and unrestricted implication for full dependencies was observed in [BV81a]. That deciding implication for full typed dependen-

makes one schema better than another? This is captured by the notion of "normal form" for relational schemas, a central notion in design theory.

Both of these approaches focus on the transformation of a schema $\mathbf{S}_1$ into a relational schema $\mathbf{S}_2$. Speaking in broad terms, three criteria are used to evaluate the result of this transformation:

(1) Preservation of data;

(2) Desirable properties of $\mathbf{S}_2$, typically described using normal forms; and

(3) Preservation of "meta-data" (i.e., information captured by schema and dependencies).

Condition (1) requires that information not be lost when instances of $\mathbf{S}_1$ are represented in $\mathbf{S}_2$. This is usually formalized by requiring that there be a "natural" mapping $\tau : Inst(\mathbf{S}_1) \to Inst(\mathbf{S}_2)$ that is one-to-one. As we shall see, the notion of "natural" can vary, depending on the data model used for $\mathbf{S}_1$.

Criterion (2) has been the focus of considerable research, especially in connection with the approach based on refining relational schemas. In this context, the notion of relational schema is generalized to incorporate dependencies, as follows: A *relation schema* is a pair (R, Σ), where R is a relation name and Σ is a set of dependencies over R. Similarly, a *database schema* is a pair $(\mathbf{R}, \Sigma)$, where $\mathbf{R}$ is a database schema as before, and Σ is a set of dependencies over $\mathbf{R}$. Some of these may be *tagged* by a single relation (i.e., have the form $R_j : \sigma$, where σ is a dependency over $R_j \in \mathbf{R}$). Others, such as ind's, may involve pairs of relations. More generally, some dependencies might range over the full set of attributes occurring in $\mathbf{R}$. (This requires a generalization of the notion of dependency satisfaction, which is discussed in Section 11.3.)

With this notation established, we return to criterion (2). In determining whether one relational schema is better than another, the main factors that have been considered are redundancy in the representation of data and update anomalies. Recall that these were illustrated in Section 8.1, using the relations *Movies* and *Showings*. We concluded there that certain schemas yielded undesirable behavior. This resulted from the nature of the information contained in the database, as specified by a set of dependencies.

Although the dependencies are in some sense the cause of the problems, they also suggest ways to eliminate them. For example, the fd

$$Movies: Title \to Director$$

suggests that the attribute *Director* is a characteristic of *Title*, so the two attributes belong together and can safely be represented in isolation from the other data. It should be clear that one always needs some form of semantic information to guide schema design; in the absence of such information, one cannot distinguish "good" schemas from "bad" ones (except for trivial cases). As will be seen, the notion of normal form captures some characteristics of "good" schemas by guaranteeing that certain kinds of redundancies and update anomalies will not occur. It will also be seen that the semantic data model approach to schema design can lead to relational schemas in normal form.

In broad terms, the intuition behind criterion (3) is that properties of data captured by schema S_1 (e.g., functional or inclusion relationships) should also be captured by schema S_2. In the context of refining relational schemas, a precise meaning will be given for this criterion in terms of "preservation" of dependencies. We shall see that there is a kind of trade-off between criteria (2) and (3).

The approach of refining relational schemas typically makes a simplifying assumption called the "pure universal relation assumption" (pure URA). Intuitively, this states that the input schema S_1 consists of a single relation schema, possibly with some dependencies. Section 11.3 briefly considers this assumption in a more general light. In addition, the "weak" URA is introduced, and the notions of dependency satisfaction and query interpretation are extended to this context.

This chapter is more in the form of a survey than the previous chapters, for several reasons. As noted earlier, more broad-based treatments of relational schema design may be found elsewhere and require a variety of tools complementary to formal analysis. The tools presented here can at best provide only part of the skeleton of a design methodology for relational schemas. Normal forms and the universal relation assumption were active research topics in the 1970s and early 1980s and generated a large body of results. Some of that work is now considered somewhat unfashionable, primarily due to the emergence of new data models. However, we mention these topics briefly because (1) they lead to interesting theoretical issues, and (2) we are never secure from a change of fashion.

11.1 Semantic Data Models

In this section we introduce semantic data models and describe how they are used in relational database design. Semantic data models provide a framework for specifying database schemas that is considerably richer than the relational model. In particular, semantic models are arguably closer than the relational model to ways that humans organize information in their own thinking. The semantic data models are precursors of the recently emerging *object-oriented database models* (presented in a more formal fashion in Chapter 21) and are thus of interest in their own right.

As a vehicle for our discussion, we present a semantic data model, called loosely the *generic semantic model* (GSM). (This is essentially a subset of the IFO model, one of the first semantic models defined in a formal fashion.) We then illustrate how schemas from this model can be translated into relational schemas. Our primary intention is to present the basic flavor of the semantic data model approach to relational schema design and some formal results that can be obtained. The presentation itself is somewhat informal so that the notation does not become overly burdensome.

In many practical contexts, the semantic model used is the *Entity-Relationship model* (ER model) or one of its many variants. The ER model is arguably the first semantic data model that appeared in the literature. We use the GSM because it incorporates several features of the semantic modeling literature not present in the ER model, and because the GSM presents a style closer to object-oriented database models.

GSM Schemas

Figure 11.1 shows the schema **CINEMA-SEM** from the GSM, which can be used to represent information on movies and theaters. The major building blocks of such schemas are abstract classes, attributes, complex value classes, and the ISA hierarchy; these will be considered briefly in turn.

The schema of Fig. 11.1 shows five classes that hold *abstract* objects: *Person*, *Director*, *Actor*, *Movie*, and *Theater*. These correspond to collections of similar objects in the world. There are two kinds of abstract class: *primary* classes, shown using diamonds, and *subclasses* shown using circles. This distinction will be clarified further when ISA relationships are discussed.

Instances of semantic schemas are constructed from the usual *printable* classes (e.g., **string**, **integer**, **float**, etc.) and "abstract" classes. The printable classes correspond to (subsets of) the domain **dom** used in the relational model. The printable classes are indicated using squares; in Fig. 11.1 we have labeled these to indicate the kind of values that populate them. Conceptually, the elements of an abstract class such as *Person* are actual persons in the world; in the formal model internal representations for persons are used. These internal representations have come to be known as *object identifiers* (OIDs). Because they are internal, it is usually assumed that OIDs cannot be presented explicitly to users, although programming and query languages can use variables that hold OIDs. The notion of instance will be defined more completely later and is illustrated in Example 11.1.1 and Fig. 11.2.

Attributes provide one mechanism for representing relationships between objects and other objects or printable values; they are drawn using arrows. For example, the *Person* class has attributes *name* and *citizenship*, which associate strings with each person object. These are examples of *single-valued* attributes. (In this schema, all attributes are assumed to be total.) *Multivalued* attributes are also allowed; these map each object to a set of objects or printable values and are denoted using arrows with double heads. For example, *acts_in* maps actors to the movies that they have acted in. It is common to permit *inverse* constraints between pairs of attributes. For example, consider the relationship between actors and movies. It can be represented using the multivalued attribute *acts_in* on *Actor* or the multivalued attribute *actors* on *Movie*. In this schema, we assume that the attributes *acts_in* and *actors* are constrained to be inverses of each other, in the sense that $m \in acts\_in(a)$ iff $a \in actor(m)$. A similar constraint is assumed between the attributes associating movies with directors.

In the schema **CINEMA-SEM**, the *Pariscope* node is an example of a *complex value class*. Members of the underlying class are triples whose coordinates are from the classes *Theater*, Time, and *Movie*, respectively. In the GSM, each complex value is the result of one application of the tuple construct. This is indicated using a node of the form $\otimes$, with components indicated using dashed arrows. The components of each complex value can be printable, abstract, or complex values. However, there cannot be a directed cycle in the set of edges used to define the complex values. As suggested by the attribute *price*, a complex value class may have attributes. Complex value classes can also serve as the range of an attribute, as illustrated by the class *Award*.

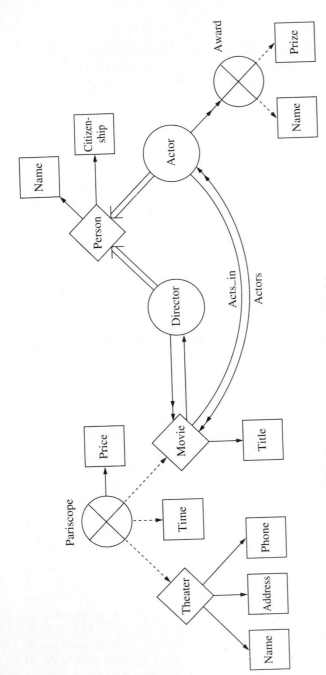

Figure 11.1: The schema **CINEMA-SEM** in the Generic Semantic Model

Complex values are of independent interest and are discussed in some depth in Chapter 20. Complex values generally include hierarchical structures built from a handful of basic constructors, including tuple (as shown here) set, and sometimes others such as bag and list. Rich complex value models are generally incorporated into object-oriented data models and into some semantic data models. Some constructs for complex values, such as set, cannot be simulated directly using the pure relational model (see Exercise 11.24).

The final building block of the GSM is the *ISA* relationship, which represents set inclusion. In the example schema of Fig. 11.1, the ISA relationships are depicted by double-shafted arrows and indicate that the set of *Director* is a subset of *Person*, and likewise that *Actor* is a subset of *Person*. In addition to indicating set inclusion, ISA relationships indicate a form of subtyping relationship, or *inheritance*. Specifically, if class *B* ISA class *A*, then each attribute of *A* is also relevant (and defined for) elements of class *B*. In the context of semantic models, this should be no surprise because the elements of *B* are elements of *A*.

In the GSM, the graph induced by ISA relationships is a directed acyclic graph (DAG). The root nodes are primary abstract classes (represented with diamonds), and all other nodes are subclass nodes (represented with circles). Each subclass node has exactly one primary node above it. Complex value classes cannot participate in ISA relationships.

In the GSM, the tuple and multivalued attribute constructs are somewhat redundant: A multivalued attribute is easily simulated using a tuple construct. Such redundancy is typical of semantic models: The emphasis is on allowing schemas that correspond closely to the way that users think about an application. On a bit of a tangent, we also note that the tuple construct of GSM is close to the relationship construct of the ER model.

GSM Instances

Let **S** be a GSM schema. It is assumed that a fixed (finite or infinite) *domain* is associated to each printable class in **S**. We also assume a countably infinite set **obj** of OIDs.

An *instance* of **S** is a function **I** whose domain is the set of primary, subclass, and complex value classes of **S** and the set of attributes of **S**. For primary class C, $\mathbf{I}(C)$ is a finite set of OIDs, disjoint from $\mathbf{I}(C')$ for each other primary class C'. For each subclass D, $\mathbf{I}(D)$ is a set of OIDs, such that the inclusions indicated by the ISA relationships of **S** are satisfied. For complex value class C with components $D_1, \ldots, D_n$, $\mathbf{I}(C)$ is a finite set of tuples $\langle d_1, \ldots, d_n \rangle$, where $d_i \in \mathbf{I}(D_i)$ if D_i is an abstract or complex value class, and d_i is in the domain of D_i if D_i is a printable class. For a single-valued attribute f from C to C', $\mathbf{I}(f)$ is a function from $\mathbf{I}(C)$ to $\mathbf{I}(C')$ (or to the domain of C', if C' is printable). For a multivalued attribute f from C to C', $\mathbf{I}(f)$ is a function from $\mathbf{I}(C)$ to finite subsets of $\mathbf{I}(C')$ (or the domain of C', if C' is printable). Given instance **I**, attribute f from C to C', and object o in $\mathbf{I}(C)$, we often write $f(o)$ to denote $[\mathbf{I}(f)](o)$.

EXAMPLE 11.1.1 Part of a very small instance $\mathbf{I}_1$ of **CINEMA-SEM** is shown in Fig. 11.2. The values of complex value *Award*, the attributes *award*, *address*, and *phone* are not shown. The symbols o_1, o_2, etc., denote OIDs.

$I_1(Person) =$ $name(o_1) = Alice$ $citizenship(o_1) = Great\ Britain$
$\quad \{o_1, o_2, o_3\}$ $name(o_2) = Allen$ $citizenship(o_2) = United\ States$
                              $name(o_3) = Keaton$ $citizenship(o_3) = United\ States$

$I_1(Director) = \{o_2\}$ $directed(o_2) = \{o_4, o_5\}$

$I_1(Actor) = \{o_2, o_3\}$ $acts\_in(o_2) = \{o_4, o_5\}$
                               $acts\_in(o_3) = \{o_5\}$

$I_1(Movie) = \{o_4, o_5\}$ $title(o_4) = Take\ the\ Money$
                               $\quad and\ Run$
                               $title(o_5) = Annie\ Hall$
                               $director(o_4) = o_2$ $actors(o_4) = \{o_2\}$
                               $director(o_5) = o_2$ $actors(o_5) = \{o_2, o_3\}$

$I_1(Theater) = \{o_6\}$ $name(o_6) = Le\ Champo$

$I_1(Pariscope) =$ $price(\langle o_6, 20{:}00, o_4 \rangle) = 30FF$
$\quad \{\langle o_6, 20{:}00, o_4 \rangle\}$

Figure 11.2:   Part of an instance I_1 of **CINEMA-SEM**

Consider an instance I' that is identical to I_1, except that o_2 is replaced by o_8 everywhere. Because OIDs serve only as internal representations that cannot be accessed explicitly, I_1 and I' are considered to be identical in terms of the information that they represent.

Let **S** be a GSM schema. An *OID isomorphism* is a function μ that is a permutation on the set **obj** of OIDs and leaves all printables fixed. Such functions are extended to *Inst*(**S**) in the natural fashion. Two instances **I** and **I**$'$ are *OID equivalent*, denoted $I \equiv_{OID} I'$, if there is an OID isomorphism μ such that $\mu(I) = I'$. This is clearly an equivalence relation. As suggested by the preceding example, if two instances are OID equivalent, then they represent the same information. The formalism of OID equivalence will be used later when we discuss the relational simulation of GSM.

The GSM is a very basic semantic data model, and many variations on the semantic constructs included in the GSM have been explored in the literature. For example, a variety of simple constraints can be incorporated, such as cardinality constraints on attributes and disjointness between subclasses (e.g., that *Director* and *Actor* are disjoint). Another variation is to require that a class be "dependent" on an attribute (e.g., that each *Award* object must occur in the image of some *Actor*) or on a complex value class. More complex constraints based on first-order sentences have also been explored. Some semantic models support different kinds of ISA relationships, and some provide "derived data" (i.e., a form of user view incorporated into the base schema).

Translating into the Relational Model

We now describe an approach for translating semantic schemas into relational database schemas. As we shall see, the semantics associated with the semantic schema will yield dependencies of various forms in the relational schema.

A minor problem to be surmounted is that in a semantic model, real-world objects such as persons can be represented using OIDs, but printable classes must be used in the pure relational model. To resolve this, we assume that each primary abstract class has a *key*, that is, a set $\{k_1, \ldots, k_n\}$ of one or more attributes with printable range such that for each instance **I** and pair o, o' of objects in the class, $o = o'$ iff $k_1(o) = k_1(o')$ and $\ldots$ and $k_n(o) = k_n(o')$. (Although more than one key might exist for a primary class, we assume that a single key is chosen.) In the schema **CINEMA-SEM**, we assume that (*person_*) *name* is the key for *Person*, that *title* is the key for *Movie*, and that (*theater_*)*name* is the key for *Theater*. (Generalizations of this approach permit the composition of attributes to serve as part of a key; e.g., including in the key for *Movie* the composition *director* ∘ *name*, which would give the name of the director of the movie.)

An alternative to the use of keys as just described is to permit the use of surrogates. Informally, a *surrogate* of an object is a unique, unchanging printable value that is associated with the object. Many real-world objects have natural surrogates (e.g., Social Security number for persons in the United States or France; or Invoice Number for invoices in a commercial enterprise). In other cases, abstract surrogates can be used.

The kernel of the translation of GSM schemas into relational ones concerns how objects in GSM instances can be represented using (tuples of) printables. For each class C occurring in the GSM schema, we associate a set of relational attributes, called the *representation* of C, and denoted $rep(C)$. For a printable class C, $rep(C)$ is a single attribute having this sort. For abstract class C, $rep(C)$ is a set of attributes corresponding to the key attributes of the primary class above C. For a complex value class $C = [C_1, \ldots, C_m]$, $rep(C)$ consists of (disjoint copies of) all of the attributes occurring in $rep(C_1), \ldots, rep(C_m)$.

Translation of a GSM schema into a relation schema is illustrated in the following example.

EXAMPLE 11.1.2   One way to simulate schema **CINEMA-SEM** in the relational model is to use the schema **CINEMA-REL**, which has the following schema:

Person	[*name, citizenship*]
Director	[*name*]
Actor	[*name*]
Acts_in	[*name, title*]
Award	[*prize, year*]
Has_Award	[*name, prize, year*]
Movie	[*title, director_name*]
Theater	[*theater_name, address, phone*]
Pariscope	[*theater_name, time, title, price*]

Person	*name*	*citizenship*
	Alice	Great Britain
	Allen	United States
	Keaton	United States

Movie	*title*	*director_name*
	Take the Money and Run	Allen
	Annie Hall	Allen

Pariscope	*theater_name*	*time*	*title*	*price*
	Le Champo	20:00	Take the Money and Run	30FF

Figure 11.3:   Part of a relational instance I_2 that simulates I_1

Figure 11.3 shows three relations in the relational simulation I_2 of the instance I_1 of Fig. 11.2.

In schema **CINEMA-REL**, both *Actor* and *Acts_in* are included in case there are one or more actors that did not act in any movie. For similar reasons, *Acts_in* and *Has_Award* are separated.

In contrast, we have assumed that each person has a citizenship (i.e., that citizenship is a total function). If not, then two relations would be needed in place of *Person*. Analogous remarks hold for directors, movies, theaters, and *Pariscope* objects.

In schema **CINEMA-REL**, we have not explicitly provided relations to represent the attributes *directed* of *Director* or *actors* of *Movie*. This is because both of these are inverses of other attributes, which are represented explicitly (by *Movie* and *Acts_in*, respectively).

If we were to consider the complex value class *Awards* of **CINEMA-SEM** to be dependent on the attribute *award*, then the relation *Award* could be omitted.

Suppose that **I** is an instance of **CINEMA-SEM** and that I' is the simulation of **I**. The semantics of **CINEMA-SEM**, along with the assumed keys, imply that I' will satisfy several dependencies. This includes the following fd's (in fact, key dependencies):

Person	:	*name* $\rightarrow$ *citizenship*
Movie	:	*title* $\rightarrow$ *director_name*
Theater	:	*theater_name* $\rightarrow$ *address, phone*
Pariscope	:	*theater_name, time, title* $\rightarrow$ *price*

A number of ind's are also implied:

Director[*name*]	$\subseteq$	*Person*[*name*]
Actor[*name*]	$\subseteq$	*Person*[*name*]
Movie[*director_name*]	$\subseteq$	*Director*[*name*]
Acts_in[*name*]	$\subseteq$	*Actor*[*name*]
Acts_in[*title*]	$\subseteq$	*Movie*[*title*]

Has_Award[*name*]	⊆	*Actor*[*name*]
Has_Award[*prize, year*]	⊆	*Award*[*prize, year*]
Pariscope[*theater_name*]	⊆	*Theater*[*theater_name*]
Pariscope[*title*]	⊆	*Movie*[*title*]

The first group of ind's follows from ISA relationships; the second from restrictions on attribute ranges; and the third from restrictions on the components of complex values. All but one of the ind's here are unary, because all of the keys, except the key for *Award*, are based on a single attribute.

Preservation of Data

Suppose that **S** is a GSM schema with keys for primary classes, and $(\mathbf{R}, \Sigma \cup \Gamma)$ is a relational schema that simulates it, constructed in the fashion illustrated in Example 11.1.2, where Σ is the set of fd's and Γ is the set of ind's. As noted in criterion (1) at the beginning of this chapter, it is desirable that there be a natural one-to-one mapping τ from instances of **S** to instances of $(\mathbf{R}, \Sigma \cup \Gamma)$. To formalize this, two obstacles need to be overcome. First, we have not developed a query language for the GSM. (In fact, no query language has become widely accepted for any of the semantic data models. In contrast, some query languages for object-oriented database models are now gaining wide acceptance.) We shall overcome this obstacle by developing a rather abstract notion of "natural" for this context.

The second obstacle stems from the fact that OID-equivalent GSM instances hold essentially the same information. Thus we would expect OID-equivalent instances to map to the same relational instance.[1] To refine criterion (1) for this context, we are searching for a one-to-one mapping from $Inst(\mathbf{S})/\equiv_{OID}$ into $Inst(\mathbf{R}, \Sigma \cup \Gamma)$.

A mapping $\tau : Inst(\mathbf{S}) \rightarrow Inst(\mathbf{R}, \Sigma \cup \Gamma)$ is *OID consistent* if $\mathbf{I} \equiv_{OID} \mathbf{I}'$ implies $\tau(\mathbf{I}) = \tau(\mathbf{I}')$. In this case, we can view τ as a mapping with domain $Inst(\mathbf{S})/\equiv_{OID}$. The mapping τ *preserves the active domain* if for each $\mathbf{I} \in Inst(\mathbf{S})$, $adom(\tau(\mathbf{I})) = adom(\mathbf{I})$. [The *active domain* of a GSM instance **I**, denoted $adom(\mathbf{I})$, is the set of all printables that occur in **I**.]

The following can be verified (see Exercise 11.3):

THEOREM 11.1.3 (Informal) Let **S** be a GSM schema with keys for primary classes, and let $(\mathbf{R}, \Sigma \cup \Gamma)$ be a relational simulation of **S**. Then there is a function $\tau : Inst(\mathbf{S}) \rightarrow Inst(\mathbf{R}, \Sigma \cup \Gamma)$ such that τ is OID consistent and preserves the active domain, and such that $\tau : Inst(\mathbf{S})/\equiv_{OID} \rightarrow Inst(\mathbf{R}, \Sigma \cup \Gamma)$ is one-to-one and onto.

Properties of the Relational Schema

We now consider criteria (2) and (3) to highlight desirable properties of relational schemas that simulate GSM schemas.

---

[1] When artificial surrogates are used to represent OIDs in the relational database, one might have to use a notion of an "equivalent" relational database instances as well.

Criterion (2) for schema transformations concerns desirable properties of the target schema. We now describe three such properties resulting from the transformation of GSM schemas into relational ones.

Suppose again that **S** is a GSM schema with keys, and $(\mathbf{R}, \Sigma \cup \Gamma)$ is a relational simulation of it. We assume as before that no constraints hold for **S**, aside from those implied by the constructs in **S** and the keys.

The three properties are as follows:

1. First, Σ is equivalent to a family of key dependencies; in the terminology of the next section, this means that each of the relation schemas obtained is in Boyce-Codd Normal Form (BCNF). Furthermore, the only mvd's satisfied by relations in **R** are implied by Σ, and so the relation schemas are in fourth normal form (4NF).

2. Second, the family Γ of ind's is acyclic (see Chapter 9). That is, there is no sequence $R_1[X_1] \subseteq R_2[Y_1]$, $R_2[X_2] \subseteq R_3[Y_2]$, ..., $R_n[X_n] \subseteq R_1[Y_n]$ of ind's in the set. By Theorem 9.4.5, this implies that logical implication can be decided for $(\Sigma \cup \Gamma)$ and that finite and unrestricted implication coincide.

3. Finally, each ind $R[X] \subseteq S[Y]$ in Γ *key based*. That is, Y is a (minimal) key of S under Σ.

Together these properties present a number of desirable features. In particular, dependency implication is easy to check. Given a database schema **R** and sets Σ of fd's and Γ of ind's over **R**, Σ and Γ are *independent* if (1) for each fd σ over **R**, $(\Sigma \cup \Gamma) \models \sigma$ implies $\Sigma \models \sigma$, and (2) for each ind γ over **R**, $(\Sigma \cup \Gamma) \models \gamma$ implies $\Gamma \models \gamma$. Suppose that **S** is a GSM schema and that $(\mathbf{R}, \Sigma \cup \Gamma)$ is a relational simulation of **S**. It can be shown that the three aforementioned properties imply that Σ and Γ are independent (see Exercise 11.4).

To conclude this section, we consider criterion (3). This criterion concerns the preservation of meta-data. We do not attempt to formalize this criterion for this context, but it should be clear that there is a close correspondence between the dependencies in $\Sigma \cup \Gamma$ and the constructs used in **S**. In other words, the semantics of the application as expressed by **S** is also captured, in the relational representation, by the dependencies $\Sigma \cup \Gamma$.

The preceding discussion assumes that no dependency holds for **S**, aside from those implied by the keys and the constructs in **S**. However, in many cases constraints will be incorporated into **S** that are not directly implied by the structure of **S**. For instance, recall Example 11.1.2, and suppose that the fd *Pariscope* : *theater_name, time* $\rightarrow$ *price* is true for the underlying data. The relational simulation will have to include this dependency and, as a result, the resulting relational schema may be missing some of the desirable features (e.g., the family of fd's is not equivalent to a set of keys and the schema is no longer in BCNF). This suggests that a semantic model might be used to obtain a coarse relational schema, which might be refined further using the techniques for improving relational schemas developed in the next section.

11.2   Normal Forms

In this section, we consider schema design based on the refinement of relational schemas and normal forms, which provide the basis for this approach. The articulation of these normal forms is arguably the main contribution of relational database theory to the realm of schema design. We begin the discussion by presenting two of the most prominent normal forms and a design strategy based on "decomposition." We then develop another normal form that overcomes certain technical problems of the first two, and describe an associated design strategy based on "synthesis." We conclude with brief comments on the relationship of ind's with decomposition.

When all the dependencies in a relational schema $(\mathbf{R}, \Sigma)$ are considered to be tagged, one can view the *database schema* as a set $\{(R_1, \Sigma_1), \ldots, (R_n, \Sigma_n)\}$, where each (R_j, Σ_j) is a relation schema and the R_j's are distinct. In particular, an *fd schema* is a relation schema (R, Σ) or database schema $(\mathbf{R}, \Sigma)$, where Σ is a set of tagged fd's; this is extended in the natural fashion to other classes of dependencies. Much of the work on refinement of relational schemas has focused on fd schemas and (fd + mvd) schemas. This is what we consider here. (The impact of the ind's is briefly considered at the end of this section.)

A normal form restricts the set of dependencies that are allowed to hold in a relation schema. The main purpose of the normal forms is to eliminate at least some of the redundancies and update anomalies that might otherwise arise. Intuitively, schemas in normal form are "good" schemas.

We introduce next two kinds of normal forms, namely BCNF and 4NF. (We will consider a third one, 3NF, later.) We then consider techniques to transform a schema into such desirable normal forms.

BCNF: Do Not Represent the Same Fact Twice

Recall the schema $(Movies[T(itle), D(irector), A(actor)], \{T \rightarrow D\})$ from Section 8.1. As discussed there, the *Movies* relation suffers from various anomalies, primarily because there is only one *Director* associated with each *Title* but possibly several *Actors*. Suppose that $(R[U], \Sigma)$ is a relation schema, $\Sigma \models X \rightarrow Y$, $Y \nsubseteq X$ and $\Sigma \nvDash X \rightarrow U$. It is not hard to see that anomalies analogous to those of *Movies* can arise in R. Boyce-Codd normal form prohibits this kind of situation.

DEFINITION 11.2.1   A relation schema $(R[U], \Sigma)$ is in *Boyce-Codd normal form* (BCNF) if $\Sigma \models X \rightarrow U$ whenever $\Sigma \models X \rightarrow Y$ for some $Y \nsubseteq X$. An fd schema $(\mathbf{R}, \Sigma)$ is in BCNF if each of its relation schemas is.

BCNF is most often discussed in cases where Σ involves only functional dependencies. In such cases, if (R, Σ) is in BCNF, the anomalies of Section 8.1 do not arise. An essential intuition underlying BCNF is, "Do not represent the same fact twice."

The question now arises: What does one do with a relation schema (R, Σ) that is not in BCNF? In many cases, it is possible to decompose this schema into subschemas $(R_1, \Sigma_1), \ldots, (R_n, \Sigma_n)$ without information loss. As a simple example, *Movies* can be decomposed into

$$\left\{ \begin{array}{l} (Movie\_director[TD], \{T \to D\}), \\ [6pt](Movie\_actors[TA], \emptyset) \end{array} \right\}$$

A general framework for decomposition is presented shortly.

4NF: Do Not Store Unrelated Information in the Same Relation

Consider the relation schema $(Studios[N(ame), D(irector), L(ocation)], \{N \twoheadrightarrow D|L\})$. A tuple $\langle n, d, l \rangle$ is in *Studios* if director d is employed by the studio with name n and if this studio has an office in location l. Only trivial fd's are satisfied by all instances of this schema, and so it is in BCNF. However, update anomalies can still arise, essentially because the D and L values are independent from each other. This gives rise to the following generalization of BCNF[2]:

DEFINITION 11.2.2   A relation schema $(R[U], \Sigma)$ is in *fourth normal form* (*4NF*) if

(a) whenever $\Sigma \models X \to Y$ and $Y \not\subseteq X$, then $\Sigma \models X \to U$

(b) whenever $\Sigma \models X \twoheadrightarrow Y$ and $Y \not\subseteq X$, then $\Sigma \models X \to U$.

An (fd + mvd) schema $(\mathbf{R}, \Sigma)$ is in 4NF if each of its relation schemas is.

It is clear that if a relation schema is in 4NF, then it is in BCNF. It is easily seen that *Studios* can be decomposed into two 4NF relations, without loss of information and that the resulting relation schemas do not have the update anomalies mentioned earlier. An essential intuition underlying 4NF is, "Do not store unrelated information in the same relation."

The General Framework of Decomposition

One approach to refining relational schemas is *decomposition*. In this approach, it is usually assumed that the original schema consists of a single wide relation containing all attributes of interest. This is referred to as the *pure universal relation assumption,* or *pure URA*. A relaxation of the pure URA, called the "weak URA," is considered briefly in Section 11.3.

The pure URA is a simplifying assumption, because in practice the original schema is likely to consist of several tables, each with its own dependencies. In that case, the design process described for the pure URA is applied separately to each table. We adopt the pure URA here. In this context, the schema transformation produced by the design process consists of decomposing the original table into smaller tables by using the projection operator. (In an alternative approach, selection is used to yield so-called *horizontal decompositions*.)

We now establish the basic framework of decompositions. Let $(U[Z], \Sigma)$ be a relation schema. A *decomposition* of $(U[Z], \Sigma)$ is a database schema $\mathbf{R} = \{R_1[X_1], \ldots, R_n[X_n]\}$ with dependencies Γ, where $\cup\{X_j \mid j \in [1, n]\} = Z$. (The relation name '$U$' is used to

---

[2] The motivation behind the names of several of the normal forms is largely historical; see the Bibliographic Notes.

suggest that it is a "universal" relation.) In the sequel, we often use relation names U (R_i) and attribute sets Z (X_i), interchangeably if ambiguity does not arise.

We now consider the three criteria for schema transformation in the context of decomposition. As already suggested, criterion (2) is evaluated in terms of the normal forms. With regard to the preservation of data (1), the "natural" mapping from R to $\mathbf{R}$ is obtained by projection: The *decomposition mapping* of $\mathbf{R}$ is the function $\pi_{\mathbf{R}} : Inst(U) \to Inst(\mathbf{R})$ such that for $I \in inst(U)$, we have $\pi_{\mathbf{R}}(I)(R_j) = \pi_{R_j}(I)$. Criterion (1) says that the decomposition should not lose information when I is replaced by its projections (i.e., it should be one-to-one).

A natural property implying that a decomposition is one-to-one is that the original instance can be obtained by joining the component relations. Formally, a decomposition is said to have the *lossless join* property if for each instance $\mathbf{I}$ of (U, Σ) the join of the projections is the original instance, i.e., $\bowtie (\pi_{\mathbf{R}}(\mathbf{I})) = \mathbf{I}$. It is easy to test if a decomposition $\mathbf{R} = \{R_1, \ldots, R_n\}$ of (U, Σ) has the lossless join property. Consider the query $q(I) = \pi_{R_1}(I) \bowtie \cdots \bowtie \pi_{R_n}(I)$. The lossless join property means that $q(I) = I$ for every instance I over (U, Σ). But $q(I) = I$ simply says that I satisfies the jd $\bowtie [\mathbf{R}]$. Thus we have the following:

THEOREM 11.2.3 Let (U, Σ) be a (full dependencies) schema and $\mathbf{R}$ a decomposition for (U, Σ). Then $\mathbf{R}$ has the lossless join property iff $\Sigma \models \bowtie [\mathbf{R}]$.

The preceding implication can be tested using the chase (see Chapter 8), as illustrated next.

EXAMPLE 11.2.4 Recall the schema (*Movies*[*TDA*], $\{T \to D\}$). As suggested earlier, a decomposition into BCNF is $\mathbf{R} = \{TD, TA\}$. This decomposition has the lossless join property. The tableau associated with the jd $\sigma = \bowtie [TD, TA]$ is as follows:

T_σ	T	D	A
	t	d	a_1
	t	d_1	a
t_σ	t	d	a

Consider the chase of $\langle T_\sigma, t_\sigma \rangle$ with $\{T \to D\}$. Because the two first tuples agree on the T column, d and d_1 are merged because of the fd. Thus $\langle t, d, a \rangle \in chase(T_\sigma, t_\sigma, \{T \to D\})$. Hence $T \to D$ implies the jd σ, so $\mathbf{R}$ has the lossless join property. (See also Exercise 11.9.)

Referring to the preceding example, note that it is possible to represent information in $\mathbf{R}$ that cannot be directly represented in *Movies*. Specifically, in the decomposed schema we can represent a movie with a director but no actors and a movie with an actor but no director. This indicates, intuitively, that a decomposed schema may have more information capacity than the original (see Exercise 11.23). In practice, this additional capacity is exploited; in fact, it provides part of the solution of so-called deletion anomalies.

REMARK 11.2.5 In the preceding example, we used the natural join operator to reconstruct decompositions. Interestingly, there are cases in which the natural join does not suffice. To show that a decomposition is one-to-one, it suffices to exhibit an inverse to the projection, called a *reconstruction mapping*. If Σ is permitted to include very general constraints expressed in first-order logic that may not be dependencies per se, then there are one-to-one decompositions whose reconstruction mappings are *not* the natural join (see Exercise 11.20).

We now consider criterion (3), the preservation of meta-data. In the context of decomposition, this is formalized in terms of "dependency preservation": Given schema (U, Σ), which is replaced by a decomposition $\mathbf{R} = \{R_1, \ldots, R_n\}$, we would like to find for each j a family Γ_j of dependencies over R_j such that $\cup_j \Gamma_j$ is equivalent to the original Σ. In the case where Σ is a set of fd's, we can make this much more precise. For $V \subseteq U$, let

$$\pi_V(\Sigma) = \{X \to A \mid XA \subseteq V \text{ and } \Sigma \models X \to A\},$$

let $\Gamma_j = \pi_{X_j}(\Sigma)$, and let $\Gamma = \cup_j \Gamma_j$. Obviously, $\Sigma \models \Gamma$. (See Proposition 10.2.4.) Intuitively, Γ consists of the dependencies in Σ^* that are local to the relations in the decomposition $\mathbf{R}$. The decomposition $\mathbf{R}$ is said to be *dependency preserving* iff $\Gamma \equiv \Sigma$. In other words, Σ can be enforced by the dependencies local in the decomposition. It is easy to see that the decomposition of Example 11.2.4 is dependency preserving.

Given an fd schema (U, Σ) and $V \subseteq U$, $\pi_V(\Sigma)$ has size exponential in V, simply because of trivial fd's. But perhaps there is a smaller set of fd's that is equivalent to $\pi_V(\Sigma)$. A *cover* of a set Γ of fd's is a set Γ' of fd's such that $\Gamma' \equiv \Gamma$. Unfortunately, in some cases the smallest cover for a projection $\pi_V(\Sigma)$ is exponential in the size of Σ (see Exercise 11.11).

What about projections of sets of mvd's? Suppose that Σ is a set of fd's and mvd's over U. Let $V \subseteq U$ and

$$\pi_V^{mvd}(\Sigma) = \{[X \twoheadrightarrow (Y \cap V)|(Z \cap V)] \mid [X \twoheadrightarrow Y|Z] \in \Sigma^* \text{ and } X \subseteq V\}.$$

Consider a decomposition $\mathbf{R}$ of (U, Σ). Viewed as constraints on U, the sets $\pi_{R_j}^{mvd}(\Sigma)$ are now embedded mvd's. As we saw in Chapter 10, testing implication for embedded mvd's is undecidable. However, the issue of testing for dependency preservation in the context of decompositions involving fd's and mvd's is rather specialized and remains open.

Fd's and Decomposition into BCNF

We now present a simple algorithm for decomposing an fd schema (U, Σ) into BCNF relations. The decomposition produced by the algorithm has the lossless join property but is not guaranteed to be dependency preserving.

We begin with a simple example.

EXAMPLE 11.2.6   Consider the schema (U, Σ), where U has attributes

$$
\begin{array}{llll}
TITLE & D\_NAME & TIME & PRICE \\
TH\_NAME & ADDRESS & PHONE &
\end{array}
$$

and Σ contains

$$
\begin{array}{ll}
FD1: & TH\_NAME \rightarrow ADDRESS, PHONE \\
FD2: & TH\_NAME, TIME, TITLE \rightarrow PRICE \\
FD3: & TITLE \rightarrow D\_NAME
\end{array}
$$

Intuitively, schema (U, Σ) represents a fragment of the real-world situation represented by the semantic schema **CINEMA-SEM**.

A first step toward transforming this into a BCNF schema is to decompose using *FD*1, to obtain the database schema

$$
\left\{
\begin{array}{l}
(\{TH\_NAME, ADDRESS, PHONE\}, \{FD1\}), \\
(\{TH\_NAME, TITLE, TIME, PRICE, D\_NAME\}, \{FD2, FD3\})
\end{array}
\right\}
$$

Next *FD*3 can be used to split the second relation, obtaining

$$
\left\{
\begin{array}{l}
(\{TH\_NAME, ADDRESS, PHONE\}, \{FD1\}) \\
(\{TITLE, D\_NAME\}, \{FD3\}) \\
(\{TH\_NAME, TITLE, TIME, PRICE\}, \{FD2\})
\end{array}
\right\}
$$

which is in BCNF. It is easy to see that this decomposition has the lossless join property and is dependency preserving. In fact, in this case, we obtain the same relational schema as would result from starting with a semantic schema.

We now present the following:

ALGORITHM 11.2.7 (BCNF Decomposition)

Input: A relation schema (U, Σ), where Σ is a set of fd's.

Output: A database schema $(\mathbf{R}, \Gamma)$ in BCNF

1. Set $(\mathbf{R}, \Gamma) := \{(U, \Sigma)\}$.
2. Repeat until $(\mathbf{R}, \Gamma)$ is in BCNF:
   (a) Choose a relation schema $(S[V], \Omega) \in \mathbf{R}$ that is not in BCNF.
   (b) Choose nonempty, disjoint $X, Y, Z \subset V$ such that
       (i) $XYZ = V$;
       (ii) $\Omega \models X \rightarrow Y$; and
       (iii) $\Omega \not\models X \rightarrow A$ for each $A \in Z$.
   (c) Replace $(S[V], \Omega)$ in $\mathbf{R}$ by $(S_1[XY], \pi_{XY}(\Omega))$ and $(S_2[XZ], \pi_{XZ}(\Omega))$.

(a) for each fd $X \rightarrow A$ in Σ, include the relational schema $(XA, \{X \rightarrow A\})$ in the output schema $(\mathbf{R}, \Gamma)$; and

(b) choose a key X of U under Σ, and include $(X, \emptyset)$ in the output.

A central aspect of this algorithm is to form a relation XA for each fd $X \rightarrow A$ in Σ. Intuitively, then, the output relations result from combining or "synthesizing" attributes rather than decomposing the full attribute set.

The following is easily verified (see Exercise 11.17):

THEOREM 11.2.14   The 3NF Synthesis Algorithm decomposes a relation schema into a database schema in 3NF that has the lossless join property and preserves dependencies.

Several improvements to the basic 3NF Synthesis Algorithm can be made easily. For example, different schemas obtained in step (2.a) can be merged if they come from fd's with the same left-hand side. Step (2.b) is not needed if step (2.a) already produced a schema whose set of attributes is a superkey for (U, Σ). In many practical situations, it may be appropriate to omit step (2.b) of the algorithm. In that case, the decomposition preserves dependencies but does not necessarily satisfy the lossless join property.

In the preceding algorithm, it was assumed that each attribute of U occurs in at least one fd of Σ. Obviously, this may not always be the case, for example, the attribute *A_NAME* in Example 11.2.15b does not participate in fd's. One approach to remedy this situation is to introduce symbolic fd's. For instance, in that example one might include the fd *TITLE, A_NAME* $\rightarrow \omega_1$, where ω_1 is a new attribute. One relation produced by the algorithm will be $\{TITLE, A\_NAME, \omega_1\}$. As a last step, attributes such as ω_1 are removed.

In Example 11.2.9 we saw that the output of a BCNF decomposition may depend on the order in which fd's are applied. In the case of the preceding algorithm for 3NF, the minimal cover chosen greatly impacts the final result.

Mvd's and Decomposition into 4NF

A fundamental problem with BCNF decomposition and 3NF synthesis as just presented is that they do not take into account the impact of mvd's.

EXAMPLE 11.2.15   (a) The schema $(Studios[N(ame), D(irector), L(ocation)], \{N \twoheadrightarrow D | L\})$ is in BCNF and 3NF but has update anomalies. The mvd suggests a decomposition into $(\{Name, Director\}, \{Name, Location\})$.

(b) A related issue is that BCNF decompositions may not separate attributes that intuitively should be separated. For example, consider again the schema of Example 11.2.6, but suppose that the attribute *A_NAME* is included to denote actor names. Following the same decomposition steps as before, we obtain the schema

$$\left\{ \begin{array}{l} (\{TH\_NAME, ADDRESS, PHONE\}, \{FD1\}), \\[2mm] (\{TITLE, D\_NAME\}, \{FD3\}), \\[2mm] (\{TH\_NAME, TITLE, TIME, PRICE, A\_NAME\}, \{FD2\}) \end{array} \right\}$$

which can be further decomposed to

$$\left\{ \begin{array}{l} (\{TH\_NAME, ADDRESS, PHONE\}, \{FD1\}), \\[2mm] (\{TITLE, D\_NAME\}, \{FD3\}), \\[2mm] (\{TH\_NAME, TITLE, TIME, PRICE\}, \{FD2\}), \\[2mm] (\{TH\_NAME, TITLE, TIME, A\_NAME\}, \emptyset) \end{array} \right\}$$

Although there is a connection in the underlying data between *TITLE* and *A_NAME*, the last relation here is unnatural. If we assume that the mvd *TITLE* $\twoheadrightarrow$ *A_NAME* is incorporated into the original schema, we can further decompose the last relation and apply a step analogous to (2d) of the BCNF Decomposition Algorithm to obtain

$$\left\{ \begin{array}{l} (\{TH\_NAME, ADDRESS, PHONE\}, \{FD1\}), \\[2mm] (\{TITLE, D\_NAME\}, \{FD3\}), \\[2mm] (\{TH\_NAME, TITLE, TIME, PRICE\}, \{FD2\}), \\[2mm] (\{TITLE, A\_NAME\}, \emptyset) \end{array} \right\}$$

Fourth normal form (4NF) was originally developed to address these kinds of situations. As suggested by the preceding example, an algorithm yielding 4NF decompositions can be developed along the lines of the BCNF Decomposition Algorithm. As with BCNF, the output of 4NF decomposition is a lossless join decomposition that is not necessarily dependency preserving.

A Note on Ind's

In relational schema design starting with a semantic data model, numerous ind's are typically generated. In contrast, the decomposition and synthesis approaches for refining relational schemas as presented earlier do not take ind's into account. It is possible to incorporate ind's into these approaches, but the specific choice of ind's is dependent on the intended semantics of the target schema.

EXAMPLE 11.2.16 Recall the schema (*Movies*[*TDA*], $\{T \rightarrow D\}$) and decomposition into ($R_1[TD]$, $\{T \rightarrow D\}$) and ($R_2[TA]$, $\emptyset$).

(a) If all movies must have a director and at least one actor, then both $R_1[T] \subseteq$

$R_2[T]$ and $R_2[T] \subseteq R_1[T]$ should be included. In this case, the mapping from *Movies* to its decomposed representation is one-to-one and onto.

(b) If the fd $T \to D$ is understood to mean that there is a *total* function from movies to directors, but movies without actors are permitted, then the ind $R_2[T] \subseteq R_1[T]$ should be included.

(c) Finally, suppose the fd $T \to D$ is understood to mean that each movie has at most one director (i.e., it is a partial function), and suppose that a movie can have no actor. Then an additional relation $R_3[T]$ should be added to hold the titles of all movies, along with ind's $R_1[T] \subseteq R_3[T]$ and $R_2[T] \subseteq R_3[T]$.

More generally, what if one is to refine a relational schema $(\mathbf{R}, \Sigma \cup \Gamma)$, where Σ is a set of tagged fd's and mvd's and Γ is a set of ind's? It may occur that there is an ind $R_i[X] \subseteq R_j[Y]$, and either X or Y is to be "split" as the result of a decomposition step. The desired semantics of the target schema can be used to select between a variety of heuristic approaches to preserving the semantics of this ind. If Γ consists of unary ind's, such splitting cannot occur. Speaking intuitively, if the ind's of Γ are key based, then the chances of such splitting are reduced.

11.3   Universal Relation Assumption

In the preceding section, we saw that the decomposition and synthesis approaches to relational schema design assume the pure URA. This section begins by articulating some of the implications that underly the pure URA. It then presents the "weak URA," which provides an intuitively natural mechanism for viewing a relational database instance $\mathbf{I}$ as if it were a universal relation.

Underlying Assumptions

Suppose that an fd schema $(U[Z], \Sigma)$ is given and that decomposition or synthesis will be applied. One of several different database schemas might be produced, but presumably all of them carry roughly the same semantics. This suggests that the attributes in Z can be grouped into relation schemas in several different ways, without substantially affecting their underlying semantics. Intuitively, then, it is the attributes themselves (along with the dependencies in Σ), rather than the attributes as they occur in different relation schemas, that carry the bulk of the semantics in the schema. The notion that the attributes can represent a substantial portion of the semantics of an application is central to schema design based on the pure URA.

When decomposition and synthesis were first introduced, the underlying implications of this notion were not well understood. Several intuitive assumptions were articulated that attempted to capture these implications. We describe here two of the most important assumptions. Any approach to relational schema design based on the pure URA should also abide by these two assumptions.

Universal Relation Scheme Assumption: This states that if an attribute name appears in two or more places in a database schema, then it refers to the same entity set in each place. For example, an attribute name *Number* should not be used for both serial numbers and employee numbers; rather two distinct attribute names *Serial#* and *Employee#* should be used.

Unique Role Assumption: This states that for each set of attributes there is a unique relationship between them. This is sometimes weakened to say that there may be several relationships, but one is deemed primary. This is illustrated in the following example.

EXAMPLE 11.3.1　(a) Recall in Example 11.2.15(b) that *D_NAME* and *A_NAME* were used for director and actor names, respectively. This is because there were two possible relationships between movies and persons.

(b) For a more complicated example, consider a schema for bank branches that includes attributes for *B(ranch)*, *L(oan)*, *(checking) A(ccount)*, and *C(ustomer)*. Suppose there are four relations

　　BL, which holds data about branches and loans they have given

　　BA, which holds data about branches and checking accounts they provide

　　CL, which holds data about customers and loans they have

　　CA, which holds data about customers and checking accounts they have.

This design does not satisfy the unique role assumption, mainly because of the cycle in the schema. For example, consider the relationship between branches and customers. In fact, there are two relationships—via loans and via accounts. Thus a request for "the" data in the relationship between banks and customers is somewhat ambiguous, because it could mean tuples stemming from either of the two relationships or from the intersection or union of both of them.

One solution to this ambiguity is to "break" the cycle. For example, we could replace the *Customer* attribute by the two attributes *L-C(ustomer)* and *A-C(ustomer)*. Now the user can specify the desired relationship by using the appropriate attribute.

The Weak Universal Relation Assumption

Suppose that schema (U, Σ) has decomposition $(\mathbf{R}, \Gamma)$ (with $\mathbf{R} = \{R_1, \ldots, R_n\}$). When studying decomposition, we focused primarily on instances $\mathbf{I}$ of $(\mathbf{R}, \Gamma)$ that were the image of some instance I of (U, Σ) under the decomposition mapping $\pi_{\mathbf{R}}$. In particular, such instances $\mathbf{I}$ are *globally consistent*. [Recall from Chapter 6 that instance $\mathbf{I}$ is *globally consistent* if for each $j \in [1, n]$, $\pi_{R_j}(\bowtie \mathbf{I}) = \mathbf{I}(R_j)$; i.e., no tuple of $\mathbf{I}(R_j)$ is dangling relative to the full join.] However, in many practical situations it might be useful to use the decomposed schema $\mathbf{R}$ to store instances $\mathbf{I}$ that are not globally consistent.

EXAMPLE 11.3.2　Recall the schema (*Movies*[*TDA*], $\{T \rightarrow D\}$) from Example 11.2.4 and its decomposition $\{TD, TA\}$. Suppose that for some movie the director is known, but no actors are known. As mentioned previously, this information is easily stored in the decomposed database, but not in the original. The impossibility of representing this information

AB	A	B
	a	b

AB	A	B
	a	b
	a'	b

AB	A	B
	a	b

BC	B	C
	b	c

BC	B	C
	b	c

BC	B	C
	b	c

ACD	A	C	D
	a	c	d

ACD	A	C	D
	a	c	d
	a'	c	d'

ACD	A	C	D
	a	c	d
	a'	c	d'

$\mathbf{I}_1$ $\mathbf{I}_2$ $\mathbf{I}_3$

Figure 11.4:   Instances illustrating weak URA

in the original schema was one of the anomalies that motivated the decomposition in the first place.

Suppose that fd schema (U, Σ) has decomposition $(\mathbf{R}, \Gamma) = \{(R_1, \Gamma_1), \ldots, (R_n, \Gamma_n)\}$. Suppose also that $\mathbf{I}$ is an instance of $\mathbf{R}$ such that (1) $\mathbf{I}(R_j) \models \Gamma_j$ for each j, but (2) $\mathbf{I}$ is not necessarily globally consistent. Should $\mathbf{I}$ be considered a "valid" instance of schema $(\mathbf{R}, \Gamma)$? More generally, given a schema (U, Σ), a decomposition $\mathbf{R}$ of U, and a (not necessarily globally consistent) instance $\mathbf{I}$ over $\mathbf{R}$, how should we define the notion of "satisfaction" of Σ by $\mathbf{I}$?

The *weak universal relation assumption* (*weak URA*) provides one approach for answering this question. Under the weak URA, we say that $\mathbf{I}$ *satisfies* Σ if there is *some* instance $J \in sat(U, \Sigma)$ such that $\mathbf{I}(R_j) \subseteq \pi_{R_j}(J)$ for each $j \in [1, n]$. In this case, J is called a *weak instance* for $\mathbf{I}$.

EXAMPLE 11.3.3   Let $U = \{ABCD\}$, $\Sigma = \{A \rightarrow B, BC \rightarrow D\}$, and $\mathbf{R} = \{AB, BC, ACD\}$. Consider the three instances of $\mathbf{R}$ shown in Fig. 11.4. The instance $\mathbf{I}_1$ satisfies Σ under the weak URA, because $J_1 = \{\langle a, b, c, d \rangle\}$ is a weak instance.

On the other hand, $\mathbf{I}_2$, which contains $\mathbf{I}_1$, does not satisfy Σ under the weak URA. To see this, suppose that J_2 is a weak instance for $\mathbf{I}_2$. Then J_2 must contain the following (not necessarily distinct) tuples:

$$t_1 = \langle a, b, c_1, d_1 \rangle$$
$$t_2 = \langle a', b, c_2, d_2 \rangle$$
$$t_3 = \langle a_3, b, c, d_3 \rangle$$
$$t_4 = \langle a, b_4, c, d \rangle$$
$$t_5 = \langle a', b_5, c, d' \rangle$$

where the subscripted constants may be new. Because $J_2 \models A \rightarrow B$, by considering the pairs $\langle t_1, t_4 \rangle$ and $\langle t_2, t_5 \rangle$, we see that $b_4 = b_5 = b$. Next, because $J_2 \models BC \rightarrow D$, and by considering the pair $\langle t_4, t_5 \rangle$, we have that $d = d'$, a contradiction.

Finally, $\mathbf{I}_3$ does satisfy Σ under the weak URA.

As suggested by the preceding example, testing whether an instance $\mathbf{I}$ over $\mathbf{R}$ is a weak instance of (U, Σ) for a set of fd's Σ can be performed using the chase. To do that, it suffices to construct a table over U by padding the tuples from each R_j with distinct new variables. The resulting table is chased with the dependencies in Σ. If the chase fails, there is no weak instance for $\mathbf{I}$. On the other hand, a successful chase provides a weak instance for $\mathbf{I}$ by simply replacing each remaining variable with a distinct new constant.

This yields the following (see Exercise 11.27):

THEOREM 11.3.4 Let Σ be a set of fd's over U and $\mathbf{R}$ a decomposition of U. Testing whether $\mathbf{I}$ over $\mathbf{R}$ satisfies Σ under the weak URA can be performed in polynomial time.

Of course, the chasing technique can be extended to arbitrary egd's, although the complexity jumps to EXPTIME-complete.

What about full tgd's? Recall that full tgd's can always be satisfied by adding new tuples to an instance. Let Σ be a set of full dependencies. It is easy to see that $\mathbf{I}$ satisfies Σ under the weak URA iff $\mathbf{I}$ satisfies $\Sigma^* \cap \{\sigma \mid \sigma$ is an egd$\}$ under the weak URA.

Querying under the Weak URA

Let (U, Σ) be a schema, where Σ is a set of full dependencies, and let $\mathbf{R}$ be a decomposition of U. Let us assume the weak URA, and suppose that database instance $\mathbf{I}$ over $\mathbf{R}$ satisfies Σ. How should queries against $\mathbf{I}$ be answered? One approach is to consider the query against all weak instances for $\mathbf{I}$ and then take the intersection of the answers. That is,

$$q_{weak}(\mathbf{I}) = \cap \{q(I) \mid I \text{ is a weak instance of } \mathbf{I}\}.$$

We develop now a constructive method for computing q_{weak}.

Given instance $\mathbf{I}$ of $\mathbf{R}$, the *representative instance* of $\mathbf{I}$ is defined as follows: For each component I_j of $\mathbf{I}$, let I'_j be the result of extending I_j to be a free instance over U by padding tuples with distinct variables. Set $I' = \cup \{I'_j \mid j \in [1, n]\}$. Now apply the chase using Σ to obtain the representative instance $rep(\mathbf{I}, \Sigma)$ (or the empty instance, if two

$(S[V], \Omega)$ is not in BCNF, then there are $A, B \in V$ such that $(V - AB) \to A$ but $(V - AB)$ is not a key.

Exercise 11.14   Recall the schema *Showings*[*Th*(*eater*), *Sc*(*reen*), *Ti*(*tle*), *Sn*(*ack*)] of Section 8.1, which satisfies the fd *Th,Sc* $\to$ *Ti* and the mvd *Th* $\twoheadrightarrow$ *Sc,Ti* | *Sn*. Consider the two decompositions

$$\mathbf{R}_1 = \{\{Th, Sc, Ti\}, \{Th, Sn\}\}$$
$$\mathbf{R}_2 = \{\{Th, Sc, Ti\}, \{Th, Sc, Sn\}\}.$$

Are they one-to-one? dependency preserving? Describe anomalies that can arise if either of these decompositions is used.

Exercise 11.15   [BB79] Verify that the schema of Example 11.2.10 has no BCNF decomposition that preserves dependencies.

Exercise 11.16   [Mai80] Develop a polynomial time algorithm that finds a minimal cover of a set of fd's.

Exercise 11.17   Prove Theorem 11.2.14.

Exercise 11.18   [Mai83] Show that a schema $(R[U], \Sigma)$ with $2n$ attributes and $2n$ fd's can have as many as 2^n keys.

Exercise 11.19   [LO78] Let $(S[V], \Omega)$ be an fd schema. Show that the following problem is NP-complete: Given $A \in V$, is there a nontrivial fd $Y \to A$ implied by Ω, where Y is not a superkey and A is not a key attribute?

★ **Exercise 11.20**   [Var82b] For this exercise, you will exhibit an example of a schema (R, Σ), where Σ consists of dependencies expressed in first-order logic (which may not be embedded dependencies) and a decomposition $\mathbf{R}$ of R such that $\mathbf{R}$ is one-to-one but does not have the lossless join property.

Consider the schema $R[ABCD]$. Given $t \in I \in inst(R)$, $t[A]$ is a *key element* for AB in I if there is no $s \in I$ with $t[A] = s[A]$ and $t[B] \neq s[B]$. The notion of $t[C]$ being a *key element* for CD is defined analogously. Let Σ consist of the constraints

(i) $\exists t \in I$ such that both $t[A]$ and $t[C]$ are key elements.
(ii) If $t \in I$, then $t[A]$ is a key element or $t[C]$ is a key element.
(iii) If $s, t \in I$ and $s[A]$ or $t[C]$ is a key element, then the tuple u is in I, where $u[AB] = s[AB]$ and $u[CD] = t[CD]$.

Let $\mathbf{R} = \{R_1[AB], R_2[CD]\}$ be a decomposition of (R, Σ).

(a) Show that the decomposition $\mathbf{R}$ for (R, Σ) is one-to-one.
(b) Exhibit a reconstruction mapping for $\mathbf{R}$. (The natural join will not work.)

Exercise 11.21   This and the following exercise provide one kind of characterization of the relative information capacity of decompositions of relation schemas. Let U be a set of attributes, let $\alpha = \{X_1, \ldots, X_n\}$ be a nonempty family of subsets of U, and let $X = \cup_{i=1}^n X_i$. The *project-join* mapping determined by α, denoted PJ_α, is a mapping from instances over U to instances over $\cup_{i=1}^n X_i$ defined by $PJ_\alpha(I) = \bowtie_{i=1}^n (\pi_{X_i}(I))$. α is *full* if $\cup_{i=1}^n = U$, in which case PJ_α is a *full* project-join mapping.

Prove the following for instances I and J over U:

(a) $\pi_X(I) \subseteq PJ_\alpha(I)$

(b) $PJ_\alpha(PJ_\alpha(I)) = PJ_\alpha(I)$

(c) if $I \subseteq J$ then $PJ_\alpha(I) \subseteq PJ_\alpha(J)$.

★ **Exercise 11.22** [BMSU81] Let U be a set of attributes. If $\alpha = \{X_1, \ldots, X_n\}$ is a nonempty full family of subsets of U, then *Fixpt*(α) denotes $\{I$ over $U \mid PJ_\alpha(I) = I\}$ (see the preceding exercise). For α and β nonempty full families of subsets of U, β *covers* α, denoted $\alpha \preceq \beta$, if for each set $X \in \alpha$ there is a set $Y \in \beta$ such that $X \subseteq Y$. Prove for nonempty full families α, β of subsets of U that the following are equivalent:

(a) $\alpha \preceq \beta$

(b) $PJ_\alpha(I) \supseteq PJ_\beta(I)$ for each instance I over U

(c) *Fixpt*$(\alpha) \subseteq$ *Fixpt*(β).

Exercise 11.23 Given relational database schemas **S** and **S'**, we say that **S'** *dominates* **S** using the calculus, denoted $\mathbf{S} \preceq_{\text{calc}} \mathbf{S}'$, if there are calculus queries $q : Inst(\mathbf{S}) \to Inst(\mathbf{S}')$ and $q' : Inst(\mathbf{S}') \to Inst(\mathbf{S})$ such that $q \circ q'$ is the identity on $Inst(\mathbf{S})$. Let schema $R = (ABC, \{A \to B\})$ and the decomposition $\mathbf{R} = \{(AB, \{A \to B\}), (AC, \emptyset)\}$. (a) Verify that $R \preceq_{\text{calc}} \mathbf{R}$. (b) Show that $\mathbf{R} \npreceq_{\text{calc}} R$. *Hint:* For schemas **S** and **S'**, **S'** *dominates* **S** *absolutely*, denoted $\mathbf{S} \preceq_{abs} \mathbf{S}'$, if there is some $n \geq 0$ such that for each finite subset $\mathbf{d} \subseteq \mathbf{dom}$ with $|\mathbf{d}| \geq n$, $|\{\mathbf{I} \in Inst(\mathbf{S}) \mid adom(\mathbf{I}) \subseteq \mathbf{d}\}| \leq |\{\mathbf{I} \in Inst(\mathbf{S}') \mid adom(\mathbf{I}) \subseteq \mathbf{d}\}|$. Show that $\mathbf{S} \preceq_{\text{calc}} \mathbf{S}'$ implies $\mathbf{S} \preceq_{abs} \mathbf{S}'$. Then show that $\mathbf{R} \npreceq_{abs} R$.

★ **Exercise 11.24** [HY84] Let A and B be relational attributes. Consider the complex value type $T = \langle A, \{B\}\rangle$, where each instance of T is a finite set of pairs having the form $\langle a, \hat{b}\rangle$, where $a \in \mathbf{dom}$ and $\hat{b}$ is a finite subset of $\mathbf{dom}$. Show that for each relational schema $\mathbf{R}$, $\mathbf{R} \preceq_{abs} T$ and $T \npreceq_{abs} \mathbf{R}$. (See Exercise 11.23 for the definition of $\preceq_{abs}$.)

♠ **Exercise 11.25** [BV84b, CP84]

(a) Let (U, Σ) be a (full dependencies) schema and $\mathbf{R}$ an acyclic decomposition of U (in the sense of acyclic joins). Then $\pi_\mathbf{R}$ is one-to-one iff $\mathbf{R}$ has the lossless join property. *Hint:* First prove the result for the case where the decomposition has two elements (i.e., it is based on an mvd). Then generalize to acyclic decompositions, using an induction based on the GYO algorithm.

(b) [CKV90] Show that (a) can be generalized to include unary ind's in Σ.

Exercise 11.26 [Hon82] Let (U, Σ) be an fd schema and $\mathbf{R} = \{R_1, \ldots, R_n\}$ a decomposition of U. Consider the following notions of "satisfaction" by $\mathbf{I}$ over $\mathbf{R}$ of Σ:

$\mathbf{I} \models_1 \Sigma$: if $I_j \models \pi_{R_j}(\Sigma)$ for each $j \in [1, n]$.

$\mathbf{I} \models_2 \Sigma$: if $\bowtie \mathbf{I} \models \Sigma$.

$\mathbf{I} \models_3 \Sigma$: if $\mathbf{I} = \pi_\mathbf{R}(I)$ for some I over U such that $I \models \Sigma$.

(a) Show that $\models_1$ and $\models_2$ are incomparable.

(b) Show that if $\mathbf{R}$ preserves dependencies, then $\models_1$ implies $\models_2$.

(c) What is the relationship of $\models_1$ and $\models_2$ to $\models_3$?

(d) What is the relationship of all of these to the notion of satisfaction based on the weak URA?

♠ **Exercise 11.27** [Hon82] Prove Theorem 11.3.4.

Exercise 11.28 [MUV84, Hon82] Prove Proposition 11.3.5.

D

Datalog and Recursion

In Part B, we considered query languages ranging from conjunctive queries to first-order queries in the three paradigms: algebraic, logic, and deductive. We did this by enriching the conjunctive queries first with union (disjunction) and then with difference (negation). In this part, we further enrich these languages by adding *recursion*. First we add recursion to the conjunctive queries, which yields *datalog*. We study this language in Chapter 12. Although it is too limited for practical use, datalog illustrates some of the essential aspects of recursion. Furthermore, most existing optimization techniques have been developed for datalog.

Datalog owes a great debt to Prolog and the logic-programming area in general. A fundamental contribution of the logic-programming paradigm to relational query languages is its elegant notation for expressing recursion. The perspective of databases, however, is significantly different from that of logic programming. (For example, in databases datalog programs define mappings from instances to instances, whereas logic programs generally carry their data with them and are studied as stand-alone entities.) We adapt the logic-programming approach to the framework of databases.

We study evaluation techniques for datalog programs in Chapter 13, which covers the main optimization techniques developed for recursion in query languages, including seminaive evaluation and magic sets.

Although datalog is of great theoretical importance, it is not adequate as a practical query language because of the lack of negation. In particular, it cannot express even the first-order queries. Chapters 14 and 15 deal with languages combining recursion and negation, which are proper extensions of first-order queries. Chapter 14 considers the issue of combining negation and recursion. Languages are presented from all three paradigms, which support both negation and recursion. The semantics of each one is defined in fundamentally operational terms, which include datalog with negation and a straightforward, fixpoint semantics. As will be seen, the elegant correspondence between languages in the three paradigms is maintained in the presence of recursion.

Chapter 15 considers approaches to incorporating negation in datalog that are closer in spirit to logic programming. Several important semantics for negation are presented, including stratification and well-founded semantics.

12 Datalog

Alice:	*What do we see next?*
Riccardo:	*We introduce recursion.*
Sergio:	*He means we ask queries about your ancestors.*
Alice:	*Are you leading me down a garden path?*
Vittorio:	*Kind of—queries related to paths in a graph call for recursion and are crucial for many applications.*

For a long time, relational calculus and algebra were considered *the* database languages. Codd even defined as "complete" a language that would yield precisely relational calculus. Nonetheless, there are simple operations on data that cannot be realized in the calculus. The most conspicuous example is graph transitive closure. In this chapter, we study a language that captures such queries and is thus more "complete" than relational calculus.[1] The language, called datalog, provides a feature not encountered in languages studied so far: *recursion*.

We start with an example that motivates the need for recursion. Consider a database for the Parisian **Metro**. Note that this database essentially describes a graph. (Database applications in which part of the data is a graph are common.) To avoid making the **Metro** database too static, we assume that the database is describing the available metro connections on a day of strike (not an unusual occurrence). So some connections may be missing, and the graph may be partitioned. An instance of this database is shown in Fig. 12.1.

Natural queries to ask are as follows:

(12.1)   What are the stations reachable from Odeon?

(12.2)   What lines can be reached from Odeon?

(12.3)   Can we go from Odeon to Chatelet?

(12.4)   Are all pairs of stations connected?

(12.5)   Is there a cycle in the graph (i.e., a station reachable in one or more stops from itself)?

Unfortunately, such queries cannot be answered in the calculus without using some *a*

---

[1] We postpone a serious discussion of completeness until Part E, where we tackle fundamental issues such as "What is a formal definition of data manipulation (as opposed to arbitrary computation)? What is a reasonable definition of completeness for database languages?"

Links	Line	Station	Next Station
	4	St.-Germain	Odeon
	4	Odeon	St.-Michel
	4	St.-Michel	Chatelet
	1	Chatelet	Louvres
	1	Louvres	Palais-Royal
	1	Palais-Royal	Tuileries
	1	Tuileries	Concorde
	9	Pont de Sevres	Billancourt
	9	Billancourt	Michel-Ange
	9	Michel-Ange	Iena
	9	Iena	F. D. Roosevelt
	9	F. D. Roosevelt	Republique
	9	Republique	Voltaire

Figure 12.1:   An instance I of the **Metro** database

priori knowledge on the **Metro** graph, such as the graph diameter. More generally, given a graph G, a particular vertex a, and an integer n, it is easy to write a calculus query finding the vertexes at distance less than n from a; but it seems difficult to find a query for all vertexes reachable from a, regardless of the distance. We will prove formally in Chapter 17 that such a query is *not* expressible in the calculus. Intuitively, the reason is the lack of recursion in the calculus.

The objective of this chapter is to extend some of the database languages considered so far with recursion. Although there are many ways to do this (see also Chapter 14), we focus in this chapter on an approach inspired by logic programming. This leads to a field called deductive databases, or database logic programming, which shares motivation and techniques with the logic-programming area.

Most of the activity in deductive databases has focused on a toy language called *datalog*, which extends the conjunctive queries with recursion. The interaction between negation and recursion is more tricky and is considered in Chapters 14 and 15. The importance of datalog for deductive databases is analogous to that of the conjunctive queries for the relational model. Most optimization techniques for relational algebra were developed for conjunctive queries. Similarly, in this chapter most of the optimization techniques in deductive databases have been developed around datalog (see Chapter 13).

Before formally presenting the language datalog, we present informally the syntax and various semantics that are considered for that language. Following is a datalog program P_{TC} that computes the transitive closure of a graph. The graph is represented in relation G and its transitive closure in relation T:

$$T(x, y) \leftarrow G(x, y)$$
$$T(x, y) \leftarrow G(x, z), T(z, y).$$

Observe that, except for the fact that relation T occurs both in the head and body of the second rule, these look like the nonrecursive datalog rules of Chapter 4.

A datalog program defines the relations that occur in heads of rules based on other relations. The definition is recursive, so defined relations can also occur in bodies of rules. Thus a datalog program is interpreted as a mapping from instances over the relations occurring in the bodies only, to instances over the relations occurring in the heads. For instance, the preceding program maps a relation over G (a graph) to a relation over T (its transitive closure).

A surprising and elegant property of datalog, and of logic programming in general, is that there are three very different but equivalent approaches to defining the semantics. We present the three approaches informally now.

A first approach is *model theoretic*. We view the rules as logical sentences stating a property of the desired result. For instance, the preceding rules yield the logical formulas

(1) $$\forall x, y(T(x, y) \leftarrow G(x, y))$$
(2) $$\forall x, y, z(T(x, y) \leftarrow (G(x, z) \land T(z, y))).$$

The result T must satisfy the foregoing sentences. However, this is not sufficient to determine the result uniquely because it is easy to see that there are many Ts that satisfy the sentences. However, it turns out that the result becomes unique if one adds the following natural minimality requirement: T consists of the smallest set of facts that makes the sentences true. As it turns out, for each datalog program and input, there is a unique minimal model. This defines the semantics of a datalog program. For example, suppose that the instance contains

$$G(a, b), G(b, c), G(c, d).$$

It turns out that $T(a, d)$ holds in each instance that obeys (1) and (2) and where these three facts hold. In particular, it belongs to the minimum model of (1) and (2).

The second *proof-theoretic* approach is based on obtaining proofs of facts. A proof of the fact $T(a, d)$ is as follows:

(i) $G(c, d)$ belongs to the instance;
(ii) $T(c, d)$ using (i) and the first rule;
(iii) $G(b, c)$ belongs to the instance;
(iv) $T(b, d)$ using (iii), (ii), and the second rule;
(v) $G(a, b)$ belongs to the instance;
(vi) $T(a, d)$ using (v), (iv), and the second rule.

A fact is in the result if there exists a proof for it using the rules and the database facts.

In the proof-theoretic perspective, there are two ways to derive facts. The first is to view programs as "factories" producing all facts that can be proven from known facts. The rules are then used *bottom up*, starting from the known facts and deriving all possible new facts. An alternative *top-down* evaluation starts from a fact to be proven and attempts to demonstrate it by deriving lemmas that are needed for the proof. This is the underlying intuition of a particular technique (called resolution) that originated in the theorem-proving field and lies at the core of the logic-programming area.

As an example of the top-down approach, suppose that we wish to prove $T(a, d)$. Then by the second rule, this can be done by proving $G(a, b)$ and $T(b, d)$. We know $G(a, b)$, a database fact. We are thus left with proving $T(b, d)$. By the second rule again, it suffices to prove $G(b, c)$ (a database fact) and $T(c, d)$. This last fact can be proven using the first rule. Observe that this yields the foregoing proof (i) to (vi). Resolution is thus a particular technique for obtaining such proofs. As detailed later, resolution permits variables as well as values in the goals to be proven and the steps used in the proof.

The last approach is the *fixpoint* approach. We will see that the semantics of the program can be defined as a particular solution of a fixpoint equation. This approach leads to iterating a query until a fixpoint is reached and is thus procedural in nature. However, this computes again the facts that can be deduced by applications of the rules, and in that respect it is tightly connected to the (bottom-up) proof-theoretic approach. It corresponds to a natural strategy for generating proofs where shorter proofs are produced before longer proofs so facts are proven "as soon as possible."

In the next sections we describe in more detail the syntax, model-theoretic, fixpoint, and proof-theoretic semantics of datalog. As a rule, we introduce only the minimum amount of terminology from logic programming needed in the special database case. However, we make brief excursions into the wider framework in the text and exercises. The last section deals with static analysis of datalog programs. It provides decidability and undecidability results for several fundamental properties of programs. Techniques for the evaluation of datalog programs are discussed separately in Chapter 13.

12.1   Syntax of Datalog

As mentioned earlier, the syntax of datalog is similar to that of languages introduced in Chapter 4. It is an extension of nonrecursive datalog, which was introduced in Chapter 4. We provide next a detailed definition of its syntax. We also briefly introduce some of the fundamental differences between datalog and logic programming.

DEFINITION 12.1.1   A *(datalog) rule* is an expression of the form

$$R_1(u_1) \leftarrow R_2(u_2), \ldots, R_n(u_n),$$

where $n \geq 1$, $R_1, \ldots, R_n$ are relation names and $u_1, \ldots, u_n$ are free tuples of appropriate arities. Each variable occurring in u_1 must occur in at least one of $u_2, \ldots, u_n$. A *datalog program* is a finite set of datalog rules.

The *head* of the rule is the expression $R_1(u_1)$; and $R_2(u_2), \ldots, R_n(u_n)$ forms the *body*.

The set of constants occurring in a datalog program P is denoted $adom(P)$; and for an instance $\mathbf{I}$, we use $adom(P, \mathbf{I})$ as an abbreviation for $adom(P) \cup adom(\mathbf{I})$.

We next recall a definition from Chapter 4 that is central to this chapter.

DEFINITION 12.1.2   Given a valuation v, an *instantiation*

$$R_1(v(u_1)) \leftarrow R_2(v(u_2)), \ldots, R_n(v(u_n))$$

of a rule $R_1(u_1) \leftarrow R_2(u_2), \ldots, R_n(u_n)$ with v is obtained by replacing each variable x by $v(x)$.

Let P be a datalog program. An *extensional* relation is a relation occurring only in the body of the rules. An *intensional* relation is a relation occurring in the head of some rule of P. The *extensional (database) schema*, denoted $edb(P)$, consists of the set of all extensional relation names; whereas the *intensional schema* $idb(P)$ consists of all the intensional ones. The *schema* of P, denoted $sch(P)$, is the union of $edb(P)$ and $idb(P)$. The semantics of a datalog program is a mapping from database instances over $edb(P)$ to database instances over $idb(P)$. In some contexts, we call the input data the extensional database and the program the intensional database. Note also that in the context of logic-based languages, the term *predicate* is often used in place of the term *relation name*.

Let us consider an example.

EXAMPLE 12.1.3   The following program P_{metro} computes the answers to queries (12.1), (12.2), and (12.3):

$$
\begin{aligned}
St\_Reachable(x, x) &\leftarrow \\
St\_Reachable(x, y) &\leftarrow St\_Reachable(x, z), Links(u, z, y) \\
Li\_Reachable(x, u) &\leftarrow St\_Reachable(x, z), Links(u, z, y) \\
Ans\_1(y) &\leftarrow St\_Reachable(Odeon, y) \\
Ans\_2(u) &\leftarrow Li\_Reachable(Odeon, u) \\
Ans\_3() &\leftarrow St\_Reachable(Odeon, Chatelet)
\end{aligned}
$$

Observe that *St_Reachable* is defined using recursion. Clearly,

$$
\begin{aligned}
edb(P_{metro}) &= \{Links\}, \\
idb(P_{metro}) &= \{St\_Reachable, Li\_Reachable, Ans\_1, Ans\_2, Ans\_3\}
\end{aligned}
$$

For example, an instantiation of the second rule of P_{metro} is as follows:

$$
\begin{aligned}
St\_Reachable(Odeon, Louvres) \leftarrow\ &St\_Reachable(Odeon, Chatelet), \\
&Links(1, Chatelet, Louvres)
\end{aligned}
$$

Datalog versus Logic Programming

Given the close correspondence between datalog and logic programming, we briefly high-light the central differences between these two fields. The major difference is that logic programming permits function symbols, but datalog does not.

EXAMPLE 12.1.4   The simple logic program P_{leq} is given by

$$leq(0, x) \leftarrow$$
$$leq(s(x), s(y)) \leftarrow leq(x, y)$$
$$leq(x, +(x, y)) \leftarrow$$
$$leq(x, z) \leftarrow leq(x, y), leq(y, z)$$

Here 0 is a constant, s a unary function sysmbol, $+$ a binary function sysmbol, and *leq* a binary predicate. Intuitively, s might be viewed as the successor function, $+$ as addition, and *leq* as capturing the less-than-or-equal relation. However, in logic programming the function symbols are given the "free" interpretation—two terms are considered nonequal whenever they are syntactically different. For example, the terms $+(0, s(0))$, $+(s(0), 0)$, and $s(0)$ are all nonequal. Importantly, functional terms can be used in logic programming to represent intricate data structures, such as lists and trees.

Observe also that in the preceding program the variable x occurs in the head of the first rule and not in the body, and analogously for the third rule.

Another important difference between deductive databases and logic programs concerns perspectives on how they are typically used. In databases it is assumed that the database is relatively large and the number of rules relatively small. Furthermore, a datalog program P is typically viewed as defining a mapping from instances over the *edb* to instances over the *idb*. In logic programming the focus is different. It is generally assumed that the base data is incorporated directly into the program. For example, in logic programming the contents of instance *Link* in the **Metro** database would be represented using rules such as *Link*(4, *St.-Germain*, *Odeon*) $\leftarrow$. Thus if the base data changes, the logic program itself is changed. Another distinction, mentioned in the preceding example, is that logic programs can construct and manipulate complex data structures encoded by terms involving function symbols.

Later in this chapter we present further comparisons of the two frameworks.

12.2   Model-Theoretic Semantics

The key idea of the model-theoretic approach is to view the program as a set of first-order sentences (also called a first-order theory) that describes the desired answer. Thus the database instance constituting the result satisfies the sentences. Such an instance is also called a *model* of the sentences. However, there can be many (indeed, infinitely many) instances satisfying the sentences of a program. Thus the sentences themselves do not uniquely identify the answer; it is necessary to specify which of the models is the *intended* answer. This is usually done based on assumptions that are external to the sentences themselves. In this section we formalize (1) the relationship between rules and logical sentences, (2) the notion of model, and (3) the concept of intended model.

We begin by associating logical sentences with rules, as we did in the beginning of this chapter. To a datalog rule

$$\rho : R_1(u_1) \leftarrow R_2(u_2), \ldots, R_n(u_n)$$

we associate the logical sentence

$$\forall x_1, \ldots, x_m (R_1(u_1) \leftarrow R_2(u_2) \wedge \cdots \wedge R_n(u_n)),$$

where $x_1, \ldots, x_m$ are the variables occurring in the rule and $\leftarrow$ is the standard logical *implication*. Observe that an instance **I** satisfies ρ, denoted $\mathbf{I} \models \rho$, if for each instantiation

$$R_1(\nu(u_1)) \leftarrow R_2(\nu(u_2)), \ldots, R_n(\nu(u_n))$$

such that $R_2(\nu(u_2)), \ldots, R_n(\nu(u_n))$ belong to **I**, so does $R_1(\nu(u_1))$. In the following, we do not distinguish between a rule ρ and the associated sentence. For a program P, the conjunction of the sentences associated with the rules of P is denoted by Σ_P.

It is useful to note that there are alternative ways to write the sentences associated with rules of programs. In particular, the formula

$$\forall x_1, \ldots, x_m (R_1(u_1) \leftarrow R_2(u_2) \wedge \cdots \wedge R_n(u_n))$$

is equivalent to

$$\forall x_1, \ldots, x_q (\exists x_{q+1}, \ldots, x_m (R_2(u_2) \wedge \cdots \wedge R_n(u_n)) \rightarrow R_1(u_1)),$$

where $x_1, \ldots, x_q$ are the variables occurring in the head. It is also logically equivalent to

$$\forall x_1, \ldots, x_m (R_1(u_1) \vee \neg R_2(u_2) \vee \cdots \vee \neg R_n(u_n)).$$

This last form is particularly interesting. Formulas consisting of a disjunction of literals of which at most one is positive are called in logic *Horn clauses*. A datalog program can thus be viewed as a set of (particular) Horn clauses.

We next discuss the issue of choosing, among the models of Σ_P, the particular model that is intended as the answer. This is not a hard problem for datalog, although (as we shall see in Chapter 15) it becomes much more involved if datalog is extended with negation. For datalog, the idea for choosing the intended model is simply that the model should not contain more facts than necessary for satisfying Σ_P. So the intended model is minimal in some natural sense. This is formalized next.

DEFINITION 12.2.1 Let P be a datalog program and **I** an instance over $edb(P)$. A *model* of P is an instance over $sch(P)$ satisfying Σ_P. The *semantics* of P on input **I**, denoted $P(\mathbf{I})$, is the minimum model of P containing **I**, if it exists.

Ans_1	Station
	Odeon
	St.-Michel
	Chatelet
	Louvres
	Palais-Royal
	Tuileries
	Concorde

Ans_2	Line
	4
	1

Ans_3	
	⟨ ⟩

Figure 12.2:   Relations of $P_{metro}(\mathbf{I})$

For P_{metro} as in Example 12.1.3, and $\mathbf{I}$ as in Fig. 12.1, the values of *Ans_1*, *Ans_2*, and *Ans_3* in $P(\mathbf{I})$ are shown in Fig. 12.2.

We briefly discuss the choice of the minimal model at the end of this section.

Although the previous definition is natural, we cannot be entirely satisfied with it at this point:

- For given P and $\mathbf{I}$, we do not know (yet) whether the semantics of P is defined (i.e., whether there exists a minimum model of Σ_P containing $\mathbf{I}$).

- Even if such a model exists, the definition does not provide any algorithm for computing $P(\mathbf{I})$. Indeed, it is not (yet) clear that such an algorithm exists.

We next provide simple answers to both of these problems.

Observe that by definition, $P(\mathbf{I})$ is an instance over $sch(P)$. A priori, we must consider all instances over $sch(P)$, an infinite set. It turns out that it suffices to consider only those instances with active domain in $adom(P, \mathbf{I})$ (i.e., a finite set of instances). For given P and $\mathbf{I}$, let $\mathbf{B}(P, \mathbf{I})$ be the instance over $sch(P)$ defined by

1. For each R in $edb(P)$, a fact $R(u)$ is in $\mathbf{B}(P, \mathbf{I})$ iff it is in $\mathbf{I}$; and
2. For each R in $idb(P)$, each fact $R(u)$ with constants in $adom(P, \mathbf{I})$ is in $\mathbf{B}(P, \mathbf{I})$.

We now verify that $\mathbf{B}(P, \mathbf{I})$ is a model of P containing $\mathbf{I}$.

LEMMA 12.2.2   Let P be a datalog program and $\mathbf{I}$ an instance over $edb(P)$. Then $\mathbf{B}(P, \mathbf{I})$ is a model of P containing $\mathbf{I}$.

Proof   Let $A_1 \leftarrow A_2, \ldots, A_n$ be an instantiation of some rule r in P such that $A_2, \ldots, A_n$ hold in $\mathbf{B}(P, \mathbf{I})$. Then consider A_1. Because each variable occurring in the head of r also occurs in the body, each constant occurring in A_1 belongs to $adom(P, \mathbf{I})$. Thus by definition 2 just given, A_1 is in $\mathbf{B}(P, \mathbf{I})$. Hence $\mathbf{B}(P, \mathbf{I})$ satisfies the sentence associated with that particular rule, so $\mathbf{B}(P, \mathbf{I})$ satisfies Σ_P. Clearly, $\mathbf{B}(P, \mathbf{I})$ contains $\mathbf{I}$ by definition 1. ∎

Thus the semantics of P on input $\mathbf{I}$, if defined, is a subset of $\mathbf{B}(P, \mathbf{I})$. This means that there is no need to consider instances with constants outside $adom(P, \mathbf{I})$.

We next demonstrate that $P(\mathbf{I})$ is always defined.

THEOREM 12.2.3 Let P be a datalog program, $\mathbf{I}$ an instance over $edb(P)$, and $\mathcal{X}$ the set of models of P containing $\mathbf{I}$. Then

1. $\cap \mathcal{X}$ is the minimal model of P containing $\mathbf{I}$, so $P(\mathbf{I})$ is defined.
2. $adom(P(\mathbf{I})) \subseteq adom(P, \mathbf{I})$.
3. For each R in $edb(P)$, $P(\mathbf{I})(R) = \mathbf{I}(R)$.

Proof   Note that $\mathcal{X}$ is nonempty, because $\mathbf{B}(P, \mathbf{I})$ is in $\mathcal{X}$. Let $r \equiv A_1 \leftarrow A_2, \ldots, A_n$ be a rule in P and ν a valuation of the variables occurring in the rule. To prove (1), we show that

(*)   if $\nu(A_2), \ldots, \nu(A_n)$ are in $\cap \mathcal{X}$ then $\nu(A_1)$ is also in $\cap \mathcal{X}$.

For suppose that (*) holds. Then $\cap \mathcal{X} \models r$, so $\cap \mathcal{X}$ satisfies Σ_P. Because each instance in $\mathcal{X}$ contains $\mathbf{I}$, $\cap \mathcal{X}$ contains $\mathbf{I}$. Hence $\cap \mathcal{X}$ is a model of P containing $\mathbf{I}$. By construction, $\cap \mathcal{X}$ is minimal, so (1) holds.

To show (*), suppose that $\nu(A_2), \ldots, \nu(A_n)$ are in $\cap \mathcal{X}$ and let $\mathbf{K}$ be in $\mathcal{X}$. Because $\cap \mathcal{X} \subseteq \mathbf{K}$, $\nu(A_2), \ldots, \nu(A_n)$ are in $\mathbf{K}$. Because $\mathbf{K}$ is in $\mathcal{X}$, $\mathbf{K}$ is a model of P, so $\nu(A_1)$ is in $\mathbf{K}$. This is true for each $\mathbf{K}$ in $\mathcal{X}$. Hence $\nu(A_1)$ is in $\cap \mathcal{X}$ and (*) holds, which in turn proves (1).

By Lemma 12.2.2, $\mathbf{B}(P, \mathbf{I})$ is a model of P containing $\mathbf{I}$. Therefore $P(\mathbf{I}) \subseteq \mathbf{B}(P, \mathbf{I})$. Hence

- $adom(P(\mathbf{I})) \subseteq adom(\mathbf{B}(P, \mathbf{I})) = adom(P, \mathbf{I})$, so (2) holds.
- For each R in $edb(P)$, $\mathbf{I}(R) \subseteq P(\mathbf{I})(R)$ [because $P(\mathbf{I})$ contains $\mathbf{I}$] and $P(\mathbf{I})(R) \subseteq \mathbf{B}(P, \mathbf{I})(R) = \mathbf{I}(R)$; which shows (3). ∎

The previous development also provides an algorithm for computing the semantics of datalog programs. Given P and $\mathbf{I}$, it suffices to consider all instances that are subsets of $\mathbf{B}(P, \mathbf{I})$, find those that are models of P and contain $\mathbf{I}$, and compute their intersection. However, this is clearly an inefficient procedure. The next section provides a more reasonable algorithm.

We conclude this section with two remarks on the definition of semantics of datalog programs. The first explains the choice of a minimal model. The second rephrases our definition in more standard logic-programming terminology.

Why Choose the Minimal Model?

This choice is the natural consequence of an implicit hypothesis of a philosophical nature: the *closed world assumption* (CWA) (see Chapter 2).

The CWA concerns the connection between the database and the world it models.

Clearly, databases are often incomplete (i.e., facts that may be true in the world are not necessarily recorded in the database). Thus, although we can reasonably assume that a fact recorded in the database is true in the world, it is not clear what we can say about facts not explicitly recorded. Should they be considered false, true, or unknown? The CWA provides the simplest solution to this problem: Treat the database as if it records complete information about the world (i.e., assume that all facts not in the database are false). This is equivalent to taking as true only the facts that must be true in all worlds modeled by the database. By extension, this justifies the choice of minimal model as the semantics of a datalog program. Indeed, the minimal model consists of the facts we know must be true in all worlds satisfying the sentences (and including the input instance). As we shall see, this has an equivalent proof-theoretic counterpart, which will justify the proof-theoretic semantics of datalog programs: Take as true precisely the facts that can be proven true from the input and the sentences corresponding to the datalog program. Facts that cannot be proven are therefore considered false.

Importantly, the CWA is not so simple to use in the presence of negation or disjunction. For example, suppose that a database holds $\{p \vee q\}$. Under the CWA, then both $\neg p$ and $\neg q$ are inferred. But the union $\{p \vee q, \neg p, \neg q\}$ is inconsistent, which is certainly not the intended result.

Herbrand Interpretation

We relate briefly the semantics given to datalog programs to standard logic-programming terminology.

In logic programming, the facts of an input instance $\mathbf{I}$ are not separated from the sentences of a datalog program P. Instead, sentences stating that all facts in $\mathbf{I}$ are true are included in P. This gives rise to a logical theory $\Sigma_{P,\mathbf{I}}$ consisting of the sentences in Σ_P and of one sentence $P(u)$ [sometimes written $P(u) \leftarrow$] for each fact $P(u)$ in the instance. The semantics is defined as a particular model of this set of sentences. A problem is that standard interpretations in first-order logic permit interpretation of constants of the theory with arbitrary elements of the domain. For instance, the constants *Odeon* and *St.-Michel* may be interpreted by the same element (e.g., *John*). This is clearly not what we mean in the database context. We wish to interpret *Odeon* by *Odeon* and similarly for all other constants. Interpretations that use the identity function to interpret the constant symbols are called *Herbrand interpretations* (see Chapter 2). (If function symbols are present, restrictions are also placed on how terms involving functions are interpreted.) Given a set Γ of formulas, a *Herbrand model* of Γ is a Herbrand interpretation satisfying Γ.

Thus in logic programming terms, the semantics of a program P given an instance $\mathbf{I}$ can be viewed as the minimum Herbrand model of $\Sigma_{P,\mathbf{I}}$.

12.3   Fixpoint Semantics

In this section, we present an operational semantics for datalog programs stemming from fixpoint theory. We use an operator called the *immediate consequence* operator. The operator produces new facts starting from known facts. We show that the model-theoretic semantics, $P(\mathbf{I})$, can also be defined as the smallest solution of a fixpoint equation involving that operator. It turns out that this solution can be obtained constructively. This approach therefore provides an alternative constructive definition of the semantics of datalog programs. It can be viewed as an implementation of the model-theoretic semantics.

Let P be a datalog program and $\mathbf{K}$ an instance over $sch(P)$. A fact A is an *immediate consequence* for $\mathbf{K}$ and P if either $A \in \mathbf{K}(R)$ for some *edb* relation R, or $A \leftarrow A_1, \ldots, A_n$ is an instantiation of a rule in P and each A_i is in $\mathbf{K}$. The *immediate consequence operator* of P, denoted T_P, is the mapping from $inst(sch(P))$ to $inst(sch(P))$ defined as follows. For each $\mathbf{K}$, $T_P(\mathbf{K})$ consists of all facts A that are immediate consequences for $\mathbf{K}$ and P.

We next note some simple mathematical properties of the operator T_P over sets of instances. We first define two useful properties. For an operator T,

- T is *monotone* if for each $\mathbf{I}, \mathbf{J}, \mathbf{I} \subseteq \mathbf{J}$ implies $T(\mathbf{I}) \subseteq T(\mathbf{J})$.
- $\mathbf{K}$ is a *fixpoint* of T if $T(\mathbf{K}) = \mathbf{K}$.

The proof of the next lemma is straightforward and is omitted (see Exercise 12.9).

LEMMA 12.3.1   Let P be a datalog program.

(i) The operator T_P is monotone.

(ii) An instance $\mathbf{K}$ over $sch(P)$ is a model of Σ_P iff $T_P(\mathbf{K}) \subseteq \mathbf{K}$.

(iii) Each fixpoint of T_P is a model of Σ_P; the converse does not necessarily hold.

It turns out that $P(\mathbf{I})$ (as defined by the model-theoretic semantics) is a fixpoint of T_P. In particular, it is the minimum fixpoint containing $\mathbf{I}$. This is shown next.

THEOREM 12.3.2   For each P and $\mathbf{I}$, T_P has a minimum fixpoint containing $\mathbf{I}$, which equals $P(\mathbf{I})$.

Proof   Observe first that $P(\mathbf{I})$ is a fixpoint of T_P:

- $T_P(P(\mathbf{I})) \subseteq P(\mathbf{I})$ because $P(\mathbf{I})$ is a model of P; and
- $P(\mathbf{I}) \subseteq T_P(P(\mathbf{I}))$. [Because $T_P(P(\mathbf{I})) \subseteq P(\mathbf{I})$ and T_P is monotone, $T_P(T_P(P(\mathbf{I}))) \subseteq T_P(P(\mathbf{I}))$. Thus $T_P(P(\mathbf{I}))$ is a model of Σ_P. Because T_P preserves the contents of the *edb* relations and $\mathbf{I} \subseteq P(\mathbf{I})$, we have $\mathbf{I} \subseteq T_P(P(\mathbf{I}))$. Thus $T_P(P(\mathbf{I}))$ is a model of Σ_P containing $\mathbf{I}$. Because $P(\mathbf{I})$ is the minimum such model, $P(\mathbf{I}) \subseteq T_P(P(\mathbf{I}))$.]

In addition, each fixpoint of T_P containing $\mathbf{I}$ is a model of P and thus contains $P(\mathbf{I})$ (which is the intersection of all models of P containing $\mathbf{I}$). Thus $P(\mathbf{I})$ is the minimum fixpoint of P containing $\mathbf{I}$. ∎

The fixpoint definition of the semantics of P presents the advantage of leading to a constructive definition of $P(\mathbf{I})$. In logic programming, this is shown using fixpoint theory (i.e., using Knaster-Tarski's and Kleene's theorems). However, the database framework is much simpler than the general logic-programming one, primarily due to the lack of function symbols. We therefore choose to show the construction directly, without the formidable machinery of the theory of fixpoints in complete lattices. In Remark 12.3.5

we sketch the more standard proof that has the advantage of being applicable to the larger context of logic programming.

Given an instance **I** over $edb(P)$, one can compute $T_P(\mathbf{I})$, $T_P^2(\mathbf{I})$, $T_P^3(\mathbf{I})$, etc. Clearly,

$$\mathbf{I} \subseteq T_P(\mathbf{I}) \subseteq T_P^2(\mathbf{I}) \subseteq T_P^3(\mathbf{I}) \ldots \subseteq \mathbf{B}(P, \mathbf{I}).$$

This follows immediately from the fact that $\mathbf{I} \subseteq T_P(\mathbf{I})$ and the monotonicity of T_P. Let N be the number of facts in $\mathbf{B}(P, \mathbf{I})$. (Observe that N depends on **I**.) The sequence $\{T_P^i(\mathbf{I})\}_i$ reaches a fixpoint after at most N steps. That is, for each $i \geq N$, $T_P^i(\mathbf{I}) = T_P^N(\mathbf{I})$. In particular, $T_P(T_P^N(\mathbf{I})) = T_P^N(\mathbf{I})$, so $T_P^N(\mathbf{I})$ is a fixpoint of T_P. We denote this fixpoint by $T_P^\omega(\mathbf{I})$.

EXAMPLE 12.3.3   Recall the program P_{TC} for computing the transitive closure of a graph G:

$$T(x, y) \leftarrow G(x, y)$$
$$T(x, y) \leftarrow G(x, z), T(z, y).$$

Consider the input instance

$$\mathbf{I} = \{G(1, 2), G(2, 3), G(3, 4), G(4, 5)\}.$$

Then we have

$$T_{P_{TC}}(I) = I \cup \{T(1, 2), T(2, 3), T(3, 4), T(4, 5)\}$$
$$T_{P_{TC}}^2(I) = T_{P_{TC}}(I) \cup \{T(1, 3), T(2, 4), T(3, 5)\}$$
$$T_{P_{TC}}^3(I) = T_{P_{TC}}^2(I) \cup \{T(1, 4), T(2, 5)\}$$
$$T_{P_{TC}}^4(I) = T_{P_{TC}}^3(I) \cup \{T(1, 5)\}$$
$$T_{P_{TC}}^5(I) = T_{P_{TC}}^4(I).$$

Thus $T_{P_{TC}}^\omega(I) = T_{P_{TC}}^4(I)$.

We next show that $T_P^\omega(\mathbf{I})$ is exactly $P(\mathbf{I})$ for each datalog program P.

THEOREM 12.3.4   Let P be a datalog program and **I** an instance over $edb(P)$. Then $T_P^\omega(\mathbf{I}) = P(\mathbf{I})$.

Proof   By Theorem 12.3.2, it suffices to show that $T_P^\omega(\mathbf{I})$ is the minimum fixpoint of T_P containing **I**. As noted earlier,

$$T_P(T_P^\omega(\mathbf{I})) = T_P(T_P^N(\mathbf{I})) = T_P^N(\mathbf{I}) = T_P^\omega(\mathbf{I}).$$

where N is the number of facts in $\mathbf{B}(P, \mathbf{I})$. Therefore $T_P^\omega(\mathbf{I})$ is a fixpoint of T_P that contains $\mathbf{I}$.

To show that it is minimal, consider an arbitrary fixpoint $\mathbf{J}$ of T_P containing $\mathbf{I}$. Then $\mathbf{J} \supseteq T_P^0(\mathbf{I}) = \mathbf{I}$. By induction on i, $\mathbf{J} \supseteq T_P^i(\mathbf{I})$ for each i, so $\mathbf{J} \supseteq T_P^\omega(\mathbf{I})$. Thus $T_P^\omega(\mathbf{I})$ is the minimum fixpoint of T_P containing $\mathbf{I}$. ∎

The smallest integer i such that $T_P^i(\mathbf{I}) = T_P^\omega(\mathbf{I})$ is called the stage for P and $\mathbf{I}$ and is denoted $stage(P, \mathbf{I})$. As already noted, $stage(P, \mathbf{I}) \leq N = |\mathbf{B}(P, \mathbf{I})|$.

Evaluation

The fixpoint approach suggests a straightforward algorithm for the evaluation of datalog. We explain the algorithm in an example. We extend relational algebra with a *while* operator that allows us to iterate an algebraic expression while some condition holds. (The resulting language is studied extensively in Chapter 17.)

Consider again the transitive closure query. We wish to compute the transitive closure of relation G in relation T. Both relations are over AB. This computation is performed by the following program:

$$T := G;$$
$$\text{while } q(T) \neq T \text{ do } T := q(T);$$

where

$$q(T) = G \cup \pi_{AB}(\delta_{B \to C}(G) \bowtie \delta_{A \to C}(T)).$$

(Recall that δ is the renaming operation as introduced in Chapter 4.)

Observe that q is an SPJRU expression. In fact, at each step, q computes the immediate consequence operator T_P, where P is the transitive closure datalog program in Example 12.3.3. One can show in general that the immediate consequence operator can be computed using SPJRU expressions (i.e., relational algebra without the difference operation). Furthermore, the SPJRU expressions extended carefully with a while construct yield exactly the expressive power of datalog. The test of the while is used to detect when the fixpoint is reached.

The while construct is needed only for recursion. Let us consider again the nonrecursive datalog of Chapter 4. Let P be a datalog program. Consider the graph $(sch(P), E_P)$, where $\langle S, S' \rangle$ is an edge in E_P if S' occurs in the head of some rule r in P and S occurs in the body of r. Then P is *nonrecursive* if the graph is acyclic. We mentioned already that nr-datalog programs are equivalent to SPJRU queries (see Section 4.5). It is also easy to see that, for each nr-datalog program P, there exists a constant d such that for each $\mathbf{I}$ over $edb(P)$, $stage(P, \mathbf{I}) \leq d$. In other words, the fixpoint is reached after a bounded number of steps, dependent only on the program. (See Exercise 12.29.) Programs for which this happens are called *bounded*. We examine this property in more detail in Section 12.5.

A lot of redundant computation is performed when running the preceding transitive closure program. We study optimization techniques for datalog evaluation in Chapter 13.

REMARK 12.3.5   In this remark, we make a brief excursion into standard fixpoint theory to reprove Theorem 12.3.4. This machinery is needed when proving the analog of that theorem in the more general context of logic programming. A partially ordered set $(U, \leq)$ is a *complete lattice* if each subset has a least upper bound and a greatest lower bound, denoted *sup* and *inf*, respectively. In particular, $inf(U)$ is denoted $\perp$ and $sup(U)$ is denoted $\top$. An operator T on U is *monotone* iff for each $x, y \in U$, $x \leq y$ implies $T(x) \leq T(y)$. An operator T on U is *continuous* if for each subset V, $T(sup(V)) = sup(T(V))$. Note that continuity implies monotonicity.

To each datalog program P and instance **I**, we associate the program $P_{\mathbf{I}}$ consisting of the rules of P and one rule $R(u) \leftarrow$ for each fact $R(u)$ in **I**. We consider the complete lattice formed with $(inst(sch(P)), \subseteq)$ and the operator $T_{P_{\mathbf{I}}}$ defined by the following: For each **K**, a fact A is in $T_{P_{\mathbf{I}}}(\mathbf{K})$ if A is an immediate consequence for **K** and $P_{\mathbf{I}}$. The operator $T_{P_{\mathbf{I}}}$ on $(inst(sch(P)), \subseteq)$ is continuous (so also monotone).

The Knaster-Tarski theorem states that a monotone operator in a complete lattice has a least fixpoint that equals $inf(\{x \mid x \in U, T(x) \leq x\})$. Thus the least fixpoint of $T_{P_{\mathbf{I}}}$ exists. Fixpoint theory also provides the constructive definition of the least fixpoint for continuous operators. Indeed, Kleene's theorem states that if T is a continuous operator on a complete lattice, then its least fixpoint is $sup(\{\mathbf{K}_i \mid i \geq 0\})$ where $\mathbf{K}_0 = \perp$ and for each $i > 0$, $\mathbf{K}_i = T(\mathbf{K}_{i-1})$. Now in our case, $\perp = \emptyset$ and

$$\emptyset \cup T_{P_{\mathbf{I}}}(\emptyset) \cup \cdots \cup T_{P_{\mathbf{I}}}^i(\emptyset) \cup \cdots$$

coincides with $P(\mathbf{I})$.

In logic programming, function symbols are also considered (see Example 12.1.4). In this context, the sequence of $\{T_{P_{\mathbf{I}}}^i(\mathbf{I})\}_{i>0}$ does not generally converge in a finite number of steps, so the fixpoint evaluation is no longer constructive. However, it does converge in countably many steps to the least fixpoint $\cup\{T_{P_{\mathbf{I}}}^i(\emptyset) \mid i \geq 0\}$. Thus fixpoint theory is useful primarily when dealing with logic programs with function symbols. It is an overkill in the simpler context of datalog. ∎

12.4   Proof-Theoretic Approach

Another way of defining the semantics of datalog is based on proofs. The basic idea is that the answer of a program P on **I** consists of the set of facts that can be proven using P and **I**. The result turns out to coincide, again, with $P(\mathbf{I})$.

The first step is to define what is meant by *proof*. A *proof tree* of a fact A from **I** and P is a labeled tree where

1. each vertex of the tree is labeled by a fact;

2. each leaf is labeled by a fact in **I**;

3. the root is labeled by A; and

4. for each internal vertex, there exists an instantiation $A_1 \leftarrow A_2, \ldots, A_n$ of a rule in P such that the vertex is labeled A_1 and its children are respectively labeled $A_2, \ldots, A_n$.

Such a tree provides a proof of the fact A.

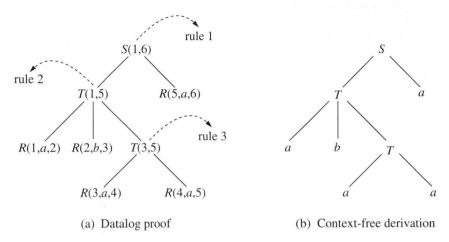

(a) Datalog proof   (b) Context-free derivation

Figure 12.3: Proof tree

EXAMPLE 12.4.1 Consider the following program:

$$S(x_1, x_3) \leftarrow T(x_1, x_2), R(x_2, a, x_3)$$
$$T(x_1, x_4) \leftarrow R(x_1, a, x_2), R(x_2, b, x_3), T(x_3, x_4)$$
$$T(x_1, x_3) \leftarrow R(x_1, a, x_2), R(x_2, a, x_3)$$

and the instance

$$\{R(1, a, 2), R(2, b, 3), R(3, a, 4), R(4, a, 5), R(5, a, 6)\}.$$

A proof tree of $S(1, 6)$ is shown in Fig. 12.3(a).

The reader familiar with context-free languages will notice the similarity between proof trees and derivation trees in context-free languages. This connection is especially strong in the case of datalog programs that have the form of the one in Example 12.4.1. This will be exploited in the last section of this chapter.

Proof trees provide proofs of facts. It is straightforward to show that a fact A is in $P(\mathbf{I})$ iff there exists a proof tree for A from $\mathbf{I}$ and P. Now given a fact A to prove, one can look for a proof either *bottom up* or *top down*.

The bottom-up approach is an alternative way of looking at the constructive fixpoint technique. One begins with the facts from $\mathbf{I}$ and then uses the rules to infer new facts, much like the immediate consequence operator. This is done repeatedly until no new facts can be inferred. The rules are used as "factories" producing new facts from already proven ones. This eventually yields all facts that can be proven and is essentially the same as the fixpoint approach.

In contrast to the bottom-up and fixpoint approaches, the top-down approach allows one to direct the search for a proof when one is only interested in proving particular facts.

For example, suppose the query *Ans_1(Louvres)* is posed against the program P_{metro} of Example 12.1.3, with the input instance of Fig. 12.1. Then the top-down approach will never consider atoms involving stations on Line 9, intuitively because they are are not reachable from *Odeon* or *Louvres*. More generally, the top-down approach inhibits the indiscriminate inference of facts that are irrelevant to the facts of interest.

The top-down approach is described next. This takes us to the field of logic programming. But first we need some notation, which will remind us once again that "To bar an easy access to newcomers every scientific domain has introduced its own terminology and notation" [Apt91].

Notation

Although we already borrowed a lot of terminology and notation from the logic-programming field (e.g., term, fact, atom), we must briefly introduce some more.

A *positive literal* is an atom [i.e., $P(u)$ for some free tuple u]; and a *negative literal* is the negation of one [i.e., $\neg P(u)$]. A formula of the form

$$\forall x_1, \ldots, x_m (A_1 \vee \cdots \vee A_n \vee \neg B_1 \vee \cdots \vee \neg B_p),$$

where the A_i, B_j are positive literals, is called a *clause*. Such a clause is written in *clausal form* as

$$A_1, \ldots, A_n \leftarrow B_1, \ldots, B_p.$$

A clause with a single literal in the head ($n = 1$) is called a *definite clause*. A definite clause with an empty body is called a *unit clause*. A clause with no literal in the head is called a *goal clause*. A clause with an empty body and head is called an *empty clause* and is denoted □. Examples of these and their logical counterparts are as follows:

definite	$T(x, y) \leftarrow R(x, z), T(z, y)$	$T(x, y) \vee \neg R(x, z) \vee \neg T(z, y)$
unit	$T(x, y) \leftarrow$	$T(x, y)$
goal	$\leftarrow R(x, z), T(z, y)$	$\neg R(x, z) \vee \neg T(z, y)$
empty	□	*false*

The empty clause is interpreted as a contradiction. Intuitively, this is because it corresponds to the disjunction of an empty set of formulas.

A *ground* clause is a clause with no occurrence of variables.

The top-down proof technique introduced here is called SLD resolution. Goals serve as the basic focus of activity in SLD resolution. As we shall see, the procedure begins with a goal such as $\leftarrow St\_Reachable(x, Concorde), Li\_Reachable(x, 9)$. A correct answer of this goal on input **I** is any value a such that $St\_Reachable(a, Concorde)$ and $Li\_Reachable(a, 9)$ are implied by $\Sigma_{P_{metro}, \mathbf{I}}$. Furthermore, each intermediate step of the top-down approach consists of obtaining a new goal from a previous goal. Finally, the procedure is deemed successful if the final goal reached is empty.

The standard exposition of SLD resolution is based on definite clauses. There is a subtle distinction between datalog rules and definite clauses: For datalog rules, we imposed the restriction that each variable that occurs in the head also appears in the body. (In particular, a datalog unit clause must be ground.) We will briefly mention some minor consequences of this distinction.

As already introduced in Remark 12.3.5, to each datalog program P and instance $\mathbf{I}$, we associate the program $P_\mathbf{I}$ consisting of the rules of P and one rule $R(u) \leftarrow$ for each fact $R(u)$ in $\mathbf{I}$. Therefore in the following we ignore the instance $\mathbf{I}$ and focus on programs that already integrate all the known facts in the set of rules. We denote such a program $P_\mathbf{I}$ to emphasize its relationship to an instance $\mathbf{I}$. Observe that from a semantic point of view

$$P(\mathbf{I}) = P_\mathbf{I}(\emptyset).$$

This ignores the distinction between *edb* and *idb* relations, which no longer exists for $P_\mathbf{I}$.

EXAMPLE 12.4.2 Consider the program P and instance $\mathbf{I}$ of Example 12.4.1. The rules of $P_\mathbf{I}$ are

1. $S(x_1, x_3) \leftarrow T(x_1, x_2), R(x_2, a, x_3)$
2. $T(x_1, x_4) \leftarrow R(x_1, a, x_2), R(x_2, b, x_3), T(x_3, x_4)$
3. $T(x_1, x_3) \leftarrow R(x_1, a, x_2), R(x_2, a, x_3)$
4. $R(1, a, 2) \leftarrow$
5. $R(2, b, 3) \leftarrow$
6. $R(3, a, 4) \leftarrow$
7. $R(4, a, 5) \leftarrow$
8. $R(5, a, 6) \leftarrow$

Warm-Up

Before discussing SLD resolution, as a warm-up we look at a simplified version of the technique by considering only ground rules. To this end, consider a datalog program $P_\mathbf{I}$ (integrating the facts) consisting only of fully instantiated rules (i.e., with no occurrences of variables). Consider a ground goal $g \equiv$

$$\leftarrow A_1, \ldots, A_i, \ldots, A_n$$

and some (ground) rule $r \equiv A_i \leftarrow B_1, \ldots, B_m$ in $P_\mathbf{I}$. A *resolvent* of g with r is the ground goal

$$\leftarrow A_1, \ldots, A_{i-1}, B_1, \ldots, B_m, A_{i+1}, \ldots, A_n.$$

Viewed as logical sentences, the resolvent of g with r is actually implied by g and r. This is best seen by writing these explicitly as clauses:

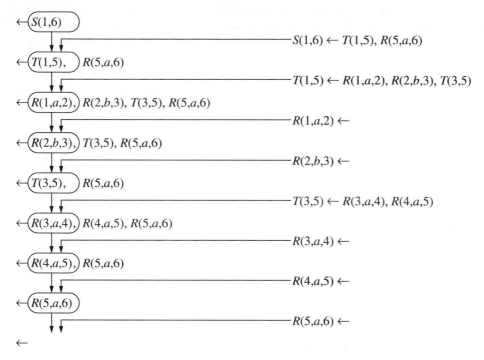

Figure 12.4: SLD ground refutation

$$(\neg A_1 \vee \cdots \vee \neg A_i \vee \cdots \vee \neg A_n) \wedge (A_i \vee \neg B_1 \vee \cdots \vee \neg B_m)$$
$$\Rightarrow (\neg A_1 \vee \cdots \vee \neg A_{i-1} \vee \neg B_1 \vee \cdots \vee \neg B_m \vee \neg A_{i+1} \vee \cdots \vee \neg A_n).$$

In general, the converse does not hold.

A *derivation* from g with $P_{\mathbf{I}}$ is a sequence of goals $g \equiv g_0, g_1, \ldots$ such that for each $i > 0$, g_i is a resolvent of g_{i-1} with some rule in $P_{\mathbf{I}}$. We will see that to prove a fact A, it suffices to exhibit a *refutation* of $\leftarrow A$—that is, a derivation

$$g_0 \equiv \leftarrow A, \quad g_1, \ldots, g_i, \ldots, \quad g_q \equiv \square.$$

EXAMPLE 12.4.3   Consider Example 12.4.1 and the program obtained by all possible instantiations of the rules of $P_{\mathbf{I}}$ in Example 12.4.2. An SLD ground refutation is shown in Fig. 12.4. It is a refutation of $\leftarrow S(1, 6)$ [i.e. a proof of $S(1, 6)$].

Let us now explain why refutations provide proofs of facts. Suppose that we wish to prove $A_1 \wedge \cdots \wedge A_n$. To do this we may equivalently prove that its negation (i.e. $\neg A_1 \vee \cdots \vee \neg A_n$) is false. In other words, we try to refute (or disprove) $\leftarrow A_1, \ldots, A_n$. The following rephrasing of the refutation in Fig. 12.4 should make this crystal clear.

EXAMPLE 12.4.4 Continuing with the previous example, to prove $S(1, 6)$, we try to refute its negation [i.e., $\neg S(1, 6)$ or $\leftarrow S(1, 6)$]. This leads us to considering, in turn, the formulas

Goal	Rule used
$\neg S(1, 6)$	(1)
$\Rightarrow \quad \neg T(1, 5) \vee \neg R(5, a, 6)$	(2)
$\Rightarrow \quad \neg R(1, a, 2) \vee \neg R(2, b, 3) \vee \neg T(3, 5) \vee \neg R(5, a, 6)$	(4)
$\Rightarrow \quad \neg R(2, b, 3) \vee \neg T(3, 5) \vee \neg R(5, a, 6)$	(5)
$\Rightarrow \quad \neg T(3, 5) \vee \neg R(5, a, 6)$	(3)
$\Rightarrow \quad \neg R(3, a, 4) \vee \neg R(4, a, 5) \vee \neg R(5, a, 6)$	(6)
$\Rightarrow \quad \neg R(4, a, 5) \vee \neg R(5, a, 6)$	(7)
$\Rightarrow \quad \neg R(5, a, 6)$	(8)
$\Rightarrow \quad false$	

At the end of the derivation, we have obtained a contradiction. Thus we have *refuted* $\neg S(1, 6)$ [i.e., proved $S(1, 6)$].

Thus refutations provide proofs. As a consequence, a goal can be thought of as a query. Indeed, the arrow is sometimes denoted with a question mark in goals. For instance, we sometimes write

$$?\text{-} S(1, 6) \text{ for } \leftarrow S(1, 6).$$

Observe that the process of finding a proof is nondeterministic for two reasons: the choice of the literal A to replace and the rule that is used to replace it.

We now have a technique for proving facts. The benefit of this technique is that it is sound and complete, in the sense that the set of facts in $P(\mathbf{I})$ coincides with the facts that can be proven from $P_{\mathbf{I}}$.

THEOREM 12.4.5 Let $P_{\mathbf{I}}$ be a datalog program and $ground(P_{\mathbf{I}})$ be the set of instantiations of rules in $P_{\mathbf{I}}$ with values in $adom(P, \mathbf{I})$. Then for each ground goal g, $P_{\mathbf{I}}(\emptyset) \models \neg g$ iff there exists a refutation of g with $ground(P_{\mathbf{I}})$.

Crux To show the "only if," we prove by induction that

(**)
$$\text{for each ground goal } g, \text{ if } T_{P_{\mathbf{I}}}^{i}(\emptyset) \models \neg g,$$
$$\text{there exists a refutation of } g \text{ with } ground(P_{\mathbf{I}}).$$

(The "if" part is proved similarly by induction on the length of the refutation. Its proof is left for Exercise 12.18.)

The base case is obvious. Now suppose that (**) holds for some $i \geq 0$, and let $A_1, \ldots, A_m$ be ground atoms such that $T_{P_{\mathbf{I}}}^{i+1}(\emptyset) \models A_1 \wedge \cdots \wedge A_m$. Therefore each A_j is in $T_{P_\mathbf{I}}^{i+1}(\emptyset)$. Consider some j. If A_j is an *edb* fact, we are back to the base case. Otherwise there exists an instantiation $A_j \leftarrow B_1, \ldots, B_p$ of some rule in $P_\mathbf{I}$ such that $B_1, \ldots, B_p$ are in $T_{P_\mathbf{I}}^i(\emptyset)$. The refutation of $\leftarrow A_j$ with $ground(P_\mathbf{I})$ is as follows. It starts with

$$\leftarrow A_j$$
$$\leftarrow B_1, B_2 \ldots, B_p.$$

Now by induction there exist refutations of $\leftarrow B_n, 1 \le n \le p$, with $ground(P_\mathbf{I})$. Using these refutations, one can extend the preceding derivation to a derivation leading to the empty clause. Furthermore, the refutations for each of the A_j's can be combined to obtain a refutation of $\leftarrow A_1, \ldots, A_m$ as desired. Therefore (**) holds for $i + 1$. By induction, (**) holds. ∎

SLD Resolution

The main difference between the general case and the warm-up is that we now handle goals and tuples with variables rather than just ground ones. In addition to obtaining the goal $\Box$, the process determines an instantiation θ for the free variables of the goal g, such that $P_\mathbf{I}(\emptyset) \models \neg\theta g$. We start with an example: An SLD refutation of $\leftarrow S(1, x)$ is shown in Fig. 12.5.

In general, we start with a goal (which does not have to be ground):

$$\leftarrow A_1, \ldots, A_i, \ldots, A_n.$$

Suppose that we selected a literal to be replaced [e.g., $A_i = Q(1, x_2, x_5)$]. Any rule used for the replacement must have Q for predicate in the head, just as in the ground case. For instance, we might try some rule

$$Q(x_1, x_4, x_3) \leftarrow P(x_1, x_2), P(x_2, x_3), Q(x_3, x_4, x_5).$$

We now have two difficulties:

(i) The same variable may occur in the selected literal and in the rule with two different meanings. For instance, x_2 in the selected literal is not to be confused with x_2 in the rule.

(ii) The pattern of constants and of equalities between variables in the selected literal and in the head of the rule may be different. In our example, for the first attribute we have 1 in the selected literal and a variable in the rule head.

The first of these two difficulties is handled easily by renaming the variables of the rules. We shall use the following renaming discipline: Each time a rule is used, a new set of distinct variables is substituted for the ones in the rule. Thus we might use instead the rule

$$Q(x_{11}, x_{14}, x_{13}) \leftarrow P(x_{11}, x_{12}), P(x_{12}, x_{13}), Q(x_{13}, x_{14}, x_{15}).$$

The second difficulty requires a more careful approach. It is tackled using unification,

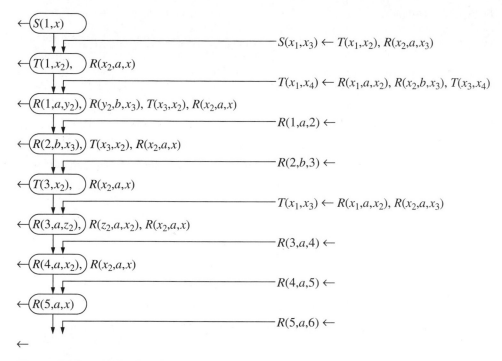

Figure 12.5:   SLD refutation

which matches the pattern of the selected literal to that of the head of the rule, if possible. In the example, unification consists of finding a substitution θ such that $\theta(Q(1, x_2, x_5)) = \theta(Q(x_{11}, x_{14}, x_{13}))$. Such a substitution is called a unifier. For example, the substitution $\theta(x_{11}) = 1$, $\theta(x_2) = \theta(x_{14}) = \theta(x_5) = \theta(x_{13}) = y$ is a unifier for $Q(1, x_2, x_5)$ and $Q(x_{11}, x_{14}, x_{13})$, because $\theta(Q(1, x_2, x_5)) = \theta(Q(x_{11}, x_{14}, x_{13})) = Q(1, y, y)$. Note that this particular unifier is unnecessarily restrictive; there is no reason to identify all of x_2, x_3, x_4, x_5.

A unifier that is no more restrictive than needed to unify the atoms is called a *most general unifier* (mgu). Applying the mgu to the rule to be used results in specializing the rule just enough so that it applies to the selected literal. These terms are formalized next.

DEFINITION 12.4.6   Let A, B be two atoms. A *unifier* for A and B is a substitution θ such that $\theta A = \theta B$. A substitution θ is *more general* than a substitution ν, denoted $\theta \hookrightarrow \nu$, if for some substitution ν', $\nu = \theta \circ \nu'$. A *most general unifier* (mgu) for A and B is a unifier θ for A, B such that, for each unifier ν of A, B, we have $\theta \hookrightarrow \nu$.

Clearly, the relation $\hookrightarrow$ between unifiers is reflexive and transitive but not antisymmetric. Let $\approx$ be the equivalence relation on substitutions defined by $\theta \approx \nu$ iff $\theta \hookrightarrow \nu$ and $\nu \hookrightarrow \theta$. If $\theta \approx \nu$, then for each atom A, $\theta(A)$ and $\nu(A)$ are the same modulo renaming of variables.

Computing the mgu

We now develop an algorithm for computing an mgu for two atoms. Let R be a relation of arity p and $R(x_1, \ldots, x_p)$, $R(y_1, \ldots, y_p)$ two literals with disjoint sets of variables. Compute $\equiv$, the equivalence relation on **var** $\cup$ **dom** defined as the reflexive, transitive closure of: $x_i \equiv y_i$ for each i in $[1, p]$. The mgu of $R(x_1, \ldots, x_p)$ and $R(y_1, \ldots, y_p)$ does not exist if two distinct constants are in the same equivalence class. Otherwise their mgu is the substitution θ such that

1. If $z \equiv a$ for some constant a, $\theta(z) = a$;
2. Otherwise $\theta(z) = z'$, where z' is the smallest (under a fixed ordering on **var**) such that $z \equiv z'$.

We show that the foregoing computes an mgu.

LEMMA 12.4.7 The substitution θ just computed is an mgu for $R(x_1, \ldots, x_p)$ and $R(y_1, \ldots, y_p)$.

Proof Clearly, θ is a unifier for $R(x_1, \ldots, x_p)$ and $R(y_1, \ldots, y_p)$. Suppose ν is another unifier for the same atoms. Let $\equiv_\nu$ be the equivalence relation on **var** $\cup$ **dom** defined by $x \equiv_\nu y$ iff $\nu(x) = \nu(y)$. Because ν is a unifier, $\nu(x_i) = \nu(y_i)$. It follows that $x_i \equiv_\nu y_i$, so $\equiv$ refines $\equiv_\nu$. Then the substitution ν' defined by $\nu'(\theta(x)) = \nu(x)$, is well defined, because $\theta(x) = \theta(x')$ implies $\nu(x) = \nu(x')$. Thus $\nu = \theta \circ \nu'$ so $\theta \hookrightarrow \nu$. Because this holds for every unifier ν, it follows that θ is an mgu for the aforementioned atoms. ■

The following facts about mgu's are important to note. Their proof is left to the reader (Exercise 12.19). In particular, part (ii) of the lemma says that the mgu of two atoms, if it exists, is essentially unique (modulo renaming of variables).

LEMMA 12.4.8 Let A, B be atoms.

(i) If there exists a unifier for A, B, then A, B have an mgu.
(ii) If θ and θ' are mgu's for A, B then $\theta \approx \theta'$.
(iii) Let A, B be atoms with mgu θ. Then for each atom C, if $C = \theta_1 A = \theta_2 B$ for substitutions θ_1, θ_2, then $C = \theta_3(\theta(A)) = \theta_3(\theta(B))$ for some substitution θ_3.

We are now ready to rephrase the notion of *resolvent* to incorporate variables. Let

$$g \equiv \leftarrow A_1, \ldots, A_i, \ldots, A_n, \qquad r \equiv B_1 \leftarrow B_2, \ldots, B_m$$

be a goal and a rule such that

1. g and r have no variable in common (which can always be ensured by renaming the variables of the rule).
2. A_i and B_1 have an mgu θ.

Then the *resolvent* of g with r using θ is the goal

$$\leftarrow \theta(A_1), \ldots, \theta(A_{i-1}), \theta(B_2), \ldots, \theta(B_m), \theta(A_{i+1}), \ldots, \theta(A_n).$$

As before, it is easily verified that this resolvent is implied by g and r.

An *SLD derivation* from a goal g with a program P_I is a sequence $g_0 = g, g_1, \ldots$ of goals and $\theta_0, \ldots$ of substitutions such that for each j, g_j is the resolvent of g_{j-1} with some rule in P_I using θ_{j_1}. An *SLD refutation* of a goal g with P_I is an SLD derivation $g_0 = g, \ldots, g_q = \square$ with P_I.

We now explain the meaning of such a refutation. As in the variable-free case, the existence of a refutation of a goal $\leftarrow A_1, \ldots, A_n$ with P_I can be viewed as a proof of the negation of the goal. The goal is

$$\forall x_1, \ldots, x_m (\neg A_1 \vee \cdots \vee \neg A_n)$$

where $x_1, \ldots, x_m$ are the variables in the goal. Its negation is therefore equivalent to

$$\exists x_1, \ldots, x_m (A_1 \wedge \cdots \wedge A_n),$$

and the refutation can be seen as a proof of its validity. Note that, in the case of datalog programs (where by definition all unit clauses are ground), the composition $\theta_1 \circ \cdots \circ \theta_q$ of mgu's used while refuting the goal yields a substitution by constants. This substitution provides "witnesses" for the existence of the variables $x_1, \ldots, x_m$ making true the conjunction. In particular, by enumerating all refutations of the goal, one could obtain all values for the variables satisfying the conjunction—that is, the answer to the query

$$\{\langle x_1, \ldots, x_m \rangle \mid A_1 \wedge \cdots \wedge A_n\}.$$

This is not the case when one allows arbitrary definite clauses rather than datalog rules, as illustrated in the following example.

EXAMPLE 12.4.9   Consider the program

$$S(x, z) \leftarrow G(x, z)$$
$$S(x, z) \leftarrow G(x, y), S(y, z)$$
$$S(x, x) \leftarrow$$

that computes in S the *reflexive* transitive closure of graph G. This is a set of definite clauses but not a datalog program because of the last rule. However, resolution can be extended to (and is indeed in general presented for) definite clauses. Observe, for instance, that the goal $\leftarrow S(w, w)$ is refuted with a substitution that does not bind variable w to a constant.

SLD resolution is a technique that provides proofs of facts. One must be sure that it produces only correct proofs (soundness) and that it is powerful enough to prove all true facts (completeness). To conclude this section, we demonstrate the soundness and completeness of SLD resolution for datalog programs.

We use the following lemma:

LEMMA 12.4.10   Let $g \equiv\leftarrow A_1, \ldots, A_i, \ldots, A_n$ and $r \equiv B_1 \leftarrow B_2, \ldots, B_m$ be a goal and a rule with no variables in common, and let

$$g' \equiv\leftarrow A_1, \ldots, A_{i-1}, B_2, \ldots, B_m, A_{i+1}, \ldots, A_n.$$

If $\theta g'$ is a resolvent of g with r using θ, then the formula r implies:

$$r' \equiv \neg\theta g' \rightarrow \neg\theta g$$
$$= \theta(A_1 \wedge \cdots \wedge A_{i-1} \wedge B_2 \wedge \cdots \wedge B_m \wedge A_{i+1} \wedge \cdots \wedge A_n) \rightarrow \theta(A_1 \wedge \cdots \wedge A_n).$$

Proof   Let $\mathbf{J}$ be an instance over $sch(P)$ satisfying r and let valuation v be such that

$$\mathbf{J} \models v[\theta(A_1) \wedge \cdots \wedge \theta(A_{i-1}) \wedge \theta(B_2) \wedge \cdots \wedge \theta(B_m) \wedge \theta(A_{i+1}) \wedge \cdots \wedge \theta(A_n)].$$

Because

$$\mathbf{J} \models v[\theta(B_2) \wedge \cdots \wedge \theta(B_m)]$$

and $\mathbf{J} \models B_1 \leftarrow B_2, \ldots, B_m$, $\mathbf{J} \models v[\theta(B_1)]$. That is, $\mathbf{J} \models v[\theta(A_i)]$. Thus

$$\mathbf{J} \models v[\theta(A_1) \wedge \cdots \wedge \theta(A_n)].$$

Hence for each v, $\mathbf{J} \models vr'$. Therefore $\mathbf{J} \models r'$. Thus each instance over $sch(P)$ satisfying r also satisfies r', so r implies r'. ∎

Using this lemma, we have the following:

THEOREM 12.4.11   (Soundness of SLD resolution) Let $P_\mathbf{I}$ be a program and $g \equiv\leftarrow A_1, \ldots, A_n$ a goal. If there exists an SLD-refutation of g with $P_\mathbf{I}$ and mgu's $\theta_1, \ldots, \theta_q$, then $P_\mathbf{I}$ implies

$$\theta_1 \circ \cdots \circ \theta_q(A_1 \wedge \cdots \wedge A_n).$$

Proof   Let $\mathbf{J}$ be some instance over $sch(P)$ satisfying $P_\mathbf{I}$. Let $g_0 = g, \ldots, g_q = \square$ be an SLD refutation of g with $P_\mathbf{I}$ and for each j, let g_j be a resolvent of g_{j-1} with some rule in $P_\mathbf{I}$ using some mgu θ_j. Then for each j, the rule that is used implies $\neg g_j \rightarrow \theta_j(\neg g_{j-1})$ by Lemma 12.4.10. Because $\mathbf{J}$ satisfies $P_\mathbf{I}$, for each j,

$$\mathbf{J} \models \neg g_j \rightarrow \theta_j(\neg g_{j-1}).$$

Clearly, this implies that for each j,

$$\mathbf{J} \models \theta_{j+1} \circ \cdots \circ \theta_q(\neg g_j) \to \theta_j \circ \cdots \circ \theta_q(\neg g_{j-1}).$$

By transitivity, this shows that

$$\mathbf{J} \models \neg g_q \to \theta_1 \circ \cdots \circ \theta_q(\neg g_0),$$

and so

$$\mathbf{J} \models \textit{true} \to \theta_1 \circ \cdots \circ \theta_q(\neg g).$$

Thus $\mathbf{J} \models \theta_1 \circ \cdots \circ \theta_q(A_1 \wedge \cdots \wedge A_n)$. ∎

We next prove the converse of the previous result (namely, the completeness of SLD resolution).

THEOREM 12.4.12 (Completeness of SLD resolution) Let $P_\mathbf{I}$ be a program and $g \equiv \leftarrow A_1, \ldots, A_n$ a goal. If $P_\mathbf{I}$ implies $\neg g$, then there exists a refutation of g with $P_\mathbf{I}$.

Proof Suppose that $P_\mathbf{I}$ implies $\neg g$. Consider the set $ground(P_\mathbf{I})$ of instantiations of rules in $P_\mathbf{I}$ with constants in $adom(P, \mathbf{I})$. Clearly, $ground(P_\mathbf{I})(\emptyset)$ is a model of $P_\mathbf{I}$, so it satisfies $\neg g$. Thus there exists a valuation θ of the variables in g such that $ground(P_\mathbf{I})(\emptyset)$ satisfies $\neg \theta g$. By Theorem 12.4.5, there exists a refutation of θg using $ground(P_\mathbf{I})$.

Let $g_0 = \theta g, \ldots, g_p = \square$ be that refutation. We show by induction on k that for each k in $[0, p]$,

(†)   there exists a derivation $g'_0 = g, \ldots, g'_k$ with $P_\mathbf{I}$ such that $g_k = \theta_k g'_k$ for some θ_k.

For suppose that (†) holds for each k. Then for $k = p$, there exists a derivation $g'_1 = g, \ldots, g'_p$ with $P_\mathbf{I}$ such that $\square = g_p = \theta_p g'_p$ for some θ_p, so $g'_p = \square$. Therefore there exists a refutation of g with $P_\mathbf{I}$.

The basis of the induction holds because $g_0 = \theta g = \theta g'_0$. Now suppose that (†) holds for some k. The next step of the refutation consists of selecting some atom B of g_k and applying a rule r in $ground(P_\mathbf{I})$. In g'_k select the atom B' with location in g' corresponding to the location of B in g_k. Note that $B = \theta_k B'$. In addition, we know that there is rule $r'' = B'' \leftarrow A''_1 \ldots A''_n$ in $P_\mathbf{I}$ that has r for instantiation via some substitution θ'' (such a pair B', r'' exists although it may not be unique). As usual, we can assume that the variables in g'_k are disjoint from those in r''. Let $\theta_k \oplus \theta''$ be the substitution defined by $\theta_k \oplus \theta''(x) = \theta_k(x)$ if x is a variable in g'_k, and $\theta_k \oplus \theta''(x) = \theta''(x)$ if x is a variable in r''. Clearly, $\theta_k \oplus \theta''(B') = \theta_k \oplus \theta''(B'') = B$ so, by Lemma 12.4.8 (i), B' and B'' have some mgu θ. Let g'_{k+1} be the resolvent of g'_k with r'', B' using mgu θ. By the definition of mgu, there exists a substitution θ_{k+1} such that $\theta_k \oplus \theta'' = \theta \circ \theta_{k+1}$. Clearly, $\theta_{k+1}(g'_{k+1}) = g_{k+1}$ and (†) holds for $k + 1$. By induction, (†) holds for each k. ∎

SLD Trees

We have shown that SLD resolution is sound and complete. Thus it provides an adequate top-down technique for obtaining the facts in the answer to a datalog program. To prove that a fact is in the answer, one must search for a refutation of the corresponding goal. Clearly, there are many refutations possible. There are two sources of nondeterminism in searching for a refutation: (1) the choice of the selected atom, and (2) the choice of the clause to unify with the atom. Now let us assume that we have fixed some golden rule, called a *selection rule*, for choosing which atom to select at each step in a refutation. A priori, such a rule may be very simple (e.g., as in Prolog, always take the leftmost atom) or in contrast very involved, taking into account the entire history of the refutation. Once an atom has been selected, we can systematically search for all possible unifying rules. Such a search can be represented in an *SLD tree*. For instance, consider the tree of Fig. 12.6 for the program in Example 12.4.2. The selected atoms are represented with boxes. Edges denote unifications used. Given $S(1, x)$, only one rule can be used. Given $T(1, x_2)$, two rules are applicable that account for the two descendants of vertex $T(1, x_2)$. The first number in edge labels denotes the rule that is used and the remaining part denotes the substitution. An SLD tree is a representation of all the derivations obtained with a fixed selection rule for atoms.

There are several important observations to be made about this particular SLD tree:

(i) It is successful because one branch yields □.

(ii) It has an infinite subtree that corresponds to an infinite sequence of applications of rule (2) of Example 12.4.2.

(iii) It has a blocking branch.

We can now explain (to a certain extent) the acronym SLD. SLD stands for <u>s</u>election rule-driven <u>l</u>inear resolution for <u>d</u>efinite clauses. *Rule-driven* refers to the rule used for selecting the atom. An important fact is that the success or failure of an SLD tree does not depend on the rule for selecting atoms. This explains why the definition of an SLD tree does not specify the selection rule.

Datalog versus Logic Programming, Revisited

Having established the three semantics for datalog, we summarize briefly the main differences between datalog and the more general logic-programming (lp) framework.

Syntax: Datalog has only relation symbols, whereas lp uses also function symbols. Datalog requires variables in rule heads to appear in bodies; in particular, all unit clauses are ground.

Model-theoretic semantics: Due to the presence of function symbols in lp, models of lp programs may be infinite. Datalog programs always have finite models. Apart from this distinction, lp and datalog are identical with respect to model-theoretic semantics.

Fixpoint semantics: Again, the minimum fixpoint of the immediate consequence operator may be infinite in the lp case, whereas it is always finite for datalog. Thus the fixpoint approach does not necessarily provide a constructive semantics for lp.

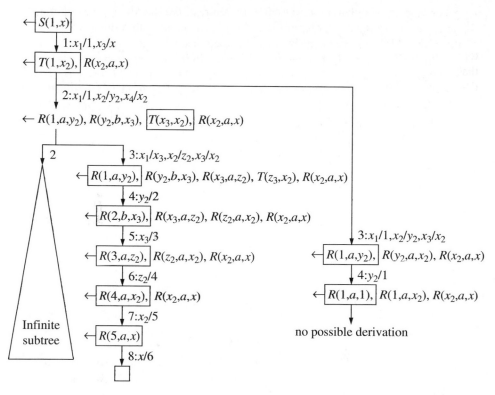

Figure 12.6: SLD tree

Proof-theoretic semantics: The technique of SLD resolution is similar for datalog and lp, with the difference that the computation of mgu's becomes slightly more complicated with function symbols (see Exercise 12.20). For datalog, the significance of SLD resolution concerns primarily optimization methods inspired by resolution (such as "magic sets"; see Chapter 13). In lp, SLD resolution is more important. Due to the possibly infinite answers, the bottom-up approach of the fixpoint semantics may not be feasible. On the other hand, every fact in the answer has a finite proof by SLD resolution. Thus SLD resolution emerges as the practical alternative.

Expressive power: A classical result is that lp can express all recursively enumerable (r.e.) predicates. However, as will be discussed in Part E, the expressive power of datalog lies within PTIME. Why is there such a disparity? A fundamental reason is that function symbols are used in lp, and so an infinite domain of objects can be constructed from a finite set of symbols. Speaking technically, the result for lp states that if S is a (possibly infinite) r.e. predicate over terms constructed using a finite language, then there is an lp program that produces for some predicate symbol exactly the tuples in S. Speaking intuitively, this follows from the facts that viewed in a bottom-up sense, lp provides composition and looping, and terms of arbitrary length can be used as scratch paper (e.g., to simulate a Turing tape). In contrast, the working space and output of range-restricted datalog programs are always contained within the active domain of the input and the program and thus are bounded in size.

Another distinction between lp and datalog in this context concerns the nature of expressive power results for datalog and for query languages in general. Specifically, a datalog program P is generally viewed as a mapping from instances of $edb(P)$ to instances of $idb(P)$. Thus expressive power of datalog is generally measured in comparison with mappings on families of database instances rather than in terms of expressing a single (possibly infinite) predicate.

12.5 Static Program Analysis

In this section, the static analysis of datalog programs is considered.[2] As with relational calculus, even simple static properties are undecidable for datalog programs. In particular, although tableau homomorphism allowed us to test the equivalence of conjunctive queries, equivalence of datalog programs is undecidable in general. This complicates a systematic search for alternative execution plans for datalog queries and yields severe limitations to query optimization. It also entails the undecidability of many other problems related to optimization, such as deciding when selection propagation (in the style of "pushing" selections in relational algebra) can be performed, or when parallel evaluation is possible.

We consider three fundamental static properties: satisfiability, containment, and a new one, boundedness. We exhibit a decision procedure for satisfiability. Recall that we showed in Chapter 5 that an analogous property is undecidable for CALC. The decidability of satisfiability for datalog may therefore be surprising. However, one must remember that, although datalog is more powerful than CALC in some respects (it has recursion), it is less powerful in others (there is no negation). It is the lack of negation that makes satisfiability decidable for datalog.

We prove the undecidability of containment and boundedness for datalog programs and consider variations or restrictions that are decidable.

Satisfiability

Let P be a datalog program. An intensional relation T is *satisfiable by* P if there exists an instance $\mathbf{I}$ over $edb(P)$ such that $P(\mathbf{I})(T)$ is nonempty. We give a simple proof of the decidability of satisfiability for datalog programs. We will soon see an alternative proof based on context-free languages.

We first consider constant-free programs. We then describe how to reduce the general case to the constant-free one.

To prove the result, we use an auxiliary result about instance homomorphisms that is of some interest in its own right. Note that any mapping θ from **dom** to **dom** can be extended to a homomorphism over the set of instances, which we also denote by θ.

---

[2] Recall that static program analysis consists of trying to detect statically (i.e., at compile time) properties of programs.

LEMMA 12.5.1 Let P be a constant-free datalog program, $\mathbf{I}, \mathbf{J}$ two instances over $sch(P)$, q a positive-existential query over $sch(P)$, and θ a mapping over **dom**. If $\theta(\mathbf{I}) \subseteq \mathbf{J}$, then (i) $\theta(q(\mathbf{I})) \subseteq q(\mathbf{J})$, and (ii) $\theta(P(\mathbf{I})) \subseteq P(\mathbf{J})$.

Proof For (i), observe that q is monotone and that $q \circ \theta \subseteq \theta \circ q$ (which is not necessary if q has constants). Because T_P can be viewed as a positive-existential query, a straightforward induction proves (ii). ■

This result does not hold for datalog programs with constants (see Exercise 12.21).

THEOREM 12.5.2 The satisfiability of an *idb* relation T by a constant-free datalog program P is decidable.

Proof Suppose that T is satisfiable by a constant-free datalog program P. We prove that $P(\mathbf{I}_a)(T)$ is nonempty for some particular instance $\mathbf{I}_a$. Let a be in **dom**. Let $\mathbf{I}_a$ be the instance over $edb(P)$ such that for each R in $edb(P)$, $\mathbf{I}_a(R)$ contains a single tuple with a in each entry. Because T is satisfiable by P, there exists $\mathbf{I}$ such that $P(\mathbf{I})(T) \neq \emptyset$. Consider the function θ that maps every constant in **dom** to a. Then $\theta(\mathbf{I}) \subseteq \mathbf{I}_a$. By the previous lemma, $\theta(P(\mathbf{I})) \subseteq P(\mathbf{I}_a)$. Therefore $P(\mathbf{I}_a)(T)$ is nonempty. Hence T is satisfiable by P iff $P(\mathbf{I}_a)(T) \neq \emptyset$. ■

Let us now consider the case of datalog programs *with* constants. Let P be a datalog program with constants. For example, suppose that b, c are the only two constants occurring in the program and that R is a binary relation occurring in P. We transform the problem into a problem without constants. Specifically, we replace R with nine new relations:

$$R_{\star\star}, R_{b\star}, R_{c\star}, R_{\star b}, R_{\star c}, R_{bc}, R_{cb}, R_{bb}, R_{cc}.$$

The first one is binary, the next four are unary, and the last four are 0-ary (i.e., are propositions). Intuitively, a fact $R(x, y)$ is represented by the fact $R_{\star\star}(x, y)$ if x, y are not in $\{b, c\}$; $R(b, x)$ with x not in $\{b, c\}$ is represented by $R_{b\star}(x)$, and similarly for $R_{c\star}, R_{\star b}, R_{\star c}$. The fact $R(b, c)$ is represented by proposition $R_{bc}()$, etc. Using this kind of transformation for each relation, one translates program P into a constant-free program P' such that T is satisfiable by P iff T_w is satisfiable by P' for some string w of $\star$ or constants occurring in P. (See Exercise 12.22a.)

Containment

Consider two datalog programs P, P' with the same extensional relations $edb(P)$ and a target relation T occurring in both programs. We say that P is *included* in P' *with respect to* T, denoted $P \subseteq_T P'$, if for each instance $\mathbf{I}$ over $edb(P)$, $P(\mathbf{I})(T) \subseteq P'(\mathbf{I})(T)$. The containment problem is undecidable. We prove this by reduction of the containment problem for context-free languages. The technique is interesting because it exhibits a correspondence between proof trees of certain datalog programs and derivation trees of context-free languages.

We first illustrate the correspondence in an example.

EXAMPLE 12.5.3   Consider the context-free grammar $G = (V, \Sigma, \Pi, S)$, where $V = \{S, T\}$, S is the start symbol, $\Sigma = \{a, b\}$, and the set Π of production rules is

$$S \to Ta$$
$$T \to abT \mid aa.$$

The corresponding datalog program P_G is the program of Example 12.4.1. A proof tree and its corresponding derivation tree are shown in Fig. 12.3.

We next formalize the correspondence between proof trees and derivation trees.

A context-free grammar is a $(\star)$ grammar if the following hold:

(1) G is ϵ free (i.e., does not have any production of the form $X \to \epsilon$, where ϵ denotes the empty string) and

(2) the start symbol does not occur in any right-hand side of a production.

We use the following:

Fact   It is undecidable, given $(\star)$ grammars G_1, G_2, whether $L(G_1) \subseteq L(G_2)$.

For each $(\star)$ grammar G, let P_G, the corresponding datalog program, be constructed (similar to Example 12.5.3) as follows: Let $G = (V, \Sigma, \Pi, S)$. We may assume without loss of generality that V is a set of relation names of arity 2 and Σ a set of elements from **dom**. Then $idb(P_G) = V$ and $edb(P_G) = \{R\}$, where R is a ternary relation. Let $x_1, x_2, \ldots$ be an infinite sequence of distinct variables. To each production in Π,

$$T \to C_1 \ldots C_n,$$

we associate a datalog rule

$$T(x_1, x_{n+1}) \leftarrow A_1, \ldots, A_n,$$

where for each i

- if C_i is a nonterminal T', then $A_i = T'(x_i, x_{i+1})$;
- if C_i is a terminal b, then $A_i = R(x_i, b, x_{i+1})$.

Note that, for any proof tree of a fact $S(a_1, a_n)$ using P_G, the sequence of its leaves is (in this order)

$$R(a_1, b_1, a_2), \ldots, R(a_{n-1}, b_{n-1}, a_n),$$

for some $a_2, \ldots, a_{n-1}$ and $b_1, \ldots, b_{n-1}$. The connection between derivation trees of G and proof trees of P_G is shown in the following.

PROPOSITION 12.5.4 Let G be a $(\star)$ grammar and P_G be the associated datalog program constructed as just shown. For each $a_1, \ldots, a_n, b_1, \ldots, b_{n-1}$, there is a proof tree of $S(a_1, a_n)$ from P_G with leaves $R(a_1, b_1, a_2), \ldots, R(a_{n-1}, b_{n-1}, a_n)$ (in this order) iff $b_1 \ldots b_{n-1}$ is in $L(G)$.

The proof of the proposition is left as Exercise 12.25. Now we can show the following:

THEOREM 12.5.5 It is undecidable, given P, P' (with $edb(P) = edb(P')$) and T, whether $P \subseteq_T P'$.

Proof It suffices to show that

(‡)
$$\text{for each pair } G_1, G_2 \text{ of } (\star) \text{ grammars,}$$
$$L(G_1) \subseteq L(G_2) \Leftrightarrow P_{G_1} \subseteq_S P_{G_2}.$$

Suppose (‡) holds and T containment is decidable. Then we obtain an algorithm to decide containment of $(\star)$ grammars, which contradicts the aforementioned fact.

Let G_2, G_2 be two $(\star)$ grammars. We show here that

$$L(G_1) \subseteq L(G_2) \Rightarrow P_{G_1} \subseteq_S P_{G_2}.$$

(The other direction is similar.) Suppose that $L(G_1) \subseteq L(G_2)$. Let $\mathbf{I}$ be over $edb(P_{G_1})$ and $S(a_1, a_n)$ be in $P_{G_1}(\mathbf{I})$. Then there exists a proof tree of $S(a_1, a_n)$ from P_{G_1} and $\mathbf{I}$, with leaves labeled by facts

$$R(a_1, b_1, a_2), \ldots, R(a_{n-1}, b_{n-1}, a_n),$$

in this order. By Proposition 12.5.4, $b_1 \ldots b_{n-1}$ is in $L(G_1)$. Because $L(G_1) \subseteq L(G_2)$, $b_1 \ldots b_{n-1}$ is in $L(G_2)$. By the proposition again, there is a proof tree of $S(a_1, a_n)$ from P_{G_2} with leaves $R(a_1, b_1, a_2), \ldots, R(a_{n-1}, b_{n-1}, a_n)$, all of which are facts in $\mathbf{I}$. Thus $S(a_1, a_n)$ is in $P_{G_2}(\mathbf{I})$, so $P_{G_1} \subseteq_S P_{G_2}$. ∎

Note that the datalog programs used in the preceding construction are very particular: They are essentially chain programs. Intuitively, in a *chain program* the variables in a rule body form a chain. More precisely, rules in chain programs are of the form

$$A_0(x_0, x_n) \leftarrow A_1(x_0, x_1), A_2(x_1, x_2), \ldots, A_n(x_{n-1}, x_n).$$

The preceding proof can be tightened to show that containment is undecidable even for chain programs (see Exercise 12.26).

The connection with grammars can also be used to provide an alternate proof of the decidability of satisfiability; satisfiability can be reduced to the emptiness problem for context-free languages (see Exercise 12.22c).

Although containment is undecidable, there is a closely related, stronger property which is decidable—namely, *uniform containment*. For two programs P, P' over the same set of intensional and extensional relations, we say that P is uniformly contained in P', denoted $P \sqsubseteq P'$, iff for each $\mathbf{I}$ over $sch(P)$, $P(\mathbf{I}) \subseteq P'(\mathbf{I})$. Uniform containment is a sufficient condition for containment. Interestingly, one can decide uniform containment. The test for uniform containment uses dependencies studied in Part D and the fundamental *chase* technique (see Exercises 12.27 and 12.28).

Boundedness

A key problem for datalog programs (and recursive programs in general) is to estimate the depth of recursion of a given program. In particular, it is important to know whether for a given program the depth is bounded by a constant independent of the input. Besides being meaningful for optimization, this turns out to be an elegant mathematical problem that has received a lot of attention.

A datalog program P is *bounded* if there exists a constant d such that for each $\mathbf{I}$ over $edb(P)$, $stage(P, \mathbf{I}) \leq d$. Clearly, if a program is bounded it is essentially nonrecursive, although it may appear to be recursive syntactically. In some sense, it is falsely recursive.

EXAMPLE 12.5.6   Consider the following two-rule program:

$$Buys(x, y) \leftarrow Trendy(x), Buys(z, y) \qquad Buys(x, y) \leftarrow Likes(x, y)$$

This program is bounded because $Buys(z,y)$ can be replaced in the body by $Likes(z,y)$, yielding an equivalent recursion-free program. On the other hand, the program

$$Buys(x, y) \leftarrow Knows(x, z), Buys(z, y) \qquad Buys(x, y) \leftarrow Likes(x, y)$$

is inherently recursive (i.e., is not equivalent to any recursion-free program).

It is important to distinguish truly recursive programs from falsely recursive (bounded) programs. Unfortunately, boundedness cannot be tested.

THEOREM 12.5.7   Boundedness is undecidable for datalog programs.

The proof is by reduction of the PCP (see Chapter 2). One can even show that boundedness remains undecidable under strong restrictions, such as that the programs that are considered (1) are constant-free, (2) contain a unique recursive rule, or (3) contain a unique intensional relation. Decidability results have been obtained for linear programs or chain-rule programs (see Exercise 12.31).

Bibliographic Notes

It is difficult to attribute datalog to particular researchers because it is a restriction or extension of many previously proposed languages; some of the early history is discussed in [MW88a]. The name *datalog* was coined (to our knowledge) by David Maier.

Many particular classes of datalog programs have been investigated. Examples are the class of *monadic* programs (all intensional relations have arity one), the class of *linear* programs (in the body of each rule of these programs, there can be at most one relation that is mutually recursive with the head relation; see Chapter 13), the class of *chain* programs [UG88, AP87a] (their syntax resembles that of context-free grammars), and the class of *single rule programs* or *sirups* [Kan88] (they consist of a single nontrivial rule and a trivial exit rule).

The fixpoint semantics that we considered in this chapter is due to [CH85]. However, it has been considered much earlier in the context of logic programming [vEK76, AvE82]. For logic programming, the existence of a least fixpoint is proved using [Tar55].

The study of stage functions $stage(d, H)$ is a major topic in [Mos74], where they are defined for finite structures (i.e., instances) as well as for infinite structures.

Resolution was originally proposed in the context of automatic theorem proving. Its foundations are due to Robinson [Rob65]. SLD resolution was developed in [vEK76]. These form the basis of logic programming introduced by Kowalski [Kow74] and [CKRP73] and led to the language Prolog. Nice presentations of the topic can be found in [Apt91, Llo87]. Standard SLD resolution is more general than that presented in this chapter because of the presence of function symbols. The development is similar except for the notion of unification, which is more involved. A survey of unification can be found in [Sie88, Kni89].

The programming language Prolog proposed by Colmerauer [CKRP73] is based on SLD resolution. It uses a particular strategy for searching for SLD refutations. Various ways to couple Prolog with a relational database system have been considered (see [CGT90]).

The undecidability of containment is studied in [CGKV88, Shm87]. The decidability of uniform containment is shown in [CK86, Sag88]. The decidability of containment for monadic programs is studied in [CGKV88]. The equivalence of recursive and nonrecursive datalog programs is shown to be decidable in [CV92]. The complexity of this problem is considered in [CV94].

Interestingly, bounded recursion is defined and used early in the context of universal relations [MUV84]. Example 12.5.6 is from [Nau86]. Undecidability results for boundedness of various datalog classes are shown in [GMSV87, GMSV93, Var88, Abi89]. Decidability results for particular subclasses are demonstrated in [Ioa85, Nau86, CGKV88, NS87, Var88].

Boundedness implies that the query expressed by the program is a positive existential query and therefore is expressible in CALC (over finite inputs). What about the converse? If infinite inputs are allowed, then (by a compactness argument) unboundedness implies nonexpressibility by CALC. But in the finite (database) case, compactness does not hold, and the question remained open for some time. Kolaitis observed that unboundedness does not imply nonexpressibility by CALC over finite structures for datalog with inequalities

$(x \neq y)$. (We did not consider comparators $\neq, <, \leq$, etc. in this chapter.) The question was settled by Ajtai and Gurevich [AG89], who showed by an elegant argument that no unbounded datalog program is expressible in CALC, even on finite structures.

Another decision problem for datalog concerns arises from the interaction of datalog with functional dependencies. In particular, it is undecidable, given a datalog program P, set Σ of fd's on $edb(P)$, and set Γ of fd's on $idb(P)$ whether $P(\mathbf{I}) \models \Gamma$ whenever $\mathbf{I} \models \Sigma$ [AH88].

The expressive power of datalog has been investigated in [AC89, ACY91, CH85, Shm87, LM89, KV90c]. Clearly, datalog expresses only monotonic queries, commutes with homomorphisms of the database (if there are no constants in the program), and can be evaluated in polynomial time (see also Exercise 12.11). It is natural to wonder if datalog expresses *precisely* those queries. The answer is negative. Indeed, [ACY91] shows that the existence of a path whose length is a perfect square between two nodes is not expressible in datalog$^{\neq}$ (datalog augmented with inequalities $x \neq y$), and so not in datalog. This is a monotonic, polynomial-time query commuting with homomorphisms. The parallel complexity of datalog is surveyed in [Kan88].

The function symbols used in logic programming are interpreted over a Herbrand domain and are prohibited in datalog. However, it is interesting to incorporate arithmetic functions such as addition and multiplication into datalog. Such functions can also be viewed as infinite base relations. If these are present, it is possible that the bottom-up evaluation of a datalog program will not terminate. This issue was first studied in [RBS87], where *finiteness dependencies* were introduced. These dependencies can be used to describe how the finiteness of the range of a set of variables can imply the finiteness of the range of another variable. [For example, the relation $+(x, y, z)$ satisfies the finiteness dependencies $\{x, y\} \rightsquigarrow \{z\}$, $\{x, z\} \rightsquigarrow \{y\}$, and $\{y, z\} \rightsquigarrow \{x\}$.] Safety of datalog programs with infinite relations constrained by finiteness dependencies is undecidable [SV89]. Various syntactic conditions on datalog programs that ensure safety are developed in [RBS87, KRS88a, KRS88b, SV89]. Finiteness dependencies were used to develop a safety condition for the relational calculus with infinite base relations in [EHJ93]. Safety was also considered in the context of *data functions* (i.e., functions whose extent is predefined).

Exercises

Exercise 12.1   Refer to the Parisian **Metro** database. Give a datalog program that yields, for each pair of stations (a, b), the stations c such that c is reachable (1) from both a and b; and (2) from a or b.

Exercise 12.2   Consider a database consisting of the **Metro** and **Cinema** databases, plus a relation *Theater-Station* giving for each theater the closest metro station. Suppose that you live near the Odeon metro station. Write a program that answers the query "Near which metro station can I see a Bergman movie?" (Having spent many years in Los Angeles, you do not like walking, so your only option is to take the metro at Odeon and get off at the station closest to the theater.)

Exercise 12.3   (Same generation) Consider a binary relation *Child_of*, where the intended meaning of *Child_of* (a, b) is that a is the child of b. Write a datalog program computing the set of pairs (c, d), where c and d have a common ancestor and are of the same generation with respect to this ancestor.

Exercise 12.4 We are given two directed graphs G_{black} and G_{white} over the same set V of vertexes, represented as binary relations. Write a datalog program P that computes the set of pairs (a, b) of vertexes such that there exists a path from a to b where black and white edges alternate, starting with a white edge.

Exercise 12.5 Suppose we are given an undirected graph with colored vertexes represented by a binary relation *Color* giving the colors of vertexes and a binary relation *Edge* giving the connection between them. (Although *Edge* provides directed edges, we ignore the direction, so we treat the graph as undirected.) Say that a vertex is *good* if it is connected to a blue vertex (blue is a constant) or if it is connected to an excellent vertex. An *excellent* vertex is a vertex that is connected to an outstanding vertex and to a red vertex. An *outstanding* vertex is a vertex that is connected to a good vertex, an excellent one, and a yellow one. Write a datalog program that computes the excellent vertexes.

Exercise 12.6 Consider a directed graph G represented as a binary relation. Show a datalog program that computes a binary relation T containing the pairs (a, b) for which there is a path of odd length from a to b in G.

Exercise 12.7 Given a directed graph G represented as a binary relation, write a datalog program that computes the vertexes x such that (1) there exists a cycle of even length passing through x; (2) there is a cycle of odd length through x; (3) there are even- and odd-length cycles through x.

Exercise 12.8 Consider the following program P:

$$R(x, y) \leftarrow Q(y, x), S(x, y)$$
$$S(x, y) \leftarrow Q(x, y), T(x, z)$$
$$T(x, y) \leftarrow Q(x, z), S(z, y)$$

Let **I** be a relation over $edb(P)$. Describe the output of the program. Now suppose the first rule is replaced by $R(x, y) \leftarrow Q(y, x)$. Describe the output of the new program.

Exercise 12.9 Prove Lemma 12.3.1.

Exercise 12.10 Prove that datalog queries are monotone.

Exercise 12.11 Suppose P is some property of graphs definable by a datalog program. Show that P is preserved under extensions and homomorphisms. That is, if G is a graph satisfying P, then (1) every supergraph of G satisfies P and (2) if h is a graph homomorphism, then $h(G)$ satisfies P.

Exercise 12.12 Show that the following graph properties are not definable by datalog programs:

  (i) The number of nodes is even.
  (ii) There is a nontrivial cycle (a trivial cycle is an edge $\langle a, a \rangle$ for some vertex a).
  (iii) There is a simple path of even length between two specified nodes.

Show that nontrivial cycles can be detected if inequalities of the form $x \neq y$ are allowed in rule bodies.

♠ **Exercise 12.13**   [ACY91] Consider the query *perfect square* on graphs: Is there a path (not necessarily simple) between nodes a and b whose length is a perfect square?

(i) Prove that *perfect square* is preserved under extension and homomorphism.

(ii) Show that *perfect square* is not expressible in datalog.

Hint: For (ii), consider "words" consisting of simple paths from a to b, and prove a pumping lemma for words "accepted" by datalog programs.

Exercise 12.14   Present an algorithm that, given the set of proof trees of depth i with a program P and instance $\mathbf{I}$, constructs all proof trees of depth $i + 1$. Make sure that your algorithm terminates.

Exercise 12.15   Let P be a datalog program, $\mathbf{I}$ an instance of $edb(P)$, and R in $idb(P)$. Let u be a vector of distinct variables of the arity of R. Demonstrate that

$$P(\mathbf{I})(R) = \{\theta R(u) \mid \text{there is a refutation of } \leftarrow R(u) \text{ using } P_{\mathbf{I}} \text{ and}$$
$$\text{substitutions } \theta_1, \ldots \theta_n \text{ such that } \theta = \theta_1 \circ \cdots \circ \theta_n\}.$$

Exercise 12.16   (Substitution lemma) Let $P_{\mathbf{I}}$ be a program, g a goal, and θ a substitution. Prove that if there exists an SLD refutation of θg with $P_{\mathbf{I}}$ and v, there also exists an SLD refutation of g with $P_{\mathbf{I}}$ and $\theta \circ v$.

Exercise 12.17   Reprove Theorem 12.3.4 using Tarski's and Kleene's theorems stated in Remark 12.3.5.

Exercise 12.18   Prove the "if part" of Theorem 12.4.5.

Exercise 12.19   Prove Lemma 12.4.8.

★ **Exercise 12.20**   (Unification with function symbols) In general logic programming, one can use function symbols in addition to relations. A *term* is then either a constant in **dom**, a variable in **var**, or an expression $f(t_1, \ldots, t_n)$, where f is an n-ary function symbol and each t_i is a term. For example, $f(g(x, 5), y, f(y, x, x))$ is a term. In this context, a substitution θ is a mapping from a subset of **var** into the set of terms. Given a substitution θ, it is extended in the natural manner to include all terms constructed over the domain of θ. Extend the definitions of unifier and mgu to terms and to atoms permitting terms. Give an algorithm to obtain the mgu of two atoms.

Exercise 12.21   Prove that Lemma 12.5.1 does not generalize to datalog programs with constants.

Exercise 12.22   This exercise develops three alternative proofs of the generalization of Theorem 12.5.2 to datalog programs with constants. Prove the generalization by

(a) using the technique outlined just after the statement of the theorem

(b) making a direct proof using as input an instance $\mathbf{I}_{C \cup \{a\}}$, where C is the set of all constants occurring in the program and a is new, and where each relation in $\mathbf{I}$ contains all tuples constructed using $C \cup \{a\}$

(c) reducing to the emptiness problem for context-free languages.

♠ **Exercise 12.23**   (datalog$^{\neq}$) The language datalog$^{\neq}$ is obtained by extending datalog with a new predicate $\neq$ with the obvious meaning.

(a) Formally define the new language.

(b) Extend the least-fixpoint and minimal-model semantics to datalog$^{\neq}$.

★ (c) Show that satisfiability remains decidable for datalog$^{\neq}$ and that it can be tested in exponential time with respect to the size of the program.

★ **Exercise 12.24** Which of the properties in Exercise 12.12 are expressible in datalog$^{\neq}$?

Exercise 12.25 Prove Proposition 12.5.4.

Exercise 12.26 Prove that containment of chain datalog programs is undecidable. *Hint:* Modify the proof of Theorem 12.5.5 by using, for each $b \in \Sigma$, a relation R_b such that $R_b(x, y)$ iff $R(x, b, y)$.

Exercise 12.27 Prove that containment does not imply uniform containment by exhibiting two programs P, Q over the same *edb*'s and with S as common *idb* such that $P \subseteq_S Q$ but $P \not\subseteq Q$.

♠ **Exercise 12.28** (Uniform containment [CK86, Sag88]) Prove that uniform containment of two datalog programs is decidable.

Exercise 12.29 Prove that each nr-datalog program is bounded.

♠ **Exercise 12.30** [GMSV87, Var88] Prove Theorem 12.5.7. *Hint:* Reduce the halting problem of Turing machines on an empty tape to boundedness of datalog programs. More precisely, have the *edb* encode legal computations of a Turing machine on an empty tape, and have the program verify the correctness of the encoding. Then show that the program is unbounded iff there are unbounded computations of the machine on the empty tape.

Exercise 12.31 (Boundedness of chain programs) Prove decidability of boundedness for chain programs. *Hint:* Reduce testing for boundedness to testing for finiteness of a context-free language.

♠ **Exercise 12.32** This exercise demonstrates that datalog is likely to be stronger than positive first order extended by generalized transitive closure.

(a) [Coo74] Recall that a single rule program (sirup) is a datalog program with one nontrivial rule. Show that the sirup

$$R(x) \leftarrow R(y), R(z), S(x, y, z)$$

is complete in PTIME. (This has been called variously the graph accessibility problem and the blue-blooded water buffalo problem; a water buffalo is blue blooded only if both of its parents are.)

(b) [KP86] Show that the in some sense simpler sirup

$$R(x) \leftarrow R(y), R(z), T(y, x), T(x, z)$$

is complete in PTIME.

(c) [Imm87b] The *generalized transitive closure* operator is defined on relations with arity $2n$ so that $TC(R)$ is the output of the datalog program

$$ans(x_1, \ldots, x_{2n}) \leftarrow R(x_1, \ldots, x_{2n})$$
$$ans(x_1, \ldots, x_n, z_1, \ldots, z_n) \leftarrow R(x_1, \ldots, x_n, y_1, \ldots, y_n),$$
$$ans(y_1, \ldots, y_n, z_1, \ldots, z_n)$$

Show that the positive first order extended with generalized transitive closure is in LOGSPACE.

13 Evaluation of Datalog

Alice:	*I don't mean to sound naive, but isn't it awfully expensive to answer datalog queries?*
Riccardo:	*Not if you use the right bag of tricks . . .*
Vittorio:	*. . . and some magical wisdom.*
Sergio:	*Well, there is no real need for magic. We will see that the evaluation is much easier if the algorithm knows where it is going and takes advantage of this knowledge.*

The introduction of datalog led to a flurry of research in optimization during the late 1980s and early 1990s. A variety of techniques emerged covering a range of different approaches. These techniques are usually separated into two classes depending on whether they focus on top-down or bottom-up evaluation. Another key dimension of the techniques concerns whether they are based on direct evaluation or propose some compilation of the query into a related query, which is subsequently evaluated using a direct technique.

This chapter provides a brief introduction to this broad family of heuristic techniques. A representative sampling of such techniques is presented. Some are centered around an approach known as "Query-Subquery"; these are top down and are based on direct evaluation. Others, centered around an approach called "magic set rewriting," are based on an initial preprocessing of the datalog program before using a fairly direct bottom-up evaluation strategy.

The advantage of top-down techniques is that selections that form part of the initial query can be propagated into the rules as they are expanded. There is no direct way to take advantage of this information in bottom-up evaluation, so it would seem that the bottom-up technique is at a disadvantage with respect to optimization. A rather elegant conclusion that has emerged from the research on datalog evaluation is that, surprisingly, there are bottom-up techniques that have essentially the same running time as top-down techniques. Exposition of this result is a main focus of this chapter.

Some of the evaluation techniques presented here are intricate, and our main emphasis is on conveying the essential ideas they use. The discussion is centered around the presentation of the techniques in connection with a concrete running example. In the cases of Query-Subquery and magic sets rewriting, we also informally describe how they can be applied in the general case. This is sufficient to give a precise understanding of the techniques without becoming overwhelmed by notation. Proofs of the correctness of these techniques are typically lengthy but straightforward and are left as exercises.

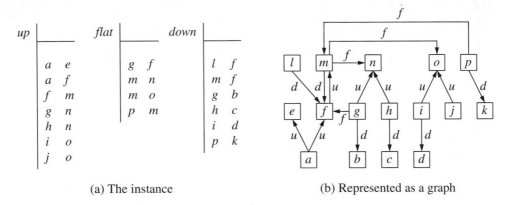

(a) The instance   (b) Represented as a graph

Figure 13.1:   Instance $\mathbf{I}_0$ for RSG example

13.1   Seminaive Evaluation

The first stop on our tour of evaluation techniques is a strategy for improving the efficiency of the bottom-up technique described in Chapter 12. To illustrate this and the other techniques, we use as a running example the program "Reverse-Same-Generation" (RSG) given by

$$rsg(x, y) \leftarrow flat(x, y)$$
$$rsg(x, y) \leftarrow up(x, x1), rsg(y1, x1), down(y1, y)$$

and the sample instance $\mathbf{I}_0$ illustrated in Fig. 13.1. This is a fairly simple program, but it will allow us to present the main features of the various techniques presented throughout this chapter.

If the bottom-up algorithm of Chapter 12 is used to compute the value of *rsg* on input $\mathbf{I}_0$, the following values are obtained:

level 0: $\emptyset$
level 1: $\{\langle g, f \rangle, \langle m, n \rangle, \langle m, o \rangle, \langle p, m \rangle\}$
level 2: $\{$level 1$\} \cup \{\langle a, b \rangle, \langle h, f \rangle, \langle i, f \rangle, \langle j, f \rangle, \langle f, k \rangle\}$
level 3: $\{$level 2$\} \cup \{\langle a, c \rangle, \langle a, d \rangle\}$
level 4: $\{$level 3$\}$

at which point a fixpoint has been reached. It is clear that a considerable amount of redundant computation is done, because each layer recomputes all elements of the previous layer. This is a consequence of the monotonicity of the T_P operator for datalog programs P. This algorithm has been termed the *naive* algorithm for datalog evaluation. The central idea of the *seminaive* algorithm is to focus, to the extent possible, on the new facts generated at each level and thereby avoid recomputing the same facts.

Consider the facts inferred using the second rule of RSG in the consecutive stages of the naive evaluation. At each stage, some new facts are inferred (until a fixpoint is reached). To infer a new fact at stage $i + 1$, one must use at least one fact newly derived at stage i. This is the main idea of seminaive evaluation. It is captured by the following "version" of RSG, called RSG':

$$\Delta^1_{rsg}(x, y) \leftarrow flat(x, y)$$

$$\Delta^{i+1}_{rsg}(x, y) \leftarrow up(x, x1), \Delta^i_{rsg}(y1, x1), down(y1, y)$$

where an instance of the second rule is included for each $i \geq 1$. Strictly speaking, this is not a datalog program because it has an infinite number of rules. On the other hand, it is not recursive.

Intuitively, Δ^i_{rsg} contains the facts in *rsg* newly inferred at the ith stage of the naive evaluation. To see this, we note a close relationship between the repeated applications of T_{RSG} and the values taken by the Δ^i_{rsg}. Let **I** be a fixed input instance. Then

- for $i \geq 0$, let $rsg^i = T^i_{RSG}(\mathbf{I})(rsg)$ (i.e., the value of *rsg* after i applications of T_{RSG} on **I**); and
- for $i \geq 1$, let $\delta^i_{rsg} = RSG'(\mathbf{I})(\Delta^i_{rsg})$ (i.e., the value of Δ^i_{rsg} when $T_{RSG'}$ reaches a fixpoint on **I**).

It is easily verified for each $i \geq 1$ that $T^{i-1}_{RSG'}(\mathbf{I})(\Delta^i_{rsg}) = \emptyset$ and $T^i_{RSG'}(\mathbf{I})(\Delta^i_{rsg}) = \delta^i_{rsg}$. Furthermore, for each $i \geq 0$ we have

$$rsg^{i+1} - rsg^i \subseteq \delta^{i+1}_{rsg} \subseteq rsg^{i+1}.$$

Therefore $RSG(\mathbf{I})(rsg) = \cup_{1 \leq i}(\delta^i_{rsg})$. Furthermore, if j satisfies $\delta^j_{rsg} \subseteq \cup_{i<j}\delta^i_{rsg}$, then $RSG(\mathbf{I})(rsg) = \cup_{i<j}\delta^i_{rsg}$, that is, only j levels of RSG' need be computed to find $RSG(\mathbf{I})(rsg)$. Importantly, bottom-up evaluation of RSG' typically involves much less redundant computation than direct bottom-up evaluation of RSG.

Continuing with the informal development, we introduce now two refinements that further reduce the amount of redundant computation. The first is based on the observation that when executing RSG', we do not always have $\delta^{i+1}_{rsg} = rsg^{i+1} - rsg^i$. Using $\mathbf{I}_0$, we have $\langle g, f \rangle \in \delta^2_{rsg}$ but not in $rsg^2 - rsg^1$. This suggests that the efficiency can be further improved by using $rsg^i - rsg^{i-1}$ in place of Δ^i_{rsg} in the body of the second "rule" of RSG'. Using a pidgin language that combines both datalog and imperative commands, the new version RSG'' is given by

$$\left\{ \begin{array}{lcl} \Delta^1_{rsg}(x, y) & \leftarrow & flat(x, y) \\ rsg^1 & := & \Delta^1_{rsg} \end{array} \right\}$$

$$\left\{ \begin{array}{lcl} temp^{i+1}_{rsg}(x, y) & \leftarrow & up(x, x1), \Delta^i_{rsg}(y1, x1), down(y1, y) \\ \Delta^{i+1}_{rsg} & := & temp^{i+1}_{rsg} - rsg^i \\ rsg^{i+1} & := & rsg^i \cup \Delta^{i+1}_{rsg} \end{array} \right\}$$

(where an instance of the second family of commands is included for each $i \geq 1$).

The second improvement to reduce redundant computation is useful when a given *idb* predicate occurs twice in the same rule. To illustrate, consider the nonlinear version of the ancestor program:

$$anc(x, y) \leftarrow par(x, y)$$
$$anc(x, y) \leftarrow anc(x, z), anc(z, y)$$

A seminaive "version" of this is

$$\left\{ \begin{array}{lcl} \Delta_{anc}^1(x, y) & \leftarrow & par(x, y) \\ anc^1 & := & \Delta_{anc}^1 \end{array} \right\}$$

$$\left\{ \begin{array}{lcl} temp_{anc}^{i+1}(x, y) & \leftarrow & \Delta_{anc}^i(x, z), anc(z, y) \\ temp_{anc}^{i+1}(x, y) & \leftarrow & anc(x, z), \Delta_{anc}^i(z, y) \\ \Delta_{anc}^{i+1} & := & temp_{anc}^{i+1} - anc^i \\ anc^{i+1} & := & anc^i \cup \Delta_{anc}^{i+1} \end{array} \right\}$$

Note here that both Δ_{anc}^i and anc^i are needed to ensure that all new facts in the next level are obtained.

Consider now an input instance consisting of $par(1, 2), par(2, 3)$. Then we have

$$\Delta_{anc}^1 = \{\langle 1, 2\rangle, \langle 2, 3\rangle\}$$
$$anc^1 = \{\langle 1, 2\rangle, \langle 2, 3\rangle\}$$
$$\Delta_{anc}^2 = \{\langle 1, 3\rangle\}$$

Furthermore, both of the rules for $temp_{anc}^2$ will compute the join of tuples $\langle 1, 2\rangle$ and $\langle 2, 3\rangle$, and so we have a redundant computation of $\langle 1, 3\rangle$. Examples are easily constructed where this kind of redundancy occurs for at an arbitrary level $i > 0$ (see Exercise 13.2).

An approach for preventing this kind of redundancy is to replace the two rules for $temp^{i+1}$ by

$$temp^{i+1}(x, y) \leftarrow \Delta_{anc}^i(x, z), anc^{i-1}(z, y)$$
$$temp^{i+1}(x, y) \leftarrow anc^i(x, z), \Delta_{anc}^i(z, y)$$

This approach is adopted below.

We now present the seminaive algorithm for the general case. Let P be a datalog program over *edb* **R** and *idb* **T**. Consider a rule

$$S(u) \leftarrow R_1(v_1), \ldots, R_n(v_n), T_1(w_1), \ldots, T_m(w_m)$$

in P, where the R_k's are *edb* predicates and the T_j's are *idb* predicates. Construct for each $j \in [1, m]$ and $i \geq 1$ the rule

$$temp_S^{i+1}(u) \leftarrow R_1(v_1), \ldots, R_n(v_n),$$

$$T_1^i(w_1), \ldots, T_{j-1}^i(w_{j-1}), \Delta_{T_j}^i(w_j), T_{j+1}^{i-1}(w_{j+1}), \ldots, T_m^{i-1}(w_m).$$

Let P_S^i represent the set of all i-level rules of this form constructed for the *idb* predicate S (i.e., the rules for $temp_S^{i+1}$, j in $[1, m]$).

Suppose now that $T_1, \ldots, T_l$ is a listing of the *idb* predicates of P that occur in the body of a rule defining S. We write

$$P_S^i(\mathbf{I}, T_1^{i-1}, \ldots, T_l^{i-1}, T_1^i, \ldots, T_l^i, \Delta_{T_1}^i, \ldots, \Delta_{T_l}^i)$$

to denote the set of tuples that result from applying the rules in P_S^i to given values for input instance $\mathbf{I}$ and for the T_j^{i-1}, T_j^i, and $\Delta_{T_j}^i$.

We now have the following:

ALGORITHM 13.1.1 (Basic Seminaive Algorithm)

Input: Datalog program P and input instance $\mathbf{I}$

Output: $P(\mathbf{I})$

    1. Set P' to be the rules in P with no *idb* predicate in the body;
    2. $S^0 := \emptyset$, for each *idb* predicate S;
    3. $\Delta_S^1 := P'(\mathbf{I})(S)$, for each *idb* predicate S;
    4. $i := 1$;
    5. do begin
        for each *idb* predicate S, where $T_1, \ldots, T_l$
        are the *idb* predicates involved in rules defining S,
          begin
            $S^i := S^{i-1} \cup \Delta_S^i$;
            $\Delta_S^{i+1} := P_S^i(\mathbf{I}, T_1^{i-1}, \ldots, T_l^{i-1}, T_1^i, \ldots, T_l^i, \Delta_{T_1}^i, \ldots, \Delta_{T_l}^i) - S^i$;
          end;
        $i := i + 1$
        end
        until $\Delta_S^i = \emptyset$ for each *idb* predicate S.
    6. $s := s^i$, for each *idb* predicate S. ∎

The correctness of this algorithm is demonstrated in Exercise 13.3. However, it is still doing a lot of unnecessary work on some programs. We now analyze the structure of datalog programs to develop an improved version of the seminaive algorithm. It turns out that this analysis, with simple control of the computation, allows us to know in advance which predicates are likely to grow at each iteration and which are not, either because they are already saturated or because they are not yet affected by the computation.

Let P be a datalog program. Form the *precedence graph* G_P for P as follows: Use the *idb* predicates in P as the nodes and include edge (R, R') if there is a rule with head predicate R' in which R occurs in the body. P is *recursive* if G_P has a directed cycle. Two predicates R and R' are *mutually recursive* if $R = R'$ or R and R' participate in the same cycle of G_P. Mutual recursion is an equivalence relation on the *idb* predicates of P, where each equivalence class corresponds to a strongly connected component of G_P. A rule of P is *recursive* if the body involves a predicate that is mutually recursive with the head.

We now have the following:

ALGORITHM 13.1.2 (Improved Seminaive Algorithm)

Input: Datalog program P and edb instance **I**

Output: $P(\mathbf{I})$

1. Determine the equivalence classes of *idb(P)* under mutual recursion.
2. Construct a listing $[R_1], \ldots, [R_n]$ of the equivalence classes, according to a topological sort of G_P (i.e., so that for each pair $i < j$ there is no path in G_P from R_j to R_i).
3. For $i = 1$ to n do
    Apply Basic Seminaive Algorithm to compute the values of predicates in $[R_i]$, treating all predicates in $[R_j]$, $j < i$, as *edb* predicates. ∎

The correctness of this algorithm is left as Exercise 13.4.

Linear Datalog

We conclude this discussion of the seminaive approach by introducing a special class of programs.

Let P be a program. A rule in P with head relation R is *linear* if there is at most one atom in the body of the rule whose predicate is mutually recursive with R. P is *linear* if each rule in P is linear. We now show how the Improved Seminaive Algorithm can be simplified for such programs.

Suppose that P is a linear program, and

$$\rho : R(u) \leftarrow T_1(v_1), \ldots, T_n(v_n)$$

is a rule in P, where T_j is mutually recursive with R. Associate with this the "rule"

$$\Delta_R^{i+1}(u) \leftarrow T_1(v_1), \ldots, \Delta_{T_j}^i(v_j), \ldots, T_n(v_n).$$

Note that this is the only rule that will be associated by the Improved Seminaive Algorithm with ρ. Thus, given an equivalence class $[T_k]$ of mutually recursive predicates of P, the rules for predicates S in $[T_k]$ use only the Δ_S^i, but not the S^i. In contrast, as seen earlier, both the Δ_S^i and S^i must be used in nonlinear programs.

13.2   Top-Down Techniques

Consider the RSG program from the previous section, augmented with a selection-based query:

$$rsg(x, y) \leftarrow flat(x, y)$$

$$rsg(x, y) \leftarrow up(x, x1), rsg(y1, x1), down(y1, y)$$

$$query(y) \leftarrow rsg(a, y)$$

where a is a constant. This program will be called the *RSG query*. Suppose that seminaive evaluation is used. Then each pair of *rsg* will be produced, including those that are not used to derive any element of *query*. For example, using $\mathbf{I}_0$ of Fig. 13.1 as input, fact $rsg(f, k)$ will be produced but not used. A primary motivation for the top-down approaches to datalog query evaluation is to avoid, to the extent possible, the production of tuples that are not needed to derive any answer tuples.

For this discussion, we define a *datalog query* to be a pair (P, q), where P is a datalog program and q is a datalog rule using relations of P in its body and the new relation *query* in its head. We generally assume that there is only one rule defining the predicate *query*, and it has the form

$$query(u) \leftarrow R(v)$$

for some *idb* predicate R.

A fact is *relevant* to query (P, q) on input **I** if there is a proof tree for *query* in which the fact occurs. A straightforward criterion for improving the efficiency of any datalog evaluation scheme is to infer only relevant facts. The evaluation procedures developed in the remainder of this chapter attempt to satisfy this criterion; but, as will be seen, they do not do so perfectly.

The top-down approaches use natural heuristics to focus attention on relevant facts. In particular, they use the framework provided by SLD resolution. The starting point for these algorithms (namely, the query to be answered) often includes constants; these have the effect of restricting the search for derivation trees and thus the set of facts produced. In the context of databases without function symbols, the top-down datalog evaluation algorithms can generally be forced to terminate on all inputs, even when the corresponding SLD-resolution algorithm does not. In this section, we focus primarily on the query-subquery (QSQ) framework.

There are four basic elements of this framework:

1. Use the general framework of SLD resolution, but do it set-at-a-time. This permits the use of optimized versions of relational algebra operations.

2. Beginning with the constants in the original query, "push" constants from goals to subgoals, in a manner analogous to pushing selections into joins.

3. Use the technique of "sideways information passing" (see Chapter 6) to pass constant binding information from one atom to the next in subgoals.

4. Use an efficient global flow-of-control strategy.

Adornments and Subqueries

Recall the RSG query given earlier. Consider an SLD tree for it. The child of the root would be $rsg(a, y)$. Speaking intuitively, not all values for *rsg* are requested, but rather only those with first coordinate a. More generally, we are interested in finding derivations for *rsg* where the first coordinate is *bound* and the second coordinate is *free*. This is denoted by the expression rsg^{bf}, where the superscript '*bf*' is called an *adornment*.

The next layer of the SLD tree will have a node holding *flat*(a, y) and a node holding $up(a, x1), rsg(y1, x1), down(y1, y)$. Answers generated for the first of these nodes are given by $\pi_2(\sigma_{1 = \text{'a'}}(flat))$. Answers for the other node can be generated by a left-to-right evaluation. First the set of possible values for $x1$ is $J = \pi_2(\sigma_{1 = \text{'a'}}(up))$. Next the possible values for $y1$ are given by $\{y1 \mid \langle y1, x1 \rangle \in rsg$ and $\langle x1 \rangle \in J\}$ (i.e., the first coordinate values of *rsg* stemming from second coordinate values in J). More generally, then, this calls for an evaluation of rsg^{fb}, where the second coordinate values are bound by J. Finally, given $y1$ values, these can be used with *down* to obtain y values (i.e., answers to the query).

As suggested by this discussion, a top-down evaluation of a query in which constants occur can be broken into a family of "subqueries" having the form (R^γ, J), where γ is an adornment for *idb* predicate R, and J is a set of tuples that give values for the columns bound by γ. Expressions of the form (R^γ, J) are called *subqueries*. If the RSG query were applied to the instance of Fig. 13.1, the first subquery generated would be $(rsg^{fb}, \{\langle e \rangle, \langle f \rangle\})$. As we shall see, the QSQ framework is based on a systematic evaluation of subqueries.

Let P be a datalog program and $\mathbf{I}$ an input instance. Suppose that R is an *idb* predicate and γ is an adornment for R (i.e., a string of b's and f's having length the arity of R). Then *bound*(R, γ) denotes the coordinates of R bound in γ. Let t be a tuple over *bound*(R, γ). Then a *completion* for t in R^γ is a tuple s such that $s[bound(R, \gamma)] = t$ and $s \in P(\mathbf{I})(R)$. The *answer* to a subquery (R^γ, J) over $\mathbf{I}$ is the set of all completions of all tuples in J.

The use of adornments within a rule body is a generalization of the technique of sideways information passing discussed in Chapter 6. Consider the rule

$$(*) \qquad R(x, y, z) \leftarrow R_1(x, u, v), R_2(u, w, w, z), R_3(v, w, y, a).$$

Suppose that a subquery involving R^{bfb} is invoked. Assuming a left-to-right evaluation, this will lead to subqueries involving R_1^{bff}, R_2^{bffb}, and R_3^{bbfb}. We sometimes rewrite the rule as

$$R^{bfb}(x, y, z) \leftarrow R_1^{bff}(x, u, v), R_2^{bffb}(u, w, w, z), R_3^{bbfb}(v, w, y, a)$$

to emphasize the adornments. This is an example of an *adorned rule*. As we shall see, the adornments of *idb* predicates in rule bodies shall be used to guide evaluations of queries and subqueries. It is common to omit the adornments of *edb* predicates.

The general algorithm for adorning a rule, given an adornment for the head and an ordering of the rule body, is as follows: (1) All occurrences of each bound variable in the rule head are bound, (2) all occurrences of constants are bound, and (3) if a variable x occurs in the rule body, then all occurrences of x in subsequent literals are bound. A different ordering of the rule body would yield different adornments. In general, we permit different orderings of rule bodies for different adornments of a given rule head. (A generalization of this technique is considered in Exercise 13.19.)

The definition of adorned rule also applies to situations in which there are repeated variables or constants in the rule head (see Exercise 13.9). However, adornments do not capture all of the relevant information that can arise as the result of repeated variables or constants that occur in *idb* predicates in rule bodies. Mechanisms for doing this are discussed in Section 13.4.

Supplementary Relations and QSQ Templates

A key component of the QSQ framework is the use of *QSQ templates* which store appropriate information during intermediate stages of an evaluation. Consider again the preceding rule (*), and imagine attempting to evaluate the subquery (R^{bfb}, J). This will result in calls to the generalized queries $(R_1^{bff}, \pi_1(J))$, (R_2^{bffb}, K), and (R_3^{bbfb}, L) for some relations K and L that depend on the evaluation of the preceding queries. Importantly, note that relation K relies on values passed from both J and R_1, and L relies on values passed from R_1 and R_2. A QSQ template provides data structures that will remember all of the values needed during a left-to-right evaluation of a subquery.

To do this, QSQ templates rely on *supplementary relations*. A total of $n + 1$ supplementary relations are associated to a rule body with n atoms. For example, the supplementary relations $sup_0, \ldots, sup_3$ for the rule (*) with head adorned by R^{bfb} are

$$R^{bfb}(x, y, z) \leftarrow R_1^{bff}(x, u, v), \quad R_2^{bffb}(u, w, w, z), \quad R_3^{bbfb}(v, w, y, a)$$

$$\uparrow \qquad\qquad\qquad \uparrow \qquad\qquad\qquad \uparrow \qquad\qquad\qquad \uparrow$$

$$sup_0[x, z] \quad sup_1[x, z, u, v] \quad sup_2[x, z, v, w] \quad sup_3[x, y, z]$$

Note that variables serve as attribute names in the supplementary relations. Speaking intuitively, the body of a rule may be viewed as a process that takes as input tuples over the bound attributes of the head and produces as output tuples over the variables (bound and free) of the head. This determines the attributes of the first and last supplementary relations. In addition, a variable (i.e., an attribute name) is in some supplementary relation if it is has been bound by some previous literal and if it is needed in the future by some subsequent literal or in the result.

More formally, for a rule body with atoms $A_1, \ldots, A_n$, the set of variables used as attribute names for the ith supplementary relation is determined as follows:

- For the 0th (i.e., zeroth) supplementary relation, the attribute set is the set X_0 of bound variables of the rule head; and for the last supplementary relation, the attribute set is the set X_n of variables in the rule head.
- For $i \in [1, n - 1]$, the attribute set of the ith supplementary relation is the set X_i of variables that occur both "before" X_i (i.e., occur in $X_0, A_1, \ldots, A_i$) and "after" X_i (i.e., occur in $A_{i+1}, \ldots, A_n, X_n$).

The *QSQ template* for an adorned rule is the sequence $(sup_0, \ldots, sup_n)$ of relation schemas for the supplementary relations of the rule. During the process of QSQ query evaluation, relation instances are assigned to these schemas; typically these instances

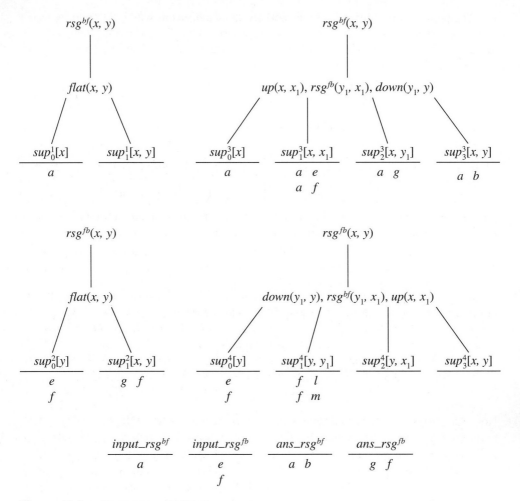

Figure 13.2:   Illustration of QSQ framework

repeatedly acquire new tuples as the algorithm runs. Figure 13.2 shows the use of QSQ templates in connection with the RSG query.

The Kernel of QSQ Evaluation

The key components of QSQ evaluation are as follows. Let (P, q) be a datalog query and let **I** be an *edb* instance. Speaking conceptually, QSQ evaluation begins by constructing an adorned rule for each adornment of each *idb* predicate in P and for the query q. In practice, the construction of these adorned rules can be lazy (i.e., they can be constructed only if needed during execution of the algorithm). Let (P^{ad}, q^{ad}) denote the result of this transformation.

The relevant adorned rules for the RSG query are as follows:

1. $rsg^{bf}(x, y) \leftarrow flat(x, y)$
2. $rsg^{fb}(x, y) \leftarrow flat(x, y)$
3. $rsg^{bf}(x, y) \leftarrow up(x, x1), \ rsg^{fb}(y1, x1), \ down(y1, y)$
4. $rsg^{fb}(x, y) \leftarrow down(y1, y), \ rsg^{bf}(y1, x1), \ up(x, x1).$

Note that in the fourth rule, the literals of the body are ordered so that the binding of y in *down* can be "passed" via $y1$ to *rsg* and via $x1$ to *up*.

A QSQ template is constructed for each relevant adorned rule. We denote the jth (counting from 0) supplementary relation of the ith adorned rule as sup_j^i. In addition, the following relations are needed and will serve as variables in the QSQ evaluation algorithm:

(a) for each *idb* predicate R and relevant adornment γ the variable ans_R^γ, with same arity as R;

(b) for each *idb* predicate R and relevant adornment γ, the variable $input\_R^\gamma$ with same arity as $bound(R, \gamma)$ (i.e., the number of b's occurring in γ); and

(c) for each supplementary relation sup_j^i, the variable sup_j^i.

Intuitively, $input\_R^\gamma$ will be used to form subqueries $(R^\gamma, input\_R^\gamma)$. The completion of tuples in $input\_R^\gamma$ will go to ans_R^γ. Thus ans_R^γ will hold tuples that are in $P(\mathbf{I})(R)$ and were generated from subqueries based on R^γ.

A QSQ algorithm begins with the empty set for each of the aforementioned relations. The query is then used to initialize the process. For example, the rule

$$query(y) \leftarrow rsg(a, y)$$

gives the initial value of $\{\langle a \rangle\}$ to $input\_rsg^{bf}$. In general, this gives rise to the subquery $(R^\gamma, \{t\})$, where t is constructed using the set of constants in the initial query.

There are essentially four kinds of steps in the execution. Different possible orderings for these steps will be considered. The first of these is used to initialize rules.

(A) Begin evaluation of a rule: This step can be taken whenever there is a rule with head predicate R^γ and there are "new" tuples in a variable $input\_R^\gamma$ that have not yet been processed for this rule. The step is to add the "new" tuples to the 0th supplementary relation for this rule. However, only "new" tuples that unify with the head of the rule are added to the supplementary relation. A "new" tuple in $input\_R^\gamma$ might fail to unify with the head of a rule defining R if there are repeated variables or constants in the rule head (see Exercise 13.9).

New tuples are generated in supplementary relations sup_j^i in two ways: Either some new tuples have been obtained for sup_{j-1}^i (case B); or some new tuples have been obtained for the *idb* predicate occurring between sup_{j-1}^i and sup_j^i (case C).

(B) Pass new tuples from one supplementary relation to the next: This step can be taken whenever there is a set T of "new" tuples in a supplementary variable sup_{j-1}^i that have not yet been processed, and sup_{j-1}^i is not the last supplementary relation of the corresponding rule. Suppose that A_j is the atom in the rule immediately following sup_{j-1}^i.

Two cases arise:

(i) A_j is $R^\gamma(u)$ for some *edb* predicate R. Then a combination of joins and projections on R and T is used to determine the appropriate tuples to be added to sup_j^i.

(ii) A_j is $R^\gamma(u)$ for some *idb* predicate R. Note that each of the bound variables in γ occurs in sup_{j-1}^i. Two actions are now taken.

    (a) A combination of joins and projections on *ans_R^γ* (the current value for R) and T is used to determine the set T' of tuples to be added to sup_j^i.

    (b) The tuples in $T[bound(R, \gamma)] - input\_R^\gamma$ are added to *input_R^γ*.

(C) Use new idb *tuples to generate new supplementary relation tuples:* This step is similar to the previous one but is applied when "new" tuples are added to one of the *idb* relation variables *ans_R^γ*. In particular, suppose that some atom A_j with predicate R^γ occurs in some rule, with surrounding supplementary variables sup_{j-1}^i and sup_j^i. In this case, use join and projection on all tuples in sup_{j-1}^i and the "new" tuples of *ans_R^γ* to create new tuples to be added to sup_j^i.

(D) Process tuples in the final supplementary relation of a rule: This step is used to generate tuples corresponding to the output of rules. It can be applied when there are "new" tuples in the final supplementary variable sup_n^i of a rule. Suppose that the rule predicate is R^γ. Add the new tuples in sup_n^i to *ans_R^γ*.

EXAMPLE 13.2.1 Figure 13.2 illustrates the data structures and "scratch paper" relations used in the QSQ algorithm, in connection with the RSG query, as applied to the instance of Fig. 13.1. Recall the adorned version of the RSG query presented on page 321. The QSQ templates for these are shown in Fig. 13.2. Finally, the scratch paper relations for the *input-* and *ans*-variables are shown.

Figure 13.2 shows the contents of the relation variables after several steps of the QSQ approach have been applied. The procedure begins with the insertion of $\langle a \rangle$ into *input_rsg^{bf}*; this corresponds to the rule

$$query(y) \leftarrow rsg(a, y)$$

Applications of step (A) place $\langle a \rangle$ into the supplementary variables sup_0^1 and sup_0^3. Step (B.i) then yields $\langle a, e \rangle$ and $\langle a, f \rangle$ in sup_1^3. Because *ans_rsg^{fb}* is empty at this point, step (B.ii.a) does not yield any tuples for sup_2^3. However, step (B.ii.b) is used to insert $\langle e \rangle$ and $\langle f \rangle$ into *input_rsg^{fb}*. Application of steps (B) and (D) on the template of the second rule yield $\langle g, f \rangle$ in *ans_rsg^{fb}*. Application of steps (C), (B), and (D) on the template of the third rule now yield the first entry in *ans_rsg^{bf}*. The reader is invited to extend the evaluation to its conclusion (see Exercise 13.10). The answer is obtained by applying $\pi_2\sigma_{1 = \text{'a'}}$ to the final contents of *ans_rsg^{bf}*.

Global Control Strategies

We have now described all of the basic building blocks of the QSQ approach: the use of QSQ templates to perform information passing both into rules and sideways through rule bodies, and the three classes of relations used. A variety of global control strategies can be used for the QSQ approach. The most basic strategy is stated simply: Apply steps (A) through (D) until a fixpoint is reached. The following can be shown (see Exercise 13.12):

THEOREM 13.2.2 Let (P, q) be a datalog query. For each input **I**, any evaluation of QSQ on (P^{ad}, q^{ad}) yields the answer of (P, q) on **I**.

We now present a more specific algorithm based on the QSQ framework. This algorithm, called *QSQ Recursive* (QSQR) is based on a recursive strategy. To understand the central intuition behind QSQR, suppose that step (B) described earlier is to be performed, passing from supplementary relation sup^i_{j-1} across an *idb* predicate R^γ to supplementary relation sup^i_j. This may lead to the introduction of new tuples into sup^i_j by step (B.ii.a) and to the introduction of new tuples into $input\_R^\gamma$ by step (B.ii.b). The essence of QSQR is that it now performs a recursive call to determine the R^γ values corresponding to the new tuples added to $input\_R^\gamma$, before applying step (B) or (D) to the new tuples placed into sup^i_j.

We present QSQR in two steps: first a subroutine and then the recursive algorithm itself. During processing in QSQR, the global state includes values for ans_R^γ and $input\_R^\gamma$ for each *idb* predicate R and relevant adornment γ. However, the supplementary relations are not global—local copies of the supplementary relations are maintained by each call of the subroutine.

Subroutine   Process subquery on one rule

Input: A rule for adorned predicate R^γ, input instance **I**, a QSQR "state" (i.e., set of values for the *input*- and *ans*-variables), and a set $T \subseteq input\_R^\gamma$. (Intuitively, the tuples in T have not been considered with this rule yet).

Action:

1. Remove from T all tuples that do not unify with (the appropriate coordinates of) the head of the rule.

2. Set $sup_0 := T$. [This is step (A) for the tuples in T.]

3. Proceed sideways across the body $A_1, \ldots, A_n$ of the rule to the final supplementary relation sup_n as follows:
   For each atom A_j
      (a) If A_j has *edb* predicate R', then apply step (B.i) to populate sup_j.
      (b) If A_j has *idb* predicate R'^δ, then apply step (B.ii) as follows:
         (i) Set $S := sup_{j-1}[bound(R', \delta)] - input\_R'^\delta$.
         (ii) Set $input\_R'^\delta := input\_R'^\delta \cup S$. [This is step (B.ii.b).]
         (iii) (Recursively) call algorithm QSQR on the query (R'^δ, S).

> [This has the effect of invoking step (A) and its consequences for the tuples in S.]
>
> (iv) Use sup_{j-1} and the current value of global variable $ans\_R'^{\delta}$ to populate sup_j. [This includes steps (B.ii.a) and (C).]

4. Add the tuples produced for sup_n into the global variable ans_R^{γ}. [This is step (D).]

The main algorithm is given by the following:

ALGORITHM 13.2.3 (QSQR)

Input: A query of the form (R^{γ}, T), input instance **I**, and a QSQR "state" (i.e., set of values for the *input*- and *ans*-variables).

Procedure:

1. Repeat until no new tuples are added to any global variable:
   Call the subroutine to process subquery (R^{γ}, T) on each rule defining R. ■

Suppose that we are given the query

$$query(u) \leftarrow R(v)$$

Let γ be the adornment of R corresponding to v, and let T be the singleton relation corresponding to the constants in v. To find the answer to the query, the QSQR algorithm is invoked with input (R^{γ}, T) and the global state where $input\_R^{\gamma} = T$ and all other *input*- and *ans*-variables are empty. For example, in the case of the *rsg* program, the algorithm is first called with argument $(rsg^{bf}, \{\langle a \rangle\})$, and in the global state $input\_rsg^{bf} = \{\langle a \rangle\}$. The answer to the query is obtained by performing a selection and projection on the final value of ans_R^{γ}.

It is straightforward to show that QSQR is correct (Exercise 13.12).

13.3   Magic

An exciting development in the field of datalog evaluation is the emergence of techniques for bottom-up evaluation whose performance rivals the efficiency of the top-down techniques. This family of techniques, which has come to be known as "magic set" techniques, simulates the pushing of selections that occurs in top-down approaches. There are close connections between the magic set techniques and the QSQ algorithm. The magic set technique presented in this section simulates the QSQ algorithm, using a datalog program that is evaluated bottom up. As we shall see, the magic sets are basically those sets of tuples stored in the relations $input\_R^{\gamma}$ and sup^i_j of the QSQ algorithm. Given a datalog query (P, q), the magic set approach transforms it into a new query (P^m, q^m) that has two important properties: (1) It computes the same answer as (P, q), and (2) when evaluated using a bottom-up technique, it produces only the set of facts produced by top-down approaches

(s1.1)	$rsg^{bf}(x, y)$	$\leftarrow input\_rsg^{bf}(x), flat(x, y)$
(s2.1)	$rsg^{fb}(x, y)$	$\leftarrow input\_rsg^{fb}(y), flat(x, y)$
(s3.1)	$sup_1^3(x, x1)$	$\leftarrow input\_rsg^{bf}(x), up(x, x1)$
(s3.2)	$sup_2^3(x, y1)$	$\leftarrow sup_1^3(x, x1), rsg^{fb}(y1, x1)$
(s3.3)	$rsg^{bf}(x, y)$	$\leftarrow sup_2^3(x, y1), down(y1, y)$
(s4.1)	$sup_1^4(y, y1)$	$\leftarrow input\_rsg^{fb}(y), down(y1, y)$
(s4.2)	$sup_2^4(y, x1)$	$\leftarrow sup_1^4(y, y1), rsg^{bf}(y1, x1)$
(s4.3)	$rsg^{fb}(x, y)$	$\leftarrow sup_2^4(y, x1), up(x, x1)$
(i3.2)	$input\_rsg^{bf}(x1) \leftarrow sup_1^3(x, x1)$	
(i4.2)	$input\_rsg^{fb}(y1) \leftarrow sup_1^4(y, y1)$	
(seed)	$input\_rsg^{bf}(a) \quad \leftarrow$	
(query)	$query(y)$	$\leftarrow rsg^{bf}(a, y)$

Figure 13.3: Transformation of RSG query using magic sets

such as QSQ. In particular, then, (P^m, q^m) incorporates the effect of "pushing" selections from the query into bottom-up computations, as if by magic.

We focus on a technique originally called "generalized supplementary magic"; it is perhaps the most general magic set technique for datalog in the literature. (An earlier form of magic is considered in Exercise 13.18.) The discussion begins by explaining how the technique works in connection with the RSG query of the previous section and then presents the general algorithm.

As with QSQ, the starting point for magic set algorithms is an adorned datalog query (P^{ad}, q^{ad}). Four classes of rules are generated (see Fig. 13.3). The first consists of a family of rules for each rule of the adorned program P^{ad}. For example, recall rule (3) (see p. 321) of the adorned program for the RSG query presented in the previous section:

$$rsg^{bf}(x, y) \leftarrow up(x, x1), rsg^{fb}(y1, x1), down(y1, y).$$

We first present a primitive family of rules corrresponding to that rule, and then apply some optimizations.

(s3.0') $\qquad$ $sup_0^3(x) \quad \leftarrow input\_rsg^{bf}(x)$

(s3.1') $\qquad$ $sup_1^3(x, x1) \leftarrow sup_0^3(x), up(x, x1)$

(s3.2) $\qquad$ $sup_2^3(x, y1) \leftarrow sup_1^3(x, x1), rsg^{fb}(y1, x1)$

(s3.3') $\qquad$ $sup_3^3(x, y) \quad \leftarrow sup_2^3(x, y1), down(y1, y)$

(S3.4') $\qquad$ $rsg^{bf}(x, y) \leftarrow sup_3^3(x, y)$

Rule (s3.0') corresponds to step (A) of the QSQ algorithm; rules (s3.1') and (s3.3') correspond to step (B.i); rule (s3.2) corresponds to steps (B.ii.a) and (C); and rule (s3.4') corresponds to step (D). In the literature, the predicate $input\_rsg^{fb}$ has usually been denoted as $magic\_rsg^{fb}$ and sup_j^i as $supmagic_j^i$. We use the current notation to stress the connection with the QSQ framework. Note that the predicate rsg^{bf} here plays the role of ans_rsg^{bf} there.

As can be seen by the preceding example, the predicates sup_0^3 and sup_3^3 are essentially redundant. In general, if the ith rule defines R^γ, then the predicate sup_0^i is eliminated, with $input\_R^\gamma$ used in its place to eliminate rule (3.0') and to form

(s3.1) $\qquad$ $sup_1^3(x, x1) \leftarrow input\_rsg^{bf}(x), up(x, x1).$

Similarly, the predicate of the last supplementary relation can be eliminated to delete rule (s3.4') and to form

(s3.3) $\qquad$ $rsg^{bf}(x, y) \leftarrow sup_2^3(x, y1), down(y1, y).$

Therefore the set of rules (s3.0') through (s3.4') may be replaced by (s3.1), (s3.2), and (s3.3). Rules (s4.1), (s4.2), and (s4.3) of Fig. 13.3 are generated from rule (4) of the adorned program for the RSG query (see p. 321). (Recall how the order of the body literals in that rule are reversed to pass bounding information.) Finally, rules (s1.1) and (s2.1) stem from rules (1) and (2) of the adorned program.

The second class of rules is used to provide values for the *input* predicates [i.e., simulating step (B.ii.b) of the QSQ algorithm]. In the RSG query, one rule for each of $input\_rsg^{bf}$ and $input\_rsg^{fb}$ is needed:

(i3.2) $\qquad$ $input\_rsg^{bf}(x1) \leftarrow sup_1^3(x, x1)$

(i4.2) $\qquad$ $input\_rsg^{fb}(y1) \leftarrow sup_1^4(y, y1).$

Intuitively, the first rule comes from rule (s3.2). In other words, it follows from the second atom of the body of rule (3) of the original adorned program (see p. 321). In general, an adorned rule with k idb atoms in the body will generate k *input* rules of this form.

The third and fourth classes of rules include one rule each; these initialize and conclude the simulation of QSQ, respectively. The first of these acts as a "seed" and is derived from the initial query. In the running example, the seed is

$$input\_rsg^{bf}(a) \leftarrow .$$

The second constructs the answer to the query; in the example it is

$$query(y) \leftarrow rsg^{bf}(a, y).$$

From this example, it should be straightforward to specify the magic set rewriting of an adorned query (P^{ad}, q^{ad}) (see Exercise 13.16a).

The example showed how the "first" and "last" supplementary predicates sup_0^3 and sup_4^3 were redundant with *input_rsg*^{bf} and *rsg*^{bf}, respectively, and could be eliminated. Another improvement is to merge consecutive sequences of *edb* atoms in rule bodies as follows. For example, consider the rule

(i) $$R^\gamma(u) \leftarrow R_1^{\gamma_1}(u_1), \ldots, R_n^{\gamma_n}(u_n)$$

and suppose that predicate R_k is the last *idb* relation in the body. Then rules $(si.k)$, $\ldots$, $(si.n)$ can be replaced with

$(si.k'')$ $$R^\gamma(u) \leftarrow sup_{k-1}^i(v_{k-1}), R_k^{\gamma_k}(u_k), R_{k+1}^{\gamma_{k+1}}(u_{k+1}), \ldots, R_n^{\gamma_n}(u_n).$$

For example, rules (s3.2) and (s3.3) of Fig. 13.3 can be replaced by

$(s3.2'')$ $$rsg^{bf}(x, y) \leftarrow sup_1^3(x, x1), rsg^{fb}(y1, x1), down(y1, y).$$

This simplification can also be used within rules. Suppose that R_k and R_l are *idb* relations with only *edb* relations occurring in between. Then rules $(i.k)$, $\ldots$, $(i.l-1)$ can be replaced with

$(si.k'')$ $$sup_{l-1}^i(v_{l-1}) \leftarrow sup_{k-1}^i(v_{k-1}), R_k^{\gamma_k}(u_k), R_{k+1}^{\gamma_{k+1}}(u_{k+1}), \ldots, R_{l-1}^{\gamma_{l-1}}(u_{l-1}).$$

An analogous simplification can be applied if there are multiple *edb* predicates at the beginning of the rule body.

To summarize the development, we state the following (see Exercise 13.16):

THEOREM 13.3.1 Let (P, q) be a query, and let (P^m, q^m) be the query resulting from the magic rewriting of (P, q). Then

(a) The answer computed by (P^m, q^m) on any input instance **I** is identical to the answer computed by (P, q) on **I**.

(b) The set of facts produced by the Improved Seminaive Algorithm of (P^m, q^m) on input **I** is identical to the set of facts produced by an evaluation of QSQ on **I**.

13.4 Two Improvements

This section briefly presents two improvements of the techniques discussed earlier. The first focuses on another kind of information passing resulting from repeated variables and constants occurring in *idb* predicates in rule bodies. The second, called counting, is applicable to sets of data and rules having certain acyclicity properties.

Repeated Variables and Constants in Rule Bodies (by Example)

Consider the program P_r:

(1) $\qquad\qquad\qquad\qquad T(x, y, z) \leftarrow R(x, y, z)$

(2) $\qquad\qquad\qquad\qquad T(x, y, z) \leftarrow S(x, y, w), T(w, z, z)$

$\qquad\qquad\qquad\qquad query(y, z) \leftarrow T(1, y, z)$

Consider as input the instance $\mathbf{I}_1$ shown in Fig. 13.4(a). The data structures for a QSQ evaluation of this program are shown in Fig. 13.4(b). (The annotations '$\$2 = \$3$', '$\$2 = \$3 = 4$', etc., will be explained later.)

A magic set rewriting of the program and query yields

$$T^{bff}(x, y, z) \quad \leftarrow input\_T^{bff}(x), R(x, y, z)$$

$$sup_1^2(x, y, w) \leftarrow input\_T^{bff}(x), S(x, y, w)$$
$$T^{bff}(x, y, z) \quad \leftarrow sup_1^2(x, y, w), T^{bff}(w, z, z)$$

$$input\_T^{bff}(w) \leftarrow sup_1^2(x, y, w)$$

$$input\_T^{bff}(1) \leftarrow$$

$$query(y, z) \quad \leftarrow T^{bff}(1, y, z).$$

On input $\mathbf{I}_1$, the query returns the empty instance. Furthermore, the SLD tree for this query on $\mathbf{I}_1$ shown in Fig. 13.5, has only 9 goals and a total of 13 atoms, regardless of the value of n. However, both the QSQ and magic set approach generate a set of facts with size proportional to n (i.e., to the size of $\mathbf{I}_1$).

Why do both QSQ and magic sets perform so poorly on this program and query? The answer is that as presented, neither QSQ nor magic sets take advantage of restrictions on derivations resulting from the repeated z variable in the body of rule (2). Analogous examples can be developed for cases where constants appear in *idb* atoms in rule bodies.

Both QSQ and magic sets can be enhanced to use such information. In the case of QSQ, the tuples added to supplementary relations can be annotated to carry information about restrictions imposed by the atom that "caused" the tuple to be placed into the left-most supplementary relation. This is illustrated by the annotations in Fig. 13.4(b). First consider the annotation '$\$2 = \$3$' on the tuple $\langle 3 \rangle$ in $input\_T^{bff}$. This tuple is included into $input\_T^{bff}$ because $\langle 1, 2, 3 \rangle$ is in sup_1^2, and the next atom considered is $T^{bff}(w, z, z)$. In particular, then, any valid tuple (x, y, z) resulting from $\langle 3 \rangle$ must have second and third coordinates equal. The annotation '$\$2 = \$3$' is passed with $\langle 3 \rangle$ into sup_0^1 and sup_0^2.

Because variable y is bound to 4 in the tuple $\langle 3, 4, 5 \rangle$ in sup_1^2, the annotation '$\$2 = \$3$' on $\langle 3 \rangle$ in sup_0^2 "transforms" into '$\$3 = 4$' on this new tuple. This, in turn, implies the annotation '$\$2 = \$3 = 4$' when $\langle 5 \rangle$ is added to $input\_T^{bff}$ and to both sup_0^1 and sup_0^2.

Now consider the tuple $\langle 5 \rangle$ in sup_0^1, with annotation ($\$2 = \$3 = 4$). This can generate a tuple in sup_1^1 only if $\langle 5, 4, 4 \rangle$ is in R. For input $\mathbf{I}_1$ this tuple is not in R, and so the annotated

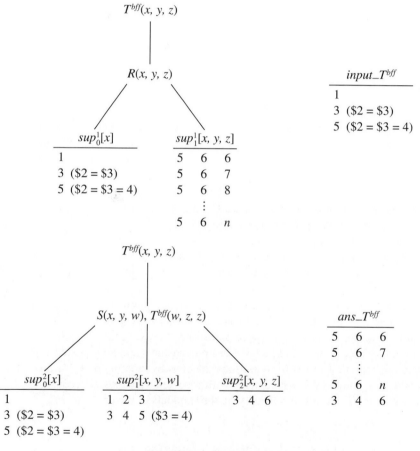

$$T^{bff}(x, y, z)$$

$$R(x, y, z)$$

$sup_0^1[x]$
1
3 ($2 = $3)
5 ($2 = $3 = 4)

$sup_1^1[x, y, z]$		
5	6	6
5	6	7
5	6	8
	⋮	
5	6	n

input_T^{bff}
1
3 ($2 = $3)
5 ($2 = $3 = 4)

$$T^{bff}(x, y, z)$$

$$S(x, y, w), \ T^{bff}(w, z, z)$$

$sup_0^2[x]$
1
3 ($2 = $3)
5 ($2 = $3 = 4)

$sup_1^2[x, y, w]$
1 2 3
3 4 5 ($3 = 4)

$sup_2^2[x, y, z]$
3 4 6

ans_T^{bff}		
5	6	6
5	6	7
	⋮	
5	6	n
3	4	6

(a) Sample input instance $\mathbf{I}_1$

	A	B	C
R	5	6	6
	5	6	7
	5	6	8
		⋮	
	5	6	n

	A	B	C
S	1	2	3
	3	4	5

$\mathbf{I}_1(R)$ $\mathbf{I}_1(S)$

(b) QSQ evaluation

Figure 13.4: Behavior of QSQ on program with repeated variables

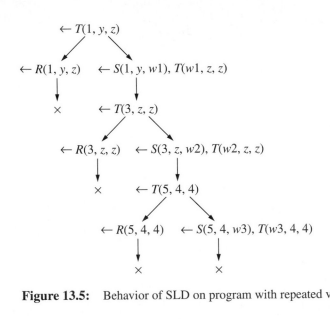

Figure 13.5:   Behavior of SLD on program with repeated variables

tuple $\langle 5 \rangle$ in sup_0^1 generates nothing (even though in the original QSQ framework many tuples are generated). Analogously, because there is no tuple $\langle 5, 4, w \rangle$ in S, the annotated tuple $\langle 5 \rangle$ of sup_0^2 does not generate anything in sup_1^2. This illustrates how annotations can be used to restrict the facts generated during execution of QSQ.

More generally, annotations on tuples are conjunctions of equality terms of the form '$\$i = \$j$' and '$\$i = a$' (where a is a constant). During step (B.ii.b) of QSQ, annotations are associated with new tuples placed into relations $input\_R^\gamma$. We permit the same tuple to occur in $input\_R^\gamma$ with different annotations. This enhanced version of QSQ is called *annotated QSQ*. The enhancement correctly produces all answers to the initial query, and the set of facts generated now closely parallels the set of facts and assignments generated by the SLD tree corresponding to the QSQ templates used.

The magic set technique can also be enhanced to incorporate the information captured by the annotations just described. This is accomplished by an initial preprocessing of the program (and query) called "subgoal rectification." Speaking loosely, a subgoal corresponding to an *idb* predicate is *rectified* if it has no constants and no repeated variables. Rectified subgoals may be formed from nonrectified ones by creating new *idb* predicates that correspond to versions of *idb* predicates with repeated variables and constants. For example, the following is the result of rectifying the subgoals of the program P_r:

$$T(x, y, z) \quad \leftarrow R(x, y, z)$$
$$T(x, y, z) \quad \leftarrow S(x, y, w), T_{\$2=\$3}(w, z)$$

$$T_{\$2=\$3}(x, z) \leftarrow R(x, z, z)$$
$$T_{\$2=\$3}(x, z) \leftarrow S(x, z, w), T_{\$2=\$3}(w, z)$$

$$query(y, z) \leftarrow T(1, y, z)$$
$$query(z, z) \leftarrow T_{\$2=\$3}(1, z).$$

It is straightforward to develop an iterative algorithm that replaces an arbitrary datalog program and query with an equivalent one, all of whose *idb* subgoals are rectified (see Exercise 13.20). Note that there may be more than one rule defining the query after rectification.

The magic set transformation is applied to the rectified program to obtain the final result. In the preceding example, there are two relevant adornments for the predicate $T_{\$2=\$3}$ (namely, *bf* and *bb*).

The following can be verified (see Exercise 13.21):

THEOREM 13.4.1 (Informal) The framework of annotated QSQ and the magic set transformation augmented with subgoal rectification are both correct. Furthermore, the set of *idb* predicate facts generated by evaluating a datalog query with either of these techniques is identical to the set of facts occurring in the corresponding SLD tree.

A tight correspondence between the assignments in SLD derivation trees and the supplementary relations generated both by annotated QSQ and rectified magic sets can be shown. The intuitive conclusion drawn from this development is that top-down and bottom-up techniques for datalog evaluation have essentially the same efficiency.

Counting (by Example)

We now present a brief sketch of another improvement of the magic set technique. It is different from the previous one in that it works only when the underlying data set is known to have certain acyclicity properties.

Consider evaluating the following SG query based on the Same-Generation program:

(1) $sg(x, y) \leftarrow flat(x, y)$
(2) $sg(x, y) \leftarrow up(x, x1), sg(x1, y1), down(y1, y)$
         $query(y) \leftarrow sg(a, y)$

on the input $\mathbf{J}_n$ given by

$$\mathbf{J}_n(up) = \{\langle a, b_i \rangle \mid i \in [1, n]\} \cup \{\langle b_i, c_j \rangle \mid i, j \in [1, n]\}$$
$$\mathbf{J}_n(flat) = \{\langle c_i, d_j \rangle \mid i, j \in [1, n]\}$$
$$\mathbf{J}_n(down) = \{\langle d_i, e_j \rangle \mid i, j \in [1, n]\} \cup \{\langle e_i, f \rangle \mid i \in [1, n]\}.$$

Instance $\mathbf{J}_2$ is shown in Fig. 13.6.

The completed QSQ template on input $\mathbf{J}_2$ for the second rule of the SG query is shown in Fig. 13.7(a). (The tuples are listed in the order in which QSQR would discover them.) Note that on input $\mathbf{J}_n$ both sup_1^2 and sup_2^2 would contain $n(n + 1)$ tuples.

Consider now the proof tree of SG having root $sg(a, f)$ shown in Fig. 13.8 (see Chapter 12). There is a natural correspondence of the children at depth 1 in this tree with the

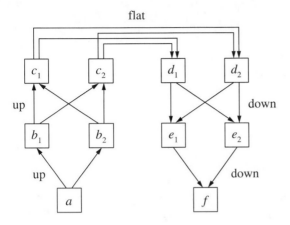

Figure 13.6: Instance $\mathbf{J}_2$ for counting

supplementary relation atoms $sup_0^2(a)$, $sup_1^2(a, b_1)$, $sup_2^2(a, e_1)$, and $sup_3^2(a, f)$ generated by QSQ; and between the children at depth 2 with $sup_0^2(b_1)$, $sup_1^2(b_1, c_1)$, $sup_2^2(b_1, d_1)$, and $sup_3^2(b_1, e_1)$.

A key idea in the counting technique is to record information about the depths at which supplementary relation atoms occur. In some cases, this permits us to ignore some of the specific constants present in the supplementary atoms. You will find that this is illustrated in Fig. 13.7(b). For example, we show atoms $count\_sup_0^2(1, a)$, $count\_sup_1^2(1, b_1)$, $count\_sup_2^2(1, e_1)$, and $count\_sup_3^2(1, f)$ that correspond to the supplementary atoms $sup_0^2(a)$, $sup_1^2(a, b_1)$, $sup_2^2(a, e_1)$, and $sup_3^2(a, f)$. Note that, for example, $count\_sup_1^2(2, c_1)$ corresponds to both $sup_1^2(b_1, c_1)$ and $sup_1^2(b_2, c_1)$.

More generally, the modified supplementary relation atoms hold an "index" that indicates a level in a proof tree corresponding to how the atom came to be created. Because of the structure of SG, and assuming that the *up* relation is acyclic, these modified supplementary relations can be used to find query answers. Note that on input $\mathbf{J}_n$, the relations $countsup_1^{2'}$ and $count\_sup_2^{2'}$ hold $2n$ tuples each rather than $n(n + 1)$, as in the original QSQ approach.

We now describe how the magic set program associated with the SG query can be transformed into an equivalent program (on acyclic input) that uses the indexes suggested by Fig. 13.7(b). The magic set rewriting of the SG query is given by

(s1.1) $\qquad\qquad sg^{bf}(x, y) \leftarrow input\_sg^{bf}(x), flat(x, y)$

(s2.1) $\qquad\qquad sup_1^2(x, x1) \leftarrow input\_sg^{bf}(x), up(x, x1)$

(s2.2) $\qquad\qquad sup_2^2(x, y1) \leftarrow sup_1^2(x, x1), sg^{bf}(x1, y1)$

(s2.3) $\qquad\qquad sg^{bf}(x, y) \leftarrow sup_2^2(x, y1), down(y1, y)$

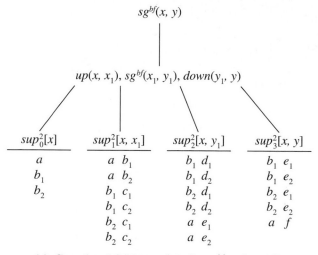

(a) Completed QSQ template for sg^{bf} on input $\mathbf{J}_2$

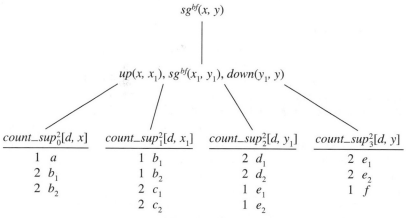

(b) Alternative QSQ "template," using indices

Figure 13.7:   Illustration of intuition behind counting

(i2.2) $input\_sg^{bf}(x1) \leftarrow sup_1^2(x, x1)$

(seed) $input\_sg^{bf}(a) \leftarrow$

(query) $query(y) \qquad \leftarrow sg^{bf}(a, y).$

The counting version of this is now given. (In other literature on counting, the seed is initialized with 0 rather than 1.)

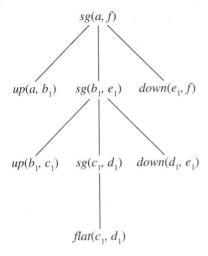

Figure 13.8:   A proof tree for $sg(a, f)$

(c-s1.1)	$count\_sg^{bf}(I, y)$	$\leftarrow count\_input\_sg^{bf}(I, x), flat(x, y)$
(c-s2.1)	$count\_sup_1^2(I, x1)$	$\leftarrow count\_input\_sg^{bf}(I, x), up(x, x1)$
(c-s2.2)	$count\_sup_2^2(I, y1)$	$\leftarrow count\_sup_1^2(I, x1), count\_sg^{bf}(I + 1, y1)$
(c-s2.3)	$count\_sg^{bf}(I, y)$	$\leftarrow count\_sup_2^2(I, y1), down(y1, y)$
(c-i2.2)	$count\_input\_sg^{bf}(I + 1, x1) \leftarrow count\_sup_1^2(I, x1)$	
(c-seed)	$count\_input\_sg^{bf}(1, a)$	$\leftarrow$
(c-query)	$query(y)$	$\leftarrow count\_sg^{bf}(1, y)$

In the preceding, expressions such as $I + 1$ are viewed as a short hand for using a variable J in place of $I + 1$ and including $J = I + 1$ in the rule body.

   In the counting version, the first coordinate of each supplementary relation keeps track of a level in a proof tree rather than a specific value. Intuitively, when "constructing" a sequence of supplementary atoms corresponding to a given level of a proof tree, each *idb* atom used must have been generated from the next deeper level. This is why *count_ sg*$^{bf}(I + 1, y1)$ is used in rule (c-s2.2). Furthermore, rule (c-i2.2) initiates the "construction" corresponding to a new layer of the proof tree.

   The counting program of the preceding example is not safe, in the sense that on some inputs the program may produce an infinite set of tuples in some predicates (e.g., $count\_sup_1^2$). For example, this will happen if there is a cycle in the *up* relation reachable from a. Analogous situations occur with most applications of counting. As a result, the counting technique can only be used where the underlying data set is known to satisfy certain restrictions.

This preceding example is a simple application of the general technique of counting. A more general version of counting uses three kinds of indexes. The first, illustrated in the example, records information about levels of proof trees. The second is used to record information about what rule is being expanded, and the third is used to record which atom of the rule body is being considered (see Exercise 13.23). A description of the kinds of programs for which the counting technique can be used is beyond the scope of this book. Although limited in applicability, the counting technique has been shown to yield significant savings in some contexts.

Bibliographic Notes

This chapter has presented a brief introduction to the research on heuristics for datalog evaluation. An excellent survey of this work is [BR88a], which presents a taxonomy of different techniques and surveys a broad number of them. Several books provide substantial coverage of this area, including [Bid91a, CGT90, Ull89b]. Experimental results comparing several of the techniques in the context of datalog are described in [BR88b]. An excellent survey on deductive database systems, which includes an overview of several prototype systems that support datalog, is presented in [RU94].

The naive and seminaive strategies for datalog evaluation underlie several early investigations and implementations [Cha81b, MS81]; the seminaive strategy for evaluation is described in [Ban85, Ban86], which also propose various refinements. The use of T^{i-1} and T^i in Algorithm 13.1.1 is from [BR87b]. Reference [CGT90] highlights the close relationship of these approaches to the classical Jacobi and Gauss-Seidel algorithms of numerical analysis.

An essential ingredient of the top-down approaches to datalog evaluation is that of "pushing" selections into recursions. An early form of this was developed in [AU79], where selections and projections are pushed into restricted forms of fixpoint queries (see Chapter 14 for the definition of fixpoint queries).

The Query-Subquery (QSQ) approach was initially presented in [Vie86]; the independently developed method of "extension tables" [DW87] is essentially equivalent to this. The QSQ approach is extended in [Vie88, Vie89] to incorporate certain global optimizations. An extension of the technique to general logic programming, called SLD-AL, is developed in [Vie87a, Vie89]. Related approaches include APEX [Loz85], Earley Deduction [PW80, Por86], and those of [Nej87, Roe87]. The connection between context-free parsing and datalog evaluation is highlighted in [Lan88].

The algorithms of the QSQ family are sometimes called "memo-ing" approaches, because they use various data structures to remember salient inferred facts to filter the work of traditional SLD resolution.

Perhaps the most general of the top-down approaches uses "rule/goal" graphs [Ull85]; these potentially infinite trees intuitively correspond to a breadth-first, set-at-a-time execution of SLD resolution. Rule/goal graphs are applied in [Van86] to evaluate datalog queries in distributed systems. Similar graph structures have also been used in connection with general logic programs (e.g., [Kow75, Sic76]). A survey of several graph-based approaches is [DW85].

Turning to bottom-up approaches, the essentially equivalent approaches of [HN84] and [GdM86] develop iterative algebraic programs for linear datalog programs. [GS87] extends these. A more general approach based on rewriting iterative algebra programs is presented in [CT87, Tan88].

The magic set and counting techniques originally appeared for linear datalog in [BMSU86]. Our presentation of magic sets is based on an extended version called "generalized supplementary magic sets" [BR87, BR91]. That work develops a general notion of sideways information passing based on graphs (see Exercise 13.19), and develops both magic sets and counting in connection with general logic programming. The Alexander method [RLK86, Ker88], developed independently, is essentially the same as generalized supplementary magic sets for datalog. This was generalized to logic programming in [Sek89]. Magic set rewriting has also been applied to optimize SQL queries [MFPR90].

The counting method is generalized and combined with magic sets in [SZ86, SZ88]. Supplementary magic is incorporated in [BR91]. Analytic comparisons of magic and counting for selected programs are presented in [MSPS87].

Another bottom-up technique is Static Filtering [KL86a, KL86b]. This technique forms a graph corresponding to the flow of tuples through a bottom-up evaluation and then modifies the graph in a manner that captures information passing resulting from constants in the initial query.

Several of the investigations just mentioned, including [BR87, KL86a, KL86b, Ull85, Vie86], emphasize the idea that sideways information passing and control are largely independent. Both [SZ88] and [BR91] describe fairly general mechanisms for specifying and using alternative sideways information passing and related message passing. A more general form of sideways information passing, which passes bounding inequalities between subgoals, is studied in [APP$^+$86]. A formal framework for studying the success of pushing selections into datalog programs is developed in [BKBR87].

Several papers have studied the connection between top-down and bottom-up evaluation techniques. One body of the research in this direction focuses on the sets of facts generated by the top-down and bottom-up techniques. One of the first results relating top-down and bottom-up is from [BR87, BR91], where it is shown that if a top-down technique and the generalized supplementary magic set technique use a given family of sideways information passing techniques, then the sets of intermediate facts produced by both techniques correspond. That research is conducted in the context of general logic programs that are range restricted. These results are generalized to possibly non-range-restricted logic programs in the independent research [Ram91] and [Sek89]. In that research, bottom-up evaluations may use terms and tuples that include variables, and bottom-up evaluation of rewritten programs uses unification rather than simple relational join. A close correspondence between top-down and bottom-up evaluation for datalog was established in [Ull89a], where subgoal rectification is used. The treatment of Program P_r and Theorem 13.4.1 are inspired by that development. This close correspondence is extended to arbitrary logic programs in [Ull89b]. Using a more detailed cost model, [SR93] shows that bottom-up evaluation asymptotically dominates top-down evaluation for logic programs, even if they produce nonground terms in their output.

A second direction of research on the connection between top-down and bottom-up approaches provides an elegant unifying framework [Bry89]. Recall in the discussion of Theorem 13.2.2 that the answer to a query can be obtained by performing the steps of the QSQ until a fixpoint is reached. Note that the fixpoint operator used in this chapter is different from the conventional bottom-up application of T_P used by the naive algorithm for datalog evaluation. The framework presented in [Bry89] is based on meta-interpreters (i.e., interpreters that operate on datalog rules in addition to data); these can be used to specify QSQ and related algorithms as bottom-up, fixpoint evaluations. (Such meta-programming is common in functional and logic programming but yields novel results in the context of datalog.) Reference [Bry89] goes on to describe several top-down and bottom-up datalog evaluation techniques within the framework, proving their correctness and providing a basis for comparison.

A recent investigation [NRSU89] improves the performance of the magic sets in some cases. If the program and query satisfy certain conditions, then a technique called factoring can be used to replace some predicates by new predicates of lower arity. Other improvements are considered in [Sag90], where it is shown in particular that the advantage of one method over another may depend on the actual data, therefore stressing the need for techniques to estimate the size of *idb*'s (e.g., [LN90]).

Extensions of the datalog evaluation techniques to stratified datalog¬ programs (see Chapter 15) include [BPR87, Ros91, SI88, KT88].

Another important direction of research has been the parallel evaluation of datalog programs. Heuristics are described in [CW89b, GST90, Hul89, SL91, WS88, WO90].

A novel approach to answering datalog queries efficiently is developed in [DT92, DS93]. The focus is on cases in which the same query is asked repeatedly as the underlying *edb* is changing. The answer of the query (and additional scratch paper relations) is materialized against a given *edb* state, and first-order queries are used incrementally to maintain the materialized data as the underlying *edb* state is changed.

A number of prototype systems based on variants of datalog have been developed, incorporating some of the techniques mentioned in this chapter. They include DedGin [Vie87b, LV89], NAIL! [Ull85, MUV86, MNS+87], LDL [NT89], ALGRES [CRG+88], NU-Prolog [RSB+87], GLUE-NAIL [DMP93], and CORAL [RSS92, RSSS93]. Descriptions of projects in this area can also be found in [Zan87], [RU94].

Exercises

Exercise 13.1 Recall the program RSG' from Section 13.1. Exhibit an instance **I** such that on this input, $\delta^i_{rsg} \neq \emptyset$ for each $i > 0$.

Exercise 13.2 Recall the informal discussion of the two seminaive "versions" of the nonlinear ancestor program discussed in Section ???. Let P_1 denote the first of these, and P_2 the second. Show the following.

   (a) For some input, P_2 can produce the same tuple more than once at some level beyond the first level.

   (b) If P_2 produces the same tuple more than once, then each occurrence corresponds to a distinct proof tree (see Section 12.5) from the program and the input.

   (c) P_1 can produce a given tuple twice, where the proof trees corresponding to the two occurrences are identical.

Exercise 13.3 Consider the basic seminaive algorithm (13.1.1).

(a) Verify that this algorithm terminates on all inputs.

(b) Show that for each $i \geq 0$ and each *idb* predicate S, after the ith execution of the loop the value of variable S^i is equal to $T_P^i(\mathbf{I})(S)$ and the value of Δ_S^{i+1} is equal to $T_P^{i+1}(\mathbf{I})(S) - T_P^i(\mathbf{I})(S)$.

(c) Verify that this algorithm produces correct output on all inputs.

(d) Give an example input for which the same tuple is generated during different loops of the algorithm.

Exercise 13.4   Consider the improved seminaive algorithm (13.1.2).

(a) Verify that this algorithm terminates and produces correct output on all inputs.

(b) Give an example of a program P for which the improved seminaive algorithm produces fewer redundant tuples than the basic seminaive algorithm.

Exercise 13.5   Let P be a linear datalog program, and let P' be the set of rules associated with P by the improved seminaive algorithm. Suppose that the naive algorithm is performed using P' on some input $\mathbf{I}$. Does this yield $P(\mathbf{I})$? Why or why not? What if the basic seminaive algorithm is used?

Exercise 13.6   A set X of relevant facts for datalog query (P, q) and input $\mathbf{I}$ is *minimal* if (1) for each answer β of q there is a proof tree for β constructed from facts in X, and (2) X is minimal having this property. Informally describe an algorithm that produces a minimal set of relevant facts for a query (P, q) and input $\mathbf{I}$ and is polynomial time in the size of $\mathbf{I}$.

Exercise 13.7   [BR91] Suppose that program P includes the rule

$$\rho : S(x, y) \leftarrow S_1(x, z), S_2(z, y), S_3(u, v), S_4(v, w),$$

where S_3, S_4 are *edb* relations. Observe that the atoms $S_3(u, v)$ and $S_4(v, w)$ are not connected to the other atoms of the rule body or to the rule head. Furthermore, in an evaluation of P on input $\mathbf{I}$, this rule may contribute some tuple to S only if there is an assignment α for u, v, w such that $\{S_3(u, v), S_4(v, w)\}[\alpha] \subseteq \mathbf{I}$. Explain why it is typically more efficient to replace ρ with

$$\rho' : S(x, y) \leftarrow S_1(x, z), S_2(z, y)$$

if there is such an assignment and to delete ρ from P otherwise. Extend this to the case when S_3, S_4 are *idb* relations. State a general version of this heuristic improvement.

Exercise 13.8   Consider the adorned rule

$$R^{bf}(x, w) \leftarrow S_1^{bf}(x, y), S_2^{bf}(y, z), T_1^{ff}(u, v), T_2^{bf}(v, w).$$

Explain why it makes sense to view the second occurrence of v as bound.

Exercise 13.9   Consider the rule

$$R(x, y, y) \leftarrow S(y, z), T(z, x).$$

(a) Construct adorned versions of this rule for R^{ffb} and R^{fbb}.

(b) Suppose that in the QSQ algorithm a tuple $\langle b, c \rangle$ is placed into $input\_R^{fbb}$. Explain why this tuple should not be placed into the 0th supplementary relation for the second adorned rule constructed in part (a).

(c) Exhibit an example analogous to part (b) based on the presence of a constant in the head of a rule rather than on repeated variables.

Exercise 13.10

(a) Complete the evaluation in Example 13.2.1.

(b) Use Algorithm 13.2.3 (QSQR) to evaluate that example.

★ **Exercise 13.11**   In the QSQR algorithm, the procedure for processing subqueries of the form (R^γ, S) is called until no global variable is changed. Exhibit an example datalog query and input where the second cycle of calls to the subqueries (R^γ, S) generates new answer tuples.

♠ **Exercise 13.12**   (a) Prove Theorem 13.2.2. (b) Prove that the QSQR algorithm is correct.

★ **Exercise 13.13**   The *Iterative QSQ (QSQI)* algorithm uses the QSQ framework, but without recursion. Instead in each iteration it processes each rule body from left to right, using the values currently in the relations ans_R^γ when computing values for the supplementary relations. As with QSQR, the variables $input\_R^\gamma$ and ans_R^γ are global, and the variables for the supplementary relations are local. Iteration continues until there is no change to the global variables.

(a) Specify the QSQI algorithm more completely.

(b) Give an example where QSQI performs redundant work that QSQR does not.

Exercise 13.14   [BR91] Consider the following query based on a nonlinear variant of the same-generation program, called here the SGV query:

(a) $sgv(x, y) \leftarrow flat(x, y)$

(b) $sgv(x, y) \leftarrow up(x, z1), sgv(z1, z2), flat(z2, z3), sgv(z3, z4), down(z4, y)$
$\quad query(y) \leftarrow sgv(a, y)$

Give the magic set transformation of this program and query.

Exercise 13.15   Give examples of how a query (P^m, q^m) resulting from magic set rewriting can produce nonrelevant and redundant facts.

♠ **Exercise 13.16**

(a) Give the general definition of the magic set rewriting technique.

(b) Prove Theorem 13.3.1.

Exercise 13.17   Compare the difficulties, in practical terms, of using the QSQ and magic set frameworks for evaluating datalog queries.

★ **Exercise 13.18**   Let (P, q) denote the SGV query of Exercise 13.14. Let (P^m, q^m) denote the result of rewriting this program, using the (generalized supplementary) magic set transformation presented in this chapter. Under an earlier version, called here "original" magic, the rewritten form of (P, q) is (P^{om}, q^{om}):

(o-m1) $sgv^{bf}(x, y)$ $\leftarrow input\_sgv^{bf}(x), flat(x, y)$

(o-m2) $sgv^{bf}(x, y)$ $\leftarrow input\_sgv^{bf}(x), up(x, z1), sgv^{bf}(z1, z2),$
$$flat(z2, z3), sgv^{bf}(z3, z4), down(z4, y)$$

(o-i2.2) $input\_sgv^{bf}(z1) \leftarrow input\_sgv^{bf}(x), up(x, z1)$

(o-i2.4) $input\_sgv^{bf}(z3) \leftarrow input\_sgv^{bf}(x), up(x, z1), sgv^{bf}(z1, z2),$
$$flat(z2, z3)$$

(o-seed) $input\_sgv(a)$ $\leftarrow$

(o-query) $query(y)$ $\leftarrow sgv^{bf}(a, y)$

Intuitively, the original magic set transformation uses the relations $input\_R^\gamma$, but not supplementary relations.

    (a) Verify that (P^{om}, q^{om}) is equivalent to (P, q).

    (b) Compare the family of facts computed during the executions of (P^m, q^m) and (P^{om}, q^{om}).

    (c) Give a specification for the original magic set transformation, applicable to any datalog query.

★ **Exercise 13.19**   Consider the adorned rule

$$R^{bbf}(x, y, z) \leftarrow T_1^{bf}(x, s), T_2^{bf}(s, t), T_3^{bf}(y, u), T_4^{bf}(u, v), T_5^{bbf}(t, v, z).$$

A *sip graph* for this rule has as nodes all atoms of the rule and a special node *exit*, and edges (R, T_1), (T_1, T_2), (R, T_3), (T_3, T_4), (T_2, T_5), (T_4, T_5), $(T_5, exit)$. Describe a family of supplementary relations, based on this sip graph, that can be used in conjunction with the QSQ and magic set approaches. [Use one supplementary relation for each edge (corresponding to the output of the tail of the edge) and one supplementary relation for each node except for R (corresponding to the input to this node—in general, this will equal the join of the relations for the edges entering the node).] Explain how this may increase efficiency over the left-to-right approach used in this chapter. Generalize the construction. (The notion of sip graph and its use is a variation of [BR91].)

♠ **Exercise 13.20**   [Ull89a] Specify an algorithm that replaces a program and query by an equivalent one, all of whose *idb* subgoals are rectified. What is the complexity of this algorithm?

♠ **Exercise 13.21**

    (a) Provide a more detailed specification of the QSQ framework with annotations, and prove its correctness.

    (b) [Ull89b, Ull89a] State formally the definitions needed for Theorem 13.4.1, and prove it.

Exercise 13.22   Write a program using counting that can be used to answer the RSG query presented at the beginning of Section 13.2.

(c-s1.1)	$count\_sgv^{bf}(I, K, L, y)$	$\leftarrow count\_input\_sgv^{bf}(I, K, L, x), flat(x, y)$
(c-s2.1)	$count\_sup_1^2(I, K, L, z1)$	$\leftarrow count\_input\_sgv^{bf}(I, K, L, x), up(x, z1)$
(c-s2.2)	$count\_sup_2^2(I, K, L, z2)$	$\leftarrow count\_sup_1^2(I, K, L, z1),$

$$count\_sgv^{bf}(I + 1, 2K + 2, 5L + 2, z2)$$

(c-s2.3)	$count\_sup_3^2(I, K, L, z3)$	$\leftarrow count\_sup_2^2(I, K, L, z2), flat(z2, z3)$
(c-s2.4)	$count\_sup_4^2(I, K, L, z4)$	$\leftarrow count\_sup_3^2(I, K, L, z3),$

$$count\_sgv^{bf}(I + 1, 2K + 2, 5L + 4, z4),$$

(c-s2.5)	$count\_sgv^{bf}(I, K, L, y)$	$\leftarrow count\_sup_4^2(I, K, L, z4), down(z4, y)$

(c-i2.2) $count\_input\_sgv^{bf}(I + 1, 2K + 2, 5L + 2, z1)$

$$\leftarrow count\_sup_1^2(I, K, L, z1)$$

(c-i2.4) $count\_input\_sgv^{bf}(I + 1, 2K + 2, 5L + 4, z3)$

$$\leftarrow count\_sup_3^2(I, K, L, z3)$$

(c-seed) $count\_input\_sgv^{bf}(1, 0, 0, a) \leftarrow$

(c-query) $query(y)$ $\leftarrow count\_sgv^{bf}(1, 0, 0, y)$

Figure 13.9:   Generalized counting transformation on SGV query

★ **Exercise 13.23**   [BR91] This exercise illustrates a version of counting that is more general than that of Exercise 13.22. Indexed versions of predicates shall have three index coordinates (occurring leftmost) that hold:

    (i) The level in the proof tree of the subgoal that a given rule is expanding.

    (ii) An encoding of the rules used along the path from the root of the proof tree to the current subgoal. Suppose that there are k rules, numbered $(1), \ldots, (k)$. The index for the root node is 0 and, given index K, if rule number i is used next, then the next index is given by $kK + i$.

    (iii) An encoding of the atom occurrence positions along the path from root to the current node. Assuming that l is the maximum number of *idb* atoms in any rule body, this index is encoded in a manner similar to item (ii).

A counting version of the SGV query of Exercise 13.14 is shown in Fig. 13.9. Verify that this is equivalent to the SGV query in the case where there are no cycles in *up* or *down*.

14 Recursion and Negation

Vittorio:	*Let's combine recursion and negation.*
Riccardo:	*That sounds hard to me.*
Sergio:	*It's no problem, just add* fixpoint *to the calculus, or* while *to the algebra.*
Riccardo:	*That sounds hard to me.*
Vittorio:	*OK—how about datalog with negation?*
Riccardo:	*That sounds hard to me.*
Alice:	*Riccardo, you are recursively negative.*

The query languages considered so far were obtained by augmenting the conjunctive queries successively with disjunction, negation, and recursion. In this chapter, we consider languages that provide both negation and recursion. They allow us to ask queries such as, *"Which are the pairs of metro stops which are **not** connected?"*. This query is not expressible in relational calculus and algebra or in datalog.

The integration of recursion and negation is natural and yields highly expressive languages. We will see how it can be achieved in the three paradigms considered so far: algebraic, logic, and deductive. The algebraic language is an extension of the algebra with a looping construct and an assignment, in the style of traditional imperative programming languages. The logic language is an extension of the calculus in which recursion is provided by a fixpoint operator. The deductive language extends datalog with negation.

In this chapter, the semantics of datalog with negation is defined from a purely computational perspective that is in the spirit of the algebraic approach. More natural and widely accepted model-theoretic semantics, such as stratified and well-founded semantics, are presented in Chapter 15.

As we consider increasingly powerful languages, the complexity of query evaluation becomes a greater concern. We consider two flavors of the languages in each paradigm: the inflationary one, which guarantees termination in time polynomial in the size of the database; and the noninflationary one, which only guarantees that a polynomial amount of space is used.[1] In the last section of this chapter, we show that the polynomial-time-bounded languages defined in the different paradigms are equivalent. The set of queries they define is called the *fixpoint queries*. The polynomial-space-bounded languages are also equivalent, and the corresponding set of queries is called the *while* queries. In Chapter 17, we examine in more detail the expressiveness and complexity of the *fixpoint* and

---

[1] For comparison, it is shown in Chapter 17 that CALC requires only logarithmic space.

while queries. Note that, in particular, the polynomial time and space bounds on the complexity of such queries imply that there are queries that are not *fixpoint* or *while* queries. More powerful languages are considered in Chapter 18.

Before describing specific languages, we present an example that illustrates the principles underlying the two flavors of the languages.

EXAMPLE   The following is based on a version of the well-known "game of life," which is used to model biological evolution. The game starts with a set of cells, some of which are alive and some dead; the alive ones are colored in blue or red. (One cell may have two colors.) Each cell has other cells as neighbors. Suppose that a binary relation *Neighbor* holds the neighbor relation (considered as a symmetric relation) and that the information about living cells and their color is held in a binary relation *Alive* (see Fig. 14.1). Suppose first that a cell can change status from dead to alive following this rule:

(α)   A dead cell becomes alive if it has at least two neighbors that are alive

and have the same color. It then takes the color of the "parents."

The evolution of a particular population for the *Neighbor* graph of Fig. 14.1(a) is given in Fig. 14.1(b). Observe that the sets of tuples keep increasing and that we reach a stable state. This is an example of inflationary iteration.

Now suppose that the evolution also obeys the second rule:

(β)   A live cell dies if it has more than three live neighbors.

The evolution of the population with the two rules is given in Fig. 14.1(c). Observe that the number of tuples sometimes decreases and that the computation diverges. This is an example of noninflationary iteration.

All languages that we consider use a fixed set of relation schemas throughout the computation. At any point in the computation, intermediate results contain only constants from the input database or that are specified in the query. Suppose the relations used in the computation have arities $r_1, \ldots, r_k$, the input database contains n constants, and the query refers to c constants. Then the number of tuples in any intermediate result is bounded by $\sum_{i=1}^{k} (n + c)^{r_i}$, which is a polynomial in n. Thus such queries can be evaluated in polynomial space. As will be seen when the formal definitions are in place, this implies that each noninflationary iteration, and hence each noninflationary query, can be evaluated in polynomial space, whether or not it terminates. In contrast, the inflationary semantics ensures termination by requiring that a tuple can never be deleted once it has been inserted. Because there are only polynomially many tuples, each such program terminates in polynomial time.

To summarize, the *inflationary* languages use iteration based on an "inflation of tuples." In all three paradigms, inflationary queries can be evaluated in polynomial time, and the same expressive power is obtained. The *noninflationary* languages use noninflationary or destructive assignment inside of iterations. In all three paradigms, noninflationary queries can be evaluated in polynomial space, and again the same expressive power is

Neighbor

a	*e*
b	*e*
c	*e*
d	*e*

(a) Neighbor

Alive

a	*blue*
b	*red*
c	*blue*
d	*red*

Alive

a	*blue*
b	*red*
c	*blue*
d	*red*
e	*blue*
e	*red*

Alive

a	*blue*
b	*red*
c	*blue*	...
d	*red*
e	*blue*
e	*red*

(b) Inflationary evolution

Alive

a	*blue*
b	*red*
c	*blue*
d	*red*

Alive

a	*blue*
b	*red*
c	*blue*
d	*red*
e	*blue*
e	*red*

Alive

a	*blue*
b	*red*
c	*blue*
d	*red*

Alive

a	*blue*
b	*red*
c	*blue*
d	*red*
e	*blue*
e	*red*

Alive

a	*blue*
b	*red*	...
c	*blue*
d	*red*

(c) Noninflationary evolution

Figure 14.1:   Game of life

obtained. (We note, however, that it remains open whether the inflationary and the non-inflationary languages have equivalent expressive power; we discuss this issue later.)

14.1   Algebra + *While*

Relational algebra is essentially a procedural language. Of the query languages, it is the closest to traditional imperative programming languages. Chapters 4 and 5 described how it can be extended syntactically using assignment (:=) and composition (;) without increasing its expressive power. The extensions of the algebra with recursion are also consistent with the imperative paradigm and incorporate a *while* construct, which calls for the iteration of a program segment. The resulting language comes in two flavors: inflationary and noninflationary. The two versions of the language differ in the semantics of the assignment statement. The noninflationary version was the one first defined historically, and we discuss it next. The resulting language is called the *while* language.

Noninflationary Semantics

Recall from Chapter 4 that assignment statements can be incorporated into the algebra using expressions of the form $R := E$, where E is an algebra expression and R a relational variable of the same sort as the result of E. (The difference from Chapter 4 is that it is no longer required that each successive assignment statement use a distinct, previously unused variable.) In the *while* language, the semantics of an assignment statement is as follows: The value of R becomes the result of evaluating the algebra expression E on the current state of the database. This is the usual destructive assignment in imperative programming languages, where the old value of a variable is overwritten.

While statements have the form

> *while change do*
>   *begin*
>   ⟨*loop body*⟩
>   *end*

There is no explicit termination condition. Instead a loop runs as long as the execution of the body causes some change to some relation (i.e., until a stable state is reached). At the end of this section, we consider the introduction of explicit terminating conditions and see that this does not affect the language in an essential manner.

Nesting of loops is permitted. A *while program* is a finite sequence of assignment or while statements. The program uses a finite set of relational variables of specified sorts, including the names of relations in the input database. Relational variables that are not in the input database are initialized to the empty relation. A designated relational variable holds the output to the program at the end of the computation. The *image* (or *value*) of program P on $\mathbf{I}$, denoted $P(\mathbf{I})$, is the value finally assigned to the designated variable if P terminates on $\mathbf{I}$; otherwise $P(\mathbf{I})$ is undefined.

EXAMPLE 14.1.1 (Transitive Closure)   Consider a binary relation $G[AB]$, specifying the edges of a graph. The following *while* program computes in $T[AB]$ the transitive closure of G.

> $T := G$
> *while change do*
>   *begin*
> $T := T \cup \pi_{AB}(\delta_{B \to C}(T) \bowtie \delta_{A \to C}(G));$
>   *end*

A computation ends when T becomes stable, which means that no new edges were added in the current iteration, so T now holds the transitive closure of G.

EXAMPLE 14.1.2 (Add-Remove)   Consider again a binary relation G specifying the edges of a graph. Each loop of the following program

- removes from G all edges $\langle a, b \rangle$ if there is a path of length 2 from a to b, and
- inserts an edge $\langle a, b \rangle$ if there is a vertex not directly connected to a and b.

This is iterated while some change occurs. The result is placed into the binary relation T. In addition, the binary relation variables *ToAdd* and *ToRemove* are used as "scratch paper." For the sake of readability, we use the calculus with active domain semantics whenever this is easier to understand than the corresponding algebra expression.

$T := G;$
while change do
    begin
    $ToRemove := \{\langle x, y \rangle \mid \exists z(T(x, z) \wedge T(z, y))\};$
    $ToAdd := \{\langle x, y \rangle \mid \exists z(\neg T(x, z) \wedge \neg T(z, x) \wedge \neg T(y, z) \wedge \neg T(z, y))\};$
    $T := (T \cup ToAdd) - ToRemove;$
    end

In the *Transitive Closure* example, the transitive closure query always terminates. This is not the case for the *Add-Remove* query. (Try the graph $\{\langle a, a \rangle, \langle a, b \rangle, \langle b, a \rangle, \langle b, b \rangle\}$.) The halting problem for *while* programs is undecidable (i.e., there is no algorithm that, given a *while* program P, decides whether P halts on each input; see Exercise 14.2). Observe, however, that for a pair $(P, \mathbf{I})$, one can decide whether P halts on input $\mathbf{I}$ because, as argued earlier, *while* computations are in PSPACE.

Inflationary Semantics

We define next an inflationary version of the *while* language, denoted by $while^+$. The $while^+$ language differs with *while* in the semantics of the assignment statement. In particular, in $while^+$, assignment is cumulative rather than destructive: Execution of the statement assigning E to R results in *adding* the result of E to the old value of R. Thus no tuple is removed from any relation throughout the execution of the program. To distinguish the cumulative semantics from the destructive one, we use the notation $P += e$ for the cumulative semantics.

EXAMPLE 14.1.3 (Transitive Closure Revisited)   Following is a $while^+$ program that computes the transitive closure of a graph represented by a binary relation $G[AB]$. The result is obtained in the variable $T[AB]$.

$T += G;$
while change do
    begin
    $T += \pi_{AB}(\delta_{B \to C}(T) \bowtie \delta_{A \to C}(G));$
    end

This is almost exactly the same program as in the *while* language. The only difference is that because assignment is cumulative, it is not necessary to add the content of T to the result of the projection.

To conclude this section, we consider alternatives for the control condition of loops. Until now, we based termination on reaching a stable state. It is also common to use explicit terminating conditions, such as tests for emptiness of the form $E = \emptyset$, $E \neq \emptyset$, or $E \neq E'$, where E, E' are relational algebra expressions. The body of the loop is executed as long as the condition is satisfied. The following example shows how transitive closure is computed using explicit looping conditions.

EXAMPLE 14.1.4   We use another relation schema $oldT$ also of sort AB.

$$T \mathrel{+}= G$$
$$while\ (T - oldT) \neq \emptyset\ do$$
$$\quad begin$$
$$\quad\quad oldT \mathrel{+}= T;$$
$$\quad\quad T \mathrel{+}= \pi_{AB}(\delta_{B \to C}(T) \bowtie \delta_{A \to C}(G));$$
$$\quad end$$

In the program, $oldT$ keeps track of the value of T resulting from the previous iteration of the loop. The computation ends when $oldT$ and T coincide, which means that no new edges were added in the current iteration, so T now holds the transitive closure of G.

It is easily shown that the use of such termination conditions does not modify the expressive power of *while*, and the use of conditions such as $E \neq E'$ does not modify the expressive power of *while*$^+$ (see Exercise 14.5).

In Section 14.4 we shall see that nesting of loops in *while* queries does not increase expressive power.

14.2 Calculus + Fixpoint

Just as in the case of the algebra, we provide inflationary and noninflationary extensions of the calculus with recursion. This could be done using assignment statements and while loops, as for the algebra. Indeed, we used calculus notation in Example 14.1.2 (*Add-Remove*). Instead we use an equivalent but more logic-oriented construct to augment the calculus. The construct, called a *fixpoint operator*, allows the iteration of calculus formulas up to a fixpoint. In effect, this allows defining relations inductively using calculus formulas. As with *while*, the fixpoint operator comes in a noninflationary and an inflationary flavor.

For the remainder of this chapter, as a notational convenience, we use active domain semantics for calculus queries. In addition, we often use a formula $\varphi(x_1, \ldots, x_n)$ as an abbreviation for the query $\{x_1, \ldots, x_n \mid \varphi(x_1, \ldots, x_n)\}$. These two simplifications do not affect the results developed.

Partial Fixpoints

The noninflationary version of the fixpoint operator is considered first. It is illustrated in the following example.

EXAMPLE 14.2.1 (Transitive Closure Revisited)   Consider again the transitive closure of a graph G. The relations J_n holding pairs of nodes at distance at most n can be defined inductively using the single formula

$$\varphi(T) = G(x, y) \lor T(x, y) \lor \exists z(T(x, z) \land G(z, y))$$

as follows:

$$J_0 = \emptyset;$$
$$J_n = \varphi(J_{n-1}), \quad n > 0.$$

Here $\varphi(J_{n-1})$ denotes the result of evaluating $\varphi(T)$ when the value of T is J_{n-1}. Note that, for each input G, the sequence $\{J_n\}_{n\geq 0}$ converges. That is, there exists some k for which $J_k = J_j$ for every $j > k$ (indeed, k is the diameter of the graph). Clearly, J_k holds the transitive closure of the graph. Thus the transitive closure of G can be defined as the limit of the foregoing sequence. Note that $J_k = \varphi(J_k)$, so J_k is also a *fixpoint* of $\varphi(T)$. The relation J_k thereby obtained is denoted by $\mu_T(\varphi(T))$. Then the transitive closure of G is defined by

$$\mu_T(G(x, y) \lor T(x, y) \lor \exists z(T(x, z) \land G(z, y))).$$

By definition, μ_T is an operator that produces a new relation (the fixpoint J_k) when applied to $\varphi(T)$. Note that, although T is used in $\varphi(T)$, T is not a database relation but rather a relation used to define inductively $\mu_T(\varphi(T))$ from the database, starting with $T = \emptyset$. T is said to be *bound* to μ_T. Indeed, μ_T is somewhat similar to a quantifier over relations. Note that the scope of the free variables of $\varphi(T)$ is restricted to $\varphi(T)$ by the operator μ_T.

In the preceding example, the limit of the sequence $\{J_n\}_{n\geq 0}$ happens to exist and is in fact the least fixpoint of φ. This is not always the case; the possibility of nontermination is illustrated next (and Exercise 14.4 considers cases in which a nonminimal fixpoint is reached).

EXAMPLE 14.2.2   Consider

$$\varphi(T) = (x = 0 \land \neg T(0) \land \neg T(1)) \lor (x = 0 \land T(1)) \lor (x = 1 \land T(0)).$$

In this case the sequence $\{J_n\}_{n\geq 0}$ is $\emptyset, \{\langle 0 \rangle\}, \{\langle 1 \rangle\}, \{\langle 0 \rangle\}, \dots$ (i.e., T flip-flops between zero and one). Thus the sequence does not converge, and $\mu_T(\varphi(T))$ is not defined. Situations in which μ is undefined correspond to nonterminating computations in the *while* language. The following nonterminating *while* program corresponds to $\mu_T(\varphi(T))$.

$T := \{\langle 0 \rangle\};$
while change do
  begin
  $T := \{\langle 0 \rangle, \langle 1 \rangle\} - T;$
  end

Because μ is only partially defined, it is called the *partial fixpoint operator*. We now define its syntax and semantics in more detail.

Partial Fixpoint Operator   Let **R** be a database schema, and let $T[m]$ be a relation schema not in **R**. Let **S** denote the schema $\mathbf{R} \cup \{T\}$. Let $\varphi(T)$ be a formula using T and relations in **R**, with m free variables. Given an instance **I** over **R**, $\mu_T(\varphi(T))$ denotes the relation that is the limit, *if it exists*, of the sequence $\{J_n\}_{n \geq 0}$ defined by

$$J_0 = \emptyset;$$
$$J_n = \varphi(J_{n-1}), \quad n > 0,$$

where $\varphi(J_{n-1})$ denotes the result of evaluating φ on the instance $\mathbf{J}_{n-1}$ over **S** whose restriction to **R** is **I** and $\mathbf{J}_{n-1}(T) = J_{n-1}$.

The expression $\mu_T(\varphi(T))$ denotes a new relation (if it is defined). In turn, it can be used in more complex formulas like any other relation. For example, $\mu_T(\varphi(T))(y, z)$ states that $\langle y, z \rangle$ is in $\mu_T(\varphi(T))$. If $\mu_T(\varphi(T))$ defines the transitive closure of G, the complement of the transitive closure is defined by

$$\{\langle x, y \rangle \mid \neg \, \mu_T(\varphi(T))(x, y)\}.$$

The extension of the calculus with μ is called *partial fixpoint logic*, denoted CALC+μ.

Partial Fixpoint Logic   CALC+μ *formulas* are obtained by repeated applications of CALC operators ($\exists, \forall, \vee, \wedge, \neg$) and the partial fixpoint operator, starting from atoms. In particular, $\mu_T(\varphi(T))(e_1, \ldots, e_n)$, where T has arity n, $\varphi(T)$ has n free variables, and the e_i are variables or constants, is a formula. Its free variables are the variables in the set $\{e_1, \ldots, e_n\}$ [thus the scope of variables occurring inside $\varphi(T)$ consists of the subformula to which μ_T is applied]. Partial fixpoint operators can be nested. CALC+μ *queries* over a database schema **R** are expressions of the form

$$\{\langle e_1, \ldots, e_n \rangle \mid \xi\},$$

where ξ is a CALC+μ formula whose free variables are those occurring in $e_1, \ldots, e_n$. The formula ξ may use relation names in addition to those in **R**; however, each occurrence P of such relation name must be bound to some partial fixpoint operator μ_P. The semantics of CALC+μ queries is defined as follows. First note that, given an instance **I** over **R** and a sentence σ in CALC+μ, there are three possibilities: σ is undefined on **I**; σ is defined on **I** and is true; and σ is defined on **I** and is false. In particular, given an instance **I** over **R**, the answer to the query

$$q = \{\langle e_1, \dots, e_n \rangle \mid \xi\}$$

is undefined if the application of some μ in a subformula is undefined. Otherwise the answer to q is the n-ary relation consisting of all valuations v of $e_1, \dots, e_n$ for which $\xi(v(e_1), \dots, v(e_n))$ is defined and true. The queries expressible in partial fixpoint logic are called the *partial fixpoint queries*.

EXAMPLE 14.2.3 (Add-Remove Revisited)   Consider again the query in Example 14.1.2. To express the query in CALC+μ, a difficulty arises: The *while* program initializes T to G before the while loop, whereas CALC+μ lacks the capability to do this directly. To distinguish the initialization step from the subsequent ones, we use a ternary relation Q and two distinct constants: 0 and 1. To indicate that the first step has been performed, we insert in Q the tuple $\langle 1, 1, 1 \rangle$. The presence of $\langle 1, 1, 1 \rangle$ in Q inhibits the repetition of the first step. Subsequently, an edge $\langle x, y \rangle$ is encoded in Q as $\langle x, y, 0 \rangle$. The *while* program in Example 14.1.2 is equivalent to the CALC+μ query

$$\{\langle x, y \rangle \mid \mu_Q(\varphi(Q))(x, y, 0)\}$$

where

$\varphi(Q) =$
$\quad [\neg Q(1, 1, 1) \wedge [(G(x, y) \wedge z = 0) \vee (x = 1 \wedge y = 1 \wedge z = 1)]]$
$\quad \vee$
$\quad [Q(1, 1, 1) \wedge [(x = 1 \wedge y = 1 \wedge z = 1) \vee$
$\qquad\qquad ((z = ((z = 0) \wedge Q(x, y, 0) \wedge \neg \exists w(Q(x, w, 0) \wedge Q(w, y, 0))) \vee$
$\qquad\qquad ((z = ((z = 0) \wedge \exists w(\neg Q(x, w, 0) \wedge \neg Q(w, x, 0) \wedge$
$\qquad\qquad\qquad \neg Q(y, w, 0) \wedge \neg Q(w, y, 0)))]].$

Clearly, this query is more awkward than its counterpart in *while*. The simulation highlights some peculiarities of computing with CALC+μ.

In Section 14.4 it is shown that the family of partial fixpoint queries is equivalent to the *while* queries. In the preceding definition of $\mu_T(\varphi(T))$, the scope of all free variables in φ is defined by μ_T. For example, if T is binary in the following

$$\exists y(P(y) \wedge \mu_T(\varphi(T, x, y))(z, w)),$$

then $\varphi(T, x, y)$ has free variables x, y. According to the definition, y is *not* free in $\mu_T(\varphi(T, x, y))(z, w)$ (the free variables are z, w). Hence the quantifier $\exists y$ applies to the y in $P(y)$ alone and has no relation to the y in $\mu_T(\varphi(T, x, y))(z, w)$. To avoid confusion, it is preferable to use distinct variable names in such cases. For instance, the preceding sentence can be rewritten as

$$\exists y (P(y) \wedge \mu_T(\varphi(T, x', y'))(z, w)).$$

A variant of the fixpoint operator can be developed that permits free variables under the fixpoint operator, but this does not increase the expressive power (see Exercise 14.11).

Simultaneous Induction

Consider the following use of nested partial fixpoint operators, where G, P, and Q are binary:

$$\mu_P(G(x, y) \wedge \mu_Q(\varphi(P, Q))(x, y)).$$

Here $\varphi(P, Q)$ involves both P and Q. This corresponds to a nested iteration. In each iteration i in the computation of $\{J_n\}_{n \geq 0}$ over P, the fixpoint $\mu_Q(\varphi(P, Q))$ is recomputed for the successive values J_i of P.

   In contrast, we now consider a generalization of the partial fixpoint that permits simultaneous iteration over two or more relations. For example, let $\mathbf{R}$ be a database schema and $\varphi(P, Q)$ and $\psi(P, Q)$ be calculus formulas using P and Q not in $\mathbf{R}$, such that the arity of P (respectively Q) is the number of free variables in φ (ψ). On input $\mathbf{I}$ over $\mathbf{R}$, one can define inductively the sequence $\{J_n\}_{n \geq 0}$ of relations over $\{P, Q\}$ as follows:

$$\mathbf{J}_0(P) = \emptyset$$
$$\mathbf{J}_0(Q) = \emptyset$$
$$\mathbf{J}_n(P) = \varphi(\mathbf{J}_{n-1}(P), \mathbf{J}_{n-1}(Q))$$
$$\mathbf{J}_n(Q) = \psi(\mathbf{J}_{n-1}(P), \mathbf{J}_{n-1}(Q)).$$

Such a mutually recursive definition of $\mathbf{J}_n(P)$ and $\mathbf{J}_n(Q)$ is referred to as *simultaneous induction*. If the sequence $\{\mathbf{J}_n(P), \mathbf{J}_n(Q)\}_{n \geq 0}$ converges, the limit is a fixpoint of the mapping on pairs of relations defined by $\varphi(P, Q)$ and $\psi(P, Q)$. This pair of values for P and Q is denoted by $\mu_{P,Q}(\varphi(P, Q), \psi(P, Q))$, and $\mu_{P,Q}$ is a *simultaneous induction partial fixpoint operator*. The value for P in $\mu_{P,Q}$ is denoted by $\mu_{P,Q}(\varphi(P, Q), \psi(P, Q))(P)$ and the value for Q by $\mu_{P,Q}(\varphi(P, Q), \psi(P, Q))(Q)$. Clearly, simultaneous induction definitions like the foregoing can be extended for any number of relations. Simultaneous induction can simplify certain queries, as shown next.

EXAMPLE 14.2.4 (Add-Remove by Simultaneous Induction) Consider again the query *Add-Remove* in Example 14.2.3. One can simplify the query by introducing an auxiliary unary relation *Off*, which inhibits the transfer of G into T after the first step in a direct fashion. T and *Off* are defined in a mutually recursive fashion by φ_{Off} and φ_T, respectively:

$$\varphi_{Off}(x) = x = 1$$
$$\varphi_T(x, y) = [\neg Off(1) \wedge G(x, y)]$$
$$\vee [Off(1) \wedge \neg\exists z(T(x, z) \wedge T(z, y)) \wedge$$
$$(T(x, y) \vee \exists z(\neg T(x, z) \wedge \neg T(z, x) \wedge \neg T(y, z) \wedge \neg T(z, y)))].$$

The *Add-Remove* query can now be written as

$$\{\langle x, y \rangle \mid \mu_{Off, T}(\varphi_{Off}(Off, T), \varphi_T(Off, T))(T)(x, y)\}.$$

It turns out that using simultaneous induction instead of regular fixpoint operators does not provide additional power. For example, a CALC+μ formula equivalent to the query in Example 14.2.4 is the one shown in Example 14.2.3. More generally, we have the following:

LEMMA 14.2.5   For some n, let $\varphi_i(R_1, \ldots, R_n)$ be CALC formulas, i in $[1..n]$, such that $\mu_{R_1, \ldots, R_n}(\varphi_1(R_1, \ldots, R_n), \ldots, \varphi_n(R_1, \ldots, R_n))$ is a correct formula. Then for each $i \in [1, n]$ there exist CALC formulas $\varphi_i'(Q)$ and tuples $\vec{e}_i$ of variables or constants such that for each i,

$$\mu_{R_1, \ldots, R_n}(\varphi_1(R_1, \ldots, R_n), \ldots, \varphi_n(R_1, \ldots, R_n))(R_i) \equiv \mu_Q(\varphi_i'(Q))(\vec{e}_i).$$

Crux   We illustrate the construction with reference to the query of Example 14.2.4. Instead of using two relations *Off* and *T*, we use a ternary relation *Q* that encodes both *Off* and *T*. The extra coordinate is used to distinguish between tuples in *T* and tuples in *Off*. A tuple $\langle x \rangle$ in *Off* is encoded as a tuple $\langle x, 1, 1 \rangle$ in *Q*. A tuple $\langle x, y \rangle$ in *T* is encoded as a tuple $\langle x, y, 0 \rangle$ in *Q*. The final result is obtained by selecting from *Q* the tuples where the third coordinate is 0 and projecting the result on the first two coordinates. ∎

Note that the use of the tuples $\vec{e}_i$ allows one to perform appropriate selections and projections on $\mu_Q(\varphi_i'(Q))$ necessary for decoding. These selections and projections are essential and cannot be avoided (see Exercise 14.17c).

Inflationary Fixpoint

The nonconvergence in some cases of the sequence $\{J_n\}_{n \geq 0}$ in the semantics of the partial fixpoint operator is similar to nonterminating computations in the *while* language with noninflationary semantics. The semantics of the partial fixpoint operator μ is essentially noninflationary because in the inductive definition of J_n, each step is a destructive assignment. As with *while*, we can make the semantics inflationary by having the assignment at each step of the induction be cumulative. This yields an inflationary version of μ, denoted by μ^+ and called the *inflationary fixpoint operator*, which is defined for all formulas and databases to which it is applied.

Inflationary Fixpoint Operators and Logic   The definition of $\mu_T^+(\varphi(T))$ is identical to that of the partial fixpoint operator except that the sequence $\{J_n\}_{n \geq 0}$ is defined as follows:

$$J_0 = \emptyset;$$
$$J_n = J_{n-1} \cup \varphi(J_{n-1}), \quad n > 0.$$

This definition ensures that the sequence $\{J_n\}_{n \geq 0}$ is increasing: $J_{i-1} \subseteq J_i$ for each $i > 0$. Because for each instance there are finitely many tuples that can be added, the sequence converges in all cases.

Adding μ^+ instead of μ to CALC yields *inflationary fixpoint logic*, denoted by CALC+μ^+. Note that inflationary fixpoint queries are always defined.

The set of queries expressible by inflationary fixpoint logic is called the *fixpoint queries*. The fixpoint queries were historically defined first among the inflationary languages in the algebraic, logic, and deductive paradigms. Therefore the class of queries expressible in inflationary languages in the three paradigms has come to be referred to as the fixpoint queries.

As a simple example, the transitive closure of a graph G is defined by the following CALC+μ^+ query:

$$\{\langle x, y \rangle \mid \mu_T^+(G(x, y) \vee \exists z(T(x, z) \wedge G(z, y))(x, y)\}.$$

Recall that datalog as presented in Chapter 12 uses an inflationary operator and yields the minimal fixpoint of a set of rules. One may also be tempted to assume that an inflationary simultaneous induction of the form $\mu_{P,Q}^+(\varphi(P, Q), \psi(P, Q))$ is equivalent to a system of equational definitions of the form

$$P = \varphi(P, Q)$$
$$Q = \psi(P, Q)$$

and that it computes the unique minimal fixpoint for P and Q. However, one should be careful because the result of the inflationary fixpoint computation is only one of the possible fixpoints. As illustrated in the following example, this may not be minimal or the "naturally" expected fixpoint. (There may not exist a unique minimal fixpoint; see Exercise 14.4.)

EXAMPLE 14.2.6   Consider the equation

$$T(x, y) \;\;= G(x, y) \vee T(x, y) \vee \exists z(T(x, z) \wedge G(z, y))$$
$$CT(x, y) = \neg T(x, y).$$

One is tempted to believe that the fixpoint of these two equations yields the complement of transitive closure. However, with the inflationary semantics

$$\mathbf{J}_0(T) \;= \emptyset$$
$$\mathbf{J}_0(CT) = \emptyset$$
$$\mathbf{J}_n(T) \;= \mathbf{J}_{n-1}(T) \cup \{\langle x, y\rangle \mid G(x, y) \vee \mathbf{J}_{n-1}(T)(x, y)$$
$$\qquad\qquad \vee\, \exists z (\mathbf{J}_{n-1}(T)(x, z) \wedge G(z, y))\}$$
$$\mathbf{J}_n(CT) = \mathbf{J}_{n-1}(CT) \cup \{\langle x, y\rangle \mid \neg \mathbf{J}_{n-1}(T)(x, y)\}$$

leads to saturating CT at the first iteration.

Positive and Monotone Formulas

Making the fixpoint operator inflationary by definition is not the only way to guarantee polynomial-time termination of the fixpoint iteration. An alternative approach is to restrict the formulas $\varphi(T)$ so that convergence of the sequence $\{J_n\}_{n\geq 0}$ associated with $\mu_T(\varphi(T))$ is guaranteed. One such restriction is monotonicity. Recall that a query q is *monotone* if for each $\mathbf{I}, \mathbf{J}, \mathbf{I} \subseteq \mathbf{J}$ then $q(\mathbf{I}) \subseteq q(\mathbf{J})$. One can again show that for such formulas, a least fixpoint always exists and that it is obtained after a finite (but unbounded) number of stages of inductive applications of the formula.

Unfortunately, monotonicity is an undecidable property for CALC. One can also restrict the application of fixpoint to positive formulas. This was historically the first track that was followed and presents the advantage that positiveness is a decidable (syntactic) property. It is done by requiring that T occur only *positively* in $\varphi(T)$ (i.e., under an even number of negations in the syntax tree of the formula). All formulas thereby obtained are monotone, and so $\mu_T(\varphi(T))$ is always defined (see Exercise 14.10).

It can be shown that the approach of inflationary fixpoint and the two approaches based on fixpoint of positive or monotone formulas are equivalent (i.e., the sets of queries expressed are identical; see Exercise 14.10).

Fixpoint Operators and Circumscription

In some sense, the fixpoint operators act as quantifiers on relational variables. This is somewhat similar to the well-known technique of *circumscription* studied in artificial intelligence. Suppose $\psi(T)$ is a calculus sentence (i.e., no free variables) that uses T in addition to relations from a database schema $\mathbf{R}$. The circumscription of $\psi(T)$ with respect to T, denoted here by $circ_T(\psi(T))$, can be thought of as an operator defining a new relation, starting from the database. More precisely, let $\mathbf{I}$ be an instance over $\mathbf{R}$. Then $circ_T(\psi(T))$ denotes the relation containing all tuples belonging to every relation T such that (1) $\psi(T)$ holds for $\mathbf{I}$, and (2) T is minimal under set inclusion[2] with this property. Consider now a fixpoint query. As stated earlier, fixpoint queries can be expressed using just fixpoint operators μ_T applied to formulas positive in T (i.e., T always appears in φ under an even number of negations). We claim that $\mu_T(\varphi(T)) = circ_T(\varphi'(T))$, where $\varphi'(T)$ is a sentence

---

[2] Other kinds of minimality have also been considered.

obtained from $\varphi(T)$ as follows:

$$\varphi'(T) = \forall x_1, \ldots \forall x_n (\varphi(T, x_1, \ldots, x_n) \rightarrow T(x_1, \ldots, x_n)),$$

where the arity of T is n. To see this, it is sufficient to note that $\mu_T(\varphi(T))$ is the unique minimal T satisfying $\varphi'(T)$. This uses the monotonicity of $\varphi(T)$ with respect to T, which follows from the fact that $\varphi(T)$ is positive in T (see Exercise 14.10). Although computing with circumscription is generally intractable, the fixpoint operator on positive formulas can always be evaluated in polynomial time. Thus the fixpoint operator can be viewed as a tractable restriction of circumscription.

14.3 Datalog with Negation

Datalog provides recursion but no negation. It defines only monotonic queries. Viewed from the standpoint of the deductive paradigm, datalog provides a form of *monotonic reasoning*. Adding negation to datalog rules permits the specification of nonmonotonic queries and hence of *nonmonotonic reasoning*.

Adding negation to datalog rules requires defining semantics for negative facts. This can be done in many ways. The different definitions depend to some extent on whether datalog is viewed in the deductive framework or simply as a specification formalism like any other query language. In this chapter, we examine the latter point of view. Then datalog with negation can essentially be viewed as a subset of the *while* or *fixpoint* queries and can be treated similarly. This is not necessarily appropriate in the deductive framework. For instance, the basic assumptions in the reasoning process may require that once a fact is assumed false at some point in the inferencing process, it should not be proven true at a later point. This idea lies at the core of stratified and well-founded semantics, two of the most widely accepted in the deductive framework. The deductive point of view is considered in depth in Chapter 15.

The semantics given here for datalog with negation follows the semantics given in Chapter 12 for datalog, but does not correspond directly to the semantics for nonrecursive datalog$^{\neg}$ given in Chapter 5. The semantics in Chapter 5 is inspired by the stratified semantics but can be simulated by (either of) the semantics presented in this chapter.

As in the previous section, we consider both inflationary and noninflationary versions of datalog with negation.

Inflationary Semantics

The inflationary language allows negations in bodies of rules and is denoted by *datalog$^{\neg}$*. Like datalog, its rules are used to infer a set of facts. Once a fact is inferred, it is never removed from the set of true facts. This yields the inflationary character of the language.

EXAMPLE 14.3.1 We present a datalog$^{\neg}$ program with input a graph in binary relation G. The program computes the relation $closer(x, y, x', y')$ defined as follows:

closer(x, y, x', y') means that the distance $d(x, y)$ from x to y in G is smaller than the distance $d(x', y')$ from x' to y' [$d(x, y)$ is infinite if there is no path from x to y].

$$
\begin{aligned}
T(x, y) &\leftarrow G(x, y) \\
T(x, y) &\leftarrow T(x, z), G(z, y) \\
Closer(x, y, x', y') &\leftarrow T(x, y), \neg T(x', y')
\end{aligned}
$$

The program is evaluated as follows. The rules are fired simultaneously with all applicable valuations. At each such firing, some facts are inferred. This is repeated until no new facts can be inferred. A negative fact such as $\neg T(x', y')$ is true if $T(x', y')$ has not been inferred so far. This does not preclude $T(x', y')$ from being inferred at a later firing of the rules. One firing of the rules is called a stage in the evaluation of the program. In the preceding program, the transitive closure of G is computed in T. Consider the consecutive stages in the evaluation of the program. Note that if the fact $T(x, y)$ is inferred at stage n, then $d(x, y) = n$. So if $T(x', y')$ has not been inferred yet, this means that the distance between x and y is less than that between x' and y'. Thus if $T(x, y)$ and $\neg T(x', y')$ hold at some stage n, then $d(x, y) \leq n$ and $d(x', y') > n$ and *closer*(x, y, x', y') is inferred.

The formal syntax and semantics of datalog$^{\neg}$ are straightforward extensions of those for datalog. A datalog$^{\neg}$ *rule* is an expression of the form

$$
A \leftarrow L_1, \ldots, L_n,
$$

where A is an atom and each L_i is either an atom B_i (in which case it is called *positive*) or a negated atom $\neg B_i$ (in which case it is called *negative*). (In this chapter we use an active domain semantics for evaluating datalog$^{\neg}$ and so do not require that the rules be range restricted; see Exercise 14.13.)

A datalog$^{\neg}$ *program* is a nonempty finite set of datalog$^{\neg}$ rules. As for datalog programs, $sch(P)$ denotes the database schema consisting of all relations involved in the program P; the relations occurring in heads of rules are the *idb* relations of P, and the others are the *edb* relations of P.

The semantics of datalog$^{\neg}$ that we present in this chapter is an extension of the fixpoint semantics of datalog. Let $\mathbf{K}$ be an instance over $sch(P)$. Recall that an (active domain) *instantiation* of a rule $A \leftarrow L_1, \ldots, L_n$ is a rule $\nu(A) \leftarrow \nu(L_1), \ldots, \nu(L_n)$, where ν is a valuation that maps each variable into $adom(P, \mathbf{K})$. A fact A' is an *immediate consequence* for $\mathbf{K}$ and P if $A' \in \mathbf{K}(R)$ for some *edb* relation R, or $A' \leftarrow L_1', \ldots, L_n'$ is an instantiation of a rule in P and each positive L_i' is a fact in $\mathbf{K}$, and for each negative $L_i' = \neg A_i'$, $A_i' \notin \mathbf{K}$. The *immediate consequence operator* of P, denoted Γ_P, is now defined as follows. For each $\mathbf{K}$ over $sch(P)$,

$$
\Gamma_P(\mathbf{K}) = \mathbf{K} \cup \{A \mid A \text{ is an immediate consequence for } \mathbf{K} \text{ and } P\}.
$$

Given an instance $\mathbf{I}$ over $edb(P)$, one can compute $\Gamma_P(\mathbf{I})$, $\Gamma_P^2(\mathbf{I})$, $\Gamma_P^3(\mathbf{I})$, etc. As suggested in Example 14.3.1, each application of Γ_P is called a *stage* in the evaluation. From the definition of Γ_P, it follows that

$$\Gamma_P(\mathbf{I}) \subseteq \Gamma_P^2(\mathbf{I}) \subseteq \Gamma_P^3(\mathbf{I}) \subseteq \ldots.$$

As for datalog, the sequence reaches a fixpoint, denoted $\Gamma_P^\infty(\mathbf{I})$, after a finite number of steps. The restriction of this to the *idb* relations (or some subset thereof) is called the *image* (or *answer*) of P on $\mathbf{I}$.

An important difference with datalog is that $\Gamma_P^\infty(\mathbf{I})$ is no longer guaranteed to be a minimal model of P containing $\mathbf{I}$, as illustrated next.

EXAMPLE 14.3.2 Let P be the program

$$R(0) \leftarrow Q(0), \neg R(1)$$
$$R(1) \leftarrow Q(0), \neg R(0).$$

Let $\mathbf{I} = \{Q(0)\}$. Then $P(\mathbf{I}) = \{Q(0), R(0), R(1)\}$. Although $P(\mathbf{I})$ is a model of P, it is not minimal. The minimal models containing $\mathbf{I}$ are $\{Q(0), R(0)\}$ and $\{Q(0), R(1)\}$.

As discussed in Chapter 12, the operational semantics of datalog based on the immediate consequence operator is equivalent to the natural semantics based on minimal models. As shown in the preceding example, there may not be a unique minimal model for a datalog¬ program, and the semantics given for datalog¬ may not yield any of the minimal models. The development of a natural model-theoretic semantics for datalog¬ thus calls for selecting a natural model from among several possible candidates. Inevitably, such choices are open to debate; Chapter 15 presents several alternatives.

Noninflationary Semantics

The language datalog¬ has inflationary semantics because the set of facts inferred through the consecutive firings of the rules is increasing. To obtain a noninflationary variant, there are several possibilities. One could keep the syntax of datalog¬ but make the semantics noninflationary by retaining, at each stage, only the newly inferred facts (see Exercise 14.16). Another possibility is to allow explicit retraction of a previously inferred fact. Syntactically, this can be done using negations in heads of rules, interpreted as deletions of facts. We adopt this solution here, in part because it brings our language closer to some practical languages that use so-called (production) rules in the sense of expert and active database systems. The resulting language is denoted by datalog¬¬, to indicate that negations are allowed in both heads and bodies of rules.

EXAMPLE 14.3.3 (Add-Remove Visited Again) The following datalog¬¬ program computes in T the *Add-Remove* query of Example 14.1.2, given as input a graph G.

$$T(x, y) \leftarrow G(x, y), \neg \textit{off}\,(1)$$
$$\textit{off}\,(1) \quad \leftarrow$$
$$\neg T(x, y) \leftarrow T(x, z), T(z, y), \textit{off}\,(1)$$
$$T(x, y) \quad \leftarrow \neg T(x, z) \neg T(z, x) \neg T(y, z) \neg T(z, y), \textit{off}\,(1)$$

Relation *off* is used to inhibit the first rule (initializing T to G) after the first step.

The immediate consequence operator Γ_P and semantics of a datalog$^{\neg\neg}$ program are analogous to those for datalog$^\neg$, with the following important proviso. If a negative literal $\neg A$ is inferred, the fact A is removed, unless A is also inferred in the same firing of the rules. This gives priority to inference of positive over negative facts and is somewhat arbitrary. Other possibilities are as follows: (1) Give priority to negative facts; (2) interpret the simultaneous inference of A and $\neg A$ as a "no-op" (i.e., including A in the new instance only if it is there in the old one); and (3) interpret the simultaneous inference of A and $\neg A$ as a contradiction that makes the result undefined. The chosen semantics has the advantage over possibility (3) that the semantics is always defined. In any case, the choice of semantics is not crucial: They yield equivalent languages (see Exercise 14.15).

With the semantics chosen previously, termination is no longer guaranteed. For instance, the program

$$T(0) \quad \leftarrow T(1)$$
$$\neg T(1) \leftarrow T(1)$$
$$T(1) \quad \leftarrow T(0)$$
$$\neg T(0) \leftarrow T(0)$$

never terminates on input $T(0)$. The value of T flip-flops between $\{\langle 0 \rangle\}$ and $\{\langle 1 \rangle\}$, so no fixpoint is reached.

Datalog$^{\neg\neg}$ and Datalog$^\neg$ as Fragments of CALC+μ and CALC+μ^+

Consider datalog$^{\neg\neg}$. It can be viewed as a subset of CALC+μ in the following manner. Suppose that P is a datalog$^{\neg\neg}$ program. The *idb* relations defined by rules can alternately be defined by simultaneous induction using formulas that correspond to the rules. Each firing of the rules corresponds to one step in the simultaneous inductive definition. For instance, the simultaneous induction definition corresponding to the program in Example 14.3.3 is the one in Example 14.2.4. Because simultaneous induction can be simulated in CALC+μ (see Lemma 14.2.5), datalog$^{\neg\neg}$ can be simulated in CALC+μ. Moreover, notice that only a single application of the fixpoint operator is used in the simulation. Similar remarks apply to datalog$^\neg$ and CALC+μ^+. Furthermore, in the inflationary case it is easy to see that the formula can be chosen to be *existential* (i.e., its prenex normal form[3] uses

---

[3] A CALC formula in prenex normal form is a formula $Q_1 x_1 \ldots Q_k x_k \varphi$ where Q_i, $1 \leq i \leq k$ are quantifiers and φ is quantifier free.

only existential quantifiers). The same can be shown in the noninflationary case, although the proof is more subtle. In summary (see Exercise 14.18), the following applies:

LEMMA 14.3.4 Each datalog$^{\neg\neg}$ (datalog$^{\neg}$) query is equivalent to a CALC+μ (CALC+μ^+) query of the form

$$\{\vec{x} \mid \mu_T^{(+)}(\varphi(T))(\vec{t})\},$$

where

    (a) φ is an existential CALC formula, and

    (b) $\vec{t}$ is a tuple of variables or constants of appropriate arity and $\vec{x}$ is the tuple of distinct free variables in $\vec{t}$.

The Rule Algebra

The examples of datalog$^{\neg}$ programs shown in this chapter make it clear that the semantics of such programs is not always easy to understand. There is a simple mechanism that facilitates the specification by the user of various customized semantics. This is done by means of the *rule algebra*, which allows specification of an order of firing of the rules as well as firing up to a fixpoint in an inflationary or noninflationary manner. For the inflationary version RA^+ of the rule algebra, the base expressions are individual datalog$^{\neg}$ rules; the semantics associated with a rule is to apply its immediate consequence operator once in a cumulative fashion. Union ($\cup$) can be used to specify simultaneous application of a pair of rules or more complex programs. The expression $P; Q$ specifies the composition of P and Q; its semantics is to execute P once and then Q once. Inflationary iteration of program P is called for by $(P)^+$. The noninflationary version of the rule algebra, denoted RA, starts with datalog$^{\neg}$ rules, but now with a noninflationary, destructive semantics, as defined in Exercise 14.16. Union and composition are generalized in the natural fashion, and the noninflationary iterator, denoted $*$, is used.

EXAMPLE 14.3.5 Let P be the set of rules

$$T(x, y) \leftarrow G(x, y)$$
$$T(x, y) \leftarrow T(x, z), G(z, y)$$

and let Q consist of the rule

$$CT(x, y) \leftarrow \neg T(x, y).$$

The RA^+ program $(P)^+; Q$ computes in CT the complement of the transitive closure of G.

It follows easily from the results of Section 14.4 that RA^+ is equivalent to datalog$^{\neg}$, and RA is equivalent to noninflationary datalog$^{\neg}$ and hence to datalog$^{\neg\neg}$ (Exercise 14.23).

Thus an RA^+ program can be compiled into a (possibly much more complicated) datalog$^-$ program. For instance, the RA^+ program in Example 14.3.5 is equivalent to the datalog$^-$ program in Example 14.4.2. The advantage of the rule algebra is the ease of expressing various semantics. In particular, RA^+ can be used easily to specify the stratified and well-founded semantics for datalog$^-$ introduced in Chapter 15.

14.4   Equivalence

The previous sections introduced inflationary and noninflationary recursive languages with negation in the algebraic, logic, and deductive paradigms. This section shows that the inflationary languages in the three paradigms, $while^+$, CALC+μ^+, and datalog$^-$, are equivalent and that the same holds for the noninflationary languages $while$, CALC+μ, and datalog^{--}. This yields two classes of queries that are central in the theory of query languages: the *fixpoint* queries (expressed by the inflationary languages) and the *while* queries (expressed by the noninflationary languages). This is summarized in Fig. 14.2, at the end of the chapter.

We begin with the equivalence of the inflationary languages because it is the more difficult to show. The equivalence of CALC+μ^+ and $while^+$ is easy because the languages have similar capabilities: Program composition in $while^+$ corresponds closely to formula composition in CALC+μ^+, and the *while change* loop of $while^+$ is close to the inflationary fixpoint operator of CALC+μ^+. More difficult and surprising is the equivalence of these languages with datalog$^-$, because this much simpler language has no explicit constructs for program composition or nested recursion.

LEMMA 14.4.1   CALC+μ^+ and $while^+$ are equivalent.

Proof   Let $\{\langle x_1, \ldots, x_m \rangle \mid \xi(x_1, \ldots, x_m)\}$ be a CALC+μ^+ query over an input database with schema **R**. It suffices to show that there exists a $while^+$ program P_ξ that defines the same result as $\xi(x_1, \ldots, x_m)$ in some m-ary relation R_ξ. The proof is by induction on the depth of nesting of the fixpoint operator in ξ, denoted $d(\xi)$. If $d(\xi) = 0$ (i.e., ξ does not contain a fixpoint operator), then ξ is in CALC and P_ξ is

$$R_\xi \; +\!= \; E_\xi,$$

where E_ξ is the relational algebra expression corresponding to ξ. Now suppose the statement is true for formulas with depth of nesting of the fixpoint operator less than d ($d > 0$). Let ξ be a formula with $d(\xi) = d$.

If $\xi = \mu_Q(\varphi(Q))(f_1, \ldots, f_k)$, then P_ξ is

$Q \; +\!= \; \emptyset;$
while change do
    begin
    $Q \; +\!= \; E_\varphi$
    end;
$R_\xi \; +\!= \; \pi(\sigma(Q)),$

where $\pi(\sigma(Q))$ denotes the selection and projection corresponding to $f_1, \ldots, f_k$.

Suppose now that ξ is obtained by first-order operations from k formulas $\xi_1, \ldots, \xi_k$, each having μ^+ as root. Let $E_\xi(R_{\xi_1}, \ldots, R_{\xi_k})$ be the relational algebra expression corresponding to ξ, where each subformula $\xi_i = \mu_Q(\varphi(Q))(e_1^i, \ldots, e_{n_i}^i)$ is replaced by R_{ξ_i}. For each i, let P_{ξ_i} be a program that produces the value of $\mu_Q(\varphi(Q))(e_1^i, \ldots, e_{n_i}^i)$ and places it into R_{ξ_i}. Then P_ξ is

$$P_{\xi_1}; \ldots; \; P_{\xi_k};$$
$$R_\xi += E_\xi(R_{\xi_1}, \ldots, R_{\xi_k}).$$

This completes the induction and the proof that CALC+μ^+ can be simulated by *while*$^+$. The converse simulation is similar (Exercise 14.20). ∎

We now turn to the equivalence of CALC+μ^+ and datalog¬. Lemma 14.3.4 yields the subsumption of datalog¬ by CALC+μ^+. For the other direction, we simulate CALC+μ^+ queries using datalog¬. This simulation presents two main difficulties.

The first involves delaying the firing of a rule until after the completion of a fixpoint by another set of rules. Intuitively, this is hard because checking that the fixpoint has been reached involves checking the *nonexistence* rather than the existence of some valuation, and datalog¬ is more naturally geared toward checking the *existence* of valuations. The solution to this difficulty is illustrated in the following example.

EXAMPLE 14.4.2 The following datalog¬ program computes the complement of the transitive closure of a graph G. The example illustrates the technique used to delay the firing of a rule (computing the complement) until the fixpoint of a set of rules (computing the transitive closure) has been reached (i.e., until the application of the transitivity rule yields no new tuples). To monitor this, the relations *old-T*, *old-T-except-final* are used. *old-T* follows the computation of T but is one step behind it. The relation *old-T-except-final* is identical to *old-T* but the rule defining it includes a clause that prevents it from firing when T has reached its last iteration. Thus *old-T* and *old-T-except-final* differ only in the iteration after the transitive closure T reaches its final value. In the subsequent iteration, the program recognizes that the fixpoint has been reached and fires the rule computing the complement in relation CT. The program is

$$T(x, y) \qquad\qquad\qquad \leftarrow G(x, y)$$
$$T(x, y) \qquad\qquad\qquad \leftarrow G(x, z), T(z, y)$$
$$old\text{-}T(x, y) \qquad\qquad \leftarrow T(x, y)$$
$$old\text{-}T\text{-}except\text{-}final(x, y) \leftarrow T(x, y), T(x', z'), T(z', y'), \neg T(x', y')$$
$$CT(x, y) \qquad\qquad\qquad \leftarrow \neg T(x, y), old\text{-}T(x', y'),$$
$$\qquad\qquad\qquad\qquad \neg old\text{-}T\text{-}except\text{-}final(x', y')$$

(It is assumed that G is not empty; see Exercise 14.3.)

The second difficulty concerns keeping track of iterations in the computation of a fixpoint. Given a formula $\mu_T^+(\varphi(T))$, the simulation of φ itself may involve numerous relations other than T, whose behavior may be "sabotaged" by an overly zealous application of iteration of the immediate consequence operator. To overcome this, we separate the internal computation of φ from the external iteration over T, as illustrated in the following example.

EXAMPLE 14.4.3   Let G be a binary relation schema. Consider the CALC+μ^+ query $\mu_{good}^+(\phi(good))(x)$, where

$$\phi = \forall y \ (G(y, x) \rightarrow good(y)).$$

Note that the query computes the set of nodes in G that are not reachable from a cycle (in other words, the nodes such that the length of paths leading to them is bounded). One application of $\varphi(good)$ is achieved by the datalog$^\neg$ program P:

$$
\begin{aligned}
bad(x) &\ \leftarrow G(y, x), \neg good(y) \\
delay &\ \leftarrow \\
good(x) &\ \leftarrow delay, \neg bad(x)
\end{aligned}
$$

Simply iterating P does not yield the desired result. Intuitively, the relations *delay* and *bad*, which are used as "scratch paper" in the computation of a single iteration of μ^+, cannot be reinitialized and so cannot be reused to perform the computation of subsequent iterations.

To surmount this problem, we essentially create a version of P for each iteration of $\varphi(good)$. The versions are distinguished by using "timestamps." The nodes themselves serve as timestamps. The timestamps marking iteration i are the values newly introduced in relation *good* at iteration $i - 1$. Relations *delay* and *delay-stamped* are used to delay the derivation of new tuples in *good* until *bad* and *bad-stamped* (respectively) have been computed in the current iteration. The process continues until no new values are introduced in an iteration. The full program is the union of the three rules given earlier, which perform the first iteration, and the following rules, which perform the iteration with timestamp t:

$$
\begin{aligned}
bad\text{-}stamped(x, t) &\leftarrow G(y, x), \neg good(y), good(t) \\
delay\text{-}stamped(t) &\leftarrow good(t) \\
good(x) &\leftarrow delay\text{-}stamped(t), \neg bad\text{-}stamped(x, t).
\end{aligned}
$$

We now embark on the formal demonstration that datalog$^\neg$ can simulate CALC+μ^+. We first introduce some notation relating to the timestamping of a program in the simulation. Let $m \geq 1$. For each relation schema Q, let $\overline{Q}$ be a new relational schema with arity$(\overline{Q}) = $ arity$(Q) + m$. If $(\neg)Q(e_1, \ldots, e_n)$ is a literal and $\vec{z}$ an m-tuple of distinct variables, then $(\neg)Q(e_1, \ldots, e_n)[\vec{z}]$ denotes the literal $(\neg)\overline{Q}(e_1, \ldots, e_n, z_1, \ldots, z_m)$. For each program P and tuple $\vec{z}$, $P[\vec{z}]$ denotes the program obtained from P by replacing each literal A by $A[\vec{z}]$. Let P be a program and $B_1, \ldots, B_q$ a list of literals. Then $P \mathbin{/\!/} B_1, \ldots, B_q$ is the program obtained by appending $B_1, \ldots, B_q$ to the bodies of all rules in P.

To illustrate the previous notation, consider the program P consisting of the following two rules:

$$S(x, y) \leftarrow R(x, y)$$
$$S(x, y) \leftarrow R(x, z), S(z, y).$$

Then $P[z] \mathbin{/\!/} \neg T(x, w, y)$ is

$$\overline{S}(x, y, z) \leftarrow \overline{R}(x, y, z), \neg T(x, w, y)$$
$$\overline{S}(x, y, z) \leftarrow \overline{R}(x, z, z), \overline{S}(z, y, z), \neg T(x, w, y).$$

LEMMA 14.4.4 $\text{CALC}+\mu^+$ and datalog$^\neg$ are equivalent.

Proof As seen in Lemma 14.3.4, datalog$^\neg$ is essentially a fragment of $\text{CALC}+\mu^+$, so we just need to show the simulation of $\text{CALC}+\mu^+$ by datalog$^\neg$. The proof is by structural induction on the $\text{CALC}+\mu^+$ formula. The core of the proof involves a control mechanism that delays firing certain rules until other rules have been evaluated. Therefore the induction hypothesis involves the capability to simulate the $\text{CALC}+\mu^+$ formula using a datalog$^\neg$ program as well as to produce concomitantly a predicate that only becomes true when the simulation has been completed. More precisely, we will prove by induction the following: For each $\text{CALC}+\mu^+$ formula φ over a database schema $\mathbf{R}$, there exists a datalog$^\neg$ program $prog(\varphi)$ whose *edb* relations are the relations in $\mathbf{R}$, whose *idb* relations include $result_\varphi$ with arity equal to the number of free variables in φ and a 0-ary relation $done_\varphi$ such that for every instance $\mathbf{I}$ over $\mathbf{R}$,

(i) $[prog(\varphi)(\mathbf{I})](result_\varphi) = \varphi(\mathbf{I})$, and

(ii) the 0-ary predicate $done_\varphi$ becomes true at the last stage in the evaluation of $prog(\varphi)$ on $\mathbf{I}$.

We will assume, without loss of generality, that no variable of φ occurs free and bound, or bound to more than one quantifier, that φ contains no $\forall$ or $\vee$, and that the initial query has the form $\{x_1, \ldots, x_n \mid \xi\}$, where $x_1, \ldots, x_n$ are distinct variables. Note that the last assumption implies that (i) establishes the desired result.

Suppose now that φ is an atom $R(\vec{e})$. Let $\vec{x}$ be the tuple of distinct variables occurring in $\vec{e}$. Then $prog(\varphi)$ consists of the rules

$$done_\varphi \quad \leftarrow$$
$$result_\varphi(\vec{x}) \leftarrow R(\vec{e}).$$

There are four cases to consider for the induction step.

1. $\varphi = \alpha \wedge \beta$. Without loss of generality, we assume that the *idb* relations of $prog(\alpha)$ and $prog(\beta)$ are disjoint. Thus there is no interference between $prog(\alpha)$ and $prog(\beta)$. Let $\vec{x}$ and $\vec{y}$ be the tuples of distinct free variables of α and β, respectively, and let $\vec{z}$ be the tuple of distinct free variables occurring in $\vec{x}$ or $\vec{y}$.

Then $prog(\varphi)$ consists of the following rules:

$$prog(\alpha)$$
$$prog(\beta)$$
$$result_{\varphi}(\vec{z}) \leftarrow done_{\alpha}, done_{\beta}, result_{\alpha}(\vec{x}), result_{\beta}(\vec{y})$$
$$done_{\varphi} \quad\quad \leftarrow done_{\alpha}, done_{\beta}.$$

2. $\varphi = \exists\, x(\psi)$. Let $\vec{y}$ be the tuple of distinct free variables of ψ, and let $\vec{z}$ be the tuple obtained from $\vec{y}$ by removing the variable x. Then $prog(\varphi)$ consists of the rules

$$prog(\psi)$$
$$result_{\varphi}(\vec{z}) \leftarrow done_{\psi}, result_{\psi}(\vec{y})$$
$$done_{\varphi} \quad\quad \leftarrow done_{\psi}.$$

3. $\varphi = \neg(\psi)$. Let $\vec{x}$ be the tuple of distinct free variables occurring in ψ. Then $prog(\varphi)$ consists of

$$prog(\psi)$$
$$result_{\varphi}(\vec{x}) \leftarrow done_{\psi}, \neg result_{\psi}(\vec{x})$$
$$done_{\varphi} \quad\quad \leftarrow done_{\psi}.$$

4. $\varphi = \mu_S(\psi(S))(\vec{e})$. This case is the most involved, because it requires keeping track of the iterations in the computation of the fixpoint as well as bookkeeping to control the value of the special predicate $done_{\varphi}$. Intuitively, each iteration is marked by timestamps. The current timestamps consist of the tuples newly inserted in the previous iteration. The program $prog(\varphi)$ uses the following new auxiliary relations:

   - Relation $fixpoint_{\varphi}$ contains $\mu_S(\psi(S))$ at the end of the computation, and $result_{\varphi}$ contains $\mu_S(\psi(S))(\vec{e})$.
   - Relation run_{φ} contains the timestamps.
   - Relation $used_{\varphi}$ contains the timestamps introduced in the previous stages of the iteration. The active timestamps are in $run_{\varphi} - used_{\varphi}$.
   - Relation $not\text{-}final_{\varphi}$ is used to detect the final iteration (i.e., the iteration that adds no new tuples to $fixpoint_{\varphi}$). The presence of a timestamp in $used_{\varphi} - not\text{-}final_{\varphi}$ indicates that the final iteration has been completed.
   - Relations $delay_{\varphi}$ and $not\text{-}empty_{\varphi}$ are used for timing and to detect an empty result.

In the following, $\vec{y}$ and $\vec{t}$ are tuples of distinct variables with the same arity as S. We first have particular rules to perform the first iteration and to handle the special case of an empty result:

$prog(\psi)$

$fixpoint_\varphi(\vec{y}) \leftarrow result_\psi(\vec{y}), done_\psi$

$delay_\varphi \quad\quad \leftarrow done_\psi$

$not\text{-}empty_\varphi \leftarrow result_\psi(\vec{y})$

$done_\varphi \quad\quad \leftarrow delay_\varphi, \neg not\text{-}empty_\varphi.$

The remainder of the program contains the following rules:

- Stamping of the database and starting an iteration: For each R in ψ different from S and a tuple $\vec{x}$ of distinct variables with same arity as R,

$$\overline{R}(\vec{x}, \vec{t}) \leftarrow R(\vec{x}), fixpoint_\varphi(\vec{t})$$

$$run_\varphi(\vec{t}) \leftarrow fixpoint_\varphi(\vec{t})$$

$$\overline{S}(\vec{y}, \vec{t}) \leftarrow fixpoint_\varphi(\vec{y}), fixpoint_\varphi(\vec{t}).$$

- Timestamped iteration:

$$prog(\psi)[\vec{t}]//run_\varphi(\vec{t}), \neg used_\varphi(\vec{t})$$

- Maintain $fixpoint_\varphi$, $not\text{-}last_\varphi$, and $used_\varphi$:

$$fixpoint_\varphi(\vec{y}) \leftarrow \overline{done}_\psi(\vec{t}), \overline{result}_\psi(\vec{y}, \vec{t}), \neg used_\varphi(\vec{t})$$

$$not\text{-}final_\varphi(\vec{t}) \leftarrow \overline{done}_\psi(\vec{t}), \overline{result}_\psi(\vec{y}, \vec{t}), \neg fixpoint_\varphi(\vec{y})$$

$$used_\varphi(\vec{t}) \quad\quad \leftarrow \overline{done}_\psi(\vec{t})$$

- Produce the result and detect termination:

$$result_\varphi(\vec{z}) \leftarrow fixpoint_\varphi(\vec{e})$$

where $\vec{z}$ is the tuple of distinct variables in $\vec{e}$,

$$done_\varphi \leftarrow used_\varphi(\vec{t}), \neg not\text{-}final_\varphi(\vec{t}).$$

It is easily verified by inspection that $prog(\varphi)$ satisfies (i) and (ii) under the induction hypothesis for cases (1) through (3). To see that (i) and (ii) hold in case (4), we carefully consider the stages in the evaluation of $prog_\varphi$. Let $\mathbf{I}$ be an instance over the relations in ψ other than S; let $J_0 = \emptyset$ be over S; and let $J_i = J_{i-1} \cup \psi(J_{i-1})$ for each $i > 0$. Then $\mu_S(\psi(S))(\mathbf{I}) = J_n$ for some n such that $J_n = J_{n-1}$. The program $prog_\varphi$ simulates the consecutive iterations of this process. The first iteration is simulated using $prog_\psi$ directly, whereas the subsequent iterations are simulated by $prog_\psi$ timestamped with the tuples added at the previous iteration. (We omit consideration of the case in which the fixpoint is $\emptyset$; this is taken care of by the rules involving $delay_\varphi$ and $not\text{-}empty_\varphi$.)

We focus on the stages in the evaluation of $prog_\varphi$ corresponding to the end of the simulation of each iteration of ψ. The stage in which the simulation of the first iteration is completed immediately follows the stage in which $done_\psi$ becomes true. The subsequent iterations are completed immediately following the stages in which

$$\exists \vec{t}\,(\overline{done_\psi(\vec{t})} \wedge \neg used_\varphi(\vec{t}))$$

becomes true. Thus let k_1 be the stage in which $done_\psi$ becomes true, and let k_i $(2 < i \le n)$ be the successive stages in which

$$\exists \vec{t}\,(\overline{done_\psi(\vec{t}) \wedge \neg used_\varphi(\vec{t})})$$

is true. First note that

- at stage k_1

$$\{\vec{y} \mid result_\psi(\vec{y})\} = \psi(J_0);$$

- at stage $k_1 + 1$

$$fixpoint_\varphi = J_1.$$

For $i > 1$ it can be shown by induction on i that

- at stage k_i $(i \le n)$

$$\{\vec{t} \mid \overline{done_\psi(\vec{t})} \wedge \neg used_\varphi(\vec{t})\} = \psi(J_{i-2}) - J_{i-2} = J_{i-1} - J_{i-2}$$
$$\{\vec{y} \mid \overline{done_\psi(\vec{t})} \wedge \overline{result_\psi(\vec{y},\vec{t})} \wedge \neg used_\varphi(\vec{t})\} = \psi(J_{i-1});$$
$$\{\vec{t} \mid \overline{done_\psi(\vec{t})} \wedge \overline{result_\psi(\vec{y},\vec{t})} \wedge \neg fixpoint_\varphi(\vec{y})\} = \psi(J_{i-1}) - J_{i-1} = J_i - J_{i-1};$$

- at stage $k_i + 1$ $(i < n)$

$$fixpoint_\varphi = J_{i-1} \cup \psi(J_{i-1}) = J_i,$$
$$used_\varphi = not\text{-}last_\varphi = \overline{done_\psi} = J_{i-1};$$

- at stage $k_i + 2$ $(i < n)$

$$\{\vec{t} \mid run_\varphi(\vec{t}) \wedge \neg used_\varphi(\vec{t})\} = J_i - J_{i-1},$$
$$\{\vec{x} \mid \overline{R(\vec{x},\vec{t})} \wedge run_\varphi(\vec{t}) \wedge \neg used_\varphi(\vec{t})\} = \mathbf{I}(R),$$
$$\{\vec{x} \mid \overline{S(\vec{x},\vec{t})} \wedge run_\varphi(\vec{t}) \wedge \neg used_\varphi(\vec{t})\} = J_i.$$

Finally, at stage $k_n + 1$

$$used_\varphi = J_{n-1},$$

$$not\text{-}last_\varphi = J_{n-2},$$

$$fixpoint_\varphi = J_n = \mu_S(\psi(S))(\mathbf{I}),$$

and at stage $k_n + 2$

$$result_\varphi = \mu_S(\psi(S))(\vec{z})(\mathbf{I}),$$

$$done_\varphi = \mathbf{true}.$$

Thus (i) and (ii) hold for $prog_\varphi$ in case (4), which concludes the induction. ■

Lemmas 14.4.1 and 14.4.4 now yield the following:

THEOREM 14.4.5 $while^+$, CALC+μ^+, and datalog¬ are equivalent.

The set of queries expressible in $while^+$, CALC+μ^+, and datalog¬ is called the *fix-point queries*. An analogous equivalence result can be proven for the noninflationary languages *while*, CALC+μ, and datalog¬¬. The proof of the equivalence of CALC+μ and datalog¬¬ is easier than in the inflationary case because the ability to perform deletions in datalog¬¬ facilitates the task of simulating explicit control (see Exercise 14.21). Thus we can prove the following:

THEOREM 14.4.6   *while*, CALC+μ, and datalog¬¬ are equivalent.

The set of queries expressible in *while*, CALC+μ, and datalog¬¬ is called the *while queries*. We will look at the *fixpoint* queries and the *while* queries from a complexity and expressiveness standpoint in Chapter 17. Although the spirit of our discussion in this chapter suggested that *fixpoint* and *while* are distinct classes of queries, this is far from obvious. In fact, the question remains open: As shown in Chapter 17, *fixpoint* and *while* are equivalent iff PTIME = PSPACE (Theorem 17.4.3).

The equivalences among languages discussed in this chapter are summarized in Fig. 14.2.

Normal Forms

The two equivalence theorems just presented have interesting consequences for the underlying extensions of datalog and logic. First they show that these languages are closed under composition and complementation. For instance, if two mappings f, g, respectively, from a schema S to a schema S' and from S' to a schema S'' are expressible in datalog¬$^{(¬)}$, then $f \circ g$ and $\neg f$ are also expressible in datalog¬$^{(¬)}$. Analogous results are true for CALC+$\mu^{(+)}$.

A more dramatic consequence concerns the nesting of recursion in the calculus and algebra. Consider first CALC+μ^+. By the equivalence theorems, this is equivalent to datalog¬, which, in turn (by Lemma 14.3.4), is essentially a fragment of CALC+μ^+. This yields a normal form for CALC+μ^+ queries and implies that a single application of

Languages		Class of queries
inflationary	*while*$^+$ CALC $+\mu^+$ *datalog*$^\neg$	*fixpoint*
noninflationary	*while* CALC $+\mu$ *datalog*$^{\neg\neg}$	*while*

Figure 14.2:   Summary of language equivalence results

the inflationary fixpoint operator is all that is needed. Similar remarks apply to CALC$+\mu$ queries. In summary, the following applies:

THEOREM 14.4.7   Each CALC$+\mu^{(+)}$ query is equivalent to a CALC$+\mu^{(+)}$ query of the form

$$\{\ \vec{x}\ \mid\ \mu_T^{(+)}(\varphi(T))(\vec{t})\},$$

where φ is an existential CALC formula.

Analogous normal forms can be shown for *while*$^{(+)}$ (Exercise 14.22) and for $RA^{(+)}$ (Exercise 14.24).

14.5   Recursion in Practical Languages

To date, there are numerous prototypes (but no commercial product) that provide query and update languages with recursion. Many of these languages provide semantics for recursion in the spirit of the procedural semantics described in this chapter. Prototypes implementing the deductive paradigm are discussed in Chapter 15.

SQL 2-3 (a norm provided by ISO/ANSII) allows **select** statements that define a table used recursively in the **from** and **where** clauses. Such recursion is also allowed in Starburst. The semantics of the recursion is inflationary, although noninflationary semantics can be achieved using deletion. An extension of SQL 2-3 is ESQL (Extended SQL). To illustrate the flavor of the syntax (which is typical for this category of languages), the following is an ESQL program defining a table SPARTS (subparts), the transitive closure of the table PARTS. This is done using a view creation mechanism.

> **create view** *SPARTS* **as**
> **select** *
> **from** *PARTS*
> **union**

select *P1.PART, P2.COMPONENT*
from *SPARTS P1, PARTS P2*
where *P1.COMPONENT = P2.PART*;

This is in the spirit of CALC+μ^+. With deletion, one can simulate CALC+μ. The system Postgres also provides similar iteration up to a fixpoint in its query language POSTQUEL.

A form of recursion closer to *while* and *while*$^+$ is provided by SQL embedded in full programming languages, such as C+SQL, which allows SQL statements coupled with C programs. The recursion is provided by while loops in the host language.

The recursion provided by datalog¬ and datalog¬¬ is close in spirit to *production-rule* systems. Speaking loosely, a production rule has the form

if ⟨condition⟩ then ⟨action⟩.

Production rules permit the specification of database updates, whereas deductive rules usually support only database queries (with some notable exceptions). Note that the deletion in datalog¬¬ can be viewed as providing an update capability. The production-rule approach been studied widely in connection with expert systems in artificial intelligence; OPS5 is a well-known system that uses this approach.

A feature similar to recursive rules is found in the emerging field of *active* databases. In active databases, the rule condition is often broken into two pieces; one piece, called the *trigger*, is usually closely tied to the database (e.g., based on insertions to or deletions from relations) and can be implemented deep in the system.

In active database systems, rules are recursively fired when conditions become true in the database. Speaking in broad terms, the noninflationary languages studied in this chapter can be viewed as an abstraction of this behavior. For example, the database language RDL1 is close in spirit to the language datalog¬¬. (See also Chapter 22 for a discussion of active databases.)

The language Graphlog, a visual language for queries on graphs developed at the University of Toronto, emphasizes queries involving paths and provides recursion specified using regular expressions that describe the shape of desired paths.

Bibliographic Notes

The *while* language was first introduced as RQ in [CH82] and as LE in [Cha81a]. The other noninflationary languages, CALC+μ and datalog¬¬, were defined in [AV91a]. The equivalence of the noninflationary languages was also shown there.

The fixpoint languages have a long history. Logics with fixpoints have been considered by logicians in the general case where infinite structures (corresponding to infinite database instances) are allowed [Mos74]. In the finite case, which is relevant in this book, the fixpoint queries were first defined using the partial fixpoint operator μ_T applied only to formulas positive in T [CH82]. The language allowing applications of μ_T to formulas monotonic, but not necessarily positive, in T was further studied in [Gur84]. An interesting difference between unrestricted and finite models arises here: Every CALC formula monotone in some predicate R is equivalent for unrestricted structures to some CALC formula positive in R (Lyndon's lemma), whereas this is not the case for finite structures [AG87]. Monotonicity is undecidable for both cases [Gur84].

The languages (1) with fixpoint over positive formulas, (2) with fixpoint over monotone formulas, and (3) with inflationary fixpoint over arbitrary formulas were shown equivalent in [GS86]. As a side-effect, it was shown in [GS86] that the nesting of μ (or μ^+) provides no additional power. This fact had been proven earlier for the first language in [Imm86]. Moreover, a new alternative proof of the sufficiency of a single application of the fixpoint in CALC+μ^+ is provided in [Lei90]. The simultaneous induction lemma (Lemma 14.2.5) was also proven in [GS86], extending an analogous result of [Mos74] for infinite structures. Of the other inflationary languages, *while*$^+$ was defined in [AV90] and datalog$^¬$ with fixpoint semantics was first defined in [AV88c, KP88].

The equivalence of datalog$^¬$ with CALC+μ^+ and *while*$^+$ was shown in [AV91a]. The relationship between the *while* and *fixpoint* queries was investigated in [AV91b], where it was shown that they are equivalent iff PTIME = PSPACE. The issues of complexity and expressivity of *fixpoint* and *while* queries will be considered in detail in Chapter 17.

The rule algebra for logic programs was introduced in [IN88].

The game of life is described in detail in [Gar70]. The normal forms discussed in this chapter can be viewed as variations of well-known folk theorems, described in [Har80].

SQL 2-3 is described in an ISO/ANSII norm [57391, 69392]). Starburst is presented in [HCL$^+$90]. ESQL (Extended SQL) is described in [GV92]. The example ESQL program in Section 14.5 is from [GV92]. The query language of Postgres, POSTQUEL, is presented in [SR86]. OPS5 is described in [For81].

The area of *active* databases is the subject of numerous works, including [Mor83, Coh89, KDM88, SJGP90, MD89, WF90, HJ91a]. Early work on database triggers includes [Esw76, BC79]. The language RDL1 is presented in [dMS88].

The visual graph language Graphlog, developed at the University of Toronto, is described in [CM90, CM93a, CM93b].

Exercises

Exercise 14.1   (Game of life) Consider the two rules informally described in Example 14.1.

(a) Express the corresponding queries in datalog$^{¬(¬)}$, *while*$^{(+)}$, and CALC+$\mu^{(+)}$.

(b) Find an input for which a vertex keeps changing color forever under the second rule.

Exercise 14.2   Prove that the termination problem for a *while* program is undecidable (i.e., that it is undecidable, given a *while* query, whether it terminates on all inputs). *Hint:* Use a reduction of the containment problem for algebra queries.

Exercise 14.3   Recall the datalog$^{¬¬}$ program of Example 14.4.2.

(a) After how many stages does the program complete for an input graph of diameter n?

(b) Modify the program so that it also handles the case of empty graphs.

(c) Modify the program so that it terminates in order of $\log(n)$ stages for an input graph of diameter n.

Exercise 14.4   Recall the definition of $\mu_T(\varphi(T))$.

(a) Exhibit a formula φ such that $\varphi(T)$ has a unique minimal fixpoint on all inputs, and $\mu_T(\varphi(T))$ terminates on all inputs but does not evaluate to the minimal fixpoint on any of them.

(b) Exhibit a formula φ such that $\mu_T(\varphi(T))$ terminates on all inputs but φ does not have a unique minimal fixpoint on any input.

Exercise 14.5

(a) Give a *while* program with explicit looping condition for the query in Example 14.1.2.

(b) Prove that $while^{(+)}$ with looping conditions of the form $E = \emptyset$, $E \neq \emptyset$, $E = E'$, and $E \neq E'$, where E, E' are algebra expressions, is equivalent to $while^{(+)}$ with the *change* conditions.

Exercise 14.6 Consider the problem of finding, given two graphs G, G' over the same vertex set, the minimum set X of vertexes satisfying the following conditions: (1) For each vertex v, if all vertexes v' such that there is a G-edge from v' to v are in X, then v is in X; and (2) the analogue for G'-edges. Exhibit a *while* program and a *fixpoint* query that compute this set.

Exercise 14.7 Recall the CALC+μ^+ query of Example 14.4.3.

(a) Run the query on the input graph G:
$\{\langle a, b\rangle, \langle c, b\rangle, \langle b, d\rangle, \langle d, e\rangle, \langle e, f\rangle, \langle f, g\rangle, \langle g, d\rangle, \langle e, h\rangle, \langle i, j\rangle, \langle j, h\rangle\}$.

(b) Exhibit a $while^+$ program that computes *good*.

(c) Write a program in your favorite conventional programming language (e.g., C or LISP) that computes the good vertexes of a graph G. Compare it with the database queries developed in this chapter.

(d) Show that a vertex a is *good* if there is no path from a vertex belonging to a cycle to a. Using this as a starting point, propose an alternative algorithm for computing the good vertexes. Is your algorithm expressible in *while*? In *fixpoint*?

★ **Exercise 14.8** Suppose that the input consists of a graph G together with a successor relation on the vertexes of G [i.e., a binary relation *succ* such that (1) each element has exactly one successor, except for one that has none; and (2) each element in the binary relation G occurs in *succ*].

(a) Give a *fixpoint* query that tests whether the input satisfies (1) and (2).

(b) Sketch a *while* program computing the set of pairs $\langle a, b\rangle$ such that the shortest path from a to b is a prime number.

(c) Do (b) using a $while^+$ query.

Exercise 14.9 (Simultaneous induction) Prove Lemma 14.2.5.

♠ **Exercise 14.10** (Fixpoint over positive formulas) Let $\varphi(T)$ be a formula positive in T (i.e., each occurrence of T is under an even number of negations in the syntax tree of φ). Let **R** be the set of relations other than T occurring in $\varphi(T)$.

(a) Show that $\varphi(T)$ is monotonic in T. That is, for all instances **I** and **J** over $\mathbf{R} \cup \{T\}$ such that $\mathbf{I}(\mathbf{R}) = \mathbf{J}(\mathbf{R})$ and $\mathbf{I}(T) \subseteq \mathbf{J}(T)$,

$$\varphi(\mathbf{I}) \subseteq \varphi(\mathbf{J}).$$

(b) Show that $\mu_T(\varphi(T))$ is defined on every input instance.

(c) [GS86] Show that the family of CALC+μ queries with fixpoints only over positive formulas is equivalent to the CALC+μ^+ queries.

★ **Exercise 14.11** Suppose CALC+μ^+ is modified so that free variables are allowed under fixpoint operators. More precisely, let

$$\varphi(T, x_1, \ldots, x_n, y_1, \ldots, y_m)$$

be a formula where T has arity n and the x_i and y_j are free in φ. Then

$$\mu_{T,x_1,\ldots,x_n}(\varphi(T, x_1, \ldots, x_n, y_1, \ldots, y_m))(e_1, \ldots, e_n)$$

is a correct formula, whose free variables are the y_j and those occurring among the e_i. The fixpoint is defined with respect to a given valuation of the y_j. For instance,

$$\exists z \exists w (P(z) \wedge \mu_{T,x,y}(\varphi(T, x, y, z)))(u, w))$$

is a well-formed formula. Give a precise definition of the semantics for queries using this operator. Show that this extension does not yield increased expressive power over CALC+μ^+. Do the same for CALC+μ.

Exercise 14.12 Let G be a graph. Give a *fixpoint* query in each of the three paradigms that computes the pairs of vertexes such that the shortest path between them is of even length.

Exercise 14.13 Let datalog$_{rr}^{\neg(\neg)}$ denote the family of datalog$^{\neg(\neg)}$ programs that are *range restricted*, in the sense that for each rule r and each variable x occurring in r, x occurs in a positive literal in the body of r. Prove that datalog$_{rr}^{\neg} \equiv$ datalog$^{\neg}$ and datalog$_{rr}^{\neg\neg} \equiv$ datalog$^{\neg\neg}$.

Exercise 14.14 Show that negations in bodies of rules are redundant in datalog$^{\neg\neg}$ (i.e., for each datalog$^{\neg\neg}$ program P there exists an equivalent datalog$^{\neg\neg}$ program Q that uses no negations in bodies of rules). *Hint:* Maintain the complement of each relation R in a new relation R', using deletions.

♠ **Exercise 14.15** Consider the following semantics for negations in heads of datalog$^{\neg\neg}$ rules:

(α) the semantics giving priority to positive over negative facts inferred simultaneously (adopted in this chapter),

(β) the semantics giving priority to negative over positive facts inferred simultaneously,

(γ) the semantics in which simultaneous inference of A and $\neg A$ leads to a "no-op" (i.e., including A in the new instance only if it is there in the old one), and

(δ) the semantics prohibiting the simultaneous inference of a fact and its negation by making the result undefined in such circumstances.

For a datalog$^{\neg\neg}$ program P, let P_ξ, denote the program P with semantics $\xi \in \{\alpha, \beta, \gamma, \delta\}$.

(a) Give an example of a program P for which P_α, P_β, P_γ, and P_δ define distinct queries.

(b) Show that it is undecidable, for a given program P, whether P_δ never simultaneously infers a positive fact and its negation for any input.

(c) Let datalog$_\xi^{\neg\neg}$ denote the family of queries P_ξ for $\xi \in \{\alpha, \beta, \gamma\}$. Prove that datalog$_\alpha^{\neg\neg} \equiv$ datalog$_\beta^{\neg\neg} \equiv$ datalog$_\gamma^{\neg\neg}$.

(d) Give a syntactic condition on datalog$^{\neg\neg}$ programs such that under the δ semantics they never simultaneously infer a positve fact and its negation, and such that the resulting query language is equivalent to $\text{datalog}_\alpha^{\neg\neg}$.

Exercise 14.16 (Noninflationary datalog$^\neg$) The semantics of datalog$^\neg$ can be made noninflationary by defining the immediate consequence operator to be destructive in the sense that only the newly inferred facts are kept after each firing of the rules. Show that, with this semantics, datalog$^\neg$ is equivalent to datalog$^{\neg\neg}$.

★ **Exercise 14.17** (Multiple versus single carriers)

(a) Consider a datalog$^\neg$ program P producing the answer to a query in an *idb* relation S. Prove that there exists a program Q with the same *edb* relations as P and just one idb relation T such that, for each *edb* instance $\mathbf{I}$,

$$[P(\mathbf{I})](S) \ = \ \pi(\sigma([Q(\mathbf{I})](T))),$$

where σ denotes a selection and π a projection.

(b) Show that the projection π and selection σ in part (a) are indispensable. *Hint:* Suppose there is a datalog$^\neg$ program with a single *edb* relation computing the complement of transitive closure of a graph. Reach a contradiction by showing in this case that connectivity of a graph is expressible in relational calculus. (It is shown in Chapter 17 that connectivity is not expressible in the calculus.)

(c) Show that the projection and selection used in Lemma 14.2.5 are also indispensable.

★ **Exercise 14.18**

(a) Prove Lemma 14.3.4 for the inflationary case.

(b) Prove Lemma 14.3.4 for the noninflationary case. *Hint:* For datalog$^{\neg\neg}$, the straightforward simulation yields a formula $\mu_T(\varphi(T))(\vec{x})$, where φ may contain negations over existential quantifiers to simulate the semantics of deletions in heads of rules of the datalog$^{\neg\neg}$ program. Use instead the noninflationary version of datalog$^\neg$ described in Exercise 14.16.

Exercise 14.19 Prove that the simulation in Example 14.4.3 works.

Exercise 14.20 Complete the proof of Lemma 14.4.1 (i.e., prove that each *while*$^+$ program can be simulated by a CALC+μ^+ program).

★ **Exercise 14.21** Prove the noninflationary analogue of Lemma 14.4.4 (i.e., that datalog$^{\neg\neg}$ can simulate CALC+μ). *Hint:* Simplify the simulation in Lemma 14.4.4 by taking advantage of the ability to delete in datalog$^{\neg\neg}$. For instance, rules can be inhibited using "switches," which can be turned on and off. Furthermore, no timestamping is needed.

Exercise 14.22 Formulate and prove a normal form for *while*$^+$ and *while*, analogous to the normal forms stated for CALC+μ^+ and CALC+μ.

Exercise 14.23 Prove that RA^+ is equivalent to datalog$^\neg$ and RA is equivalent to noninflationary datalog$^\neg$, and hence to datalog$^{\neg\neg}$. *Hint:* Use Theorems 14.4.5 and 14.4.6 and Exercise 14.16.

Exercise 14.24 Let the *star height* of an RA program be the maximum number of occurrences of * and $^+$ on a path in the syntax tree of the program. Show that each RA program is equivalent to an RA program of star height one.

15 Negation in Datalog

Alice:	*I thought we already talked about negation.*
Sergio:	*Yes, but they say you don't think by fixpoint.*
Alice:	*Humbug, I just got used to it!*
Riccardo:	*So we have to tell you how you* really *think.*
Vittorio:	*And convince you that our explanation is well founded!*

As originally introduced in Chapter 12, datalog is a toy language that expresses many interesting recursive queries but has serious shortcomings concerning expressive power. Because it is monotonic, it cannot express simple relational algebra queries such as the difference of two relations. In the previous chapter, we considered one approach for adding negation to datalog that led to two procedural languages—namely, inflationary datalog¬ and datalog¬¬. In this chapter, we take a different point of view inspired by non-monotonic reasoning that attempts to view the semantics of such programs in terms of a natural reasoning process.

This chapter begins with illustrations of how the various semantics for datalog do not naturally extend to datalog¬. Two semantics for datalog¬ are then considered. The first, called *stratified*, involves a syntactic restriction on programs but provides a semantics that is natural and relatively easy to understand. The second, called *well founded*, requires no syntactic restriction on programs, but the meaning associated with some programs is expressed using a 3-valued logic. (In this logic, facts are true, false, or unknown.) With respect to expressive power, well-founded semantics is equivalent to the *fixpoint* queries, whereas the stratified semantics is strictly weaker. A proof-theoretic semantics for datalog¬, based on *negation as failure*, is discussed briefly at the end of this chapter.

15.1 The Basic Problem

Suppose that we want to compute the pairs of disconnected nodes in a graph G (i.e., we are interested in the *complement* of the transitive closure of a graph whose edges are given by a binary relation G). We already know how to define the transitive closure of G in a relation T using the datalog program P_{TC} of Chapter 12:

$$T(x, y) \leftarrow G(x, y)$$
$$T(x, y) \leftarrow G(x, z), T(z, y).$$

To define the complement CT of T, we are naturally tempted to use negation as we did in Chapter 5. Let $P_{TC comp}$ be the result of adding the following rule to P_{TC}:

$$CT(x, y) \leftarrow \neg T(x, y).$$

To simplify the discussion, we generally assume an active domain interpretation of datalog¬ rules.

In this example, negation appears to be an appealing addition to the datalog syntax. The language datalog¬ is defined by allowing, in bodies of rules, literals of the form $\neg R_i(u_i)$, where R_i is a relation name and u_i is a free tuple. In addition, the equality predicate is allowed, and $\neg = (x, y)$ is denoted by $x \neq y$.

One might hope to extend the model-theoretic, fixpoint, and proof-theoretic semantics of datalog just as smoothly as the syntax. Unfortunately, things are less straightforward when negation is present. We illustrate informally the problems that arise if one tries to extend the least-fixpoint and minimal-model semantics of datalog. We shall discuss the proof-theoretic aspect later.

Fixpoint Semantics: Problems

Recall that, for a datalog program P, the fixpoint semantics of P on input $\mathbf{I}$ is the unique minimal fixpoint of the immediate consequence operator T_P containing $\mathbf{I}$. The immediate consequence operator can be naturally extended to a datalog¬ program P. For a program P, T_P is defined as follows[1]: For each $\mathbf{K}$ over $sch(P)$, A is $T_P(\mathbf{K})$ if $A \in \mathbf{K}|edb(P)$ or if there exists some instantiation $A \leftarrow A_1, \ldots, A_n$ of a rule in P for which (1) if A_i is a positive literal, then $A_i \in \mathbf{K}$; and (2) if $A_i = \neg B_i$ where B_i is a positive literal, then $B_i \notin \mathbf{K}$. [Note the difference from the immediate consequence operator Γ_P defined for datalog¬ in Section 14.3: Γ_P is inflationary by definition, (that is, $\mathbf{K} \subseteq \Gamma_P(\mathbf{K})$ for each $\mathbf{K}$ over $sch(P)$, whereas T_P is not.] The following example illustrates several unexpected properties that T_P might have.

EXAMPLE 15.1.1

(a) T_P may not have any fixpoint. For the propositional program $P_1 = \{p \leftarrow \neg p\}$, T_{P_1} has no fixpoint.

(b) T_P may have several minimal fixpoints containing a given input. For example, the propositional program $P_2 = \{p \leftarrow \neg q, q \leftarrow \neg p\}$ has two minimal fixpoints (containing the empty instance): $\{p\}$ and $\{q\}$.

(c) Consider the sequence $\{T_P^i(\emptyset)\}_{i>0}$ for a given datalog¬ program P. Recall that for datalog, the sequence is increasing and converges to the least fixpoint of T_P. In the case of datalog¬, the situation is more intricate:

    1. The sequence does not generally converge, even if T_P has a least fixpoint. For example, let $P_3 = \{p \leftarrow \neg r; r \leftarrow \neg p; p \leftarrow \neg p, r\}$. Then

---

[1] Given an instance $\mathbf{J}$ over a database schema $\mathbf{R}$ with $\mathbf{S} \subseteq \mathbf{R}$, $\mathbf{J}|\mathbf{S}$ denotes the restriction of $\mathbf{J}$ to $\mathbf{S}$.

T_{P_3} has a least fixpoint $\{p\}$ but $\{T_{P_3}^i(\emptyset)\}_{i>0}$ alternates between $\emptyset$ and $\{p, r\}$ and so does not converge (Exercise 15.2).

2. Even if $\{T_P^i(\emptyset)\}_{i>0}$ converges, its limit is not necessarily a minimal fixpoint of T_P, even if such fixpoints exist. To see this, let $P_4 = \{p \leftarrow p, q \leftarrow q, p \leftarrow \neg p, q \leftarrow \neg p\}$. Now $\{T_{P_4}^i(\emptyset)\}_{i>0}$ converges to $\{p, q\}$ but the least fixpoint of T_{P_4} equals $\{p\}$.

REMARK 15.1.2 (Inflationary fixpoint semantics)   The program P_4 of the preceding example contains two rules of a rather strange form: $p \leftarrow p$ and $q \leftarrow q$. In some sense, such rules may appear meaningless. Indeed, their logical forms [e.g., $(p \vee \neg p)$] are tautologies. However, rules of the form $R(x_1, \ldots, x_n) \leftarrow R(x_1, \ldots, x_n)$ have a nontrivial impact on the immediate consequence operator T_P. If such rules are added for each *idb* relation R, this results in making T_P inflationary [i.e., $\mathbf{K} \subseteq T_P(\mathbf{K})$ for each $\mathbf{K}$], because each fact is an immediate consequence of itself. It is worth noting that in this case, $\{T_P^i(\mathbf{I})\}_{i>0}$ always converges and the semantics given by its limit coincides with the inflationary fixpoint semantics for datalog¬ programs exhibited in Chapter 14.

To see the difference between the two semantics, consider again program P_{TCcomp}. The sequence $\{T_{P_{TCcomp}}^i(I)\}_{i>0}$ on input I over G converges to the desired answer (the complement of transitive closure). With the inflationary fixpoint semantics, CT becomes a complete graph at the first iteration (because T is initially empty) and P_{TCcomp} does not compute the complement of transitive closure. Nonetheless, it was shown in Chapter 14 that there is a different (more complicated) datalog¬ program that computes the complement of transitive closure with the inflationary fixpoint semantics. ∎

Model-Theoretic Semantics: Problems

As with datalog, we can associate with a datalog¬ program P the set Σ_P of CALC sentences corresponding to the rules of P. Note first that, as with datalog, Σ_P always has at least one model containing any given input $\mathbf{I}$. $B(P, \mathbf{I})$ is such a model. [Recall that $B(P, \mathbf{I})$, introduced in Chapter 12, is the instance in which the idb relations contain all tuples with values in $\mathbf{I}$ or P.]

For datalog, the model-theoretic semantics of a program P was given by the unique minimal model of Σ_P containing the input. Unfortunately, this simple solution no longer works for datalog¬, because uniqueness of a minimal model containing the input is not guaranteed. Program P_2 in Example 15.1.1(b) provides one example of this: $\{p\}$ and $\{q\}$ are distinct minimal models of P_2. As another example, consider the program P_{TCcomp} and an input I for predicate G. Let $\mathbf{J}$ over $sch(P_{TCcomp})$ be such that $\mathbf{J}(G) = I$, $\mathbf{J}(T) \supseteq I$, $\mathbf{J}(T)$ is transitively closed, and $\mathbf{J}(CT) = \{\langle x, y \rangle \mid x, y \text{ occur in } \mathbf{I}, \langle x, y \rangle \notin \mathbf{J}(T)\}$. Clearly, there may be more than one such $\mathbf{J}$, but one can verify that each one is a minimal model of $\Sigma_{P_{TCcomp}}$ satisfying $\mathbf{J}(G) = I$.

It is worth noting the connection between T_P and models of Σ_P: An instance $\mathbf{K}$ over $sch(P)$ is a model of Σ_P iff $T_P(\mathbf{K}) \subseteq \mathbf{K}$. In particular, every fixpoint of T_P is a model of Σ_P. The converse is false (Exercise 15.3).

When for a program P, Σ_P has several minimal models, one must specify which

among them is the model intended to be the solution. To this end, various criteria of "nice-
ness" of models have been proposed that can distinguish the intended model from other
candidates. We shall discuss several such criteria as we go along. Unfortunately, none of
these criteria suffices to do the job. Moreover, upon reflection it is clear that no criteria
can exist that would always permit identification of a unique intended model among several minimal models. This is because, as in the case of program P_2 of Example 15.1.1(b),
the minimal models can be completely symmetric; in such cases there is no property that
would separate one from the others using just the information in the input or the program.

In summary, the approach we used for datalog, based on equivalent least-fixpoint
or minimum-model semantics, breaks down when negation is present. We shall describe
several solutions to the problem of giving semantics to datalog¬ programs. We begin with
the simplest case and build up from there.

15.2   Stratified Semantics

This section begins with the restricted case in which negation is applied only to *edb* relations. The semantics for negation is straightforward in this case. We then turn to stratified
semantics, which extends this simple case in an extremely natural fashion.

Semipositive Datalog¬

We consider now *semipositive* datalog¬ programs, which only apply negation to *edb* relations. For example, the difference of R and R' can be defined by the one-rule program

$$Diff(x) \leftarrow R(x), \neg R'(x).$$

To give semantics to $\neg R'(x)$, we simply use the closed world assumption (see Chapter 2):
$\neg R'(x)$ holds iff x is in the active domain and $x \notin R'$. Because R' is an *edb* relation, its
content is given by the database and the semantics of the program is clear. We elaborate on
this next.

DEFINITION 15.2.1   A datalog¬ program P is *semipositive* if, whenever a negative literal
$\neg R'(x)$ occurs in the body of a rule in P, $R' \in edb(P)$.

As their name suggests, semipositive programs are almost positive. One could eliminate negation from semipositive programs by adding, for each *edb* relation R', a new *edb*
relation $\overline{R'}$ holding the complement of R' (with respect to the active domain) and replacing
$\neg R'(x)$ by $\overline{R'}(x)$. Thus it is not surprising that semipositive programs behave much like
datalog programs. The next result is shown easily and is left for the reader (Exercise 15.7).

THEOREM 15.2.2   Let P be a semipositive datalog¬ program. For every instance $\mathbf{I}$ over
$edb(P)$,

    (i) Σ_P has a unique minimal model $\mathbf{J}$ satisfying $\mathbf{J}|edb(P) = \mathbf{I}$.

    (ii) T_P has a unique minimal fixpoint $\mathbf{J}$ satisfying $\mathbf{J}|edb(P) = \mathbf{I}$.

(iii) The minimum model in (i) and the least fixpoint in (ii) are identical and equal to the limit of the sequence $\{T_P^i(\mathbf{I})\}_{i>0}$.

REMARK 15.2.3   Observe that in the theorem, we use the formulation "minimal model satisfying $\mathbf{J}|edb(P) = \mathbf{I}$," whereas in the analogous result for datalog we used "minimal model containing $\mathbf{I}$." Both formulations would be equivalent in the datalog setting because adding tuples to the *edb* predicates would result in larger models because of monotonicity. This is not the case here because negation destroys monotonicity. ■

Given a semipositive datalog¬ program P and an input $\mathbf{I}$, we denote by $P^{semi-pos}(\mathbf{I})$ the minimum model of Σ_P (or equivalently, the least fixpoint of T_P) whose restriction to $edb(P)$ equals $\mathbf{I}$.

An example of a semipositive program that is neither in datalog nor in CALC is given by

$$T(x, y) \leftarrow \neg G(x, y)$$
$$T(x, y) \leftarrow \neg G(x, z), T(z, y).$$

This program computes the transitive closure of the complement of G. On the other hand, the foregoing program for the complement of transitive closure is not a semipositive program. However, it can naturally be viewed as the composition of two semipositive programs: the program computing the transitive closure followed by the program computing its complement. Stratification, which is studied next, may be viewed as the closure of semipositive programs under composition. It will allow us to specify, for instance, the composition just described, computing the complement of transitive closure.

Syntactic Restriction for Stratification

We now consider a natural extension of semipositive programs. In semipositive programs, the use of negation is restricted to *edb* relations. Now suppose that we use some *defined* relations, much like views. Once a relation has been defined by some program, other programs can subsequently treat it as an *edb* relation and apply negation to it. This simple idea underlies an important extension to semipositive programs, called stratified programs.

Suppose we have a datalog¬ program P. Each *idb* relation is defined by one or more rules of P. If we are able to "read" the program so that, for each *idb* relation R', the portion of P defining R' comes before the negation of R' is used, then we can simply compute R' before its negation is used, and we are done. For example, consider program P_{TCcomp} introduced at the beginning of this chapter. Clearly, we intended for T to be defined by the first two rules before its negation is used in the rule defining CT. Thus the first two rules are applied before the third. Such a way of "reading" P is called a stratification of P and is defined next.

DEFINITION 15.2.4   A *stratification* of a datalog¬ program P is a sequence of datalog¬ programs $P^1, \ldots, P^n$ such that for some mapping σ from $idb(P)$ to $[1..n]$,

(i) $\{P^1, \ldots, P^n\}$ is a partition of P.

(ii) For each predicate R, all the rules in P defining R are in $P^{\sigma(R)}$ (i.e., in the same program of the partition).

(iii) If $R(u) \leftarrow \ldots R'(v) \ldots$ is a rule in P, and R' is an *idb* relation, then $\sigma(R') \leq \sigma(R)$.

(iv) If $R(u) \leftarrow \ldots \neg R'(v) \ldots$ is a rule in P, and R' is an *idb* relation, then $\sigma(R') < \sigma(R)$.

Given a stratification $P^1, \ldots, P^n$ of P, each P^i is called a *stratum* of the stratification, and σ is called the *stratification mapping*.

Intuitively, a stratification of a program P provides a way of parsing P as a sequence of subprograms $P^1, \ldots, P^n$, each defining one or several *idb* relations. By (iii), if a relation R' is used positively in the definition of R, then R' must be defined earlier or simultaneously with R (this allows recursion!). If the negation of R' is used in the definition of R, then by (iv) the definition of R' must come strictly before that of R.

Unfortunately, not every datalog$^\neg$ program has a stratification. For example, there is no way to "read" program P_2 of Example 15.1.1 so that p is defined before q and q before p. Programs that have a stratification are called *stratifiable*. Thus P_2 is not stratifiable. On the other hand, P_{TCcomp} is clearly stratifiable: The first stratum consists of the first two rules (defining T), and the second stratum consists of the third rule (defining CT using T).

EXAMPLE 15.2.5   Consider the program P_7 defined by

$$r_1 \quad S(x) \leftarrow R'_1(x), \neg R(x)$$
$$r_2 \quad T(x) \leftarrow R'_2(x), \neg R(x)$$
$$r_3 \quad U(x) \leftarrow R'_3(x), \neg T(x)$$
$$r_4 \quad V(x) \leftarrow R'_4(x), \neg S(x), \neg U(x).$$

Then P_7 has 5 distinct stratifications, namely,

$$\{r_1\}, \{r_2\}, \{r_3\}, \{r_4\}$$
$$\{r_2\}, \{r_1\}, \{r_3\}, \{r_4\}$$
$$\{r_2\}, \{r_3\}, \{r_1\}, \{r_4\}$$
$$\{r_1, r_2\}, \{r_3\}, \{r_4\}$$
$$\{r_2\}, \{r_1, r_3\}, \{r_4\}.$$

These lead to five different ways of reading the program P_7. As will be seen, each of these yields the same semantics.

There is a simple test for checking if a program is stratifiable. Not surprisingly, it involves testing for an acyclicity condition in definitions of relations using negation. Let P be a datalog$^\neg$ program. The *precedence graph* G_P of P is the labeled graph whose nodes are the *idb* relations of P. Its edges are the following:

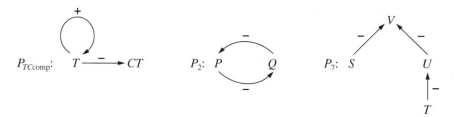

Figure 15.1:   Precedence graphs for P_{CT}, P_2, and P_7

- If $R(u) \leftarrow \ldots R'(v) \ldots$ is a rule in P, then $\langle R', R \rangle$ is an edge in G_P with label $+$ (called a *positive edge*).
- If $R(u) \leftarrow \ldots \neg R'(v) \ldots$ is a rule in P, then $\langle R', R \rangle$ is an edge in G_P with label $-$ (called a *negative edge*).

For example, the precedence graphs for program P_{TCcomp}, P_2, and P_7 are represented in Fig. 15.1. It is straightforward to show the following (proof omitted):

LEMMA 15.2.6   Let P be a program with stratification σ. If there is a path from R' to R in G_P, then $\sigma(R') \leq \sigma(R)$; and if there is a path from R' to R in G_P containing some negative edge, then $\sigma(R') < \sigma(R)$.

We now show how the precedence graph of a program can be used to test the stratifiability of the program.

PROPOSITION 15.2.7   A datalog$^\neg$ program P is stratifiable iff its precedence graph G_P has no cycle containing a negative edge.

Proof   Consider the "only if" part. Suppose P is a datalog$^\neg$ program whose precedence graph has a cycle $R_1, \ldots R_m, R_1$ containing a negative edge, say from R_m to R_1. Suppose, toward a contradiction, that σ is a stratification mapping for P. By Lemma 15.2.6, $\sigma(R_1) < \sigma(R_1)$, because there is a path from R_1 to R_1 with a negative edge. This is a contradiction, so no stratification mapping σ exists for P.

Conversely, suppose P is a program whose precedence graph G_P has no cycle with negative edges. Let $\prec$ be the binary relation among the strongly connected components of G_P defined as follows: $C \prec C'$ if $C \neq C'$ and there is a (positive or negative) edge in G_P from some node of C to some node of C'.

We first show that

(*) $\prec$ is acyclic.

Suppose there is a cycle in $\prec$. Then by construction of $\prec$, this cycle must traverse two *distinct* strongly connected components, say C, C'. Let A be in C. It is easy to deduce that there is a path in G_P from some vertex in C' to A and from A to some vertex in C'.

Because C' is a strongly connected component of G_P, A is in C'. Thus $C \subseteq C'$, so $C = C'$, a contradiction. Hence (*) holds.

In view of (*), the binary relation $\prec$ induces a partial order among the strongly connected components of G_P, which we also denote by $\prec$, by abuse of notation. Let $C^1, \ldots, C^n$ be a topographic sort with respect to $\prec$ of the strongly connected components of G_P; that is, $C^1 \ldots C^n$ is the set of strongly connected components of G_P and if $C^i \prec C^j$, then $i \leq j$. Finally, for each i, $1 \leq i \leq n$, let Q^i consist of all rules defining some relation in C^i. Then $Q^1, \ldots, Q^n$ is a stratification of P. Indeed, (i) and (ii) in the definition of stratification are clearly satisfied. Conditions (iii) and (iv) follow immediately from the construction of G_P and $\prec$ and from the hypothesis that G_P has no cycle with negative edge.

∎

Clearly, the stratifiability test provided by Proposition 15.2.7 takes time polynomial in the size of the program P.

Verification of the following observation is left to the reader (Exercise 15.4).

LEMMA 15.2.8 Let $P^1, \ldots, P^n$ be a stratification of P, and let $Q^1, \ldots, Q^m$ be obtained as in Proposition 15.2.7. If $Q^j \cap P^i \neq \emptyset$, then $Q^j \subseteq P^i$. In particular, the partition $Q^1, \ldots, Q^m$ of P refines all other partitions given by stratifications of P.

Semantics of Stratified Programs

Consider a stratifiable program P with a stratification $\sigma = P^1, \ldots, P^n$. Using the stratification σ, we can now easily give a semantics to P using the well-understood semipositive programs. Notice that for each program P^i in the stratification, if P^i uses the negation of R', then $R' \in edb(P^i)$ [note that $edb(P^i)$ may contain some of the *idb* relations of P]. Furthermore, R' is either in $edb(P)$ or is defined by some P^j preceding P^i [i.e., $R' \in \bigcup_{j<i} idb(P^j)$]. Thus each program P^i is semipositive relative to previously defined relations. Then the semantics of P is obtained by applying, in order, the programs P^i. More precisely, let **I** be an instance over $edb(P)$. Define the sequence of instances

$$\mathbf{I}_0 = \mathbf{I}$$
$$\mathbf{I}_i = \mathbf{I}_{i-1} \cup P^i(\mathbf{I}_{i-1}|edb(P^i)), 0 < i \leq n.$$

Note that $\mathbf{I}_i$ extends $\mathbf{I}_{i-1}$ by providing values to the relations defined by P^i; and that $P^i(\mathbf{I}_{i-1}|edb(P^i))$, or equivalently, $P^i(\mathbf{I}_{i-1})$, is the semantics of the semipositive program P^i applied to the values of its *edb* relations provided by $\mathbf{I}_{i-1}$. Let us denote the final instance $\mathbf{I}_n$ thus obtained by $\sigma(\mathbf{I})$. This provides the *semantics of* a datalog⁻ program *under a stratification* σ.

Independence of Stratification

As shown in Example 15.2.5, a datalog⁻ program can have more than one stratification. Will the different stratifications yield the same semantics? Fortunately, the answer is yes.

To demonstrate this, we use the following simple lemma, whose proof is left to the reader (Exercise 15.10).

LEMMA 15.2.9   Let P be a semipositive datalog$^\neg$ program and σ a stratification for P. Then $P^{semi-pos}(\mathbf{I}) = \sigma(\mathbf{I})$ for each instance $\mathbf{I}$ over $edb(P)$.

Two stratifications of a datalog$^\neg$ program are *equivalent* if they yield the same semantics on all inputs.

THEOREM 15.2.10   Let P be a stratifiable datalog$^\neg$ program. All stratifications of P are equivalent.

Proof   Let G_P be the precedence graph of P and $\sigma_{G_P} = Q^1, \ldots, Q^n$ be a stratification constructed from G_P as in the proof of Theorem 15.2.7. Let $\sigma = P^1, \ldots, P^k$ be a stratification of P. It clearly suffices to show that σ is equivalent to σ_{G_P}. The stratification σ_{G_P} is used as a reference because, as shown in Lemma 15.2.8, its strata are the finest possible among all stratifications for P.

As in the proof of Theorem 15.2.7, we use the partial order $\prec$ among the strongly connected components of G_P and the notation introduced there. Clearly, the relation $\prec$ on the C^i induces a partial order on the Q^i, which we also denote by $\prec$ ($Q^i \prec Q^j$ if $C^i \prec C^j$). We say that a sequence $Q^{i_1}, \ldots, Q^{i_r}$ of some of the Q^i is *compatible* with $\prec$ if for every $l < m$ it is *not* the case that $Q^{i_m} \prec Q^{i_l}$.

We shall prove that

1. If σ' and σ'' are permutations of σ_{G_P} that are compatible with $\prec$, then σ' and σ'' are equivalent stratifications of P.

2. For each P^i, $1 \le i \le k$, there exists $\sigma_i = Q^{i_1}, \ldots, Q^{i_r}$ such that σ_i is a stratification of P^i, and the sequence $Q^{i_1}, \ldots, Q^{i_r}$ is compatible with $\prec$.

3. $\sigma_1, \ldots, \sigma_k$ is a permutation of $Q^1, \ldots, Q^n$ compatible with $\prec$.

Before demonstrating these, we argue that the foregoing statements (1 through 3) are sufficient to show that σ and σ_{G_P} are equivalent. By statement 2, each σ_i is a stratification of P^i. Lemma 15.2.9 implies that P^i is equivalent to σ_i. It follows that $\sigma = P^1, \ldots, P^k$ is equivalent to $\sigma_1, \ldots, \sigma_k$ which, by statement 3, is a permutation of σ_{G_P} compatible with $\prec$. Then $\sigma_1, \ldots, \sigma_k$ and σ_{G_P} are equivalent by statement 1, so σ and σ_{G_P} are equivalent.

Consider statement 1. Note first that one can obtain σ'' from σ' by a sequence of exchanges of adjacent Q^i, Q^j such that $Q^i \not\prec Q^j$ and $Q^j \not\prec Q^i$ (Exercise 15.9). Thus it is sufficient to show that for every such pair, Q^i, Q^j is equivalent to Q^j, Q^i. Because $Q^i \not\prec Q^j$ and $Q^j \not\prec Q^i$, it follows that no *idb* relation of Q^i occurs in Q^j and conversely. Then $Q^i \cup Q^j$ is a semipositive program [with respect to $edb(Q^i \cup Q^j)$] and both Q^i, Q^j and Q^j, Q^i are stratifications of $Q^i \cup Q^j$. By Lemma 15.2.9, Q^i, Q^j and Q^j, Q^i are both equivalent to $Q^i \cup Q^j$ (as a semipositive program), so Q^i, Q^j and Q^j, Q^i are equivalent.

Statement 2 follows immediately from Lemma 15.2.8.

Finally, consider statement 3. By statement 2, each σ_i is compatible with $\prec$. Thus it remains to be shown that, if Q^m occurs in σ_i, Q^l occurs in σ_j, and $i < j$, then $Q^l \not\prec Q^m$.

Note that Q^l is included in P^j, and Q^m is included in P^i. It follows that for all relations R defined by Q^m and R' defined by Q^l, $\sigma(R) < \sigma(R')$, where σ is the stratification function of $P^1, \ldots, P^k$. Hence $R' \nprec R$ so $Q^l \nprec Q^m$. ∎

Thus all stratifications of a given stratifiable program are equivalent. This means that we can speak about the semantics of such a program independently of a particular stratification. Given a stratifiable datalog¬ program P and an input $\mathbf{I}$ over $edb(P)$, we shall take as the semantics of P on $\mathbf{I}$ the semantics $\sigma(\mathbf{I})$ of any stratification σ of P. This semantics, well defined by Theorem 15.2.10, is denoted by $P^{strat}(\mathbf{I})$. Clearly, $P^{strat}(\mathbf{I})$ can be computed in time polynomial with respect to $\mathbf{I}$.

Now that we have a well-defined semantics for stratified programs, we can verify that for semipositive programs, the semantics coincides with the semantics already introduced. If P is a semipositive datalog¬ program, then P is also stratifiable. By Lemma 15.2.9, $P^{semi-pos}$ and P^{strat} are equivalent.

Properties of Stratified Semantics

Stratified semantics has a procedural flavor because it is the result of an ordering of the rules, albeit implicit. What can we say about $P^{strat}(\mathbf{I})$ from a model-theoretic point of view? Rather pleasantly, $P^{strat}(\mathbf{I})$ is a minimal model of Σ_P containing $\mathbf{I}$. However, no precise characterization of stratified semantics in model-theoretic terms has emerged. Some model-theoretic properties of stratified semantics are established next.

PROPOSITION 15.2.11 For each stratifiable datalog¬ program P and instance $\mathbf{I}$ over $edb(\mathbf{I})$,

    (a) $P^{strat}(\mathbf{I})$ is a minimal model of Σ_P whose restriction to $edb(P)$ equals $\mathbf{I}$.

    (b) $P^{strat}(\mathbf{I})$ is a minimal fixpoint of T_P whose restriction to $edb(P)$ equals $\mathbf{I}$.

Proof For part (a), let $\sigma = P^1, \ldots, P^n$ be a stratification of P and $\mathbf{I}$ an instance over $edb(P)$. We have to show that $P^{strat}(\mathbf{I})$ is a minimal model of Σ_P whose restriction to $edb(P)$ equals $\mathbf{I}$. Clearly, $P^{strat}(\mathbf{I})$ is a model of Σ_P whose restriction to $edb(P)$ equals $\mathbf{I}$. To prove its minimality, it is sufficient to show that, for each model $\mathbf{J}$ of Σ_P,

$$(**) \qquad \text{if } \mathbf{I} \subseteq \mathbf{J} \subseteq P^{strat}(\mathbf{I}) \text{ then } \mathbf{J} = P^{strat}(\mathbf{I}).$$

Thus suppose $\mathbf{I} \subseteq \mathbf{J} \subseteq P^{strat}(\mathbf{I})$. We prove by induction on k that

$$(\dagger) \qquad P^{strat}(\mathbf{I})|sch(\cup_{i \leq k} P^i) = \mathbf{J}|sch(\cup_{i \leq k} P^i)$$

for each k, $1 \leq k \leq n$. The equality of $P^{strat}(\mathbf{I})$ and $\mathbf{J}$ then follows from ($\dagger$) with $k = n$.
    For $k = 1$, $edb(P^1) \subseteq edb(P)$ so

$$P^{strat}(\mathbf{I})|edb(P^1) = \mathbf{I}|edb(P^1) = \mathbf{J}|edb(P^1).$$

By the definition of stratified semantics and Theorem 15.2.2, $P^{strat}(\mathbf{I})|sch(P^1)$ is the minimum model of Σ_{P^1} whose restriction to $edb(P^1)$ equals $P^{strat}(\mathbf{I})|edb(P^1)$. On the other hand, $\mathbf{J}|sch(P^1)$ is also a model of Σ_{P^1} whose restriction to $edb(P^1)$ equals $P^{strat}(\mathbf{I})|edb(P^1)$. From the minimality of $P^{strat}(\mathbf{I})|sch(P^1)$, it follows that

$$P^{strat}(\mathbf{I})|sch(P^1) \subseteq \mathbf{J}|sch(P^1).$$

From (**) it then follows that $P^{strat}(\mathbf{I})|sch(P^1) = \mathbf{J}|sch(P^1)$, which establishes (†) for $k = 1$. For the induction step, suppose (†) is true for k, $1 \le k < n$. Then (†) for $k + 1$ is shown in the same manner as for the case $k = 1$. This proves (†) for $1 \le k \le n$. It follows that $P^{strat}(\mathbf{I})$ is a minimal model of Σ_P whose restriction to $edb(P)$ equals $\mathbf{I}$.

The proof of part (b) is left for Exercise 15.12. ∎

There is another appealing property of stratified semantics that takes into account the syntax of the program in addition to purely model-theoretic considerations. This property is illustrated next.

Consider the two programs

$$P_5 = \{p \leftarrow \neg q\}$$
$$P_6 = \{q \leftarrow \neg p\}$$

From the perspective of classical logic, Σ_{P_5} and Σ_{P_6} are equivalent to each other and to $\{p \vee q\}$. However, T_{P_5} and T_{P_6} have different behavior: The unique fixpoint of T_{P_5} is $\{p\}$, whereas that of T_{P_6} is $\{q\}$. This is partially captured by the notion of "supported" as follows.

Let datalog$^\neg$ program P and input $\mathbf{I}$ be given. As with pure datalog, $\mathbf{J}$ is a model of P iff $\mathbf{J} \supseteq T_P(\mathbf{J})$. We say that $\mathbf{J}$ is a *supported* model if $\mathbf{J} \subseteq T_P(\mathbf{J})$ (i.e., if each fact in $\mathbf{J}$ is "justified" or supported by being the head of a ground instantiation of a rule in P whose body is all true in $\mathbf{J}$). (In the context of some input $\mathbf{I}$, we say that $\mathbf{J}$ is supported *relative* to $\mathbf{I}$ and the definition is modified accordingly.) This condition, which has both syntactic and semantic aspects, captures at least some of the spirit of the immediate consequence operator T_P. As suggested in Remark 15.1.2, its impact can be annulled by adding rules of the form $p \leftarrow p$.

The proof of the following is left to the reader (Exercise 15.13).

PROPOSITION 15.2.12   For each stratifiable program P and instance $\mathbf{I}$ over $edb(P)$, $P^{strat}(\mathbf{I})$ is a supported model of P relative to $\mathbf{I}$.

We have seen that stratification provides an elegant and simple approach to defining semantics of datalog$^\neg$ programs. Nonetheless, it has two major limitations. First, it does not provide semantics to *all* datalog$^\neg$ programs. Second, stratified datalog$^\neg$ programs are not entirely satisfactory with regard to expressive power. From a computational point of view, they provide recursion and negation and are inflationary. Therefore, as discussed in Chapter 14, one might expect that they express the *fixpoint* queries. Unfortunately, stratified datalog$^\neg$ programs fall short of expressing all such queries, as will be shown in Section 15.4. Intuitively, this is because the stratification condition prohibits recursive application of negation, whereas in other languages expressing *fixpoint* this computational restriction does not exist.

For these reasons, we consider another semantics for datalog¬ programs called *well founded*. As we shall see, this provides semantics to all datalog¬ programs and expresses all *fixpoint* queries. Furthermore, well-founded and stratified semantics agree on stratified datalog¬ programs.

15.3 Well-Founded Semantics

Well-founded semantics relies on a fundamental revision of our expectations of the answer to a datalog¬ program. So far, we required that the answer must provide information on the truth or falsehood of every fact. Well-founded semantics is based on the idea that a given program may not necessarily provide such information on all facts. Instead some facts may simply be indifferent to it, and the answer should be allowed to say that the truth value of those facts is *unknown*. As it turns out, relaxing expectations about the answer in this fashion allows us to provide a natural semantics for *all* datalog¬ programs. The price is that the answer is no longer guaranteed to provide total information.

Another aspect of this approach is that it puts negative and positive facts on a more equal footing. One can no longer assume that $\neg R(u)$ is true simply because $R(u)$ is not in the answer. Instead, both negative and positive facts must be inferred. To formalize this, we shall introduce 3-valued instances, in which the truth value of facts can be **true, false,** or **unknown**.

This section begins by introducing a largely declarative semantics for datalog¬ programs. Next an equivalent fixpoint semantics is developed. Finally it is shown that stratified and well-founded semantics agree on the family of stratified datalog¬ programs.

A Declarative Semantics for Datalog¬

The aim of giving semantics to a datalog¬ program P will be to find an appropriate 3-valued model **I** of Σ_P. In considering what *appropriate* might mean, it is useful to recall the basic motivation underlying the logic-programming approach to negation as opposed to the purely computational approach. An important goal is to model some form of natural reasoning process. In particular, consistency in the reasoning process is required. Specifically, one cannot use a fact and later infer its negation. This should be captured in the notion of appropriateness of a 3-valued model **I**, and it has two intuitive aspects:

- the positive facts of **I** must be inferred from P assuming the negative facts in **I**; and
- all negative facts that can be inferred from **I** must already be in **I**.

A 3-valued model satisfying the aforementioned notion of appropriateness will be called a 3-stable model of P. It turns out that, generally, programs have several 3-stable models. Then it is natural to take as an answer the certain (positive and negative) facts that belong to all such models, which turns out to yield, in some sense, the smallest 3-stable model. This is indeed how the well-founded semantics of P will be defined.

EXAMPLE 15.3.1   The example concerns a game with states, $a, b, \ldots$. The game is between two players. The possible moves of the games are held in a binary relation *moves*. A
tuple $\langle a, b \rangle$ in *moves* indicates that when in state a, one can choose to move to state b. A
player loses if he or she is in a state from which there are no moves. The goal is to compute
the set of winning states (i.e., the set of states such that there exists a winning strategy for
a player in this state). These are obtained in a unary predicate *win*.

Consider the input **K** with the following value for *moves*:

$$\mathbf{K}(moves) = \{\langle b, c \rangle, \langle c, a \rangle, \langle a, b \rangle, \langle a, d \rangle, \langle d, e \rangle, \langle d, f \rangle, \langle f, g \rangle\}$$

Graphically, the input is represented as

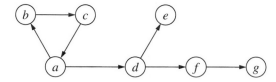

It is seen easily that there are indeed winning strategies from states d (move to e) and
f (move to g). Slightly more subtle is the fact that there is no winning strategy from any of
states a, b, or c. A given player can prevent the other from winning, essentially by forcing
a nonterminating sequence of moves.

Now consider the following nonstratifiable program P_{win}:

$$win(x) \leftarrow moves(x, y), \neg win(y)$$

Intuitively, P_{win} states that a state x is in *win* if there is at least one state y that one can
move to from x, for which the opposing player loses. We now exhibit a 3-valued model **J**
of P_{win} that agrees with **K** on *moves*. As will be seen, this will in fact be the well-founded
semantics of P_{win} on input **K**. Instance **J** is such that $\mathbf{J}(moves) = \mathbf{K}(moves)$ and the values
of *win*-atoms are given as follows:

true	$win(d), win(f)$
false	$win(e), win(g)$
unknown	$win(a), win(b), win(c)$

We now embark on defining formally the well-founded semantics. We do this in three
steps. First we define the notion of 3-valued instance and extend the notion of truth value
and satisfaction. Then we consider datalog and show the existence of a minimum 3-valued
model for each datalog program. Finally we consider datalog¬ and the notion of 3-stable
model, which is the basis of well-founded semantics.

3-valued Instances   Dealing with three truth values instead of the usual two requires
extending some of the basic notions like instance and model. As we shall see, this is
straightforward. We will denote **true** by 1, **false** by 0, and **unknown** by 1/2.

Consider a datalog¬ program P and a classical 2-valued instance $\mathbf{I}$. As was done in the discussion of SLD resolution in Chapter 12, we shall denote by $P_{\mathbf{I}}$ the program obtained from P by adding to P unit clauses stating that the facts in $\mathbf{I}$ are true. Then $P(\mathbf{I}) = P_{\mathbf{I}}(\emptyset)$. For the moment, we shall deal with datalog¬ programs such as these, whose input is included in the program. Recall that $\mathbf{B}(P)$ denotes all facts of the form $R(a_1, \ldots, a_k)$, where R is a relation and $a_1, \ldots, a_k$ constants occurring in P. In particular, $\mathbf{B}(P_{\mathbf{I}}) = \mathbf{B}(P, \mathbf{I})$.

Let P be a datalog¬ program. A *3-valued instance* $\mathbf{I}$ over $sch(P)$ is a total mapping from $\mathbf{B}(P)$ to $\{0, 1/2, 1\}$. We denote by $\mathbf{I}^1$, $\mathbf{I}^{1/2}$, and $\mathbf{I}^0$ the set of atoms in $\mathbf{B}(P)$ whose truth value is $1, 1/2$, and 0, respectively. A 3-valued instance $\mathbf{I}$ is *total*, or *2-valued*, if $\mathbf{I}^{1/2} = \emptyset$. There is a natural ordering $\prec$ among 3-valued instances over $sch(P)$, defined by

$$\mathbf{I} \prec \mathbf{J} \text{ iff for each } A \in \mathbf{B}(P), \ \mathbf{I}(A) \leq \mathbf{J}(A).$$

Note that this is equivalent to $\mathbf{I}^1 \subseteq \mathbf{J}^1$ and $\mathbf{I}^0 \supseteq \mathbf{J}^0$ and that it generalizes containment for 2-valued instances.

Occasionally, we will represent a 3-valued instance by listing the positive and negative facts and omitting the undefined ones. For example, the 3-valued instance $\mathbf{I}$, where $\mathbf{I}(p) = 1, \mathbf{I}(q) = 1, \mathbf{I}(r) = 1/2, \mathbf{I}(s) = 0$, will also be written as $\mathbf{I} = \{p, q, \neg s\}$.

Given a 3-valued instance $\mathbf{I}$, we next define the truth value of Boolean combinations of facts using the connectives $\vee, \wedge, \neg, \leftarrow$. The truth value of a Boolean combination α of facts is denoted by $\hat{\mathbf{I}}(\alpha)$, defined by

$$\hat{\mathbf{I}}(\beta \wedge \gamma) = \min\{\hat{\mathbf{I}}(\beta), \hat{\mathbf{I}}(\gamma)\}$$
$$\hat{\mathbf{I}}(\beta \vee \gamma) = \max\{\hat{\mathbf{I}}(\beta), \hat{\mathbf{I}}(\gamma)\}$$
$$\hat{\mathbf{I}}(\neg\beta) = 1 - \hat{\mathbf{I}}(\beta)$$
$$\hat{\mathbf{I}}(\beta \leftarrow \gamma) = 1 \text{ if } \hat{\mathbf{I}}(\gamma) \leq \hat{\mathbf{I}}(\beta), \text{ and } 0 \text{ otherwise.}$$

The reader should be careful: Known facts about Boolean operators in the 2-valued context may not hold in this more complex one. For instance, note that the truth value of $p \leftarrow q$ may be different from that of $p \vee \neg q$ (see Exercise 15.15). To see that the preceding definition matches the intuition, one might want to verify that with the specific semantics of $\leftarrow$ used here, the instance $\mathbf{J}$ of Example 15.3.1 does satisfy (the ground instantiation of) $P_{win,\mathbf{K}}$. That would not be the case if we define the semantics of $\leftarrow$ in a more standard way; by using $p \leftarrow q \equiv p \vee \neg q$.

A 3-valued instance $\mathbf{I}$ over $sch(P)$ *satisfies* a Boolean combination α of atoms in $\mathbf{B}(P)$ iff $\hat{\mathbf{I}}(\alpha) = 1$. Given a datalog$^{(\neg)}$ program P, a *3-valued model* of Σ_P is a 3-valued instance over $sch(P)$ satisfying the set of implications corresponding to the rules in $ground(P)$.

EXAMPLE 15.3.2 Recall the program P_{win} of Example 15.3.1 and the input instance $\mathbf{K}$ and output instance $\mathbf{J}$ presented there. Consider these ground sentences:

$$win(a) \leftarrow moves(a, d), \neg win(d)$$
$$win(a) \leftarrow moves(a, b), \neg win(b).$$

The first is true for **J**, because $\hat{\mathbf{J}}(\neg win(d)) = 0$, $\hat{\mathbf{J}}(moves(a, d)) = 1$, $\hat{\mathbf{J}}(win(a)) = 1/2$, and $1/2 \geq 0$. The second is true because $\hat{\mathbf{J}}(\neg win(b)) = 1/2$, $\hat{\mathbf{J}}(moves(a, b)) = 1$, $\hat{\mathbf{J}}(win(a)) = 1/2$, and $1/2 \geq 1/2$.

Observe that, on the other hand,

$$\hat{\mathbf{J}}(win(a) \vee \neg(moves(a, b) \wedge \neg win(b))) = 1/2.$$

3-valued Minimal Model for Datalog   We next extend the definition and semantics of datalog programs to the context of 3-valued instances. Although datalog programs do not contain negation, they will now be allowed to infer positive, unknown, and false facts. The syntax of a *3-extended datalog program* is the same as for datalog, except that the truth values $0, 1/2$, and 1 can occur as literals in bodies of rules. Given a 3-extended datalog program P, the *3-valued immediate consequence operator 3-T_P* of P is a mapping on 3-valued instances over $sch(P)$ defined as follows. Given a 3-valued instance **I** and $A \in \mathbf{B}(P)$, *3-T_P*(**I**)(A) is

1 if there is a rule $A \leftarrow body$ in $ground(P)$ such that $\hat{\mathbf{I}}(body) = 1$,

0 if for each rule $A \leftarrow body$ in $ground(P)$, $\hat{\mathbf{I}}(body) = 0$ (and, in particular, if there is no rule with A in head),

1/2 otherwise.

EXAMPLE 15.3.3   Consider the 3-extended datalog program $P = \{p \leftarrow 1/2; p \leftarrow q, 1/2; q \leftarrow p, r; q \leftarrow p, s; s \leftarrow q; r \leftarrow 1\}$. Then

$$\begin{aligned} 3\text{-}T_P(\{\neg p, \neg q, \neg r, \neg s\}) &= \{\neg q, r, \neg s\} \\ 3\text{-}T_P(\{\neg q, r, \neg s\}) &= \{r, \neg s\} \\ 3\text{-}T_P(\{r, \neg s\}) &= \{r\} \\ 3\text{-}T_P(\{r\}) &= \{r\}. \end{aligned}$$

In the following, 3-valued instances are compared with respect to $\prec$. Thus "least," "minimal," and "monotonic" are with respect to $\prec$ rather than the set inclusion used for classical 2-valued instances. In particular, note that the minimum 3-valued instance with respect to $\prec$ is that where all atoms are false. Let $\perp$ denote this particular instance.

With the preceding definitions, extended datalog programs on 3-valued instances behave similarly to classical programs. The next lemma can be verified easily (Exercise 15.16):

LEMMA 15.3.4   Let P be a 3-extended datalog program. Then

1. $3 - T_P$ is monotonic and the sequence $\{3\text{-}T_P^i(\perp)\}_{i > 0}$ is increasing and converges to the least fixpoint of $3\text{-}T_P$;

    2. *P* has a unique minimal 3-valued model that equals the least fixpoint of *3-T_P*.

The semantics of an extended datalog program is the minimum 3-valued model of *P*. Analogous to conventional datalog, we denote this by *P*($\perp$).

3-stable Models of Datalog⁻

We are now ready to look at datalog⁻ programs and formally define 3-stable models of a datalog⁻ program *P*. We "bootstrap" to the semantics of programs with negation, using the semantics for 3-extended datalog programs described earlier. Let **I** be a 3-valued instance over *sch(P)*. We reduce the problem to that of applying a positive datalog program, as follows. The *positivized ground version* of *P* given **I**, denoted *pg(P, **I**)*, is the 3-extended datalog program obtained from *ground(P)* by replacing each negative premise $\neg A$ by $\hat{I}(\neg A)$ (i.e., 0, 1, or 1/2). Because all negative literals in *ground(P)* have been replaced by their truth value in **I**, *pg(P, **I**)* is now a 3-extended datalog program (i.e, a program without negation). Its least fixpoint *pg(P, **I**)*($\perp$) contains all the facts that are consequences of *P* by assuming the values for the negative premises as given by **I**. We denote *pg(P, **I**)*($\perp$) by *conseq_P(**I**)*. Thus the intuitive conditions required of 3-stable models now amount to *conseq_P(**I**)* = **I**.

DEFINITION 15.3.5 Let *P* be a datalog⁻ program. A 3-valued instance **I** over *sch(P)* is a *3-stable model* of *P* iff *conseq_P(**I**)* = **I**.

Observe an important distinction between *conseq_P* and the immediate consequence operator used for inflationary datalog⁻. For inflationary datalog⁻, we assumed that $\neg A$ was true as long as *A* was not inferred. Here we just assume in such a case that *A* is unknown and try to prove new facts. Of course, doing so requires the 3-valued approach.

EXAMPLE 15.3.6 Consider the following datalog⁻ program *P*:

$$p \leftarrow \neg r$$
$$q \leftarrow \neg r, p$$
$$s \leftarrow \neg t$$
$$t \leftarrow q, \neg s$$
$$u \leftarrow \neg t, p, s$$

The program has three 3-stable models (represented by listing the positive and negative facts and leaving out the unknown facts):

$$\mathbf{I}_1 = \{p, q, t, \neg r, \neg s, \neg u\}$$
$$\mathbf{I}_2 = \{p, q, s, \neg r, \neg t, \neg u\}$$
$$\mathbf{I}_3 = \{p, q, \neg r\}$$

Let us check that **I**₃ is a 3-stable model of *P*. The program *P′* = *pg(P, **I**₃)* is

$$p \leftarrow 1$$
$$q \leftarrow 1, p$$
$$s \leftarrow 1/2$$
$$t \leftarrow q, 1/2$$
$$u \leftarrow 1/2, p, s$$

The minimum 3-valued model of $pg(P, \mathbf{I}_3)$ is obtained by iterating $3\text{-}T_{P'}(\bot)$ up to a fixpoint. Thus we start with $\bot = \{\neg p, \neg q, \neg r, \neg s, \neg t, \neg u\}$. The first application of $3\text{-}T_{P'}$ yields $3\text{-}T_{P'}(\bot) = \{p, \neg q, \neg r, \neg t, \neg u\}$. Next $(3\text{-}T_{P'})^2(\bot) = \{p, q, \neg r, \neg t\}$. Finally $(3\text{-}T_{P'})^3(\bot) = (3\text{-}T_{P'})^4(\bot) = \{p, q, \neg r\}$. Thus

$$conseq_P(\mathbf{I}_3) = pg(P, \mathbf{I}_3)(\bot) = (3\text{-}T_{P'})^3(\bot) = \mathbf{I}_3,$$

and $\mathbf{I}_3$ is a 3-stable model of P.

The reader is invited to verify that in Example 15.3.1, the instance $\mathbf{J}$ is a 3-stable model of the program $P_{win, \mathbf{K}}$ for the input instance $\mathbf{K}$ presented there.

As seen from the example, datalog¬ programs generally have several 3-stable models. We will show later that each datalog¬ program has at least one 3-stable model. Therefore it makes sense to let the final answer consist of the positive and negative facts belonging to all 3-stable models of the program. As we shall see, the 3-valued instance so obtained is itself a 3-stable model of the program.

DEFINITION 15.3.7   Let P be a datalog¬ program. The *well-founded semantics* of P is the 3-valued instance consisting of all positive and negative facts belonging to all 3-stable models of P. This is denoted by $P^{wf}(\emptyset)$, or simply, P^{wf}. Given datalog¬ program P and input instance $\mathbf{I}$, $P_{\mathbf{I}}^{wf}(\emptyset)$ is denoted $P^{wf}(\mathbf{I})$.

Thus the well-founded semantics of the program P in Example 15.3.6 is $P^{wf}(\emptyset) = \{p, q, \neg r\}$. We shall see later that in Example 15.3.1, $P_{win}^{wf}(\mathbf{K}) = \mathbf{J}$.

A Fixpoint Definition

Note that the preceding description of the well-founded semantics, although effective, is inefficient. The straightforward algorithm yielded by this description involves checking all possible 3-valued instances of a program, determining which are 3-stable models, and then taking their intersection. We next provide a simpler, efficient way of computing the well-founded semantics. It is based on an "alternating fixpoint" computation that converges to the well-founded semantics. As a side-effect, the proof will show that each datalog¬ program has at least one 3-stable model (and therefore the well-founded semantics is always defined), something we have not proven. It will also show that the well-founded model is itself a 3-stable model, in some sense the smallest.

The idea of the computation is as follows. We define an alternating sequence $\{\mathbf{I}_i\}_{i \geq 0}$ of 3-valued instances that are underestimates and overestimates of the facts known in every

3-stable model of P. The sequence is as follows:

$$\mathbf{I}_0 \quad = \perp$$
$$\mathbf{I}_{i+1} = conseq_P(\mathbf{I}_i).$$

Recall that $\perp$ is the least 3-valued instance and that all facts have value 0 in $\perp$. Also note that each of the $\mathbf{I}_i$ just defined is a total instance. This follows easily from the following facts (Exercise 15.17):

- if $\mathbf{I}$ is total, then $conseq_P(\mathbf{I})$ is total; and
- the $\mathbf{I}_i$ are constructed starting from the total instance $\perp$ by repeated applications of $conseq_P$.

The intuition behind the construction of the sequence $\{\mathbf{I}_i\}_{i \geq 0}$ is the following. The sequence starts with $\perp$, which is an overestimate of the negative facts in the answer (it contains all negative facts). From this overestimate we compute $\mathbf{I}_1 = conseq_P(\perp)$, which includes all positive facts that can be inferred from $\perp$. This is clearly an overestimate of the positive facts in the answer, so the set of negative facts in $\mathbf{I}_1$ is an underestimate of the negative facts in the answer. Using this underestimate of the negative facts, we compute $\mathbf{I}_2 = conseq_P(\mathbf{I}_1)$, whose positive facts will now be an underestimate of the positive facts in the answer. By continuing the process, we see that the even-indexed instances provide underestimates of the positive facts in the answer and the odd-indexed ones provide underestimates of the negative facts in the answer. Then the limit of the even-indexed instances provides the positive facts in the answer and the limit of the odd-indexed instances provides the negative facts in the answer. This intuition will be made formal later in this section.

It is easy to see that $conseq_P(\mathbf{I})$ is antimonotonic. That is, if $\mathbf{I} \prec \mathbf{J}$, then $conseq_P(\mathbf{J}) \prec conseq_P(\mathbf{I})$ (Exercise 15.17). From this and the facts that $\perp \prec \mathbf{I}_1$ and $\perp \prec \mathbf{I}_2$, it immediately follows that, for all $i > 0$,

$$\mathbf{I}_0 \prec \mathbf{I}_2 \ldots \prec \mathbf{I}_{2i} \prec \mathbf{I}_{2i+2} \prec \ldots \prec \mathbf{I}_{2i+1} \prec \mathbf{I}_{2i-1} \prec \ldots \prec \mathbf{I}_1.$$

Thus the even subsequence is increasing and the odd one is decreasing. Because there are finitely many 3-valued instances relative to a given program P, each of these sequences becomes constant at some point. Let $\mathbf{I}_*$ denote the limit of the increasing sequence $\{\mathbf{I}_{2i}\}_{i \geq 0}$, and let $\mathbf{I}^*$ denote the limit of the decreasing sequence $\{\mathbf{I}_{2i+1}\}_{i \geq 0}$. From the aforementioned inequalities, it follows that $\mathbf{I}_* \prec \mathbf{I}^*$. Moreover, note that $conseq_P(\mathbf{I}_*) = \mathbf{I}^*$ and $conseq_P(\mathbf{I}^*) = \mathbf{I}_*$. Finally let $\mathbf{I}_*^*$ denote the 3-valued instance consisting of the facts known in both $\mathbf{I}_*$ and $\mathbf{I}^*$; that is,

$$\mathbf{I}_*^*(A) = \begin{cases} 1 & \text{if } \mathbf{I}_*(A) = \mathbf{I}^*(A) = 1 \\ 0 & \text{if } \mathbf{I}_*(A) = \mathbf{I}^*(A) = 0 \text{ and} \\ 1/2 & \text{otherwise.} \end{cases}$$

Equivalently, $\mathbf{I}_*^* = (\mathbf{I}_*)^1 \cup (\mathbf{I}^*)^0$. As will be seen shortly, $\mathbf{I}_*^* = P^{wf}(\emptyset)$. Before proving this, we illustrate the alternating fixpoint computation with several examples.

EXAMPLE 15.3.8

(a) Consider again the program in Example 15.3.6. Let us perform the alternating fixpoint computation described earlier. We start with $\mathbf{I}_0 = \perp = \{\neg p, \neg q, \neg r, \neg s, \neg t, \neg u\}$. By applying $conseq_P$, we obtain the following sequence of instances:

$$\mathbf{I}_1 = \{p, q, \neg r, s, t, u\},$$
$$\mathbf{I}_2 = \{p, q, \neg r, \neg s, \neg t, \neg u\},$$
$$\mathbf{I}_3 = \{p, q, \neg r, s, t, u\},$$
$$\mathbf{I}_4 = \{p, q, \neg r, \neg s, \neg t, \neg u\}.$$

Thus $\mathbf{I}_* = \mathbf{I}_4 = \{p, q, \neg r, \neg s, \neg t, \neg u\}$ and $\mathbf{I}^* = \mathbf{I}_3 = \{p, q, \neg r, s, t, u\}$. Finally $\mathbf{I}_*^* = \{p, q, \neg r\}$, which coincides with the well-founded semantics of P computed in Example 15.3.6.

(b) Recall now P_{win} and input $\mathbf{K}$ of Example 15.3.1. We compute $\mathbf{I}_*^*$ for the program $P_{win,\mathbf{I}}$. Note that for $\mathbf{I}_0$ the value of all *move* atoms is **false**, and for each $j \geq 1$, $\mathbf{I}_j$ agrees with the input $\mathbf{K}$ on the predicate *moves*; thus we do not show the *move* atoms here. For the *win* predicate, then, we have

$$\mathbf{I}_1 = \{win(a), win(b), win(c), win(d), \neg win(e), win(f), \neg win(g)\}$$
$$\mathbf{I}_2 = \{\neg win(a), \neg win(b), \neg win(c), win(d), \neg win(e), win(f), \neg win(g)\}$$
$$\mathbf{I}_3 = \mathbf{I}_1$$
$$\mathbf{I}_4 = \mathbf{I}_2.$$

Thus

$$\mathbf{I}_* = \mathbf{I}_2 = \{\neg win(a), \neg win(b), \neg win(c), win(d), \neg win(e), win(f), \neg win(g)\}$$
$$\mathbf{I}^* = \mathbf{I}_1 = \{win(a), win(b), win(c), win(d), \neg win(e), win(f), \neg win(g)\}$$
$$\mathbf{I}_*^* = \{win(d), \neg win(e), win(f), \neg win(g)\},$$

which is the instance $\mathbf{J}$ of Example 15.3.1.

(c) Consider the database schema consisting of a binary relation G and a unary relation *good* and the following program defining *bad* and *answer*:

$$bad \quad \leftarrow G(y, x), \neg good(y)$$
$$answer(x) \leftarrow \neg bad(x)$$

Consider the instance $\mathbf{K}$ over G and *good*, where

$$\mathbf{K}(G \quad = \{\langle b, c\rangle, \langle c, b\rangle, \langle c, d\rangle, \langle a, d\rangle, \langle a, e\rangle\}, \text{ and}$$
$$\mathbf{K}(good) = \{\langle a\rangle\}.$$

We assume that the facts of the database are added as unit clauses to P, yielding $P_{\mathbf{K}}$. Again we perform the alternating fixpoint computation for $P_{\mathbf{K}}$. We start with $\mathbf{I}_0 = \bot$ (containing all negated atoms). Applying $conseq_{P_K}$ yields the following sequence $\{\mathbf{I}_i\}_{i>0}$:

	bad	answer
$\mathbf{I}_0$	$\emptyset$	$\emptyset$
$\mathbf{I}_1$	$\{\neg a, b, c, d, e\}$	$\{a, b, c, d, e\}$
$\mathbf{I}_2$	$\{\neg a, b, c, d, \neg e\}$	$\{a, \neg b, \neg c, \neg d, \neg e\}$
$\mathbf{I}_3$	$\{\neg a, b, c, d, \neg e\}$	$\{a, \neg b, \neg c, \neg d, e\}$
$\mathbf{I}_4$	$\{\neg a, b, c, d, \neg e\}$	$\{a, \neg b, \neg c, \neg d, e\}$

We have omitted [as in (b)] the facts relating to the *edb* predicates G and *good*, which do not change after step 1.

Thus $\mathbf{I}_*^* = \mathbf{I}_* = \mathbf{I}^* = \mathbf{I}_3 = \mathbf{I}_4$. Note that P is stratified and its well-founded semantics coincides with its stratified semantics. As we shall see, this is not accidental.

We now show that the fixpoint construction yields the well-founded semantics for datalog$^{\neg}$ programs.

THEOREM 15.3.9 For each datalog$^{\neg}$ program P,

1. $\mathbf{I}_*^*$ is a 3-stable model of P.
2. $P^{wf}(\emptyset) = \mathbf{I}_*^*$.

Proof For statement 1, we need to show that $conseq_P(\mathbf{I}_*^*) = \mathbf{I}_*^*$. We show that for every fact A, if $\mathbf{I}_*^*(A) = \epsilon \in \{0, 1/2, 1\}$, then $conseq_P(\mathbf{I}_*^*)(A) = \epsilon$. From the antimonotonicity of $conseq_P$, the fact that $\mathbf{I}_* \prec \mathbf{I}_*^* \prec \mathbf{I}^*$ and $conseq_P(\mathbf{I}_*) = \mathbf{I}^*$, $conseq_P(\mathbf{I}^*) = \mathbf{I}_*$, it follows that $\mathbf{I}_* \prec conseq_P(\mathbf{I}_*^*) \prec \mathbf{I}^*$. If $\mathbf{I}_*^*(A) = 0$, then $\mathbf{I}^*(A) = 0$ so $conseq_P(\mathbf{I}_*^*)(A) = 0$; similarly for $\mathbf{I}_*^*(A) = 1$. Now suppose that $\mathbf{I}_*^*(A) = 1/2$. It is sufficient to prove that $conseq_P(\mathbf{I}_*^*)(A) \geq 1/2$. [It is not possible that $conseq_P(\mathbf{I}_*^*)(A) = 1$. If this were the case, the rules used to infer A involve only facts whose value is 0 or 1. Because those facts have the same value in $\mathbf{I}_*$ and $\mathbf{I}^*$, the same rules can be used in both $pg(P, \mathbf{I}_*)$ and $pg(P, \mathbf{I}^*)$ to infer A, so $\mathbf{I}_*(A) = \mathbf{I}^*(A) = \mathbf{I}_*^*(A) = 1$, which contradicts the hypothesis that $\mathbf{I}_*^*(A) = 1/2$.]

We now prove that $conseq_P(\mathbf{I}_*^*)(A) \geq 1/2$. By the definition of $\mathbf{I}_*^*$, $\mathbf{I}_*(A) = 0$ and $\mathbf{I}^*(A) = 1$. Recall that $conseq_P(\mathbf{I}_*) = \mathbf{I}^*$, so $conseq_P(\mathbf{I}_*)(A) = 1$. In addition, $conseq_P(\mathbf{I}_*)$ is the limit of the sequence $\{3\text{-}T^i_{pg(P,\mathbf{I}_*)}\}_{i>0}$. Let $stage(A)$ be the minimum i such that $3\text{-}T^i_{pg(P,\mathbf{I}_*)}(A) = 1$. We prove by induction on $stage(A)$ that $conseq_P(\mathbf{I}_*^*)(A) \geq 1/2$. Suppose that $stage(A) = 1$. Then there exists in $ground(P)$ a rule of the form $A \leftarrow$, or one of the form $A \leftarrow \neg B_1, \ldots, \neg B_n$, where $\mathbf{I}_*(B_j) = 0, 1 \leq j \leq n$. However, the first case cannot occur, for otherwise $conseq_P(\mathbf{I}^*)(A)$ must also equal 1 so $\mathbf{I}_*(A) = 1$ and therefore $\mathbf{I}_*^*(A) = 1$, contradicting the fact that $\mathbf{I}_*^*(A) = 1/2$. By the same argument, $\mathbf{I}^*(B_j) = 1$, so $\mathbf{I}_*^*(B_j) = 1/2, 1 \leq j \leq n$. Consider now $pg(P, \mathbf{I}_*^*)$. Because $\mathbf{I}_*^*(B_j) =$

$1/2$, $1 \leq j \leq n$, the second rule yields $conseq_P(\mathbf{I}^*_*)(A) \geq 1/2$. Now suppose that the statement is true for $stage(A) = i$ and suppose that $stage(A) = i + 1$. Then there exists a rule $A \leftarrow A_1 \ldots A_m \neg B_1 \ldots \neg B_n$ such that $\mathbf{I}_*(B_j) = 0$ and $3\text{-}T^i_{pg(P, \mathbf{I}_*)}(A_k) = 1$ for each j and k. Because $\mathbf{I}_*(B_j) = 0$, $\mathbf{I}^*_*(B_j) \leq 1/2$ so $\mathbf{I}^*_*(\neg B_j) \geq 1/2$. In addition, by the induction hypothesis, $conseq_P(\mathbf{I}^*_*)(A_k) \geq 1/2$. It follows that $conseq_P(\mathbf{I}^*_*)(A) \geq 1/2$, and the induction is complete. Thus $conseq_P(\mathbf{I}^*_*) = \mathbf{I}^*_*$ and $\mathbf{I}^*_*$ is a 3-stable model of P.

Consider statement 2. We have to show that the positive and negative facts in $\mathbf{I}^*_*$ are those belonging to every 3-stable model $\mathbf{M}$ of P. Because $\mathbf{I}^*_*$ is itself a 3-stable model of P, it contains the positive and negative facts belonging to every 3-stable model of P. It remains to show the converse (i.e., that the positive and negative facts in $\mathbf{I}^*_*$ belong to every 3-stable model of P). To this end, we first show that for each 3-stable model $\mathbf{M}$ of P and $i \geq 0$,

$$(\ddagger) \qquad \mathbf{I}_{2i} \prec \mathbf{M} \prec \mathbf{I}_{2i+1}.$$

The proof is by induction on i. For $i = 0$, we have

$$\mathbf{I}_0 = \perp \prec \mathbf{M}.$$

Because $conseq_P$ is antimonotonic, $conseq_P(\mathbf{M}) \prec conseq_P(\mathbf{I}_0)$. Now $conseq_P(\mathbf{I}_0) = \mathbf{I}_1$ and because $\mathbf{M}$ is 3-stable, $conseq_P(\mathbf{M}) = \mathbf{M}$. Thus we have

$$\mathbf{I}_0 \prec \mathbf{M} \prec \mathbf{I}_1.$$

The induction step is similar and is omitted.

By ($\ddagger$), $\mathbf{I}_* \prec \mathbf{M} \prec \mathbf{I}^*$. Now a positive fact in $\mathbf{I}^*_*$ is in $\mathbf{I}_*$ and so is in $\mathbf{M}$ because $\mathbf{I}_* \prec \mathbf{M}$. Similarly, a negative fact in $\mathbf{I}^*_*$ is in $\mathbf{I}^*$ and so is in $\mathbf{M}$ because $\mathbf{M} \prec \mathbf{I}^*$. ∎

Note that the proof of statement 2 above formalizes the intuition that the $\mathbf{I}_{2i}$ provide underestimates of the positive facts in all acceptable answers (3-stable models) and the $\mathbf{I}_{2i+1}$ provide underestimates of the negative facts in those answers. The fact that $P^{wf}(\emptyset)$ is a minimal model of P is left for Exercise 15.19.

Variations of the alternating fixpoint computation can be obtained by starting with initial instances different from $\perp$. For example, it may make sense to start with the content of the *edb* relations as an initial instance. Such variations are sometimes useful for technical reasons. It turns out that the resulting sequences still compute the well-founded semantics. We show the following:

PROPOSITION 15.3.10   Let P be a datalog$^\neg$ program. Let $\{\bar{\mathbf{I}}_i\}_{i \geq 0}$ be defined in the same way as the sequence $\{\mathbf{I}_i\}_{i \geq 0}$, except that $\bar{\mathbf{I}}_0$ is some total instance such that

$$\perp \prec \bar{\mathbf{I}}_0 \prec P^{wf}(\emptyset).$$

Then

$$\bar{\mathbf{I}}_0 \prec \bar{\mathbf{I}}_2 \ldots \prec \bar{\mathbf{I}}_{2i} \prec \bar{\mathbf{I}}_{2i+2} \prec \ldots \prec \bar{\mathbf{I}}_{2i+1} \prec \bar{\mathbf{I}}_{2i-1} \prec \ldots \prec \bar{\mathbf{I}}_1$$

and (using the same notation as before),

$$\bar{\mathbf{I}}_*^* = P^{wf}(\emptyset).$$

Proof Let us compare the sequences $\{\mathbf{I}_i\}_{i\geq0}$ and $\{\bar{\mathbf{I}}_i\}_{i\geq0}$. Because $\bar{\mathbf{I}}_0 \prec P^{wf}(\emptyset)$ and $\bar{\mathbf{I}}_0$ is total, it easily follows that $\bar{\mathbf{I}}_0 \prec \mathbf{I}_*$. Thus $\perp = \mathbf{I}_0 \prec \bar{\mathbf{I}}_0 \prec \mathbf{I}_*$. From the antimonotonicity of the *conseq $_P$* operator and the fact that $conseq_P^2(\mathbf{I}_*) = \mathbf{I}_*$, it follows that $\mathbf{I}_{2i} \prec \bar{\mathbf{I}}_{2i} \prec \mathbf{I}_*$ for all i, $i \geq 0$. Thus $\bar{\mathbf{I}}_* = \mathbf{I}_*$. Then

$$\bar{\mathbf{I}}^* = conseq_P(\bar{\mathbf{I}}_*) = conseq_P(\mathbf{I}_*) = \mathbf{I}^*$$

so $\bar{\mathbf{I}}_*^* = \mathbf{I}_*^* = P^{wf}(\emptyset)$. ∎

As noted earlier, the instances in the sequence $\{\mathbf{I}_i\}_{i\geq0}$ are total. A slightly different alternating fixpoint computation formulated only in terms of positive and negative facts can be defined. This is explored in Exercise 15.25.

Finally, the alternating fixpoint computation of the well-founded semantics involves looking at the ground rules of the given program. However, one can clearly compute the semantics without having to explicitly look at the ground rules. We show in Section 15.4 how the well-founded semantics can be computed by a *fixpoint* query.

Well-Founded and Stratified Semantics Agree

Because the well-founded semantics provides semantics to all datalog¬ programs, it does so in particular for stratified programs. Example 15.3.8(c) showed one stratified program for which stratified and well-founded semantics coincide. Fortunately, as shown next, stratified and well-founded semantics are always compatible. Thus if a program is stratified, then the stratified and well-founded semantics agree.

A datalog¬ program P is said to be *total* if $P^{wf}(\mathbf{I})$ is total for each input $\mathbf{I}$ over *edb(P)*.

THEOREM 15.3.11 If P is a stratified datalog¬ program, then P is total under the well-founded semantics, and for each 2-valued instance $\mathbf{I}$ over *edb(P)*, $P^{wf}(\mathbf{I}) = P^{strat}(\mathbf{I})$.

Proof Let P be stratified, and let input $\mathbf{I}_0$ over *edb(P)* be fixed. The idea of the proof is the following. Let $\mathbf{J}$ be a 3-stable model of $P_{\mathbf{I}_0}$. We shall show that $\mathbf{J} = P^{strat}(\mathbf{I}_0)$. This will imply that $P^{strat}(\mathbf{I}_0)$ is the unique 3-stable model for $P_{\mathbf{I}_0}$. In particular, it contains only the positive and negative facts in all 3-stable models of $P_{\mathbf{I}_0}$ and is thus $P^{wf}(\mathbf{I}_0)$.

For the proof, we will need to develop some notation.

Notation for the stratification: Let $P^1, \ldots, P^n$ be a stratification of P. Let $P^0 = \emptyset_{\mathbf{I}_0}$ (i.e., the program corresponding to all of the facts in $\mathbf{I}_0$). For each k in $[0, n]$,

- let $\mathbf{S}_k = idb(P^k)$ ($\mathbf{S}_0$ is *edb(P)*);

- $\mathbf{S}_{[0,k]} = \cup_{i \in [0,k]} \mathbf{S}_i$; and
- $\mathbf{I}_k = (P^1 \cup \cdots \cup P^k)^{strat}(\mathbf{I}_0) = \mathbf{I}_n | \mathbf{S}_{[0,k]}$ (and, in particular, $P^{strat}(\mathbf{I}_0) = \mathbf{I}_n$).

Notation for the 3-stable model: Let $\hat{P} = pg(P_{\mathbf{I}_0}, \mathbf{J})$. Recall that because $\mathbf{J}$ is 3-stable for $P_{\mathbf{I}_0}$,

$$\mathbf{J} = conseq_{\hat{P}}(\mathbf{J}) = \lim_{i \geq 0} 3\text{-}T_{\hat{P}}^i(\emptyset).$$

For each k in $[0, n]$,

- let $\mathbf{J}_k = \mathbf{J} | \mathbf{S}_{[0,k]}$; and
- $\hat{P}^{k+1} = pg(P_{\mathbf{J}_k}^{k+1}, \mathbf{J}_k) = pg(P_{\mathbf{J}_k}^{k+1}, \mathbf{J})$.

[Note that $pg(P_{\mathbf{J}_k}^{k+1}, \mathbf{J}_k) = pg(P_{\mathbf{J}_k}^{k+1}, \mathbf{J})$ because all the negations in P^{k+1} are over predicates in $\mathbf{S}_{[0,k]}$.]

To demonstrate the result, we will show by induction on $k \in [0, n]$ that

(*) $\qquad\qquad \exists l_k \geq 0$ such that $\forall i \geq 0$, $\mathbf{J}_k = 3\text{-}T_{\hat{P}}^{l_k+i}(\emptyset) \mid \mathbf{S}_{[0,k]} = \mathbf{I}_k$.

Clearly, for $k = n$, (*) demonstrates the result.

The case where $k = 0$ is satisfied by setting $l_0 = 1$, because $\mathbf{J}_0 = 3\text{-}T_{\hat{P}}^{1+i}(\emptyset) | \mathbf{S}_0 = \mathbf{I}_0$ for each $i \geq 0$.

Suppose now that (*) is true for some $k \in [0, n-1]$. Then for each $i \geq 0$, by the choice of $\hat{P}^{k+1}$, the form of P^{k+1}, and (*),

(1) $\qquad\qquad T_{P^{k+1}}^i(\mathbf{I}_k) | \mathbf{S}_{k+1} \subseteq 3\text{-}T_{\hat{P}^{k+1}}^{i+1}(\emptyset) | \mathbf{S}_{k+1} \subseteq T_{P^{k+1}}^{i+1}(\mathbf{I}_k) | \mathbf{S}_{k+1}.$

(Here and later, $\subseteq$ denotes the usual 2-valued containment between instances; this is well defined because all instances considered are total, even if $\mathbf{J}$ is not.) In (1), the $3\text{-}T_{\hat{P}^{k+1}}^{i+1}$ and $T_{P^{k+1}}^{i+1}$ terms may not be equal, because the positive atoms of $\mathbf{I}_k = \mathbf{J}_k$ are available when applying $T_{P^{k+1}}$ the first time but are available only during the second application of $3\text{-}T_{\hat{P}^{k+1}}$. On the other hand, the $T_{P^{k+1}}^i$ and $3\text{-}T_{\hat{P}^{k+1}}^{i+1}$ terms may not be equal (e.g., if there is a rule of the form $A \leftarrow$ in P^{k+1}).

By (1) and finiteness of the input, there is some $m \geq 0$ such that for each $i \geq 0$,

(2) $\qquad\qquad \mathbf{I}_n | \mathbf{S}_{k+1} = T_{P^{k+1}}^{m+i}(\mathbf{I}_k) | \mathbf{S}_{k+1} = 3\text{-}T_{\hat{P}^{k+1}}^{m+i}(\emptyset) | \mathbf{S}_{k+1}.$

This is almost what is needed to complete the induction, except that $\hat{P}^{k+1}$ is used instead of $\hat{P}$. However, observe that for each $i \geq 0$,

(3) $\qquad\qquad 3\text{-}T_{\hat{P}}^i(\emptyset) | \mathbf{S}_{k+1} \subseteq 3\text{-}T_{\hat{P}^{k+1}}^i(\emptyset) | \mathbf{S}_{k+1}$

because $3\text{-}T_{\hat{P}}^i(\emptyset) | \mathbf{S}_{[0,k]} \subseteq \mathbf{J}_k$ for each $i \geq 0$ by the induction hypothesis. Finally observe that for each $i \geq 0$,

(4) $\qquad\qquad 3\text{-}T_{\hat{P}^{k+1}}^i(\emptyset) | \mathbf{S}_{k+1} \subseteq 3\text{-}T_{\hat{P}}^{i+l_k}(\emptyset) | \mathbf{S}_{k+1}$

because $3\text{-}T_{\hat{P}}^{l_k}(\emptyset)|\mathbf{S}_{[0,k]}$ contains all of the positive atoms of $\mathbf{J}_k$.

Then for each $i \geq 0$ we have

$$3\text{-}T_{\hat{P}k+1}^{m+i}(\emptyset)|\mathbf{S}_{k+1} \subseteq 3\text{-}T_{\hat{P}}^{m+i+l_k}(\emptyset)|\mathbf{S}_{k+1} \qquad \text{by (4)}$$

$$\subseteq 3\text{-}T_{\hat{P}k+1}^{m+i+l_k}(\emptyset)|\mathbf{S}_{k+1} \qquad \text{by (3)}$$

$$\subseteq 3\text{-}T_{\hat{P}k+1}^{m+i}(\emptyset)|\mathbf{S}_{k+1} \qquad \text{by (2)}.$$

It follows that

(5) $$3\text{-}T_{\hat{P}k+1}^{m+i}(\emptyset)|\mathbf{S}_{k+1} = 3\text{-}T_{\hat{P}}^{m+i+l_k}(\emptyset)|\mathbf{S}_{k+1}.$$

Set $l_{(k+1)} = l_k + m$. Combining (2) and (5), we have, for each $i \geq 0$,

$$\mathbf{J}|\mathbf{S}_{k+1} = 3\text{-}T_{\hat{P}}^{l_{(k+1)}+i}(\emptyset)|\mathbf{S}_{k+1} = \mathbf{I}_n|\mathbf{S}_{k+1}.$$

Together with the inductive hypothesis, we obtain for each $i \geq 0$ that

$$\mathbf{J}|\mathbf{S}_{[0,k+1]} = 3\text{-}T_{\hat{P}}^{l_{(k+1)}+i}(\emptyset)|\mathbf{S}_{[0,k+1]} = \mathbf{I}_n|\mathbf{S}_{[0,k+1]},$$

which concludes the proof. ∎

As just seen, each stratifiable program is total under the well-founded semantics. However, as indicated by Example 15.3.8(b), a datalog¬ program P may yield a 3-valued model $P^{wf}(\mathbf{I})$ on some inputs. Furthermore, there are programs that are not stratified but whose well-founded models are nonetheless total (see Exercise 15.22). Unfortunately, there can be no effective characterization of those datalog¬ programs whose well-founded semantics is total for all input databases (Exercise 15.23). One can find sufficient syntactic conditions that guarantee the totality of the well-founded semantics, but this quickly becomes a tedious endeavor. It remains open whether, for each datalog¬ program P, one can find another program whose well-founded semantics is total on all inputs and that produces the same positive facts as P.

15.4 Expressive Power

In this section, we examine the expressive power of datalog¬ with the various semantics for negation we have considered. More precisely, we focus on semipositive, stratified, and well-founded semantics. We first look at the relative power of these semantics and show that semipositive programs are weaker than stratified, which in turn are weaker than well founded. Then we look at the connection with languages studied in Chapter 14 that also use recursion and negation. We prove that well-founded semantics can express precisely the *fixpoint* queries.

Finally we look at the impact of *order* on expressive power. An ordered database contains a special binary relation *succ* that provides a successor relation on all constants in the active domain. Thus the constants are ordered by *succ* and in fact can be viewed as integers. The impact of assuming that a database is ordered is examined at length in Chapter 17. Rather surprisingly, we show that in the presence of order, semipositive programs are as powerful as programs with well-founded semantics. In particular, all three semantics are equivalent and express precisely the *fixpoint* queries.

We begin by briefly noting the connection between stratified datalog¬ and relational calculus (and algebra). To see that stratified datalog¬ can express all queries in CALC, recall the nonrecursive datalog¬ (nr-datalog¬) programs introduced in Chapter 5. Clearly, these are stratified datalog¬ programs in which recursion is not allowed. Theorem 5.3.10 states that nr-datalog¬ (with one answer relation) and CALC are equivalent. It follows that stratified datalog¬ can express all of CALC. Because transitive closure of a graph can be expressed in stratified datalog¬ but not in CALC (see Proposition 17.2.3), it follows that stratified datalog¬ is strictly stronger than CALC.

Stratified Datalog Is Weaker than *Fixpoint*

Let us look at the expressive power of stratified datalog¬. Computationally, stratified programs provide recursion and negation and are inflationary. Therefore one might expect that they express the *fixpoint* queries. It is easy to see that all stratified datalog¬ are *fixpoint* queries (Exercise 15.28). In particular, this shows that such programs can be evaluated in polynomial time. Can stratified datalog¬ express all *fixpoint* queries? Unfortunately, no. The intuitive reason is that in stratified datalog¬ there is no recursion through negation, so the number of applications of negation is bounded. In contrast, *fixpoint* queries allow recursion through negation, so there is no bound on the number of applications of negation. This distinction turns out to be crucial. We next outline the main points of the argument, showing that stratified datalog¬ is indeed strictly weaker than *fixpoint*.

The proof uses a game played on so-called game trees. The game is played on a given tree. The nodes of the tree are the possible positions in the game, and the edges are the possible moves from one position to another. Additionally, some leaves of the tree are labeled black. The game is between two players. A round of the game starting at node x begins with Player I making a move from x to one of its children y. Player II then makes a move from y, etc. The game ends when a leaf is reached. Player I wins if Player II picks a black leaf. For a given tree (with labels), Player I has a winning strategy for the game starting at node x if he or she can win starting at x no matter how Player II plays. We are interested in programs determining whether there is such a winning strategy.

The game tree is represented as follows. The set of possible moves is given by a binary relation *move* and the set of black nodes by a unary relation *black*. Consider the query *winning* (not to be confused with the predicate *win* of Example 15.3.1), which asks if Player I has a winning strategy starting at the root of the tree. We will define a set of game trees $\mathcal{G}$ such that

     (i) the query *winning* on the game trees in $\mathcal{G}$ is definable by a *fixpoint* query, and

     (ii) for each stratified program P, there exist game trees $G, G' \in \mathcal{G}$ such that *winning* is true on G and false on G', but P cannot distinguish between G and G'.

Clearly, (ii) shows that the *winning* query on game trees is not definable by a stratified datalog¬ program. The set $\mathcal{G}$ of game trees is defined next. It consists of the $G_{l,k}$ and $G'_{l,k}$ defined by induction as follows:

- $G_{0,k}$ and $G'_{0,k}$ have no moves and just one node, labeled black in $G_{0,k}$ and not labeled in $G'_{0,k}$.
- $G_{i+1,k}$ consists of a copy of $G'_{i,k}$, k disjoint copies of $G_{i,k}$, and a new root d_{i+1}. The moves are the union of the moves in the copies of $G'_{i,k}$ and $G_{i,k}$ together with new moves from the root d_{i+1} to the roots of the copies. The labels remain unchanged.
- $G'_{i+1,k}$ consists of $k + 1$ disjoint copies of $G_{i,k}$ and a new root d'_{i+1} from which moves are possible to the roots of the copies of $G_{i,k}$.

The game trees $G_{4,1}$ and $G'_{4,1}$ are represented in Fig. 15.2. It is easy to see that *winning* is true on the game trees $G_{2i,k}$ and false on game trees $G'_{2i,k}$, $i > 0$ (Exercise 15.30).

We first note that the query *winning* on game trees in $\mathcal{G}$ can be defined by a *fixpoint* query. Consider

$$\varphi(T) = (\exists y)[Move(x, y) \wedge (\forall z)(Move(y, z) \rightarrow Black(z))]$$
$$\vee (\exists y)[Move(x, y) \wedge (\forall z)(Move(y, z) \rightarrow T(z))].$$

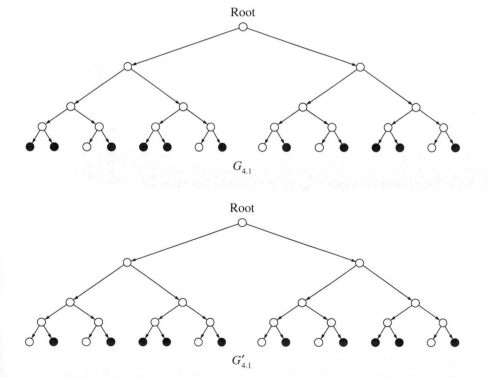

Figure 15.2:   Game trees

It is easy to verify that *winning* is defined by $\mu_T(\varphi(T))(root)$, where *root* is the root of the game tree (Exercise 15.30). Next we note that the *winning* query is not expressible by any stratified datalog$^\neg$ program. To this end, we use the following result, stated without proof.

LEMMA 15.4.1   For each stratified datalog$^\neg$ program P, there exist i, k such that

$$P(G_{i,k})(winning) = P(G'_{i,k})(winning).$$

The proof of Lemma 15.4.1 uses an extension of Ehrefeucht-Fraissé games (the games are described in Chapter 17). The intuition of the lemma is that, to distinguish between $G_{i,k}$ and $G'_{i,k}$ for i and k sufficiently large, one needs to apply more negations than the fixed number allowed by P. Thus no stratified program can distinguish between all the $G_{i,k}$ and $G'_{i,k}$. In particular, it follows that the *fixpoint* query *winning* is not equivalent to *any* stratified datalog$^\neg$ program. Thus we have the following result, settling the relationship between stratified datalog$^\neg$ and the *fixpoint* queries.

THEOREM 15.4.2   The class of queries expressible by stratified datalog$^\neg$ programs is strictly included in the *fixpoint* queries.

REMARK 15.4.3   The game tree technique can also be used to prove that the number of strata in stratified datalog$^\neg$ programs has an impact on expressive power. Specifically, let $Strat_i$ consist of all queries expressible by stratified datalog$^\neg$ programs with i strata. Then it can be shown that for all i, $Strat_i \subset Strat_{i+1}$. In particular, semipositive datalog$^\neg$ is weaker than stratified datalog$^\neg$.

Well-Founded Datalog$^\neg$ Is Equivalent to *Fixpoint*

Next we consider the expressive power of datalog$^\neg$ programs with well-founded semantics. We prove that well-founded semantics can express precisely the *fixpoint* queries. We begin by showing that the well-founded semantics can be computed by a *fixpoint* query. More precisely, we show how to compute the set of false, true, and undefined facts of the answer using a *while*$^+$ program (see Chapter 14 for the definition of *while*$^+$ programs).

THEOREM 15.4.4   Let P be a datalog$^\neg$ program. There exists a *while*$^+$ program w with input relations $edb(P)$, such that

1. w contains, for each relation R in $sch(P)$, three relation variables R^ϵ_{answer}, where $\epsilon \in \{0, 1/2, 1\}$;
2. for each instance $\mathbf{I}$ over $edb(P)$, $u \in w(\mathbf{I})(R^\epsilon_{answer})$ iff $P^{wf}(\mathbf{I})(R(u)) = \epsilon$, for $\epsilon \in \{0, 1/2, 1\}$.

Crux   Let P be a datalog$^\neg$ program. The *while*$^+$ program mimics the alternating fixpoint computation of P^{wf}. Recall that this involves repeated applications of the operator $conseq_P$, resulting in the sequence

$$\mathbf{I}_0 \prec \mathbf{I}_2 \ldots \prec \mathbf{I}_{2i} \prec \mathbf{I}_{2i+2} \prec \ldots \prec \mathbf{I}_{2i+1} \prec \mathbf{I}_{2i-1} \prec \ldots \prec \mathbf{I}_1.$$

Recall that the $\mathbf{I}_i$ are all total instances. Thus 3-valued instances are only required to produce the final answer from $\mathbf{I}_*$ and $\mathbf{I}^*$ at the end of the computation, by one last first-order query.

It is easily verified that *while*$^+$ can simulate one application of *conseq*$_P$ on total instances (Exercise 15.27). The only delicate point is to make sure the computation is inflationary. To this end, the program w will distinguish between results of even and odd iterations of *conseq*$_P$ by having, for each R, an odd and even version R^0_{odd} and R^1_{even}. R^0_{odd} holds at iteration $2i + 1$ the negative facts of R in $\mathbf{I}_{2i+1}$, and R^1_{even} holds at iteration $2i$ the positive facts of R in $\mathbf{I}_{2i}$. Note that both R^0_{odd} and R^1_{even} are increasing throughout the computation.

We elaborate on the simulation of the operator *conseq*$_P$ on a total instance $\mathbf{I}$. The program w will have to distinguish between facts in the input $\mathbf{I}$, used to resolve the negative premises of rules in P, and those inferred by applications of *3-T*$_P$. Therefore for each relation R, the *while*$^+$ program will also maintain a copy $\bar{R}_{even}$ and $\bar{R}_{odd}$ to hold the facts produced by consecutive applications of *3-T*$_P$ in the even and odd cases, respectively. More precisely, the $\bar{R}_{odd}$ hold the positive facts inferred from input $\mathbf{I}_{2i}$ represented in R^1_{even}, and the $\bar{R}_{even}$ hold the positive facts inferred from input $\mathbf{I}_{2i+1}$ represented in R^0_{odd}. It is easy to write a first-order query defining one application of *3-T*$_P$ for the even or odd cases. Because the representations of the input are different in the even and odd cases, different programs must be used in the two cases. This can be iterated in an inflationary manner, because the set of positive facts inferred in consecutive applications of *3-T*$_P$ is always increasing. However, the $\bar{R}_{odd}$ and $\bar{R}_{even}$ have to be initialized to $\emptyset$ at each application of *conseq*$_P$. Because the computation must be inflationary, this cannot be done directly. Instead, timestamping must be used. The initialization of the $\bar{R}_{odd}$ and $\bar{R}_{even}$ is simulated by timestamping each relation with the current content of R^1_{even} and R^0_{odd}, respectively. This is done in a manner similar to the proofs of Chapter 14. ∎

We now exhibit a converse of Theorem 15.4.4, showing that any *fixpoint* query can essentially be simulated by a datalog$^\neg$ program with well-founded semantics. More precisely, the positive portion of the well-founded semantics yields the same facts as the *fixpoint* query. It is open whether this can be achieved with a total datalog$^\neg$ program.

Example 15.4.6 illustrates the proof of this result.

THEOREM 15.4.5 Let q be a *fixpoint* query over input schema $\mathbf{R}$. There exists a datalog$^\neg$ program P such that $edb(P) = \mathbf{R}$, P has an *idb* relation *answer*, and for each instance $\mathbf{I}$ over $\mathbf{R}$, the positive portion of *answer* in $P^{wf}(\mathbf{I})$ coincides with $q(\mathbf{I})$.

Crux We will use the definition of *fixpoint* queries by iterations of positive first-order formulas. Let q be a *fixpoint* query. As discussed in Chapter 14, there exists a CALC formula $\varphi(T)$, positive in T, such that q is defined by $\mu_T(\varphi(T))(u)$, where u is a vector of variables and constants. Consider the CALC formula $\varphi(T)$. As noted earlier in this section, there is an nr-datalog$^\neg$ program P_φ with one answer relation R' such that P_φ is equivalent to $\varphi(T)$. Because $\varphi(T)$ is positive in T, along any path in the syntax tree of $\varphi(T)$ ending with atom T there is an even number of negations. This is also true of paths in G_{P_φ}.

Consider the precedence graph G_{P_φ} of P_φ. Clearly, one can construct P_φ such that each *idb* relation except T is used in the definition of exactly one other *idb* relation, and all idb relations are used eventually in the definition of the answer R'. In other words, for each *idb* relation R other than T, there is a unique path in G_{P_φ} from R to R'. Consider the paths from T to some *idb* relation R in P_φ. Without loss of generality, we can assume that all paths have the same number of negations (otherwise, because all paths to T have an even number of negations, additional *idb* relations can be introduced to pad the paths with fewer negations, using rules that perform redundant double negations). Let the *rank* of an *idb* relation R in P_φ be the number of negations on each path leading from T to R in G_{P_φ}. Now let P be the datalog$^\neg$ program obtained from P_φ as follows:

- replace the answer relation R' by T;
- add one rule *answer*$(v) \leftarrow T(u)$, where v is the vector of distinct variables occurring in u, in order of occurrence.

The purpose of replacing R' by T is to cause program P_φ to iterate, yielding $\mu_T(\varphi(T))$. The last rule is added to perform the final selection and projection needed to obtain the answer $\mu_T(\varphi(T))(u)$. Note that, in some sense, P is almost stratified, except for the fact that the result T is fed back into the program.

Consider the alternating fixpoint sequence $\{\mathbf{I}_i\}_{i \geq 0}$ in the computation of $P^{wf}(\mathbf{I})$. Suppose R' has rank q in P_φ, and let R be an *idb* relation of P_φ whose rank in P_φ is $r \leq q$. Intuitively, there is a close correspondence between the sequence $\{\mathbf{I}_i\}_{i \geq 0}$ and the iterations of φ, along the following lines: Each application of *conseq*$_P$ propagates the correct result from relations of rank r in P_φ to relations of rank $r + 1$. There is one minor glitch, however: In the fixpoint computation, the *edb* relations are given, and even at the first iteration, their negation is taken to be their complement; in the alternating fixpoint computation, all negative literals, including those involving *edb* relations, are initially taken to be true. This results in a mismatch. To fix the problem, consider a variation of the alternating fixpoint computation of $P^{wf}(\mathbf{I})$ defined as follows:

$$\bar{\mathbf{I}}_0 = \mathbf{I} \cup \neg.\{R(a_1, \ldots, a_n) \mid R \in idb(P), R(a_1, \ldots, a_n) \in \mathbf{B}(P, \mathbf{I})\}$$
$$\bar{\mathbf{I}}_{i+1} = conseq_P(\bar{\mathbf{I}}_i).$$

Clearly, $\perp \prec \bar{\mathbf{I}}_0 \prec P^{wf}(\mathbf{I})$. Then, by Proposition 15.3.10, $\bar{\mathbf{I}}_*^* = P^{wf}(\mathbf{I})$.

Now the following can be verified by induction for each *idb* relation R of rank r:

For each i, $(\bar{\mathbf{I}}_{iq+r})^1$ contains exactly the facts of R true in $P_\varphi(\varphi^i(\emptyset))$.

Intuitively, this is so because each application of *conseq*$_P$ propagates the correct result across one application of negation to an *idb* predicate. Because R' has rank q, it takes q applications to simulate a complete application of P_φ. In particular, it follows that for each i, $(\bar{\mathbf{I}}_{iq})^1$ contains in T the facts true in $\varphi^i(\emptyset)$.

Thus $(\bar{\mathbf{I}}_*)^1$ contains in T the facts true in $\mu_T(\varphi(T))$. Finally *answer* is obtained by a

simple selection and projection from T using the last rule in P and yields $\mu_T(\varphi(T))(u)$.
∎

In the preceding theorem, the *positive* portion of *answer* for $P^{wf}(\mathbf{I})$ coincides with $q(\mathbf{I})$. However, $P^{wf}(\mathbf{I})$ is not guaranteed to be total (i.e., it may contain unknown facts). It remains open whether a program can be constructed that always provides a total answer and whose positive portion coincides with the answer of q.

Recall from Chapter 14 that datalog⁻ with inflationary semantics also expresses precisely the *fixpoint* queries. Thus we have converged again, this time by the deductive database path, to the *fixpoint* queries. This bears witness, once more, to the naturalness of this class. In particular, the well-founded and inflationary semantics, although very different, have the same expressive power (modulo the difference between 3-valued and 2-valued models).

EXAMPLE 15.4.6 Consider the *fixpoint* query $\mu_{good}(\varphi(good))(x)$, where

$$\varphi(good) = \forall y(G(y, x) \rightarrow good(y)).$$

Recall that this query, also encountered in Chapter 14, computes the "good" nodes of the graph G (i.e., those that cannot be reached from a cycle). The nr-datalog⁻ program P_φ corresponding to one application of $\varphi(good)$ is the one exhibited in Example 15.3.8(c):

$$bad(x) \leftarrow G(y, x), \neg good(y)$$
$$R'(x) \;\;\leftarrow \neg bad(x)$$

Note that *bad* is negative in P_φ and has rank one, and *good* is positive. The answer R' has rank two. The program P is as follows:

$$bad(x) \qquad \leftarrow G(y, x), \neg good(y)$$
$$good(x) \quad \leftarrow \neg bad(x)$$
$$answer(x) \leftarrow good(x)$$

Consider the input graph

$$G = \{\langle b, c\rangle, \langle c, b\rangle, \langle c, d\rangle, \langle a, d\rangle, \langle a, e\rangle\}.$$

The consecutive values of $\varphi^i(\emptyset)$ are

$$\varphi(\emptyset) \;\;= \{a\},$$
$$\varphi^2(\emptyset) = \{a, e\},$$
$$\varphi^3(\emptyset) = \{a, e\}.$$

Thus $\mu_{good}(\varphi(good))(x)$ yields the answer $\{a, e\}$. Consider now the alternating fixpoint sequence in the computation of P^{wf} on the same input (only the positive facts of *bad* and *good* are listed, because G does not change and *answer* = *good*).

	bad	*good*
$\bar{\mathbf{I}}_0$	$\emptyset$	$\emptyset$
$\bar{\mathbf{I}}_1$	$\{b, c, d, e\}$	$\{a, b, c, d, e\}$
$\bar{\mathbf{I}}_2$	$\emptyset$	$\{a\}$
$\bar{\mathbf{I}}_3$	$\{b, c, d\}$	$\{a, b, c, d, e\}$
$\bar{\mathbf{I}}_4$	$\emptyset$	$\{a, e\}$
$\bar{\mathbf{I}}_5$	$\{b, c, d\}$	$\{a, b, c, d, e\}$
$\bar{\mathbf{I}}_6$	$\emptyset$	$\{a, e\}$

Thus

$$\varphi(\emptyset) \; = (\bar{\mathbf{I}}_2)^1(good),$$
$$\varphi^2(\emptyset) = (\bar{\mathbf{I}}_4)^1(good)$$

and

$$(\bar{\mathbf{I}}_4)^1(answer) = \mu_{good}(\varphi(good))(x).$$

The relative expressive power of the various languages discussed in this chapter is summarized in Fig. 15.3. The arrows indicate strict inclusion. For a view of these languages in a larger context, see also Figs. 18.4 and 18.5 at the end of Part E.

The Impact of Order

Finally we look at the impact of order on the expressive power of the various datalog¬ semantics. As we will discuss at length in Chapter 17, the assumption that databases are ordered can have a dramatic impact on the expressive power of languages like *fixpoint* or *while*. The datalog¬ languages are no exception. The effect of order is spectacular. With this assumption, it turns out that semipositive datalog¬ is (almost) as powerful as stratified

well-founded semantics datalog¬ $\equiv$ fixpoint semantics datalog¬

⇑

stratified datalog¬

⇑

semipositive datalog¬

⇑

datalog

Figure 15.3:   Relative expressive power of datalog$^{(\neg)}$ languages

datalog¬ and datalog¬ with well-founded semantics. The "almost" comes from a technicality concerning the order: We also need to assume that the minimum and maximum constants are explicitly given. Surprisingly, these constants, which can be computed with a first order query if *succ* is given, cannot be computed with semipositive programs (see Exercise 15.29).

The next lemma states that semipositive programs express the *fixpoint* queries on ordered databases with *min* and *max* (i.e., databases with a predicate *succ* providing a successor relation among all constants, and unary relations *min* and *max* containing the smallest and the largest constant).

LEMMA 15.4.7 The semipositive datalog¬ programs express precisely the *fixpoint* queries on ordered databases with *min* and *max*.

Crux Let q be a *fixpoint* query over database schema **R**. Because q is a *fixpoint* query, there is a first-order formula $\varphi(T)$, positive in T, such that q is defined by $\mu_T(\varphi(T))(u)$, where u is a vector of variables and constants. Because T is positive in $\varphi(T)$, we can assume that $\varphi(T)$ is in prenex normal form $Q_1 x_1 Q_2 x_2 \ldots Q_k x_k(\psi)$, where ψ is a quantifier free formula in disjunctive normal form and T is not negated in ψ. We show by induction on k that there exists a semipositive datalog¬ program P_φ with an *idb* relation *answer*$_\varphi$ defining $\mu_T(\varphi(T))$ [the last selection and projection needed to obtain the final answer $\mu_T(\varphi(T))(u)$ pose no problem]. Suppose $k = 0$ (i.e., $\varphi = \psi$). Then P_φ is the nr-datalog¬ program corresponding to ψ, where the answer relation is T. Because ψ is quantifier free and T is not negated in ψ, P_φ is clearly semipositive. Next suppose the statement is true for some $k \geq 0$, and let $\varphi(T)$ have quantifier depth $k + 1$. There are two cases:

(i) $\varphi = \exists x \psi(x, v)$, where ψ has quantifier depth k. Then P_φ contains the rules of P_ψ, where T is replaced in heads of rules by a new predicate T' and one additional rule

$$T(v) \leftarrow T'(x, v).$$

(ii) $\varphi = \forall x \psi(x, v)$, where ψ has quantifier depth k. Then P_φ consists, again, of P_ψ, where T is replaced in heads of rules by a new predicate T', with the following rules added:

$$R'(x, v) \leftarrow T'(x, v), min(x)$$
$$R'(x', v) \leftarrow R'(x, v), succ(x, x'), T'(x', v)$$
$$T(v) \qquad \leftarrow R'(x, v), max(x),$$

where R' is a new auxiliary predicate. Thus the program steps through all x's using the successor relation *succ*, starting from the minimum constant. If the maximum constant is reached, then $T'(x, v)$ is satisfied for all x, and $T(v)$ is inferred.

This completes the induction. ∎

As we shall see in Chapter 17, *fixpoint* expresses on ordered databases exactly the queries computable in time polynomial in the size of the database (i.e., QPTIME). Thus we obtain the following result. In comparing well-founded semantics with the others, we take the positive portion of the well-founded semantics as the answer.

THEOREM 15.4.8   Stratified datalog⁻ and datalog⁻ with well-founded semantics are equivalent on ordered databases and express exactly QPTIME. They are also equivalent to semipositive datalog⁻ on ordered databases with *min* and *max* and express exactly QPTIME.

15.5   Negation as Failure in Brief

In our presentation of datalog in Chapter 12, we saw that the minimal model and least fixpoint semantics have an elegant proof-theoretic counterpart based on SLD resolution. One might naturally wonder if such a counterpart exists in the case of datalog⁻. The answer is yes and no. Such a proof-theoretic approach has indeed been proposed and is called negation as failure. This was originally developed for logic programming and predates stratified and well-founded semantics. Unfortunately, the approach has two major drawbacks. The first is that it results in a proof-building procedure that does not always terminate. The second is that it is not the exact counterpart of any other existing semantics. The semantics that has been proposed as a possible match is "Clark's completion," but the match is not perfect and Clark's completion has its own problems. We provide here only a brief and informal presentation of negation as failure and the related Clark's completion.

The idea behind negation as failure is simple. We would like to infer a negative fact $\neg A$ if A cannot be proven by SLD resolution. Thus $\neg A$ would then be proven by the failure to prove A. Unfortunately, this is generally noneffective because SLD derivations may be arbitrarily long, and so one cannot check in finite time[2] that there is no proof of A by SLD resolution. Instead we have to use a weaker notion of negation by failure, which can be checked. This is done as follows. A fact $\neg A$ is proven if all SLD derivations starting from the goal $\leftarrow A$ are finite and none produces an SLD refutation for $\leftarrow A$. In other words, *A finitely fails*. This procedure applies to ground atoms A only. It gives rise to a proof procedure called SLDNF resolution. Briefly, SLDNF resolution extends SLD resolution as follows. Refutations of positive facts proceed as for SLD resolution. Whenever a negative ground goal $\leftarrow \neg A$ has to be proven, SLD resolution is applied to $\leftarrow A$, and $\neg A$ is proven if the SLD resolution finitely fails for $\leftarrow A$. The idea of SLDNF seems appealing as the proof-theoretic version of the closed world assumption. However, as illustrated next, it quickly leads to significant problems.

EXAMPLE 15.5.1   Consider the usual program P_{TC} for transitive closure of a graph:

$$T(x, y) \leftarrow G(x, y)$$
$$T(x, y) \leftarrow G(x, z), T(z, y)$$

---

[2] Because databases are finite, one can develop mechanisms to bound the expansion. We ignore this aspect here.

Consider the instance **I** where G has edges $\{\langle a, b \rangle, \langle b, a \rangle, \langle c, a \rangle\}$. Clearly, $\{\langle a, c \rangle\}$ is not in the transitive closure of G, and so not in T, by the usual datalog semantics. Suppose we wish to prove the fact $\neg T(a, c)$, using negation as failure. We have to show that SLD resolution finitely fails on $T(a, c)$, with the preceding program and input. Unfortunately, SLD resolution can enter a negative loop when applied to $\leftarrow T(a, c)$. One obtains the following SLD derivation:

1. $\leftarrow T(a, c)$;
2. $\leftarrow G(a, z), T(z, c)$, using the second rule;
3. $\leftarrow T(b, c)$, using the fact $G(a, b)$;
4. $\leftarrow G(b, z), T(z, c)$ using the second rule;
5. $\leftarrow T(a, c)$ using the fact $G(b, a)$.

Note that the last goal is the same as the first, so this can be extended to an infinite derivation. It follows that SLD resolution does not finitely fail on $\leftarrow T(a, c)$, so SLDNF does not yield a proof of $\neg T(a, c)$. Moreover, it has been shown that this does not depend on the particular program used to define transitive closure. In other words, there is *no* datalog$^{\neg}$ program that under SLDNF can prove the positive and negative facts true of the transitive closure of a graph.

The preceding example shows that SLDNF can behave counterintuitively, even in some simple cases. The behavior is also incompatible with all the semantics for negation that we have discussed so far. Thus one cannot hope for a match between SLDNF and these semantics.

Instead a semantics called Clark's completion has been proposed as a candidate match for negation as failure. It works as follows. For a datalog$^{\neg}$ program P, the *completion of P, comp(P)*, is constructed as follows. For each *idb* predicate R, each rule

$$\rho : R(u) \leftarrow L_1(v_1), \dots, L_n(v_n)$$

defining R is rewritten so there is a uniform set of distinct variables in the rule head and so all free variables in the body are existentially quantified:

$$\rho' : R(u') \leftarrow \exists v'(x_1 = t_1 \wedge \cdots \wedge x_k = t_k \wedge L_1(v_1) \wedge \cdots \wedge L_n(v_n)).$$

(If the head of ρ has distinct variables for all coordinates, then the equality atoms can be avoided. If repeated variables or constants occur, then equality must be used.) Next, if the rewritten rules for R are $\rho'_1, \dots, \rho'_l$, the *completion* of R is formed by

$$\forall u'(R(u') \leftrightarrow body(\rho'_1) \vee \cdots \vee body(\rho'_l)).$$

Intuitively, this states that ground atom $R(w)$ is true iff it is supported by one of the rules defining R. Finally the completion of P is the set of completions of all *idb* predicates of P, along with the axioms of equality, if needed.

The semantics of P is now defined by the following: A is true iff it is a logical consequence of $comp(P)$. A first problem now is that $comp(P)$ is not always consistent; in fact, its consistency is undecidable. What is the connection between SLDNF and Clark's completion? Because SLDNF is consistent (it clearly cannot prove A and $\neg A$) and $comp(P)$ is not so always, SLDNF is not always complete with respect to $comp(P)$. For consistent $comp(P)$, it can be shown that SLDNF resolution is sound. However, additional conditions must be imposed on the datalog$^\neg$ programs for SLDNF resolution to be complete.

Consider again the transitive closure program P_{TC} and input instance $\mathbf{I}$ of Example 15.5.1. Then the completion of T is equivalent to

$$T(x, y) \leftrightarrow G(x, y) \vee \exists z(G(x, z) \wedge T(z, y)).$$

Note that neither $T(a, c)$ nor $\neg T(a, c)$ are consequences of $comp(P_{TC,\mathbf{I}})$.

In summary, negation as failure does not appear to provide a convincing proof-theoretic counterpart to the semantics we have considered. The search for more successful proof-theoretic approaches is an active research area. Other proposals are described briefly in the Bibliographic Notes.

Bibliographic Notes

The notion of a stratified program is extremely natural. Not surprisingly, it was proposed independently by quite a few investigators [CH85, ABW88, Lif88, VanG86]. The independence of the semantics from a particular stratification (Theorem 15.2.10) was shown in [ABW88].

Research on well-founded semantics, and the related notion of a 3-stable model, has its roots in investigations of stable and default model semantics. Although formulated somewhat differently, the notion of a stable/default model is equivalent to that of a total 3-stable model [Prz90]. Stable model semantics was introduced in [GL88], and default model semantics was introduced in [BF87, BF88]. Stable semantics is based on Moore's autoepistemic logic [Moo85], and default semantics is based on Reiter's default logic [Rei80]. The equivalence between autoepistemic and default logic in the general case has been shown in [Kon88]. The equivalence between stable model semantics and default model semantics was shown in [BF88].

Several equivalent definitions of the well-founded semantics have been proposed. The definition used in this chapter comes from [Prz90]. The alternating fixpoint computation we described is essentially the same as in [VanG89]. Alternative procedures for computing the well-founded semantics are exhibited in [BF88, Prz89]. Historically, the first definition of well-founded semantics was proposed in [VanGRS88, VanGRS91]. This is described in Exercise 15.24.

The fact that well-founded and stratified semantics agree on stratifiable datalog$^\neg$ programs (Theorem 15.3.11) was shown in [VanGRS88].

Both the stratified and well-founded semantics were originally introduced for general logic programming, as well as the more restricted case of datalog. In the context of logic programming, both semantics have expressive power equivalent to the arithmetic hierarchy [AW88] and are thus noneffective.

The result that datalog⁻ with well-founded semantics expresses exactly the *fixpoint* queries is shown in [VanG89]. The fact that stratified datalog⁻ is weaker than *fixpoint*, and therefore weaker than well-founded semantics, was shown in [Kol91], making use of earlier results from [Dal87] and [CH82]. In particular, Lemma 15.4.1 is based on Lemma 3.9 in [CH82]. The result that semipositive datalog⁻ expresses QPTIME on ordered databases with *min* and *max* is due to [Pap85].

The investigation of negation as failure was initiated in [Cla78], in connection with general logic programming. In particular, SLDNF resolution as well as Clark's completion are introduced there. The fact that there is no datalog⁻ program for which the positive and negative facts about the transitive closure of the graph can be proven by SLDNF resolution was shown in [Kun88]. Other work related to Clark's completion can be found in [She88, Llo87, Fit85, Kun87].

Several variations of SLDNF resolutions have been proposed. SLS resolution is introduced in [Prz88] to deal with stratified programs. An exact match is achieved between stratified semantics and the proof procedure provided by SLS resolution. Although SLS resolution is effective in the context of (finite) databases, it is not so when applied to general logic programs, with function symbols. To deal with this shortcoming, several restrictions of SLS resolution have been proposed that are effective in the general framework [KT88, SI88].

Several proof-theoretic approaches corresponding to the well-founded semantics have been proposed. SLS resolution is extended from stratified to arbitrary datalog⁻ programs in [Prz88], under well-founded semantics. Independently, another extension of SLS resolution called global SLS resolution is proposed in [Ros89], with similar results. These proposals yield noneffective resolution procedures. An effective procedure is described in [BL90].

In [SZ90], an interesting connection between nondeterminism and stable models of a program (i.e., total 3-stable models; see also Exercise 15.20) is pointed out. Essentially, it is shown that the stable models of a datalog⁻ program can be viewed as the result of a natural nondeterministic choice. This uses the choice construct introduced earlier in [KN88]. Another use of nondeterminism is exhibited in [PY92], where an extension of well-founded semantics is provided, which involves the nondeterministic choice of a fixpoint of a datalog⁻ program. This is called *tie-breaking* semantics. A discussion of nondeterminism in deductive databases is provided in [GPSZ91].

Another semantics in the spirit of well-founded is the valid model semantics introduced in [BRSS92]. It is less conservative than well-founded semantics, in the sense that all facts that are positive in well-founded semantics are also positive in the valid model semantics, but the latter generally yields more positive facts than well-founded semantics.

There are a few prototypes (but no commercial system) implementing stratified datalog⁻. The language LDL [NT89, BNR+87b, NK88] implements, besides the stratified semantics for datalog⁻, an extension to complex objects (see also Chapter 20). The implementation uses heuristics based on the magic set technique described in Chapter 13. The language NAIL! (Not Yet Another Implementation of Logic!), developed at Stanford, is another implementation of the stratified semantics, allowing function symbols and a set construct. The implementation of NAIL! [MUG86, Mor88] uses a battery of evaluation techniques, including magic sets. The language EKS [VBKL89], developed at

the negated complement $\neg.\overline{P}(\mathbf{N})$ is an overestimate of the negative facts. Using this overestimate, one can infer an overestimate of the positive facts, $P(\neg.\overline{P}(\mathbf{N}))$. Therefore $\neg.\overline{P}(\neg.\overline{P}(\mathbf{N}))$ is now a new underestimate of the negative facts containing the previous underestimate. So $\{\mathbf{N}_i\}_{i \geq 0}$ is an increasing sequence of underestimates of the negative facts, which converges to the negative facts in the well-founded model. Formally prove the following:

(a) The sequence $\{\mathbf{N}_i\}_{i \geq 0}$ is increasing.

(b) Let $\mathbf{N}$ be the limit of the sequence $\{\mathbf{N}_i\}_{i \geq 0}$ and $\mathbf{K} = \mathbf{N} \cup P(\mathbf{N})$. Then $\mathbf{K} = P^{wf}$.

(c) Explain the connection between the sequence $\{\mathbf{N}_i\}_{i \geq 0}$ and the sets of negative facts in the sequence $\{\mathbf{I}_i\}_{i \geq 0}$ defined in the alternating fixpoint computation of P^{wf} in the text.

(d) Suppose the definition of the sequence $\{\mathbf{N}_i\}_{i \geq 0}$ is modified such that $\mathbf{N}_0 = \neg.\mathbf{B}(P)$ (i.e., all facts are negative at the start). Show that for each $i \geq 0$, $\mathbf{N}_i = \neg.(\mathbf{I}_{2i})^0$.

Exercise 15.26   Let P be a datalog$^\neg$ program. Let T_P be the immediate consequence operator on sets of ground literals, defined in Exercise 15.24, and let $\bar{T}_P$ be defined by $\bar{T}_P(\mathbf{I}) = \mathbf{I} \cup T_P(\mathbf{I})$. Given a set $\mathbf{I}$ of ground literals, let $P(\mathbf{I})$ denote the limit of the increasing sequence $\{\bar{T}_P^i(\mathbf{I})\}_{i>0}$. A set $\mathbf{I}^-$ of negative ground literals is *consistent with respect to P* if $P(\mathbf{I}^-)$ is consistent. $\mathbf{I}^-$ is *maximally consistent with respect to P* if it is maximal among the sets of negative literals consistent with P. Investigate the connection between maximal consistency, 3-stable models, and well-founded semantics:

(a) Is $\neg.\mathbf{I}^0$ maximally consistent for every 3-stable model $\mathbf{I}$ of P?

(b) Is $P(\mathbf{I}^-)$ a 3-stable model of P for every $\mathbf{I}^-$ that is maximally consistent with respect to P?

(c) Is $\neg.(P^{wf})^0$ the intersection of all sets $\mathbf{I}^-$ that are maximally consistent with respect to P?

Exercise 15.27   Refer to the proof of Lemma 15.4.4.

(a) Outline a proof that $conseq_P$ can be simulated by a $while^+$ program.

(b) Provide a full description of the timestamping technique outlined in the proof of Lemma 15.4.4.

Exercise 15.28   Show that every query definable by stratified datalog$^\neg$ is a *fixpoint* query.

Exercise 15.29   Consider an ordered database (i.e., with binary relation $succ$ providing a successor relation on the constants). Prove that the minimum and maximum constants cannot be computed using a semipositive program.

★ **Exercise 15.30**   Consider the game trees and *winning* query described in Section 15.4.

(a) Show that *winning* is true on the game trees $G_{2i,k}$ and false on the game trees $G'_{2i,k}$, for $i > 0$.

(b) Prove that the *winning* query on game trees is defined by the *fixpoint* query exhibited in Section 15.4.

E Expressiveness and Complexity

Various query languages were presented in Parts B and D. Simple languages like conjunctive queries were successively augmented with various constructs such as union, negation, and recursion. The primary motivation for defining increasingly powerful languages was the need to express useful queries not captured by the simpler languages. In the presentation, the process was primarily example driven. The following chapters present a more advanced and global perspective on query languages. In addition to their ability to express specific queries, we consider more broadly the capability of languages to express queries of a given complexity. This leads to establishing formal connections between languages and complexity classes of queries. This approach lies on the border between databases, complexity theory, and logic. It is closely related to *descriptive complexity*, which attempts to characterize complexity classes in terms of logic.

The basic framework for the formal development is presented in Chapter 16, in which we discuss the notion of a query and produce a formal definition. It turns out that it is relatively easy to define languages expressing *all* queries. Such languages are called *complete*. However, the real challenge for the language designer is not simply to define increasingly powerful languages. Instead an important aspect of language design is to achieve a good balance between expressiveness and the complexity of evaluating queries. The ideal language would allow expression of most useful queries while guaranteeing that *all* queries expressible in the language can be evaluated with reasonable complexity. To formalize this, we raise the following basic question: How does one evaluate a query language with respect to expressiveness and complexity? In an attempt to answer this question, we discuss the issue of sizing up languages in Chapter 16.

Chapter 17 considers some of the classes of queries discussed in Part B from the viewpoint of expressiveness and complexity. The focus is on the relational calculus of Chapter 5 and on its extensions *fixpoint* and *while* defined in Chapter 14. We show the connection of these languages to complexity classes. Several techniques for showing the nonexpressibility of queries are also presented, including *games* and 0-1 laws.

Chapter 17 also explores the intriguing theoretical implications of one of the basic assumptions of the pure relational model—namely, that the underlying domain **dom** consists of uninterpreted, unordered elements. This assumption can be viewed as a metaphor for the data independence principle, because it implies using only logical properties of data as opposed to the underlying implementation (which would provide additional information, such as an order).

Chapter 18 presents highly expressive (and complex) languages, all the way up to complete languages. In particular, we discuss constructs for value invention, which are similar to the object creation mechanisms encountered in object languages (see Chapter 21).

For easy reference, the expressiveness and complexity of relational query languages are summarized at the end of Chapter 18.

16 Sizing Up Languages

Alice: *Do you ever worry about how hard it is to answer queries?*
Riccardo: *Sure — my laptop can only do conjunctive queries.*
Sergio: *I can do the* while *queries on my Sun.*
Vittorio: *I don't worry about it — I have a Cray in my office.*

This chapter lays the groundwork for the study of the complexity and expressiveness of query languages. First the notion of query is carefully reconsidered and formally defined. Then, the complexity of individual queries is considered. Finally definitions that allow comparison of query languages and complexity classes are developed.

16.1   Queries

The goal of Part E is to develop a general understanding of query languages and their capabilities. The first step is to formulate a precise definition of what constitutes a query. The focus is on a fairly high level of abstraction and thus on the mappings expressible by queries rather than on the syntax used to specify them. Thus, unlike Part B, in this part we use the term *query* primarily to refer to mappings from instances to instances rather than to syntactic objects. Although there are several correct definitions for the set of permissible queries, the one presented here is based on three fundamental assumptions: *well-typedness*, *computability*, and *genericity*.

The first assumption involves the schemas of the input and the answer to a query. A query is over a particular database schema, say **R**. It takes as input an instance over **R** and returns as answer a relation over some schema S. In principle, it is conceivable that the schema of the result may be data dependent. However, to simplify, it is assumed here (as in most query languages) that the schema of the result is fixed for a given query. This assumption is referred to as *well-typedness*. Thus, for us, a query is a partial mapping from $inst(\mathbf{R})$ to $inst(S)$ for *fixed* **R** and S. By allowing partially defined mappings, we account for queries expressed by programs that may not always terminate.

Because we are only interested in effective queries, we also make the natural assumption that query mappings are *computable*. Query computability is defined using classical models of computation, such as Turing machines (TM). The basic idea is that the query must be "implementable" by a TM. Thus there must exist a TM that, given as input a natural encoding of a database instance on the tape, produces an encoding of the output. The formalization of these notions requires some care and is done next.

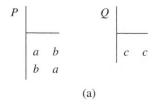

(a)

P[0#1][1#0]Q[10#10]

(b)

Figure 16.1: An instance **I** and its TM encoding with respect to $\alpha = abc$

The first question in developing the formalization is, How can input and output in-stances be represented on a TM tape that has finite alphabet when the underlying domain **dom** is infinite? We resolve this by using standard encodings for **dom**. As we shall see later on, although this permits us to use conventional complexity theory in our study of query language expressiveness, it also takes us a bit outside of the pure relational model.

We focus on encodings of both **dom** and of subsets of **dom**, and we use the symbols 0 and 1. Let $\mathbf{d} \subseteq \mathbf{dom}$ and let $\alpha = \{d_0, d_1, \ldots, d_i, \ldots\}$ be an enumeration of **d**. The *encoding* of **d** relative to α is the function enc_α, which maps d_i to the binary representation of i (with no leading zeros) for each $d_i \in \mathbf{d}$. Note that $|enc_\alpha(d_i)| \leq \lceil \log i \rceil$ for each i.

We can now describe the encoding of instances. Suppose that a set $\mathbf{d} \subseteq \mathbf{dom}$, enu-meration α for **d**, source schema $\mathbf{R} = \{R_1, \ldots, R_m\}$, and target schema S are given. The encoding of instances of **R** uses the alphabet $\{0, 1, [,], \#\} \cup \mathbf{R} \cup \{S\}$. An instance **I** over **R** with $adom(\mathbf{I}) \subseteq \mathbf{d}$ is encoded relative to α as follows:

1. $enc_\alpha(\langle a_1, \ldots, a_k \rangle)$ is $[enc_\alpha(a_1)\# \ldots \#enc_\alpha(a_k)]$.
2. $enc_\alpha(\mathbf{I}(R))$, for $R \in \mathbf{R}$, is $R\ enc_\alpha(t_1) \ldots enc_\alpha(t_l)$, where $t_1, \ldots, t_l$ are the tuples in $\mathbf{I}(R)$ in the lexicographic order induced by the enumeration α.
3. $enc_\alpha(\mathbf{I}) = enc_\alpha(\mathbf{I}(R_1)) \ldots enc_\alpha(\mathbf{I}(R_m))$.

EXAMPLE 16.1.1 Let $\mathbf{R} = \{P, Q\}$, **I** be the instance over **R** in Fig. 16.1(a), and let $\alpha = abc$. Then $enc_\alpha(\mathbf{I})$ is shown in Fig. 16.1(b).

Let α be a fixed enumeration of **dom**. In this case the encoding enc_α described earlier is one-to-one on instances and thus has an inverse enc_α^{-1} when considered as a mapping on instances. We are now ready to formalize the notion of computability *relative to an encoding* of **dom**.

DEFINITION 16.1.2 Let α be an enumeration of **dom**. A mapping q from $inst(\mathbf{R})$ to $inst(S)$ is *computable* relative to α if there exists a TM M such that for each instance **I** over **R**

(a) if $q(\mathbf{I})$ is undefined, then M does not terminate on input $enc_\alpha(\mathbf{I})$, and

(b) if $q(\mathbf{I})$ is defined, M halts on input $enc_\alpha(\mathbf{I})$ with output $enc_\alpha(q(\mathbf{I}))$ on the tape.

As will be seen shortly, the third assumption about queries (namely, genericity) will permit us to reformulate the preceding definition to be independent of the encoding of **dom** used. Before introducing that notion, we consider more carefully the representation of database instances on TM tapes. In some sense, TM encodings on the tape are similar to the internal representation of the database on some physical storage. In both cases, the representation contains more information than the database itself. In the case of the TM representation, the extra information consists primarily of the enumeration α of constants necessary to define enc_α. In the pure relational model, this kind of information is not part of the database. Instead, the database is an abstraction of its internal (or TM) representation. This additional information can be viewed as noise associated with the internal representation and thus should not have any visible impact for the user at the conceptual level. This is captured by the *data independence* principle in databases, which postulates that a database provides an abstract interface that hides the internal representation of data.

We can now state the intuition behind the third and last requirement of queries, which formalizes the data independence principle. Although computations performed on the internal representation may take advantage of all information provided at this level, it is explicitly prohibited, in the definition of a query, that the result depend on such information. (In some cases this restriction may be relaxed; see Exercise 16.4.)

For example, consider a database that consists of a binary relation specifying the edges of a directed graph. Consider a query that returns as answer a subset of the vertexes in the graph. One can imagine queries that extract (1) all vertexes with positive in-degree, or (2) all vertexes belonging to some cycle, or (3) the first vertex of the graph as presented in the TM tape representation. Speaking intuitively, (1) and (2) are independent of the internal representation used, whereas (3) depends on it. Queries such as (3) will be excluded from the class of queries.

The property that a query depends only on information provided by the input instance is called genericity and is formalized next. The idea is that the constants in the database have no properties other than the relationships with each other specified by the database. (In particular, their internal representation is irrelevant.) Thus the database is essentially unchanged if all constants are consistently renamed. Of course, a query can always explicitly name a finite set of constants, which can then be treated differently from other constants. (The set of such constants is the set C in Definition 16.1.3.)

A *permutation* of **dom** is a one-to-one, onto mapping from **dom** to **dom**. As done before, each mapping ρ over **dom** is extended to tuples and database instances in the obvious way.

DEFINITION 16.1.3 Let $\mathbf{R}$ and S be database schemas, and let C be a finite set of constants. A mapping q from $inst(\mathbf{R})$ to $inst(S)$ is $C = generic$ iff for each $\mathbf{I}$ over $\mathbf{R}$ and each permutation ρ of **dom** that is the identity on C, $\rho(q(\mathbf{I})) = q(\rho(\mathbf{I}))$. When C is empty, we simply say that the query is *generic*.

The previous definition is best visualized using the following commuting diagram:

$$
\begin{array}{ccc}
\mathbf{I} & \overset{q}{\rightarrow} & q(\mathbf{I}) \\
\downarrow\rho & & \downarrow\rho \\
\rho(\mathbf{I}) & \overset{q}{\rightarrow} & \rho(q(\mathbf{I})) = q(\rho(\mathbf{I})).
\end{array}
$$

In other words, a query is (C) = generic if it commutes with permutations (that leave C fixed).

Genericity states that the query is insensitive to renaming of the constants in the database (using the permutation ρ). It uses only the relationships among constants provided by the database and is independent of any other information about the constants. The set C specifies the exceptional constants named explicitly in the query. These cannot be renamed without changing the effect of the query.

Permutations ρ for which $\rho(\mathbf{I}) = \mathbf{I}$ are of special interest. Such ρ are called *automorphisms* for $\mathbf{I}$. If ρ is an automorphism for $\mathbf{I}$ and $\rho(a) = b$, this says intuitively that a and b cannot be distinguished using the structure of $\mathbf{I}$. Let q be a generic query, $\mathbf{I}$ an instance, and ρ an automorphism for $\mathbf{I}$. Then, by genericity,

$$
\rho(q(\mathbf{I})) = q(\rho(\mathbf{I})) = q(\mathbf{I}),
$$

so ρ is also an automorphism for $q(\mathbf{I})$. In particular, a generic query cannot distinguish between constants that are undistinguishable in the input (see Exercise 16.5). Of course, this is not the case if the query explicitly names some constants.

We illustrate these various aspects of genericity in an example.

EXAMPLE 16.1.4   Consider a database over a binary relation G holding the edges of a directed graph. Let $\mathbf{I}$ be the instance $\{\langle a, b\rangle, \langle b, a\rangle, \langle a, c\rangle, \langle b, c\rangle\}$.

Let σ be the CALC query

$$
\{\langle x\rangle \mid \exists y G(x, y)\}.
$$

Note that $\sigma(\mathbf{I}) = \{\langle a\rangle, \langle b\rangle\}$. Let ρ be the permutation defined by $\rho(a) = b$, $\rho(b) = c$, and $\rho(c) = d$. Then $\rho(\mathbf{I}) = \{\langle b, c\rangle, \langle c, b\rangle, \langle b, d\rangle, \langle c, d\rangle\}$. Genericity requires that $\sigma(\rho(\mathbf{I})) = \{\langle b\rangle, \langle c\rangle\}$. This is true in this case.

Note also that a and b are undistinguishable in $\mathbf{I}$. Formally, the renaming ρ defined by $\rho(a) = b$, $\rho(b) = a$, and $\rho(c) = c$ has the property that $\rho(\mathbf{I}) = \mathbf{I}$ and thus is an automorphism of $\mathbf{I}$. Let q be a generic query on G. By genericity of q, either a and b both belong to $q(\mathbf{I})$, or neither does. Thus a generic query cannot distinguish between a and b. Of course, this is not true for C-generic queries (for C nonempty). For instance, let $q_b = \pi_1(\sigma_{2=b}(G))$. Now q_b is $\{b\}$-generic, and $q_b(\mathbf{I}) = \{\langle a\rangle\}$. Thus q_b distinguishes between a and b.

It is easily verified that if a database mapping q is C = generic, then for each input instance $\mathbf{I}$, $adom(q(\mathbf{I})) \subseteq C \cup adom(\mathbf{I})$ (see Exercise 16.1).

In most cases we will ignore the issue of constants in queries because it is not central. Note that a C-generic query can be viewed as a generic query by including the constants in C in the input, using one relation for each constant. For instance, the $\{b\}$-generic query q_b over G in Example 16.1.4 is reduced to a generic query q' over $\{G, R_b\}$, where $R_b = \{\langle b \rangle\}$, defined as follows:

$$q' = \pi_1(\sigma_{2=3}(G \times R_b)).$$

In the following, we will usually assume that queries have no constants unless explicitly stated.

Suppose now that α and β are two enumerations of **dom** and that a generic mapping q from $\mathbf{R}$ to S is computed by a TM M using enc_α. It is easily verified that the same query is computed by M if enc_β is used in place of enc_α (see Exercise 16.2). This permits us to adopt the following notion of computable, which is equivalent to "computable relative to enumeration α" in the case of generic queries. This definition has the advantage of relying on finite rather than infinite enumerations.

DEFINITION 16.1.5   A generic mapping q from $inst(\mathbf{R})$ to $inst(S)$ is *computable* if there exists a TM M such that for each instance $\mathbf{I}$ over $\mathbf{R}$ and each enumeration α of $adom(\mathbf{I})$,

    (a) if $q(\mathbf{I})$ is undefined, then M does not terminate on input $enc_\alpha(\mathbf{I})$, and

    (b) if $q(\mathbf{I})$ is defined, M halts on input $enc_\alpha(\mathbf{I})$ with output $enc_\alpha(q(\mathbf{I}))$ on the tape.

We are now ready to define queries formally.

DEFINITION 16.1.6   Let $\mathbf{R}$ be a database schema and S a relation schema. A *query* from $\mathbf{R}$ to S is a partial mapping from $inst(\mathbf{R})$ to $inst(S)$ that is generic and computable.

Note that all queries discussed in previous chapters satisfy the preceding definition (modulo constants in queries).

Queries and Query Languages

We are usually interested in queries specified by the expressions (i.e., syntactic queries or programs) of a given query language. Given an expression E in query language L, the mapping between instances that E describes is called the *effect* of E. Depending on the language, there may be several alternative semantics (e.g., inflationary versus noninflationary) for defining the query expressed by an expression. A related issue concerns the specification of the output schema of an expression. In calculus-based languages, the output schema is unambiguously specified by the form of the expression. The situation is more ambiguous for other languages, such as datalog and *while*. Programs in these languages typically manipulate several relations and may not specify explicitly which is to be taken as the answer to the query. In such cases, the concepts of *input*, *output*, and *temporary relations* may become important. Thus, in addition to semantically significant input and output relations, the programs may use temporary relations whose content is immaterial outside the computation. We will state explicitly which relations are temporary and which constitute the output whenever this is not clear from the context.

A query language or computing device is called *complete* if it expresses all queries. We will discuss such languages in Chapter 18.

16.2   Complexity of Queries

We now develop a framework for measuring the complexity of queries. This is done by reference to TMs and classical complexity classes defined using the TM model.

There are several ways to look at the complexity of queries. They differ in the parameters with respect to which the complexity is measured. The two main possibilities are as follows:

- *data complexity*: the complexity of evaluating a *fixed query* for variable database inputs; and

- *expression complexity*: the complexity of evaluating, on a *fixed database instance*, the various queries specifiable in a given query language.

Thus in the data complexity perspective, the complexity is with respect to the database input and the query is considered constant. Conversely, with expression complexity, the database input is fixed and the complexity is with respect to the size of the query expression. Clearly, the measures provide different information about the complexity of evaluating queries. The usual situation is that the size of the database input dominates by far the size of the query, and so data complexity is typically most relevant. This is the primary focus of Part E, and we use the term *complexity* to refer to data complexity unless otherwise stated.

The complexity of queries is defined based on the *recognition problem* associated with the query. For a query q, the recognition problem is as follows: Given an instance $\mathbf{I}$ and a tuple u, determine if u belongs to the answer $q(\mathbf{I})$. To be more precise, the recognition problem of a query q is the language

$$\{enc_\alpha(\mathbf{I}) \# enc_\alpha(u) \mid u \in q(\mathbf{I}), \alpha \text{ an enumeration of } adom(\mathbf{I})\}.$$

The (*data*) *complexity* of q is the (conventional) complexity of its recognition problem. Technically, the complexity is with respect to the size of the input [i.e., the length of the word $enc_\alpha(\mathbf{I}) \# enc_\alpha(u)$]. Because for an instance $\mathbf{I}$ the size (number of tuples) in $\mathbf{I}$ is closely related to the length of $enc_\alpha(\mathbf{I})$ (see Exercise 16.12), the size of $\mathbf{I}$ is usually taken as the measure of the input.

For each Turing time or space complexity class C, one can define a corresponding *complexity class of queries*, denoted by QC . The class of queries QC consists of all queries whose recognition problem is in C. For example, the class QPTIME consists of all queries for which the recognition problem is in PTIME.

There is another way to define the complexity of queries that is based on the complexity of actually *constructing the result* of the query rather than the recognition problem for individual tuples. The two definitions are in most cases interchangeable (see Exercise 16.13). In particular, for complexity classes insensitive to a polynomial factor, the definitions are equivalent. In general, the definition based on constructing the result distinguishes between a query with a large answer and one with a small answer, which is irrelevant to the definition based on recognition. On the other hand, the definition based on constructing the result may not distinguish between easy and hard queries with large results.

EXAMPLE 16.2.1   Consider a database consisting of one binary relation G and the three queries *cross*, *path*, and *self* on G defined as follows:

$$cross(G) = \pi_1(G) \times \pi_2(G),$$
$$path(G) \ = \{\langle x, y \rangle \mid x \text{ and } y \text{ are connected by a path in } G\},$$
$$self(G) \ = G.$$

Consider first *cross* and *path*. Both have potentially large answers, but *cross* is clearly easier than *path*, even though the time complexity of constructing the result is $O(n^2)$ for both *cross* and *path*. The time complexity of the recognition problem is $O(n)$ for *cross* and $O(n^2)$ for *path*. Thus the measure based on constructing the result does not detect a difference between *cross* and *path*, whereas this is detected by the complexity of the recognition problem. Next consider *cross* and *self*. The time complexity of the recognition problem is in both cases $O(n)$, but the complexity of computing the result is $O(n)$ for *self* whereas it is $O(n^2)$ for *cross*. Thus the complexity of the recognition problem does not distinguish between *cross* and *self*, although *cross* can potentially generate a much larger answer. This difference is detected by the complexity of constructing the result.

In Part E, we will use the definition of query complexity based on the associated recognition problem.

16.3 Languages and Complexity

In the previous section we studied a definition of the complexity of an *individual query*. To measure the complexity of a query language L, we need to establish a correspondence between

- the class of queries expressible in L, and
- a complexity class QC of queries.

Expressiveness with Respect to Complexity Classes

The most straightforward connection between L and a class of queries QC is when L and

QC are precisely the same.[1] In this case, it is said that *L expresses* QC. In every case, each query in *L* has complexity c, and conversely *L* can express every query of complexity c.

Ideally, one would be able to perform complexity-tailored language design; that is, for a desired complexity c, one would design a language expressing precisely QC. Unfortunately, we will see that this is not always possible. In fact, there are no such results for the pure relational model for complexity classes of polynomial time and below, that are of most interest. We consider this phenomenon at length in the next chapter. Intuitively, the shapes of classes of queries of low complexity do not match those of classes of queries defined by any known language. Therefore we are led to consider a less straightforward way to match languages to complexity classes.

Completeness with Respect to Complexity Classes

Consider a language *L* that does not correspond precisely to any natural complexity class of queries. Nonetheless we would like to say something about the complexity of queries in *L*. For instance, we may wish to guarantee that all queries in *L* lie within some complexity class c, even though *L* may not express *all* of QC. For the bound to be meaningful, we would also like that c is, in some sense, a tight upper bound for the complexity of queries in *L*. In other words, *L* should be able to express at least some queries that are among the hardest in QC. The property of a problem being hardest in a complexity class c is captured, in complexity theory, by the notion of *completeness* of the problem in the class (see Chapter 2). By extension to a language, this leads to the following:

DEFINITION 16.3.1   A language *L* is *complete with respect to a complexity class* c if

    (a) each query in *L* is also in QC, and

    (b) there exists a query in *L* for which the associated recognition problem is complete with respect to the complexity class c.

As in the classical definition of completeness of a problem in a complexity class, we qualify, when necessary, the notion of a completeness in a complexity class by the complexity of the reduction. For instance, *L is logspace complete with respect to* c qualifies (b) by stating that the query expressible in *L* whose recognition problem is complete in c is in fact *logspace complete* in c.

In some sense, completeness without expressiveness says something negative about the language *L*. *L* can express some queries that are as hard as any query in QC; on the other hand, there may be *easy* queries in QC that are not expressible in *L*. This may at first appear contradictory because *L* expresses some queries that are complete in c, and any problem in c can be reduced to the complete problem. However, there is no contradiction. The *reduction* of the "easy" query to the complete query may be computationally easy but nevertheless not expressible in *L*. Examples of this situation involve the familiar languages *fixpoint* and *while*. As will be shown in Section 17.3, these languages are complete in

---

[1] By abuse of notation, we also denote by *L* the set of queries expressible in *L*.

PTIME and PSPACE, respectively. However, neither can express the simple parity query on a unary relation R:

$$even(R) = true \text{ if } |R| \text{ is even, and } false \text{ otherwise.}$$

Complexity and Genericity

To conclude this chapter, we consider the delicate impact of genericity on complexity. The foregoing query *even* illustrates a fundamental phenomenon relating genericity to the complexity of queries. As stated earlier, *even* cannot be computed by *fixpoint* or by *while*, both of which are powerful languages. The difficulty in computing *even* is due to the lack of information about the elements of the set. Because the database only provides a set of undifferentiated elements, genericity implies that they are treated uniformly in queries. This rules out the straightforward solution of repeatedly extracting one arbitrary element from the set until the set is empty while keeping a binary counter: How does one specify the first element to be extracted?

On the other hand, consider the problem of computing *even* with a TM. The additional information provided by the encoding of the input on the tape makes the problem trivial and allows a linear-time solution.

This highlights the interesting fact that genericity may complicate the task of computing a query, whereas access to the internal representation may simplify this task considerably. Thus this suggests a trade-off between genericity and complexity. This can be formalized by defining complexity classes based on a computing device that is generic by definition in place of a TM. Such a device cannot take advantage of the representation of data in the same manner as a TM, and it treats data generically at all points in the computation. It can be shown that *even* is hard with respect to complexity measures based on such a device. The query *even* will be used repeatedly to illustrate various aspects of the complexity of queries.

Bibliographic Notes

The study of computable queries originated in the work of Chandra and Harel [CH80b, Cha81a, CH82]. In addition to well-typed languages, they also considered languages defining queries with data-dependent output schemas. The data and expression complexity of queries were introduced and studied in [CH80a, CH82] and further investigated in [Var82a]. Data complexity is most widely used and is based on the associated recognition problem. Data complexity based on constructing the result of the query is discussed in [AV90].

The notion of genericity was formalized in [AU79, CH80b] with different terminology. The term *C-genericity* was first used in [HY84]. Other notions related in spirit to genericity are studied in [Hul86]. The definition of genericity is extended in [AK89] to object-oriented queries that can produce new constants in the result (arising from new object identifiers); see also [VandBGAG92, HY90]. This is further discussed in Chapters 18 and 21.

A modified notion of Turing machine is introduced in [HS93] that permits domain elements to appear on the Turing tape, thus obviating the need to encode them. However, this device still uses an ordered representation of the input instance. A device operating directly on relations is the on-site acceptor of [Lei89a]. This extends the formal algorithmic procedure (FAP) proposed in [Fri71] in the context of recursion theory. Another variation of this device is presented in [Lei89b]. Further generalizations of TMs, which do not assume an ordered input, are introduced in [AV91b, AV94]. These are used to define nonstandard complexity classes of queries and to investigate the trade-off between genericity and complexity.

Informative discussions of the connection between query languages and complexity classes are provided in [Gur84, Gur88, Imm87b, Lei89a].

Exercises

Exercise 16.1 Let q be a C-generic mapping. Show that, for each input instance $\mathbf{I}$, $adom(q(\mathbf{I})) \subseteq C \cup adom(\mathbf{I})$.

Exercise 16.2 (Genericity) Let q be a generic database mapping from $\mathbf{R}$ to S.

(a) Let α and β be enumerations of **dom**, and suppose that M computes q using enc_α. Prove that for each instance $\mathbf{I}$ over $\mathbf{R}$,

$$enc_\alpha \circ M \circ enc_\alpha^{-1} = enc_\beta \circ M \circ enc_\beta^{-1}.$$

Conclude that M computes q using enc_β.

(b) Verify that the definitions of *computable relative to* α and *computable* are equivalent for generic database mappings.

★ **Exercise 16.3** Let $\mathbf{R}$ be a database schema and S a relation schema.

(a) Prove that it is undecidable to determine, given TM M that computes a mapping q from $inst(\mathbf{R})$ to $inst(S)$ relative to enumeration α of **dom**, whether q is generic.

(b) Show that the set of TMs that compute queries from $\mathbf{R}$ to S is co-r.e.

Exercise 16.4 In many practical situations the underlying domains used (e.g., strings, integers) have some structure (e.g., an ordering relationship that is visible to both user and implementation). For each of the following, develop a natural definition for *generic* and exhibit a nongeneric query, if there is one.

(a) **dom** is partitioned into several sorts $\mathbf{dom}_1, \ldots, \mathbf{dom}_n$.

(b) **dom** has a dense total order $\leq$. [A total order $\leq$ is *dense* if $\forall x, y(x < y \rightarrow \exists z(x < z \wedge z < y))$.]

(c) **dom** has a discrete total order $\leq$. [A total order $\leq$ is *discrete* if $\forall x[\exists y(x < y \rightarrow \exists z(x < z \wedge \neg \exists w(x < w \wedge w < z))) \wedge \exists y(y < x \rightarrow \exists z(z < x \wedge \neg \exists w(z < w \wedge w < x)))].$]

(d) **dom** is the set of nonnegative integers and has the usual ordering $\leq$.

Exercise 16.5 Let q be a C-generic query, and let $\mathbf{I}$ be an input instance. Let ρ be an automorphism of $\mathbf{I}$ that is the identity on C, and let a, b be constants in $\mathbf{I}$, such that $\rho(a) = b$. Show that a occurs in $q(\mathbf{I})$ iff b occurs in $q(\mathbf{I})$.

The next several exercises use the following notions. Let **R** be a database schema. Let k be a positive integer and **I** an instance over **R**. $\Delta_k^{\mathbf{I}}$ denotes the set of k-tuples that can be formed using just constants in **I**. Define the following relation $\equiv_k^{\mathbf{I}}$ on $\Delta_k^{\mathbf{I}}$: $u \equiv_k^{\mathbf{I}} v$ iff there exists an automorphism ρ of **I** such that $\rho(u) = v$. The k-*type index* of **I**, denoted $\#_k(\mathbf{I})$, is the number of equivalence classes of $\equiv_k^{\mathbf{I}}$.

Exercise 16.6 (Equivalence induced by automorphisms) Let **R** be a database schema and **I** an instance of R.

(a) Show that $\equiv_k^{\mathbf{I}}$ is an equivalence relation on $\Delta_k^{\mathbf{I}}$.

(b) Let q be a generic query on **R**, whose output is a k-ary relation. Show that $q(\mathbf{I})$ is a union of equivalence classes of $\equiv_k^{\mathbf{I}}$.

♠ **Exercise 16.7** (Type index) Let G be a binary relation schema corresponding to the edges of a directed graph. Show the following:

(a) The k-type index of a complete graph is a constant independent of the size of the graph, as long as it has at least k vertexes.

(b) The k-type index of graphs consisting of a simple path is polynomial in the size of the graph.

(c) [Lin90, Lin91] The k-type index of a complete binary tree is polynomial in the *depth* of the tree.

Exercise 16.8 Let k, n be integers, $0 < n < k$, and **I** an instance over schema **R**.

(a) Show how to compute $\equiv_n^{\mathbf{I}}$ from $\equiv_k^{\mathbf{I}}$.

(b) Prove that $\#_n(\mathbf{I}) < \#_k(\mathbf{I})$, unless **I** has just one constant.

★ **Exercise 16.9** (Fixpoint queries and type index) Let φ be a *fixpoint* query on database schema **R**. Show that there exists a polynomial p such that, for each instance **I** over **R**, φ on input **I** terminates after at most $p(\#_k(\mathbf{I}))$ steps, for some $k > 0$.

♠ **Exercise 16.10** (Fixpoint queries on special graphs) Show that every *fixpoint* query terminates in

(a) constant number of steps on complete graphs;

(b) [Lin90, Lin91] $p(\log(|\mathbf{I}|))$ number of steps on complete binary trees **I**, for some polynomial p. *Hint:* Use Exercises 16.7 and 16.9.

♠ **Exercise 16.11** [Ban78, Par78] Let **R** be a schema, **I** a fixed instance over **R**, and $a_1, \ldots, a_n$ an enumeration of $adom(\mathbf{I})$. For each automorphism ρ on **I**, let $t_\rho = \langle \rho(a_1), \ldots, \rho(a_n) \rangle$, and let

$$auto(\mathbf{I}) = \{t_\rho \mid \rho \text{ an automorphism of } \mathbf{I}\}.$$

(a) Prove that there is a CALC query q with no constants (depending on **I**) such that $q(\mathbf{I}) = auto(\mathbf{I})$.

(b) Prove that for each relation schema S and instance J over S with $adom(J) \subseteq adom(\mathbf{I})$,

there is a CALC query q with no constants
(depending on **I** and J)

$$\text{such that } q(\mathbf{I}) = J$$
$$\text{iff}$$
$$\text{for each automorphism } \rho \text{ of } \mathbf{I}, \rho(J) = J.$$

A query language is called BP-*complete* if it satisfies the "if" direction of part (b).

Exercise 16.12   (Tape encoding of instances) Let $\mathbf{I}$ be a nonempty instance of a database schema $\mathbf{R}$. Let n_c be the number of constants in $\mathbf{I}$, n_t the number of tuples, and α an enumeration of the constants in $\mathbf{I}$. Show that there exist integers k_1, k_2, k_3 depending only on $\mathbf{R}$ such that

(a) $n_c \leq k_1 n_t \leq |enc_\alpha(\mathbf{I})|$,

(b) $|enc_\alpha(\mathbf{I})| \leq k_2 n_t \log(n_t)$,

(c) $|enc_\alpha(\mathbf{I})| \leq (n_c)^{k_3}$.

Exercise 16.13   (Recognition versus construction complexity) Let f be a time or space bound for a TM, and let q be a query. The notation *r-complexity* abbreviates the complexity based on recognition, and *a-complexity* stands for complexity based on constructing the answer. Show the following:

(a) If the time r-complexity of q is bounded by f, then there exists $k, k > 0$, such that the time a-complexity of q is bounded by $n^k f$, where n is the number of constants in the input instance.

(b) If the space r-complexity of q is bounded by f, then there exists $k, k > 0$, such that the space a-complexity of q is bounded by $n^k + f$, where n is the number of constants in the input instance.

(c) If the time a-complexity of q is bounded by f, then there exists $k, k > 0$, such that the time r-complexity of q is bounded by kf.

(d) If the space a-complexity of q is bounded by f, then the space r-complexity of q is bounded by f.

Exercise 16.14   (Data complexity of algebra) Determine the time and space complexity of each of the relational algebra operations (show the lowest complexity you can).

★ **Exercise 16.15**

(a) Develop an algorithm for computing the transitive closure of a graph that uses only the information provided by the graph (i.e., a generic algorithm).

(b) Develop algorithms for a TM to compute the transitive closure of a graph (starting from a standard encoding of the graph on the tape) that use as little time (space) as you can manage.

(c) Write a datalog program defining the transitive closure of a graph so that the number of stages in the bottom-up evaluation is as small as you can manage.

17 First Order, Fixpoint, and While

Alice: *I get it, now we'll match languages to complexity classes.*
Sergio: *It's not that easy—data independence adds some spice.*
Riccardo: *You can think of it as not having order.*
Vittorio: *It's a lot of fun, and we'll play some games along the way.*

In Chapter 16, we laid the framework for studying the expressiveness and complexity of query languages. In this chapter, we evaluate three of the most important classes of languages discussed so far—CALC, *fixpoint*, and *while*—with respect to expressiveness and complexity. We show that CALC is in LOGSPACE and AC_0, that *fixpoint* is complete in PTIME, and that *while* is complete in PSPACE.[1] We also investigate the impact of the presence of an ordering of the constants in the input.

We first show that CALC can be evaluated in LOGSPACE. This complexity result partly explains the success of relational database systems: Relational queries can be evaluated efficiently. Furthermore, it implies that these queries are within NC and thus that they have a high potential of intrinsic parallelism (not yet fully exploited in actual systems). We prove that CALC queries can be evaluated in constant time in a particular (standard) model of parallel computation based on circuits.

While looking at the expressive power of CALC and the other two languages, we study their limitations by examining queries that cannot be expressed in these languages. This leads us to introduce important tools that are useful in investigating the expressive power of query languages. We first present an elegant characterization of CALC based on *Ehrenfeucht-Fraïssé games*. This is used to show limitations in the expressive power of CALC, such as the nonexpressibility of the transitive closure query on a graph. A second tool related to expressiveness, which applies to all languages discussed in this chapter, consists of proving *0-1 laws* for languages. This powerful approach, based on probabilities, allows us to show that certain queries (such as *even*) are not expressible in *while* and thus not in *fixpoint* or CALC.

As discussed in Section 16.3, there are simple queries that these languages cannot express (e.g., the prototypical example of *even*). Together with the completeness of *fixpoint* and *while* in PTIME and PSPACE, respectively, this suggests that there is an uneasy relationship between these languages and complexity classes. As intimated in Section 16.3, the problem can be attributed to the fact that a generic query language cannot take advantage of the information provided by the internal representation of data used by Turing

---

[1] AC_0 and NC are two parallel complexity classes defined later in this chapter.

machines, such as an ordering of the constants. For instance, the query *even* is easily expressible in *while* if an order is provided.

A fundamental result of this chapter is that *fixpoint* expresses exactly QPTIME under the assumption that queries can access an order on the constants. It is especially surprising that a complexity class based on such a natural resource as time coincides with a logic-based language such as *fixpoint*. However, this characterization depends on the order in a crucial manner, and this highlights the importance of order in the context of generic computation. No language is known that expresses QPTIME without the order assumption; and the existence of such a language remains one of the main open problems in the theory of query languages.

This chapter concludes with two recent developments that shed further light on the interplay of order and expressiveness. The first shows that a *while* query on an unordered database can be reduced to a *while* query on an ordered database via a *fixpoint* query. The *fixpoint* query produces an ordered database from a given unordered one by grouping tuples into a sequence of blocks that are never split in the computation of the *while query*; the blocks can then be thought of as elements of an ordered database. This also allows us to clarify the connection between *fixpoint* and *while*: They are distinct, unless PTIME = PSPACE.

The second recent development considers nondeterminism as a means for overcoming limitations due to the absence of ordering of the domain. Several nondeterministic extensions of CALC, *fixpoint*, and *while* are shown.

The impact of order is a constant theme throughout the discussion of expressive power. As discussed in Chapter 16, the need to consider computation without order is a consequence of the data independence principle, which is considered important in the database perspective. Therefore computation *with* order is viewed as a metaphor for an (at least partial) abandonment of the data independence principle.

17.1   Complexity of First-Order Queries

This section considers the complexity of first-order queries and shows that they are in QLOGSPACE. This result is particularly significant given its implications about the *parallel* complexity of CALC and thus of relational languages in general. Indeed, LOGSPACE ⊆ NC. As will be seen, this means that every CALC query can be evaluated in polylogarithmic time using a polynomial number of processors. Moreover, as described in this section, a direct proof shows the stronger result that the first-order queries can in fact be evaluated in AC_0. Intuitively, this says that first-order queries can be evaluated in *constant* time with a polynomial number of processors.

We begin by showing the connection between CALC and QLOGSPACE.

THEOREM 17.1.1   CALC is included in QLOGSPACE.

Proof   Let φ be a query in CALC over some database schema **R**. We will describe a TM M_φ, depending on φ, that solves the recognition problem for φ and uses a work tape with length logarithmic in the size of the read-only input tape.

Suppose that M_φ is started with input $enc_\alpha(\mathbf{I}) \# enc_\alpha(u)$ for some instance $\mathbf{I}$ over $\mathbf{R}$, some enumeration α of the constants, and some tuple u over $adom(\mathbf{I})$ whose arity is the same as that of the result of φ. M_φ should accept the input iff $u \in \varphi(\mathbf{I})$. We assume w.l.o.g. that φ is in prenex normal form. We show by induction on the number of quantifiers of φ that the computation can be performed using $k \cdot \log(|enc_\alpha(\mathbf{I}) \# enc_\alpha(u)|)$ cells of the work tape, for some constant k.

Basis. If φ has no quantifiers, then all the variables of φ are free. Let ν be the valuation mapping the free variables of φ to u. M_φ must determine whether $\mathbf{I} \models \varphi[\nu]$. To determine the truth value of each literal L under ν occurring in φ, one needs only scan the input tape looking for $\nu(L)$. This can be accomplished by considering each tuple of $\mathbf{I}$ in turn, comparing it with relevant portions of u. For each such tuple, the address of the beginning of the tuple should be stored on the tape along with the offset to the current location of the tuple being scanned. This can be accomplished within logarithmic space.

Induction. Now suppose that each prenex normal form CALC formula with less than n quantifiers can be evaluated in LOGSPACE, and let φ be a prenex normal form formula with n quantifiers. Suppose φ is of the form $\exists x \ \psi$. (The case when φ is of the form $\forall x \ \psi$ is similar.)

All possible values of x are tried. If some value is found that makes ψ true, then the input is accepted; otherwise it is rejected. The values used for x are all those that appear on the input tape in the order in which they appear. To keep track of the current value of x, one needs $\log(n_c)$ work tape cells, where n_c is the number of constants in $\mathbf{I}$. Because n_c is less than the length of the input, the number of cells needed is no more than $\log(|enc_\alpha(\mathbf{I}) \# enc_\alpha(u)|)$. The problem is now reduced to evaluating ψ for each value of x. By the induction hypothesis, this can be done using $k \cdot \log(|enc_\alpha(\mathbf{I}) \# enc_\alpha(u)|)$ work tape cells for some k. Thus the entire computation takes $(k+1)\log(|enc_\alpha(\mathbf{I}) \# enc_\alpha(u)|)$ work tape cells; which concludes the induction. ■

Unfortunately, CALC does not express all of QLOGSPACE. It will be shown in Section 17.3 that *even*, although clearly in QLOGSPACE, is not a first-order query.

We next consider informally the *parallel* complexity of CALC. We are concerned with two parallel complexity classes: NC and AC_0. Intuitively, NC is the class of problems that can be solved using polynomially many processors in time polynomial in the logarithm of the input size; AC_0 also allows polynomially many processors but only *constant* time. The formal definitions of NC and AC_0 are based on a circuit model in which time corresponds to the depth of the circuit and the number of gates corresponds to its size. The circuits use *and*, *or*, and *not* gates and have unbounded fan-in.[2] Thus AC_0 is the class of problems definable using circuits where the depth is constant and the size polynomial in the input.

The fact that the complexity of CALC is LOGSPACE implies that its parallel complexity is NC, because it is well known that LOGSPACE $\subseteq$ NC. However, one can prove a tighter result, which says that the parallel complexity of CALC is in fact AC_0. So only constant time is needed to evaluate CALC queries. More than any other known complexity result on CALC, this captures the fundamental intuition that first-order queries can be evaluated

---

[2] The *fan-in* is the number of wires going into a gate.

in parallel very efficiently and that they represent, in some sense, primitive manipulations of relations.

We sketch only the proof and leave the details for Exercise 17.2.

THEOREM 17.1.2   Every CALC query is in AC_0.

Crux   Let us first provide an intuition of the result independent of the circuit model. We will use the relational algebra. We will argue that each of the operations $\pi, \sigma, \times, -, \cup$ can be performed in constant parallel time using only polynomially many processors.

Let e be an expression in the algebra over some database schema **R**. Consider the following infinite space of processors. There is one processor for each pair $\langle f, u \rangle$, where f is a subexpression of e and u is a tuple of the same arity as the result of f, using constants from **dom**. Let us denote one such processor by $p_{f,u}$. Note that, in particular, for each relation name Q occurring in f and each u of the arity of Q, $p_{Q,u}$ is one of the processors. Each processor has two possible states, *true* or *false*, indicating whether u is in the result of f.

At the beginning, all processors are in state *false*. An input instance is specified by turning on the processors corresponding to tuples in the input relations (i.e., processors $p_{R,u}$ if u is in input relation R). The result consists of the tuples u for which $p_{e,u}$ is in state *true* at the end of the computation. For a given input, we are only concerned with the processors formed from tuples with constants occurring in the input. Clearly, no more than polynomially many processors will be relevant during the computation.

It remains to show that each algebra operation takes constant time. Consider, for instance, cross product. Suppose $f \times g$ is a subexpression of e. To compute $f \times g$, the processors $p_{f,u}$ and $p_{g,v}$ send the message *true* to processor $p_{(f \times g),uv}$ if their state is *true*. Processor $p_{(f \times g),uv}$ goes to state *true* when receiving two *true* messages. The other operations are similar. Thus e is evaluated in constant time in our informal model of parallel computation.

To formalize the foregoing intuition using the circuit model, one must construct, for each n, a circuit B_n that, for each input of length n consisting of an encoding over the alphabet $\{0, 1\}$ of an instance **I** and a tuple u, outputs 1 iff $u \in e(\mathbf{I})$. The idea for constructing the circuit is similar to the informal construction in the previous paragraph except that processors are replaced by wires (edges in the graph representing the circuit) that carry either the value 1 or 0. Moreover, each B_n has polynomial size. Thus only wires that can become active for some input are included. Figure 17.1 represents fragments of circuits computing some relational operations. In the figure, f is the cross product of g and h (i.e., $g \times h$); f' is the difference $g - h$; and f'' is the projection of h on the first coordinate. Observe that projection is the most tricky operation. In the figure, it is assumed that the active domain consists of four constants. Note also that because of projection, the circuits have unbounded fan-in.

We leave the details of the construction of the circuits B_n to the reader (see Exercise 17.2). In particular, note that one must use a slightly more cumbersome encoding than that used for Turing machines because the alphabet is now restricted to $\{0, 1\}$. ■

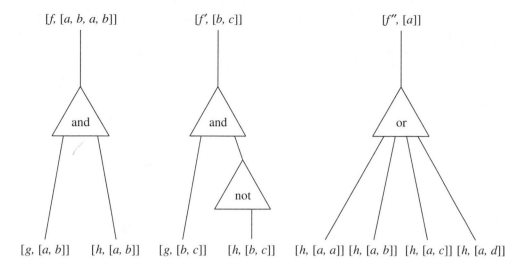

Figure 17.1: Some fragments of circuits

One might naturally wonder if CALC expresses *all* queries in AC_0. It turns out that there are queries in AC_0 that are not first order. This is demonstrated in Section 17.4.

17.2 Expressiveness of First-Order Queries

We have seen that first-order queries have desirable properties with respect to complexity. However, there is a price to pay for this in terms of expressiveness: There are many useful queries that are not first order. Typical examples of such queries are *even* and transitive closure of a graph. This section presents an elegant technique based on a two-player game that can be used to prove that certain queries (including *even* and transitive closure) are not first order. Although the game we describe is geared toward first-order queries, games provide a general technique that is used in conjunction with many other languages.

The connection between CALC sentences and games is, intuitively, the following. Consider as an example a CALC sentence of the form

$$\forall x_1\, \exists x_2\, \forall x_3\, \psi(x_1, x_2, x_3).$$

One can view the sentence as a statement about a game with two players, 1 and 2, who alternate in picking values for x_1, x_2, x_3. The sentence says that Player D can always force a choice of values that makes $\psi(x_1, x_2, x_3)$ true. In other words, no matter which value Player S chooses for x_1, Player D can pick an x_2 such that, no matter which x_3 is chosen next by Player S, $\psi(x_1, x_2, x_3)$ is true.

The actual game we use, called the *Ehrenfeucht-Fraissé* game, is slightly more involved, but is based on a similar intuition. It is played on two instances. Suppose that **R** is a database schema. Let **I** and **J** be instances over **R**, with disjoint sets of constants. Let r be

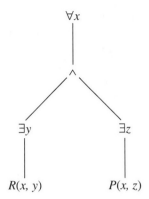

Figure 17.2: A syntax tree

a positive integer. The *game of length r associated with **I** and **J*** is played by two players called S and D, making r choices each. Player S starts by picking a constant occurring in **I** or **J**, and Player D picks a constant in the opposite instance. This is repeated r times. At each move, Player S has the choice of the instance and a constant in it, and Player D must respond in the opposite instance.

Let a_i be the ith constant picked in **I** (respectively, b_i in **J**). The set of pairs $\{(a_1, b_1), \ldots, (a_r, b_r)\}$ is a *round* of the game. The *subinstance* of **I** generated by $\{a_1, \ldots, a_r\}$, denoted $\mathbf{I}/\{a_1, \ldots, a_r\}$, consists of all facts in **I** using only these constants, and similarly for **J**, $\{b_1, \ldots, b_r\}$ and $\mathbf{J}/\{b_1, \ldots, b_r\}$.

Player D *wins the round* $\{(a_1, b_1), \ldots, (a_r, b_r)\}$ iff the mapping $a_i \to b_i$ is an isomorphism of the subinstances $\mathbf{I}/\{a_1, \ldots, a_r\}$ and $\mathbf{J}/\{b_1, \ldots, b_r\}$.

Player D *wins the game of length r* associated with **I** and **J** if he or she has a winning strategy (i.e., Player D can always win any game of length r on **I** and **J**, no matter how Player S plays). This is denoted by $\mathbf{I} \equiv_r \mathbf{J}$. Note that the relation $\equiv_r$ is an equivalence relation on instances over **R** (see Exercise 17.3).

Intuitively, the equivalence $\mathbf{I} \equiv_r \mathbf{J}$ says that **I** and **J** cannot be distinguished by looking at just r constants at a time in the two instances. Recall that the *quantifier depth* of a CALC formula is the maximum number of quantifiers in a path from the root to a leaf in the representation of the sentence as a tree. The main result of Ehrenfeucht-Fraïssé games is that the ability to distinguish among instances using games of length r is equivalent to the ability to distinguish among instances using some CALC sentence of quantifier depth r.

EXAMPLE 17.2.1   Consider the sentence $\forall x\ (\exists y\ R(x, y) \land \exists z\ P(x, z))$. Its syntax tree is represented in Fig. 17.2. The sentence has quantifier depth 2. Note that, for a sentence in prenex normal form, the quantifier depth is simply the number of quantifiers in the formula.

The main result of Ehrenfeucht-Fraïssé games, stated in Theorem 17.2.2, is that if **I** and **J** are two instances such that Player D has a winning strategy for the game of length

r on the two instances, then **I** and **J** cannot be distinguished by any CALC sentence of quantifier depth r. Before proving this theorem, we note that the converse of that result also holds. Thus if two instances are undistinguishable using sentences of quantifier depth r, then they are equivalent with respect to $\equiv_r$. Although interesting, this is of less use as a tool for proving expressibility results, and we leave it as a (nontrivial!) exercise. The main idea is to show that each equivalence class of $\equiv_r$ is definable by a sentence of quantifier depth r (see Exercises 17.9 and 17.10).

THEOREM 17.2.2 Let **I** and **J** be two instances over a database schema **R**. If $\mathbf{I} \equiv_r \mathbf{J}$, then for each CALC sentence φ over **R** with quantifier depth r, **I** and **J** both satisfy φ or neither does.

Crux Suppose that $\mathbf{I} \models \varphi$ and $\mathbf{J} \not\models \varphi$ for some φ of quantifier depth r. We prove that $\mathbf{I} \not\equiv_r \mathbf{J}$. We provide only a sketch of the proof in an example.

Let φ be the sentence $\forall x_1 \exists x_2 \forall x_3 \, \psi(x_1, x_2, x_3)$, where ψ has no quantifiers, and let **I** and **J** be two instances such that $\mathbf{I} \models \varphi$, $\mathbf{J} \not\models \varphi$. Then

$$\mathbf{I} \models \forall x_1 \exists x_2 \forall x_3 \, \psi(x_1, x_2, x_3) \quad \text{and} \quad \mathbf{J} \models \exists x_1 \forall x_2 \exists x_3 \, \neg\psi(x_1, x_2, x_3).$$

We will show that Player S can prevent Player D from winning by forcing the choice of constants a_1, a_2, a_3 in **I** and b_1, b_2, b_3 in **J** such that $\mathbf{I} \models \psi(a_1, a_2, a_3)$ and $\mathbf{J} \models \neg\psi(b_1, b_2, b_3)$. Then the mapping $a_i \to b_i$ cannot be an isomorphism of the subinstances $\mathbf{I}/\{a_1, a_2, a_3\}$ and $\mathbf{J}/\{b_1, b_2, b_3\}$, contradicting the assumption that Player D has a winning strategy. To force this choice, Player S always picks "witnesses" corresponding to the existential quantifiers in φ and $\neg\varphi$ (note that the quantifier for each variable is either $\forall$ in φ and $\exists$ in $\neg\varphi$, or vice versa).

Player S starts by picking a constant b_1 in **J** such that

$$\mathbf{J} \models \forall x_2 \exists x_3 \, \neg\psi(b_1, x_2, x_3).$$

Player D must respond by picking a constant a_1 in **I**. Due to the universal quantification in φ,

$$\mathbf{I} \models \exists x_2 \forall x_3 \, \psi(a_1, x_2, x_3),$$

regardless of which a_1 was picked. Next Player S picks a constant a_2 in **I** such that

$$\mathbf{I} \models \forall x_3 \, \psi(a_1, a_2, x_3).$$

Regardless of which constant b_2 in **J** Player D picks,

$$\mathbf{J} \models \exists x_3 \, \neg\psi(b_1, b_2, x_3).$$

Finally Player S picks b_3 in **J** such that $\mathbf{J} \models \neg\psi(b_1, b_2, b_3)$; Player D picks some a_3 in **I**, and $\mathbf{I} \models \psi(a_1, a_2, a_3)$. ∎

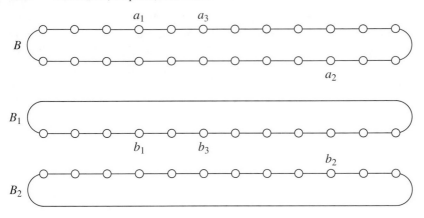

Figure 17.3: Two undistinguishable graphs

Theorem 17.2.2 provides an important tool for proving that certain properties are not definable by CALC. It is sufficient to exhibit, for each r, two instances $\mathbf{I}_r$ and $\mathbf{J}_r$ such that $\mathbf{I}_r$ has the property, $\mathbf{J}_r$ does not, and $\mathbf{I}_r \equiv_r \mathbf{J}_r$. In the next proposition, we illustrate the use of this technique by showing that graph connectivity, and therefore transitive closure, is not expressible in CALC.

PROPOSITION 17.2.3   Let $\mathbf{R}$ be a database schema consisting of one binary relation. Then the query *conn* defined by

$$conn(\mathbf{I}) = true \text{ iff } \mathbf{I} \text{ is a connected graph}$$

is not expressible in CALC.

Crux   Suppose that there is a CALC sentence φ checking graph connectivity. Let r be the quantifier depth of φ. We exhibit a connected graph $\mathbf{I}_r$ and a disconnected graph $\mathbf{J}_r$ such that $\mathbf{I}_r \equiv_r \mathbf{J}_r$. Then, by Theorem 17.2.2, the two instances satisfy φ or none does, a contradiction.

For a sufficiently large n (depending only on r; see Exercise 17.5), the graph $\mathbf{I}_r$ consists of a cycle B of $2n$ nodes and the graph $\mathbf{J}_r$ of two disjoint cycles B_1 and B_2 of n nodes each (see Fig. 17.3). We outline the winning strategy for Player D. The main idea is simple: Two nodes a, a' in $\mathbf{I}_r$ that are far apart behave in the same way as two nodes b, b' in $\mathbf{J}_r$ that belong to different cycles. In particular, Player S cannot take advantage of the fact that a, a' are connected but b, b' are not. To do so, Player S would have to exhibit a path connecting a to a', which Player D could not do for b and b'. However, Player S cannot construct such a path because it requires choosing more than r nodes.

For example, if Player S picks an element a_1 in $\mathbf{I}_r$, then Player D picks an arbitrary element b_1, say in B_1. Now if Player S picks an element b_2 in B_2, then Player D picks an element a_2 in $\mathbf{I}_r$ far from a_1. Next, if Player S picks a b_3 in B_1 close to b_1, then Player D picks an element a_3 in $\mathbf{I}_r$ close to a_1. The graphs are sufficiently large that this can proceed for r moves with the resulting subgraphs isomorphic. The full proof requires a complete case analysis on the moves that Player S can make. ∎

The preceding technique can be used to show that many other properties are not expressible in CALC—for instance, *even*, 2-colorability of graphs, or Eulerian graphs (i.e., graphs for which there is a cycle that passes through each edge exactly once) (see Exercise 17.7).

17.3 *Fixpoint* and *While* Queries

That transitive closure is not expressible in CALC has been the driving force behind extending relational calculus and algebra with recursion. In this section we discuss the expressiveness and complexity of the two main extensions of these languages with recursion: the *fixpoint* and *while* queries.

It is relatively easy to place an upper bound on the complexity of *fixpoint* and *while* queries. Recall that the main distinction between languages defining *fixpoint* queries and those defining *while* queries is that the first are inflationary and the second are not (see Chapter 14). It follows that *fixpoint* queries can be implemented in polynomial time and *while* queries in polynomial space. Moreover, these bounds are tight, as shown next.

THEOREM 17.3.1

    (a) The *fixpoint* queries are complete in PTIME.

    (b) The *while* queries are complete in PSPACE.

Crux The fact that each *fixpoint* query is in PTIME follows immediately from the inflationary nature of languages defining the *fixpoint* queries and the fact that the total number of tuples that can be built from constants in a given instance is polynomial in the size of the instance (see Chapter 14). For *while*, inclusion in PSPACE follows similarly (see Exercise 17.11). The completeness follows from an important result that will be shown in Section 17.4. The result, Theorem 17.4.2, states that if an order on the constants of the domain is available, *fixpoint* expresses exactly QPTIME and *while* expresses exactly QPSPACE. The completeness then follows from the fact that there exist problems that are complete in PTIME and problems that are complete in PSPACE (see Exercise 17.11). ∎

The Parity Query

As was the case for the first-order queries, *fixpoint* and *while* do not match precisely with complexity classes of queries. Although they are powerful, neither *fixpoint* nor *while* can express certain simple queries. The typical example is the parity query *even* on a unary relation. We next provide a direct proof that *while* (and therefore *fixpoint*) cannot express *even*. The result also follows using 0-1 laws, which are presented later. We present the direct proof here to illustrate the proof technique of hyperplanes.

PROPOSITION 17.3.2   The query *even* is not a *while* query.

Proof   Let R be a unary relation. Suppose that there exists a *while* program w that computes the query *even* on input R. We can assume, w.l.o.g., that R contains a unary relation *ans* so that, on input $\mathbf{I}$, $w(\mathbf{I})(ans) = \emptyset$ if $|\mathbf{I}|$ is even, and $w(\mathbf{I}) = \mathbf{I}$ otherwise. Let $\mathbf{R}$ be the schema of w (so $\mathbf{R}$ contains R and *ans*). We will reach a contradiction by showing that the computation of w on a given input is essentially independent of its size. More precisely, for n large enough, the computations of w on all inputs of size greater than n will in some sense be identical. This contradicts the fact that *ans* should be empty at the end of some computations but not others.

To show this, we need a short digression related to computations on unary relations. We assume here that w does not use constants, but the construction can be generalized to that case (see Exercise 17.14). Let $\mathbf{I}$ be an input instance and k an integer. We consider a partition of the set of k-tuples with entries in *adom*($\mathbf{I}$) into hyperplanes based on patterns of equalities and inequalities between components as follows. For each equivalence relation $\simeq$ over $\{1, \ldots, k\}$, the corresponding *hyperplane* is defined by[3]

$$H_{\simeq}(\mathbf{I}) = \{\langle u_1, \ldots, u_k \rangle \mid \text{for each } i, j \in [1, k],$$
$$u_i, u_j \in adom(\mathbf{I}) \text{ and } u_i = u_j \Leftrightarrow i \simeq j\}.$$

For instance, let $adom(\mathbf{I}) = \{a, b, c\}$, $k = 3$ and

$$\simeq = \{\langle 1, 1 \rangle, \langle 2, 2 \rangle, \langle 1, 2 \rangle, \langle 2, 1 \rangle, \langle 3, 3 \rangle\}.$$

Then

$$H_{\simeq}(\mathbf{I}) = \{\langle a, a, b \rangle, \langle a, a, c \rangle, \langle b, b, a \rangle, \langle b, b, c \rangle, \langle c, c, a \rangle, \langle c, c, b \rangle\}.$$

Finally there are two 0-ary hyperplanes, denoted *true* and *false*, that evaluate to $\{\langle \rangle\}$ and $\{\}$, respectively.

We will see that a *while* computation cannot distinguish between two k-tuples in the same hyperplane, and so intermediate relations of arity k will always consist of a union of hyperplanes.

Now consider the *while* program w. We assume that the condition guarding each *while* loop has the form $R \neq \emptyset$ for some $R \in \mathbf{R}$, and that in each assignment $R := E$, E involves a single application of some unary or binary algebra operator. We label the statements of the program so we can talk about the program state (i.e., the label) after some number of computation steps on input $\mathbf{I}$. We include two labels in a *while* statement in the following manner:

label1 *while* $\langle condition \rangle$ *do* **label2** $\langle statement \rangle$.

---

[3] Note that, in logic terminology, $\simeq$ corresponds to the notion of *equality type*, and hyperplanes correspond to realizations of equality types.

Let N be the maximum arity of any relation in **R**. To conclude the proof, we will show by induction on the steps of the computation that there is a number b_w such that for each input **I** with size $\geq N$, w terminates on **I** after exactly b_w steps. Furthermore,

(*) for each step $m \leq b_w$, there exists a label j_m and for each relation T of arity k a set $E_{T,m}$ of equivalence relations over $\{1, \ldots, k\}$ such that for each input **I** of size greater than N

  1. the control is at label j_m after m steps of the computation; and
  2. each T then contains $\cup\{H_{\simeq}(\mathbf{I}) \mid \simeq \text{ in } E_{T,m}\}$.

To see that this yields the result, suppose that it is true. Then for each **I** with size $\geq N$, w terminates with *ans* always empty or always nonempty, regardless of whether the size of **I** is even or odd (a contradiction).

The claim follows from an inductive proof of (*). It is clear that this holds at the 0th step. At the start of the computation, all T are empty except for the input unary relation R, which contains all constants and so consists of the hyperplane $H_{\simeq}$, where $\simeq = \{\langle 1, 1 \rangle\}$. Suppose now that (*) holds for each step less than m and that the program has not terminated on any **I** with size $\geq N$. We prove that (*) also holds for m. There are two cases to consider:

- Label j_{m-1} occurs before the keyword *while*. By induction, the relation controlling the loop is empty after the $(m-1)^{\text{st}}$ step, for all inputs large enough, or nonempty for all such inputs. Thus at step m, the control will be at the same label for all instances large enough, so (*1) holds. No relations have been modified, so (*2) also holds.

- Otherwise j_{m-1} labels an assignment statement. Then after the $(m-1)^{\text{st}}$ step, the control will clearly be at the label of the next statement for all instances large enough, so (*1) holds. With regard to (*2), we consider the case where the assignment is $T := Q_1 \times Q_2$ for some variables T, Q_1, and Q_2; the other relation operators are handled in a similar fashion (see Exercise 17.12). By induction, (*2) holds for all relations distinct from T because they are not modified. Consider T. After step m, T contains

$$\bigcup\{H_{\simeq_1}(\mathbf{I}) \mid \simeq_1 \text{ in } E_{Q_1,m-1}\} \times \bigcup\{H_{\simeq_2}(\mathbf{I}) \mid \simeq_2 \text{ in } E_{Q_2,m-1}\} =$$
$$\bigcup\{H_{\simeq_1}(\mathbf{I}) \times H_{\simeq_2}(\mathbf{I}) \mid \simeq_1 \text{ in } E_{Q_1,m-1}, \simeq_2 \text{ in } E_{Q_2,m-1}\}.$$

Let k, l be the arities of Q_1, Q_2, respectively, and for each $\simeq_2$ in $E_{Q_2,m-1}$, let

$$\simeq_2^{+k} = \{(x+k, y+k) \mid (x, y) \in \simeq_2\}.$$

For an arbitrary binary relation $\gamma \subseteq [1, k+l] \times [1, k+l]$, let γ^* denote the reflexive, symmetric, and transitive closure of γ. For $\simeq_1, \simeq_2$ in $E_{Q_1,m-1}, E_{Q_2,m-1}$, respectively, set

$$\simeq_1 \otimes \simeq_2 = \{(\simeq_1 \cup \simeq_2^{+k} \cup \Lambda)^* \mid \Lambda \subseteq [1, k] \times [k+1, k+l],$$

and for all i, i', j, j' such that $[i, j] \in \Lambda$

and $[i', j'] \in \Lambda, i \simeq_1 i'$ iff $j \simeq_2^{+k} j'\}.$

It is straightforward to verify that for each pair $\simeq_1, \simeq_2$ in $E_{Q_1,m-1}, E_{Q_2,m-1}$, respectively, and $\mathbf{I}$ with size $\geq N$,

$$H_{\simeq_1}(\mathbf{I}) \times H_{\simeq_2}(\mathbf{I}) = H_{\simeq_1 \otimes \simeq_2}(\mathbf{I}).$$

Note that this uses the assumption that the size of $\mathbf{I}$ is greater than N, the maximum arity of relations in w. It follows that

$$E_{T,m} = \bigcup \{\simeq_1 \otimes \simeq_2 \mid \simeq_1 \text{ in } E_{Q_1,m-1} \text{ and } \simeq_2 \text{ in } E_{Q_2,m-1}\}.$$

Thus (*2) also holds for T at step m, and the induction is completed. ∎

The hyperplane technique used in the preceding proof is based on the fact that in the context of a (sufficiently large) unary relation input, there are families of tuples (in this case the different hyperplanes) that "travel together" and hence that the intermediate and final results are unions of these families of tuples. Although there are other cases in which the technique of hyperplanes can be applied (see Exercise 17.15), in the general case the input is not a union of hyperplanes, and so the members of a hyperplane do not travel together. However, there is a generalization of hyperplanes based on automorphisms that yields the same effect. Recall that an *automorphism* of $\mathbf{I}$ is a one-to-one mapping ρ on $adom(\mathbf{I})$ such that $\rho(\mathbf{I}) = \mathbf{I}$. For fixed $\mathbf{I}$, consider the following equivalence relation $\equiv_k^{\mathbf{I}}$ on k-tuples of $adom(\mathbf{I})$: $u \equiv_k^{\mathbf{I}} v$ iff there exists an automorphism ρ of $\mathbf{I}$ such that $\rho(u) = v$. (See Exercises 16.6 and 16.7 in the previous chapter.) It can be shown that if w is a *while* query (without constants), then the members of equivalence classes $\equiv_k^{\mathbf{I}}$ travel together when w is executed on input $\mathbf{I}$. More precisely, suppose that $\mathbf{J}$ is an instance obtained at some point in the computation of w on input $\mathbf{I}$. The genericity of *while* programs implies that if ρ is an automorphism of $\mathbf{I}$, it is also an automorphism of $\mathbf{J}$. Thus for each k-tuple u in some relation of $\mathbf{J}$ and each v such that $u \equiv_k^{\mathbf{I}} v$, v also belongs to that relation. Thus each relation in $\mathbf{J}$ of arity k is a union of equivalence classes of $\equiv_k^{\mathbf{I}}$. The equivalence relation $\equiv_k^{\mathbf{I}}$ will be used in our development of 0-1 laws, presented next.

0-1 Laws

We now develop a powerful tool that provides a uniform approach to resolving in the negative a large spectrum of expressibility problems. It is based on the probability that a property is true in instances of a given size. We shall prove a surprising fact: All properties expressible by a *while* query are "almost surely" true, or "almost surely" false. More precisely, we prove the result for *while* sentences:

DEFINITION 17.3.3 A *sentence* is a total query that is Boolean (i.e., returns as answer either *true* or *false*).

Let q be a sentence over some schema **R**. For each n, let $\mu_n(q)$ denote the fraction of instances over **R** with entries in $\{1, \ldots, n\}$ that satisfy q. That is,

$$\mu_n(q) = \frac{|\{\mathbf{I} \mid q(\mathbf{I}) = true \text{ and } adom(\mathbf{I}) \subseteq \{1, \ldots, n\}\}|}{|\{\mathbf{I} \mid adom(\mathbf{I}) \subseteq \{1, \ldots, n\}\}|}.$$

DEFINITION 17.3.4 A sentence q is *almost surely true (false)* if $\lim_{n \to \infty} \mu_n(q)$ exists and equals 1 (0). If every sentence in a language L is almost surely true or almost surely false, the language *L has a 0-1 law*.

To simplify the discussion of 0-1 laws, we continue to focus exclusively on constant-free queries (see Exercise 17.19).

We will show that CALC, *fixpoint*, and *while* sentences have 0-1 laws. This provides substantial insight into limitations of the expressive power of these languages and can be used to show that they cannot express a variety of properties. For example, it follows immediately that *even* is not expressible in either of these languages. Indeed, $\mu_n(even)$ is 1 if n is even and 0 if n is odd. Thus $\mu_n(even)$ does not converge, so *even* is not expressible in a language that has a 0-1 law.

While 0-1 laws provide an elegant and powerful tool, they require the development of some nontrivial machinery. Interestingly, this is one of the rare occasions when we will need to consider *infinite* instances even though we aim to prove something about finite instances only.

We start by proving that CALC has a 0-1 law and then extend the result to *fixpoint* and *while*. For simplicity, we consider only the case when the input to the query is a binary relation G (representing edges in a directed graph with no edges of the form $\langle a, a \rangle$). It is straightforward to generalize the development to arbitrary inputs (see Exercise 17.19).

We will use an infinite set $\mathcal{A}$ of CALC sentences called *extension axioms*, which refer to graphs. They say, intuitively, that every subgraph can be extended by one node in all possible ways. More precisely, $\mathcal{A}$ contains, for each k, all sentences of the form

$$\forall x_1 \ldots \forall x_k ((\bigwedge_{i \neq j} (x_i \neq x_j)) \Rightarrow \exists y (\bigwedge_i (x_i \neq y) \wedge connections(x_1, \ldots, x_k; y))),$$

where $connections(x_1, \ldots, x_k; y)$ is some conjunction of literals containing, for each x_i, one of $G(x_i, y)$ or $\neg G(x_i, y)$, and one of $G(y, x_i)$ or $\neg G(y, x_i)$. For example, for $k = 3$, one of the 2^6 extension axioms is

$$\forall x_1, x_2, x_3 ((x_1 \neq x_2 \wedge x_2 \neq x_3 \wedge x_3 \neq x_1) \Rightarrow$$
$$\exists y (x_1 \neq y \wedge x_2 \neq y \wedge x_3 \neq y \wedge$$
$$G(x_1, y) \wedge \neg G(y, x_1) \wedge \neg G(x_2, y) \wedge \neg G(y, x_2) \wedge G(x_3, y) \wedge G(y, x_3)))$$

specifying the pattern of connections represented in Fig. 17.4.

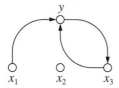

Figure 17.4:   A connection pattern

A graph G satisfies this particular extension axiom if for each triple x_1, x_2, x_3 of distinct vertexes in G, there exists a vertex y connected to x_1, x_2, x_3, as shown in Fig. 17.4.

Note that $\mathcal{A}$ consists of an infinite set of sentences and that each finite subset of $\mathcal{A}$ is satisfied by some infinite instance. (The instance is obtained by starting from one node and repeatedly adding nodes required by the extension axioms in the subset.) Then by the compactness theorem there is an infinite instance satisfying all of $\mathcal{A}$, and by the Löwenheim-Skolem theorem (see Chapter 2) there is a countably infinite instance $\mathcal{R}$ satisfying $\mathcal{A}$.

The following lemma shows that $\mathcal{R}$ is unique up to isomorphism.

LEMMA 17.3.5   If $\mathcal{R}$ and $\mathcal{P}$ are two countably infinite instances over G satisfying all sentences in $\mathcal{A}$, then $\mathcal{R}$ and $\mathcal{P}$ are isomorphic.

Proof   Suppose that $a_1 a_2 \ldots$ is an enumeration of all constants in $\mathcal{R}$, and $b_1 b_2 \ldots$ is an enumeration of those in $\mathcal{P}$. We construct an isomorphism between $\mathcal{R}$ and $\mathcal{P}$ by alternatingly picking constants from $\mathcal{R}$ and from $\mathcal{P}$. We construct sequences $a_{i_1} \ldots a_{i_k} \ldots$ and $b_{i_1} \ldots b_{i_k} \ldots$ such that $a_{i_k} \to b_{i_k}$ is an isomorphism from $\mathcal{R}$ to $\mathcal{P}$. The procedure for picking the kth constants a_{i_k} and b_{i_k} in these sequences is defined inductively as follows. For the base case, let $a_{i_1} = a_1$ and $b_{i_1} = b_1$. Suppose that sequences $a_{i_1} \ldots a_{i_k}$ and $b_{i_1} \ldots b_{i_k}$ have been defined. If k is even, let $a_{i_{k+1}}$ be the first constant in $a_1, a_2, \ldots$ that does not occur so far in the sequence. Let σ_k be the sentence in $\mathcal{A}$ describing the way $a_{i_{k+1}}$ extends the subgraph with nodes $a_{i_1} \ldots a_{i_k}$. Because $\mathcal{P}$ also satisfies σ_k, there exists a constant b in $\mathcal{P}$ that extends the subgraph $b_{i_1} \ldots b_{i_k}$ in the same manner. Let $b_{i_{k+1}} = b$. If k is odd, the procedure is reversed (i.e., it starts by choosing first a new constant from $b_1, b_2, \ldots$). This back-and-forth procedure ensures that (1) all constants from both $\mathcal{R}$ and $\mathcal{P}$ occur eventually among the chosen constants, and (2) the mapping $a_{i_k} \to b_{i_k}$ is an isomorphism. ■

Thus the foregoing proof shows that there exists a unique (up to isomorphism) countable graph $\mathcal{R}$ satisfying $\mathcal{A}$. This graph, studied extensively by Rado [Rad64] and others, is usually referred to as the *Rado graph*. We can now prove the following crucial lemma. The key point is the equivalence between (*a*) and (*c*), called the *transfer property*: It relates satisfaction of a sentence by the Rado graph to the property of being almost surely true.

LEMMA 17.3.6   Let $\mathcal{R}$ be the Rado graph and σ a CALC sentence. The following are equivalent:

(a) $\mathcal{R}$ satisfies σ;

(b) $\mathcal{A}$ implies σ; and

(c) σ is almost surely true.

Proof $(a) \Rightarrow (b)$: Suppose (a) holds but (b) does not. Then there exists some instance $\mathcal{P}$ satisfying $\mathcal{A}$ but not σ. Because $\mathcal{P}$ satisfies $\mathcal{A}$, $\mathcal{P}$ must be infinite. By the Lowënheim-Skolem theorem (see Chapter 2), we can assume that $\mathcal{P}$ is countable. But then, by Lemma 17.3.5, $\mathcal{P}$ is isomorphic to $\mathcal{R}$. This is a contradiction, because $\mathcal{R}$ satisfies σ but $\mathcal{P}$ does not.

$(b) \Rightarrow (c)$: It is sufficient to show that each sentence in $\mathcal{A}$ is almost surely true. Suppose this is the case and $\mathcal{A}$ implies σ. By the compactness theorem, σ is implied by some finite subset $\mathcal{A}'$ of $\mathcal{A}$. Because every sentence in $\mathcal{A}'$ is almost surely true, the conjunction $\bigwedge \mathcal{A}'$ of these sentences is almost surely true. Because σ is true in every instance where $\bigwedge \mathcal{A}'$ is true, $\mu_n(\sigma) \geq \mu_n(\bigwedge \mathcal{A}')$, so $\mu_n(\sigma)$ converges to 1 and σ is almost surely true.

It remains to show that each sentence in $\mathcal{A}$ is almost surely true. Consider the following sentence σ_k in $\mathcal{A}$:

$$\forall x_1 \ldots \forall x_k ((\bigwedge_{i \neq j} (x_i \neq x_j)) \rightarrow \exists y (\bigwedge_i (x_i \neq y) \wedge connections(x_1, \ldots, x_k; y))).$$

Then $\neg \sigma_k$ is the sentence

$$\exists x_1 \ldots \exists x_k ((\bigwedge_{i \neq j} (x_i \neq x_j)) \wedge$$

$$\forall y (\bigwedge_i (x_i \neq y) \rightarrow \neg connections(x_1, \ldots, x_k; y))).$$

We will show the following property on the probability that an instance with n constants *does not* satisfy σ_k:

(**) $\qquad \mu_n(\neg \sigma_k) \leq n \cdot (n-1) \cdot \ldots \cdot (n-k) \cdot (1 - \frac{1}{2^{2k}})^{(n-k)}.$

Because $\lim_{n \to \infty} [n \cdot (n-1) \cdot \ldots \cdot (n-k) \cdot (1 - \frac{1}{2^{2k}})^{(n-k)}] = 0$, it follows that $\lim_{n \to \infty} \mu_n(\neg \sigma_k) = 0$, so $\neg \sigma_k$ is almost surely false, and σ_k is almost surely true.

Let N be the number of instances with constants in $\{1, \ldots, n\}$. To prove (**), observe the following:

1. For some fixed distinct $a_1, \ldots, a_k, b$ in $\{1, \ldots, n\}$, the number of **I** satisfying some fixed literal in $connections(a_1, \ldots, a_k; b)$ is $\frac{1}{2} \cdot N$.

2. For some fixed distinct $a_1, \ldots, a_k, b$ in $\{1, \ldots, n\}$, the number of **I** satisfying $connections(a_1, \ldots, a_k; b)$ is $\frac{1}{2^{2k}} \cdot N$ (because there are $2k$ literals in *connections*).

3. The number of **I** *not* satisfying *connections*$(a_1, \ldots, a_k; b)$ is therefore $N - \frac{1}{2^{2k}} \cdot N = (1 - \frac{1}{2^{2k}}) \cdot N$.

4. For some fixed $a_1, \ldots, a_k$ in $\{1, \ldots, n\}$, the number of **I** satisfying

$$\forall y (\bigwedge_i (a_i \neq y) \rightarrow \neg connections(a_1, \ldots, a_k; y))$$

is $(1 - \frac{1}{2^{2k}})^{n-k} \cdot N$ [because there are $(n - k)$ ways of picking b distinct from $a_1, \ldots, a_k$)].

5. The number of **I** satisfying $\neg \sigma_k$ is thus at most

$$n \cdot (n - 1) \cdot \ldots \cdot (n - k) \cdot (1 - \frac{1}{2^{2k}})^{(n-k)} \cdot N$$

(from the choices of $a_1, \ldots, a_k$). Hence (**) is proven.

(See Exercise 17.16.)

$(c) \Rightarrow (a)$: Suppose that $\mathcal{R}$ does not satisfy σ (i.e., $\mathcal{R} \models \neg \sigma$). Because $(a) \Rightarrow (c)$, $\neg \sigma$ is almost surely true. Then σ cannot be almost surely true (a contradiction). ∎

The 0-1 law for CALC follows immediately.

THEOREM 17.3.7   Each sentence in CALC is almost surely true or almost surely false.

Proof   Let σ be a CALC sentence. The Rado graph $\mathcal{R}$ satisfies either σ or $\neg \sigma$. By the transfer property $[(a) \Rightarrow (c)$ in Lemma 17.3.6], σ is almost surely true or $\neg \sigma$ is almost surely true. Thus σ is almost surely true or almost surely false. ∎

The 0-1 law for CALC can be extended to *fixpoint* and *while*. We prove it next for *while* (and therefore *fixpoint*). Once again the proof uses the Rado graph and extends the transfer property to the *while* sentences.

THEOREM 17.3.8   Every *while* sentence is almost surely true or almost surely false.

Proof   We use as a language for the *while* queries the partial fixpoint logic CALC+μ. The main idea of the proof is to show that every CALC+μ sentence that is defined on all instances is in fact equivalent almost surely to a CALC sentence, and so by the previous result is almost surely true or almost surely false. We show this for CALC+μ sentences. By Theorem 14.4.7, we can consider w.l.o.g. only sentences involving one application of the partial fixpoint operator μ. Thus consider a CALC+μ sentence ξ of the form

$$\xi = \exists \vec{x} \, (\mu_T(\varphi(T))(\vec{t}))$$

over schema **R**, where

(a) φ is a CALC formula, and

(b) $\vec{t}$ is a tuple of variables or constants of appropriate arity, and $\vec{x}$ is the tuple of distinct free variables in $\vec{t}$.

(We need the existential quantification for binding the free variables. An alternative is to have constants in $\vec{t}$ but, as mentioned earlier we do not consider constants when discussing 0-1 laws.)

Essentially, a computation of a query ξ consists of iterating the CALC formula φ until convergence occurs (if ever). Consider the sequence $\{\varphi^i(\mathbf{I})\}_{i>0}$, where $\mathbf{I}$ is an input. If $\mathbf{I}$ is finite, the sequence is periodic [i.e., there exist N and p such that, for each $n \geq N$, $\varphi^n(\mathbf{I}) = \varphi^{n+p}(\mathbf{I})$]. If $p = 1$, then the sequence converges (it becomes constant at some point); otherwise it does not. Now consider the sequence $\{\varphi^i(\mathcal{R})\}_{i>0}$, where $\mathcal{R}$ is the Rado graph. Because the set of constants involved is no longer finite, the sequence may or may not be periodic. A key point in our proof is the observation that the sequence $\{\varphi^i(\mathcal{R})\}_{i>0}$ is indeed periodic, just as in the finite case.

To see this, we use a technique similar to the hyperplane technique in the proof of Lemma 17.3.5. Let k be some integer. We argue next that for each k, there is a finite number of equivalence classes of k-tuples induced by automorphisms of $\mathcal{R}$. For each pair u, v of k-tuples with entries in $adom(\mathcal{R})$, let $u \equiv_k^{\mathcal{R}} v$ iff there exists an automorphism ρ of $\mathcal{R}$ such that $\rho(u) = v$.

Let $u \simeq_k^{\mathcal{R}} v$ if both the patterns of equality and the patterns of connection within u and v are identical. More formally, for each $u = \langle a_1, \dots, a_k \rangle$, $v = \langle b_1, \dots, b_k \rangle$ (where a_i and b_i are constants in $\mathcal{R}$), $u \simeq_k^{\mathcal{R}} v$ if

- for each i, j, $a_i = a_j$ iff $b_i = b_j$, and
- for each i, j, $\langle a_i, a_j \rangle$ is an edge in $\mathcal{R}$ iff $\langle b_i, b_j \rangle$ is an edge in $\mathcal{R}$.

We claim that

$$u \equiv_k^{\mathcal{R}} v \text{ iff } u \simeq_k^{\mathcal{R}} v.$$

The "only if" part follows immediately from the definitions. For the "if" part, suppose that $u \simeq_k^{\mathcal{R}} v$. To show that $u \equiv_k^{\mathcal{R}} v$, we must build an automorphism ρ of $\mathcal{R}$ such that $\rho(u) = v$. This is done by a back-and-forth construction, as in Lemma 17.3.5, using the extension axioms satisfied by $\mathcal{R}$ (see Exercise 17.18).

Because there are finitely many patterns of connection and equality among k vertexes, there are finitely many equivalence classes of $\simeq_k^{\mathcal{R}}$, so of $\equiv_k^{\mathcal{R}}$. Due to genericity of the *while* computation, each $\varphi^i(\mathcal{R})$ is a union of such equivalence classes (see Exercise 16.6 in the previous chapter). Thus there must exist $m, l, 0 \leq m < l$, such that $\varphi^m(\mathcal{R}) = \varphi^l(\mathcal{R})$. Let $N = m$ and $p = l - m$. Then for each $n \geq N$, $\varphi^n(\mathcal{R}) = \varphi^{n+p}(\mathcal{R})$. It follows that:

(1) $\{\varphi^i(\mathcal{R})\}_{i>0}$ is periodic.

Using this fact, we show the following:

(2) The sequence $\{\varphi^i(\mathcal{R})\}_{i>0}$ converges.

(3) The sentence ξ is equivalent almost surely to some CALC sentence σ.

Before proving these, we argue that (2) and (3) will imply the statement of the theorem. Suppose that (2) and (3) holds. Suppose also that σ is false in $\mathcal{R}$. By Lemma 17.3.6, σ is almost surely false. Then $\mu_n(\xi) \leq \mu_n(\xi \not\equiv \sigma) + \mu_n(\sigma)$ and both $\mu_n(\xi \not\equiv \sigma)$ and $\mu_n(\sigma)$ converge to 0, so $\lim_{n\to\infty}(\mu_n(\xi)) = 0$. Thus ξ is also almost surely false. By a similar argument, ξ is almost surely true if σ is true in $\mathcal{R}$.

We now prove (2). Let Σ_{ij} be the CALC sentence stating that φ^i and φ^j are equivalent. Suppose $\{\varphi^i(\mathcal{R})\}_{i>0}$ does not converge. Thus the period of the sequence is greater than 1, so there exist $m, j, l, m < j < l$, such that

$$\varphi^m(\mathcal{R}) = \varphi^l(\mathcal{R}) \neq \varphi^j(\mathcal{R}).$$

Thus $\mathcal{R}$ satisfies the CALC sentence

$$\chi = \Sigma_{ml} \wedge \neg\Sigma_{mj}.$$

Let $\mathbf{I}$ range over finite databases. Because ξ is defined on all finite inputs, $\{\varphi^i(\mathbf{I})\}_{i \geq 0}$ converges. On the other hand, by the transfer property (Lemma 17.3.6), χ is almost surely true. It follows that the sequence $\{\varphi^i(\mathbf{I})\}_{i>0}$ diverges almost surely. In particular, there exist finite $\mathbf{I}$ for which $\{\varphi^i(\mathbf{I})\}_{i>0}$ diverges (a contradiction).

The proof of (3) is similar. By (1) and (2), the sequence $\{\varphi^i(\mathcal{R})\}_{i>0}$ becomes constant after finitely many iterations, say N. Then ξ is equivalent on $\mathcal{R}$ to the CALC sentence $\sigma = \exists \vec{x}(\varphi^N(\vec{t}))$. Suppose $\mathcal{R}$ satisfies ξ. Thus $\mathcal{R}$ satisfies σ. Furthermore, $\mathcal{R}$ satisfies $\Sigma_{N(N+1)}$ because $\{\varphi^i(\mathcal{R})\}_{i>0}$ becomes constant at the Nth iteration. Thus $\mathcal{R}$ satisfies $\sigma \wedge \Sigma_{N(N+1)}$. By the transfer property for CALC, $\sigma \wedge \Sigma_{N(N+1)}$ is almost surely true. For each finite instance $\mathbf{I}$ where $\Sigma_{N(N+1)}$ holds, $\{\varphi^i(\mathbf{I})\}_{i>0}$ converges after N iterations, so ξ is equivalent to σ. It follows that ξ is almost surely equivalent to σ. The case where $\mathcal{R}$ does not satisfy ξ is similar. ∎

Thus we have shown that *while* sentences have a 0-1 law. It follows immediately that many queries, including *even*, are not *while* sentences. The technique of 0-1 laws has been extended successfully to languages beyond *while*. Many languages that do not have 0-1 laws are also known, such as *existential second-order logic* (see Exercise 17.21). The precise border that separates languages that have 0-1 laws from those that do not has yet to be determined and remains an interesting and active area of research.

17.4   The Impact of Order

In this section, we consider in detail the impact of order on the expressive power of query languages. As mentioned at the beginning of this chapter, we view the assumption of order as, in some sense, suspending the data independence principle in a database. Because data independence is one of the main guiding principles of the pure relational model, it is important to understand its consequences in the expressiveness and complexity of query languages.

As illustrated by the *even* query, order can considerably affect the expressiveness of a language and the difficulty of computing some queries. Without the order assumption, no expressiveness results are known for the complexity classes of PTIME and below; that is, no

P			$succ$	
b	a	c	a	b
b	b	d	b	c
c	a	d	c	d
d	b	a		

Figure 17.5:   An ordered instance

languages are known that express precisely the queries of those complexity classes. With order, there are numerous such results. We present two of the most prominent ones.

At the end of this section, we present two recent developments that further explore the interplay of order and expressiveness. The first is a normal form for *while* queries that, speaking intuitively, separates a *while* query into two components: one unordered and the second ordered. The second development increases expressive power on unordered input by introducing nondeterminism in queries.

We begin by making the notion of an ordered database more precise. A database is said to be *ordered* if it includes a designated binary relation *succ* that provides a successor relation on the constants occurring in the database. A *query on an ordered database* is a query whose input database schema contains *succ* and that ranges only over the ordered instances of the input database schema.

EXAMPLE 17.4.1   Consider the database schema $\mathbf{R} = \{P, succ\}$, where P is ternary. An ordered instance of $\mathbf{R}$ is represented in Fig. 17.5. According to *succ*, a is the first constant, b is the successor of a, c is the successor of b, and d is the successor of c. Thus a, b, c, d can be identified with the integers 1, 2, 3, 4, respectively.

We now consider the power of *fixpoint* and *while* on ordered databases. In particular, we prove the fundamental result that *fixpoint* expresses precisely QPTIME on ordered databases, and *while* expresses precisely QPSPACE on ordered databases. This shows that order has a far-reaching impact on expressiveness, well beyond isolated cases such as the *even* query. More broadly, the characterization of QPTIME by *fixpoint* (with the order assumption) provides an elegant logical description of what have traditionally been considered the tractable problems. Beyond databases, this is significant to both logic and complexity theory.

THEOREM 17.4.2

   (a) *Fixpoint* expresses QPTIME on ordered databases.

   (b) *While* expresses QPSPACE on ordered databases.

Proof   Consider (a). We have already seen that *fixpoint* $\subseteq$ QPTIME (see Exercise 17.11), and so it remains to show that all QPTIME queries on ordered databases are expressible in *fixpoint*. Let q be a query on a database with schema $\mathbf{R}$ that includes *succ*, such that q is in

QPTIME on the ordered instances of $\mathbf{R}$. Thus there is a polynomial p and Turing machine M' that, on input $enc(\mathbf{I})\#enc(u)$, terminates in time $p(|enc(\mathbf{I})\#enc(u)|)$ and accepts the input iff $u \in q(\mathbf{I})$. (In this section, encodings of ordered instances are with respect to the enumeration of constants provided by *succ*; see also Chapter 16.) Because $q(\mathbf{I})$ has size polynomial in $\mathbf{I}$, a TM M can be constructed that runs in polynomial time and that, on input $enc(\mathbf{I})$, produces as output $enc(q(\mathbf{I}))$. We now describe the construction of a CALC$+\mu^+$ query q_M that is equivalent to q on ordered instances of $\mathbf{R}$.

The fixpoint query q_M we construct, when given ordered input $\mathbf{I}$, will operate in three phases: (α) construct an encoding of $\mathbf{I}$ that can be used to simulate M; (β) simulate M; and (γ) decode the output of M. A key point throughout the construction is that q_M is inflationary, and so it must compute without ever deleting anything from a relation. Note that this restriction does not apply to (b), which simplifies the simulation in that case.

We next describe the encoding used in the simulation of M. The encoding is centered around a relation that holds the different configurations reached by M.

Representing a tape. Because the tape is infinite, we only represent the finite portion, polynomial in length, that is potentially used. We need a way to identify each cell of the tape. Let n_c be the number of constants in $\mathbf{I}$. Because M runs in polynomial time, there is some k such that M on input $enc(\mathbf{I})$ takes time $\leq n_c^k$, and thus $\leq n_c^k$ tape cells (see also Exercise 16.12 in the previous chapter). Consider the world of k-tuples with entries in the constants from $\mathbf{I}$. Note that there are n_c^k such tuples and that they can be lexicographically ordered using *succ*. Thus each cell can be uniquely identified by a k-tuple of constants from $\mathbf{I}$. One can define by a *fixpoint* query a $2k$-ary relation $succ_k$ providing the successor relation on k-tuples, in the lexicographic order induced by *succ* (see Exercise 17.23a). The ordered k-tuples thus allow us to represent a sequence of cells and hence M's tape.

Representing all the configurations. Note that one cannot remove the tuples representing old configurations of M due to the inflationary nature of *fixpoint* computations. Thus one represents all the configurations in a single relation. To distinguish a particular configuration (e.g., that at time i, $i \leq n_c^k$), k-columns are used as timestamp. Thus to keep track of the sequence of configurations in a computation of M, one can use a $(2k + 2)$-ary relation R_M where

1. the first k columns serve as a timestamp for the configuration,
2. the next k identify the tape cells,
3. column $(2k + 1)$ holds the content of the cell, and
4. column $(2k + 2)$ indicates the state and position of the head.

Note that now we are dealing with a double encoding: The database is encoded on the tape, and then the tape is encoded back into R_M.

To illustrate this simple but potentially confusing situation, we consider an example. Let $\mathbf{R} = \{P, succ\}$, and let $\mathbf{I}$ be the ordered instance of $\mathbf{R}$ represented in Fig. 17.5. Then $enc(\mathbf{I})$ is represented in Fig. 17.6. We assume, without loss of generality, that symbols in the tape alphabet and the states of M are in **dom**. Parts of the first two configurations are represented in the relation shown in Fig. 17.7. The representation assumes that $k = 4$, so the arity of the relation is 10. Because this is a single-volume book, only part of the relation is shown. More precisely, we show the first tuples from the representation of the

P[1#0#10][1#1#11][10#0#11][11#1#0]*succ*[0#1][1#10][10#11]

Figure 17.6: Encoding of **I** and *u* on a TM tape

first two configurations. It is assumed that the original state is *s* and the head points to the first cell of the tape; and that in that state, the head moves to the right, changing *P* to 0, and the machine goes to state *r*. Observe that the timestamp for the first configuration is $\langle a, a, a, a \rangle$, and $\langle a, a, a, b \rangle$ for the second. Observe also the numbering of tape cells: $\langle a, a, a, a \rangle, \ldots, \langle a, a, c, d \rangle$, etc.

We can now describe the three phases of the operation of q_M more precisely: For a given ordered instance **I**, q_M

(α) computes, in R_M, a representation of the initial configuration of *M* on input *enc*(**I**);

(β) computes, also in R_M, the sequence of consecutive configurations of *M* until termination; and

(γ) decodes the final tape contents of *M*, as represented in R_M, into the output relation.

We sketch the construction of the *fixpoint* queries realizing (α) and (β) here, and we leave (γ) as an exercise (17.23).

Consider phase (α). Recall that each constant is encoded on the tape of *M* as the binary representation of its rank in the successor relation *succ* (e.g., *c* as 10). To perform the encoding of the initial configuration, it is useful first to construct an auxiliary relation that provides the encoding of each constant. Because there are n_c constants, the code of each constant requires $\leq \lceil \log(n_c) \rceil$ bits, and thus less than n_c bits. We can therefore use a ternary relation *constant_coding* to record the encoding. A tuple $\langle x, y, z \rangle$ in that relation indicates that the kth bit of the encoding of constant *x* is *z*, where *k* is the rank of constant *y* in the *succ* relation. For instance, the relation *constant_coding* corresponding to the *succ* in Fig. 17.5 is represented in Fig. 17.8. The tuples $\langle c, a, 1 \rangle$ and $\langle c, b, 0 \rangle$ indicate, for instance, that *c* is encoded as 10. It is easily seen that *constant_coding* is definable from *succ* by a *fixpoint* query (see Exercise 17.23b).

With relation *constant_coding* constructed, the task of computing the encoding of **I** and *u* into R_M is straightforward. We will illustrate this using again the example in Fig. 17.5. To encode relation *P*, one steps through all 3-tuples of constants and checks if a tuple in *P* has been reached. To step through the 3-tuples, one first constructs the successor relation $succ_3$ on 3-tuples. The first tuple in *P* that is reached is $\langle b, a, c \rangle$. Because this is the first tuple encoded, one first inserts into R_M the identifying information for *P* (the first tuple in Fig. 17.7). This proceeds, yielding the next tuples in Fig. 17.7. The binary representation for each of *b*, *a*, *c* is obtained from relation *constant_coding*. This proceeds by moving to the next 3-tuple. It is left to the reader to complete the details of the *fixpoint* query constructing R_M (see Exercise 17.23c). Several additional relations have to be used for bookkeeping purposes. For instance, when stepping through the tuples in $succ_3$, one must keep track of the last tuple that has been processed.

We next outline the construction for (β). One must simulate the computation of *M* starting from the initial configuration represented in R_M. To construct a new configuration from the current one, one must simulate a move of *M*. This is repeated until *M* reaches

R_M

a	a	a	a	a	a	a	a	P	s
a	a	a	a	a	a	a	b	[	0
a	a	a	a	a	a	a	c	1	0
a	a	a	a	a	a	a	d	#	0
a	a	a	a	a	a	b	a	0	0
a	a	a	a	a	a	b	b	#	0
a	a	a	a	a	a	b	c	1	0
a	a	a	a	a	a	b	d	0	0
a	a	a	a	a	a	c	a	]	0
a	a	a	a	a	a	c	b	[	0
a	a	a	a	a	a	c	c	1	0
a	a	a	a	a	a	c	d	#	0
.	.	.	.	.	.	.	.	.	.
.	.	.	.	.	.	.	.	.	.
.	.	.	.	.	.	.	.	.	.
a	a	a	b	a	a	a	a	0	0
a	a	a	b	a	a	a	b	[	r
a	a	a	b	a	a	a	c	1	0
a	a	a	b	a	a	a	d	#	0
a	a	a	b	a	a	b	a	0	0
a	a	a	b	a	a	b	b	#	0
a	a	a	b	a	a	b	c	1	0
a	a	a	b	a	a	b	d	0	0
a	a	a	b	a	a	c	a	]	0
a	a	a	b	a	a	c	b	[	0
a	a	a	b	a	a	c	c	1	0
a	a	a	b	a	a	c	d	#	0
.	.	.	.	.	.	.	.	.	.
.	.	.	.	.	.	.	.	.	.
.	.	.	.	.	.	.	.	.	.

Figure 17.7:   Coding of part of the (first two) configurations

a final state (accepting or rejecting), which, as we assumed earlier, happens after at most n_c^k steps. The iteration can be performed using the fixpoint operator in $CALC + \mu^+$. Each step consists of defining the new configuration from the current one, timestamping it, and adding it to R_M. This can be done with a CALC formula. For instance, suppose the current state of M is q, the content of the current cell is 0, and the corresponding move of M is to change 0 to 1, move right, and change states from q to r. Suppose also that

constant_coding

a	a	0
b	a	1
c	a	1
c	b	0
d	a	1
d	b	1

Figure 17.8:   The relation *constant_coding* corresponding to *a,b,c,d*

- $\vec{t}$ is the timestamp (in the example this is a 4-tuple) identifying the current configuration,
- R_M contains the tuple $\langle \vec{t}, \vec{j}, 0, q \rangle$, where $\vec{j}$ specifies a tape cell (in the example again with a 4-tuple), and
- $\vec{t'}$ is the next timestamp and $\vec{j'}$ the next cell [i.e., $succ_k(\vec{t}, \vec{t'})$ and $succ_k(\vec{j}, \vec{j'})$].

The tuples describing the new configuration of M are

- (a) $\langle \vec{t'}, \vec{i}, x, y \rangle$ if $\vec{i} \neq \vec{j}, \vec{i} \neq \vec{j'}$ and $\langle \vec{t}, \vec{i}, x, y \rangle \in R_M$;
- (b) $\langle \vec{t'}, \vec{j}, 1, 0 \rangle$;
- (c) $\langle \vec{t'}, \vec{j'}, x, r \rangle$ if $\langle \vec{t}, \vec{j'}, x, 0 \rangle \in R_M$.

In other words, (a) says that the cells other than the jth cell and the next cell remain unchanged; (b) says that the content of cell j changes from 0 to 1, and the head no longer points to the jth cell; finally, (c) says that the head points to the right adjacent cell, the new state is r, and the content of that cell is unchanged. Clearly, (a) through (c) can be expressed by a CALC formula (Exercise 17.23d). One such formula is needed for each move of M, and the formula corresponding to the finite set of possible moves is obtained by their disjunction.

We have outlined queries that realize (α) and (β) (i.e., perform the encoding needed to run M and then simulate the run of M). Using these *fixpoint* queries and their analog for phase (γ), it is now easy to construct the *fixpoint* query q_M that carries out the complete computation of q. This completes the proof of (a).

The construction for (b) is similar. The difference lies in the fact that a *while* computation need not be inflationary, unlike *fixpoint* computations. This simplifies the simulation. For instance, only the tuples corresponding to the current configuration of M are kept in R_M (Exercise 17.24). ∎

Although PTIME is considered synonymous with tractability in many circumstances, complexity classes lower than PTIME are most useful in practice in the context of potentially large databases. There are numerous results that extend the logical characterization of QPTIME to lower complexity classes for ordered databases. For instance, by limiting the fixpoint operator in *fixpoint* to simpler operators based on various forms of transitive closure, one can obtain languages expressing QLOGSPACE and QNLOGSPACE on ordered databases.

Theorem 17.4.2 implies that the presence of order results in increased expressive power for the *fixpoint* and *while* queries. For these languages, this is easily seen (for instance, *even* can be expressed by *fixpoint* when an order is provided). For weaker languages, the impact of order may be harder to see. For instance, it is not obvious whether the presence of order results in increased expressive power for CALC. The query *even* is of no immediate help, because it cannot be expressed by CALC even in the presence of order (Exercise 17.8). However, a more complicated query based on *even* can be used to show that CALC does indeed become more expressive with an order (Exercise 17.27). Because the CALC queries on ordered instances remain in AC$_0$, this shows in particular that there are queries in AC$_0$ that CALC cannot express.

From Chaos to Order: A Normal Form for *While*

We next discuss informally a normal form for the *while* queries that provides a bridge between computations without order and computations with order. This helps us understand the impact of order and the cost of computation without order.

The normal form says, intuitively, that each *while* query on an unordered instance can be reduced to a *while* query over an *ordered* instance via a *fixpoint* query. More precisely, a *while* program in the normal form consists of two phases. The first is a *fixpoint* query that performs an analysis of the input. It computes an equivalence relation on tuples that is a congruence with respect to the rest of the computation, in that equivalent tuples are treated identically throughout the computation. Thus each equivalence class is treated as an indivisible block of tuples that is never split later in the computation. The *fixpoint* query outputs the equivalence classes in some order, so that each class can be thought of abstractly as an integer. The second phase consists of a *while* query that can be viewed as computing on an *ordered* database obtained by replacing each equivalence class produced in the analysis phase by its corresponding integer.

The normal form also allows the clarification of the relationship between *fixpoint* and *while*. Because on ordered databases the two languages express QPTIME and QPSPACE, respectively, the languages are equivalent on ordered databases iff PTIME = PSPACE. What about the relationship of these languages without the order assumption? It turns out that the normal form can be used to extend this result to the general case when no order is present.

We do not describe the normal form in detail, but we provide some intuition on how a query on an unordered database reduces to a query on an ordered database.

Consider a *while* program q and a particular instance. There are only finitely many CALC queries that are used in q, and the number of their variables is bounded by some integer, say k. To simplify, assume that the input instance consists of a single relation I of arity k and that all relations used in q also have arity k. We can further assume that all queries used in assignment statements are either conjunctive queries or the single algebra operations $-$, $\cup$, and that no relation name occurs twice in a query. For a query φ in q, $\varphi(R_1, \ldots, R_n)$ indicates that $R_1, \ldots, R_n$ are the relation names occurring in φ.

Consider the set J of k-tuples formed with the constants from I. First we can distinguish between tuples based on their presence in (or absence from) I. This yields a first partition of J. Now using the conjunctive queries occurring in q, we can iteratively refine this partition in the following way: If for some conjunctive query $\varphi(R_1, \ldots, R_n)$ occurring in q and some blocks $B_1, \ldots, B_n$ of the current partition $\varphi(B_1, \ldots, B_n)$ and $\neg\varphi(B_1, \ldots, B_n)$ have nonempty intersection with some block B' of the current partition, we refine the partition by splitting the block B' into $B' \cap \varphi(B_1, \ldots, B_n)$ and $B' \cap \neg\varphi(B_1, \ldots, B_n)$. This is repeated until no further refinement occurs, yielding a final partition of J. Furthermore, the blocks can be numbered as they are produced, which provides an ordering $\langle J_1, \ldots, J_m \rangle$ of the blocks of the partition. The entire computation can be performed by a *fixpoint* query constructed from q.

It is important to note that two tuples u, v in one block of the final partition cannot be separated by the computation of q on input I (i.e., at each step of this computation, each relation either contains both u and v or none). In other words, each relation contains a union of blocks of the final partition. Then one can reduce the original computation to an abstract computation q' on the integers by replacing the ith block of the partition by integer i. Thus the original query q can be rewritten as the composition of a *fixpoint* query f followed by a *while* query q' that essentially operates on an ordered input.

Using this normal form, one can show the following:

THEOREM 17.4.3 *While* = *fixpoint* iff PTIME = PSPACE.

Crux The "only if" part follows from Theorem 17.4.2. The normal form is used for the "if" part as follows. Suppose PTIME = PSPACE. Then QPTIME = QPSPACE. Let q be a *while* query. By the normal form, $q = fq'$, where f is a *fixpoint* query and q' is a *while* query whose computation is isomorphic to that of a *while* query on an ordered domain. Because q' is in PSPACE and PSPACE = PTIME, q' is in PTIME. By Theorem 17.4.2(a), there exists a *fixpoint* query f' equivalent to q' on the ordered domain. Thus q is equivalent to ff' and is a *fixpoint* query. ∎

An Alternative to Order: Nondeterminism

Results such as Theorem 17.4.2 show that the presence of order can solve some of the problems of expressiveness of query languages. This can be interpreted as a trade-off between expressiveness and the data independence provided by the abstract interface to the database system. We conclude this section by considering an alternative to order for increasing expressive power. It is based on the use of nondeterminism.

We will use the following terminology. A *deterministic* query is a classical query that always produces at most one output for each input instance. A *nondeterministic* query is a query that may have more than one possible outcome on a given input instance. Generally we assume that all possible outcomes are acceptable as answers to the query. For example, the query "Find *one* cinema showing *Casablanca*" is nondeterministic.

Consider again the query *even*, which is not expressible by *fixpoint* or *while*. The query *even* is easily computed by *fixpoint* in the presence of order (see Exercise 17.25). Another way to circumvent the difficulty of computing *even* is to relax the *determinism*

R	A	B
	a	b
	a	c
	b	b
	b	c

I

R	A	B
	a	b
	b	b

I_1

R	A	B
	a	b
	b	c

I_2

R	A	B
	a	c
	b	b

I_3

R	A	B
	a	c
	b	c

I_4

Figure 17.9:   An application of *witness*

of the query language. If one could choose, whenever desired, an *arbitrary* element from the set, this would provide another way of enumerating the elements of the set and computing *even*. The drawback is that, with such a nondeterministic construct in the language, determinism of queries can no longer be guaranteed.

The trade-offs based on order and nondeterminism are not unrelated, as it may seem at first. Suppose that an order is given. As argued earlier, this comes down to suspending the data independence principle and accessing the internal representation. In general, the computation may depend on the particular order accessed. Then at the conceptual level, where the order is not visible, the mapping defined by the query appears as nondeterministic. Different outcomes are possible for the same conceptual-level view of the input. Thus the trade-offs based on order and on relaxing determinism are intimately connected.

To illustrate this, we exhibit nondeterministic versions of the $while^{(+)}$ and $CALC+\mu^{(+)}$ queries. In both cases we obtain exactly the (deterministic and nondeterministic) queries computable in polynomial space (time). Analogous results can be shown for lower complexity classes of queries.

Consider first the algebraic setting. We introduce a new operator called *witness* that provides the nondeterminism. To illustrate the use of this operator, consider the relation I in Fig. 17.9. An application of $witness_B$ to I may lead to several results [i.e., $witness_B(I)$ is either I_1, I_2, I_3 or I_4]. Intuitively, for each x occurring in the A column, $witness_B$ selects some tuple $\langle x, y \rangle$ in I, thus choosing nondeterministically a B value y for x. More generally, for each relation J over some schema $U = XY$, $X \cap Y = \emptyset$, $witness_Y(I)$ selects one tuple $\langle \vec{x}, \vec{y} \rangle$ for each $\langle \vec{x} \rangle$ occurring in $\Pi_X(J)$. Observe that from this definition, $witness_U(J)$ selects one tuple in J (if any).

It is also possible to describe the semantics of the *witness* operator using functional dependencies: For each instance J over some schema XY, $X \cap Y = \emptyset$, a possible result of $witness_Y(J)$ is a maximal subinstance J' of J satisfying $X \to Y$ (i.e., such that the attributes in X form a key).

The *witness* operator provides, more generally, a uniform way of obtaining nondeterministic counterparts for traditional deterministic languages.

The extension of $while^{(+)}$ with *witness* is denoted by $while^{(+)}+W$. Following is a useful example that shows that an arbitrary order can be constructed using the *witness* operator.

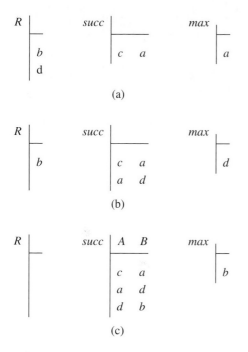

Figure 17.10:   Some steps in the computation of an ordering

EXAMPLE 17.4.4   Consider an input instance over some unary relation schema R. The following *while+W* query defines *all possible* successor relations on the constants from the input (i.e., each run constructs some ordering of the constants from the input; we use the unnamed perspective):

$succ := witness_{12}(\sigma_{1 \neq 2}(R \times R));$
$max := \pi_2(succ);\ R := R - (\pi_1(succ) \cup \pi_2(succ));$
while change do
  begin
  $succ := succ \cup witness_{12}(max \times R);$
  $max := \pi_2(succ) - \pi_1(succ);$
  $R := R - max$
  end

The result is constructed in a binary relation *succ*. A unary relation *max* contains the current maximum element in *succ*. Some steps of a possible computation on input $R = \{a, b, c, d\}$ are shown in Fig. 17.10: (a) shows the state before the loop is first entered, (b) the state after the first execution of the loop, and (c) the final state. Note that the output is empty if R contains fewer than two constants. It is of interest to observe that the program uses only the ability of *witness* to pick an arbitrary tuple from a relation.

This query can also be expressed in *while*$^+$+W. (See Exercise 17.31.)

To continue with the nondeterministic languages, we next consider the language CALC+$\mu^{(+)}$. The nondeterminism is again provided by a logical operator called *witness*[4] and denoted W. Suppose $\varphi(\vec{x}, \vec{y})$ is a formula with free variables $\vec{x}, \vec{y}$. Intuitively, $W\vec{y}\varphi(\vec{x}, \vec{y})$ indicates that one "witness" $\vec{y}_x$ is chosen for each $\vec{x}$ satisfying $\exists \, \vec{y} \, \varphi(\vec{x}, \vec{y})$. For example, if R consists of the relation I in Fig. 17.9, the formula $W_y R(x, y)$ defines the possible answers I_1, I_2, I_3, I_4 in the same figure. [Thus $W_y R(x, y)$ is equivalent to *witness*$_B(R)$.] More precisely, for each formula $\varphi(\vec{x}, \vec{y})$ (where $\vec{x}$ and $\vec{y}$ are vectors of the variables that are free in φ), $W\vec{y}\varphi(\vec{x}, \vec{y})$ is a formula (where the $\vec{y}$ remain free) defining the *set* of relations $\mathbf{I}$ such that for some $\mathbf{J}$ defined by φ: $\mathbf{I} \subseteq \mathbf{J}$; and for each $\vec{x}$ for which $\langle \vec{x}, \vec{y} \rangle$ is in $\mathbf{J}$ for some $\vec{y}$, there exists a *unique* $\vec{y}_x$ such that $\langle \vec{x}, \vec{y}_x \rangle$ is in $\mathbf{I}$.

The extension of CALC+$\mu^{(+)}$ with the *witness* operator is denoted by CALC+$\mu^{(+)}$+W. Following is a useful example that shows that an arbitrary order can be constructed using CALC+μ^++W.

EXAMPLE 17.4.5   Consider the (unary) relation schema R of Example 17.4.4. The following CALC+μ^++W query defines, on each instance I of R, *all possible* successor relations on the constants in I. (The output is empty if I contains fewer than two constants.) The query uses a binary relation schema *succ*, which is used to construct the successor relation iteratively. The query is $\mu_{succ}^+(\varphi(succ))(x, y)$, where $\varphi = \varphi_1 \vee \varphi_2$ and

$\varphi_1(x, y) = \neg \exists x \exists y(succ(xy)) \; \wedge \; Wxy(R(x) \wedge R(y) \wedge x \neq y),$

$\varphi_2(x, y) = Wy(R(y) \wedge \neg \exists z(succ(yz) \vee succ(zy))) \wedge \exists z(succ(zx)) \wedge \neg \exists z(succ(xz)).$

The formula φ_1 initializes the iteration when *succ* is empty; φ_2 adds to *succ* a tuple $\langle x, y \rangle$, where y is an arbitrarily chosen element of $I(R)$ not yet in *succ* and x is the current maximum element in *succ*.

The ability of *while*$^+$+W and CALC+μ^++W to define nondeterministically a successor relation on the constants suggests that the impact of nondeterminism on expressive power is similar to that of order. This is confirmed by the following result.

THEOREM 17.4.6   The set of deterministic queries that are expressed by *while*$^+$+W or CALC+μ^++W is QPTIME.

Proof   It is easy to verify that each deterministic query expressed by *while*$^+$ + W is in QPTIME. Conversely, let q be a query in QPTIME. By Theorem 17.4.2, there exists a *while*$^+$ query w that expresses q if a successor relation *succ* on the constants is given. Then the *while*$^+$+W query expressing q consists of the following:

(i) construct a successor relation *succ* on the constants, as in Example 17.4.5;

---

[4] The *witness* operator is related to Hilbert's ε-symbol [Lei69], but its semantics is different. In particular, the ε-symbol does not yield nondeterminism.

(ii) apply query w to the input instance together with *succ*. ∎

An analogous result holds for *while*$+W$ and CALC$+\mu+W$. Specifically, the set of deterministic queries expressible by these languages is precisely QPSPACE.

Note that Theorem 17.4.6 does *not* provide a *language* that expresses precisely QPTIME, because nondeterministic queries can also be expressed and it is undecidable if a *while*$^{+}+W$ or CALC$+\mu^{+}+W$ query defines a deterministic query (Exercise 17.32). Instead the result shows the power of nondeterministic constructs and so points to a trade-off between expressive power and determinism.

Bibliographic Notes

The sequential data complexity of CALC was investigated by Vardi [Var82a], who showed that CALC is included in LOGSPACE. The parallel complexity of CALC, specifically the connection with AC$_0$, was studied by Immerman [Imm87a]. In [DV91], a database model for parallel computation is defined, and CALC is shown to coincide *exactly* with its restriction to constant time and polynomial size. This differs from AC$_0$ in that the match is precise. Intuitively, this is due to the fact that the model in [DV91] is generic and does not assume an ordered encoding of the input.

The first results on the expressiveness and complexity of *fixpoint* and *while* were obtained by Chandra and Harel, Vardi, and Immerman. In [CH80b] it is shown by a direct proof that *fixpoint* cannot express *even*. The result is extended to *while* in [Cha81a]. The fundamental result that *fixpoint* expresses QPTIME on ordered instances was obtained independently by Immerman [Imm86] and Vardi [Var82a]. The fact that *while* on ordered instances expresses QPSPACE is shown in [Var82a].

Languages expressing complexity classes of queries below QPTIME are investigated in [Imm87b]. They are based on augmenting CALC with operators providing limited recursion, such as various forms of transitive closure. The classes of queries expressed by the resulting languages on ordered databases include deterministic logspace, denoted LOGSPACE, nondeterministic logspace, denoted NLOGSPACE, and symmetric logspace, denoted SLOGSPACE.

There has been a long quest for a language expressing precisely QPTIME on arbitrary (unordered) databases. The problem is formalized in a general setting in [Gur88], where it is also conjectured that no such language exists. The issue is further investigated in [Daw93], where, in particular, it is shown that there exists a language for QPTIME iff there exists some problem complete in P via an extended kind of first-order reductions. To date, the problem of the existence of a language for QPTIME remains open.

In the absence of a language for QPTIME, there have been several proposals to extend the *fixpoint* queries to capture more of QPTIME. Recall that queries involving counting (such as *even*) are not in *fixpoint*. Therefore it is natural to consider extensions of *fixpoint* with counting constructs. An early proposal by Chandra [Cha81a] is to add a *bounded looping* construct of the form *For* $|R|$ *do*, which iterates the body of the loop $|R|$ times. Clearly, this construct allows us to express *even*. However, it has been shown that bounded looping is not sufficient to yield all of QPTIME, because tests $|R_1| = |R_2|$ cannot be expressed (see [Cha88]). More recently, extensions of *fixpoint* with counting constructs have been considered and studied in [CFI89, GO93]. They allow access to the cardinality of relations as well as limited integer manipulation. These languages are more powerful than *fixpoint* but, as shown in [CFI89], still fall short of expressing all of QPTIME. Other results of this flavor are proven in [Daw93, Hel92]. They show that extending *fixpoint* with a finite set of polynomial-time computable constructs of certain forms (generalized quantifiers acting much like oracles) cannot yield a language expressing exactly QPTIME (see Exercise 17.35 for a simplified version of this result).

The normal form for *while* was proven in [AV91b, AV94]. It was also shown there, using the normal form, that *fixpoint* and *while* are equivalent iff PTIME = PSPACE. The cost of computing without an order is also investigated in [AV91b, AV94]. This is formalized using an alternative model of computation called *generic machine* (GM). Unlike Turing machines, GMs do not require an ordered encoding of the input and use only the information provided by the input instance. Based on GM, *generic* complexity classes of queries are defined. For example, GEN-PTIME and GEN-PSPACE are obtained by taking polynomial time and space restrictions of GM. As a typical result, it is shown that *even* is not in GEN-PSPACE, which captures the intuition that this query is hard to compute without order. Another more restricted device, also operating without encodings, is the *relational machine*, also considered in [AV91b, AV94]. There is a close match between complexity classes defined using this device, called *relational complexity classes*, and various languages. For example, relational polynomial time coincides with *fixpoint* and relational polynomial space with *while*. Further connections between languages and relational complexity classes are shown in [AVV92].

Nondeterministic languages and their expressive power are investigated in [ASV90, AV91a, AV91c]. The languages include nondeterministic extensions of CALC+μ^+ and CALC+μ and of rule-based languages such as datalog$^\neg$. Strong connections between these languages are shown (see Exercise 17.33). Nondeterministic languages that can express all the QPTIME queries are exhibited.

A construct related to the witness operator described in this chapter is the *choice* operator, first presented in [KN88]. This construct has been included in the language LDL, an implementation of datalog$^\neg$ [NT89] (see also Chapter 15). Variations of the choice operator, and its connection with stable models of datalog$^\neg$ programs, are further studied in [SZ90, GPSZ91]. The expressive power of the choice operator in the context of datalog is investigated in [CGP93] (see Exercise 17.34).

The Ehrenfeucht-Fraïssé games are due to Ehrenfeucht [Ehr61] and Fraïssé [Fra54]. Since their work, extensions of the games have been proposed and related to various languages such as datalog [LM89], fragments of infinitary logic [KV90c], *fixpoint* queries, and second-order logic [dR87]. In [Imm82, CFI89], games are used to prove lower bounds on the number of variables needed to express certain graph properties. Typically, in the extensions of Ehrenfeucht-Fraïssé games, choosing a constant in an instance is thought of as placing a pebble over that constant (the games are often referred to as *pebble games*). Like the Ehrenfeucht-Fraïssé games, these are two-player games in which one player attempts to prove that the instances are not the same and the other attempts to prove the contrary by placing the pebbles such that the corresponding subinstances are isomorphic. The games differ in the rules for taking turns among players and instances, the number of pebbles placed in one move, whether the pebbles are colored, etc. In games correspond-

G[00#01][10#00][10#01][01#01]#[10]

Figure 17.11: Encoding of an instance and tuple

ing to languages with recursion, players have more than one chance for achieving their objective by removing some of the pebbles and restarting the game. Our presentation of Ehrenfeucht-Fraissé games was inspired by Kolaitis's excellent lecture notes [Kol83].

The study of 0-1 laws was initiated by Fagin and Glebskiĭ. The 0-1 law for CALC was proven in [Fag72, Fag76] and independently by Glebskiĭ et al. [GKLT69]. The 0-1 law for *fixpoint* was shown by Blass, Gurevich, and Kozen [BGK85] and Talanov and Knyazev [TK84]. This was extended to *while* by Kolaitis and Vardi, who proved further extensions of 0-1 laws for certain fragments of second-order logic [KV87, KV90b] and for *infinitary logic* with finitely many variables [KV92], both of which subsume *while*. For instance, 0-1 laws were proven for existential second-order sentences $\exists Q_1 \ldots \exists Q_k \sigma$, where the Q_i are relation variables and σ is a CALC formula in prenex form, whose quantifier portion has one of the shapes $\exists^* \forall^*$ or $\exists^* \forall \exists^*$. It is known that arbitrary existential second-order sentences do not have a 0-1 law (see Exercise 17.21). Infinitary logic is an extension of CALC that allows infinite disjunctions and conjunctions. Kolaitis and Vardi proved that the language consisting of infinitary logic sentences that use only finitely many variables has a 0-1 law. Note that this language subsumes *while* (Exercise 17.22). Another aspect of 0-1 laws that has been studied involves the difficulty of deciding whether a sentence in a language that has a 0-1 law is almost surely true or whether it is almost surely false. For instance, Grandjean proved that the problem is PSPACE complete for CALC [Gra83]. The problem was investigated for other languages by Kolaitis and Vardi [KV87]. A comprehensive survey of 0-1 laws is provided by Compton [Com88].

Fagin [Fag93] presents a survey of finite model theory including 0-1 laws that inspired our presentation of this topic.

Exercises

Exercise 17.1 Consider the CALC query on a database schema with one binary relation G:

$$\varphi = \{x \mid \exists y \forall z (G(x, y) \land \neg G(z, x))\}.$$

Consider the instance **I** over G and tuple encoded on a Turing input tape, as shown in Fig. 17.11. Describe in detail the computation of the Turing machine M_φ, outlined in the proof of Theorem 17.1.1, on this input.

♠ **Exercise 17.2** Prove Theorem 17.1.2.

Exercise 17.3 Prove that $\equiv_r$ is an equivalence relation on instances.

Exercise 17.4 Outline the crux of Theorem 17.2.2 for the case where

$$\varphi = \forall x \, (\exists y \, (R(xy)) \lor \forall z \, (R(zx))).$$

(Note that the quantifier depth of φ is 2, so this case involves games with two moves.)

★ **Exercise 17.5**   Provide a complete description of the winning strategy outlined in the crux of Proposition 17.2.3. *Hint:* For the game with r moves, choose cycles of size at least $r(2^{r+1} - 1)$.

Exercise 17.6   Extend Proposition 17.2.3 by showing that connectivity of graphs is not first-order definable even if an order $\leq$ on the constants is provided. More precisely, let **R** be the database schema consisting of two binary relations G and $\leq$. Let $\mathcal{I}_\leq$ be the family of instances **I** over **R** such that $\mathbf{I}(\leq)$ provides a total order on the constants of $\mathbf{I}(G)$. Outline a proof that there is no CALC sentence σ such that, for each $\mathbf{I} \in \mathcal{I}_\leq$,

$$\sigma(\mathbf{I}) \text{ is true iff } \mathbf{I}(G) \text{ is a connected graph.}$$

♠ **Exercise 17.7**   [Kol83] Use Ehrenfeucht-Fraïssé games to show that the following properties of graphs are not first-order definable:

    (i) the number of vertexes is even;

    (ii) the graph is 2-colorable;

    (iii) the graph is Eulerian (i.e., there exists a cycle that passes through each edge exactly once).

★ **Exercise 17.8**   Show that the property that the number of elements in a unary relation is even is not first-order definable even if an order on the constants is provided.

The following two exercises lead to a proof of the converse of Theorem 17.2.2. It states that instances that are undistinguishable by CALC sentences of quantifier depth r are equivalent with respect to $\equiv_r$. This is shown by proving that each equivalence class of $\equiv_r$ is definable by a special CALC sentence of quantifier depth r, called the r-type of the equivalence class. Intuitively, the r-type sentence describes all patterns that can be detected by playing games of length r on pairs of instances in the equivalence class.

To define the r-types, one first defines formulas with m free variables, called (m, r)-types. An r-type is defined as a $(0, r)$-type. The set of (m, r)-types is defined by backward induction on m as follows.

An (r, r)-type consists of all satisfiable formulas φ with variables $x_1, \ldots, x_r$ such that φ is a conjunction of literals over R and for each $i_1, \ldots, i_k$, either $R(x_{i_1}, \ldots, x_{i_k})$ or $\neg R(x_{i_1}, \ldots, x_{i_k})$ is in φ. Suppose the set of $(m + 1, r)$-types has been defined. Each set S of $(m + 1, r)$-types gives rise to one (m, r)-type defined by

$$\bigvee \{ \exists x_{m+1} \, \varphi \mid \varphi \in S \} \vee \bigvee \{ \forall x_{m+1} \, (\neg(\varphi)) \mid \varphi \notin S \}.$$

♠ **Exercise 17.9**   [Kol83] Let r and m be positive integers such that $0 \leq m \leq r$. Prove that

    (a) every (m, r)-type is a CALC formula with free variables $x_1, \ldots, x_m$ and quantifier depth $(r - m)$;

    (b) there are only finitely many distinct (m, r)-types; and

    (c) for every instance **I** and sequence $a_1, \ldots, a_m$ of constants in **I**, there is exactly one (m, r)-type φ such that **I** satisfies $\varphi(a_1, \ldots, a_m)$.

♠ **Exercise 17.10**   [Kol83] Prove that each equivalence class of $\equiv_r$ is definable by a CALC sentence of quantifier depth r. *Hint:* For a given equivalence class of $\equiv_r$, consider an instance in the class and the unique r-type satisfied by the instance.

Exercise 17.11   Complete the proof of Theorem 17.3.1; specifically show that

(a) *fixpoint* $\subseteq$ QPTIME and *while* $\subseteq$ QPSPACE, and

(b) *fixpoint* is complete in PTIME and *while* is complete in PSPACE.

Exercise 17.12 In the proof of Proposition 17.3.2, the case of assignments of the form $T :=Q_1 \times Q_2$ was discussed. Describe the constructions needed for the other algebra operators. Point out where the assumption that the size of **I** is greater than N is used.

★ **Exercise 17.13** Prove that the *while* queries collapse to CALC on unary relation inputs. More precisely, let **R** be a database schema consisting of unary relations. Show that for each *while* query w on **R** there exists a CALC query φ equivalent to it. *Hint:* Use the same approach as in the proof of Proposition 17.3.2 to show that there is a constant bound on the length of runs of a given *while* program on unary inputs.

★ **Exercise 17.14** Describe how to generalize the proof of Proposition 17.3.2 so that it handles *while* queries that have constants. In particular, describe how the notion of hyperplanes needs to be generalized.

Exercise 17.15 Recall the technique of hyperplanes used in the proof of Proposition 17.3.2.

(a) Let $D \subseteq \mathbf{dom}$ be finite. For a relation schema R, the *cross-product instance* of R over D is $I^R_{\times D} = D \times \cdots \times D$ (arity of R times). The *cross-product instance* of database schema **R** over D is the instance $\mathbf{I^R}_{\times D}$, where $\mathbf{I^R}_{\times D}(R) = I^R_{\times D}$ for each $R \in \mathbf{R}$. Let P be a datalog$^\neg$ program with no constants, input schema **R**, and output schema S with arity k. Prove that there is an $N > 0$ and a set E_P of equivalence relations over $[1, k]$ such that for each set $D \subseteq \mathbf{dom}$: if $|D| \geq N$ then

$$P(\mathbf{I^R}_{\times D}) = \bigcup \{H_{\simeq}(D) \mid \simeq \in E_P\}.$$

(b) Prove (a) for datalog$^{\neg\neg}$ programs.

(c) Generalize your proofs to permit constants in P.

Exercise 17.16 In the proof of Lemma 17.3.6, prove more formally the bound on $\mu_n(\neg \sigma_k)$. Prove that its limit is 0 when n goes to ∞.

Exercise 17.17 Determine whether the following properties of graphs are almost surely true or whether they are almost surely false.

(a) Existence of a cycle of length three

(b) Connectivity

(c) Being a tree

Exercise 17.18 Prove that there is a finite number of equivalence classes of k-tuples induced by automorphisms of the Rado graph. *Hint:* Each class is completely characterized by the pattern of connection and equality among the coordinates of the k-tuple. To see this, show that for all tuples u and v satisfying this property, one can construct an automorphism ρ of the Rado graph such that $\rho(u) = v$. The automorphism is constructed using the extension axioms, similar to the proof of Lemma 17.3.5.

♠ **Exercise 17.19** Describe how to generalize the development of 0-1 laws for arbitrary input and for queries involving constants.

Exercise 17.20 Prove or disprove: The properties expressible in *fixpoint* are exactly the PTIME properties that have a 0-1 law.

Exercise 17.21   The language *existential second-order logic*, denoted ($\exists SO$), consists of sentences of the form $\exists Q_i \dots \exists Q_k \sigma$, where Q_i are relations and σ is a first-order sentence using the relations Q_i (among others). Show that $\exists SO$ does not have a 0-1 law. *Hint:* Exhibit a property expressible in $\exists SO$ that is neither almost surely true nor almost surely false.

★ **Exercise 17.22**   Infinitary logic with finitely many variables, denoted $L^\omega_{\infty\omega}$, is an extension of CALC that allows formulas with infinitely long conjunctions and disjunctions but using only a finite number of variables. Show that each *while* query can be expressed in $L^\omega_{\infty\omega}$. *Hint:* Start with a specific example, such as transitive closure.

Exercise 17.23   The following refer to the proof of Theorem 17.4.2.

(a) Describe a *fixpoint* query that, given a successor relation *succ* on constants, constructs a $2k$-ary successor relation $succ_k$ on k-tuples of constants, in the lexicographical order induced on k-tuples by *succ*.

(b) Show that the relation *constant_coding* can be defined from *succ* using a *fixpoint* query.

(c) Complete the details of the construction of R_M by a *fixpoint* query.

(d) Describe in detail the CALC formula corresponding to the move of M considered in the proof of Theorem 17.4.2.

(e) Describe in detail the CALC formula used to perform phase γ in the computation of q_M.

(f) Show where the proof of Theorem 17.4.2 breaks down if it is not assumed that the input instance is ordered.

Exercise 17.24   Spell out the differences in the proofs of (a) and (b) in Theorem 17.4.2.

Exercise 17.25   Write a *fixpoint* query that computes the parity query *even* on ordered databases.

Exercise 17.26   Consider queries of the form

Does the diameter of G have property P?

where P is an EXPTIME property of the integers (i.e., a property that can be checked, for integer n, in time exponential in $\log n$, or polynomial in n). Show that each query as above is a *fixpoint* query.

♠ **Exercise 17.27**   [Gur] This exercise shows that there is a query expressible in CALC in the presence of order that is not expressible in CALC without order. Let $\mathbf{R} = \{D, S\}$, where D is unary and S is binary. Consider an instance $\mathbf{I}$ of $\mathbf{R}$. Suppose the second column of $\mathbf{I}(S)$ contains only constants from $\mathbf{I}(D)$. Then one can view each constant s in the first column of $\mathbf{I}(S)$ as denoting a subset of $\mathbf{I}(D)$, namely $\{x \mid S(s, x)\}$. Call an instance $\mathbf{I}$ of $\mathbf{R}$ *good* if for each subset of $\mathbf{I}(D)$, there exists a constant representing it. In other words, for each subset T of $\mathbf{I}(D)$, there exists a constant s such that

$$T = \{x \mid S(s, x)\}.$$

Consider the query q defined by $q(\mathbf{I}) = \mathbf{true}$ iff $\mathbf{I}$ is a good input and $|\mathbf{I}(D)|$ is even.

(a) Show that q is not expressible by CALC.

(b) Show that q is expressible on instances extended with an order relation $\le$ on the constants.

(c) Note that in (b), an order is used instead of the usual successor relation on constants. Explain the difficulty of proving (b) if a successor relation is used instead of $\le$.

Hint: For (a), use Ehrenfeucht-Fraissé games. Consider (b). To check that the input is good, check that (1) all singleton subsets of $\mathbf{I}(D)$ are represented, and (2) if T_1 and T_2 are represented, so is $T_1 \cup T_2$. To check evenness of $|\mathbf{I}(D)|$ on good inputs, define first from $\le$ a successor relation $succ_D$ on the constants in $\mathbf{I}(D)$; then check that there exists a subset T of $\mathbf{I}(D)$ consisting of the even constants according to $succ_D$ and that the last element in $succ_D$ is in T.

♠ **Exercise 17.28**   (Expression complexity [Var82a])

(a) Show that the *expression* complexity of CALC is within PSPACE. That is, consider a fixed instance $\mathbf{I}$ and tuple u, and a TM $M_{\mathbf{I},u}$ depending on $\mathbf{I}$ and u that, given as input some standard encoding of a query φ in CALC, decides if $u \in \varphi(\mathbf{I})$. Show that there is such a TM $M_{\mathbf{I},u}$ whose complexity is within PSPACE with respect to $|enc(\varphi)|$, when φ ranges over CALC.

(b) Prove that in terms of expression complexity, CALC is complete in PSPACE. *Hint:* Use a reduction to quantified propositional calculus (see Chapter 2 and [GJ79]).

(c) Let $CALC^-$ consist of the quantifier-free queries in CALC. Show that the expression complexity of $CALC^-$ is within LOGSPACE.

Exercise 17.29   Show that

(a) $Wx(WyR(x, y))$ is not equivalent[5] to $Wxy\varphi(x, y)$;

(b) $Wx(WyR(x, y))$ is not equivalent to $Wy(WxR(x, y))$.

Exercise 17.30   Write a $CALC+\mu^++W$ formula defining the query *even*.

Exercise 17.31   Express the query of Example 17.4.4 in $while^++W$.

♠ **Exercise 17.32**   [ASV90] Show that it is undecidable whether a given $CALC+\mu^++W$ formula defines a deterministic query. *Hint:* Use the undecidability of satisfiability of CALC sentences.

♠ **Exercise 17.33**   [AV91a, AV91c]. As seen, the *witness* operator can be used to obtain nondeterministic versions of $while^{(+)}$ and $CALC+\mu^{(+)}$. One can obtain nondeterministic versions of $datalog^{\neg(\neg)}$ as follows. The syntax is the same, except that heads of rules may contain several literals, and equality may be used in bodies of rules. The rules of the program are fired one rule at a time and one instantiation at a time. The nondeterminism is due to the choice of rule and instantiation used in each firing. The languages thus obtained are denoted $N\text{-}datalog^{\neg(\neg)}$.

(a) Prove that $N\text{-}datalog^{\neg\neg}$ is equivalent to $CALC+\mu+W$ and $while+W$ and expresses all nondeterministic queries computable in polynomial space.[6]

(b) Show that $N\text{-}datalog^\neg$ cannot compute the query $P - \pi_A(Q)$, where Q is of sort AB and P of sort A.

---

[5] Two formulas are *equivalent* iff they define the same set of relations for each given instance.

[6] This includes QPSPACE, the *deterministic* queries computable in polynomial space.

other. However, in our context of value invention, it is practical to have the more direct control on loops provided by *while R*.

Note that the *new* construct is, strictly speaking, nondeterministic. The new values are arbitrary, so several possible outcomes are possible depending on the choice of values. However, the different outcomes differ *only* in the choice of new values. This is formalized by the following:

LEMMA 18.2.1   Let w be a *while_new* program with input schema **R**, and let R be a relation variable in w. Let **I** be an instance over **R**, and let J, J' be two possible values of R at the same point during the execution of w on **I**. Then there exists an isomorphism ρ from J to J' that is the identity on the constants occurring in **I** or w.

The proof of Lemma 18.2.1 is done by a straightforward induction on the number of steps in a partial execution of w on **I** (Exercise 18.7).

Recall that our definition of *query* requires that the answer be unique (i.e., the query must be deterministic). Therefore we must consider only *while_new* programs whose answer never contains values introduced by the *new* statements. Such programs are called *well-behaved while_new* programs. It is possible to give a syntactic restriction on *while_new* programs that guarantees good behavior, can be checked, and yields a class of programs equivalent to all well-behaved *while_new* programs (see Exercises 18.8 and 18.9).

We wish to show that well-behaved *while_new* programs can express all queries. First we have to make sure that well-behaved *while_new* programs do in fact express queries. This is shown next.

LEMMA 18.2.2   Each well-behaved *while_new* program with input schema **R** and output schema *answer* expresses a query from *inst(**R**)* to *inst(answer)*.

Proof   We need to show that well-behaved *while_new* programs define *mappings* from *inst(**R**)* to *inst(answer)* (i.e., they are deterministic with respect to the final answer). Computability and genericity are straightforward. Let w be a well-behaved *while_new* program with input schema **R** and output *answer*. Let I, I' be two possible values of *answer* after the execution of w on an instance **I** of **R**. By Lemma 18.2.1, there exists an isomorphism ρ from I to I' that is the identity on values in **I** or w. Because w is well behaved, *answer* contains *only* values from **I** or w. Thus ρ is the identity and $I = I'$. ∎

Note that although well-behaved programs are deterministic with respect to their final answer, they are not deterministic with respect to intermediate results that may contain new values.

We next show that well-behaved *while_new* programs express all queries. The basic idea is simple. Recall that *while_N* is complete on *ordered* databases. That is, for each query q, there is a *while_N* program w that, given an enumeration of the input values in a relation *succ*, computes q. If, given an input, we were able to construct such an enumeration, we could then simulate *while_N* to compute any desired query. Because of genericity, we cannot hope to construct *one* such enumeration. However, constructing *all* enumerations of values in the input would not violate genericity. Both *while_new* and the language with variable arities considered in the next section can compute arbitrary queries precisely in this fashion: They first compute all possible enumerations of the input values and then simulate a *while$_N$* program on the ordered database corresponding to each enumeration. These computations yield the same result for all enumerations because queries are generic, so the result is independent of the particular enumeration used to encode the database (see Chapter 16).

Before proving the result, we show how we can construct all the possible enumerations of the elements in the active domain of the input.

Representation

Let **I** be an instance over **R**. Let *Success* be the set of all binary relations defining a successor relation over *adom*(**I**). We can represent all the enumerations in *Success* with a 3-ary relation:

$$\overline{succ} = \bigcup_{I \in Success} I \times \{\alpha_I\},$$

where $\{\alpha_I \mid I \in Success\}$ is a set of distinct new values. [Each such α_I is used to denote a particular enumeration of *adom*(**I**).] For example, Fig. 18.2 represents an instance **I** and the corresponding $\overline{succ}$.

Computation of $\overline{succ}$

We now argue that there exists a *while$_{new}$* program w that, given **I**, computes $\overline{succ}$. Clearly, there is a *while$_{new}$* program that, given **I**, produces a unary relation D containing all values

I		$\overline{succ}$			$\widehat{succ}$				
a	b	a	b	α_1	a	b	a	b	c
a	c	b	c	α_1	b	c	a	b	c
c	a	a	c	α_2	a	c	a	c	b
		c	b	α_2	c	b	a	c	b
		b	a	α_3	b	a	b	a	c
		a	c	α_3	a	c	b	a	c
		b	c	α_4	b	c	b	c	a
		c	a	α_4	c	a	b	c	a
		c	a	α_5	c	a	c	a	b
		a	b	α_5	a	b	c	a	b
		c	b	α_6	c	b	c	b	a
		b	a	α_6	b	a	c	b	a

Figure 18.2: An example of $\overline{succ}$ and $\widehat{succ}$

in **I**. Following is a *while_new* program $w_{\overline{succ}}$ that computes the relation $\overline{succ}$ starting from D (using a query q explained next):

$$\overline{succ} := new(\sigma_{1 \neq 2}(D \times D));$$
$$\Delta \quad := q;$$
$$while \ \Delta \ do$$
$$\qquad begin$$
$$\qquad\qquad S := new(\Delta);$$
$$\qquad\qquad \overline{succ} := \left\{ \langle x, y, \alpha' \rangle \; \middle| \; \begin{array}{l} \exists \alpha, x', y'[S(x', y', \alpha, \alpha') \wedge \overline{succ}(x, y, \alpha)] \\ \qquad \vee \ \exists \alpha[S(x, y, \alpha, \alpha')] \end{array} \right\};$$
$$\qquad\qquad \Delta := q;$$
$$\qquad end$$

The intuition is that we construct in turn enumerations of subsets of size 2, 3, etc., until we obtain the enumerations of D. (To simplify, we assume that D contains more than two elements.) An enumeration of a subset of D consists of a successor (binary) relation over that subset. As mentioned earlier, the program associates a marking (invented value) with each such successor relation.

During the computation, $\overline{succ}$ contains the successor relation of subsets of size i computed so far. A triple $\langle a, b, \alpha \rangle$ indicates that b follows a in enumeration denoted α.

The first instruction computes the enumerations of subsets of size 2 (i.e., the distinct pairs of elements of D) and marks them with new values. At each iteration, Δ indicates for each enumeration the elements that are missing in this enumeration. More precisely, relation Δ must contain the following set of triples:

$$\left\{ \langle a, b, \alpha \rangle \; \middle| \; \begin{array}{l} b \ \text{does not occur in the successor relation corresponding to } \alpha \\ \\ \text{and the last element of } \alpha \text{ is } a. \end{array} \right\}$$

The relational query q computes the set Δ given a particular relation $\overline{succ}$. If Δ is not empty, for each α a new value α' is created for each element missing in α (i.e., the enumeration α is extended in all possible ways with each of the missing elements). This yields as many new enumerations from each α as missing elements.

This is iterated until Δ becomes empty, at which point all enumerations are complete. Note that if D contains n elements, the final result $\overline{succ}$ contains $n!$ enumerations.

THEOREM 18.2.3   The well-behaved *while_new* programs express all queries.

Crux   Let q be a query from *inst*(**R**) to *inst*(*answer*). Assume the query is generic (i.e., C-generic with $C = \emptyset$). The proof is easily modified for the case when the query is C-generic with $C \neq \emptyset$. It is sufficient to observe that

(*)   for each *while_N* program,
there exists an equivalent well-behaved *while_new* program.

Suppose that (*) holds. Let $w_{\overline{succ}}$ be the *while_new* program computing $\overline{succ}$ from given

I over **R**. By Theorem 18.1.2 and (*), there exists a *while$_{new}$* program $w(succ)$ that computes q using a successor relation *succ*. We construct another *while$_{new}$* program $\overline{w}(\overline{succ})$ that computes q given **I** and $\overline{succ}$. Intuitively, $w(succ)$ is run in parallel for *all* possible enumerations *succ* provided by $\overline{succ}$. All computations produce the same result and are placed in *answer*. The computations for different enumerations in $\overline{succ}$ are identified by the α marking the enumeration in $\overline{succ}$. To this end, each relation R of arity k in $w(succ)$ is replaced by a relation $\overline{R}$ of arity $k + 1$. The extended database relations are first initialized by statements of the form $\overline{R} := R \times \pi_3(\overline{succ})$. Next the instructions of $w(succ)$ are modified as follows:

- $R := \{\langle u \rangle \mid \phi(u)\}$ becomes $\overline{R} := \{\langle u, \alpha \rangle \mid \exists y \exists z \overline{succ}(y, z, \alpha) \wedge \overline{\phi}(u, \alpha)\}$, where $\overline{\phi}(u, \alpha)$ is obtained from $\phi(u)$ by replacing each atom $S(v)$ by $\overline{S}(v, \alpha)$;
- *while change do* remains unchanged.

Finally the instruction *answer* $:= \pi_{1..n}(\overline{answer})$, where $n = arity(answer)$, is appended at the end of the program. The following can be shown by induction on the steps of a partial execution of $\overline{w}(\overline{succ})$ on **I** (Exercise 18.10):

(**) At each point in the computation of $\overline{w}(\overline{succ})$ on **I**, the set of tuples in relation $\overline{R}$ marked with α coincides with the value of R at the same point in the computation when $w(succ)$ is run on **I** and *succ* is the successor relation corresponding to α.

In particular, at the end of the computation of $\overline{w}(\overline{succ})$ on **I**,

$$\overline{answer} = \bigcup_\alpha w(\alpha)(\mathbf{I}) \times \{\alpha\},$$

where α ranges over the enumeration markers. Because $w(\alpha)(\mathbf{I}) = q(\mathbf{I})$ for each α, it follows that *answer* contains $q(\mathbf{I})$ at the end of the computation. Thus query q is computable by a well-behaved *while$_{new}$* program.

Thus it remains to show (*). Integer variables are easily simulated as follows. An integer variable i is represented by a binary variable R_i. If i contains the integer n, then R_i contains a successor relation for $n + 1$ distinct new values:

$$\{\langle \alpha_j, \alpha_{j+1} \rangle \mid 0 \le j < n\}.$$

(The integer 0 is represented by an empty relation and the integer 1 by a singleton $\{\langle \alpha_0, \alpha_1 \rangle\}$.) It is easy to find a *while$_{new}$* program for *increment* and *decrement* of i. ∎

We showed that well-behaved *while$_{new}$* programs are complete with respect to our definition of query. Recall that *while$_{new}$* programs that are not well behaved can compute a different kind of query that we excluded deliberately, which contains new values in the answer. It turns out, however, that such queries arise naturally in the context of object-oriented databases, where new object identifiers appear in query results (see Chapter 21). This requires extending our definition of query. In particular, the query is nondeterministic but, as discussed earlier, the different answers differ only in the particular choice of new values. This leads to the following extended notion of query:

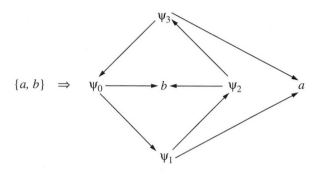

Figure 18.3:   A query not expressible in *while_new*

DEFINITION 18.2.4   A *determinate query* is a relation Q from *inst(**R**)* to *inst(answer)* such that

- Q is computable;
- if $\langle I, J \rangle \in Q$ and ρ is a one-to-one mapping on constants, then $\langle \rho(I), \rho(J) \rangle \in Q$; and
- if $\langle I, J \rangle \in Q$ and $\langle I, J' \rangle \in Q$, then there exists an isomorphism from J to J' that is the identity on the constants in I.

A language is *determinate complete* if it expresses only determinate queries and all determinate queries.

Let Q be a determinate query. If $\langle I, J \rangle \in Q$ and ρ is a one-to-one mapping on constants leaving I fixed, then $\langle I, \rho(J) \rangle \in Q$.

The question arises whether *while_new* remains complete with respect to this extended notion of query. Surprisingly, the answer is negative. Each *while_new* query is determinate. However, we exhibit a simple determinate query that *while_new* cannot express. Let q be the query with input schema $\mathbf{R} = \{S\}$, where S is unary, and output G, where G is binary. Let q be defined as follows: For each input I over S, if $I = \{a, b\}$ then $q(I) = \{\langle \psi_0, \psi_1 \rangle, \langle \psi_1, \psi_2 \rangle, \langle \psi_2, \psi_3 \rangle, \langle \psi_3, \psi_0 \rangle, \langle \psi_0, b \rangle, \langle \psi_1, a \rangle, \langle \psi_2, b \rangle, \langle \psi_3, a \rangle\}$ for some new elements $\psi_0, \psi_1, \psi_2, \psi_3$, and $q(I) = \emptyset$ otherwise (Fig. 18.3).

THEOREM 18.2.5   The query q is not expressible in *while_new*.

Proof   The proof is by contradiction. Suppose w is a *while_new* program expressing q. Consider the sequence of steps in the execution of w on an input $I = \{a, b\}$. We can assume without loss of generality that no invented value is ever deleted from the database (otherwise modify the program to keep all invented values in some new unary relation). For each invented value occurring in the computation, we define a trace that records how the value was invented and uniquely identifies it. More precisely, *trace(α)* is defined inductively as follows. If α is a constant, then *trace(α)* = $\langle \alpha \rangle$. Suppose α is a new value created at step i with a *new* statement associating it with tuple $\langle x_1, \ldots, x_k \rangle$. Then

$trace(\alpha) = \langle i, trace(x_1), \ldots, trace(x_k) \rangle$. Clearly, one can extend *trace* to tuples and relations in the natural manner. It is easily shown (Exercise 18.11) by induction on the number of steps in a partial execution of *w* on *I* that

(†) $trace(\alpha) = trace(\beta)$ iff $\alpha = \beta$;

(‡) for each instance *J* computed during the execution of *w* on input *I*, $trace(J)$ is closed under each automorphism ρ of *I*. In particular, for each α occurring in *J*, $\rho(trace(\alpha))$ equals $trace(\beta)$ for some β also occurring in *J*.

Consider now $trace(q(I))$ and the automorphism ρ of *I* [and therefore of $trace(q(I))$] defined by $\rho(a) = b$, $\rho(b) = a$. Note that $\rho^2 = id$ (the identity) and $\rho = \rho^{-1}$. Consider $\rho(trace(\psi_0))$. Because $\langle \psi_0, b \rangle \in q(I)$, it follows that $\langle trace(\psi_0), b \rangle \in trace(q(I))$. Because $\rho(b) = a$, it further follows that $\langle \rho(trace(\psi_0)), a \rangle \in trace(q(I))$ so $\rho(trace(\psi_0))$ is either $trace(\psi_1)$ or $trace(\psi_3)$. Suppose $\rho(trace(\psi_0)) = trace(\psi_1)$ (the other case is similar). From the fact that ρ is an automorphism of $trace(q(I))$ it follows that $\rho(trace(\psi_3)) = trace(\psi_0)$, $\rho(trace(\psi_2)) = trace(\psi_3)$, and $\rho(trace(\psi_1)) = trace(\psi_2)$. Consider now ρ^2. First, because $\rho^2 = id$, $\rho^2(trace(\psi_i)) = trace(\psi_i)$, $0 \leq i \leq 3$. On the other hand, $\rho^2(trace(\psi_0)) = \rho(\rho(trace(\psi_0))) = \rho(trace(\psi_1)) = trace(\psi_2)$. This is a contradiction. Hence *q* cannot be computed by *while_{new}*. ∎

The preceding example shows that the presence of new values in the answer raises interesting questions with regard to completeness. There exist languages that express all queries with invented values in answers (see Exercise 18.14 for a complex construct that leads to a determinate-complete language). Value invention is common in object-oriented languages, in the form of object creation constructs (see Chapter 21).

18.3 *While_{uty}*—An Untyped Extension of *while*

We briefly describe in this section an alternative complete language obtained by relaxing the fixed-arity requirement of the languages encountered so far. This relaxation is done using an *untyped* version of relational algebra instead of the familiar typed version. We will obtain a language allowing us to construct relations of variable, data-dependent arity in the course of the computation. Although strictly speaking they are not needed, we also allow integer variables and integer manipulation, as in *while_N*. Intuitively, it is easy to see why this yields a complete language. Variable arities allow us to construct all enumerations of constants in the input, represented by sufficiently long tuples containing all constants. The ability to construct the enumerations and manipulate integers yields a complete language.

The first step in defining the untyped version of *while* is to define an untyped version of relational algebra. This means that operations must be defined so that they work on relations of arbitrary, unknown arity. Expressions in the untyped algebra are built from relation variables and constants and can also use *integer* variables and constants. Let *i*, *j* be integer variables, and for each integer *k*, let $\emptyset^k$ denote the empty relation of arity *k*. Untyped algebra expressions are built up using the following operations:

- If e, e' are expressions, then $e \cap e'$ and $e \cup e'$ are expressions; if $arity(e) = arity(e')$ the semantics is the usual; otherwise the result is $\emptyset^0$.

- If e is an expression, then $\neg e$ is an expression; the complement is with respect to the active domain (not including the integers).

- If e, f are expressions, then $e \times f$ is an expression; the semantics is the usual cross-product semantics.

- If e is an expression, then $\sigma_{i=j}(e)$ is an expression, where i, j are integer variables or constants; if $arity(e) \geq max\{i, j\}$ the semantics is the usual; otherwise the result is $\emptyset^0$.

- If e is an expression, then $\pi_{ij}(e)$ is an expression, where i, j are integer variables or constants; if $i \leq j$ and $arity(e) \geq max\{i, j\}$, this projects e on columns i through j; otherwise the result is $\emptyset^{|j-i|}$.

- If e is an expression, then $ex_{ij}(e)$ is an expression; if $arity(e) \geq max\{i, j\}$, this exchanges in each tuple in the result of e the i and j coordinates; otherwise the result is $\emptyset^0$.

We may also consider an untyped version of tuple relational calculus (see Exercise 18.15).

We can now define $while_{uty}$ programs. They are concatenations of statements of the form

- $i := j$, where i is an integer variable and j an integer variable or constant.

- $increment(i)$, $decrement(i)$, where i is an integer variable.

- $while\ i > 0\ do\ t$, where i is an integer variable and t a program.

- $R := e$, where R is a relational variable and e an untyped algebra expression; the semantics here is that R is assigned the content *and arity* of e.

- $while\ R\ do\ t$, where R is a relational variable and t a program; the semantics is that the body of the loop is repeated as long as R is nonempty.

All relational variables that are not database relations are initialized to $\emptyset^0$; integer variables are initialized to 0.

EXAMPLE 18.3.1   Following is a $while_{uty}$ program that computes the arity of a nonempty relation R in the integer variable n:

$S_0 := \{\langle\rangle\}; S_1 := S_0 \cup R; S_2 := \neg S_1;$
$while\ S_2\ do$
   $begin$
   $n := n + 1;$
   $S_0 := S_0 \times D;$
   $S_1 := S_0 \cup R;$
   $S_2 := \neg S_1;$
   end

where D abbreviates an algebra expression computing the active domain [e.g., $\pi_{11}(R) \cup \neg\pi_{11}(R)$]. The program tries out increasing arities for R starting from 0. Recall that whenever R and S_0 have different arities, the result of $S_0 \cup R$ is $\emptyset^0$. This allows us to detect when the appropriate arity has been found.

REMARK 18.3.2 There is a much simpler set of constructs that yields the same power as $while_{uty}$. In general, programs are much harder to write in the resulting language, called QL, than in $while_{uty}$. One can show that the set of constructs of QL is minimal. The language QL is described next; it does not use integer variables. QL expressions are built from relational variables and constant relations as follows (D denotes the active domain):

- *equal* is an expression denoting $\{\langle a, a \rangle \mid a \in D\}$.
- $e \cap e'$ and $\neg e$ are defined as for $while_{uty}$; the complement is with respect to the active domain.
- If e is an expression, then $e \downarrow$ is an expression; this projects out the last coordinate of the result of e (and is $\emptyset^0$ if the arity is already zero).
- If e is an expression, then $e \uparrow$ is an expression; this produces the cross-product of e with D.
- If e is an expression, then $e \sim$ is an expression; if $arity(e) \geq 2$, then this exchanges the last two coordinates in each tuple in the result of e. Otherwise the answer is $\emptyset^0$.

Programs are built by concatenations of assignment statements ($R := e$) and *while* statements (*while R do s*). The semantics of the *while* is that the loop is iterated as long as R is nonempty.

We leave it to the reader to check that QL is equivalent to $while_{uty}$ (Exercise 18.17). We briefly describe the simulation of integers by QL. Let Z denote the constant 0-ary relation $\{\langle\rangle\}$. We can have Z represent the integer 0 and $Z \uparrow^n$ represent the integer n. Then *increment*(n) is simulated by one application of $\uparrow$, and *decrement*(n) is simulated by one application of $\downarrow$. A test of the form $x = 0$ becomes $e \downarrow = \emptyset$, where e is the untyped algebra expression representing the value of x. Thus we can simulate arbitrary computations on the integers.

Recall that our definition of query requires that both the input and output be instances over *fixed* schemas. On the other hand, in $while_{uty}$ relation arities are variable, so in general the arity of the answer is data dependent. This is a problem analogous to the one we encountered with $while_{new}$, which generally produces new values in the result. As in the case of $while_{new}$, we can define semantic and syntactic restrictions on $while_{uty}$ programs that guarantee that the programs compute queries. Call a $while_{uty}$ program *well behaved* if its answer is always of the same arity regardless of the input. Unfortunately, it can be shown that it is undecidable if a $while_{uty}$ program is well behaved (Exercise 18.19). However, there is a simple syntactic condition that guarantees good behavior and covers all well-behaved programs. A $while_{uty}$ program with answer relation *answer* is *syntactically well behaved* if the last instruction of the program is of the form *answer* $:= \pi_{mn}(R)$, where m, n are integer constants. Clearly, syntactic good behavior guarantees good behavior and can be checked. Furthermore, it is obvious that each well-behaved *while$_{uty}$* program is equivalent to some syntactically well-behaved program (Exercise 18.19).

We now prove the completeness of well-behaved *while$_{uty}$* programs.

THEOREM 18.3.3   The well-behaved *while$_{uty}$* programs express all queries.

Crux   It is easily verified that all well-behaved *while$_{uty}$* programs define queries. The proof that every query can be expressed by a well-behaved *while$_{uty}$* program is similar to the proof of Theorem 18.2.3. Let q be a query with input schema **R**. We proceed in two steps: First construct all orderings of constants from the input. Next simulate the *while$_N$* program computing q on the ordered database corresponding to each ordering. The main difference with *while$_{new}$* lies in how the orderings are computed. In *while$_{uty}$*, we use the arbitrary arity to construct a relation $R_<$ containing sufficiently long tuples each of which provides an enumeration of all constants. This is done by the following *while$_{uty}$* program, where D stands for an algebra expression computing the active domain:

$$R_< := \emptyset^0;$$
$$C := D; \, arityC := 1;$$
$$while \ C \ do$$
$$\quad begin$$
$$\quad R_< := C;$$
$$\quad C := C \times D; \, increment(arityC);$$
$$\quad for \ i := 1 \ to \ (arityC - 1) \ do$$
$$\quad\quad C := C \cap \neg\sigma_{i=arity(C)}(C);$$
$$\quad end$$

Clearly, the looping construct *for $i := 1$ to $\ldots$* can be easily simulated. If the size of D is n, the result of the program is the set of n-tuples with distinct entries in $adom(D)$. Note that each such tuple t in $R_<$ provides a complete enumeration of the constants in D. Next one can easily construct a *while$_{uty}$* program that constructs, for each such tuple t in $R_<$, the corresponding successor relation. More precisely, one can construct

$$\widehat{succ} = \bigcup_{t \in R_<} succ_t \times \{t\},$$

where $succ_t = \{\langle t(i), t(i+1)\rangle \mid 1 \leq i < n\}$ (see Fig. 18.2 and Exercise 18.20). ∎

Untyped languages allow us to relax the restriction that the output schema is fixed. This may have a practical advantage because in some applications it may be necessary to have the output schema depend on the input data. However, in such cases one would likely prefer a richer type system rather than no typing at all.

The overall results on the expressiveness and complexity of relational query languages are summarized in Figs. 18.4 and 18.5. The main classes of queries and their inclusion structure are represented in Fig. 18.4 (solid arrows indicate strict inclusion; the dotted arrow indicates strict inclusion if PTIME $\neq$ PSPACE). Languages expressing each class of

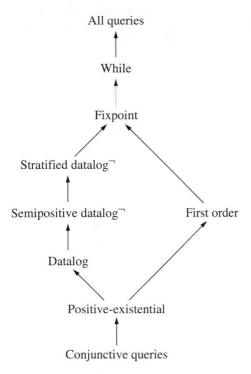

Figure 18.4: Main classes of queries

queries are listed in Fig. 18.5, which also contains information on complexity (first without assumptions, then with the assumption of an order on the database). In Fig. 18.5, $CALC(\exists, \wedge)$ denotes the conjunctive calculus and $CALC(\exists, \wedge, \vee)$ denotes the positive-existential calculus.

Bibliographic Notes

The first complete language proposed was the language QL of Chandra and Harel [CH80b]. Chandra also considered a language equivalent to $while_N$, which he called LC [Cha81a]. It was shown that LC cannot compute *even*. Several other primitives are considered in [Cha81a] and their power is characterized. The language $while_{new}$ was defined in [AV90], where its completeness was also shown.

The languages considered in this chapter can be viewed as formalizing practical languages, such as C+SQL or O_2C, used to develop database applications. These languages combine standard computation (C) with database computation (SQL in the relational world or O_2 in the object-oriented world). In this direction, several computing devices were defined in [AV91b], and complexity-theoretic results are obtained using the devices. First an extension of Turing machines with a relational store, called *relational*

Class of queries	Languages	Complexity	Complexity with order
conjunctive	CALC($\exists$, $\wedge$)	$\subset$ LOGSPACE	$\subset$ LOGSPACE
	SPJR algebra	$\subset$ AC$_0$	$\subset$ AC$_0$
positive-existential	CALC($\exists$, $\wedge$, $\vee$)		
	SPJUR algebra	$\subset$ LOGSPACE	$\subset$ LOGSPACE
	nr-datalog	$\subset$ AC$_0$	$\subset$ AC$_0$
datalog	datalog	$\subset$ monotonic PTIME	$\subset$ monotonic PTIME
semipositive datalog$^\neg$	semipositive datalog$^\neg$	$\subset$ PTIME	$=$ PTIME (with *min*, *max*)
first order	CALC		
	ALG	$\subset$ LOGSPACE	$\subset$ LOGSPACE
	nr-stratified datalog$^\neg$	$\subset$ AC$_0$	$\subset$ AC$_0$
stratified datalog$^\neg$	stratified datalog$^\neg$	$\subset$ PTIME	$=$ PTIME
fixpoint	CALC$+\mu^+$		
	while$^+$		
	datalog$^\neg$ (fixpoint and well-founded semantics)	$\subset$ PTIME	$=$ PTIME
while	CALC$+\mu$		
	while		
	datalog$^{\neg\neg}$ (fixpoint semantics)	$\subset$ PSPACE	$=$ PSPACE
all queries	*while$_{uty}$*	no bound	no bound
	while$_{new}$		

Figure 18.5:   Languages and complexity

machine, was shown to be equivalent to *while$_N$*. A further extension of relational machines equivalent to *while$_{new}$* and *while$_{uty}$*, called *generic machine*, was also defined. In the generic machine, *parallelism* is used to allow simultaneous computations with all possible successor relations.

Queries with new values in their answers were first considered in [AK89], in the context of an object-oriented deductive language with object creation, called IQL. The notion of determinate query [VandBGAG92] is a recasting of the essentially equivalent notion of db transformation, formulated in [AK89]. In [AK89], the query in Theorem 18.2.5 is also exhibited, and it is shown that IQL without duplicate elimination cannot express it. Because IQL is more powerful than *while$_{new}$*, their result implies the result of Theorem 18.2.5. The issue of completeness of languages with object creation was further investigated in [AP92, VandBG92, VandBGAG92, VandBP91, DV91, DV93].

Finally it is easy to see that each (determinate) query can be computed in some natural *nondeterministic* extension of *while_new* (e.g., with the witness operator of Chapter 17) [AV91c]. However, such programs may be nondeterministic so they do not define only determinate queries.

Exercises

Exercise 18.1   Let G be a graph. Consider a query "*Does the shortest path from a to b in G have property P?*" where G is a graph, P is a recursive property of the integers, and a, b are two particular vertexes of the graph. Show that such a query can be expressed in *while_N*.

Exercise 18.2   Prove that the query in Example 18.1.1 can be expressed (a) in *while*; (b) in *fixpoint*.

Exercise 18.3   Sketch a direct proof that *even* cannot be expressed by *while_N* by extending the hyperplane technique used in the proof of Proposition 17.3.2.

♠ **Exercise 18.4**   [AV94] Consider the language $\mathcal{L}$ augmenting *while_N* by allowing mixing of integers with data. Specifically, the following instruction is allowed in addition to those of *while_N*: $R := \{\langle i_1, \ldots, i_k \rangle\}$, where R is a k-ary relation variable and $i_1, \ldots, i_k$ are integer variables. It is assumed that the domain of input values is disjoint from the integers. Complement (or negation) is taken with respect to the domain formed by all values in the database or program, including the integer values present in the database. The *well-behaved* $\mathcal{L}$ programs are those whose outputs never contain integers. Show that well-behaved $\mathcal{L}$ and *while_N* are equivalent.

Exercise 18.5   Complete the proof of Theorem 18.1.2.

♠ **Exercise 18.6**   [AV90] Consider a variation of the language *while_new* where the $R := new(S)$ instruction is replaced by the simpler instruction "$R := new$" where R is unary. The semantics of this instruction is that R is assigned a singleton $\{\langle \alpha \rangle\}$, where α is a new value. Denote the new language by *while_{unary-new}*.

    (a) Show that each query expressible in *while_N* is also expressible in *while_{unary-new}*. *Hint:* Use new values to represent integers. Specifically, to represent the integers up to n, construct a relation $succ_{int}$ containing a successor relation on n new values. The value of rank i with respect to *succ* represents integer i.

    (b) Show that each query expressible in *while_{unary-new}* is also expressible in *while_N*. *Hint:* Again establish a correspondence between new values and integers. Then use Exercise 18.4.

Exercise 18.7   Prove Lemma 18.2.1.

Exercise 18.8   Prove that it is undecidable if a given *while_new* program is well behaved.

★ **Exercise 18.9**   In this exercise we define a syntactic restriction on *while_new* programs that guarantees good behavior. Let w be a *while_new* program. Without loss of generality, we can assume that all instructions contain at most one algebraic operation among $\cup, -, \pi, \times, \sigma$. Let the *not-well-behaved set of* w, denoted $Bad(w)$, be the smallest set of pairs of the form $\langle R, i \rangle$, where R is a relation in w and $1 \leq i \leq arity(R)$, such that

(a) if $S := new(R)$ is an instruction in w and $arity(S) = k$, then $\langle S, k \rangle \in Bad(w)$;

(b) if $S := T \cup R$ is in w and $\langle T, i \rangle \in Bad(w)$ or $\langle R, i \rangle \in Bad(w)$, then $\langle S, i \rangle \in Bad(w)$;

(c) if $S := T - R$ is in w and $\langle T, i \rangle \in Bad(w)$, then $\langle S, i \rangle \in Bad(w)$;

(d) if $S := T \times R$ is in w and $\langle T, i \rangle \in Bad(w)$, then $\langle S, i \rangle \in Bad(w)$; and if $\langle R, j \rangle \in Bad(w)$, then $\langle S, arity(T) + j \rangle \in Bad(w)$;

(e) if $S := \pi_{i_1 \ldots i_k}(T)$ is in w and $\langle T, i_j \rangle \in Bad(w)$, then $\langle S, j \rangle \in Bad(w)$;

(f) if $S := \sigma_{cond}(T)$ is in w and $\langle T, i \rangle \in Bad(w)$, then $\langle S, i \rangle \in Bad(w)$.

A *while$_{new}$* program w is *syntactically well behaved* if

$$\{\langle answer, i \rangle \mid 1 \leq i \leq arity(answer)\} \cap Bad(w) = \emptyset.$$

(a) Outline a procedure to check that a given *while$_{new}$* program is syntactically well behaved.

(b) Show that each syntactically well-behaved *while$_{new}$* program is well behaved.

(c) Show that for each well-behaved *while$_{new}$* program, there exists an equivalent syntactically well-behaved *while$_{new}$* program.

Exercise 18.10   Prove (*) in the proof of Theorem 18.2.3.

Exercise 18.11   Prove (†) and (‡) in the proof of Theorem 18.2.5.

Exercise 18.12   Consider the query q exhibited in the proof of Theorem 18.2.5. Let q_2 be the query that, on input $I = \{a, b\}$, produces as answer two copies of $q(I)$. More precisely, for each ψ_i in $q(I)$, let ψ_i' be a distinct new value. Let $q'(I)$ be obtained from $q(I)$ by replacing ψ_i by ψ_i', and let $q_2(I) = q(I) \cup q'(I)$. Prove that q_2 can be expressed by a *while$_{new}$* program.

♠**Exercise 18.13**   [DV91, DV93] Consider the instances I, J of Fig. 18.6. Consider a query q that, on input of the same pattern as I, returns J (up to an arbitrary choice of distinct β, θ_i) and otherwise returns the empty instance. Show that q is not expressible in *while$_{new}$*.

♠**Exercise 18.14**   (*Choose* [AK89]) Let *while$_{new}^{choose}$* be obtained by augmenting *while$_{new}$* with the following (determinate) *choose* construct. A program w may contain the instruction $choose(R)$ for some unary relation R. On input $\mathbf{I}$, when $choose(R)$ is applied in a state $\mathbf{J}$, the next state $\mathbf{J}'$ is defined as follows:

(a) if for each a, b in $\mathbf{J}(R)$, there is an automorphism of $\mathbf{J}$ that is the identity over $adom(\mathbf{I}, w)$ and maps a to b, $\mathbf{J}'$ is obtained from $\mathbf{J}$ by eliminating one arbitrary element in $\mathbf{J}(R)$;

(b) otherwise $\mathbf{J}'$ is just $\mathbf{J}$.

Show that *while$_{new}^{choose}$* is determinate complete.

Exercise 18.15   One may consider an untyped version of tuple relational calculus. Untyped relations are used just like typed relations, except that terms of the form $t(i)$ are allowed, where t is a tuple variable and i an integer variable. Equivalence of queries now means that the queries yield the same answers given the same relations and values for the integer variables. Show that untyped relational calculus and untyped relational algebra are equivalent.

$$
\begin{array}{ccc}
\alpha_1 & a & \psi_1 \\
\alpha_1 & b & \psi_1 \\
\alpha_1 & b & \psi_2 \\
\alpha_1 & c & \psi_2 \\
\alpha_1 & c & \psi_3 \\
\alpha_1 & d & \psi_3 \\
\alpha_1 & d & \psi_4 \\
\alpha_1 & a & \psi_4 \\
\alpha_2 & a & \psi_5 \\
\alpha_2 & b & \psi_5 \\
\alpha_2 & b & \psi_6 \\
\alpha_2 & c & \psi_6 \\
\alpha_2 & c & \psi_7 \\
\alpha_2 & d & \psi_7 \\
\alpha_2 & d & \psi_8 \\
\alpha_2 & a & \psi_8 \\
\end{array}
\qquad
\begin{array}{ccc}
\beta & a & \theta_1 \\
\beta & b & \theta_1 \\
\beta & b & \theta_2 \\
\beta & c & \theta_2 \\
\beta & c & \theta_3 \\
\beta & d & \theta_3 \\
\beta & d & \theta_4 \\
\beta & a & \theta_4 \\
\end{array}
$$

The $\Longrightarrow$ appears between the two tables.

$$I \qquad\qquad J$$

Figure 18.6: Another query not expressible in $while_{new}$

Exercise 18.16 Show that ex_{ij} is not redundant in the untyped algebra.

♠ **Exercise 18.17** Sketch a proof that $while_{uty}$ and the language QL described in Remark 18.3.2 are equivalent.

Exercise 18.18 Write a QL program computing the transitive closure of a binary relation.

♠ **Exercise 18.19** This exercise concerns well-behaved $while_{uty}$ programs. Show the following:

(a) It is undecidable whether a given $while_{uty}$ program is well behaved.

(b) Each syntactically well-behaved $while_{uty}$ program is well behaved.

(c) For each well-behaved $while_{uty}$ program, there exists an equivalent syntactically well-behaved $while_{uty}$ program.

Exercise 18.20 Write a $while_{uty}$ program that constructs the relation $\widehat{succ}$ from $R_<$ in the proof of Theorem 18.3.3.

♠ **Exercise 18.21** [AV91b] Prove that any query on a unary relation computed by a $while_{new}$ or $while_{uty}$ program in polynomial space is in FO. (For the purpose of this exercise, define the space used in a program execution as the maximum number of occurrences of constants in some instance produced in the execution of the program.) Note that, in particular, *even* cannot be computed in polynomial space in these languages.

♠ **Exercise 18.22** [AV91a] Consider the following extension of datalog$^{\neg\neg}$ with the ability to create new values. The rules are of the same form as datalog$^{\neg\neg}$ rules, but with a different semantics than the active domain semantics used for datalog$^{\neg\neg}$. The new semantics is the following. When rules are fired, all variables that occur in heads of rules but do not occur positively in the body are assigned distinct new values, not present in the input database, program, or any of the other relations in the program. A distinct value is assigned for each applicable valuation of the variables positively bound in the body in each firing. This is similar to the *new* construct in *while$_{new}$*. For example, one firing of the rule

$$R(x, y, \alpha) \leftarrow P(x, y)$$

has the same effect as the $R := new(P)$ instruction in *while$_{new}$*. The resulting extension of datalog$^{\neg\neg}$ is denoted datalog$^{\neg\neg}_{new}$. The *well-behaved* datalog$^{\neg\neg}_{new}$ programs are those that never produce new values in the answer. Sketch a proof that well-behaved datalog$^{\neg\neg}_{new}$ programs express all queries.

F Finale

In this part, we consider four advanced topics. Two of them (incomplete information and dynamic aspects) have been studied for a while, but for some reason (perhaps their difficulty) they have never reached the maturity of more established areas such as dependency theory. Interest in the other two topics (complex values and object databases) is more recent, and our understanding of them is rudimentary. In all cases, no clear consensus has yet emerged. Our choice of material, as well as our presentation, are therefore unavoidably more subjective than in other parts of this book. However, the importance of these issues for practical systems, as well as the interesting theoretical issues they raise, led us to incorporate a discussion of them in this book.

In Chapter 19, we address the issue of incomplete information. In many database applications, the knowledge of the real world is incomplete. It is crucial to be able to handle such incompleteness and, in particular, to be able to ask queries and perform updates. Chapter 19 surveys various models of incomplete databases, research directions, and some results.

In Chapter 20, we present an extension of relations called complex values. These are obtained from atomic elements using tuple and set constructors. The richer structure allows us to overcome some limitations of the relational model in describing complex data. We generalize results obtained for the relational model; in particular, we present a calculus and an equivalent algebra.

Chapter 21 looks at another way to enrich the relational model by introducing a number of features borrowed and adapted from object-oriented programming, such as objects, classes, and inheritance. In particular, objects consist of a structural part (a data repository) and a behavioral part (pieces of code). Thus the extended framework encompasses behavior, a notion conspicuously absent from relational databases.

Chapter 22 deals with dynamic aspects. This is one of the less settled areas in databases, and it raises interesting and difficult questions. We skim through a variety of issues: languages and semantics for updates; updating views; updating incomplete information; and active and temporal databases.

A comprehensive vision of the four areas discussed in Part F is lacking. The reader should therefore keep in mind that some of the material presented is in flux, and its importance pertains more to the general flavor than the specific results.

19 Incomplete Information

Somebody:	*What are we doing next?*
Alice:	*Who are we? Who are you?*
Somebody:	We *are you and the authors of the book, and* I *am one of them. This is an instance of incomplete information.*
Somebody:	*It's not much, but we can still tell that* surely *one of us is Alice and that there are* possibly *up to three "Somebodies" speaking.*

In the previous parts, we have assumed that a database always records information that is completely known. Thus a database has consisted of a completely determined finite instance. In reality, we often must deal with incomplete information. This can be of many kinds. There can be missing information, as in "John bought a car but I don't know which one." In the case of John's car, the information exists but we do not have it. In other cases, some attributes may be relevant only to some tuples and irrelevant to others. Alice is single, so the spouse field is irrelevant in her case. Furthermore, some information may be imprecise: "Heather lives in a large and cheap apartment," where the values of *large* and *cheap* are fuzzy. Partial information may also arise when we cannot completely rely on the data because of possible inconsistencies (e.g., resulting from merging data from different sources).

As soon as we leave the realm of complete databases, most issues become much more intricate. To deal with the most general case, we need something resembling a theory of knowledge. In particular, this quickly leads to logics with modalities: Is it *certain* that John lives in Paris? Is it *possible* that he may? What is the *probability* that he does? Does John *know* that Alice is a good student? Does he *believe* so? etc.

The study of knowledge is a fascinating topic that is outside the scope of this book. Clearly, there is a trade-off between the expressivity of the model for incomplete information used and the difficulty of answering queries. From the database perspective, we are primarily concerned with identifying this trade-off and understanding the limits of what is feasible in this context. The purpose of this chapter is to make a brief foray into this topic. We limit ourselves mostly to models and results of a clear database nature. We consider simple forms of incompleteness represented by null values. The main problem we examine is how to answer queries on such databases. In relation to this, we argue that for a representation system of incomplete information to be adequate in the context of a query language, it must also be capable of representing *answers* to queries. This leads to a desirable closure property of representations of incomplete information with respect to query languages. We observe the increase of complexity resulting from the use of nulls.

We also consider briefly two approaches closer to knowledge bases. The first is based on the introduction of disjunctions in deductive databases, which also leads to a form of incompleteness. The second is concerned with the use of modalities. We briefly mention the language KL, which permits us to talk about knowledge of the world.

19.1   Warm-Up

As we have seen, there are many possible kinds of incomplete information. In this section, we will focus on databases that partially specify the state of the world. Instead of completely identifying one state of the world, the database contents are compatible with many possible worlds. In this spirit, we define an *incomplete database* simply as a set of possible worlds (i.e., a set of instances). What is actually stored is a *representation* of an incomplete database. Choosing appropriate representations is a central issue.

We provide a mechanism for representing incomplete information using *null values*. The basic idea is to allow occurrences of variables in the tuples of the database. The different possible values of the variables yield the possible worlds.

The simplest model that we consider is the Codd table (introduced by Codd), or *table* for short. A table is a relation with constants and variables, in which no variable occurs twice. More precisely, let U be a finite set of attributes. A *table T* over U is a finite set of free tuples over U such that each variable occurs at most once. An example of a table is given in Fig. 19.1. The figure also illustrates an alternative representation (using @) that is more visual but that we do not adopt here because it is more difficult to generalize.

The preceding definition easily extends to database schemas. A database table **T** over a database schema **R** is a mapping over **R** such that for each R in **R**, $\mathbf{T}(R)$ is a table over $sort(R)$. For this generalization, we assume that the sets of variables appearing in each table are *pairwise disjoint*. Relationships between the variables can be stated through

R	A	B	C
	0	1	x
	y	z	1
	2	0	v

Table T

R	A	B	C
	0	1	@
	@	@	1
	2	0	@

Alternative representation of T

R	A	B	C
	0	1	2
	2	0	1
	2	0	0

I_1

R	A	B	C
	0	1	2
	3	0	1
	2	0	5

I_2

R	A	B	C
	0	1	2
	2	0	1
	2	0	0

I_3

R	A	B	C
	0	1	1
	2	0	1

I_4

Figure 19.1:   A table and examples of corresponding instances

global conditions (which we will introduce in the next section). In this section, we will focus on single tables, which illustrate well the main issues.

To specify the semantics of a table, we use the notion of valuation (see Chapter 4). The incomplete database represented by a table is defined as follows:

$$rep(T) = \{v(T) \mid v \text{ a valuation of the variables in } T\}.$$

Consider the table T in Fig. 19.1. Then $I_1, \ldots, I_4$ all belong to $rep(T)$ (i.e., are possible worlds).

The preceding definition assumes the Closed World Assumption (CWA) (see Chapter 2). This is because each tuple in an instance of $ref(T)$ must be justified by the presence of a particular free tuple in T. An alternative approach is to use the Open World Assumption (OWA). In that case, the incomplete database of T would include all instances that contain an instance of $rep(T)$. In general, the choice of CWA versus OWA does not substantially affect the results obtained for incomplete databases.

We now have a simple way of representing incomplete information. What next? Naturally, we wish to be able to query the incomplete database. Exactly what this means is not clear at this point. We next look at this issue and argue that the simple model of tables has serious shortcomings with respect to queries. This will naturally lead to an extension of tables that models more complicated situations.

Let us consider what querying an incomplete database might mean. Consider a table T and a query q. The table T represents a set of possible worlds $rep(T)$. For each $I \in rep(T)$, q would produce an answer $q(I)$. Therefore the set of possible answers of q is $q(rep(T))$. This is, again, an incomplete database. The answer to q should be a representation of this incomplete database.

More generally, consider some particular representation system (e.g., tables). Such a system involves a language for describing representations and a mapping *rep* that associates a set of instances with each representation. Suppose that we are interested in a particular query language $\mathcal{L}$ (e.g., relational algebra). We would always like to be capable of representing the result of a query in the same system. More precisely, for each representation T and query q, there should exist a computable representation $\overline{q}(T)$ such that

$$rep(\overline{q}(T)) = q(rep(T)).$$

In other words, $\overline{q}(T)$ represents the possible answers of q [i.e., $\{q(I) \mid I \in rep(T)\}$].

If some representation system τ has the property described for a query language $\mathcal{L}$, we will say that τ is a *strong representation system* for $\mathcal{L}$. Clearly, we are particularly interested in strong representation systems for relational algebra and we shall develop such a system later.

Let us now return to tables. Unfortunately, we quickly run into trouble when asking queries against them, as the following example shows.

EXAMPLE 19.1.1   Consider T of Fig. 19.1 and the algebraic query $\sigma_{A=3}(T)$. There is no table representing the possible answers to this query. A possible answer (e.g., for I_1) is the empty relation, whereas there are nonempty possible answers (e.g., for I_2). Suppose that there exists a table T' representing the set of possible answers. Either T' is empty and $\sigma_{A=3}(I_2)$ is not in $rep(T')$; or T' is nonempty and the empty relation is not in $rep(T')$. This is a contradiction, so no such T' can exist.

The problem lies in the weakness of the representation system of tables; we will consider richer representation systems that lead to a complete representation system for all of relational algebra. An alternative approach is to be less demanding; we consider this next and present the notion of *weak* representation systems.

19.2   Weak Representation Systems

To relax our expectations, we will no longer require that the answer to a query be a representation of the set of all possible answers. Instead we will ask which are the tuples that are surely in the answer (i.e., that belong to *all* possible answers). (Similarly, we may ask for the tuples that are possibly in the answer (i.e., that belong to *some* possible answer). We make this more precise next.

For a table T and a query q, the set of sure facts, $sure(q, T)$, is defined as

$$sure(q, T) = \cap\{q(I) \mid I \in rep(T)\}.$$

Clearly, a tuple is in $sure(q, T)$ iff it is in the answer for every possible world. Observe that the sure tuples in a table T [i.e., the tuples in every possible world in $rep(T)$] can be computed easily by dropping all free tuples with variables. One could similarly define the set $poss(q, T)$ of possible facts.

One might be tempted to require of a weak system just the ability to represent the set of tuples surely in the answer. However, the definition requires some care due to the following subtlety. Suppose T is the table in Fig. 19.1 and q the query $\sigma_{A=2}(R)$, for which $sure(q, T) = \emptyset$. Consider now the query $q' = \pi_{AB}(R)$ and the query $q \circ q'$. Clearly, $q'(sure(q, T)) = \emptyset$; however, $sure(q'(q(rep(T))) = \{\langle 2, 0\rangle\}$. So $q \circ q'$ cannot be computed by first computing the tuples surely returned by q and then applying q'. This is rather unpleasant because generally it is desirable that the semantics of queries be compositional (i.e., the result of $q \circ q'$ should be obtained by applying q' to the result of q). The conclusion is that the answer to q should provide more information than just $sure(q, T)$; the incomplete database it specifies should be equivalent to $q(rep(T))$ with respect to its ability to compute the sure tuples of any query in the language applied to it. This notion of equivalence of two incomplete databases is formalized as follows.

If $\mathcal{L}$ is a query language, we will say that two incomplete databases $\mathcal{I}, \mathcal{J}$ are $\mathcal{L}$ equivalent, denoted $\mathcal{I} \equiv_{\mathcal{L}} \mathcal{J}$, if for each q in $\mathcal{L}$ we have

$$\cap\{q(I) \mid I \in \mathcal{I}\} = \cap\{q(I) \mid I \in \mathcal{J}\}.$$

In other words, the two incomplete databases are undistinguishable if all we can ask for is the set of sure tuples in answers to queries in $\mathcal{L}$.

We can now define weak representation systems. Suppose $\mathcal{L}$ is a query language. A representation system is *weak* for $\mathcal{L}$ if for each representation T of an incomplete database, and each q in $\mathcal{L}$, there exists a representation denoted $\overline{q}(T)$ such that

$$rep(\overline{q}(T)) \equiv_{\mathcal{L}} q(rep(T)).$$

With the preceding definition, $\overline{q}(T)$ does not provide precisely $sure(q, T)$ for tables T. However, note that $sure(q, T)$ can be obtained at the end simply by eliminating from the answer all rows with occurrences of variables.

The next result indicates the power of tables as a weak representation system.

THEOREM 19.2.1 Tables form a weak representation system for selection-projection (SP) [i.e., relational algebra limited to selection (involving only equalities and inequalities) and projection]. If union or join are added, tables no longer form a weak representation system.

Crux It is easy to see that tables form a weak representation system for SP queries. Selections operate conservatively on tables. For example,

$$\overline{\sigma_{cond}}(T) = \{t \mid t \in T \text{ and } cond(\nu(t)) \text{ holds}$$
$$\text{for all valuations } \nu \text{ of the variables in } t\}.$$

Projections operate like classical projections. For example, if T is again the table in Fig. 19.1, then

$$\overline{\sigma_{A=2}}(T) = \{\langle 2, 0, v \rangle\}$$

and

$$\overline{(\pi_{AB}(R) \circ \sigma_{A=2}(R))}(T) = \{\langle 2, 0 \rangle\}.$$

Let us show that tables are no longer a weak representation system if join or union are added to SP. Consider join first. So the query language is now SPJ. Let T be the table

R	A	B	C
	a	x	c
	a'	x'	c'

where x, x' are variables and a, a', c, c' are constants.

Let $q = \pi_{AC}(R) \bowtie \pi_B(R)$. Suppose there is table W such that

$$rep(W) \equiv_{SPJ} q(rep(T)),$$

and consider the query $q' = \pi_{AC}(\pi_{AB}(R) \bowtie \pi_{BC}(R))$. Clearly, $sure(q \circ q', T)$ is

A	C
a	c
a'	c
a	c'
a'	c'

Therefore $sure(q', W)$ must be the same. Because $\langle a', c \rangle \in sure(q', W)$, for each valuation v of variables in W there must exist tuples $u, v \in W$ such that $u(A) = a', v(C) = c$, $v(u)(B) = v(v)(B)$. Let v be a valuation such that $v(z) \neq v(y)$ for all variables $z, y, z \neq y$. If $u = v$, then $u(A) = a'$ and $u(C) = c$ so $\langle a', c \rangle \in sure(\pi_{AC}(R), W)$. This cannot be because, clearly, $\langle a', c \rangle \notin sure(\pi_{AC}(R), q(rep(T)))$. So, $u \neq v$. Because $v(u)(B) = v(v)(B)$ and W has no repeated variables, it follows that $u(B)$ and $v(B)$ equal some constant k. But then $\langle a', k \rangle \in sure(\pi_{AB}(R), W)$, which again cannot be because one can easily verify that $sure(\pi_{AB}(R), q(rep(T))) = \emptyset$.

The proof that tables do not provide a weak representation system for SPU follows similar lines. Just consider the table T

R	A	B
	x	b

and the query q outputting two relations: $\sigma_{A=a}(R)$ and $\sigma_{A \neq a}(R)$. It is easily seen that there is no pair of tables W_1, W_2 weakly representing $q(rep(T))$ with respect to SPU. To see this, consider the query $q' = \pi_B(W_1 \cup W_2)$. The details are left to the reader (Exercise 19.7). ∎

Naive Tables

The previous result shows the limitations of tables, even as weak representation systems. As seen from the proof of Theorem 19.2.1, one problem is the lack of repeated variables. We next consider a first extension of tables that allows repetitions of variables. It will turn out that this will provide a weak representation system for a large subset of relational algebra.

A *naive* table is like a table except that variables may repeat. A naive table is shown in Fig. 19.2. Naive tables behave beautifully with respect to positive existential queries (i.e., conjunctive queries augmented with union). Recall that, in terms of the algebra, this is SPJU.

THEOREM 19.2.2   Naive tables form a weak representation system for positive relational algebra.

Crux   Given a naive table T and a positive query q, the evaluation of $\overline{q}(T)$ is extremely simple. The variables are treated as distinct new constants. The standard evaluation of q is then performed on the table. Note that incomplete information yields no extra cost in this case. We leave it to the reader to verify that this works. ∎

$$
\begin{array}{c|ccc}
R & A & B & C \\
\hline
 & 0 & 1 & x \\
 & x & z & 1 \\
 & 2 & 0 & v \\
\end{array}
$$

Figure 19.2:   A naive table

Naive tables yield a nice representation system for a rather large language. But the representation system is weak and the language does not cover all of relational algebra. We introduce in the next section a representation that is a strong system for relational algebra.

19.3   Conditional Tables

We have seen that Codd tables and naive tables are not rich enough to provide a strong representation system for relational algebra. To see what is missing, recall that when we attempt to represent the result of a selection on a table, we run into the problem that the presence or absence of certain tuples in a possible answer is conditioned by certain properties of the valuation. To capture this, we extend the representation with conditions on variables, which yields conditional tables. We will show that such tables form a strong representation system for relational algebra.

A *condition* is a *conjunct* of *equality atoms* of the form $x = y$, $x = c$ and of *inequality atoms* of the form $x \neq y$, $x \neq c$, where x and y are variables and c is a constant. Note that we only use conjuncts of atoms and that the Boolean *true* and *false* can be respectively encoded as atoms $x = x$ and $x \neq x$.

If formula Φ is a condition, we say that a valuation v *satisfies* Φ if its assignment of constants to variables makes the formula true.

Conditions may be associated with table T in two ways: (1) A *global* condition Φ_T is associated with the entire table T; (2) a *local* condition φ_t is associated with one tuple t of table T. A *conditional table* (*c-table* for short) is a triple (T, Φ_T, φ), where

- T is a table,
- Φ_T is a global condition,
- φ is a mapping over T that associates a local condition φ_t wich each tuple t of T.

A c-table is shown in Fig. 19.3. If we omit listing a condition, then it is by default the atom *true*. Note also that conditions Φ_T and φ_t for t in T may contain variables not appearing respectively in T or t.

For our purposes, the global conditions in c-tables could be distributed at the tuple level as local conditions. However, they are convenient as shorthand and when dependencies are considered.

For brevity, we usually refer to a c-table (T, Φ_T, φ) simply as T. A given c-table T represents a set of instances as follows (again adopting the CWA):

$$
\begin{array}{c|cc}
T' & A & B \\
\hline
\end{array}
$$

T'	A	B	
	$x \neq 2, y \neq 2$		
	0	1	$z = z$
	1	x	$y = 0$
	y	x	$x \neq y$

J_1	A	B		J_2	A	B		J_3	A	B		J_4	A	B
	0	1			0	1			0	1			0	1
	0	0			1	0							0	3

Figure 19.3:   A c-table and some possible instances

$rep(T) = \{I \mid$ there is a valuation v satisfying Φ_T such that relation I
consists exactly of those facts $v(t)$ for which v satisfies $\varphi_t\}$.

Consider the table T' in Fig. 19.3. Then J_1, J_2, J_3, J_4 are obtained by valuating x, y, z to $(0,0,0)$, $(0,1,0)$, $(1,0,0)$, and $(3,0,0)$, respectively.

The next example illustrates the considerable power of the local conditions of c-tables, including the ability to capture disjunctive information.

EXAMPLE 19.3.1   Suppose we know that Sally is taking math or computer science (CS) (but not both) and another course; Alice takes biology if Sally takes math, and math or physics (but not both) if Sally takes physics. This can be represented by the following c-table:

Student	Course	
		$(x \neq math) \wedge (x \neq CS)$
Sally	math	$(z = 0)$
Sally	CS	$(z \neq 0)$
Sally	x	
Alice	biology	$(z = 0)$
Alice	math	$(x = physics) \wedge (t = 0)$
Alice	physics	$(x = physics) \wedge (t \neq 0)$

Observe that there may be several c-table representations for the same incomplete database. Two representations T, T' are said to be equivalent, denoted $T \equiv T'$, if $rep(T) = rep(T')$. Testing for equivalence of c-tables is not a trivial task. Just testing membership of an instance in $rep(T)$, apparently a simpler task, will be shown to be NP-complete. To test equivalence of two c-tables T and T', one must show that for each valuation v of the variables in T there exists a valuation v' for T' such that $v(T) = v'(T')$, and conversely. Fortunately, it can be shown that one need only consider valuations to a set C of constants containing all constants in T or T' and whose size is at most the number of variables in the two tables (Exercise 19.11). This shows that equivalence of c-tables is decidable.

In particular, finding a minimal representation can be hard. This may affect the computation of the result of a query in various ways: The complexity of computing the answer may depend on the representation of the input; and one may require the result to be somewhat compact (e.g., not to contain tuples with unsatisfiable local conditions).

It turns out that c-tables form a strong representation system for relational algebra.

THEOREM 19.3.2 For each c-table T over U and relational algebra query q over U, one can construct a c-table $\overline{q}(T)$ such that $rep(\overline{q}(T)) = q(rep(T))$.

Crux The proof is straightforward and is left as an exercise (Exercise 19.13). The example in Fig. 19.4 should clarify the construction.[1] For projection, it suffices to project the columns of the table. Selection is performed by adding new conjuncts to the local conditions. Union is represented by the union of the two tables (after making sure that they use distinct sets of variables) and choosing the appropriate local conditions. Join and intersection involve considering all pairs of tuples from the two tables. For difference, we consider a tuple in the first table and add a huge conjunct stating that it does not match any tuple from the second table (disjunctions may be used as shorthand; they can be simulated using new variables, as illustrated in Example 19.3.1). ∎

To conclude this section, we consider (1) languages with recursion, and (2) dependencies. In both cases (and for related reasons) the aforementioned representation system behaves well. The presentation is by examples, but the formal results can be derived easily.

Languages with Recursion

Consider an incomplete database and a query involving fixpoint. For instance, consider the table in Fig. 19.5. The representation $\overline{tc}(T)$ of the answer to the transitive closure query tc is also given in the same figure. One can easily verify that

$$rep(\overline{tc}(T)) = tc(rep(T)).$$

This can be generalized to arbitrary languages with iteration. For example, consider a c-table T and a relational algebra query q that we want to iterate until a fixpoint is reached.

---

[1] The representations in the tables can be simplified; they are given in rough form to illustrate the proof technique.

T_1	B	C
	x	c

T_2	B	C	
	y	c	$(y = b)$
	z	w	

$\overline{\pi_B(T_2)}$	B	
	y	$(y = b)$
	z	

T_3	A	B
	a	y

$\overline{\sigma_{B=b}(T_1 \bowtie T_3)}$	A	B	C	
	a	y	c	$(y = x) \wedge (y = b)$

$T_1 \cup T_2$	B	C	
	x	c	
	y	c	$(y = b)$
	z	w	

$T_1 \bowtie T_3$	A	B	C	
	a	y	c	$(y = x)$

$T_1 - T_2$	B	C	
	x	c	$(y \neq b) \wedge (x \neq z)$
	x	c	$(y \neq b) \wedge (w \neq c)$
	x	c	$(y = b) \wedge (x \neq b) \wedge (x \neq z)$
	x	c	$(y = b) \wedge (x \neq b) \wedge (w \neq c)$

Figure 19.4:   Computing with c-tables

Then we can construct the sequence of c-tables:

$$\overline{q}(T), \overline{q}^2(T), \ldots, \overline{q}^i(T), \ldots.$$

Suppose now that q is a positive query. We are guaranteed to reach a fixpoint on every single complete instance. However, this does not a priori imply that the sequence of representations $\{\overline{q}^i(T)\}_{i>0}$ converges. Nonetheless, we can show that this is in fact the case. For some i,

$$rep(\overline{q}^i(T)) = rep(\overline{q}^{i+1}(T)).$$

T	A	B	$\overline{tc}(T)$	A	B	
	a	b		a	b	
	x	c		x	c	
	c	d		c	d	
				a	c	$x = b$
				x	d	
				c	c	$x = d$
				a	d	$x = b$

Figure 19.5:   Transitive closure of a table

(See Exercise 19.17.) It can also be shown easily that for such i, every $I \in rep(\overline{q}^i(T))$ is a fixpoint of q. The proof is by contradiction: Suppose there is $I \in rep(\overline{q}^i(T))$ such that $q(I) \neq I$, and consider one such I with a minimum number of tuples. Because $rep(\overline{q}^i(T)) = rep(\overline{q}^{i+1}(T))$, $I = q(J)$ for some $J \in rep(\overline{q}^i(T))$. Because q is positive, $J \subseteq I$; so because $q(I) \neq I$, $J \subset I$. This contradicts the minimality of I. So $\overline{q}^i(T))$ is indeed the desired answer.

Thus to find the table representing the result, it suffices to compute the sequence $\{\overline{q}^i(T)\}_{i>0}$ and stop when two consecutive tables are equivalent.

Dependencies

In Part B, we studied dependencies in the context of complete databases. We now reconsider dependencies in the context of incomplete information. Suppose we are given an incomplete database (i.e., a set $\mathcal{I}$ of complete databases) and are told, in addition, that some set Σ of dependencies is satisfied. The question arises: How should we interpret the combined information provided by $\mathcal{I}$ and by Σ?

The answer depends on our view of the information provided by an incomplete database. Dependencies should add to the information we have. But how do we compare incomplete databases with respect to information content? One common-sense approach, in line with our discussion so far, is that more information means reducing further the set of possible worlds. Thus an incomplete database $\mathcal{I}$ (i.e., a set of possible worlds) is more informative than $\mathcal{J}$ iff $\mathcal{I} \subset \mathcal{J}$. In this spirit, the natural use of dependencies would be to eliminate from $\mathcal{I}$ those possible worlds not satisfying Σ. This makes sense for egd's (and in particular fd's).

A different approach may be more natural in the context of tgd's. This approach stems from a relaxation of the CWA that is related to the OWA. Let $\mathcal{I}$ be an incomplete database, and let Σ be a set of dependencies. Recall that tgd's imply the presence of certain tuples based on the presence of other tuples. Suppose that for some $I \in \mathcal{I}$, a tuple t implied by a tgd in Σ is not present in I. Under the relaxation of the CWA, we conclude that t should be viewed as present in I, even though it is not represented explicitly. More generally, the chase (see Chapter 8), suitably generalized to operate on instances rather than tableaux,

I_1

A	B	C
a	b	c
a	b'	c'

I_2

A	B	C
e	f	g
e	f'	g'
e	f	g'
e	f'	g

I_3

A	B	C
a	b	c
g	b	h

J_1

A	B	C
a	b	c
a	b'	c'
a	b	c'
a	b'	c

J_2

A	B	C
e	f	g
e	f'	g'
e	f	g
e	f'	g

Figure 19.6:   Incomplete databases and dependencies

can be used to complete the instance by adding all missing tuples implied by the tgd's in Σ. (See Exercise 19.18.)

In fact, the chase can be used for both egd's and tgd's. In contrast to tgd's, the effect of chasing with egd's (and, in particular, fd's) may be to eliminate possible worlds that violate them. Note that tuples added by tgd's may lead to violations of egd's. This suggests that an incomplete database $\mathcal{I}$ with a set Σ of dependencies represents

$$\{chase(I, \Sigma) \mid I \in \mathcal{I} \text{ and the chase of } I \text{ by } \Sigma \text{ succeeds}\}.$$

For example, consider Fig. 19.6, which shows the incomplete database $\mathcal{I} = \{I_1, I_2, I_3\}$. Under this perspective, the incorporation of the dependencies $\Sigma = \{A \twoheadrightarrow B, B \to A\}$ in this incomplete database leads to $\mathcal{J} = \{J_1, J_2\}$.

Suppose now that the incomplete database $\mathcal{I}$ is represented as a c-table T. Can the effect of a set Σ of full dependencies on T be represented by another c-table T'? The answer is yes, and T' is obtained by extending the chase to c-tables in the straightforward way. For example, a table T_1 and its completion T_2 by $\Sigma = \{A \twoheadrightarrow B, C \to D\}$ are given in Fig. 19.7. The reader might want to check that

$$chase_\Sigma(rep(T_1)) = rep(T_2).$$

T_1

A	B	C	D
a	b	c	d
x	e	y	g
a	b	c	z

T_2

A	B	C	D	
a	b	c	d	
x	e	y	g	
a	b	y	g	$(x = a)$
a	e	c	d	$(x = a)$

Figure 19.7:   c-tables and dependencies

19.4   The Complexity of Nulls

Conditional tables may appear to be a minor variation from the original model of complete relational databases. However, we see next that the use of nulls easily leads to intractability. This painfully highlights the trade-off between modeling power and resources.

We consider some basic computational questions about incomplete information databases. Perhaps the simplest question is the *possibility* problem: "Given a set of possible worlds (specified, for instance, by a c-table) and a set of tuples, is there a possible world where these tuples are all true?" A second question is the *certainty* problem: "Given a set of possible worlds and a set of tuples, are these tuples all true in every possible world?" Natural variations of these problems involve queries: Is a given set of tuples possibly (or certainly) in the answer to query q?

Consider a (c-) table T, a query q, a relation I, and a tuple t. Some typical questions include the following:

(Membership) Is I a possible world for T [i.e., $I \in rep(T)$]?

(Possibility) Is t possible [i.e., $\exists I \in rep(T)(t \in I)$]?

(Certainty) Is t certain [i.e., $\forall I \in rep(T)(t \in I)$]?

(q-Membership) Is I a possible answer for q and T [i.e., $I \in q(rep(T))$]?

(q-Possibility) Is t possibly in the answer [i.e., $\exists I \in rep(T)(t \in q(I))$]?

(q-Certainty) Is t certainly in the answer [i.e., $\forall I \in rep(T)(t \in q(I))$]?

Finally we may consider the following generalizations of the q-membership problem:

(q-Containment) Is T contained in $q(T')$ [i.e., $rep(T) \subseteq q(rep(T'))$]?

(q, q'-Containment) Is $q(T)$ contained in $q'(T)$ [i.e., $rep(q(T)) \subseteq rep(q'(T))$]?

The crucial difference between complete and incomplete information is the large number of possible valuations for the latter case. Because of the finite number of variables in a set of c-tables, only a finite number of valuations are nonisomorphic (see Exercise 19.10). However, the number of such valuations may grow exponentially in the input size. By simple reasoning about all valuations and by guessing particular valuations, we have some easy upper bounds. For a query q that can be evaluated in polynomial time on complete databases, deciding whether $I \in q(rep(T))$, or whether I is a set of possible answers, can be answered in NP; checking whether $q(rep(T)) = \{I\}$, or if I is a set of certain tuples, is in CO-NP.

To illustrate such complexity results, we demonstrate one lower bound concerning the q-membership problem for (Codd) tables.

PROPOSITION 19.4.1   There exists a positive existential query q such that checking, given a table T and a complete instance I, whether $I \in q(rep(T))$ is NP-complete.

Proof   The proof is by reduction of graph 3-colorability. For simplicity, we use a query mapping a two-relation database into another two-relation database. (An easy modification of the proof shows that the result also holds for databases with one relation. In particular, increase the arity of the largest relation, and use constants in the extra column to encode several relations into this one.)

We will use (1) an input schema **R** with two relations R, S of arity 5 and 2, respectively; (2) an output schema **R'** with two relations R', S' of arity 3 and 1, respectively; and (3) a positive existential query q from **R** to **R'**. The query q [returning, on each input **I** over **R**, two relations $q_1(\mathbf{I})$ and $q_2(\mathbf{I})$ over R' and S'] is defined as follows:

$$q_1 = \{\langle x, z, z' \rangle \mid \exists y([\exists vw(R(x, y, v, w, z) \vee R(v, w, x, y, z))]$$
$$\wedge \, [\exists vw(R(x, y, v, w, z') \vee R(v, w, x, y, z'))])\}$$
$$q_2 = \{z \mid \exists xyvw(R(x, y, v, w, z) \wedge S(y, w))\}.$$

For each input $G = (V, E)$ to the graph 3-colorability problem, we construct a table **T** over the input schema **R** and an instance **I'** over the output schema **R'**, such that G is 3-colorable iff $\mathbf{I'} \in q(rep(\mathbf{T}))$.

Without loss of generality, assume that G has no self-loops and that E is a binary relation, where we list each edge once with an arbitrary orientation.

Let $V = \{a_i \mid i \in [1..n]\}$ and $E = \{(b_j, c_j) \mid j \in [1..m]\}$. Let $\{x_j \mid j \in [1..m]\}$ and $\{y_j \mid j \in [1..m]\}$ be two disjoint sets of distinct variables. Then **T** and **I'** are constructed as follows:

(a) $\mathbf{T}(R) = \{t_j \mid j \in [1..m]\}$, where t_j is the tuple $\langle b_j, x_j, c_j, y_j, j \rangle$;

(b) $\mathbf{T}(S) = \{\langle i, j \rangle \mid i, j \in \{1, 2, 3\}, i \neq j\}$;

(c) $\mathbf{I'}(R') = \{\langle a, j, k \rangle \mid a \in \{b_j, c_j\} \cap \{b_k, c_k\}$, where each (b, c) pair is an edge in $E\}$; and

(d) $\mathbf{I'}(S') = \{j \mid j \in [1..m]\}$.

Intuitively, for each tuple in $\mathbf{I}(R)$, the second column contains the color of the vertex in the first column, and the fourth column contains the color of the vertex in the third column. The edges are numbered in the fifth column. The role of query q_2 is to check whether this provides an assignment of the three colors $\{1, 2, 3\}$ to vertexes such that the colors of the endpoints of each edge are distinct. Indeed, q_2 returns the edges z for which the colors y, w of its endpoints are among $\{1, 2, 3\}$. So if $q(\mathbf{I})(S') = \mathbf{I'}(S')$, then all edges have color assignments among $\{1, 2, 3\}$ to their endpoints. Next query q_1 checks whether a vertex is assigned the same color consistently in all edges where it occurs. It returns the $\langle x, z, z' \rangle$, where x is a vertex, z and z' are edges, x occurs as an endpoint, and x has the same color assignment y in both z and z'. So if $q_1(\mathbf{I})(R') = \mathbf{I'}(R')$, it follows that the color assignment is consistent everywhere for all vertexes.

For example, consider the graph G given in Fig. 19.8; the corresponding **I'** and **T** are exhibited in Fig. 19.9. Suppose that f is a 3-coloring of G. Consider the valuation σ defined by $\sigma(x_j) = f(b_j)$ and $\sigma(y_j) = f(c_j)$ for all j. It is easily seen that $\mathbf{I'} = q(\sigma(T))$. Moreover, it is straightforward to show that G is 3-colorable iff **I'** is in $q(rep(\mathbf{T}))$. ∎

1	2
2	3
3	4
4	1
3	1

Figure 19.8: Graph G

T(R)				T(S)		I'(R')			I'(S')
1	x_1	2	y_1 1	1	2	1	1	1	1
2	x_2	3	y_2 2	1	3	1	1	4	2
3	x_3	4	y_3 3	2	1	1	1	5	3
4	x_4	1	y_4 4	2	3	1	4	1	4
3	x_5	1	y_5 5	3	1	1	4	4	5
				3	2	1	4	5	
						2	1	1	
						2	1	2	
						2	2	1	
						2	2	2	
							$\vdots$		
						4	3	3	
						4	3	4	
						4	4	3	
						4	4	4	

Figure 19.9: Encoding for the reduction of 3-colorability

19.5 Other Approaches

Incomplete information often arises naturally, even when the focus is on complete data-bases. For example, the information in a view is by nature incomplete, which in particular leads to problems when trying to update the view (as discussed in Chapter 22); and we already considered relations with nulls in the weak universal relations of Chapter 11.

In this section, we briefly present some other aspects of incomplete information. We consider some alternative kinds of null values; we look at disjunctive deductive data-bases; we mention a language that allows us to address directly in queries the issue of incompleteness; and we briefly mention several situations in which incomplete informa-tion arises naturally, even when the database itself is complete. An additional approach to representing incomplete information, which stems from using explicit logical theories, will be presented in connection with the view update problem in Chapter 22.

Other Nulls in Brief

So far we have focused on a specific kind of null value denoting values that are unknown. Other forms of nulls may be considered. We may consider, for instance, *nonexisting* nulls. For example, in the tuple representing a CEO, the field DirectManager has no meaning and therefore contains a nonexisting null. Nonexisting nulls are at the core of the weak universal model that we considered in Chapter 11.

It may also be the case that we do not know for a specific field if a value exists. For example, if the database ignores the marital status of a particular person, the spouse field is either unknown or nonexisting. It is possible to develop a formal treatment of such *no-information* nulls. An incomplete database consists of a set of sets of tuples, where each set of tuples is closed under projection. This closure under projection indicates that if a tuple is known to be true, the projections of this tuple (although less informative) are also known to be true. (The reader may want to try, as a nontrivial exercise, to define tables formally with such nulls and obtain a closure theorem analogous to Theorem 19.3.2.)

For each new form of null values, the game is to obtain some form of representation with clear semantics and try to obtain a closure theorem for some reasonable language (like we did for unknown nulls). In particular, we should focus on the most important algebraic operations for accessing data: projection and join. It is also possible to establish a lattice structure with the different kinds of nulls so that they can be used meaningfully in combination.

Disjunctive Deductive Databases

Disjunctive logic programming is an extension of standard logic programming with rules of the form

$$A_1 \vee \cdots \vee A_i \leftarrow B_1, \ldots, B_j, \neg C_1, \ldots, \neg C_k.$$

In datalog, the answer to a query is a set of valuations. For instance, the answer to a query $\leftarrow Q(x)$ is a set of constants a such that $Q(a)$ holds. In disjunctive deductive databases, an answer may also be a disjunction $Q(a) \vee Q(b)$.

Disjunctions give rise to new problems of semantics for logic programs. Although in datalog each program has a unique minimal model, this is no longer the case for datalog with disjunctions. For instance, consider the database consisting of a single statement $\{Q(a) \vee Q(b)\}$. Then there are clearly two minimal models: $\{Q(a)\}$ and $\{Q(b)\}$. This leads to semantics in terms of *sets of minimal models*, which can be viewed as incomplete databases. We can develop a fixpoint theory for disjunctive databases, extending naturally the fixpoint approach for datalog. To do this, we use an ordering over *sets of minimal interpretations* (i.e., sets $\mathcal{I}$ of instances such that there are no I, J in $\mathcal{I}$ with $I \subset J$).

DEFINITION 19.5.1   Let $\mathcal{I}, \mathcal{J}$ be sets of minimal interpretations. Then

$$\mathcal{J} \sqsubseteq \mathcal{I} \text{ iff } \forall I \in \mathcal{I} \, (\exists J \in \mathcal{J} \, (J \subseteq I)).$$

Consider the following immediate consequence operator. Let P be a datalog program with disjunctions, and let $\mathcal{I}$ be a set of minimal interpretations. A new set $\mathcal{J}$ of interpretations is obtained as follows. For each I in $\mathcal{I}$, $state_P(I)$ is the set of disjunctions of the form $A_1 \vee \cdots \vee A_i$ that are immediate consequences of some facts in I using P. Then $\mathcal{J}$ is the set of of instances J such that for some $I \in \mathcal{I}$, J is a model of $state_P(I)$ containing I. Clearly, $\mathcal{J}$ is not a set of minimal interpretations. The immediate consequence of $\mathcal{I}$, denoted $T_P(\mathcal{I})$, is the set of minimal interpretations in $\mathcal{J}$. Now consider the sequence

$$\mathcal{I}_0 = \emptyset$$
$$\mathcal{I}_i = T_P(\mathcal{I}_{i-1}).$$

It is easy to see that the sequence $\{\mathcal{I}_i\}_{i \geq 0}$ is nondecreasing with respect to the ordering $\sqsubseteq$, so it becomes constant at some point. The semantics of P is the limit of the sequence.

When negation is introduced, the situation, as usual, becomes more complicated. However, it is possible to extend semantics, such as stratified and well founded, to disjunctive deductive databases.

Overall, the major difficulty in handling disjunction is the combinatorial explosion it entails. For example, the fixpoint semantics of datalog with disjunctions may yield a set of interpretations exponential in the input.

Logical Databases and KL

The approach to null values adopted here is essentially a *semantic* approach, because the meaning of an incomplete database is a set of possible instances. One can also use a *syntactic*, proof-theoretic approach to modeling incomplete information. This is done by regarding the database as a set of sentences, which yields the *logical database* approach.

As discussed in Chapter 2, in addition to statements about the real world, logical databases consider the following:

1. *Uniqueness axioms*: State that distinct constants stand for distinct elements in the real world.

2. *Domain closure axiom*: Specify the universe of constants.

3. *Completion axiom*: Specify that no fact other than recorded holds.

Missing in both the semantic and syntactic approaches is the ability to make more refined statements about what the database knows. Such capabilities are particularly important in applications where the real world is slowly discovered through imprecise data. In such applications, it is general impossible to wait for a complete state to answer queries, and it is often desirable to provide the user with information about the current state of knowledge of the database.

To overcome such limitations, we may use languages with modalities. We briefly mention one such language: KL. The language KL permits us to distinguish explicitly between the real world and the knowledge the database has of it. It uses the particular modal symbol K. Intuitively, whereas the sentence φ states the truth of φ in the real world, $K\varphi$ states that the database knows that φ holds.

For instance, the fact that the database knows neither that Alice is a student nor that she is not is expressed by the statement

$$\neg K\,Student(Alice) \wedge \neg K\,(\neg Student(Alice)).$$

The following KL statement says that there is a teacher who is unknown:

$$\exists x\,(Teacher(x) \wedge \neg K\,(Teacher(x))).$$

This language allows the database to reason and answer queries about its own knowledge of the world.

Incomplete Information in Complete Databases

Incomplete information often arises naturally even when the focus is on complete databases. The following are several situations that naturally yield incomplete information:

- *Views*: Although a view of a database is usually a complete database, the information it contains is incomplete relative to the whole database. For a user seeing the view, there are many possible underlying databases. So the view can be seen as a representation for the set of possible underlying databases. The incompleteness of the information in the view is the source of the difficulty in view updating (see Chapter 22).

- *Weak universal relations*: We have already seen how relations with nulls arise in the weak universal relations of Chapter 11.

- *Nondeterministic queries*: Recall from Chapter 17 that nondeterministic languages have several possible answers on a given input. Thus we can think of nondeterministic queries as producing as an answer a set of possible worlds (see also Exercise 19.20).

- *Semantics of negation*: As seen in Chapter 15, the well-founded semantics for datalog¬ involves 3-valued interpretations, where some facts are neither true nor false but unknown. Clearly, this is a form of incomplete information.

Bibliographic Notes

It was accepted early on that database systems should handle incomplete information [Cod75]. After some interesting initial work on the topic (e.g., [Cod75, Gra77, Cod79, Cod82, Vas79, Vas80, Bis81, Lip79, Lip81, Bis83]), the landmark paper [IL84] laid the formal groundwork for incomplete databases with nulls of the unknown kind and introduced the notion of representation system. That paper assumed the OWA, as opposed to the CWA that was assumed in this chapter. Since then, there has been considerable work on querying incomplete information databases. The focus of most of this work has been a search for the correct semantics for queries applied to incomplete information databases (e.g., [Gra84, Imi84, Zan84, AG85, Rei86, Var86b]).

Much of the material presented in this chapter is from [IL84] (although it was presented there assuming the OWA), and we refer the reader to it for a detailed treatment.

Tables form the central topic of the monograph [Gra91]. Examples in Section 19.1 are taken from there. The naive tables have been called "V-tables" and "e-tables" in [AG85, Gra84, IL84]. The c-tables with local conditions are from [IL84]; they were augmented with global conditions in [Gra84]. The fact that c-tables provide a strong representation system for relational algebra is shown in [IL84]. That this strong representation property extends to query languages with fixpoint on positive queries is reported in [Gra91]. Chasing is applied to c-tables in [Gra91].

There are two main observations in the literature on certainty semantics. The first observation follows from the results of [IL84] (based on c-tables) and [Rei86, Var86b] (based on logical databases). Namely, under particular syntactic restrictions on c-tables and using positive queries, the certainty question can be handled exactly as if one had a complete information database. The second observation deals with the negative effects of the many possible instantiations of the null values (e.g., [Var86b]).

Comprehensive data-complexity analysis of problems related to representing and querying databases with null values is provided in [IL84, Var86b, AKG91]. The program complexity of evaluation is higher by an exponential than the data complexity [Cos83, Var82a]. Such problems were first noted in [HLY80, MSY81] as part of the study of nulls in weak universal instances.

Early investigations suggesting the use of orderings in the spirit of denotational semantics for capturing incomplete information include [Vas79, Bis81]. The first paper to develop this approach is [BJO91], which focused on fd's and universal relations. This has spawned several papers, including an extension to complex objects (see Chapter 20) [BDW88, LL90], mvd's [Lib91], and bags [LW93b]. An important issue in this work concerns which power domain ordering is used (Hoare, Smyth, or Plotkin); see [BDW91, Gun92, LW93a].

The logical database approach has been largely influenced by the work of Reiter [Rei78, Rei84, Rei86] and by that of Vardi [Var86a, Var86b]. The extension of the fixpoint operator of logic programs to disjunctive logic programs is shown in [MR90]. Disjunctive logic programming is the topic of [LMR92]. A survey on deductive databases with disjunctions can be found in [FM92]. The complexity of datalog with disjunction is investigated in [EGM94].

A related but simpler approach to incomplete information is the use of "or-sets." As a simple example, a tuple ⟨*Joe*, {20, 21}⟩ might be used to indicate that Joe has age either 20 or 21. This approach is introduced in [INV91a, INV91b] in the context of complex objects; subsequent works include [Rou91, LW93a].

One will find in [Lev84b, Lev84a] entry points to the interesting world of knowledge bases (from the viewpoint of incompleteness of information), including the language KL. A related, active area of research, called reasoning about knowledge, extends modal operators to talk about the knowledge of several agents about facts in the world or about each other's knowledge. This may be useful in distributed databases, where sites may have different knowledge of the world. The semantics of such statements is in terms of an extension of the possible worlds semantics, based on Kripke structures. An introduction to reasoning about knowledge can be found in [Hal93, FHMV94].

Finally, nonapplicable nulls are studied in [LL86]; open nulls are studied in [GZ88]; and weak instances with nonapplicable nulls are studied in [AB87b].

Exercises

Exercise 19.1   Consider the c-table in Example 19.3.1. Give the c-tables for the answers to these queries: (1) Which students are taking Math? (2) Which students are not taking Math? (3) Which students are taking Biology? In each case, what are the sets of sure and possible tuples of the answer?

Exercise 19.2   Consider the c-table T' in Fig. 19.3. Show that each I in $rep(T')$ has two tuples. Is T' equivalent to some 2-tuple c-table?

Exercise 19.3   Consider the naive table in Fig. 19.2. In the weak representation system described in Section 19.1, compute the naive tables for the answers to the queries $\sigma_{A=C}(R)$, $\pi_{AB}(R) \bowtie \pi_{AC}(R)$. What are the tuples surely in the answers to these queries?

Exercise 19.4   A ternary c-table T represents a directed graph with blue, red, and yellow edges. The first two columns represent the edges and the last the colors. Some colors are unknown. The local conditions are used to enforce that a blue edge cannot follow a red one on a path. Give a datalog query q stating that there is a cycle with no two consecutive edges of the same color. Give c-tables such that (1) there is surely such a cycle; and (2) there may be one but it is not sure. In each case, compute the table strongly representing the answer to q.

Exercise 19.5   Let T be the Codd table in Fig. 19.1. Compute strong representations of the results of the following queries, using c-tables: (a) $\sigma_{A=3}(R)$; (b) $q_1 = \delta_{BC \to AB}(\pi_{BC}(R))$; (c) $q_1 \cup \pi_{AB}(R)$; (d) $q_1 \cap \pi_{AB}(R)$; (e) $q_1 - \pi_{AB}(R)$; (f) $q_1 \bowtie \pi_{BC}(R)$.

Exercise 19.6   Consider the c-table $T_4 = T_1 \cup T_2$ of Fig. 19.4. Compute a strong representation of the transitive closure of T_4.

Exercise 19.7   Complete the proof that Codd tables are not a weak representation system with respect to SPU, in Theorem 19.2.1.

Exercise 19.8   Example 19.1.1 shows that one cannot strongly represent the result of a selection on a table with another table. For which operations of relational algebra applied to tables is it possible to strongly represent the result?

Exercise 19.9   Prove that naive tables are not a weak representation system for relational algebra.

Exercise 19.10   Prove that, given a c-table T without constants, $rep(T)$ is the closure under isomorphism of a finite set of instances. Extend the result for the case with constants.

Exercise 19.11   Provide an algorithm for testing equivalence of c-tables.

★**Exercise 19.12**   Show that there exists a datalog query q such that, given a naive table T and a tuple t, testing whether t is possibly in the answer is NP-complete.

Exercise 19.13   Prove Theorem 19.3.2.

Exercise 19.14   Prove that for each c-table T_1 and each set of fd's and mvd's, there exists a table T_2 such that $chase_\Sigma(rep(T_1)) = rep(T_2)$. *Hint:* Use the chase on c-tables.

★**Exercise 19.15**   Show that there is a query q in polynomial time for which deciding, given I and a c-table T, (a) whether $I \in q(rep(T))$, or whether I is possible, are NP-complete; and (b) whether $q(rep(T)) \subseteq \{I\}$, or whether I is certain, are co-NP-complete.

Exercise 19.16 Give algorithms to compute, for a c-table T and a relational algebra query q, the set of tuples $sure(q, T)$ surely in the answer and the set of tuples $poss(q, T)$ possibly in the answer. What is the complexity of your algorithms?

Exercise 19.17 Let T be a c-table and q a positive existential query of the same arity as T. Show that the sequence $\bar{q}^i(T)$ converges [i.e., that for some i, $\bar{q}^i(T) \equiv \bar{q}^{i+1}(T)$]. *Hint:* Show that the sequence converges in at most m stages, where $m = max\{i \mid q^i(I) = q^{i+1}(I), I \in \mathcal{I}\}$ and where $\mathcal{I}$ is a finite set of relations representing the nonisomorphic instances in $rep(T)$.

Exercise 19.18 Describe how to generalize the technique of chasing by full dependencies to apply to instances rather than tableau. If an egd can be applied and calls for two distinct constants to be identified, then the chase ends in failure. Show that for instance I, if the chase of I by Σ succeeds, then $chase(I, \Sigma) \models \Sigma$.

Exercise 19.19 Show that for datalog programs with disjunctions in heads of rules, the sequence $\{\mathcal{I}_i\}_{i \geq 0}$ of Section 19.5 converges. What can be said about the limit in model-theoretic terms?

♠ **Exercise 19.20** [ASV90] There is an interesting connection between incomplete information and *nondeterminism*. Recall the nondeterministic query languages based on the *witness* operator W, in Chapter 17. One can think of nondeterministic queries as producing as an answer a set of possible worlds. In the spirit of the sure and possible answers to queries on incomplete databases, one can define for a nondeterministic query q the deterministic queries $sure(q)$ and $poss(q)$ as follows:

$$sure(q)(I) = \cap\{J \mid J \in q(I)\}$$
$$poss(q)(I) = \cup\{J \mid J \in q(I)\}$$

Consider the language $FO + W$, where a program consists of a finite sequence of assignment statements of the form $R := \varphi$, where φ is a relational algebra expression or an application of W to a relation. Let $sure(FO + W)$ denote all deterministic queries that can be written as $sure(q)$ for some $FO + W$ query q, and similarly for $poss(FO + W)$. Prove that

(a) $poss(FO + W) = $NP, and
(b) $sure(FO + W) = $CO-NP.

20 Complex Values

Alice:	*Complex values?*
Riccardo:	*We could have used a different title: nested relations, complex objects, structured objects ...*
Vittorio:	*... NINF, NFNF, NF², NF2, V-relation ... I have seen all these names and others as well.*
Sergio:	*In a nutshell, relations are nested within relations; something like Matriochka relations.*
Alice:	*Oh, yes. I love Matriochkas.*

Although we praised the simplicity of the data structure in the relational model, this simplicity becomes a severe limitation when designing many practical database applications. To overcome this problem, the complex value model has been proposed as a significant extension of the relational one. This extension is the topic of this chapter.

Intuitively, complex values are relations in which the entries are not required to be atomic (as in the relational model) but are allowed to be themselves relations. The data structure in the relational model (the relation) can be viewed as the result of applying to atomic values two constructors: a *tuple constructor* to make tuples and a *set constructor* to make sets of tuples (relations). Complex values allow the application of the tuple and set constructor recursively. Thus they can be viewed as finite trees whose internal nodes indicate the use of the tuple and finite set constructors. Clearly, a relation is a special kind of complex value: a set of tuples of atomic values.

At the schema level, we will specify a set of complex *sorts* (or types). These indicate the structure of the data. At the instance level, sets of complex values corresponding to these sorts are provided. For example, we have the following:

Sort	*Complex Value*
dom	a
{**dom**}	$\{a, b, c\}$
$\langle A : \textbf{dom}, B : \textbf{dom}\rangle$	$\langle A : a, B : b\rangle$
$\{\langle A : \textbf{dom}, B : \textbf{dom}\rangle\}$	$\{\langle A : a, B : b\rangle, \langle A : b, B : a\rangle\}$
{{**dom**}}	$\{\{a, b\}, \{a\}, \{\}\}$

An example of a more involved complex value sort and of a value of that sort is shown in Fig. 20.1(a). The tuple constructor is denoted by $\times$ and the set constructor by $*$. An

508

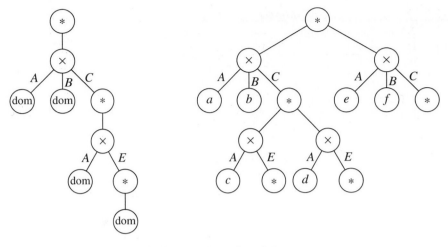

(a) A sort and a value of that sort

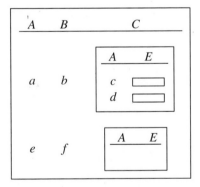

(b) Another representation of the same value

Figure 20.1:   Complex value

alternative representation more in the spirit of our representations of relations is shown in
Fig. 20.1(b). Another complex value (for a **CINEMA** database) is shown in Fig. 20.2.

We will see that, whereas it is simple to add the tuple constructor to the traditional
relational data model, the set constructor requires a number of interesting new ideas. There
are similarities between this set construct and the set constructs used in general-purpose
programming languages such as Setl.

In this chapter, we introduce complex values and present a many-sorted algebra and
an equivalent calculus for complex values. The focus is on the use of the two constructors
of complex values: tuples and (finite) sets. (Additional constructors, such as list, bags, and

Director	Movies	
	Title	**Actors**
Hitchcock	The Trouble with Harry	John Forsythe Edmund Gwenn Shirley MacLaine Alfred Hitchcock
	The Birds	Tippi Hedren Rod Taylor Suzanne Pleshette Alfred Hitchcock
	Psycho	Anthony Perkins Janet Leigh Alfred Hitchcock
	Title	**Actors**
Bergman	Cries and Whispers	Harriet Andersson Kari Sylwan Ingrid Thulin Liv Ullman
	The Seventh Seal	Max von Sydow Gunnar Björnstrand Bengt Ekerot Mils Poppe

Figure 20.2: The **CINEMA** database revisited (with additional data shown)

union, have also been incorporated into complex values but are not studied here.) After introducing the algebra and calculus, we present examples of these interesting languages. We then comment on the issues of expressive power and complexity and describe equivalent languages with fixpoint operators, as well as languages in the deductive paradigm. Finally we briefly examine a subset of the commercial query language O_2SQL that provides an elegant SQL-style syntax for querying complex values.

The theory described in this chapter serves as a starting point for object-oriented databases, which are considered in Chapter 21. However, key features of the object-oriented paradigm, such as objects and inheritance, are still missing in the complex value framework and are left for Chapter 21.

20.1 Complex Value Databases

Like the relational model, we will use relation names in **relname**, attributes in **att**, and constants in **dom**. The sorts are more complex than for the relational model. Their abstract syntax is given by

$$\tau = \mathbf{dom} \mid \langle B_1 : \tau, \ldots, B_k : \tau \rangle \mid \{\tau\},$$

where $k \geq 0$ and $B_1, \ldots, B_k$ are distinct attributes. Intuitively, an element of **dom** is a constant; an element of $\langle B_1 : \tau_1, \ldots, B_k : \tau_k \rangle$ is a k-tuple with an element of sort τ_i in entry B_i for each i; and an element of sort $\{\tau\}$ is a finite set of elements of sort τ.

Formally, the set of values of sort τ (i.e., the interpretation of τ), denoted $[\![\tau]\!]$, is defined by

1. $[\![\mathbf{dom}]\!] = \mathbf{dom}$,
2. $[\![\{\tau\}]\!] = \{\{v_1, \ldots, v_j\} \mid j \geq 0, v_i \in [\![\tau]\!], i \in [1, j]\}$, and
3. $[\![\langle B_1 : \tau_1, \ldots, B_k : \tau_k \rangle]\!] = \{\langle B_1 : v_1, \ldots, B_k : v_k \rangle \mid v_j \in [\![\tau_j]\!], j \in [1, k]\}$.

An element of a sort is called a *complex value*. A complex value of the form $\langle B_1 : a_1, \ldots, B_k : a_k \rangle$ is said to be a *tuple*, whereas a complex value of the form $\{a_1, \ldots, a_j\}$ is a set.

REMARK 20.1.1 For instance, consider the sort

$$\{\langle A : \mathbf{dom}, B : \mathbf{dom}, C : \{\langle A : \mathbf{dom}, E : \{\mathbf{dom}\}\rangle\}\rangle\}$$

and the value

$$\{ \; \langle A : a, B : b, C : \{ \; \langle A : c, E : \{\}\rangle,$$
$$\langle A : d, E : \{\}\rangle\}\rangle,$$
$$\langle A : e, B : f, C : \{ \; \}\rangle \; \}$$

of that sort. This is yet again the value of Fig. 20.1. It is customary to omit **dom** and for instance write this sort $\{\langle A, B, C : \{\langle A, E : \{\}\rangle\}\rangle\}$.

As mentioned earlier, each complex value and each sort can be viewed as a finite tree. Observe the tree representation. Outgoing edges from tuple vertexes are labeled; set vertexes have a single child in a sort and an arbitrary (but finite) number of children in a value.

Finally note that (because of the empty set) a complex value may belong to more than one sort. For instance, the value of Fig. 20.1 is also of sort

$$\{\langle A : \mathbf{dom}, B : \mathbf{dom}, C : \{\langle A : \mathbf{dom}, E : \{\{\mathbf{dom}\}\}\rangle\}\rangle\}.$$

Relational algebra deals with *sets* of tuples. Similarly, complex value algebra deals with sets of complex values. This motivates the following definition of sorted relation (this definition is frequently a source of confusion):

> A (complex value) *relation* of sort τ is a finite set of values of sort τ.

We use the term *relation* for complex value relation. When we consider the classical relational model, we sometimes use the phrase *flat relation* to distinguish it from complex value relation. It should be clear that the flat relations that we have studied are special cases of complex value relations.

We must be careful in distinguishing the sort of a complex value relation and the sort of the relation viewed as one complex value. For example, a complex value relation of sort $\langle A, B, C \rangle$ is a set of tuples over attributes ABC. At the same time, the entire relation can be viewed as one complex value of sort $\{\langle A, B, C \rangle\}$. There is no contradiction between these two ways of viewing a relation.

We now assume that the function *sort* (of Chapter 3) is from **relname** to the set of sorts. We also assume that for each sort, there is an infinite number of relations having that sort.

Note that the sort of a relation is not necessarily a tuple sort (it can be a set sort). Thus relations do not always have attributes at the top level. Such relations whose sort is a set are essentially unary relations without attribute names.

A *(complex value) schema* is a relation name; and a *(complex value) database schema* is a finite set of relation names. A *(complex value) relation* over relation name R is a finite set of values of sort $sort(R)$—that is, a finite subset of $[\![sort(R)]\!]$. A *(complex value database) instance* **I** of a schema **R** is a function from **R** such that for each R in **R**, $\mathbf{I}(R)$ is a relation over R.

EXAMPLE 20.1.2   To illustrate this definition, an instance **J** of $\{R_1, R_2, R_3\}$ where

$$sort(R_1) = sort(R_3) = \langle A : \mathbf{dom}, B : \{\langle A_1 : \mathbf{dom}, A_2 : \mathbf{dom} \rangle\} \rangle \text{ and}$$
$$sort(R_2) = \langle A : \mathbf{dom}, A_1 : \mathbf{dom}, A_2 : \mathbf{dom} \rangle$$

is shown in Fig. 20.3.

Variations

To conclude this section, we briefly mention some variations of the complex value model. The principal one that has been considered is the *nested relation model*. For nested relations, set and tuple constructors are required to alternate (i.e., set of sets and tuple with a tuple component are prohibited). For instance,

$$\tau_1 = \langle A, B, C : \{\langle D, E : \{\langle F, G \rangle\} \rangle\} \rangle \quad \text{and}$$
$$\tau_2 = \langle A, B, C : \{\langle E : \{\langle F, G \rangle\} \rangle\} \rangle$$

are nested relation sorts whereas

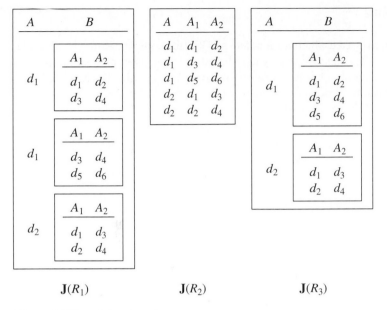

$$\mathbf{J}(R_1) \qquad\qquad \mathbf{J}(R_2) \qquad\qquad \mathbf{J}(R_3)$$

Figure 20.3:   A database instance

$$\tau_3 = \langle A, B, C : \langle D, E : \{\langle F, G \rangle\}\rangle\rangle \quad \text{and}$$
$$\tau_4 = \langle A, B, C : \{\{\langle F, G \rangle\}\}\rangle$$

are not. (For τ_3, observe two adjacent tuple constructors; there are two set constructors for τ_4.)

The restriction imposed on the structure of nested relations is mostly cosmetic. A more fundamental constraint is imposed in so-called Verso-relations (V-relations).

As with nested relations, set and tuple constructors in V-relations are required to alternate. A relation is defined recursively to be a set of tuples, such that each component may itself be a relation but at least one of them must be atomic. The foregoing sort τ_1 would be acceptable for a V-relation whereas sort τ_2 would not because of the sort of tuples in the C component.

A further (more radical) assumption for V-relations is that for each set of tuples, the atomic attributes form a key. Observe that as a consequence, the cardinality of each set in a V-relation is bounded by a polynomial in the number of atomic elements occurring in the V-relation. This bound certainly does not apply for a relation of sort $\{\mathbf{dom}\}$ (a set of sets) or for a nested relation of sort

$$\langle A : \{\langle B : \mathbf{dom}\rangle\}\rangle,$$

which is also essentially a set of sets. The V-relations are therefore much more limited data structures. (See Exercise 20.1.) They can be viewed essentially as flat relational instances.

20.2   The Algebra

We now define a many-sorted algebra, denoted ALG^{cv} (for *complex values*). Like relational algebra, ALG^{cv} is a functional language based on a small set of operations. This section first presents a family of core operators of the algebra and then an extended family of operators that can be simulated by them. At the end of the section we introduce an important subset of ALG^{cv}, denoted ALG^{cv-}.

The Core of ALG^{cv}

Let $I, I_1, I_2, \ldots$ be relations of sort $\tau, \tau_1, \tau_2, \ldots$ respectively. It is important to keep in mind that a relation of sort τ is a *set* of values of sort τ.

Basic set operations: If $\tau_1 = \tau_2$, then $I_1 \cap I_2$, $I_1 \cup I_2$, $I_1 - I_2$, are relations of sort τ_1, and their values are defined in the obvious manner.

Tuple operations: If I is a relation of sort $\tau = \langle B_1 : \tau_1, \ldots, B_k : \tau_k \rangle$, then

- $\sigma_\gamma(I)$ is a relation of sort τ.
  The selection condition γ is (with obvious restrictions on sorts) of the form $B_i = d$, $B_i = B_j$, $B_i \in B_j$ or $B_i = B_j.C$, where d is a constant, and it is required in the last case that τ_j be a tuple sort with a C field. Then

$$\sigma_\gamma(I) = \{v \mid v \in I, v \models \gamma\},$$

  where $\models$ is defined by

  - $\langle \ldots, B_i : v_i, \ldots \rangle \models B_i = d$ if $v_i = d$,
  - $\langle \ldots, B_i : v_i, \ldots, B_j : v_j, \ldots \rangle \models B_i = B_j$ if $v_i = v_j$, and
  - $\langle \ldots, B_i : v_i, \ldots, B_j : v_j, \ldots \rangle \models B_i \in B_j$ if $v_i \in v_j$.
  - $\langle \ldots, B_i : v_i, \ldots, B_j : \langle \ldots, C : v_j, \ldots \rangle, \ldots \rangle \models B_i = B_j.C$ if $v_i = v_j$.

- $\pi_{B_1, \ldots, B_l}(I), l \leq k$ is a relation of sort $\langle B_1 : \tau_1, \ldots, B_l : \tau_l \rangle$ with

$$\pi_{B_1, \ldots, B_l}(I) = \{ \; \langle B_1 : v_1, \ldots, B_l : v_l \rangle \mid$$
$$\exists v_{l+1}, \ldots, v_k (\langle B_1 : v_1, \ldots, B_k : v_k \rangle \in I)\}.$$

Constructive operations

- *powerset*(I) is a relation of sort $\{\tau\}$ and

$$powerset(I) = \{v \mid v \subseteq I\}.$$

- If $A_1, \ldots, A_n$ are distinct attributes, *tup_create*$_{A_1 \ldots A_n}(I_1, \ldots, I_n)$ is of sort $\langle A_1 : \tau_1, \ldots, A_n : \tau_n \rangle$, and

$$tup\_create_{A_1, \ldots, A_n}(I_1, \ldots, I_n) = \{\langle A_1 : v_1, \ldots, A_n : v_n \rangle \mid \forall i \; (v_i \in I_i)\}.$$

- *set_create*(I) is of sort $\{\tau\}$, and *set_create*$(I) = \{I\}$.

Destructive operations

- If $\tau = \{\tau'\}$, then *set_destroy*(I) is a relation of sort τ' and

$$set\_destroy(I) = \cup I = \{w \mid \exists v \in I, w \in v\}.$$

- If I is of sort $\langle A : \tau' \rangle$, *tup_destroy*$(I)$ is a relation of sort τ', and

$$tup\_destroy(I) = \{v \mid \langle A : v \rangle \in I\}.$$

We are now prepared to define the (core of the) language ALG^{cv}. Let **R** be a database schema. A query returns a set of values of the same sort. By analogy with relations, a query of sort τ returns a *set* of values of sort τ. ALG^{cv} queries and their answers are defined as follows. There are two base cases:

Base values: For each relation name R in **R**, R is an algebraic query of sort *sort*(R). The answer to query R is $\mathbf{I}(R)$.

Constant values: For each element a, $\{a\}$ is a (constant) algebraic query of sort **dom**. The answer to query $\{a\}$ is simply $\{a\}$.

Other queries of ALG^{cv} are obtained as follows. If $q_1, q_2, \ldots$ are queries, γ is a selection condition, and $A_1, \ldots$ are attributes,

$q_1 \cap q_2,$ $q_1 \cup q_2,$ $q_1 - q_2,$
$\sigma_\gamma(q_1),$ $\pi_{A_1,\ldots,A_k}(q_1),$ $tup\_create_{A_1,\ldots,A_k}(q_1,\ldots,q_k),$
powerset$(q_1),$ *tup_destroy*$(q_1),$ *set_destroy*$(q_1),$
set_create(q_1)

are queries if the appropriate restrictions on the sorts apply. (Note that because of the sorting constraints, *tup_destroy* and *set_destroy* cannot both be applicable to a given q_1.) The sort of a query and its answer are defined in a straightforward manner.

To illustrate these definitions, we present two examples. We then consider other algebraic operators that are expressible in the algebra. In Section 20.4 we provide several more examples of algebraic queries.

EXAMPLE 20.2.1   Consider the instance **J** of Fig. 20.3. Then one can find in Fig. 20.4

$$J_1 = [\sigma_{A=d_2}(R_1)](\mathbf{J}), \qquad J_2 = \pi_B(J_1),$$
$$J_3 = tup\_destroy(J_2), \qquad J_4 = set\_destroy(J_3),$$
$$J_5 = powerset(J_4), \qquad J_6 = tup\_create_C(J_4).$$

Also observe that

$$J_5 = [powerset(set\_destroy(tup\_destroy(\pi_B(\sigma_{A=d_2}(R_1)))))](\mathbf{J}).$$

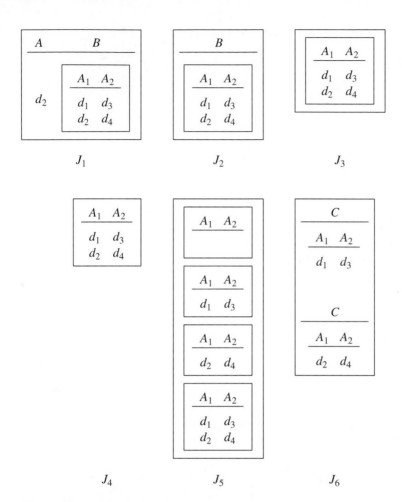

Figure 20.4: Algebraic operations

EXAMPLE 20.2.2 In this example, we illustrate the destruction and construction of a complex value. Consider the relation

$$I = \{\langle A : a, B : \{b, c\}, C : \langle A : d, B : \{e, f\}\rangle\rangle\}.$$

Then

$$[(\pi_A \circ tup\_destroy)$$
$$\cup (\pi_B \circ tup\_destroy \circ set\_destroy)$$
$$\cup (\pi_C \circ tup\_destroy \circ \pi_A \circ tup\_destroy)$$
$$\cup (\pi_C \circ tup\_destroy \circ \pi_B \circ tup\_destroy \circ set\_destroy)](I)$$
$$= \{a, b, c, d, e, f\}.$$

We next reconstruct I from singleton sets:

$$I = tup\_create_{A,B,C}(\{a\}, set\_create(\{b\} \cup \{c\}),$$
$$tup\_create_{A,B}(\{d\}, set\_create(\{e\} \cup \{f\}))).$$

Additional Algebraic Operations

There are infinite possibilities in the choice of algebraic operations for complex values. We chose to incorporate in the core algebra only a few basic operations to simplify the formal presentation and the proof of the equivalence between the algebra and calculus. However, making the core *too* reduced would complicate that proof. (For example, the operator *set_create* can be expressed using the other operations but is convenient in the proof.) We now present several additional algebraic operations. It is important to note that all these operations can be expressed in complex value algebra. (In that sense, they can be viewed as macro operations.) Furthermore, all but the *nest* operator can be expressed without using the powerset operator.

We first generalize constant queries.

Complex constants: It is easy to see that the technique of Example 20.2.2 can be generalized. So instead of simply $\{a\}$ for a atomic, we use as constant queries arbitrary complex value sets.

We also generalize relational operations.

Renaming: Renaming can be computed using the other operations, as illustrated in Section 20.4 (which presents examples of queries).

Cross-product: For i in [1,2], let I_i be a relation of sort

$$\tau_i = \langle B_1^i : \tau_1^i, \ldots, B_{j_i}^i : \tau_{j_i}^i \rangle$$

and let the attribute sets in τ_1, τ_2 be disjoint. Then $I_1 \times I_2$ is the relation defined by

$$sort(I_1 \times I_2) = \langle B_1^1 : \tau_1^1, \ldots, B_{j_1}^1 : \tau_{j_1}^1, B_1^2 : \tau_1^2, \ldots, B_{j_2}^2 : \tau_{j_2}^2 \rangle$$

and

$$I_1 \times I_2 = \{ \langle B_1^1 : x_1^1, \ldots, B_{j_1}^1 : x_{j_1}^1, B_1^2 : x_1^2, \ldots, B_{j_2}^2 : x_{j_2}^2 \rangle \mid$$
$$\langle B_1^i : x_1^i, \ldots, B_{j_i}^i : x_{j_i}^i \rangle \in I_i \text{ for } i \in [1, 2] \}.$$

It is easy to simulate cross-product using the operations of the algebra. This is also illustrated in Section 20.4.

Join: This can be defined in the natural manner and can be simulated using cross-product, renaming, and selection.

It should now be clear that complex value algebra subsumes relational algebra when applied to flat relations. We also have new set-oriented operations.

N-ary set_create: We introduced *tup_create* as an *n*-ary operation. We also allow *n*-ary *set_create* with the meaning that

$$set\_create(I_1, \ldots, I_n) \equiv set\_create(I_1) \cup \cdots \cup set\_create(I_n).$$

Singleton: This operator transforms a set of values $\{a_1, \ldots, a_n\}$ into a set $\{\{a_1\}, \ldots, \{a_n\}\}$ of singletons.

Nest, unnest: Less primitive interesting operations such as *nest, unnest* can be considered. For example, for $\mathbf{J}$ of Fig. 20.3 we have

$$unnest_B(\mathbf{J}(R_1)) = \mathbf{J}(R_2) \qquad \text{and}$$
$$nest_{B=(A_1 A_2)}(\mathbf{J}(R_2)) = \mathbf{J}(R_3).$$

More formally, suppose that we have R and S with sorts

$$sort(R) = \langle A_1 : \tau_1, \ldots, A_k : \tau_k, B : \{\langle A_{k+1} : \tau_{k+1}, \ldots, A_n : \tau_n \rangle\} \rangle$$
$$sort(S) = \langle A_1 : \tau_1, \ldots, A_k : \tau_k, A_{k+1} : \tau_{k+1}, \ldots, A_n : \tau_n \rangle.$$

Then for instances I of R and J of S, we have

$$unnest_B(I) = \{\langle A_1 : x_1, \ldots, A_n : x_n \rangle \mid \exists y$$
$$\langle A_1 : x_1, \ldots, A_k : x_k, B : y \rangle \in I \text{ and } \langle A_{k+1} : x_{k+1}, \ldots, A_n : x_n \rangle \in y\}$$
$$nest_{B=(A_{k+1}, \ldots, A_n)}(J) = \{\langle A_1 : x_1, \ldots, A_k : x_k, B : y \rangle \mid$$
$$\emptyset \neq y = \{\langle A_{k+1} : x_{k+1}, \ldots, A_n : x_n \rangle \mid \langle A_1 : x_1, \ldots, A_n : x_n \rangle \in J\}\}.$$

Observe that

$$unnest_B(nest_{B=(A_1 A_2)}(\mathbf{J}(R_2))) = \mathbf{J}(R_2).$$
$$nest_{B=(A_1 A_2)}(unnest_B(\mathbf{J}(R_1))) \neq \mathbf{J}(R_1).$$

This is indeed not an isolated phenomenon. *Unnest* is in general the right inverse of *nest* ($nest_{B=\alpha} \circ unnest_B$ is the identity), whereas *unnest* is in general not information preserving (one-to-one) and so has no right inverse (see Exercise 20.8).

Relational projection and selection were filtering operations in the sense that intuitively they scan a set and keep only certain elements, possibly modifying them in a uniform way. The filters in complex value algebra are more general. Of course, we shall allow Boolean expressions in selection conditions. More interestingly, we also allow set comparators in addition to $\in$, such as $\ni, \subset, \subseteq, \supset, \supseteq$ and negations of these comparators (e.g., $\not\subseteq$). The inclusion comparator $\subseteq$ plays a special role in the calculus. We will see in Section 20.4 how to simulate selection with $\subseteq$.

Selection is a *predicative filter* in the sense that a predicate allows us to select some elements, leaving them unchanged. Other filters, such as projection, are *map filters*. They transform the elements. Clearly, one can combine both aspects and furthermore allow more complicated selection conditions or restructuring specifications. For instance, suppose I is a set of tuples of sort

$$\langle A : \textbf{dom}, \ B : \langle C : \langle E : \{\textbf{dom}\}, \ E' : \textbf{dom} \rangle, \ C' : \{\textbf{dom}\}\rangle \rangle.$$

We could use an operation that first filters all the values matching the pattern

$$\langle A : x, \ B : \langle C : \langle E : y, \ E' : z \rangle, \ C' : \{x\}\rangle \rangle;$$

and then transforms them into

$$\langle A : (y \cup \{x\}), \ B : y, \ C : z \rangle.$$

This style of operations is standard in functional languages (e.g., *apply-to-all* in fp).

REMARK 20.2.3   As mentioned earlier, all of the operations just introduced are expressible in ALG^{cv}. We might also consider an operation to *iterate* over the elements of a set in some order. Such an operation can be found in several systems. As we shall see in Section 20.6, iteration is essentially expressible within ALG^{cv}. On the other hand, an iteration that depends on a specific ordering of the underlying domain of elements cannot be simulated using ALG^{cv} unless the ordering is presented as part of the input. ∎

In the following sections, we (informally) call *extended algebra* the algebra consisting of the operations of ALG^{cv} and allowing complex constants, renaming, cross-product, join, n-ary *set_create*, singleton, *nest*, and *unnest*.

An important subset of ALG^{cv}, denoted ALG^{cv-}, is formed from the core operators of ALG^{cv} by removing the *powerset* operator and adding the *nest* operator. As will be seen in Section 20.7, although the *nest* operator has the ability to construct sets, it is much weaker than *powerset*. When restricted to nested relations, the language ALG^{cv-} is usually called *nested relation algebra*.

20.3   The Calculus

The calculus is modeled after a standard, first-order, many-sorted calculus. However, as we shall see, calculus variables may denote sets, so the calculus will permit quantification over sets (something normally considered to be a second-order feature). For complex value calculus, the separation between first and second order (and higher order as well) is somewhat blurred. As with the algebra, we first present a core calculus and then extend it. The issues of domain independence and safety are also addressed.

For each sort, we assume the existence of a countably infinite set of variables of that sort. A variable is *atomic* if it ranges over the sort **dom**. Let **R** be a schema. A *term* is an atomic element, a variable, or an expression $x.A$, where x is a tuple variable and A is an attribute of x. We do not consider (yet) fancier terms. A *positive literal* is an expression of the form

$$R(t), \quad t = t', \quad t \in t', \quad \text{or} \quad t \subseteq t',$$

where $R \in \mathbf{R}$, t, t' are terms and the appropriate sort restrictions apply.[1] *Formulas* are defined from atomic formulas using the standard connectives and quantifiers: $\wedge, \vee, \neg, \forall, \exists$. A *query* is an expression $\{x \mid \varphi\}$, where formula φ has exactly one free variable (i.e. x). We sometimes denote it by $\varphi(x)$. The calculus is denoted CALC^{cv}.

The following example illustrates this calculus.

EXAMPLE 20.3.1   Consider the schema and the instance of Fig. 20.3. We can verify that $\mathbf{J}(R_2)$ is the answer on instance $\mathbf{J}$ to the query

$$\{x \mid \exists y, z, z', u, v, w \ (R_1(y) \wedge y.A = u \wedge y.B = z$$
$$\wedge z' \in z \wedge z'.A_1 = v \wedge z'.A_2 = w$$
$$\wedge x.A = u \wedge x.A_1 = v \wedge x.A_2 = w) \},$$

where the sorts of the variables are as follows:

$sort(x) = \langle A, A_1, A_2 \rangle$, $sort(y) = \langle A, B : \{\langle A_1, A_2 \rangle\} \rangle$,

$sort(u) = sort(v) = sort(w) = \mathbf{dom}$, $sort(z') = \langle A_1, A_2 \rangle$,

$sort(z) = \{\langle A_1, A_2 \rangle\}$.

We could also have used an unsorted alphabet of variables and sorted them inside the formula, as in

$$\{x : \langle A, A_1, A_2 \rangle \ \mid \ \exists y : \langle A, B : \{\langle A_1, A_2 \rangle\} \rangle,$$
$$z : \{\langle A_1, A_2 \rangle\}, z' = \langle A_1, A_2 \rangle,$$
$$u : \mathbf{dom}, v : \mathbf{dom}, w : \mathbf{dom}$$
$$(R_1(y) \wedge y.A = u \wedge y.B = z$$
$$\wedge z' \in z \wedge z'.A_1 = v \wedge z'.A_2 = w$$
$$\wedge x.A = u \wedge x.A_1 = v \wedge x.A_2 = w) \}.$$

The key difference with relational calculus is the presence of the predicates $\in$ and $\subseteq$, which are interpreted as the standard set membership and inclusion. Another difference (of a more cosmetic nature) is that we allow only one free variable in relation atoms and in query formulas. This comes from the stronger sorts: A variable may represent an n-tuple.

The *answer* to a query q on an instance $\mathbf{I}$, denoted $q(\mathbf{I})$, is defined as for the relational model. As in the relational case, we may define various interpretations, depending on the underlying domain of base values used. As with relational calculus, the basis for defining the semantics is the notion

$$\mathbf{I} \text{ satisfies } \varphi \text{ for } \nu \text{ relative to } \mathbf{d}.$$

---

[1] Strictly speaking, the symbols $=$, $\subseteq$ and $\in$ are also many sorted.

[Recall that v is a valuation of the free variables of φ and **d** is an arbitrary set of elements containing $adom(\varphi, \mathbf{I})$.]

Consider the definition of this notion in Section 5.3. Cases (a) through (g) remain valid for the complex object calculus. We have to consider two supplementary cases. Recall that for equality, we had case (b):

(b) $\qquad\qquad \mathbf{I} \models_{\mathbf{d}} \varphi[v]$ if $\varphi = (s = s')$ and $v(s) = v(s')$.

In the same spirit, we add

(h-1) $\qquad\qquad \mathbf{I} \models_{\mathbf{d}} \varphi[v]$ if $\varphi = (s \in s')$ and $v(s) \in v(s')$

(h-2) $\qquad\qquad \mathbf{I} \models_{\mathbf{d}} \varphi[v]$ if $\varphi = (s \subseteq s')$ and $v(s) \subseteq v(s')$.

This formally states that $\in$ is interpreted as set membership and $\subseteq$ as set inclusion (in the same sense that as $=$ is interpreted as equality).

The issues surrounding domain independence for relational calculus also arise with CALC^{cv}. We develop a syntactic condition ensuring domain independence, but we also occasionally use an active domain interpretation.

Extensions

As in the case of the algebra, we now consider extensions of the calculus that can be simulated by the core syntax just given.

The standard abbreviations used for relational calculus, such as the logical connectives $\rightarrow$, $\leftarrow$, $\leftrightarrow$, can be incorporated into CALC^{cv}. Using these connectives, it is easy to see the nonminimality of the calculus: Each literal $x \subseteq y$ can be replaced by $\forall z(z \in x \rightarrow z \in y)$, where z is a fresh variable.

Arity In the core calculus, only relation atoms of the form $R(t)$ are permitted. Suppose that the sort of R is $\langle A_1 : \tau_1, \ldots, A_n : \tau_n \rangle$ for some n. Then $R(u_1, \ldots, u_n)$ is a shorthand for

$$\exists y(R(y) \wedge y.A_1 = u_1 \wedge \cdots \wedge y.A_n = u_n),$$

where y is a new variable. In particular, if R_0 is a relation of sort $\langle\, \rangle$ ($n = 0$), observe that the only value of that sort is the empty tuple. Thus a variable y of that sort has only one possible value, namely $\langle\, \rangle$. Thus for such y, we can use the following expression:

$$R_0(\,) \quad \text{for} \quad \exists y(R_0(y)).$$

Constructed Terms Next we allow constructed terms in the calculus such as

$$\{x, b\}, \quad x.A.C, \quad \langle B_1 : a, B_2 : y \rangle.$$

More formally, if $t_1, \ldots, t_k$ are terms and $B_1, \ldots, B_k$ are distinct attributes, then $\langle B_1 : t_1, \ldots, B_k : t_k \rangle$ is a term. Furthermore, if the t_i are of the same sort, $\{t_1, \ldots, t_k\}$ is a term;

and if t_1 is a tuple term with attribute C, then $t_1.C$ is a term. The sorts of terms are defined in the obvious way. Note that a term may have several sorts because of the empty set. (We ignore this issue here.)

The use of constructed terms can be viewed as syntactic sugaring. For instance, suppose that the term $\{a, y\}$ occurs in a formula ψ. Then ψ is equivalent to

$$\exists x(\psi' \wedge \forall z(z \in x \leftrightarrow (z = a \vee z = y))),$$

where ψ' is obtained from ψ by replacing the term $\{a, y\}$ by x (a fresh variable).

Complex Terms   We can also view relations as terms. For instance, if R is a relation of sort $\langle A, B \rangle$, then R can be used in the language as a term of sort $\{\langle A, B \rangle\}$. We may then consider literals such as $x \in R$, which is equivalent to $R(x)$; or more complex ones such as $S \in T$, which essentially means

$$\exists y(T(y) \wedge \forall x(x \in y \leftrightarrow S(x))).$$

The previous extension is based on the fact that a relation (in our context) can be viewed as a complex value. This is again due to the stronger sort system. Now the answer to a query q is also a complex value. This suggests considering the use of queries as terms of the language. We consider this now: A query $q \equiv \{y \mid \psi(y)\}$ is a legal term that can be used in the calculus like any other term. More generally, we allow terms of the form

$$\{y \mid \psi(y, y_1, \ldots, y_n)\},$$

where the free variables of ψ are $y, y_1, \ldots, y_n$. Intuitively, we obtain queries by providing bindings for $y_1, \ldots, y_n$. We will call such an expression a *parameterized query* and denote it $q(y_1, \ldots, y_n)$ (where $y_1, \ldots, y_n$ are the parameters).

For instance, suppose that a formula $liked(x, y)$ computes the films y that person x liked; and another one $saw(x, y)$ computes those that x has seen. The set of persons who liked all the films that they saw is given by

$$\{ x \mid \{y \mid liked(x, y)\} \subseteq \{y \mid saw(x, y)\} \}.$$

The following form of literals will play a particular role when we study safety for this calculus:

$$x = \{y \mid \psi(y, y_1, \ldots, y_n)\},$$
$$x' \in \{y \mid \psi(y, y_1, \ldots, y_n)\}, \text{ and}$$
$$x'' \subseteq \{y \mid \psi(y, y_1, \ldots, y_n)\},$$

where y is a free variable of ψ. Like the previous extensions, the parameterized queries can be viewed simply as syntactic sugaring. For instance, the three last formulas are, respectively, equivalent to

$$\forall y(y \in x \leftrightarrow \psi),$$
$$\exists y(x' = y \wedge \psi), \text{ and}$$
$$\forall y(y \in x'' \rightarrow \psi).$$

In the following sections, we (informally) call *extended calculus* the calculus consisting of CALC^{cv} extended with the abbreviations described earlier (such as constructed and complex terms and, notably, parameterized queries).

20.4 Examples

We illustrate the previous two sections with a series of examples. The queries in the examples apply to schema $\{R, S\}$ with

$$sort(R) = \langle A : \mathbf{dom}, A' : \mathbf{dom}\rangle,$$
$$sort(S) = \langle B : \mathbf{dom}, B' : \{\mathbf{dom}\}\rangle.$$

For each query, we give an algebraic and a calculus expression.

EXAMPLE 20.4.1 The union of R and a set of two constant tuples is given by

$$\{r \mid R(r) \vee r = \langle A : 3, A' : 5\rangle \vee r = \langle A : 0, A' : 0\rangle\}$$

or

$$R \cup \{\langle A : 3, A' : 5\rangle, \langle A : 0, A' : 0\rangle\}.$$

EXAMPLE 20.4.2 The selection of the tuples from S, where the first component is a member of the second component, is obtained with

$$\{s \mid S(s) \wedge s.B \in s.B'\} \quad \text{or} \quad \sigma_{B \in B'}(S).$$

EXAMPLE 20.4.3 The (classical) cross-product of R and S is the result of

$$\{t \mid \exists r, s(R(r) \wedge S(s) \wedge t = \langle A : r.A, A' : r.A', B : s.B, B' : s.B'\rangle)\}$$

or

$$\pi_{AA'BB'}(\sigma_{A=A''.A}(\sigma_{A'=A''.A'}(\sigma_{B=B''.B}(\sigma_{B'=B''.B'}(q))))),$$

where q is

$$tup\_create_{AA'BB'A''B''}(tup\_destroy(\pi_A(R)),$$
$$tup\_destroy(\pi_{A'}(R)),$$
$$tup\_destroy(\pi_B(S)),$$
$$tup\_destroy(\pi_{B'}(S)), R, S).$$

EXAMPLE 20.4.4   The join of R and S on $A = B$. This query is the composition of the cross-product of Example 20.4.3, with a selection. In Example 20.4.3, let the formula describing the cross-product be φ_3 and let $(R \times S)$ be the algebraic expression. Then the $(A = B)$ join of R and S is expressed by

$$\{t \mid \varphi_3(t) \wedge t.A = t.B\} \quad \text{or} \quad \sigma_{A=B}(R \times S).$$

EXAMPLE 20.4.5   The renaming of the attributes of R to A_1, A_2 is obtained in the calculus by

$$\{t \mid \exists r(R(r) \wedge t.A_1 = r.A \wedge t.A_2 = r.A')\}$$

with t of sort $\langle A_1 : \mathbf{dom}, A_2 : \mathbf{dom} \rangle$. In the algebra, it is given by

$$\pi_{A_1 A_2}(\sigma_{A_0.A=A_1}(\sigma_{A_0.A'=A_2}(tup\_create_{A_0 A_1 A_2}$$
$$(R, tup\_destroy(\pi_A(R)), tup\_destroy(\pi_{A'}(R))))))).$$

EXAMPLE 20.4.6   Flattening S means producing a set of flat tuples, each of which contains the first component of a tuple of S and one of the elements of the second component. This is the unnest operation $unnest_{B'}(\cdot)$ in the extended algebra, or in the calculus

$$\{t \mid \exists s(S(s) \wedge t.B = s.B \wedge t.C \in s.B')\},$$

where t is of sort $\langle B, C \rangle$. In the core algebra, this is slightly more complicated. We first obtain the set of values occurring in the B' sets using

$$E_1 = tup\_create_C(set\_destroy(tup\_destroy(\pi_{B'}(S)))).$$

We can next compute $(E_1 \times S)$ (using the same technique as in Example 20.4.3). Then the desired query is given by

$$\pi_{BC}(\sigma_{C \in B'}(E_1 \times S)).$$

Flattening can be extended to sorts with arbitrary nesting depth.

EXAMPLE 20.4.7   The next example is a selection using $\subseteq$. Consider a relation T of sort $\langle C : \{\mathbf{dom}\}, C' : \{\mathbf{dom}\} \rangle$. We want to express the query

$$\{t \mid T(t) \wedge t.C \subseteq t.C'\}$$

in the algebra. We do this in stages:

$$F_1 = \sigma_{C'' \in C}(T \times tup\_create_{C''}(set\_destroy(tup\_destroy(\pi_C(T))))),$$
$$F_2 = \sigma_{C'' \in C'}(F_1),$$
$$F_3 = F_1 - F_2,$$
$$F_4 = T - \pi_{CC'}(F_3).$$

Observe that

1. A tuple $\langle C : U, C' : V, C'' : u \rangle$ is in F_1 if $\langle C : U, C' : V \rangle$ is in T and u is in U.
2. A tuple $\langle C : U, C' : V, C'' : u \rangle$ is in F_2 if $\langle C : U, C' : V \rangle$ is in T and u is in U and V.
3. A tuple $\langle C : U, C' : V, C'' : u \rangle$ is in F_3 if $\langle C : U, C' : V \rangle$ is in T and u is in $U - V$.
4. A tuple $\langle C : U, C' : V \rangle$ is in F_4 if it is in T and there is no u in $U - V$ (i.e., $U \subseteq V$).

EXAMPLE 20.4.8 This example illustrates the use of nesting and of sets. Consider the algebraic query

$$nest_{C=(A)} \circ nest_{C'=(A')} \circ \sigma_{C=C'} \circ unnest_C \circ unnest_{C'}(R).$$

It is expressed in the calculus by

$$\{\langle x, y \rangle \mid \exists u (x \in u \wedge y \in u$$
$$\wedge \, u = \{x' \mid R(x', y)\}$$
$$\wedge \, u = \{y' \mid \{x' \mid R(x', y')\} = u\})\}.$$

A consequence of Theorem 20.7.2 is that this query is expressible in relational calculus or algebra. It is a nontrivial exercise to obtain a relational query for it. (See Exercise 20.24.)

EXAMPLE 20.4.9 Our last example highlights an important difference between the flat relational calculus and CALC^{cv}. As shown in Proposition 17.2.3, the flat calculus cannot express the transitive closure of a binary relation. In contrast, the following CALC^{cv} query does:

$$\{y \mid \forall x (closed(x) \wedge contains\_R(x) \rightarrow y \in x)\},$$

where

- $closed(x) \equiv$

$$\forall u, v, w (\langle A : u, A' : v \rangle \in x \wedge \langle A : v, A' : w \rangle \in x \rightarrow \langle A : u, A' : w \rangle \in x);$$

- $contains\_R(x) \equiv \forall z (R(z) \rightarrow z \in x)$;
- $sort(x) = \{sort(R)\}$, $sort(y) = sort(z) = sort(R)$; and
  $sort(u) = sort(v) = sort(w) = \textbf{dom}$.

Intuitively, the formula specifies the set of pairs y such that y belongs to each binary relation x containing R and transitively closed. This construction will be revisited in Section 20.6.

20.5 Equivalence Theorems

This section presents three results that compare the complex value algebra and calculus. First we establish the equivalence of the algebra and the domain-independent calculus. Next we develop a syntactic safeness condition for the calculus and show that it does not reduce expressive power. Finally we develop a natural syntactic condition on CALC^{cv} that yields a subset equivalent to ALG^{cv-}.

Our first result is as follows:

THEOREM 20.5.1 The algebra and the domain independent calculus for complex values are equivalent.

In the sketch of the proof, we present a simulation of the core algebra by the extended calculus and the analogous simulation in the opposite direction. An important component of this proof—namely, that the extended algebra (calculus) is no stronger than the core algebra (calculus)—is left for the reader (see Exercises 20.6, 20.7, 20.8, 20.10, and 20.11).

From Algebra to Calculus

We now show that for each algebra query, there is a domain-independent calculus query equivalent to it.

Let q be a named algebra query. We construct a domain-independent query $\{x \mid \varphi_q\}$ equivalent to q. The formula φ_q is constructed by induction on subexpressions of q. For a subexpression E of q, we define φ_E as follows:

(a) E is R for some $R \in \mathbf{R}$: φ_E is $R(x)$.

(b) E is $\{a\}$: φ_E is $x = a$.

(c) E is $\sigma_\gamma(E_1)$: φ_E is $\varphi_{E_1}(x) \wedge \Gamma$, where Γ is

$$x.A_i = x.A_j \text{ if } \gamma \equiv A_i = A_j; \quad x.A_i = a \text{ if } \gamma \equiv A_i = a;$$
$$x.A_i \in x.A_j \text{ if } \gamma \equiv A_i \in A_j; \quad x.A_i = x.A_j.C \text{ if } \gamma \equiv A_i = A_j.C.$$

(d) E is $\pi_{A_{i_1}, \dots, A_{i_k}}(E_1)$: φ_E is

$$\exists y (x = \langle A_{i_1} : y.A_{i_1}, \dots, A_{i_k} : y.A_{i_k} \rangle \wedge \varphi_{E_1}(y)).$$

(e) For the basic set operations, we have

$$\varphi_{E_1 \cap E_2}(x) = \varphi_{E_1}(x) \wedge \varphi_{E_2}(x),$$
$$\varphi_{E_1 \cup E_2}(x) = \varphi_{E_1}(x) \vee \varphi_{E_2}(x),$$
$$\varphi_{E_1 - E_2}(x) = \varphi_{E_1}(x) \wedge \neg\varphi_{E_2}(x).$$

(f) E is *powerset*(E_1): φ_E is $x \subseteq \{y \mid \varphi_{E_1}(y)\}$.

(g) E is *set_destroy*(E_1): φ_E is $\exists y(x \in y \wedge \varphi_{E_1}(y))$.

(h) E is *tup_destroy*(E_1): φ_E is $\exists y(\langle A : x \rangle = y \wedge \varphi_{E_1}(y))$, where A is the name of the field (of y).

(i) E is *tup_create*$_{A_1,\ldots,A_n}$($E_1, \ldots, E_n$): φ_E is

$$\exists y_1, \ldots, y_n(x = \langle A_1 : y_1, \ldots, A_n : y_n \rangle \wedge \varphi_{E_1}(y_1) \wedge \cdots \wedge \varphi_{E_n}(y_n)).$$

(j) E is *set_create*(E_1): $x = \{y \mid \varphi_{E_1}(y)\}$.

We leave the verification of this construction to the reader (see Exercise 20.13). The domain independence of the obtained calculus query follows from the fact that algebra queries are domain independent.

From Calculus to Algebra

We now show that for each domain-independent query, there is a named algebra query equivalent to it.

Let $q = \{x \mid \varphi\}$ be a domain-independent query over **R**. As in the flat relational case, we assume without loss of generality that associated with each variable x occurring in q (and also variables used in the following proof) is a unique, distinct attribute A_x in **att**. We use the active domain interpretation for the query, denoted as before with a subscript *adom*.

The crux of the proof is to construct, for each subformula ψ of φ, an algebra formula E_ψ that has the property that for each input **I**,

$$E_\psi(\mathbf{I}) = \{y \mid \exists x_1, \ldots, x_n(y = \langle A_{x_1} : x_1, \ldots, A_{x_n} : x_n \rangle \wedge \psi(x_1, \ldots, x_n))\}_{adom}(\mathbf{I}),$$

where $x_1, \ldots, x_n$ is a listing of *free*(ψ).

This construction is accomplished in three stages.

Computing the Active Domain   The first step is to construct an algebra query E_{adom} having sort **dom** such that on input instance **I**, $E_{adom}(\mathbf{I}) = adom(q, \mathbf{I})$. The construction of E_{adom} is slightly more intricate than the similar construction for the relational case. We prove by induction that for each sort τ, there exists an algebra operation F_τ that maps a set I of values of sort τ to $adom(I)$. This induction was not necessary in the flat case because the base relations had fixed depth. For the base case (i.e., $\tau = $ **dom**), it suffices to use for F_τ an identity operation (e.g., *tup_create*$_A$ ∘ *tup_destroy*). For the induction, the following cases occur:

1. τ is $\langle A_1 : \tau_1, \ldots, A_n : \tau_n \rangle$ for $n \geq 2$. Then F_τ is

$$F_{\langle A_1:\tau_1 \rangle}(\pi_{A_1}) \cup \cdots \cup F_{\langle A_n:\tau_n \rangle}(\pi_{A_n}).$$

2. τ is $\langle A_1 : \tau_1 \rangle$. Then F_τ is $F_{\tau_1}(tup\_destroy)$.
3. τ is $\{\tau_1\}$. Then F_τ is $F_{\tau_1}(set\_destroy)$.

Now consider the schema **R**. Then for each R in **R**, $F_{sort(R)}$ maps a relation I over R to $adom(I)$. Thus $adom(q, \mathbf{I})$ can be computed with the query

$$E_{adom} = F_{sort(R_1)}(R_1) \cup \cdots \cup F_{sort(R_m)}(R_m) \cup \{a_1\} \cup \cdots \cup \{a_p\},$$

where $R_1, \ldots, R_m$ is the list of relations in **R** and $a_1, \ldots, a_p$ is the list of elements occurring in q.

Constructing Complex Values   In the second stage, we prove by induction that for each sort τ, there exists an algebra query G_τ that constructs the set of values I of sort τ such that $adom(I) \subseteq adom(q, \mathbf{I})$. For $\tau = \mathbf{dom}$, we can use E_{adom}. For the induction, two cases occur:

1. τ is $\langle A_1 : \tau_1, \ldots, A_n : \tau_n \rangle$. Then G_τ is $tup\_create_{A_1,\ldots,A_n}(G_{\tau_1}, \ldots, G_{\tau_n})$.
2. τ is $\{\tau_1\}$. Then G_τ is $powerset(G_{\tau_1})$.

Last Stage   We now describe the last stage, an inductive construction of the queries E_ψ for subformulas ψ of φ. We assume without loss of generality that the logical connectives $\vee$ and $\forall$ do not occur in φ. The proof is similar to the analogous proof for the flat case. We also assume that relation atoms in φ do not contain constants or repeated variables. We only present the new case (the standard cases are left as Exercise 20.13). Let ψ be $x \in y$. Suppose that x is of sort τ, so y is of sort $\{\tau\}$. The set of values of sort τ (or $\{\tau\}$) within the active domain is returned by query G_τ, or $G_{\{\tau\}}$. The query

$$\sigma_{A_x \in A_y}(tup\_create_{A_x, A_y}(G_\tau, G_{\{\tau\}}))$$

returns the desired result.

Observe that with this construction, E_φ returns a set of tuples with a single attribute A_x. The query q is equivalent to $tup\_destroy(E_\varphi)$.

As we did for the relational model, we can define a variety of syntactic restrictions of the calculus that yield domain-independent queries. We consider such restrictions next.

Safe Queries

We now turn to the development of syntactic conditions, called safe range, that ensure domain independence. These conditions are reminiscent of those presented for relational calculus in Chapter 5. As we shall see, a variant of safe range, called strongly safe range, will yield a subset of CALC^{cv}, denoted CALC^{cv-}, that is equivalent to ALG^{cv-}.

We could define safe range on the core calculus. However, such a definition would be cumbersome. A much more elegant definition can be given using the extended calculus. In particular, we consider here the calculus augmented with (1) constructed terms and (2) parameterized queries.

Recall that intuitively, if a formula is safe range, then each variable is bounded, in the sense that it is restricted by the formula to lie within the active domain of the query or the input. We now define the notions of safe formulas and safe terms. To give these definitions, we define the set of *safe-range variables* of a formula using the following procedure, which returns either the symbol $\perp$ (which indicates that some quantified variable is not bounded) or the set of free variables that are bounded. In this discussion, we consider only formulas in which universal quantifiers do not occur.

In the following procedure, if several rules are applicable, the one returning the largest set of safe-range variables (which always exists) is chosen.

procedure *safe-range* (sr)

input: a calculus formula φ

output: a subset of the free variables of φ or $\perp$. (In the following, for each Z, $\perp \cup Z = \perp \cap Z = \perp - Z = Z - \perp = \perp$.)

begin
(*pred* is a predicate in $\{=, \in, \subseteq\}$)
if for some parameterized query $\{x \mid \psi\}$ occurring as a term in φ, $x \notin sr(\psi)$ **then**
return $\perp$
case φ **of**

$$
\begin{array}{ll}
R(t) & : sr(\varphi) = free(t); \\
(t \ pred \ t' \wedge \psi) & : \textbf{if } \psi \text{ is safe and } free(t') \subseteq free(\psi) \\
& \qquad \textbf{then } sr(\varphi) = free(t) \cup free(\psi); \\
t \ pred \ t' & : \textbf{if } free(t') = sr(t') \textbf{ then } sr(\varphi) = free(t') \cup free(t); \\
& \qquad \textbf{else } sr(\varphi) = \emptyset; \\
\varphi_1 \wedge \varphi_2 & : sr(\varphi) = sr(\varphi_1) \cup sr(\varphi_2); \\
\varphi_1 \vee \varphi_2 & : sr(\varphi) = sr(\varphi_1) \cap sr(\varphi_2); \\
\neg\varphi_1 & : sr(\varphi) = \emptyset; \\
\exists x \varphi_1 & : \textbf{if } x \in sr(\varphi_1) \\
& \qquad \textbf{then } sr(\varphi) = sr(\varphi_1) - \{x\} \\
& \qquad \textbf{else return } \perp
\end{array}
$$

end;

We say that a formula φ is *safe* if $sr(\varphi) = free(\varphi)$; and a query q is safe if its associated formula is safe.

It is important to understand how new sets are created in a safe manner. The next example illustrates two essential techniques for such creation.

EXAMPLE 20.5.2   Let R be a relation of sort $\langle A, B \rangle$. The powerset of R can be obtained in a safe manner with the query

$$\{x \mid x \subseteq \{y \mid R(y)\}\}.$$

For $\{y \mid R(y)\}$ is clearly a safe query (by the first case). Now letting $t \equiv x, t' \equiv \{y \mid R(y)\}$, the formula is safe (by the third case).

Now consider the nesting of the B column of R. It is achieved by the following query:

$$\{x \mid x = \langle z, \{y \mid R(z, y)\}\rangle \wedge \exists y'(R(z, y'))\}.$$

Let $t \equiv x, t' \equiv \langle z, \{y \mid R(z, y)\}\rangle$ and $\psi \equiv \exists y'(R(z, y'))$. First note that $sr(R(z, y))$ contains y, so the parameterized query $\{y \mid R(z, y)\}$ can be used safely. Next the formula ψ is safe. Finally the only free variable in t' is z, which is also free in ψ. Thus x is safe range (by the second case) and the query is safe.

As detailed in Section 20.7, the complex value algebra and calculus can express mappings with complexity corresponding to arbitrarily many nestings of exponentiation. In contrast, as discussed in that section, the nested relation algebra ALG^{cv-}, which uses the nest operator but not powerset, has complexity in PTIME. Interestingly, there is a minor variation of the safe-range condition that yields a subset of the calculus equivalent to ALG^{cv-}. Specifically, a formula is *strongly safe range* if it is safe range and the inclusion predicate does not occur in it. In the previous example, the nesting is strongly safe range whereas *powerset* is not.

We now have the following:

THEOREM 20.5.3

   (a) The safe-range calculus, the domain-independent calculus, and ALG^{cv} coincide.

   (b) The strongly safe-range calculus and ALG^{cv-} coincide.

Crux   Consider (a). By inspection of the construction in the proof that $\text{ALG}^{cv} \sqsubseteq \text{CALC}^{cv}$, each algebra query is equivalent to a safe-range calculus query. Clearly, each safe-range calculus query is a domain-independent calculus query. We have already shown that each domain-independent calculus query is an algebra query.

Now consider (b). Observe that in the proof that $\text{ALG}^{cv} \sqsubseteq \text{CALC}^{cv}$, $\subseteq$ is used only for powerset. Thus each query in ALG^{cv-} is a strongly safe-range query. Now consider a strongly safe-range query; we construct an equivalent algebra query. We cannot use the construction from the proof of the equivalence theorem, because *powerset* is crucial for constructing complex domains. However, we can show that this can be avoided using the ranges of variables. (See Exercise 20.16.) More precisely, the brute force construction of the domain of variables using powerset is replaced by a careful construction based on the strongly safe-range restriction. The remainder of the proof stays unchanged. ∎

Because of part (b) of the previous result, we denote the strongly safe-range calculus by CALC^{cv-}.

20.6   Fixpoint and Deduction

Example 20.4.9 suggests that the complex value algebra and calculus can simulate iteration. In this section, we examine iteration in the spirit of both fixpoint queries and datalog. In both cases, they do not increase the expressive power of the algebra or calculus. However, they allow us to express certain queries more efficiently.

Fixpoint for Complex Values

Languages with fixpoint semantics were considered in the context of the relational model to overcome limitations of relational algebra and calculus. In particular, we observed that transitive closure cannot be computed in relational calculus. However, as shown by Example 20.4.9, transitive closure can be expressed in the complex value algebra and calculus. Although transitive closure can be expressed in that manner, the use of *powerset* seems unnecessarily expensive. More precisely, it can be shown that *any* query in the complex value algebra and calculus that expresses transitive closure uses exponential space (assuming the straightforward evaluation of the query). In other words, the blowup caused by the *powerset* operator cannot be avoided. On the other hand, a fixpoint construct allows us to express transitive closure in polynomial space (and time). It is thus natural to develop fixpoint extensions of the calculus and algebra.

We can provide inflationary and noninflationary extensions of the calculus with recursion. As in the relational case, an *inflationary fixpoint operator* μ_T^+ allows the iteration of a CALC^{cv} formula $\varphi(T)$ up to a fixpoint. This essentially permits the inductive definition of relations, using calculus formulas. The calculus CALC^{cv} augmented with the inflationary fixpoint operator is defined similarly to the flat case (Chapter 14) and yields CALC$^{cv} + \mu^+$. We only consider the inflationary fixpoint operator. (Exercise 20.19 explores the noninflationary version.)

THEOREM 20.6.1   CALC$^{cv} + \mu^+$ is equivalent to ALG^{cv} and CALC^{cv}.

The proof of this theorem is left for Exercise 20.18. It involves simulating a fixpoint in a manner similar to Example 20.4.9.

Before leaving the fixpoint extension, we show how powerset can be computed by iterating a ALG^{cv-} formula to a fixpoint. (We will see later that powerset cannot be computed in ALG^{cv-} alone.)

EXAMPLE 20.6.2   Consider a relation R of sort **dom** (i.e., a set of atomic elements). The powerset of R is computed by $\{x \mid \mu_T(\varphi(T))(x)\}$, where T is of sort $\{$**dom**$\}$ and

$$\varphi(T)(y) \equiv [y = \emptyset \vee \exists x', y' (R(x') \wedge T(y') \wedge y = y' \cup \{x'\}.]$$

This formula is in fact equivalent to a query in ALG^{cv-}. (See Exercise 20.15.) For example, suppose that R contains $\{2, 3, 4\}$. The iteration of φ yields

$$
\begin{aligned}
J_0 &= \emptyset \\
J_1 &= \varphi(\emptyset) &&= \{\emptyset\} \\
J_2 &= \varphi(J_1) &&= J_1 \cup \{\{2\}, \{3\}, \{4\}\} \\
J_3 &= \varphi(J_2) &&= J_2 \cup \{\{2, 3\}, \{2, 4\}, \{3, 4\}\} \\
J_4 &= \varphi(J_3) &&= J_3 \cup \{\{2, 3, 4\}\},
\end{aligned}
$$

and J_4 is a fixpoint and coincides with $powerset(\{2, 3, 4\})$.

Datalog for Complex Values

We now briefly consider an extension of datalog to incorporate complex values. The basic result is that the extension is equivalent to the complex value algebra and calculus. We also consider a special grouping construct, which can be used for set construction in this context.

In the datalog extension considered here, the predicates $\subseteq$ and $\in$ are permitted. A rule is *safe range* if each variable that appears in the head also appears in the body, and the body is safe (i.e., the conjunction of the literals of the body is a safe formula). We assume henceforth that rules are safe. Stratified negation will be used. The language is illustrated in the following example.

EXAMPLE 20.6.3   The input is a relation R of sort $\langle A, B : \{\langle C, C'\rangle\}\rangle$. Consider the query defining an *idb* relation T, which contains the tuples of R, with the B-component replaced by its transitive closure. Let us assume that we have a ternary relation *ins*, where $ins(w, y, z)$ is interpreted as "z is obtained by inserting w into y." We show later how to define this relation in the language. The program consists of the following rules:

$(r1)$ $S(x, y) \leftarrow R(x, y)$

$(r2)$ $S(x, z) \leftarrow S(x, y), u \in y, v \in y, u.C' = v.C, ins(\langle u.C, v.C'\rangle, y, z)$

$(r3)$ $S'(x, z) \leftarrow S(x, z), S(x, z'), z \subseteq z', z \neq z'$

$(r4)$ $T(x, z) \leftarrow S(x, z), \neg S'(x, z).$

The first two rules compute in S pairs corresponding to pairs from R, such that the second component of a pair contains the corresponding component from the pair in R and possibly additional elements derived by transitivity. Obviously, for each pair $\langle x, y \rangle$ of R, there is a pair $\langle x, z \rangle$ in S, such that z is the transitive closure of y, but there are other tuples as well. To answer the query, we need to select for each x the unique tuple $\langle x, z \rangle$ of S, where z is maximal.[2] The third rule puts into S' tuples $\langle x, z \rangle$ such that z is not maximal for that x. The last rule then selects those that are maximal, using negation.

---

[2] We assume, for simplicity, that the first column of R is a key. It is easy to change the rules for the case when this does not hold.

We now show the program that defines *ins* for some given sort τ (the variables are of sort $\{\tau\}$ except for w, which is of sort τ):

$$super(w, y, z) \qquad\qquad \leftarrow w \in z,\ y \subseteq z$$
$$not\text{-}min\text{-}super(w, y, z) \leftarrow super(w, y, z),\ super(w, y, z'),\ z' \subseteq z,\ z' \neq z$$
$$ins(w, y, z) \qquad\qquad \leftarrow super(w, y, z),\ \neg not\text{-}min\text{-}super(w, y, z)$$

Note that the program is sort specific only through its dependence on the sorts of the variables. The same program computes *ins* for another sort τ', if we assume that the sort of w is τ' and that of the other variables is $\{\tau'\}$. Note also that the preceding program is not safe. To make it safe, we would have to use derived relations to range restrict the various variables.

We note that although we used $\subseteq$ in the example as a built-in predicate, it can be expressed using membership and stratified negation.

The proof of the next result is omitted but can be reconstructed reasonably easily using the technique of Example 20.6.3.

THEOREM 20.6.4 A query is expressible in datalog^{cv} with stratified negation if and only if it is expressible in CALC^{cv}.

The preceding language relies heavily on negation to specify the new sets. We could consider more set-oriented constructs. An example is the *grouping* construct, which is closely related to the algebraic nest operation. For instance, in the language $\mathcal{LDL}$, the rule:

$$S(x, \langle y \rangle) \leftarrow R(x, y)$$

groups in S, for each x, all the y's related to it in R (i.e., S is the result of the nesting of R on the second coordinate).

The grouping construct can be used to simulate negation. Consider a query q whose input consists of two unary relations R, S not containing some particular element a and that computes $R - S$. Query q can be answered by the following $\mathcal{LDL}$ program:

$$Temp(x, a) \leftarrow R(x)$$
$$Temp(x, x) \leftarrow S(x)$$
$$T(x, \langle y \rangle) \leftarrow Temp(x, y)$$
$$Res(x) \qquad \leftarrow T(x, \{a\})$$

Note that for an x in $R - S$, we derive $T(x, \{a\})$; but for x in $R \cap S$, we derive $T(x, \{x, a\}) \neq T(x, \{a\})$ because a is not in R.

From the previous example, it is clear that programs with grouping need not be monotone. This gives rise to semantic problems similar to those of negation. One possiblity, adopted in $\mathcal{LDL}$, is to define the semantics of programs with grouping analogously to stratification for negation.

20.7   Expressive Power and Complexity

This section presents two results. First the expressive power and complexity of ALG^{cv}/CALC^{cv} is established—it is the family of queries computable in hyperexponential time. Second, we consider the expressive power of ALG^{cv-}/CALC^{cv-} (i.e., in algebraic terms the expressive power of permitting the *nest* operator, but not *powerset*). Surprisingly, we show that the *nest* operator can be eliminated from ALG^{cv-} queries with flat input/ouput.

Complex Value Languages and Elementary Queries

We now characterize the queries in ALG^{cv} in terms of the set of computable queries in a certain complexity class. First the notion of computable query is extended to the complex value model in the straightforward manner. The complexity class of interest is the class of *elementary queries*, defined next.

The *hyperexponential* functions hyp_i for i in N are defined by

1. $hyp_0(m) = m$; and
2. $hyp_{i+1}(m) = 2^{hyp_i(m)}$ for $i \geq 0$.

A query is an *elementary query* if it is a computable query and has hyperexponential time data complexity[3] w.r.t. the database size. By database size we mean the amount of space it takes to write the content of the database using some natural encoding. Note that, for complex value databases, size can be very different from cardinality. For example, the database could consist of a single but very large complex value.

It turns out that a query is in ALG^{cv}/CALC^{cv} iff it is an elementary query.

THEOREM 20.7.1   A query is in ALG^{cv}/CALC^{cv} iff it is an elementary query.

Crux   It is trivial to see that each query in ALG^{cv}/CALC^{cv} is elementary. All operations can be evaluated in polynomial time in the size of their arguments except for powerset, which takes exponential time.

Conversely, let q be of complexity hyp_n. We show how to compute it in CALC^{cv}.

Suppose first that an enumeration of $adom(\mathbf{I})$ is provided in some binary relation *succ*. (We explain later how this is done.) We prove that q can then be computed in CALC$^{cv}+\mu^+$. Let $X^0 = adom(I)$ and for each i, $X^i = powerset(X^{i-1})$. Observe that for each X^i, we can provide an enumeration as follows: First *succ* provides the enumeration for X^0; and for each i, we define $V <_i U$ for U, V in X^i if there exists x in $U - V$ such that each element larger than x (under $<_{i-1}$) is in both or neither of U, V. Clearly, there exists a query in CALC$^{cv}+\mu^+$ that constructs X^n and a binary relation representing $<_n$.

Now we view each element of X^n as an atomic element. The input instance together with X^n and the enumeration can be seen as an ordered database with size the order of hyp_n. Query q is now polynomial in this new (much larger) instance. Finally we can easily

---

[3] We are concerned exclusively with the *data* complexity. Observe that when considering the union of hyperexponential complexities, time and space coincide.

extend to complex values the result from the flat case that CALC+μ^+ can express QPTIME on ordered databases (Theorem 17.4.2). Thus CALC^{cv}+μ^+ can also express all QPTIME queries on ordered complex value databases, so q can be computed in CALC^{cv}+μ^+ using $<_n$ on X_n. By Theorem 20.6.1, CALC^{cv}+μ^+ is equivalent to CALC^{cv}, so there exists a CALC^{cv} query φ computing q if an (arbitrary) enumeration of the active domain is given in some binary relation *succ*.

To conclude the proof, it remains to remove the restriction on the existence of an enumeration of the active domain. Let φ' be the formula obtained from φ by replacing

1. *succ* by some fresh variable y (the sort of y is set of pairs); and
2. each literal $succ(t, t')$ by $\langle t, t' \rangle \in y$.

Then q can be computed by

$$\exists y(\varphi' \wedge \psi).$$

where ψ is the CALC^{cv} formula stating that y is the representation in a binary relation of an enumeration of the active domain. (Observe that it is easy to state in CALC^{cv} that the content of a binary relation is an enumeration.) ∎

On the Power of the *nest* Operator

The *set-height* of a complex sort is the maximum number of set constructors in any branch of the sort. We can exhibit hierarchies of classes of queries in CALC^{cv} based on the set-height of the sorts of variables used in the query. For example, consider all queries that take as input a flat relational schema and produce as output a flat relation. Then for each $n > 0$, the family of CALC^{cv} queries using variables that have sorts with set-height $\leq n$ is strictly weaker than the family of CALC^{cv} queries using variables that have sorts with set-height $\leq n + 1$. A similar hierarchy exists for ALG^{cv}, based on the sorts of intermediate types used. Intuitively, these results follow from the use of the powerset operator, which essentially provides an additional exponential amount of scratch paper for each additional level of set nesting.

The bottom of this hierarchy is simply relational calculus. Recall that ALG^{cv-} can use the *nest* operator but not the powerset operator. It is thus natural to ask, Where do ALG^{cv-}/CALC^{cv-} (assuming flat input and output) lie relative to the relational calculus and the first level of the hierarchy? Rather surprisingly, it turns out that the *nest* operator alone does not increase expressive power. Specifically, we show now that with flat input and output, ALG^{cv-}/CALC^{cv-} is equivalent to relational calculus.

THEOREM 20.7.2   Let φ be a CALC^{cv-}/ALG^{cv-} query over a relational database schema **R** with output of relational sort S. Then there exists a relational calculus query φ' equivalent to φ.

Crux   The basic intuition underlying the proof is that with a flat input in CALC^{cv-} or ALG^{cv-}, each set constructed at an intermediate stage can be identified by a tuple of atomic values. In terms of ALG^{cv-}, the intuitive reason for this is that sets can be created only in two ways:

- by *nest*, which builds a relation whose nonnested coordinates form a key for the nested one, and
- by *set_create*, which can build only singleton sets.

Thus all created sets can be identified using some flat key of bounded length. The sets can then be simulated in the computation by their flat representations. The proof consists of

- providing a careful construction of the flat representation of the sets created in the computation, which reflects the history of their creation; and
- constructing a new query, equivalent to the original one, that uses only the flat representations of sets.

The details of the proof are omitted. ■

Observe that an immediate consequence of the previous result is that transitive closure or powerset are *not* expressible in ALG^{cv-}.

REMARK 20.7.3   The previous results focus on relational queries. The same technique can be used for nonflat inputs. An arbitrary input $\mathbf{I}$ can be represented by a flat database $\mathbf{I}_f$ of size polynomial in the size of the input. Now an arbitrary ALG^{cv-} query on $\mathbf{I}$ can be simulated by a relational query on $\mathbf{I}_f$ to yield a flat database representing the result. Finally the complex object result is constructed in polynomial time. This shows in particular that ALG^{cv-} is in PTIME. ■

20.8   A Practical Query Language for Complex Values

We conclude our discussion of languages for complex values with a brief survey of a fragment of the query language O_2SQL supported by the commercial object-oriented database system O_2 (see Chapter 21). This fragment provides an elegant syntax for accessing and constructing deeply nested complex values, and it has been incorporated into a recent industrial standard for object-oriented databases.

For the first example we recall the query

(4.4)   What are the address and phone number of the Le Champo?

In O_2SQL this can be expressed as

> **element select tuple** (t.address, t.phone)
>   **from** t **in** Theater
>   **where** t.name $=$ "Le Champo"

The *select-from-where* clause has semantics analogous to those for SQL. Unlike SQL, the *select* part can specify an essentially arbitrary complex value, not just tuples. A *select-from-where* clause returns a set[4]; the keyword **element** here is a desetting operator that returns a runtime error if the set does not have exactly one element.

The next example illustrates how O_2SQL can work inside nested structures. Recall the complex value shown in Fig. 20.2, which represents a portion of the **CINEMA** database. Let the full complex value be named *Films*. The following query returns all movies for which the director does not participate as an actor. (We assume that the same name is used for a director who is also an actor.)

> **select** m.Title
> **from**   f **in** Films
>   m **in** f.Movies
> **where** f.Director **not in select** a
>   **from** a **in** m.Actors

O_2SQL also provides a mechanism for collapsing nested sets. Again using the complex value *Films* of Fig. 20.2, the following gives the set of all directors that have not acted in any Hitchcock film.

> **select** f.Director
> **from**   f **in** Films
> **where** f.Director **not in flatten select** m.Actors
>   **from** g **in** Films
>   m **in** g.Movies
>   **where** g.Director = "Hitchcock"

Here the inner *select-from-where* clause returns a set of sets of actors. The keyword **flatten** has the effect of forming the union of these sets to yield a set of actors.

We conclude with an illustration of how O_2SQL can be used to construct a deeply nested complex value. The following query builds, from components of the schema of Fig. 21.1, a complex value with the same type as *Films* that holds information about all movies for which the director does not serve as an actor.

> **select** tuple (Director: d.Name,
>   Movies: **select** tuple (Title: m.Name,
>   Actors: **select** a.Name
>   **from** a **in** m.Actors)
>   **from** m **in** d.Directs
>   **where** d **not in** m.Actors)
> **from** d **in** Director

---

[4] In the full language O_2SQL, a list or bag might also be returned; we do not discuss that here. Furthermore, we do not include the keyword **unique** in our queries, although technically it should be included to remove duplicates from answer sets.

Bibliographic Notes

The original proposal for generalizing the relational model to allow entries in relations to be sets is often attributed to Makinouchi [Mak77]. Our presentation is strongly influenced by [AB88]. An extensive coverage of the field can be found in [Hul87]. The nested relation model is studied in [JS82, TF86, RKS86]. The V-relation model is studied in [BRS82, AB86, Ver89], and the essentially equivalent partition normal form (PNF) nested relation model is studied in [RKS86]. The connection of the PNF nested relations with dependencies has also been studied (e.g., in [TF86, OY87]).

There have been many proposals of algebras. In general, the earlier ones have essentially the power of ALG^{cv-} (due to obvious complexity considerations). The powerset operation was first proposed for the Logical Data Model of [KV84, KV93b].

The calculus presented in this chapter is based on Jacobs's calculus [Jac82]. This original proposal allowed noncomputable queries [Var83]. We use in this chapter a computable version of that calculus that is also used (with minor variations) in [KV84, KV93b, AB88, RKS86, Hul87].

Parameterized queries are close to the commonly used mathematical concept of *set comprehension*.

The equivalence of the algebra and the calculus has been shown in [AB88]. An equivalence result for a more general model had been previously given in [KV84, KV93b]. The equivalence result is preserved with oracles. In particular, it is shown in [AB88] that if the algebra and the calculus are extended with an identical set of oracles (i.e., sorted functions that are evaluated externally), the equivalence result still holds.

The strongly safe-range calculus, and the equivalence of ALG^{cv-} and $CALC^{cv-}$, are based on [AB88].

The fact that transitive closure can be computed in the calculus was noted in [AB88]. The result that any algebra query computing transitive closure requires exponential space (with the straightforward evaluation model) was shown in [SP94]. The equivalence between the calculus and various rule-based languages is from [AB88]. In the rule-based paradigm, nesting can be expressed in many ways. A main difference between various proposals of logic programming with a set construct is in their approach to nesting: grouping in $\mathcal{LDL}$ [BNR$^+$87a], data functions in COL [AG91], and a form of universal quantification in [Kup87]. In [Kup88], equivalence of various rule-based languages is proved. In [GG88], it is shown that various programming primitives are interchangeable: powerset, fixpoint, various iterators.

The correspondence between $ALG^{cv}/CALC^{cv}$ queries and elementary queries is studied in [HS93, KV93a]. Hierarchies of classes of queries based on the level of set nesting are considered in [HS93, KV93a]. Exact complexity characterizations are obtained with fixpoint, which is no longer redundant when the level of set nesting is bounded [GV91].

Theorem 20.7.2 is from [PG88], which uses a proof based on a strongly safe calculus. The proof of Theorem 20.7.2 outlined in this chapter suggests a strong connection between ALG^{cv-} and the V-relation model.

Reference [BTBW92] introduces a rich family of languages for complex objects, extended to include lists and bags, that is based on structural recursion. One language in this family corresponds to the nested algebra presented in this chapter. Using this, an elegant family of generalizations of Theorem 20.7.2 is developed in [Won93].

An extension of complex values, called *formats* [HY84], includes a marked union construct in addition to tuple and finitary set. Abstract notions of relative information capacity are developed there; for example, it can be shown that two complex value types have equivalent information capacity iff they are isomorphic.

Exercises

Exercise 20.1 (V-relations) Consider the schema R of sort

$$\langle A, B : \{\langle C, D\rangle\}\rangle.$$

Furthermore, we impose the fd $A \to B$ (more precisely, the generalization of a functional dependency). (a) Prove that for each instance I of R, the size of I is bounded by a polynomial in $adom(I)$. (b) Show how the same information can be naturally represented using two flat relations. (One suffices with some coding.) (c) Formalize the notion of V-relation of Section 20.1 and generalize the results of (a) and (b).

Exercise 20.2 Consider a (flat) relation R of sort

$$name\ age\ address\ car\ child\_name\ child\_age$$

and the multivalued dependency *name age address* $\twoheadrightarrow$ *car*. Prove that the same information can be stored in a complex value relation of sort

$$\langle name, age, address, cars : \{\mathbf{dom}\}, children : \{\langle child\_name, child\_age\rangle\}\rangle$$

Discuss the advantages of this alternative representation. (In particular, show that for the same data, the size of the instance in the second representation is smaller. Also consider update anomalies.)

Exercise 20.3 Consider the value

$$\{\ \langle A : a, B : \langle A : \{a, b\}, B : \langle A : a\rangle\rangle, C : \langle\ \rangle\rangle,$$
$$\langle A : a, B : \langle A : \{\}, B : \langle A : a\rangle\rangle, C : \langle\ \rangle\rangle\ \}.$$

Show how to construct it in the core algebra from $\{a\}$ and $\{b\}$.

Exercise 20.4 Prove that for each complex value relation I, there exists a constant query in the core algebra returning I.

Exercise 20.5 Let $\mathbf{R}$ be a database schema consisting of a relation R of sort

$$\langle A : \mathbf{dom}, B : \langle A : \{\mathbf{dom}\}, B : \langle A : \mathbf{dom}\rangle\rangle, C : \langle\ \rangle\rangle;$$

and let $\tau = \{\langle A : \mathbf{dom}, B : \{\{\mathbf{dom}\}\}\rangle\}$.

  (a) Give a query computing for each $\mathbf{I}$ over $\mathbf{R}$, $adom(\mathbf{I})$.
  (b) Give a query computing the set of values J of sort τ such that $adom(J) \subseteq adom(\mathbf{I})$.

Exercise 20.6   Prove that *set_create* can be expressed using the other operations of the core algebra. *Hint:* Use *powerset*.

Exercise 20.7   Formally define the following operations: (a) renaming, (b) singleton, (c) cross-product, and (d) join. In each case, prove that the operation is expressible in ALG^{cv}. Which of these can be expressed without powerset?

Exercise 20.8   (Nest,unnest)

    (a) Show that *nest* is expressible in ALG^{cv}.

    (b) Show that *unnest* is expressible in ALG^{cv} without using the powerset operator.

    (c) Prove that *unnest*$_A$ is a right inverse of *nest*$_{A=(A_1 \ldots A_k)}$ and that *unnest*$_A$ has no right inverse.

Exercise 20.9   (Map) The operation *map*$_{C,q}$ is applicable to relations of sort τ where τ is of the form $\{\langle C : \{\tau'\}, \ldots \rangle\}$ and q is a query over relations of sort τ'. For instance, let

$$I = \{\langle C : I_1, C' : J_1 \rangle, \langle C : I_2, C' : J_2 \rangle, \langle C : I_3, C' : J_3 \rangle\}.$$

Then

$$map_{C,q}(I) = \{\langle C : q(I_1), C' : J_1 \rangle, \langle C : q(I_2), C' : J_2 \rangle, \langle C : q(I_3), C' : J_3 \rangle\}.$$

    (a) Give an example of *map* and show how the query of this example can be expressed in ALG^{cv}.

    (b) Give a formal definition of *map* and prove that the addition of *map* does not change the expressive power of the algebra.

Exercise 20.10   Show how to express

$$\{x \mid \{y \mid liked(x, y)\} = \{y \mid saw(x, y)\}\}$$

in the core calculus.

Exercise 20.11   The calculus is extended by allowing terms of the form $z \cup z'$ and $z - z'$ for each set term z, z' of identical sort. Prove that this does not modify the expressive power of the language. More generally, consider introducing in the calculus terms of the form $q(t_1, \ldots, t_n)$, where q is an n-ary algebraic operation and the t_i are set terms of appropriate sort.

Exercise 20.12   Give five queries on the **CINEMA** database expressed in ALG^{cv}. Give the same queries in CALC^{cv}.

Exercise 20.13   Complete the proof that ALG$^{cv} \sqsubseteq$ CALC^{cv} for Theorem 20.5.1. Complete the proof of "Last Stage" for Theorem 20.5.1.

Exercise 20.14   This exercise elaborates the simulation of CALC^{cv} by ALG^{cv} presented in the proof of Theorem 20.5.1. In particular, give the details of

    (a) the construction of E_{adom}

    (b) the construction of G_τ for each τ

    (c) the last stage of the construction.

Exercise 20.15 Show that the query in Example 20.6.2 is strongly safe range (e.g., give a query in ALG^{cv-} or CALC^{cv-} equivalent to it).

Exercise 20.16 Show that every strongly safe-range query is in ALG^{cv-} [one direction of (b) of Theorem 20.5.3].

Exercise 20.17 Sketch a program expressing the query *even* in CALC$^{cv}+\mu^{+}$.

Exercise 20.18 Prove that CALC$^{cv}+\mu^{+}$ =ALG^{cv}.

Exercise 20.19 Define a *while* language based on ALG^{cv}. Show that it does not have more power than ALG^{cv}.

Exercise 20.20 Consider a query q whose input consists of two relations *blue*, *red* of sort $\langle A, B \rangle$ (i.e., consists of two graphs). Query q returns a relation of sort $\langle A, B : \{\textbf{dom}\} \rangle$ with the following meaning. A tuple $\langle x, X \rangle$ is in the result if x is a vertex and X is the set of vertexes y such that there exists a path from x to y alternating blue and red edges. Prove in one line that q is expressible in ALG^{cv}. Show how to express q in some complex value language of this chapter.

Exercise 20.21 Generalize the construction of Example 20.6.2 to prove Theorem 20.6.1.

Exercise 20.22 Datalog with stratified negation was shown to be weaker than datalog with inflationary negation. Is the situation similar for datalog^{cv} with negation?

Exercise 20.23 Exhibit a query that is not expressible in CALC^{cv-} but is expressible in CALC^{cv}, and one that is not expressible in CALC^{cv}.

Exercise 20.24 Give a relational calculus formula or algebra expression for the query in Example 20.4.8.

★ **Exercise 20.25** Recall the language *while*$_N$ from Chapter 18. The language allows assignments of relational algebra expressions to relational variables, looping, and integer arithmetic. Let *while*$_N^{cv}$ be like *while*$_N$, except that the relational algebra expressions are in ALG^{cv}. Prove that *while*$_N^{cv}$ can express all queries from flat relations to flat relations.

21 Object Databases

> *Minkisi are complex objects clearly not the product of a momentary impulse. . . . To do justice to objects, a theory of them must be as complex as them.*[1]
>
> —Wyatt MacGaffey in *Astonishment and Power*

Alice: *What is a Minkisi?*
Sergio: *It is an African word that translates somewhat like "things that do things."*
Vittorio: *It is art, religion, and magic.*
Riccardo: *Oh, this sounds to me very object oriented!*

In this chapter, we provide a brief introduction to object-oriented databases (OODBs). A complete coverage of this new and exciting area is beyond the scope of this volume; we emphasize the new modeling features of OODBs and some of the preliminary theoretical research about them. On the one hand, we shall see that some of the most basic issues concerning OODBs, such as the design of query languages or the analysis of their expressive power, can be largely resolved using techniques already developed in connection with the relational and complex value models. On the other hand, the presence of new features (such as object identifiers) and methods brings about new questions and techniques.

As mentioned previously, the simplicity of the data structure in the relational model often hampers its use in many database applications. A relational representation can obscure the intention and intricate semantics of a complex data structure (e.g., for holding the design of a VLSI chip or an airplane wing). As we shall see, OODBs remedy this situation by borrowing a variety of data structuring constructs from the complex value model (Chapter 20) and from semantic data models (considered in Chapter 11). At a more fundamental level, the relational data model and all of the data models presented so far impose a sharp distinction between data storage and data processing: The DBMS provides data storage, but data processing is provided by a host programming language with a relatively simple language such as SQL embedded in it. OODBs permit the incorporation of behavioral portions of the overall data management application directly into the database schema, using methods in the sense of object-oriented programming languages.

This chapter begins with an informal presentation of the underlying constructs of OODBs. Next a formal definition for a particular OODB model is presented. Two directions of theoretical research into OODBs are then discussed. First a family of languages

---

[1] Reprinted with permission. Smithsonian Institution Press ©1993.

for data access is presented, with an emphasis on how the languages interact with the novel modeling constructs (of particular interest is the impact of generalizing the notion of complete query language to accommodate the presence of object identifiers, OIDs). Next two languages for methods are described. The first is an imperative language allowing us to specify methods with side effects.[2] The second language brings us to a functional perspective on methods and database languages and allows us to specify side-effect-free methods. In both cases, we present some results on type safety and expressive power. Checking type safety is generally undecidable; we identify a significant portion of the functional language, monadic method schemas, for which type safety is decidable. With respect to expressive power, the imperative language is complete in an extended sense formalized in this chapter. The functional language expresses precisely QPTIME on ordered inputs and so turns out to express the by-now-famous *fixpoint* queries. The chapter concludes with a brief survey of additional research issues raised by OODBs.

21.1 Informal Presentation

Object-oriented database models stem from a synthesis of three worlds: the complex value model, semantic database models, and object-oriented programming concepts. At the time of writing, there is not widespread agreement on a specific OODB model, nor even on what components are required to constitute an OODB model. In this section, we shall focus on seven important ingredients of OODB models:

1. objects and object identifiers;
2. complex values and types;
3. classes;
4. methods;
5. ISA hierarchies;
6. inheritance and dynamic binding;
7. encapsulation.

In this section, we describe and illustrate these interrelated notions informally; a more formal definition is presented in the following section. We will also briefly discuss alternatives.

As a running example for this discussion, we shall use the OODB schema specified in Fig. 21.1. This schema is closely related to the semantic data model schema of Fig. 11.1, which in turn is closely related to the **CINEMA** example of Chapter 3.

As discussed in Chapter 11, a significant shortcoming of the relational model is that it must use printable values, often called *keys*, to refer to entities or objects-in-the-world. As a simple example, suppose that the first and last names of a person are used as a key to identify that person. From a physical point of view, it is then cumbersome to refer to a person, because the many bytes of his or her name must be used. A more fundamental

---

[2] Methods are said to have side-effects if they cause updates to the database.

(* schema and base definitions *)

create schema *PariscopeSchema* ;
create base *PariscopeBase*;

(* class definitions *)

class *Person*
    type tuple (name: string, citizenship: string, gender: string);
class *Director* inherit *Person*
    type tuple (directs: set (*Movie*));
class *Actor* inherit *Person*
    type tuple (acts_in: { *Movie* },
            award: { tuple (prize: string, year: integer) });
class *Actor_Director* inherit *Director*, *Person*
class *Movie*
    type tuple (title: string, actors: set (*Actor*);
            director: *Director*);
class *Theater*
    type tuple (name: string, address: string, phone: string);

(* name definitions *)

name *Pariscope*: set (tuple (theater: *Theater*, time: string, *price*: integer,
            movie: *Movie*));
name *Persons_I_like*: set (*Person*);
name *Actors_I_like*, *Actors_you_like*: set (*Actor*);
name *My_favorite_director* : *Director*

(* method definitions *)

method *get_name* in class *Person* : string
    { if (gender = "male")
        return "Mr." + self.name;
      else
        return "Ms." + self.name }

method *get_name* in class *Director* : string
    { return ("Director" + self.name) };

method *get_name* in class *Actor_Director* : string
    { return ("Director" + self.name) };

(* we assume here that '+' denotes a string concatenation operator *)

Figure 21.1:   An OODB Schema

problem arises if the person changes his or her name (e.g., as the result of marriage). When performing this update, conceptually there is a break in the continuity in the representation of the person. Furthermore, care must be taken to update all tuples (typically arising in a number of different relations) that refer to this person, to reflect the change of name.

Following the spirit of semantic data models, OODB models permit the explicit representation of physical and conceptual objects through the use of object identifiers (OIDs). Conceptually, a unique OID is assigned to each object that is represented in the database, and this association between OID and object remains fixed, even as attributes of the object (such as name or age) change in value. The use of objects and OIDs permits OODBs to share information gracefully; a given object o is easily shared by many other objects simply by referencing the OID of o. This is especially important in the context of updates; for example, the name of a person object o need be changed in only one place even if o is shared by many parts of the database.

In an OODB, a complex value is associated with each object. This complex value may involve printables and/or OIDs (i.e., references to the same or other objects). For example, each object in the class *Movie* in Fig. 21.1 has an associated triple whose second coordinate contains a set of OIDs corresponding to actors. In this section, we focus on complex values constructed using the tuple and set construct. In practical OODB models, other constructs are also supported (including, for example, bags and lists). Some commercial OODBs are based on an extension of C++ that supports persistence; in these models essentially any C++ structure can serve as the value associated with an object.

Objects that have complex values with the same type may be grouped into classes, as happens in semantic data models. In the running example, these include *Person*, *Director*, and *Movie*. Classes also serve as a natural focal point for associating some of the behavioral (or procedural) components of a database application. This is accomplished by associating with each class a family of methods for that class. Methods might be simple (e.g., producing the name of a person) or arbitrarily complex (e.g., displaying a representation of an object to a graphical interface or performing a stress analysis of a proposed wing design). A method has a name, a signature, and an implementation. The name and signature serve as an external interface to the method. The implementation is typically written in a (possibly extended) programming language such as C or C++. The choice of implementation language is largely irrelevant and is generally not considered to be part of the data model.

As with semantic models, OODB models permit the organization of classes into a hierarchy based on what have been termed variously ISA, specialization, or class-subclass relationships. The term *hierarchy* is used loosely here: In many cases any directed acyclic graph (DAG) is permitted. In Fig. 21.1 the ISA hierarchy has *Director* and *Actor* as (immediate) specializations of *Person* and *Actor_Director* as a specialization of both *Director* and *Actor*. Following the tradition of object-oriented programming languages, a virtual class **any** is included that serves as the unique root of the ISA hierarchy.

In OODB models, there are two important implications of the statement that class c' is a subclass of c. First it is required that the complex value type associated with c' be a subtype (in the sense formally defined later) of the complex value type associated with c. Second it is required that if there is a method with name m associated with c, then there is also a method with name m associated with c'. In some cases, the implementation (i.e., the actual code) of *m* for c' is identical to that for c; in this case the code of *m* for c' need not be explicitly specified because it is *inherited* from c. In other cases, the implementation of *m* for c' is different from that for c; in which case we say that the implementation of *m* for c' *overrides* the implementation of *m* for c. (See the different implementations for method *get_name* in Fig. 21.1.) The determination of what implementation is associated with a given method name and class is called *method resolution*. A method is invoked with respect to an object o, and the class to which o belongs determines which implementation is to be used. This policy is called *dynamic binding*. As we shall see, the interaction of method calls and dynamic binding in general makes type checking for OODB schemas undecidable. (It is undecidable to check whether such a schema would lead to a runtime type error; on the other hand, it is clearly possible to find decidable sufficient conditions that will guarantee that no such error can arise.)

In the particular OODB model presented here, both values (in the style of complex values) and objects are supported. For example, in Fig. 21.1 a persistent set of triples called *Pariscope* is supported (see also Fig. 11.1). The introduction of values not directly associated with OIDs is a departure from the tradition of object-oriented programming, and not all OODBs in the literature support it. However, in databases the use of explicit values often simplifies the design and use of a schema. Their presence also facilitates expressing queries in a declarative manner.

The important principle of encapsulation in object orientation stems from the field of abstract data types. Encapsulation is used to provide a sharp boundary between how information about objects is accessed by database users and how that information is actually stored and provided. The principle of encapsulation is most easily understood if we distinguish two categories of database use: *dba mode*, which refers to activities unique to database administrators (including primarily creating and modifying the database schema), and *user mode*, which refers to activities such as querying and updating the actual data in the database. Of course, some users may operate in both of these modes on different occasions. In general, application software is viewed as invoked from the user mode.

Encapsulation requires that when in user mode, a user can access or modify information about a given object only by means of the methods defined for that object; he or she cannot directly examine or modify the complex value or the methods associated with the object. In particular, then, essentially all application software can access objects only through their methods. This has two important implications. First, as long as the same set of methods is supported, the underlying implementation of object methods, and even of the complex value representation of objects, can be changed without having to modify any application software. Second, the methods of an object often provide a focused and abstracted interface to the object, thus making it simpler for programmers to work with the objects.

In object-oriented programming languages, it is typical to enforce encapsulation except in the special case of rewriting method implementations. In some OODB models, there is an important exception to this in connection with query languages. In particular, it is generally convenient to permit a query language to examine explicitly the complex values associated with objects.

The reader with no previous exposure to object-oriented languages may now be utterly overwhelmed by the terminology. It might be helpful at this point to scan through a book or manual about an object-oriented programming language such as C++, or an OODB such as O$_2$ or ObjectStore. This will provide numerous examples and the overall methodology of object-oriented programming, which is beyond the scope of this book.

21.2 Formal Definition of an OODB Model

This section presents a formal definition of a particular OODB model, called the *generic OODB model*. (This model is strongly influenced by the IQL and O$_2$ models. Many features are shared by most other OODB models. While presenting the model, we also discuss different choices made in other models.) The presentation essentially follows the preceding informal one, beginning with definitions for the types and class hierarchy and then introducing methods. It concludes with definitions of OODB schema and instance.

Types and Class Hierarchy

The formal definitions of object, type, and class hierarchy are intertwined. An object consists of a pair (*identifier, value*). The identifiers are taken from a specific sort containing OIDs. The values are essentially standard complex values, except that OIDs may occur within them. Although some of the definitions on complex values and types are almost identical to those in Chapter 20, we include them here to make precise the differences from the object-oriented context. As we shall see, the class hierarchy obeys a natural restriction based on subtyping.

To start, we assume a number of atomic types and their pairwise disjoint corresponding domains: **integer**, **string**, **bool**, **float**. The set **dom** of atomic values is the (disjoint) union of these domains; as before, the elements of **dom** are called *constants*. We also assume an infinite set **obj** $= \{o_1, o_2, \dots\}$ of *object identifiers* (OIDs), a set **class** of class names, and a set **att** of *attribute names*. A special constant *nil* represents the undefined (i.e., null) value.

Given a set O of OIDs, the family of *values* over O is defined so that

(a) *nil*, each element of **dom**, and each element of O are values over O; and

(b) if $v_1, \dots, v_n$ are values over O, and $A_1, \dots, A_n$ distinct attributes names, the tuple $[A_1 : v_1, \dots, A_n : v_n]$ and the set $\{v_1, \dots, v_n\}$ are values over O.

The set of all values over O is denoted **val**(O). An *object* is a pair (o, v), where o is an OID and v a value.

In general, object-oriented database models also include constructors other than tuple and set, such as list and bag; we do not consider them here.

EXAMPLE 21.2.1   Letting *oid7, oid22*, etc. denote OIDs, some examples of values are as follows:

[*theater* : *oid*7, *time* : "16:45", *price* : 45, *movie* : *oid*22]
{"H. Andersson", "K. Sylwan", "I. Thulin", "L. Ullman"}
[*title* : "The Trouble with Harry", *director* : *oid*77,
actors : {*oid*81, *oid*198, *oid*265, *oid*77}]

An example of an object is

(*oid*22 , [*title* :"The Trouble with Harry", *director* : *oid*77,
actors : {*oid*81, *oid*198, *oid*265, *oid*77}])

As discussed earlier, objects are grouped in classes. All objects in a class have complex values of the same type. The type corresponding to each class is specified by the OODB schema.

Types are defined with respect to a given set C of class names. The family of *types* over C is defined so that

1. **integer, string, bool, float,** are types;
2. the class names in C are types;
3. if τ is a type, then[3] $\{\tau\}$ is a (set) type;
4. if $\tau_1, \ldots, \tau_n$ are types and $A_1, \ldots, A_n$ distinct attribute names,
then $[A_1 : \tau_1, \ldots, A_n : \tau_n]$ is a (tuple) type.

The set of types over C together with the special class name **any** are denoted **types**(C). (The special name **any** is a type but may not occur inside another type.) Observe the close resemblance with types used in the complex value model.

EXAMPLE 21.2.2   An example of a type over the classes of the schema in Fig. 21.1 is

[*name* : **string**, *citizenship* : **string**, *gender* : **string**]

One may want to give a name to this type (e.g., *Person_type*). Other examples of types (with names associated to them) include

Director_type = [*name* : **string**, *citizenship* : **string**, *gender* : **string**,
directs : {*Movie*}]
Theater_type   = [*name* : **string**, *address* : **string**, *phone* : **string**]
Pariscope_type = [*theater* : *Theater*, *time* : **string**, *price* : **integer**, *movie* : *Movie*]
Movie_type   = [*title* : **string**, *actors* : {*Actor*}, *director* : *Director*]
Award_type   = [*prize* : **string**, *year* : **integer**]

---

[3] In Fig. 21.1 we use keywords **set** and **tuple** as syntactic sugar when specifying the set and tuple constructors.

In an OODB schema we associate with each class c a type $\sigma(c)$, which dictates the type of objects in this class. In particular, for each object (o, v) in class c, v must have the exact structure described by $\sigma(c)$.

Recall from the informal description that an OODB schema includes an ISA hierarchy among the classes of the schema. The class hierarchy has three components: (1) a set of classes, (2) the types associated with these classes, and (3) a specification of the ISA relationships between the classes. Formally, a *class hierarchy* is a triple $(C, \sigma, \prec)$, where C is a finite set of class names, σ a mapping from C to **types**(C), and $\prec$ a partial order on C.

Informally, in a class hierarchy the type associated with a subclass should be a refinement of the type associated with its superclass. For example, a class *Student* is expected to refine the information on its superclass *Person* by providing additional attributes. To capture this notion, we use a subtyping relationship ($\leq$) that specifies when one type refines another.

DEFINITION 21.2.3   Let $(C, \sigma, \prec)$ be a class hierarchy. The *subtyping relationship* on **types**(C) is the smallest partial order $\leq$ over **types**(C) satisfying the following conditions:

    (a) if $c \prec c'$, then $c \leq c'$;

    (b) if $\tau_i \leq \tau_i'$ for each $i \in [1, n]$ and $n \leq m$, then
$$[A_1 : \tau_1, \ldots, A_n : \tau_n, \ldots, A_m : \tau_m] \leq [A_1 : \tau_1', \ldots, A_n : \tau_n'];$$

    (c) if $\tau \leq \tau'$, then $\{\tau\} \leq \{\tau'\}$; and

    (d) for each τ, $\tau \leq$ **any** (i.e., **any** is the top of the hierarchy).

A class hierarchy $(C, \sigma, \prec)$ is *well formed* if for each pair c, c' of classes, $c \prec c'$ implies $\sigma(c) \leq \sigma(c')$.

By way of illustration, it is easily verified that

$$Director\_type \leq Person\_type \qquad Director\_type \nleq Movie\_type.$$

Thus the schema obtained by adding the constraint *Director* $\prec$ *Movie* would not be well formed.

Henceforth we consider only well-formed class hierarchies.

EXAMPLE 21.2.4   Consider the class hierarchy $(C, \sigma, \prec)$ of the schema of Fig. 21.1. The set of classes is

$$C = \{Person, Director, Actor, Actor\_Director, Theater, Movie\}$$

with *Actor* $\prec$ *Person*, *Director* $\prec$ *Person*, *Actor_Director* $\prec$ *Director*, *Actor_Director* $\prec$ *Actor*, and (referring to Example 21.2.2 for the definitions of *Person_type*, *Theater_type*, etc.)

$$\sigma(Person) \qquad = Person\_type,$$

$$\sigma(Theater) \qquad = Theater\_type,$$

$$\sigma(Movie) \qquad = Movie\_type,$$

$$\sigma(Director) \qquad = Director\_type,$$

$$\sigma(Actor) \qquad = [name : \textbf{string}, \ citizenship : \textbf{string},$$
$$gender : \textbf{string}, \ acts\_in : \{Movie\},$$
$$award : \{Award\_type\}]$$

$$\sigma(Actor\_Director) = [name : \textbf{string}, \ citizenship : \textbf{string},$$
$$gender : \textbf{string}, \ acts\_in : \{Movie\},$$
$$award : \{Award\_type\}, \ directs : \{Movie\}]$$

The use of type names here is purely syntactic. We would obtain the same schema if we replaced, for instance, *Person_type* with the value of this type.

Observe that $\sigma(Director) \leq \sigma(Person)$ and $\sigma(Actor) \leq \sigma(Person)$, etc.

The Structural Semantics of a Class Hierarchy

We now describe how values can be associated with the classes and types of a class hierarchy. Because the values in an OODB instance may include OIDs, the semantics of classes and types must be defined simultaneously. The basis for these definitions is the notion of OID assignment, which assigns a set of OIDs to each class.

DEFINITION 21.2.5   Let $(C, \sigma, \prec)$ be a (well-formed) class hierarchy. An *OID assignment* is a function π mapping each name in C to a disjoint finite set of OIDs. Given OID assignment π, the *disjoint extension* of c is $\pi(c)$, and the *extension* of c, denoted $\pi^*(c)$, is $\cup\{\pi(c') \mid c' \in C, c' \prec c\}$.

If π is an OID assignment, then $\pi^*(c') \subseteq \pi^*(c)$ whenever $c' \prec c$. This should be understood as a formalization of the fact that an object of a subclass c' may be viewed also as an object of a superclass c of c'. From the perspective of typing, this suggests that operations that are type correct for members of c are also type correct for members of c'.

Unlike the case for many semantic data models, the definition of OID assignment for OODB schemas implies that extensions of classes of an ISA hierarchy without common subclasses are necessarily disjoint. In particular, extensions of all leaf classes of the hierarchy are disjoint (see Exercise 21.2). This is a simplifying assumption that makes it easier to associate objects to classes. There is a unique class to whose disjoint extension each object belongs.

The semantics for types is now defined relative to a class hierarchy $(C, \sigma, \prec)$ and an OID assignment π. Let $O = \cup\{\pi(c) \mid c \in C\}$, and define $\pi(\textbf{any}) = O$. The *disjoint interpretation* of a type τ, denoted $dom(\tau)$, is given by

(a) for each atomic type τ, $dom(\tau)$ is the usual interpretation of that type;

(b) $dom(\textbf{any})$ is $\textbf{val}(O)$;

(c) for each $c \in C$, $dom(c) = \pi^*(c) \cup \{nil\}$;

(d) $dom(\{\tau\}) = \{\{v_1, \ldots, v_n\} \mid n \geq 0,$ and $v_i \in dom(\tau), i \in [1, n]\}$; and

(e) $dom([A_1 : \tau_1, \ldots, A_k : \tau_k]) = \{[A_1 : v_1, \ldots, A_k : v_k] \mid v_i \in dom(\tau_i), i \in [1, k]\}$.

REMARK 21.2.6 In the preceding interpretation, the type determines precisely the structure of a value of that type. It is interesting to replace (e) by

(e′)
$$dom([A_1 : \tau_1, \ldots, A_k : \tau_k]) =$$
$$\{[A_1 : v_1, \ldots, A_k : v_k, A_{k+1} : v_{k+1}, \ldots A_l : v_l] \mid$$
$$v_i \in dom(\tau_i), i \in [1, k], v_j \in \mathbf{val}(O), j \in [k + 1, l]\}.$$

Under this alternative interpretation, for each τ, τ' in $\mathbf{types}(C)$, if $\tau' \leq \tau$ then $dom(\tau') \subseteq dom(\tau)$. This is why this is sometimes called the *domain-inclusion semantics*. From a data model viewpoint, this presents the disadvantage that in a correctly typed database instance, a tuple may have a field that is not even mentioned in the database schema. For this reason, we do not adopt the domain-inclusion semantics here. On the other hand, from a linguistic viewpoint it may be useful to adopt this more liberal semantics in languages to allow variables denoting tuples with more attributes than necessary. ∎

Adding Behavior

The final ingredient of the generic OODB model is *methods*. A method has three components:

(a) a *name*

(b) a *signature*

(c) an *implementation* (or *body*).

There is no problem in specifying the names and signatures of methods in an OODB schema. To specify the implementation of methods, a language for methods is needed. We do not consider specific languages in the generic OODB model. Therefore only names and signatures of methods are specified at the schema level in this model. In Section 21.4, we shall consider several languages for methods and shall therefore be able to add the implementation of methods to the schema.

Without specifying the implementation of methods, the generic OODB model specifies their semantics (i.e., the effect of each method in the context of a given instance). This effect, which is a function over the domains of the types corresponding to the signature of the method, is therefore specified at the instance level.

We assume the existence of an infinite set **meth** of method names. Let $(C, \sigma, \prec)$ be a class hierarchy. For method name m, a *signature* of m is an expression of the form $m : c \times \tau_1 \times \cdots \times \tau_{n-1} \rightarrow \tau_n$, where c is a class name in C and each τ_i is a type over C. This signature is associated with the class c; we say that method m *applies* to objects of class c and to objects of classes that inherit m from c. It is common for the same method name to have different signatures in connection with different classes. (Some restrictions shall be specified later.) The notion of signature here generalizes the one typically found in object-oriented programming languages, because we permit the τ_i's to be types rather than only classes.

It is easiest to describe the notions of overloading, method inheritance, and dynamic binding in terms of an example. Consider the methods defined in the schema of Fig. 21.1. All three share the name *get_name*. The signatures are given by

$$get\_name : Person \to \textbf{string}$$

$$get\_name : Director \to \textbf{string}$$

$$get\_name : Actor\_Director \to \textbf{string}$$

Note that *get_name* has different implementations for these classes; this is an example of *overloading* of a method name.

Recall that *Actor* is a subclass of *Person*. According to the informal discussion, if *get_name* applies to elements of *Person*, then it should also apply to members of *Actor*. Indeed, in the object-oriented paradigm, if a method m is defined for a class c but not for a subclass c' of c (and it is not defined anywhere else along a path from c' to c), then the definition of m for c' is *inherited* from c. In particular, the signature of m on c' is identical to the one of m for c, except that the first c is replaced by c'. The implementation of m for c' is identical to that for c. In the schema of Fig. 21.1, the signature of *get_name* for *Actor* is

$$get\_name : Actor \to \textbf{string}$$

and the implementation is identical to the one for *Person*. The determination of the correct method implementation to use for a given method name m and class c is called *method resolution*; the selected implementation is called the *resolution* of m for c.

Suppose that π is an OID assignment, that *oid25* is in the extension $\pi^*(Person)$ of *Person*, and that *get_name* is called on *oid25*. What implementation of *get_name* will be used? In our OODB model we shall use *dynamic binding* (also called *late binding*, or *value-dependent binding*). This means that the specific implementation chosen for *get_name* on *oid25* depends on the most specific class that *oid25* belongs to, that is, the class c such that $oid25 \in \pi(c)$.

(An alternative to dynamic binding is *static binding*, or *context-dependent binding*. Under this discipline, the implementation used for *get_name* depends on the type associated with the variable holding *oid25* at the point in program where *get_name* is invoked. This can be determined at compile time, and so static binding is generally much cheaper than dynamic binding. In the language C++, the default is static binding, but dynamic binding can be obtained by using the keyword **virtual** when specifying the method.)

Consider a call $m(o, v_1, \ldots, v_{n-1})$ to method m. This is often termed a *message*, and o is termed the *receiver*. As described here, the implementation of m associated with this message depends exclusively on the class of o. To emphasize the importance of the receiver for finding the actual implementation, in some languages the message is denoted $o \to m[v_1, \ldots v_{n-1}]$. In some object-oriented programming languages, such as CommonLoops (an object-oriented extension of LISP), the implementation depends on

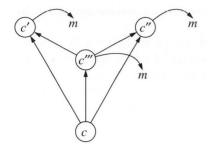

Figure 21.2:   Unambiguous definition

all of the parameters of the call, not just the first. This is also the approach of the method schemas introduced in Section 21.4.

The set of methods applicable to an object is called the *interface* of the object. As noted in the informal description of OODB models, in most cases objects are accessed only via their interface; this philosophy is called *encapsulation*.

As part of an OODB schema, a set M of method signatures is associated to a class hierarchy $(C, \sigma, \prec)$. Note that a signature $m : c \times \tau_1 \times \cdots \times \tau_{n-1} \to \tau_n$ can be viewed as giving a particular meaning to m for class c, at least at a syntactic level. Because of inheritance, a meaning for method m need not be given explicitly for each class of C nor even for subclasses of a class for which m has been given a meaning. However, we make two restrictions on the family of method signatures: The set M is *well formed* if it obeys the following two rules:

Unambiguity: If c is a subclass of c' and c'' and there is a definition of m for c' and c'', then there is a definition of m for a subclass of c' and c'' that is either c itself, or a superclass of c. (See Fig. 21.2.)

Covariance[4]: If $m : c \times \tau_1 \times \cdots \times \tau_n \to \tau$ and $m : c' \times \tau'_1 \times \cdots \times \tau'_m \to \tau'$ are two definitions and $c \prec c'$, then $n = m$ for each i, $\tau_i \leq \tau'_i$ and $\tau \leq \tau'$.

The first rule prevents ambiguity resulting from the presence of two method implementations both applicable for the same object. A primary motivation for the second rule is intuitive: We expect the argument and result types of a method on a subclass to be more refined than those of the method on a superclass. This also simplifies the writing of type-correct programs, although type checking leads to difficulties even in the presence of the covariance assumption (see Section 21.4).

Database Schemas and Instances

We conclude this section by presenting the definitions of schemas and instances in the generic OODB model. An important subtlety here will be the role of OIDs in instances

---

[4] In type theory, *contravariance* is used instead. Contravariance is the proper notion when functions are passed as arguments, which is not the case here.

as placeholders; as will be seen, the specific OIDs present in an instance are essentially irrelevant.

As indicated earlier, a schema describes the structure of the data that is stored in a database, including the types associated with classes and the ISA hierarchy and the signature of methods (i.e., the interfaces provided for objects in each class).

In many practical OODBs, it has been found convenient to allow storage of complex values that are not associated with any objects and that can be accessed directly using some name. This also allows us to subsume gracefully the capabilities of value-based models, such as relations and complex values. It also facilitates writing queries. To reflect this feature, we allow a similar mechanism in schemas and instances. Thus schemas may include a set of value names with associated types. Instances assign values of appropriate type to the names. Method implementations, external programming languages, and query languages may all use these names (to refer to their current values) or a class name (to refer to the set of objects currently residing in that class). In this manner, named values and class names are analogous to relation names in the relational model and to complex value relation names in the complex value model.

In the schema of Fig. 21.1, examples of named values are *Pariscope* (holding a set of triples); *Persons_I_like*, *Actors_I_like*, and *Actors_you_like* (referring to sets of person objects and actor objects; and, finally, *My_favorite_director* (referring to an individual object as opposed to a set). These names can be used explicitly in method implementations and in external query and programming languages.

We now have the following:

DEFINITION 21.2.7   A *schema* is a 5-tuple $\mathbf{S} = (C, \sigma, \prec, M, G)$ where

- G is a set of *names* disjoint from C;
- σ is a mapping from $C \cup G$ to **types**(C);
- $(C, \sigma, \prec)$ is a well-formed class hierarchy[5]; and
- M is a well-formed set of method signatures for $(C, \sigma, \prec)$.

An instance of an OODB schema populates the classes with OIDs, assigns values to these OIDs, gives meaning to the other persistent names, and assigns semantics to method signatures. The semantics of method signatures are mappings describing their effect. From a practical viewpoint, the population of the classes, the values of objects, and the values of names are kept extensionally; whereas the semantics of the methods are specified by pieces of code (intensionally). However, we ignore the code of methods for the time being.

DEFINITION 21.2.8   An *instance* of schema $(C, \sigma, \prec, M, G)$ is a 4-tuple $\mathbf{I} = (\pi, \nu, \gamma, \mu)$, where

    (a) π is an OID assignment (and let $O = \cup\{\pi(c) \mid c \in C\}$);

    (b) ν maps each OID in O to a value in **val**(O) of correct type [i.e., for each c and $o \in \pi(c)$, $\nu(o) \in dom(\sigma(c))$];

---

[5] By abuse of notation, we use here and later σ instead of $\sigma|_C$.

(c) γ associates to each name in G of type τ a value in $dom(\tau)$;

(d) μ assigns semantics to method names in agreement with the method signatures in M. More specifically, for each signature $m : c \times \vec{\alpha} \rightarrow \tau$,

$$\mu(m : c \times \vec{\alpha} \rightarrow \tau) : dom(c \times \vec{\alpha}) \rightarrow dom(\tau);$$

that is, $\mu(m : c \times \vec{\alpha} \rightarrow \tau)$ is a partial function from $dom(c \times \vec{\alpha})$ to $dom(\tau)$.

Recall that a method m can occur with different signatures in the same schema. The mapping μ can assign different semantics to each signature of m. The function $\mu(m : c \times \vec{\alpha} \rightarrow \tau)$ is only relevant on objects associated with c and subclasses of c for which m is not redefined.

In the preceding definitions, the assignment of semantics to method signatures is included in the instance. As will be seen in Section 21.4, if method implementations are included in the schema, they induce the semantics of methods at the instance level (this is determined by the semantics of the particular programming language used in the implementation).

Intuitively, it is generally assumed that elements of the atomic domains have universally understood meaning. In contrast, the actual OIDs used in an instance are not relevant. They serve essentially as placeholders; it is only their relationship with other OIDs and constants that matters. This arises in the practical perspective in two ways. First, in most practical systems, OIDs cannot be explicitly created, examined, or manipulated. Second, in some object-oriented systems, the actual OIDs used in a physical instance may change over the course of time (e.g., as a result of garbage collection or reclustering of objects).

To capture this aspect of OIDs in the formal model, we introduce the notion of OID isomorphism. Two instances **I**, **J** are *OID isomorphic*, denoted $\mathbf{I} \equiv_{OID} \mathbf{J}$, if there exists a bijection on **dom** $\cup$ **obj** that maps **obj** to **obj**, is the identity on **dom**, and transforms **I** into **J**. To be precise, the term *object-oriented instance* should refer to an equivalence class under OID isomorphism of instances as defined earlier. However, it is usually more convenient to work with representatives of these equivalence classes, so we follow that convention here.

REMARK 21.2.9 In the model just described, a class encompasses two aspects:

1. at the schema level, the class definition (its type and method signatures); and
2. at the instance level, the class extension (the set of objects currently in the class).

It has been argued that one should not associate explicit class extensions with classes. To see the disadvantage of class extensions, consider object deletion. To be removed from the database, an object has to be deleted *explicitly* from its class extension. This is not convenient in some cases. For instance, suppose that the database contains a class *Polygon* and polygons are used only in figures. When a polygon is no longer used in any figure of the current database, it is no longer of interest and should be deleted. We would like this deletion to be implicit. (Otherwise the user of the database would have to search all possible places in which a reference to a polygon may occur to be able to delete a polygon.)

To capture this, some OODBs use an integrity constraint, which states that

every object should be accessible from some named value.

This integrity constraint is enforced by an automatic deletion of all objects that become unreachable from the named values. In the polygon example, this approach would allow defining the class *Polygon*, thus specifying the structure and methods proper to polygons. However, the members of class *Polygon* would only be those polygons that are currently relevant. Relevance is determined by membership in (or accessibility from) the named values (e.g., *My-Figures, Your-Figures*) that refer to polygons. From a technical viewpoint, this involves techniques such as garbage collection.

In these OODBs, the set of objects in a class is not directly accessible. For this reason, the corresponding models are sometimes called models without class extension. Of course, it is always possible, given a schema, to compute the class extensions or to adapt object creation in a given class to maintain explicitly a named value containing that class extension. In these OODBs, the named values are also said to be roots of persistence, because the persistence of an object is dependent on its accessibility from these named values. ∎

21.3 Languages for OODB Queries

This section briefly introduces several languages for querying OODBs. These queries are formulated against the database as a whole; unlike methods, they are not associated with specific classes. In the next section, we will consider languages intended to provide implementations for methods.

In describing the OODB query languages, we emphasize how OODB features are incorporated into them. The first language is an extension of the calculus for complex values, which incorporates such object-oriented components as OIDs, different notions of equality, and method calls. The second is an extension of the *while* language, initially introduced in Chapter 14. Of primary interest here is the introduction of techniques for creating new OIDs as part of a query. At this point we examine the notion of completeness for OODB access languages. We also briefly look at a language introducing a logic-based approach to object creation. Finally, we mention a practical language, O_2SQL. This is a variant of SQL for OODBs that provides elegant object-oriented features.

Although the languages discussed in this section do provide the ability to call methods and incorporate the results into the query processing and answer, we focus primarily on access to the extensional structural portion of the OODB. The intensional portion, provided by the methods, is considered in the following section. Also, we largely ignore the important issue of typing for queries and programs written in these languages. The issue of typing is considered, in the context of languages for methods, in the next section.

An Object-Oriented Calculus

The object-oriented calculus presented here is a straightforward generalization of the complex value calculus of Chapter 20, extended to incorporate objects, different notions of equality, and methods.

Let $(C, \sigma, \prec, M, G)$ be an OODB schema, and let us ignore the object-oriented features for a moment. Each name in G can be viewed as a complex value; it is straightforward to generalize the complex value calculus to operate on the values referred to by G. (The fact that in the complex value model all relations are sets whereas some names in G might refer to nonset values requires only a minor modification of the language.)

Let us now consider objects. OIDs may be viewed as elements of a specific sort. If viewed in isolation from their associated values, this suggests that the only primitive available for comparing OIDs is equality. Recall from the schema of Fig. 21.1 the names *Actors_I_like* and *Actors_you_like*. The query[6]

(21.1) $\exists x, y(x \in Actors\_I\_like \land y \in Actors\_you\_like \land x = y)$

asks whether there is an actor we both like. To obtain the names of such actors, we need to introduce dereferencing, a mechanism to obtain the value of an object. Dereferencing is denoted by $\uparrow$. The following query yields the names of actors we both like:

(21.2) $\{y \mid \exists x(x \in Actors\_I\_like \land x \in Actors\_you\_like \land x \uparrow .name = y)\}$

In the previous query, $x \uparrow$ denotes the value of x, in this case, a tuple with four fields. The dot notation (.) is used as before to obtain the value of specific fields.

In query (21.1), we tested two objects for equality, essentially testing whether they had the same OID. Although it does not increase the expressive power of the language, it is customary to introduce an alternative test for equality, called *value equality*. This tests whether the values of two objects are equal regardless of whether their OIDs are distinct. To illustrate, consider the three objects having *Actor_type*:

$$(oid50, [name : \text{``Martin''}, citizenship : \text{``French''}, gender : \text{``male''},$$
$$award : \{ \}, acts\_in : \{oid33\}])$$
$$(oid51, [name : \text{``Martin''}, citizenship : \text{``French''}, gender : \text{``male''},$$
$$award : \{ \}, acts\_in : \{oid33\}])$$
$$(oid52, [name : \text{``Martin''}, citizenship : \text{``French''}, gender : \text{``male''},$$
$$award : \{ \}, acts\_in : \{oid34\}])$$

Then $oid50$ and $oid51$ are value equal, whereas $oid50$ and $oid52$ are not. Yet another form of equality is *deep equality*. If $oid33$ and $oid34$ are value equal, then $oid50$ and $oid52$ are deep equal. Intuitively, two objects are deep equal if the (possibly infinite) trees

---

[6] In this example, if *name* is a key for *Actor*, then one can easily obtain an equivalent query not using object equality; this may not be possible if there is no key for *Actor*.

obtained by recursively replacing each object by its value are equal. The infinite trees that we obtain are called the *expansions*. They present some regularity; they are regular trees (see Exercise 21.10).

The notion of deep equality highlights a major difference between value-based and object-based models. In a value-based model (such as the relational or complex value models), the database can be thought of as a collection of (finite) trees. The connections between trees arise as a result of the contents of atomic fields. That is, they are implicit (e.g., the same string may appear twice). In the object-oriented world, a database instance can be thought of as graph. Paths in the database are more explicit. That is, one may view an (*oid*, *value*) pair as a form of logical pointer and a path as a sequence of pointer dereferencing.

This graph-based perspective leads naturally to a navigational form of data access (e.g., using a sequence such as $o \uparrow .director \uparrow .citizenship$ to find the citizenship of the director of a given movie object o). This has led some to view object-oriented models as less declarative than value-based models such as the relational model. This is inaccurate, because declarativeness is more a property of access languages than models. Indeed, the calculus for OODBs described here illustrates that a highly declarative language can be developed for the OODB model.

We conclude the discussion of the object-oriented calculus by incorporating methods. For this discussion, it is irrelevant how the methods are specified or evaluated; this evaluation is external to the query. The query simply uses the method invocations as oracles. Method resolution uses dynamic binding. The value of an expression of the form $m(t_1, \ldots, t_n)$ under a given variable assignment v is obtained by evaluating (externally) the implementation of m for the class of $v(t_1)$ on input $v(t_1, \ldots, t_n)$. In this context, it is assumed that m has no side-effects. Although not defined formally here, the following illustrates the incorporation of methods into the calculus:

(21.3) $\{y \mid \exists x (x \in Persons\_I\_like \land y = get\_name(x))\}$

If the set *Persons_I_like* contains Bergman and Liv Ullman, the answer would be

$$\{\text{"Ms. Ullman", "Liv Ullman"}\}$$

The use of method names within the calculus raises a number of interesting typing and safety issues that will not be addressed here.

Object Creation and Completeness

Relational queries take relational instances as input and produce relational instances as output. The preceding calculus fails to provide the analogous capability because the output of a calculus query is a set of values or objects. Two features are needed for a query language to produce the full-fledged structural portion of an object-oriented instance: the ability to create OIDs, and the ability to populate a family of named values (rather than producing a single set).

We first introduce an extension of the *while* language of Chapter 14 that incorporates both of these capabilities. This language leads naturally to a discussion of completeness of OODB access languages. After this we mention a second approach to object creation that stems from the perspective of logic programming.

The extension of *while* introduced here is denoted $while_{obj}$. It will create new OIDs in a manner reminiscent of how the language $while_{new}$ of Chapter 18 invented new constants.

The language $while_{obj}$ incorporates object-oriented features such as dereferencing and method calls, as in the calculus. To illustrate, we present a $while_{obj}$ program that collects all actors reachable from an actor I like—Liv Ullman. In this query, *v_movies* and *v_directors* serve as variables, and *reachable* serves as a new name that will hold the output.

> *reachable* := $\{x \mid x \in Actors\_I\_like \land x \uparrow .name =$ "Liv Ullman"$\}$;
> *v_movies* := { }; *v_directors* := { };
> *while change do*
>   *begin*
>   *reachable* := *reachable* $\cup \{x \mid \exists y(y \in v\_movies \land x \in y \uparrow .actors)\}$;
>   *v_directors* := *v_directors*
> $\cup \{x \mid \exists y(y \in v\_movies \land x \in y \uparrow .director)\}$;
>   *v_movies* := *v_movies*
> $\cup\{x \mid \exists y(y \in reachable \land x \in y \uparrow .acts\_in)\}$
> $\cup\{x \mid \exists y(y \in v\_directors \land x \in y \uparrow .directs)\}$;
>   *end*;

We now introduce object creation. The operator **new** works as follows. It takes as input a set of values (or objects) and produces one new OID for each value in the set. As a simple example, suppose that we want to objectify the triples in the named value *Pariscope* of the schema of Fig. 21.1. This may be accomplished with the commands

> *add_class Pariscope_obj*
>   *type tuple* (*theater* : *Theater*, *time* : **string**, *price* : **integer**, *movie* : *Movie*);
> *Pariscope_obj* := **new**(*Pariscope*)

Of course, the **new** operator can be used in conjunction with arbitrary expressions that yield a set of values, not just a named value.

The **new** operator used here is closely related to the *new* operator of the language $while_{new}$ of Chapter 18. Given that $while_{obj}$ has iteration and the ability to create new OIDs, it is natural to ask about the expressive power of this language. To set the stage, we introduce the following analogue of the notion of (computable) query, which mimics the one of Chapter 18. The definition focuses on the structural portion of the OODB model; methods are excluded from consideration.

DEFINITION 21.3.1 Let **R** and **S** be two OODB schemas with no method signatures. A *determinate query* is a relation Q from *inst*(**R**) to *inst*(**S**) such that

(a) Q is computable;

(b) (Genericity) if $\langle \mathbf{I}, \mathbf{J} \rangle \in Q$ and ρ is a one-to-one mapping on constants, then $\langle \rho(\mathbf{I}), \rho(\mathbf{J}) \rangle \in Q$;

(c) (Functionality) if $\langle \mathbf{I}, \mathbf{J} \rangle \in Q$, and $\langle \mathbf{I}, \mathbf{J}' \rangle \in Q$, then $\mathbf{J}$ and $\mathbf{J}'$ are OID isomorphic; and

(d) (Well defined) if $\langle \mathbf{I}, \mathbf{J} \rangle \in Q$ and $\langle \mathbf{I}', \mathbf{J}' \rangle$ is OID isomorphic to $\langle \mathbf{I}, \mathbf{J} \rangle$, then $\langle \mathbf{I}', \mathbf{J}' \rangle \in Q$.

A language is *determinate complete* (for OODBs) if it expresses exactly the determinate queries.

The essential difference between the preceding definition and the definition of determinate query in Chapter 18 is that here only OIDs can be created, not constants. Parts (c) and (d) of the definition ensure that a determinate query Q can be viewed as a *function* from OID equivalence classes of instances over $\mathbf{R}$ to OID equivalence classes of instances over $\mathbf{S}$. So OIDs serve two purposes here: (1) They are used to compute in the same way that invented values were used to break the polynomial space barrier; and (2) they are now essential components of the data structure and in particular of the result. With respect to (2), an important aspect is that we are not concerned with the actual value of the OIDs, which motivates the use of the equivalence relation. (Two results are viewed as identical if they are the same up to the renaming of the OIDs.)

Like $while_{new}$, $while_{obj}$ is not determinate complete. There is an elegant characterization of the determinate queries expressible in $while_{obj}$. This result, which we state next, uses a *local* characterization of input-output pairs of $while_{obj}$ programs. That characterization is in the spirit of the notion of BP-completeness, relating input-output pairs of relational calculus queries (see Exercise 16.11). For each input-output pair $\langle I, J \rangle$, the characterization of $while_{obj}$ queries requires a simple connection between the automorphism group of I and that of J. For an instance K, let $Aut(K)$ denote the set of automorphisms of K. For a pair of instances K, K', $Aut(\langle K, K' \rangle)$ denotes the bijections on $\mathbf{adom}(K \cup K')$ that are automorphisms of both K and K'.

THEOREM 21.3.2 A determinate query q is expressible in $while_{obj}$ iff for each input-output pair $\langle I, J \rangle$ in q there exists a mapping h from $Aut(I)$ to $Aut(\langle I, J \rangle)$ such that for each $\tau, \mu \in Aut(I)$,

(i) τ and $h(\tau)$ coincide on I;

(ii) $h(\tau \circ \mu) = h(\tau) \circ h(\mu)$; and

(iii) $h(\mathbf{id}_I) = \mathbf{id}_{\langle I, J \rangle}$.

The "only if" part of the theorem is proven by an extension of the trace technique developed in the proof of Theorem 18.2.5 (Exercise 21.14). The "if" part is considerably more complex and is based on a group-theoretic argument.

A mapping h just shown is called an *extension homomorphism* from $Aut(I)$ to $Aut(\langle I, J \rangle)$. To see an example of the usefulness of this characterization, consider the query q in Fig. 21.3. Recall that q was shown as not expressible in the language $while_{new}$ by Theorem 18.2.5. The language $while_{obj}$ is more powerful than $while_{new}$, so in principle it may be able to express that query. However, we show that this is not the case, so $while_{obj}$ is not determinate complete.

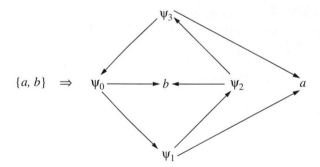

Figure 21.3: A query not expressible in *while*$_{obj}$

PROPOSITION 21.3.3 Query q (of Fig. 21.3) is not expressible in *while*$_{obj}$.

Proof Let $\langle I, J \rangle$ be the input-output pair of Fig. 21.3. The proof is by contradiction. Suppose there is a *while*$_{obj}$ query that produces J on input I. By Theorem 21.3.2, there is an extension homomorphism h from $Aut(I)$ to $Aut(\langle I, J \rangle)$. Let μ be the automorphism of I exchanging a and b. Note that $\mu^{-1} = \mu$, so $\mu \circ \mu = \mathbf{id}_I$. Consider $h(\mu)(\psi_0)$. Clearly, $h(\mu)(\psi_0) \in \{\psi_1, \psi_3\}$. Suppose $h(\mu)(\psi_0) = \psi_1$ (the other case is similar). Then clearly, $h(\mu)(\psi_1) = \psi_2$. Consider now $h(\mu \circ \mu)(\psi_0)$. We have, on one hand,

$$h(\mu \circ \mu)(\psi_0) = (h(\mu) \circ h(\mu))(\psi_0)$$
$$= h(\mu)(\psi_1)$$
$$= \psi_2$$

and on the other hand

$$h(\mu \circ \mu)(\psi_0) = h(\mathbf{id}_I)(\psi_0)$$
$$= \mathbf{id}_{\langle I, J \rangle}(\psi_0)$$
$$= \psi_0,$$

which is a contradiction because $\psi_0 \neq \psi_2$. So q is not expressible in *while*$_{obj}$. ∎

It is possible to obtain a language expressing all determinate queries by adding to *while*$_{obj}$ a *choose* operator that allows the selection (nondeterministically but in a determinate manner) of one object out of a set of objects that are isomorphic (see Exercise 18.14). However, this is a highly complex construct because it requires the ability to check for isomorphism of graphs. The search for simpler, local constructs that yield a determinate-complete language is an active area of research.

A Logic-Based Approach to Object Creation

We now briefly introduce an alternative approach for creating OIDs that stems from the perspective of datalog and logic programming. Suppose that a new OID is to be created for each pair $\langle t, m \rangle$, where movie m is playing at theater t according to the current value of *Pariscope*. Consider the following dataloglike rule:

    1. *create_tm_object*$(x, t, m) \leftarrow Pariscope(t, s, m)$

Note that x occurs in the rule head but not in the body, so the rule is not safe. Intuitively, we would like to attach semantics to this rule so that a new OID is associated to x for each distinct pair of (t, m) values. Using the symbol $\exists!$ to mean "exists a unique," the following versions of (1) intuitively captures the semantics.

    2. $\forall t \forall m \exists! x \forall s [create\_tm\_object(x, t, m) \leftarrow Pariscope(t, s, m)]$

    3. $\forall t \forall m \exists! x [create\_tm\_object(x, t, m) \leftarrow \exists s(Pariscope(t, s, m))]$

This suggests that Skolem functions might be used. Specifically, let f_{tm} be a function symbol associated with the predicate *create_tm_object*. We rewrite (2) as

$$\forall t \forall m \forall s [create\_tm\_object(f_{tm}(t, m), t, m) \leftarrow Pariscope(t, s, m)]$$

or, leaving off the universal quantifiers as traditional in datalog,

    4. *create_tm_object*$(f_{tm}(t, m), t, m) \leftarrow Pariscope(t, s, m)$

    Under this approach, the Skolem terms resulting from rule (4) are to be interpreted as new, distinct OIDs. Under some formulations of the approach, syntactic objects such as $f_{tm}(oid7, oid22)$ (where $oid7$ is the OID of some theater and $oid22$ the OID of some movie) serve explicitly as OIDs. Under other formulations, such syntactic objects are viewed as placeholders during an intermediate stage of query evaluation and are (nondeterministically) replaced by distinct new OIDs in the final stage of query evaluation (see Exercise 21.13).

    The latter approach to OID creation, incorporated into complex value datalog extended to include also OID dereferencing, yields a language equivalent to *while*$_{obj}$. As with *while*$_{obj}$, this language is not determinate complete.

A Practical Language for OODBs

We briefly illustrate some object-oriented features of the language O_2SQL, which was introduced in Section 20.8. Several examples are presented there, that show how O_2SQL can be used to access and construct deeply nested complex values. We now indicate how the use of objects and methods is incorporated into the language. It is interesting to note that methods and nested complex values are elegantly combined in this language, which has the appearance of SQL but is essentially based on the functional programming paradigm.

    For this example, we again assume the complex value *Films* of Fig. 20.2, but we assume that *Age* is a method defined for the class *Person* (and thus for *Director*).

    select tuple (f.Director, f.Director.Age)
    from f **in** Films
    where f.Director **not in flatten select** m.Actors
                          from g **in** Films,

m **in** g.Movies
where g.Director = "Hitchcock"

(Recall that here the inner *select-from-where* clause returns a set of sets of actors. The keyword **flatten** has the effect of forming the union of these sets to yield a set of actors.)

21.4 Languages for Methods

So far, we have used an abstraction of methods (their signature) and ignored their implementations. In this section, we present two abstract programming languages for specifying method implementations. Method implementations will be included in the specification of methods in OODB schemas. In studying these languages, we emphasize two important issues: type safety and expressive power. This focus largely motivates our choice of languages and the particular abstractions considered.

The first language is an imperative programming language. The second, method schemas, is representative of a functional style of database access. In the first language, we will gather a number of features present in practical object-oriented database languages (e.g., side-effect, iteration, conditionals). We will see that with these features, we get (as could be expected) completeness, and we pay the obvious price for it: the undecidability of many questions, such as type safety. With method schemas, we focus on the essence of inheritance and methods. We voluntarily consider a limited language. We see that the undecidability of type safety is a consequence of recursion in method calls. (We obtain decidability in the restricted case of monadic methods.) With respect to expressiveness, we present a surprising characterization of QPTIME in terms of a simple language with methods.

For both languages, we study type safety and expressive power. We begin by discussing briefly the meaning of these notions in our context, and then we present the two languages and the results.

An OODB schema **S** (with method implementations assigned to signatures) is type safe if for each instance **I** of **S** and each syntactically correct method call on **I**, the execution of this method does not result in a runtime type error (an illegal method call). When the imperative programming language is used in method implementations, type safety is undecidable. (It is possible, however, to obtain decidable sufficient conditions for type safety.) For method schemas, type safety remains undecidable. Surprisingly, type safety is decidable for monadic method schemas.

To evaluate the expressive power of OODB schemas using a particular language for method implementation, a common approach is to simulate relational queries and then ask what family of relational queries can be simulated. If OID creation is permitted, then all computable relational queries can be simulated using the imperative language. The expressive power of imperative methods without OID creation depends on the complex types permitted in OODB schemas. We also present a result for the expressive power of method schemas, showing that the family of method schemas using an ordered domain of atomic elements expresses exactly QPTIME.

A Model with Imperative Methods

To consider the issue of type safety in a general context, we present the *imperative (OODB) model*, which incorporates imperative method implementations. This model simplifies the OODB model presented earlier by assuming that the type of each class is a tuple of values and OIDs. However, a schema in this model will include an assignment of implementations to method signatures.

The syntax for method implementations is

par: $u_1, \ldots, u_n$;
var: $x_1, \ldots, x_l$;
body: $s_1; \ldots; s_q$;
return x_1

where the u_i's are parameters ($n \geq 1$), the x_j's are internal variables ($l \geq 1$), and for each $p \in [1, q]$, s_p is a statement of one of the following forms (where w, y, z range over parameters and internal variables):

Basic operations

   (i) $w := self$.
   (ii) $w := self.a$ for some field name a.
   (iii) $w := y$.
   (iv) $w := m(y, \ldots, z)$, for some method name m.
   (v) $self.a := w$, for some field name a.

Class operations

   (vi) $w := \textbf{new}(c)$, where c is a class.
   (vii) $\textbf{delete}(c, w)$, where c is a class.
   (viii) **for each** w **in** c **do** $s_1'; \ldots; s_t'$ **end**, where c is a class and $s_1', \ldots, s_t'$ are statements having forms from this list.

Conditional

   (ix) **if** $y \theta z$ **then** s, where θ is $=$ or $\neq$ and s is a statement having a form in this list except for the conditional.

It is assumed that all internal variables are initialized before used to some default value depending on their type. The intended semantics for the forms other than (viii) should be clear. (Here *clear* does not mean "easy to implement." In particular, object deletion is complex because all references to this object have to be deleted.) The looping construct executes for each element of the extension (not disjoint extension) of class c. The execution of the loop is viewed as nondeterministic, in the sense that the particular ordering used for the elements of c is not guaranteed by the implementation. In general, we focus on OODB schemas in which different orders of execution of the loops yield OID-equivalent results (note, however, that this property is undecidable, so it must be ensured by the programmer).

An imperative *schema* is a 6-tuple $\mathbf{S} = (C, \sigma, \prec, M, G, \mu)$, where $(C, \sigma, \prec, M, G)$ is a schema as before; where the range of σ is tuples of atomic and class types; and where μ is an assignment of implementations to signatures. The notion of *instance* for this model is defined in the natural fashion.

It is straightforward to develop operational semantics for this model, where the execution of a given method call might be *successful, nonterminating*, or *aborted* (as the result of a runtime type error) (Exercise 21.15a).

Type Safety in the Imperative Model   There are two ways that a runtime type error can arise: (1) if the type of the result of an execution of method m does not lie within the type specified by the relevant method signature of m; or (2) if a method is called on a tuple of parameters that does not satisfy the domain part of the appropriate signature of m. We assume that the range of all method signatures is **any**, and thus we focus on case (2).

A schema $\mathbf{S}$ is *type safe* if for each instance over $\mathbf{S}$ and each $m(o, v_1, \ldots, v_n)$ method call that satisfies the signature of m associated with the class of o, execution of this call is either successful or nonterminating.

Given a Turing machine M, it is easy to develop a schema S in this model that can simulate the operation of M on a suitable encoding of an input tape (Exercise 21.15c). This shows that such schemas are computationally powerful and implies the usual undecidability results. With regard to type safety, it is easy to verify the following (Exercise 21.16):

PROPOSITION 21.4.1   It is undecidable, given an imperative schema $\mathbf{S}$, whether $\mathbf{S}$ is type safe. This remains true, even if in method implementations conditional statements and the **new** operator are prohibited and all methods are monadic (i.e., have only one argument).

A similar argument can be used to show that it is undecidable whether a given method terminates on all inputs. Finally, a method m' on class c' is *reachable* from method m on class c in OODB schema $\mathbf{S}$ if there is some instance $\mathbf{I}$ of $\mathbf{S}$ and some tuple $o, v_1, \ldots$ with o in c such that the execution of $m(o, v_1, \ldots)$ leads to a call of m' on some object in c'. Reachability is also undecidable for imperative schemas.

Expressive Power of the Imperative Model

As discussed earlier, we measure the expressive power of OODB schemas in terms of the relational queries they can simulate. A relational schema $\mathbf{R} = \{R_1, \ldots, R_n\}$ is *simulated by* an OODB schema $\mathbf{S}$ of this model if there are leaf classes $c_1, \ldots, c_n$ in $\mathbf{S}$, where the number of attributes of c_i is the arity of R_i for $i \in [1, n]$ and where the type of each of these attributes is atomic. We focus on instances in which no null values appear for such attributes. Let $\mathbf{R}$ be a relational schema and $\mathbf{S}$ be an OODB schema that simulates $\mathbf{R}$. An instance $\mathbf{I}$ of $\mathbf{R}$ is *simulated* by instance $\mathbf{J}$ of $\mathbf{S}$ if for each tuple $\vec{v} \in \mathbf{I}(R_i)$ there is exactly one object o in the extension of c_i such that the value associated with o is $\vec{v}$ and all other classes of $\mathbf{S}$ are empty. Following this spirit, it is straightforward to define what it means for a method call in schema $\mathbf{S}$ to simulate a relational query from $\mathbf{R}$ to relation schema R.

We consider only schema $\mathbf{S}$ for which different orders of evaluation of the looping construct yield the same final result (i.e., generic mappings). We now have the following (see Exercise 21.20):

THEOREM 21.4.2   The family of generic queries corresponding to imperative schemas coincides with the family of all relational queries.

The preceding result relies on the presence of the **new** operator. It is natural to ask about the expressive power of imperative schemas that do not support **new**. As discussed in Exercise 21.21, the expressive power depends on the complex types permitted for objects.

Note also that imperative schemas can express all determinate queries. This uses the nondeterminism of the **for each** construct. Naturally, nondeterministic queries that are not determinate can also be expressed.

Method Schemas

We now present an abstract model for side-effect-free methods, called method schemas. In this model, we focus almost exclusively on methods and their implementations. Two kinds of methods are distinguished: base and composite. The base methods do not have implementations: Their semantics is specified explicitly at the instance level. The implementations of composite methods consist of a composition of other methods.

We now introduce method schemas. In the next definition, we make the simplifying assumption that there are no named values (only class names) in database schemas. In fact, data is only stored in base methods. In the following, $\sigma_{[\,]}$ denotes the type assignment $\sigma_{[\,]}(c) = [\,]$ for every class c. Because the type assignment provides no information in method schemas (it is always $\sigma_{[\,]}$), this assignment is not explicitly specified in the schemas.

DEFINITION 21.4.3   A *method schema* is a 5-tuple $\mathbf{S} = (C, \prec, M_{base}, M_{comp}, \mu)$, where $(C, \sigma_{[\,]}, \prec)$ is a well-formed class hierarchy, $M_{base} \cup M_{comp}$ is a well-formed set of method signatures for $(C, \sigma_{[\,]}, \prec)$, and

- no method name occurs in both M_{base} and M_{comp};
- each method signature in M_{comp} is of the form $m : c_1, \ldots, c_n \to$ **any** (method signatures for M_{base} are unrestricted, i.e., can have any class as range);
- μ is an assignment of implementations to the method signatures of M_{comp}, as follows: For a signature $m : c_1, \ldots, c_n \to$ **any** in M_{comp}, $\mu(m : c_1, \ldots, c_n \to$ **any**$)$ is a term obtained by composing methods in M_{base} and M_{comp}.

An example of an implementation for a method $m : c_1, c_2 \to$ **any** is

$$m(x, y) \equiv m_1(m_2(x), m_1(x, y)).$$

The semantics of methods is defined in the obvious way. For instance, to compute $m(o, o')$, one computes first $o_1 = m_2(o)$ and then $o_2 = m_1(o, o')$; the result is $m_1(o_1, o_2)$. The range of composite methods is left unspecified (it is **any**) because it is determined by the domain and the method implementation as a composition of methods. Because the range of composite methods is always **any**, we will sometimes only specify their domain.

Let $\mathbf{S} = (C, \prec, M_{base}, M_{comp}, \mu)$ be a method schema. An *instance* of $\mathbf{S}$ is a pair $\mathbf{I} = (\pi, \nu)$, where π is an OID assignment for $(C, \prec)$ and where ν assigns a semantics to the base methods. Note the difference from the imperative schemas of the previous section, where π together with the method implementations was sufficient to determine the semantics of methods. In contrast, the semantics of the base methods must be specified in instances of method schemas.

Inheritance of method implementations for method schemas is defined slightly differently from that for the OODB model given earlier. Specifically, given an n-ary method m and invocation $m(o_1, \ldots, o_n)$, where o_i is in disjoint class c_i for $i \in [1, n]$, the implementation for m is inherited from the implementation of signature $m : c'_1, \ldots, c'_n \to c'$, where this is the unique signature that is pointwise least above $c_1, \ldots, c_n$. [Otherwise m is undefined on input $(o_1, \ldots, o_n)$.]

An important special case is when methods take just *one* argument. Method schemas using only such methods are called *monadic*. To emphasize the difference, unrestricted method schemas are sometimes called *polyadic*.

EXAMPLE 21.4.4 Consider the following monadic method schema. The classes in the schema are

$$class\ c$$
$$class\ c' \prec c$$

The base method signatures are

$$method\ m_1 : c \to c'$$
$$method\ m_2 : c \to c$$
$$method\ m_2 : c' \to c'$$
$$method\ m_3 : c' \to c$$

The composite method definitions are

$$method\ m : c = m_2(m_2(m_1(x)))$$
$$method\ m' : c = m_3(m'(m_2(x)))$$
$$method\ m' : c' = m_1(x)$$

Note that m' is recursive and that calls to m' on elements in c' break the recursion.

Type Safety for Method Schemas As before, a method schema $\mathbf{S}$ is *type safe* if for each instance $\mathbf{I}$ of $\mathbf{S}$ no method call on $\mathbf{I}$ leads to a runtime type error.

The following example demonstrates that the schema of Example 21.4.4 is not type safe. Note how the interpretation ν for base methods can be viewed as an assignment of values for objects.

EXAMPLE 21.4.5   Recall the method schema of Example 21.4.4. An instance of this is $\mathbf{I} = (\pi, \nu)$, where[7]

$$\pi(c) = \{p, q\}$$
$$\pi(c') = \{r\}$$

and

$$
\begin{array}{lll}
\nu(m_1)(p) = r & \nu(m_2)(p) = q & \\
\nu(m_1)(q)l = \perp & \nu(m_2)(q) = r & \nu(m_3)(r) = p. \\
\nu(m_1)(r) = r & \nu(m_2)(r) = r &
\end{array}
$$

Consider the execution of $m(p)$. This calls for the computation of $m_2(m_2(m_1(p))) = m_2(m_2(r)) = r$. Thus the execution is successful. On the other hand, $m'(p)$ leads to a runtime type error: $m'(p) = m_3(m'(m_2(p))) = m_3(m'(q)) = m_3(m_3(m'(m_2(q)))) = m_3(m_3(m'(r))) = m_3(m_3(m_1(r))) = m_3(m_3(r)) = m_3(p)$, which is undefined and raises a runtime type error. Thus the schema is not type safe.

It turns out that type safety of method schemas permitting polyadic methods is undecidable (Exercise 21.19). Interestingly, type safety is decidable for monadic method schemas. We now sketch the proof of this result.

THEOREM 21.4.6   It is decidable in polynomial time whether a monadic method schema is type safe.

Crux   Let $\mathbf{S} = (C, \prec, M_{base}, M_{comp}, \mu)$ be a monadic method schema. We construct a context-free grammar (see Chapter 2) that captures possible executions of a method call over all instances of $\mathbf{S}$. The grammar is $G_{\mathbf{S}} = (V_n, V_t, A, P)$, where the set V_t of terminals is the set of base method names (denoted N_{base}) along with the symbols $\{\langle error \rangle, \langle ignore \rangle\}$, and the set V_n of nonterminals includes start symbol A and

$$\{[c, m, c'] \mid c, c' \text{ are classes, and } m \text{ is a method name}\}$$

The set P of production rules includes

    (i) $A \rightarrow [c, m, c']$, if m is a composite method name and it is defined at c or a superclass of c.

    (ii) $[c, m, c'] \rightarrow \langle error \rangle$, if m is not defined at c or a superclass of c.

    (iii) $[c, m, c'] \rightarrow m$, if m is a base method name, the resolution of m for c is $m : c_1 \rightarrow c_2$, and $c' \prec c_2$. (Note that $c' = c_2$ is just a particular case.)

---

[7] We write $\nu(m_1)(p)$ rather than $\nu(m_1, c)(p)$ to simplify the presentation.

(iv) $[c, m, c] \rightarrow \epsilon$, if m is a composite method name and the resolution of m for c is the identity mapping.

(v) $[c, m, c_n] \rightarrow [c, m_1, c_1][c_1, m_2, c_2]\ldots[c_{n-1}, m_n, c_n]$, if m is a composite method, m on c resolves to a method with implementation $m_n(m_{n-1}(\ldots(m_2(m_1(x)))\ldots))$, and $c_1, \ldots, c_n$ are arbitrary classes.

(vi) $[c, m, c'] \rightarrow \langle ignore \rangle$, for all classes c, c' and method names m.

Given a successful execution of a method call $m(o)$, it is easy to construct a word in $L(G_{\mathbf{S}})$ of the form $m_1 \ldots m_n$, where the m_i's list the sequence of base methods called during the execution. On the other hand, if the execution of $m(o)$ leads to a runtime error, a word of the form $m_1 \ldots m_i \langle error \rangle \ldots$ can be formed. The terminal $\langle ignore \rangle$ can be used in cases where a nonterminal $[c, m, c']$ arises, such that m is a base method name and c' is outside the range of m for c. The productions of type (vi) are permitted for all nonterminals $[c, m, c']$, although they are needed only for some of them.

It can be shown that **S** is type safe iff

$$L(G_{\mathbf{S}}) \cap N^*_{base}\langle error \rangle V^*_t = \emptyset.$$

Because it can be tested if the intersection of a context-free language with a regular language is empty, the preceding provides an algorithm for checking type safety. However, a modification of the grammar $G_{\mathbf{S}}$ is needed to obtain the polynomial time test (see Exercise 21.18). ∎

Expressive Power of Method Schemas   We now argue that method schemas (with order) simulate precisely the relational queries in QPTIME. The object-oriented features are not central here: The same result can be shown for functional data models without such features.

As for imperative schemas, we show that method schemas can simulate relational queries. The encoding of these queries assumes an ordered domain, as is traditional in the world of functional programming.

A relational database is encoded as follows:

(a) a class **elem** contains objects representing the elements of the domain, and it has **zero** as a subclass containing a unique element, say 0;

(b) a function *pred*, which is included as a base method,[8] provides the predecessor function over **elem** ∪ **zero** [$pred(0)$ is, for instance, 0]; a base method 0 returns the least element and another base method N the largest object in **elem**;

(c) to have the Booleans, we think of 0 as the value *false* and all objects in **elem** as representations of *true*;

(d) an n-ary relation R is represented by an n-ary base method m_R of signature $m_R : \mathbf{elem}, \ldots, \mathbf{elem} \rightarrow \mathbf{elem}$, the characteristic function of R. [For a tuple t, $m_R(t)$ is *true* iff t is in R.]

---

[8] The function *pred* is a functional analog of the relation *succ*, which we have assumed is available in every ordered database (a successor function could also have been used).

Next we represent queries by composite methods. A query q is computed by method m_q if $m_q(t)$ is true (not in **zero**) iff t is in the answer to query q.

The following illustrates how to compute with this simple language.

EXAMPLE 21.4.7   Consider relation R with $R = \{R(1, 1), R(1, 2)\}$. The class **zero** is populated with the object 0 and the class **elem** with 1, 2. The base method *pred* is defined by $pred(2) = 1, pred(0) = pred(1) = 0$. The base method m_R is defined by $m_R(1, 1) = m_R(1, 2) = 1$ and $m_R(x, y) = 0$ otherwise.

Recall that each object in class **elem** is viewed as *true* and object 0 as *false*. We can code the Boolean function *and* as follows:

$$\text{for } x, y \text{ in } \textbf{zero}, \textbf{zero} \quad and(x, y) \equiv 0$$
$$\text{for } x, y \text{ in } \textbf{elem}, \textbf{zero} \quad and(x, y) \equiv 0$$
$$\text{for } x, y \text{ in } \textbf{zero}, \textbf{elem} \quad and(x, y) \equiv 0$$
$$\text{for } x, y \text{ in } \textbf{elem}, \textbf{elem} \quad and(x, y) \equiv N.$$

The other standard Boolean functions can be coded similarly. We can code the intersection between two binary relations R and S with $and(m_R(x, y), m_S(x, y))$. As a last example, the projection of a binary relation R over the first coordinate can be coded by a method $\pi_{R,1}$ defined by

$$\pi_{R,1} \equiv m(x, N),$$

where m is given by

$$\text{for } x, y \text{ in } \textbf{elem}, \textbf{zero} \quad m(x, y) \equiv m_R(x, y)$$
$$\text{for } x, y \text{ in } \textbf{elem}, \textbf{elem} \quad m(x, y) \equiv or(m_R(x, y), m(x, pred(y))).$$

We now state the following:

THEOREM 21.4.8   Method schemas over ordered databases express exactly QPTIME.

Crux   As indicated in the preceding example, we can construct composite methods for the Boolean operations *and*, *or*, and *not*. For each k, we can also construct k k-ary functions $pred_k^i$ for $i \in [1, k]$ that compute for each k tuple u the k components of the predecessor (in lexicographical ordering) of u. Indeed, we can simulate an arbitrary relational operation and more generally an arbitrary inflationary fixpoint. To see this, consider the transitive closure query. It is computed with a method tc defined (informally) as follows. Intuitively, a method $tc(x, y)$ asks, "Is $\langle x, y \rangle$ in the transitive closure?" Execution of $tc(x, y)$ first calls a method $m_1(x, y, N)$, whose intuitive meaning is "Is there a path of length N from x to y?" This will be computed by asking whether there is a path of length $N - 1$ (a recursive call to m_1), etc. This can be generalized to a construction that simulates an arbitrary inflationary fixpoint query. Because the underlying domain is ordered, we have captured all QPTIME queries. The converse follows from the fact that there are only polynomially many possible method calls in the context of a given instance, and each method call in this model can be answered in QPTIME. Moreover, loops in method calls can be detected in polynomial time; calls giving rise to loops are assumed to output some designated special value. (See Exercise 21.25.) ■

We have presented an object-oriented approach in the applicative programming style. There exists another important family of functional languages based on typed λ calculi. It is possible to consider database languages in this family as well. These calculi present additional advantages, such as being able to treat functions as objects and to use higher-order functions (i.e., functions whose arguments are functions).

21.5   Further Issues for OODBs

As mentioned at the beginning of this chapter, the area of OODB is relatively young and active. Much research is needed to understand OODBs as well as we understand relational databases. A difficulty (and richness) is that there is still no well-accepted model. We conclude this chapter with a brief look at some current research issues for OODBs. These fall into two broad categories: advanced modeling features and dynamic aspects.

Advanced Modeling Features

This is not an exhaustive list of new features but a sample of some that are being studied:

Views: Views are intended to increase the flexibility of database systems, and it is natural to extend the notion of relational view to the OODB framework. However, unlike relational views, OODB views might redefine the behavior of objects in addition to restructuring their associated types. There are also significant issues raised by the presence of OIDs. For example, to maintain incrementally a materialized view with created OIDs, the linkage between the base data and the created OIDs must be maintained. Furthermore, if the view is virtual, then how should virtual OIDs be specified and manipulated?

Object roles: The same entity may be involved in several roles. For instance, a director may also be an actor. It is costly, if not infeasible, to forecast all cases in which this may happen. Although not as important in object-oriented programming, in OODBs it would be useful to permit the same object to live in several classes (a departure from the disjoint OID assignment from which we started) and at least conceptually maintain distinct repositories, one for each role. This feature is present in some semantic data models; in the object-oriented context, it raises a number of interesting typing issues.

Schema design: Schema design techniques (e.g., based on dependencies and normal forms) have emerged for the relational model (see Chapter 11). Although the richer model in the OODB provides greater flexibility in selecting a schema, there is a concomitant need for richer tools to facilitate schema design. The scope of schema design is enlarged in the OODB context because of the interaction of methods within a schema and application software for the schema.

Querying the schema: In many cases, information may be hidden in an OODB schema. Suppose, for example, that movies were assigned categories such as "drama," "western," "suspense," etc. In the relational model, this information would typically be represented using a new column in the *Movies* relation. A query such as "list all categories of movie that Bergman directed" is easily answered. In an OODB, the category information might be represented using different subclasses of the *Movie* class. Answering this query now requires the ability of the query language to return class names, a feature not present in most current systems.

Classification: A related problem concerns how, given an OODB schema, to classify new data for this schema. This may arise when constructing a view, when merging two databases, or when transforming a relational database into an OODB one by objectifying tuples. The issue of classification, also called taxonomic reasoning, has a long history in the field of knowledge representation in artificial intelligence, and some research in this direction has been performed for semantic and object-oriented databases.

Incorporating deductive capabilities: The logic-programming paradigm has offered a tremendous enhancement of the relational model by providing an elegant and (in many cases) intuitively appealing framework for expressing a broad family of queries. For the past several years, researchers have been developing hybrids of the logic-programming and object-oriented paradigms. Although it is very different in some ways (because the OO paradigm has fundamentally imperative aspects), the perspective of logic programming provides alternative approaches to data access and object creation.

Abstract data types: As mentioned earlier, OODB systems come equipped with several constructors, such as set, list, or bag. It is also interesting to be able to extend the language and the system with application-specific data types. This involves language and typing issues, such as how to gracefully incorporate access mechanisms for the new types into an existing language. It also involves system issues, such as how to introduce appropriate indexing techniques for the new type.

Dynamic Issues

The semantics of updates in relational systems is simple: Perform the update if the result complies with the dependencies of the schema. In an OODB, the issue is somewhat trickier. For instance, can we allow the deletion of an object if this object is referred to somewhere in the database (the dangling reference problem)? This is prohibited in some systems, whereas other systems will accept the deletion and just mark the object as dead. Semantically, this results in viewing all references to this object as *nil*.

Another issue is object migration. It is easy to modify the value of an object. But changing the status of an object is more complicated. For example, a person in the database may act in a movie and overnight be turned into an actor. In object-oriented programming languages, objects are often not allowed to change classes. Although such limitations also exist in most present OODBs, object migration is an important feature that is needed in many database applications. One approach, followed by some semantic data models, is to permit objects to be associated with multiple classes or roles and also permit them to migrate to different classes over time. This raises fundamental issues with regard to typing. For example, how do we treat a reference to the manager of a department (that should be of type *Employee*) when he or she leaves the company and is turned into a "normal" person?

Finally, as with the relational model, we need to consider evolution of the schema itself. The OODB context is much richer than the relational, because there are many more kinds of changes to consider: the class hierarchy, the type of a class, additions or deletions of methods, etc.

Bibliographic Notes

Collections of papers on object-oriented databases can be found in [BDK92, KL89, ZM90]. The main characteristics of object-oriented database systems are described in [ABD⁺89]. An influential discussion of some foundational issues around the OODB paradigm is [Bee90]. An important survey of subtyping and inheritance from the perspective of programming languages, including the notion of domain-inclusion semantics, is [CW85].

Object-oriented databases are, of course, closely related to object-oriented programming languages. The first of these is Smalltalk [GR83], and C++ [Str91] is fast becoming the most widely used object-oriented programming language. Several commercial OODBs are essentially persistent versions of C++. Several object-oriented extensions of Lisp have been proposed; the article [B⁺86] introduces a rich extension called CommonLoops and surveys several others.

There have been a number of approaches to provide a formal foundation [AK89, Bee90, HTY89, KLW93] for OODBs. We can also cite as precursors attempts to formalize semantic data models [AH87] and object-based models [KV84, HY84]. Recent graph-oriented models, although they do not stress object orientation, are similar in spirit (e.g., [GPG90]).

The generic OODB model used here is directly inspired from the IQL model [AK89] and that of O₂ [BDK92, LRV88]. The model and results on imperative method implementations are inspired by [HTY89, HS89a]. A similar model of imperative method implementation, which avoids nondeterminism and introduces a parallel execution model, is developed in [DV91]. Method schemas and Theorem 21.4.6 are from [AKRW92]; the functional perspective and Theorem 21.4.8 are from [HKR93].

OIDs have been part of many data models. For example, they are called *surrogates* in [Cod79], *l-values* in [KV93a], or *object identifiers* in [AH87]. The notion of object and the various forms of equalities among objects form the topic of [KC86]. Type inheritance and multiple inheritance are studied in [CW85, Car88].

Since [KV84], various languages for models with objects have been proposed in the various paradigms: calculus, algebra, rule based, or functional. Besides standard features found in database languages without objects, the new primitives are centered around object creation. Language-theoretic issues related to object creation were first considered in the context of IQL [AK89]. Object creation is an essential component of IQL and is the main reason for the completeness of the language. The need for a primitive in the style of copy elimination to obtain determinate completeness was first noticed in [AK89]. The IQL language is rule based with an inflationary fixpoint semantics in the style of datalog$^\neg$ of Chapter 14.

The logic-based perspective on object creation based on Skolem was first informally discussed in [Mai86] and refined variously in [CW89a, HY90, KLW93, KW89]. In particular, F-logic [KLW93] considers a different approach to inheritance. In our framework, the classification of objects is explicit; in particular, when an object is created, it is within an explicit class. In [KLW93], data organization is also specified by rules and thus may depend on the properties of the objects involved. For instance, reasoning about the hierarchy becomes part of the program.

Algebraic and imperative approaches to object creation are developed in [Day89]. Since then, object creation has been the center of much interesting research (e.g., [DV93, HS89b, HY92, VandBG92, VandBGAG92, VandB93]). The characterization of queries expressible in *while*$_{obj}$ (Theorem 21.3.2) is from [VandBG92]; this extends a previous result from [AP92]. The proof of Proposition 21.3.3 is also from [VandBG92]. In [VandBG92, VandB93], it is argued that the notion of determinate query may not be the most appropriate one for the object-based context, and alternative notions, such as semideterministic queries, are discussed. A tractable construct yielding a determinate-complete language is exhibited in [DV93]. However, the construct proposed there is global in nature and is involved. The search for simpler and more natural local constructs continues.

As mentioned earlier, the OODB calculus and algebra presented here are mostly variations of languages for non object-based models and, in particular, of the languages for complex values of Chapter 20. There have been several proposals of SQL extensions. In particular, as indicated in Section 21.3, O_2SQL [BCD89] retains the flavor of SQL but incorporates object orientation by adopting an elegant functional programming style. This approach has been advanced as a standard in [Cat94].

Functional approaches to databases have been considered rather early but attracted only modest interest in the past [BFN82, Shi81]. The functional approach has become more popular recently, both because of the success of object-oriented databases and due to recent results of complex objects and types emphasizing the functional models [BTBN92, BTBW92]. The use of a typed functional language similar to λ calculus as a formalism to express queries is adapted from [HKM93]. Characterizations of QPTIME in functional terms are from [HKM93, LM93]. The work in [AKRW92, HKM93, HKR93] provides interesting bridges between (object-oriented) databases and well-developed themes in computer science: applicative program schemas [Cou90, Gre75] and typed λ calculi [Chu41, Bar84, Bar63].

This chapter presented both imperative and functional perspectives on OODB methods. A different approach (based on rules and datalog with negation) has been used in [ALUW93] to provide semantics to a number of variations of schemas with methods. The connection between methods and rule-based languages is also considered in [DV91].

Views for OODBs are considered in [AB91, Day89, HY90, KKS92, KLW93]. The merging of OODBs is considered in [WHW90]. Incremental maintenance of materialized object-oriented views is considered in [Cha94]. The notion of object roles, or sharing objects between classes, is found in some semantic data models [AH87, HK87] and in recent research on OODBs [ABGO93, RS91]. A query language that incorporates access to an

OODB schema is presented in [KKS92]. Classification has been central to the field of knowledge representation in artificial intelligence, based on the central notion of taxonomic reasoning (e.g., see [BGL85, MB92], which stem from the KL-ONE framework of [BS85]); this approach has been carried to the context of OODBs in, for example, [BB92, BS93, BBMR89, DD89]. Deductive object-oriented database is the topic of a conference (namely, the *Intl. Conf. on Deductive and Object-Oriented Databases*). Properties of object migration between classes in a hierarchy are studied in [DS91, SZ89, Su92].

Exercises

Exercise 21.1 Construct an instance for the schema of Fig. 21.1 that corresponds to the **CINEMA** instance of Chapter 3.

Exercise 21.2 Suppose that the class *Actor_Director* were removed from the schema of Fig. 21.1. Verify that in this case there is no OID assignment for the schema such that there is an actor who is also a director.

Exercise 21.3 Design an OODB schema for a bibliography database with articles, book chapters, etc. Use inheritance where possible.

Exercise 21.4 Exhibit a class hierarchy that is not well formed.

Exercise 21.5 Add methods to the schema of Fig. 21.1 so that the resulting family of methods violates rules *unambiguous* and *covariance*.

Exercise 21.6 Show that testing whether $\mathbf{I} \equiv_{OID} \mathbf{J}$ is in NP and at least at hard as the graph isomorphism problem (i.e., testing whether two graphs are isomorphic).

Exercise 21.7 Give an algorithm for testing value equality. What is the data complexity of your algorithm?

Exercise 21.8 In this exercise, we consider various forms of equality. Value equality as discussed in the text is denoted $=_1$. Two objects o, o' are 2-value equal, denoted $o =_2 o'$, if replacing each object in $\nu(o)$ and $\nu(o')$ by its value yields values that are equal. The relations $=_i$ for each i are defined similarly. Show that for each i, $=_{i+1}$ refines $=_i$. Let n be a positive integer. Give a schema and an instance over this schema such that for each i in $[1, n]$, $=_i$ and $=_{i+1}$ are different.

Exercise 21.9 Design a database schema to represent information about persons, including males and females with names and husbands and wives. Exhibit a cyclic instance of the schema and an object o that has an infinite expansion. Describe the infinite tree representing the expansion of o.

★ **Exercise 21.10** Consider a database instance $\mathbf{I}$ over a schema $\mathbf{S}$. For each o in $\mathbf{I}$, let *expand*(o) be the (possibly infinite) tree obtained by replacing each object by its value recursively. Show that *expand*(o) is a *regular* tree (i.e., that it has a finite number of distinct subtrees). Derive from this observation an algorithm for testing deep equality of objects.

Exercise 21.11 In this exercise, we consider the schema $\mathbf{S}$ with a single class c that has type $\sigma(c) = [A : c, B : \textbf{string}]$. Exhibit an instance $\mathbf{I}$ over $\mathbf{S}$ and two distinct objects in $\mathbf{I}$ that have the same expansion. Exhibit two distinct instances over $\mathbf{S}$ with the same set of object expansions.

Exercise 21.12 Sketch an extension of the complex value algebra to provide an algebraic simulation of the calculus of Section 21.3. Give algebraic versions of the queries of that section.

♠ **Exercise 21.13** Recall the approach to creating OIDs by extending datalog to use Skolem function symbols. Consider the following programs:

$$
\begin{array}{ll}
T(f_1(x, y), x) \leftarrow S(x, y) & T(f_3(x, y), x) \leftarrow S(x, y) \\
T(f_2(x, y), x) \leftarrow S(x, y) & T(f_3(y, x), x) \leftarrow S(x, y) \\
T(f_1(x, y), y) \leftarrow S(x, y), S(y, x) & T(f_4(x, y), x) \leftarrow S(x, y), S(y, x) \\
\qquad\qquad P & \qquad\qquad Q
\end{array}
$$

(a) Two programs P_1, P_2 involving Skolem terms such as the foregoing are *exposed equivalent*, denoted $P_1 \sim_{exp} P_2$, if for each input instance **I** having no OIDs, $P_1(\mathbf{I}) = P_2(\mathbf{J})$. Show that $P \sim_{exp} Q$ does not hold.

(b) Following the ILOG languages [HY92], given an instance **J** possibly with Skolem terms, an *obscured* version of **J** is an instance $\mathbf{J}'$ obtained from **J** by replacing each distinct nonatomic Skolem term with a new OID, where multiple occurrences of a given Skolem term are replaced by the same OID. (Intuitively, this corresponds to hiding the history of how each OID was created.) Two programs P_1, P_2 are *obscured equivalent*, denoted $P_1 \sim_{obs} P_2$, if for each input instance **I** having no OIDs, if $\mathbf{J}_1$ is an obscured version of $P_1(\mathbf{I})$ and $\mathbf{J}_2$ is an obscured version of $P_2(\mathbf{I})$, then $\mathbf{J}_1 \equiv_{OID} \mathbf{J}_2$. Show that $P \sim_{obs} Q$.

(c) Let P and Q be two nonrecursive datalog programs, possibly with Skolem terms in rule heads. Prove that it is decidable whether $P \sim_{exp} Q$. *Hint:* Use the technique for testing containment of unions of conjunctive queries (see Chapter 4).

★ (d) A nonrecursive datalog program with Skolem terms in rule heads has *isolated OID invention* if in each target relation at most one column can include nonatomic Skolem terms (OID). Give a decision procedure for testing whether two such programs are obscured equivalent. (Decidability of obscured equivalence of arbitrary nonrecursive datalog programs with Skolem terms in rule heads remains open.)

♠ **Exercise 21.14** [VandBGAG92] Prove the "only if" part of Theorem 21.3.2. *Hint:* Associate traces to new object id's, similar to the proof of Theorem 18.2.5. The extension homomorphism is obtained via the natural extension to traces of automorphisms of the input.

Exercise 21.15 [HTY89]

(a) Define an operational semantics for the imperative model introduced in Section 21.4.

(b) Describe how a method in this model can simulate a *while*loop of arbitrary length. *Hint:* Use a class c with associated type **tuple**$(a : c, \ldots)$, and let $c' \prec c$. Construct the implementation of method m on c so that on input o if the loop is to continue, then it creates a new object o' in c, sets $o.a = o'$, and calls m on o'. To terminate the loop, create o' in c', and define m on c' appropriately.

(c) Show how the computation of a Turing machine can be simulated by this model.

Exercise 21.16 Prove Proposition 21.4.1. *Hint:* Use a reduction from the PCP problem, similar in spirit to the one used in the proof of Theorem 6.3.1. The effect of conditionals can be simulated by putting objects in different classes and using dynamic binding.

Exercise 21.17   Describe how monadic method schemas can be simulated in the imperative model.

Exercise 21.18   [AKRW92]

    (a) Verify that the grammar $G_\mathbf{S}$ described in the proof of Theorem 21.4.6 has the stated property.

    (b) How big is $G_\mathbf{S}$ in terms of $\mathbf{S}$?

    (c) Find a variation of $G_\mathbf{S}$ that has size polynomial in the size of $\mathbf{S}$. *Hint:* Break production rules having form (v) into several rules, thereby reducing the overall size of the grammar.

    (d) Complete the proof of the theorem.

Exercise 21.19   [AKRW92]

    ★ (a) Show that it is undecidable whether a polyadic method schema is type safe. *Hint:* You might use undecidability results for program schemas (see Bibliographic Notes), or you might use a reduction from the PCP.

    ★ (b) A schema is *recursion free* if there are no two methods m, m' such that m occurs in some code for m' and conversely. Show that type safety is decidable for recursion-free method schemas.

Exercise 21.20

    (a) Complete the formal definition of an imperative schema simulating a relational query.

    (b) Prove Theorem 21.4.2.

♠ **Exercise 21.21**

    (a) Suppose that the imperative model were extended to include types for classes that have one level of the set construct (so tuple of set of tuple of atomic of class types is permitted) and that the looping construct is extended to the sets occurring in these types. Assume that the **new** command is not permitted. Prove that the family of relational queries that this model can simulate is QPSPACE. *Hint:* Intuitively, because the looping operates object at a time, it permits the construction of a nondeterministic ordering of the database.

    (b) Suppose that n levels of set nesting are permitted in the types of classes. Show that this simulates $\text{QEXP}^{n-1}\text{SPACE}$.

Exercise 21.22

    (a) Describe how the form of method inheritance used for polyadic method schemas can be simulated using the originally presented form of method inheritance, which is based only on the class of the first argument.

    (b) Suppose that a base method m_R in an instance of a polyadic method schema is used to simulate an n-ary relation R. In a simulation of this situation by an instance of a conventional OODB schema, how many OIDs are present in the class on which m_R is simulated?

Exercise 21.23   Show how to encode *or*, *not*, and *equal* using method schemas.

Exercise 21.24   Show how to encode $pred_k^i$ and the join operation using method schemas.

♠ **Exercise 21.25**   [HKR93] Prove Theorem 21.4.8. *Hint:* Show first that method schemas can simulate relational algebra and then inflationary fixpoint. For the fixpoint, you might want to use $pred_k$. For the other direction, you might want to simulate method schemas over ordered databases by inflationary fixpoint.

22 Dynamic Aspects

Alice: *How come we've waited so long to talk about something so important?*
Riccardo: *Talking about change is hard.*
Sergio: *We're only starting to get a grip on it.*
Vittorio: *And still have a long way to go.*

At a fundamental level, updating a database is essentially imperative programming. However, the persistence, size, and long life cycle of a database lead to perspectives somewhat different from those found in programming languages. In this chapter, we briefly examine some of these differences and sketch some of the directions that have been explored in this area. Although it is central to databases, this area has received far less attention from the theoretical research community than other topics addressed in this book. The discussion in this chapter is intended primarily to give an overview of the important issues raised concerning the dynamic aspects of databases. It therefore emphasizes examples and intuitions much more than results and proofs.

This chapter begins by examining database update languages, including a simple language that corresponds to the update capabilities of practical languages such as SQL, and more complex ones expressed within a logic-based framework. Next optimization and semantic properties of transactions built from simple update commands are considered, including a discussion of the interaction of transactions and static integrity constraints.

The impact of updates in richer contexts is then considered. In connection with views, we examine the issue of how to propagate updates incrementally from base data to views and the much more challenging issue of propagating an update on a view back to the base data. Next updates for incomplete information databases are considered. This includes both the conditional tables studied in Chapter 19 and more general frameworks in which databases are represented using logical theories.

The emerging field of active databases is then briefly presented. These incorporate mechanisms for automatically responding to changes in the environment or the database, and they often use a rule-based paradigm of specifying the responses.

This chapter concludes with a brief discussion of temporal databases, which support the explicit representation of the time dimension and thus historical information.

A broad area related to dynamic aspects of databases (namely, concurrency control) will not be addressed. This important area concerns mechanisms to increase the throughput of a database system by interleaving multiple transactions while guaranteeing that the semantics of the individual transactions is not lost.

22.1   Update Languages

Before embarking on a brief excursion into update languages, we should answer the following natural question: Why are update languages necessary? Could we not use query languages to specify updates?

The difference between query and update languages is subtle but important. To specify an update, we could indeed define the new database as the answer to a query posed against the old database. However, this misses an essential characteristic of updates: Most often, they involve small changes to the current database. Query languages are not naturally suited to speak explicitly about *change*. In contrast, update languages use as building blocks simple statements expressing change, such as insertions, deletions, and modifications of tuples in the database.

In this section, we outline several formal update languages and point to some theoretical issues that arise in this context.

Insert-Delete-Modify Transactions

We begin with a simple procedural language to specify insertions, deletions, and modifications. Most commercial relational systems provide at least these update capabilities.

To simplify the presentation, we suppose that the database consists of a single relation schema R. Everything can be extended to the multirelational case. An *insertion* is an expression $ins(t)$, where t is a tuple over $att(R)$. This inserts the tuple t into R. [We assume set-based semantics, under which $ins(t)$ has no effect if t is already present in R.] A deletion removes from R all tuples satisfying some stated set of conditions. More precisely, a *condition* is an (in)equality of the form $A = c$ or $A \neq c$, where $A \in att(R)$ and c is a constant. A *deletion* is an expression $del(C)$, where C is a finite set of conditions. This removes from R all tuples satisfying each condition in C. Finally, a *modification* is an expression $mod(C \rightarrow C')$, where C, C' are sets of conditions, with C' containing only equalities $A = c$. This selects all tuples in R satisfying C and then, for each such tuple and each $A = c$ in C', sets the value of A to c. An *update* over R is an insertion, deletion, or modification over R. An IDM transaction (for insert, delete, modify) over R is a finite sequence of updates over R. This is illustrated next.

EXAMPLE 22.1.1   Consider the relation schema *Employee* with attributes *N (Name), D (Department), R (Rank)*. The following IDM transaction fires the manager of the parts department, transfers the manager of the sales department to the parts department, and hires Moe as the new manager for the sales department:

$$del(\{D = parts, R = manager\});$$
$$mod(\{D = sales, R = manager\} \rightarrow \{D = parts\});$$
$$ins(Moe, sales, manager)$$

The same update can be expressed in SQL as follows:

delete from Employee

        where D = "parts" **and** R = "manager";
update Employee
        set D = "parts"
        where D = "sales" **and** R = "manager";
   insert **into** Employee **values** ⟨ "Moe","sales","manager"⟩

As for queries, a question of central interest to update languages is optimization. To see how IDM transactions can be optimized, it is useful to understand when two such transactions are equivalent. It turns out that equivalence of IDM transactions has a sound and complete axiomatization. Following are some simple axioms:

$$mod(C \to C'); del(C') \quad \equiv del(C); del(C')$$

$$ins(t); mod(C \to C') \quad \equiv mod(C \to C'); ins(t')$$

$$\text{where } t \text{ satisfies } C \text{ and } \{t'\} = mod(C \to C')(\{t\})$$

and a slightly more complex one:

$$del(C_3); mod(C_1 \to C_3); mod(C_2 \to C_1); mod(C_3 \to C_2)$$
$$\equiv del(C_3); mod(C_2 \to C_3); mod(C_1 \to C_2); mod(C_3 \to C_1),$$

where C_1, C_2, C_3 are mutually exclusive sets of conditions.

We can define criteria for the optimization of IDM transactions along two main lines:

Syntactic: We can take into account the length of the transaction as well as the kind of operations involved (for example, it may be reasonable to assume that insertions are simpler than modifications).

Semantic: This can be based on the number of tuple operations actually performed when the transaction is applied.

Various definitions are possible based on the preceeding criteria. It can be shown that there exists a polynomial-time algorithm that optimizes IDM transactions, with respect to a reasonable definition based on syntactic and semantic criteria. The syntactic criteria involve the number of insertions, deletions, and modifications. The semantic criteria are based on the number of tuples touched at runtime by the transaction. We omit the details here.

EXAMPLE 22.1.2   Consider the IDM transaction over a relational schema R of sort AB:

$$mod(\{A \neq 0, B = 1\} \to \{B = 2\}); ins(0, 1); ins(3, 2);$$
$$mod(\{A = 0, B = 1\} \to \{B = 2\}); mod(\{A \neq 0, B = 0\} \to \{B = 1\});$$
$$mod(\{A = 0, B = 0\} \to \{B = 1\}); mod(\{A \neq 0, B = 2\} \to \{B = 0\});$$
$$mod(\{A = 0, B = 2\} \to \{B = 0\}); del(\{A \neq 0, B = 0\}).$$

Assuming that insertions are less expensive than deletions, which are less expensive than modifications, an optimal IDM transaction equivalent to the foregoing is

$$del(\{A \neq 0, B = 1\}); \; del(\{A \neq 0, B = 2\});$$
$$mod(\{A = 0, B = 1\} \rightarrow \{B = 2\});$$
$$mod(\{B = 0\} \rightarrow \{B = 1\});$$
$$mod(\{A = 0, B = 2\} \rightarrow \{B = 0\});$$
$$ins(0, 0).$$

Thus the six modifications, one deletion, and two insertions of the original transaction were replaced by three modifications, two deletions, and one insertion.

Another approach to optimization is to turn some of the axioms of equivalence into simplification rules, as in

$$mod(C \rightarrow C'); \; del(C') \Rightarrow del(C); \; del(C').$$

It can be shown that such a set of simplification rules can be used to optimize a restricted set of IDM transactions that satisfy a syntactic acyclicity condition. For the other transactions, applications of the simplification rules yield a simpler, but not necessarily optimal, transaction. The simplification rules have the advantage that they are local and can be easily applied even online, whereas the complete optimization algorithm is global and has to know the entire transaction in advance.

Rule-Based Update Languages

The IDM transactions provide a simple update language of limited power. This can be extended in many ways. One possibility is to build another procedural language based on tuple insertions, deletions, and modifications, which includes relation variables and an iterative construct. Another, which we illustrate next, is to use a rule-based approach. For example, consider the language datalog$^{\neg\neg}$ described in Chapter 17, with its fixpoint semantics. Recall that rules allow for both positive and negative atoms in heads of rules; consistently with the fixpoint semantics, the positive atoms can be viewed as insertions of facts and the negative atoms as deletions of facts. For example, the following program removes all cycles of length one or two from the graph G:

$$\neg G(x, y) \leftarrow G(x, y), G(y, x).$$

In the usual fixpoint semantics, rules are fired in parallel with all possible instantiations for the variables. This yields a deterministic semantics. Some practical rule-based update languages take an alternative approach, which yields a nondeterministic semantics: The rules are fired one instantiation at a time. With this semantics, the preceeding program provides *some* orientation of the graph G. Note that generally there is no way to obtain an orientation of a graph deterministically, because a nondeterministic choice of edges to be removed may be needed.

A deterministic language expressing *all* updates can be obtained by extending datalog$^{\neg\neg}$ with the ability to invent new values, in the spirit of the language *while*$_{new}$

in Chapter 18. This can be done in the manner described in Exercise 18.22. The same language with nondeterministic semantics can be shown to express all nondeterministic updates.

The aforementioned languages yield a bottom-up evaluation procedure. The body of the rule is first checked, and then the actions in the head are executed. Another possibility is to adopt a top-down approach, in the spirit of the *assert* in Prolog. Here the actions to be taken are specified in rule bodies. A good example of this approach is provided by *Dynamic Logic Programming* (DLP). Interestingly, this language allows us to test hypothetical conditions of the form "Would φ hold if t was inserted?" This, and the connection of DLP with Prolog, is illustrated next.

EXAMPLE 22.1.3 Consider a database schema with relations *ES* of sort *Emp,Sal* (employees and their salaries), *ED* of sort *Emp,Dep* (employees and their departments), and *DA* of sort *Dep,Avg* (average salary in each department).

Suppose that an update is intended to hire John in the toys department with a salary of $200K$, under the condition that the average salary of the department stays below $50K$. In the language DLP, this update is expressed by

$$\langle hire(emp1, sal1, dep1) \rangle \leftarrow$$
$$\langle +ES(emp1, sal1) \rangle (\langle +ED(emp1, dep1) \rangle (DA(dep1, avg1) \ \& \ avg1 < 50k)).$$

(Other rules are, of course, needed to define *DA*.) A call *hire*(John,200K,Toys) hires John in the toys department only if, after hiring him, the average salary of the department remains below $50K$. The $+$ symbol indicates an insertion. Here the conditions in parentheses should hold after the two insertions have been performed; if not, then the update is not realized. Testing a condition under the assumption of an update is a form of hypothetical reasoning.

It is interesting to contrast the semantics of DLP with that of Prolog. Consider the following Prolog program:

$$: - \quad assert(ES(john, 200)), assert(ED(john, toys)),$$
$$DA(toys, Avg1), Avg1 < 50.$$

In this program, the insertions into *ES* and *ED* will be performed even if the conditions are not satisfied afterward. (The reader familiar with Prolog is encouraged to write a program that has the desired semantics.)

A similar top-down approach to updates is adopted in Logical Data Language (LDL).

Updates concern not only instances of a fixed schema. Sometimes the schema itself needs to be changed (e.g., by adding an attribute). Some practical update languages include constructs for schema change. The main problem to be resolved is how the existing data can be fit to the new schema.

In deductive databases, some relations are defined using rules. Occasionally these definitions may have to be changed, leading to updates of the "rule base." There are languages that can be used to specify such updates.

22.2   Transactional Schemas

Typically, database systems restrict the kinds of updates that users can perform. There are three main ways of doing this:

   (a) Specify constraints (say, fd's) that the database must satisfy and reject any update that leads to a violation of the constraints.

   (b) Restrict the updates themselves by only allowing the use of a set of prespecified, valid updates.

   (c) Permit users to request essentially arbitrary updates, but provide an automatic mechanism for detecting and repairing constraint violations.

Object-oriented databases essentially embrace option (b); updates are performed only by *methods* specified at the schema level, and it is assumed that these will not violate the constraints (see Chapter 21). Both options (a) and (b) are present in the relational model. Several commercial systems can recognize and abort on violation of simple constraints (typically key and simple inclusion dependencies). However, maintenance of more complex constraints is left to the application software. Option (c) is supported by the emerging field of active databases, which is discussed in the following section.

We now briefly explore some issues related to approach (b) in connection with the relational model. To illustrate the issues, we use simple procedures based on IDM transactions. The procedures we use are *parameterized IDM transactions*, obtained by allowing variables in addition to constants in conditions of IDM transactions. The variables are used as parameters. A database schema **R** together with a finite set of parameterized IDM transactions over **R** is called an *IDM transactional schema*.

EXAMPLE 22.2.1   Consider a database schema **R** with two relations, *TA* (Teaching Assistant) of sort *Name,Course*, and *PHD* (Ph.D. student) of sort *Name, Address*. The following IDM-parameterized transactions allow the hiring and firing of TAs (subscripts indicate the relation to which each update applies):

$$hire(x, y, z) = del_{TA}(Name = x); ins_{TA}(x, y)$$
$$del_{PHD}(Name = x); ins_{PHD}(x, z)$$
$$fire(x) \qquad = del_{TA}(Name = x)$$

The pair $\mathbf{T} = \langle \mathbf{R}, \{hire, fire\} \rangle$ is an IDM transactional schema. Note in this simple example that once a name n is incorporated into the *PHD* relation, it can never be removed.

Clearly, we could similarly define transactional schemas in conjunction with any update language.

Suppose **T** is an IDM transactional schema. To apply the parameterized transactions, values must be supplied to the variables. A transaction obtained by replacing the variables of a parameterized transaction t in **T** by constants is a *call* to t. The only updates allowed by an IDM transactional schema are performed by calls to its parameterized transactions.

The set of instances that can be generated by such calls (starting from the empty instance) is denoted $Gen(\mathbf{T})$.

Transactional schemas offer an approach for constraint enforcement, essentially by preventing updates that violate them. So it is important to understand to what extent they can do so. First we need to clarify the issue. Suppose $\mathbf{T}$ is an IDM transactional schema and Σ is a set of constraints over a database schema $\mathbf{R}$; $Sat(\Sigma)$ denotes all instances over $\mathbf{R}$ satisfying Σ. If $\mathbf{T}$ is to replace Σ, we would expect the following properties to hold:

- *soundness* of $\mathbf{T}$ with respect to Σ: $Gen(\mathbf{T}) \subseteq Sat(\Sigma)$; and
- *completeness* of $\mathbf{T}$ with respect to Σ: $Gen(\mathbf{T}) \supseteq Sat(\Sigma)$.

Thus $\mathbf{T}$ is sound and complete with respect to Σ iff it generates precisely the instances satisfying Σ.

EXAMPLE 22.2.2 Consider again the IDM transactional schema $\mathbf{T}$ in Example 22.2.1. Let Σ be the following constraints:

$$
\begin{aligned}
TA &: Name &&\rightarrow Course \\
PHD &: Name \rightarrow Address \\
TA&[Name] &&\subseteq PHD[Name]
\end{aligned}
$$

It is easily seen that $\mathbf{T}$ in Example 22.2.1 is sound and complete with respect to Σ. That is, $Gen(\mathbf{T}) = Sat(\Sigma)$ (Exercise 22.7).

This example also highlights a limitation in the notion of completeness: It can be seen that there are pairs $\mathbf{I}$ and $\mathbf{J}$ of instances in $Sat(\Sigma)$ where $\mathbf{I}$ cannot be transformed into $\mathbf{J}$ using $\mathbf{T}$. In other words, there are valid database states $\mathbf{I}$ and $\mathbf{J}$ such that when in state $\mathbf{I}$, $\mathbf{J}$ is never reachable. Such forbidden transitions are also a means of enriching the model, because we can view them as temporal constraints on the database evolution. We will return to temporal constraints later in this chapter.

Of course, the ability of transaction schemas to replace constraints depends on the update language used. For IDM transactional schemas, we can show the following (Exercise 22.8):

THEOREM 22.2.3 For each database schema $\mathbf{R}$ and set Σ of fd's and acyclic inclusion dependencies over $\mathbf{R}$, there exists an IDM transactional schema $\mathbf{T}$ that is sound and complete with respect to Σ.

Thus IDM transactional schemas are capable of replacing a significant set of constraints. The kind of difficulty that arises with more general constraints is illustrated next.

EXAMPLE 22.2.4 Consider a relation R of sort ABC and the following set Σ of constraints:

- the embedded join dependency

$$\forall xyzx'y'z'(R(xyz) \wedge R(x'y'z') \Rightarrow \exists z'' R(xy'z')),$$

- the functional dependency AB → C,
- the inclusion dependency R[A] ⊆ R[C],
- the inclusion dependency R[B] ⊆ R[A],
- the inclusion dependency R[A] ⊆ R[B].

It is easy to check that, for each relation satisfying the constraints, the number of constants in the relation is a perfect square (n^2, $n \geq 0$). Thus there are unbounded gaps between instances in $Sat(\Sigma)$. There is no IDM transactional schema **T** such that $Sat(\Sigma) = Gen(\textbf{T})$, because the gaps cannot be crossed using calls to parameterized transactions with a bounded number of parameters. Moreover, this problem is not specific to IDM transactional schemas; it arises with any language in which procedures can only introduce a bounded number of new constants into the database at each call.

Another natural question relating updates and constraints is, What about *checking* soundness and/or completeness of IDM transactional schemas with respect to given constraints? Even in the case of IDM transactional schemas, such questions are generally undecidable. There is one important exception: Soundness of IDM transactional schemas with respect to fd's is decidable. These questions are explored in Exercise 22.12.

22.3 Updating Views and Deductive Databases

We now turn to the impact of updates on views. Views are an important aspect of databases. The interplay between views and updates is intricate. We can mention in particular two important issues. One is the *view maintenance* problem: A view has been materialized and the problem is to maintain it incrementally when the database is updated. An important variation of this is in the context of deductive databases when the view consists of idb relations. The other is known as the *view update* problem: Given a view and an update against a view, the problem is to translate the update into a corresponding update against the base data. This section considers these two issues in turn.

View Maintenance

Suppose that a base schema **B** and view schema **V** are given along with a (total) view mapping $f : Inst(\textbf{B}) \rightarrow Inst(\textbf{V})$. Suppose further that a materialized view is to be maintained [i.e., whenever the base database holds an instance $\textbf{I}_B$, then the view schema should be holding $f(\textbf{I}_B)$].

For this discussion, an *update* for a schema **R** is considered to be a mapping from $Inst(\textbf{R})$ to $Inst(\textbf{R})$. If constraints are present, it is assumed that an update cannot map to instances violating the constraints. The updates considered here might be based on IDM transactions or might be more general. We shall often speak of "the" update μ that maps

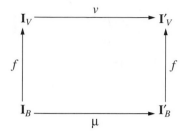

Figure 22.1: Relationship of views and updates

instance **I** to instance **I′**, and by this we shall mean the set of insertions and deletions that need to be made to **I** to obtain **I′**.

Suppose that the base database **B** is holding $\mathbf{I}_B$ and that update μ maps this to $\mathbf{I}'_B$ (see Fig. 22.1). A naive way to keep the view up to date is to simply compute $f(\mathbf{I}'_B)$. However, $\mathbf{I}'_B$ is typically large relative to the difference between $\mathbf{I}_V$ and $\mathbf{I}'_V$. It is thus natural to search for more efficient ways to find the update v that maps $\mathbf{I}_V$ to $\mathbf{I}'_V = f(\mu(\mathbf{I}_B))$. This is the *view maintenance problem*.

There are generally two main components to solutions of the view maintenance problem. The first involves developing algorithms to test whether an update to the base data can affect the view. Given such an algorithm, an update is said to be *irrelevant* if the algorithm certifies that the update cannot affect the view, and it is said to be *relevant* otherwise.

EXAMPLE 22.3.1 Let the base database schema be $\mathbf{B} = (R[AB], S[BC])$, and consider the following views:

$$V_1 = (R \bowtie \sigma_{C>50}S)$$
$$V_2 = \pi_A R$$
$$V_3 = R \bowtie S$$
$$V_4 = \pi_{AC}(R \bowtie S).$$

Inserting $\langle b, 20 \rangle$ into S cannot affect views V_1 or V_2. On the other hand, whether or not this insertion affects V_3 or V_4 depends on the data already present in the database.

Various algorithms have been developed for determining relevance with varying degrees of precision. A useful technique involves maintaining auxiliary information, as illustrated next.

EXAMPLE 22.3.2 Recall view V_2 of Example 22.3.1, and suppose that R currently holds

R	A	B
	a	20
	a	30
	a'	80

Deleting $\langle a, 20 \rangle$ has no impact on the view, whereas deleting $\langle a', 80 \rangle$ has the effect of deleting $\langle a' \rangle$ from the view. One way to monitor this is to maintain a count on the number of distinct ways that a value can arise; if this count ever reaches 0, then the value should be deleted from the view.

The other main component of solutions to the view maintenance problem concerns the development of *incremental evaluation algorithms*. This is closely related to the seminaive algorithm for evaluating datalog programs (see Chapter 13).

EXAMPLE 22.3.3   Recall view V_3 from Example 22.3.1, and let Δ_R^+ and Δ_S^+ denote sets of tuples that are to be inserted into R and S, respectively. It is easily verified that

$$(R \cup \Delta_R^+) \bowtie (S \cup \Delta_S^+) = (R \bowtie S) \cup (R \bowtie \Delta_S^+) \cup (\Delta_R^+ \bowtie S) \cup (\Delta_R^+ \bowtie \Delta_S^+).$$

Thus the new join can be found by performing three (typically smaller) joins followed by some unions.

It is relatively straightforward to develop incremental evaluation expressions, such as in the preceeding example, for all of the relational algebra operators (see Exercise 22.13). In some cases, these expressions can be refined by using information about constraints, such as key and functional dependencies, on the base data.

Incremental Update of Deductive Views

The view maintenance problem has also been studied in connection with views constructed with (stratified) datalog$^{(\neg)}$. In general, the techniques used are analogous to those discussed earlier but are generalized to incorporate recursion. In the context of stratified datalog$^{\neg}$, various heuristics have been adapted from the field of belief revision for incrementally maintaining supports (i.e., auxiliary information that holds the justifications for the presence of a fact in the materialized output of the program).

An interesting research direction that has recently emerged focuses on the ability of first-order queries to express incremental updates on views defined using datalog. The framework for these problems is as follows. The base schema **B** and view schema **V** are as before, except that **V** contains only one relation and the view f is defined in terms of a datalog program P. A basic question is, Given P, is there a first-order query φ such that $\varphi(\mathbf{I}_B, \mathbf{I}_V, +R(t)) = P(\mathbf{I}_B \cup \{R(t)\})$ for each choice of $\mathbf{I}_B, \mathbf{I}_V = P(\mathbf{I}_B)$ and insertion $+R(t)$ where $R \in \mathbf{B}$? If this holds, then P is said to be *first-order incrementally definable* (FOID) (without auxiliary relations).

EXAMPLE 22.3.4 Consider a binary relation $G[AB]$ and the usual datalog program P that computes the transitive closure of G in $T[AB]$. Suppose that I is an instance of G, and J is $P(I)$. Suppose that tuple $\langle a, b \rangle$ is inserted into I. Then a tuple $\langle a', b' \rangle$ will be inserted into J iff one of the following occurs:

(a) $a' = a$ and $b = b'$;

(b) $a' = a$ and $\langle b, b' \rangle \in J$;

(c) $\langle a', a \rangle \in J$ and $b = b'$; or

(d) $\langle a', a \rangle \in J$ and $\langle b, b' \rangle \in J$.

The preceeding conditions can clearly be specified by a first-order query. It easily follows that P is FOID (see Exercise 22.21).

Several variations of FOIDs have been studied. These include FOIDs with auxiliary relations (i.e., that permit the maintenance of derived relations not in the original datalog program) and FOIDs that support incremental updates for sets of insertions and/or deletions. FOIDs have been found for a number of restricted classes of datalog programs. However, it remains open whether there is a datalog program that is not FOID with auxiliary relations.

Basic Issues in View Update

The view update problem is essentially the inverse of the view maintenance problem. Referring again to Fig. 22.1, the problem now is, Given $\mathbf{I}_B$, $\mathbf{I}_V$, and update v on $\mathbf{I}_V$, find an update μ so that the diagram commutes.

The first obvious problem here is the potential for ambiguity.

EXAMPLE 22.3.5 Recall the view V_2 of Example 22.3.1. Suppose that the base value of R is $\{\langle a, b \rangle\}$ (and the base value of S is $\emptyset$). Thus the view holds $\{\langle a \rangle\}$. Now consider an update v to the view that inserts $\langle a' \rangle$. Some possible choices for μ include

(a) Insert $\langle a', b \rangle$ into R.

(b) Insert $\langle a', b' \rangle$ into R for some $b' \in \mathbf{dom}$.

(c) Insert $\{\langle a', b' \rangle \mid b' \in X\}$ into R, where X is a finite subset of $\mathbf{dom}$.

(d) Insert $\langle a', b' \rangle$ into R for some $b' \in \mathbf{dom}$, and replace $\langle a, b \rangle$ by $\langle a, b' \rangle$.

Possibility (d) seems undesirable, because it affects a tuple in a base relation that is, intuitively speaking, independent of the view update. Possibilities (a) and (b) seem more appealing than (c), but (c) cannot be ruled out. In any case, it is clear that there are a large number of updates μ that correspond to v.

The fundamental problem, then, is how to select one update μ to the base data given that many possibilities may exist. One approach to resolving the ambiguity involves examining the intended semantics of the database and the view.

EXAMPLE 22.3.6 Consider a schema *Employee*[*Name, Department, Team_position*], which records an employee's department and the position he or she plays in the corporate baseball league. It is assumed that *Name* is a key. The value "no" indicates that the employee does not play in the league. It is assumed that *Name* is a key. Consider the views defined by

$$Sales = \sigma_{Department="Sales"}(Employee)$$

$$Baseball = \pi_{Employee, Team\_position}(\sigma_{Team\_position \neq "no"}(Employee))$$

Typically, if tuple ⟨"Joe", "Sales", "shortstop"⟩ is deleted from the *Sales* view, then this tuple should also be deleted from the underlying *Employee* relation. In contrast, if tuple ⟨"Joe", "shortstop"⟩ is deleted from the *Baseball* view, it is typically most natural to replace the underlying tuple ⟨"Joe", d, "shortstop"⟩ in *Employee* by ⟨"Joe", d, "no"⟩ (i.e., to remove Joe from the baseball league rather than forcing him out of the company).

As just illustrated, the correct translation of a view update can easily depend on the semantics associated with the view as well as the syntactic definition. Research in this area has developed notions of update translations that perform a *minimal* change to the underlying database. Algorithms that generate families of acceptable translations of views have been developed, so that the database administrator may choose at view definition time the most appropriate one.

Another issue in view update is that a requested update may not be permitted on the view, essentially because of constraints implicit to the view definition and algorithm for choosing translations of updates.

EXAMPLE 22.3.7 Recall the view V_4 of Example 22.3.1, and suppose that the base data is

R	A	B
	a	20
	a'	20

S	B	C
	20	c
	20	c'

In this case the view contains $\{\langle a, c \rangle, \langle a, c' \rangle, \langle a', c \rangle, \langle a', c' \rangle\}$.

Suppose that the user requests that $\langle a, c \rangle$ be deleted. Typically, this deletion is mapped into one or more deletions against the base data. However, deleting $R(a, 20)$ results in a side-effect (namely, the deletion of $\langle a, c' \rangle$ from the view). Deletion of $S(20, c)$ also yields a side-effect.

Formal issues surrounding such side-effects of view updates are largely unexplored.

Complements of Views

We now turn to a more abstract formulation of the view update problem. Although it is relatively narrow, it provides an interesting perspective.

In this framework, a *view* over a base schema **B** is defined to be a (total) function f from *Inst*(**B**) into some set. In practice this set is typically *Inst*(**V**) for some view schema **V**; however, this is not required for this development. [The proof of Theorem 22.3.10, which presents a completeness result, uses a view whose range is not *Inst*(**V**) for any schema **V**.] A binary relation $\leq$ on views is defined so that $f \leq g$ if for all base instances **I** and **I'**, $g(\mathbf{I}) = g(\mathbf{I}')$ implies $f(\mathbf{I}) = f(\mathbf{I}')$. Intuitively, $f \leq g$ if g can distinguish more instances that f. For view f, let $\equiv_f$ be the equivalence relation on *Inst*(**B**) defined by $\mathbf{I} \equiv_f \mathbf{I}'$ iff $f(\mathbf{I}) = f(\mathbf{I}')$. It is clear that $f \leq g$ iff $\equiv_g$ is a refinement of $\equiv_f$ and thus $\leq$ can be viewed as a partial order on the equivalence relations over *Inst*(**B**).

Two views f, g are *equivalent*, denoted $f \equiv g$, if $f \leq g$ and $g \leq f$. This is an equivalence relation on views. In the following, the focus is primarily on the equivalence classes under $\equiv$. Let $\top$ denote the view that is simply the identity, and let $\bot$ denote a view that maps every base instance to $\emptyset$. It is clear that (the equivalence classes represented by) $\top$ and $\bot$ are the maximal and minimal elements of the partial order $\leq$. We use cross-product as a binary operator to create views: The product of views f and g is defined so that $(f \times g)(\mathbf{I}) = (f(\mathbf{I}), g(\mathbf{I}))$. View g is a *complement* of view f if $f \times g \equiv \top$. Intuitively, this means that the base relations can be completely identified if both f and g are available. Clearly, each view f has a trivial complement: $\top$.

EXAMPLE 22.3.8 (a) Let $\mathbf{B} = \{R[ABC]\}$ along with the fd $R : A \to B$, and consider the view $f = \pi_{AB} R$. Let $g = \pi_{AC} R$. It follows from Proposition 8.2.2 that g is a complement of f.

(b) Let $\mathbf{B} = \{R[AB]\}$ and $f = \pi_A R$. As mentioned earlier, $\top$ is a complement of f. It turns out that there are other complements of f, but they cannot be expressed using the relational algebra (see Exercise 22.25).

(c) Let $\mathbf{B} = \{Employee(Name, Salary, Bonus, Total\_pay)\}$, with the constraints that *Name* is a key and that for each tuple $\langle n, s, b, t \rangle$ in *Employee* we have $s + b = t$. Consider the view $f = \pi_{Name,Salary}(Employee)$. Consider the views

$$g_1 = \pi_{Name,Bonus}(Employee)$$
$$g_2 = \pi_{Name,Total\_pay}(Employee).$$

Both g_1 and g_2 are complements of f.

Thus each view has at least one complement (namely, $\top$) and may have more than one minimal complement.

In some cases, complements can be used to resolve ambiguity in the view update problem in the following way. Suppose that view f has complement g, and suppose that $\mathbf{I}_V = f(\mathbf{I}_B)$ and update v on $\mathbf{I}_V$ are given. An update μ is a g-*translation* of v if $f(\mu(\mathbf{I}_B)) = v(f(\mathbf{I}_B))$ and $g(\mu(\mathbf{I}_B)) = g(\mathbf{I}_B)$ (see Fig. 22.2). Intuitively, a g-translation

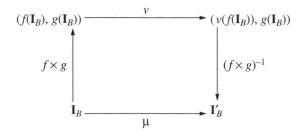

Figure 22.2:   Properties of a g-translation μ of view update ν on view f

accomplishes the update but leaves $g(\mathbf{I}_B)$ fixed. By the properties of complements, for an update ν there is at most one g-translation of ν.

EXAMPLE 22.3.9   (a) Recall the base schema $\{R[ABC]\}$, view f, and complement g of Example 22.3.8(a). Suppose that $\langle a, b \rangle$ is in the view, and consider the update ν on the view that modifies $\langle a, b \rangle$ to $\langle a, b' \rangle$. The update μ defined to modify all tuples $\langle a, b, c \rangle$ of R into $\langle a, b', c \rangle$ is a g-translation of ν. On the other hand, given an insertion or deletion ν to the view, there is no g-translation of ν.

(b) Recall the base schema, view f, and complementary views g_1 and g_2 of Example 22.3.8(c). Suppose that $\langle Joe, 200, 50, 250 \rangle$ is in *Employee*. Consider the update ν that replaces $\langle Joe, 200 \rangle$ by $\langle Joe, 210 \rangle$ in the view. Consider the updates

$$\mu_1 = \text{replace } \langle Joe, 200, 50, 250 \rangle \text{ by } \langle Joe, 210, 50, 260 \rangle$$
$$\mu_2 = \text{replace } \langle Joe, 200, 50, 250 \rangle \text{ by } \langle Joe, 210, 40, 250 \rangle.$$

Then μ_1 is the g_1-translation of ν, and μ_2 is the g_2-translation of ν.

Finally, we state a result showing that a restricted class of view updates can be translated into base updates using complementary views. To this end, we focus on *updates* of a schema $\mathbf{R}$ that are total functions from *Inst*$(\mathbf{R})$ to *Inst*$(\mathbf{R})$. A family U of updates on $\mathbf{R}$ is said to be *complete* if

(a) it is closed under composition (i.e., if μ and μ' are in U, then so is $\mu \circ \mu'$);

(b) it is closed under inverse in the following sense: $\forall \mathbf{I} \in inst(\mathbf{R}) \ \forall \mu \in U \ \exists \mu' \in U$ such that $\mu'(\mu(\mathbf{I})) = \mathbf{I}$.

Intuitively, condition (b) says that a user can always undo an update just made. It is certainly natural to focus on complete sets of updates.

Let base schema $\mathbf{B}$ and view f be given, and let U_f be a family of updates on the view. Let U_B denote the family of all updates on the base schema. A *translator* for U_f is a mapping $t : U_f \to U_B$ such that for each base instance $\mathbf{I}_B$ and update $\nu \in U_f$, $f(t(\nu)(\mathbf{I}_B)) = \nu(f(\mathbf{I}_B))$. Clearly, solving the view update problem consists of coming up with a translator.

If g is a complement for f, then a translator t is a *g-translator* if $t(v)$ is a g-translation of v for each $v \in U_f$.

We can now state the following (see Exercise 22.26):

THEOREM 22.3.10 Let base schema **B** and view f be given, and let U_f be a complete set of updates on the view. Suppose that t is a translator for U_f. Then there is a complement g of f such that t is a g-translator for U_f.

Thus to find a translator for a complete set of view updates, it is sufficient to specify an appropriate complementary view g and take the corresponding g-translator. The theorem says that one can find such g if a translator exists at all.

The preceeding framework provides an abstract, elegant perspective on the view update problem. Forming bridges to the more concrete frameworks in which views are defined by specific languages (e.g., relational algebra) remains largely unexplored.

22.4 Updating Incomplete Information

In a sense, an update to a view is an incompletely specified update whose completion must be determined or selected. In this section, we consider more general settings for studying updates and incomplete information.

First we return to the conditional tables of Chapter 19 and show a system for updating such databases. We then introduce formulations of incomplete information that use theories (i.e., sets of propositional or first-order sentences) to represent the (partial) knowledge about the world. Among other benefits, this approach offers an interesting alternative to resolving the view update problem. This section concludes by comparing these approaches to belief revision.

Updating Conditional Tables

The problems posed by updating a c-table are similar to those raised by queries. A representation T specifies a set of possible worlds $rep(T)$. Given an update u, the possible outcomes of the update are

$$u(rep(T)) = \{u(\mathbf{I}) \mid \mathbf{I} \in rep(T)\}.$$

As for queries, it is desirable to represent the result in the same representation system. If the representation system is always capable of representing the answer to any update in a language $\mathcal{L}$, it is a *strong representation system with respect to* $\mathcal{L}$.

Let us consider c-tables and simple insertions, deletions, and modifications, as in the language of IDM transactions. We know from Chapter 19 that c-tables form a strong representation system for relational algebra; and it is easily seen that IDM transactions can be expressed in the algebra (see Exercise 22.3). It follows that c-tables are a strong representation system for IDM transactions. In other words, for each c-table T and IDM transaction t, there exists a c-table $\bar{t}(T)$ such that $rep(\bar{t}(T)) = t(rep(T))$.

EXAMPLE 22.4.1   Consider the c-table in Example 19.3.1. Insertions $ins(t)$ are straight-forward: t is simply inserted in the table. Consider the deletion $d = del(\{Student = Sally, Course = Physics\})$. The c-table $\bar{t}(T)$ representing the result of the deletion is

Student	Course	
	$(x \neq Math) \wedge (x \neq CS)$	
Sally	Math	$(z = 0)$
Sally	CS	$(z \neq 0)$
Sally	x	$(x \neq Physics)$
Alice	Biology	$(z = 0)$
Alice	Math	$(x = Physics) \wedge (t = 0)$
Alice	Physics	$(x = Physics) \wedge (t \neq 0)$

Consider again the original c-table T in Example 19.3.1 and the modification

$$m = mod(\{Student = Sally, Course = Music\} \to \{Course = Physics\}).$$

The c-table $\bar{m}(T)$ representing the result of the modification is

Student	Course	
	$(x \neq Math) \wedge (x \neq CS)$	
Sally	Math	$(z = 0)$
Sally	CS	$(z \neq 0)$
Sally	Physics	$(x = Music)$
Sally	x	$(x \neq Music)$
Alice	Biology	$(z = 0)$
Alice	Math	$(x = Physics) \wedge (t = 0)$
Alice	Physics	$(x = Physics) \wedge (t \neq 0)$

In the context of incomplete information, it is natural to consider updates that themselves have partial information. For c-tables, it seems appropriate to define updates with the same kind of incomplete information, using tuples with variables subject to conditions. We can define extensions of insertions, deletions, and modifications in this manner. It can be shown that c-tables remain a strong representation system for such updates.

Representing Databases Using Logical Theories

Conditional tables provide a stylized, restricted framework for representing incomplete information and are closed under a certain class of updates. We now turn to more general frameworks for representing and updating incomplete information. These are based on representing databases as logical theories.

Given a logical theory **T** (i.e., set of sentences), the set of *models* of **T** is denoted by $Mod(\mathbf{T})$. In our context, each model corresponds to a different possible instance. If $|Mod(\mathbf{T})| > 1$, then $\mathbf{T}$ can be viewed as representing incomplete information.

In general, these approaches use the *open world assumption* (OWA). Recall from Chapter 2 that under the closed world assumption (CWA), a fact is viewed as false unless it can be proved from explicitly stated facts or sentences. In contrast, under the OWA if a fact is not implied or contradicted by the underlying theory, then the fact may be true or false. As a simple example, consider the theory $\mathbf{T} = \{p\}$ over a language with two propositional constants p and q. Under the CWA, there is only one model of $\mathbf{T}$ (namely, $\{p\}$), but under the OWA, there are two models (namely, $\{p\}$ and $\{p, q\}$).

Model-Based Approaches to Updating Theories

One natural approach to updating a logical theory $\mathbf{T}$ is *model based*; it focuses on how proposed updates affect the elements of $Mod(\mathbf{T})$. Given an update u and instance $\mathbf{I}$, let $u(\mathbf{I})$ denote the set of possible instances that could result from applying u to $\mathbf{I}$. We use a set for the result to accommodate the case in which u itself involves incomplete information.

Now let $\mathbf{T}$ be a theory and u an update. Under the model-based approach, the result $u(\mathbf{T})$ of applying u to $\mathbf{T}$ should be a theory $\mathbf{T}'$ such that

$$Mod(\mathbf{T}') = \cup\{u(\mathbf{I}) \mid \mathbf{I} \in Mod(\mathbf{T})\}.$$

EXAMPLE 22.4.2

(a) Consider the theory $\mathbf{T} = \{p \wedge q\}$, where p and q are propositional constants, and the update [*insert* $\neg p$]. There is only one model of $\mathbf{T}$ (namely, $\{p, q\}$). If we take the meaning of *insert* $\neg p$ to be "make p false and leave other things unchanged," then updating this model yields the single model $\{q\}$. Thus the result of applying [*insert* $\neg p$] to $\mathbf{T}$ yields the theory $\{q\}$.

(b) Consider $\mathbf{T}' = \{p \vee q\}$ and the update [*insert* $\neg p$]. The models of $\mathbf{T}'$ and the impact of the update are given by

$$\{p\} \quad \longmapsto \varnothing$$
$$\{q\} \quad \longmapsto \{q\}$$
$$\{p, q\} \longmapsto \{q\}.$$

Thus the result of applying the update to $\mathbf{T}'$ is $\{\neg p\}$.

The approach to updating c-tables presented earlier falls within the model-based paradigm (see Exercise 22.14). A family of richer model-based frameworks that supports null values and disjunctive updates has also been developed. An interesting dimension of variation in this approach concerns how permissive or restrictive a given update semantics is. This essentially amounts to considering how many models are associated with $u(\mathbf{I})$ for given update u and instance $\mathbf{I}$. As a simple example, consider starting with an empty database $\mathbf{I}_{\emptyset}$ and the update [*insert* $(p \vee q)$]. Under a restrictive semantics, only $\{p\}$ and $\{q\}$

are in $u(\mathbf{I}_\emptyset)$, but under a permissive semantics, $\{p, q\}$ might also be included. The update semantics for c-tables given earlier is very permissive: All possible models corresponding to an update are included in the result.

Formula-Based Approaches to Updating Theories

Another approach to updating theories is to apply updates directly to the theories themselves. As we shall see, a disadvantage of this approach is that the same update may have a different effect on equivalent but distinct theories. On the other hand, this approach does allow us to assign priorities to different sentences (e.g., so that constraints are given higher priority than atomic facts).

We consider two forms of update: [*insert* φ] and [*delete* φ], where φ is a sentence (i.e., no free variables). Given theory $\mathbf{T}$, a theory $\mathbf{T}'$ *accomplishes* the update [*insert* φ] for $\mathbf{T}$ if $\varphi \in \mathbf{T}'$, and it *accomplishes* [*delete* φ] for $\mathbf{T}$ if[1] $\varphi \notin \mathbf{T}'^*$. Observe that there is a difference between [*insert* $\neg\varphi$] and [*delete* φ]: In the former case $\neg\varphi$ is true for all models of $\mathbf{T}'$, whereas in the latter case φ may hold in some model of $\mathbf{T}'$.

In general, we are interested in accomplishing an update for $\mathbf{T}$ with minimal impact on $\mathbf{T}$. Given theory $\mathbf{T}$, we define a partial order $\leq_{\mathbf{T}}$ on theories with respect to the degree of change from $\mathbf{T}$. In particular, we define $\mathbf{T}' \leq_{\mathbf{T}} \mathbf{T}''$ if $\mathbf{T} - \mathbf{T}' \subset \mathbf{T} - \mathbf{T}''$, or if $\mathbf{T} - \mathbf{T}' = \mathbf{T} - \mathbf{T}''$ and $\mathbf{T}' - \mathbf{T} \subseteq \mathbf{T}'' - \mathbf{T}$. Intuitively, $\mathbf{T}' \leq_{\mathbf{T}} \mathbf{T}''$ if $\mathbf{T}'$ has fewer deletions (from $\mathbf{T}$) than $\mathbf{T}''$, or both $\mathbf{T}'$ and $\mathbf{T}''$ have the same deletions but $\mathbf{T}'$ has no more insertions than $\mathbf{T}''$. (Exercise 22.16 considers the opposite ordering, where insertions are given priority over deletions.)

Intuitively, we are interested in theories $\mathbf{T}'$ that accomplish a given update u for $\mathbf{T}$ and are minimal under $\leq_{\mathbf{T}}$. We say that such theories $\mathbf{T}'$ accomplish u for $\mathbf{T}$ *minimally*. The following characterizes such theories (see Exercise 22.15):

PROPOSITION 22.4.3   Let $\mathbf{T}$, $\mathbf{T}'$ be theories and φ a sentence. Then

    (a) $\mathbf{T}'$ accomplishes [*delete* φ] for $\mathbf{T}$ minimally iff $\mathbf{T}'$ is a maximal subset of $\mathbf{T}$ that is consistent with $\neg\varphi$.

    (b) $\mathbf{T}' \cup \varphi$ accomplishes [*insert* φ] for $\mathbf{T}$ minimally iff $\mathbf{T}'$ is a maximal subset of $\mathbf{T}$ that is consistent with φ.

Thus $\mathbf{T}'$ accomplishes [*delete* φ] for $\mathbf{T}$ minimally iff $\mathbf{T}' \cup \neg\varphi$ accomplishes [*insert* $\neg\varphi$] for $\mathbf{T}$ minimally.

The following example shows that equivalent but distinct theories can be affected differently by updates.

EXAMPLE 22.4.4   (a) Consider the theory $\mathbf{T}_0 = \{p, q\}$ and the update [*insert* $\neg p$]. Then $\{\neg p, q\}$ is the unique minimal theory that accomplishes this update.

---

[1] For a theory $\mathbf{S}$, the (*logical*) *closure* of $\mathbf{S}$, denoted $\mathbf{S}^*$, is the set of all sentences implied by $\mathbf{S}$.

(b) Let $\mathbf{T}_1 = \{p \wedge q\}$ and consider [*insert* $\neg p$]. The unique minimal theory that accomplishes this update for $\mathbf{T}_1$ is $\{\neg p\}$ [i.e., $(\emptyset \cup \{\neg p\})$]. Note how this differs from the model-based update in Example 22.4.2(a).

A problem at this point is that, in general, there are several theories that minimally accomplish a given update. Thus an update to a theory may yield a set of theories, and so the framework is not closed under updates. Given a set $\mathbf{T}_1, \mathbf{T}_2, \ldots$, we would like to find a theory $\mathbf{T}$ whose models are exactly the union of all models of the set of theories. In general, it is not clear that there is a theory that has this property. However, if there is only a finite number of theories that are possible answers, then we can use the *disjunction* operator $\bigvee$ defined by

$$\bigvee\{\mathbf{T}_i \mid i \in [1, n]\} = \{\tau_1 \vee \cdots \vee \tau_n \mid \tau_i \in \mathbf{T}_i \text{ for } i \in [1, n]\}.$$

It is easily verified that $Mod(\bigvee\{\mathbf{T}_i \mid i \in [1, n]\}) = \cup\{Mod(\mathbf{T}_i) \mid i \in [1, n]\}$. Of course, there is a great likelihood of a combinatorial explosion if the disjunction operator is applied repeatedly.

Assigning Priorities to Sentences

We now explore a mechanism for giving priority to some sentences in a theory over other sentences. Let $n \geq 0$ be fixed. A *tagged sentence* is a pair (i, φ), where $i \in [0, n]$ and φ is a sentence. A *tagged theory* is a set of tagged sentences. Given tagged theory $\mathbf{T}$ and $i \in [1, n]$, $\mathbf{T}_i$ denotes $\{\varphi \mid (i, \varphi) \in \mathbf{T}\}$.

The partial order for comparing theories is extended in the following natural fashion. Given tagged theories $\mathbf{T}, \mathbf{T}'$ and $\mathbf{T}''$, define $\mathbf{T}' \leq_{\mathbf{T}} \mathbf{T}''$ if for some $i \in [1, n]$ we have

$$\mathbf{T}_j - \mathbf{T}'_j = \mathbf{T}_j - \mathbf{T}''_j, \text{ for each } j \in [1, i-1]$$

and

$$\mathbf{T}_i - \mathbf{T}'_i \subset \mathbf{T}_i - \mathbf{T}''_i$$

or we have

$$\mathbf{T}_j - \mathbf{T}'_j = \mathbf{T}_j - \mathbf{T}''_j, \text{ for each } j \in [1, n]$$

and

$$\mathbf{T}' - \mathbf{T} \subset \mathbf{T}'' - \mathbf{T}.$$

Intuitively, $\mathbf{T}' \leq_{\mathbf{T}} \mathbf{T}''$ if the deletions of $\mathbf{T}'$ and $\mathbf{T}''$ agree up to some level i and then $\mathbf{T}'$ has fewer deletions at level i; or if the deletions match and $\mathbf{T}'$ has fewer insertions. In this manner, higher priority is given to the sentences having lower numbers.

EXAMPLE 22.4.5   Consider a relation $R[ABC]$ that satisfies the functional dependency $A \rightarrow B$, and consider the instance

R	A	B	C
	a	b	c
	a	b	c'
	a'	b'	c''
	a''	b'	c'''

We now construct a tagged theory **T** to represent this situation and show how changing a B value of a tuple is accomplished.

We assume three tag values and describe the contents of $\mathbf{T}_0$, $\mathbf{T}_1$, and $\mathbf{T}_2$ in turn. $\mathbf{T}_0$ holds the functional dependency and the unique name axiom (see Chapter 2). That is,

$$\left\{ \begin{array}{l} (0, \forall x, y, y', z, z'(R(x, y, z) \wedge R(x, y', z') \rightarrow y = y')), \\ (0, a \neq a'), (0, a \neq a''), \ldots, (0, a \neq b), \ldots, (0, c'' \neq c''') \end{array} \right\}$$

$\mathbf{T}_1$ holds the following existential sentences:

$$\left\{ \begin{array}{l} (1, \exists x (R(a, x, c))), \\ (1, \exists x (R(a, x, c'))), \\ (1, \exists x (R(a', x, c''))), \\ (1, \exists x (R(a'', x, c'''))) \end{array} \right\}$$

Finally, $\mathbf{T}_2$ holds

$$\left\{ \begin{array}{l} (2, R(a, b, c)), \\ (2, R(a, b, c')), \\ (2, R(a', b', c'')), \\ (2, R(a'', b', c''')) \end{array} \right\}$$

Consider now the update $u = [insert\ \varphi]$, where $\varphi = \exists y R(a, b'', y)$. Intuitively, this insertion should replace all $\langle a, b \rangle$ pairs occurring in $\pi_{AB} R$ by $\langle a, b'' \rangle$. More formally, it is easy to verify that the unique tagged theory (up to choice of i) that accomplishes u is (see Exercise 22.17)

$$\{(i, \varphi)\} \cup \mathbf{T}_0 \cup \mathbf{T}_1 \cup \left\{ \begin{array}{l} (2, R(a, b'', c)) \\ (2, R(a, b'', c')) \\ (2, R(a', b', c'')) \\ (2, R(a'', b', c''')) \end{array} \right\}$$

Thus the choice of sentences and tags included in the theory can influence the result of an update.

The approach of tagged theories can also be used to develop a framework for accomplishing view updates. The underlying database and the view are represented using a tagged theory, and highest priority is given to ensuring that the complement of the view remains fixed. Exercise 22.18 explores a simple example of this approach.

In the approach described here, a set of theories is combined using the disjunction operator. In this case, multiple deletions can lead to an exponential blowup in the size of the underlying theory, and performing insertions is NP-hard (see Exercise 22.19). This provided one motivation for developing a generalization of the approach, in which families of theories, called flocks, are used to represent a database with incomplete information.

Update versus Revision

The idea of representing knowledge using theories is not unique to the field of databases. The field of belief revision takes this approach and considers the issue of revising a knowledge base. Here we briefly compare the approaches to updating database theories described earlier with those found in belief revision.

A starting point for belief revision theory is the set of *rationality postulates* of Alchourrón, Gärdenfors, and Makinson, often referred to as the *AGM* postulates. These present a general family of guidelines for when a theory accomplishes a revision, and they include postulates such as

(R1) If $\mathbf{T}'$ accomplishes [*insert* φ] for $\mathbf{T}$, then $\mathbf{T}' \models \varphi$.
(R2) If φ is consistent with $\mathbf{T}$, then the result of [*insert* φ] on $\mathbf{T}$ should be equivalent to $\mathbf{T} \cup \{\varphi\}$.
(R3) If $\mathbf{T} \equiv \mathbf{T}'$ and $\varphi \equiv \varphi'$, then the result of [*insert* φ] on $\mathbf{T}$ is equivalent to the result of [*insert* φ'] on $\mathbf{T}'$.

(This is a partial listing of the eight AGM postulates.) Other postulates focus on maintaining satisfiability, relationships between the effects of different updates, and capturing some aspects of minimal change.

It is clear from postulate (R3) that the formula-based approaches to updating database theories do not qualify as belief revision systems. The relationship of the formula-based approaches and belief revision is largely unexplored.

A key difference between belief revision and the model-based approach to updating database theories stems from different perspectives on what a theory $\mathbf{T}$ is intended to represent. In the former context, $\mathbf{T}$ is viewed as a set of beliefs about the state of the world. If a new fact φ is to be inserted, this is a modification (and, it is hoped, improvement) of our knowledge about the state of the world, but the world itself is considered to remain unchanged. In contrast, in the model-based approaches, the theory $\mathbf{T}$ is used to identify a set of worlds that are possible given the limited information currently available. If a fact φ is inserted, this is understood to mean that the world itself has been modified. Thus $\mathbf{T}$ is modified to identify a different set of possible worlds.

EXAMPLE 22.4.6   Suppose that the world of interest is a room with a table in it. There is an abacus and a (hand-held, electronic) calculator in the room. Let proposition a mean that the abacus is on the table, and let proposition c mean that the calculator is on the table. Finally, let **T** be $(a \wedge \neg c) \vee (\neg a \wedge c)$.

From the perspective of belief revision, **T** indicates that according to our current knowledge, either the abacus or the calculator is on the table, but not both. Suppose that we are informed that the calculator is on the table (i.e., [*insert c*]). This is viewed as additional knowledge about the unchanging world. Combining **T** with c, we obtain the new theory $\mathbf{T}_1 = ((a \wedge \neg c) \vee (\neg a \wedge c)) \wedge c \equiv (\neg a \wedge c)$. [Note that this outcome is required by postulate (R2).]

From the model-based perspective, **T** indicates that either the world is $\{a\}$ or it is $\{c\}$. The request [*insert c*] is understood to mean that the world has been modified so that c has become true. This can be envisioned in terms of having a robot enter the room and place the calculator on the table (if it isn't already there) without reporting on the status of anything except that the robot has been successful. As a result, the world $\{a\}$ is replaced by $\{a, c\}$, and the world $\{c\}$ is replaced by itself. The resulting theory is $\mathbf{T}_2 = c$ (which is interpreted under the OWA).

A set of postulates for updates, analogous to the AGM postulates for revision, has been developed. The postulate analogous to (R2) is

(U2) If **T** implies φ, then the result of [*insert φ*] on **T** should be equivalent to **T**.

This is strictly weaker than (R2). Other postulates enforce the intuition that the effect of an update on a possible model is independent of the other possible models of a theory, maintaining satisfiability and relationships between the effects of different updates.

22.5   Active Databases

As we have seen, object orientation provides one paradigm for incorporating behavioral information into a database schema. This has the effect of separating a portion of the behavioral information from the application software and providing a more structured representation and organization for that portion. In this section, we briefly consider a second, essentially orthogonal, paradigm for separating a portion of the behavioral information from the application software. This emerging paradigm, called activeness, stems from a synthesis of techniques from databases, on the one hand, and expert systems and artificial intelligence, on the other.

Active databases generally support the automatic triggering of updates in response to internal or external events (e.g., a clock tick, a user-requested update, or a change in a sensor reading). In a manner reminiscent of expert systems, forward chaining of *rules* is generally used to accomplish the response. However, there are several differences between classical expert systems and active databases. At the conceptual and logical level, the differences are centered around the expressive power of rule conditions and the semantics of rule application. (Some active database systems, such as POSTGRES, also support a form of backward chaining or query rewriting; this is not considered here.)

Active databases have been shown to be useful in a variety of areas, including con-

Suppliers	Sname	Address		Prices	Part	Sname	Price
	The Depot	1210 Broadway			nail	The Depot	.02
	Builder's Mart	100 Main			bolt	The Depot	.05
					bolt	Builder's Mart	.04
					nut	Builder's Mart	.03

Figure 22.3:   Sample instance for active database examples

straint maintenance, incremental update of materialized views, mapping view updates to the base data, and supporting database interoperability.

Rules and Rule Application

There are three distinguishing components in an active database: (1) a subsystem for monitoring events, (2) a set of rules, often called a *rule base*, and (3) a semantics for rule application, typically called an *execution model*.

Rules typically have the following so-called ECA form:

$$\textbf{on } \langle event \rangle \textbf{ if } \langle condition \rangle \textbf{ then } \langle action \rangle.$$

Depending on the system and application, the *event* may range over external phenomena and/or over internal events (such as a method call or inserting a tuple to a relation). Events may be atomic or *composite*, where these are built up from atomic events using, say, regular expressions or a process algebra. Events may be essentially Boolean or may return a tuple of values that indicate what triggered the event.

Conditions typically involve parameters passed in by the events, and the contents of the database. As will be described shortly, several systems permit conditions to look at more than one version of the database state (e.g., corresponding to the state before the event and the state after the event). In some systems, events are not explicitly specified; essentially any change to the database makes the event true and leads to testing of all rule conditions.

In principle, the *action* may be a call to an arbitrary routine. In many cases in relational systems, the action will involve a sequence of insertions, deletions, and modifications; and in object-oriented systems it will involve one or more method calls. Note that this may in turn trigger other rules.

The remainder of this discussion focuses on the relational model. A short example is given, followed by a brief discussion of execution models.

EXAMPLE 22.5.1   Suppose that the *Inventory* database includes the following relations:

$$Suppliers[Sname, Address]$$
$$Prices[Part, Sname, Price]$$

Suppliers and the parts they supply are represented in *Suppliers* and *Prices*, respectively. It is assumed that *Sname* is a key of *Suppliers* and *Part*, *Sname* is a key of *Prices*. An example instance is shown in Fig. 22.3.

We now list some example rules. These rules are written in a pidgin language that uses tuple variables. The variable T ranges over sets of tuples and is used to pass them from the condition to the action. As detailed shortly, both (r1) considered in isolation and the set (r2.a) ... (r2.d) taken together can be used to enforce the inclusion dependency *Prices*[*Sname*] $\subseteq$ *Suppliers*[*Sname*].

(r1)   **on** true
      if *Prices*(*p*) and *p.Sname* $\notin \pi_{Sname}$(*Suppliers*)
      then *Prices* := *Prices* $-$ {*p*}

(r2.a)   **on** delete *Sname*(*s*)
        if $T := \sigma_{Sname=s.Sname}$(*Prices*) is not empty
        then *Prices* := *Prices* $-$ *T*

(r2.b)   **on** modify *Sname*(*s*)
        if *old*(*s*).*Sname* $\neq$ *new*(*s*).*Sname*
           and $T = \sigma_{Sname=old(s).Sname}$(*Prices*)
        then *set p.Sname* = *new*(*s*).*Sname*
           for each *p* in *Prices*
           where $p \in T$

(r2.c)   **on** insert *Prices*(*p*)
        if $\langle p.Sname \rangle \notin \pi_{Sname}$(*Suppliers*)
        then issue `supplier_warning`(*p*)

(r2.d)   **on** modify *Prices*(*p*)
        if $\langle new(p).Sname \rangle \notin \pi_{Sname}$(*Suppliers*)
        then issue `supplier_warning`(*new*(*p*))

Consider rule (r1). If ever a state arises that violates the inclusion dependency, then the rule deletes violating tuples from the *Prices* relation. The event of (r1) is always true; in principle the database must check the condition whenever an update is made. It is easy to see in this case that such checking need only be done if the relations *Supplies* or *Prices* are updated, and so the event "**on** *Supplies* or *Prices* is updated" could be incorporated into (r1). Although this does not change the effect of the rule, it provides a hint to the system about how to implement it efficiently.

Rules (r2.a) ... (r2.d) form an alternative mechanism for enforcing the inclusion dependency. In this case, the cause of the dependency violation determines the reaction of the system. Here a deletion from (r2.a) or modification (r2.b) to *Suppliers* will result in deletions from or modifications to *Prices*. In (r2.b), variable *s* ranges over tuples that have been modified, *old*(*s*) refers to the original value of the tuple, and *new*(*s*) refers to the modified value. On the other hand, changes to *Prices* that cause a violation [rules (r2.c) and (r2.d))] call a procedure `supplier_warning`; this might abort the transaction and warn the user or dba of the constraint violation, or it might attempt to use heuristics to modify the offending *Sname* value.

Execution Models

Until now, we have considered rules essentially in isolation from each other. A fundamental issue concerns the choice of an execution model, which specifies how and when rules will be applied. As will be seen, a wide variety of execution models are possible. The true semantics of a rule base stems both from the rules themselves and from the execution model for applying them.

We assume for this discussion that there is only one user of the system, or that a concurrency control protocol is enforced that hides the effect of other users.

Suppose that a user transaction $t = c_1; \dots; c_n$ is issued, where each of the c_i's is an atomic command. In the absence of active database rules, application of t will yield a sequence

$$\mathbf{I}_0, \mathbf{I}_1, \dots, \mathbf{I}_n$$

of database states, starting with the original state $\mathbf{I}_0$ and where each state $\mathbf{I}_{i+1}$ is the result of applying c_{i+1} to state $\mathbf{I}_i$. If rules are present, then a different sequence of states might arise.

One dimension of variation between execution models concerns when rules are fired. Under *immediate* firing, a rule is essentially fired as soon as its event and condition become true; under *deferred* firing, rule application is delayed until after the state $\mathbf{I}_n$ is reached; and under *concurrent* firing, a separate process is spawned for the rule action and is executed concurrently with other processes. In the most general execution models, each rule is assigned its own coupling mode (i.e., immediate, deferred, or concurrent), which may be further refined by associating a coupling mode between event and condition testing and between condition testing and action execution.

We now examine the semantics of immediate and deferred firing in more detail. We assume for this discussion that the event of each rule is simply *true*.

To illustrate immediate firing, suppose that a rule r with action $d_1; \dots; d_m$ is triggered (i.e., its condition has become true) in state $\mathbf{I}_1$ of the preceeding sequence of states. Then the sequence of databases states might start with

$$\mathbf{I}_0, \mathbf{I}_1, \mathbf{I}'_1, \mathbf{I}'_2, \dots, \mathbf{I}'_m, \dots,$$

where $\mathbf{I}'_1$ is the result of applying d_1 to $\mathbf{I}_1$ and $\mathbf{I}'_{j+1}$ is the result of applying d_{j+1} to $\mathbf{I}'_j$. After $\mathbf{I}'_m$, the command c_2 would be applied. The semantics of intermediate rule firing is in fact more complex, for two reasons. First, another rule might be triggered during the execution of the action of the first triggered rule. In general, this calls for a recursive style of rule application, where the command sequences of each triggered rule are placed onto a stack. Second, several rules might be triggered at the same time. It is common in this case to assume that the rules are ordered and that rules triggered simultaneously are considered in that order.

In the case of deferred firing, the full user transaction is completed before any rules are fired, and each rule action is executed in its entirety before another rule action is initiated. This gives rise to a sequence of states having the form

$$\mathbf{I}^{orig}, \mathbf{I}^{user}, \mathbf{I}_2, \mathbf{I}_3, \ldots, \mathbf{I}^{curr},$$

where now $\mathbf{I}^{orig}$ is the original state, $\mathbf{I}^{user}$ is the result of applying the user-requested transaction, and the states $\mathbf{I}_2, \mathbf{I}_3, \ldots, \mathbf{I}^{curr}$ are the results of applying the actions of fired rules. The sequence shown here might be extended if additional rules are to be fired.

Several intricacies arise. As before, the order of rule firing must be considered if multiple rules are triggered at a given state. Recall the (r2) rules of Example 22.5.1, whose events where based on transitions between some former state and some latter state. What states should be used? It is natural to use $\mathbf{I}^{curr}$ as the latter state. With regard to the former state, some systems advocate using $\mathbf{I}^{orig}$, whereas other systems support the use of one of the intermediate states (where the choice may depend on a complex condition).

Suppose that two rules r and r' are triggered at some state $\mathbf{I}^{curr} = \mathbf{I}_i$ and that r is fired first to reach state $\mathbf{I}_{i+1}$. The event and/or condition of r' may no longer be true. This raises the question, Should r' be fired? A consensus has not emerged in the literature.

As should be clear from the preceeding discussion, there is a wide variety of choices for execution models. A more subtle dimension of flexibility concerns the expressive power of rule events and conditions: In addition to accessing the current state, should they be able to access one or more previous ones? Several prototype active database systems have been implemented; each uses a different execution model, and several permit access to both current and previous states. It has been argued that different execution models may be appropriate for different applications. This has given rise to systems that include a choice of execution models and to languages that permit the specification of customized execution models. An open problem at the time this book was written is to develop a natural syntax that can be used to specify easily a broad range of execution models, including a substantial subset of those described in the literature.

The *while* languages studied in Part E can serve as the kernel of an active database. These languages do not use events; restrict rule actions to insertions, deletions, and value creation; and examine only the current state in a rule firing sequence. If value creation is supported, then these languages are complete for database mappings and so in some sense can simulate all active databases. However, richer rules and execution models permit the possibility of developing rule bases that enforce a desired set of policies in a more intuitive fashion than a *while* program.

An Execution Model That Reaches a Unique Fixpoint

It should be clear that whatever execution model and form for rules is selected, most questions about the behavior of an active database are undecidable. It is thus interesting to consider more restricted execution models that behave in predictable ways. We now present one such execution model, called the *accumulating* model; this forms a portion of the execution model of AP5, a main-memory active database system that has been used in research for over a decade.

To describe the accumulating execution model, we first introduce the notion of a *delta*. Let $\mathbf{R} = \{R_1, \ldots, R_n\}$ be a database schema. An *atomic update* over $\mathbf{R}$ is an expression of the form $+R_i(t)$ or $-R_i(t)$, where $i \in [1, n]$ and t is a tuple having the arity of R_i. A *delta* over $\mathbf{R}$ is a finite set of atomic updates over $\mathbf{R}$ that does not contain both $+R(t)$ and $-R(t)$ for any R and t or the special value *fail*. (Modifies could also be incorporated into deltas, but we do not consider that here.) A delta not containing the value *fail* is *consistent*. For delta Δ, we define

$$\Delta^+ = \{R(t) \mid +R(t) \in \Delta\}$$
$$\Delta^- = \{R(t) \mid -R(t) \in \Delta\}.$$

Given instance $\mathbf{I}$ and consistent delta Δ over $\mathbf{R}$, the result of *applying* Δ to $\mathbf{I}$ is

$$apply(\mathbf{I}, \Delta) = (\mathbf{I} \cup \Delta^+) - \Delta^- = (\mathbf{I} - \Delta^-) \cup \Delta^+.$$

Finally, the *merge* of two consistent deltas Δ_1, Δ_2 is defined by

$$\Delta_1 \& \Delta_2 = \begin{cases} \Delta_1 \cup \Delta_2 & \text{if this is consistent} \\ fail & \text{otherwise.} \end{cases}$$

The accumulating execution model uses deferred rule firing. Each rule action is viewed as producing a consistent delta. The user-requested transaction is also considered to be the delta Δ_0. Thus a sequence of states

$$\mathbf{I}^{orig} = \mathbf{I}_0, \mathbf{I}^{user} = \mathbf{I}_1, \mathbf{I}_2, \mathbf{I}_3, \ldots, \mathbf{I}^{curr}$$

is produced, where $\mathbf{I}^{user} = apply(\mathbf{I}^{orig}, \Delta_0)$ and, more generally, $\mathbf{I}_{i+1} = apply(\mathbf{I}_i, \Delta_i)$ for some Δ_i produced by a rule firing.

At this point the accumulating model is quite generic. We now restrict the model and develop some interesting theoretical properties. First we assume that rules have only conditions and actions (i.e., that the event part is always *true*). Second, as noted before, we assume that the action of each rule can be viewed as a delta. Furthermore, we assume that these deltas use only constants from $\mathbf{I}^{orig}$ (i.e., there is no invention of constants). Third we insist that for each $i \geq 0$, $\Delta_0 \& \ldots \& \Delta_i$ is consistent. More precisely, we modify the execution model so that if for some i we have $\Delta_0 \& \ldots \& \Delta_i = fail$, then the execution is aborted. For each $i \geq 0$, let $\Delta'_i = \Delta_0 \& \ldots \& \Delta_i$.

Suppose that we are now in state $\mathbf{I}^{curr}$ with delta Δ^{curr}. We assume that rule conditions can access only $\mathbf{I}^{orig}$ and Δ^{curr}. (If the rule conditions have the power of, for example, the relational calculus, this means they can in effect access $\mathbf{I}^{curr}$.) Given rule r, state $\mathbf{I}$, and delta Δ, the *effect* of r on $\mathbf{I}$ and Δ, denoted *effect*$(r, \mathbf{I}, \Delta)$, is the delta corresponding to the firing of r on $\mathbf{I}$ and Δ, if the condition of r is satisfied, and is $\emptyset$ otherwise.

Execution proceeds as follows. The sequence $\Delta'_0, \Delta'_1, \ldots$ is constructed sequentially. At the ith step, if there is no rule whose condition is satisfied by $\mathbf{I}^{orig}$ and Δ'_i, then execution terminates successfully. Otherwise a rule r with condition satisfied by $\mathbf{I}^{orig}$ and Δ'_i

is selected nondeterministically. If $\Delta_i' \& effect(r, \mathbf{I}^{orig}, \Delta_i')$ is *fail*, then execution terminates with an abort; otherwise set $\Delta_{i+1}' = \Delta_i' \& effect(r, \mathbf{I}^{orig}, \Delta_i')$ and continue.

A natural question at this point is, Will execution always terminate? It is easy to see that it does, because constants are not invented and the sequence of deltas being constructed is monotonically increasing under set containment.

It is also natural to ask, Does the order of rule firing affect the outcome? In general, the answer is yes. We now develop a semantic condition on rules that ensures independence of rule firing order. A rule r is *monotonic* if for each instance $\mathbf{I}$ and pair $\Delta_1 \subseteq \Delta_2$ of deltas, $effect(r, \mathbf{I}, \Delta_1) \subseteq effect(r, \mathbf{I}, \Delta_2)$. The following can now be shown (see Exercise 22.23):

THEOREM 22.5.2   If each rule in a rule base is monotonic, then the outcome of the accumulating execution model on this rule base is independent of rule firing order.

Monitoring Events and Conditions

In Example 22.5.1, the events that triggered rules were primitive, in the sense that each one corresponded to an atomic occurrence of some phenomenon. There has been recent interest in developing languages for specifying and recognizing composite events, which might involve the occurrence of several primitive events. For example, composite event specification is supported by the ODE system, a recently released prototype object-oriented active database system. The ODE system supports a rich language for specifying composite events, which has essentially the power of regular expressions (see also Section 22.6 for examples of composite events specified by regular expressions). An implementation technique based on finite state automata has been developed for recognizing composite events specified in this language.

Other formalisms can also be used for specifying composite events (e.g., using Petri nets or temporal logics). There appears to be a trade-off between the expressiveness of triggers in rules and conditions. For example, some Petri-net-based languages for composite events can be simulated using additional relations and rules based on simple events. The details of such trade-offs are largely unexplored.

22.6   Temporal Databases and Constraints

Classical databases model *static* aspects of data. Thus the information in the database consists of data currently true in the world. However, in many applications, information about the history of data is just as important as static information. When history is taken into account, queries can ask about the evolution of data through time; and constraints may restrict the way changes occur. We briefly discuss these two aspects.

Temporal Databases

Suppose we are interested in a database over some schema $\mathbf{R}$. Thus we wish to model and query information about the content of the database through time. Conceptually, we can associate to each time t the state $\mathbf{I}_t$ of the database at time t. Thus the database appears as a sequence of states—*snapshots*—indexed by some time domain. Two basic questions come up immediately:

- What is the meaning of $\mathbf{I}_t$? Primarily two possible answers have been proposed. The first is that $\mathbf{I}_t$ represents the data that was true in the world at time t; this view of time is referred to as *valid time*. The second possibility is that time represents the moment when the information was recorded in the database; this is called *transaction time*.

  Clearly, using valid time requires including time as a first-class citizen in the data model. In many applications transaction time might be hidden and dealt with by the system; however, in time-critical applications, such as air-traffic control or monitoring a power plant, transaction time may be important and made explicit. A particular database may use valid time, transaction time, or both. In our discussion, we will consider valid time only.

- What is the time domain? This can be discrete (isomorphic to the integers), continuous (isomorphic to the reals), or dense and countable (isomorphic to the rationals). In databases, time is usually taken to be discrete, with some fixed granularity for the time unit. However, several distinct time domains with different granularities are often used (e.g., years, months, days, hours, etc.). The time domain is usually equipped with a total order and sometimes with arithmetic operations. A temporal variable **now** may be used to refer to the present time.

To query a temporal database, relational languages must be extended to take into account the time coordinate. To say that a tuple u is in relation R at time t, we could simply extend R with one temporal coordinate and write $R(u, t)$. Then we could use CALC or ALG on the extended relations. This is illustrated next.

EXAMPLE 22.6.1 Consider the **CINEMA** database, indexed by a time domain consisting of dates of the form month/day/year. The query

"What were the movies shown at La Pagode in May, 1968?"

is expressed in CALC by

$$\{m \mid \exists s, t\, (Pariscope(\text{La Pagode}, m, s, t) \wedge 5/1/68 \leq t \leq 5/31/68)\}.$$

The query

"Since when has La Pagode been showing the current movie?"

is expressed by

$$\{t \mid \exists m[\exists s\,(Pariscope(\text{"La Pagode"}, m, s, \mathbf{now})) \wedge$$
$$since(t, m) \wedge \forall t''(since(t'', m) \rightarrow t \leq t'')]\},$$

where

$$since(t, m) = \forall t'[t \leq t' \leq \textbf{now} \rightarrow \exists s'(Pariscope(\text{"La Pagode"}, m, s', t'))].$$

Classical logics augmented with a temporal coordinate have been studied extensively, mostly geared toward specification and verification of concurrent programs. Such logics are usually referred to as *temporal logics*. There is a wealth of mathematical machinery developed around temporal logics; unfortunately, little of it seems to apply directly to databases.

Although the view of a temporal database as a sequence of instances is conceptually clean, it is extremely inefficient to represent a temporal database in this manner. In practice, this information is summarized in a single database in which data is timestamped to indicate the time of validity. The timestamps can be placed at the tuple level or at the attribute level. Typically, timestamps are unions of intervals of the temporal domain. Such representations naturally lead to nested structures, as in the nested relation, semantic, and object-oriented data models.

EXAMPLE 22.6.2   Figure 22.4 is a representation of temporal information about *Pariscope* using attribute timestamps with nested relations. It would also be natural to represent this using a semantic or object-oriented model.

The same information can be represented by timestamping at the tuple level, as follows:

Pariscope	Theater	Title	Schedule	
	La Pagode	Sleeper	19:00	[5/1/68–5/31/68]
	La Pagode	Sleeper	19:00	[7/15/74–7/31/74]
	La Pagode	Sleeper	19:00	[12/1/93–**now**]
	La Pagode	Sleeper	22:00	[8/1/74–8/14/75]
	La Pagode	Sleeper	22:00	[10/1/93–11/30/93]
	La Pagode	Psycho	19:00	[8/1/93–11/30/93]
	La Pagode	Psycho	22:00	[2/15/78–10/14/78]
	La Pagode	Psycho	22:00	[12/1/93–**now**]
	Kinopanorama	Sleeper	19:30	[4/1/90–10/31/90]
	Kinopanorama	Sleeper	19:30	[2/1/92–8/31/92]

In this representation, the time intervals are more fragmented. This may have some drawbacks. For example, retrieving the information about when "Sleeper" was playing at La Pagode (using a selection and projection) yields time intervals that are more fragmented than needed. To obtain a more concise representation of the answer, we must merge some of these intervals.

Note also the difference between the timestamps and the attribute *Schedule*, which also conveys some temporal information. The value of *Schedule* is user defined, and the database may not know that this is temporal information. Thus from the point of view of

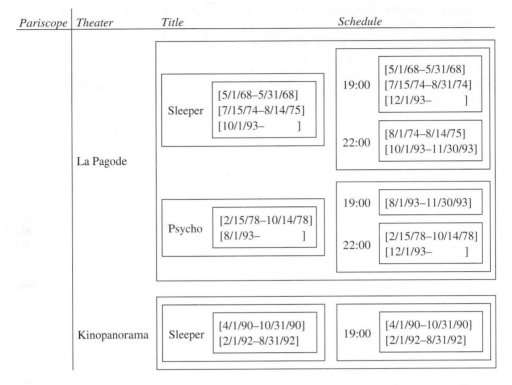

Figure 22.4:   A representation of temporal information using attribute timestamps with nested relations

the temporal database, the value of *Schedule* is treated just like any other nontemporal value in the database.

Much of the research in temporal databases has been devoted to finding extensions of SQL and other relational languages suitable for temporal queries. Most proposals assume some representation based on tuple timestamping by intervals and introduce intuitive linguistic constructs to compare and manipulate these temporal intervals. Sometimes this is done without explicit reference to time, in the spirit of modal operators in temporal logic. One such operator is illustrated next.

EXAMPLE 22.6.3   Several temporal extensions of SQL use a **when** clause to express a temporal condition. For example, consider the query on the **CINEMA** database:

"Find the pairs of theaters that have shown some movie at the same date and hour."

This can be expressed using the **when** clause as follows:

> **select** $t_1.theater, t_2.theater$
> **from**   *Pariscope* t_1 t_2
> **where** $t_1.title = t_2.title$ **and** $t_1.schedule = t_2.schedule$
> **when** $t_1.interval$ **overlaps** $t_2.interval$

The **when** clause is true for tuples t_1, t_2 iff the intervals indicating their validity have nonempty intersection. Other Boolean tests on intervals include **before, after, during, follows, precedes**, etc., with the obvious semantics. The expressive power of such constructs is not always well elucidated in the literature, beyond the fact that they can clearly be expressed in CALC. A review of the many constructs proposed in the literature on temporal databases is beyond the scope of this book. For the time being, it appears that a single well-accepted temporal language is far from emerging, although there are several major prototypes.

Temporal Deductive Databases

An interesting recent development involves the use of deductive databases in the temporal framework, yielding temporal extensions of datalog. This can be used in two main ways.

- As a specification mechanism: Datalog-like rules allow the specification of some temporal databases in a concise fashion. In particular, this allows us to specify *infinite* temporal databases, with both past and future information.

- As a query mechanism: Rules can be used to express recursive temporal queries.

EXAMPLE 22.6.4   We first illustrate the use of rules in the specification of an infinite temporal database. The database holds information on a professor's schedule—more precisely, the times she meets her two Ph.D. students. The facts

$$meets\text{-}first(Emma, 0), follows(Emma, John), follows(John, Emma)$$

say that the professor's first meeting is with Emma, and then John and Emma take turns. Consider the rules

$$
\begin{aligned}
meets(x, t) \quad &\leftarrow meets\text{-}first(x, t)\\
meets(y, t+1) &\leftarrow meets(x, t), follows(x, y)
\end{aligned}
$$

The rules define the following infinite sequence of facts providing the professor's schedule:

$$meets(Emma, 0)$$
$$meets(John, 1)$$
$$meets(Emma, 2)$$
$$meets(John, 3)$$

$$\vdots$$

Another way to use temporal rules is for querying. Consider the query

"Find the times t such that La Pagode showed 'Sleeper' on date t and continued to show it at least until the Kinopanorama started showing it."

The answer (given in the unary relation *until*) is defined by the following stratified program:

$$date(x, y, t) \leftarrow Pariscope(x, y, s, t)$$
$$until(t) \quad \leftarrow date(\text{``Kinopanorama''}, \text{``Sleeper''}, t + 1),$$
$$\neg\, date(\text{``Kinopanorama''}, \text{``Sleeper''}, t),$$
$$date(\text{``La Pagode''}, \text{``Sleeper''}, t)$$
$$until(t) \quad \leftarrow date(\text{``La Pagode''}, \text{``Sleeper''}, t), until(t + 1)$$

The expressiveness of several datalog-like temporal languages and the complexity of query evaluation using such languages are active areas of research.

Temporal Constraints

Classical constraints in relational databases are static: They speak about properties of the data seen at some moment in time. This does not allow modeling the *behavior* of data. Temporal (or dynamic) constraints place restrictions on how the data changes in time. They can arise in the context of classical databases as well as in temporal databases. In temporal databases, we can specify restrictions on the sequence of time-indexed instances using temporal logics (extensions of CALC, or modal logics). These are essentially Boolean (yes/no) temporal queries. For example, we might require that "La Pagode" not be a first-run theater (i.e., every movie shown there must have been shown in some other theater at some earlier time). An important question is how to enforce such constraints efficiently. A step in this direction is suggested by the following example.

EXAMPLE 22.6.5 Suppose that *Pariscope* is extended with a time domain ranging over days, as in Example 22.6.1. The constraint that "La Pagode" is not a first-run theater can be expressed in CALC as

$$\forall m, s, t\, (Pariscope(\text{``La Pagode''}, m, s, t)$$
$$\rightarrow \exists x, s', t'(Pariscope(x, m, s', t') \land x \neq \text{``La Pagode''} \land t' < t))$$

A naive way to enforce this constraint involves maintaining the full history of the relation *Pariscope*; this would require unbounded storage. A more efficient way involves storing only the current value of *Pariscope* and maintaining a unary relation *Shown_Before*[*Title*], which holds all movie titles that have been shown in the past at a theater other than "La Pagode." Note that the size of *Shown_Before* is bounded by the number of titles that have occurred through the history of the database but is independent of how long the database has been in existence. (Of course, if a new title is introduced each day, then *Shown_Before* will have size comparable to the full history.)

A systematic approach has been developed to maintain temporal constraints in this fashion.

For classical databases, in which no history is kept, temporal constraints can only involve transitions from the current instance to the next; this gives rise to a subset of temporal constraints, called *transition* constraints

For instance, a transition constraint can state that "salaries do not decrease" or that "the new salary of an employee is determined by the old salary and the seniority." Such transition constraints are by far the most common kind of temporal constraint considered for databases. We discuss some ways to specify transition constraints. Clearly, these can be stated using a temporal version of CALC that can refer to the previous and next state. A notion of identity similar to object identity is useful here; otherwise we may have difficulty speaking about the old and new versions of some tuple or entity. Such identity may be provided by a key, assuming that it does not change in time.

Besides CALC, transition constraints may be stated in various other ways, including

- pre- and postconditions associated with transitions;
- extensions of classical static constraints, such as dynamic fd's;
- computational constraints on sequences of consecutive versions of tuples.

Restrictions on updates—say, by transactional schemas—also induce temporal constraints. For instance, consider again the transactional schema in Example 22.2.1. It can be verified that all possible sequences of instances obtained by calls to the transactions of that schema satisfy the temporal constraint:

"Nobody can be a PhD student without having been a TA at some point."

The following less desirable temporal constraint is also satisfied:

"Once a PhD student, always a PhD student."

Overall, the connection between canned updates and temporal constraints remains largely unexplored.

A related means of specifying temporal constraints is to identify a set of update events and impose restrictions on valid sequences of events. This can be done using regular expressions. For example, suppose that the events concerning an employee are

hire, transfer, promote, raise, fire, retire

The valid sequences of events are all prefixes of sequences specified by the regular expression

$$\textbf{hire}[(\textbf{transfer}) + (\textbf{promote} + \epsilon)(\textbf{raise})]^*[(\textbf{retire}) + (\textbf{fire})]$$

Thus an employee is first hired, receives some number of promotions and raises, may be transferred, and finally either retires or is fired. Everybody who is promoted must also receive a raise, but raises may be received even without promotion. Such constraints appear to be particularly well suited to object-oriented databases, in which events can naturally be associated with method invocations. Some active databases (Section 22.5) can also enforce constraints on sequences of events.

Bibliographic Notes

The properties of IDM transactions were formally studied in [AV88b]. The sound and complete axiomatization for IDM transactions is provided in [KV91]. The results on simplification rules are also presented there. The language datalog¬¬ and other rule-based and imperative update languages are studied in [AV88c]. Dynamic Logic Programming is discussed in [MW88b]. In particular, Example 22.1.3 is from there. The language LDL, including its update capabilities, is presented in [NT89].

IDM transactional schemas are investigated in [AV89]. Transactional schemas based on more powerful languages are discussed in [AV87, AV88a]. Patterns of object migration in object-oriented databases are studied in [Su92], using results on IDM transactional schemas. A simple update language is shown there to express the family of migration patterns characterized by regular languages; richer families of patterns are obtained by permitting conditionals in this language.

One of the earliest works on the view maintenance problem is [BC79], which focuses on determining whether an update is relevant or not. References [KP81, HK89] study the maintenance of derived data in the context of semantic data models, and [SI84] studies the maintenance of a universal relation formed from an acyclic database family. Additional works that use the approach of incremental evaluation include [BLT86, GKM92, Pai84, QW91]. Heuristics for maintaining the materialized output of a stratified datalog¬ program are developed in [AP87b, Küc91]. A comprehensive approach, which handles views defined using the stratified datalog and aggregate operators, is developed in [GMS93]. Reference [Cha94] addresses the issue of incremental update to materialized views in the presence of OIDs.

Testing for relevance of updates in connection with view maintenance is related to the problem of incremental maintenance of integrity constraints. References [BBC80, HMN84] develop general techniques for this problem, and approaches for deductive databases include [BDM88, LST87, Nic82].

The issue of first-order incremental definability of datalog programs was first raised in [DT92]. Subsequent research in this area includes [Don92, DS92, DS93, DST94]. A more general perspective on these kinds of problems is presented in [PI94].

An informative survey of research on the view update problem is [FC85]. One practical approach to the view update problem is to consider the underlying database and the view to be abstract data types, with the updating operations predefined by the dba [SF78, RS79]. The other practical approach is to perform a careful analysis of the syntax and semantics of a view definition to determine a unique or a small set of update translation(s) that satisfy a family of natural properties. This approach is pioneered in [DB82] and further developed in [Kel85, Kel86]. Example 22.3.6 is inspired by [Kel86]. Reference [Kel82] considers the issue of unavoidable side-effects from view updates.

The discussion of view complements and Theorem 22.3.10 is from [BS81]. Reference [CP84] studies complexity issues in this area; for example, in the context of projective views over a single relation possibly having functional dependencies, finding a minimal complement is NP-complete. Reference [KU84] examines some of the practical shortcomings of the approach based on complementary views.

The semantics of updates on incomplete databases is investigated in [AG85] and [Gra91].

The idea of representing a database as a logical theory, as opposed to a set of atomic facts, has roots in [Kow81, NG78, Rei84]. A survey of approaches to updating logical theories, which articulates the distinction between model-based and formula-based approaches, is [Win88]. Reference [Win86] develops a model-based approach for updating theories that extends the framework of [Rei84]. Complexity and expressiveness issues related to this approach are studied in [GMR92, Win86]. A model-based approach has recently been applied in connection with supporting object migration in object-oriented databases in [MMW94].

An early formula-based approach to updating is discussed in [Tod77]. This chapter's discussion of the formula-based approach is inspired largely by [FUV83]. The notion of using flocks (i.e., families of theories) to describe incomplete information databases is developed in [FKUV86]. Reference [Var85] investigates the complexity of querying databases that are logical theories and shows that even in restricted cases, the complexity of, for example, the relational calculus goes from LOGSPACE to CO-NP-complete.

References on belief revision include [AGM85], where the AGM postulates are developed, and [Gär88, Mak85]. The contrast between belief revision and knowledge update was articulated informally in [KW85] and formally in [KM91a], where postulates for updating theories under the model-based perspective were developed; see also [GMR92, KM91b]. The discussion in this chapter is inspired by [KM91a].

Active databases generally support the automatic triggering of updates as a response to user-requested or system-generated updates. Most active database systems (e.g., [CCCR$^+$90, Coh86, MD89, Han89, SKdM92, SJGP90, WF90]) use a paradigm of *rules* to specify the actions to be taken, in a manner reminiscent of expert systems.

Active databases and techniques have been shown to be useful for constraint maintenance [Mor83, CW90, CTF88], incremental update of materialized views [CW91], and database security [SJGP90]; and they hold the promise of providing a new family of solutions to the view and derived data update problem [CHM94] and issues in database interoperability [CW93, Cha94, Wie92]. Another functionality associated with some active databases is query rewriting [SJGP90], whereby a query q might be transformed into a related query q' before being executed.

As discussed in Section 22.5 (see also [HJ91b, HW92, Sto92]), each of the active database systems described in the literature uses a different approach for event specification and a different execution model. The execution models of several active database systems are specified using deltas, either implicitly or explicitly [Coh86, SKdM92, WF90]. The Heraclitus language [HJ91a, JH91, GHJ$^+$93] elevates deltas to be first-class citizens in a database programming language based on C and the relational model, thereby enabling the specification, and thus implementation, of a wide variety of execution models. Execution models that support immediate, deferred, and concurrent firing include [BM91, HLM88, MD89].

The accumulating execution model forms part of the semantics of the AP5 active database model [Coh86, Coh89] (see also [HJ91a]). Theorem 22.5.2 is from [ZH90], which goes on to present syntactic conditions on rules that ensure the Church-Rosser property for rule bases that are not necessarily monotonic.

An early investigation of composite events in connection with active databases is [DHL91]. Reference [GJS92c] describes the event specification language of the ODE active database system [GJ91]. Reference [GJS92b] presents the equivalence of ODE's composite event specification language and regular expressions, and [GJS92a] develops an implementation technique based on finite state automata for recognizing composite events in the case where parameters are omitted. Reference [GD94] uses an alternative formalism for composite events based on Petri nets and can support parameters.

A crucial issue with regard to efficient implementation of active databases is determining incrementally when a condition becomes true. Early work in this area is modeled after the RETE algorithm from expert systems [For82]. Enhancements of this technique biased toward active database applications include [WH92, Coh89]. Reference [CW90] describes a mechanism for analyzing rule conditions to infer triggers for them.

There is a vast amount of literature on temporal databases. The volume [TCG$^+$93] provides a survey of current research in the area. In particular, several temporal extensions of SQL can be found there. Bibliographies on temporal databases are provided in [Sno90, Soo91]. A survey of temporal database research, emphasizing theoretical aspects, is provided in [Cho94]. Deductive temporal databases are presented in [BCW93]. Example 22.6.4 is from [BCW93].

Specification of transition constraints by pre- and postconditions is studied in [CCF82, CF84]. Transition constraints based on a dynamic version of functional dependencies are investigated in [Via87], where the interaction between static and dynamic fd's is discussed. Constraints of a computational flavor on sequences of objects (*object histories*) are considered in [Gin93]. Temporal constraints specified by regular languages of events (where the events refer to object migration in object-oriented databases) are studied in [Su92]. References [Cho92a, LS87] develop the approach of "history-less" checking of temporal constraints, as illustrated in Example 22.6.5. This technique is applied to testing real-time temporal constraints in [Cho92b], providing one approach to monitoring complex events in an active database system.

Temporal databases are intimately related to temporal logic. Informative overviews of temporal logic can be found in [Eme91, Gal87].

A survey of dynamic aspects in databases is provided in [Abi88].

Exercises

Exercise 22.1 Show that there are updates expressible by IDM transactions that are not expressible by ID transactions (i.e., transactions with just insertions and deletions).

Exercise 22.17   [FUV83] Verify the claim of Example 22.4.5.

Exercise 22.18   [FUV83] Let $R[ABC]$ be a relation schema with functional dependency $A \to B$, and let $\mathbf{I}$ be the instance of Example 22.4.5.

Consider the view f over $S[AB]$ defined by $\pi_{AB}(R)$. A complement of this view is $\pi_{AC}(R)$. The idea of keeping this complement unchanged while updating the view is captured by the sentences

$$\left\{ \begin{array}{l} \exists x(R(a, x, c)), \\ \exists x(R(a, x, c')) \\ \exists x(R(a', x, c'')) \\ \exists x(R(a'', x, c''')) \end{array} \right\}$$

Let $\mathbf{T}_0$ be that set of sentences. Let $\mathbf{T}_1$ include the functional dependency and the unique name axioms. Finally, let $\mathbf{T}_2$ include the four atoms of $\mathbf{I}$. Verify that there is a unique tagged theory that accomplishes the view update [*insert* $S(a, b'')$] with minimal change.

Exercise 22.19   [FUV83] Show that under the formula-based approach to updating theories presented in Section 22.4,

(a) A sequence of deletions can lead to an exponential blowup in the size of the theory.

(b) Determining the result of an insertion is NP-hard.

Exercise 22.20   [DT92, DS93] Give a formal definition of FOID and of FOID with auxiliary relations. Include the cases in which sets of insertions and/or deletions are permitted.

♠ **Exercise 22.21**   [DT92]

(a) Verify the claim of Example 22.3.4, that the transitive closure query is FOID.

(b) Consider the datalog program

$$\begin{array}{l} R(z) \leftarrow R(x), S(x, y, z) \\ R(z) \leftarrow R(y), S(x, y, z) \\ R(x) \leftarrow T(x) \end{array}$$

An intuitive interpretation of this is that the variables range over nodes in a graph, and the predicate $S(a, b, c)$ indicates that nodes a and b are connected by an *or*-gate to node c. The relation R contains all nodes that have value *true*, assuming that the nodes in the input relation T are initially set to *true*.

Prove that there is a FOID with auxiliary relations for R. *Hint:* Define a new derived relation Q that holds paths of nodes with value *true*.

(c) Prove that there is no FOID without auxiliary relations for R.

★ (d) A *regular chain* program consists of a finite set of chain rules of the form

$$R(x, z) \leftarrow R_1(x, y_1), R_2(y_1, y_2), \ldots, R_n(y_{n-1}, z),$$

where the only idb predicate occurring in the body (if any) is R_n. Show that each regular chain program is FOID with auxiliary relations. In particular, describe an algorithm that produces, for each regular chain program defining a predicate R, a first-order query with auxiliary relations that incrementally evaluates the program.

Exercise 22.22   Specify in detail an active database execution model based on immediate rule firing.

Exercise 22.23   [ZH90] Recall the accumulating execution model for active databases.

   (a) Exhibit a rule base for which the outcome of execution depends on the order of rule firing.

   (b) Prove Theorem 22.5.2.

★ **Exercise 22.24**   [HJ91a] Recall that in the accumulating semantics, rule conditions can access $\mathbf{I}^{orig}$ and Δ^{curr}. Consider an alternative semantics that differs from the accumulating semantics only in that the rule conditions can access only $\mathbf{I}^{orig}$ and $\mathbf{I}^{curr}$. Suppose that rule conditions have the expressive power of the relational calculus (and in the case of the accumulating semantics, the ability to access the sets $\Delta_R^+ = \{R(t) \mid +R(t) \in \Delta\}$ and $\Delta_R^- = \{R(t) \mid -R(t) \in \Delta\}$). Show that the accumulating semantics is more expressive than the alternative semantics. *Hint:* It is possible that Δ^{curr} may have "redundant" elements, e.g., an update $+R(t)$, where $R(t) \in \mathbf{I}^{orig}$. Such redundant elements are not accessible to the alternative semantics.

Exercise 22.25   Consider a base schema $\mathbf{B} = \{R[AB]\}$ and a view $f = \pi_A R$, as in Example 22.3.8(b).

   (a) Describe a complement g of f that is not equivalent to $\top$.

   (b) Show that each complement g of f expressible in the relational algebra is equivalent to $\top$.

Exercise 22.26   [BS81] Prove Theorem 22.3.10. *Hint:* Consider the equivalence relation on $Inst(\mathbf{B})$ defined by $\mathbf{I} \equiv \mathbf{I}'$ iff $\exists$ update $v \in U_f$ such that $\mathbf{I}' = t(v)(\mathbf{I})$. Now define the mapping $g : Inst(\mathbf{I}) \to Inst(\mathbf{I})/\equiv$ so that $g(\mathbf{I})$ is the equivalence class of $\mathbf{I}$ under $\equiv$.

Bibliography

[57391] ISO/IEC JTC1/SC21 N 5739. Database language SQL, April 1991.

[69392] ISO/IEC JTC1/SC21 N 6931. Database language SQL (SQL3), June 1992.

[A+76] M. M. Astrahan et al. System R: a relational approach to data management. *ACM Trans. on Database Systems*, 1(2):97–137, 1976.

[AA93] P. Atzeni and V. De Antonellis. *Relational Database Theory*. Benjamin/Cummings Publishing Co., Menlo Park, CA, 1993.

[AABM82] P. Atzeni, G. Ausiello, C. Batini, and M. Moscarini. Inclusion and equivalence between relational database schemata. *Theoretical Computer Science*, 19:267–285, 1982.

[AB86] S. Abiteboul and N. Bidoit. Non first normal form relations: An algebra allowing restructuring. *Journal of Computer and System Sciences*, 33(3):361–390, 1986.

[AB87a] M. Atkinson and P. Buneman. Types and persistence in database programming languages. *ACM Computing Surveys*, 19(2):105–190, June 1987.

[AB87b] P. Atzeni and M. C. De Bernardis. A new basis for the weak instance model. In *Proc. ACM Symp. on Principles of Database Systems*, pages 79–86, 1987.

[AB88] S. Abiteboul and C. Beeri. On the manipulation of complex objects. Technical Report, INRIA and Hebrew University, 1988. (To appear, *VLDB Journal*.)

[AB91] S. Abiteboul and A. Bonner. Objects and views. In *Proc. ACM SIGMOD Symp. on the Management of Data*, 1991.

[ABD+89] M. Atkinson, F. Bancilhon, D. DeWitt, K. Dittrich, D. Maier, and S. Zdonik. The object-oriented database system manifesto. In *Proc. of Intl. Conf. on Deductive and Object-Oriented Databases (DOOD)*, pages 40–57, 1989.

[ABGO93] A. Albano, R. Bergamini, G. Ghelli, and R. Orsini. An object data model with roles. In *Proc. of Intl. Conf. on Very Large Data Bases*, pages 39–51, 1993.

[Abi83] S. Abiteboul. Algebraic analogues to fundamental notions of query and dependency theory. Technical Report, INRIA, 1983.

[Abi88] S. Abiteboul. Updates, a new frontier. In *Proc. of Intl. Conf. on Database Theory*, 1988.

[Abi89] S. Abiteboul. Boundedness is undecidable for datalog programs with a single recursive rule. *Information Processing Letters*, 32(6):281–289, 1989.

[Abr74] J.R. Abrial. Data semantics. In *Data Base Management*, pages 1–59. North Holland, Amsterdam, 1974.

[ABU79] A. V. Aho, C. Beeri, and J. D. Ullman. The theory of joins in relational databases. *ACM Trans. on Database Systems*, 4(3):297–314, 1979.

[ABW88] K. R. Apt, H. Blair, and A. Walker. Towards a theory of declarative knowledge. In J. Minker, editor, *Foundations of Deductive Databases and Logic Programming*, pages 89–148. Morgan Kaufmann, Inc., Los Altos, CA, 1988.

[AC78] A. K. Arora and C. R. Carlson. The information preserving properties of relational data base transformations. In *Proc. of Intl. Conf. on Very Large Data Bases*, pages 352–359, 1978.

[AC89] F. Afrati and S. S. Cosmadakis. Expressiveness of restricted recursive queries. In *Proc. ACM SIGACT Symp. on the Theory of Computing*, pages 113–126, 1989.

[ACO85] A. Albano, L. Cardelli, and R. Orsini. Galileo: A strongly-typed, interactive conceptual language. *ACM Trans. on Database Systems*, 10:230–260, June 1985.

[ACY91] F. Afrati, S. Cosmadakis, and M. Yannakakis. On datalog vs. polynomial time. In *Proc. ACM Symp. on Principles of Database Systems*, pages 13–25, 1991.

[ADM85] G. Ausiello, A. D'Atri, and M. Moscarini. Chordality properties on graphs and minimal conceptual connections in semantic data models. In *Proc. ACM Symp. on Principles of Database Systems*, pages 164–170, 1985.

[AG85] S. Abiteboul and G. Grahne. Update semantics for incomplete databases. In *Proc. of Intl. Conf. on Very Large Data Bases*, pages 1–12, 1985.

[AG87] M. Ajtai and Y. Gurevich. Monotone versus positive. *J. ACM*, 34(4):1004–1015, 1987.

[AG89] M. Ajtai and Y. Gurevich. Datalog versus first order. In *focs*, pages 142–148, 1989.

[AG91] S. Abiteboul and S. Grumbach. A rule-based language with functions and sets. *ACM Trans. on Database Systems*, 16(1):1–30, 1991.

[AGM85] C. E. Alchourrón, P. Gärdenfors, and D. Makinson. On the logic of theory change: partial meet contraction and revision functions. *Journal of Symbolic Logic*, 50:510–530, 1985.

[AGSS86] A. K. Aylamazan, M. M. Gigula, A. P. Stolboushkin, and G. F. Schwartz. Reduction of the relation model with infinite domains to the finite domain case. In *Proceedings of USSR Academy of Science (Dokl. Akad. Nauk. SSSR)*, vol. 286,(2), pages 308–311, 1986. (In Russian.)

[AH87] S. Abiteboul and R. Hull. IFO: A formal semantic database model. *ACM Trans. on Database Systems*, 12(4):525–565, 1987.

[AH88] S. Abiteboul and R. Hull. Data functions, datalog and negation. In *Proc. ACM SIGMOD Symp. on the Management of Data*, pages 143–153, 1988.

[AH91] A. Avron and Y. Hirshfeld. Safety in the presence of function and order symbols. In *Proc. IEEE Conf. on Logic in Computer Science*, 1991.

[AK89] S. Abiteboul and P. C. Kanellakis. Object identity as a query language primitive. In *Proc. ACM SIGMOD Symp. on the Management of Data*, pages 159–173, 1989. To appear in *J. ACM*.

[AKG91] S. Abiteboul, P. Kanellakis, and G. Grahne. On the representation and querying of sets of possible worlds. *Theoretical Computer Science*, 78:159–187, 1991.

[AKRW92] S. Abiteboul, P. Kanellakis, S. Ramaswamy, and E. Waller. Method schemas. Technical Report CS-92-33, Brown University, 1992. (An earlier version appeared in Proceedings 9th ACM PODS, 1990.)

[ALUW93] S. Abiteboul, G. Lausen, H. Uphoff, and E. Waller. Methods and rules. In *Proc. ACM SIGMOD Symp. on the Management of Data*, pages 32–41, 1993.

[AP82] P. Atzeni and D. S. Parker. Assumptions in relational database theory. In *Proc. ACM Symp. on Principles of Database Systems*, pages 1–9, 1982.

[AP87a] F. Afrati and C. H. Papadimitriou. The parallel complexity of simple chain queries. In *Proc. ACM Symp. on Principles of Database Systems,* pages 210–213, 1987.

[AP87b] K. R. Apt and J. -M. Pugin. Maintenance of stratified databases viewed as a belief revision system. In *Proc. ACM Symp. on Principles of Database Systems*, pages 136–145, 1987.

[AP92] M. Andries and J. Paredaens. A language for generic graph-transformations. In *Proc. Intl. Workshop WG 91*, pages 63–74. Springer-Verlag, Berlin, 1992.

[APP⁺86] F. Afrati, C. H. Papadimitriou, G. Papageorgiou, A. Roussou, Y. Sagiv, and J. D. Ullman. Convergence of sideways query evaluation. In *Proc. ACM Symp. on Principles of Database Systems*, pages 24–30, 1986.

[Apt91] K. R. Apt. Logic programming. In J. Van Leeuwen, editor, *Handbook of Theoretical Computer Science*, pages 493–574. Elsevier, Amsterdam, 1991.

[Arm74] W. W. Armstrong. Dependency structures of data base relationships. In *Proc. IFIP Congress*, pages 580–583. North Holland, Amsterdam, 1974.

[ASSU81] A. V. Aho, Y. Sagiv, T. G. Szymanski, and J. D. Ullman. Inferring a tree from the lowest common ancestors with an application to the optimization of relational expressions. *SIAM J. on Computing*, 10:405–421, 1981. Extended abstract appears in *Proc. 16th Ann. Allerton Conf. on Communication, Control and Computing*, Monticello, Ill., Oct. 1978, pp. 54–63.

[ASU79a] A. V. Aho, Y. Sagiv, and J. D. Ullman. Efficient optimization of a class of relational expressions. *ACM Trans. on Database Systems*, 4(4):435–454, 1979.

[ASU79b] A. V. Aho, Y. Sagiv, and J. D. Ullman. Equivalence of relational expressions. *SIAM J. on Computing*, 8(2):218–246, 1979.

[ASV90] S. Abiteboul, E. Simon, and V. Vianu. Non-deterministic languages to express deterministic transformations. In *Proc. ACM Symp. on Principles of Database Systems*, pages 218–229, 1990.

[AT93] P. Atzeni and R. Torlone. A metamodel approach for the management of multiple models and the translation of schemas. *Information Systems*, 18:349–362, 1993.

[AU79] A. V. Aho and J. D. Ullman. Universality of data retrieval languages. In *Proc. ACM Symp. on Principles of Programming Languages*, pages 110–117, 1979.

[AV87] S. Abiteboul and V. Vianu. A transaction language complete for database update and specification. In *Proc. ACM Symp. on Principles of Database Systems*, pages 260–268, 1987.

[AV88a] S. Abiteboul and V. Vianu. The connection of static constraints with boundedness and determinism of dynamic specifications. In *3rd Intl. Conf. on Data and Knowledge Bases*, pages 324–334, Jerusalem, 1988.

[AV88b] S. Abiteboul and V. Vianu. Equivalence and optimization of relational transactions. *J. ACM*, 35(1):130–145, 1988.

[AV88c] S. Abiteboul and V. Vianu. Procedural and declarative database update languages. In *Proc. ACM Symp. on Principles of Database Systems*, pages 240–250, 1988.

[AV89] S. Abiteboul and V. Vianu. A transaction-based approach to relational database specification. *J. ACM*, 36(4):758–789, October 1989.

[AV90] S. Abiteboul and V. Vianu. Procedural languages for database queries and updates. *Journal of Computer and System Sciences*, 41:181–229, 1990.

[AV91a] S. Abiteboul and V. Vianu. Datalog extensions for database queries and updates. *Journal of Computer and System Sciences*, 43:62–124, 1991.

[AV91b] S. Abiteboul and V. Vianu. Generic computation and its complexity. In *Proc. ACM SIGACT Symp. on the Theory of Computing*, pages 209–219, 1991.

[AV91c] S. Abiteboul and V. Vianu. Non-determinism in logic-based languages. *Annals of Math. and Artif. Int.*, 3:151–186, 1991.

[AV94] S. Abiteboul and V. Vianu. Computing with first-order logic. *Journal of Computer and System Sciences*, 1994. To appear.

[AvE82] K. Apt and M. van Emden. Contributions to the theory of logic programming. *J. ACM*, 29(3):841–862, 1982.

[AVV92] S. Abiteboul, M. Y. Vardi, and V. Vianu. Fixpoint logics, relational machines, and computational complexity. In *Conf. on Structure in Complexity Theory*, pages 156–168, 1992.

[AW88] K. R. Apt and H. A. Walker. Arithmetic classification of perfect models of stratified programs. Technical Report TR-88-09, University of Texas at Austin, 1988.

[B+86] D. G. Bobrow et al. CommonLoops: Merging lisp and object-oriented programming. In *Proc. ACM Conf. on Object-Oriented Programming Systems, Languages, and Applications*, pages 17–29, 1986.

[B+88] D. S. Batory et al. Genesis: An extensible database management system. *IEEE Transactions on Software Engineering*, SE-14(11):1711–1730, 1988.

[Ban78] F. Bancilhon. On the completeness of query languages for relational data bases. In *7th Symposium on the Mathematical Foundations of Computer Science*, pages 112–123. Springer-Verlag, Berlin, LNCS 64, 1978.

[Ban85] F. Bancilhon. A note on the performance of rule based systems. Technical Report DB-022-85, MCC, 1985.

[Ban86] F. Bancilhon. Naive evaluation of recursively defined relations. In M. L. Brodie and J. L. Mylopoulos, editors, *On Knowledge Base Management Systems—Integrating Database and AI Systems*, pages 165–178. Springer-Verlag, Berlin, 1986.

[Bar63] H. Barendregt. Functional programming and lambda calculus. In J. Van Leeuwen, editor, *Handbook of Theoretical Computer Science, vol. B*, pages 321–363. Elsevier, Amsterdam, 1990.

[Bar84] H. Barendregt. *The Lambda Calculus: Its Syntax and Semantics*. North Holland, Amsterdam, 1984.

[BB79] C. Beeri and P. A. Bernstein. Computational problems related to the design of normal form relational schemas. *ACM Trans. on Database Systems*, 4(1):30–59, March 1979.

[BB91] J. Berstel and L. Boasson. Context-free languages. In J. Van Leeuwen, editor, *Handbook of Theoretical Computer Science*, pages 102–163. Elsevier, Amsterdam, 1991.

[BB92] D. Beneventano and S. Bergamaschi. Subsumption for complex object data models. In *Proc. of Intl. Conf. on Database Theory*, pages 357–375, 1992.

[BBC80] P. A. Bernstein, B. T. Blaustein, and E. M. Clarke. Fast maintenance of semantic integrity assertions using redundant aggregate data. In *Proc. of Intl. Conf. on Very Large Data Bases*, pages 126–136, 1980.

[BBG78] C. Beeri, P. A. Bernstein, and N. Goodman. A sophisticate's introduction to database normalization theory. In *Proc. of Intl. Conf. on Very Large Data Bases*, pages 113–124, 1978.

[BBMR89] A. Borgida, R. J. Brachman, D. L. McGuinness, and L. A. Resnick. CLASSIC: A structural data model for objects. In *Proc. ACM SIGMOD Symp. on the Management of Data*, pages 58–67, 1989.

[BC79] O. P. Buneman and G. K. Clemons. Efficiently monitoring relational databases. *ACM Trans. on Database Systems*, 4(3):368–382, September 1979.

[BC81] P. A. Bernstein and D. W. Chiu. Using semi-joins to solve relational queries. *J. ACM*, 28(1):25–40, 1981.

[BCD89] F. Bancilhon, S. Cluet, and C. Delobel. Query languages for object-oriented database systems: the O_2 proposal. In *Proc. Second Intl. Workshop on Data Base Programming Languages*, 1989.

[BCW93] M. Baudinet, J. Chomicki, and P. Wolper. Temporal deductive databases. In A. U. Tansel et al., editors, *Temporal Databases—Theory, Design, and Implementation*, pages 294–320. Benjamin/Cummings Publishing Co., Menlo Park, CA, 1993.

[BDB79] J. Biskup, U. Dayal, and P. A. Bernstein. Synthesizing independent database schemas. In *Proc. ACM SIGMOD Symp. on the Management of Data*, pages 143–152, 1979.

[BDFS84] C. Beeri, M. Dowd, R. Fagin, and R. Statman. On the structure of Armstrong relations for functional dependencies. *J. ACM*, 31(1):30–46, 1984.

[BDK92] F. Bancilhon, C. Delobel, and P. Kanellakis, editors. *Building an Object-Oriented Database System: The Story of O_2*. Morgan Kaufmann, Inc., Los Altos, CA, 1992.

[BDM88] F. Bry, H. Decker, and R. Manthey. A uniform approach to constraint satisfaction and constraint satisfiability in deductive databases. In *Proc. of Intl. Conf. on Extending Data Base Technology*, pages 488–505, 1988.

[BDW88] P. Buneman, S. Davidson, and A. Watters. A semantics for complex objects and approximate queries. In *Proc. ACM Symp. on Principles of Database Systems*, pages 302–314, 1988.

[BDW91] P. Buneman, S. Davidson, and A. Watters. A semantics for complex objects and approximate answers. *Journal of Computer and System Sciences*, 43:170–218, 1991.

[Bee80] C. Beeri. On the membership problem for functional and multivalued dependencies in relational databases. *ACM Trans. on Database Systems*, 5:241–259, 1980.

[Bee90] C. Beeri. A formal approach to object-oriented databases. *Data and Knowledge Engineering*, 5(4):353–382, 1990.

[Ber76a] C. Berge. *Graphs and Hypergraphs*. North Holland, Amsterdam, 1976.

[Ber76b] P. A. Bernstein. Synthesizing third normal form relations from functional dependencies. *ACM Trans. on Database Systems*, 1(4):277–298, 1976.

[BF87] N. Bidoit and C. Froidevaux. Minimalism subsumes default logic and circumscription. In *Proc. IEEE Conf. on Logic in Computer Science*, pages 89–97, 1987.

[BF88] N. Bidoit and C. Froidevaux. General logic databases and programs: Default logic semantics and stratification. Technical Report, LRI, Université de Paris-Sud, Orsay, 1988. To appear in *J. Information and Computation*.

[BFH77] C. Beeri, R. Fagin, and J. H. Howard. A complete axiomatization for functional and multivalued dependencies. In *Proc. ACM SIGMOD Symp. on the Management of Data*, pages 47–61, 1977.

[BFM$^+$81] C. Beeri, R. Fagin, D. Maier, A. O. Mendelzon, J. D. Ullman, and M. Yannakakis. Properties of acyclic database schemes. In *Proc. ACM SIGACT Symp. on the Theory of Computing*, pages 355–362, 1981.

[BFMY83] C. Beeri, R. Fagin, D. Maier, and M. Yannakakis. On the desirability of acyclic database schemes. *J. ACM*, 30(3):479–513, 1983.

[BFN82] P. Buneman, R. Frankel, and R. Nikhil. An implementation technique for database query languages. *ACM Trans. on Database Systems*, 7:164–186, 1982.

[BG81] P. A. Bernstein and N. Goodman. The power of natural semi-joins. *SIAM J. on Computing*, 10(4):751–771, 1981.

[BGK85] A. Blass, Y. Gurevich, and D. Kozen. A zero-one law for logic with a fixed point operator. *Information and Control*, 67:70–90, 1985.

[BGL85] R. J. Brachman, V. P. Gilbert, and H. J. Levesque. An essential hybrid reasoning system: Knowledge and symbol level accounts of KRYPTON. In *Intl. Joint Conf. on Artificial Intelligence*, pages 532–539, 1985.

[BGW+81] P. A. Bernstein, N. Goodman, E. Wong, et al. Query processing in a system for distributed databases (SDD-1). *ACM Trans. on Database Systems*, 6:602–625, 1981.

[BHG87] P. A. Bernstein, V. Hadzilacos, and N. Goodman. *Concurrency Control and Recovery in Database Systems*. Addison-Wesley, Reading, MA, 1987.

[Bid91a] N. Bidoit. *Bases de Données Déductives (Présentation de Datalog)*. Armand Colin, Paris, 1991.

[Bid91b] N. Bidoit. Negation in rule-based database languages: A survey. *Theoretical Computer Science*, 78:3–83, 1991.

[Bis80] J. Biskup. Inferences of multivalued dependencies in fixed and undetermined universes. *Theoretical Computer Science*, 10:93–105, 1980.

[Bis81] J. Biskup. A formal approach to null values in database relations. In H. Gallaire, J. Minker, and J.M. Nicolas, editors, *Advances in Data Base Theory, vol. 1*, pages 299–341. Plenum Press, New York, 1981.

[Bis83] J. Biskup. A foundation of Codd's relational maybe-operations. *ACM Trans. on Database Systems*, 8(4):608–636, 1983.

[BJO91] P. Buneman, A. Jung, and A. Ohori. Using powerdomains to generalize relational databases. *Theoretical Computer Science*, 91:23–55, 1991.

[BK86] C. Beeri and M. Kifer. An integrated approach to logical design of relational database schemes. *ACM Trans. on Database Systems*, 11:134–158, 1986.

[BKBR87] C. Beeri, P. C. Kanellakis, F. Bancilhon, and R. Ramakrishnan. Bounds on the propagation of selection into logic programs. In *Proc. ACM Symp. on Principles of Database Systems*, pages 214–226, 1987.

[BL90] N. Bidoit and P. Legay. Well! an evaluation procedure for all logic programs. In *Proc. of Intl. Conf. on Database Theory*, pages 335–348. Springer-Verlag, Berlin, LNCS 470, 1990.

[BLN86] C. Batini, M. Lenzerini, and S. B. Navathe. A comparative analysis of methodologies for database schema integration. *ACM Computing Surveys*, 18:323–364, 1986.

[BLT86] J. A. Blakeley, P.-A. Larson, and F. W. Tompa. Efficiently updating materialized views. In *Proc. ACM SIGMOD Symp. on the Management of Data*, pages 61–71, 1986.

[BM91] C. Beeri and T. Milo. A model for active object oriented databases. In *Proc. of Intl. Conf. on Very Large Data Bases*, pages 337–349, 1991.

[BMG93] J. A. Blakeley, W. J. McKenna, and G. Graefe. Experiences building the open OODB query optimizer. In *Proc. ACM SIGMOD Symp. on the Management of Data*, pages 287–296, 1993.

[BMSU81] C. Beeri, A. O. Mendelzon, Y. Sagiv, and J. D. Ullman. Equivalence of relational database schemes. *SIAM J. on Computing*, 10(2):352–370, 1981.

[BMSU86] F. Bancilhon, D. Maier, Y. Sagiv, and J. D. Ullman. Magic sets and other strange ways to implement logic programs. In *Proc. ACM Symp. on Principles of Database Systems*, pages 1–15, 1986.

[BNR+87a] C. Beeri, S. Naqvi, R. Ramakrishnan, O. Shmueli, and S. Tsur. Sets and negation in a logic database language (LDL1). In *Proc. ACM Symp. on Principles of Database Systems*, pages 21–37, 1987.

[Bor85] A. Borgida. Features of languages for the development of information systems at the conceptual level. *IEEE Software*, 2:63–72, 1985.

[BP83] P. De Bra and J. Paredaens. Conditional dependencies for horizontal decompositions. In *Proc. Intl. Conf. on Algorithms, Languages and Programming*, pages 67–82. Springer-Verlag, Berlin, LNCS 154, 1983.

[BPR87] I. Balbin, B. S. Port, and K. Ramamohanarao. Magic set computation for stratified databases. Technical Report TR 87/3, Dept. of Computer Science, University of Melbourne, 1987.

[BR80] C. Beeri and J. Rissanin. Faithful representation of relational database schemes. Technical Report RJ2722, IBM Research Laboratory, San Jose, CA, 1980.

[BR87a] C. Beeri and R. Ramakrishnan. On the power of magic. In *Proc. ACM Symp. on Principles of Database Systems*, pages 269–283, 1987.

[BR87b] I. Balnbin and K. Ramamohanarao. A generalization of the differential approach to recursive query evaluation. In *Journal of Logic Programming*, 4(3), 1987.

[BR88a] F. Bancilhon and R. Ramakrishnan. An amateur's introduction to recursive query processing strategies. In M. Stonebraker, editor, *Readings in Database Systems*, pages 507–555. Morgan Kaufmann, Inc., Los Altos, CA, 1988. An earlier version of this work appears in *Proc. ACM SIGMOD Conf. on Management of Data*, pp. 16–52, 1986.

[BR88b] F. Bancilhon and R. Ramakrishnan. Performance evaluation of data intensive logic programs. In J. Minker, editor, *Foundations of Deductive Databases and Logic Programming*, pages 439–517. Morgan Kaufmann, Inc., Los Altos, CA, 1988.

[BR91] C. Beeri and R. Ramakrishnan. On the power of magic. *J. Logic Programming*, 10(3&4):255–300, 1991.

[BRS82] F. Bancilhon, P. Richard, and M. Scholl. On line processing of compacted relations. In *Proc. of Intl. Conf. on Very Large Data Bases*, pages 263–269, 1982.

[BRSS92] C. Beeri, R. Ramakrishnan, D. Srivastava, and S. Sudarshan. The valid model semantics for logic programs. In *Proc. ACM Symp. on Principles of Database Systems*, pages 91–104, 1992.

[Bry89] F. Bry. Query evaluation in recursive databases: Bottom-up and top-down reconciled. In *Proc. of Intl. Conf. on Deductive and Object-Oriented Databases (DOOD)*, pages 20–39, 1989.

[BS81] F. Bancilhon and N. Spyratos. Update semantics of relational views. *ACM Trans. on Database Systems*, 6(4):557–575, 1981.

[BS85] R. J. Brachman and J. G. Schmolze. An overview of the KL-ONE knowledge representation system. *Cognitive Science*, 9:171–216, 1985.

[BS93] S. Bergamaschi and C. Sartori. On taxonomic reasoning in conceptual design. *ACM Trans. on Database Systems*, 17:385–422, 1993.

[BST75] P. A. Bernstein, J. R. Swenson, and D. C. Tzichritzis. A unified approach to functional dependencies and relations. In *Proc. ACM SIGMOD Symp. on the Management of Data*, pages 237–245, 1975.

[BTBN92] V. Breazu-Tannen, P. Buneman, and S. Naqvi. Structural recursion as a query language. In *Proc. of Intl. Workshop on Database Programming Languages*, pages 9–19. Morgan Kaufmann, Inc., Los Altos, CA, 1992.

[BTBW92] V. Breazu-Tannen, P. Buneman, and L. Wong. Naturally embedded query languages. In *Proc. of Intl. Conf. on Database Theory*, pages 140–154. Springer-Verlag, Berlin, LNCS, 1992.

[BV80a] C. Beeri and M. Y. Vardi. On the complexity of testing implications of data dependencies. Technical Report, Department of Computer Science, Hebrew University of Jerusalem, 1980.

[BV80b] C. Beeri and M. Y. Vardi. A proof procedure for data dependencies (preliminary report). Technical Report, Department of Computer Science, Hebrew University of Jerusalem, August 1980.

[BV81a] C. Beeri and M. Y. Vardi. The implication problem for data dependencies. In *Proc. Intl. Conf. on Algorithms, Languages and Programming*, pages 73–85, 1981. Springer-Verlag, Berlin, LNCS 115.

[BV81b] C. Beeri and M. Y. Vardi. On the properties of join dependencies. In H. Gallaire, J. Minker, and J. M. Nicolas, editors, *Advances in Data Base Theory, vol. 1*, pages 25–72. Plenum Press, New York, 1981.

[BV84a] C. Beeri and M. Y. Vardi. Formal systems for tuple and equality generating dependencies. *SIAM J. on Computing*, 13(1):76–98, 1984.

[BV84b] C. Beeri and M. Y. Vardi. On acyclic database decompositions. *Inf. and Control*, 61(2):75–84, 1984.

[BV84c] C. Beeri and M. Y. Vardi. A proof procedure for data dependencies. *J. ACM*, 31(4):718–741, 1984.

[BV85] C. Beeri and M. Y. Vardi. Formal systems for join dependencies. *Theoretical Computer Science*, 38:99–116, 1985.

[C$^+$76] D. D. Chamberlin et al. Sequel 2: a unified approach to data definition, manipulation and control. *IBM J. Research and Development*, 20(6):560–575, 1976.

[Cam92] M. Campbell. *Microsoft Access – Inside and Out*. Osborne McGraw-Hill, New York, 1992.

[Car88] L. Cardelli. A semantics of multiple inheritance. *Information and Computation*, 76:138–164, 1988.

[Cat94] R. G. G. Cattell, editor. *The Object Database Standard: ODMB-93*. Morgan Kaufmann, Inc., Los Altos, CA, 1994.

[CCCR$^+$90] F. Cacace, S. Ceri, S. Crespi-Reghizzi, L. Tanca, and R. Zicari. Integrating object-oriented data modeling with a rule-based programming paradigm. In *Proc. ACM SIGMOD Symp. on the Management of Data*, pages 225–236, 1990.

[CCF82] I. M. V. Castillo, M. A. Casanova, and A. L. Furtado. A temporal framework for database specification. In *Proc. of Intl. Conf. on Very Large Data Bases*, pages 280–291, 1982.

[CF84] M. A. Casanova and A. L. Furtado. On the description of database transition constraints using temporal logic. In H. Gallaire, J. Minker, and J. -M. Nicolas, editors, *Advances in Data Base Theory, vol. 2*. Plenum Press, New York, 1984.

[CFI89] J. Cai, M. Fürer, and N. Immerman. An optimal lower bound on the number of variables for graph identification. In *IEEE Conf. on Foundations of Computer Science*, pages 612–617, 1989.

[CFP84] M. A. Casanova, R. Fagin, and C. H. Papadimitriou. Inclusion dependencies and their interaction with functional dependencies. *Journal of Computer and System Sciences*, 28(1):29–59, 1984.

[CGKV88] S. S. Cosmadakis, H. Gaifman, P. C. Kanellakis, and M. Y. Vardi. Decidable optimization problems for database logic programs. In *Proc. ACM SIGACT Symp. on the Theory of Computing*, 1988.

[CGP93] L. Corciulo, F. Giannotti, and D. Pedreschi. Datalog with non-deterministic choice computes NDB-PTIME. In *Proc. of Intl. Conf. on Deductive and Object-Oriented Databases (DOOD)*, 1993.

[CGT90] S. Ceri, G. Gottlob, and L. Tanca. *Logic Programming and Databases*. Springer-Verlag, Berlin, 1990.

[CH80a] A. K. Chandra and D. Harel. Structure and complexity of relational queries. In *IEEE Conf. on Foundations of Computer Science*, pages 333–347, 1980.

[CH80b] A. K. Chandra and D. Harel. Computable queries for relational data bases. *Journal of Computer and System Sciences*, 21(2):156–178, 1980.

[CH82] A. K. Chandra and D. Harel. Structure and complexity of relational queries. *Journal of Computer and System Sciences*, 25(1):99–128, 1982.

[CH85] A. K. Chandra and D. Harel. Horn clause queries and generalizations. *J. Logic Programming*, 2(1):1–15, 1985.

[Cha81a] A. K. Chandra. Programming primitives for database languages. In *Proc. ACM Symp. on Principles of Programming Languages*, pages 50–62, 1981.

[Cha81b] C. Chang. On the evaluation of queries containing derived relations in relational databases. In H. Gallaire, J. Minker, and J.-M. Nicolas, editors, *Advances in Database Theory, vol. 1*, pages 235–260. Plenum Press, New York, 1981.

[Cha88] A. K. Chandra. Theory of database queries. In *Proc. ACM Symp. on Principles of Database Systems*, pages 1–9, 1988.

[Cha94] T. -P. Chang. *On Incremental Update Propagation Between Object-based Databases*. Ph.D. thesis, University of Southern California, Los Angeles, 1994.

[Che76] P. P. Chen. The entity-relationship model – Toward a unified view of data. *ACM Trans. on Database Systems*, 1:9–36, 1976.

[CHM94] I-M. A. Chen, R. Hull, and D. McLeod. Local ambiguity and derived data update. In *Fourth Intl. Workshop on Research Issues in Data Engineering: Active Database Systems*, pages 77–86, 1994.

[Cho92a] J. Chomicki. History-less checking of dynamic integrity constraints. In *Proc. IEEE Intl. Conf. on Data Engineering*, 1992.

[Cho92b] J. Chomicki. Real-time integrity constraints. In *Proc. ACM Symp. on Principles of Database Systems*, 1992.

[Cho94] J. Chomicki. Temporal query languages: A survey. In *Proc. 1st Intl. Conf. on Temporal Logic*, 1994.

[Chu41] A. Church. *The Calculi of Lambda-Conversion*. Princeton University Press, Princeton, NJ, 1941.

[CK73] C. C. Chang and H. J. Keisler. *Model Theory*. North Holland, Amsterdam, 1973.

[CK85] S. S. Cosmadakis and P. C. Kanellakis. Equational theories and database constraints. In *Proc. ACM SIGACT Symp. on the Theory of Computing*, pages 73–284, 1985.

[CK86] S. S. Cosmadakis and P. C. Kanellakis. Functional and inclusion dependencies: A graph theoretic approach. In P. C. Kanellakis and F. Preparata, editors, *Advances in Computing Research, vol. 3: The Theory of Databases*, pages 164–185. JAI Press, Inc., Greenwich, CT, 1986.

[CKRP73] A. Colmerauer, H. Kanoui, P. Roussel, and R. Pasero. Un système de communication homme-machine en français. Technical Report, Groupe de Recherche en Intelligence Artificielle, Université Aix-Marseille, 1973.

[CKS86] S. S. Cosmadakis, P. C. Kanellakis, and S. Spyratos. Partition semantics for relations. *Journal of Computer and System Sciences*, 32(2):203–233, 1986.

[CKV90] S. S. Cosmadakis, P. C. Kanellakis, and M. Y. Vardi. Polynomial-time implications problems for unary inclusion dependencies. *J. ACM*, 37:15–46, 1990.

[CL73] C. L. Chang and R. C. T. Lee. *Symbolic Logic and Mechanical Theorem Proving*. Academic Press, New York, 1973.

[CL94] D. Calvanese and M. Lenzerini. Making object-oriented schemas more expressive. In *Proc. ACM Symp. on Principles of Database Systems*, 1994.

[Cla78] K. L. Clark. Negation as failure logic and databases. In H. Gallaire and J. Minker, editors, *Logic and Databases*, pages 293–322. Plenum Press, New York, 1978.

[CLM81] A. K. Chandra, H. R. Lewis, and J. A. Makowsky. Embedded implicational dependencies and their inference problem. In *Proc. ACM SIGACT Symp. on the Theory of Computing*, pages 342–354, 1981.

[CM77] A. K. Chandra and P. M. Merlin. Optimal implementation on conjunctive queries in relational data bases. In *Proc. ACM SIGACT Symp. on the Theory of Computing*, pages 77–90, 1977.

[CM90] M. Consens and A. Mendelzon. GraphLog: A visual formalism for real life recursion. In *Proc. ACM Symp. on Principles of Database Systems*, pages 404–416, 1990.

[CM93a] M. Consens and A. Mendelzon. The hy+ hygraph visualization system. In *Proc. ACM SIGMOD Symp. on the Management of Data*, 1993.

[CM93b] M. Consens and A. Mendelzon. Low complexity aggregation in GraphLog and Datalog. *Theoretical Computer Science*, 116(1):95–116, 1993. A preliminary version was published in the Proceedings of the Third International Conference on Database Theory, Springer-Verlag, Berlin, LNCS 470, 1990.

[Cod70] E. F. Codd. A relational model of data for large shared data banks. *Comm. of the ACM*, 13(6):377–387, 1970.

[Cod71] E. F. Codd. Normalized database structure: A brief tutorial. In *ACM SIGFIDET Workshop on Data Description, Access and Control*, November 1971.

[Cod72a] E. F. Codd. Further normalization of the data base relational model. In R. Rustin, editor, *Courant Computer Science Symposium 6: Data Base Systems*, pages 33–64. Prentice-Hall, Englewood Cliffs, NJ, 1972.

[Cod72b] E. F. Codd. Relational completeness of database sublanguages. In R. Rustin, editor, *Courant Computer Science Symposium 6: Data Base Systems*, pages 65–98. Prentice-Hall, Englewood Cliffs, NJ, 1972.

[Cod74] E. F. Codd. Recent investigations in relational data base systems. In *Information Processing 74*, pages 1017–1021. North Holland, Amsterdam, 1974.

[Cod75] T. Codd. Understanding relations (installment #7). In *FDT Bull. of ACM Sigmod 7*, pages 23–28, 1975.

[Cod79] E. F. Codd. Extending the data base relational model to capture more meaning. *ACM Trans. on Database Systems*, 4(4):397–434, 1979.

[Cod82] E. F. Codd. Relational databases: A practical foundation for productivity. *Comm. of the ACM*, 25(2):102–117, 1982.

[Coh86] D. Cohen. Programming by specification and annotation. In *Proc. of AAAI*, 1986.

[Coh89] D. Cohen. Compiling complex database transition triggers. In *Proc. ACM SIGMOD Symp. on the Management of Data*, pages 225–234, 1989.

[Coh90] J. Cohen. Constraint logic programming languages. *Comm. of the ACM*, 33(7):69–90, 1990.

[Com88] K. Compton. 0-1 laws in logic and combinatorics. In *1987 NATO Adv. Study Inst. on Algorithms and Order*, pages 353–383, 1988.

[Coo74] S. A. Cook. An observation on a time-storage trade-off. *Journal of Computer and System Sciences*, 9:308–316, 1974.

[Cos83] S. S. Cosmadakis. The complexity of evaluating relational queries. *Inf. and Control*, 58:101–112, 1983.

[Cos87] S. S. Cosmadakis. Database theory and cylindric lattices. In *IEEE Conf. on Foundations of Computer Science*, pages 411–420, 1987.

[Cou90] B. Courcelle. Recursive applicative program schemes. In J. Van Leeuwen, editor, *Handbook of Theoretical Computer Science, vol. B*, pages 459–492. Elsevier, Amsterdam, 1990.

[CP84] S. S. Cosmadakis and C. H. Papadimitriou. Updates of relational views. *J. ACM*, 31(4):742–760, 1984.

[CRG$^+$88] S. Ceri, S. Crespi Reghizzi, G. Gottlob, F. Lamperti, L. Lavazza, L. Tanca, and R. Zicari. The algres project. In *Proc. of Intl. Conf. on Extending Data Base Technology*. Springer-Verlag, Berlin, 1988.

[CT48] L. H. Chin and A. Tarski. Remarks on projective algebras. *Bulletin AMS*, 54:80–81, 1948.

[CT87] S. Ceri and L. Tanca. Optimization of systems of algebraic equations for evaluating datalog queries. In *Proc. of Intl. Conf. on Very Large Data Bases*, 1987.

[CTF88] M. A. Casanova, L. Tucherman, and A. L. Furtado. Enforcing inclusion dependencies and referential integrity. In *Proc. of Intl. Conf. on Very Large Data Bases*, pages 38–49, 1988.

[CV81] T. Connors and V. Vianu. Tableaux which define expression mappings. Technical Report, Computer Science Department, University of Southern California, 1981. Presented at XP2 Conf. on Theory of Relational Databases, Pennsylvania State University, June 1981.

[CV83] M. A. Casanova and V. M. P. Vidal. Towards a sound view integration methodology. In *Proc. ACM Symp. on Principles of Database Systems*, pages 36–47, 1983.

[CV85] A. K. Chandra and M. Y. Vardi. The implication problem for functional and inclusion dependencies is undecidable. *SIAM J. on Computing*, 14(3):671–677, 1985.

[CV92] S. Chaudhuri and M. Y. Vardi. On the equivalence of datalog programs. In *Proc. ACM Symp. on Principles of Database Systems*, pages 55–66, 1992.

[CV93] S. Chaudhuri and M. Y. Vardi. Optimization of *real* conjunctive queries. In *Proc. ACM Symp. on Principles of Database Systems*, pages 59–70, 1993.

[CV94] S. Chaudhuri and M. Y. Vardi. On the complexity of equivalence between recursive and nonrecursive datalog programs. In *Proc. ACM Symp. on Principles of Database Systems*, pages 107–116, 1994.

[CW85] L. Cardelli and P. Wegner. On understanding types, data abstraction and polymorphism. *ACM Computing Surveys*, 17:471–522, December 1985.

[CW89a] W. Chen and D. S. Warren. C-Logic of complex objects. In *Proc. ACM Symp. on Principles of Database Systems*, pages 369–378, 1989.

[CW89b] S. R. Cohen and O. Wolfson. Why a single parallelization strategy is not enough in knowledge bases. In *Proc. ACM Symp. on Principles of Database Systems*, pages 200–216, 1989.

[CW90] S. Ceri and J. Widom. Deriving production rules for constraint maintenance. In *Proc. of Intl. Conf. on Very Large Data Bases*, pages 566–577, 1990.

[CW91] S. Ceri and J. Widom. Deriving production rules for incremental view maintenance. In *Proc. of Intl. Conf. on Very Large Data Bases*, pages 577–589, 1991.

[CW92] W. Chen and D. S. Warren. A goal oriented approach to computing well founded semantics. In *Proc. of the Joint Intl. Conf. and Symp. on Logic Programming*, pages 589–606, 1992.

[CW93] S. Ceri and J. Widom. Managing semantic heterogeneity with production rules and persistent queues. In *Proc. of Intl. Conf. on Very Large Data Bases*, pages 108–119, 1993.

[DA83] C. Delobel and M. Adiba. *Bases de Données et Systèmes Relationnels*. Dunod Informatique, Paris, 1983.

[Dal87] E. Dalhaus. Skolem normal forms concerning the least fixpoint. In E. Börger, editor, *Computation Theory and Logic, vol. 270*, pages 101–106. Springer-Verlag, Berlin, LNCS, 1987.

[Dat81] C. J. Date. Referential integrity. In *Proc. of Intl. Conf. on Very Large Data Bases*, pages 2–12, 1981.

[Dat86] C. J. Date. *An Introduction to Database Systems*. Addison-Wesley, Reading, MA, 1986.

[Daw93] A. Dawar. *Feasible Computation through Model Theory*. Ph.D. thesis, University of Pennsylvania, 1993.

[Day89] U. Dayal. Queries and views in an object-oriented data model. In *Proc. of Intl. Workshop on Database Programming Languages*, pages 80–102, 1989.

[DB82] U. Dayal and P. A. Bernstein. On the correct translation of update operations on relational views. *ACM Trans. on Database Systems*, 8(3):381–416, 1982.

[DC72] C. Delobel and R. C. Casey. Decomposition of a database and the theory of boolean switching functions. *IBM J. Research and Development*, 17(5):370–386, 1972.

[DD89] L. M. L. Delcambre and K. C. Davis. Automatic validation of object-oriented database structures. In *Proc. IEEE Intl. Conf. on Data Engineering*, pages 2–9, 1989.

[Dec86] H. Decker. Extending and restricting deductive databases. Technical Report KB-21, ECRC, Munich, 1986.

[Del78] C. Delobel. Normalization and hierarchical dependencies in the relational data model. *ACM Trans. on Database Systems*, 3(3):201–222, 1978.

[Dem82] R. Demolombe. Syntactical characterization of a subset of domain independent formulas. Technical Report, ONERA–CERT, Toulouse, 1982.

[DF92] C. J. Date and R. Fagin. Simple conditions for guaranteeing higher normal forms in relational databases. *ACM Trans. on Database Systems*, 17:465–476, 1992.

[DG79] B. S. Dreben and W. D. Goldfarb. *The Decision Problem: Solvable Classes of Qualificational Formulas*. Addison-Wesley, Reading, MA, 1979.

[DHL91] U. Dayal, M. Hsu, and R. Ladin. A transaction model for long-running activities. In *Proc. of Intl. Conf. on Very Large Data Bases*, pages 113–122, 1991.

[DiP69] R. A. DiPaola. The recursive unsolvability of the decision problem for a class of definite formulas. *J. ACM*, 16(2):324–327, 1969.

[DM86a] E. Dahlhaus and J. A. Makowsky. Computable directory queries. In *11th CAAP 86*, pages 254–265, Springer-Verlag, Berlin, LNCS 214, 1986.

[DM86b] A. D'Atri and M. Moscarini. Recognition algorithms and design methodologies for acyclic database. In P. C. Kanellakis and F. Preparata, editors, *Schemes Advances in Computing Research, vol. 3*, pages 164–185. JAI Press, Inc., Greenwich, CT, 1986.

[DM92] E. Dalhaus and J. A. Makowsky. Query languages for hierarchic databases. *Information and Computation*, 101(1):1–32, November 1992.

[DMP93] M. A. Derr, S. Morishita, and G. Phipps. Design and implementation of the Glue-Nail database system. In *Proc. ACM SIGMOD Symp. on the Management of Data*, pages 147–156, 1993.

[dMS88] C. de Maindreville and E. Simon. Modelling non-deterministic queries and updates in deductive databases. In *Proc. of Intl. Conf. on Very Large Data Bases*, 1988.

[Don92] G. Dong. Datalog expressiveness of chain queries: Grammar tools and characterizations. In *Proc. ACM Symp. on Principles of Database Systems*, pages 81–90, 1992.

[DP84] P. DeBra and J. Paredaens. Horizontal decompositions for handling exceptions to functional dependencies. In H. Gallaire, J. Minker, and J. -M. Nicolas, editors, *Advances in Database Theory, vol. 2*, pages 123–144. Plenum Press, New York, 1984.

[dR87] M. de Rougemont. Second-order and inductive definability of finite structures. *Zeitschr. Math. Logik und Grundlagen d. Math.*, 33:47–63, 1987.

[DS91] G. Dong and J. Su. Object behaviors and scripts. In *Proc. of Intl. Workshop on Database Programming Languages*, pages 27–30, 1991.

[DS92] G. Dong and J. Su. Incremental and decremental evaluation of transitive closure by first-order queries. Technical Report TRCS 92-18, University of California, Santa Barbara, 1992. To appear in *Information and Computation*.

[DS93] G. Dong and J. Su. First-order incremental evaluation of datalog queries (extended abstract). In *Proc. of Intl. Workshop on Database Programming Languages*, 1993.

[DST93] G. Dong, J. Su, and R. Topor. First-order incremental evaluation of datalog queries. Technical Report, Department of Computer Science, University of Melbourne, Australia, 1993.

[DT92] G. Dong and R. Topor. Incremental evaluation of datalog queries. In *Proc. of Intl. Conf. on Database Theory*, pages 282–296, 1992.

[DV91] K. Denninghoff and V. Vianu. The power of methods with parallel semantics. In *Proc. of Intl. Conf. on Very Large Data Bases*, pages 221–232, 1991.

[DV93] K. Denninghoff and V. Vianu. Database method schemas and object creation. In *Proc. ACM Symp. on Principles of Database Systems*, pages 265–275, 1993.

[DW85] S. W. Dietrich and D. S. Warren. Dynamic programming strategies for the evaluation of recursive queries. Technical Report TR 85-31, Computer Science Department, SUNY at Stony Brook, New York, 1985.

[DW87] S. W. Dietrich and D. S. Warren. Extension tables: Memo relations in logic programming. In *Proc. of the Symposium on Logic Programming*, 1987.

[DW94] U. Dayal and J. Widom. *Active Database Systems*. Morgan Kaufmann Publishers, Inc., Los Altos, CA. In preparation, to appear in 1994.

[EFT84] H. D. Ebbinghaus, J. Flum, and W. Thomas. *Mathematical Logic*. Springer-Verlag, Berlin, 1984.

[EGM94] T. Eiter, G. Gottlob, and H. Mannila. Adding disjunction to Datalog. In *Proce. ACM Symp. on Principles of Database Systems*, pages 267–278, 1994.

[EHJ93] M. Escobar-Molano, R. Hull, and D. Jacobs. Safety and translation of calculus queries with scalar functions. In *Proc. ACM Symp. on Principles of Database Systems*, pages 253–264, 1993.

[Ehr61] A. Ehrenfeucht. An application of games to the completeness problem for formalized theories. *Fund. Math.*, 49:129–141, 1961.

[Eme91] E. A. Emerson. Temporal and modal logic. In J. Van Leeuwen, editor, *Handbook of Theoretical Computer Science*, pages 997–1072. Elsevier, Amsterdam, 1991.

[EN89] R. Elmasri and S. B. Navathe. *Fundamentals of Database Systems*. Benjamin/Cummings Publishing Co., Menlo Park, CA, 1989.

[End72] H. B. Enderton. *A Mathematical Introduction to Logic*. Academic Press, New York, 1972.

[Esw76] K. P. Eswaran. Aspects of a trigger subsystem in an integrated data base system. In *Proceedings of the 2nd International Conference in Software Engineering*, San Francisco, CA, pages 243–250, 1976.

[ESW79] R. Epstein, M. Stonebraker, and E. Wong. Distributed query processing in a relational database system. In *Proc. ACM SIGMOD Symp. on the Management of Data*, pages 169–180, 1979.

[Fag72] R. Fagin. Probabilities on finite models. *Notices of the American Mathematical Society*, October: *A714*, 1972.

[Fag76] R. Fagin. Probabilities on finite models. *Journal of Symbolic Logic*, 41(1):50–58, 1976.

[Fag77a] R. Fagin. The decomposition versus synthetic approach to relational database design. In *Proc. of Intl. Conf. on Very Large Data Bases*, pages 441–446, 1977.

[Fag77b] R. Fagin. Multivalued dependencies and a new normal form for relational databases. *ACM Trans. on Database Systems*, 2:262–278, 1977.

[Fag79] R. Fagin. Normal forms and relational database operators. In *Proc. ACM SIGMOD Symp. on the Management of Data*, pages 153–160, 1979.

[Fag81] R. Fagin. A normal form for relational databases that is based on domains and keys. *ACM Trans. on Database Systems*, 6(3):387–415, 1981.

[Fag82a] R. Fagin. Armstrong databases. In *Proc. IBM Symp. on Mathematical Foundations of Computer Science*, 1982.

[Fag82b] R. Fagin. Horn clauses and database dependencies. *J. ACM*, 29(4):952–985, 1982.

[Fag83] R. Fagin. Degrees of acyclicity for hypergraphs and relational database schemes. *J. ACM*, 30(3):514–550, 1983.

[Fag93] R. Fagin. Finite-model theory—A personal perspective. *Theoretical Computer Science*, 116:3–31, 1993.

[FC85] A. L. Furtado and M. A. Casanova. Updating relational views. In W. Kim, D. S. Reiner, and D. S. Batory, editors, *Query Processing in Database Systems*. Springer-Verlag, Berlin, 1985.

[FHMV94] R. Fagin, J. Y. Halpern, Y. Moses, and M. Y. Vardi. *Reasoning about Knowledge*. MIT Press, Cambridge, MA, 1994.

[Fit85] M. Fitting. A Kripke-Kleene semantics of logic programs. *Logic Programming*, 4:295–312, 1985.

[FJT83] P. C. Fischer, J. H. Jou, and D. M. Tsou. Succinctness in dependency systems. *Theoretical Computer Science*, 24:323–329, 1983.

[FKUV86] R. Fagin, G. Kuper, J. D. Ullman, and M. Y. Vardi. Updating logical databases. In P. C. Kanellakis and F. Preparata, editors, *Advances in Computing Research, vol. 3*, pages 1–18. JAI Press, Inc., Greenwich, CT, 1986.

[FM92] J. A. Fernandez and J. Minker. Semantics of disjunctive deductive databases. In *Proc. of Intl. Conf. on Database Theory*, pages 21–50. Springer-Verlag, Berlin, LNCS 646, 1992.

[FMU82] R. Fagin, A. O. Mendelzon, and J. D. Ullman. A simplified universal relational assumption and its properties. *ACM Trans. on Database Systems*, 7(3):343–360, 1982.

[FNS91] C. Faloutsos, R. Ng, and T. Sellis. Predictive load control for flexible buffer allocation. In *Proc. of Intl. Conf. on Very Large Data Bases*, pages 265–274, 1991.

[For81] C. L. Forgy. OPS5 user's manual. Technical Report CMU-CS-81-135, Carnegie-Mellon University, 1981.

[For82] C. L. Forgy. Rete: A fast algorithm for the many pattern/many object pattern match problem. *Artificial Intelligence*, 19:17–37, 1982.

[Fra54] R. Fraissé. Sur les classifications des systèmes de relations. *Publ. Sci. Univ. Alger*, I:1, 1954.

[Fre87] J. C. Freytag. A rule-based view of query optimization. In *Proc. ACM SIGMOD Symp. on the Management of Data*, pages 173–180, 1987.

[Fri71] H. Friedman. Algorithmic procedures, generalized Turing algorithms, and elementary recursion theory. In R. O.Gangy and C. M. E.Yates, editors, *Logic Colloquium '69*, pages 361–389. North Holland, Amsterdam, 1971.

[FT83] P. C. Fischer and D. -M. Tsou. Whether a set of multivalued dependencies implies a join dependency is np-hard. *SIAM J. on Computing*, 12:259–266, 1983.

[FUMY83] R. Fagin, J. D. Ullman, D. Maier, and M. Yannakakis. Tools for template dependencies. *SIAM J. on Computing*, 12(1):36–59, 1983.

[FUV83] R. Fagin, J. D. Ullman, and M. Y. Vardi. On the semantics of updates in databases. In *Proc. ACM Symp. on Principles of Database Systems*, pages 352–365, 1983.

[FV86] R. Fagin and M. Y. Vardi. The theory of data dependencies: A survey. In M. Anshel and W. Gewirtz, editors, *Mathematics of Information Processing: Proceedings of Symposia in Applied Mathematics*, vol. 34, pages 19–71. American Mathematical Society, Providence, RI, 1986.

[Fv89] C. C. Fleming and B. von Halle. *Handbook of Relational Database Design*. Addison-Wesley, Reading, MA, 1989.

[Gal87] A. Galton. *Temporal logics and their applications*. Academic Press, New York, 1987.

[Gar70] M. Gardner. The game of life. *Sci. American*, 223, 1970.

[Gär88] P. Gärdenfors. *Knowledge in Flux: Modeling the Dynamics of Epistemic States*. MIT Press, Cambridge, MA, 1988.

[GD87] G. Graefe and D. J. DeWitt. The EXODUS optimizer generator. In *Proc. ACM SIGMOD Symp. on the Management of Data*, pages 160–172, 1987.

[GD94] S. Gatziu and K. R. Dittrich. Detecting composite events in active database systems using petri nets. In *Proc. Fourth Intl. Workshop on Research Issues in Data Engineering: Active Database Systems*, pages 2–9, 1994.

[GdM86] G. Gardarin and C. de Maindreville. Evaluation of database recursive logic programs as recurrent function series. In *Proc. ACM SIGMOD Symp. on the Management of Data*, pages 177–186, 1986.

[GG88] M. Gyssens and D. Van Gucht. The powerset algebra as a result of adding programming constructs to the nested relational algebra. In *Proc. ACM SIGMOD Symp. on the Management of Data*, pages 225–232, 1988.

[GH83] S. Ginsburg and R. Hull. Characterizations for functional dependency and Boyce-Codd normal form families. *Theoretical Computer Science*, 27:243–286, 1983.

[GH86] S. Ginsburg and R. Hull. Sort sets in the relational model. *J. ACM*, 33:465–488, 1986.

[Gin66] S. Ginsburg. *The Mathematical Theory of Context-Free Languages*. McGraw-Hill, New York, 1966.

[Gin93] S. Ginsburg. Object and spreadsheet histories. In A. U. Tansel et al., editors, *Temporal Databases – Theory, Design, and Implementation*, pages 272–293. Benjamin/Cummings Publishing Co., Menlo Park, 1993.

[GJ79] M. R. Garey and D. S. Johnson. *Computers and Intractibilitiy: A Guide to the Theory of NP-Completeness*. Freeman, San Francisco, 1979.

[GJ82] J. Grant and B. E. Jacobs. On the family of generalized dependency constraints. *J. ACM*, 29(4):986–997, 1982.

[GJ91] N. H. Gehani and H. V. Jagadish. ODE as an active database: Constraints and triggers. In *Proc. of Intl. Conf. on Very Large Data Bases*, pages 327–336, 1991.

[GHJ+93] S. Ghandeharizadeh, R. Hull, D. Jacobs, et al. On implementing a language for specifying active database execution models. In *Proc. of Intl. Conf. on Very Large Data Bases*, pages 441–454, 1993.

[GHJ94] S. Ghandeharizadeh, R. Hull, and D. Jacobs. [Alg,C]: Elevating deltas to be first-class citizens in a database programming language. Technical report USC–CS–94–581, Computer Science Dept., University of Southern California, Los Angeles, September, 1994.

[GJS92a] N. H. Gehani, H. V. Jagadish, and O. Shmueli. Composite event specification in active databases: Model & implementation. In *Proc. of Intl. Conf. on Very Large Data Bases*, pages 327–338, 1992.

[GJS92b] N. H. Gehani, H. V. Jagadish, and O. Shmueli. Event specification in an active object-oriented database. Technical memorandum, Bell Labs, Holmdel, NJ, 1992.

[GJS92c] N. H. Gehani, H. V. Jagadish, and O. Shmueli. Event specification in an active object-oriented database. In *Proc. ACM SIGMOD Symp. on the Management of Data*, 1992.

[GKLT69] Y. V. Glebskiĭ, D. I. Kogan, M. I. Liogonkiĭ, and V. A. Talanov. Range and degree of realizability of formulas in the restricted predicate calculus. *Kibernetika*, 2:17–28, 1969.

[GKM92] A. Gupta, D. Katiyar, and I. S. Mumick. Counting solutions to the view maintenance problem. In K. Ramamohanarao, J. Harland, and G. Dong, editors, *Proc. of the JICSLP Workshop on Deductive Databases*, 1992.

[GL82] Y. Gurevich and H. R. Lewis. The inference problem for template dependencies. In *Proc. ACM Symp. on Principles of Database Systems*, pages 221–229, 1982.

[GL88] M. Gelfond and V. Lifschitz. The stable model semantics for logic programs. In *Intl. Conf. on Logic Programming*, pages 1070–1080, 1988.

[GM78] H. Gallaire and J. Minker. *Logic and Databases*. Plenum Press, New York, 1978.

[GMN84] H. Gallaire, J. Minker, and J. -M. Nicolas. Logic and databases: A deductive approach. *ACM Computing Surveys*, 16(2):153–185, 1984.

[GMR92] G. Grahne, A. O. Mendelzon, and P. Z. Revesz. Knowledgebase transformations. In *Proc. ACM Symp. on Principles of Database Systems*, pages 246–260, 1992.

[GMS93] A. Gupta, I. S. Mumick, and V. S. Subrahmanian. Maintaining views incrementally. In *Proc. ACM SIGMOD Symp. on the Management of Data*, pages 157–166, 1993.

[GMSV87] H. Gaifman, H. Mairson, Y. Sagiv, and M. Y. Vardi. Undecidable optimization problems for database logic programs. In *Proc. IEEE Conf. on Logic in Computer Science*, pages 106–115, 1987.

[GMSV93] H. Gaifman, H. Mairson, Y. Sagiv, and M. Y. Vardi. Undecidable optimization problems for database logic programs. *J. ACM*, 40:683–713, 1993.

[GMV86] M. H. Graham, A. O. Mendelzon, and M. Y. Vardi. Notions of dependency satisfaction. *J. ACM*, 33(1):105–129, 1986.

[GO93] E. Grädel and M. Otto. Inductive definability with counting on finite structures. In *6th Workshop on Computer Science Logic CSL 92*, pages 231–247. Springer-Verlag, Berlin, LNCS 702, 1993.

[Goo70] L. A. Goodman. The multivariate analysis of qualitative data: Interactions among multiple classifications. *J. Amer. Stat. Assn.*, 65:226–256, 1970.

[Got87] G. Gottlob. Computing covers for embedded functional dependencies. In *Proc. ACM Symp. on Principles of Database Systems*, pages 58–69, 1987.

[GPG90] M. Gyssens, J. Paredaens, and D. Van Gucht. A graph-oriented object database model. In *Proc. ACM Symp. on Principles of Database Systems*, pages 417–424, 1990.

[GPSZ91] F. Giannotti, D. Pedreschi, D. Saccà, and C. Zaniolo. Nondeterminism in deductive databases. In *Proc. of Intl. Conf. on Deductive and Object-Oriented Databases (DOOD)*, pages 129–146. Springer-Verlag, Berlin LNCS 566, 1991.

[GR83] A. Goldberg and D. Robson. *Smalltalk-80: The Language and Its Implementation*. Addison-Wesley, Reading, MA, 1983.

[GR86] G. Grahne and K. -J. Raiha. Characterizations for acyclic database schemes. In P. C. Kanellakis and F. Preparata, editors, *Advances in Computing Research, vol. 3: The Theory of Databases*, pages 19–42. JAI Press, Inc., Greenwich, CT, 1986.

[Gra77] J. Grant. Null values in relational databases. In *Inf. Proc. Letters*, pages 156–157, 1977.

[Gra79] M. H. Graham. On the universal relation. Technical Report, University of Toronto, Toronto, Ontario, Canada, 1979.

[Gra83] E. Grandjean. Complexity of the first-order theory of almost all structures. *Information and Control*, 52:180–204, 1983.

[Gra84] G. Grahne. Dependency satisfaction in databases with incomplete information. In *Proc. of Intl. Conf. on Very Large Data Bases*, pages 37–45, 1984.

[Gra91] G. Grahne. *The Problem of Incomplete Information in Relational Databases*. Springer-Verlag, Berlin, 1991.

[Gra93] G. Graefe. Query evaluation techniques for large databases. *ACM Computing Surveys*, 25(2):73–170, 1993.

[Gre75] S. Greibach. *Theory of Program Structures: Schemes, Semantics, Verification*. Springer-Verlag, Berlin, LCNS 36, 1975.

[GS82] N. Goodman and O. Shmueli. Tree queries: A simple class of queries. *ACM Trans. on Database Systems*, 7(4):653–677, 1982.

[GS84] N. Goodman and O. Shmueli. The tree projection theorem and relational query processing. *Journal of Computer and System Sciences*, 28(1):60–79, 1984.

[GS86] Y. Gurevich and S. Shelah. Fixed-point extensions of first-order logic. *Annals of Pure and Applied Logic*, 32:265–280, 1986.

[GS87] G. Gardarin and E. Simon. Les systèmes de gestion de bases de données deductives. *Technique et Science Informatiques*, 6(5), 1987.

[GS94] S. Grumbach and J. Su. Finitely representable databases. In *Proc. ACM Symp. on Principles of Database Systems*, 1994.

[GST90] S. Ganguly, A. Silberschatz, and S. Tsur. A framework for the parallel processing of datalog queries. In *Proc. ACM SIGMOD Symp. on the Management of Data*, pages 143–152, 1990.

[GT83] N. Goodman and Y. C. Tay. Synthesizing fourth normal form relations from multivalued dependencies. Technical Report, Harvard University , 1983.

[Gun92] C. Gunter. The mixed powerdomain. *Theoretical Computer Science*, 103:311–334, 1992.

[Gur] Y. Gurevich. Personal communication.

[Gur66] Y. Gurevich. The word problem for certain classes of semigroups (In Russian.). *Algebra and Logic*, 5:25–35, 1966.

[Gur84] Y. Gurevich. Toward a logic tailored for computational complexity. In M. M. Richter et al., editor, *Computation and Proof Theory*, pages 175–216. Springer-Verlag, Berlin, LNM 1104, 1984.

[Gur88] Y. Gurevich. Logic and the challenge of computer science. In E. Borger, editor, *Trends in Theoretical Computer Science*, pages 1–57. Computer Science Press, Rockville, MD, 1988.

[GV84] M. H. Graham and M. Y. Vardi. On the complexity and axiomatizability of consistent database states. *Proc. ACM Symp. on Principles of Database Systems*, pages 281–289, 1984.

[GV91] S. Grumbach and V. Vianu. Tractable query languages for complex object databases. In *Proc. ACM Symp. on Principles of Database Systems*, 1991.

[GV92] G. Gardarin and P. Valduriez. ESQL2: An object-oriented SQL with F-logic semantics. In *Intl. Conf. on Data Engineering*, 1992.

[GW89] G. Graefe and K. Ward. Dynamic query evaluation plans. In *Proc. ACM SIGMOD Symp. on the Management of Data*, pages 358–366, 1989.

[GW90] J. R. Groff and P. N. Weinberg. *Using SQL*. Osborne McGraw-Hill, New York, 1990.

[GZ82] S. Ginsburg and S. M. Zaiddan. Properties of functional dependency families. *J. ACM*, 29(4):678–698, 1982.

[GZ88] G. Gottlob and R. Zicari. Closed world databases opened through null values. In *Proc. of Intl. Conf. on Very Large Data Bases*, pages 50–61, 1988.

[Hab70] S. J. Haberman. *The general log-linear model*. Ph.D. thesis, Department of Statistics, University of Chicago, 1970.

[Hal93] J. Y. Halpern. Reasoning about knowledge: a survey circa 1991. In A. Kent and J. G. Williams, editors, *Encyclopedia of Computer Science and Technology, Vol. 27 (Supplement 12)*. Marcel Dekker, New York, 1993.

[Han89] E. H. Hanson. An initial report on the design of ariel: a dbms with an integrated production rule system. In *SIGMOD Record*, 18(3):12–19, 1989.

[Har78] M. A. Harrison. *Introduction to Formal Language Theory*. Addison-Wesley, Reading, MA, 1978.

[Har80] D. Harel. On folk theorems. *Comm. of the ACM*, 23:379–385, 1980.

[HCL$^+$90] L. Haas, W. Chang, G. M. Lohman, J. McPherson, P. F. Wilms, G. Lapis, B. Lindsay, H. Pirahesh, M. Carey, and E. Shekita. Starburst midflight: As the dust clears. *IEEE Transactions on Knowledge and Data Engineering*, 2(1):143–160, 1990.

[Hel92] L. Hella. Logical hierarchies in PTIME. In *Proc. IEEE Conf. on Logic in Computer Science*, 1992.

[Her92] C. Herrmann. On the undecidability of implications between embedded multivalued database dependencies. Technical Report, Technische Hochschule Darmstadt, Germany. February 24, 1992.

[HH93] T. Hirst and D. Harel. Completeness results of recursive data bases. In *Proc. ACM Symp. on Principles of Database Systems*, pages 244–252, 1993.

[HJ91a] R. Hull and D. Jacobs. Language constructs for programming active databases. In *Proc. of Intl. Conf. on Very Large Data Bases*, pages 455–468, 1991.

[HJ91b] R. Hull and D. Jacobs. On the semantics of rules in database programming languages. In J. Schmidt and A. Stogny, editors, *Next Generation Information System Technology: Proc. of the First International East/West Database Workshop, Kiev, USSR, October 1990*, pages 59–85. Springer-Verlag, Berlin, LNCS 504, 1991.

[HK81] M. S. Hecht and L. Kerschberg. Update semantics for the functional data model. Technical Report, Bell Laboratories, Holmdel, NJ, January 1981.

[HK87] R. Hull and R. King. Semantic database modeling: Survey, applications, and research issues. *ACM Computing Surveys*, 19:201–260, 1987.

[HK89] S. E. Hudson and R. King. Cactis: A self-adaptive, concurrent implementation of an object-oriented database management system. *ACM Trans. on Database Systems*, 14:291–321, 1989.

[HKM93] G. Hillebrand, P. Kanellakis, and H. Mairson. Database query languages embedded in the typed lambda calculus. In *Proc. IEEE Conf. on Logic in Computer Science*, pages 332–343, 1993.

[HKR93] G. Hillebrand, P. Kanellakis, and S. Ramaswamy. Functional programming formalisms for OODB methods. In *Proc. NATO ASI Summer School on OODBs*, Kasadaci, Turkey, 1993.

[HLM88] M. Hsu, R. Ladin, and D. R. McCarthy. An execution model for active data base management systems. In *Intl. Conf. on Data and Knowledge Bases: Improving Usability and Responsiveness*, pages 171–179, 1988.

[HLY80] P. Honeyman, R. E. Ladner, and M. Yannakakis. Testing the universal instance assumption. *Inf. Proc. Letters*, 10(1):14–19, 1980.

[HM81] M. Hammer and D. McLeod. Database description with SDM: A semantic database model. *ACM Trans. on Database Systems*, 6(3):351–386, 1981.

[HMN84] L. J. Henschen, W. W. McCune, and S. A. Naqvi. Compiling constraint-checking programs from first-order formulas. In H. Gallaire, J. Minker, and J. -M. Nicolas, editors, *Advances in Data Base Theory, vol. 2*, pages 145–169. Plenum Press, New York, 1984.

[HMT71] L. Henkin, J. D. Monk, and A. Tarski. *Cylindric Algebras*. North Holland, Amsterdam, 1971.

[HN84] L. J. Henschen and S. A. Naqvi. On compiling queries in recursive first-order databases. *J. ACM*, 31(1):47–85, 1984.

[Hon82] P. Honeyman. Testing satisfaction of functional dependencies. *J. ACM*, 29(3):668–677, 1982.

[HS89a] R. Hull and J. Su. On accessing object-oriented databases: Expressive power, complexity, and restrictions. In *Proc. ACM SIGMOD Symp. on the Management of Data*, pages 147–158, 1989.

[HS89b] R. Hull and J. Su. Untyped sets, invention, and computable queries. In *Proc. ACM Symp. on Principles of Database Systems*, pages 347–359, March 1989.

[HS91] R. Hull and J. Su. Domain independence and the relational calculus. Technical Report 88-64 (September, 1991, revision), Computer Science Department, University of Southern California, 1991. To appear, *Acta Informatica*.

[HS93] R. Hull and J. Su. Algebraic and calculus query languages for recursively typed complex objects. *Journal of Computer and System Sciences*, 47:121–156, 1993.

[HTY89] R. Hull, K. Tanaka, and M. Yoshikawa. Behavior analysis of object-oriented databases: Method structure, execution trees and reachability. In *Proceedings 3rd International Conference on Foundations of Data Organization and Algorithms*, pages 372–388, 1989.

[Hul83] R. Hull. Acyclic join dependency and data base projections. *Journal of Computer and System Sciences*, 27(3):331–349, 1983.

[Hul84] R. Hull. Finitely specifiable implicational dependency families. *J. ACM*, 31(2):210–226, 1984.

[Hul85] R. Hull. Non-finite specifiability of projections of functional dependency families. In *Theoretical Computer Science*, 39:239–265, 1985.

[Hul86] R. Hull. Relative information capacity of simple relational schemata. *SIAM J. on Computing*, 15(3):856–886, August 1986.

[Hul87] R. Hull. A survey of theoretic research on typed complex database objects. In J. Paredaens, editor, *Databases*, pages 193–256. Academic Press, London, 1987.

[Hul89] G. Hulin. Parallel processing of recursive queries in distributed architectures. In *Proc. of Intl. Conf. on Very Large Data Bases*, pages 87–96, 1989.

[HW92] E. N. Hanson and J. Widom. An overview of production rules in database systems. Technical Report RJ 9023 (80483), IBM Almaden Research, October 1992.

[HY84] R. Hull and C. K. Yap. The Format model: A theory of database organization. *Journal of the ACM*, 31(3):518–537, 1984.

[HY90] R. Hull and M. Yoshikawa. ILOG: Declarative creation and manipulation of object identifiers (extended abstract). In *Proc. of Intl. Conf. on Very Large Data Bases*, pages 455–468, 1990.

[HY92] R. Hull and M. Yoshikawa. On the equivalence of data restructurings involving object identifiers. In J. D. Ullman, editor, *Studies in Theoretical Computer Science (a festschrift for Seymour Ginsburg)*, pages 253–286. Academic Press, New York, 1992. See also article of same title in *Proc. ACM Symp. on Principles of Data Base Systems*, 1991.

[IK90] Y. E. Ioannidis and Y. C. Kang. Randomized algorithms for optimizing large join queries. In *Proc. ACM SIGMOD Symp. on the Management of Data*, pages 312–321, 1990.

[IL84] T. Imielinski and W. Lipski. The relational model of data and cylindric algebras. *Journal of Computer and System Sciences*, 28(1):80–102, 1984.

[Imi84] T. Imielinski. On algebraic query processing in logical databases. In H. Gallaire and J. Minker, editors, *Advances in Data Base Theory, vol. 2*. Plenum Press, New York, 1984.

[Imm82] N. Immerman. Upper and lower bounds for first-order definability. *Journal of Computer and System Sciences*, 25:76–98, 1982.

[Imm86] N. Immerman. Relational queries computable in polynomial time. *Inf. and Control*, 68:86–104, 1986.

[Imm87a] N. Immerman. Expressibility as a complexity measure: Results and directions. Technical Report DCS-TR-538, Yale University, New Haven, CT, 1987.

[Imm87b] N. Immerman. Languages which capture complexity classes. *SIAM J. on Computing*, 16(4):760–778, 1987.

[IN88] T. Imielinski and S. Naqvi. Explicit control of logic programs through rule algebra. In *Proc. ACM Symp. on Principles of Database Systems*, pages 103–116, 1988.

[INSS92] Y. E. Ioannidis, R. T. Ng, K. Shim, and T. K. Sellis. Parametric query optimization. In *Proc. of Intl. Conf. on Very Large Data Bases*, pages 103–114, 1992.

[INV91a] T. Imielinski, S. Naqvi, and K. Vadaparty. Incomplete objects – A data model for design and planning applications. In *Proc. ACM SIGMOD Symp. on the Management of Data*, pages 288–197, 1991.

[INV91b] T. Imielinski, S. Naqvi, and K. Vadaparty. Querying design and planning databases. In *Proc. of Intl. Conf. on Deductive and Object-Oriented Databases (DOOD)*, pages 524–545, 1991.

[Ioa85] Y. E. Ioannidis. A time bound on the materialization of some recursively defined views. In *Proc. of Intl. Conf. on Very Large Data Bases*, pages 219–226, 1985.

[Jac82] B. E. Jacobs. On database logic. *J. ACM*, 29(2):310–332, 1982.

[JH91] D. Jacobs and R. Hull. Database programming with delayed updates. In *Proc. of Intl. Workshop on Database Programming Languages*, pages 416–428, 1991.

[JK84a] M. Jarke and J Koch. Query optimization in database systems. *ACM Computing Surveys*, 16(2):111–152, 1984.

[JK84b] D. S. Johnson and A. Klug. Testing containment of conjunctive queries under functional and inclusion dependencies. *Journal of Computer and System Sciences*, 28:167–189, 1984.

[JL87] J. Jaffar and J. L. Lassez. Constraint logic programming. In *Proc. ACM Symp. on Principles of Programming Languages*, pages 111–119, 1987.

[Joh91] D. S. Johnson. A catalog of complexity classes. In J. Van Leeuwen, editor, *Handbook of Theoretical Computer Science*, pages 67–162. Elsevier, Amsterdam, 1991.

[Joy76] W. H. Joyner Jr. Resolution strategies as decision procedures. *J. ACM*, 23:398–417, 1976.

[JS82] G. Jaeschke and H. -J. Schek. Remarks on the algebra on non first normal form relations. In *Proc. ACM Symp. on Principles of Database Systems*, pages 124–138, 1982.

[Kam81] Y. Kambayashi. *Database: A Bibliography*. Computer Science Press, Rockville, MD, 1981.

[Kan88] P. C. Kanellakis. Logic programming and parallel complexity. In J. Minker, editor, *Foundations of Deductive Databases and Logic Programming*, pages 547–586. Morgan Kaufmann, Inc., Los Altos, CA, 1988.

[Kan91] P. C. Kanellakis. Elements of relational database theory. In J. Van Leeuwen, editor, *Handbook of Theoretical Computer Science*, pages 1074–1156. Elsevier, Amsterdam, 1991.

[KC86] S. Khoshafian and G. Copeland. Object identity. In *Proc. OOPSALA*, 1986.

[KDM88] A. M. Kotz, K. R. Dittrich, and J. A. Mülle. Supporting semantic rules by a generalized event/trigger mechanism. In *Intl. Conf. on Extending Data Base Technology*, pages 76–91, 1988.

[Kel82] A. M. Keller. Updates to relational databases through views involving joins. In Peter Scheuermann, editor, *Improving Database Usability and Responsiveness*. Academic Press, New York, 1982.

[Kel85] A. Keller. Algorithms for translating view updates to database updates for views involving selections, projections and joins. In *Proc. ACM Symp. on Principles of Database Systems*, pages 154–163, 1985.

[Kel86] A. M. Keller. The role of semantics in translating view updates. *IEEE Computer*, 19(1):63–73, January 1986.

[Ken78] W. Kent. *Data and Reality*. North Holland, Amsterdam, 1978.

[Ken79] W. Kent. Limitations of record-based information models. *ACM Trans. on Database Systems*, 4:107–131, 1979.

[Ken89] W. Kent. The many forms of a single fact. In *Proc. of the IEEE Compcon Conf.*, 1989.

[Ker88] J-M. Kerisit. *La Méthode d'Alexander: Une Technique de Déduction*. Ph.D. thesis, Université Paris VII, 1988.

[KG94] P. Kanellakis and D. Goldin. Constraint programming and database query languages. To appear in Springer-Verlag, Berlin, editor, *Proc. 2nd Conference on Theoretical Aspects of Computer Software (TACS)*, 1994.

[Kif88] M. Kifer. On safety, domain independence, and capturability of database queries. In C. Beeri, J. W. Schmidt, and U. Dayal, editors, *Proc. 3rd Intl. Conf. on Data and Knowledge Bases*, pages 405–415. Morgan Kaufmann, Inc., Los Altos, CA, 1988.

[KKR90] P. Kanellakis, G Kuper, and P. Revesz. Constraint query languages. In *Proc. 9th ACM Symp. on Principles of Database Systems*, pages 299–313, Nashville, 1990.

[KKS92] M. Kifer, W. Kim, and Y. Sagiv. Querying object-oriented databases. In *Proc. ACM SIGMOD Symp. on the Management of Data*, pages 393–402, 1992.

[KL86a] M. Kifer and E. Lozinskii. A framework for an efficient implementation of deductive databases. In *Proc. of the Advanced Database Symposium*, Tokyo, 1986.

[KL86b] M. Kifer and E. L. Lozinskii. Filtering data flow in deductive databases. In *Proc. of Intl. Conf. on Database Theory*, 1986.

[KL89] W. Kim and F. Lochovsky, editors. *Object-Oriented Concepts, Databases, and Applications*. Addison-Wesley, Reading, MA, 1989.

[Kle67] S. C. Kleene. *Mathematical Logic*. North Holland, Amsterdam, 1967.

[Klu80] A. Klug. Caculating constraints on relational tableaux. In *ACM Trans. on Database Systems*, 5:260–290, 1980.

[Klu82] A. Klug. Equivalence of relational algebra and relational calculus query languages having aggregate functions. *J. ACM*, 29(3):699–717, 1982.

[Klu88] A. Klug. On conjunctive queries containing inequalities. *J. ACM*, 35(1):146–160, 1988.

[KLW93] M. Kifer, G. Lausen, and J. Wu. Logical foundations of object-oriented and frame-based languages. Technical Report 93/06, Computer Science Department, SUNY at Stony Brook, NY, 1993.

[KM91a] H. Katsuno and A. O. Mendelzon. On the difference between updating a knowledge base and revising it. In *Proc. of the Second Intl. Conf. on Principles of Knowledge Representation and Reasoning*, pages 387–394, 1991.

[KM91b] H. Katsuno and A. O. Mendelzon. Propositional knowledgebase revision and minimal change. *Artificial Intelligence*, 52:263–294, 1991.

[KN88] R. Krishnamurthy and S. A. Naqvi. Nondeterministic choice in datalog. In *5th Intl. Conf. on Data and Knowledge Bases*, pages 416–424. Morgan Kaufmann, Inc., Los Altos, CA, 1988.

[Kni89] K. Knight. Unification: a multidisciplinary survey. *ACM Computing Surveys*, 21(1):93–124, 1989.

[Kol83] P. G. Kolaitis. Lecture notes on finite model theory, 1983.

[Kol91] P. G. Kolaitis. The expressive power of stratified logic programs. *Information and Computation*, 90(1):50–66, 1991.

[Kon88] S. Konolige. On the relation between default and autoepistemic logic. *Artificial Intelligence*, 35(3):343–382, 1988.

[Kow74] R. A. Kowalski. Predicate logic as a programming language. In *Proc. IFIP.'74*, pages 569–574, 1974.

[Kow75] R. A. Kowalski. A proof procedure using connection graphs. *J. ACM*, 22:572–595, 1975.

[Kow81] R. Kowalski. Logic as database language. Unpublished manuscript, Dept. of Computing, Imperial College, London, 1981.

[KP81] S. Koenig and R. Paige. A transformational framework for the automatic control of derived data. In *Proc. of Intl. Conf. on Very Large Data Bases*, pages 306–318, 1981.

[KP82] A. Klug and R. Price. In determining view dependencies using tableaux. In *ACM Trans. on Database Systems*, 7:361–381, 1982.

[KP86] P. Kanellakis and C. H. Papadimitriou. Notes on monadic sirups. Unpublished manuscript, 1986.

[KP88] P. G. Kolaitis and C. H. Papadimitriou. Why not negation by fixpoint? In *Proc. ACM Symp. on Principles of Database Systems*, pages 231–239, 1988.

[KRS88a] M. Kifer, R. Ramakrishnan, and A. Silberschatz. An axiomatic approach to deciding query safety in deductive databases. In *Proc. ACM Symp. on Principles of Database Systems*, pages 52–60, 1988.

[KRS88b] R. Krishnamurthy, R. Ramakrishnan, and O. Shmueli. A framework for testing safety and effective computability of extended Datalog. In *Proc. ACM SIGMOD Symp. on the Management of Data*, pages 154–163, 1988.

[KS91] H. F. Korth and A. Silberschatz. *Database System Concepts, 2d ed*. McGraw-Hill, New York, 1991.

[KT88] D. B. Kemp and R. W. Topor. Completeness of a top-down query evaluation procedure for stratified databases. In *Proc. Fifth Intl. Symp. on Logic Programming*, pages 195–211, 1988.

[KU84] A. Keller and J. D. Ullman. On complementary and independent mappings. In *Proc. ACM SIGMOD Symp. on the Management of Data*, pages 143–148, 1984.

[Küc91] V. Küchenhoff. On the efficient computation of the difference between consecutive database states. In *Proc. of Intl. Conf. on Deductive and Object-Oriented Databases (DOOD)*, pages 478–502, 1991.

[Kuh67] J. L. Kuhns. Answering questions by computer: a logical study. Technical Report RM-5428-PR, Rand Corp., 1967.

[Kun87] K. Kunen. Negation in logic programming. *Logic Programming*, 4:289–308, 1987.

[Kun88] K. Kunen. Some remarks on the completed database. In *Intl. Conf. on Logic Programming*, pages 978–992, 1988.

[Kup87] G. M. Kuper. Logic programming with sets. In *Proc. ACM Symp. on Principles of Database Systems*, pages 11–20, 1987.

[Kup88] G. M. Kuper. On the expressive power of logic programming languages with sets. In *Proc. ACM Symp. on Principles of Database Systems*, pages 10–14, 1988.

[Kup93] G. M. Kuper. Aggregation in constraint databases. In *Proc. First Workshop on Principles and Practice of Constraint Programming*, 1993.

[KV84] G. Kuper and M. Y. Vardi. A new approach to database logic. In *Proc. ACM Symp. on Principles of Database Systems*, pages 86–96, 1984.

[KV87] P. Kolaitis and M. Y. Vardi. The decision problem for the probabilities of higher-order properties. In *Proc. ACM SIGACT Symp. on the Theory of Computing*, pages 425–435, 1987.

[KV90a] D. Karabeg and V. Vianu. Parallel update transactions. *Theoretical Computer Science*, 76:93–114, 1990.

[KV90b] P. G. Kolaitis and M. Y. Vardi. 0-1 laws and decision problems for fragments of second-order logic. *Information and Computation*, 87:302–338, 1990.

[KV90c] P. G. Kolaitis and M. Y. Vardi. On the expressive power of Datalog: tools and a case study. In *Proc. ACM Symp. on Principles of Database Systems*, pages 61–71, 1990.

[KV91] D. Karabeg and V. Vianu. Simplification rules and axiomatization for relational update transactions. *ACM Trans. on Database Systems*, 16(3):439–475, 1991.

[KV92] P. G. Kolaitis and M. Y. Vardi. Infinitary logics and 0-1 laws. *Information and Computation*, 98:258–294, 1992.

[KV93a] G. Kuper and M. Y. Vardi. On the complexity of queries in the logical data model. *Theoretical Computer Science*, 116:33–58, 1993.

[KV93b] G. M. Kuper and M. Y. Vardi. The logical data model. *ACM Trans. on Database Systems*, 18:379–413, 1993.

[KW85] A. M. Keller and M. Winslett Wilkins. On the use of an extended relational model to handle changing incomplete information. *IEEE Transactions on Software Engineering*, SE-11:620–633, 1985.

[KW89] M. Kifer and J. Wu. A logic for object-oriented logic programming (Maier's O-logic revisited). In *Proc. ACM Symp. on Principles of Database Systems*, pages 379–393, 1989.

[Lan88] B. Lang. Datalog automata. In *Proc. 3rd Intl. Conf. on Data and Knowledge Bases*, pages 389–404. Morgan Kaufmann, Inc., Los Altos, CA, 1988.

[Lee91] J. Van Leeuwen, editor. *Handbook of Theoretical Computer Science*. Elsevier, Amsterdam, 1991.

[Lei69] A. C. Leisenring. *Mathematical Logic and Hilbert's ε-symbol*. Gordon and Breach, New York, 1969.

[Lei89a] D. Leivant. Descriptive characterization of computational complexity. *Journal of Computer and System Sciences*, 39:51–83, 1989.

[Lei89b] D. Leivant. Monotonic use of space and computational complexity over abstract structures. Technical Report CMU-CS-89-212, Carnegie-Mellon University, 1989.

[Lei90] D. Leivant. Inductive definitions over finite structures. *Information and Computation*, 89:95–108, 1990.

[Lel87] W. Leler. *Constraint Programming Languages*. Addison-Wesley, Reading, MA, 1987.

[Lev84a] H. J. Levesque. The logic of incomplete knowledge bases. In M. L. Brodie, J. L. Mylopoulos, and J. W. Schmidt, editors, *On Conceptual Modeling*, pages 165–189. Springer-Verlag, Berlin, 1984.

[Lev84b] H. J. Levesque. Foundations of a functional approach to knowledge representation. *AI J.*, 23:155–212, 1984.

[Lib91] L. Libkin. A relational algebra for complex objects based on partial information. In *LNCS 495: Proceedings of Symp. on Mathematical Fundamentals of Database Systems*, pages 36–41. Springer-Verlag, Berlin, 1991.

[Lie80] Y. E. Lien. On the semantics of the entity-relationship model. In P. P. Chen, editor, *Entity-Relationship Approach to Systems Analysis and Design*, pages 155–167, 1980.

[Lie82] E. Lien. On the equivalence of database models. *J. ACM*, 29(2):333–363, 1982.

[Lif88] V. Lifschitz. On the declarative semantics of logic programs with negation. In J. Minker, editor, *Foundations of Deductive Databases and Logic Programming*, pages 177–192. Morgan Kaufmann, Inc., Los Altos, CA, 1988.

[Lin90] S. Lindell. *An analysis of fixed-point queries on binary trees*. Ph.D. thesis, University of California at Los Angeles, 1990.

[Lin91] S. Lindell. An analysis of fixed-point queries on binary trees. *Theoretical Computer Science*, 85:75–95, 1991.

[Lip79] W. Lipski. On semantic issues connected with incomplete information databases. *ACM Trans. on Database Systems*, 4(3):262–296, 1979.

[Lip81] W. Lipski. On databases with incomplete information. *J. ACM*, 28(1):41–70, 1981.

[LL86] N. Lerat and W. Lipski. Nonapplicable nulls. *Theoretical Computer Science*, 46:67–82, 1986.

[LL90] M. Leven and G. Loizou. The nested relation type model: An application of domain theory to databases. *The Computer Journal*, 33:19–30, 1990.

[Llo87] J. W. Lloyd. *Foundations of logic programming, 2d ed.*, Springer-Verlag, Berlin, 1987.

[LM89] V. S. Lakshmanan and A. O. Mendelzon. Inductive pebble games and the inductive power of Datalog. In *Proc. ACM Symp. on Principles of Database Systems*, pages 301–311, 1989.

[LM93] D. Leivant and J. -Y. Marion. Lambda calculus characterizations of polytime. In *Proceedings of the International Conference on Typed Lambda Calculi and Applications*, 1993. (To appear in *Fundamenta Informaticae*.)

[LMG83] K. Laver, A. O. Mendelzon, and M. H. Graham. Functional dependencies on cyclic database schemes. In *Proc. ACM SIGMOD Symp. on the Management of Data*, pages 79–91, 1983.

[LN90] R. J. Lipton and J. F. Naughton. Query size estimation by adaptive sampling (extended abstract). In *Proc. ACM Symp. on Principles of Database Systems*, pages 40–46, 1990.

[LO78] C. L. Lucchesi and S. L. Osborn. Candidate keys for relations. *Journal of Computer and System Sciences*, 17(2):270–279, 1978.

[Loh88] G. M. Lohman. Grammar-like functional rules for representing query optimization alternatives. In *Proc. ACM SIGMOD Symp. on the Management of Data*, pages 18–27, 1988.

[Low15] L. Lowenheim. Uber Möglichkeiten im relativekalkul. *Math. Ann.*, 76:447–470, 1915.

[Loz85] E. Lozinskii. Evaluating queries in deductive databases by generating. In *Proc. 11th Intl. Joint Conf. on Artificial Intelligence*, pages 173–177, 1985.

[LP81] H. R. Lewis and C. H. Papadimitriou. *Elements of the Theory of Computation*. Prentice-Hall, Englewood Cliffs, NJ, 1981.

[LMR92] J. Lobo, J. Minker, and A. Rajasekar. *Foundations of Disjunctive Logic Programming*. MIT Press, Cambridge, MA, 1992.

[LRV88] C. Lecluse, P. Richard, and F. Velez. O_2, an object-oriented data model. In *Proc. ACM SIGMOD Symp. on the Management of Data*, pages 424–434, 1988.

[LS87] U. W. Lipeck and G. Saake. Monitoring dynamic integrity constraints based on temporal logic. *Information Systems*, 12(3):255–269, 1987.

[LST87] J. W. Lloyd, E. A. Sonenberg, and R. W. Topor. Integrity constraint checking in stratified databases. *Journal of Logic Programming*, 4:331–343, 1987.

[LTK81] T. Ling, F. Tompa, and T. Kameda. An improved third normal form for relational databases. *ACM Trans. on Database Systems*, 6(2):326–346, 1981.

[LV87] P. Lyngbaek and V. Vianu. Mapping a semantic database model to the relational model. In *Proc. ACM SIGMOD Symp. on the Management of Data*, 1987.

[LV89] A. Lefevre and L. Vieille. On deductive query evaluation in the DedGin* system. In *Proc. 1st Internat. Conf. on Deductive and Object-Oriented Databases*, pages 225–246, 1989.

[LW93a] L. Libkin and L. Wong. Semantic representations and query languages for or-sets. In *Proc. ACM Symp. on Principles of Database Systems*, pages 37–48, 1993.

[LW93b] L. Libkin and L. Wong. Some properties of query languages for bags. In *Proc. of Intl. Workshop on Database Programming Languages*, pages 97–114, 1993.

[Mai80] D. Maier. Minimum covers in the relational database model. *J. ACM*, 27(4):664–674, 1980.

[Mai83] D. Maier. *The Theory of Relational Databases*. Computer Science Press, Rockville, MD, 1983.

[Mai86] D. Maier. A logic for objects. From a Workshop on Foundations of Deductive Databases and Logic Programming held in Washington, D.C., pages 6–26, 1986.

[Mak77] A. Makinouchi. A consideration of normal form of not-necessarily-normalized relations in the relational data model. In *Proc. of Intl. Conf. on Very Large Data Bases*, pages 447–453, 1977.

[Mak81] J. A. Makowsky. Characterizing data base dependencies. In *8th Colloquium on Automata, Languages and Programming*. Springer-Verlag, Berlin, 1981.

[Mak85] D. Makinson. How to give it up: A survey of some formal aspects of the logic of theory change. *Synthèse*, 62:347–363, 1985.

[Mal86] F. M. Malvestuto. Modelling large bases of categorical data with acyclic schemes. In *Proc. of Intl. Conf. on Database Theory*, 1986.

[MB92] R. M. MacGregor and D. Brill. Recognition algorithms for the Loom classifier. In *Proc. Natl. Conf. on Artificial Intelligence*, 1992.

[MBW80] J. Mylopoulos, P. A. Bernstein, and H. K. T. Wong. A language facility for designing database-intensive applications. *ACM Trans. on Database Systems*, 5:185–207, June 1980.

[MD89] D. McCarthy and U. Dayal. The architecture of an active database management system. In *Proc. ACM SIGMOD Symp. on the Management of Data*, pages 215–224, 1989.

[ME92] P. Mishra and M. H. Eich. Join processing in relational databases. *ACM Computing Surveys*, 24:63–113, 1992.

[MFPR90] I. S. Mumick, S. Finkelstein, H. Pirahesh, and R. Ramakrishnan. Magic is relevant. In *Proc. ACM SIGMOD Symp. on the Management of Data*, 1990.

[Min88a] J. Minker, editor. *Foundations of Deductive Databases and Logic Programming*. Morgan Kaufmann, Inc., Los Altos, CA, 1988.

[Min88b] J. Minker. Perspectives in deductive databases. *J. Logic Programming*, 5(1):33–60, 1988.

[MIR93] R. Miller, Y. Ioannidis, and R. Ramakrishnan. The use of information capacity in schema integration and translation. In *Proc. of Intl. Conf. on Very Large Data Bases*, pages 120–133, 1993.

[MIR94] R. Miller, Y. Ioannidis, and R. Ramakrishnan. Schema equivalence in heterogeneous systems: bridging theory and practice, in *Information Systems*, 19:3–31, 1994.

[Mit83a] J. C. Mitchell. The implication problem for functional and inclusion dependencies. *Information and Control*, 56:154–173, 1983.

[Mit83b] J. C. Mitchell. Inference rules for functional and inclusion dependencies. In *Proc. ACM Symp. on Principles of Database Systems*, pages 58–69, 1983.

[MM79] A. O. Mendelzon and D. Maier. Generalized mutual dependencies and the decomposition of database relations. In *Proc. of Intl. Conf. on Very Large Data Bases*, pages 75–82, 1979.

[MMS79] D. Maier, A. O. Mendelzon, and Y. Sagiv. Testing implications of data dependencies. *ACM Trans. on Database Systems*, 4(4):455–469, 1979.

[MMSU80] D. Maier, A. O. Mendelzon, F. Sadri, and J. D. Ullman. Adequacy of decompositions of relational databases. *Journal of Computer and System Sciences*, 21(3):368–379, 1980.

[MMW94] A. O. Mendelzon, T. Milo, and E. Waller. Object migration. In *Proc. ACM Symp. on Principles of Database Systems*, 1994.

[MNS⁺87] K. Morris, J. F. Naughton, Y. Saraiya, J. D. Ullman, and A. Van Gelder. YAWN! (yet another window on NAIL!). *Data Engineering*, 10(4), 1987.

[Moo85] R. C. Moore. Semantics considerations on non-monotonic logic. *Artificial Intelligence*, 25:75–94, 1985.

[Mor83] M. Morgenstern. Active databases as a paradigm for enhanced computing environments. In *Proc. of Intl. Conf. on Very Large Data Bases*, pages 34–42, 1983.

[Mor88] K. Morris. An algorithm for ordering subgoals in NAIL! In *Proc. ACM Symp. on Principles of Database Systems*, pages 82–88, 1988.

[Mos74] Y. N. Moschovakis. *Elementary Induction on Abstract Structures*. North Holland, Amsterdam, 1974.

[MR85] H. Mannila and K. -J. Räihä. Small Armstrong relations for database design. In *Proc. ACM Symp. on Principles of Database Systems*, pages 245–250, 1985.

[MR88] H. Mannila and K. -J. Räihä. Generating Armstrong databases for sets of functional and inclusion dependencies. Technical Report A-1988-7, University of Tampere, Department of Computer Science, Tampere, Finland, 1988.

[MR90] J. Minker and A. Rajasekar. A fixpoint semantics for disjunctive logic programs. In *J. Logic Programming*, 1990.

[MR92] H. Mannila and K. -J. Räihä. *The Design of Relational Databases*. Addison-Wesley, Wokingham, England, 1992.

[MRW86] D. Maier, D. Rozenshtein, and D. S. Warren. Window functions. In P. C. Kanellakis and F. Preparata, editors, *Advances in Computing Research, vol. 3*, pages 213–246. JAI Press, Inc., Greenwich, CT, 1986.

[MS81] D. McKay and S. Shapiro. Using active connection graphs for reasoning with recursive rules. In *Proc. 7th Intl. Joint Conf. on Artificial Intelligence*, pages 368–374, 1981.

[MS92] V. M. Markowitz and A. Shoshani. Represented extended Entity-Relationship structures in relational databases. *ACM Trans. on Database Systems*, 17:385–422, 1992.

[MSPS87] A. Marchetti-Spaccamela, A. Pelaggi, and D. Saccà. Worst-case complexity analysis of methods for logic query implementation. In *Proc. ACM Symp. on Principles of Database Systems*, pages 294–301, 1987.

[MSY81] D. Maier, Y. Sagiv, and M. Yannakakis. On the complexity of testing implications of functional and join dependencies. *J. ACM*, 28(4):680–695, 1981.

[MUG86] K. Morris, J. D. Ullman, and A. Van Gelder. Design overview of the NAIL! system. In *3rd Int. Conf. on Logic Programming*, LNCS 225, pages 554–568, Springer-Verlag, Berlin, 1986.

[MUV84] D. Maier, J. D. Ullman, and M. Y. Vardi. On the foundations of the universal relation model. *ACM Trans. on Database Systems*, 9(2):283–308, 1984.

[MUV86] K. Morris, J. D. Ullman, and A. Van Gelder. Design overview of the NAIL! system. In *Proc. Third Intl. Conf. on Logic Programming*, pages 554–568, 1986.

[MV86] J. A. Makowsky and M. Y. Vardi. On the expressive power of data dependencies. *Acta Informatica*, 23:231–244, 1986.

[MW88a] D. Maier and D. S. Warren. *Computing with Logic: Logic Programming with Prolog*. Benjamin/Cummings Publishing Co., Menlo Park, CA, 1988.

[MW88b] S. Manchanda and D. S. Warren. A logic-based language for database updates. In J. Minker, editor, *Foundations of Deductive Databases and Logic Programming*, pages 363–394. Morgan Kaufmann, Inc., Los Altos, CA, 1988.

[Nau86] J. F. Naughton. Data independent recursion in deductive databases. In *Proc. ACM Symp. on Principles of Database Systems*, pages 267–279, 1986.

[NCS91] R. Ng, C. Caloutsos, and T. Sellis. Flexible buffer allocation based on marginal gains. In *Proc. ACM SIGMOD Symp. on the Management of Data*, pages 387–396, 1991.

[ND82] J. -M. Nicolas and R. Demolombe. On the stability of relational queries. Technical Report, ONERA-CERT, Toulouse, 1982.

[Nej87] W. Nejdl. Recursive strategies for answering recursive queries – The RQA/FQI strategy. In *Proc. of Intl. Conf. on Very Large Data Bases*, 1987.

[NG78] J. -M. Nicolas and H. Gallaire. Database – Theory vs. interpretation. In H. Gallaire and J. Minker, editors, *Logic and Databases*, pages 33–54. Plenum Press, New York, 1978.

[Nic78] J -M. Nicolas. First order logic formalization for functional, multivalued, and mutual dependencies. In *Proc. ACM SIGMOD Symp. on the Management of Data*, pages 40–46, 1978.

[Nic82] J. -M. Nicolas. Logic for improving integrity checking in relational databases. *Acta Informatica*, 18(3):227–253, 1982.

[Nij76] G. M. Nijssen, editor. *Modelling in Data Base Management Systems*. North Holland, Amsterdam, 1976.

[NK88] S. Naqvi and R. Krishnamurthy. Database updates in logic programming. In *Proc. ACM Symp. on Principles of Database Systems*, 1988.

[NPS91] M. Negri, S. Pelagatti, and L. Sbattella. Formal semantics of SQL queries. *ACM Trans. on Database Systems*, 16(3):513–535, 1991.

[NRSU89] J. F. Naughton, R. Ramakrishnan, Y. Sagiv, and J. D. Ullman. Argument reduction by factoring. In *Proc. of Intl. Conf. on Very Large Data Bases*, 1989. To appear in *Theoretical Computer Science*.

[NS87] J. F. Naughton and Y. Sagiv. A decidable class of bounded recursions. In *Proc. ACM Symp. on Principles of Database Systems*, pages 227–236, 1987.

[NT89] S. Naqvi and S. Tsur. *A language for data and knowledge bases*. Computer Science Press, Rockville, MD, 1989.

[Ora89] *SQL Language Reference: ORACLE Server for OS/2*. Oracle Corp. Redwood Shores, CA, 1989.

[Osb79] S. L. Osborn. Towards a universal relation interface. In *Proc. of Intl. Conf. on Very Large Data Bases*, pages 52–60, 1979.

[OW93] G. Özsoyoğlu and H. Wang. A survey of QBE languages. *Computer*, 26, 1993.

[OY87] Z. M. Özsoyoğlou and L. -Y. Yuan. A new normal form for nested relations. *ACM Trans. on Database Systems*, 12(1):111–136, 1987.

[Pai84] R. Paige. Applications of finite differencing to database integrity control and query/transaction optimization. In H. Gallaire, J. Minker, and J. -M. Nicolas, editors, *Advances in Data Base Theory, vol. 2*, pages 171–209. Plenum Press, New York, 1984.

[Pap85] C. P. Papadimitriou. A note on the expressive power of prolog. *Bulletin of the EATCS*, 26:21–23, 1985.

[Pap86] C. H. Papadimitriou. *The Theory of Concurrency Control*. Computer Science Press, Rockville, MD, 1986.

[Pap94] C. Papadimitriou. *Computational Complexity*. Addison-Wesley, Reading, MA, 1994.

[Par78] J. Paredaens. On the expressive power of the relational algebra. *Inf. Proc. Letters*, 7(2):107–111, 1978.

[Par79] J. Paredaens. Transitive dependencies in a database scheme. Technical Report R387, MBLE, Brussels, 1979.

[PBGG89] J. Paredaens, P. De Bra, M. Gyssens, and D. Van Gucht. *The Structure of the Relational Database Model*. EATCS Monographs on Theoretical Computer Science No. 17. Springer-Verlag, Berlin, 1989.

[Pea88] J. Pearl. *Probabilistic Reasoning in Intelligent Systems*. Morgan Kaufmann, Inc., Los Altos, CA, 1988.

[Per91] D. Perrin. Finite automata. In J. Van Leeuwen, editor, *Handbook of Theoretical Computer Science*, pages 1–58. Elsevier, Amsterdam, 1991.

[Pet89] S. V. Petrov. Finite axiomatization of languages for representation of system properties. *Information Sciences*, 47:339–372, 1989.

[PG88] J. Paredaens and D. Van Gucht. Possibilities and limitations of using flat operators in nested algebra expressions. In *Proc. ACM Symp. on Principles of Database Systems*, pages 29–38, 1988.

[PI94] S. Patnaik and N. Immerman. Dyn-FO: A parallel, dynamic complexity class. In *Proc. ACM Symp. on Principles of Database Systems*, 1994.

[PJ81] J. Paredaens and D. Janssens. Decompositions of relations: a comprehensive approach. In H. Gallaire, J. Minker, and J. -M. Nicolas, editors, *Advances in Data Base Theory, vol. 1*, pages 73–100. Plenum Press, New York, 1981.

[PM88] J. Peckham and F. Maryanski. Semantic data models. *ACM Computing Surveys*, 20:153–190, 1988.

[Por86] H. H. Porter. Earley deduction. Technical Report TR CS/E-86-002, Oregon Graduate Center, Beaverton, OR, 1986.

[Pos47] E. L. Post. Recursive unsolvability of a problem of Thue. *J. of Symbolic Logic*, 12:1–11, 1947.

[PPG80] D. S. Parker and K. Parsaye-Ghomi. Inference involving embedded multivalued dependencies and transitive dependencies. In *Proc. ACM SIGMOD Symp. on the Management of Data*, pages 52–57, 1980.

[Prz86] T. Przymusinski. On the semantics of stratified deductive databases. In *Proc. Workshop on the Foundations of Deductive Databases and Logic Programming*, pages 433–443, 1986.

[Prz88] T. Przymusinski. Perfect model semantics. In *Intl. Conf. on Logic Programming*, pages 1081–1096, 1988.

[Prz89] T. Przymusinski. Every logic program has a natural stratification and an iterated least fixpoint model. In *Proc. ACM Symp. on Principles of Database Systems*, pages 11–21, 1989.

[Prz90] T. Przymusinski. Well-founded semantics coincides with three-valued stable semantics. *Fundamenta Informaticae*, XIII:445–463, 1990.

[PSV92] D. S. Parker, E. Simon, and P. Valduriez. SVP – A model capturing sets, streams, and parallelism. In *Proc. of Intl. Conf. on Very Large Data Bases*, pages 115–126, 1992.

[PV88] J. Pearl and T. Verma. The logic of representing dependencies by directed graphs. In *Proceedings, AAAI Conference, Seattle, WA. July, 1987*, pages 374–379, 1988.

[PW80] F. C. N. Pereira and D. H. D. Warren. Definite clause grammars for language analysis – A survey of the formalism and a comparison with augmented transition networks. *Artificial Intelligence*, 13:231–278, 1980.

[PY92] C. H. Papadimitriou and M. Yannakakis. Tie-breaking semantics and structural totality. In *Proc. ACM Symp. on Principles of Database Systems*, pages 16–22, 1992.

[QW91] X. Qian and G. Wiederhold. Incremental recomputation of active relational expressions. *IEEE Trans. on Knowledge and Data Engineering*, 3:337–341, 1991.

[Rad64] R. Rado. Universal graphs and universal functions. *Acta Arith.*, 9:331–340, 1964.

[Ram91] R. Ramakrishnan. Magic templates: A spellbinding approach to logic programs. *J. Logic Programming*, 11:189–216, 1991. See also *Proc. Joint Symp. and Intl. Conf. on Logic Programming*, 1988.

[RBS87] R. Ramakrishnan, R. Bancilhon, and A. Silberschatz. Safety of recursive horn clauses with infinite relations (extended abstract). In *Proc. ACM Symp. on Principles of Database Systems*, pages 328–339, 1987.

[RD75] J. Rissanen and C. Delobel. Decomposition of files, a basis for data storage and retrieval. Technical Report RJ1220, IBM Res. Lab, San Jose, CA, 1975.

[Rei78] R. Reiter. On closed world databases. In H. Gallaire and J. Minker, editors, *Logic and Databases*, pages 56–76. Plenum Press, New York, 1978.

[Rei80] R. Reiter. A logic for default reasoning. *Artificial Intelligence*, 13(1):80–132, 1980.

[Rei84] R. Reiter. Towards a logical reconstruction of relational database theory. In M. L. Brodie, J. L. Mylopoulos, and J. W. Schmidt, editors, *On Conceptual Modeling*, pages 191–238. Springer-Verlag, Berlin, 1984.

[Rei86] R. Reiter. A sound and sometimes complete query evaluation algorithm for relational databases with null values. *J. ACM*, 33(2):349–370, 1986.

[Ris77] J. Rissanen. Independent components of relations. *ACM Trans. on Database Systems*, 2(4):317–325, 1977.

[Ris78] J. Rissanen. Theory of relations for databases – A tutorial survey. In *Proc. 7th Symp. on Mathematical Foundations of Computer Science*, pages 536–551. Zadopane, Springer-Verlag, Berlin, LNCS 64, 1978.

[Ris82] J. Rissanen. On equivalence of database schemes. In *Proc. ACM Symp. on Principles of Database Systems*, pages 23–26, 1982.

[RKS86] M. A. Roth, H. F. Korth, and A. Silberschatz. Theory of non-first-normal-form relational databases. Technical Report TR-84-36, University of Texas, Austin, 1986.

[RLK86] J. Rohmer, R. Lescoeur, and J. M. Kerisit. The Alexander method – A technique for the processing of recursive axioms in deductive databases. *New Generation Computing*, 4(3):273–286, 1986.

[Rob65] J. A. Robinson. A machine oriented logic based on the resolution principle. *J. ACM*, 12(1):23–41, 1965.

[Roe87] D. Roelants. Recursive rules in logic databases. Technical Report R513, Philips Research Laboratories, Bruxelles, 1987.

[Ros89] K. Ross. A procedural semantics for the well-founded negation in logic programs. In *Proc. ACM Symp. on Principles of Database Systems*, pages 22–33, 1989.

[Ros91] K. A. Ross. *The Semantics of Deductive Databases*. Ph.D. thesis, Stanford University, 1991.

[Rou91] B. Rounds. Situation-theoretic aspects of databases. In *Proc. of Conf. on Situation Theory and Applications; CSLI vol. 26*, pages 229–256, 1991.

[RS79] L. Rowe and K. A. Schoens. Data abstractions, views and updates in RIGEL. In *Proc. ACM SIGMOD Symp. on the Management of Data*, pages 71–81, 1979.

[RS91] J. Richardson and P. Schwartz. Aspects: Extending objects to support multiple independent roles. In *Intl. Conf. on Principles of Knowledge Representation and Reasoning*, pages 298–307, 1991.

[RSB+87] K. Ramamohanarao, J. Shepherd, I. Balbin, G. Port, L. Naish, J. Thom, J. Zobel, and P. Dart. The NU-Prolog deductive database system. *Data Engineering*, 10(4):10–19, 1987.

[RSS92] R. Ramakrishnan, D. Srivastava, and S. Sudarshan. CORAL: control, relations and logic. In *Proc. of Intl. Conf. on Very Large Data Bases*, 1992.

[RSSS93] R. Ramakrishnan, D. Srivastava, S. Sudarshan, and P. Seshadri. Implementation of the CORAL deductive database system. In *Proc. ACM SIGMOD Symp. on the Management of Data*, pages 167–176, 1993.

[RSUV89] R. Ramakrishnan, Y. Sagiv, J. D. Ullman, and M. Y. Vardi. Proof-tree transformations and their applications. In *Proc. ACM Symp. on Principles of Database Systems*, pages 172–182, 1989.

[RSUV93] R. Ramakrishnan, Y. Sagiv, J. D. Ullman, and M. Y. Vardi. Logical query optimization by proof-tree transfomation. *J. Computer and System Sciences*, 47, pages 222–248, 1993.

[RU94] R. Ramakrishnan and J. D. Ullman. A survey of research on deductive database systems. In *J. of Logic Programming*, to appear.

[SAC+79] P. Selinger, M. M. Astrahan, D. D. Chamberlin, R. A. Lorie, and T. G. Price. Access path selection in a relational database management system. In *Proc. ACM SIGMOD Symp. on the Management of Data*, pages 23–34, 1979.

[Sag81] Y. Sagiv. Can we use the universal assumption without using nulls? In *Proc. ACM SIGMOD Symp. on the Management of Data*, pages 108–120, 1981.

[Sag83] Y. Sagiv. A characterization of globally consistent database and their correct access paths. *ACM Trans. on Database Systems*, 8(2):266–286, 1983.

[Sag88] Y. Sagiv. Optimizing datalog programs. In J. Minker, editor, *Foundations of Deductive Databases and Logic Programming*, pages 659–698. Morgan Kaufmann, Inc., Los Altos, CA, 1988.

[Sag90] Y. Sagiv. Is there anything better than magic? In *Proc. North American Conf. on Logic Programming*, pages 235–254, 1990.

[Sci81] E. Sciore. Real-world MVDs. In *Proc. ACM SIGMOD Symp. on the Management of Data*, pages 121–132, 1981.

[Sci82] E. Sciore. A complete axiomatization of full join dependencies. *J. ACM*, 29:373–393, 1982.

[Sci83] E. Sciore. Inclusion dependencies and the universal instance. In *Proc. ACM Symp. on Principles of Database Systems*, pages 48–57, 1983.

[Sci86] E. Sciore. Comparing the universal instance and relational data models. In P. C. Kanellakis and F. Preparata, editors, *Advances in Computing Research, vol. 3: The Theory of Databases*, pages 139–163. JAI Press, Inc., Greenwich, CT, 1986.

[SDPF81] Y. Sagiv, C. Delobel, D. S. Parker, Jr., and R. Fagin. An equivalence between relational database dependencies and a fragment of propositional logic. *J. ACM*, 28:435–453, 1981.

[Sek89] H. Seki. On the power of Alexander templates. In *Proc. ACM Symp. on Principles of Database Systems*, pages 150–159, 1989.

[SF78] K. C. Sevcik and A. L. Furtado. Complete and compatible sets of update operations. In *Intl. Conf. on Management of Data (ICMOD)*, Milan, Italy, 1978.

[SG85] D. E. Smith and M. R. Genesereth. Ordering conjunctive queries. *Artificial Intelligence*, 26:171–215, 1985.

[She88] J. Shepherdson. Negation in logic programming. In J. Minker, editor, *Foundations of Deductive Databases and Logic Programming*, pages 19–88. Morgan Kaufmann, Inc., Los Altos, CA, 1988.

[Shi81] D. Shipman. The functional data model and the data language daplex. *ACM Trans. on Database Systems*, 6:140–173, 1981.

[Shm87] O. Shmueli. Decidability and expressiveness aspects of logic queries. In *Proc. ACM Symp. on Principles of Database Systems*, pages 237–249, 1987.

[SI88] H. Seki and H. Itoh. A query evaluation method for stratified programs under the extended CWA. In *Proc. Fifth Intl. Symp. on Logic Programming*, pages 195–211, 1988.

[SI84] O. Shmueli and A. Itai. Maintenance of views. In *Proc. ACM SIGMOD Symp. on the Management of Data*, pages 240–255, 84.

[Sic76] S. Sickel. A search technique for clause interconnectivity graphs. *IEEE Trans. on Computers*, C-25:72–80, 1976.

[Sie88] J. H. Siekmann. Unification theory. *J. Symbolic Computation*, 7:207–274, 1988.

[SJGP90] M. Stonebraker, A. Jhingran, J. Goh, and S. Potamianos. On rules, procedures, caching and views in data base systems. In *Proc. ACM SIGMOD Symp. on the Management of Data*, pages 281–290, 1990.

[SKdM92] E. Simon, J. Kiernan, and C. de Maindreville. Implementing high level active rules on top of a relational dbms. In *Proc. of Intl. Conf. on Very Large Data Bases*, pages 315–326, 1992.

[SL90] A. P. Sheth and J. A. Larson. Federated database systems for managing distributed, heterogeneous, and autonomous databases. *ACM Computing Surveys*, 22:184–236, 1990.

[SL91] J. Seib and G. Lausen. Parallelizing datalog programs by generalized pivoting. In *Proc. ACM Symp. on Principles of Database Systems*, pages 78–87, 1991.

[SLRD93] W. Sun, Y. Ling, N. Rishe, and Y. Deng. An instant and accurate size estimation method for joins and selection in a retrieval-intensive environment. In *Proc. ACM SIGMOD Symp. on the Management of Data*, pages 79–88, 1993.

[SM81] A. M. Silva and M. A. Melkanoff. A method for helping discover the dependencies of a relation. In *Advances in Data Base Theory*, ed. by H. Gallaire, J. Minker, and J. -M. Nicolas, pages 115–133. Plenum Press, New York, 1981.

[Sno90] R. Snodgrass. Temporal databases: status and research directions. *ACM SIGMOD Record*, 19(4):83–89, December 1990.

[Soo91] M. Soo. Bibliography on temporal databases. In *Proc. ACM SIGMOD Symp. on the Management of Data*, pages 14–23, 1991.

[SP94] D. Suciu and J. Paredaens. Any algorithm in the complex object algebra with powerset needs exponential space to compute transitive closure. In *Proc. ACM Symp. on Principles of Database Systems*, pages 171–179, 1994.

[SR86] M. Stonebraker and L. Rowe. The design of Postgres. In *Proc. ACM SIGMOD Symp. on the Management of Data*, pages 340–355, 1986.

[SR93] S. Sudarshan and R. Ramakrishnan. Optimizations of Bottom-up evaluation with non-ground terms. In *Proc. of Intl. Logic Programming Symp*, 1993.

[SS86] Y. Sagiv and O. Shmueli. The equivalence of solving queries and producing tree projections. In *Proc. ACM Symp. on Principles of Database Systems*, pages 160–172, 1986.

[Sto81] M. Stonebraker. Operating system support for database management. *Comm. of the ACM*, 24:412–418, 1981.

[Sto88] M. Stonebraker, editor. *Readings in Database Systems*. Morgan Kaufmann, Inc., Los Altos, CA, 1988.

[Sto92] M. Stonebraker. The integration of rule systems and database systems. *IEEE Transactions on Knowledge and Data Engineering*, 4:415–423, 1992.

[Str91] B. Stroustrup. *The C++ Programming Language, 2d ed*. Addison-Wesley, Reading, MA, 1991.

[SU82] U. F. Sadri and J. D. Ullman. Template dependencies: A large class of dependencies in relational database and their complete axiomatization. *J. ACM*, 29(2):363–372, 1982.

[Su92] J. Su. Dynamic constraints and object migration. Technical Report TRCS-9202, Computer Science Department, University of California, Santa Barbara, 1992. To appear, *Theoretical Computer Science*; see also *Proc. of Intl. Conf. on Very Large Data Bases*, 1991.

[SV89] Y. Sagiv and M. Y. Vardi. Safety of datalog queries over infinite databases. In *Proc. ACM Symp. on Principles of Database Systems*, pages 160–172, 1989.

[SW82] Y. Sagiv and S. Walecka. Subset dependencies and a completeness result for a subclass of embedded multivalued dependencies. *J. ACM*, 29(1):103–117, 1982.

[SWKH76] M. Stonebraker, E. Wong, P. Kreps, and G. Held. The design and implementation of Ingres. *ACM Trans. on Database Systems*, 1(3):189–222, 1976.

[SY80] Y. Sagiv and M. Yannakakis. Equivalence among expressions with the union and difference operators. *J. ACM*, 27(4):633–655, 1980.

[SZ86] D. Saccà and C. Zaniolo. On the implementation of a simple class of logic queries for databases. In *Proc. ACM Symp. on Principles of Database Systems*, pages 16–23, 1986.

[SZ88] D. Saccà and C. Zaniolo. The generalized counting method for recursive logic queries. *Theoretical Computer Science*, 62:187–220, 1988.

[SZ89] L. A. Stein and S. B. Zdonik. Clovers: The dynamic behavior of type and instances. Technical Report CS-89-42, Computer Science Department, Brown University, 1989.

[SZ90] D. Saccà and C. Zaniolo. Stable models and non-determinism in logic programs with negation. In *Proc. ACM Symp. on Principles of Database Systems*, pages 205–217, 1990.

[Tan88] L. Tanca. *Optimization of Recursive Logic Queries to Relational Databases*. Ph.D. thesis, Politecnico di Milano and Universita' di Napoli, 1988.

[Tar55] A. Tarski. A lattice theoretical fixpoint theorem and its applications. *Pacific J. Math*, 5(2):285–309, 1955.

[TCG+93] A. U. Tansel, J. Clifford, S. Gadia, S. Jajodia, A. Segev, and R. Snodgrass. *Temporal Databases – Theory, Design, and Implementation*. Benjamin/Cummings Publishing Co., Menlo Park, CA, 1993.

[TF82] D. -M. Tsou and P. C. Fischer. Decomposition of a relation scheme into Boyce-Codd normal form. *SIGACT News*, 14(3):23–29, 1982.

[TF86] S. J. Thomas and P. C. Fischer. Nested relational structures. In P. C. Kanellakis and F. Preparata, editors, *Advances in Computing Research, vol. 3*, pages 269–307. JAI Press, Inc., Greenwich, CT, 1986.

[Tha91] B. Thalheim. *Dependencies in Relational Databases*. Teubner Verlagsgesellschaft, Stuttgart and Leipzig, 1991.

[TK84] V. A. Talanov and V. V. Knyazev. The asymptotic truth value of infinite formulas. In *All-union seminar on discrete mathematics and its applications*, pages 56–61, 1984.

[TL82] D. C. Tsichritzis and F. H. Lochovsky. *Data Models*. Prentice-Hall, Englewood Cliffs, NJ, 1982.

[Tod77] S. Todd. Automatic constraint maintenance and updating defined relations. In B. Gilchrist, editor, *Proc. IFIP 77*, pages 145–148. North Holland, Amsterdam, 1977.

[Top87] R. Topor. Domain independent formulas and databases. *Theoretical Computer Science*, 52(3):281–307, 1987.

[Top91] R. Topor. Safe database queries with arithmetic relations. Technical Report, Computer Science Department, University of Melbourne, 1991. Abstract appears as *Safe Database Queries with Arithmetic Relations*, Proc. 14th Australian Computer Science Conf., Sydney, 1991, pp. 1–13.

[TS88] R. W. Topor and E. A. Sonenberg. On domain independent databases. In J. Minker, editor, *Foundations of Deductive Databases and Logic Programming*, pages 217–240. Morgan Kaufmann, Inc., Los Altos, CA, 1988.

[TT52] A. Tarski and F. B. Thompson. Some general properties of cylindric algebras. *Bulletin of the AMS*, 58:65, 1952.

[TY84] R. E. Tarjan and M. Yannakakis. Simple linear-time algorithms to test chordality of graphs, test acyclicity of hypergraphs, and selectively reduce acyclic hypergraphs. *SIAM J. on Computing*, 13(3):566–579, 1984.

[TYF86] T. J. Teorey, D. Yand, and J. P. Fry. A logical design methodology for relational databases using the extended entity-relationship model. In *ACM Computing Surveys*, pages 197–222, 1986.

[UG88] J. D. Ullman and A. Van Gelder. Parallel complexity of logical query programs. *Algorithmica*, 3(1):5–42, 1988.

[Ull82a] J. D. Ullman. The U.R. strikes back. In *Proc. ACM Symp. on Principles of Database Systems*, pages 10–22, 1982.

[Ull82b] J. D. Ullman. *Principles of Database Systems, 2d ed*. Computer Science Press, Rockville, MD, 1982.

[Ull85] J. D. Ullman. Implementation of logical query languages for databases. *ACM Trans. on Database Systems*, 10(3):289–321, 1985.

[Ull88] J. D. Ullman. *Principles of Database and Knowledge Base Systems, vol. I*. Computer Science Press, Rockville, MD, 1988.

[Ull89a] J. D. Ullman. Bottom-up beats top-down for datalog. In *Proc. ACM Symp. on Principles of Database Systems*, pages 140–149, 1989.

[Ull89b] J. D. Ullman. *Principles of Database and Knowledge Base Systems, vol. II: The New Technologies*. Computer Science Press, Rockville, MD, 1989.

[Van86] A. Van Gelder. A message passing framework for logical query evaluation. In *Proc. ACM SIGMOD Symp. on the Management of Data*, pages 155–165, 1986.

[VandB93] J. Van den Bussche. *Formal Aspects of Object Identity*. Ph.D. thesis, University of Antwerp, 1993.

[VandBG92] J. Van den Bussche and D. Van Gucht. Semi-determinism. In *Proc. ACM Symp. on Principles of Database Systems*, pages 191–201, 1992.

[VandBGAG92] J. Van den Bussche, D. Van Gucht, M. Andries, and M. Gyssens. On the completeness of object-creating query languages. In *IEEE Conf. on Foundations of Computer Science*, pages 372–379, 1992.

[VandBP91] J. Van den Bussche and J. Paredaens. The expressive power of structured values in pure OODBS. In *Proc. ACM Symp. on Principles of Database Systems*, pages 291–299, 1991.

[VanG86] A. Van Gelder. Negation as failure using tight derivations for general logic programs. In *IEEE Symp. on Logic Programming*, pages 127–139, 1986.

[VanG89] A. Van Gelder. The alternating fixpoint of logic programs with negation. In *Proc. ACM Symp. on Principles of Database Systems*, pages 1–11, 1989.

[VanGRS88] A. Van Gelder, K. A. Ross, and J. S. Schlipf. The well-founded semantics for general logic programs. In *Proc. ACM Symp. on Principles of Database Systems*, pages 221–230, 1988.

[VanGRS91] A. Van Gelder, K. A. Ross, and J. S. Schlipf. The well-founded semantics for general logic programs. *J. ACM*, 38:620–650, 1991.

[VanGT91] A. Van Gelder and R. Topor. Safety and translation of relational calculus queries. *ACM Trans. on Database Systems*, 16:235–278, 1991.

[Var81] M. Y. Vardi. The decision problem for database dependencies. *Inf. Proc. Letters*, 12(5):251–254, 1981.

[Var82a] M. Y. Vardi. The complexity of relational query languages. In *Proc. ACM SIGACT Symp. on the Theory of Computing*, pages 137–146, 1982.

[Var82b] M. Y. Vardi. On decomposition of relational databases. In *IEEE Conf. on Foundations of Computer Science*, pages 176–185, 1982.

[Var83] M. Y. Vardi. Inferring multivalued dependencies from functional and join dependencies. *Acta Informatica*, 19:305–324, 1983.

[Var84] M. Y. Vardi. The implication and finite implication problems for typed template dependencies. *Journal of Computer and System Sciences*, 28:3–28, 1984.

[Var85] M. Y. Vardi. Querying logical databases. In *Proc. ACM Symp. on Principles of Database Systems*, pages 57–65, 1985.

[Var86a] M. Y. Vardi. On the integrity of databases with incomplete information. In *Proc. ACM Symp. on Principles of Database Systems*, pages 252–266, 1986.

[Var86b] M. Y. Vardi. Querying Logical Databases. *J. Computer and Systems Sciences*, 33, pages 142–160, 1986.

[Var87] M. Y. Vardi. Fundamentals of dependency theory. In E. Borger, editor, *Trends in Theoretical Computer Science*, pages 171–224. Computer Science Press, Rockville, MD, 1987.

[Var88] M. Y. Vardi. Decidability and undecidablity results for boundedness of linear recursive queries. In *Proc. ACM Symp. on Principles of Database Systems*, pages 341–351, 1988.

[Vas79] Y. Vassiliou. Null values in database management, A denotational semantics approach. In *Proc. ACM SIGMOD Symp. on the Management of Data*, pages 162–169, 1979.

[Vas80] Y. Vassiliou. *A Formal Treatment of Imperfect Information in Data Management*. Ph.D. thesis, University of Toronto, 1980.

[VBKL89] L. Vieille, P. Bayer, V. Kuchenoff, and A. Lefebvre. Eks-v1: A short overview. In *Proc. ACM SIGMOD Symp. on the Management of Data*, 1989. Technical exhibition.

[vEK76] M. H. van Emden and R. A. Kowalski. The semantics of predicate logic as a programming language. *J. ACM*, 23(4):733–742, 1976.

[Ver89] J. Verso. Verso: a database machine based on non-1nf relations. In H. Schek, S. Abiteboul,

P. Fisher, editors, *Nested Relations and Complex Objects*, LNCS, page 361. Springer-Verlag, Berlin, 1989.

[Via87] V. Vianu. Dynamic functional dependencies and database aging. *J. ACM*, 34(1):28–59, 1987.

[Via88] V. Vianu. Database survivability under dynamic constraints. *Acta Informatica*, 25:55–84, 1988.

[Vie86] L. Vieille. Recursive axioms in deductive databases: The Query/Subquery approach. In L. Kerschberg, editor, *Proc. First Intl. Conf. on Expert Database Systems*, pages 179–193, 1986.

[Vie87a] L. Vieille. A database-complete proof procedure based on sld-resolution. In *Proc. of the Fourth Intl. Conf. on Logic Programming*, pages 74–103, 1987.

[Vie87b] L. Vieille. Recursion in deductive databases: DedGin, a recursive query evaluator. In *Des Bases de Données aux Bases de Connaissances*, Sophia-Antipolis, France, 1987. Also available as Technical Report TR-KB-14, ECRC, Munich.

[Vie88] L. Vieille. From QSQ towards QaSSaQ: Global optimization of recursive queries. In L. Kerschberg, editor, *Proc. Second Intl. Conf. on Expert Database Systems*, pages 421–436, 1988.

[Vie89] L. Vieille. Recursive query processing: The power of logic. *Theoretical Computer Science*, 69:1–53, 1989.

[Vos91] G. Vossen. *Data Models, Database Languages and Database Management Systems*. Addison-Wesley, Wokingham, England, 1991.

[VV92] V. Vianu and G. Vossen. Conceptual-level concurrency control for relational update transactions. *Theoretical Computer Science*, 95:1–42, 1992.

[WF90] J. Widom and S. J. Finkelstein. Set-oriented production rules in relational database systems. In *Proc. ACM SIGMOD Symp. on the Management of Data*, pages 259–264, 1990.

[WH92] Y. -W. Wang and E. N. Hanson. A performance comparison of the Rete and TREAT algorithms for testing database rule conditions. In *IEEE Conf. on Data Engineering*, pages 88–97, 1992.

[WHW90] S. Widjojo, R. Hull, and D. S. Wile. A specificational approach to merging persistent object bases. In A. Dearle, G. Shaw, and S. Zdonik, editors, *Implementing Persistent Object Bases: Proc. of Fourth Intl. Workshop on Persistent Object Systems*, pages 267–278. Morgan Kaufmann, Inc., Los Altos, CA, 1990.

[Wie92] G. Wiederhold. Mediators in the architecture of future information systems. *IEEE Computer*, 25(3):38–49, March 1992.

[Win86] M. Winslett. A model-theoretic approach to updating logical databases. In *Proc. ACM Symp. on Principles of Database Systems*, pages 224–234, 1986.

[Win88] M. Winslett. A framework for comparison of update semantics. In *Proc. ACM Symp. on Principles of Database Systems*, pages 315–324, 1988.

[WO90] O. Wolfson and A. Ozeri. A new paradigm for parallel and distributed rule-processing. In *Proc. ACM SIGMOD Symp. on the Management of Data*, pages 133–142, 1990.

[Won93] L. Wong. Normal forms and conservative properties for query languages over collection types. In *Proc. ACM Symp. on Principles of Database Systems*, pages 26–36, 1993.

[WS88] O. Wolfson and A. Silberschatz. Distributed processing of logic programming. In *Proc. ACM SIGMOD Symp. on the Management of Data*, pages 329–336, 1988.

[WW75] C. P. Wang and H. H. Wedekind. Segment synthesis in logical data base design. *IBM J. Res. and Develop.*, 19:71–77, 1975.

[WY76] E. Wong and K. Youssefi. Decomposition—A strategy for query processing. *ACM Trans. on Database Systems*, 1(3):223–241, 1976.

[Yan81] M. Yannakakis. Algorithms for acyclic database schemes. In *Proc. of Intl. Conf. on Very Large Data Bases*, pages 82–94, 1981.

[YC84] C. T. Yu and C. C. Chang. Distributed query processing. *ACM Computing Surveys*, 16, 1984.

[YO79] C. T. Yu and M. Z. Özsoyoğlu. An algorithm for tree-query membership of a distributed query. In *Proc. IEEE COMPSAC*, pages 306–312, 1979.

[YP82] M. Yannakakis and C. Papadimitriou. Algebraic dependencies. *Journal of Computer and System Sciences*, 25(2):3–41, 1982.

[Zan76] C. Zaniolo. *Analysis and Design of Relational Schemata for Database Systems*. Ph.D. thesis, University of California at Los Angeles, 1976. Technical Report UCLA-Eng-7669, Department of Computer Science.

[Zan82] C. Zaniolo. A new normal form for the design of relational database schemata. *ACM Trans. on Database Systems*, 7:489–499, 1982.

[Zan84] C. Zaniolo. Database relations with null values. *Journal of Computer and System Sciences*, 28(1):142–166, 1984.

[Zan87] C. Zaniolo, editor. *IEEE Data Engineering 10(4)*, 1987. Special issue on databases and logic.

[ZH90] Y. Zhou and M. Hsu. A theory for rule triggering systems. In *Intl. Conf. on Extending Data Base Technology*, pages 407–421, 1990.

[Zlo77] M. Zloof. Query-by-example: A data base language. *IBM Systems Journal*, 16:324–343, 1977.

[ZM90] S. B. Zdonik and D. Maier, editors. *Readings in Object-Oriented Database Systems*. Morgan Kaufmann, Inc., Los Altos, CA, 1990.

Symbol Index

Index

Page numbers in italics indicate the location of definitions of terms.